Lecture Notes in Computer Science 4294

Commenced Publication in 1973
Founding and Former Series Editors:
Gerhard Goos, Juris Hartmanis, and Jan van Leeuwen

Asit Dan Winfried Lamersdorf (Eds.)

Service-Oriented Computing – ICSOC 2006

4th International Conference
Chicago, IL, USA, December 4-7, 2006
Proceedings

Springer

Volume Editors

Asit Dan
IBM T.J. Watson Research Center
19, Skyline Drive, Hawthorne, NY, 10532, USA
E-mail: asit@us.ibm.com

Winfried Lamersdorf
University of Hamburg
Distributed Systems and Information Systems, Computer Science Department
Vogt-Kölln-Str. 30, 22527 Hamburg, Germany
E-mail: lamersdorf@informatik.uni-hamburg.de

Library of Congress Control Number: 2006937445

CR Subject Classification (1998): C.2, D.2, D.4, H.4, H.3, K.4.4

LNCS Sublibrary: SL 2 – Programming and Software Engineering

ISSN 0302-9743
ISBN-10 3-540-68147-7 Springer Berlin Heidelberg New York
ISBN-13 978-3-540-68147-2 Springer Berlin Heidelberg New York

Springer is a part of Springer Science+Business Media

springer.com

Printed in Germany

Typesetting: Camera-ready by author, data conversion by Scientific Publishing Services, Chennai, India
Printed on acid-free paper SPIN: 11948148 06/3142 5 4 3 2 1 0

Preface

This volume contains the proceedings of the 4th International Conference on Service-Oriented Computing (ICSOC 2006), which took place in Chicago, USA, December 4–7, 2006. ICSOC 2006 followed on the success of three previous editions of the International Conference on Service-Oriented Computing in Amsterdam, Netherlands (2005), New York City, USA (2004) and Trento, Italy (2003). ICSOC is recognized as the main conference for service-oriented computing research that covers the entire spectrum from theoretical and foundational results to empirical evaluations as well as practical and industrial experiences. ICSOC 2006 built on that foundation while introducing several innovations in furthering this goal.

Service-oriented computing brings together ideas and technologies from many different fields in an evolutionary manner to address research challenges such as service composition, discovery, integration, monitoring and management of services, service quality and security, methodologies for supporting service development, governances in their evolution, as well as their overall life-cycle management. ICSOC 2006 strengthened the link to two important communities, *Software Engineering* and *Grid Computing*, with well-known leaders from these communities serving in important organizing roles such as general chairs in shaping the conference.

In order to provide a balanced coverage and equal emphasis on all SOC topics, these topics are divided into six major areas. They include *Business Service Modeling, Service Assembly, Service Deployment, and Management* – covering the research issues in the four primary life-cycle phases of a service, modeling, assembly, deployment, and management. Additionally, the runtime architectural issues are covered by the *SOA Runtime*, and quality of service issues – spanning all life-cycle stages, i.e., specification to autonomic management – are covered by the *Quality of Service* area. Finally, the *Grid Services* area covers application of service-oriented computing in managing infrastructural resources.

Organizationally, for each of these areas, respective *Area Coordinators* have the key role of defining topics, reaching out to the scientific communities and supporting the evaluation and selection of papers related to the diverse communities.

The paper selection process was very thorough. Matching diversity of paper topics and reviewer expertise is definitely a challenge. Therefore, we worked closely with the Area Coordinators, i.e., two experts representing each of the areas, to assign reviewers to submitted papers, and also to sort out the differences in opinions from different reviewers by weighing in their expert opinion. Since the content of a paper may be identified by multiple areas, reviewers were drawn from all the associated areas. Overall in the selection process, we sought a diversity of papers and balance across the areas while selecting the top papers in each of the areas. ICSOC 2006 received over 200 contributions in the research track, accepting only 34 full and 16 short papers.

This year we also enhanced the industrial track by attracting many industry leaders – representing the gamut of software middleware vendors, consulting analysts, solution integrators and practitioners of service-oriented architecture (SOA) – both to serve on the Program Committee and to submit papers sharing valuable hands-on experiences and key challenges in practicing service-oriented computing. The industrial papers highlight lessons learned, analysis of technology gap, methodology used in practice, noteworthy and innovative application scenarios, need for new standardization, and major improvements to the state of practice. The industry track received more than 60 submissions, out of which only 9 full papers were selected. It also features two invited vision papers discussing the evolution of service-oriented computing.

In addition to the regular, industry, and short presentations, the ICSOC 2006 conference featured three tutorials, two panels examining the role of open-source software and research challenges, and – as customary in ICSOC conferences – top-notch keynotes, given by leaders in the industrial and academic community.

The excellent program that we assembled for presentation at the conference is a reflection of the hard and dedicated work of numerous people. We would like to thank the members of the Program Committee and the reviewers for their great efforts in selecting the papers, and the Area Coordinators in making an extra effort in looking over the reviews and sorting out differences in opinions. We also acknowledge the great contributions of Julie Wulf-Knoerzer in the local organization, of Vincenzo D'Andrea for handling finances, of Matei Ripeanu in handling the publicity, of Boualem Benatallah for handling publication of the conference proceedings, and of Martin Swany for handling registration. We also thank Dimitrios Georgakopoulos, Norbert Ritter (Workshop Chairs), Frank Leymann and Heiko Ludwig (Tutorial Chairs) for organizing associated workshops and tutorials. We would also like to thank some individuals for their special help and contributions: Sonja Zaplata for assisting the Program Chairs in tracking various issues that arose throughout the review process, and for being prompt in responding to queries from authors, reviewers and other conference chairs, Harald Weinreich, who created and adapted the conftool for us several times – often without anyone really noticing—and Anne Awizen for her support. And last but not the least, we would like to thank the Steering Committee members, Fabio Casati, Paco Curbera, Mike Papazoglou, and Paolo Traverso, for their guidance, and our partners, ACM SIGWeb and SIGSoft.

We hope you find the papers in this volume interesting and stimulating.

December 2006

Ian Foster and Carlo Ghezzi (General Chairs)
Asit Dan and Winfried Lamersdorf (Program Chairs)
Robert Johnson, and Jeff Mischkinsky (Industrial Track Chairs)

Organization

ICSOC 2006 Conference Chairs

General Chairs	Ian Foster, University of Chicago, USA Carlo Ghezzi, Politecnico di Milano, Italy
Program Chairs	Asit Dan, IBM, USA Winfried Lamersdorf, Hamburg University, Germany
Industrial Track Chairs	Robert Johnson, IBM, USA Jeff Mischkinsky, Oracle, USA
Workshop Coordination	Dimitrios Georgakopoulos, Telcordia, USA Norbert Ritter, Hamburg University, Germany
Tutorial Chairs	Frank Leymann, University of Stuttgart, Germany Heiko Ludwig, IBM, USA
Local Arrangements Chair	Julie Wulf, Univa Corporation, USA
Financial Chair	Vincenzo D'Andrea, University of Trento, Italy
Registration Chair	Martin Swany, University of Delaware, USA
Publicity Chair	Matei Ripeanu, University of British Columbia, Canada
Publication Chair	Boualem Benatallah, UNSW, Australia
Steering Committee	Fabio Casati, Hewlett-Packard Labs, USA Paco Curbera, IBM Research, Hawthorne, UK Mike Papazoglou, Tilburg University, Netherlands Paolo Traverso, ITC-IRST, Italy

Area Coordinators

Service Modeling	Wolfgang Emmerich, UCL, UK Mathias Weske, University of Potsdam, Germany
Service Assembly	Barbara Pernici, Politecnico di Milano, Italy Munindar Singh, North Carolina State University, USA
Service Management	Luciano Baresi , Politecnico di Milano, Italy Hiro Kishimoto, Jujitsu, Japan
SOA Runtime	Douglas Schmidt, Vanderbilt University, USA Steve Vinoski, Iona, USA
Quality of Service	Priya Narasimhan, CMU, USA Jim Pruyne, HP, USA
Grid Services	Dennis Gannon, Indiana University, USA Paul Watson, Univ. of Newcastle upon Tyne, UK

Program Committee

Research Track

Nabil R. Adam	Rutgers University, USA
Jose Luis Ambite	USC/ISI, USA
Mikio Aoyama	NISE, Japan
Alistair Barros	SAP, Australia
Boualem Benatallah	University of New South Wales, Australia
Walter Binder	EPFL, Switzerland
Athman Bouguettaya	Virginia Tech, USA
Sjaak Brinkkemper	Utrecht University, Netherlands
Tevfik Bultan	UCSB, USA
Fabio Casati	HP, USA
Malu Castellanos	HP, USA
Bruno Crispo	Vrije University Amsterdam, Netherlands
Paco Curbera	IBM Research, USA
Vincenzo D'Andrea	Università di Trento, Italy
Umesh Dayal	HP, USA
Flavio De Paoli	Università di Milano, Italy
Tommaso Di Noia	University of Bari, Italy
Jens-Peter Dittrich	ETH Zurich, Switzerland
John Domingue	KMI, UK
Schahram Dustdar	University of Technology Vienna, Austria
Boi Faltings	EPFL, Switzerland
Dieter Fensel	University of Innsbruck, Austria
Gianluigi Ferrari	University of Pisa, Italy
George Feuerlicht	University of Technology Sydney, Australia
Ioannis Fikouras	Ericsson, Germany
Geoffrey Fox	Indiana University, USA
Alex Galis	UCL, UK
Dimitrios Georgakopoulos	Telcordia, USA
Paolo Giorgini	University of Trento, Italy
Claude Godart	Université Henri Poincaré Nancy, France
Paul Grefen	Eindhoven University of Technology, Netherlands
John Grundy	University of Auckland, New Zealand
Mohand-Said Hacid	Université Lyon, France
Hakan Hacigumus	Almaden IBM, USA
Kate Keahey	Argonne National Laboratory, USA
Alfons Kemper	Technische Universität München, Germany
Roger Kilian-Kehr	SAP Karlsruhe, Germany
Jana Koehler	IBM Zurich Research Lab, Switzerland
Bernd Kraemer	Fernuniversität Hagen, Germany
Brian LaMacchia	Microsoft, USA
Frank Leymann	University of Stuttgart, Germany

Ling Liu	Georgia Institute of Technology, USA
Heiko Ludwig	IBM Research, USA
Neil Maiden	City University London, UK
Tiziana Margarina	Potsdam University, Germany
Ioana Manolescu	INRIA, France
David Martin	SRI, USA
Eugene M. Maximilien	IBM Almaden, USA
Massimo Mecella	Università di Roma, Italy
Brahim Medjahed	Michigan University, USA
Toshiyuki Nakata	NEC, Japan
Christos Nikolaou	University of Crete, Greece
David O'Hallaron	Carnegie Mellon University, USA
Guadalupe Ortiz	Universidad de Extremadura, Spain
Mike Papazoglou	Tilburg University, Netherlands
Anna Perini	ITC-IRST Trento, Italy
Marco Pistore	Università di Trento, Italy
Axel Polleres	Universidad Rey Juan Carlos, Spain
Jean Pierre Prost	IBM Montpellier, France
Omer Rana	Cardiff University, UK
Thomas Risse	Fraunhofer Gesellschaft, Germany
Norbert Ritter	Hamburg University, Germany
Colette Rolland	Université de Paris I, France
Rainer Ruggaber	SAP, Germany
Akhil Sahai	HP, USA
Volker Sander	Jülich Research Centre, Germany
Vladimiro Sassone,	University of Southampton, UK
Dimitrios N. Serpanos	University of Patras, Greece
Jun Shen	University of Wollongong, Australia
Santosh Srivastava	University of New Castle, UK
Maarten Steen	Telematica Enschede, Netherlands
Tony Storey	IBM, UK
Jianwen Su	UCSB, USA
Ravi Subramaniam	Intel, USA
Angelo Susi	ITC-IRST Trento, Italy
Katia Sycara	CMU, USA
Stefan Tai	IBM New York, USA
Kian-Lee Tan	National University of Singapore, Singapore
Paolo Tonella	ITC-IRST Trento, Italy
Farouk Toumani	ISIMA Autiere, France
Don Towsley	University of Massachusetts, USA
Paolo Traverso	ITC-RST, Italy
Aphrodite Tsalgatidou	University of Athens, Greece
Karthikeyan Umapathy	Penn State University, USA
Will van der Aalst	Eindhoven University of Technology, Netherlands
Jos van Hillegersberg	University of Twente, Netherlands
Aad Van Moorsel	University of Newcastle, UK
Vijay Varadharajan	Macquarie University, Australia
John Wilkes	HP Labs Palo Alto, USA
Martin Wirsing	Technische Universität München, Germany

Jian Yang	Macquiri University, Australia
Arkady Zaslavsky	Monash University Melbourne, Australia
Gianluigi Zavattaro	University of Bologna, Italy
Yanchun Zhang	Victoria University, Australia
Christian Zirpins	University College London, UK

Industry Track

Anne Anderson	Sun, USA
Paul Fremantle	WSO2, UK
Steve Graham	IBM, USA
Frederick Hirsch	Nokia, USA
Kerrie Holley	IBM, USA
Philippe Le Hégaret	W3C, USA
Mark Little	Redhat, USA
Ashok Malhotra	Oracle, USA
Andy Mulholland	CapGemini, UK
Srinivas Narayanan	Tavant, USA
Eric Newcomer	Iona Technology, USA
Mark Nottingham	Yahoo, USA
Sanjay Patil	SAP, USA
Greg Pavlik	Oracle, USA
Harini Srinivasan	IBM, USA
William Vambenepe	HP, USA
Sanjiva Weerawarana	WSO2, Sri Lanka
Bobbi Young	Unisys, USA

Additional Referees

Grigoris Antoniou
Andrei Arion
George Athanasopoulos
Michael Averstegge
Donald Baker
Venkat Balakrishnan
Piergiorgio Bertoli
Aliaksandr Birukou
Lars Braubach
Volha Bryl
Andrzej Cichocki
Francesco Colasuonno
Marco Comerio
Nick Cook
Eugenio Di Sciascio
Remco Dijkman
Nicola Dragoni
Christian Drumm
Cu Nguyen Duy
Paul El-Khoury
Rik Eshuis
Reza Eslami
Pascal Fenkam
Eugen Freiter
Keisuke Fukui
GR Gangadaran
Steffen Göbel
Jan Goossenaerts
Simone Grega
Claudio Guidi
Michael Harrison
Martin Husemann
Hiroshi Igaki
Yuji Imai
Sarath Indrakanti
Marijke Janssen

Rim Samia Kaabi
Raman Kazhamiakin
Natallia Kokash
Jacek Kopecky
Iryna Kozlowa
Kathleen Krebs
Christian P. Kunze
Jens Lemcke
Ching Lin
Xumin Liu
Roberto Lucchi
Matteo Maffei
Daniele Maggiore
Zaki Malik
Manolis Marazakis
Annapaola Marconi
Bogdan Marinoiu
Andrea Maurino
Harald Meyer
Stefano Modafferi
Carlos Molina-Jimenez
Graham Morgan
Enrico Mussi
Marian Nodine
Michael Pantazoglou
Panayiotis Periorellis
Marinella Petrocchi
Christian Platzer
Dimitris Plexousakis
Alexander Pokahr
Stanislav Pokraev
Frank Puhlmann
Azzurra Ragone
Claudia Raibule
Claudia Raibulet
Chun Ruan
Yacine Sam
Andreas Savva
Alberto Siena
Jim Smith
Luca Spalazzi
Alexander Stuckenholz
Ioan Toma
Martin Treiber
Uday Kiran Tupakula
Harald Vogt
Michael von Riegen
Jochem Vonk
Jim Webber
Stuart Wheater
Simon Woodman
Xu Yang
Qi Yu
Nicola Zannone
Sonja Zaplata
Uwe Zdun
Yi Zhang
Weiliang Zhao
George Zheng

Table of Contents

Part 1: Research Track Full Papers

Service Mediation

Grid Services and Scheduling

Mobile and P2P Services

Service Composition

Adaptive Services

Data Intensive Services

Service Management: Registry, Reliability

XML Processing

Service Modeling

Business Services: Transaction, Licensing and SLA Assessment

Service Discovery and Selection

Part 2: Research Track Short Papers

Quality of Service (Policy, Transaction and Monitoring)

Business Service Modeling

Service Assembly

Part 3: Industrial Track Vision and Full Papers

Vision Papers

Experience with Deployed SOA

SOA Architectures

Early Adoption of SOA Technology

Requirements and Method for Assessment of Service Interoperability

Stanislav Pokraev[1], Dick Quartel[2], Maarten W.A. Steen[1], and Manfred Reichert[2]

[1] Telematica Instituut, The Netherlands, P.O. Box 589
7500 AN Enschede, The Netherlands
Centre for Telematics and Information Technology,
[2] University of Twente, P.O. Box 217, 7500 AE, Enschede, The Netherlands
Stanislav.Pokraev@telin.nl, D.A.C.Quartel@ewi.utwente.nl,
Maarten.Steen@telin.nl, M.U.Reichert@ewi.utwente.nl

Abstract. Service interoperability is a major obstacle in realizing the SOA vision. Interoperability is the capability of multiple, autonomous and heterogeneous systems to use each other's services effectively. It is about the meaningful sharing of functionality and information that leads to the achievement of a common goal. In this paper we systematically explain what interoperability means and analyze possible interoperability problems. Further, we define requirements for service interoperability and present a method to assess whether a composite system meets the identified requirements.

Keywords: service modeling, service interoperability, formal verification.

1 Introduction

The integration of software systems is a major challenge for companies today. Both organizational forces, such as *business process integration (BPI)*, and technology drivers, such as the move towards *service-oriented architectures (SOA)*, put increasing pressure on software engineers to reuse and integrate existing system services, rather than building new systems from scratch. However, the lack of interoperability forms a major stumbling block in the integration process. To address this issue a lot of efforts are currently being invested in standardizing service description languages and protocols for service interactions such as WSDL, BPEL, WS-CDL. Unfortunately, these efforts mainly address what we call *syntactic interoperability*, whereas *semantic interoperability* is just starting to be addressed by initiatives such as the SWSI[1] and the WSMO[2] working groups.

In this paper we analyze what it means for software systems to be *interoperable*. Based on the results of this analysis we identify possible interoperability problems and define requirements for appropriate solutions. Next, we propose a conceptual framework for service modeling as well as a method for formally verifying the interoperability of an integrated system, starting with an integration goal. The latter

[1] http://www.swsi.org/
[2] http://www.wsmo.org/

A. Dan and W. Lamersdorf (Eds.): ICSOC 2006, LNCS 4294, pp. 1 – 14, 2006.

qualification becomes necessary because a composite system has properties that emerge due to the interaction of its components. Assessing interoperability of such a system means that one can check if a desired goal (i.e., a number of emerging properties) can be achieved by the elements of that system in concert.

The paper is organized as follows: Section 2 presents our conceptual framework for service modeling. Section 3 explains what interoperability means, analyze possible interoperability problems, and define requirements for service interoperability. Section 4 presents our method for formal verification whether a composite system meets the identified interoperability requirements. Section 5 gives an overview of the state-of-the art and the related work. Finally, Section 6 presents our conclusions and discusses some future research directions.

2 A Conceptual Framework for Service Modeling

This section presents our conceptual framework for service modeling. The framework defines concepts and a notation to model interactions between systems from a *communication, behavioral* and *information* perspective. The presented concepts are generic in that they can be applied in different application domains and at successive abstraction levels. This helps limiting the number of required concepts. The core concept in our framework is the *interaction* concept. It supports a *constraint-oriented style* of service specification, which facilitates the addressing of interoperability requirements by modeling the participation of interacting entities as separate constraints and by reasoning about satisfiability of the logical conjunction of these constraints. The conceptual framework is based on earlier work [12][13].

The ***communication perspective*** is concerned with modeling the interacting systems and their interconnection structure. For that purpose we introduce two basic concepts, namely *Entity* and *Interaction point*.

An *Entity* models the existence of some system, while abstracting from its properties. An *Interaction point* models the existence of some mechanism that enables interaction between two or more systems, while abstracting from the properties of the mechanism. In general, the interaction mechanism is identified by its location (e.g., the combination of an IP address and port number can be used to identify a TCP/UDP socket).

We adopt Webster's definition of a system, which defines a system as "*a regularly interacting or interdependent group of items, components or parts, forming a unified whole*". This definition distinguishes between two system perspectives: an *internal* perspective, i.e., the "*regularly interacting or interdependent group of items, components or parts*", and an *external* perspective, i.e., the "*unified whole*". Fig. 1 illustrates both perspectives.

From an external perspective a system is modeled as a single entity (e.g., *System A*) having one or more interaction points (e.g., IP_1, IP_2 and IP_3). From an internal perspective a system is modeled as a structure of interconnected system parts (e.g., *Systems* A_1, *System* A_2 and *System* A_3).

The ***behavioral perspective*** is concerned with modeling the behavioral properties of a system, i.e., the activities that are performed by the system as well as the relations among them. For that purpose we introduce four basic concepts, namely, *Action, Interaction, Interaction contribution* and one relation, namely, *Causality relation.*

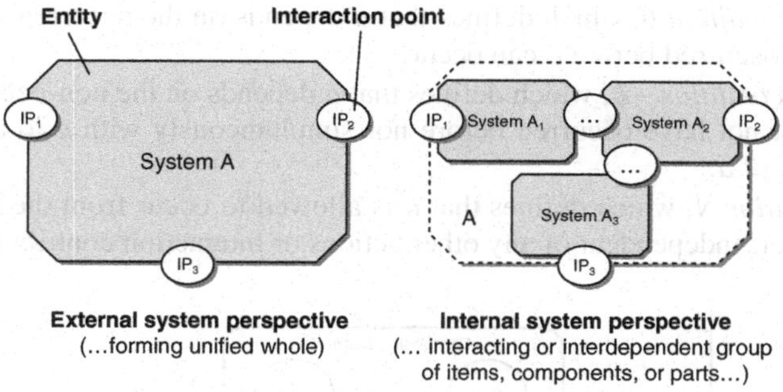

Fig. 1. Communication perspective

An *Action* represents a unit of activity that either occurs (completes) or does not occur (complete) during the execution of a system. Furthermore, an action only represents the activity result (effect) that is established upon completion, and abstracts from the way this result is achieved.

An *Interaction* represents a common activity of two or more entities. An interaction can be considered as a refinement of an action, defining the contribution of each entity involved in the interaction. Therefore, an interaction inherits the properties of an action. In addition, an interaction either occurs for all entities that are involved, or does not occur for any of them. In case an interaction occurs, the same result is established for all involved entities.

An *Interaction contribution* represents the participation (or responsibility) of an entity that is involved in an interaction. An interaction can only occur if each involved entity can participate. An entity can participate if the causality condition of its interaction contribution is satisfied (see below). In addition, an interaction contribution may define constraints on the possible results that can be established in the interaction. This means that an interaction represents a negotiation among the involved entities, only defining the potential results of the interaction, while abstracting from how they are established. We distinguish three basic types of negotiation between two entities *A* and *B*.

- *Value checking:* entity A proposes a single value x as interaction result and entity B proposes a single value y. The interaction can only occur if $x = y$, in which case the interaction result is x;
- *Value passing:* entity A proposes a single value x as interaction result and entity B accepts a set of values Y. The interaction can only occur if $x \in Y$, in which case the interaction result is x;
- *Value generation:* entity A accepts a set of values X as interaction result and entity B accepts a set of values Y. The interaction can only occur if $X \cap Y \neq \emptyset$, in which case the interaction result is a value from the intersection of X and Y (while abstracting from the choice of the particular value).

For an action or interaction contribution, say a, a *Causality relation* defines the condition that must be satisfied to enable the occurrence of a. Three basic conditions are distinguished:

- *Enabling condition b*, which defines that *a* depends on the occurrence of *b*, i.e., *b* must have occurred before *a* can occur;
- *Disabling condition ¬b*, which defines that *a* depends on the non-occurrence of *b*, i.e., *b* must not have occurred before nor simultaneously with *a* to allow for the occurrence of *a*;
- *Start condition* √, which defines that *a* is allowed to occur from the beginning of the behavior, independent of any other actions or interaction contributions.

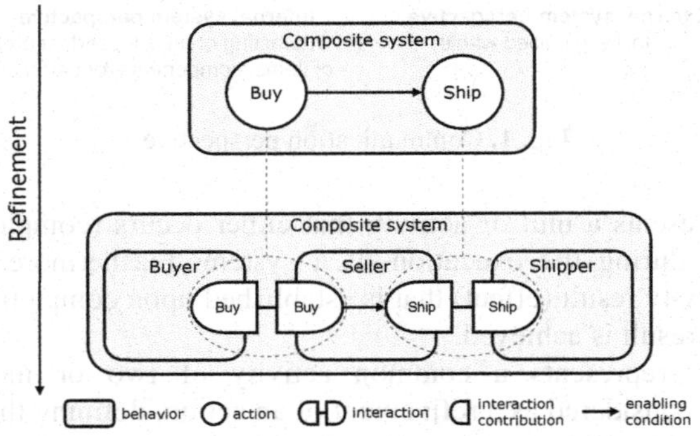

Fig. 2. Refinement of an action

The behavioral concepts are illustrated in Fig. 2. At the higher abstraction level action Buy is followed by action Ship. At the lower level the actions are refined by assigning actors (e.g., Buyer, Seller and Shipper) that contribute to the result of these actions. Constraints on the results of interactions that systems may define are discussed later after having introduced the information perspective.

Basic conditions can be combined to represent more complex causality conditions. For this we provide the *AND* and the *OR* operators, which define that a conjunction and disjunction of conditions must be satisfied, respectively.

The ***information perspective*** is concerned with modeling the *subject domain* of a system. First, we explain what subject domain is and then we introduce five basic modeling concepts.

Software systems manage a domain of *lexical* items. These items represent entities and phenomena in the real world that are *identifiable* by the system (e.g., people, companies or locations). In this context we denote the part of the world that is identifiable by the systems as *subject domain* of the system.

Software systems interact with their environment by exchanging *messages*. Messages that enter the system request or update the state of its lexical domain. Messages that leave the system request information about the system's subject domain or provide information about the lexical domain of the system.

Messages consist of *data* that represent property values of entities or phenomena from the subject domain. The data in the messages have meaning only when interpreted in terms of the subject domain model of the system.

To model the information perspective we provide five basic concepts, namely *Individual*, *Class*, *Property*, *Result constraint* and *Causality constraint*.

An *Individual* represents an entity or phenomenon in the subject domain of the system, e.g., the person "*John*", the hospital "*Saint Joseph*" or the city "*London*".

A *Class* represents an abstract type of entities or phenomena in the subject domain of the system, e.g., "*Patient*", "*Hospital*" or "*City*".

A *Property* represent possible relations that can exist between entities or phenomena in the system's subject domain, e.g., "*admitted to*", "*is a*" or "*is located in*".

A *Result constraint* models a condition on the result of an action or interaction contribution that must be satisfied after the occurrence of the action or interaction contribution.

A *Causality constraint* models a condition on the results established in causal predecessors (i.e., actions or interaction contributions) that must be satisfied to enable the occurrence of an action or interaction contribution.

Fig. 3 shows how information concepts are related to interactions.

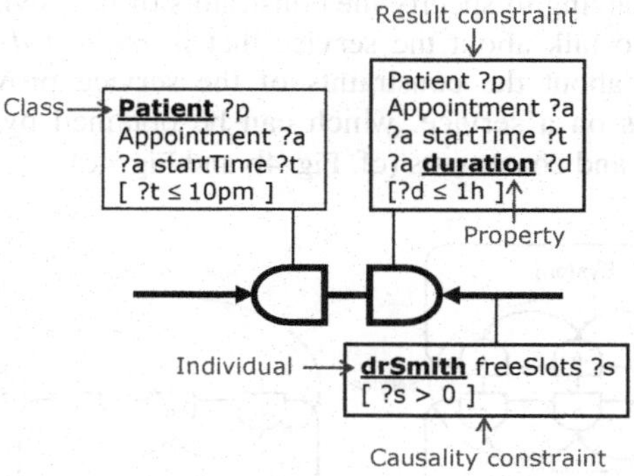

Fig. 3. Relating information concepts to an interaction

In the example a system requests an appointment for a patient starting not later than 10pm. The hospital system accepts any appointments with duration less or equal than 1 hour. In addition, the interaction can only happen if Dr. Smith (the healthcare professional responsible for this case) has free slots in his calendar. Indeed, this is a causality constraint if the individual drSmith has been established as a result of a preceding (inter)action.

We use *Description Logics (DL)*[6], more specifically *OWL-DL*[7] to represent our information concepts by a concrete formalism. DL ontologies consist of *concepts*, *roles* and *individuals*. *Individuals* represent entities of phenomena from the real world, *concepts* represent abstract classes of entities or phenomena, and *roles* represent relations between entities or phenomena.

A concept can be *atomic*, i.e., denoted by its name (e.g., *Patient*, *Room* or *Hospital*) or defined as an expression that contains other concepts, roles and composition operators such as *union* or *intersection*.

Besides concepts, individuals and relations, DL ontologies consist of a set of *axioms* specifying the properties of the concepts, roles and individuals. Examples of such axioms are concept inclusion $(C(x) \wedge C \subseteq D \rightarrow D(x))$, role inclusion

$(R(x, y) \wedge R \subseteq S \rightarrow S(x, y))$, transitive role $(R(x, y) \wedge R(y, z) \rightarrow R(x, z))$, etc. For the formal semantics of OWL-DL we refer to [7].

Putting together the three modeling perspectives yields an *integrated service model.* A *service* is a set of related interactions between the system and its environment. An example is given in Fig. 4a. It shows two interacting behaviors, representing the behaviors the one of a system and another one of its environment. These entities can engage in three interactions *a*, *b* and *c*, which are related by causality relations. The interaction contributions can be adorned with result constraints and the causality relations with causality constraints respectively. Taken together, the interactions, their causal relations and the information constraints define the service between the system and the environment.

Our definition of service does not include a sense of direction. It is an interaction that models a common activity of two or more entities in which some results (values) can be established, but abstracts from who takes the initiative or the direction in which values flow. However, often it is useful to talk about the service that is *offered* by a system without having to specify the constraints of the environment. Likewise, it is also often useful to talk about the service that is *requested* by an entity without making assumptions about the constraints of the service provider. These are two complementary views on a service, which can be obtained by only specifying one entity's contributions and constraints (cf. Fig. 4b and Fig. 4c).

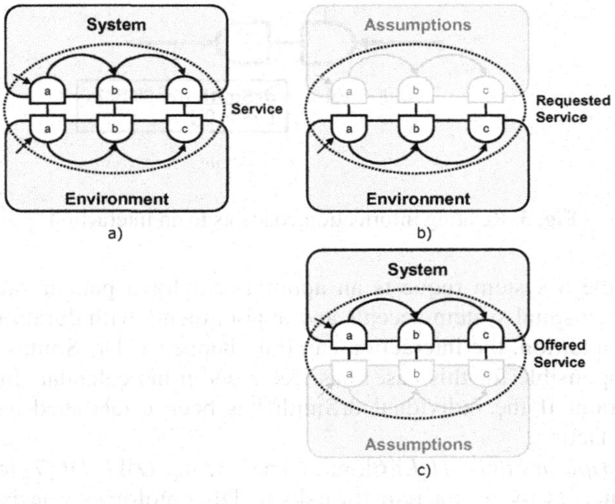

Fig. 4. Service model

3 Requirements for Interoperability

In our approach we distinguish three different levels of interoperability, namely *syntactic*, *semantic* and *pragmatic*.

Syntactic interoperability is concerned with ensuring that data from the exchanged messages are in compatible formats. The message sender encodes data in a message using syntactic rules, specified in some grammar. The message receiver decodes the received message using syntactic rules defined in the same or some other grammar. Syntactic interoperability problems arise when the sender's encoding rules are incompatible with the receiver's decoding rules, which leads to (construction of) mismatching message parse trees.

Web Services standards address syntactic interoperability by providing XML-based standards such as SOAP, WSDL and BPEL. XML is a platform-independent markup language capable of describing both data and data structure. This way, different systems can parse each other's messages, check if these messages are well-formed, and validate if the messages adhere to a specific syntactic schema. In our approach we adopt XML to deal with syntactic interoperability and only focus on semantic and pragmatic interoperability.

Semantic interoperability is concerned with ensuring that the exchanged information has the same meaning for both message sender and receiver. The data in the messages have meaning only when interpreted in terms of the respective subject domain models. However, the message sender does not always know the subject domain model of the message receiver. Depending on its knowledge, the message sender makes assumptions about the subject domain model of the receiver and uses this assumed subject domain model to construct a message and to communicate it. Semantic interoperability problems arise when the message sender and receiver have a different *conceptualization* or use a different *representation* of the entity types, properties and values from their subject domains. Examples of such differences are *naming conflicts* (same representation is used to designate different entities, entity types or properties, or different representations are used to designate the same entity, entity type or property), *generalization conflicts* (the meaning of an entity type or a property is more general than the meaning of the corresponding entity type or property), *aggregation conflicts* (an entity type aggregates two or more corresponding entity types), *overlapping conflicts* (an entity type or a property partially overlaps a corresponding entity type or a property), *isomorphism conflicts* (the same entity type or property is defined differently in different subject domain models), *identification conflicts* (the same entity is identified by different properties), *entity-property conflicts* (an entity type in modeled as a property), etc.

To address the identified semantic conflicts we define the following requirement:

> *Requirement 1:* A necessary condition for the semantic interoperability of two systems is the existence of a translation function that maps the entity types, properties and values of the subject domain model of the first system to the respective entity types, properties and values of the subject domain model of the second system.

Pragmatic interoperability is concerned with ensuring that message sender and receiver share the same expectation about the effect of the exchanged messages.

When a system receives a messages it changes its state, sends a message back to the environment, or both[18]. In most cases, messages sent to the system change or request the system state, and messages sent from the system change or request the state of the environment. That is, the messages are always sent with some *intention* for achieving some desired effect. In most of the cases the effect is realized not only by a single message but by a number of messages send in some order. Pragmatic interoperability problems arise when the intended effect differs from the actual effect.

> *Requirement 2:* A necessary condition for pragmatic interoperability of a single interaction is that at least one result that satisfies the constraints of all contributing systems can be established.

As said earlier, a service is a set of related interactions between the system and its environment.

> *Requirement 3:* A necessary condition for pragmatic interoperability of a service is that Requirement 2 is met for all of its interactions and they can occur in a causal order, allowed by all participating systems.

The requirements are discussed in more details in the next section.

4 Formal Verification of Service Designs

In this section we present a formal method for checking if a service design meets the requirements identified in the previous section.

To address *Requirement 1* we need a method to establish mappings between values, concepts and relations from subject domains of the systems being integrated. This method requires understanding of the meaning of values, concepts and relations from the respective subject domains and cannot be fully automated. However, tools exist that use sophisticated heuristic algorithms to discover possible mappings and provide mechanisms for specifying these mappings. Besides mapping there are two other relevant approaches: alignment and merging of the subject domain models. Alignment is the process of making the subject domain models consistent and coherent with one another while keeping them separate. Merging is the process of creating a single subject domain model that includes the information from all source subject domain models.

To address the semantic conflicts identified in the previous section we need a formal language capable of expressing mappings. In the following we show how some of the identified problems can be addressed using OWL-DL axioms. In the explanation below we use the prefixes `a:` and `b:` to identify a concept or a relation in the subject domain model of *System A* and *System B* respectively.

Naming conflicts can be addressed using axioms that assert sameness (e.g., `a:Medicine` ≡ `b:Drug`) or difference (`a:Employee` ≠ `b:Employee`). Aggregation conflicts can be addressed using axioms that define a new concept as aggregation of the corresponding concepts (e.g., `a:Address` ≡ `List (b:StreetNo, b:Street, b:City)`. Generalization conflicts can be addressed using axioms that assert the generalization (or specialization) relation between the respective concepts (`a:Human` ⊆ `b:Patient`). Overlapping conflicts can be addressed using axioms that assert that corresponding concepts are not disjoint (e.g., ¬(`a:Man` ∩ `b:Adult`) ⊆ ⊥).

Unfortunately, not all types of mappings can be expressed using OWL. For example, OWL does not allow for property chaining (e.g., `a:hasUncle` ≡ `b:hasBrother` • `b:hasFather`) and qualified cardinality restrictions `a:SafeBuilding = b:Building ∩ ≥2b:hasStairs.b:FireEscapeStairs` which makes it difficult (in some cases impossible) to deal with isomorphic and cardinality conflicts. However, some of these issues are being dealt with in the upcoming version of OWL 1.1.

To address *Requirement 2* we define a class as an intersection of the classes that define the admissible results of an interaction for all participating interaction contributions, and check if the concept that represents the class is satisfiable.

As said earlier, we use OWL-DL as a representation system for individuals, classes and properties as well as to define result and causality constraints. This way, we can describe the subject domains of the system, define classes that represent the conditions and results of actions and interaction contributions and reason if these classes can have instances or not.

The basic reasoning task in OWL-DL is *subsumption check* – a task of checking if a concept D is more general than a concept C. In other words, subsumption is checking if the criteria for being individual of type C imply the criteria for being individual of type D. The concept D is called subsumer and the concept C is called subsumee. If C subsumes D and D subsumes C, then we can conclude that class C and D are equivalent.

Checking concept satisfiability is a special case of subsumption reasoning. In this case the subsumer is the empty concept (⊥). If a concept C is subsumed by the empty concept we say that the concept *C* is not satisfiable. This means that no individual can be of type C.

Requirement 2 is illustrated in Fig. 5. In this example, any appointment not earlier than 10pm with duration no longer that 1 hour is a possible result of the interaction *a*.

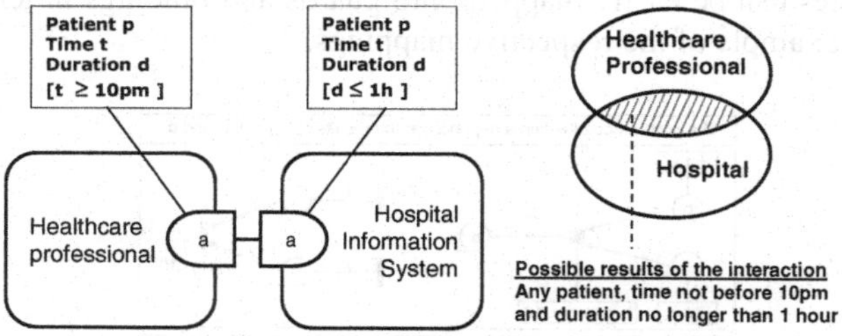

Fig. 5. Example of Requirement 2

To check if a composite system meets *Requirement 3* we translate a model of a composite service described in our language to a Coloured Petri Net (CPN)[8][9]. This way we can construct the corresponding occurrence graph and reason about the dynamic properties of the model. The presented mapping is partially based on previous work [16].

A classical Petri Net (PN) consists of a set of *places* (represented by circles), a set of *transitions* (represented by black bars), *directed arcs* connecting places to transitions or transitions to places, and *markings* assigning one or more *tokens* (represented by black dots) to some places. CPNs extend the classical PNs by providing a mechanism for associating a *value* of a certain type to each token. In addition, a transition can be enabled only if its input tokens satisfy certain conditions (*guards*) and produce output tokens that represent new values (*bindings*). In this way, a transition can be seen as a function that maps input values to output values in a certain context.

An action in our language maps to a transition in terms of PNs. A transition can be executed when all incoming places contain at least one token. On execution it consumes a token from all incoming places and produces a token in all outgoing places. Similar to actions, enabled transitions may execute in parallel. Nets that correspond to some elementary causality relations from our language are depicted in Fig. 6:

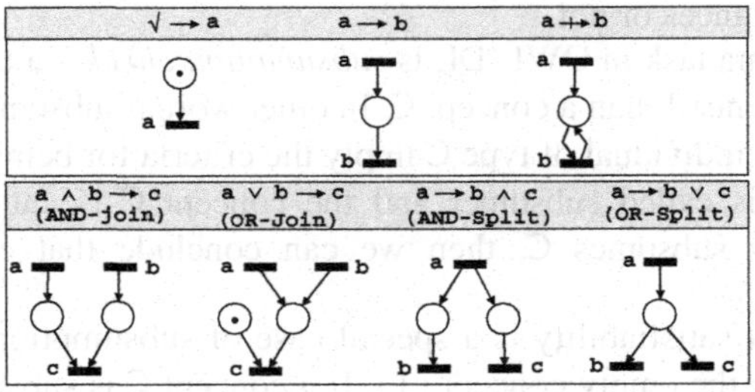

Fig. 6. Mapping to Petri Nets

As said earlier, the occurrence or the result of an action (or interaction) may depend on the result of one or more causal predecessors (actions or interactions). Such dependences can be easily mapped onto guards and bindings in terms of CPNs. Fig. 7 shows an example of the respective mappings.

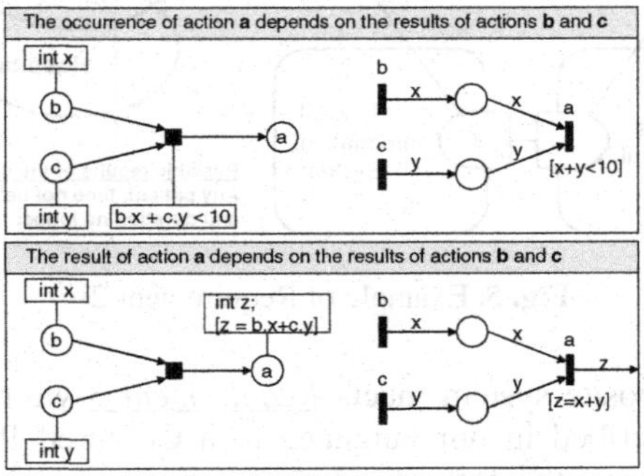

Fig. 7. Mapping to Coloured Petri Nets

The presented mappings allow models expressed in our language to be translated into CPN and analyzed using existing tools.

To check if the composition from our example meets <u>*Requirement 3*</u>, we translate the model to the corresponding CPN using the presented mapping and construct the occurrence graph of that net. We use the constructed graph to check for the existence of a marking in which the results defined by the participating systems can be established. Next, we check if the order of the results establishment meets the causality constraints of the participating systems. The requirement is illustrated in Fig. 8 and explained in an example below.

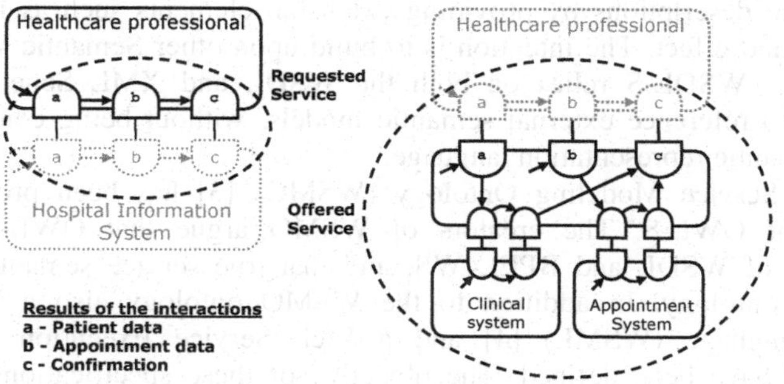

Fig. 8. Example of Requirement 3

Consider a healthcare professional who wants to refer a patient to a specialist. His system allows him to send the patient's clinical data, followed by the appointment data and finally to receive a confirmation from the hospital information system. I.e., the allowed interaction order of the healthcare professional is *a, b, c.* The hospital information system can either first receive the patient's clinical data or the appointment data. Once it has both it registers the data in the clinical and appointment systems and sends back a confirmation to the healthcare professional. I.e., the allowed interaction order of the hospital information system is *a, b, c*, or *b, a, c*. In the example, the systems are interoperable because the order *a, b, c* meets the constraints of both the healthcare professional and the hospital information system.

To validate our conceptual framework, we implemented a prototype that checks if a composite system meets the identified requirements. Our prototype uses Racer[14] Renew[10] and CPNTools[15].

5 State-of-the Art and Related Work

OWL-S[11] is an OWL ontology for Web Services, aiming at making them computer-interpretable, to enable automatic service discovery and invocation, i.e., breaking down interoperability barriers through precise service semantics. For that reason OWL-S defines a class *Service*, where all service properties are very general. The idea is to provide a conceptual basis for building service taxonomies, but it is expected that taxonomies will be created according to functional and domain-specific needs. A service has a *ServiceProfile*. This is a high level description of the service and its provider. A *ServiceProfile* describes the functional and non-functional service properties in a human readable way. The service is formally described by a *ServiceModel*. It provides means for describing the data and control flow in case of a composite service. Finally, a service has a *ServiceGrounding*, which is a specification of service access information such as communication protocols, and transport mechanisms.

IBM together with LSDIS Lab at University Of Georgia has proposed lightweight approach for adding semantics to Web Service descriptions, WSDL-S[1]. It is based in the work done in METEOR-S[17]. WSDL-S provides a mechanism to annotate WSDL service descriptions by providing extension elements such as input, output, precondition and effect. The intention is to build upon other Semantic Web Services related efforts. WSDL-S relies on both the WSDL and XML Schema extension mechanisms to reference external semantic models, without being constrained to a particular semantic representation language.

The Web Service Modeling Ontology (WSMO) [3] has been proposed as an alternative for OWL-S. The creators of WSMO argue that OWL-S is only a formalization of WSDL and BPEL4WS, and that true service semantics require a much richer ontology. In addition to the WSMO ontology also a Web Service Modeling Language (WSML) [4] and a Web Service Execution Environment (WSMX) [5] have been defined. The objective of these specifications is to allow automatic service discovery, composition, execution and interoperation in the context of Web and Grid.

The Semantic Web Services Framework [2] is a relatively new initiative, which addresses interoperability by proposing a language and ontology for specifying the semantics of Web services. The language consists of two parts, namely, a first order logic language for describing web services (SWSL-FOL) and a rule-based language with non-monotonic semantics (SWSL-Rules). SWSL-FOL is used to formally specify service characteristics whereas SWSL-Rules is used to reason about those characteristics and execute services. SWSF also defines a formal ontology for representing service characteristics called First-Order Logic Ontology for Web Services (FLOWS).

6 Conclusions

The main contributions of this work are the definition of a conceptual framework for service modeling, the identification of requirements for semantic and pragmatic interoperability and a method for assessing whether a composite system meets the identified requirements. We did this by first analyzing and defining what it means for software systems to be interoperable. We identified three different levels of interoperability – the *syntactic*, *semantic* and *pragmatic* level – and defined the requirements for assessing interoperability at each of these levels. Since we feel that syntactic interoperability is sufficiently addressed by existing standards and initiatives, we focused on the semantic and pragmatic interoperability requirements.

What makes our work different from the related work in the area is that our method is based on a new service modeling framework which provides generic concepts that can be applied in different application domains and at successive abstraction levels. The key concept in our framework (the concept *Interaction)* supports a *constraint-oriented style* of service specification. This style allows service requestors and providers to *explicitly* specify their assumptions about the environment of their systems. This in turn enables formal verification of the interoperability of the composite system by checking constraint satisfiability.

Our approach combines the precise, but abstract, definition of the behavior of services and their compositions with a formal definition of the information being exchanged between services. Once we have specified services in this formalism, we are able to apply a combination of a formal logic reasoner and a formal behavior analysis tool to verify the semantic and the pragmatic interoperability of a given set of services.

There are a number of issues that we still need to address to make our method more practical.

First, we cannot assume that existing services are specified using our modeling notation. Therefore, we are working on providing mappings from existing service description languages and tools for the (semi)-automatic transformations of service models from descriptions in WSDL and BPEL.

Second, we plan to investigate ways of presenting the verification results back into the original models. Currently, the outcome of applying our method is a yes/no-answer. However, it is not very satisfactory to find out that a particular composition of services is not interoperable. In that case more feedback is required as to the cause of the interoperability problem.

Finally, we would like to investigate ways to (semi)-automatically derive mediators capable of solving detected semantic and pragmatic interoperability problems. Such mediators should implement mappings between the information and behavioral models to overcome semantic and pragmatic interoperability problems.

Acknowledgments. The presented work has been done in the Freeband Communication project A-Muse (http://a-muse.freeband.nl). Freeband Communication (http://www.freeband.nl) is sponsored by the Dutch government under contract BSIK 03025.We would like to thank Henk Jonkers, Patrick Strating and Rogier Brussee from the Telematica Instituut, the Netherlands for their valuable comments on this work.

References

1. Akkiraju, R., Farrell, J., Miller, J., Nagarajan, M., Schmidt, M.-T., Sheth, A., Verma, K. Web Service Semantics - WSDL-S. W3C Member Submission 7 November 2005, Version 1.0, http://www.w3.org/Submission/2005/SUBM-WSDL-S-20051107/
2. Battle, S., Bernstein, A., Boley, H., Grosof, B., Gruninger, M., Hull, R., Kifer, M., Martin, D., McIlraith, S., McGuinness, D., Su, J., Tabet, S. Semantic Web Services Framework (SWSF) Overview, W3C Member Submission 9 September 2005, http://www.w3.org/Submission/SWSF/
3. Bruijn, J. de, Bussler, C., Domingue, J., Fensel, D., Hepp, M., Keller, U., Kifer, M., König-Ries, B., Kopecky, J., Lara, R., Lausen, H., Oren, E., Polleres, A., Roman, D., Scicluna, J., Stollberg, M. Web Service Modeling Ontology (WSMO), W3C Member Submission 3 June 2005, http://www.w3.org/Submission/WSMO/
4. Bruijn, J. de, Fensel, D., Keller, U., Kifer, M., Lausen, H., Krummenacher, R., Polleres, A., Predoiu, L. Web Service Modeling Language (WSML), W3C Member Submission 3 June 2005, http://www.w3.org/Submission/WSML/
5. Bussler, C., Cimpian, E., Fensel, D., Gomez, J. M., Haller, A., Haselwanter, T., Kerrigan, M., Mocan, A., Moran, M., Oren, E., Sapkota, B., Toma, I., Viskova, J., Vitvar, T., Zaremba, M. Web Service Execution Environment (WSMX), W3C Member Submission 3 June 2005, http://www.w3.org/Submission/WSMX/

6. Calvanese, D., McGuinness, D., Nardi, D., Patel-Schneider, P. The Description Logic Handbook: Theory, Implementation and Applications, Cambridge University Press, 2003. http://www.cambridge.org/uk/catalogue/catalogue.asp?isbn=0521781760
7. Dean, M (eds.), Schreiber, G.(eds.), Bechhofer, S., van Harmelen, F., Hendler, J., Horrocks, I., McGuinness, D. L., Patel-Schneider, P. F., Stein, L. A. OWL Web Ontology Language Reference, W3C Recommendation 10 February 2004, http://www.w3.org/TR/owl-ref/
8. Jensen, K. Coloured Petri Nets. Basic Concepts, Analysis Methods and Practical Use. Volume 1, Basic Concepts. Monographs in Theoretical Computer Science, Springer-Verlag, 1992. ISBN: 3-540-60943-1.
9. Jensen, K. Coloured Petri Nets. Basic Concepts, Analysis Methods and Practical Use. Volume 2, Analysis Methods. Monographs in Theoretical Computer Science, Springer - Verlag, 1994. ISBN: 3 -540-58276-2
10. Kummer, O., Wienberg, F., Duvigneau, M., Köhler, M., Moldt, D., Rölke, H. Renew - The Reference Net Workshop. In Veerbeek, E. (editor), Tool Demonstrations. 24th International Conference on Application and Theory of Petri Nets (ATPN 2003). International Conference on Business Process Management (BPM 2003)., pages 99-102.
11. Martin, D., Burstein, M., Hobbs, J., Lassila, O., McDermott, D., McIlraith, S., Narayanan, S., Paolucci, M., Parsia, B., Payne, T., Sirin, E., Srinivasan, N., Sycara, K. OWL-S: Semantic Markup for Web Services W3C Member Submission 22 November 2004, http://www.w3.org/Submission/OWL-S/
12. Quartel, D.A.C., Dijkman R.M., Sinderen van M. J. Methodological support for service-oriented design with ISDL. In: Proceedings of the 2nd International Conference on Service Oriented Computing (ICSOC 2004), New York City, NY, USA, 2004.
13. Quartel, D.A.C., Ferreira Pires, L., Sinderen, van M. J. On Architectural Support for Behaviour Refinement in Distributed Systems Design. In: Journal of integrated design and process science online, 06(01) ISNN 1092-0617.
14. Racer Systems, Racer Reasoner, http://www.racer-systems.com/, 2005
15. Ratzer, A. V., Wells, L., Lassen, H. M., Laursen, M., Qvortrup, J. F., Stissing, M. S., Westergaard, M., Christensen, S., Jensen, K. CPN Tools for Editing, Simulating, and Analysing Coloured Petri Net, In: Proceedings of the 24th International Conference on Applications and Theory of Petri Nets (ICATPN 2003), Eindhoven, The Netherlands, June 23-27, 2003, pages 450-462. Volume 2679 of Lecture Notes in Computer Science / Wil M. P. van der Aalst and Eike Best (Eds.) Springer-Verlag, June 2003.
16. Sinderen, M. J. van, Ferreira Pires, L., Vissers, C. A., Katoen, J.P. A design model for open distributed processing systems. Computer Networks and ISDN Systems, Vol. 27, 1995, pp. 1263-1285. ISSN 0169-7552.
17. Verma, K., Gomadam, K., Sheth, A., Miller, J., Wu, Z. The METEOR-S Approach for Configuring and Executing Dynamic Web Processes", Technical Report . Date: 6-24-05.
18. Wieringa, R. J. Design Methods for Reactive Systems: Yourdon, Statemate, and the UML. Morgan Kaufmann, 2003. http://www.mkp.com/dmrs

An Aspect-Oriented Framework for Service Adaptation

Woralak Kongdenfha[1], Régis Saint-Paul[1], Boualem Benatallah[1], and Fabio Casati[2]

[1] SCSE, University of New South Wales, Sydney, NSW, 2052, Australia
{woralakk, regiss, boualem}@cse.unsw.edu.au
[2] DIT, University of Trento, Via Sommarive 14, I-38050 POVO (TN), Italy
casati@dit.unitn.it

Abstract. Web services are emerging technologies for integrating heterogeneous applications. In application integration, the internal services are interconnected with other external resources to form a virtual enterprise. This puts new requirements on the standardization in terms of external specification, i.e., a combination of service interfaces and business protocols, that interconnected services have to obey. However, previously developed service implementations do not always conform to the standard and require adjustment.

In this paper, we characterize the problem of aligning internal service implementation to a standardized external specification. We propose an Aspect oriented framework as a solution to provide support for service adaptation. In particular, the framework consists of i) a taxonomy of the different possible types of mismatch between external specification and service implementation, ii) a repository of aspect-based templates to automate the task of handling mismatches, and iii) a tool to support template instantiation and their execution together with the service implementation.

1 Introduction

The essence of service-oriented computing (SOC) lies in the creation of loosely coupled, reusable components that can be invoked and composed by clients. In a successful SOC environment, a service may invoke several other services as part of its execution, and may in turn be invoked by several clients. The creation of such modular components and of the infrastructure for their secure and reliable invocation is a challenging endeavor that is being tackled by scores of companies and researchers through novel technologies, methodologies, and standards.

The realization of SOC raises the need for methodologies and tools to manage *service adaptation*. Service adaptation refers to the problem of modifying a service so that it can correctly interact with another service, overcoming functional and non-functional mismatches and incompatibilities.

There are two main situations in which adaptation is needed, both likely to be fairly common in SOC. In a first scenario, the ACME company offers

A. Dan and W. Lamersdorf (Eds.): ICSOC 2006, LNCS 4294, pp. 15–26, 2006.

a service that implements some business process (e.g., a quotation and ordering process). As part of exposing a service to clients, the company also provides the *external specifications* of the service, that is, the description of the service interface (typically in WSDL), the business protocol supported by the service (i.e., the order in which the interface methods can be invoked), and possibly other non-functional attributes. The external specifications are used at development time to write clients that can correctly interact with a service, and at run time by the middleware that supports service selection and interoperability. In some cases, external specifications are mandated by standardization consortia (such as RosettaNet), that define how services in a certain industry sector should behave. Such standardization is important as it simplifies interoperability and promotes competition (if many services support the same external specifications, it is technically easy for clients to switch between providers based on economical convenience). If ACME wants many customers to use its Web service, then it has to make its Web service as interoperable as possible. This implies the need of being compliant with a variety of different external specification requirements, provided by different standardization consortia or different customers. Hence, while the service functionality remains to a large extent the same, a service needs to adapt to different external specifications. As the number of services provided by ACME grows, and as the number of customers grows, managing adaptation quickly becomes a daunting effort.

In a second scenario, ACME runs (composite) services which are themselves implemented by invoking other services, possibly offered by third parties. It is not infrequent to have many ACME services invoke a same third-party service, e.g., a payment service offered by a financial institution. Hence, a version change of the external service would have a deep impact on the collection of composite services, possibly preventing some or all of them from performing their task. In this case, some or all of the composite services need to be adapted to interact with the new version of the invoked service. Again, as scale increases, so does the complexity of the adaptation management effort.

This paper presents a framework and a tool for managing service adaptation. We argue that, to simplify adaptation, it is important to separate the adaptation logic from the business logic. Such separation helps to avoid the need of developing and maintaining several versions of a service implementation and isolates the adaptation logic in a single place. We further argue that adaptation can be seen as a cross-cutting concern, i.e., it is, from the developer and project architecture point of view, transversal to the other functional concerns of the service. This is particularly evident in the second scenario above: if the invoked service changes the interface or protocol, then all the composite services invoking it will have to undergo analogous changes to interact with the new version of the invoked service. Consistently with this vision, we propose the use of an aspect-oriented programming (AOP) approach to weave adaptation solutions into the different composite services that need to be modified. To the best of our knowledge, this is the first work to identify service adaptation as a cross-cutting concern and to propose an aspect oriented approach to tackle it.

In a nutshell, the proposed approach works as follows. First, we provide a taxonomy of mismatches that can occur between two services. We specifically focus on service interfaces and protocols, the two most commonly used parts of external specifications. The reasoning behind having a taxonomy of mismatches is because we argue that similar mismatches can be addressed with similar modifications to the service implementation. Then, for each mismatch, we provide a template that embodies the AOP approach to adaptation. Specifically, the template contains a set of <pointcut, advice> pairs that define where the adaptation logic is to be applied, and what this logic is. As a very simple example, if the base service changed the signature of an operation, the pointcuts will be the activities in the composite services where the operation is invoked, and the adaptation logic consists in modifying the invoked message so that it can be made compatible with the new interface. In our approach, pointcuts are specified as queries over business process execution, that is, over the execution of composite services. In this paper, and in the tool we developed, we assume that services are implemented in BPEL, though the concepts are independent of the specific language adopted. The advices are therefore also specified in BPEL, as snippets that modify the behavior of the services at the specified pointcuts. In fact, since, as we will see, adaptation needs arise from the conjunction of a given service composition and a particular client interaction, weaving adaptation code at runtime is more suited than static weaving done at the code level as it allows for query expressed on particular execution contexts.

Finally, we present the development and runtime tools we have implemented to support aspect-oriented adaptation. All of the above ingredients of the solution correspond to contributions of this paper, with the exception of the identification of the mismatch taxonomy, which is part of our earlier work [3].

2 Service Mismatches

We illustrate an instance of service adaptation problem as it occurs in the first scenario discussed in the introduction through a supply chain example. Figure 1 shows a model of the interactions that take place in a supply chain process. This model is expressed using the Business Process Modeling Notation [15], which is a high-level equivalent of BPEL [11]. In this supply chain process, the client follows a standardized External Specification (ES) which specifies a protocol that allows the client to performs operations in one of the two sequences, namely S_1 (top part of the client flow) or S_2 (bottom part of the client flow).

In this example, the implementation of the Business Process (BP) (bottom part of the figure), differs from the target ES, and therefore is incompatible with the client, in several respects:

(a) Signature mismatch: The BP allows a client to order products through an operation named `OrderProduct` that requires an input parameter named `order` whose type is `ProductOrderInfo`. The ES specifies the same functionality via the `SubmitOrder` operation with the same input parameter but the data type is `OrderDetail`.

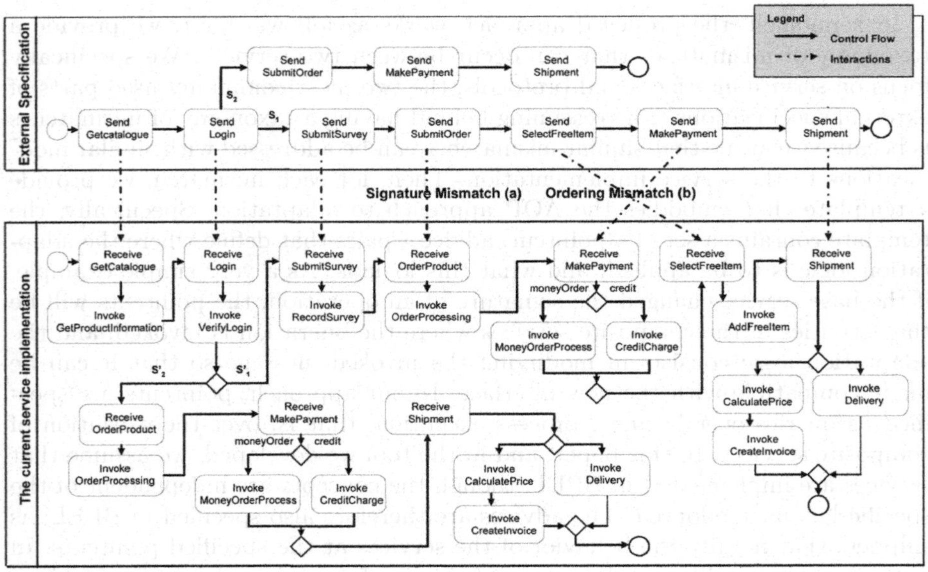

Fig. 1. A Supply Chain Example showing the Differences between an ES and a BP

(b) Ordering Mismatch: After an order has been submitted, the BP requires the client to send a `makePayment` message, while the ES specifies that the client has also the possibility of using `selectFreeItem`. This possibility can create an ordering mismatch when the client choses to follow the execution path S_2 of the ES.

To be able to interact with clients of this supply chain community, the external behavior of this BP has to be modified so that it complies with the community's ES. At the same time, since the BP might participate in some other companies' workflow and interact with various internal partners, we have to make sure that any modification will not prejudice those interactions.

Mismatch Types. In our previous work [3], we identified a taxonomy of possible mismatches at the interface and protocol levels. To make this paper self-contained, we briefly introduce the mismatch types, in addition to the signature and ordering mismatches above, as follows:

– Parameter constraint: Two services have different constraints on an input parameter, where the value range of the ES parameter is not a subset of the BP parameter, therefore values sent by the client are not accepted by the BP. For output parameters, mismatch occurs when value range of the BP parameter is not a subset of the ES parameter.
– Extra message: The BP issues a message that is not specified in the ES.
– Missing message: The BP does not issue a message specified in the ES.

– Message split: The ES specifies a single message to achieve a functionality, while the BP requires several messages for the same functionality.
– Message merge: The ES specifies several messages to achieve a functionality, while the BP requires only one message for the same functionality.

3 Aspect Oriented Service Adaptation

To address mismatches such as the ones mentioned above, we introduce adaptation templates. An example of template for the ordering mismatch is presented in Figure 2. In the following we detail this template structure: we first introduce joinpoint queries and discuss the alternatives and rationale for their design. We then present the advices and, finally, we show how the ordering template, as well as an other example of template corresponding to the signature mismatch, are applied to perform adaptation.

Ordering Template	
Query	**Generic Adaptation Advice**
query(<operation>,<sequence>) executes *before receive* when O_j^{bp} = <operation> AND S_i = <sequence>	OrderingPart1() { Receive $msgO_i^{bp}$; Assign $msgO_i^{tmp} \longleftarrow msgO_i^{bp}$; }
query(<operation>,<sequence>) executes *before receive* when O_i^{bp} = <operation> AND S_j = <sequence>	OrderingPart2() { Assign $msgO_i^{bp} \longleftarrow msgO_i^{tmp}$; Reply $msgO_i^{bp}$; }

Fig. 2. Template corresponding to the ordering mismatch

3.1 Joinpoints

The key part in the aspect-oriented approach to adaptation lies in understanding the requirements for the joinpoint query language. To this end, we first observe that the need of adaptation advice is determined not only by the BPEL code, but also by the actual messages received from the client, and in general by runtime service execution data. For instance, the ordering mismatch (b) of Figure 1 only happens when the interaction path follows sequence $S_2^{'}$. In this situation, it is the client choice of using one particular interaction pattern among the possible ones (i.e. sending `SubmitSurvey` after sending the `login` message) that triggers the adaptation need.

In general, aspect oriented programming can be done using various approaches for query language. A first approach consists in tailoring the query language for the identification, within the BPEL code, of locations where advices should be inserted. This limits the query expressiveness to conditions on the BPEL code only. As observed above, adaptation advice execution is also conditioned by runtime context, i.e. by how the service is actually used by a client or how it executes. Using a query language that focuses on the identification of code location would force us to include, as part of the advice, some code to evaluate those runtime conditions. A second approach consists in directly expressing, in the query language, not only code location but also runtime conditions. This approach has been preferred since it groups together all advice execution conditions in the query and frees the advice code from any runtime condition evaluations. The net result is a more readable code and advices that are more generic.

Note that we are discussing here the query language syntax, not the actual deployment of the solution. Choosing a query language that incorporates runtime conditions still allows for aspect weaving done either at compile-time or at runtime. At compile-time, a new BPEL code would be generated with advices weaved preceded by runtime conditions. In a runtime deployment model, a specially modified query engine evaluates execution conditions based on the execution context it maintains, leaving the original code unmodified. While both deployment models are viable, the first one (compile-time) imposes to incorporate in the BPEL code some additional logic, not part of advices, that is needed to maintain execution context informations (e.g. the interaction pattern used by the client). In this paper, we therefore chose the second (runtime) deployment model which, in addition to its greater simplicity, also allows to dynamically plug and unplug adaptation aspects. The special runtime environment needed for this deployment model is presented in section 4.

Intuitively, we expect the query language to be able to perform i) identification of operations with (or without) a certain signature (this is to handle interface-level mismatches), and ii) identification of paths that are or are not present in a protocol, that is the query language must be able to discriminate between the various execution paths that lead to or follow this activity (this is to handle protocol-level mismatches). Due to space limitations we only present here the intuition rather than the detailed analysis which is based on the mismatch types discussed earlier. In both cases, what is done is the identification of a BPEL activity where adaptation is needed, e.g., the activity where a signature mismatch occurs, or the first activity of a sequence that does not have any correspondence at the protocol level in the client. In addition, we need the language to be able to define the location of the joinpoint, i.e. whether the advice is to be performed *before*, *after* or *around* (i.e. in place of) the BPEL activity.

In addition, the query needs to be able to handle runtime conditions, and to this end it can take parameters that are matched against execution context at the time of query evaluation. Parameters are given by the user and correspond to BPEL construct or operations sequences. For example, in the first query of Figure 2, parameters corresponding to the ordering mismatch above would be <operation>=`makePayment` and <sequence>=S_2'. This query will be evaluated by the runtime environment before each receive activity, as indicated by the `executes` statement, and the two variables O_j^{bp} and S_i are valued according to the current operation and the sequence of operations that lead to the receive activity under consideration.

Figure 3 presents, in a semi-formal way, the syntax for a query specification language that satisfies the above requirements. This query language shares some common characteristics with query languages that operate at the code level such as BPQL[2]. The main differences are that i) conditions on BP executions can be expressed and ii) the language also incorporates the location of the advice relative to the joinpoint (i.e. the *before*, *after* or *around* keywords). As explained above, those modifications are needed to achieve a self contained query language able to express all the conditions for advice execution. Examples of queries are given in Figure 2 and in Figure 5.

```
<query>            ::= query( [<param>[,<param>]*] )
                       executes <location> <activity>
                       when <condition>
<param>            ::= id[;id]*
<location>         ::= before|after|around
<activity>         ::= receive|reply|invoke
<condition>        ::= <pred>[AND<pred>]
<pred>             ::= <context object>=<param> |<context object>!=<param>
<context object>   ::= partnerLink|portType|operation|inputParameter
                       |outputParameter|type|executionPath
```

Fig. 3. Semi-formal syntax for query language

Finally, we observe that mismatches of different types may occur at the same point in a process. In this case, many queries may need to be evaluated. We have prioritized the query evaluation based on the mismatch types. For example, signature mismatches need to be addressed before a message is stored and forwarded to the BP by an ordering template.

3.2 Advices

An advice corresponds to the code that is executed when its associated query conditions are satisfied. We call this code *generic* since it requires parameters that are specific to an adaptation situation. We choose BPEL as a language to express template advices for consistency with the original BPEL service implementation, although any other languages commonly used to implement web services could be a choice. Moreover, the activities required for adapting business processes, such as receiving messages, storing messages, transforming message data, and invoking service operations, are very well modeled by BPEL.

As an example, consider the ordering template (Figure 2). Figure 4 presents how this template behaves at runtime: upon receiving a message, the runtime environment triggers the execution of the OrderingPart1 if this message is not desired at this stage of the BP execution, i.e. if message `selectFreeItemIn` is received. When executed, the OrderingPart1 advice assigns the `selectFreeItemIn` into a temporary variable, i.e. `freeItemTmp` for later use. When the message `selectFreeItemIn` is required by the BP, the orderingPart2 advice copies its value from the `freeItemTmp` variable and forwards it to the BP. Note that for the sake of clarity, we omitted the acknowledgment of the `selectFreeItemIn` message in this

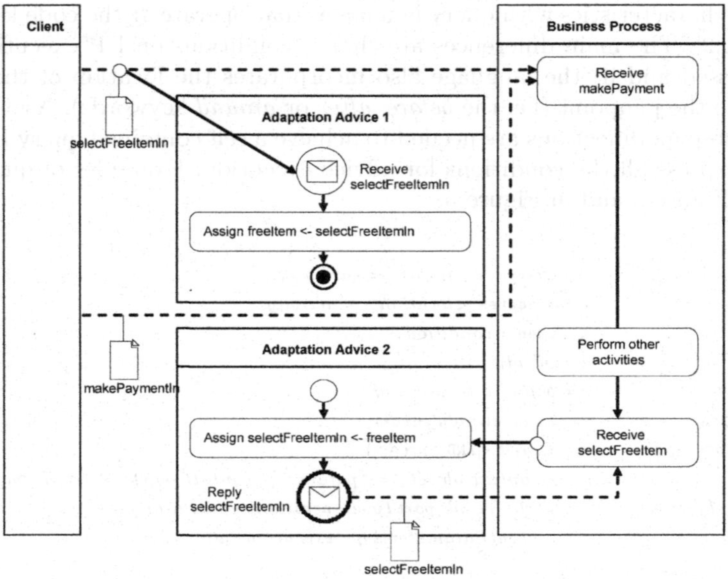

Fig. 4. Sample Usage of the Ordering Template

mismatch template. In a situation where the client requires an acknowledgment, the adaptation logic will be more complex. We refer the reader to [3] where this situation is discussed.

As another example, consider the template to address the signature mismatch, given in Figure 5. It also consists of two adaptation advices: SignaturePart1 and SignaturePart2. The SignaturePart1 first intercepts an incoming message $msgO^{es}$ of an operation O^{es} specified by the ES, then transforms the data type $type^{es}$ of a message parameter into $type^{bp}$ required by the BP, and finally sends the resulted message $msgO^{bp}$ to the BP. Similar actions are specified in the SignaturePart2 to solve mismatch for the outgoing messages of the BP.

Due to space limitations, it is not possible here to present the full set of templates, but the general method described above can easily be applied in the other mismatch situations.

4 Template Usage and Tool Support

The generic mismatch handling procedures encapsulated in templates allows for i) generation of the adaptation logic, and ii) integration of the generated adaptation logic into the business process. All the developer has left to do is to identify the mismatches and instantiate their corresponding templates. For example, once a signature mismatch has been identified between two services, the user retrieves the corresponding template and provides parameters for the queries and advices of SignturePart1 and SignaturePart2. Both queries of this template take a data

Signature Template	
Query	**Generic Adaptation Advice**
query(<inputType>) executes *before receive* when $type^{bp}$= <inputType>	SignaturePart1($<T_i>$) { Receive $msgO^{es}$; Assign $msgO^{bp}.inPara^{bp}.type^{bp}$ $\longleftarrow <T_i>(msgO^{es}.inPara^{es}.type^{es})$; Reply $msgO^{bp}$; }
query(<outputType>) executes *before reply* when $type^{bp}$ = <outputType>	SignaturePart2($<T_o>$) { Receive $msgO^{bp}$; Assign $msgO^{es}.outPara^{es}.type^{es}$ $\longleftarrow <T_o>(msgO^{bp}.outPara^{bp}.type^{bp})$; Reply $msgO^{es}$; }

Fig. 5. Template corresponding to the signature mismatch

type as input and express that their corresponding advices should be executed for each receive (resp. reply) of the BP that involves a message parameter of that type. In addition, SignaturePart1 and Signaturepart2 advices each takes a *Transformation Function* (denoted $< T_i >$ and $< T_o >$) that is responsible of actually transforming the data types of the message parameters. One of the benefits of using those precise templates is that the developer's task is limited to the identification of the mismatch (i.e. checking the compatibility of the data models as used in the BP and as specified by the ES) and, when those types do not correspond, to write the mapping between them. For mapping authoring, third party tools (e.g. Biztalk) already provide efficient schema matching functionality. In our implementation, we used XQuery[4] functions to perform those transformations, though other languages can be used.

The developer is assisted in this task by a tool that we have developed. The tool consists of a development and runtime environment.

Development Environment. The development environment assists the developer in instantiating the adaptation templates. To this end, the user has to provide the parameters for queries and advices. As discussed in section 3.1, the query parameters correspond to BPEL construct identifiers (i.e. their names as found in the BPEL source). The user has to look through the process specification which could be large in its size. We intend to provide a query support that allows the user to query over process specifications and give parameters to template queries. On the other hand, advice parameters are transformation functions that can be authored using third party softwares.

Once both the query and advice parameters are provided, the Development Environment generates two outputs: the Aspect Definition Document and a collection of adaptation advices. An example of the Aspect Definition Document is shown below. It is an XML file that consists of a set of mismatch elements, each specifying a template and its corresponding parameters. Used together, the Aspect Definition Document and Adaptation Advices (template instances with their query and advice parameters) allow the Runtime Environment, discussed in the next section, to adapt the BP in compliance with the ES.

```
<aspect>
  <mismatch template="Signature">
    <advice name="SignaturePart1" location="before" activity="receive">
      <queryParameter name="inputType" value="ProductOrderInfo"/>
      <adviceParameter name="Ti" value"TransformProductOrderInfo"/> </advice>
    <advice name="SignaturePart2" location="before" activity="reply">
      <queryParameter name="outputType" value"OrderConfirmation"/>
      <adviceParameter name="To" value"TransformOrderConfirmation"/> </advice>
  </mismatch>  ... </aspect>
```

Runtime Environment. The Runtime is implemented on top of the ActiveBPEL engine [1], and enables the dynamic weaving of adaptation advices with the business process. Similar extensions can be considered for other types of business process implementation (e.g. J2EE). During process execution, the runtime environment uses query information in the Aspect Definition Document to identify if an adaptation advice needs to be executed, based on the current execution context. If it is the case, the adaptation advice, which is also specified in the Aspect Definition document, is loaded and executed according to its definition. After the completion of the adaptation advice execution, ActiveBPEL continues to process the BPEL instance. Interestingly, this extension has itself been implemented using an aspect weaved with the ActiveBPEL code using AspectJ.

The runtime environment supports the inclusion of multiple adaptations for the same BP. To make this possible, each adaptation aspect is associated with a specific virtual URL. When the BP is first invoked by a client, the URL is used to determine which adaptation aspect (i.e. which Aspect Definition document) should be used. Hence, the same business process can be adapted to different ESs.

5 Related Work

In the software engineering area, few approaches exist for analyzing and solving software component mismatches. [9] proposes an algorithm to identify mismatches between different versions of architectural models and generates an edit script to solve those mismatches. This approach can be extended to identify mismatches between business protocols. Several efforts recognize the importance of protocol specification in component-based models [5,12,17]. They provide models for component interface specifications (based on formal approaches e.g. process algebra) and algorithms (e.g. compatibility checking) that can be used for web service protocol specification and analysis.

In the context of web services, [13] proposed a technique called chain of adapters, that satisfies their identified requirements, to manage different versions of services. In our previous work [3], we argued that mismatches between service interfaces and protocols are recurring, hence we complemented the adapter approach by providing a taxonomy of mismatches. [8] also supports this argument and provides visual operators for adaptations. However, in our previous work, we made no contribution on the actual implementation of the adaptation logic and how to integrate them with the service implementation. In this paper, we design, for each mismatch, an aspect based template that consists of a collection of adaptation logic expressed in BPEL, and query to support weaving of the adaptation logic with the business process.

A large amount of work has been done in the area of AOP, however they mostly address non-functional concerns of software [10]. We focus on previous work that applies AOP to the adaptation problem. [14] proposes an aspect oriented platform to support adaptation of services according to changes in the environment, while we focus on the adaptation of processes to be compatible with external specifications. In addition, their focus on services implemented in Java prompts them to identify joinpoints on methods and field accesses rather than BPEL activities as in our framework. Work of [6,7] also supports aspect oriented adaptation of BPEL processes according to changes in the environment. They use XPath to identify pointcuts which restrict to queries on individual process execution events. Our query on execution paths differentiate our framework from this previous work. Another work that also focuses on adaptation for compatibility is presented in [16]. They propose a framework for transforming XML messages where pointcuts are defined on document contents using XPath. We differ from this work in terms of the mismatch taxonomy and our focus on business protocol mismatches.

6 Conclusion

In this paper we proposed the use of AOP for service adaptation to interface and protocol mismatches. We have argued for adaptation as a cross-cutting concern and for the separation of business and adaptation logic. This modularization facilitates the maintenance of the BP when the target ES evolves since only the adaptation logic needs to be changed. A further benefit of our framework consists in the precise input parameters required from the user that can be built from third party tools or supported by a graphical interface. The notion of template also promotes reusability of adaptation logic that occurs repetitively across different locations in an implementation of a service. In this paper, we exemplified the application of our framework into the first scenario discussed in the introduction where adaptation needs to be performed at the level of individual web services. The benefits become even greater when considering situations where adaptation needs to be performed across several composite services since, in this case, considering adaptation as a cross cutting concern becomes critical.

We have developed a proof-of-concept implementation of the proposed framework. In particular, we have implemented the Runtime Environment that takes an Aspect Definition Document and Adaptation Advices as inputs to adapt a business process in accordance to an external specification. Our experience with the framework has been primarily example driven. For the Development Environment, we have provided a GUI support for the instantiation of adaptation advices.

In the current framework, users have to look at the protocol definition and the BP model to identify the mismatches and provide query parameters. When the model grows large, this task can become significant. In the future, we plan to extend the Development Environment to offer a semi-automated identification of mismatches and a graphical interface that allows the user to create queries over process specifications and navigate through the results in order to identify query parameters.

References

1. ActiveBPEL Engine 2.0. http://www.activebpel.org/.
2. C. Beeri, A. Eyal, S. Kamenkovich, and T. Milo. Querying Business Processes with BP-QL. In *VLDB'05*.
3. B. Benatallah, F. Casati, D. Grigori, H.R. Motahari Nezhad, and Farouk Toumani. Developing Adapters for Web Services Integration. In *CAISE'05*, pages 415–429.
4. S. Boag, D. Chamberlin, M. Fernández, D. Florescu, J. Robie, and J. Siméon. XML Query Language (XQuery 1.0), November 2005. http://www.w3.org/TR/xquery/.
5. A. Bracciali, A. Brogi, and C. Canal. A Formal Approach to Component Adaptation. *Journal of System and Software*, 74(1):45–54, 2005.
6. A. Charfi and M. Mezini. Aspect-Oriented Web Service Composition with AO4BPEL. In *ECOWS'04*, pages 168–182.
7. C. Courbis and A. Finkelstein. Towards Aspect Weaving Applications. In *ICSE'05*, pages 69–77.
8. M. Dumas, M.Spork, and K.Wang. Adapt or Perish: Algebra and Visual Notation for Service Interface Adaptation. In *accepted to BPM'06*.
9. M. Abi-Antoun et.al. Differencing and Merging of Architectural Views. Technical report, Carnegie Mellon University, CMU-ISRI-05-128R, August 2005.
10. N. Loughran et.al. Survey of aspect-oriented middleware research. Technical report, Lancaster University, June 2005.
11. T. Andrews et.al. Business Process Execution Language for Web Services 1.1. Technical Report TUV-1841-2004-16, BEA, IBM, Microsoft, SAP, Siebel, 2003.
12. P. Inverardi and M. Tivoli. Deadlock-free software architectures for COM/DCOM applications. *Journal of Systems and Software*, 65(3):173–183, 2003.
13. P. Kaminski, H. Muller, and M. Litoiu. A design for adaptive web service evolution. In *SEAMS'06*, pages 86–92.
14. A. Nicoara and G. Alonso. Dynamic AOP with PROSE. In *CAISE'05*, pages 125–138.
15. Stephen A. White. Business Process Modeling Notation (BPMN 1.0), May 2004. http://www.bpmn.org.
16. E. Wohlstadter and K. Volder. Doxpects: aspects supporting XML transformation interfaces. In *AOSD'06*, pages 99–108.
17. D. Yellin and R. Strom. Protocol Specifications and Component Adaptors. *ACM TOPLAS*, 19(2):292–333, 1997.

Automated Generation of BPEL Adapters*

Antonio Brogi and Razvan Popescu

Computer Science Department, University of Pisa, Italy

Abstract. The heterogeneous, dynamic, distributed, and evolving nature of Web services calls for adaptation techniques to overcome various types of mismatches that may occur among services developed by different parties. In this paper we present a methodology for the automated generation of (service) adapters capable of solving behavioural mismatches among BPEL processes. The adaptation process, given two communicating BPEL processes whose interaction may lock, builds (if possible) a BPEL process that allows the two processes to successfully interoperate. A key ingredient of the adaptation methodology is the transformation of BPEL processes into YAWL workflows.

1 Introduction

BPEL [2] is currently used to (manually) compose WSDL [15] services into complex business applications. A main problem to achieve automated service composition is that the composite application may lock due to interaction mismatches among the participant services. One possibility to overcome such mismatches is a disciplined use of *adapters*, as services "in-the-middle" capable of mediating the information exchanged by the involved parties.

Service adaptation may be tackled at various levels of the Web services stack [10]. For example, signature-based adaptation [9,12] addresses issues due to syntactic differences among the exchanged messages (e.g., different orderings of the message parts), ontology-based adaptation [8,11] mediates semantic mismatches among the exchanged messages (e.g., messages belonging to different ontology concepts), and behaviour-based adaptation [1,3] handles the integration of services into a lock-free aggregate due to mismatches in their communicating protocols (e.g., different orderings of message exchanges). However, Web service adaptation is in its early stages and current approaches feature only partial solutions to the issues of adaptation.

Our long term objective is to develop a general methodology for service adaptation capable of suitably overcoming signature, ontology and behaviour mismatches in view of business application integration within and across organisational boundaries. In this paper we present a methodology for the automated generation of (service) adapters capable of solving *behavioural mismatches* among BPEL processes. The adaptation process, given two communicating BPEL processes whose interaction may lock, builds (if possible) a BPEL process that allows the two processes to

* This work has been partially supported by the SMEPP project (EU-FP6-IST 0333563) and by the F.I.R.B. project TOCAI.IT.

A. Dan and W. Lamersdorf (Eds.): ICSOC 2006, LNCS 4294, pp. 27–39, 2006.

successfully interoperate. Three strong motivations for adapting services are the need to develop adapters for service composition, for ensuring backwards compatibility of new service versions, as well as the need to develop adapters for each class of clients a service may have. A key ingredient of the adaptation methodology is the use of service contracts [6] including WSDL *signatures* and YAWL *behaviour*, where YAWL [13] is used as intermediate (formal) language to provide a (partial) description of the service behaviour. Immediate advantages of using such an abstract language are the possibility of adapting services written in different service description languages, multiple deployment of the adapter as a real-world service, as well as developing formal analyses and transformations independently of the different languages used by providers to describe the behaviour of their services. Moreover, integration with the YAWL-based service customisation [5] and aggregation of Web services [4,6] becomes straightforward.

Regrettably, space limitations do not allow us to introduce BPEL and YAWL. Detailed descriptions of the two languages are to be found in [2] and [13], respectively.

2 Motivating Example

Consider the following example consisting of two interacting BPEL processes: *Command Centre* (CC) and *Mars Explorer* (ME). The former provides a Web service interface for the assignment of exploration tasks. The latter is a Web service interface to the robot performing the tasks. Hereafter we present a simplification of the BPEL processes (e.g., in order to express the message exchanges we simply use service names instead of *partnerLinks* and *portTypes*). Although fairly simple, the example illustrates various interactions among services. On the one hand, *CC* communicates with its client, as well as with the *ME* service. On the other hand, *ME* interacts with *CC* (viz., its client), as well as with the *Logger* and *Explorer* services.

```
<process name="CommandCentre"><sequence>
  <receive op="ExecTask" from Client var="taskInfo" createInst="yes"/>
  <invoke op="Login" of MarsExplorer var="loginInfo"/>
  <assign><copy> from="/taskInfo/coords" to="coords"></copy></assign>
  <invoke op="SetCoords" of MarsExplorer var="coords"/>
  <assign><copy> from="/taskInfo/job" to="jobDetails"></copy></assign>
  <invoke op="SetJob" of MarsExplorer var="jobDetails"/>
  <pick>
    <onMsg op="SubmitRep" from MarsExplorer var="report"><sequence>
      <receive op="JobID" from MarsExplorer var="id"/>
      <invoke op="Logout" of MarsExplorer/>
      <reply op="ExecTask" of Client var="report"/></sequence></onMsg>
    <onMsg op="SubmitErr" from MarsExplorer var="error"><sequence>
      <invoke op="Logout" of MarsExplorer/>
      <assign><copy> from="error" to="report"></copy></assign>
      <reply op="ExecTask" of Client var="report" faultName="Task_Error"/>
    </sequence></onMsg></pick></sequence></process>
```

The CC service[1] first receives the task information from its client. It then logs in with the ME, to which it forwards the location and the job details. It waits

[1] We use "process" and "service" interchangeably to denote BPEL processes.

next either a report or an error message from the ME. In the former case, it first receives the job id from the ME, then it closes the connection with the ME, and finally, it forwards the report to the client. In the latter case, it first logs out from the ME, and then it replies to the client with the error message.

```
<process name="MarsExplorer"><sequence>
  <receive op="Login" from CommandCentre var="loginInfo" createInst="yes"/>
  <invoke op="JobID" of CommandCentre var="id"/>
  <receive op="SetJob" from CommandCentre var="jobDetails"/>
  <receive op="SetCoords" from CommandCentre var="coords"/>
  <invoke op="ValidateLocation" of LoggerService inVar="coords" outVar="rep1"/>
  <invoke op="Explore" of ExplorerService inVar="jobDetails" outVar="rep2"/>
  <assign><copy> from="concat(rep1,rep2)" to="report"></copy></assign>
  <invoke op="SubmitRep" of CommandCentre var="report"/>
  <receive op="Logout" from CommandCentre/></sequence>
<faultHandlers>
  <catch faultName="Task_Error" faultVar="error"><sequence>
    <invoke op="SubmitErr" of CommandCentre var="error"/>
    <receive op="Logout" from CommandCentre/>
  </sequence></catch></faultHandlers></process>
```

The ME service starts by waiting for the CC to log in, to which it sends immediately the job's id. It receives next from the CC the job description and the location of the exploration site. In order to carry out the task, the ME first validates the coordinates (e.g., by checking previous exploration logs) and moves the robot to the respective location by (synchronously) invoking the *Logger Service* (LS), and then, it delegates the *Explorer Service* (ES) for the actual execution of the job (again, through a synchronous invocation). If the latter two invocations return successfully, the ME generates the final report, sends it to the CC, and waits for the CC to log out. Note that, although not represented in the example, the invocations to the LS and to the ES may return a "Task_Error" fault. (This information has to be specified in the WSDL file(s) defining the respective operations). In that case, the ME service catches the fault, forwards to the CC the error, and finally, it waits for the CC to close the connection.

It is easy to see that the two services, CC and ME, cannot successfully interact because of mismatches between their behaviour. Immediately after the login information exchange, while the CC sends the location of the exploration site to the ME, the ME sends the job id to the CC. Furthermore, the CC first sends the location, and then the details of the job to the ME, which expects them in the reversed order. A further mismatch is the fact that, while the CC expects the job id only when the exploration is successful, the ME always sends it, and moreover, at a different moment.

The following Section 3 shows how we automatically generate BPEL adapters to cope with such behabioural mismatches.

3 Adaptation Methodology

The adaptation methodology inputs two communicating BPEL processes, C and S, whose interaction may lock, and it builds (if possible) a BPEL process adapter A, which allows the two processes to successfully interoperate. The four adaptation phases are: **(1.) Service Translation**. This phase is in charge of translating the BPEL descriptions of C and S into corresponding YAWL workflows [7]. **(2.) Adapter Generation**. This phase builds the YAWL workflow of A from the workflows of C and S. It first generates the *Service Execution Trees* (SETs) of C with respect to S ($SET(C_S)$), as well as of S with respect to C ($SET(S_C)$), followed by the generation of the SETs of their duals ($SET(\overline{C_S})$ and $SET(\overline{S_C})$). Informally, when a service X outputs a message m, a dual of X is a service that inputs m, and vice-versa. Next, $SET(A)$ is obtained by suitably merging $SET(\overline{C_S})$ and $SET(\overline{S_C})$. Finally, the YAWL workflow of A is derived from $SET(A)$. **(3.) Lock Analysis**. This phase verifies whether the YAWL-based aggregation [4,6] of C, A, and S locks. If it does, we consider that the adaptation has failed. Otherwise, we consider that the adaptation is successful. **(4.) Adapter Deployment**. If the adaptation is successful, this phase deploys the YAWL workflow of A as a BPEL process, which can be used as a service-in-the-middle between C and S.

3.1 Service Translation

In [7] we present a methodology for translating BPEL processes into YAWL workflows. Its main strengths are that (1) it defines YAWL patterns for all BPEL activities, (2) it provides a compositional approach to construct structured patterns from suitably interconnecting other patterns, and (3) it handles events, faults and (explicit) compensation.

On the one hand, the pattern of each BPEL basic activity (with the exception of *assign* and *compensate*) is obtained by suitably instantiating the *Basic Pattern Template* (BPT). The BPT is a template of YAWL tasks, which serves both for identifying the translated activity (through an *Activity Specific Task*, or AST for short), as well as the control-logic of executing or skipping the activity. On the other hand, the pattern of each BPEL structured activity (together with *assign*, *compensate*, and *process*) is obtained from the *Structured Pattern Template* (SPT) template. The SPT consists of a *Begin* (logically marking the initiation of the structured activity) and of an *End* pattern (logically marking the termination of the structured activity), as well as a pattern template (BPT or SPT) for each child activity. Furthermore, the *Scope* and *Process* patterns add SPTs for handling exceptional behaviour. Each pattern inputs and outputs at most three types of control-flow links, called *green*, *blue*, and *red* lines. The green lines serve for translating the structural dependencies among BPEL activities. The blue lines are used for translating the BPEL synchronisation links, and the red lines are necessary for implementing the fault handling mechanism. As space limitations do not allow us to go into further details, please see [7] for more (in-depth) details on the BPEL2YAWL translator.

The YAWL workflows of the CC and ME services of our example can be seen in Figure 1.[2] In the workflow of ME, *Begin(Process)* and *End(Process)*, logically

[2] The two workflows are represented in a slightly simplified form w.r.t. the description given in [7] (e.g., the default *faultHandlers* of the process, as well as redundant *green gates* are not represented, the *assign* is represented in a compact form, etc.).

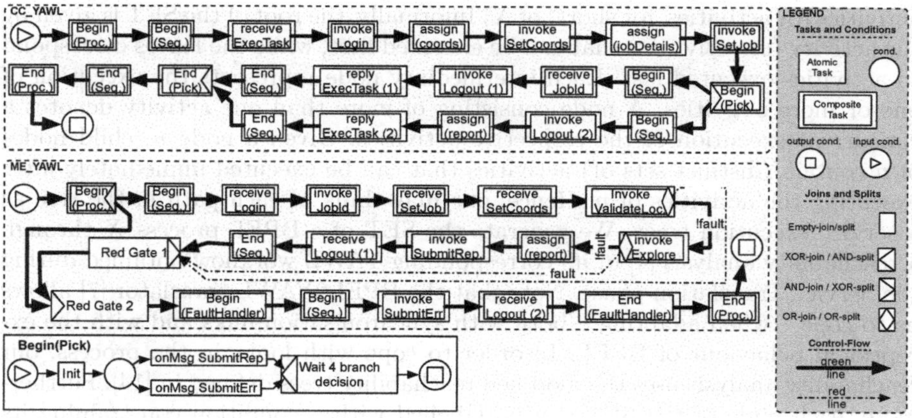

Fig. 1. YAWL workflows corresponding to the *CC* and *ME* BPEL processes

mark the initiation and the termination, respectively, of the BPEL process. The process activity, a *sequence* leads to generating the *Begin(Sequence)* as well as the *End(Sequence)* tasks. The first activity in the sequence is a *receive*, which gives the *Receive* task. Furthermore, the rest of the activities are translated correspondingly. (The numbers inside some of the task labels are used for disambiguation purposes only.) Note however the translation of the BPEL *pick*. The *Begin(Pick)* task contains the branch selection logic (basically a deferred choice construct [13]), and it outputs two tokens[3]. One leads to executing the chosen branch, while the second leads to skipping the other branch (so as to achieve the dead-path-elimination).

The workflow of *CC* is built in a similar manner. However, the composite tasks representing the *invoke ValidateLocation* and *invoke Explore* activities output *either* green tokens, if the invocations succeed, *or* red tokens, if the invocations fail (i.e., faults are being raised). In the former case, the execution of the workflow continues normally, and the green output of *End(Sequence)* leads to skipping the tasks inside the *Begin(FaultHandler)* → *End(FaultHandler)* zone (so as to achieve the dead-path-elimination). In the latter case, the execution of the faulty invocation is (immediately) followed by the execution of the tasks in the fault handling zone.

3.2 Adapter Generation

The Adapter Generation phase consists of the four steps discussed hereafter.

Service Execution Trees. This step automatically generates the Service Execution Trees (SETs) of the two services to be adapted. The SET of a BPEL process X is a tree describing all the possible scenarios of executing the basic

[3] The semantics of executing YAWL workflows is quite similar to executing PNs.

activities (or activities, for short) of X. Informally, the root of the SET is given by the activity (or activities) that can be executed first, while the leaves correspond to activities executed last. Each intermediary node represents the execution of one or more activities. A node consisting of more than one activity denotes a concurrent execution of the respective activities. Given a node n, child nodes of n contain (distinct sets of) activities that can be executed immediately after executing the activities of n. Hence, one may think of each path in the tree as a service execution trace. We generate the SET of a BPEL process X through a reachability analysis [4] of its corresponding YAWL workflow obtained during the Service Translation phase. Note that the BPEL2YAWL translator [7] allows us to cope – when adapting – both with synchronisation links and with the exceptional behaviour of BPEL. In order to cope with loops in the process, our reachability analysis uses the modified reachability trees defined in [14]. Furthermore, each node of the SET can be labelled with a condition constraining its execution. Such conditions are due to guards employed by *switch* activities and synchronisation links. In [4,5] we show how to generate the logical expression constraining the fulfilment of a service execution trace. However, in order to ease the description of the methodology, and due to space limitations, we do not detail this issue here. The SET one obtains for a service X contains all message exchanges of X with other services. We call this the *full-form* of the SET, and we denote it by $SET(X)$. $SET(ME)$ is given in Figure 2(a). For example, the execution of the (synchronous) *invoke ValidateLocation* can be followed *either* by the *invoke Explore*, *or* by the *invoke SubmitErr*. The former is due to a successful execution of the *invoke ValidateLocation*, while the latter is executed in the case of a fault being received by the *invoke ValidateLocation*. Furthermore, the successful termination of the sequence activity of the BPEL process leads to employing the dead-path-elimination inside the pattern implementing the *faultHandler* of the BPEL process [7]. This is indicated in $SET(ME)$ by the dark coloured *invoke SubmitErr* and *rcv Logout* nodes.

From (the full-form of) $SET(X)$ we derive next the (*compact-form* of) SET of X with respect to another service Y, with which X interacts. We denote it by $SET(X_Y)$. Informally, from the original $SET(X)$ we keep only message exchanges between X and Y. First, all message exchanges (viz., receive/reply/invoke) of X with services other than Y, as well as all other basic activities (e.g., assign), and all skipped activities are replaced by *empty* activities. We denote the resulting SET as $SET(X^*_Y)$. For example, the *invoke ValidateLocation* and the *invoke Explore*, which ME performs on the *Logger Service* and *Explorer Service*, respectively, are set to *empty* when computing $SET(ME_{CC})$. ($SET(ME^*_{CC})$ is given in Figure 2(b).) Second, each *empty* node in $SET(X^*_Y)$ (with the exception of the root) is removed from the tree, and its sub-trees (if any) are merged with its parent nodes. We denote the resulting tree by $SET(X_Y)$. Note that the merge process applied at a node n of $SET(X^*_Y)$ also removes duplicate subtrees of n. For instance, by removing the three empty nodes of $SET(ME^*_{CC})$, we get two identical subtrees (*invoke SubmitErr* → *receive Logout*) at the *receive SetCoords* node. The merge at *receive SetCoords* will then remove one duplicate. $SET(ME_{CC})$ is represented in

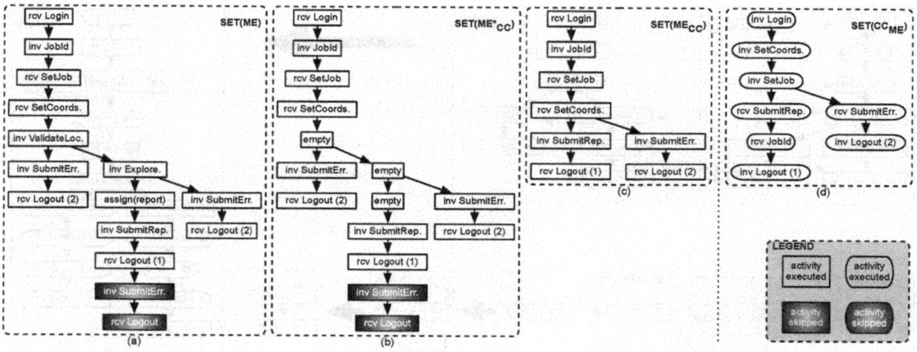

Fig. 2. (a) $SET(ME)$, (b) $SET(ME^*_{CC})$, (c) $SET(ME_{CC})$, and (d) $SET(CC_{ME})$

Figure 2(c). Due to space limitations, we present only the $SET(CC_{ME})$ – which is built analogously – in Figure 2(d).

Dual SETs. This step generates for each service X (to be adapted), the SET of a dual of X with respect to another service Y. Basically, when X receives a message m from Y, a dual of X with respect to Y (denoted by $SET(\overline{X_Y})$) acts somewhat "as Y should" and sends a message m to X, and vice-versa. One obtains $SET(\overline{X_Y})$ from $SET(X_Y)$ by replacing asynchronous *invokes* with *receives* (and vice-versa), and synchronous *invokes* with pairs *receive* → *reply* (and vice-versa). $SET(\overline{ME_{CC}})$ and $SET(\overline{CC_{ME}})$ are depicted in Figure 3(a) and (b), respectively.

Adapter SET. The SET of an adapter A ($SET(A)$) mediating the interaction of two services, C and S, is obtained by suitably merging $SET(\overline{C_S})$ with $SET(\overline{S_C})$. This process consists of two steps, as follows.

During the first step, we *match* the activities of $SET(\overline{C_S})$ with the activities of $SET(\overline{S_C})$ with the following two rules: (1) An asynchronous *invoke Op* of $SET(\overline{C_S})$ matches a *receive Op* of $SET(\overline{S_C})$, and vice-versa, and (2) a synchronous *invoke Op* of $SET(\overline{C_S})$ matches a pair *receive Op* → *reply Op* of $SET(\overline{S_C})$, and vice-versa. Then, we express each match as a *data-flow dependency* (or dependency, for short), which emerges at the *receive* and targets the *invoke*, in the case of asynchronous message exchanges, or as a pair of dependencies, one emerging at the *receive* and targeting the *invoke*, and another one emerging at the *invoke* and targeting the *reply*, in the case of synchronous message exchanges. We call an activity that is target of at least one dependency as *constrained*. Otherwise, we say that the activity is *unconstrained* (with respect to the data-flow dependencies between the two SETs). For example, *invoke Login* and *receive JobId* of $SET(\overline{ME_{CC}})$ match *receive Login* and *invoke JobId*, respectively, of $SET(\overline{CC_{ME}})$. (See Figure 3(a) and (b).) Informally, a dependency indicates that the adapter has to wait first a message from one of the two services, and then (possibly at a later moment) it forwards it to the other service. In other

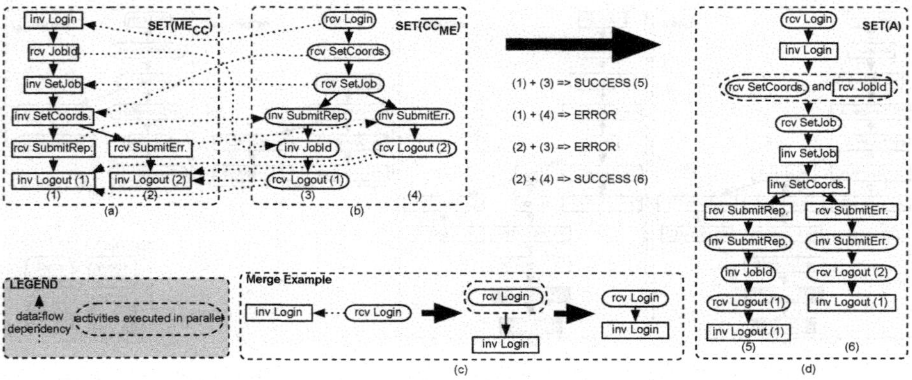

Fig. 3. (a) $SET(\overline{ME_{CC}})$, (b) $SET(\overline{CC_{ME}})$, (c) Generating $SET(A)$ nodes, (d) $SET(A)$

words, a dependency from X to Y says that the adapter has to execute X before executing Y. Note that the interpretation in the case of multiple dependencies emerging from different activities X_k and targeting an activity Y, is that for the execution of Y it suffices to execute only one activity X_k. This is the case for *invoke Logout (1)* and *invoke Logout (2)* of $SET(\overline{ME_{CC}})$.

As previously mentioned, each path in $SET(X)$ is an execution trace of X. During the second step, we compute the merge of all possible pairs of traces $(\overline{c}, \overline{s})$, where $\overline{c} =< \overline{c_1}, \overline{c_2}, \ldots, \overline{c_n} >$ is a trace of $SET(\overline{C_S})$, and $\overline{s} =< \overline{s_1}, \overline{s_2}, \ldots, \overline{s_m} >$ is a trace of $SET(\overline{S_C})$. Such a merge can lead either to a success, or to a failure. In the former case, the merge of $\overline{c}$ and $\overline{s}$ gives a (successful) trace a of the adapter A (and consequently a path in $SET(A)$). At each step, the merge process compares nodes $\overline{c_i}$ and $\overline{s_j}$, by starting from the roots of the two traces, and it produces a node a_k. In terms of BPEL activities, one may think of the node a_k as a sequence containing a flow. The merge algorithm basically adds activities of the two nodes ($\overline{c_i}$ and $\overline{s_j}$) either inside the flow, or inside the sequence yet following the flow. For simplicity, we informally describe hereafter the algorithm of merging two nodes containing each one activity only, and each being the target of at most one dependency. (The general case of merging nodes with multiple activities and multiple constraints is analogous.) If $\overline{c_i}$ is unconstrained, then add $\overline{c_i}$ to the flow inside a_k (e.g., merging *receive JobId* and *receive SetCoords*). Please note that in the case of an unconstrained *invoke* activity, the merge process (of the two traces) returns with a *failure*. We do so in order to avoid the generation of (arbitrary) messages by the adapter. Otherwise, if $\overline{c_i}$ is constrained by $\overline{s_J}$ such that $J < j$ (i.e., from the point of view of executing the trace $\overline{s}$, activity of $\overline{s_J}$ has already been executed), then add $\overline{c_i}$ to the flow (e.g., merging *invoke SetCoords* and *invoke SubmitRep*). Otherwise, if $\overline{c_i}$ is constrained by $\overline{s_J}$ such that $J = j$ (i.e., activity of $\overline{s_J}$ is ready to be executed), then add $\overline{c_i}$ to the sequence, following the flow (e.g., merging *invoke Login* and *receive Login*). Otherwise, if $\overline{c_i}$ is constrained by $\overline{s_J}$ such that $j < J$ (i.e., activity of $\overline{s_J}$ is not executable yet), then we say that the trace $\overline{c}$ is "stalled" (e.g., assume merging *invoke SetJob* and *receive SetCoords*). Next, the algorithm does the same for $\overline{s_j}$. For example, one may see in Figure 3(c) the result of merging the roots of $\overline{ME_{CC}}$, and $\overline{CC_{ME}}$. (The elimination of the flow is due to the fact that it contains one activity only.) If both traces are stalled, then we have a lock between the two traces, and hence a *failure* in merging the two traces. Otherwise, the algorithm continues by comparing the node $\overline{c_i}$ (if $\overline{c}$ is stalled) or $\overline{c_{i+1}}$ (if $\overline{c}$ is not stalled) with the node $\overline{s_j}$ (if $\overline{s}$ is stalled) or $\overline{s_{j+1}}$ (if $\overline{s}$ is not stalled). If the merge has added to the trace a all nodes of one of the two traces ($\overline{c}/\overline{s}$), it simply appends at the end of a the remaining sequence of nodes of the other trace ($\overline{s}/\overline{c}$). If all nodes of both $\overline{c}$ and $\overline{s}$ have been added to a, then we have a *success*, and a represents a (successful) trace of the adapter A.

Next, we derive $SET(A)$ by merging all successful traces a of A. If no such successful traces exist, then the algorithm generating the adapter fails, as the mismatches between the two interacting processes cannot be solved. For example, if the root of $SET(\overline{C_S})$ consists of an *invoke Op1* and if the root of $SET(\overline{S_C})$ consists of another *invoke Op2*, then we have a deadlock as each service is waiting to receive a message from the other. Consider a set $\{a^1, a^2, \ldots, a^p\}$ of successful adapter traces. The merge algorithm, in this case, starts by considering $SET(A)$ to be a^1. Then, for all nodes a_i^k of the other traces a^k, it checks whether a_i^k is contained in $SET(A)$ at depth i. If so, it marks the respective position in the tree, and it choses the next node in the sequence (i.e., a_{i+1}^k). Otherwise, it adds the rest of the trace a^k, including the node a_i^k, as a branch splitting from the last marked node in $SET(A)$. For our example, we get only two successful traces of the adapter. The first one, denoted by (5) in Figure 3(d) is obtained by merging the traces denoted by (1) and (3) of $SET(\overline{ME_{CC}})$ and $SET(\overline{CC_{ME}})$, respectively, while the second one, denoted by (6) is obtained by merging traces denoted by (2) and (4). These two adapter traces are then merged into the adapter given in Figure 3(d).

Adapter Workflow. If the adapter has at least one successful trace, then the adaptation process generates next the YAWL workflow of the adapter A from $SET(A)$ as described hereafter. Initially, it generates the *Begin(Process)* and the *Begin(Sequence)*, as well as the *End(Sequence)* and the *End(Process)* patterns [7], which logically mark the initiation of the business process and of its activity, as well as their termination, respectively. The former two, as well as the last two are to be linked in a sequence. (See Figure 4.) Basically, generating the pattern of a basic activity simply consists of instantiating the *Basic Pattern Template* defined in [7] (e.g., setting the name, inputs, and outputs of its *Activity Specific Task*), while generating the pattern of a structured one reduces to instantiating its *Begin* and its *End* patterns, and the pattern of each child activity (, as well as the patterns for handling the exceptional behaviour, if any). For each node n in $SET(A)$, starting with its root, the algorithm generates and adds to the workflow the pattern(s) corresponding to the activity (activities) contained in n. If n consists of one activity only, then the pattern of its (basic) activity is produced and suitably linked in the workflow as output of the pattern corresponding to

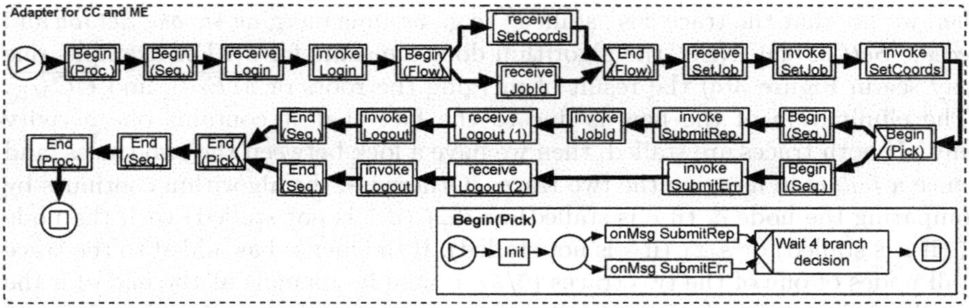

Fig. 4. YAWL workflow of an adapter for CC and ME

the parent node of n (or to *Begin(Sequence)* if n is the root). For example, the *receive Login* root of $SET(A)$ leads to a *Receive* pattern linked as output of *Begin(Sequence)*. If n consists of multiple activities, then the pattern given by the node is a *Flow*, which includes the patterns of each activity in the node. Next, if n has one child node only, the adaptation process continues with its child. Otherwise, if n has more than one successor, then we have three possibilities: (1) If all child nodes of n contain each one *receive* only, and if there are no conditions constraining their execution[4] then the resulting pattern is a *Pick* having the respective *receives* as *onMessage* tasks in *Begin(Pick)*, and for each branch is generated a *Sequence* pattern. The generation process continues then on each subtree having as root a child of n (excluding the child of n already considered as *onMessage* inside the *Pick*). (2) If all child nodes of n are constrained by (disjoint) conditions, then a *Switch* pattern is produced with the respective conditions as guards, and for each branch of the *Switch*, a *Sequence* pattern is generated. The algorithm continues next on each branch of the subtree with the root n. (3) In all other cases, the adaptation process aborts, as the adapter cannot be successfully constructed due to a non-deterministic (other than *pick*) behaviour. For example, if n has two unconstrained children, one *invoke Op1* and one *receive Op2*, then the adapter cannot "know" whether it should wait for a message, or whether it should send a message. The YAWL adapter one obtains for our example is presented in Figure 4.

3.3 Lock Analysis

In [4] we show how reachability graphs (or modified reachability trees) can be employed to check the lock-freedom of aggregations of YAWL workflows (e.g., a non-final node of the reachability graph/tree without outgoing links corresponds to a deadlock). Hence, through this methodology one may check whether the aggregation [4,6] of the workflows of C, A, and S locks. If all traces of the aggregate are lock-free, then A is a *full adapter* for C and S. Otherwise, if

[4] We recall that such conditions are due to the guards of *switch* activities and synchronisation links.

some (yet not all) of the traces of the aggregate are lock-free, then A is a *partial adapter*, as there are interaction scenarios that cannot be resolved. Finally, if the aggregate does not have lock-free traces, then we consider that the adaptation has failed. (Although space limitations do not allow us to demonstrate it, note that the adapter for CC and ME given in Figure 4 is a full adapter.)

3.4 Adapter Deployment

If the Lock Analysis phase has validated A as a full/partial adapter, then the Adapter Deployment phase generates the BPEL process of the adapter A from its YAWL workflow. The deployment process works by parsing the YAWL workflow with respect to the patterns defined in our BPEL2YAWL translator [7]. For example, the *Pick* pattern in Figure 4 leads to the generation of a BPEL *pick* with two branches guarded by *onMessage SubmitRep*, and *onMessage SubmitErr*, where each branch activity is a *sequence*. Although not explicitly represented in the figures, the YAWL patterns translating BPEL activities contain all the necessary information for the inverse, YAWL2BPEL translator (e.g., *partnerLink*, *portType*, *operation*, and *variable* attributes in the case of a *receive*, and so on). The YAWL workflow of the adapter in Figure 4, leads to the following BPEL (adapter) process:

```
<process name="Adapter_for_CC_and_ME"><sequence>
  <receive op="Login" from CommandCentre var="loginInfo"/>
  <invoke op="Login" of MarsExplorer var="loginInfo"/>
  <flow>
    <receive op="SetCoords" from CommandCentre var="coords"/>
    <receive op="JobID" from MarsExplorer var="id"/></flow>
  <receive op="SetJob" from CommandCentre var="jobDetails"/>
  <invoke op="SetJob" of MarsExplorer var="jobDetails"/>
  <invoke op="SetCoords" of MarsExplorer var="coords"/>
  <pick>
    <onMsg op="SubmitRep" from MarsExplorer var="report"><sequence>
      <invoke op="SubmitRep" of CommandCentre var="report">
      <invoke op="JobID" of CommandCentre var="id"/>
      <receive op="Logout" from CommandCentre/>
      <invoke op="Logout" of MarsExplorer/></sequence></onMsg>
    <onMsg op="SubmitErr" from MarsExplorer var="error"><sequence>
      <invoke op="SubmitErr" of CommandCentre var="error">
      <receive op="Logout" from CommandCentre/>
      <invoke op="Logout" of MarsExplorer/>
    </sequence></onMsg></pick></sequence></process>
```

4 Concluding Remarks

In this paper we have outlined a methodology for the automated generation of (service) adapters capable of solving behavioural mismatches between BPEL processes. Its main features are: (1) It automatically synthesises a full/partial BPEL adapter (if possible) from two input BPEL processes, (2) it generates the YAWL workflow of the adapter, which can be used to check properties (e.g., lock-freedom, reachability, liveness, and so on) of the interaction with the adapted services, as well as (3) it can be straightforward integrated with the ontology-enriched service customisation [5] and service aggregation [4,6] approaches, as all use service contracts with YAWL as intermediate language to represent the service behaviour.

Web *service adaptation* is in its early stages and current approaches feature only partial solutions to the issues of adaptation. Iyer et al. [9] employ XML scripts and XSL to (manually) achieve the signature-level interoperability of SOAP services. Syu [12] describes an OWL-S based approach to deal with only three cases of adaptation of input parameters: permutation, modification, and combination. Hau et al. [8] provide a framework for semantic matchmaking and service adaptation, which deals with signature mismatches, yet not with behavioural ones. Ponnekanti and Fox [11] propose a framework for coping with structural, value, encoding, and semantic incompatibilities among services. Yet, their approach – as [8,9,12] – relies on black-box (viz., behaviour-less) views of services. A methodology for generating service adapters to solve behavioural mismatches was presented by Brogi et al. in [3], yet it assumes the availability of an adapter specification to be manually generated. Benatallah et al. [1] describe an approach for the generation of replaceability adapters based on mismatch patterns. However, their approach cannot capture complex behavioural mismatches (through pattern compositions), and the generation of the adapter code relies on the designer (e.g., the provision of the template parameters).

It is worth noting that our adaptation methodology can be successfully employed to generate *replaceability adapters*, viz., adapters that wrap Web services so that they become compliant with other services (e.g., wrapping new service versions for backwards compatibility). Given two services, S and S^*, wrapping S^* so as to behave like S with respect to clients C can be achieved by computing $SET(A)$ as the merge of $SET(S_C)$ and $SET(\overline{S^*_C})$. Furthermore, *behavioural service customisation*, viz., the generation of adapters that wrap services S^* into exposing to clients C a partial behaviour S, can be achieved again by computing $SET(A)$ as the merge of $SET(S_C)$ and $SET(\overline{S^*_C})$.

Two main lines of future work are the development of adapters capable of solving behavioural mismatches among several interacting BPEL processes, as well as enhancing the adaptation methodology to cope with ontology mismatches along the lines of [4,5].

References

1. B. Benatallah, F. Casati, D. Grigori, H. R. M. Nezhad, and F. Toumani. Developing Adapters for Web Services Integration. In *Proc. of CAiSE, LNCS vol. 3520*, pages 415–429, 2005.
2. BPEL4WS Coalition. Business Process Execution Language for Web Services v1.1.
3. A. Brogi, C. Canal, E. Pimentel, and A. Vallecillo. Formalizing Web Service Choreographies. In *Proc. of WS-FM'04, ENTCS 105*, pages 73–94, 2004.
4. A. Brogi and R. Popescu. Contract-based Service Aggregation. Technical Report, University of Pisa, Sep. 2006. (`http://www.di.unipi.it/~popescu/CoSA.pdf`).
5. A. Brogi and R. Popescu. Service Adaptation through Trace Inspection. In *Proc. of SOBPI'05*, pages 44–58, 2005.
6. A. Brogi and R. Popescu. Towards Semi-automated Workflow-Based Aggregation of Web Services. In *Proc. of ICSOC'05, LNCS vol. 3826*, pages 214–227, 2005.

7. A. Brogi and R. Popescu. From BPEL Processes to YAWL Workflows. In *Proc. of WS-FM'06, LNCS vol. 4184*, pages 107–122, 2006.
8. J. Hau, W. Lee, and S. Newhouse. The ICENI Semantic Service Adaptation Framework. In UK e-Science All Hands Meeting, 2003. (`http://www.nesc.ac.uk/events/ahm2003/AHMCD/pdf/017.pdf`).
9. A. Iyer, G. Smith, P. Roe, and J. Pobar. An Example of Web Service Adaptation to Support B2B Integration. (`http://ausweb.scu.edu.au/aw02/papers/refereed/smith2/paper.html`).
10. M. P. Papazoglou and D. Georgakopoulos. Service-Oriented Computing. *Communications of the ACM*, 46(10):24–28, 2003.
11. S. R. Ponnekanti and A. Fox. Interoperability among independently evolving web services. In *Proc. of the 5th ACM Int. Conf. on Middleware*, pages 331–351, 2004.
12. J.-Y. Syu. *An Ontology-Based Approach to Automatic Adaptation of Web Services*. Department of Information Management National Taiwan University, 2004. (`http://www.im.ntu.edu.tw/IM/Theses/r92/R91725051.pdf`).
13. W. M. P. van der Aalst and A. H. M. ter Hofstede. YAWL: Yet Another Workflow Language. *Inf. Syst.*, 30(4):245–275, 2005.
14. F.-Y. Wang, Y. Gao, and M. Zhou. A Modified Reachability Tree Approach to Analysis of Unbounded Petri Nets. *IEEE Transactions on Systems, Man and Cybernetics – Part B*, 34(1):303–308, 2004.
15. WSDL Coalition. Web Service Description Language (WSDL) v1.1.

Division of Labor: Tools for Growing and Scaling Grids

T. Freeman[2], K. Keahey[2,3], I. Foster[1,2,3], A. Rana[4], B. Sotomoayor[1], and F. Wuerthwein[4]

[1] Department of Computer Science, University of Chicago, Chicago, IL, USA
[2] Computation Institute, University of Chicago & Argonne National Lab, Chicago, IL, USA
[3] Math & Computer Science Division, Argonne National Lab, Argonne, IL, USA
[4] Department of Physics, University of California, San Diego, CA, USA
{foster, freeman, keahey, borja}@mcs.anl.gov,
{rana, fkw}@ucsd.edu

Abstract. To enable Grid scalability and growth, a usage model has evolved whereby resource providers make resources available not to individual users directly, but rather to larger units, called virtual organizations. In this paper, we describe abstractions that allow resource providers to delegate the usage of remote resources dynamically to virtual organizations in application-independent ways, and present and evaluate an implementation of this abstraction using the Xen virtual machine and Linux networking tools. We also describe how our implementation is being used in a specific context, namely the enforcement of resource allocations in the Edge Services Framework, currently deployed in the Open Science Grid.

Keywords: virtualization, grid computing, resource management, distributed computing.

1 Introduction

Over the last decade of successful Grid usage, a model has evolved whereby a number of resources federated by a large *resource provider* such as Grid3 [1] (and its successor Open Science Grid (OSG) [2]) and TeraGrid [3] make resources available not to individual users directly but rather to larger communities, called *virtual organizations* (VOs) [4]. Each VO then enables its users to use the resources according to VO-specific policies. This interaction model allows Grids to scale—a fundamental condition of growth—since instead of providing for the needs of each of many thousands of users directly, a resource provider need interact only with a smaller number of VOs.

To function correctly, this VO-based scheduling model requires the development of tools that can ensure that the resources provided to each client (i.e., VO) are delivered in a controlled manner, so that clients obtain the resources they need, and one client cannot interfere with others, for example by acquiring excess resources or damaging data. In addition, it is frequently important that individual clients be able to deploy specialized software not supported by the resource provider. In short, the growth and scalability of Grids requires the development of mechanisms that allow

A. Dan and W. Lamersdorf (Eds.): ICSOC 2006, LNCS 4294, pp. 40–51, 2006.

for a clear separation of concerns between resource providers and the clients that consume resources, and thus enable a *division of labor* [5].

We argue that to address management issues arising from this "division of labor," we must develop abstractions and tools that allow clients to dynamically configure, deploy, and manage required execution environments in application-independent ways, as well as to negotiate enforceable resource allocations for the execution of these environments. We have previously defined the *virtual workspace* abstraction [6] that meets many of these requirements. In this paper, we refine this abstraction to address dynamic resource allocation and management issues. In so doing, we provide a tool satisfying the separation of concerns requirements between resource provider and a client.

More specifically, in this paper we show how a workspace implementation based on virtual machines (VMs) can be extended to respond to negotiated resource allocations. We also quantify via experimental studies how well such allocations can be enforced. Finally, we report on the use of our workspace mechanisms to provide a platform for Edge Services [7]—VO-specific infrastructure services particularly sensitive to resource sharing—and discuss how workspaces are being used to support Edge Services on the OSG production grid.

In summary, our contributions in this paper are as follows:

- We describe an abstraction for providing mechanisms for dynamically negotiated resource usage as seen from the client's perspective.
- We show an implementation of this abstraction using the Globus Toolkit [8], the Xen virtual machine tools [9], and Linux networking tools.
- We describe how this abstraction and implementation has been used to realize Edge Services on the Open Science Grid.
- We evaluate our abstraction and implementation experimentally.

2 Related Work

The need for abstractions and mechanisms that enable a separation of resource provider and VO enforcement functions has been argued elsewhere [10, 11]. Our work here focuses on the management of such resource "slots," with a particular focus on issues that arise when managing more than one slot attribute at a time.

Several projects have explored the of VMs in distributed computing [12-15]. In particular, the Cluster-On-Demand (COD) [16] and VIOLIN [17] projects are relevant to our effort as they address resource management issues arising when overlaying virtual machines over physical resources. However, while these projects focus on simulating coarse-grain management of large numbers of VMs, we develop fine-grain abstractions and enforcement methods that provide detailed low-level management. We also model virtual resources in terms of allocations directly available to the resource user, requiring that overhead be accounted for separately. The Virtuoso Project [18] builds a VM scheduler and their approach is complementary to our work.

The interfaces we propose are informed by the standards work at the Open Grid Forum, specifically the work on WS-Agreement [19] and the Job Submission Definition Language (JSDL) [20]. We focus on the implementation of such interfaces to negotiating Grid abstractions and on demonstrating their relevance.

3 Requirements and Focus

Our argument for enabling "division of labor" between resource providers and VOs is driven by the need to provide mechanisms for flexible and scalable behavior in the Grid. It is impossible for a resource provider to provide every bit of configuration for a VO, much less to arbitrate between competing demands from different VOs for different configurations. Instead, we want to allow resource providers to focus on providing and maintaining resources. In general, we want to enable a *provider* (e.g., a resource owner) to delegate the usage of a well-constrained resource quantum to a *consumer* (e.g., a VO) such that this consumer in turn can further distribute those resources among its customers (e.g., VO users). As we have explained elsewhere [6], this situation may involve many resource layers and employ different workspace implementations to achieve the desired fairness and granularity of sharing.

A compelling illustration of the need for division of labor between resource providers and VOs is provided by *Edge Services*, Grid middleware services that run at a site to enable remote access to site resources. Examples of Edge Services include job management services, storage brokers, and database caches. Edge Service implementations must often perform multiple privileged and unprivileged actions, such as data staging and registration, security processing, monitoring, and resource procurement. The variety of possible implementations means that Edge Services are often VO-specific. Different VOs upgrade them on a different schedule and may use conflicting versions of the software.

Further, each VO works with an often large and dynamically changing pool of users and has to mold its policies to changing objectives (e.g., research vs. development). In addition, since all requests for site use come through Edge Services, they easily become a bottleneck as request rates increase. Because of their variety and complexity (combination of differently owned processes and threads, network and disk traffic, and memory demands) it is hard for a resource provider to track, account, and enforce resource usage and thus ensure quality of service for any particular VO. This leads to situations where some users cannot use a site at all due to excessive traffic from others. Last but not least, the relationship between an organization and resource provider evolves constantly reflecting the need for potentially frequent and dynamic change in the configuration and policy assigned to Edge Services.

Without a mechanism enabling a resource provider to effectively delegate bulk resource usage to a VO, the provider takes on a significant burden affecting its ability to scale – and to prevent any one VO from impacting another. In a general case, such mechanism should provide separation along the following dimensions:

1) *Environment and configuration*: a VO should be able to obtain the configuration it needs independently of the resource provider.
2) *Isolation*: a VO's internal activities should not impact the resource provider, and thus should do not need to be under the provider's control.
3) *Resource usage and accounting*: a provider needs to be able to provide a resource in a way that is independent of how the resource is consumed.

We focus here on the third concern; the other two concerns are the subject of our ongoing research [6, 21].

4 Allocating Resources to Workspaces

The term Virtual Workspaces [21] a customized and isolated execution environment that can be dynamically deployed in the Grid. This environment is implemented by a workspace image, typically provided by the client, that contains all information necessary for its deployment. In addition, the client provides a resource allocation request that describes resources bound to the workspace at deployment time. The workspace service also provides management interfaces based on the Web Services Resource Framework (WSRF) [22], such as inspection and lifetime management. Workspaces can be implemented by various means, such as software imaging on physical resources as well as virtual machines. Here, we explain how the workspace service is used to assign resources to activities contained in the workspace.

4.1 Negotiating Resource Allocations

We define a workspace's *resource allocation* as those resources *directly* available to the workspace. This allocation does not include additional (overhead) resources that the resource provider requires to support the workspace's execution.

We model a resource allocation as a `ResourceAllocation` element, based on the JSDL [20] `Resources` element, with extensions as highlighted in Figure 1. Time is specified as start time and duration of deployment (in practice, only current start time is supported). Memory size is also specified as single value. CPU type is specified as a list of architectures (e.g., x86, IA64, x86_64) and percentage pairs to accommodate workspaces with multiple CPUs. Storage and networking are also specified as potentially multiple resource slots with salient characteristics; for example, in the Edge Services example, the two networking slots are used for private and public connection, respectively. The `Storage` element may describe one or more partitions in terms of size and read/write speeds. (This information may determine if partitions need to reside in local storage or may be remote.) The networking element specifies the incoming and outgoing bandwidth, as measured by the iperf program for a virtual NIC. The values of duration, CPU percentage, size, read/write speed and bandwidth can be specified as JSDL RangeValue term. Currently, only exact values (JSDL Exact) and lower-bound open-ended ranges (JSDL LowerBoundedRange, interpreted to mean "the assigned value or more") are supported.

All values specified as part of `ResourceAllocation` can be specified as a ranges of acceptable values in a request (e.g., 50-60% of CPU), thus allowing a client to pose open-ended resource requests to be concretized by the workspace service on acceptance. Feasible resource allocation ranges are published by the workspace factory service, much like WS-Agreement agreement templates [19]. Information about feasible ranges takes into account resource coordination; for example, the current workspace service policy does not allow clients to specify resource allocations that cannot be realized as in the case where not enough CPU is requested for a certain network bandwidth.

Shaping resource assignment policy for a specific workspace has four stages: (1) a client defines a requested resource allocation, (2) the resource allocation is assigned based on negotiation with the resource provider, (3) the assigned resource allocation is published, and (4) the resource allocation is potentially renegotiated. Our current implementation uses a simple all-or-nothing negotiation strategy: a *requested resource allocation* is sent as part of the Workspace Service's create operation and is either accepted or rejected based on resource availability. If accepted, the *assigned resource allocation* (which concretizes value ranges of the requested resource allocation) is published as a WSRF resource property of the workspace.

Renegotiation is achieved by updating the resource property values. This updating can be performed either by sending a completely new resource property description or by requesting the adjustment of a specific value (e.g., CPU percentage). In the latter case, the request is interpreted as if the existing resource allocation value was sent with the adjusted value. As with workspace creation, the result of this operation is subject to the same all-or-nothing strategy. If the request cannot be satisfied the workspace deployment is not disrupted; if it can, new resources are assigned.

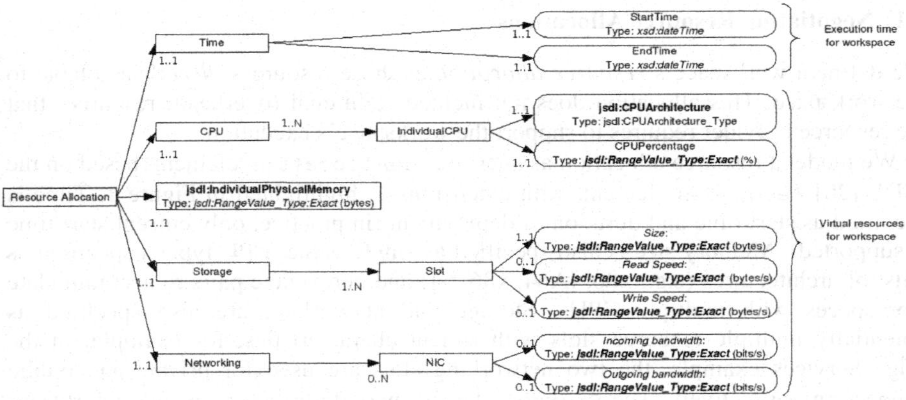

Fig. 1. The Resource Allocation Element

A client request may specify requirements for only some of the resources: for example, only memory and CPU. In such cases, default values for other resources are assigned by the workspace service. These default policies are published as resource properties by the workspace factory service. The current implementation provides only a "best effort" policy, we are experimenting with more controllable defaults, e.g. preventing service starvation through overbooking of memory or other qualities.

4.2 Enforcing the Resource Allocation

Our current VM-based workspace implementation deploys workspaces on a pool of resources configured with a hypervisor, and interacts with those workspaces through a configurable back-end. We focus in this paper on an implementation based on the Xen hypervisor [9]. In Xen, privileged hypervisor interaction usually takes place in domain 0, which allows a client to create and manage other virtual machines (called user or guest domains).

The physical memory size allocated to a Xen domain is specified when the domain is created. This memory size can be adjusted after startup using Xen's balloon driver. Two flavors of disk allocation are needed: obtaining storage for disk partitions that form a part of a VM image, and providing extra writing space for the VM. We address the former requirement by mounting the VM partition as a loopback device. (A physical partition on the local disk could also be mounted, but those are already allocated.) We address the latter requirement by allocating space from network filesystems or by creating new, blank loopback images. For best access and write times, both read and write partitions should be mounted from whichever site disk can offer the best performance within the requested allocation. In order to accomplish this goal of best performance, the workspace service keeps track of available local disk space on various resources and uses the "size" element in partition meta-data to schedule workspace deployment.

To enforce the CPU allocation we used the Xen Simple-Earliest Deadline First (SEDF) [23] scheduler, which provides weighted (i.e., percentage based) CPU sharing between domains. Weights can be specified exactly, or alternatively the scheduler can be allowed to give a domain extra CPU cycles if they are available, in which case it provides *at least* the specified weight. In practice, the latter policy results in better overall performance and was used throughout our experiments. The assigned CPU share as well as the policy can be changed dynamically. For CPU-intensive domains, we found that an assignment of 5-10% to domain 0 gave a good balance.

Effective resource allocation frequently requires coordinating more than one resource dimension. For example, when requesting a bandwidth allocation to a workspace, we have to ensure not only that the incoming/outgoing message rate is limited but also that the CPU share assigned to both the workspace and hypervisor overhead is sufficient to process messages. Since domain 0 in Xen acts like a switch, switching traffic to user domains, we have to maintain a balance between weights allocated to domain 0 and the guest domains: while domain 0 needs to process all incoming messages, giving it more weight at the cost of guest domains may result in poor performance as the guest domains are unable to process traffic in a timely fashion. In addition, while scheduling a domain more often improves the latency of this domain (as it is able to receive messages faster), it also results in higher context switching and thus CPU cost.

To develop rough guidelines for managing these tradeoffs, we conducted a parameter sweep over different CPU allocations for up to eight deployed domains, with the goal of obtaining an aggregate bandwidth to those domains within 1% of the maximum bandwidth achievable for our hardware (described in Section 6). We found that while CPU allocations for both the hypervisor and guest domains can vary due to various factors, it was possible to obtain acceptable bandwidth (within 1% of maximum for our hardware) by using bounds on those settings. Specifically, we adopted a bound of 20% of CPU for the domain 0 setting and guest bounds dependent on the number of guest domains. (For example, for the two domains case described in Section 6, the aggregate bound was 20%.)

The workspace service then bases its allocation decisions on those bounds and admits only allocations that can be supported within them. We find in our experiments that there is often a substantial difference between actual CPU utilization and the CPU weight assigned (typically less CPU gets used). However, weights are important to obtain the desired bandwidth. In addition, we find that while our bounds on CPU weights simplify resource management, they also allow further inefficiency to burden the system. Thus, our present SEDF-based resource management strategy for CPU allocations is approximate and sacrifices much utilization to compensate for the relative lack of control that SEDF provides over CPU allocations for I/O intensive operations. Work on alternative schedulers that address the SEDF shortcomings leading to this inefficiency is underway [24, 25] and we plan to explore such alternatives in the future.

Xen does not implement controlled bandwidth sharing itself, so we rely on Linux network shaping tools [26] for that purpose. We again take advantage of the facts that the network interface of each domain is connected to a virtual network interface in domain 0 by a point-to-point link and that traffic on these virtual interfaces is handled in domain 0 using standard Linux mechanisms for bridging, routing and rate limiting. To implement bandwidth sharing (for both incoming and outgoing bandwidth) we limit the rate of network traffic going to and from the respective domains using the Hierarchical Token Bucket queuing discipline [27]. To implement this behavior, we needed to recompile the domain 0 kernel. We developed an API to the Linux tools that allows us to set the bandwidth rates for created domains. We also increase the domain 0 CPU allocation by 2% to manage bandwidth splitting for user domains.

5 Case Study: Edge Services Framework

The Edge Services Framework (ESF) has been developed to decouple the tasks of (a) configuring and managing VO service nodes and (b) providing resources, thus allowing for division of labor between VO administrator and site administrator. ESF achieves this decoupling by leveraging the workspace abstraction to allow a VO administrator to configure an Edge Service image and deploy it based on need and resource availability.

ESF consists of a workspace image library, image transport and storage mechanisms, and the workspace service. The image library contains base images (basic OS configuration, at present including Scientific Linux 3/4, CentOS 3/4, and Fedora Core 4) and fully configured Edge Services images, currently including the ATLAS DASH service [28] and CMS FroNtier [29]. Since Edge Service images can be large in size (5 to ~10 GB), ESF uses compression and fast transport mechanisms (GridFTP [30]) as well as high-end Storage Elements (SEs) such as dCache [31].

The role of a VO administrator is to prepare, configure, and test an ES image. The image can then be shared within the VO, transported to deployment sites, and stored within the local site SE, where it can be retrieved for deployment by any VO administrator. In the current deployment, images stored on a site are further manually configured with required IP addresses and a pre-generated credential. We are working to automating those latter tasks as part of workspace deployment [21].

The role of a site administrator is to provision hardware resources that can be used for Edge Services and to ensure the proper configuration and maintenance of those hardware resources. In our testbed these tasks include configuring hardware resources with Xen, and providing one deployment of the workspace service per site. A site administrator also provisions storage space in a local Storage Element for storage and retrieval of ES images.

During site operation, Edge Service workspaces are dynamically retrieved, provisioned, and deployed by a VO administrator authorized using their VOMS credentials [32]. For example, when working with ATLAS analysis jobs requiring a database cache of a specific type, an ATLAS administrator deploys the DASH Edge Service. On deployment, the cache initializes using remote data repositories over its public network connection and is then available on the private network to the jobs submitted by ATLAS users to the site.

The current ESF deployment spans both integration-level testbed sites and production-level sites on OSG. Integration-level sites include Argonne National Laboratory, Fermilab, University of Chicago, and UCSD. The production-level deployment is at DISUN [33] at SDSC.

6 Experimental Evaluation

To evaluate the usefulness of our approach, we performed experiments in a configuration comprising two VOs, VO1 and VO2. Each VO deployed an Edge Service on the same physical node, an AMD Athlon MP 2200 (booted in single CPU mode) with 2GB memory and a GB NIC over a 100 Mbps switch. The machine was configured with Linux 2.6.12 and Xen 3.0. The Edge Services were managed using our workspace service deployed on a different node than the services themselves and receiving requests from VO clients running on separate nodes.

6.1 Managing Execution Request Throughput

We first examined to what extent running within workspaces helps implement policy-regulated sharing between VOs. For this experiment, we modeled the work of a Compute Element (CE) by configuring an Edge Service with the GT4.0 GRAM service receiving non-staging requests (/bin/date) from the two VO clients. To simulate high load on VO1, we used an additional load client that submitted to VO1 a job performing 2 million square root operations every 10 seconds.

We considered a scenario in which one VO receives high request load in two different settings: (1) a physical machine setting in which the CE is deployed directly on the physical machine and used by both VOs (reflecting the situation in most current deployments), and (2) the workspace setting in which each VO deploys the CE in a Xen workspace, and each negotiates a resource allocation of at least 45% CPU weight and 896 MB of memory (domain 0 is set to 10% of CPU and 256 MB).

In both the physical and workspace setting, we measured the end-to-end job throughput of VO1 and VO2 clients. The job submission throughput was calculated over a period starting after the CE was saturated with load to a period when the VO2 client stopped submitting. As expected, the physical scenario resulted in roughly the same (low) request throughput for both VO clients (7.83 jobs/minute for VO1 and 8.0 jobs/minute for VO2), as the pre-existing VO1 load impacted both equally. In the workspace scenario, all VO1 request load is confined to VM1. Thus, we see worse throughput for VM1—4.18 jobs/minute—but observe that the request throughput for VO2 is now unimpacted by VO1 load and increases to 22.36 jobs/minute.

To observe CE behavior more closely over time, we summed the number of completed requests for VO1 and VO2 clients respectively during regular intervals (every 30 seconds) and plotted this number against time. (The values shown are an average of 5 trials and all fall within 10% of the average.) Figure 2 (left) shows the comparison: VO2 has consistently high throughput while VO1 has low throughput until VO2 client stops sending requests, causing VM2 to temporarily stop consuming resources. VO1 is then able to claim a larger CPU weight and obtain more processing power (at 600 seconds the load client ceases to submit and the throughput improves further). Even when we varied the load coming from the load client by doubling or tripling its operations, the VO2 request throughput was unimpacted (right side of Figure 2) and stayed at the same level independently of the load on VO2.

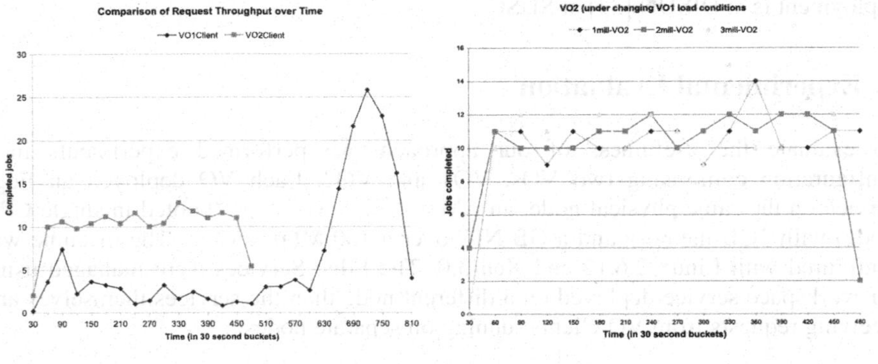

Fig. 2. Request throughput for VO1 and VO2. The graph on the left compares request throughput for VO1 and VO2 over time. The graph on the right shows that the VO2 request throughput remains unimpacted in the presence of increasing load on the physical machine.

6.2 Managing Network Traffic

In this experiment we model a situation that might be experienced during the operation of a Storage Element (SE), in which two VOs run services requiring heavy network traffic. As in the previous example, running the SE inside one workspace does not result in fair sharing. Unlike our previous example, effectively managing such traffic requires simultaneous management of two qualities: the bandwidth leased to each workspace assigned to the respective VOs, and the CPU share required to support the processing of message arrival rates.

Our experimental scenario is the same as in the previous experiment. To isolate network performance, we modeled the work of an SE with a GridFTP 4.0.1 performing memory-to-memory transfers. In our scenario both VO1 and VO2 have each negotiated a resource allocation of 128 MB memory, 6% CPU weight and 4.1 MB/s raw bandwidth (the CPU weight is the minimum needed to process this bandwidth as per our baseline). The workspace service allocates a weight of 22% to domain 0; all remaining CPU share is always taken up by an additional CPU-intensive domain to ensure enforcement.

Figure 3 shows a time trace of the behavior of the two workspaces. VO2 processes a steady stream of requests and saturates its bandwidth from the beginning of the trace. VO1 performs transfers of various sizes for a while and then it too begins to saturate its bandwidth (~150 seconds of the trace). Note that neither domain achieves the raw 4.1 MB/s bandwidth due to application (GridFTP) overhead. After about 240 seconds (first arrow mark on the graph), the VO1 renegotiates its allocation to request a higher bandwidth of 8.2 MB/s requiring at least 14% of CPU (as per our baseline transfer utility measurements). As a result the workspace service adjusts the CPU settings (from 6 to 14) as well as bandwidth settings (from 4.1 to 8.2) on the hypervisor node and the bandwidth for VO1 goes up. To compensate for application overhead, the VO then further renegotiates just the CPU weight from 14 to 34 which brings performance closer to the desired bandwidth.

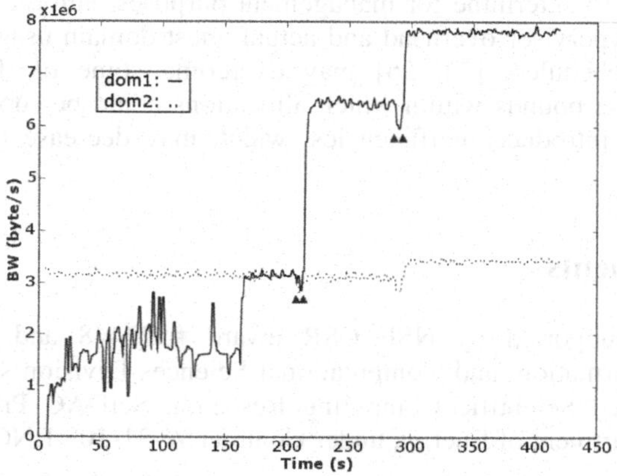

Fig. 3. Isolating SE for VO1 and VO2; the arrows indicate renegotiation points

Renegotiation (Figure 3) takes about 7 seconds. Most of this time (~5 seconds) is taken by SEDF weight adjustments, a factor that is responsible for the indentation in the graph during negotiation time. Increasing the domain 0 allocation speeds up this processing, at a cost of lower guarantees offered to user domains. The times taken by bandwidth adjustment and end-to-end request processing are ~400 ms and ~300ms (WS overhead), respectively.

7 Conclusions

Our deployment and experimental experiences lead us to conclude that workspaces are a promising "division of labor" tool for providers and consumers. We believe that this conclusion is especially true in situations in which the task of understanding interdependencies among various load-causing factors is complex, and indeed potentially impossible to manage at the application level. Load management on OSG service nodes is an example of such a situation, due to the complex and time-varying workloads that may be generated by different clients.

The ability to negotiate and renegotiate resource allocations is particularly important, both to the client and the provider. This ability allows both client and provider to react to changing load conditions and optimize their provisioning to satisfy targets, for example by requesting more CPU to account for application overhead in the GridFTP example. Additional flexibility can be obtained by using migration, as demonstrated by Clark et al. [34] for an application similar to ours.

Our results indicate that it is useful to support "aggregate" resource allocations that combine, for example, bandwidth and CPU allocations, for the reason that an allocation of one resource (e.g., bandwidth) may be wasteful unless matched by at another (e.g., at least a minimal CPU allocation to match a bandwidth allocation). It is a useful aid, and potentially a useful policy, for the resource provider to publish offers of such "bundled" allocations.

Finally, while we managed to obtain reasonable results in bandwidth-related allocations with the SEDF scheduler, we also found that tractable allocations with this scheduler are hard to determine for management purposes, enforce, and account for, both in terms of hypervisor overhead and actual guest domain usage. Ongoing work on credit-based schedulers [24, 25] may overcome some of those issues. Our approach was to use bounds within which allocations could be supported. However, this approach can introduce inefficiencies, which may decrease utilization for the resource provider.

Acknowledgements

This work was supported by NSF CSR award #527448 and, in part, by the Mathematical, Information, and Computational Sciences Division subprogram of the Office of Advanced Scientific Computing Research, SciDAC Program, Office of Science, U.S. Department of Energy, under Contract W-31-109-ENG-38.

References

1. Foster, I. and others. The Grid2003 Production Grid: Principles and Practice. in HPDC 2004: IEEE Computer Science Press.
2. Open Science Grid (OSG). 2004: www.opensciencegrid.org.
3. The TeraGrid Project 2005: www.taragrid.org
4. Foster, I., C. Kesselman, and S. Tuecke, The Anatomy of the Grid: Enabling Scalable Virtual Organizations. International Journal of Supercomputer Applications, 2001. 15(3): p. 200-222.
5. Smith, A., The Wealth of Nations. 1776
6. Keahey, K., I. Foster, T. Freeman, and X. Zhang, Virtual Workspaces: Achieving Quality of Service and Quality of Life in the Grid. Scientific Progamming Journal, 2005.
7. ESF: http://osg.ivdgl.org/twiki/bin/view/EdgeServices/WebHome.
8. Foster, I., Globus Toolkit version 4: Software for Service-Oriented Systems. International Conference on Network and Parallel Computing, 2005.
9. Barham, P., B. Dragovic, K. Fraser, S. Hand, T. Harris, A. Ho, R. Neugebar, I. Pratt, and A. Warfield. Xen and the Art of Virtualization. in SOSP 2003
10. Foster, I., K. Keahey, C. Kesselman, E. Laure, M. Livny, S. Martin, M. Rynge, and G. Singh, Embedding Community-Specific Resource Managers in General-Purpose Grid Infrastructure. White Paper, 2005.
11. Bavier, A., M. Bowman, B. Chun, D. Culler, S. Karlin, S. Muir, L. Peterson, T. Roscoe, T. Spalink, and M. Wawrzoniak. Operating System Support for Planetary-Scale Services. in 1st Symposium on Network Systems Design and Implementation. 2004.
12. Figueiredo, R., P. Dinda, and J. Fortes. A Case for Grid Computing on Virtual Machines. 23rd International Conference on Distributed Computing Systems. 2003.

13. Adabala, S., V. Chadha, P. Chawla, R. Figueiredo, J. Fortes, I. Krsul, A. Matsunaga, M. Tsugawa, J. Zhang, M. Zhao, L. Zhu, and X. Zhu, From Virtualized Resources to Virtual Computing Grids: The In-VIGO System. Future Generation Computer Systems, 2004.
14. Xu, M., Z. Hu, W. Long, and W. Liu, Service Virtualization: Infrastructure and Applications, The Grid: Blueprint for a New Computing Infrastructure. 2004, Morgan Kaufmann.
15. Reed, D., I. Pratt, P. Menage, S. Early, and N. Stratford. Xenoservers: Accountable Execution of Untrusted Programs. in 7th Workshop on Hot Topics in Operating Systems. 1999.
16. Irwin, D., J. Chase, L. Grit, A. Yunerefendi, D. Decker, and K. Yocum, Sharing Networked Resources with Brokered Leases. 2006: in submission, available at http://issg.cs.duke.edu/publications/sisyphus.pdf.
17. Ruth, P., J. Rhee, D. Xu, S. Kennell, and S. Goasguen. Autonomic Live Adaptation of Virtual Computational Environments in a Multi-Domain Infrastructure. in ICAC. 2006.
18. Lin, B. and P. Dinda, VSched: Mixing Batch And Interactive Machines Using Periodic Real-time Scheduling. Supercomputing, 2005.
19. Andrieux, A., K. Czajkowski, A. Dan, K. Keahey, H. Ludwig, J. Pruyne, J. Rofrano, S. Tuecke, and M. Xu, Web Services Agreement Specification (WS-Agreement) 2004: https://forge.gridforum.org/projects/graap-wg/.
20. Andrieux, A., K. Czajkowski, J. Lam, C. Smith, and M. Xu, Standard Terms for Specifying Computational Jobs. http://www.epcc.ed.ac.uk/%7Eali/WORK/GGF/JSDL-WG/DOCS/WS-Agreement_job_terms_for_JSDL_print.pdf, 2003.
21. Lu, W., T. Freeman, K. Keahey, and F. Siebenlist, Making your workspace secure: establishing trust with VMs in the Grid. SC05 Posters, 2005.
22. Czajkowski, K., D. Ferguson, I. Foster, J. Frey, S. Graham, I. Sedukhin, D. Snelling, S. Tuecke, and W. Vambenepe, The WS-Resource Framework. 2004: www.globus.org/wsrf.
23. Xen Scheduling: http://wiki.xensource.com/xenwiki/Scheduling.
24. Gupta, D., L. Cherkasova, R. Gardner, and A. Vahadat, Enforcing Performance Isolation Across Virtual Machines in Xen. HP-2006-77, 2006.
25. Xen CPU Scheduler w/SMP Load Balancer: http://lists.xensource.com/archives/html/xen-devel/2006-05/msg01315.html.
26. Linux Advanced Routing and Traffic Control: http://lartc.org.
27. Devera, M., Hierarchical Token Bucket Queuing. 2005: http://luxik.cdi.cz/~devik/qos/htb/.
28. Vaniachine, A., DASH: Database Access for Secure Hyperinfrastructure: OSG document 307. http://osg-docdb.opensciencegrid.org/cgi-bin/ShowDocument?docid=307.
29. Lueking, L., FroNtier project: http://lynx.fnal.gov/ntier-wiki.
30. Allcock, W., J. Bester, J. Bresnahan, A.L. Chervenak, I. Foster, C. Kesselman, S. Meder, V. Nefedova, D. Quesnel, and S. Tuecke. Secure, Efficient Data Transport and Replica Management for High-Performance Data-Intensive Computing. in Mass Storage Conference. 2001.
31. The dCache Project: http://www.dcache.org.
32. The Virtual Organization Management System: http://infnforge.cnaf.infn.it/projects/voms.
33. Data Intensive Sciences University Network: http://disun.org.
34. Clark, C., K. Fraser, S. Hand, J.G. Hansen, E. Jul, C. Limpach, I. Pratt, and A. Warfield, Live Migration of Virtual Machines. NSDI, 2005.

DECO: Data Replication and Execution CO-scheduling for Utility Grids

Vikas Agarwal, Gargi Dasgupta, Koustuv Dasgupta,
Amit Purohit, and Balaji Viswanathan

IBM, India Research Lab
{avikas, gdasgupt, kdasgupta, ampurohi, bviswana}@in.ibm.com

Abstract. Vendor strategies to standardize grid computing as the IT backbone for service-oriented architectures have created business opportunities to offer grid as a utility service for compute and data–intensive applications. With this shift in focus, there is an emerging need to incorporate agreements that represent the QoS expectations (e.g. response time) of customer applications and the prices they are willing to pay. We consider a utility model where each grid application (job) is associated with a function, that captures the revenue accrued by the provider on servicing it within a specified deadline. The function also specifies the penalty incurred on failing to meet the deadline. Scheduled execution of jobs on appropriate sites, along with timely transfer of data closer to compute sites, collectively work towards meeting these deadlines. To this end, we present DECO, a grid meta-scheduler that tightly integrates the compute and data transfer times of each job. A unique feature of DECO is that it enables differentiated QoS – by assigning profitable jobs to more powerful sites and transferring the datasets associated with them at a higher priority. Further, it employs replication of popular datasets to save on transfer times. Experimental studies demonstrate that DECO earns significantly better revenue for the grid provider, when compared to alternative scheduling methodologies.

1 Introduction

Grid computing is a form of distributed computing in which the use of heterogeneous resources (computation, storage, applications and data), spread across geographic locations and administrative domains, is optimized through virtualization and collective management. Initially conceived to support compute–intensive scientific applications and to share massive datasets, enterprises of all sizes and shapes are slowly beginning to recognize the technology as a foundation for management of IT resources, enabling them to better meet business objectives. Rapid advances in Web services technology have further provided an evolutionary path from the "stovepipe" architecture of traditional grids to a standardized, service–oriented, enterprise class grid of the future. The convergence of SOA and grid computing is embodied by the Global Grid Forum's Open Grid Services Architecture (OGSA) [1] that describes a service–oriented

A. Dan and W. Lamersdorf (Eds.): ICSOC 2006, LNCS 4294, pp. 52–65, 2006.

grid. The specifications provide various capabilities like job execution, data management, resource management, and security, some of which are illustrated in Fig.1(a).

It is of little surprise that the IT infrastructure of the future is being dubbed as the network grid, a universal computing paradigm that takes the ubiquitous connectivity of the Internet to its next logical step–ubiquitous *utility computing.* Grid providers will now store and manage customer data and run their applications in exchange of a usage fee. Today, a number of major vendors are advocating utility computing– for example Sun Grid, HP Utility Data Center, and IBM Deep Computing Capacity On Demand offerings, all promise its customers the choice and control on how to purchase and leverage IT power for competitive advantage. What is interesting about this computing model is its fiscal impact. With the utility grid, IT dollars and resources are not tied up in hardware and administrative costs. Instead, the focus shifts to the more strategic aspects of IT, such as Service Level Agreements (SLAs). These agreements specify QoS–based pricing policies for applications requiring access to computation referred to as compute in rest of the paper and data resources, and enable grid customers to delineate and prioritize business deliverables. From the provider's point of view, SLAs provide endless possibilities for business revenue maximization, based on differentiated quality–of–service.

1.1 Towards a Utility Framework for Grids

In a service-oriented grid, several heterogeneous cluster sites are inter-connected by WAN routers and links. Each cluster site is associated with some compute power and some storage space. The grid hosts customer data and provides compute capabilities. It charges each customer application (job) for usage of compute and storage resources. The conditions for service payments can be captured by a utility model that guarantees a certain QoS level for the price associated with it. Utility models have been proposed for scheduling and resource management in computational grids [2,3].

Since the response time of an application (job) serves as a common service–level objective for providers, we consider a *revenue function* illustrated in Fig.1(b), that captures the QoS requirements in terms of the response time expected by the job and the price it is willing to pay for it. If a job finishes within a deadline T, then the provider earns a revenue R. Otherwise, the revenue decays linearly at a constant rate δ. Eventually, the revenue may decay to a negative number, indicating a *penalty.* The penalty may or may not be unbounded. Each job submitted to the grid is associated with a revenue function. The revenue functions capture a rich space of policy choices by capturing the importance of a task (maximum revenue) as well as its urgency (decay) as separate measures. Each job has some compute requirements in terms of CPU time, and some data requirements, in terms of data files (objects) required for the computation. The total response time of a job is dependent on its execution time, as well as the time taken to transfer its data to the compute site. The execution time depends on the nature of the job and the compute power of the site assigned to it. The

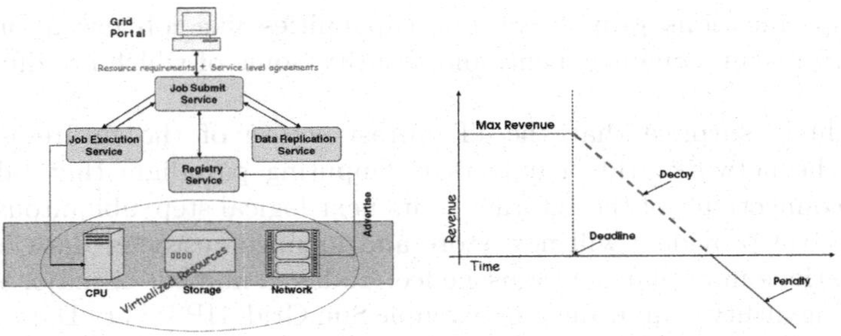

(a) High–level architecture of service–oriented grids (b) Revenue function for utility grids

Fig. 1. Utility framework for grids

transfer time depends on the network connectivity and the location of the data objects. Because of the large number and size of data objects, it is unlikely that a site will have all the data required to execute any job. For data–intensive jobs, the time taken to complete the data transfers to the compute sites over WAN links, can thus be potentially significant. Hence, it is of critical importance that data objects are placed closer to the jobs accessing them. Further, a job needs to transfer all its data before it can execute. It is, however, possible to overlap the transfer time of a job with the execution of other jobs that have their data available locally. Finally, in a utility framework, the order in which the job executions and data transfers are scheduled have implications on the completion time of each job and, hence, the revenue earned by the provider.

Traditional grid solutions have inherently decoupled the execution of jobs from data transfer (and placement) decisions. The *Job Execution Service* handles the scheduling of a batch of jobs at different compute sites. The choice of a site for each job depends upon factors like load on the site, availability of datasets locally etc. Approaches for assigning job execution have been proposed in [4,5]. Multiple transfers of the same data object is avoided by creating replicas of the object at selected sites. The *Data Replication Service* of the grid provides this functionality. A number of algorithms have been proposed in the literature [6,7] for data replication in grids. In each case, changes in data placement are prescribed by a long–term replication process, that studies the history of accesses to data objects. Data objects are transferred (replicated) across sites using transfer protocols like GridFTP [8]. However, decoupling execution assignment from data transfer (and replication) often leads to poor and in-efficient response time for jobs. Since the finish time of jobs translates directly to dollars earned or lost, it is very critical to consider both the execution and transfer times of each job. To do so, job execution service needs to work in close co–ordination with the data replication service. Asynchronous replication of historically popular objects is no longer enough— placement decisions need to be based on the compute locations of jobs, and vice versa. Finally, it is imperative that job and data transfer scheduling policies incorporate service differentiation, i.e. jobs that have

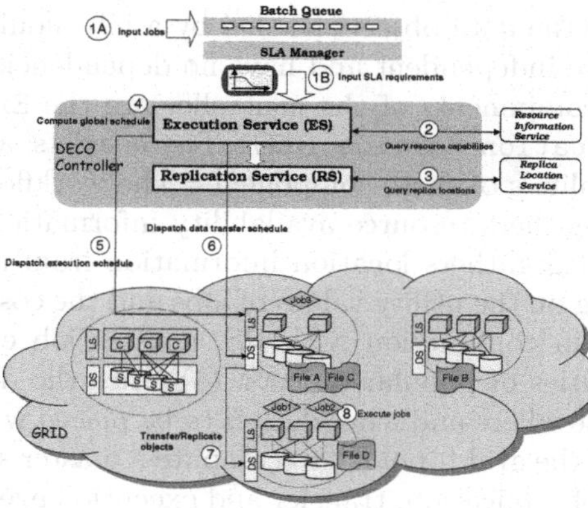

Fig. 2. DECO Architecture

higher revenues and/or harsher penalties need to be assigned higher priorities. This leads towards a *utility–based co–scheduling* framework for grids.

1.2 Contributions

We present **DECO**, a system for **D**ata replication and **E**xecution **CO**-scheduling in utility grids. DECO is designed for business revenue maximization of the grid service provider. DECO decides which job to assign to which site, which objects to replicate at which site, when to execute each job, and finally when to transfer (or replicate) data across the sites. A unique feature of DECO is that it enables differentiated QoS based on the revenue functions of the jobs and their compute/data requirements. Our main contributions include: (i) a co-scheduling framework that tightly couples the job execution and data replication services in a utility grid; (ii) a (meta)scheduling system that co-ordinates the placements of jobs and data objects, and (iii) a differentiated approach for scheduling job executions and data transfers (replications) aimed at maximizing the revenue earned by the provider.

2 DECO Architecture

We propose a co–scheduling framework for integrating the execution and data transfer times of compute and data–intensive applications in grids. Fig.2 gives a detailed view of the proposed framework. We consider as input a batch of grid jobs along with compute and data requirements, and SLA descriptions managed by an `SLA Manager`. Admission controller selects and places jobs in the `Batch Queue` based on business policies, current system state etc. The `DECO Controller` is a single point of submission for all jobs. It computes an offline schedule periodically (for e.g. every 24 hrs), for all unfinished jobs in the queue. The controller works on the following assumptions: every job needs to execute at one cluster site; all the data objects needed by a job should be present at its execution site; jobs are independent and have no dependencies on other jobs.

The two primary components of the controller are the `Execution Service (ES)` and the `Replication Service (RS)`. There exists a tight integration between the functionalities of these components. The workflow of the controller is as follows: (1) ES gathers resource availability information from a Resource Information Service. RS gathers location information from a Replica Location Service. (2) Depending on the utility values of jobs and the cost benefits obtained from replication, ES in conjunction with RS, advises job execution sites and replica creation activities of popular objects. (3) Once the decision is made on which jobs will execute where and what data is to be placed where, the controller uses its global view of the grid topology to compute a master schedule containing an ordered sequence of replication, transfer and execution events across clusters. (4) From the master schedule, DECO extracts the corresponding cluster-specific schedule and dispatches it to each cluster site. Finally, at each cluster site, there is a local job scheduler responsible for intra-cluster job scheduling and management of resources and a data scheduler responsible for handling data transfers to and from the site.

3 Utility–Based Data Replication and Execution Co-scheduling

Assume that the time horizon can be divided into L discrete time intervals, all not necessarily of equal length. If a job finishes in an interval within its completion time deadline T_j, it earns a revenue of Rev_j, else incurs penalty at the rate of Pen_j per hour. Let Z denote the net business revenue earned by all jobs in the workload. The overall approach for maximizing Z is summarized in two steps:

- **Step 1:** Weigh the reward of scheduling each job with the risk of delaying it. Based on these weights decide on which jobs to execute in which time interval and meet their completion time goals by (a) assigning them to appropriate cluster sites and (b) replicating their data objects.
- **Step 2:** Given the entire topology of the provider's network, determine a time schedule of when the job executions and the data transfers (replications) should begin/end.

3.1 Step 1: Integrated Job Assignment and Data Placement

Consider a set of M cluster sites, N data objects and K jobs. Each site i has an associated compute capacity A_i and a storage capacity S_i. Cluster sites a and b are connected by a WAN link of available bandwidth bw_{ab}. Each object o is of size s_o and is associated with a replica set R_o that specifies the clusters at which the object is currently placed. Each job j submitted to the batch queue specifies a compute requirement e_j, and a set of data objects F_j that it will operate on.

WAN transfer times are assumed to be dominant over the LAN parameters. Let β_{io} denote 1 if the data object o is replicated at site i, and 0 otherwise. For job j executing at cluster site i, let te_{ij} denote the job execution time, tr_{ij} denote the total transfer time of all objects in F_j that are not locally present at i, tr_{io} denote the transfer time of the data object o to site i, and bestReplica(i,o) $\in R_o$, denote the cluster site that holds the replica of o and is connected by the highest bandwidth link to i. Then the total time taken to execute job j at site i, t_{ij}, is given by

$$t_{ij} = te_{ij} + tr_{ij} \tag{1}$$

where

$$tr_{ij} = \sum_{o \in F_j} tr_{io} \tag{2}$$

and

$$tr_{io} = (1 - \beta_{io}) s_o / bw(i, bestReplica(i, o)) \tag{3}$$

Let α_{ijl} be an indicator variable denoting 1 if job j is assigned to site i and finishes execution in time interval l, and 0 otherwise. Let U_{jl} denote the utility value of job j finishing at time l. If $\alpha_{ijl} = 1$ and $l \leq T_j$, then $U_{jl} = Rev_j$, else $U_{jl} = Rev_j - (l - T_j) * Pen_j$. The optimal assignment of jobs to sites and objects to sites such that Z is maximized, can be found by solving for the α and β assignments in the following program:
Maximize

$$T = \sum_{i=1}^{M} \sum_{j=1}^{K} \sum_{l=1}^{L} \alpha_{ijl} U_{jl} \tag{4}$$

subject to
Feasibility constraint:

$$\sum_{i=1}^{M} \sum_{l=1}^{L} \alpha_{ijl} = 1, \quad \forall j \tag{5}$$

Compute execution constraint:

$$\sum_{p=1}^{l} \sum_{j=1}^{K} \alpha_{ijp} (te_{ij} + \sum_{o \in F_j} tr_{io}) \leq A_i l, \quad \forall i, l \tag{6}$$

The feasibility constraint ensures that each job finishes in exactly one time interval at a site. The compute execution constraint makes sure that the number of jobs that can complete in time l at a site is atmost A_i times l. The above problem is Max-SNP hard[9] and hence is difficult even to approximate. To obtain a solution we present a simplification of the above problem. We begin with an initial placement $\hat{P}$ of data objects and consider the following two sub–problems: **AssignJobs**:- given the placement of objects, solve the problem for optimal assignment of jobs to cluster sites that maximizes the earned revenue. This reduces to solving the above problem in eqn. 4 for the α variables only (with β equal to 0 or 1). This problem is NP-hard and we design a linear-relaxation

based heuristic for solving it. We relax α to take real values and then round the α values to nearest integers. **AssignReplicas**:- given the job assignments, determine an optimal assignment of replicas to sites such that the replication benefit is maximized. The benefit for replication considered here is the increase in total business profit due to creation of a replica. Consider a replica of object o created at site i. From among the set of jobs assigned to site i and incurring penalties, some of them will be able to now meet their deadline. For each such job j that was paying a penalty of Pen_j, the increment in revenue obtained is $Rev_j - Pen_j$. Let c_{io} denote the total increment in revenue obtained by placing a replica of o at site i. The goal is determine additional replicas of objects such that the increase in business revenue is maximized:
Maximize

$$\sum_{i=1}^{M} \sum_{o=1}^{N} \beta_{io} c_{io} \tag{7}$$

subject to storage constraint:

$$\sum_{o=1}^{N} \beta_{io} s_o \leq S_i, \quad \forall i \tag{8}$$

We relax β to take real values and solve the linear program. The β values returned by the LP are always integral and hence the solution is optimal.

The combination of steps **AssignJobs** and **AssignReplicas** returns an approximate solution to the integrated job assignment and data placement problem. To bring the solution closer to the optimal, we suggest an iterative approach where the placement assignments from **AssignReplicas** serve as input to step **AssignJobs** and the procedure is repeated for k iterations. After the final iteration, an assignment of jobs and data objects to sites is obtained along with the start-time d_j for each job execution at cluster site i.

3.2 Step 2: Computing the Master Schedule

In this step, we derive the time to replicate objects across sites and determine a master schedule that specifies 1) selection of source replicas from which to initiate transfers/replications, and 2) computing a master schedule that specifies when (and where) all data transfers and job executions occur.

Selection of source replicas and computing master schedule. As before, we consider the time horizon can be divided into discrete time intervals, all not necessarily of equal length. Let t_{io} denote the time taken to transfer object o on link i. Let x_{iol} be 1 if transfer of object o on link i completes in the time interval $(l-1, l]$. The deadlines before which each data transfer should complete is given by d_o. These deadlines represent the maximum time before which the object o needs to be present at site i, and are obtained from the start time of jobs (d_j) in job execution schedule obtained from the final iteration of Step 1. When object o is required by multiple jobs with different start times, the earliest start time (minimum d_j) represents the deadline d_o. The problem of selecting source replicas such that these deadlines are satisfied is then essentially finding a feasible assignment of x_{iol} subject to the constraints:

$$\sum_{i=1}^{TotalLinks} \sum_{l=1}^{L} x_{iol} = 1, \quad \forall o \tag{9}$$

$$\sum_{o=1}^{N} \sum_{k=1}^{l} x_{iok} t_{io} \leq l, \quad \forall i, \forall l \tag{10}$$

$$\sum_{i=1}^{TotalLinks} \sum_{l=1}^{L} x_{iol} l \leq d_o, \quad \forall o \tag{11}$$

Eqn. 9 makes sure that a transfer finishes in exactly one time interval on one link; eqn. 10 ascertains that there is no more than one simultaneous transfer on a link; eqn. 11 guarantees all transfers finish before their respective job start times. The resulting LP is essentially the one considered by Shmoys [9] and is known to be NP-hard. We use a rounding heuristic to solve the problem in polynomial time based on the one outlined in [9]. The heuristic returns a selection of links on which to schedule the transfer such that the deadlines are met. Finally, we compute a master schedule that specifies the assignment and ordering of all job executions and replication/data transfer activities.

4 Performance Evaluation

In this section, we evaluate the performance of the proposed two–step algorithm and compare it with alternative heuristics. We use the GridSim toolkit with its new Data Grid capabilities [10], to simulate a compute and data–intensive grid environment. For evaluation, we use a network topology based on the EU DataGrid TestBed topology with 11 sites and 23 links . Each site in the topology is modeled as a cluster site with finite compute and storage resources. The resource settings are obtained from a real testbed scenario outlined in [10]. To make the simulation feasible, we scaled down the compute and storage capacities of all sites while ignoring a few sites with very low compute and network resources. The network link bandwidths are used as specified.

Utility model: The batch of jobs is divided into three classes of Gold, Silver and Bronze jobs depending on their response time requirements (deadlines) and the corresponding revenue they are willing to pay. These jobs also differ in the penalty charged for missing the deadline. Each job has a revenue function associated with it, as described in Section 1, with unbounded penalty. The maximum revenue for a job and its penalty rate are picked from normal distributions with mean dependent on the class that the job belongs to. For the set of results presented here, the ratio

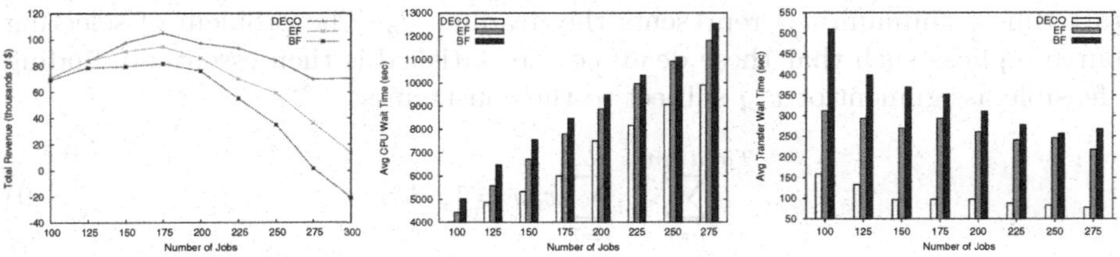

(a) (b) (c)

Fig. 3. Performance of all algorithms (a) Total revenue earned as number of jobs increase (b) Average CPU wait time of jobs before they are granted CPU (c) Average transfer wait time of jobs before all their files are available

of the means for Gold, Silver and Bronze is 5:3:2. The mix of Gold, Silver and Bronze jobs is 20%, 60%, and 20% respectively.

Job distribution: Each job specifies an execution time and a set of files required to execute the job. The number of files per job follows a normal distribution with a variance of 0.25. We vary the mean of the distribution between 3 and 6 to simulate various data-intensive scenarios. To model a realistic workload, the files for a job are chosen based on a Zipf distribution . The execution time for each job is approximately 20 minutes ± 30%. The job deadline time is a factor of its execution time and number of file dependencies. In our experimental setting, gold jobs have smaller (and hence) stricter deadlines than Silver and Bronze jobs. The ratio of the deadlines for Gold, Silver and Bronze jobs is 3:5:7.

Data distribution: Data objects considered in the experiments have an average file size of 1 GB, where file sizes follow a power-law(Pareto) distribution. We begin with a random placement of files at the cluster sites, with each file placed at exactly one site. Files are replicated as long as storage space is available at a site. The file replacement policy of the storage manager at a site is assumed to be LRU.

4.1 Alternative Heuristics

Previous approaches exist that use heuristics for value-based scheduling in computation grids, however they do not consider data requirements. Similarly, approaches in traditional data grids for compute and data assignments do not have an associated utility notion. To obtain competitive alternatives, we combine the best known utility–based scheduling policy [2,3], with the best known heuristics for compute and data assignment.

For each job j delayed by l hours beyond its deadline T_j, its utility value is given by $U_j = (l * Pen_j)/T_j$, where Pen_j is the penalty rate. The list of jobs is sorted based on their utility values. We consider two compute assignment techniques, earliest fit (EF) and best fit (BF). Starting with the first job in the sorted list, EF assigns it to the site that can satisfy it at the earliest time interval. This is a greedy approach, based on the generic Min-Min algorithm

[4,5], that aims at finishing jobs as early as possible. On the other hand, BF assigns the job to the site that can satisfy it at the latest time interval but still meets its deadline [3]. This approach keeps earlier time slots free for later jobs in the list. Both EF and BF, first transfer the required non-local files before it begins execution.

Previous work [11,6] outlines a Threshold based replication scheme, where each site records the number of local data transfers it needs to do for a globally popular file. When number of local transfers exceed a specified threshold, a replica is created locally. This Threshold based scheme is used in EF and BF to replicate files at cluster sites. Note that, both these heuristics have loose coupling of data replication and job execution. We compare DECO's tightly coupled replication and job execution algorithm with the above heuristics. For all the algorithms, we measure the following: (a) total revenue earned by a batch of jobs, including the revenues from satisfied jobs and penalties from those missing their deadlines (b) average time a job has to wait in the queue before it begins execution (c) business revenue earned by creating replicas.

4.2 Experimental Results

In the first set of experiments, we compare the revenue earned by DECO in comparison with EF and BF as shown in Fig.3(a). We increase the number of jobs in a batch, while keeping the system resources constant. We note that for all the approaches, the revenue steadily increases reaching a *peak*, and then dips beyond a *knee* point. The resource contention is low in the beginning with fewer jobs entering the system. With increasing number of jobs, system utilization improves leading to higher revenue. The peak of the curve represents an optimal system state when the revenue earned is the maximum. Increasing jobs beyond this point leads to greater resource contention and causes more jobs to miss their deadlines. Continual increase in the delay incurred by jobs is indicative of an overloaded system state and leads to reduction in revenue. This is captured by the zone beyond the knee of the curve. In an under-utilized system state all algorithms achieve comparable performance. But as the number of jobs is increased, DECO shows sustained significant improvement over EF and BF. Even in high resource contention conditions, revenue drop of DECO is less as compared to the alternative heuristics. This is observed by the sharp fall in EF and BF beyond the knee point as opposed to graceful degradation of DECO. On an average, DECO has (30-40)% improvement in revenue earnings over alternative approaches.

Fig.3(b) and Fig.3(c) report the average wait time of jobs, divided into CPU wait time and transfer wait time, for increasing number of jobs. The first component represents the cpu utilization and captures benefits of scheduling some jobs ahead of others. The second component, represents data availability and captures the benefits of replication and transfer scheduling. CPU wait time reduces when a job is assigned to a compute site with low queue lengths. Similarly, transfer wait time reduces with smart scheduling and parallelizing data transfers with job executions. With a batch size of 200 jobs, DECO shows about

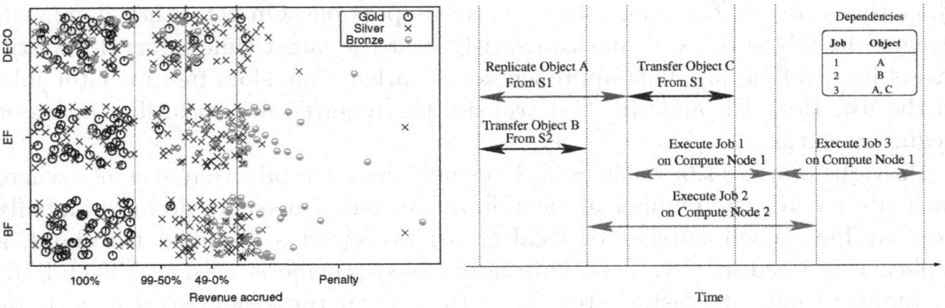

(a) (b)

Fig. 4. (a) Scatter plot showing the revenue accrued by jobs (b) Illustration of master schedule

30% reduction in CPU wait time over EF and LF. With an average requirement of 5 files/job, DECO reduces the transfer wait time by as much as 40%.

Fig.4(a) sheds light on the superior performance of DECO over alternative heuristics. The experiment was conducted with a batch of 200 jobs. For each job, we determine the total response time and the corresponding revenue earned. (Note that, the revenue may be positive or negative depending on the scheduled time interval). The entire region is divided into four revenue zones. From left to right the vertical regions mean the following: the first vertical represents revenues earned by jobs that finish within the deadline. The second and third for jobs that miss their deadlines, but earn 50-99% and 0-49% of their maximum revenue respectively. The last contains jobs that incur penalties for finishing late.

Fig.4(a) reports the distribution of Gold, Silver and Bronze jobs in the four revenue zones. The alternative heuristics try to accommodate the heavy penalty incurring Gold and Silver jobs in the earlier time intervals, so as to avoid missing their deadlines. As a result most of the Bronze jobs are forced in the penalty zone and a significant number of Silver jobs earn less than a third of their maximum revenue. They fail to capture the possibility that the penalty from a large number of Bronze jobs can overshadow the revenue earned from Gold and Silver jobs. DECO intelligently chooses the right balance of placing the different types of jobs in suitable time intervals by weighing both their revenues and penalties, and thereby accrues significantly higher revenue than its competitors. Fig.4(b) show the actual data transfers, replications and executions scheduled by DECO along the timeline. The schedule is shown for three representative jobs (executing on the a compute site with two compute nodes). The jobs and their dependencies are as shown in Fig.4(b). In the schedule, replication of object A from site S1 is initiated along with transfer of object B from site S2. Jobs 1 and 2 begin execution in parallel with the transfer of object C from site S1. Job 3 however executes only after C's transfer completes and either of Job 1 or Job 2 finishes execution. This snapshot illustration demonstrates how DECO utilizes the available resources (network links, compute resources) to minimize idle time.

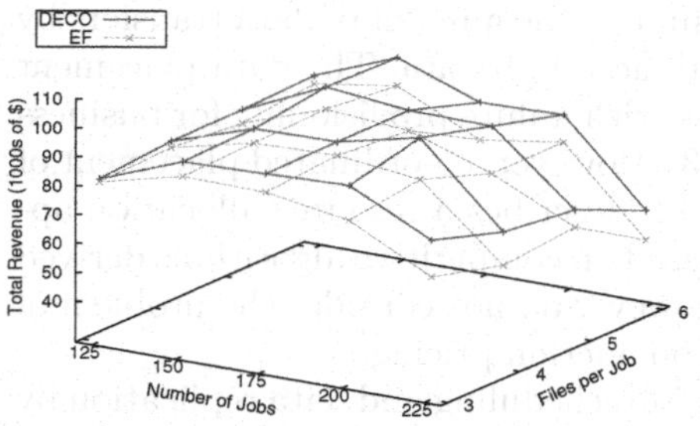

Fig. 5. Surface plot showing change in revenue as number of jobs and number of dependencies is varied

Table 1. Replica Utility showing Files per Job (FJ), Avg Replicas per File (AR) and Avg Replica Utility (ARU)

FJ	AR			ARU		
	DECO	EF	BF	DECO	EF	BF
3	1.3	1.1	1.1	99.7	43.1	35.3
4	1.4	1.2	1.3	88.0	68.6	53.5
5	1.5	1.3	1.3	116.3	62.8	60.0
6	1.7	1.4	1.4	130.2	65.7	61.3

In Fig.5, we compare the revenue earned as the number of jobs and their file dependencies are scaled for DECO and EF. When a job requires a larger set of files for its execution, job wait times are more pronounced as transfer times tend to be larger. The raised surface for DECO can be attributed to the fact that it creates more beneficial replicas when compared to EF, and achieves better parallelization of execution and data transfers. We additionally note that for 3–5 files per job, the revenue accrued by DECO steadily increases. Finally, for larger batch sizes and a larger number of file dependencies, the revenues begin to dip. This is because the system enters an overloaded state, as explained earlier.

Table-1 shows the replication statistics for each algorithm. We report the average number of replicas created per object, which captures the degree of replication. The table also reports the average utility of the replicated objects, which is defined as the revenue gain per new replica. Table–1 shows that the algorithms create 1.09–1.68 replicas per object, which is within acceptable limits for given storage constraints. Though more replicas are created by DECO, they contribute to significant revenue growth as reflected by the replica utility values. The replica utility of DECO is much better than the alternative heuristics(87.95–130.15 vs 43.14–68.55). This indicates that tight coupling of replication with compute allocation creates more meaningful replicas which are more effectively utilized while doing job assignment. Decoupled replication as adopted in the alternative heuristics fails to influence the job assignment directly, resulting in less optimal utilization of the replicas.

5 Related Work

Market–based economy models have recently received much attention in the grid utility computing domain [2,3]. [2] presents value-based scheduling heuristics that attempt to balance risk and reward of a job. [3] presents heuristics for admission control and resource allocation when jobs come with their own SLA requirements. However, both approaches do not consider the data transfer/replication as a part of the schedule. [12] presents a grid service broker for discovery of resources and scheduling of jobs. Here, the scheduler minimizes the amount of data transfers by executing jobs at sites which have "nearer" access to data. The data placement however remains static. Resource allocation with failure provisioning for business profit maximization has been studied in [13]. However, co-ordinated placement of data with jobs has not been addressed. [14] describes a resource allocation approach for distributed computer systems based on competitive algorithms derived from Microeconomics. These algorithms however do not consider the problem of dynamic creation of replicas and its effect on auction pricing.

Among approaches that try to integrate job scheduling and data replication by incorporating network latencies and data transfer times are the Close-To-Files [4] and the Time-Budget constrained [5]. However, none of these approaches consider dynamic replication of data across sites. [6] looks at a number of techniques to dynamically replicate data across sites and assign jobs to sites. In this scheme, local monitors keep track of popular objects and preemptively replicates them at other sites. However, the work assumes homogeneous network conditions and single input files, both of which may not hold in case of globally distributed grids. [11,7] consider decoupled approach wherein the replication is controlled by an asynchronous process and looks at long-term history of access patterns. Stork [15] introduces a specialized scheduler for data placement activities and mentions the need for tighter integration between data placement and job execution. [16] presents an approach for co-scheduling by combining the Condor scheduler with a storage resource manager (SRM). Although, match-making is influenced by file placement, replication is performed without considering compute assignments. The co-scheduling problem addressed in [17] assumes single data object only. Finally, [18] solves the co-scheduling problem in a data grids using a genetic algorithm based heuristic. The work however, does not address the problem of optimal replica source selection and the time sequencing of job executions and replication/data transfers.

6 Conclusion

In this paper, we propose DECO, a co–scheduling framework for compute and data–intensive applications in utility grids. DECO employs a two–step algorithm for maximizing the business revenue of the grid provider. In Step 1, decisions are made on the assignment of jobs and replication of data objects. Step 2 schedules the data transfers (and replications) along with the job executions. The main highlight is that by integrating execution and data transfer times, DECO delivers significant improvements, both in terms of higher business revenues and lower job wait times, when compared to alternative approaches. As a part of future work, we will consider peer-to-peer approaches for resource-sharing among meta-schedulers. In this perspective, we plan to investigate distributed competitive algorithms [14]. Further, we are investigating application performance analysis techniques to help DECO make more up-to-date co-scheduling decisions. Finally, we plan to enhance the system with failure handling mechanisms.

References

1. Foster, I., Kesselman, C., Nick, J., Tuecke, S.: The physiology of the grid: An open grid services architecture for distributed systems integration (2002)
2. Irwin, D.E., Grit, L.E., Chase, J.S.: Balancing risk and reward in a market-based task service. In: Proc. of HPDC'04. (2004)
3. Yeo, C.S., Buyya, R.: Service level agreement based allocation of cluster resources: Handling penalty to enhance utility. In: Proc. of Cluster 2005. (2005)
4. Mohamed, H., Epema, D.: An evaluation of the close-to-files processor and data co-allocation policy in multiclusters. In: Proc. of IEEE International Conference on Cluster Computing. (2004)
5. Venugopal, S., Buyya, R.: A deadline and budget constrained scheduling algorithm for e-science applications on data grids. In: Proc. of 6th International Conference on Algorithms and Architectures for Parallel Processing. (2005)
6. Ranganathan, K., Foster, I.: Computation scheduling and data replication algorithms for data grids. Grid resource management: state of the art and future trends (2004) 359–373
7. A. Chakrabarti, R.A.D., Sengupta, S.: Integration of scheduling and replication in data grids. In: Proc. of HiPC. (2004)
8. Allcock, W.: Gridftp protocol specification (global grid forum recommendation gfd.20). In: Globus Project: http://www.globus.org/alliance/publications/papers/GFD-R.0201.pdf. (2003)
9. Hall, L., Schulz, A., Shmoys, D.B., Wein, J.: Scheduling to minimize average completion time: off-line and on-line algorithms. In: Proc. of ACM-SIAM Symposium on Discrete Algorithms. (1996)
10. Sulistio, A., Cibej, U., Buyya, R., Robic, B.: A toolkit for modeling and simulation of data grids with integration of data storage, replication and analysis. In: Technical Report, GRIDS-TR-2005-13, GRIDS Lab, University of Melbourne, Australia. (2005)
11. Ranganathan, K., Foster, I.: Decoupling computation and data scheduling in distributed data-intensive applications. In: Proc. of the 11 th IEEE International Symposium on High Performance Distributed Computing. (2002)
12. Venugopal, S., Buyya, R., Winton, L.: A grid service broker for scheduling distributed data-oriented applications on global grids. In: Proc. of the 2nd workshop on Middleware for grid computing. (2004)
13. Dasgupta, G., Dasgupta, K., Purohit, A., Viswanathan, B.: Qos-graf: A framework for qos based grid resource allocation with failure provisioning. In: Proc. of 14th IEEE IWQoS. (2006)
14. Ferguson, D.F., Yemini, Y., Nikolaou, C.: Microeconomic algorithms for load balancing in distributed computer systems. In: Proc. of ICDCS. (1988)
15. Kosar, T., Livny, M.: Stork: Making data placement a first class citizen in the grid. In: Proc. of the 24th Int. Conference on Distributed Computing Systems. (2004)
16. Romosan, A., Rotem, D., Shoshani, A., Wright, D.: Co-scheduling of computation and data on computer clusters. In: SSDBM'2005: Proceedings of the 17th SSDBM'2005. (2005)
17. H. Liu, M.B., Huang, J.: Dynamic co-scheduling of distributed computation and replication. In: Proc. of 6th IEEE Int. Symposium on Cluster Computing and the Grid (to appear). (2006)
18. Phan, T., Ranganathan, K., Sion, R.: Evolving toward the perfect schedule: Co-scheduling job assignments and data replication in wide-area systems using a genetic algorithm. In: Proc. of Job Scheduling Strategies for Parallel Processing. (2005)

Coordinated Co-allocator Model for Data Grid in Multi-sender Environment

R.S. Bhuvaneswaran, Yoshiaki Katayama, and Naohisa Takahashi

Department of Computer Science and Engineering,
Graduate School of Engineering, Nagoya Institute of Technology, Japan
{bhuvan, katayama, naohisa}@moss.elcom.nitech.ac.jp

Abstract. We propose a model, which simultaneously allocates a data block request to the multiple sites, termed as co-allocation, to enable parallel data transfer in a grid environment. The model comprises of co-allocator, monitor and control mechanisms. The co-allocation scheme adapts well to the highly inconsistent network performances of the sites concerned. The scheme initially obtains the bandwidth parameter from the monitor module to fix the partition size and the data transfer tasks are allocated onto the servers in duplication. The scheme is found to be tolerant despite the situation that the link to servers under consideration is broken or become idle. We used Globus toolkit for our framework and utilized the partial copy feature of GridFTP. We compared our schemes with the existing schemes and the results show notable improvement in overall completion time of data transfer.

Keywords: Data grid, co-allocation, parallel data transfer, GridFTP.

1 Introduction

Applications designed to execute on grids frequently require the simultaneous co-allocation of multiple resources in order to meet performance requirements [7][1][5]. For instance, several computers and network elements may be required in order to achieve real-time re-construction of experimental data, while a large numerical simulation may require simultaneous access to multiple supercomputers. Motivated by these concerns, several researchers [1][5][3][8] developed general resource management architecture for Grid environments, in which resource co-allocation is an integral component. Data store is one of the important resources and this paper deals about it. Several applications considered distributed data stores as resources [8][9]. Most of these data grid applications are executed simultaneously and access a large number of data files in a grid, termed as data grid. The data grid infrastructure is to integrate the data storage devices and data management service into the grid environment. Data grid consists of scattered computing and storage resources located dispersedly in the global network accessible to the users. These large sized data sets are replicated in more than one site for the better availability to the other nodes in

A. Dan and W. Lamersdorf (Eds.): ICSOC 2006, LNCS 4294, pp. 66 – 77, 2006.

a grid. For instance, in the multi tiered data grid architecture high energy physics experiments[9], replicated data stores are considered. Hence, any popular dataset is likely to have replicas located in multiple sites.

Instead of downloading the entire high volume dataset from a single server, the technique of downloading the data set parts from multiple servers in parallel that are consolidated at the client end, is of more theoretical and practical interest. This co-allocation of data transfer has alleviated most of the bottlenecks in downloading and improves the performance compared to the single server selection one. Many researchers realized this factor, discussed its advantages and proposed variety of techniques in different contexts [14][3][15]. We propose a model, which simultaneously allocates a data block request to the multiple sites, termed as co-allocation, to enable parallel data transfer in a grid environment. The model comprises of co-allocator, monitor and control mechanisms, naturally blended with feedback loop. The co-allocator scheme adapts well to the highly inconsistent network performances of the sites concerned.

We have experimented our schemes with Globus toolkit as the middleware and GridFTP. The results are compared with the existing approaches and the initial results outlast the existing ones performance. The rest of the paper is organized as follows: the problem is defined with the co-allocation model in section 2 and the related works in the same area are discussed in Section 3. We presented our proposed algorithm in Section 4 with assumptions and the experiments. Section 5 describes the analyses and Section 6 concludes the paper.

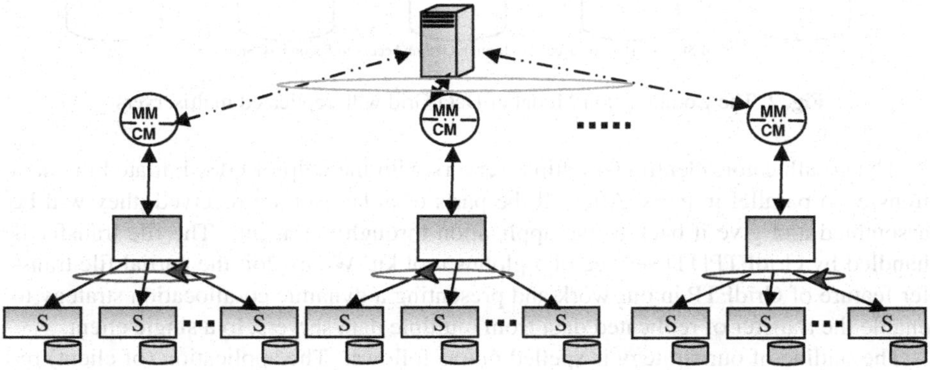

Fig. 1. Integrated Co-allocation Model of Data Grid with replicated multiservers

2 Co-allocation Model with Globus

The integrated coallocation model comprises of coallocation, monitoring and control components, discussed in detail in the subsequent sections.

2.1 Coallocation Mechanism and the Overall Architecture

The dynamic collacotor module integrated with monitor is shown in Fig.1. The model is presented from the client perspective. Each client has a coallocator agent (CM) and the periodical execution of monitor agent (MM).We used Globus Toolkit [11] which is an open source software toolkit used for building grid. The major component of a globus tool kit is GIS (Globus Information Service) which provide necessary information about the data stores in a grid. With help of GIS, the co-allocator adopted dynamic strategy to transfer data from multiple servers to the intended client. Fig. 2 depicts a single client point of view. The agent accepts the request from an application about the data solicited and its description is passed on to the co-allocator.

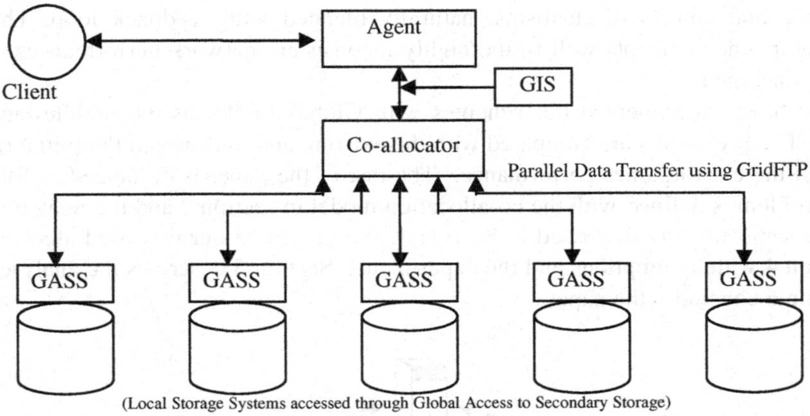

Fig. 2. The Co-allocation Model of Data Grid with replicated multiservers

The co-allocator, identifies multiple servers with the help of GIS, initiated the data transfer in parallel in parts. After all the parts of a data set are received, they will be assembled and give it back to the application through the agent. The file transfer is handled by GridFTP[11] service of a globus tool kit. We exploit the partial file transfer feature of GridFTP in our work and presenting a dynamic co-allocation strategy to enable the transfer of replicated data from multiple data servers, to a single client.

The outline of our strategy is spelled out as follows: The application (of client) requests the data with its description to co-allocator agent. Based on the information provided by GIS, the dataset is replicated and available in the servers scattered in the network. The dataset to be downloaded is divided into blocks. The co-allocator sends multiple requests to the server and the download process taken place in parallel. At the beginning, every server is assigned to transfer exactly one block respectively. When the requested block is received from a server, then, one of the yet unassigned blocks is assigned to the server. Co-allocator repeats this process until all the blocks of the dataset are assigned. Obviously, good performance servers transfer more blocks than the slow servers. There may be duplication of blocks among the servers thereby reducing the waiting time from the slower servers and thus the fault tolerant factor can also be achieved.

2.2 Monitoring and Control Mechanisms

The allocation and configuration phases of the coallocation process result in the data transfer tasks on set of servers. During the data transfer, it is desirable to monitor and control the ensemble as a collective unit. The monitoring and control operations that we defined have this property. Monitoring operations allow a client program to receive notification when the resource set changes state. In addition to the obvious global state transitions of failure and termination, the complex failure modes encountered in Grid applications lead to a need to support and respond to individual process state transitions as well. Hence, the interface should allow for signaling operation (algorithm in Sec. 4) to the monitoring program, which can then act upon this transition in a manner that is appropriate for the coallocation. Similarly, control operations allow for the manipulation of the resource set as a whole. One required control operation is to check whether the received data is corrupted or not and the other one is killing the duplicate processes, which will be discussed in Sec. 4. Before we discuss about our strategy in detail, let us present the related works in this aspect.

3 Related Works

Few research works have been reported in the literature about parallel data transfer for the grid environment. They can be categorized into static and dynamic based on the allocation strategy. Once the allocation is made, it can never be changed during execution is termed as static, whereas, in dynamic allocations the allocations may be altered based on bandwidth or other performance criteria. t al [15] used past history of data to forecast the current data transfer speed. The same authors [14] proposed co-allocation architecture for grid data transfers across multiple connections. They provided brute-force, history-based and other techniques. Brute force works by dividing the file size equally among available flows. It does not address the bandwidth differences among the various client-server links. Past history-based co-allocation schemes not exhibit consistent performance, since performance (speed) of the each processor varies over time [13]. Many algorithms and schemes found in the literature [3][7][14][15] make the decision based on the past history, heuristics, performance in the first allocation, etc. But, in practical, server and network performance cannot be forecasted in full guarantee. Hence, several researchers proposed dynamic strategies [14][3][13].

The dynamic co-allocation mechanisms of [14] were noteworthy. In the conservative load balancing, the dataset requested is divided into disjoint blocks of equal size. Each available server is assigned one block to deliver in parallel. Once the server finishes delivering the block, another block is requested and so on, till the entire file is downloaded. There exists a shortcoming of the faster servers that must wait for the slower server to deliver the final block. Another strategy by the same authors is the aggressive load balancing, which progressively increase the amount of data requested from faster servers and reduce the amount of data requested from slower servers or stop requesting data altogether. These schemes are calculating bandwidth at the time of delivering the block and thereby allocating the next block under the motive of utilizing faster servers. But, the idle time of faster servers awaiting the slowest server to deliver the last block is one of factor, which affects total efficiency. The other technique, Recursive Adjustment co-allocation [3] was designed under the objective of reducing the waiting time.

In all these techniques, the data set is divided into block size according to each server's bandwidth and the co-allocator assigns the blocks to each server for transferring. But, after assigning the block size, there is no guarantee that the bandwidth of the server remains constant. In other words, this technique does not cope up with the highly dynamic performance behavior of the multiple servers and their networks. Moreover, when any one of the servers becomes idle or link is broken, the alternative is not suggested in none of the existing methods.

Our proposed scheme takes care of all these factors. It neither uses predictions nor heuristics, instead dynamically co-allocate with duplication assignments and coping up nicely with the changing speed performance of the servers. The idea of duplication in allocation has already been used in multiprocessor scheduling in the yester years and applied in computational grid environments in recent years [13]. But, there are quite number of variations between computational grid and data grid, where the former one is constrained by precedence constraints, task partitioning, dependency, interprocess communication, resource reservation & allocation, process control, etc. The next section describes our strategy which alleviates the problems mentioned afore.

4 Dynamic Co-allocation Scheme with Duplicate Assignments (DCDA)

Let D be the dataset, k be the number of blocks of a dataset of fixed block size and m be the available number of servers having replicated data content. First, D is divided into k disjoint blocks (B_i) of equal size and each one of the available server is assigned to deliver, in parallel, in other words, $D = \{B_1, B_2, \ldots, B_k\}$. The strategy for partitioning the dataset into data blocks is analyzed in section 5. When the requested block is received from a server, one of the yet unassigned blocks is assigned to the server. Co-allocator repeats this process until all the blocks of a dataset are assigned. Hence, good performance servers transfer more blocks than the slow servers, which take more time deliver. In this case, the block assigned to that server is again assigned to the faster server; In other words, there may be duplication of blocks among the servers and thereby reducing the waiting time from the slower servers. Moreover, when the server becomes idle or the link to the server is broken, the entire data process is safeguarded from disruption. A data structure of circular queue is maintained here, with k (number of blocks) as the size of the queue. The complete scheme is presented here:

---

coalloc(m, k, D)

1. [Initialization]
   1a) Partition the dataset D into k equal sized blocks B_j, $j = [1..k]$.
   1b) All the blocks are numbered and placed in a circular queue $CQ(k)$.
   1c) CQ pointer p is initialized with 1 so as to point to its first element.
2. [Initial allocation of blocks on to the servers]
   for (i = 1 to m)
   2a) fetch block B_p from CQ and assign to server S_i
   2b) $p = (p + 1) \bmod k$
3. When a block B_j (any j, $1 \le j \le k$) is delivered by the server S_l (any l, $1 \le l \le m$),
   3a) remove block B_j from CQ, $k = k - 1$
   3b) signal the servers to stop processing of block B_j
   3c) fetch block B_p from CQ and assign to server S_l
   If CQ is empty, Go to step 6.
   3d) $p = (p + 1) \bmod k$
4. When a server S_l ($1 \le l \le m$) is signalled,
   4a) fetch block B_p from CQ and assign to server S_l
   If CQ is empty, Go to Step 6.
   4b) $p = (p + 1) \bmod k$
5. [Waiting for delivery or free signal from servers]
   Go to Step 3
6. [At the completion of transfer of dataset]
   When the CQ is empty, kill all the assigned data transfer processes in other servers.

For the purpose of explaining the scheme, initially, let us consider the constant rate of transfer and the data set is divided equally into k disjoint blocks. The scheme is illustrated as follows: Let us consider the example of data set of size 100 MB replicated in five servers (s1 to s5) and hence the block size is 20 MB. Also assume that the speeds of the data transfer of the five servers are 200, 70, 150, 80, 200 Kbps, respectively. Note that, when same blocks are received by co-allocator, it considers the one with the earliest timestamp and discards other.

Note that in this first example, $k = m$, for simplicity. Initially, a block numbered 1 to 5 is assigned to each server, respectively in the same order. Naturally, servers 1 and 5 delivered data much faster than others. After the blocks 1 and 5 are received, blocks 2 and 3 are assigned to servers 1 and 5. In due course, block 3 is delivered by server 3 and hence the block request to the server 5 is cancelled and block 4 is assigned to server 3 and block 2 is assigned to server 5. Note that the block 2 is duplicated in servers 1, 2 and 5. Finally, block 4 is assigned duplicated in all the sites. This is illustrated in the Gantt chart (Fig. 3a). The total time taken is 273.0 seconds. The allocation of blocks on to the servers, for every reception of delivery signal in succession is shown as in Fig. 4a along with the status of the queue. At the end of the execution, the blocks delivered by the servers are shown in Fig. 4b.

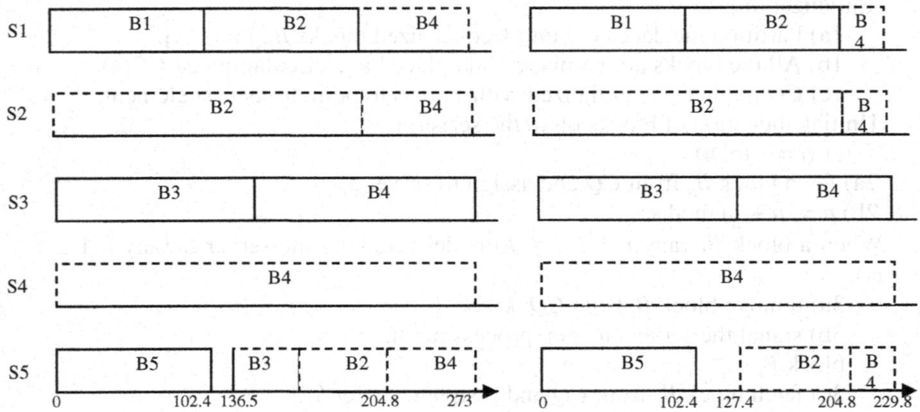

Fig. 3. Gantt Chart showing Co-allocated Behavior with a)Constant and b) varying bandwidth

The allocation of blocks on to the servers, for every reception of delivery signal in succession is shown below (Fig. 4a) along with the status of the queue. At the end of the execution, the blocks delivered by the servers are shown in Fig. 4b.

S_1	S_2	S_3	S_4	S_5
B_1	B_2	B_3	B_4	B_5
B_2	B_2	B_3	B_4	B_3
B_2	B_2	B_4	B_4	B_2
B_4	B_4	B_4	B_4	B_4

B_1 B_2 B_3 B_4 B_5 $CQ(5)$
$B_2 B_3 B_4$ $CQ(3)$
$B_2 B_4$ $CQ(2)$
B_4 $CQ(1)$

(a)

B_1	B_2	B_3	B_4	B_5
S_1	S_1	S_3	S_1	S_5

(b)

Fig. 4. Status of the circular queue during execution and the final allocation

5 Experiment and Analysis

5.1 General Analysis

In order to analyze the scheme, let us consider the next case (case 2) of change in network performance. Let the data transfer rate, be represented as a pair (a, b) where, a is the rate of transfer in the first 100 seconds and b represents after first 100 seconds. In this way, rate of transfer for five servers are considered as (200,200), (70,50),(150,200),(80,0), and (200,150) respectively. Rate of transfer 0 specifies nil or no data transfer, which may be due to the broken link or idle server (here, site 4 detoriate, after 100 seconds). In this case, the total time taken will be 229.8. Note that the performance can further be improved, when the frequency of change-in-transfer rate is more. Now, consider the same case with more number of blocks. In the same example cited above, partition the data set into ten blocks, each of size 10 MB. The total completion time is drastically reduced to 204.8 and the blocks delivered by the appropriate servers are tabulated as Table 1.

Table 1. Performance of Dynamic Duplicate Assignment Scheme with $k > m$

Sites	Rate of transfer (interval of 100 secs)	Blocks assigned	Blocks delivered
1	200, 200	1, 6, 9, 4	1, 6, 9, 4
2	50, 70	2, 4	-
3	150, 200	3, 8, 2, 10	3, 8, 2
4	70, 0	4	---
5	200, 150	5, 7, 10, 4	5, 7, 10

The performances of the three cases mentioned above are shown as bar chart in the Fig. 5. Numbers of blocks considered are mentioned along with the case. Thus, from the figure, it is apparent that the varying speed performances of the replicated sites are utilized which results in minimal completion time of the download process of a data set.

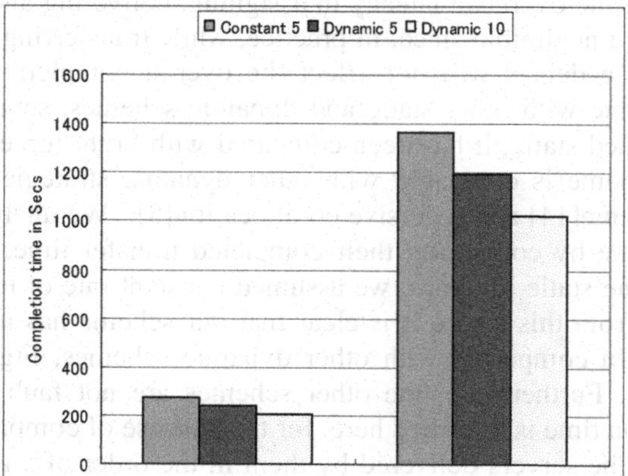

Fig. 5. Performances of Static and Dynamic bandwidth for 100M & 500M file sizes

We used Globus toolkit 2.4 in our experiment, and in order to study the performance of our scheme in varying network performance, we conducted our experiment by changing the network and server loads, apart from normal traffic. In order to evaluate our scheme in dynamic environment, we used frequency table of data transfer rate. For example, Table 2 shows one such frequency table when the case 2 above is extended with more frequency of data transfer in the interval of 20 seconds.

We can study the behavior of our algorithm with frequency tables like this. We used several file sizes as 2GB, 1.5 GB, 1GB, 500MB, 100MB and 10MB and the expected completion time threshold is assumed as 5 minutes, which is required by the 3 schemes mentioned above. We fixed a constant L=5 in the formula of finding *k*.

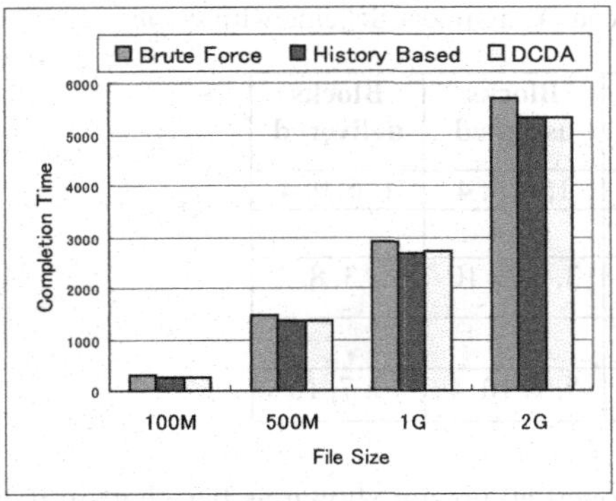

a) with Static schemes

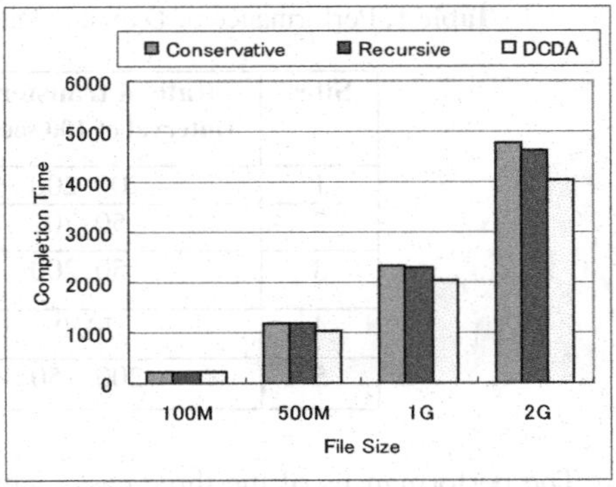

b) with Dynamic schemes

Fig. 6. Comparative Performance with $k > m$

We assumed that the overhead latency in assigning, delivering and killing of duplicate assignments are negligible since, in practice, while transferring giga, peta or tera bytes of sizes, these delays will not affect the overall completion time. We have evaluated our scheme with other static and dynamic schemes, separately. When the bandwidth is assumed static, it has been compared with brute force[14] and our proposed dynamic scheme is compared with other dynamic strategies of conservative load balancing scheme[14] and recursive co-allocation[3]. We analyzed the performance of each scheme by comparing their completed transfer time, shown in Fig. 6. When comparing the static schemes, we assumed constant rate of transfer (as in case 1), as in Fig. 6a. From this figure it is clear that our scheme has marginal improvement over others. In comparing with other dynamic schemes, Fig. 6b, our scheme outperforms others. Furthermore, the other schemes are not fault tolerant, and the expected completion time is specified here, for the purpose of comparison.

The blocks and the servers delivered by them in the order of arrival (left to right) for the case 2 are :

B_1	B_5	B_3	B_6	B_7	B_8	B_9	B_{10}	B_4	B_2
S_1	S_5	S_3	S_1	S_7	S_3	S_1	S_3	S_1	S_3

Fig. 7. Final Allocation of Blocks on to servers

One of the factors, which influence the scheme, is data set portioning; that is the manner in which the data set is partitioned. The question now is whether to have small number of blocks with greater size or more number of blocks with smaller size. The later one is better since more number of blocks may brighten the scope of dynamicity; in other words, there is a possibility of assigning more blocks to the faster servers. But, at the same time, more number of blocks may have the overhead of communication latency and the block management. Next subsection discusses about fixing the block size *k*.

5.2 Finding the Optimal Number of Blocks

One of the factors, which influence the overall performance, is data set portioning; that is the manner in which the data set is partitioned. The question now is whether to have small number of blocks with greater size or more number of blocks with smaller size. The later one is better since more number of blocks may brighten the scope of dynamicity; in other words, there is a possibility of assigning more blocks to the faster servers. But, at the same time, more number of blocks may have the overhead of communication latency and the block management. The partitioning factor in turn based on block size and the number of replicated sites available. Choosing the optimal block may yield significant performance with our scheme. In general, smaller number of blocks may yield poor completion time and on the other hand, more number of blocks results in switchover overheads and thereby showing poor completion time.

Hence, it is highly important to partition the data set into optimal number of blocks. The specialty of the algorithm is independent of any estimating measures under the motive of adapting to the natural dynamicity of network behavior. Without compromising this objective let us fix the number of blocks, based on the function of bandwidth. Before executing the algorithm, assume that the bandwidths of all the servers are known from the client perspective. These metrics can easily be obtained from the monitoring module, which is executing periodically by using the tools such as *iperf* [12].

Let the ratio of coefficient of variation of set of bandwidths be, $C_v = (\sigma / \mu)*100$, where, σ is the standard deviation and μ is the average of the bandwidths from client to all the sites having replicated data. Further, the set of bandwidths in a network of multisender scenario aggregates normal distribution [10]. Hence, if set of bandwidth values aggregates normal distribution, C_v can be used to compare the amount of variance between populations with different means.Based on the basic statistics, it can be interpreted that, the lower percentage is closer to the average and the higher percentage depicts the farther distance from average. The number of fixed sized blocks can be fixed as, $k = m *([C_v / [100/L]] + 1)$, (or can be simplified as $k = m ([\sigma L/ \mu] + 1)$) for any constant L (> 0) which is used to divide the range of distributions. For example, for normal distribution curve with μ=140 and σ=2.007638, the entire range of distribution is divided in to 4(=L) portions. Note that, for this example, $k = 2m$.

5.3 Improvement of the Algorithm

Note that the sequentiality is not maintained in this method. In other words, the blocks are not received in the partitioning order. For example, the blocks and the servers delivered by them in the order of arrival (left to right) for the case 2 as in Fig.7 is not block sequential. This may not be the problem with the applications considering insensitive with sequentiality. On the other hand, for the applications like streaming, the sequential delivery of partitioned blocks is matters a lot. Hence the algorithm is modified to ensure the sequential delivery to the client and at the same time exploiting the parallel feature enriched in the co-allocated model.

The data file is divided into blocks and each block is further partitioned into sub-blocks to exploit the parallelism in downloading. This is illustrated in the Fig. 8. The dashed lines indicate the sub-blocks.

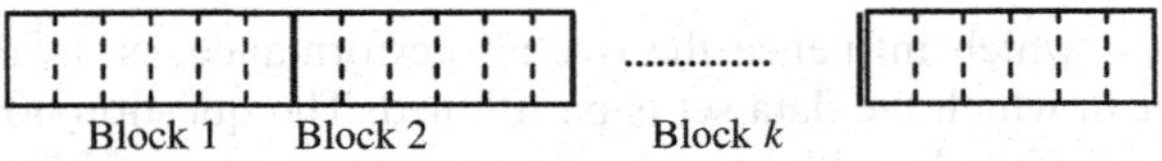

Fig. 9. Partitioning of a Data file

For each block, the basic algorithm in section 4 is executed as, *coalloc(m, s, B_i)*, where *s* is the number of sub-blocks and B_i is the block *i* of the dataset *D*, for any *i*, $1 \leq i \leq k$. After all the sub-blocks of a block are delivered, rearranged the sub-blocks, execute for the next block *coalloc(m, s, B_{i+1})* and this process is repeated for all the blocks of a dataset. Hence, the blocks will be received in the sequential order.

Table 2. Sample Frequency Table of Data Transfer Rate

	Rate of transfer in K/Second in the interval 20 seconds												
S1	200	200	80	190	210	220	205	180	150	120	180	185	200
S2	50	50	80	80	90	70	70	80	80	90	70	80	80
S3	150	160	50	150	170	180	200	210	210	190	200	210	200
S4	70	80	70	60	40	60	50	0	0	0	0	0	0
S5	200	210	190	200	200	190	170	160	150	160	150	140	150

For example, consider the simple example of case 2, discussed in section 5.1. Let the number of blocks as 4 and each block has 5 sub-blocks. Thus, the size of sub-block is 5MB. Only 4 servers S_1, S_2, S_3 & S_5 are considered, eliminating server S_4. For the purpose of explanation, we denote the sub-block with double index, as SB_{ij}, where *j* refers to the sub-block number within a block *i*. Now, with the improved sequential algorithm, the sub-blocks will be delivered in the following order, (from left to right). $SB_{11}, SB_{15}, SB_{13}, SB_{12}, SB_{14}, SB_{21}, SB_{25}, SB_{23}, SB_{22}, SB_{24} \ldots SB_{41}, SB_{45}, SB_{43}, SB_{42}, SB_{44}$

Note that there is a necessity of rearrangement of sub-blocks, before the next iteration of a block. This scheme ensures the ordered delivery of data file and thus highly suitable for the applications like streaming.

6 Conclusion

We have designed a dynamic co-allocation model, to enable parallel download of replicated data from multiple servers. The coallocation scheme is presented which initially fix the number of data blocks based on bandwidth obtained from monitor. Our scheme uses neither past history nor heuristics but fully compliant with high dynamicity in the network / server performance. The scheme works fine, even when the link to servers is broken (or servers become idle) during the process, whereas, none of the existing algorithms considered this situation. It is compared with the existing schemes and shows significant improvement in overall completion time of data transfer. The scheme may yield significant performance when choosing optimal block size.

Acknowledgment

This research was partially supported by the Ministry of Education, Culture, Sports, Science and Technology, Grant-in-Aid for JSPS Fellows 1604285, Scientific Research on Priority Areas 18049038 and Scientific Research (C) 18500050.

References

1. Allcock B, Bester J, et al, "Data Management and Transfer in High Performance Computational Grid Environments", Parallel Computing, May 2002.
2. Bhuvaneswaran R.S, Katayama Y, Takahashi N ,"Dynamic Co-allocation Scheme for Parallel Data Transfer in Grid Environment", Semantics, Knowledge and Grid, Beijing, pp 178-188, 2005.
3. Chao-Tung Yang, I Hsien Yang, Chun Hsiang Chen, "Improve Dynamic Adjustment Mechanism in Co-allocation data Grid Environments", Proceedings of the 11th Workshop on Compiler Techniques for High-Performance Computing (CTHPC 05), 189-194, 2005
4. Chervenak A, et al ,"A Framework for Constructing Scalable Replica Location Services", Proceedings of Super Computing Conference 2002, Baltimore, 2002.
5. Chervenak A, Foster I, et al, "The Data Grid: Towards an Architecture for the Distributed Management and Analysis of Large Scientific Datasets," Journal of Network and Computer Applications, 23:187-200, 2001.
6. Chun Hsiang Chen, Chao-Tung Yang, Chuan-Lin Lai, "Towards an Efficient Replica selection for Data Grid", Workshop on Grid Technologies and Applications, Dec 2004.
7. Czakowski K, Foster I, Kesselman C, "Resource Co-allocation in Computational Grids", Proc. IEEE International Symposium on High Performance Distributed Computing 1999.
8. Data Grid Project (EU Data Grid), http://www.eu-datagrid.org
9. GridPhyN project (Grid Physics Network), http://www.griphyn.org
10. Hui,S.C and Jack Y. B. Lee, "Modeling of Aggregate Available Bandwidth in Many-to-One Data Transfer," Proc. of the Fourth International Conference on Intelligent Multimedia Computing and Networking, July 21-26, 2005, Utah.
11. Introduction to Grids and the Globus Toolkit, The Globus Project, http://www.globus.org.
12. Iperf Homepage : http://dast.nlanr.net/Projects/Iperf/ .
13. Noriyuki Fujimoto, Kenichi Hagihara, "Near Optimal Dynamic Task Scheduling of Independent Coarse Grained Tasks onto a Computational Grid", International Conference on Parallel Processing (ICPP-03), pp.391-398, October 6-9, 2003.
14. Vazhkudai S, "Enabling the Co-allocation of Grid Data Transfers", International Workshop on Grid Computing, Nov 2003, pp 44-51.
15. Vazhkudai S, Tuecke S, Foster I, "Replica Selection in the Globus Data Grid", IEEE/ACM International Symposium on Cluster Computing and the Grid, May 2001, pp 106-113

Adaptive Preference Specifications for Application Sessions

Christine Julien

Mobile and Pervasive Computing Group
The Center for Excellence in Distributed Global Environments
The University of Texas at Austin
c.julien@mail.utexas.edu

Abstract. In ubiquitous computing applications, mobile participants must be empowered to opportunistically connect to services available in their local environments. Our previous work has elucidated a model for allowing applications to specify the functional properties of the services to which they need to connect. Our framework then connects applications to dynamic resources through the use of a novel suite of *application sessions*. In this paper, we revisit this framework to devise a mechanism for applications to specify preferences for one service provider over another. In this investigation, we argue that these preferences are actually provided by a set of session participants: the application itself, the service provider, and, more surprisingly, the network that connects the application and the provider. We develop a framework for each of these parties to specify preferences among various allowable connections. We demonstrate not only what kinds of properties can be expressed in our framework but also implementation paths for integrating them into the communication and application support infrastructure.

1 Introduction

In ubiquitous computing, software and hardware resources are available embedded in a user's environment. The service concept provides an intuitive abstraction through which applications can gain access to remote resources. In dynamic ubiquitous computing environments such as aware homes [1] or first responder situations [2], applications opportunistically connect to a set of locally available resources that change due to the application's (or user's) mobility. Such environments commonly rely on *mobile ad hoc networks* to provide network connectivity. In mobile ad hoc networks, devices are disconnected from any wired infrastructure and instead communicate directly with one another using wireless radio signals. Such networks employ multihop routing protocols that use intermediate devices as routers for communicating partners that are not directly connected.

Application sessions [3] enable applications to select resources from the immediate environment based on their functional properties. The approach is simple in that it uses non-deterministic selection to connect the service requester to *any* available resource that matches the request. However, it only accounts for the static properties that define the capabilities of a particular resource; it does

A. Dan and W. Lamersdorf (Eds.): ICSOC 2006, LNCS 4294, pp. 78–89, 2006.

not allow applications to express the fact that a resource with particular non-functional properties is preferable to another resource.

In this paper, we create an expressive preference function that we incorporate into the application sessions framework. The function allows all parties that participate in the service interaction to express their non-functional requirements regarding a particular service binding. This includes the resource user, the resource provider, and the devices that support the connection between the provider and user. Characteristics that are likely to have an impact on the selection of a particular resource include: the relative mobility of the user and the resource, the proximity of the user to the resource, the reliability of a resource, the battery power of the devices involved, etc.

This work differs from previous work because connections and the preferences associated with them are determined dynamically in a changing environment. In addition, all policy evaluations must be accomplished in a distributed and ad hoc fashion because no infrastructure exists to facilitate service selection. The specific novel contributions of this work fall in two categories. First, we define a framework for preference specification. Second, we provide implementation paths for incorporating these preferences into the application sessions framework.

This paper is organized as follows. First we overview the original application sessions model. We then extend the model to include preference functions. Section 4 describes related work, and Section 5 concludes.

2 The Application Sessions Model

The application sessions model [3] defined a set of interactions between ubiquitous computing applications and services available in the applications' immediate surroundings. Our model explicitly separates the user program (i.e, the *application*) from the session management infrastructure that manages coordination with available providers. The only knowledge shared between the two are a specification (*spec*) that describes the desired service, and a provider handle (p) that allows the application to access the provider the infrastructure connects it to.

Services and requests are described using semi-structured data [4], an approach common among description languages [5] and tuple based systems [6]. We use ELIGHTS [7], a flexible, lightweight tuple space implementation. Each device maintains a local *tuple space* where it stores information in *tuples*. Service providers describe service properties using tuples; a location service that provides readings once a second may be described as:

$$\langle(\mathit{service}, \text{location}), (\mathit{frequency}, 1\,\text{sec})\rangle$$

A service description may include additional tuple fields, e.g., format of information, error rate, etc. Service requests are encoded as templates (or patterns) over the description tuples. Content-based matching determines whether a description tuple matches a request template. An example template is:

$$\langle(\mathit{service}, = \text{location}), (\mathit{frequency}, < 30\,\text{sec})\rangle$$

This request matches location services that have a frequency of less than 30 seconds. A communication protocol underlying the application session framework delivers request templates to providers [8], where matches are evaluated against tuples in the provider's local tuple space. No intermediate lookup service aids in this process; providers respond directly to requests they receive. This autonomy afforded by mobile ad hoc networks allows the framework to apply to dynamic ubiquitous computing environments.

We focus on three specific session types from our model: the *query session*, *provider session*, and *type session*. Detailed application examples that motivate each session type can be found in [3]; they are omitted here for brevity. Each session is represented as an assignment to a local handle that the requestor subsequently uses as a proxy for the discovered service. Throughout our description, the *entails* ($\models$) relation indicates that a resource satisfies a specification, i.e., in $p \models spec$, service p satisfies *spec*. The selection of a matching provider uses *non-deterministic assignment* [9] to indicate that a provider is selected from any that satisfy the specification. A statement $x := x'.Q$ assigns to x a value x' nondeterministically selected from among the values satisfying the predicate Q. If an assignment is not possible, the statement aborts; we assume this results in assigning ϵ (a null value) to x.

A *query session* is a simple, one-time request for data from some remote service. The application should be connected to a single matching service for the duration of this interaction. The session provides no long-lived interaction with the selected provider. We write the semantics of a query session as:

$$\boxed{p = spec}$$
$$\triangleq \; p = p'.(p' \models spec \wedge p'.\texttt{reachable})$$

The expression in the box denotes the particular session semantic. In this case, the query semantic is expressed by assigning the specification to the handle p. The value assigned is nondeterministically selected from all services that satisfy the specification and are reachable. The reachable relationship models the requirement that the two devices can communicate with each other, perhaps using a multihop path in the ad hoc network.

The *provider session* supports applications that connect to a remote service and perform several operations with that specific provider. This is useful, for example, when an interaction produces state at both endpoints that is necessary for subsequent interactions. The operational semantics can be written as:

$$\boxed{p \twoheadleftarrow spec}$$
$$\begin{array}{ll} \triangleq & p = p'.(p' \models spec \wedge p'.\texttt{reachable}) \\ & \textbf{if } p \neq \epsilon \textbf{ then} \\ & \quad \langle \textbf{await } \neg p.\texttt{reachable} \rightarrow p = \epsilon \rangle^1 \\ & \textbf{fi} \end{array}$$

[1] The $\langle$**await** $B \rightarrow S\rangle$ construct [10] allows a program to delay execution until the condition B holds. When B is true, the statements in S are executed in order. The angle brackets enclosing the construct indicate that the statement is executed atomically, i.e., no state internal to S is visible outside the execution of S.

In a provider session, the infrastructure maintains the connection to a particular resource given network dynamics. As long as the infrastructure can maintain a connection to the initial provider, the provider session is maintained. When the connection fails, the handle is assigned ϵ, which effectively notifies the application that the requested resource is no longer available.

In contrast to the previous sessions, the particular service provider supplying the resource in a *type session* can change during the session, as long as the new provider also satisfies the request specification. An example is a connection to a location server; the particular provider servicing a mobile device's requests for location readings is likely to change over time, but programming the application is simplified if this dynamic binding is transparent to the application. We express the type session formally as:

$$\boxed{p \Leftarrow spec}$$

$$\begin{array}{l} \triangleq\ p = p'.(p' \models spec \land p'.\texttt{reachable}) \\ \textbf{while}\ p \neq \epsilon\ \textbf{do} \\ \qquad \langle \textbf{await}\ \neg p.\texttt{reachable} \rightarrow p = p'.(p' \models spec \land p'.\texttt{reachable})\rangle \\ \textbf{od} \end{array}$$

If an attached provider becomes unreachable, the infrastructure attempts to locate a new provider that *is* reachable and matches the specification. As long as such a provider is available, the application remains connected to one, nondeterministically chosen from those that meet the requirements.

These session types do not completely address the needs of ubiquitous computing applications. What an application truly wants is the ability to request that it is connected to the best available provider for some measure of "best" (for example, the closest provider). We rectify this problem by introducing an expressive preference function as an extension to the existing framework that continues to hide the complexity of creating highly interactive ubiquitous applications.

3 Specifying Preference

The framework described above assumes that each provider that matches the functional specification is equally well suited. In this work, we introduce a function (f) that evaluates properties of a potential matching service and its hosting device, properties of the application and its hosting device, and properties of the network that connects the two. The latter is important because our framework supports dynamic connections between applications and services in mobile ad hoc networks where ordinary devices must serve as routers for communication among other hosts in the network. As such, the cost of supporting communication between two peers in the network (i.e., the application host and the service provider) has impact on other devices in a manner that is not commonly captured by end-to-end quality of service approaches such as [11,12].

Our general framework for defining the preference function f relies on three partial cost functions: $f_a(p)$, which defines the cost to application a of selecting a particular provider p; $f_p(a)$, which defines the cost to provider p of servicing application a; and $f_n(a,p)$, which defines the cost of a network path between the devices hosting the application (a) and the potential provider (p). In combination, the overall "global" preference function can be defined as:

$$f(a,p) = \alpha f_a(p) + \rho f_p(a) + \nu f_n(a,p)$$

where α, ρ, and ν are system-specified constants that can place varying emphasis on the three different components under different operating conditions. The provider that best satisfies this function at any given instant has a cost of:

$$c_{optimal} = \langle \min a,p : p \models spec :: f(a,p) \rangle^2.$$

All of the partial cost functions ($f_a(p)$, $f_p(a)$, and $f_n(a,p)$) return values between 0 and 1, as described below, and $\alpha + \rho + \nu = 1$, so that the result of evaluating the global preference function for any application/provider pair is a value between 0 and 1. Each of the partial cost functions is also allowed to return ∞, which effectively vetoes that party's participation in the session.

In the remainder of this section, we first revisit the model to show the revised semantics of sessions with preferences. We then explore each of the partial cost functions in more detail, describing how its behavior is implemented within our tuple-based model. This is especially important in the case of network costs, where our approach allows $f_n(a,p)$ to be computed as part of the underlying communication protocol, thereby incurring minimal additional overhead.

3.1 Preference Based Application Sessions

Incorporating preferences into the application sessions model requires augmenting the operational semantics listed in Section 2 to ensure that the "best" provider is chosen based on the global cost function. In this section, we express the semantics in terms of the global cost function; in the subsequent sections we show how these global semantics are implemented using the partial cost functions described above. We abuse our own notation slightly here by writing $f(p)$ to indicate the global preference function $f(a,p)$ because these definitions are written from the application's perspective (i.e., a is fixed in all cases). If p is not reachable from a in the mobile ad hoc network, then the cost function has a value of ∞, that is, $\neg p.\mathtt{reachable} \Rightarrow f(p) = \infty$. How this is implemented is described in Section 3.4.

The preference-aware query session simply selects the service provider to connect based on minimizing the preference function:

[2] In the *three-part notation*: $\langle \textbf{op}\ quantified\_variables : range :: expression \rangle$, the variables from *quantified_variables* take on all possible values permitted by *range*. Each instantiation of the variables is substituted in *expression*, producing a multiset of values to which **op** is applied, yielding the value of the three-part expression. If no instantiation of the variables satisfies *range*, then the value of the three part expression is the identity element for **op**, e.g., *true* if **op** is $\forall$ or 0 when **op** is min.

$\boxed{p = spec/f}$

$$\triangleq \; p = p'.(p' \models spec \land p'.\texttt{reachable} \land \langle \forall \pi : \pi \models spec :: f(p') < f(\pi) \rangle)$$

The provider session is similar; the best provider is selected, and no subsequent reselection is performed:

$\boxed{p \leftarrow spec/f}$

$$\begin{array}{l} \triangleq \; p = p'.(p' \models spec \land p'.\texttt{reachable} \land \langle \forall \pi : \pi \models spec :: f(p') < f(\pi) \rangle) \\ \quad \textbf{if } p \neq \epsilon \textbf{ then} \\ \quad\quad \langle \textbf{await } \neg p.\texttt{reachable} \rightarrow p = \epsilon \rangle \\ \quad \textbf{fi} \end{array}$$

The preference-aware type session is more complicated because not only must it ensure that it initially selects the best match, but it has to constantly monitor the available providers to ensure that this match remains the best one available:

$\boxed{p \Leftarrow spec/f}$

$$\begin{array}{l} \triangleq \; p = p'.(p' \models spec \land p'.\texttt{reachable} \land \langle \forall \pi : \pi \models spec :: f(p') < f(\pi) \rangle) \\ \textbf{while } p \neq \epsilon \textbf{ do} \\ \quad \langle \textbf{await } \neg p.\texttt{reachable} \lor \langle \exists \pi : \pi.\texttt{reachable} \land \pi \models spec \;\land\; f(\pi) < f(p) \rangle \rightarrow \\ \quad\quad p = p'.(p' \models spec \land p'.\texttt{reachable} \land \langle \forall \pi : \pi \models spec :: f(p') < f(\pi) \rangle) \\ \textbf{od} \end{array}$$

The statement inside the loop ensures that the application is reconnected if a better provider is available. As above, this assignment ultimately sets the handle to ϵ if no satisfactory provider is available.

3.2 Implementing Application Preferences

The most obvious of the three components of the preference function is the application requesting access to the service. Factors that influence the application include aspects such as:

- service fidelity (i.e., the error rate in responses from the provider)
- service availability (i.e., the percentage of time the provider is responsive)
- proximity of the provider (i.e., location-dependent interactions tend to favor closer providers)
- relative mobility (i.e., if both the application's host and the provider's host can move, stable connections will involve low *relative* mobility)

The portion of the global preference function related to application preferences is $\alpha f_a(p)$. Effectively, the application provides a function that takes as a parameter a provider (or more specifically, attributes of a provider) and generates a cost value. This is done for every potential provider, enabling the application to select the lowest cost provider. Service providers generate attribute tuples in their local tuple spaces that provide up-to-date information about the attributes described above. As an example, a provider may output a velocity tuple:

$$\langle(\mathit{speed}, \text{my\_speed}), (\mathit{direction}, \text{my\_direction})\rangle$$

As the provider's velocity changes, it removes this tuple and inserts a new tuple representing the updated velocity. Service requests evaluating the cost for this provider can access this information asynchronously to generate values for the cost to this provider. The provider may not have a tuple for every attribute; if a client request requires information about an attribute but the provider does not provide it, the connection cannot be made.

The application's cost function is provided as an *active tuple* as was introduced in the Linda model [6]. An active tuple differs from the previously described *passive tuples* in that it can contain uncompleted computation. In our case, the active tuple encapsulates the computation that calculates the cost function's value for a particular provider:

$$\langle(\mathit{source}, \text{requester\_id}), (\mathit{cost}_a, \mathtt{cost_a}(\ldots))\rangle$$

where the *source* field's value indicates the unique id of the requesting device, and the $cost_a$ field's value actually calculates the cost for the application to use a particular provider. The communication protocol broadcasts this active tuple to every host reachable in the network. This is excessive, since the network could be very large; Section 3.4 shows how this broadcast is restricted to only provider devices that are in a reasonable range to service the request.

The code implementing $\mathtt{cost}_a(\ldots)$ for our example based on the relative mobility between the service requester and the service provider has the form:

```
costa(my_velocity)
  rd( [spec] )
  v = rdp( ⟨(speed, ? ), (direction ? )⟩ )
  if(v == null)
    return ∞
  else
    return relative_velocity(v, my_velocity)
```

The first line is a blocking tuple space operation, a `rd`, which waits until it encounters a tuple matching its argument (in this case the template representing the service request). When the active tuple encounters such a match, the blocking `rd` operation returns, allowing the cost function to continue. At this point, the active tuple knows that it is at a location hosting a service provider that matches the request. The second line is a probing (non-blocking) `rdp` operation that looks for a tuple matching the provided template; in this case, a tuple containing speed and direction information (where the values for the fields are unrestricted, as indicated by the "?"). If no matching tuple exists, the operation returns `null`, and the cost cannot be computed. If a matching tuple does exist, the result is used to compute the relative velocity of the two devices (normalized to be between 0 and 1). This example uses only one attribute of the provider, but more attributes can be incorporated by looking for additional attribute tuples. When the function returns, it automatically replaces the function portion of the active tuple (the second field) with the returned value, resulting in a passive tuple:

$$\langle(source, \text{requester\_id}), (cost_a, \texttt{relative\_velocity})\rangle$$

The underlying communication protocol responds to the presence of this tuple and returns it to the requester. Each device within the network receives a copy of the original active tuple; each device that supports a matching service executes the active tuple, generating a cost for that service. Therefore, the requester receives a cost tuple for each potential provider, allowing the application to select the best option.

3.3 Implementing Provider Preferences

The second participant in the session that desires to to influence service selection is the service provider itself. Factors that might influence whether or not a provider wants to participate in a session include:

- current provider load
- current battery level of provider device
- announced intended length of usage by the application requesting access (or duration of session)
- periodicity of requests from the application

The portion of the global preference function related to the provider specified preferences is $\rho f_p(a)$. When a provider makes a service remotely available, it also specifies a preference function that takes as a parameter an application (or more specifically, attributes of a particular application and its request) and generates a cost value for servicing that request.

The implementation of the provider preference adds to the process elucidated in the previous section. Instead of the communication protocol responding to a two-field passive tuple (the tuple containing the requester's id and the application cost value), the protocol responds only to a three-field active tuple:

$$\langle(source, \text{requester\_id}), (cost_a, \text{cost\_value}), (cost_p, \texttt{cost}_{\texttt{p}}(\ldots))\rangle$$

Before the communication protocol responds to this tuple, the provider device removes the two-field tuple generated by evaluating the application's cost function and replaces it with the above three-field tuple by inserting its own cost function. This cost function is partially evaluated with respect to having values filled in for needed provider attributes (e.g., current load), and when it arrives at the requester, it reads attributes about the application requesting the service (e.g., the frequency of requests). Once the communication protocol transports this three-field tuple back to the requester (using the tuple's first field, which uniquely identifies the requester), the provider's cost function completes its execution using tuples read from the requester's local tuple space.

3.4 Implementing Network Preferences

While the first two stakeholders (the application and the service provider) are obvious, a third, often overlooked component is the network. Ubiquitous computing applications like those mentioned in Section 1 are supported by mobile ad hoc networks in which the nodes themselves serve as routers for connections between devices that are not directly connected. These intermediate nodes have a vested interest in ensuring the connections selected ensure the longevity of the network as a whole. Factors that play into network preferences include:

– aggregate bandwidth available on potential transmission path
– number of network hops
– battery power available on intermediate nodes
– latency of the network connection

The portion of the global preference function related to the network is $\nu f_n(a,p)$. This function has a static definition applicable across the entire network and known to all applications, but the values that influence the cost calculated for a path are themselves dynamic. We have so far assumed a broadcast-based communication protocol in which every request is delivered to every other device in the network. Our communication protocol that incorporates the network cost function embodies additional intelligence. A mobile ad hoc network is made up of a set of devices connected by a graph in which vertices in the graph are wireless devices and edges in the graph are direct connections between devices that are physically close enough to be within communication range. A mobile ad hoc network routing protocol can dynamically impose a tree on this graph where the root of the tree is the requesting device and paths to other devices emanate out from the root. Our resource requests move along these paths, recalculating the network cost at every hop. If the network cost ever exceeds its allowable threshold (provided statically by the network deployer to each node), the message kills itself. Our network cost function allows more sophisticated definitions, though the simple definitions can still be used to halt propagation.

When using all three cost functions in conjunction, the process changes slightly again from the previous section. The static network cost function is provided to every device, and any requesting device must place this cost function in its request tuple:

$$\langle (source, \text{requester\_id}), (cost_n, \mathtt{cost_n}(\mathtt{cost_a}(\ldots), \ldots)\rangle$$

where the network cost function ($\mathtt{cost_n}(\ldots)$) is the active portion of the tuple, and the application's cost function is invoked when a match is encountered. The first line of the application's cost function defined above is no longer necessary; this matching of the application's specification against the provider's description is performed within the network cost function.

The implementation of the network cost function has the following structure:

```
costn(costa(...), ...)
  current_cost = 0
  max_net_cost = threshold
  while(true)
    if rdp( [spec]) != null
      out(⟨(source, requester_id), (costn, current_cost), (costa, costa(...))⟩
    update_cost(current_cost)
    if current_cost < max_net_cost
      forward_self
    else
      out([garbage collecting active tuple])
      return ∞
```

The rdp operation checks to see if the current device has a service that matches the application's request. If so, the function generates a dedicated tuple for responding from this provider and places it in the provider's local tuple space. Processing of this tuple proceeds as described above; the application's cost function is evaluated first. When it finishes, the provider removes the tuple and replaces it with a tuple containing its unevaluated cost function. The result tuple now contains four fields, including a value for the network cost function.

Whether the current provider matched or not, the network cost function continues by updating the network cost stored within the active tuple. The single statement update_cost(current_cost) encodes a more complicated process that may involve carrying some state from one node to another and/or reading values stored in local tuples (e.g., local available bandwidth information or remaining battery power). When the network cost function generates a cost value that exceeds a specified threshold, it performs a sequence of steps that ensure that the request no longer propagates and that it leaves no residue on the current provider. This process suffices completely for query and provider sessions; type sessions require the active tuple to remain resident and send updates back to the requester if any of the cost values change. This allows the requester to reconnect to a better provider as soon as one becomes available.

4 Related Work

Research projects have increasingly focused on providing applications dynamic access to a changing set of resources. We highlight the most relevant projects, especially with respect to how applications specify constraints or preferences on selected resources. Many projects have focused on mediating quality of service requirements by leveraging object mobility [13,14] to enhance application responsiveness and network-wide performance metrics. These approaches focus on bringing objects closer to clients instead of on the notion that the clients themselves are mobile and resource usage may be inherently location-dependent.

Network sensitive service selection [15] observed the differences between performing user-side resource selection (where the user collects necessary information about available providers) and provider-side resource selection (where a provider collects information about potential users). Work founded on these observations introduced the ability for applications to include network parameters and requirements in resource requests.

In moving from network-sensitivity to awareness of quality of service (QoS), service efficiency has been defined as a tradeoff between service coverage and cost [16]. This work is extended in [17] which provides guaranteed availability of a multimedia service in dynamic ad hoc networks using a combination of algorithms that includes predicting network partitions. This work focuses on optimal creation and placement of service instances in dynamic ad hoc networks, and therefore is sufficient only for non-location-dependent software services. Our approach addresses the discovery of resources (both physical and software resources) that are available in a local environment.

Work more closely related to our approach [11] differentiates QoS parameters into metrics and policies and considers both constraints on the user of a resource and constraints on the provider of that resource. This work does not naturally accommodate dynamically changing QoS measurements and is limited to traditional performance-style measurements (like bandwidth, reliability, load, etc.). Our approach handles application-level requirements (e.g., location, mobility, etc.) and defines three categories of constraints (application-, provider-, and network-specific constraints) instead of just two. This allows us to consider the impact that a peer-to-peer interaction has on the rest of the network, not just its impact on the direct participants. Other work [18] introduces formal modeling tools that enable optimal service compositions to be selected given a static set of QoS requirements. Our approach focuses on the ability of an infrastructure to dynamically adapt such selections in response to changes in the underlying network and service infrastructure.

A final important component of the work that was described in this paper is its ambition to simplify the development of adaptive ubiquitous computing applications. Along that same vein, previous work has created middleware solutions to enable developers to easily specify the relationships between their applications and QoS metrics [12]. In a similar manner, DySOA [19] enables service compositions to dynamically evaluate the network status and adapt the system at runtime to maintain a set of specified QoS parameters.

5 Conclusions

Our approach explicitly separates preferences into three categories, allowing the application, the resource provider, and the network to each specify preferences with regard to a potential resource interaction. At runtime, these preferences are dynamically evaluated, and connections between applications and resource providers are automatically maintained to ensure that these preference functions are maximized and that no constraints are violated. This style of interaction is essential to applications which function in long-lived ubiquitous computing environments where applications' interactions are inherently location, environment, and task-dependent.

Acknowledgments

The author would like to thank the Center for Excellence in Distributed Global Environments for providing research facilities and the collaborative environment. This research was funded, in part, by the NSF, Grant # CNS-0620245. The views and conclusions herein are those of the authors and do not necessarily reflect the views of the sponsoring agencies.

References

1. Kidd, C., Orr, R., Abowd, G., Atkeson, C., Essa, I., MacIntyre, B., Mynatt, E., Starner, T., Newstetter, W.: The aware home: A living laboratory for ubiquitous computing research. In: Proc. of CoBuild. (1999)
2. Malan, D., Fulford-Jones, T., Welsh, M., Moulton, S.: CodeBlue: An ad hoc sensor network infrastructure for emergency medical care. In: Proc. of BSN. (2004)
3. Julien, C., Stovall, D.: Enabling ubiquitous coordination using application sessions. In: Proc. of Coordination. (2006)
4. Abiteboul, S.: Querying semi-structured data. In: Proc. of ICDT. (1997) 1–18
5. Christensen, E., Gubera, F., Meredith, G., Weerawarana, S.: Web services description language (WSDL) 1.1 (2001) Current as of 2005.
6. Carriero, N., Gelernter, D.: Linda in context. Communications of the ACM **32**(4) (1989) 444–458
7. Julien, C., Roman, G.C.: Egocentric context-aware programming in ad hoc mobile environments. In: Proc. of FSE. (2002) 21–30
8. Julien, C., Venkataraman, M.: Resource-directed discovery and routing in mobile ad hoc networks. Technical Report TR-UTEDGE-2005-01, Univ. of Texas (2005)
9. Back, R., Sere, K.: Stepwise refinement of parallel algorithms. Science of Computer Prog. **13**(2-3) (1990) 133–180
10. Andrews, G.: Foundations of Multithreaded, Parallel, and Distributed Programming. Addison Wesley (1999)
11. Liu, J., Issarny, V.: QoS-aware service location in mobile ad hoc networks. In: Proc. of MDM. (2004) 224–235
12. Nahrstedt, K., Xu, D., Wichadakul, D., Li, B.: Qos-aware middleware for ubiquitous and heterogeneous environments. IEEE Comm. Magazine (2001) 140–148
13. Grimm, R., Davis, J., Lemar, E., MacBeth, A., Swanson, S., Anderson, T., Bershad, B., Borriello, G., Gribble, S., Wetherall, D.: System support for pervasive applications. ACM Trans. on Computer Systems **22**(4) (2004) 421–486
14. Holder, O., Ben-Shaul, I., Gazit, H.: Dynamic layout of distributed applications in FarGo. In: Proc. of ICSE. (1999) 163–173
15. Huang, A.C., Steenkiste, P.: Network-sensitive service discovery. Journal of Grid Comput. **1**(3) (2003) 309–326
16. Li, B.: QoS-aware adaptive services in mobile networks. In: Proc. of IWQoS. Volume 2092 of LNCS. (2001) 251–268
17. Li, B., Wang, K.: Nonstop: Continuous multimedia streaming in wireless ad hoc networks with node mobility. IEEE Journal on Selected Areas in Comm. **21**(10) (2003) 1627–1641
18. Yu, T., Lin, K.J.: Service selection algorithms for composing complex services with multiple QoS constraints. In: Proc. of ICSOC. (2005) 130–143
19. Siljee, J., Bosloper, I., Nijhuis, J., Hammer, D.: DySOA: Making service systems self-adaptive. In: Proc. of ICSOC. (2005) 255–268

Mobile Ad Hoc Services: Semantic Service Discovery in Mobile Ad Hoc Networks

Andronikos Nedos, Kulpreet Singh, and Siobhán Clarke

Distributed Systems Group, Trinity College Dublin, Ireland

Abstract. Mobile ad hoc networks (MANETs) are a class of networks where autonomous mobile devices with wireless communication capabilities cooperate to provide spontaneous, multi-hop connectivity. The opportunistic and dynamic characteristics of these networks make discovery of services difficult as they preclude the use of agreed, predefined service interfaces. Using semantic services and permitting their description with multiple domain ontologies is more realistic in this environment because it increases service expressiveness and does not require consensus on a common representation. However, the techniques used in resource-rich, globally connected environments to relate different ontologies and discover semantic services are inappropriate in MANETs. We present here a model for semantic service discovery that facilitates distributed ontology matching and provides scalable discovery of service provider nodes. It uses a gossip protocol to randomly disseminate ontology concepts and a random walk mechanism to identify candidate providers. The model requires no central coordination and the use of randomisation gives it good scalability properties.

1 Introduction

Mobile ad hoc networks are composed of autonomous, wireless nodes which act as mobile routers to provide communication without the need for fixed infrastructure. These networks have an opportunistic aspect as they can form anywhere with little or no coordination. The resulting unpredictability is both appealing and problematic. While these networks require no existing infrastructure, their decentralised topologies make resource identification challenging. In this paper we examine the issue of service discovery in MANETs given the assumption of service role symmetry in nodes, that is, each node has the potential to be both a service provider and a consumer.

Current service description and discovery mechanisms in MANETs [1,2], rely on standardised interfaces to achieve the necessary consensus that makes advertising and discovery possible. While this is usually sufficient in environments that are centrally administered, it poses a serious problem for serendipitous application interoperability in open, distributed systems. For uncoordinated service interaction in MANETs, service based applications would benefit from an expressive service specification language, increased autonomy in the description of individual services and distributed discovery mechanisms.

The use of ontologies in the description of services has already been proposed as a solution for more flexible discovery [3,4]. However, most semantic service description languages and architectures require a globally connected network such as the web. In ad hoc networks, assumptions of global connectivity do not hold because the properties

A. Dan and W. Lamersdorf (Eds.): ICSOC 2006, LNCS 4294, pp. 90–103, 2006.

of the environment are drastically different. One core difference in our model is that nodes do not share a common semantic representation for their services but instead it is assumed that semantic agreement can be derived through node interaction. We believe that this a more appropriate assumption that is in line with the network's uncoordinated and spontaneous formation. Violating this assumption would require either one global ontology to describe all services or maintenance of all potential ontologies in each node. The former is restrictive while the latter is not practical. The idea of semantic decentralisation is also present in decentralised P2P networks [4,5] but has not yet appeared in the domain of mobile ad hoc networks. Below we present a summary of MANET characteristics that form the assumptions of our proposed model:

- Nodes can be both providers and consumers of services. This symmetry precludes the use of centralised brokering architectures. Instead, discovery facilities should be distributed across the participating mobile nodes.
- Nodes are autonomous and consist of small, low-powered devices that can belong in different administrative domains. The implications of this are that applications will be coming from different sources and can be developed independently without a central distribution channel.
- Connectivity is local to the network with no guarantees for Internet availability. This characteristic enforces designs where applications are both self-contained and reactive. Applications will need to function in the absence of any service but also be able to discover and use any desired services as provider nodes connect to the network.
- Connectivity is also intermittent with nodes appearing and disappearing at any moment. Assuming that participating nodes have similar processing capabilities, any load imposed by service discovery has to be shared uniformly. Increasing the processing overhead in select nodes is not desirable and it also leads to extra protocol complexity caused by node election and mandatory fault-tolerant behaviour.

The contribution of this paper is the description of a network model for the discovery of autonomous semantic services in MANET environments. An evaluation based on simulation demonstrates good scalability characteristics as the number of nodes and ontology sizes increase. Although this paper is focused on the network support for the discovery part, the tight dependency to a gossip protocol that is used to facilitate discovery and match heterogeneous ontologies necessitates a brief description presented in section 2.2.

The paper is organised as follows. Section 2 introduces the model and the underlying gossip-based protocol. Section 3 describes how we specify services and discusses the ontology matching algorithm. In Section 4 we present the random walk protocol for semantic service discovery in MANETs. Section 5 presents the evaluation results while we conclude with the state of the art and final remarks in Sections 6 and 7.

2 A Model for Semantic Service Discovery in MANETs

Recent standards for semantic web services, e.g., WSMO, OWL-S, WSDL-S, specify how services are described but are independent of any concrete mechanisms for the discovery of services. To enable the use of such standards in an environment where provider nodes are autonomous and no fixed infrastructure exists, we have identified two problems that discovery has to address:

Discovery queries must be interpreted by nodes with heterogeneous ontologies – So far a single domain ontology has been assumed for the description of MANET services. This makes possible the direct evaluation of discovery queries between different mobile nodes. We argue that given the opportunistic and unpredictable interaction patterns in MANETs, it is inappropriate to assume that a global ontology is available in every mobile node. Rather, each autonomous node will maintain its own ontology to describe its own services. Since a shared understanding is still required for meaningful semantic interpretation and service interaction, an ontology matching process is needed.

Lack of persistent and centralised service registries – In connected, fixed networks, certain assumptions can be made about longevity of ontology references. Usually, a URI reference is enough for clients to obtain an ontology from a central repository. Resource availability and infrastructure support in these environments also means that ontology matching and semantic service discovery can employ sophisticated techniques that make use of central facilities. In MANETs, transient communication renders brokering architectures harder to support. In addition, the self-contained nature of ad hoc networks means that only ontologies in the participating nodes can be used.

Part of the proposed solution is based on a gossip protocol that exchanges randomised subsets of concepts between nodes. On each node, received concepts are stored in a buffer until certain conditions are met. As a consequence, this buffer holds a constantly evolving and randomised set of concepts. A lightweight ontology matching mechanism in each node matches received concepts with those stored in the node's buffer. We consider this random set of concepts maintained by each node to be a view on all ontologies that has the following properties: It is *partial*, since no view contains the union of all concepts of all ontologies; it is *evolving*, the gossip protocol constantly inserts and removes concepts from this view while the matching algorithm in each node establishes associations between received and stored concepts; it is *randomised* since each view does not contain a set of concepts that concretely describe a knowledge domain, rather it contains randomised concepts that can belong to any of the available ontologies.

2.1 System Model

We consider an ad hoc network $N = \{n_1, n_2, \cdots, n_m\}$ as a set of mobile nodes $n_i \in N$ of size m. Each mobile node is considered to be an active participant that provides services described by an ontology. Each node maintains three different views. The *ontology view*, the *concept view* and the *node view*. We denote each of the three views at node n_i as V_i^O, V_i^C and V_i^N correspondingly.

The ontology view represents an ontology in each node as a fixed set of concepts, $V_i^O = \{c_{i1}, \cdots, c_{ig}\}$. Here, $c_{il} \in V_i^O, 1 \leq l \leq g$ is a concept in the ontology of source node n_i while g represents the maximum number of concepts. We assume that these ontologies are static so this view allows no additions or deletions of concepts for the duration of the protocol execution. This assumption is reasonable as ontologies are structured metadata, meaning they are specified during application design and don't change often. In contrast, services are described as metadata instances and their description can change at any time.

The concept view includes the set of concepts that are received from other nodes and does not allow duplicate concepts or concepts that exist already in the same node's ontology view. We represent this view as $V_i^C = \{c_{kl} \,| c_{kl} \in V_k^O, k \in N - \{n_i\}, 1 \leq l \leq g\}$, where c_{kl} represents any concept from any ontology view other than the one in node n_i. The concept view has variable size, i.e., concepts are added and removed during the execution of the protocol but the gossip protocol guarantees that V^C only contains a subset of the overall concepts.

The node view is composed by a set of node identifiers, $V_i^N = \{n_k | k \in N - \{n_i\}\}$. It maintains a uniform, randomised, partial and fixed-size set of node ids and is populated during a bootstrap phase. Like the concept view it does not allow duplicate node identifiers and does not contain the node's own id.

The consequences of maintaining the two partial views (V^N and V^C) is that no node holds the complete knowledge of all participating nodes or all ontology concepts. This helps applicability in a large scale setting. The gossip protocol is completely characterised by the following parameters:

- F_c: The concept fanout specifies the number of concepts a source node includes in a gossip transmission,
- F_n: The node fanout specifies the number of target nodes a gossip message is sent to,
- $age_{\text{threshold}}$: Specifies the number of times a node transmits a received concept before the concept is removed from V^C. For convenience, we define function $age(c)$ that takes concept c as input and returns its age.
- ttl_{gossip}: This value is assigned by each source node to any concepts from V^O that are selected for transmission. It specifies the number of hops that c will traverse before being discarded when $c.ttl$ reaches zero.

2.2 Gossip Protocol

We describe here a gossip protocol that transmits random subsets of concepts between the participating mobile nodes. The protocol is executed in every node and is described in terms of the actions taken during the reception and transmission of a gossip message.

On reception, a node executes the algorithm described in Listing 1. The algorithm first matches the set of concepts included in the transmission against its stored concepts. This is shown in line 3. Subsequent to matching, lines 4 – 6 show that if a concept is not found in either the concept or the ontology view and the concept's ttl is greater to one, it will be stored at the receiver's concept view.

Each gossip reception results in progressing the system's shared semantic knowledge in an incremental fashion. Through an ontology matching algorithm, described in section 3.1, each message has the potential to create new associations between concepts from different ontologies. A concept view size that is bound by the protocol and a fixed concept fanout ensure that nodes are not overwhelmed with matching large ontologies. Although the redundancy that is inherent in gossip protocols can seem excessive, it is this very feature that allows progressive matching through concept transmission and scalable discovery through concept replication. A gossip approach also avoids flooding, which in multi-hop networks can significantly increase traffic as the network size grows.

Listing 1. Gossip Reception

On reception of *gossip* at node j
for all $c \in gossip.concepts$ **do**
    Execute ontology matching algorithm between c and $V_j^O \bigcup V_j^C$
    if $c \notin V_j^O \wedge c \notin V_j^C \wedge c.ttl > 1$ **then**
        $c.ttl \leftarrow c.ttl - 1$
        $V_j^C = V_j^C \bigcup \{c\}$
    end if
end for

Listing 2. Gossip Transmission

Every t ms at node j
Choose $X = \{c_{j1}, \ldots, c_{jl}\}$ *random concepts from* $V_j^O \bigcup V_j^C$ *, with* $l = F_c$
for all $c \in X$ **do**
    if $c \in V_j^O$ **then**
        $c.ttl \leftarrow ttl_{\text{gossip}}$
    end if
    if $c \in V_j^C \wedge age(c) = age_{\text{threshold}}$ **then**
        $V_j^C \leftarrow V_j^C - \{c\}$
    else if $c \in V_j^C$ **then**
        $c.age \leftarrow age(c) + 1$
    end if
end for
$gossip.concepts \leftarrow X$
Choose $Y = \{n_1, \ldots, n_{F_n}\}$ *random nodes from* V_j^N
for all $r \in Y$ **do**
    $\mathbf{send}(r, gossip)$
end for

Listing 2 describes the transmission of a gossip message. In each timeout, a node selects F_c concepts at random from the union of the ontology and concept views. Any item from the concept view that has been transmitted $age_{threshold}$ times is removed from that view. This selection algorithm is simple and exhibits a desirable adaptive behaviour. During the initial stages of gossip transmission, a node's priority is to disseminate its own ontology so that its semantic information is diffused throughout the network. Since the concept view contains few elements during the initial rounds, concepts from a node's ontology have a higher probability of being selected for transmission. A more in-depth description and analysis of the gossip protocol together with experimental results can be found in [6]. It is omitted here for space considerations.

With the dissemination of concepts by the gossip protocol, we can now discover services based on their semantic description. Concept based service discovery has been used previously in the context of P2P networks by [7] and [8]. It corresponds to discovery of services not by mere syntax but by their semantic properties. In the distributed setting that we consider here, concept discovery can provide an ideal method to identify relevant services.

3 Semantic Service Description

We have chosen the Resouce Description Framework Schema (RDFS) [9] to model ontologies and to represent service description and queries. RDFS, although limited in its modelling constructs, can provide adequate expressiveness for our demo prototype and the scenario types we consider. There is currently no service standard in RDFS, so we have defined a minimal service specification based on the service profile of OWL-S. An example of an RDFS-based service instance is shown in Fig. 1a.

In the proposed model it is concepts rather than services that are advertised and discovered. This provides the required flexibility to enable the progressive ontology matching and the concept-based discovery of services. However, the decomposition of ontologies into concepts and the distribution of concepts across the network imposes certain requirements on the concept's syntax. Ontology languages like RDFS and OWL were not designed for this task so the syntax of advertised concepts had to be augmented. We call this syntax the *network representation* of a concept to distinguish it from the normal representation a concept has in an ontology. Figure 1b shows an instance of a concept network representation. This advertised syntax needs to contain enough information to satisfy two distinct requirements:

1. *Discovery of service providers*. A first step to service discovery is the identification of nodes with ontologies compatible to the ontology of the node that initiated the discovery query. To achieve this we use the following properties. First, the gossip protocol enables the dissemination of concepts to any of the participating nodes. Second, as we show in Section 4, a discovery query can be formulated as a set of concepts. If we now embed the source node identifier in each concept network representation, we can facilitate the discovery of service provider nodes.
2. *Pair-wise concept matching*. Properties in most ontology languages (e.g. object or datatype properties in OWL) are first-class entities and are usually defined outside the scope of concepts. For the semantic interpretation of discovery queries we rely on concept matching and specifically on the name and property correspondence between concepts from different ontologies. By embedding concept properties in the network representation we can facilitate matching in any participating node. Section 3.1 elaborates on the issue.

3.1 Ontology Matching

Scarcity of computational resources and transient communication necessitates a lightweight and practical approach for matching heterogeneous ontologies. Syntactical matching is more appropriate because it requires less resources. Semantic matching on the other hand can produce more accurate integration, but requires complex inferencing over the candidate ontologies. For the initial implementation described in this paper we have used an algorithm similar to *intermediate matching* of H-Match [10]. We assume that all participating nodes share the same matching algorithm. Each node records a match between two concepts when their respective names are syntactically equal and each of their properties match in type and name. We note however that details of ontology matching are outside the scope of this work. What is of interest is the utilisation of the matching relationship after it has been established.

```
<rdf:RDF xml:lang="en"
<om:Service rdf:ID="aService">
  <om:hasInput rdf:resource="#ConceptA"/>
  ...
  <om:hasOutput rdf:resource="#ConceptB"/>
  ...
</om:Service>
</rdf:RDF>
```

a. A service instance in XML.

```
<rdfs:Class rdf:ID="C">
  <om:source rdf:resource="192.168.1.2"
  <om:isSubClassOf rdf:resource="#C"/>
  ...
  <om:hasProperty rdf:resource="P1"/>
  <om:hasProperty rdf:resource"P2"/>
  ...
</rdfs:Class>
```

b. A concept's network representation in XML.

Fig. 1. Representation of a service and a concept's advertised syntax

We define the concept matching relationship as a transitive and symmetric relation. For example, if c_i, c_j and c_k represent concepts in V_i^O, V_j^O, V_k^O; **M** the matching relation, and a match exists between c_i, c_j and also between c_j, c_k, the following matches are inferred:

1. $c_i\mathbf{M}c_j \Leftrightarrow c_j\mathbf{M}c_i$,
2. $c_j\mathbf{M}c_k \Leftrightarrow c_k\mathbf{M}c_j$
3. $c_i\mathbf{M}c_j \wedge c_j\mathbf{M}c_k \Rightarrow c_i\mathbf{M}c_k$.

The exact semantics of the matching relationship depend on the strength of the matching mechanism. Here, we have reduced the scope of matching to an equivalence relationship that is similar to the `owl:equivalentClass` property in OWL. Other relationship types are also possible, for example `kindOf` or `partOf` relationships.

There is a dependency between the network representation of concepts and the accuracy of the matching algorithm. If the network representation of a concept contains only its name, it is difficult for any algorithm to produce an accurate match between concepts. In the current prototype, the concept network representation includes any properties that have the specific concept as their domain concept in addition to properties inherited through the RDFS `subClassOf` and `subPropertyOf` relations.

4 Discovery and Matchmaking of Services in a Distributed Environment

In centralised architectures like UDDI or where broadcast facilities are available (e.g., LANs), mechanisms for service discovery can use existing infrastructure. A query to a well known URL or a broadcast request can return any available services that match certain criteria. Neither of these facilities are available in MANETs.

Our proposed mechanism for service discovery is distributed and is overlayed on top of the gossip protocol described previously. The discovery process has two phases: 1) the identification of candidate nodes with compatible ontologies and 2) the redirection of the discovery query to the candidate nodes for the final service matchmaking. During the first phase, a random walk mechanism aggregates the addresses of nodes that have ontologies with concepts that match the concepts in the discovery query. These are addresses of potential service providers since matching relationships indicate partially compatible ontologies. Depending on the matching progress and the number of hops before the discovery query expires, it is expected that candidate nodes will be identified

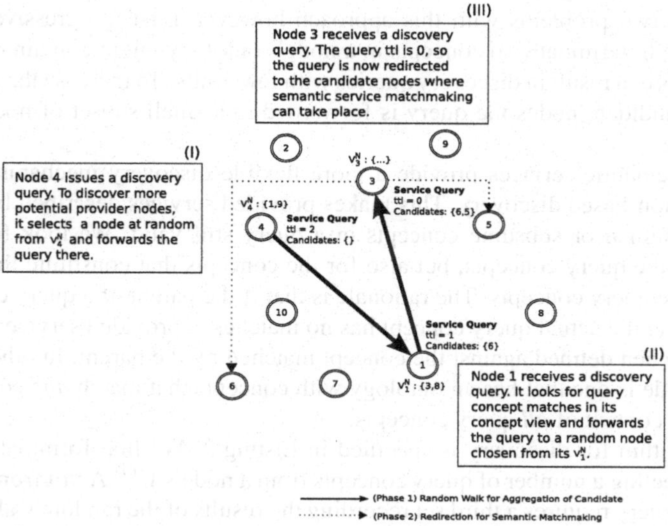

Fig. 2. The two phase semantic service discovery

with high probability. In the second phase, the query is redirected to the discovered nodes where semantic matchmaking of available services can take place. Figure 2 illustrates the process.

4.1 Aggregation of Candidate Nodes

We introduce the following definitions:

- We call a node that initiates a discovery query, the query's *source* node.
- We formulate a service query as a set of `In` and `Out` concepts. We represent such a query as:
$$Q = \{(c, T), \ldots, | c \in V^O, T = \{In, Out\}\},$$
where T is a parameter type and c a *query concept* from a node's ontology view.
- We define the *semantic context* of a concept as its super and sub-concepts.
- As the semantic context of a concept can be the complete ontology, we bound the context with a parameter τ.
- If $super_\tau(c)$ and $sub_\tau(c)$ give the set of super and sub-concepts for concept c, then we represent the semantic context of all query concepts in Q using the set:

$$H_\tau = \{super_\tau(c) \cup sub_\tau(c) | \forall c \in Q\}$$

The first step to service discovery is to identify nodes with concepts that match all the concepts in a query. A simple mechanism would identify candidate nodes by examining only the source's V^O and would immediately redirect the query to the identified nodes. This is straightforward since each concept embeds predicates for any matching concepts and their corresponding source node identifiers.

There are two problems with this approach however. First, progressive matching can take time to terminate, so concepts in a node's ontology might contain only partial matches. This can result in discovery queries with fewer hits. To increase the probability of finding candidate nodes the query is forwarded to a small subset of nodes using a random walk.

Second, semantic services provide a more flexible discovery mechanism because of subsumption-based discovery. This makes provided services described by concepts that are subsumed or subsume concepts in a query still valid. We look for matches not only for the query concepts, but also for the concepts that constitute the semantic context of the query concepts. The rationale is that if the parent of a query concept has a match, while the actual query concept has no matches, a provided service can still be compatible when defined against the concept matched by the parent. In other words, a candidate node is one that has an ontology with concepts that match *any* concept from the semantic context of *all* query concepts.

The algorithm for discovery is specified in Listing 3. We first formulate a service query by selecting a number of query concepts from a node's V^O. Apart from Q and H, a discovery query requires a third set recording the results of the random walk protocol. Note that Q and H need not contain the complete concept representation. If the qualified name of a concept includes the node's address, e.g., a URI of the form `node://<node address>/<concept name>`, that would be enough to uniquely identify concepts and avoid name clashes.

Matches are stored in $R = \{(c, \{id_1, \ldots, id_n\}), \ldots, | c \in Q \cup H\}$, where id is the identifier of a node that has an ontology with a concept matching c. To simplify our description we define a function $f_S(c)$ where c is a concept with $c \in S$ and S can be either of the two views, i.e., V^O, V^C or R. This function returns the set of node identifiers of all matched concepts currently embedded in c.

After formulating the discovery query, line 2 shows a first set of matches being recorded at the source node. In a situation where matching has been completed between all ontologies, this first set would represent all possible matches. We take the general case however and assume that matching is still ongoing (i.e., gossip protocol continues to execute). The query is then forwarded to a small number of nodes to increase the probability that all potential matches are identified. These nodes are selected using a random walk. To avoid visiting all nodes, we bound the random walk with a ttl_{query} parameter. This parameter can be set independently by each source and is necessary because the distributed nature of matching makes it hard to devise adaptive termination criteria (e.g., terminate the query when all matches are found).

Until the query's ttl reaches zero, each receiving node will augment R with any extra information it might contain and will forward the query to another random node selected from V^N. To avoid visiting a node multiple times the query records the id of each node in the random walk.

For clarity, in line 6, we omit the extra step of recording node ids by transitively following matched relationships. The condition shown, is that if the receiving node contains new matches for the query concepts, R is updated with the new matches. Line 11 is the condition to identify the set of nodes that have concepts compatible with all the query concepts or their semantic context.

Listing 3. Discovery of Service Provider Nodes

$discovery \leftarrow \{Q, H, R\}$
At source node: $R \leftarrow f_{V^O}(c), \forall c \in Q \cup H$
$discovery.ttl \leftarrow ttl_{\text{query}}$
At each node receiving discovery during the random walk:
for all $c \in Q \cup H$ **do**
  if $c \in V^C$ and $f_R(c) \subset f_{V^C}(c)$ **then**
    $R \leftarrow f_R(c) \cup f_{V^C}(c)$
  end if
end for
if $discovery.ttl = 0$ **then**
  $D = \bigcap_{c \in Q}(f_R(c) \cup \forall x \in sub_\tau(c).f_R(x) \cup \forall x \in super_\tau(c).f_R(x))$
  $\forall i \in D$: *redirect query to node i*
else
  Choose a random node id r *from* V^N
  $discovery.ttl \leftarrow discovery.ttl - 1$
  Forward query to r
end if

5 Evaluation

We have implemented the gossip protocol and the first phase of the discovery protocol. For evaluation purposes we simulated networks of 20, 40 and 60 nodes. We are interested in the evaluation of the random walk mechanism, so to simplify the simulations we used complete node views. Each node now contains the complete set of participating nodes, rather than a partial one. This simplification does not alter the correct functioning of the algorithm.

Each node maintains its own unique ontology composed of 10 concepts, i.e., $|V^O| = 10$. These are test ontologies in RDFS that are generated automatically for evaluation purposes and have no semantics. Matching between these generated ontologies is guaranteed by randomly specifying predefined matching relationships. In these predefined relationships, each concept can select another concept with a certain probability and can also be selected by other concepts provided they are not from the same ontology. Predefined matching is only an indication for the real matching relationship. Matching still materialises only when two concepts are actually compared.

We want to investigate the scalability properties of the system as the number of nodes and the number of concepts increase. We also want to investigate whether the number of concepts in $Q \cup H$ have an impact on discovery. To this effect, we have conducted repeated trials with varying network and query sizes. The following parameters held constant values: $F_c = 4, F_n = 2, ttl_{\text{gossip}} = 2, age_{\text{threshold}} = 2$.

Each of the 3 experimental setups corresponding to the different network sizes were run 20 times. In each setup, different discovery queries are run at certain system rounds. A system round is counted after every node transmits a gossip message. Every 5 rounds, the following process is repeated 30 times. A node is selected at random and a discovery query is initiated from that node. Query concepts are also randomly selected from each source node. We issue two types of queries:

1. To assess discovery as the network size grows, we fix the query concepts to 2 and the value of ttl_{query} to 3.
2. For the evaluation of query sizes, we initiate successive queries with an increasing number of concepts that range from 1 – 4 and keep the ttl_{query} value constant at 2.

Overall, 150 queries are initiated every five rounds with each experimental setup lasting for 200 rounds.

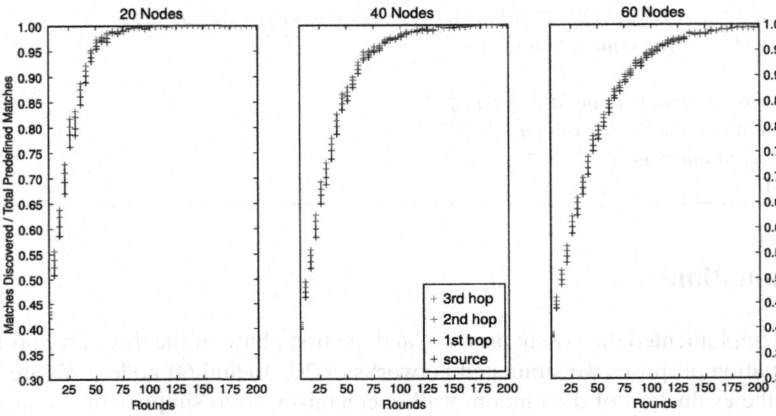

Fig. 3. Total discovery ratio vs. rounds

Figure 3 shows the mean discovery ratio between the matches discovered during the random walk and the *total* predefined matches for the query concepts. For each query and in each hop we divide the number given by $|f_R(c)|, \forall c \in Q \cup H$ against the number of predefined matches for each c. *This ratio indicates the degree to which all predefined matches have been discovered.* Any query concepts not belonging to a matching relationship are excluded from the calculation. Crosses represent the hops in the random walk. In each vertical line, the lowest cross represents the discovery ratio at the source node.

We observe that the difference in the discovery ratio between hops increases, albeit by a small percentage, as rounds progress. The overall ratio though increases exponentially with the number of rounds, until it reaches 1. This shows the strong dependency between discovery and matching. During the initial rounds, matching associations have not yet being established, so the discovery ratio is low. As more concepts are progressively disseminated across nodes, the network augments its shared knowledge.

Figure 4 shows the mean discovery ratio between the matches discovered during the random walk and the *network* matches. This ratio is calculated by dividing the number given by $|f_R(c)|$ in each hop against the number of matches that exist for concept c across the network. In other words, if c is replicated across k nodes, the network matches

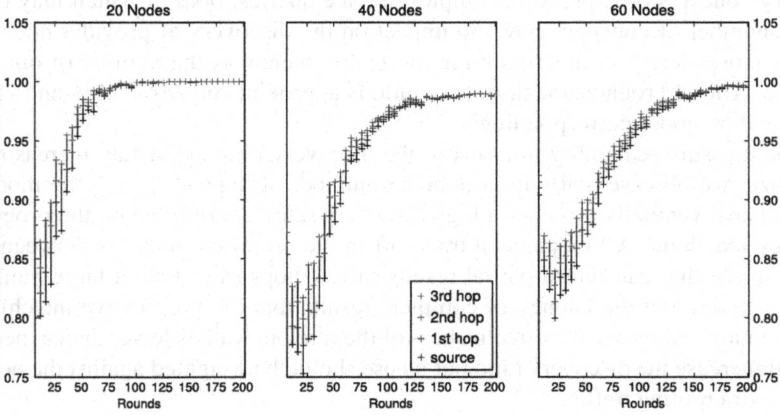

Fig. 4. Network discovery ratio vs. rounds

are calculated as: $|\bigcup_{i\in k} f_{V_i^C}(c)|$. This is an alternative measure for the performance of the random walk since it reflects the current state of ontology matching rather than the ideal state. In that respect we expect this ratio to be high in the beginning when matching associations are low, drop as more matching associations become available in the network and finally stabilise close to 1. We observe this behaviour in all cases. It is also possible for this ratio to exceed 1, as transitive matching means that a query might record more matches than what is found in the replicated query concepts.

Finally, Fig. 5 depicts the discovery ratio for queries with a varying number of query concepts. In this experiment, the discovery ratio is the value recorded on the last hop. There does not appear to be a significant difference in discovery when increasing the number of concepts. This is a good result indicating that including the semantic context

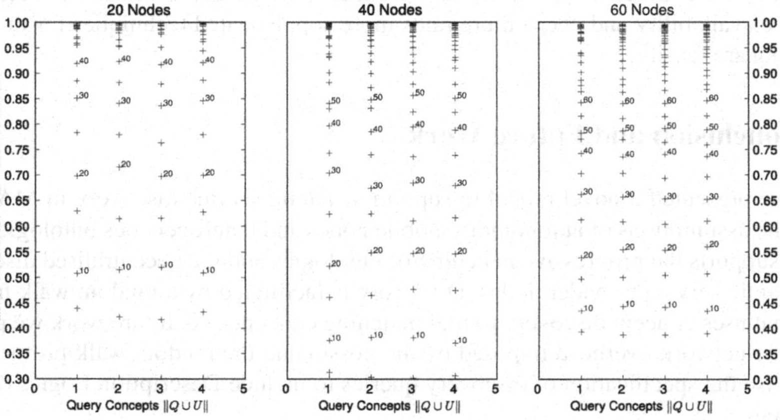

Fig. 5. Total discovery ratio vs. query concepts

of query concepts or expressing complex service queries, both of which may contain a large number of concepts, have no impact on the discovery of provider nodes. One can see more clearly in this figure the discovery latency as the number of ontologies increase. After 40 rounds, the discovery ratio is approximately 90%, 80% and 75% for 20, 40 and 60 nodes correspondingly.

If we measure scalability in terms of the discovery ratio against an increasing network size, we observe that with a bounded number of hops (ttl_{query}) the model described here eventually provides a high discovery ratio, *conditional* on the progress of ontology matching. A fundamental trade-off in the proposed model is between a discovery query that can return partial results in few hops even with a large number of provider nodes and the latency of complete results that the progressive matching approach entails. Although the effectiveness of the random walk is lower than expected, it can still increase the discovery ratio but its use should be weighted against the potential cost of extra routing traffic.

6 Related Work

The work presented here stands at the intersection of decentralised mechanisms for data dissemination and semantic services with an emphasis on scale and autonomy of interaction. Initial research in service discovery for MANET environments was mainly focused on distributed discovery protocols, e.g., [11]. This however assumed strict assumptions on service names and interfaces so that services could interoperate. Subsequent work, such as GSD [1] developed a service framework based on the semantic description of services. However, it was based upon the implicit assumption that nodes maintain a common global ontology. Current research is beginning to accept that in open distributed systems knowledge will be decentralised.

The assumption of heterogeneous domain ontologies for semantic services follows closely the evolution of semantic P2P networks. Networks such as EDUTELLA [7] assume that not only data is distributed but metadata descriptions are also decentralised and not uniform. Since in P2P networks a broader set of assumptions can be made about resource availability and peer failure rates more sophisticated techniques for ontology matching are feasible.

7 Conclusion and Future Work

We have presented a novel model to support semantic service discovery in MANETs given the assumptions of autonomous mobile nodes and heterogeneous ontologies. The model supports the progressive matching of ontologies and the decentralised discovery of semantic service provider nodes. Discovery is facilitated by a random walk mechanism that uses concept discovery to find matching concepts. As future work we plan to study the network overhead imposed by the gossip and the random walk protocol and generalise the specification of discovery queries to include Description Logics derived languages.

References

1. Chakraborty, D., Joshi, A., Finin, T., Yesha, Y.: Gsd: A Novel Group Based Service Discovery Protocol for MANETs. In: Proceedings of the 4th IEEE Conference on Mobile and Wireless Communications Networks (MWCN'02), IEEE Press (2002)
2. Kozat, U.C., Tassiulas, L.: Network layer support for service discovery in mobile ad hoc networks. In: IEEE INFOCOM. Volume 22. (2003) 1965–1975
3. McGuinness, D.L., van Harmelen, F.: Owl web ontology language overview (2004) W3C Recommendation.
4. Aberer, K., Cudré-Mauroux, P., Ouksel, A.M., Catarci, T., Hacid, M.S., Illarramendi, A., Kashyap, V., Mecella, M., Mena, E., Neuhold, E.J., De Troyer, O., Risse, T., Scannapieco, M., Saltor, F., de Santis, L., Spaccapietra, S., Staab, S., Studer, R.: Emergent Semantics Principles and Issues. In: DASFAA 2004. (2004) 25–38
5. Aberer, K., Cudré-Mauroux, P., Hauswirth, M.: A framework for semantic gossiping. SIGMOD Rec. **31** (2002) 48–53
6. Nedos, A., Singh, K., Cunningham, R., Clarke, S.: A Gossip Protocol to Support Service Discovery with Heterogeneous Ontologies in manets. Technical Report TCD-CS-2006-34, Distributed Systems Group, Computer Science Department, Trinity College Dublin (2006)
7. Nejdl, W., Wolf, B., Qu, C., Decker, S., Sintek, M., Naeve, A., Nilsson, M., Palmér, M., Risch, T.: Edutella: A P2P Networking Infrastructure Based on RDF. In: Proceedings of the 11th International Conference on World Wide Web (WWW'02), New York, NY, USA, ACM Press (2002) 604–615
8. Castano, S., Ferrara, A., Montanelli, S., Pagani, E., Rossi, G.: Ontology-Addressable Contents in P2P Networks. In: Proceedings of the 1st WWW International Workshop on Semantics in Peer-to-Peer and Grid Computing (SemPGRID '03), Budapest, Hungary (2003)
9. Brickley, D., Guha, R.: Resource Description Framework RDF Schema Specification 1.0 (2000) W3C.
10. Castano, S., Ferrara, A., Montanelli, S.: H-match: an algorithm for dynamically matching ontologies in peer-based systems. In: SWDB. (2003) 231–250
11. Kozat, U.C., Tassiulas, L.: Service discovery in mobile ad hoc networks: an overall perspective on architectural choices and network layer support issues. Ad Hoc Networks **2** (2004) 23–44

Discovering Web Services and JXTA Peer-to-Peer Services in a Unified Manner

Michael Pantazoglou, Aphrodite Tsalgatidou, and George Athanasopoulos

Department of Informatics & Telecommunications,
National & Kapodistrian University of Athens, 15784, Greece
{michaelp, atsalga, gathanas}@di.uoa.gr

Abstract. Web services constitute the most prevailing instantiation of the service-oriented computing paradigm. Recently however, representatives of other computing technologies, such as peer-to-peer (p2p), have also adopted the service-oriented approach and expose functionality as services. Thus the service-oriented community could be greatly assisted, if these heterogeneous services were integrated and composed. A key towards achieving this integration is the establishment of a unified approach in service discovery. In this paper, we describe some features of a unified service query language and focus on its associated engine, which is used to discover web and p2p services in a unified manner. We exemplify how our unified approach is applied in the case of web and p2p service discovery in UDDI and JXTA, respectively. Additionally, we demonstrate how our service search engine is able to process heterogeneous service advertisements and thus to exploit the advertised syntactic, semantic, and quality-of-service properties during matchmaking.

1 Introduction

The service-oriented computing (SOC) paradigm has been successfully instantiated by the technology of web services. To date, most of the core aspects of web services have been standardized and, specifically with regard to their discovery, the *Universal Description, Discovery and Integration (UDDI)* [1] specification has been established as the preferred model of choice. Recently however, other types of services have also emerged such as peer-to-peer (p2p) services [2], fostering a new model for service sharing, discovery and reuse. Among the most well known p2p technologies currently supporting the notion of service is JXTA [3], an open peer-to-peer infrastructure which enables any connected device on the network to act as a *peer* and interact with other peers. Peers in a JXTA network are expected to interact through the services they offer/consume. Peers are organized in *peer groups,* where each peer group establishes its own policies and a set of services that all peer members should implement. Usually, peer groups are used to organize peers offering services in a specific application domain.

The established p2p infrastructure and core services of JXTA have been used in a number of cases to deploy, publish and compose p2p services. In [4], a distributed and decentralized market of p2p services was proposed, also facilitating their automatic

A. Dan and W. Lamersdorf (Eds.): ICSOC 2006, LNCS 4294, pp. 104 – 115, 2006.

composition. In [5], an approach was proposed for the semantic annotation of p2p services that could assist their automatic discovery and selection. Utilized from a different point of view, the p2p architecture was also used as the underlying infrastructure for grouping service registries into domain-specific federations [6]. Such organization provided a significant enhancement to the course of service discovery.

Even though many well known p2p technologies (e.g. [19] [20]) have not yet embraced the service-oriented architecture, the results of the aforementioned efforts could provide a strong motivation for doing so in the near future. Hence, there is an emerging need for the integration and interoperability of web and p2p services technologies. A significant step towards achieving such integration involves the establishment of a unified approach in service discovery. Currently, the existing web or p2p services can be discovered only through the underlying discovery mechanisms of the registry or the p2p network where they have been published. Thus, developers are either confined to search in a specific type of registry / network, or they are forced to employ separately the different approaches and mechanisms in order to locate services which are appropriate for their application.

In this paper, we propose a solution for discovering web and p2p services in a unified way. Our solution comprises a query language which supports the creation of queries for discovering heterogeneous services in a unified manner and its associated search engine, which tackles the heterogeneity among the existing web and p2p service discovery mechanisms and description protocols. Among the key contributions of the search engine, which is the main focus of this paper, are: (1) the provision of a unified search interface, which alleviates requesters from the burden of conducting separate service lookups in the various heterogeneous registries and p2p networks; (2) the established level of abstraction, which hides the underlying complexity and heterogeneity from the users; (3) the ability to support existing and emerging standards in service description and discovery.

Briefly, the rest of the paper is structured as follows: in Section 2, we describe a motivating scenario which underlines the need for integration of web and p2p services and also highlights the heterogeneity that hinders their unified discovery; in Section 3, we briefly describe the *Unified Service Query Language (USQL)*, which is used by our search engine for the formulation of the queries and their corresponding responses; Section 4 describes the architecture and some of the main components of the search engine; in Section 5, we demonstrate how the engine is used to discover web and p2p services in UDDI registries and JXTA networks, respectively; Section 6 compares our approach to related work and, finally, we conclude in Section 7 with a discussion on future work.

2 Motivating Scenario

In order to reveal the need for integration of web and p2p services, let us consider the following scenario from the domain of Healthcare.

The IT department of a private clinic has decided to develop a service-oriented application to enable direct interactions between doctors, patients, as well as other partners. The clinic has already established partnerships with external doctors and the

IT departments of other hospitals. Specifically, a p2p network has been established to support communication and exchange of data between the clinic and external doctors, while the partner hospitals offer a number of specialized web services to the clinic. Fig. 1 depicts an excerpt of this application, where a second opinion is requested for a specific medical episode.

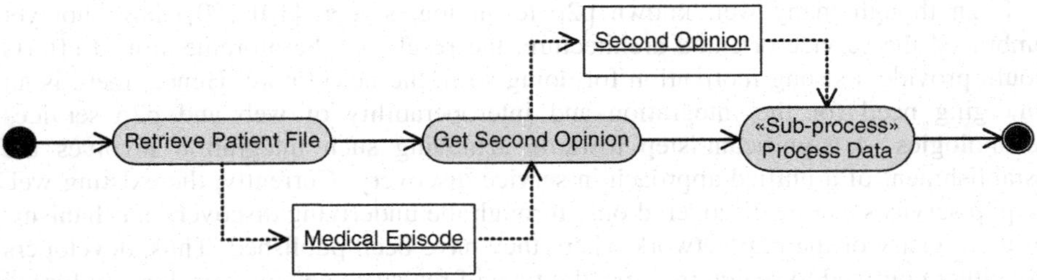

Fig. 1. A service composition requiring the integration of web and p2p services

In the above example, the patient file retrieval functionality could be offered by a web service, while doctors could communicate and exchange second opinions on specific medical incidents with the use of specialized p2p services running on their PDAs. Alternatively, partner hospitals could provide web services which offer diagnoses for specific medical episodes.

In order to implement the above service composition, the developers of the clinic's IT department have to first discover the required services from the established registries and the p2p network. Alas, the current state of the art produces a number of implications: (1) the IT department has to use separate discovery tools, which increase the development cost; (2) the developers need to acquire thorough knowledge on the technical details of the underlying discovery mechanisms and protocols, and thus fail to focus on the business part of the application.

The scenario reveals the need for integration of web and p2p services and, moreover, shows that a unified approach towards the discovery of such services would very much simplify and facilitate the work of developers. In the following sections, we describe how our search engine addresses these issues. First, we provide a very brief description of the language used by the search engine for the formulation of the queries and their respective responses.

3 The Unified Service Query Language (USQL)

The *Unified Service Query Language (USQL)* is an XML-based language enabling requesters to create meaningful queries for heterogeneous services in a unified manner, while at the same time it keeps technical details transparent. The USQL specification defines two types of messages, namely the *USQLRequest* and *USQLResponse*. To better capture real-world requirements, the language blends the flavors of syntactic, semantic and quality-of-service (QoS) search criteria. Moreover, it defines a set of operators, which can be explicitly applied to the search criteria and determine the matchmaking process. This departure is particularly useful when applying service discovery at design time, where requirements should be expressed in a more relaxed fashion.

The snippet below illustrates a USQL request in accordance to the motivating scenario discussed in Section 2.

```
<USQL version="1.0" xmlns="urn:sodium:USQL">
 <USQLRequest>
  <ViewAdditionalProperties>
   <property>Availability</property>
  </ViewAdditionalProperties>
  <Where>
   <Service>
    <ServiceDescription valueIs="contain"> medical diagnosis</ServiceDescription>
    <ServiceDomain ontologyURI="http://onthealth#">Healthcare</ServiceDomain>
    <Operation>
     <Inputs><input>
       <type>http://www.w3.org/2001/XMLSchema#string</type>
       <semantics ontologyURI="http://onthealth#">MedicalEpisode</semantics>
      </input>
     </Inputs>
     <Outputs><output>
       <type>http://www.w3.org/2001/XMLSchema#string</type>
       <semantics ontologyURI="http://onthealth#">Diagnosis</semantics>
      </output>
     </Outputs>
     <QoS><Availability valueIs="equalOrGreater">0.9999</Availability></QoS>
    </Operation>
   </Service>
  </Where>
  <OrderBy direction="descending">Availability</OrderBy>
 </USQLRequest>
</USQL>
```

Fig. 2. A USQL request for *"get second opinion"* services

The query contains a number of syntactic, semantic and QoS requirements at various levels. Specifically, the requester is looking for *"medical diagnosis"* services in the domain of *Healthcare*. The desired operation should accept a string as input (the *medical episode*) and return a string as output (the *diagnosis*). Due to its very nature, the service should be *at least 99.99% available*. The requester has specified that the availability property should be included in the matching services (with the use of the *<ViewAdditionalProperties>* element), and moreover its value should be used for sorting the results (via the *<OrderBy>* element).

A closer look to the USQL request example reveals that all requirements were specified in a service type-agnostic manner. Indeed, the message contains no indication or requirement regarding the type of the candidate service(s). Moreover, requirements were expressed at a relatively high level, based on the intuitive knowledge of what is required for the specific task. No technical details were required or imposed by the USQL language in formulating the request, besides the need for a basic knowledge of XML.

For the sake of brevity, we refer to [7] for a detailed description of the various structures and elements of the USQL language. Nevertheless, the provided information is considered adequate for the purposes of this paper, allowing us to proceed with the description of our service search engine.

4 The Unified Service Search Engine

The *Unified Service Search Engine* is an extensible framework used for applying service discovery in heterogeneous registries and networks. It is characterized by an open architecture enabling the smooth accommodation of various registry and service description standards, for the purposes of service discovery and matchmaking. More specifically, plug-ins are used for supporting access to the various service registries and networks, while appropriate document handlers are introduced to deal with the various syntactic, semantic and QoS service advertisements. The engine was briefly discussed in [8] and [10]; here, we will elaborate on the functionality of its various components and provide technical details regarding its implementation.

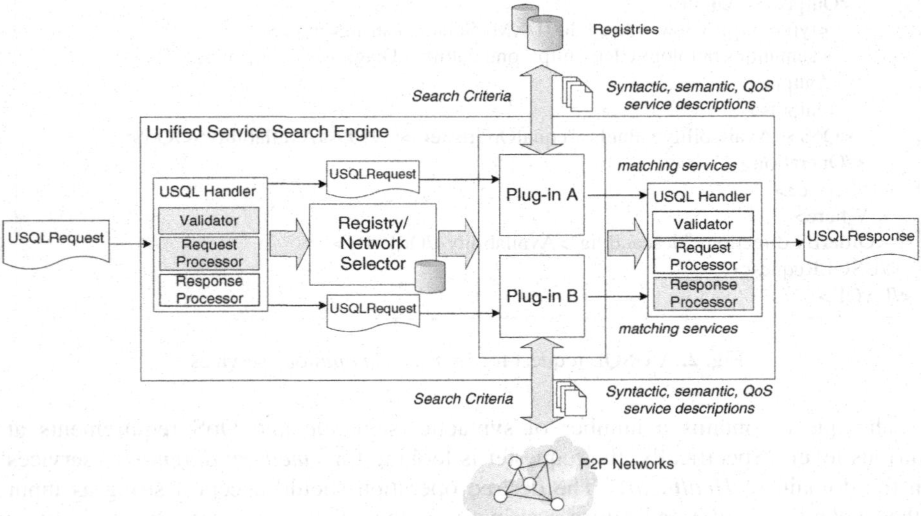

Fig. 3. Basic components of the service search engine

Fig. 3 depicts the internal structure of the search engine. Upon receiving a USQL request, the engine employs the *USQL Handler* to validate it against the USQL schema. The USQL Handler is divided into three logical parts: the *Validator*, responsible for the validation of USQL messages; the *Request Processor*, responsible for processing the content of USQL request messages; and the *Response Processor*, responsible for constructing and properly formatting the USQL response messages.

The USQL Handler component contributes significantly to the overall flexibility and maintainability of the search engine; it abstracts the rest of the components from language-specific details, thus making them resilient to potential changes in the USQL specification.

After the USQL request has been found to be valid, the request processor is activated to extract the specified service domain value from the message. The specified domain is then used by the *Registry Selector* component in identifying the target registries and/or networks for the query. As it was described in [10], the engine makes use of an upper ontology –implemented with the use of OWL (see http://www.w3.org/2004/OWL/)– which associates registries with application domains. The ontology is instantiated by a forest of domains (there is a tree for each addressed domain); also, there are registry and p2p network instances (both instantiating the *Registry* class in the upper ontology), each one of which is associated with one or more domains, and a set of related properties that are stored by the engine. These properties include the id of the plug-in to be used, along with other parameters necessary for successfully accessing the respective registry or network (e.g. JXTA peer groups might require authentication for a peer to be able to join). Note that, maintaining the ontology's instances and associating registries with domains are human-triggered tasks and form part of the search engine's configuration process.

Having identified the target registries and/or networks, the search engine configures and instantiates the respective *Plug-ins* which accept the USQL request as input and run in separate threads, thus allowing for a form of parallelism during the execution of the query. This multi-thread implementation inside the engine contributes to the improvement of its overall performance. To better explain how each registry plug-in works, we illustrate its internal structure in Fig. 4:

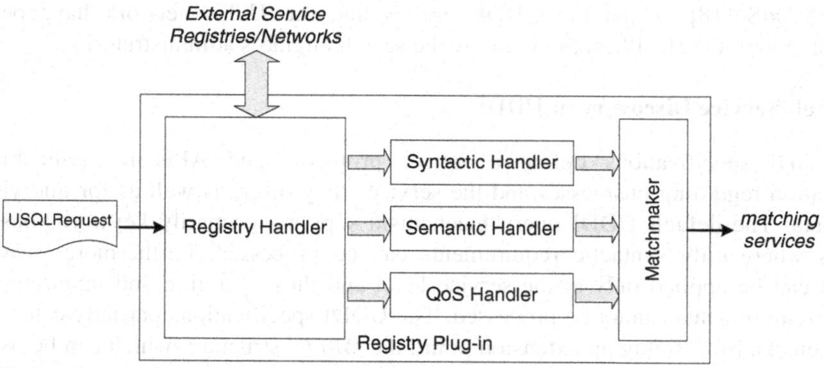

Fig. 4. Internal structure of the search engine's registry plug-ins

The *Registry Handler* component is responsible for extracting the registry-supported search criteria from the original USQL request and utilizes the specific registry type-supported discovery mechanisms and APIs to find the requested services. The process of querying the registry results in a set of service advertisements which are processed by the appropriate *Syntactic, Semantic,* and *QoS Handlers* to extract the values of the properties that were constrained in the USQL request. Thanks to the decoupling of syntactic, semantic and QoS service description handling from the rest of the plug-in, the latter can be seamlessly extended and use different document handlers in many combinations. In this way, the search engine is capable of dealing with the various heterogeneous service description protocols.

Next, the registry plug-in employs the USQL *Matchmaker* in order to apply extended, semantically enhanced and QoS-based matchmaking to each service. The matchmaker implements a sophisticated matchmaking algorithm [9] which however goes beyond the scope of this paper. Briefly described, the algorithm calculates the overall degree of match for a given service and its operations, based on the individual degrees of match of each specified requirement. The degree of match value is a normalized float number ranging between 0 and 1. Going back to Fig. 3, the outcome of the matchmaking process, i.e. the matching services, is forwarded to the USQL Handler component, which employs the response processor to consolidate the output from all registry plug-ins into a single USQL response message.

5 Example: Unified Service Discovery in UDDI & JXTA

In accordance to the use case described in Section 2, in the following paragraphs we will demonstrate how our service search engine applies service discovery in UDDI and JXTA for *"get second opinion"* services, with the use of a single USQL request (the one that was described in Section 3). In this example, we assume that the established p2p network between the clinic and the external doctors is based on JXTA, while the web services being offered by the clinic's partners have been published to a UDDI registry. Moreover, all web and p2p services have been described with the use of WSDL-S (see http://www.w3.org/Submission/WSDL-S/) and WS-QoS [18], whilst the UDDI registry and the JXTA network have been associated with the Healthcare domain by the search engine's administrator.

5.1 Web Service Discovery in UDDI

The UDDI specifications define a set of protocols and APIs for publishing information regarding businesses and the services they offer, as well as for querying such data. The default UDDI query mechanism supports primarily keywords-based queries where only syntactic requirements can be processed. Furthermore, search criteria can be applied only at the service level and thus operation and input/output related requirements cannot be processed. The UDDI specifications partially cater for these defects, by defining an extension point, the *tModel* structure, which can be used to reference external information (e.g. WSDL or WSDL-S service descriptions). The use of the tModel facility in service discovery with UDDI is described in [11]. Our approach also exploits tModels, as we will see next.

The search engine gains access and queries the UDDI registry that has been associated with the Healthcare domain, by employing the respective UDDI plug-in. If the USQL request contains criteria which are supported by the primitive discovery mechanism of UDDI, such as the service name/description or the service provider, these are used accordingly to narrow the lookup range. The query yields a number of tModels containing references to the WSDL-S descriptions of the published web services, as shown in the example below:

```
<tModel ...>
  <overviewDoc>
    <overviewURL>WSDL-S document URL here</overviewURL>
  </overviewDoc>
  <categoryBag>
    <keyedReference tModelKey="..." keyName="uddi-org:types" keyValue="wsdlSpec"/>
  </categoryBag>
</tModel>
```

Fig. 5. An example tModel structure with reference to an external WSDL-S document

These descriptions are retrieved and parsed with the use of the appropriate WSDL-S document handler, employed by the UDDI plug-in of the search engine. In a similar way, the WS-QoS document handler provided by the search engine is used to parse the referenced WS-QoS offers included in the WSDL-S documents. The extracted information is mapped to a unified, USQL-like service advertisement according to the rules given in Table 1, which is then dispatched to the USQL matchmaker component along with the USQL request for matchmaking.

Table 1. Rules for mapping WSDL-S & WS-QoS to USQL

WSDL, WSDL-S & WS-QoS	USQL
wsdl:service @name	Service /ServiceName
wsdl:operation /wsdl:input /wsdl:output @name	Service/Operation /Inputs /Outputs /name
wsdl:message/wsdl:part @name @type @wssem:modelReference	Service/Operation/Inputs/input Service/Operation/Outputs/output /name /type /semantics
wsqos:qosOffer /defaultQoSInfo/serverQoSMetrics/availability /defaultQoSInfo/serverQoSMetrics/reliability /defaultQoSInfo/serverQoSMetrics/processingTime	Service/Operation/QoS /Availability /Reliability /ProcessingTime

5.2 P2P Service Discovery in JXTA

Services in a JXTA network are advertised through a specific type of XML-based advertisement, namely the *ModuleSpecAdvertisement (MSA)*, which provides limited information regarding the service, the service provider, etc. Nevertheless, as it has already been proposed in [5], JXTA service advertisements can be extended to support rich-content service descriptions, and thus substantially facilitate the task of service discovery. Our approach takes advantage of this extensibility in order to perform advanced service discovery in JXTA networks.

Upon its instantiation, the JXTA plug-in provided by our search engine – acting as a minimal edge peer – joins the peer group specified by configuration and submits a *"getRemoteAdvertisements"* query to the peer group's *rendezvous peer(s)*, by using the peer group's established discovery service. These special types of super peers maintain indices of peers and advertisements in the peer group, which they use in order to propagate the query to the appropriate peer(s). Like in the case of UDDI, criteria such as service name / description or provider can be used to narrow the lookup range. The rendezvous peers respond by sending to the plug-in the MSAs which were found to meet the query. Similar to the tModels, the MSAs contain links to WSDL-S documents, as the following snippet illustrates.

```
<jxta:MSA xmlns:jxta="http://jxta.org">
  <MSID>...</MSID>
  <Name>GetDiagnosisService</Name>
  <SURI>WSDL-S document URL here</SURI>
</jxta:MSA>
```

Fig. 6. An example JXTA ModuleSpecAdvertisement (MSA)

At this point, the JXTA plug-in needs not be part of the p2p network any more and therefore disconnects. By accessing the referenced WSDL-S descriptions and applying the mapping rules described in Table 1, a USQL-like advertisement is generated for each service and is consequently checked against the USQL request by the USQL matchmaker.

5.3 Shaping the Service Discovery Results

As it was described in Section 4, the response processor consolidated the results (i.e. the matching services) from the UDDI and JXTA plug-ins and generated the USQL response shown in Fig. 7. Apparently two services were found to meet the search criteria: a JXTA p2p service and a web service. The service entries in the response appear sorted in descending order according to the value of their availability. The web service availability advertised in the respective WS-QoS offer was less than what was originally requested, resulting in a smaller degree of match. Note that, both service entities contain all the necessary information for their immediate invocation. The referenced WSDL documents provide the details and bindings of the services' operations. The binding information depends on the specific service type. For instance, the WSDL document of the JXTA service includes information regarding the JXTA pipes used for communicating with the service, while the WSDL document of the web service provides the service endpoint address, encoding style, communication protocol, etc.

```
<USQL version="1.0" xmlns="urn:sodium:USQL" xmlns:srv="urn:sodium:USQL:services">
 <USQLResponse>
  <srv:Services>
   <srv:Service type="P2PService" degreeOfMatch="1.0" networkType="JXTA">
    <srv:name>GetDiagnosis</srv:name>
    <srv:descriptionDocUrl>
     http://jemini.di.uoa.gr:8080/sodium/wsdl/SecondOpinion.wsdl
    </srv:descriptionDocUrl>
    <srv:interface name="GetDiagnosisInterface">
     <srv:Operation degreeOfMatch="1.0">
      <srv:name>getDiagnosis</srv:name>
      <Availability>0.9999</Availability>
     </srv:Operation>
    </srv:interface>
   </srv:Service>
   <srv:Service type="WebService" degreeOfMatch="0.9999">
    <srv:name>GetDiagnosisWS</srv:name>
    <srv:descriptionDocUrl>
     http://jemini.di.uoa.gr:8080/sodium/wsdl/GetDiagnosis.wsdl
    </srv:descriptionDocUrl>
    <srv:interface name="GetDiagnosisIF">
     <srv:Operation degreeOfMatch="0.9999">
      <srv:name>getMedicalDiagnosis</srv:name>
      <Availability>0.9998</Availability>
     </srv:Operation>
    </srv:interface>
   </srv:Service>
  </srv:Services>
 </USQLResponse>
</USQL>
```

Fig. 7. The USQL response containing alternative *"get second opinion"* services

This concludes our example.

6 Related Work

A lot of research has revolved around service discovery over the last years and a number of service search engines and matchmakers have been proposed. In [12], a novel search engine is described which enables searching for web service operations that are similar to a given one. The underlying idea of this approach is the grouping of inputs and outputs into semantically meaningful concepts. Thus, syntactic information in service advertisements attains semantics and can be exploited in a more fruitful manner. Yet, the approach does not consider existing semantic service descriptions and thus, as opposed to our search engine, it does not exploit their rich content. In [11], Paolucci et al. describe how the UDDI infrastructure can be extended to support OWL-S based semantic annotations for services. The main drawback of this approach lies in that a significant update to the UDDI specifications is required. Moreover, discovery is confined to web services only. Another framework that makes use of OWL-S for automating the matchmaking process during web service discovery is the

WSML middleware, as described in [13]. However, the proposed matchmaking algorithm seems to be bound with that specific semantic description protocol and thus is not able to apply semantic matchmaking to services described with other protocols, e.g. WSDL-S. The same shortcoming also characterizes similar efforts in JXTA service discovery, such as the Oden framework [5]. As opposed to those approaches, our service search engine remains independent from the various service description protocols. Thanks to its flexible design, it can leverage existing or emerging standards, such as OWL-S and WSDL-S, and thus it can operate in a wide range of service-oriented settings.

Integration of web services with p2p networks has been extensively examined in the sense of using a p2p infrastructure to enhance the various web service activities. In METEOR-S [6], a JXTA-based p2p network is utilized to organize web service registries, in order to facilitate the tasks of service publication and discovery. Yet, to the best of our knowledge, there is no approach other than the one presented in this paper, which attempts to integrate the web service and p2p worlds in terms of unified service discovery.

7 Concluding Summary

In this paper, we briefly described the Unified Service Query Language (USQL) and some of the functional details of our service search engine supporting the unified discovery of web and p2p services. The engine is characterized by its flexible and extensible design, which renders it capable of accommodating different discovery mechanisms and service description protocols. At the same time, the technical details are kept transparent to the user, thus simplifying the task of service discovery.

Experience has revealed a number of challenges that need to be addressed by our search engine prototype. The restriction imposed by the matchmaker as regards the use of the same ontology to semantically annotate service queries and service advertisements is planned to be overcome with the utilization of a semi-automatic ontology mapping mechanism, like the one presented in [14]. Further, we are leaning towards ultimately replacing our custom upper ontology with more standardized efforts, such as the *Suggested Upper Merged Ontology (SUMO)* [15].

The matchmaker component of our search engine employs a set of distance measure functions for the calculation of the degree of match. Similarity distance measure is a very popular technique in matchmaking and has been successfully applied to similar technological areas, such as data mining and web information retrieval [16] [17]. In the future, we plan to utilize some of the already established efforts in syntactic, semantic, and QoS matchmaking, in order to enhance the precision of our search engine. Finally, to enhance the engine's performance, we are in the process of developing a caching mechanism, which will also allow us to experiment on the engine's recall.

Acknowledgement. This work is partially supported by the Special Account of Research Funds of the National and Kapodistrian University of Athens under contract 70/4/5829 and by the European Commission under contract IST-FP6-004559 for the SODIUM project (website: http://www.atc.gr/sodium).

References

1. Organization for the Advancement of Structured Information Standards (OASIS), *Universal Description, Discovery and Integration, UDDI.* http://www.uddi.org/
2. Broekstra, J., Ehrig, M. et al. (2004) *Bibster - A Semantics-Based Bibliographic Peer-to-Peer System.* WWW'04 Workshop on Semantics in Peer-to-Peer and Grid Computing
3. Traversat, B., Arora, A. et al. (2003) *Project JXTA 2.0 Super-Peer Virtual Network,* Sun Microsystems, Inc., Palo Alta, California
4. Gerke, J., Reichl, P., Stiller, B. (2005) *Strategies for Service Composition in P2P Networks.* In Proceedings of ICETE 2005, Reading, UK
5. Elenius, D., Ingmarsson, M. (2004) *Ontology-based Service Discovery in P2P Networks.* International Workshop on Peer-to-Peer Knowledge Management, P2PKM 2004
6. Verma, K., Sivashanmugam, et al (2005) *METEOR-S WSDI: A Scalable Infrastructure of Registries for Semantic Publication and Discovery of Web Services.* Journal of Information Technology and Management, Vol. 6 (1), pp. 17-39
7. Tsalgatidou, A. et al. (2006) *Specification of the Unified Service Query Language (USQL).* Technical Report, available online at http://cgi.di.uoa.gr/~michaelp/TR/usql-1.0-spec.pdf
8. Tsalgatidou, A. et al. (2005) *Semantically Enhanced Unified Service Discovery.* W3C Workshop on Frameworks for Semantics in Web Services, Innsbruck, Austria
9. Pantazoglou, M., Tsalgatidou, A., Athanasopoulos, G. (2006) *Quantified Matchmaking of Heterogeneous Services.* In Proceedings of the 7th International Conference on Web Information Systems Engineering, WISE 2006
10. Tsalgatidou, A. et al. (2005) *Semantically Enhanced Discovery of Heterogeneous Services.* 1st International IFIP/WG12.5 Working Conference on Industrial Applications of Semantic Web, IASW2005, Jyväskylä, Finland
11. Paolucci, M. et al. (2002) *Importing the Semantic Web in UDDI.* In Proceedings of Web Services, E-business and Semantic Web Workshop
12. Dong, X., Halevy, A. et al. (2004) *Similarity Search for Web Services.* In Proc. of VLDB
13. Cibran, M. A. et al (2004) *Automatic Service Discovery and Integration using Semantic Descriptions in the Web Services Management Layer.* Proc. of 3rd Nordic Conf. on Web Services, Vaxjo, Sweden
14. Li, J. (2004) *LOM: A Lexicon-based Ontology Mapping Tool.* Performance Metrics for Intelligent Systems Workshop, PerMIS 2004, Gaithersburg, MD
15. Niles, I., Pease, A. (2001) *Towards a Standard Upper Ontology.* In Proceedings of the International Conference on Formal Ontology in Information Systems
16. Sahami, M. Mittal, V. et al. (2004) *The Happy Searcher: Challenges in Web Information Retrieval.* Trends in Artificial Intelligence, 8th Pacific Rim International Conference on Artificial Intelligence, PRICAI 2004
17. D. Lin (1998) *An Information-Theoretic Definition of Similarity.* In International Conference on Machine Learning
18. Tian, M., Gramm, A. et al. (2004) *Efficient Selection and Monitoring of QoS-Aware Web Services with the WS-QoS Framework.* IEEE/WIC/ACM International Conference on Web Intelligence, WI 2004
19. Ion Stoica, Robert Morris et al (2001) *Chord: Scalable Peer-to-peer Lookup Service for Internet Applications.* In Proceedings of ACM SIGCOMM, San Diego, CA
20. Ben Y. Zhao, Ling Huang et al. (2003) *Tapestry: A resilient global-scale overlay for service deployment.* IEEE Journal on Selected Areas in Communications

A Hierarchical Framework for Composing Nested Web Processes

Haibo Zhao and Prashant Doshi

LSDIS Lab., Department of Computer Science
University of Georgia
Athens, GA 30602
{zhao, pdoshi}@cs.uga.edu

Abstract. Many of the previous methods for composing Web processes utilize either classical planning techniques such as hierarchical task networks (HTNs), or decision-theoretic planners such as Markov decision processes (MDPs). While offering a way to automatically compose a desired Web process, these techniques do not scale to large processes. In addition, classical planners assume away the uncertainties involved in service invocations such as service failure. In this paper, we present a hierarchical approach for composing Web processes that may be nested - some of the components of the process may be Web processes themselves. We model the composition problem using a semi-Markov decision process (SMDP) that generalizes MDPs by allowing actions to be temporally extended. We use these actions to represent the invocation of lower level Web processes whose execution times are uncertain and different from simple service invocations.

1 Introduction

Service-oriented architectures (SOAs) aim to provide a rapid, flexible, and loosely-coupled way to seamlessly integrate the intra- and inter-enterprise resources into business processes. As the fundamental building blocks of processes, Web services (WS) are seen as self-contained, self-describing, and platform-independent applications which can be published, discovered, and invoked over the Web. We refer to business processes with WSs as their components as *Web processes* [1].

Contemporary business processes are composed primarily by human system designers in a manual and tedious manner. However, SOA offers an opportunity to compose the business processes with varying levels of automation. In this regard, several preliminary planning based approaches exist [2,3,4] that automatically compose the Web process given a model of the business problem. While these methods offer a way to automatically compose the Web process, many of them do not scale efficiently to large processes. This precludes their applicability to real-world business processes.

Planning techniques for automatically composing a Web process may be grouped into classical planning [2] or decision-theoretic planning [3]. Decision-theoretic planners such as Markov decision processes (MDPs) generalize classical

A. Dan and W. Lamersdorf (Eds.): ICSOC 2006, LNCS 4294, pp. 116–128, 2006.

planning techniques to nondeterministic environments, where actions outcomes may be uncertain, and associate a cost to the different plans thereby allowing the selection of an optimal plan. These techniques are especially relevant in the context of SOA where services may fail and processes must minimize costs.

In this paper, we adopt a hierarchical approach for composing complex Web processes. In many cases, a Web process may be seen as nested – a higher level Web process may be composed of WSs and lower level Web processes – which induces a natural hierarchy over the process. We provide a method of composition that exploits the hierarchical decomposition; We model each level of the hierarchy using a semi-Markov decision process (SMDP) [5] that generalizes a MDP [5] by allowing temporally extended actions. Specifically, the lowest levels of the hierarchy (leaves) are modeled using a SMDP containing *primitive* actions, which are invocations of the WSs. Higher levels of the process are modeled using SMDPs that contain *abstract* actions, which represent the execution of lower level Web processes. We represent their invocations as *temporally extended* actions in the higher level SMDPs. These are actions whose durations are probabilistically distributed and an accumulating cost is associated with them that depends on their duration. Since information about only the individual WSs is usually available, we provide methods for deriving the model parameters of the higher level SMDP from the parameters of the lower level ones. Thus, our approach is applicable to Web processes that are nested to an arbitrary depth. Also, our experimental results show that our method performs favorably in terms of cost effectiveness and robustness to uncertainty compared to another hierarchical composition technique, hierarchical task networks (HTNs) [2].

2 Related Work

There are several approaches proposed to address the automatic Web process composition problem. McIlraith et al. [6] adapt and extend the Golog language for representing service constraints. WSs that satisfy the constraint are discovered at runtime and bound to the abstract process. Medjahed et al. [7] present a technique to generate composite services from high level declarative descriptions of the individual services. Traverso and Pistore [4] propose a MBP (a model checking planner) based framework to do automated WS composition, where WSs are modeled as stateful, nondeterministic and partially observable behaviors. Our approach differs from their work in that we take into account scalability and optimality of the plan/policy. SHOP2 [8], a classical planner based on HTNs, is utilized for automatic composition of Web processes in [2]. The final plan generated by SHOP2 is a sequence of WS invocations, which is not robust to external events. Recent work on HTN approach [9] tries to deal with this issue by gathering information during planning, which can decrease the probability of service failure during execution when information used to generate a plan does not change much during execution time. In comparison, our approach explicitly models uncertainty in WS outcomes, and generates a policy which specifies an optimal action no matter the state of the problem.

This paper also generalizes our previous work [3] on using MDPs for dynamic process composition by taking into account scalability. We utilize a hierarchical structure to address the scalability problem and provide a new method to formulate hierarchical SMDPs, whose model parameters are derived from lower level ones. This allows its application to processes that are nested to an arbitrary depth.

3 Examples of Hierarchical Decompositions

We briefly describe two scenarios that benefit from a nested structure. Our first example is a typical scenario for handling orders that in a supply chain (Fig. 1).

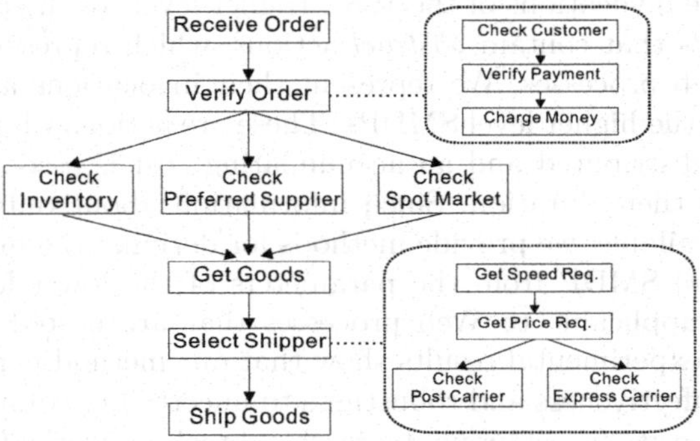

Fig. 1. A supply chain scenario in which the services *Verify Order* and *Select Shipper* are Web processes themselves. This problem is *singly* nested.

An instance of the business process is created when a customer sends in an order. The order specifics first need to be verified, in that the customer's payment needs to be processed. Subsequently, the manufacturer choose one from three possible supplies to complete the order based on their satisfactory rates and invocation costs. On receiving the supplies, the manufacturer may ship the completed order to the customer using ground postal (slow and inexpensive but with good coverage) or express air (fast and expensive but with limited coverage) carriers, depending on the customer's requirement.

The second example (Fig. 2) is a patient transfer clinical pathway. Patients first check in with the primary care giver followed by the patient's insurance verification step. If the primary care giver can give the needed physical care, patients will stay with the primary care giver and receive the proper care; otherwise, the patients will be transferred to one of the four possible secondary care givers based on the vacancy and other factors like distance, cost and reputation. In this case, the patient must be checked into the secondary care giver and her insurance validated.

Within a SOA, each step of the scenarios is an invocation of WSs, which in some cases represent lower level Web processes. For example, in order to verify

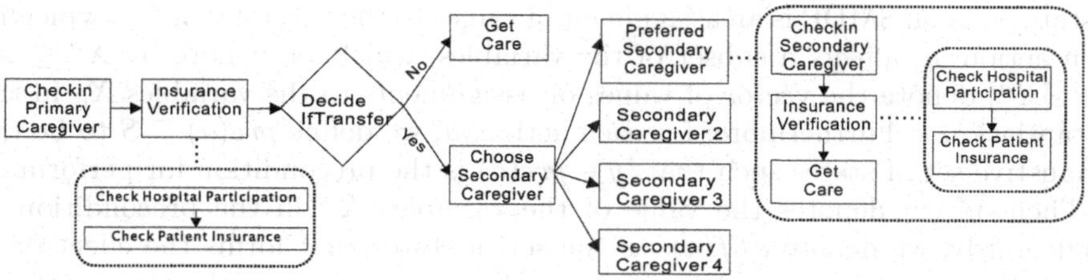

Fig. 2. A patient transfer pathway illustrating a *double* nesting of Web processes

the customer and her payment, the manufacturer may invoke a *Verify Order* WS, which is itself a composite Web process composed of *Customer Checker*, *Verify Payment*, and *Charge Money* WSs. This nested nature of Web processes could extend to more levels as the patient transfer scenario shows in Fig. 2.

4 Background: Semi-Markov Decision Processes

A semi-Markov decision process (SMDP) [5] is a temporal generalization of the MDP. Instead of assuming that the durations of all actions are identical and therefore ignoring them while planning, a SMDP explicitly models the system evolution in continuous time and models the time spent in a particular state while performing an action to follow a pre-specified probability distribution. Solution to a SMDP produces a *policy*. A policy assigns to each state of the process an action that is expected to be optimal over the period of consideration. We formally define a SMDP below:

Definition 1 (SMDP). *A SMDP is defined as a tuple,*

$$SMDP = \langle S, A, T, K, F, C, s_0 \rangle \qquad where:$$

• $S = \Pi_{i=1}^{n} X^i$, *where* S *is the set of all possible states factored into a set,* X, *of* n *variables,* $X = \{X^1, X^2, \ldots, X^n\}$
• A *is the set of all possible actions*
• T *is the transition function,* $T : S \times A \rightarrow \Delta(S)$, *where* $\Delta(\cdot)$ *specifies a probability distribution. The transition function captures the uncertain effect of performing an action on particular variables*
• K *is the lump sum reward,* $K : A \rightarrow \mathbb{R}$. *This specifies the reward (or cost) obtained on performing an action*
• F *is the sojourn time distribution for each pair of state and action,* $F : S \times A \rightarrow \Delta(t)$, *where* $t \in [0, t_{max}]$, t_{max} *is the maximum time duration of any action. Given the current state,* s, *and action,* a, *the system will remain in the state for a certain amount of time,* t, *which follows a density described by* $f(t|s,a)$
• C *is the reward accumulating rate,* $C : S \times A \rightarrow \mathbb{R}$, *which specifies the rate at which the reward (or cost) is obtained when performing an action from some state*
• $s_0 \in S$ *is the start state of the process*

A state, s, in an SMDP is an assignment of values to the variables in X. Typically, each action, a, affects a subset of the variables, which we denote by $X^a \subseteq X$. Let $s[X^a]$ denote the vector of values or assignments to the variables X_a in the instantiation s. Furthermore, for each action, a, we define $pre(a) \subseteq S$ to be the exhaustive set of states such that, $y \in pre(a)$ is the precondition for performing a. Then, $y[X^a]$ denotes the value of the variables X^a in the precondition y. Analogously, we denote $eff(a)$, as the set of states that forms the effect of a. Because the action is non-deterministic, there may be more than one state in $eff(a)$. The lump sum reward, K, and the reward accumulating rate, C, are not necessarily positive; negative values imply a cost. Finally, we assume that the sojourn times of all actions follow Gaussian densities with different means and standard deviations.

When performing an action, a, from a state, $s \in pre(a)$, the system will gain a lump sum reward $K(a)$, and as long as the sojourn time is not over, the system will accumulate reward at the accumulating rate, $C(s,a)$. The total reward for a state action pair is:

$$R(s,a) = K(a) + C(s,a) \int_0^{T_{max}} e^{-\alpha t} f(t|s,a)dt \tag{1}$$

In order to solve the SMDP and compute the policy, we associate a value function, $V : S \to \mathbb{R}$, with each state. This function quantifies the desirability of a state over the long term.The solution of a SMDP is a policy, $\pi : S \to A$, which, for each state of the process, prescribes an action that is expected to be optimal. If the period of consideration is infinite then:

$$V_\pi(s) = \underset{a \in A}{argmax}\ R(s,a) + \sum_{s' \in eff(a)} M(s'|s,a)V(s') \tag{2}$$

$$\text{where}: M(s'|s,a) = \int_0^{T_{max}} e^{-\alpha t} Q(dt, s'|s,a) = \int_0^{T_{max}} e^{-\alpha t} T(s'|s,a)F(t|s,a)dt$$

and $R(s,a)$ is as defined in Eq. 1.

Standard SMDP solution techniques for arriving at the optimal policy involve repeatedly iterating over Eq. 2 until the function, V, approximately converges. Another technique for computing the policy requires formulating and solving a linear program (LP). In this paper, we use the LP method to solve SMDPs.

5 Hierarchical Semi-Markov Decision Processes

We define a framework called hierarchical SMDPs for composing nested Web processes. For the lowest levels of the process, the framework uses the standard SMDP, defined in Section 4, to model the composition problem. Let us label these SMDPs as *primitive*. In primitive SMDPs, actions are WS invocations, and sojourn times are the response times of the WSs. We compose the higher levels of the Web processes using a composite SMDP (C-SMDP). Within a C-SMDP, the actions are either abstract and represent lower level Web processes, which in turn are modeled using either composite or primitive SMDPs, or simple WS invocations. In this section, we will take the Order Handling scenario as the example to explain how we extract and derive model parameters for both primitive SMDPs and composite SMDPs.

5.1 Eliciting the Model of Primitive SMDPs

We briefly describe ways in which the model parameters of the primitive SMDP may be obtained. The actions, A, are the WS operations that compose the Web process. The variables constituting the state space, S, of the process are those that form the preconditions and effects of the component WSs, found in their OWL-S or WSDL-S descriptions. The probabilities of the different responses from service invocations that make up transition function, T, may be found in either the *serviceParameter* section of the OWL-S description of the WS or in the *SLAparameter* section of the WSLA specification [10](see Fig. 3). These probabilities quantify contracted service reliability rates. The parameter, K, which models the cost of using a service, may also be obtained from the serviceParameter section of the OWL-S description or from the agreement between the service users and providers. The sojourn time distribution, F, and the cost rate, C, are typically selected by the system designer from past experience.

```
<ServiceLevelObjective name="InventoryAvailabilityRate">
<Obligated>InventoryProvider</Obliged>
  <Expression>
    <Predicate xsi:type="Eual">
      <SLAParameter>InventoryAvailability</SLAParameter>
      <Value>0.4</Value>
    </Predicate>
  </Expression>
  ......
<ServiceLevelObjective>
```

Fig. 3. A WSLA snippet illustrating the specification of inventory availability rate

5.2 Definition of a Composite SMDP

We formally define a C-SMDP below:

Definition 2 (C-SMDP). *A C-SMDP is defined as a tuple,*

$$C\text{-}SMDP = \langle S_c, A_c, T_c, K_c, F_c, C_c, s_0 \rangle \qquad where:$$

• $S_c = \Pi_{i=1}^{n} X_c^i$ *is the set of all possible states factored into a set,* X_c*, of* n *variables,* $X_c = \{X_c^1, X_c^2, \ldots, X_c^n\}$
• A_c *is the set of all possible actions,* $A_c = A \cup \bar{A}$*, and includes primitive actions,* A*, as well as abstract actions,* $\bar{A}$
The remaining parameters are defined analogously to Def. 1 but with the above mentioned state and action spaces.

Using the order handling scenario introduced in Section 3, we illustrate the state and action spaces of the high-level C-SMDP.

Example 1. For the order handling scenario, $X_c = \{$*Order Received (OR), Order Verified (OV), Inventory Availability (IA), Preferred Supplier Availability (PSA), Spot Market Availability (SMA), Goods Received (GR), Shipper Selected (SS), and Goods Shipped (GS)*$\}$. Each of these variables assumes a value of Y, N or U, where U signifies an unexpected service operation (e.g. failure), while Y and N are straightforward. $A_c = A \cup \bar{A}$, where $A = \{$Receive Order, Check Inventory, Check Preferred Supplier, Check Spot Market, Get Goods, Ship Goods$\}$ and $\bar{A} = \{$Verify Order, Select Shipper$\}$. We observe that performing an action affects the value of the corresponding state variable.

While the model parameters for primitive actions are available, we need methods to derive those that involve abstract actions from the lower level SMDP parameters. We describe these methods next.

5.3 C-SMDP Model Parameters for Abstract Actions

A C-SMDP is so far not well-defined because meaningful parameters for the abstract actions in the model are not given. For example, in the order handling scenario, the composite WS Verify Order is composed of three primitive WSs: Check Customer, Verify Payment, and Charge Money. Transition probabilities associated with the abstract action Verify Order are not available, but instead must be derived from the transition probabilities associated with the primitive actions. In particular, we derive the transition probability, T_c, lump sum reward, K_c, sojourn time distribution, F_c, and accumulating rate, C_c, for abstract actions.

For the sake of simplicity, we focus on deriving the model parameters for a process that is singly-nested. Our methods generalize to a multiply-nested process in a straightforward manner. We utilize the correspondence between the high level abstract actions and the corresponding low-level primitive actions. Let the abstract action, $\bar{a}$, represent the sequential execution, in some order, of primitive actions, $\{a_1, a_2\}$, of the underlying primitive SMDP. As per our notation introduced in Section 4, let $pre(\bar{a}) = \{\bar{s}_p\}$ be the precondition state for performing $\bar{a}$, $X_c^{\bar{a}}$ denotes the variables affected by $\bar{a}$, and $\bar{s}_p[X_c^{\bar{a}}]$ are the precondition values of these variables. We use analogous notation for the effect of $\bar{a}$, $eff(\bar{a}) = \{\bar{s}_e\}$. Then, the precondition values of the state variables affected by $\bar{a}$ ($\bar{s}_p[X_c^{\bar{a}}]$) are a mathematical or logical function of the precondition values for the primitive actions, and analogously for the effects. In other words,

$$\bar{s}_p[X_c^{\bar{a}}] \equiv \Psi_p(s_p^1[X^{a_1}], s_p^2[X^{a_2}]) \text{ and } \bar{s}_e[X_c^{\bar{a}}] \equiv \Psi_e(s_e^1[X^{a_1}], s_e^2[X^{a_2}]) \quad (3)$$

where $pre(a_1) = \{s_p^1\}$, $pre(a_2) = \{s_p^2\}$ and analogously for effects, and X^{a_1} and X^{a_2} denote the variables affected by the actions a_1 and a_2, respectively. The correspondences Ψ_p and Ψ_e are constructed using domain knowledge, and we give an example below.

Example 2. Let us consider the abstract action Verify Order ($\bar{a}$), which corresponds to the primitive actions Check Customer (a_{cc}) , Verify Payment (a_{vp}) and

Charge Money (a_{cm}) in the lower level SMDP. Let, pre(Verify Order) $= \{\bar{s}_p\}$, and eff(Verify Order) $= \{\bar{s}_e^1, \bar{s}_e^2, \bar{s}_e^3\}$, where:
$\bar{s}_p = (OR{=}Y, OV{=}U, IA{=}U, PSA{=}U, SMA{=}U, GR{=}U, SS{=}U, GS{=}U)$,
$\bar{s}_e^1 = (OR{=}Y, \mathbf{OV}{=}\mathbf{Y}, IA{=}U, PSA{=}U, SMA{=}U, GR{=}U, SS{=}U, GS{=}U)$,
$\bar{s}_e^2 = (OR = Y, \mathbf{OV} = \mathbf{N}, IA = U, PSA = U, SMA = U, GR = U, SS = U, GS = U)$, and $\bar{s}_e^3 = (OR = Y, \mathbf{OV} = \mathbf{U}, IA = U, PSA = U, SMA = U, GR = U, SS = U, GS = U)$. Then, in the C-SMDP: $X_c^{\bar{a}} = \{OV\}$, $\bar{s}_p[X_c^{\bar{a}}] = \langle OV = U \rangle$, $\bar{s}_e^1[X_c^{\bar{a}}] = \langle OV = Y \rangle$, $\bar{s}_e^2[X_c^{\bar{a}}] = \langle OV = N \rangle$, $\bar{s}_e^3[X_c^{\bar{a}}] = \langle OV = U \rangle$

In the associated primitive SMDP, let, $X^{a_{cc}} = \{\textit{Customer Verified (CV)}\}$, $X^{a_{vp}} = \{\textit{Payment Valid (PV)}\}$, and $X^{a_{cm}} = \{\textit{Account Charged (AC)}\}$. In the table below we define the correspondences:

Correspondence	Instantiation of the Correspondence
Ψ_p	$\langle OV = U \rangle \equiv \langle CV = U \rangle$ and $\langle PV = U \rangle$ and $\langle AC = U \rangle$
Ψ_e^1	$\langle OV = Y \rangle \equiv \langle CV = Y \rangle$ and $\langle PV = Y \rangle$ and $\langle AC = Y \rangle$
Ψ_e^2	$\langle OV = N \rangle \equiv \langle CV = N \rangle$ or $\langle PV = N \rangle$ or $\langle AC = N \rangle$
Ψ_e^3	$\langle OV = U \rangle \equiv \langle CV = U \rangle$ or $\langle PV = U \rangle$ or $\langle AC = U \rangle$

Based on such associations, we can identify the corresponding low-level states for the composite states, $\bar{s}_p$, $\bar{s}_e^1$, $\bar{s}_e^2$ and $\bar{s}_e^3$. We derive the C-SMDP parameters in the following way:

Transition probability, $T_c(\bar{s}_e^1|\bar{a}, \bar{s}_p)$: As an example, we focus on computing $T_c(\bar{s}_e^1|\bar{a}, \bar{s}_p)$, where $\bar{s}_e^1$, $\bar{s}_p$, and $\bar{a}$ are as defined before. The approach for computing the other transition probabilities is analogous. Because the abstract action, $\bar{a}$, affects only the variable(s), $X_c^{\bar{a}}$, we may rewrite $T_c(\bar{s}_e^1|\bar{a}, \bar{s}_p)$ as,

$$\begin{aligned} T_c(\bar{s}_e^1|\bar{a}, \bar{s}_p) &= Pr(\bar{s}_e^1[X_c^{\bar{a}}] \mid \bar{a}, \bar{s}_p[X_c^{\bar{a}}]) \\ &= Pr(\Psi_e(s_e^1[X^{a_1}], s_e^2[X^{a_2}]) \mid \bar{a}, \Psi_p(s_p^1[X^{a_1}], s_p^2[X^{a_2}])) \qquad \text{from Eq. 3} \end{aligned}$$

Let the state of the primitive SMDP satisfying $\Psi_p(s_p^1[X^{a_1}], s_p^2[X^{a_2}])$ be s_p – this is the initial state of the lower level Web process – and that containing $\Psi_e(s_e^1[X^{a_1}], s_e^2[X^{a_2}])$ be s_e – this is one of the terminal states. Then, we may rewrite, $Pr(\Psi_e(s_e^1[X^{a_1}], s_e^2[X^{a_2}]) \mid \bar{a}, \Psi_p(s_p^1[X^{a_1}], s_p^2[X^{a_2}])) = Pr(s_e|s_p)$, which is the probability of reaching s_e from state s_p. Because the order in which the primitive actions a_1 and a_2 are performed is not known from beforehand, there may be multiple ways to start from the state s_p and reach the state, s_e. Let $s_p \xrightarrow{a_1} s_1 \xrightarrow{a_2} s_e$ be one such path, then, $T(s_1|a_1, s_p) \times T(s_e|a_2, s_1)$ is the probability of following this path, where T is the transition function of the primitive SMDP. The required probability $Pr(s_e|s_p)$ is the sum of the probabilities of following all such paths.

Example 3. We again consider the abstract action Verify Order ($\bar{a}$), its precondition state $\bar{s}_p$ and one of the effect states $\bar{s}_e^1$, as in Example 2.

$$\begin{aligned} T_c(\bar{s}_e^1|\bar{a}, \bar{s}_p) &= Pr(\langle OV = Y \rangle \mid \bar{a}, \langle OV = U \rangle) \\ &= Pr(\langle CV = Y, PV = Y, AC = Y \rangle \mid \bar{a}, \langle CV = U, PV = U, AC = U \rangle) \end{aligned}$$

We denote $(CV = U, PV = U, AC = U)$ as primitive state s_p and $(CV = Y, PV = Y, AC = Y)$ as primitive effect state s_e. Then we have, $T_c(\bar{s}_e^1|\bar{a}, \bar{s}_p) = Pr(s_e \mid s_p)$. Given the associated primitive actions, Check Customer (a_{cc}) , Verify Payment (a_{vp}) , and Charge Money (a_{cm}) , one of the paths is, $s_p \xrightarrow{a_{cc}} s_1 \xrightarrow{a_{vp}} s_2 \xrightarrow{a_{mc}} s_e$, where $s_1 = (CV = Y, PV = U, AC = U), s_2 = (CV = Y, PV = Y, AC = U)$. The probability of following this path is, $T(s_1|s_p, a_{cc}) \times T(s_2|s_1, a_{pv}) \times T(s_e|s_2, a_{mc}) = 0.95 * 0.95 * 0.90 = 0.81225$; we calculate probabilities for other action sequences in the same way. In this example, they are all 0.81225. The desired transition probability is: $T_c(\bar{s}_e^1|\bar{a}, \bar{s}_p) = Pr(s_e \mid s_p) = \sum_{i=1}^{6} 0.81225 * \frac{1}{6} = 0.81225$

Lump sum reward, $K_c(\bar{a})$: Because the abstract action represents the execution of all the primitive actions, the lump sum reward for an abstract action is a summation of the lump sum rewards of the associated low-level primitive actions and an overhead which denotes the cost of combining the primitive actions. The overhead may assume a zero value.

$$K_c(\bar{a}) = \sum_{i=1}^{2} K(a_i) + \kappa$$

where K is the lump sum reward of the primitive SMDP and κ is the overhead.

Sojourn time distribution, $F_c(t|\bar{s}_p, \bar{a})$: Let the sojourn time of a_1 be distributed according to the Gaussian, $\mathcal{N}(t; \mu_2, \sigma_1)$, and that of a_2 be $\mathcal{N}(t; \mu_2, \sigma_2)$. The sojourn time distribution of $\bar{a}$ is a linear combination of the Gaussian densities of a_1 and a_2 This is a Gaussian, $\mathcal{N}(t; \mu, \sigma)$, whose mean and deviation is:

$$\mu = \sum_{i=1}^{2} \mu_i \qquad \sigma = \sqrt{\sum_{i=1}^{2} \sigma_i^2}$$

Accumulating rate, $C_c(\bar{s}_p, \bar{a})$: The accumulated reward of an abstract action is the total accumulated reward of all the corresponding primitive actions. Using the sojourn time distributions of the primitive actions, we compute the expected sojourn time of each, and use it to derive the rate:

$$C(\bar{s}_p, \bar{a}) = \frac{\sum_{i=1}^{2} C(s_p^i, a_i) \times E_{a_i}(F)}{\sum_{i=1}^{2} E_{a_i}(F)}$$

where, $E_{a_i}(F) = \int_0^{T_{max}} tF(t|s_p^i, a_i)dt$, F is the sojourn distribution of the primitive SMDP.

By providing general methods for deriving the C-SMDP model parameters from those of the lower level ones, we allow C-SMDPs at any level to be formulated and solved using the standard solution methods.

5.4 Composing and Executing the Nested Web Process

The algorithm for composing the nested Web process takes as input the policy obtained by solving the top most C-SMDP in the hierarchical framework and the start state. Our algorithm is recursive, using the policy prescriptively to guide the selection of the next WS to invoke. If the policy prescribes an abstract action, we invoke the algorithm with the policy and start state of the lower level Web process. We show the algorithm in Fig. 4.

```
Algorithm for Composing and Executing Nested Web Process
    Input: π //Policy, s0 //Initial state

    s ← s0
    while terminal state not reached
          a ← π(s)  //the optimal action of current state s
          if a is a primitive action then
             Invoke WS representing a
             Get response of WS and form the next state s'
             s ← s'
          else  //a is an abstract action
             s_initial ← initial state of the lower level process   //lower level state satisfying Ψ_p^{-1}(s)
             π' ← corresponding policy for abstract action a
             (s_final, a_final) ← recursively call this algorithm with policy π', s_initial
             s ← state satisfying Ψ_e(s_final[X^{a_final}])  //effect of executing the lower level process
    end while
    if policy π is not a policy for the top-level SMDP then
        return (s, a)
end algorithm
```

Fig. 4. Algorithm for composing and executing a nested Web process modeled using the hierarchical SMDP framework

6 Experimental Results

Within our SOA, we provide the policies as input to the algorithm of Fig. 4 implemented as a WS-BPEL Web process. We show the partial WS-BPEL document highlighting the various steps of the algorithm when the WS *Verify Order* is invoked in Fig. 5. We specify each of the lower level Web processes using WS-BPEL documents of their own, while the external WSs are described using WSDL. We used IBM's BPWS4J engine for executing the WS-BPEL files and Axis 1.2 for deploying individual Web services.

We experimentally evaluate our framework using the two examples mentioned in Section 3 and use the HTN method as a benchmark for purpose of comparison. Our methodology for evaluation consisted of running 1000 instances of both scenarios, while varying the uncertainty of the process environment. We plot the average total reward in Fig. 6.

For low probabilities of the inventory satisfying the order, the manufacturer's Web process chooses to bypass the inventory and instead invokes the preferred supplier. However, as we increase the probability, at 0.68, the policy changes and the process first asks the inventory. Since the manufacturer's own inventory is less expensive than the preferred supplier, the expected utility of using the inventory exceeds that of the supplier when the inventory availability is sufficiently high, causing the change in the policy. Because the process tries the less expensive inventory first, the average reward obtained on running the process

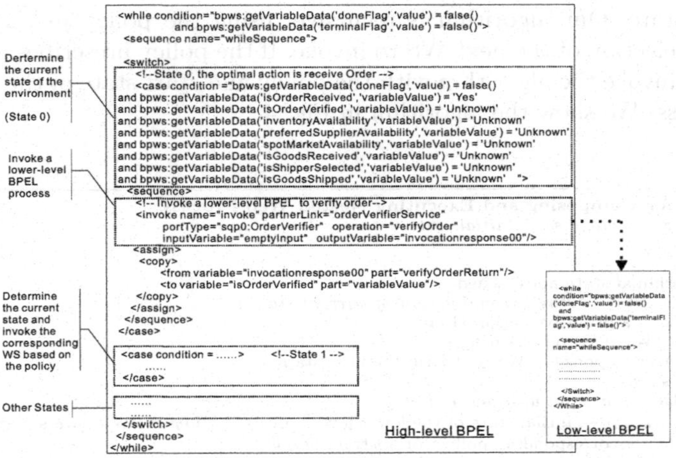

Fig. 5. A snippet of the WS-BPEL flow for the supply chain process. The *verifyOrder* operation is an abstract action whose invocation leads to the execution of a lower level Web process.

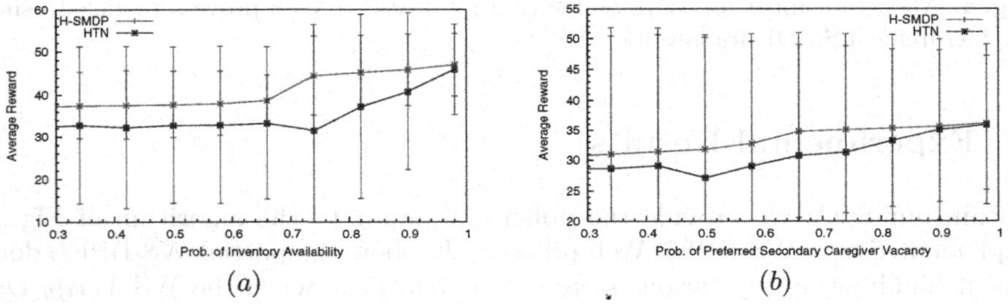

Fig. 6. Average reward and standard deviations from running processes generated using H-SMDP approach and HTN approach for the (*a*) order handling scenario, and (*b*) patient transfer pathway. As we increase the probability of inventory availability(the environment becomes less uncertain),the performance of HTN approaches that of ours.

increases from this point onwards. We observe an analogous behavior for the patient transfer process.

Because the HTN method does not account for the fact that the inventory may not always satisfy the order while planning (as with other classical planning techniques, it assumes that all services are deterministic), the execution of the HTN generated process stops prematurely when the inventory or the preferred supplier is unable to satisfy the order. For lower rates of inventory satisfaction, this happens frequently, and is responsible for the lower average reward of the process. As the probability increases, this behavior reduces and average reward increases. An interesting observation is the subsequent catch-up of the HTN generated process with the one generated using the SMDP framework, when

Table 1. Run times of generating the compositions for the two scenarios

Problem	Hier. SMDP	HTN
Supply Chain scenario	16ms	11ms
Patient Transfer scenario	31ms	17ms

the inventory is assumed to satisfy all the orders. This demonstrates the applicability of classical planning approaches like HTNs: they perform well only in a deterministic environment. We point out that the improvement in overall rewards within our framework comes at a computational price. We show the run times of two approaches in Table 1.

7 Discussion

Existing planning methods for automatically composing Web processes do not scale well to large and uncertain process environments. Many real world business processes are amenable to a hierarchical decomposition into lower level processes and primitive service invocations. We presented a new framework for modeling, composing, and executing large Web processes by exploiting such a hierarchy. We model the composition problem using a probabilistic planning technique, SMDP, that allows an explicit representation of the uncertain reliability and cost of services. In addition, SMDPs allow temporally extended actions of uncertain duration, which are used as abstractions for the lower level Web processes. We introduced the framework of hierarchical SMDPs that is characterized by composite SMDPs for composing high level Web processes, and primitive SMDPs for the lowest level Web processes. Because, we provide ways for deriving the parameters of the composite SMDPs from lower level ones, our framework may be used to compose processes nested to an arbitrary depth. Our experimental results on the supply chain and patient transfer clinical pathway demonstrate that the approach performs better in comparison to the other hierarchical planning technique, HTN, in environments of varying uncertainty. As part of future work, we will extend our framework to support concurrent actions, which are common in realistic Web processes.

Acknowledgements. This research was supported by a grant from UGARF.

References

1. Cardoso, J., Sheth, A.P.: Introduction to semantic web services and web process composition. In: SWSWPC, San Diego, CA, USA (2004)
2. Wu, D., Parsia, B., Sirin, E., Hendler, J., , Nau, D.: Automating daml-s web services composition using shop2. In: ICWC, Sanibel Island, Florida (2003)
3. Doshi, P., Goodwin, R., Akkiraju, R., Verma, K.: Dynamic workflow composition: Using markov decision processes. JWSR (2005)
4. Traverso, P., Pistore, M.: Automated composition of semantic web services into executable processes. (2004)

5. Puterman, M.L.: Markov Decision Processes: Discrete Stochastic Dynamic Programming. Wiley-Interscience (1994)
6. McIlraith, S., Son, T.C.: Adapting golog for composition of semantic web services. In: Proceedings of the 8th International Conference on Knowledge Representation and Reasoning (KR2002), Toulouse, France (2002)
7. Medjahed, B., Bouguettaya, A., Elmagarmid, A.K.: Composing web services on the semantic web. The VLDB Journal (2003)
8. Nau, D.S., Au, T.C., Ilghami, O., Kuter, U., Murdock, J.W., Wu, D., Yaman, F.: Shop2: An htn planning system. Journal of Artificial Intelligence Research (2003)
9. Kuter, U., Sirin, E., Nau, D., Parsia, B., Hendler, J.: Information gathering during planning for web serivce composition. Journal of Web Semantics (2005)
10. Ludwig, H., Keller, A., Dan, A., King, R.P., Franck, R.: Web Service Level Agreeement(WSLA) Language Specification. (2003)

Using Dynamic Asynchronous Aggregate Search for Quality Guarantees of Multiple Web Services Compositions

Xuan Thang Nguyen, Ryszard Kowalczyk, and Jun Han

Swinburne University of Technology, Faculty of Information and Communication Technologies,Melbourne VIC 3122, Australia
{xnguyen, rkowalczyk, jhan}@ict.swin.edu.au

Abstract. With the increasing impact and popularity of Web service technologies in today's World Wide Web, composition of Web services has received much interest to support enterprise-to-enterprise application integrations. As for service providers and their partners, the Quality of service (QoS) offered by a composite Web service is important. The QoS guarantee for composite services has been investigated in a number of works. However, those works consider only an individual composition or take the viewpoint of a single provider. In this paper, we focus on the problem of QoS guarantees for multiple inter-related compositions and consider the global viewpoints of all providers engaged in the compositions. The contributions of this paper are two folds. We first formalize the problem of QoS guarantees for multi-compositions and show that it can be modelled as a Distributed Constraint Satisfaction Problem (DisCSP). We also take into account the dynamic nature of the Web service environment of which compositions may be formed or dissolved any time. Secondly, we present a dynamic DisCSP algorithm to solve the problem and discuss our initial experiment to show the feasibility of our approach for multiple Web service compositions with QoS guarantees.

1 Introduction

During the past few years, in an effort to improve the collaborations between organizations, the Web service framework has been emerging as a de-facto choice for integrating distributed and heterogeneous applications across organizational boundaries. Consequently, much research has been carried out in various areas including Web service discovery, composition, and management. Web service composition in general focuses on building a new value-added *composite* Web service from a number of existing *component* Web services. A Web service composition can be considered as a *choreography* or an *orchestration* of Web services from different viewpoints. A *choreography* describes a composition from a global viewpoint of all participants (i.e. Web service providers who participate in the composition) whereas an *orchestration* has the local viewpoint of a single provider. While Web service orchestration has enjoyed its popularity with an

A. Dan and W. Lamersdorf (Eds.): ICSOC 2006, LNCS 4294, pp. 129–140, 2006.

increasing number of support tools and implementations [13], Web service choreography standards emerge rather late with the replacement of WSCI/WSCL [17] by WS-CDL [18]. Without choreography, Web services compositions' examples [8,6] are often restricted to a model which we call the *single provider* composition model. For a *single provider* composition, a provider searches for available Web services, combines them together to form a new composite Web service that it can offer. The major characteristic of a *single provider* composition is that it is planned and composed solely by a single provider or QoS broker. The composition may even not be noticed by component service providers. With the increasing popularity of Web service choreography as a mechanism for *multi-party* contracts [18], Web services choreography opens up the possiblities for *multi-provider* compositions in which every participant has some vested interest in the composite service and actively engages in composing the service. QoS guarantees for an individual *single provider* composition has been well investigated in a number of works [3,6,8]. However, to our knowledge, there has not been any works on the same problem for multiple related *multi-provider* compositions in which multiple providers collaborate to guarantee the QoS levels of composite services.

In parallel to the advancement of Web services, the MAS and AI communities have shown an increasing interest in the Distributed Constraint Satisfaction Problem (DisCSP) in the past few years. DisCSP has been widely viewed as a powerful paradigm for solving combinatorial problems arising in distributed, multi-agent environments. A DisCSP is a problem with finite number of variables, each of which has a finite and discrete set of possible values and a set of constraints over the variables. These variables and constraints are distributed among a set of autonomous and communicating agents. A solution in DisCSP is an instantiation of all variables such that all the constraints are satisfied. In this paper, we investigate the application of DisCSP techniques to the QoS guarantee problem and propose a new DisCSP based algorithm for multiple multi-provider Web service compositions. The rest of the paper is organized as follows. In the next section we present some important related work. We discuss how the QoS guarantee for Web service composition problems can be modelled as Dynamic DisCSP problems in Section 3. We also present formal descriptions of the QoS guarantee for multi-provider compositions, DisCSP and Dynamic DisCSP frameworks in that section. We review the AAS (Asynchronous Aggregate Search) algorithm for its application in the problem of QoS guarantees and describe our proposed DynAAS (Dynamic Asynchronous Aggregate Search) algorithm in Section 4. Section 5 present our experiment on the algorithm's performance. Finally, conclusions and future work are discussed in Section 6.

2 Related Work and Open Issues

There have been several studies on QoS of Web service compositions. QoS guarantees for compositions are discussed in [8,7,6]. In [7], the authors discuss an approach for QoS aggregation based on Web service composition patterns [14].

More related work on QoS planning can be found in [8], in which a method for selecting optimal sub-providers from a list of service providers is proposed. In [3], the authors model the QoS requirements as an optimization problem and employ a special centralized CSP technique to solve it. However, we argue that there are three major issues that have not been addressed in those works:

- QoS guarantees for multi-provider compositions: As we explained before, choreography offers a new service model in which a number of component service providers may share common goals and hence *collaborate* together to offer a composite service. Most of the current QoS composition research focus on *single provider* composition. Therefore they look at a composition from a local view of a single provider, as for orchestration. The QoS composition for multi-provider compositions, as for choreography, requires a global view.
- Multiple inter-related compositions: Some services or service providers may engage in many compositions and hence there is a relationship between these compositions through the shared services and providers. This relationship needs to be taken into account in the composition planning.
- Discovery of supported QoS levels: Most of current QoS composition research assume that service providers *publicly* advertise precisely their supported QoS levels. This can be done by categorizing different *classes of service* and embedding the supported QoS values directly into WSDL interfaces or UDDI registries [11]. However, such a *public* advertisement requires disclosure of private information and is not the only way for QoS discovery. Works on negotiation [5] suggest that QoS discovery can be achieved by direct negotiation between a client and a service provider. By doing this, supported QoS levels can be kept private.

In addition, we argue that public advertisement is more suitable for *atomic* services (i.e services which do not use third party component services). For a composite service which uses a third party service, supported QoS can be better negotiated because the composite service provider might replace the third pary service with a better one at runtime. Of course here we assume that self-reconfiguration can be done within the composite service and this is the subject of research in [1]. The dynamic runtime change in the structure of a composite service suggests that a set of pre-defined QoS levels for that service may not be desirable. Align to this argument, there are works on "services on demand" [4,1] platforms which attempt to satisfy any QoS requirements from clients. In the remaining part of this paper, we introduce a framework to handle the above three issues. Our framework focuses on a global view as opposed to work in [1,8,11,6].

3 Formalization of the QoS Guarantee Problem for Web Service Compositions

We present a motivation example in Figure 1 which shows four composite services: Mel(burne)-Tourist, Aus(tralia)-Tourist, Syd(ney)-Tourist, and Aus-Attraction which make up the set $\mathbf{S}_{composite}$. The composite services are composed from six

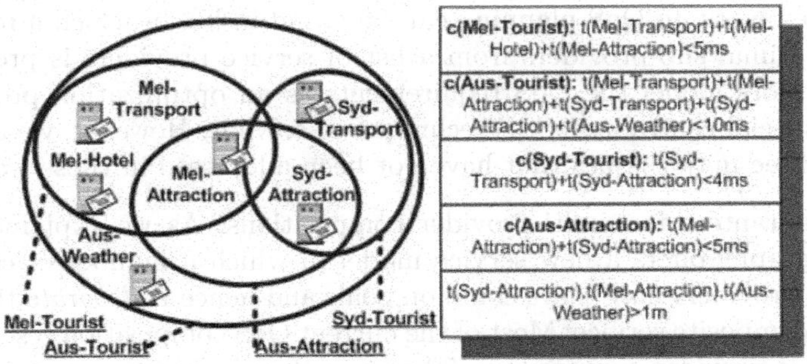

Fig. 1. An example of multiple compositions for tourist related services

individual services: Mel-Transport, Mel-Hotel, Mel-Attraction, Syd-Transport, Syd-Attraction, and Aus-Weather which make up the set $\mathbf{S}_{component}$.

Since a service provider must allocate necessary resources to live up to the QoS guarantees, if its service engages in a number of compositions, there will be a dependency between the levels of QoS that service can contribute to these compositions. Consequently, there is a mutual relationship between the compositions. Here we assume that this relationship can be formally expressed as constraints. For the sake of clarity, we assume the response time is our only interested QoS parameter. The t(S) variable in Figure 1 represents the response time of a Web service S, $S \in \mathbf{S}_{composite} \cup \mathbf{S}_{component}$. We also assume that every composition in $\mathbf{S}_{composite}$ is a sequential combination of its component services and hence its E2E (end-to-end) response time can be computed as a sum of the component services' response time. For other QoS parameters and composition patterns, the E2E QoS can be computed with different aggregation operators [7]. The QoS requirements on the values of these sums form the set of constraints $\{c(S){:}S \in \mathbf{S}_{composite}\}$. We note that these constraints c(S) are only *shared* among service providers who engage in the composition S(i.e. not all providers). In addition to these shared constraints, each provider has its private constraints as shown in the last row of the table in Figure 1. These constraints might be shaped by the provider's resource limitations, business rules, organizational policies or even conditions in contracts with a third party. The providers have a choice to reveal them or not by making the constraints *shared* (i.e. known to a number of or all other providers) or *private* respectively. Here we focus on a general problem in which multiple providers engage in multi-Web service compositions. The final goal of the QoS guarantee for multiple Web service compositions is to satisfy the E2E QoS requirements of all compositions. Formally, the problem can be stated as:

Definition 1. *Given m service providers participate in n compositions and a set of pre-defined E2E QoS requirements for those compositions. The problem of QoS guarantee for multi-Web service compositions is to assign QoS values to each component service so that these values can be supported by the service's provider and all the compositions meet their QoS requirements.*

Some main characteristics of the QoS guarantee problem for multi-Web service compositions that makes it more complex and difficult than the single-provider QoS composition problem are:

- **Prop$_1$:** Many providers engage in the composition process. They may publish their supported QoS levels or require direct negotiations.
- **Prop$_2$:** Many compositions need to be considered concurrently. QoS planning in one composition may affect another composition.

In a real world Web services environment, there are two main sources of dynamism regarding the compositions and the constraints. They are also important characteristics of the QoS guarantee problem for multi-Web service compositions:

- **Prop$_3$:** Compositions can be formed and disbanded any time, e.g. compositions in $\mathbf{S}_{composite}$ do not appear and disappear at the same time. They might be formed or dropped one after one.
- **Prop$_4$:** Service providers might have their own constraints changed during their service lifetime. QoS requirements for a composition might also change (e.g. changes in user's requests).

The characteristic **Prop$_3$** reflects many possibilities. One of them is that some providers may realize that the final goal to satisfy the QoS requirements of all compositions may not be achieved. They then drop less important compositions (according to their own ratings) and hence the original problem of QoS guarantee for Web service compositions is transformed into a new easier one to solve.

4 Modelling the QoS Guarantee Problem for Web Service Compositions as an Instance of DisCSP

Based on the above discussion, it is proposed that DisCSP techniques can be well suited for modelling and solving the QoS guarantee problem for Web service composition. More specifically:

- The distributed nature of the Web environment and the engagement of many participants in multi-provider services suggest that a distributed approach is best suited.
- Constraints in the QoS guarantee for multi-Web service composition problem can be either private or shared. Distributed constraints with different visibility levels have been one of the main focuses of DisCSP techniques.

To apply DisCSP techniques for solving the problem of QoS guarantee for multi-Web services compositions, each service provider can be considered as an agent (an autonomously processing entity) in a constraint network. Each QoS parameter is mapped into a variable in the constraint network; the set of providers' constraints is mapped into the network's constraint set. For the rest of this paper, we will use the terms *service providers* and *agents* interchangeably. More formally, the problem of QoS guarantee for Web service compositions can be considered as an instance of DisCSP problems of which the general definition is:

Definition 2. *A static distributed constraint satisfaction problem P is a tuple* $\langle V,D,C,A \rangle$ *where* $V=\{x_1,...,x_n\}$ *is a set of variables,* $D=\{D_1,...,D_n\}$ *is a set of discrete finite domains for each of the variables , and* $C=\{C_1,...,C_m\}$ *is a set of constraints on possible values of variables. These variables and constraints are distributed among a set of agents* $A=\{A_1,...,A_k\}$. *If an agent* A_l *knows a constraint* C_q, *it also must know all variables contained in* C_q. *A solution is an assignment of values in the domains to all variables such that every constraint is satisfied.*

To take into account the dynamic nature of Web services environment, we consider the implications of the properties **Prop**$_3$, and **Prop**$_4$ discussed in the previous section. In the DisCSP framework, the appearance of a new composition indicates that new constraints and possiblly new variables and agents are added into the constraint network. Dissolving of a composition means that some existing constraints are removed and possibly some existing variables or agents are also removed. In general, there are introductions or reductions of new variables, constraints, and agents.

Traditionally, Dynamic CSP (DynCSP) is a branch of CSP. Its goal is to effectively handle CSP problems with dynamic changes instead of restarting a static search every time a change is detected. DynCSP has been modestly extended into distributed environments [9].A formal description of dynamic DisCSP followed by a dynamic CSP definition in [16] can be given as:

Definition 3. *A dynamic distributed constraint satisfaction problem P is a sequence* $P^0 ...,P^i ...$ *of static DisCSPs, where each one resulting from a change in the preceding one. This change may be a restriction or a relaxation.*

A restriction can be caused by more agents, variables, or new constraints. A relaxation results from removing agents, variables, or constraints. Note that a change rate is important to measure and specify how fast a DynDisCSP changes over time. This rate, defined as Δ can be measured as the total of added or removed constraints between any two P^i and P^j over the time distance between them.

5 DisCSP Algorithms to Solve the QoS Guarantee Problem for Web Service Compositions

There have recently been many publications on DisCSP algorithms. Traditionally these algorithms are developed and demonstrated in the context of the Meeting Scheduling and Sensor Network [2]. However, there are some characteristics that make the QoS guarantee for Web service composition problem different from those problems: Firstly each agent holds a set (often more than one) of variables to represent QoS parameters; secondly local constraints in QoS problem can be very complex; and thirdly service providers are heterogeneous and hence flexibility in algorithm implementations is desireable. In searching for a suitable DisCSP algorithm, these characteristics are the most important criteria for us.

Whilst most DisCSP algorithms can be extended so that one agent can hold more than one variable, substantial effort is required for that and for handling complex private constraints. The originial DisCSP model [20] and most of the solving algorithms focus on shared constraints instead of private constraints and hence is more suitable for distributed control but not negotiation. A notable exception is Asynchronous Aggregate Search (AAS) [12] that allows one agent to maintain a set of variables and these variables can be shared and hence is suitable for negotiation. Also all constraints are private in AAS (shared constraints can be modeled as duplicated private constraints). However, in the current version of AAS, private constraints at each agent are assumed to be simple and hence there is no attention in solving these local constraints. Also, AAS is designed only for static environments. In this section, we introduce AAS and suggest to use a centralized CSP solver inside each agent to handle complex local constraints. We also propose an extension of AAS called DynAAS to handle the dynamic nature of Web services environment.

5.1 Asynchronous Aggregate Search and Local CSP Solvers

Here we briefly introduce AAS in the Web services context. A complete explanation of AAS can be found in [12] where its termination, correctness and completeness are proven. Asynchronous Aggregate Search (AAS) is a DisCSP search technique based on the classical Asynchronous Backtrack (ABT) algorithm [20]. In AAS, each agent (service provider) maintains a set of variables (relevant QoS variables in our Web services QoS guarantee problem) which can be shared with others and a set of private constraints on the values of these variables. AAS differs from most of existing methods in that it exchanges aggregated consistent values (in contrast to a single value in ABT) of partial solutions during the solving process. The aggregated consistent values are the Cartesian products of domains which represent a set of possible valuations. This aggregate significantly reduces the number of backtracks. At the beginning, AAS agents are (randomly) assigned with priorities and generate random assignments (i.e. proposals). Two agents are neighbors if they share some variables. During search, each agent A sends assignments in *ok?* messages to A^+ or rejections in *nogood* messages to A^-. Here we denote A^+ the set of neighboring agents whose priorities are higher, and A^- the set of neighboring agents whose priorities are lower than A's priority. V^+ is the set of variables the agent share with A^+, and V^- is with A^-. An agent can also send *addneighbor* to ask another agent to become its neighbor. Each agent keeps a view (current assignments of its variables and variables in V^+) and a list of nogoods (assignments rejected by A^-).

In AAS, an agent implements three main procedures *process-ok*, *process-nogood*, and *process-addneighbor* to handle incoming *ok?*, *nogood*, and *addneighbor* messages. These procedures check whether the information of a partial solution in the messages is still compatible with the agent's own assignment of its variables. The procedures may invoke a *check-agent-view* procedure to find out a new compatible assignment for the agent's local variables. In particular, the procedure *process-ok* updates the agent-view and nogood list from the remaining valid assignments before possibly invoking the *check-agent-view* procedure. The procedure *process-nogood* updates its view according to new assignments found in the nogood content. If the nogood invalidates the current instantiation and contains new variables then the agent will try to establish new links with agents in $A^+{}_k$ which hold these variables. The procedure *check-agent-view* is used to find a new instantiation and sends updated values in this instantiation to appropriate agents in $A^-{}_k$. To effectively handle the complexity of local constraints, we introduce a local CSP solver into each agent. Instead of carrying out a simple local search as in the originial version of AAS, our *check-agent-view* employs a local CSP solver to find an aggregate V over the Cartesian product of domains of the agent's variables so that the current agent-view and V are consistent and satisfy the agent's local constraints. In general, the CSP solver of an agent A takes assignments from A^- and generates solutions for V^+. If a solution cannot be found for an assignment from an agent in A^+, a *nogood* message is backtracked to this agent. Otherwise, new assignments generated by A and sent to A^-.

5.2 Dynamic Asynchronous Aggregate Search

Our new extension of AAS for dynamic environment is based on an indexing technique called *eliminating explanation* which had been proposed in centralized DynCSP [15]. Note that (nogood based) CSP algorithms in general generate and test solutions, and record nogoods (invalid solutions). The main idea of the *eliminating explanation* technique is simple enough: to index every nogood against the minimal set of constraints that create the nogood, and remove the nogood if a constraint in the constraint set is removed. In DynAAS, an agent creates and stores an *eliminating explanation* before it sends a nogood. The sent nogood is tagged with an identity number and kept by both the sender and the receiver so that the sender, due to some changes later, can ask the receiver to remove this nogood. It does this by sending the receiver a *remove-nogood* message that contains the nogood's identity.

Algorithm 1 shows a procedure *add-constraints* used by an agent to handle a newly added constraint set C_{new}. In the algorithm, the agent first tries a local repair of the partial assignments of variables contained in both those constraints and V^+ (line 2). If it fails, the agent then attempts to repair the assignments of the whole V^+ (line 4). New assignments if exist are used to update the view and sent to A^+, otherwise a backtrack occurs.

Algorithm 2 explains a procedure *remove-constraints* which handles the removal of a constraint set $C_{removed}$. The agent bases on its eliminating explanation set (E) to detect which nogood it sent to a parent in the past is no longer a nogood (line 2). It then sends a *remove-nogood* message to ask the parent for the removal of this nogood. The nogood is a constraint from the parent's perspective. Therefore, the parent handles the message by invoking Algorithm 2. Adding and removing constraints are the same as calling *add-constraints* and *remove-constraints* sequentially.

Algorithm 1. Add-Constraints(C_{new})

1: update neighbor list, variable list, and constraint list
2: *assgmts* =re-assign($v(C_{new}) \cap V^+$)
3: **if** *assgmts* $= \emptyset$ **then**
4: *assigmts* =re-assign(V^+)
5: **end if**
6: **if** *assgmts* $= \emptyset$ **then**
7: send nogoods to A^-
8: **else**
9: update view and send ok to A^+
10: **end if**

Algorithm 2. Remove-Constraints($C_{removed}$)

1: update neighbor list, variable list, and constraint list
2: **for all** $e \in E$ and $c(e) \cap C_{removed} \neq \emptyset$ **do**
3: send *remove-nogood* message to parent to remove c
4: delete e from E
5: **end for**

It is important to note that adding or removing of variables or domain values can be modeled as constraints [16], therefore can be handled by the two above algorithms. If a new agent is added to the network, it is given the lowest priority. For every type of changes, affected agent must update its lists of neighbors, variables, and constraints (e.g. line 1 of Algorithm 1 and 2) first. As we have seen so far, the key idea of DynAAS is to reuse partial solutions to achieve stability. If we model the whole environment as a discrete-event system where events are constraint additions or removals, then during the interval between any two consecutive events the system can be viewed as a static DisCSP using AAS. This is because DynAAS reacts to maintain consistent views and nogood storages whenever constraints are added or removed.

6 Experiments

We have built a prototype for experiment, in which we uses Axis 2 for SOAP engine running on Windows platforms. We develop a DisCSP module with 2 supported protocols: AAS and DynAAS. The module is implemented as a Web service that has an one-way operation to receive messages sent from other DisCSP modules. The endpoint reference implementation of a DisCSP module supports four different WS-Addressing actions with local names: *ok*, *nogood*, *add-neighbor*, and *remove-nogood*. These actions are used to identify a message type sent between two Web services. We use XPATH to present the constraints. We use NSolver [10] as the Local Solver module. We developed an adaptor to invoke NSolver engine (.NET process) from the Web services. The adapter transforms XPath expression into NSolver native constraints and can be downloaded from [19]. For our experiment, 10 Web services are used. A list of prefetched constraints on QoS parameters, and neighbors (i.e addresses of other DisCSP Web services) are stored in a mySQL database. These data are modified by a simulator with the varying rate σ of adding/removing constraints. In particular, compositions are randomly formed and removed among any 3 agents. For the sake of clarity, each of our compositions consists of exactly three component services and introduces maximum two constraints on the E2E QoS parameters of the composition. The QoS parameters that we use are response time and cost which both have simple aggregation formulas [7]. Each parameter has a domain of 10 discrete values. The average of all constraint tightness (the probability that there is not a valid assignment within a constraint) is 30% . 20 instances are run for each test.

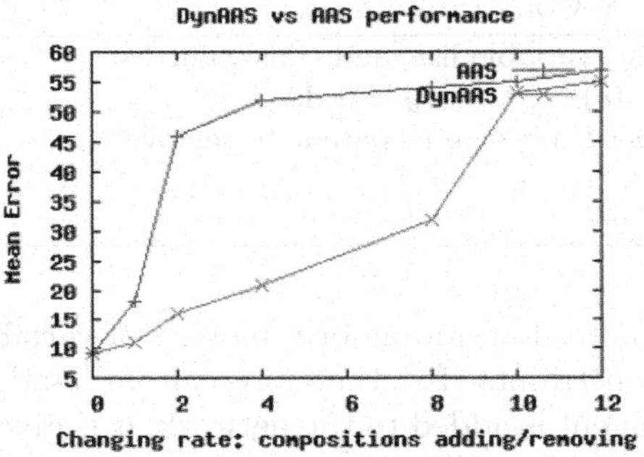

Fig. 2. Mean Error of DynAAS versus Static AAS for 10 providers with dynamic number of compositions

Before an explaining experiments' result, we first introduce some important metrics. Most of current DisCSP algorithms use *processing cycles* as a measurement of time due to its good approximation and the asynchronously distributed nature of the search (i.e. there is no global clock). A processing cycle of an agent consists of receiving a message, processing it and sending out new messages. Also for DynDisCSP, it is important to measure the rate of environmental changes. We adopt the rate function σ defined in [9]. It is defined as the first deriviative of the change rate Δ that measures how reactive an algorithm is to changes. The time unit to calculate Δ and σ is one *processing cycle*. For example, at a rate σ=4, four constraints are added or removed at each *processing cycle*. Note that because sometimes an algorithm might not keep up with the change rate, completion time is not an appropriate indicator for performance of DynDisCSP algorithms. Instead, accuracy in approximating a valid solution is used. The metric is *instantaneous error* [9] which is calculated as the distance from a current solution found by the algorithm and the valid solution bounds. Note that these valid solution bounds are computed by our simulator everytime it adds or removes a constraint.

In the experiments, we have used both static AAS and our new DynAAS algorithm. Static AAS restarts the search from scratch every time a change is detected. Figure 4 shows the performance of DynAAS and static AAS in terms of mean values of normalized *instantaneous errors* vesus rate of change. The graph shows that the error rate of DynAAS is significant lower than AAS for low changed rates and increased for larger values of σ. This can be explained as the the change rate is greater than the adaptive rate at which DynAAS can handle. However it shows that DynAAS offers significant reduction in solution errors if the change rate is reasonable. This reduction is greater than 50% for $\sigma \leq 8$. In other words, for the current setup, as long as there are no more than 8 constraints added or removed at each processing cycle then DynAAS gives twice of the level of solution accuracy over static AAS.

7 Conclusions

We have discussed in this paper the limitations of current approaches in solving general QoS composition problems and outlined a new approach for modelling and solving the QoS guarantees for multi-provider compositions as a DisCSP problem. We also describe a new extension of AAS called DynAAS for dynamic environment where unexpected events and changes can happen. Experiments show that the QoS guarantee problem for multiple Web service can efficiently be solved with DisCSP. Our future work focuses on QoS guarantees for Web service compositions and optimization of a joint interest function among all providers, such as the joint satisfaction levels of the DisCSP solution quality.

References

1. V. Agarwal, K. Dasgupta, N. Karnik, A. Kumar, A. Kundu, S. Mittal, and B. Srivastava. A service creation environment based on end to end composition of web services. In *WWW '05: Proceedings of the 14th international conference on World Wide Web*, pages 128–137, New York, NY, USA, 2005. ACM Press.
2. R. Bejar, B. Krishnamachari, C. Gomes, and B. Selman. Distributed constraint satisfaction in a wireless sensor tracking system. In *Workshop on Distributed Constraints, IJCAI*, 2001.
3. B. Benatallah, F. Casati, and P. Traverso, editors. *Service-Oriented Computing - ICSOC 2005, Third International Conference, Amsterdam, The Netherlands, December 12-15, 2005, Proceedings*, volume 3826 of *Lecture Notes in Computer Science*. Springer, 2005.
4. A. Dan, D. Davis, R. Kearney, A. Keller, R. King, D. Kuebler, H. Ludwig, M. Polan, M. Spreitzer, and A. Youssef. Web services on demand: Wsla-driven automated management. *IBM Syst. J.*, 43(1):136–158, 2004.
5. A. Elfatatry and P. Layzell. Negotiating in service-oriented environments. *Commun. ACM*, 47(8):103–108, 2004.
6. X. Gu, K. Nahrstedt, R. Chang, and C. Ward. Qos-assured service composition in managed service overlay networks, 2003.

7. M. C. Jaeger, G. Rojec-Goldmann, and Mühl. QoS aggregation for service composition using workflow patterns. In *Proceedings of the 8th International Enterprise Distributed Object Computing Conference (EDOC 2004)*, pages 149–159, Monterey, California, USA, 2004. IEEE CS Press.
8. Y. Liu, A. H. Ngu, and L. Z. Zeng. Qos computation and policing in dynamic web service selection. In *WWW Alt. '04: Proceedings of the 13th international World Wide Web conference on Alternate track papers & posters*, pages 66–73, New York, NY, USA, 2004. ACM Press.
9. R. Mailler. Comparing two approaches to dynamic, distributed constraint satisfaction. In *AAMAS '05: Proceedings of the fourth international joint conference on Autonomous agents and multiagent systems*, pages 1049–1056, New York, NY, USA, 2005. ACM Press.
10. *NSolver home page.* http://www.cs.cityu.edu.hk/ hwchun/nsolver/, 2005.
11. S. Ran. A model for web services discovery with qos. *SIGecom Exch.*, 4(1):1–10, 2003.
12. M. C. Silaghi and B. Faltings. Asynchronous aggregation and consistency in distributed constraint satisfaction. In *Artificial Intelligence Journal Vol.161*, pages 25–53, New York, NY, USA, 2005. ACM Press.
13. W. M. P. van der Aalst. Don't go with the flow: web services composition standards exposed. *IEEE Intelligent Systems*, 18(1):72–76, 2003.
14. W. M. P. van der Aalst, A. H. M. ter Hofstede, B. Kiepuszewski, and A. P. Barros. Workflow patterns. *Distrib. Parallel Databases*, 14(1):5–51, 2003.
15. G. Verfaillie and T. Schiex. Dynamic backtracking for dynamic constraint satisfaction problems. In *Proceedings of the ECAI'94 Workshop on Constraint Satisfaction Issues Raised by Practical Applications, Amsterdam, The Netherlands*, pages 1–8, 1994.
16. G. Verfaillie and T. Schiex. Solution reuse in dynamic constraint satisfaction problems. In *National Conference on Artificial Intelligence*, pages 307–312, 1994.
17. *Web Service Choreography Interface (WSCI) 1.0.* http://www.w3.org/TR/wsci/, 2005.
18. *Web Services Choreography Description Language Version 1.0.* http://www.w3.org/TR/2004/WD-ws-cdl-10-20041217/, 2006.
19. *XPath Adapter for NSolver.* http://www.it.swin.edu.au/centres/ciamas/tiki-index.php?page=xpath2nsolver, 2005.
20. M. Yokoo, E. H. Durfee, T. Ishida, and K. Kuwabara. Distributed constraint satisfaction for formalizing distributed problem solving. In *International Conference on Distributed Computing Systems*, pages 614–621, 1992.

Service Composition (re)Binding Driven by Application–Specific QoS

Gerardo Canfora, Massimiliano Di Penta, Raffaele Esposito, Francesco Perfetto, and Maria Luisa Villani

RCOST - Research Centre on Software Technology
University of Sannio
Palazzo ex Poste, Via Traiano 82100 Benevento, Italy
{canfora, dipenta, r.esposito, villani}@unisannio.it, ggperf@libero.it

Abstract. QoS–aware service composition and binding are among the most challenging and promising issues for service–oriented architectures. The aim of QoS–aware service composition is to determine the set of services that, once composed, will perform the required functionality, and will best contribute to achieve the level of QoS promised in Service Level Agreements (SLAs). While the existing works focus on cross–domain QoS attributes, it would be useful to support service composition and binding according to some characteristics on the borderline between functional and non–functional attributes, often specific to the service domain.

The paper describes a QoS evaluator that, integrated with our previously developed binder, allows the use of application specific QoS attributes for composite service binding and re–binding. The applicability of the proposed approach and tool is shown through a case study related to the image processing domain.

Keywords: Quality of Service, Dynamic binding, Re–binding, Composite Web Services.

1 Introduction

Late, dynamic binding of service compositions constitutes one of the most interesting and relevant challenges for service–oriented architectures. In this scenario, a service composition can contain some abstract service specifications – e.g., indicating that a hotel booking service is needed at a particular point of the workflow – without specifying the binding to some existing services. When the functionality offered by more available services is equivalent, the binding is driven by some non–functional, Quality of Service (QoS) criteria, such as minimizing the cost, the time or achieving a tradeoff between the two.

In case the bindings need to fulfill some global constraints imposed over the workflow and (near) optimize a global fitness function, proper aggregation formulae have been proposed to estimate the QoS of the composition from the QoS attributes of invoked services and from some properties of the workflow [4]. Finding a solution of the aforementioned problem is NP–hard: this was addressed by

A. Dan and W. Lamersdorf (Eds.): ICSOC 2006, LNCS 4294, pp. 141–152, 2006.

various authors: Cardoso *et al.* [5] and Zeng *et al.* [11] proposed to use Integer Programming, while, in past work, we used Genetic Algorithms (GAs), that resulted to be more scalable and allowed the use of non–linear QoS aggregation formulae [2].

While most of the existing works focus on cross–domain QoS attributes – e.g., response time, cost, availability, reputation, reliability, etc. – it would be useful to also consider other attributes, that are specific of the service domain/purpose. For example, if the service composition returns a photo, one would try to maximize the photo resolution or the number of colors, keeping low, if possible, the cost and the response time. Much in the same way, a travel booking composite service – involving flight and hotel booking – would try to achieve a compromise between the cost and the hotel category, favoring hotels and airlines encompassing the maximum possible number of priority clubs.

This paper presents the use of application–specific QoS attributes for the purpose of QoS–aware composition and re–binding. In particular, this work enhances our framework for service (re)binding [3] by:

- introducing constructs, and a tool, to define new QoS attributes (specifying type, scale and domain) and to annotate services with these attributes;
- specifying a language for defining QoS attribute aggregation formulae, i.e., formulae similar to those defined by Cardoso [4] for domain–independent attributes. The formulae specification is supported by a guided editor and a type–checker;
- realizing an interpreter for the aforementioned formulae; the interpreter is integrated in our service binder described in [3] and is used to evaluate the QoS of a composite service at binding–time and at run–time (to trigger re–binding if necessary).

The remainder of this paper is organized as follows. Section 2 defines the language for specifying QoS attributes and aggregation formulae. Section 3 describes the QoS–attribute definition tool, highlighting its architecture, its features and how it is integrated with our binder. Section 4 shows the approach at work in the context of a image processing workflow. After a review of the literature in Section 5, Section 6 concludes the paper and outlines the directions for future work.

2 QoS Definition Language

Let us consider a composite service S of n *abstract services*, $S \equiv \{s_1, s_2, \ldots, s_n\}$, whose structure is defined through a workflow description language (e.g., WS-BPEL). Each abstract service s_i can be bound to one of the m *concrete services* $cs_{i,1}, \ldots, cs_{i,m}$, which are functionally equivalent, while exhibiting different QoS values. As said in the introduction, the choice of bindings can depend on an objective function and on a set of constraints. Determining the (near) optimal solution requires to evaluate each solution, estimating the QoS of a concrete workflow, i.e., bound to a set of concrete services. Cardoso *et al.* [5] defined QoS aggregation formulae for each pair QoS attribute–workflow construct. For example, the cost (or the response time) of a sequence of service invocations is given by the sum of each cost (response time), while the cost of a *switch* is given by the weighted sum of costs for each *case*, where weights are the probabilities that cases will be followed.

In most cases, the aforementioned aggregation formulae are cabled in the optimization algorithm the binder is using. However, as mentioned in the introduction, in many cases it is useful to consider QoS attributes, sometimes specific of a particular domain, sometimes specific of a particular application, for which the aggregation formulae have not been defined yet. Therefore, it is necessary to provide a language and a tool to specify aggregation formulae, and to allow the QoS–aware binder to interpret such formulae for estimating the QoS of the whole composition. To this aim, we developed a language that permits to specify a new QoS attribute, defining:

1. *The type:* supported types are primitive types (integer, real, Boolean), strings and collection types (*Set*, *Bag* and *Sequence*). For integer and real it is either possible to define a range of possible values, or to specify an enumeration of admissible values. For strings it is necessary to enumerate values (thus imposing an order relationship among them). Collection types can be used when the QoS value for a service is constituted of sets of atomic values. In particular, *Set* indicates the mathematical set (no order relationship, no repeated values), *Bag* admits repetitions and *Sequence* imposes an order relationship. The chosen type limits the set of operations that can be used when defining the aggregation formulae. For example, a set supports operations such as union, intersection, while it is not possible to apply arithmetic operators. If necessary, it is possible to get the set cardinality and then apply on it any operator supported for the integer type.
2. *The scale:* ordinal, interval, ratio, absolute. As for the type, the scale limits the set of admissible operations. Since the QoS attribute must be able, at least, to establish an order relationship between two services (i.e., indicate which service is better from a particular QoS perspective), the nominal scale is not considered.

For example, if we consider the photo domain, the *color depth* (defined as the number of bits encoding colors) QoS attribute is of type integer and its scale is ordinal. For any service involving a payment, the *accepted credit cards* attribute is a set, containing strings indicating the various credit cards accepted. The scale for this type of attribute is the ordinal scale where the order relationship is defined over the set cardinality (i.e., the more credit card are accepted, the better is the service). Finally, the *refresh rate* attribute of a webcam service can be considered a real value in the ratio scale.

Our approach for specifying types is similar to what available in the WSLA language [6]. However, WSLA does not consider Collection types nor it defines how QoS attributes values can be aggregated. Similarly to Cardoso, who defined aggregation formulae for domain–independent attributes (cost, response time, etc.), we can compute overall workflow QoS, specifying, for each workflow control construct, aggregation formulae for domain-specific attributes too. In order to

Table 1. Aggregation formulae for some domain–specific QoS attributes

Attribute	Workflow construct	QoS aggregation formula
Color Depth	Sequence	$min(Ai)$
	Switch	$maxProbability(Ai, pi)$
	Flow	$min(Ai)$
	Loop	Ai
Credit Cards	Sequence	$intersection(Ai)$
	Switch	$maxProbability(Ai, pi)$
	Flow	$intersection(Ai)$
	Loop	Ai
Refresh Rate	Sequence	$min(Ai)$
	Switch	$sum(pi \cdot Ai)$
	Flow	$min(Ai)$
	Loop	Ai

obtain that, the language we propose offers a set of operators and functions, most of them inherited from the Object Constraint Language (OCL) [9]. In particular, the language includes mathematical operators, Boolean operators, collection operators, and finally *keywords* proper of the aggregation language. These indicate parameters to be used in aggregation formulae, i.e.:

- k, the number of iterations for a *Loop*;
- pi, the probability of following the i–th case in a *Switch*;
- Ai, the QoS of the inner node of a workflow constructs. For a *Sequence*, Ai is the array of QoS for nodes belonging to the sequence; for a *Switch* it is the array of QoS for all cases; for a *Flow* it is the array of QoS for all the children; for a *Loop* is the QoS of the *Loop* inner node.

Table 1 shows examples of aggregation formulae for some domain–specific QoS attributes, i.e. *color depth* of a photo service, number of *credit cards* accepted from a payment service and *refresh rate* of a temperature service. For the *Sequence* and the *Flow*, the *color depth* is the minimum among the values Ai of the inner nodes. For the *Switch* it can be defined as the color depth Ai for the case having maximum probability pi. Finally, for the *Loop* it is just the value computed for the inner node. For the *credit card* attribute, the aggregation is made through the set intersection operator over *Sequences* and *Flows* (i.e., considering the set of credit cards common to all the services), while for a *Switch* it is the value of the branch having highest probability, and for the *Loop* the value computed for the inner node. The *refresh rate* aggregates similarly to *color depth* for all workflow construct, except for the *Switch*, where an averaged weight is computed. Finally, it is worth to point out that, even in our example we considered only the most common workflow constructs, the language can be used to define formulae for further constructs.

Besides the aggregation formulae, it is necessary to specify the function to be used for evaluating the attribute and to impose an order relationship between services (thus permitting their comparison). Let A be the value of our QoS attribute for a given service. For attributes (e.g., *color depth*) for which the type already imposes an order relationship, the function is the identify function, while for *credit card* – for which the order relationship is not imposed – the function is $size(A)$, where the function $size$ returns the cardinality of the set A.

As detailed in Section 3, the formulae specification is supported by a guided editor and a type–checker.

3 The QoS Aggregation Tool

The workflow QoS-aggregation mechanism has been implemented as part of the WS–Binder Tool [3]. The previous release of the binder supported composite service (re)binding considering cross–domain attributes such as Cost, Response Time and Availability. As shown in Fig. 2, the binder has been extended with the following modules:

- *A QoS Aggregation Function Editor:* it is a web–based editor (see Fig. 1) that a service integrator can use to define new QoS attributes and their aggregation formulae.
- *A Type Checker:* at design time, the *Type Checker* is used to verify the type–correctness of the aggregation formulae specified by the service integrator, according to the language rules and the type scales.
- *A QoS Formulae Interpreter:* at run–time, given a composite service workflow and a possible set of bindings, the *Interpreter* evaluates the workflow global QoS.

The whole environment is realized in Java. Services are deployed using the Axis container[1] while WS–BPEL composite services are executed using the *ActiveBPEL* engine. The QoS aggregator is also realized in Java using the Java Compiler Compiler (JavaCC) Parser Generator[2]. The tool GUI has been developed using the JSP technology.

3.1 Development Time

When designing a composite service abstract workflow, the system integrator may want to specify an objective function and some QoS constraints that will drive the binding. It can happen that either the objective function or the constraints involve some application–dependent QoS attributes. To support binding based on these attributes, it is necessary to have aggregation formulae defined for them. From the preference settings user interface, the system integrator may select the attributes of interest for the composition. The tool provides a support to (i) choose and insert the attributes to be considered for the objective function and (ii) define constraints for some of the attributes, according to their type.

In addition, the user may decide to add new attributes. Of course, this is needed whenever, in the context of a composition, a QoS attribute has to be considered, for which an aggregation function has not been defined before. In

[1] *http://xml.apache.org/axis*
[2] *https://javacc.dev.java.net/*

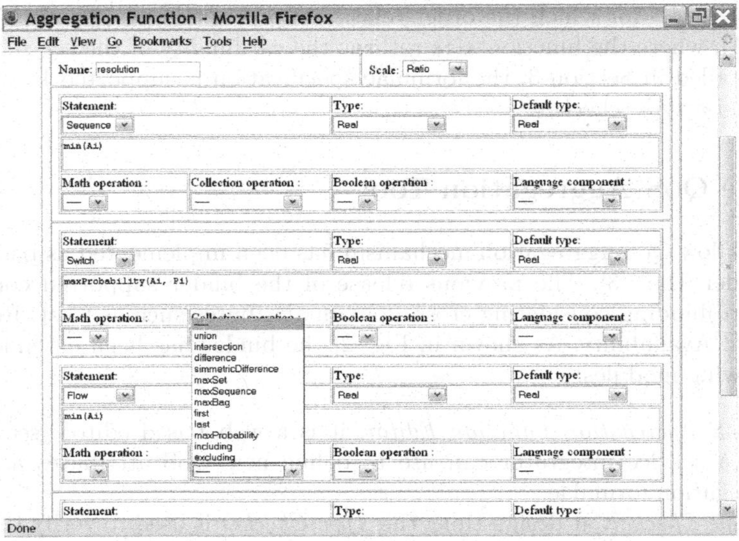

Fig. 1. QoS Aggregation Function Definition Interface

this case, its definition could be specific for the particular composite service being designed. A service integrator can, for example, define his/her own way to aggregate image resolution, while others could do it differently for services having different purposes. Finally, it can happen that the attribute definition is more generic, thus reusable for other service compositions within the same (or related) domain. This is especially the case when attributes are defined by domain experts.

To add new QoS attributes, and to specify aggregation formulae using the language described in Section 2, a guided editor is available. Fig. 1 shows a screenshot of the editor interface. Given the QoS attribute, with the indication of scale and type, the user is required to edit a function for each workflow construct, in a guided fashion. This is achieved by specifying the return type and the aggregation formula.

3.2 Binding Time

At binding time, the QoS Formulae Interpreter allows to estimate the QoS of a concrete workflow (i.e., a workflow for which the abstract services have been bound to some possible concrete services). This is done by applying the defined aggregation formulae over the workflow topology and the QoS values of the services composing it. This permits, using optimization techniques such as those defined in [2], the QoS-aware (re)binding of a workflow according to domain–oriented attributes. In this case, the QoS Aggregator component is used by the Binder in the selection process of the solution services to the optimization problem. The next subsection explains their interaction.

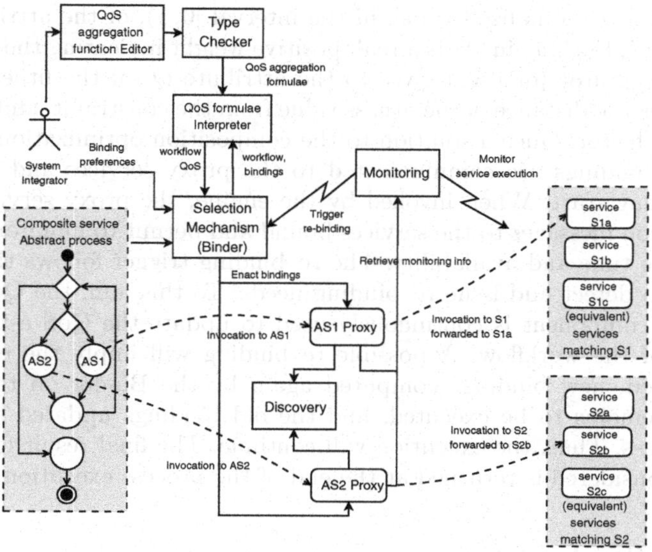

Fig. 2. WS-Binder extended architecture

Integration with the WS–Binder. Fig. 2 shows the extended architecture of the WS–Binder. Specifically, the abstract workflow is a WS–BPEL process definition containing invocations to proxy services. These represent the abstract services and are used to realize the bindings with the final services at run–time and allow re–binding. Indeed, just before the execution, each proxy service allows to retrieve, through some discovery mechanism, and maintain a list of candidate services for the binding, together with their QoS information. This consists of estimated values from monitoring data for attributes like response time and availability, and declared values by the service provider at publication time for the other QoS characteristics of each service. These lists of services are passed to the Binder to determine the (near) optimal concretization for the abstract workflow. In our tool, this is accomplished using GAs, as described in [2]. The genome is represented by an integer array with a number of items equals to the number of distinct abstract services present in the process specification. Each item, in turn, contains an index to the array of the services matching that abstract service. The two–points crossover and a mutation operator that randomly changes a binding are used to generate new individuals. In this generation process towards convergence, the QoS Aggregator module is used to evaluate the individuals. Indeed, the individuals with the best value of the fitness function will reproduce. The fitness function for a genome g is:

$$F(g) = \sum_{i=1}^{n} (w_i \cdot V_i(g)) + w_d\, D(g) \tag{1}$$

where $V_i(g)$ is a normalized value, in the interval $[0, 1)$, of the attribute Q_i for the workflow[3]. Each w_i in (1) is a real, positive weight indicating the importance a service integrator (or user) gives to the attribute Q_i of the fitness function, while $D(g)$ is the distance of the fitness value from the constraint, and w_d weights the penalty factor. Once a solution to the composition optimization problem is found, the bindings are communicated to the proxy services and the process execution may start. When invoked by the engine, the proxy services forward the invocation messages to the services bound and permit to monitor them, e.g., the response time and availability. The re–binding trigger follows the workflow execution to detect and issue re–binding needs. To this aim, the QoS formulae Interpreter component is continuously used to update the QoS estimations at each step of the workflow. A possible re–binding will imply the execution to be suspended, new bindings computed again by the Binder on the workflow slice that remains to be executed, and the old bindings updated through the proxy services. Thus, the execution will continue. The final result for each QoS attribute considered is returned at the end of the process execution.

4 Case Study

This section presents the approach at work over an image manipulation process. The process (shown in Fig. 3) takes as an input one or two images, plus some options. In case a rotation is requested, the image is properly rotated. Then, the *addConstant* operation makes changes to the image basic colors, while the *executeMedian* smoothens the image. Subsequently, a sum, or a difference (e.g., adding a frame or removing a background) is computed with the second image. Finally, the image is properly scaled. The QoS attributes considered for this process are:

1. *the cost*, with aggregation formulae defined as in the paper [3];
2. *the color depth* (values contained in the enumeration $\{16, 24, 32\}$ bits), having aggregation formulae defined in Table 1; and
3. *the resolution*, in terms of image number of pixels, having aggregation formulae similar to color depth.

As a first step, we evaluate how the GA is able to search for a (near) optimal solution according to a given fitness function and a constraint set. Let us suppose one wants to maximize *resolution* and *color depth* while keeping *cost* ≤ 11. We set our GA with a population of 50 individuals, 100 generations, a crossover probability of 0.7 and a mutation probability of 0.01. Fig. 4 shows how the fitness (a), the cost (b), the resolution (c) and the color depth (d) evolve over the GA generations. In particular, Fig. 4(a) shows the averaged fitness over 30 runs of the GA, indicating how the fitness is able to drive the search towards a (near) optimal solution.

[3] Note that attributes are normalized (see Zeng *et al.* [11] for details) so that higher values of $V_i(g)$ always correspond to better QoS.

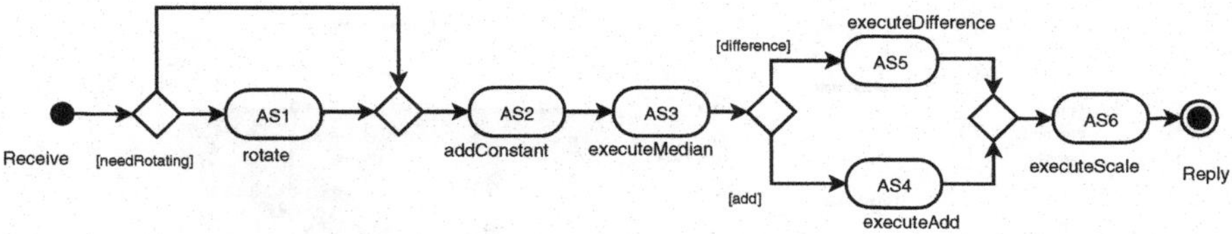

Fig. 3. Image transformation process

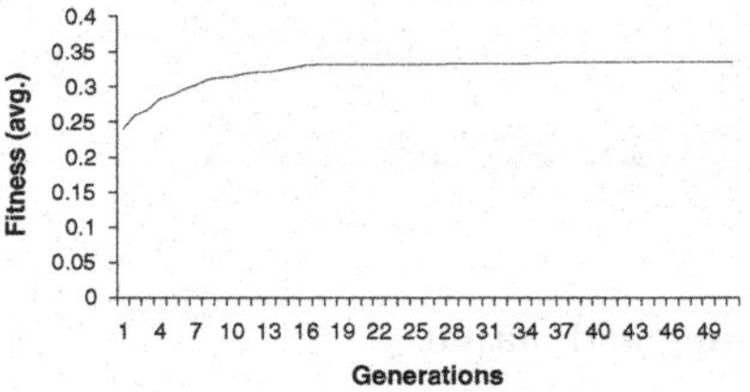

(a) Fitness

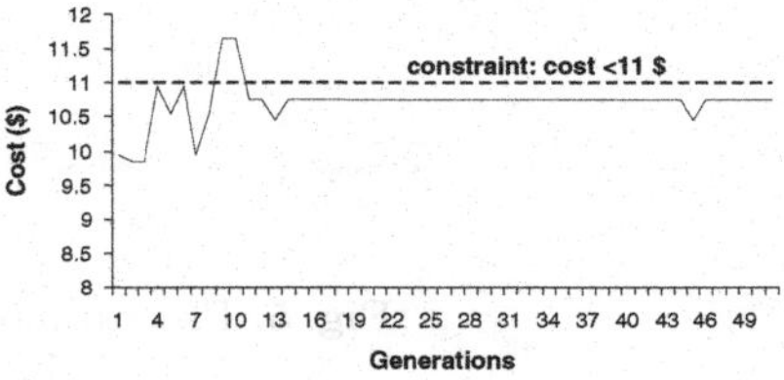

(b) Cost

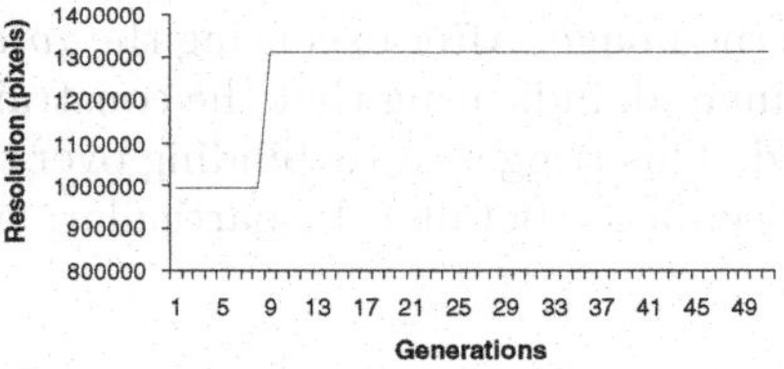

(c) Resolution

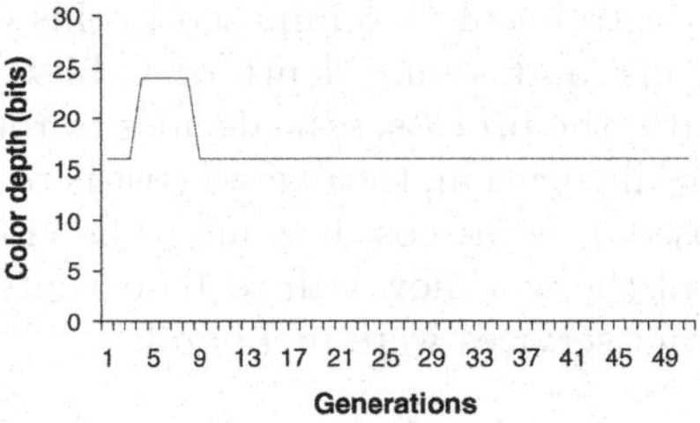

(d) Color depth

Fig. 4. GA evolution

The other figures show how, for a particular run of the GA and the best individual, the different QoS attributes evolve. After 5 generations, the algorithm tries to increase the color depth from 16 to 24 bits. This produces an increase of the cost, however still within the constraint. After 9 generations, a solution with a higher resolution is found. However, this produces an unacceptable increase of the cost, violating the constraint. Alternative solutions are therefore selected: the resolution is kept high, while accepting to reduce again the color depth. In this particular case, the weights chosen on the fitness function and the tradeoff between the resolution increase and the color depth decrease balances in favor of a better resolution (reached at generation 10).

As described in [3], it may happen that the actual QoS measured at run–time differs from the initial estimates. For example, when estimating the overall QoS of the image processing workflow shown in Fig. 3, the cost of the *rotate* service does not highly contribute to the overall cost, since the probability of executing it, declared from the service provider, is of 20%. Because of that, the workflow

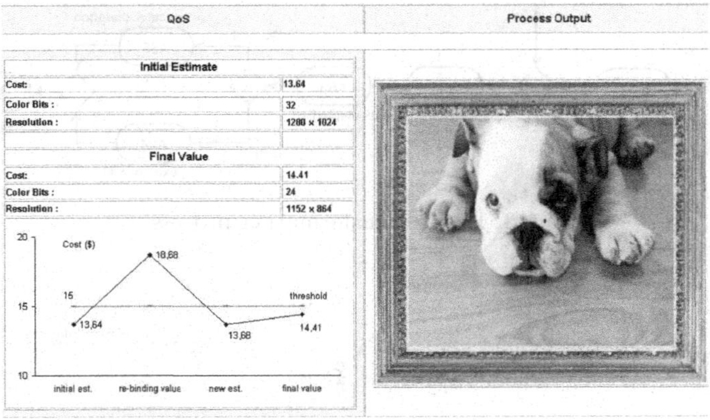

Fig. 5. Process monitoring and output

is bound to a set of services that guarantees an overall cost of 13.64 $, within the constraint of 15 $ imposed in this case, a resolution of 1280 × 1024 (i.e., 1.3 M pixels) and a color depth of 32 bits. However, it happens that, when the user executes the process, s/he decides to rotate the image. After executing the *rotate* service invocation, the overall cost is re–estimated, indicating that the constraint imposed over the cost is going to be violated. This triggers a re–binding over the slice of the workflow still to be executed (see [3] for details). In particular, two abstract services were re–bound:

1. *rotate (AS1):* from a service having cost=8.40 $, color depth=32 and Resolution= 1280 × 1024 to a service having cost=4.40 $, color depth=24 and Resolution= 1152 × 864;
2. *executeMedian (AS3):* from a service having cost=2.80 $, color depth=32 and Resolution= 1280 × 1024 to a service having cost=1.80 $, color depth=24 and Resolution=1152 × 864.

The new bindings guarantee a cost within the constraint (13.88 $), while lowering the resolution at 1152 × 864 and the color depth to 24 bits. Details on the QoS initial estimates, the final QoS values, and the dynamics of the cost attribute (i.e., initial estimate, run–time estimate triggering the re–binding, new estimate and final value measured) are shown in the monitoring view of WS–Binder (Fig. 5), together with the output, i.e., the picture produced by the process.

5 Related Work

To support a QoS-aware composition, models and techniques for workflow QoS estimation and optimization are being developed. In [4,5] a mathematical model is proposed for workflow QoS computation, using metrics aggregation functions which are defined for time, cost, reliability and fidelity. In our work, we propose to precisely identify domain–wide attributes in order to have consistent ways to aggregate them within workflows.

Aggarwal *et al.* [1] focus on the QoS–driven selection and composition features of the tool METEOR-S. QoS attributes are numerical and formally defined as an ontology that represents generic metrics is used, which also includes the concept of domain-specific QoS metrics. To express process–level QoS constraints, the aggregation operator must be specified for each attribute. The objective function for optimization is a linear combination of the parameters and solved through an integer programming tool, which outputs a set of feasible (sub)optimal solutions, among which the service integrator may choose. In our knowledge, this is the first work where it is explicitly foreseen the possibility of defining domain–specific QoS attributes. Nevertheless, the case studies reported in the work are limited to cross–domain attributes and it is not discussed how different domain–specific QoS attributes can aggregate over workflow constructs. The same authors [8] mentioned that the integrator could specify how the global value for a QoS attribute is computed for a specific process. Differently from them, our approach does not require to necessarily specify aggregation formulae for each process: it would only suffice to define aggregation formulae for pairs QoS–attribute/workflow constructs. Then, the estimated QoS for the whole process is computed automatically. Zeng *et al.* [11] focus more on the optimization problem for workflow bindings based on QoS criteria, which is solved through integer programming techniques. Another work on these issues is by Yu and Lin [10], where a different optimization algorithm is presented. Serhani *et al.* [7] propose a QoS broker-based architecture to support the client in selecting web services based on his/her required QoS.

6 Conclusions

QoS–aware composition and binding represents a challenging mechanism for service–oriented architectures. This paper describes how such a composition can involve not only cross-domain QoS attributes, but also attributes specifically defined for a particular domain or even for a particular application. In that case the service integrator can define domain–specific attributes together with customized aggregation formulae. This permits to estimate the attribute value over a workflow, to determine the (near) optimal bindings and, if necessary, trigger re–binding at run–time.

Work–in–progress is devoted to apply the proposed approach to further case studies and to exploit it to automatically generate test cases, using evolutionary testing techniques, with the aim of violating the SLA in case the latter includes some constraints over domain–specific QoS attributes.

Acknowledgments

This work is framed within the European Commission VI Framework IP Project SeCSE (Service Centric System Engineering) (*http://secse.eng.it*), Contract No. 511680.

References

1. R. Aggarwal, K. Verma, J. Miller, and W. Milnor. Constraint driven web service composition in METEOR-S. In *Proc. IEEE International Conference on Services Computing (SCC'04)*, pages 23–30, Shanghai, China, Sept. 2004.
2. G. Canfora, M. Di Penta, R. Esposito, and M. L. Villani. An Approach for QoS-aware Service Composition based on Genetic Algorithms. In *Proc. of the Genetic and Computation Conference (GECCO'05)*, pages 1069–1075, Washington, USA, June 2005. ACM.
3. G. Canfora, M. Di Penta, R. Esposito, and M. L. Villani. QoS-Aware Replanning of Composite Web Services. In *Proc. International Conference on Web Services (ICWS'05)*, pages 121–129, Orlando, FL, Jul. 2005. IEEE.
4. J. Cardoso. *Quality of Service and Semantic Composition of Workflows.* PhD thesis, Univ. of Georgia, 2002.
5. J. Cardoso, A. P. Sheth, J. A. Miller, J. Arnold, and K. J. Kochut. Modeling quality of service for workflows and web service processes. *Web Semantics Journal: Science, Services and Agents on the World Wide Web Journal*, 1(3):281–308, 2004.
6. H. Ludwig, A. Keller, A. Dan, R. King, and R. Franck. Web Service Level Agreement (WSLA) language specification. *http://www.research.ibm.com/wsla/WSLASpecV1-20030128.pdf.*
7. M. Serhani, R. Dssouli, A. Hafid, and H. Sahraoui. A QoS broker based architecture for efficient web services selection. In *Proc. International Conference on Web Services (ICWS'05)*, pages 113–120, Orlando, FL, Jul. 2005. IEEE.
8. K. Verma, K. Gomadam, J. Lathem, A. P. Sheth, and J. A. Miller. Semantics enabled dynamic process configuration. Technical report, LDIS, University of Georgia, 2006.
9. J. Warmer and A. Kleppe. *The Object Constraint Language.* AW, 1999.
10. T. Yu and K. Lin. Service Selection Algorithms for Composing Complex Services with Multiple QoS Constraints. In *Proc. 3rd International Conference on Service Oriented Computing (ICSOC'05)*, pages 130–143, Amsterdam, The Netherlands, December 2005. Springer.
11. L. Zeng, B. Benatallah, A. H. H. Ngu, M. Dumas, J. Kalagnanam, and H. Chang. QoS-aware middleware for web services composition. *IEEE Transactions on Software Engineering*, 30(5):311–327, May 2004.

Design of Quality-Based Composite Web Services

F. De Paoli, G. Lulli, and A. Maurino

Università degli Studi di Milano Bicocca
Dipartimento di Informatica, Sistemistica e Comunicazione
{depaoli, lulli, maurino}@disco.unimib.it

Abstract. One of the key factors for successful SOC-based systems is the ability to assure the achievement of Quality of Services. The knowledge and the enforcement of the Quality of Services allows for the definition of agreements that are the basis for any business process. In this paper we discuss a method for the evaluation of qualities associated with services. This method is based on a set of quality evaluation rules that state the relations between Web services quality dimensions and process structure. The method is part of a design methodology that addresses quality issues along the service life-cycle. A case study in the e-placement field is presented to illustrate a practical use of the approach.

1 Introduction

Service Oriented Architecture (SOA) is rapidly evolving to become a business integration architecture that supports the dynamic composition of Web services to enact business processes. For the enactment of business processes the conditions under which certain features are provided are as important as the features themselves. Therefore, models and tools to address the non-functional aspects of a service, such as privacy, security, exception handling, performance, and so on, should be defined for effective service composition.

Traditional approaches to service composition focus on service operations, while there is little attention dedicated to the possibility of composing services with, for instance, different security models. A service is usually implemented by a Web service described by means of a WSDL (Web Service Description Language) interface that includes information on operation signatures and access points. Currently a major effort is devoted to the definition of descriptions that deal with issues beyond WSDL. SLA (Service Level Agreement) [1] and WS-Policy [2] are examples of descriptions of the mutual understandings and expectations of both the service provider and the service requester. These contracts regulate and define matters such as contents, price, delivery process, acceptance and quality criteria, penalties and so on. Semantic descriptions are related to the definition of what a service provides in terms of functionality and how the provided services are supplied in terms of behavior and non-functional properties. Emerging proposals are OWL-S [3] and WSMO [4]. Their aim is to define architectural abstractions and description languages that supply machine

A. Dan and W. Lamersdorf (Eds.): ICSOC 2006, LNCS 4294, pp. 153–164, 2006.

interpretable semantics to facilitate dynamic interoperability, composability, and substitutability.

In this paper, we propose a method for Web service composition to address quality evaluation in composed services. The work is part of an effort in the development of a quality-based design methodology that addresses the non-functional requirements of (composite) services [5]. According to the model-driven development approach [17], the goal is to deliver an enhanced platform independent model (PIM, in Model Driven Architecture terminology) that includes non-functional descriptions.

The methodology includes a customization phase that takes into account the actual profiles of target end-users and service providers. Technical characteristics and user profiles are evaluated with manifold objectives: select a set of candidate services that fulfill the requirements, tune-up the service specification and/or identify the target users for the service. The designer, with the support of the rules discussed in this paper, composes and evaluates the qualities of candidate services that satisfy classes of requests so to be able to support future agreements on the base of specific user requirements. The result is a set of (composite) services that differs on quality attributes, each one depending on the specific set of requirements and composing services.

A composite Web service is composed of a number of Web services that are invoked according to a given execution flow described in a language such as Ws-BPEL. Starting from the distinction proposed in WSDL 1.1 between abstract and concrete service, we introduce the term *abstract service* to represent a service which is only the description of its interface, and the term *concrete service* to refer to fully implemented and described Web services. It is important to underline that only concrete services can be invoked. According with this taxonomy, the proposed quality-based composition model refers to abstract processes that is composed of abstract services only. In our vision each abstract service represents a prototype of a set of concrete services that share the same functional description, but provide different implementations and QoSs. The substitution of each abstract service with a concrete Web service, provides a concrete composite Web service that can be invoked. We identify this activity with the term *concretization*. It is worth noting that successful concretization activities are influenced, at the same time, by the desired quality dimensions and by the process execution flows. To address the issue, we propose a set of metrics (called *quality evaluation rules*) that can be used to evaluate specific QoS dimensions according to specific process language constructs (such as sequence, parallel, switch and loop).

The paper is organized as follow: in Section 2 we present the mathematical formulation of the concretization activity, then Section 3 presents a set of quality evaluation rules that are used according with specific quality dimensions and process language structures. Section 4 discusses the method in a case study that is under development as part of the IST project SEEMP. Section 5 is dedicated to related works and, finally, Section 6 draws some conclusions and outlines future works.

2 Mathematical Model

The structure of a composite abstract Web service can be described as a direct graph $\mathcal{G} = (\mathcal{N}, \mathcal{E})$; where $\mathcal{N}$ is the set of nodes representing abstract services, and $\mathcal{E}$ is the set of arcs that define the execution flow. The abstract process is composed of smaller and homogeneous parts according to their structure. Each part can be classified as a simple service or a group of services, which are structured to form a sequence, a parallel, a switch or a loop. According to [6], a process graph can be collapsed into a single node (i.e., single composite service) by substituting each process-language structure with a Web service that exposes the same functional and QoS description of the original set.

Illustrating with an example, let us consider a generic quality dimension q_i and the Ws-BPEL process in Fig.1(a). The first transformation considers the parallel execution of OperationB, OperationC, and OperationD. The three Web services can be substituted by a new one called OperationBCD (Fig.1(b)) whose quality value is the one obtained by applying the quality evaluation rule (see next) to the three Web services. Then the transformation of the switch structure generates another Web service, OperationFG (Fig.1(c)). Finally, by means of another quality evaluation rule, we obtain the quality dimension q_i of the composite service (Fig.1(d)).

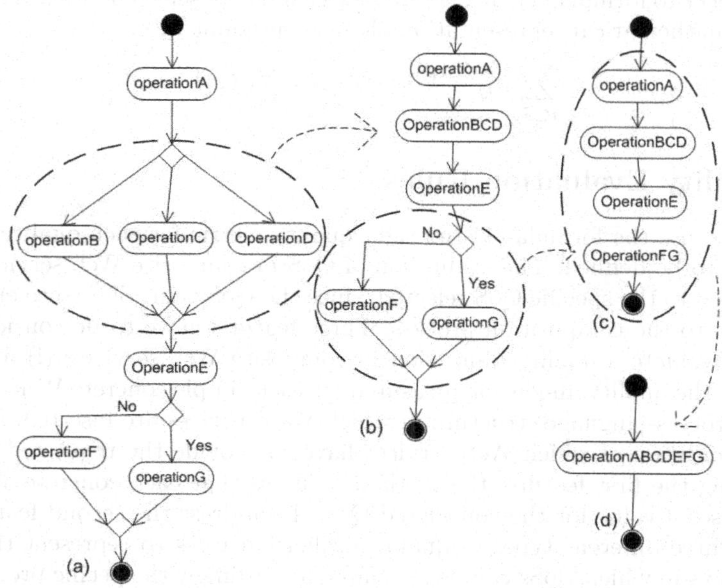

Fig. 1. A stepwise graph transformation

The notation of the model adopted in the sequel is the following:

$\mathcal{S} \equiv$ the set of concrete services;
$\mathcal{A} \equiv$ the set of abstract services;
$\mathcal{C} \equiv$ the set of clients;
$\mathcal{S}_a \subseteq \mathcal{S} \equiv$ the set of concrete services which may implement the abstract one $a \in A$;
$w_c \equiv$ weights assigned by customer c to qualities (vector);
$f_s \equiv$ qualities of the concrete service $s \in \mathcal{S}$ (vector);
$r_c \equiv$ qualities of client $c \in \mathcal{C}$ (vector).

The decision variables are:

$$x_{ij}^c = \begin{cases} 1 & \text{if the abstract service } j \text{ for customer } c \text{ is concretized by the concrete service } i; \\ 0 & \text{otherwise.} \end{cases}$$

The mathematical formulation of the concretization activity is the following:

$$Min \sum_{c \in \mathcal{C}} w_c \cdot (r_c - \theta_c)^+ \quad (1)$$

where θ_c are auxiliary variables representing the vector of the value of the features guaranteed to the client c. $(\cdot)^+$ denotes the positive part of the argument. With respect to formula (1), a concrete service must be selected for each abstract one; the mathematical representation of this constraint is:

$$\sum_{i \in \mathcal{S}_j} x_{ij}^c \geq 1 \qquad \forall c \in \mathcal{C}, \ \forall j \in \mathcal{A}. \quad (2)$$

3 Quality Evaluation Rules

In order to use the formula (1) the right quality metric for each quality dimension need to be defined. The evaluation of QoS in composite Web service is not only related to the specific QoS selected, since the QoS value offered to end users refers also to the composition process. Three features have to be considered in order to evaluate a quality dimension in composite Web services: (i) a quality metric for the quality dimension measured for each simple concrete Web services, (ii) the process-language structure in which Web services are inserted, and (iii) the identification of which Web services have to provide the requested quality. Concerning the first feature, the method assumes that each concrete Web service exposes a value for the considered QoS. To address the second feature, we propose three different types of quality evaluation rules to represent the most typical ways in which QoSs can be evaluated according with specific process language primitives. Finally, according with the specific application domain, quality dimensions can be classified as *local*, if the QoS is provided by a subset of concrete Web services or *global*, if all Web services contribute in the definition of the quality dimension.

The three quality evaluation rules are explained in the next sub sections.

Additive Quality. This quality evaluation rule can be used by designers to evaluate qualities exposing an additive behavior, in a composite Web service. An example of additive QoS is the completion time of a Web service. For a concrete composite service to compute the value of an additive quality, the QoS values of all the service's components are added (in formula, $\sum_{k\in\mathcal{K}} t_c^k$). According to the composition structure, for each component k, the additive quality is computed by one of the following sets of constraints:

$$\text{Sequence } (\mathcal{S}eq_k) \qquad t_c^k = \sum_{j\in\mathcal{S}eq_k, i\in\mathcal{S}_j} t_{ij}\cdot x_{ij}^c \tag{3}$$

$$\text{Parallel } (\mathcal{P}_k) \qquad t_c^k \geq \sum_{i\in\mathcal{S}_j} t_{ij}\cdot x_{ij}^c \qquad \forall j\in\mathcal{P}_k. \tag{4}$$

$$\text{Switch } (\mathcal{S}w_k) \qquad t_c^k \geq t_{ij}\cdot x_{ij}^c \qquad \forall j\in\mathcal{S}w_k,\ \forall i\in\mathcal{S}_j. \tag{5}$$

$$\text{Loop } (\mathcal{L}_k) \qquad t_c^k = l_k\cdot \sum_{j\in\mathcal{L}_k, i\in\mathcal{S}_j} t_{ij}\cdot x_{ij}^c \tag{6}$$

where t_{ij} is the completion time of the concrete service i in executing the abstract service j, and l_k is the expected number of loops executed.

For instance, referring to the example depicted in Figure 1, the service completion time for customer c is given by

$$t_c^A + t_c^{BCD} + t_c^E + t_c^{FG}$$

where t_c^{BCD} is the completion time of the Web services *OperationBCD*, which is the result of a parallel structure. In this case, the completion time corresponds to the longest completion time of *OperationB, OperationC* and *OperationD*. In fact, according with the Ws-BPEL specification, it is not possible, to proceed in the process execution before *OperationsB, OperationsC* and *OperationsD* have been completed. In the formula, t_c^{BCD} is given by the following constraints:

$$t_c^{BCD} \geq \sum_{i\in\mathcal{S}_B} t_{iB}\cdot x_{iB}^c$$

$$t_c^{BCD} \geq \sum_{i\in\mathcal{S}_C} t_{iC}\cdot x_{iC}^c$$

$$t_c^{BCD} \geq \sum_{i\in\mathcal{S}_D} t_{iD}\cdot x_{iD}^c$$

Full Additive Quality. This quality evaluation rule is similar to the previous one. It can be applied to quality dimensions, such as the cost, that involve all concrete Web services. To compute the value of a full additive quality, the constraints given above are still valid, but the one for parallel composition that it needs to be re-formulated as follows:

$$\text{Parallel } (\mathcal{P}_k) \qquad C_c^k = \sum_{j \in \mathcal{P}_k} C_{ij} \cdot x_{ij}^c \tag{7}$$

In this case, all QoS values exposed by concrete services involved in the parallel execution are considered.

Non-additive Quality. It represents quality dimensions that involve a subset of Web services that affect the whole composite service. For example, if a composite Web service is requested to support multichannel provisioning, it is mandatory that at least one of the Web services is able to interact with the users in a multichannel way. Another example is security. In this case, every component has to contribute to the global security, which is represented here as a boolean value (i.e., $0, 1$). The following set of constraints captures this case:

$$\theta_c^{sec} \geq f_s^{sec} \cdot x_{si}^c \qquad \forall s \in \mathcal{S}^i, \ \forall c \in \mathcal{C}, \ \ , \forall i \in \mathcal{N} \setminus \{\mathcal{S}w\}. \tag{8}$$

The sets of constraints presented so far refer to global features of the Web service. On the other hand, some of the requirements can be specific of a service, i.e., local requirements. For instance, by fixing the value of a decision variable $x_{ij} = 1$, an abstract service j is executed by the concrete service i. The following constraint declares that specific features are met by the concrete service s concretizing the abstract service j:

$$\sum_{s \in \mathcal{S}_j} x_{sj}^c \cdot f_s \geq \bar{f}_j \qquad \forall j \in \mathcal{I}, \ \forall c \in \mathcal{C}. \tag{9}$$

4 The Case Study

In this section, an example of Web service composition is discussed. The case study is derived from a larger case study developed within the IST SEEMP project [7], whose goal is to develop a European ePlacement market place.

Public Employment Services (PESes) are becoming more and more important for Public administrations since social implications on sustainability, workforce mobility and equal opportunities are of strategic importance for any central or local government. In our case, we are interested in the development of a service to search for jobs in European countries (e.g., Italy, Ireland and Great Britain). Such a service, *FindJob*, has the following functionalities:

- search for job vacancies in a specified country;
- glue together and rank retrieved job vacancies;

– translate vacancies in different languages; and
– notify end-users of results via different communication channels.

Note that these are *added-value* features that go beyond the simple functionalities to enrich the service in order to fulfill advanced customer requirements better. Users are requested to specify the kind of job he/she is seeking, along with languages spoken and personal contact information (email addresses, mobile phone numbers ...). Language and the job being searched are parameters of the searching job functionality. Contact information is used to identify and use the proper notification channel.

Besides the above functionalities, *FindJob* is requested to meet a set of quality requirements. In particular, we are interested in:

– the duration time to perform the process;
– the cost of the composite service invocation;
– the number of distribution channels on which the answer can be delivered.

Figure 2 shows a possible UML activity diagram representing the Ws-BPEL process including six different abstract Web services. Three kinds of information are supplied: the native language, the job description (MyRequest in the figure) and the communication preferences (MyData).

The service starts with the orchestration engine that registers the user by sending his/her contact information to a *Notification* service that will be in charge

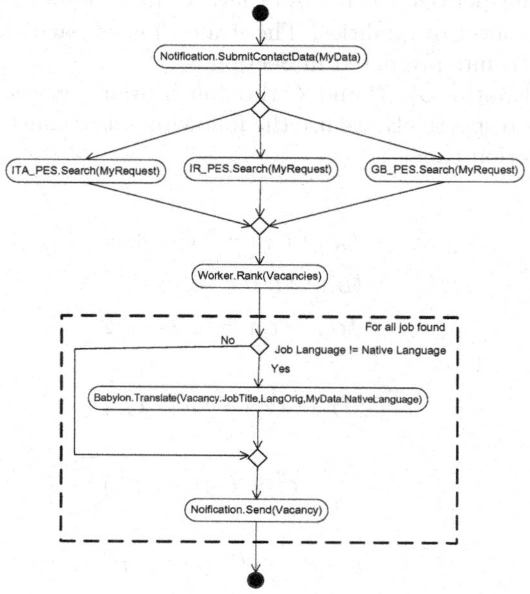

Fig. 2. The case study

of delivering the results. Such a registration might end-up with a failure, which is not discussed here to keep the example simple. Then the orchestration engine invokes the *search* operation on three different PESes, one for each country. These services discover job vacancies according to job descriptions. Discovered job vacancies are inputs for a Web service that sorts the results according to certain criteria (the discussion of which is not of interest in this context). Then for each job vacancy, the process checks the language in which it is written, and, when necessary, invokes a translation Web service. At the end of this operation, the engine invokes the *send* operation of the *Notification* Web service by passing the job vacancy.

Table 1. List of concrete services

ID	Virtual Service	Type	Cost	Answers	Time	Accuracy
1	Job Search	Regular	33	25	100	-
2	//	Premium	100	60	20	-
3	Translation	High Accuracy	100	-	15	1.0
4	//	Low Accuracy	50	-	20	0.0
5	Notification	2 channels	20	-	1	-
6	//	3 channels	50	-	1	-

In Table 1, the available concrete services that implement the abstract services and their qualities are listed. For each abstract service, we consider two possible concrete ones, a cheaper one with a lower level of qualities and a more expensive one with a higher level of qualities. The evaluation of each quality is handled using sets of constraints presented in Section 3.

For instance, denoting A, B and C the Job Search services in Italy, Ireland and Great Britain respectively, we use the following set of constraints to evaluate the service completion time:

$$t^{JS} \geq t_{A,1} \cdot x_{A,1} + t_{A,2} \cdot x_{A,2}$$
$$t^{JS} \geq t_{B,1} \cdot x_{B,1} + t_{B,2} \cdot x_{B,2}$$
$$t^{JS} \geq t_{C,1} \cdot x_{C,1} + t_{C,2} \cdot x_{C,2}$$

$$t^{T} \geq t_{T,3} \cdot x_{T,3} + t_{T,4} \cdot x_{T,4}$$

$$t^{\mathcal{L}} = l \cdot (t_T + t^N)$$

$$t = t^{\mathcal{L}} + t^{JS} + t^N + t^R$$

where t^{JS}, t^T, t^R, t^N are the execution times of search, translation, rank and notification activities, respectively. $t^{\mathcal{L}}$ is the execution time of the loop which depends on the number l of iterations. Finally, t is the completion time of the composite Web service. Similar constraints (see Section 3) should be added to the mathematical definition in order to evaluate the full set of qualities.

In this case study, we identified 8 possible processes. For instance, a process can be composed of the following concrete services: the 2-channel service for the Notification, the High-Accuracy service for the Translation and the Premium service for the Job Search (service pattern P-HA-2ch). In this case, by applying the computational formulas presented in Section 2, the cost and the time of the process are 420 and 2409 respectively. In Table 2, the global qualities for each process are reported.

Table 2. Computed qualities of the alternative processes

Service Pattern	Time	Cost	Channel	Accuracy
R-HA-2ch	1381	220	2	1
R-HA-3ch	1381	250	3	1
R-LA-2ch	1781	170	2	0
R-LA-3ch	1781	200	3	0
P-HA-2ch	2409	420	2	1
P-HA-3ch	2409	450	3	1
P-LA-2ch	3149	370	2	0
P-LA-3ch	3149	400	3	0

According to the weights assigned by each customer or class of customers to the qualities, the customer can be served by a specific process. For instance, a customer who is interested only in minimizing the cost will be served with the services R-LA-2ch (Regular Job Search service, Low-Accuracy Translation service and 2-channel Notification service), which deliver the cheapest process.

5 Related Works

The issue of quality of services is getting increasing consideration in the service-oriented literature (for example [8], and [9]); the focus, however, is often in modeling issues rather than in the design process. The problem of evaluating QoS dimensions in composite Web services is faced in [10], [11], and [12] where a set of composition rules is defined to evaluate the global value of a QoS dimension according to specific workflow patterns. However, the problem of joint design of services and their qualities is not addressed.

Concerning papers addressing QoS issues in design processes, [13] presents the ADD (Attibute-Drived Design) method, which is based on understanding the relationship between software qualities and the architectural mechanisms used to achieve these qualities. The lack of a quality model that can help the designer to identify and relate qualities is a drawback. Moreover, ADD is tailored for generic software development, without specific focus on SOA. Dealing with web services, [14] presents a QoS model, addressing time, cost, and reliability dimensions. The model computes the quality of service for workflows automatically based on QoS attributes of an atomic task. This QoS model is then implemented on the top of the METEOR workflow system. [15] presents a fixed QoS model for the Self-serv model-driven design and an approach to select the optimal set of Web services according to QoS. The limited and fixed number of QoS dimensions considered reduces the possibility of adopting this approach in different application domains. Finally, QoS is considered in [16] to improve the outcome of web services discovery.

6 Conclusions

The non-functional properties, often referred to Quality of Services, are one of the most relevant issues in service-oriented architectures. In fact, the capability of describing, composing, evaluating and monitoring qualities associated with services is critical to the effective enactment of business processes.

This paper proposed and discussed a method to support the design processes to deliver (composite) services augmented with quality descriptions which can be exploited for service and agreement descriptions. The method helps in describing and evaluating generic qualities.

The scope of the mathematical model presented can be twofold. First, the model can be used to define a set of processes according to the desired qualities. The mathematical model suggests which concrete services have to be selected to implement the abstract services. The selection of concrete services depends on the classes of customers that will use the composite Web service and other requirements established by the Web service designer, such us budget constraints, service-level agreements, etc. Once the concrete services have been selected, many alternative processes can be identified.

Second, the model addresses the issue related to process selection. It supports the selection of the process to be supplied to each class of customers according to their quality requirements and the weights assigned to each quality by the customer.

The work presented here needs to be further developed to reach maturation, but we believe that the path is promising. We are studying the integration of the quality model presented in this paper with WSMoD [5] a methodology for the design of QoS-aware Web service. In particular we want to enrich the ontology approach adopted in WSMoD to facilitate both the understanding and the sharing of concepts. The aim is to let independent organizations, developers, and providers rely on common understandings, which is the basis for every future development. This understanding should go beyond the syntax barriers of XML/RDF dialects in order to enable semantic, and possibly automatic enactment of business processes. The association of evaluation rules with concepts (i.e. qualities) enhances the computing capabilities of the approach. Moreover, we are currently developing a visual tool which is implemented as part of the Eclipse development environment to support WSMoD. The capabilities of expressing and evaluating qualities will allow the different players -business clients, developers and providers- to understand each others and build tools to support aspects other than design, such as discovery and selection of services, contracts definition and monitoring.

Acknowledgements

The work presented in this paper has been partially supported by the European IST project n. 27347 SEEMP - Single European Employment Market-Place and the Italian FIRB project RBNE05XYPW NeP4B - Networked Peers for Business.

References

1. Dan, A., Davis, D., Kearney, R., Keller, A., King, R.P., Kuebler, D., Ludwig, H., Polan, M., Spreitzer, M., Youssef, A.: Web services on demand: Wsla-driven automated management. IBM Systems Journal **43**(1) (2004) 136–158
2. VA: Web services policy framework (ws-policy). Technical report, BEA Systems Inc., International Business Machines Corporation, Microsoft Corporation, Inc., SAP AG, Sonic Software, and VeriSign Inc (2006)
3. Martin, D.L., Paolucci, M., McIlraith, S.A., Burstein, M.H., McDermott, D.V., McGuinness, D.L., Parsia, B., Payne, T.R., Sabou, M., Solanki, M., Srinivasan, N., Sycara, K.P.: Bringing semantics to web services: The owl-s approach. In Cardoso, J., Sheth, A.P., eds.: SWSWPC. Volume 3387 of Lecture Notes in Computer Science., Springer (2004) 26–42
4. Lausen, H., Roman, D., Keller, U.: Web service modeling ontology (wsmo). Technical report, DERI (2004)
5. Comerio, M., De Paoli, F., Grega, S., Maurino, A., Batini, C.: Wsmod: a methodology for qos-based web services design. International Journal of Web Services Research (2007)
6. Jaeger, M.C., Rojec-Goldmann, G., Mühl, G.: Qos aggregation for web service composition using workflow patterns. [17] 149–159
7. VA: Single European Employment Market-Place. http://www.seemp.org/, (IST SEEMP project n. 27347)
8. Menascé, D.A.: Composing web services: A qos view. IEEE Internet Computing **8**(6) (2004) 88–90
9. Patil, A.A., Oundhakar, S.A., Sheth, A.P., Verma, K.: Meteor-s web service annotation framework. In Feldman, S.I., Uretsky, M., Najork, M., Wills, C.E., eds.: WWW, ACM (2004) 553–562
10. Raje, R.R., Bryant, B.R., Olson, A.M., Auguston, M., Burt, C.C.: A quality-of-service-based framework for creating distributed heterogeneous software components. Concurrency and Computation: Practice and Experience **14**(12) (2002) 1009–1034
11. Ulbrich, A., Weis, T., Geihs, K.: Qos mechanism composition at design-time and runtime. In: ICDCS Workshops, IEEE Computer Society (2003) 118–
12. Weis, T., Ulbrich, A., Geihs, K., Becker, C.: Quality of service in middleware and applications: A model-driven approach. [17] 160–171
13. Bachmann, F., Bass, L.J.: Introduction to the attribute driven design method. In: ICSE, IEEE Computer Society (2001) 745–746

14. Cardoso, J., Sheth, A.P., Miller, J.A., Arnold, J., Kochut, K.: Modeling quality of service for workflows and web service processes. J. Web Sem. **1**(3) (2004) 281–308
15. Zeng, L., Benatallah, B., Ngu, A.H.H., Dumas, M., Kalagnanam, J., Chang, H.: Qos-aware middleware for web services composition. IEEE Trans. Software Eng. **30**(5) (2004) 311–327
16. Ran, S.: A framework for discovering web services with desired quality of services attributes. In Zhang, L.J., ed.: ICWS, CSREA Press (2003) 208–213
17. 8th International Enterprise Distributed Object Computing Conference (EDOC 2004), 20-24 September 2004, Monterey, California, USA, Proceedings. In: EDOC, IEEE Computer Society (2004)

AMPol-Q: Adaptive Middleware Policy to Support QoS

Raja Afandi, Jianqing Zhang, and Carl A. Gunter

University of Illinois Urbana-Champaign, Urbana, IL 61801, USA
afandi@illinoisalumni.org, {jzhang24, cgunter}@cs.uiuc.edu

Abstract. There are many problems hindering the design and development of Service-Oriented Architectures (SOAs), which can dynamically discover and compose multiple services so that the quality of the composite service is measured by its End-to-End (E2E) quality, rather than that of individual services in isolation. The diversity and complexity of QoS constraints further limit the wide-scale adoption of QoS-aware SOA. We propose extensions to current OWL-S service description mechanisms to describe QoS information of all the candidate services. Our middleware based solution, *AMPol-Q*, enables clients to discover, select, compose, and monitor services that fulfil E2E QoS constraints. Our implementation and case studies demonstrate how AMPol-Q can accomplish these goals for web services that implement messaging.

Keywords: AMPol-Q, WSEmail, Adaptive Middleware, Policy, Service Oriented Architecture, QoS, Dynamic Service Discovery, Security, Ontologies.

1 Introduction

Although there has been considerable attention devoted to the composition of functional properties in Service Oriented Architectures (SOAs), more work is needed to deal with *non-functional* Quality of Service (QoS) properties such as reliability, performance and security required by clients. Issues that need attention include providing QoS features at the level of the individual service and client, discovering and composing candidate services on the basis of QoS features, monitoring and ensuring that a promised QoS is actually provided during execution, and adopting and using QoS-aware SOAs on a large scale. At least three problems must be overcome. First, current approaches [1,2,3] for dynamic service discovery and composition do not provide a *global* view of QoS features about all candidate services prior to invocation. They are limited to discovering first-level immediate services, and each individual service is responsible for discovering other services independently. They also lack the comprehensive specification of QoS features. Second, QoS is not compositional in the sense that functional features expressed through interfaces or functional components are composed to achieve a composite functionality (*e.g.* workflow systems). QoS-based composition requires complex calculations of *aggregate* QoS values of multiple entities involved in a transaction. Participants are interested in the final aggregate value of the runtime global QoS (*e.g.* end-to-end delay, overall cost, global integrity and confidentiality). However, current QoS-aware systems are not able to support global QoS behavior. Third, and finally, QoS-aware service composition and negotiation may not be effective without monitoring. Most QoS-aware systems do not guarantee that an agreed quality of service is

A. Dan and W. Lamersdorf (Eds.): ICSOC 2006, LNCS 4294, pp. 165–178, 2006.

actually provided during execution. Existing QoS-monitoring approaches [4,5] rely on trusted third parties to centrally monitor QoS delivered by service providers. This is technically difficult and limited to QoS features like availability and performance, while security and privacy cannot be covered. Moreover, monitoring involves complex and domain-specific logic for measuring and verifying QoS, which make the task harder.

To address these problems, we have developed an *Adaptive Middleware Policy to Support QoS (AMPol-Q)*. Our approach is based on an integrated collection of reference frameworks for description, discovery, and monitoring that are specially suited to handle QoS features in a SOA. The *description framework* includes semantic model for capturing QoS requirements, constraints and capabilities. We extend current service description and advertisement mechanisms (OWL-S and UDDI) to gather QoS information about all the candidate services. For efficient implementation, we represent these QoS requirements as policy rules. In the *discovery framework*, AMPol-Q serves as a broker (at the client end) for dynamically discovering and composing matched services on the basis of functional as well as non-functional features. The candidate services are first discovered on the basis of their functional capabilities and the final set of services is selected according to their QoS features. This approach is capable of evaluating global quality requirements and applying different types of optimizations (such as context-aware optimizations) to select the best-matched services. It negotiates the QoS properties between service providers and consumers to create an agreement. The *monitoring framework* provides an agile and adaptive mechanism to automatically plug in customized modules for measuring, verifying and ensuring QoS features without modifying the baseline system. We use a technique [6] in which the QoS contracts are monitored at each individual participant. Furthermore we improve on distributed monitoring approaches by providing support for two-way specialization.

We validated AMPol-Q with a prototype implementation and a case study on WSEmail [7] that shows how AMPol-Q can enhance the function of email messaging systems by enabling automatic deployment and use of complex QoS features like cycle exhaustion puzzles, reverse Turing tests and identity based encryption without the need for global deployment or changes to the baseline system. This case study shows how SOA can support QoS-aware service discovery, selection and monitoring.

2 Description Framework

The AMPol-Q *description* framework is a collection of interoperable semantic models used to represent QoS features of all entities in SOA. These QoS ontology and policy models, which are extensions to current service description frameworks [8,9,10,11], are intended for global discovery and selection of candidate services on the basis of QoS features. They are based on layered semantic models (*QoS Ontology, Policy* and *Entity Profile*). The steps of describing QoS features are a series of bottom up instantiations of these models. We use semantic models because they can be easily extended with new concepts. Furthermore, existing reasoning tools can be applied on the semantic models to detect ambiguity or inconsistency. Our discussion focus on novel features related to capturing global QoS behavior and to achieve support for E2E Global QoS.

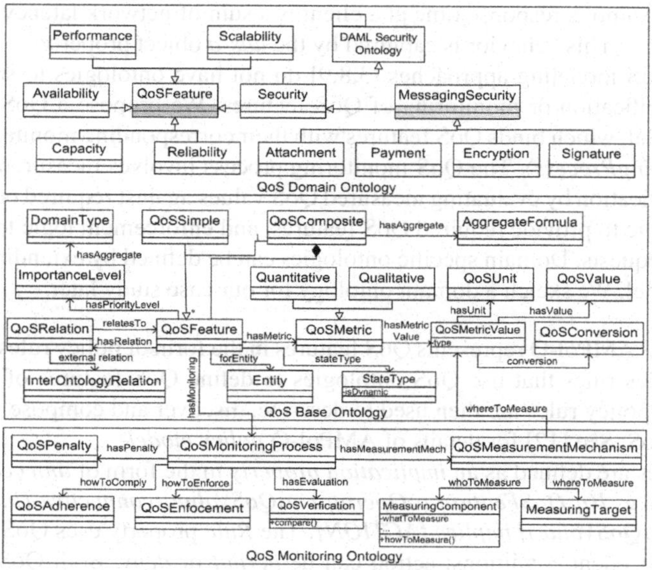

Fig. 1. AMPol-Q QoS Model

Semantic QoS Ontology Model. Our semantic QoS ontology model provides a standard generic ontology 2for arbitrary QoS features. It defines the nature of associations between QoS concepts, QoS metrics, and the way they are measured and monitored. Figure 1 shows the detailed ontology model. To facilitate reusability and extensibility, the ontology has a modular design and is categorized into three models: *base, monitoring* and *domain*.

In the QoS base ontology model, each QoS feature is an instance of a class *QoSFeature*, and it is associated to a *Quantitative* or *Qualitative* property. *Quantitative* relates the attributes which can be measured by numbers with a particular unit. For example, the percentage availability of a service. *Qualitative* relates to attributes which cannot necessarily be measured by exact amount. For example, the obligation features such as requirement of data encryption or providing an X.509 certificate.

In the context of global QoS, we define *QoSSimple* and *QoSCopmosite* as subclasses of *QoSFeature*. *QoSComposite* represents complex global QoS features which are drawn from calculation of aggregate QoS values. For example, the formula for composite service availability is the *product* of availability measure of each participant service. The computational logic is captured by *AggregateFormula*. Different entities may specify QoS values (*QoSMetricValue*) with different units (*e.g.* 90% versus 0.90 or 50F versus 10C). The unit conversion is done by *QoSConversion*, which captures the conversion logic. In global QoS, there are dependencies and correlations between QoS features. For example, some QoS values are inversely proportional each other, *e.g.* the service response time and the throughput; some are directly proportional, *e.g.* accessibility and availability. *QoSRelation* class captures these relationship types. Some composite QoS is measured from aggregate values of different types of related QoS feature. For example, response time at a client is a sum of network latency and service processing time. This behavior is captured by the *has-a* object property.

Current QoS modeling approaches [3,8,9] do not have ontologies to support measurement, verification or monitoring of QoS features. We propose a QoS monitoring ontology model, which binds QoS features with their corresponding monitoring process (*QoSMonitoringProcess*). The QoS monitoring process involves measurement of QoS features, verification by evaluating measured QoS values against required policy values, adherence logic to provide required QoS features, and enforcement logic to *e.g.* permit or deny the requests. Domain specific ontologies can be defined by extending QoS base ontology model. We sketch a domain ontology for our case study later.

Policy Model. AMPol-Q represents QoS features in the form of policy rules. The policy model specifies rules that use QoS ontologies to define QoS features of a particular entity. These policy rules are then used to describe, discover and compose services and to monitor QoS. See [12] for details of AMPol-Q *policy model.*

Policy rules are defined as an *implication property* in the form of *antecedent implies consequent, e.g. [(a:QoSFeature o:Operator a:QoSValue) connective (b:QoSFeature o:Operator b:QoSValue)] implies [ACTION]*. The *Rule* property uses QoS ontology to represent antecedent conditions; action can be *permit* or *deny*. Both QoS constraints and capabilities are described as rules.

For dynamic service composition based on global QoS, the advertised QoSValue can be calculated only if the QoS values of all dependent services are determined. For example, a loan processing service LP provides functionality for acquiring loans from banks. In order to process loan requests it talks to credit reporting agency CR to verify a client credit history and coordinate with bank B for loan processing. Processing time for acquiring a loan (the functionality of the LP service) can be calculated by adding its processing time (*P:QoSFeature*) and processing times of all the dependent services (CR and B). If CR and B are dynamically discovered then LP's processing time cannot be calculated beforehand. Current description languages are not able to handle these kinds of complex QoS features. To solve this problem we introduce a concept of *rule templates*. Rule templates can specify antecedents containing unresolved *template variables*. Antecedents can be evaluated only if all the template variables are determined (during runtime). In the above scenario, say, LA processing time is *50ms*, the capability rule of LA can be represented as *[P:QoSFeature = (50ms:QoSValue + p1:T1 + p2:T2)]*, where *p1* and *p2* are template variables, *T1* and *T2* are templates which are defined as *T1 = ((B.P):QoSValue)* and *T2=((CR.P):QoSValue)*. This problem can also be solved by modeling each QoS feature as a *QoSComposite* object with a *has-a* object property to represent dependent QoS feature values and an *AggregrateFormula* object to represent aggregation logics. But our policy engine implementation has shown that rule templates are simpler to construct and more efficient to evaluate.

AMPol uses meta-specification (the policies of a policy) to specify how polices are evaluated and enforced. For example, in a service oriented environment for monitoring global QoS, the policy model should be able to specify which entities the policy is applied to and which entities enforce them. In a distributed system, the creator of the rule or the policy might not be the entity who will check the enforcement of the policy. So it is necessary to indicate the subject and target of the policies explicitly. Furthermore, by explicitly relating rules to their enforcement and adherence components (QoS monitoring components), our adaptive policy model can take the policy conformance and enforcement logics for each individual quality requirement out of the core application. This is beneficial for monitoring QoS features in a flexible and dynamic manner. Each *Rule* or *RuleSet* has associated meta-information, which is captured through the class *MetaSpecification*. *MetaSpecification* has *Subject*, which is the entity the rule or rules set will be applicable to (entity providing QoS feature), and *Target*, which is the entity enforcing the rule or rules set (entity assuring QoS is met). It uses *Transformation* and *QoSMonitoringProcess* for policy enforcement.

The policy model aids wide-scale adoption of complex and dynamic QoS features. The policy language is generic enough so that the policy semantic schema and core components (policy engine, inference engine, merging, comparison, conflict resolution and so on) do not need to be modified by the addition of new assertions. Addition and execution of associated third-party components is also policy driven (*extension policies*).

Entity Profile Model. Finally, we propose a construct named *profile* which captures everything required to specify QoS features. It can be associated with a system entity and can be advertised. Thus, clients can use it to discover desired services. Entity profiles represents entities' QoS capabilities, constraints, extension constraints, service dependencies and dependent request templates. The client profile contains only QoS capabilities, QoS constraints, and extension constraints.

The entity profile model supports end-to-end global QoS better than current service description and advertisement mechanisms such as OWL-S. Unlike current approaches, every service description in AMPol-Q explicitly specifies a list of its dependent services so that the discovery mechanisms can gather global QoS information about all the candidate services. Furthermore, we propose *service request templates*, a functional request based on IOPE attributes [13], to enhance dynamic services discovery. These templates have static IOPE attributes and dynamic IOPE template variables which can be instantiated using the client functional request's IOPE attributes. Each service provides the templates for their dependent services and the third party can use them to discover other services.

We use OWL to implement the QoS model and core policy model constructs. Policy rules are written using SWRL language constructs, which use an ontology vocabulary described by the QoS model in OWL. The benefit of using this two layer approach is that, first by using OWL, it is possible to perform reasoning over the knowledge model (QoS model) and the policy rules, and second, by the use of SWRL policy rules and underlying policy framework, the system's QoS behavior can be controlled without any ambiguity. Details of the implementation are given in [12].

3 Discovery Framework

Discovery framework consists of *Service Discovery and Chaining*, *Global QoS Analysis and Policy Agreement* and *Contract Negotiation*. It provides mechanisms for discovering global QoS information about all the candidate services, selecting best matched

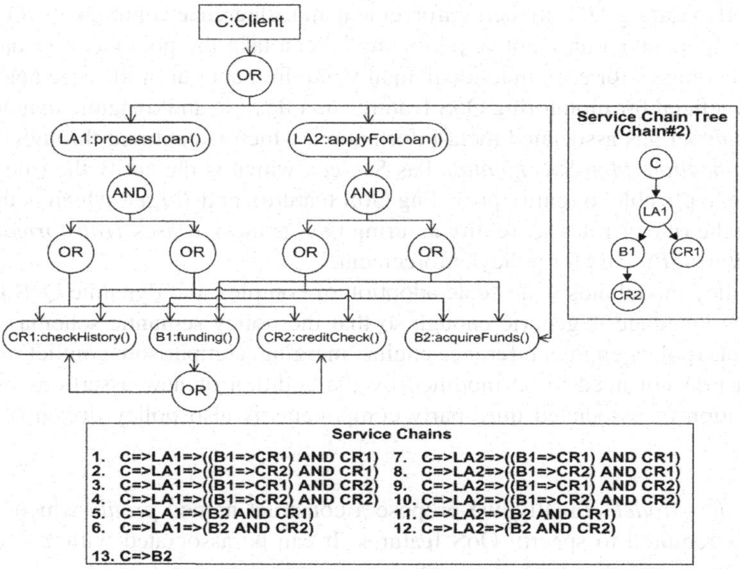

Fig. 2. Service Chain Graph

services and binding selected parties in a QoS contract. As mentioned in Section 1, QoS based service composition requires complex calculations of aggregate and global QoS values, which makes it hard to work with QoS features without global analysis. We will show how this section addresses issues related toGlobal QoS based service composition.

Service Discovery and Chaining. The framework initiates a discovery process on behalf of a client. First the immediate-level services are discovered by using conventional IOPE based discovery approach. IOPE based request is send to a registry or directory service, which returns a list of services matched on the basis of functional IOPE attributes. We extend the discovery approach proposed by [14] to return AMPol-Q entity profile for the selected services. For each first-level service, the IOPE base discovery process is re-run to gather profiles of its dependent services. The IOPE request for discovering dependant services is generated from the request templates associated with a dependent service. The template variables are first assigned values from the available IOPE information of client or other services and then fully populated request is used for discovering profiles of dependent services.

Service discovery process continues until the profiles of all the candidate services are discovered. This global information can be modeled as an AND-OR graph called Service Chain Graph (SCG). In the SCG, an OR combination shows the option of choosing one of the candidate service and an AND combination represents dependent services which must be composed. Figure 2 shows a SCG for the example of loan processing agency we discussed before. In this example, we have an option of two candidate services for each type. Client has an option of getting loan either from loan processing agencies or directly from a bank. Only bank B2 directly deals with small business clients. Loan processing agencies are dependant on credit reporting agencies and banks. Bank B1 independently verifies the credit score of a client from an external credit reporting service, while bank B2 has its own internal credit reporting department. By doing a traversal on SCG we can easily extract service chains (SC). Service chain represents a set of services which can provide a required service functionality. Global QoS analysis is done on each service chain to select a best candidate chain for final execution. For the above example, we have thirteen possible service chains. Service chain are further modeled as a tree to simplify the global QoS analysis and policy matching.

Global QoS Analysis and Policy Agreement. Global QoS analysis has two steps: 1) pre-process QoS information; 2) match the policies and create a contract. These steps are repeated for each service chain in a SCG to create a list of policy contracts with associated agreement value.

Pre-processing is to map the global QoS requirements and capabilities to each individual node so that policy matching and agreement can be done independently between two nodes. It involves normalizing ontologies, filling rule templates, calculating aggregate QoS values, propagating rules and associating different entities with constraint rules. For example, for service chain 5 in Fig 2, the aggregate availability of the composite services (LA1, B2 and CR2) will be calculated by the product of availability value of each individual service, and then either a new capability rule is added to represent this value (e.g. in case of a broker) or the capability value of first level service (LA1) is replaced by the calculated aggregate value. Similarly, suppose client has a requirement of end-to-end message confidentiality then this constraint is propagated to all the services in the chain, so that during policy matching phase it can be compared against capabilities of each service.

Next, to find out whether a node fulfills the QoS requirements or not, QoS constraints are matched with QoS capabilities. For any constraint, if there is no matching capability (or capability is not sufficient enough) then there must be an associated capability module (adherence logic). Every rule can have associated adherence, verification and enforcement modules. If external capability is required then it must be checked against extension policy restrictions of that node. QoS requirement rule can only be satisfied if there is a matching capability rule available or there is an extension module available to provide the QoS capability and there are no extension restrictions on this module.

At last, a policy contract is created and an agreement value is assigned. Policy contract contains all entities in a service chain along with their capabilities and imposed constraints. Agreement value is penalized for every non-resolvable conflict, missing associated capability, no associated monitoring module, restricted extension modules *etc.* The service chains in which entities cannot fulfill the QoS requirements of each other are heavily penalized and hence have less chance of getting selected.

Contract Negotiation. The contract with maximum agreement value in the policy contract list is selected, verified and signed from each entity in the service chain. The terms of the contract imply that the entities in question will comply with all the QoS constraints and will provide agreed upon QoS behavior. Policy contract is sent to each party in a service chain. Each individual entity verifies the contract policies against its private policies (if any). If a contract is rejected by any entity in a service chain then a next best contract is chosen for agreement. Negotiation process continues until all the entities agree on a particular contract. Because our service selection approach is based on global QoS information, it is able to select best set of services, while most existing approaches [14,13,15,3,1] can only select the first available matched service(s). Contract negotiation phase is optional but it provides assurance of a desired QoS from all entities even if capabilities or constraints are not advertised.

The discovery framework uses the Jena ontology inference engine and SWRL virtual machine to parse, normalize and compare policies. More implementation details are given in the [12].

4 QoS Monitoring Framework

Adaptive Middleware for QoS Monitoring. Monitoring involves measuring delivered QoS, verifying QoS features and taking enforcement actions. AMPol-Q is an agile and adaptive middleware framework that enables the participants to adapt to QoS features of others during runtime. It is realized by two-way specialization, which extracts the logic of measuring QoS values and verifying and enforcing QoS policies by third party customized and pluggable components. These components are called *extensions*. This is executed in the way described by *extension policies*. The QoS features in a policy contract are associated with these extensions and can be dynamically added or removed per collaboration. In order to support a new QoS behavior, we do not need to change the core of the application. Instead AMPol-Q middleware can locate, load and execute new extensions automatically. The whole procedure is called *system extension*. We have used a middleware approach to mask problems of heterogeneity and distribution. Its flexibility and extensibility helps to support dynamic QoS, fine-grained policy control and seamless system evolution. It hides the implementation complexity from the core application logic and the functionality provided can be re-used by different applications. The discovery framework is also a part of the AMPol-Q middleware, which acts as a broker at the client end for discovering and selecting services. Figure 3shows different components of the AMPol-Q middleware.

Entities in a service chain must be capable of providing requested QoS features, fulfilling QoS requirements, or complying with QoS constraints. We call this an *adherence logic*. First we need to distinguish between two types of QoS features, pluggable and non-pluggable. Pluggable QoS can be supported independently without any significant change to the core application, *e.g.* an encryption algorithm. Non-pluggable QoS features that cannot be supported by just adding an external capability, *e.g.* processing time or network bandwidth. Generally, qualitative features (capabilities) are likely to be pluggable more often than quantitative ones. A specialization can only be applied to a pluggable QoS feature. QoS capabilities may be pluggable through adherence components, while logic for QoS measurements, verification and enforcement for both qualitative and quantitative QoS features are easily pluggable.

The monitoring framework has three core components: QoS measurement, policy verification, and policy enforcement. Each component is heavily reliant on extensions.

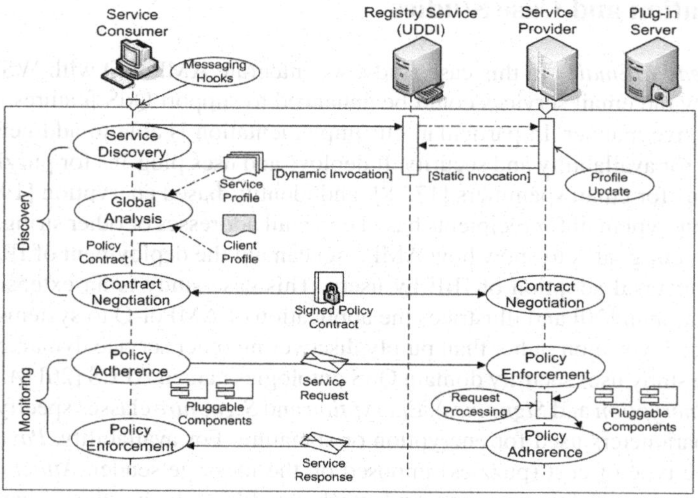

Fig. 3. AMPol-Q Middleware

The service invocation process starts with the interpretation of policy contract at the client side. It executes a series of verification and adherence extensions on a request message to provide required QoS for a target service. On receiving a request, the service middleware first verifies the QoS constraint imposed by a service on the client. According to verification result the enforcement logic either rejects the request or forwards it to the service. Once the response is ready, the verification logic verifies that a response complies with client constraints. If the verification fails, the pluggable adherence logic is executed to conform the response message with the client constraints. On receiving a response, the client verifies the QoS delivered by the service, which may involve measuring QoS through extensions. If verification fails, then the enforcement mechanism will take actions accordingly. The QoS policies are verified, adhered or enforced on a point-to-point basis, but eventually they all comply with global QoS constraint and requirements.

Extension Manager. The extension manager manages extension components and the system extension process. Extension management is controlled by extension policies, in which extensions are downloaded and executed only if extension policies allow doing so. Extension policies may restrict a type of extension to be only downloadable from a particular trusted extension server or may restrict the execution of an extension to allow limited access to the system resources (such as sandbox execution). Additionally, The system extension has a meta-level control over the adaptation process to ensure that the changes are effective.

Modules of the monitoring framework are implemented in C# and the extensions are packaged in separate DLLs. Details are given in the [12].

5 Validation and Case Studies

Policy-Based WSEmail. In this case study, we integrate AMPol-Q with WSEmail [7] to show how the email services could be enhanced to support QoS features in an end-to-end adaptive manner. In particular, our implementation is able to add new QoS requirements for availability and security. It deploys and uses plug-ins for puzzles [16] to raise burdens for email spammers [17,18], and identity-based encryption [19] to allow senders to encrypt mail for recipients based on email addresses or other strings. As with the puzzles, our goal is to show how AMPol-Q can aid the deployment of IBE without requiring universal adoption of IBE by users. This case study is an extension of our implementation in [20] and illustrates the application of AMPol-Q to systems based on static service invocation rather than purely discovering other service dynamically.

The case study uses security domain QoS ontologies named APES [20] (*Attachment, Payment, Encryption* and *Signature*). *Encryption* and *Signature* classes specify the cryptographic parameters used for encryption or signature. For availability, *Payment* class specifies the type of cost (puzzles) imposed on the message sender. *Attachment* class specifies the patterns of the messages and attachment files, which is the primary medium for spreading viruses.

There are four entities involved in the system, the Sender Mail User Agent (SMUA), the Sender Mail Transfer Agent (SMTA), the Recipient MTA (RMTA) and the Recipient MUA (RMUA). MTAs advertise their clients and their own entity profiles, which are merged with client profiles for simplicity. MTAs entity profiles also contain dependent services (Relays or RMTAs) and their request templates, which can be used to dynamically discover dependent MTAs. These request templates also specify a mechanism to discover relaying MTAs by providing a reference to an extension e.g. a plugin for querying local DNS server for finding next hop MTA. In the example settings we map a MTA to a single relay per email address domain, which is in fact a target RMTA. So in this case we only have one service chain with three entities (SMUA $\Longrightarrow$ SMTA $\Longrightarrow$ RMTA). Also there is a third-party trusted plugin-server which hosts the extensions. For the current setup we show how the SMUA can automatically adapt to the QoS constraints of the target services (SMTA, RMTA and RMUA).

The MUA's AMPol-Q middleware is configured as a broker for discovering profiles of other entities. AMPol-Q first requests an SMTA entity profile and then fills in the dependency request templates; this only requires email addresses for the users. It invokes a pluggable discovery component to retrieve the merged entity profile of the RMTA. Because there is only one service chain, a single contract is created with an agreement value and simply send to other entities for QoS monitoring. Messages sent by the SMUA are verified against the contract and accordingly adherence extensions are downloaded and executed to conform the message with required QoS constraints. At the SMTA, the received message is first verified by the middleware and then processed by the SMTA application (if the verification succeeds). When the message is relayed to the RMTA, it is again verified and then forwarded to the RMUA. QoS discovery, verification, measurement, adherence and enforcement mechanisms are provided through pluggable extensions which are automatically downloaded from a trusted third party plug-in servers.

Web Based WSEmail. Based on WSEmail, this case study realizes AMPol-Q for typical web-based applications. Here a web browser client (CB) and a web application server (AS) adapt themselves to accommodate QoS aware service discovery and monitoring. The motivation behind this case study is that most of the client applications in SOA are web based and we try to show that how easily AMPol-Q can enable these client applications to be QoS aware.

We extended WSEmail by providing an application server and a browser-based MUA instead of the WSEmail MUA. We also extended it to provide a multi-hop and multi-relay topology to dynamically discover relays. Profiles are advertised on a UDDI-based server instead of relying on DNS entries. On receiving an HTTP request from a MUA browser, the application server internally talks to the WSEmail MTA and replies with an HTML page. In contrast to previous case study, it is not possible for the web client to do dynamic discovery and selection of services and to publish or advertise its QoS policies.

Our implementation considers AS and CB to be two independent entities with their own QoS features. CB does not need to discover any services as it statically invokes AS, while AS dynamically discovers other services. HTTP request from a CB is intercepted by AMPol-Q middleware and it first sends a modified HTTP request for service selection along with CB's QoS policies and functional intent to AS. The corresponding AMPol-Q middleware component at AS receives the request and initiates the service discovery based on CB request. We consider each AS application (for example, servlet or asp pages) to be a service interface and like other services, AS should also provide a complete entity profile including request templates to discover other dependent services. In the web-based scenario these profiles do not need to be advertised at registry service as the AS is never dynamically invoked by clients. The final service chain is selected and the contract is negotiated by AS. The communication between AS and CB is done through HTTP requests and responses. Finally the original HTTP request from CB is evaluated against an agreed contract and the final modified HTTP request is sent to AS. On receiving a response message, it is monitored by verifying against agreed contract.

We used Firefox Mozilla v1.5 as the browser and Apache Tomcat (v4.1) as AS. See [12] for the implementation details and video demonstration.

6 Related Work

Different service description (*e.g.* OWL/OWLS, Web Service Modeling Ontology) and QoS models [1,8,9] represent services with both functional and non-functional requirements, but they do not provide explicit support for compositional QoS and E2E service discovery. The OWL-S process model has implicit information about dependent services, but this information is not useful for discovering other services. Additionally, the QoS models in these works do not capture monitoring and compositional aspects. There are studies [2,3,14,21] on QoS aware dynamic discovery and composition of services, but these are not able to discover or compose services on the basis of E2E global QoS features and do not provide sufficient support for continuously changing QoS requirements. There is no comprehensive specification that states how dynamic selection and invocation of services is to be performed on the bases of QoS features.

There are efforts on contract monitoring [5,6] and mediating services [4,15] through trusted third parties, but these approaches are based on local criteria and do not address the global end-to-end QoS assurance problem of the composite business services. Different policy frameworks [10,11] are used to enforce requirements for individual entities. Adaptability is achieved by adding, customizing or replacing entities such as aspects [22], components, or concerns [23]. Existing efforts assume a built-in logic to support and ensure QoS policy constraints (QoS requirements) or have a static binding with external processing components to handle policy rules. AMPol-Q provides a more flexible approach because it takes the QoS logic out of the core application and provides it in a form of pluggable extensions.

There is a work [24] on a broker-based framework for QoS-aware Web Service (QCWS) composition. It is based on several service selection algorithms used to ensure the E2E QoS of a composite web services. This work addresses the problem of evaluating E2E QoS, but leaves open questions about how to support and ensure them. It also does not address the issue of how to dynamically discover E2E global QoS information.

There is work [25,26] on dynamic adaptation in a service-oriented framework that addresses entities that have different QoS requirements on a per session basis. This work does not provide concrete negotiation protocols and does not explicitly specify which system entity will enforce the policy. [27] is another policy-based effort to achieve E2E adaptability, but it also does not support negotiation of requirements and focuses more on system extensibility and policy framework. DySOA [28] provides a framework for monitoring the application system, evaluating acquired data against the QoS requirements, and adapting the application configuration at runtime. It has a simple manual policy negotiation between the requester and the provider but does not support runtime negotiation. It does not address system extensibility beyond the capability of reconfiguring system parameters. GlueQoS [29] proposes a declarative language based on WS-Policy to specify QoS features and a policy mediation meta-protocol for exchanging and negotiating QoS features. One obvious limitation of GlueQoS is that it does not support dynamic system extensibility. All of above efforts only can handle simple QoS features because WS-Policy framework they use is not generic and adaptive enough to support new types of QoS constraints.

In a related work [30] on messaging systems we explored using XACML to model policies for email systems. In this work policies are used for controlling access to mailing lists. A related effort [20] on adaptive policies uses a 'non-semantic' policy language to model security features. AMPol-Q uses a semantic approach to support more complex policies. [20] is similar to AMPol-Q but it is based on systems with static binding and a more domain-specific focus, while AMPol-Q has a more generic formulation. In other work [31], we explored more sophisticated policy merging mechanisms than the ones in AMPol-Q, but these could perhaps be used for AMPol-Q policies as well.

7 Conclusion

We have introduced AMPol-Q, a policy-driven adaptive middleware for providing E2E support for dynamic QoS features in SOA. Its main contributions are its E2E solution, its adaptive middleware framework for supporting and monitoring QoS features, its generic semantics-aware reference architecture for describing, discovering and composing services on the basis of their non-functional features, and its application of this middleware to the systems based on web services. AMPol-Q differs from other work on adaptation in its focus on exploring an E2E solution for QoS features that incorporates all of the necessary support features. This work also provides one of the most complete studies to date of a proof-of-concept QoS-aware policy system based on Web services. Our future work includes formal security analysis, improved security measures such as sandbox protection, features to support privacy, models for negotiating policies, policy conflict resolution and performance testing.

Acknowledgements

We are grateful for help and encouragement we received from Anne Anderson, Noam Artz, Mike Berry, Jodie Boyer, Rakesh Bobba, Jon Doyle, Omid Fatemieh, Munawar Hafiz, Fariba Khan, Himanshu Khurana, Steve Lumetta, Adam Lee, Kevin D. Lux, Michael J. May, Anoop Singhal, Kaijun Tan. This research was partially supported by NSF CCR02-08996, CNS05-5170, CNS05-09268, and CNS05-24695 and ONR N00014-04-1-0562 and N00014-02-1-0715.

References

1. Zeng, L., Benatallah, B., Ngu, A., Dumas, M., Kalagnanam, J., Chang, H.: Qos-aware middleware for web services composition. In: ITSE'04: IEEE Trans. on Software Engr. (2004)
2. Casati, F., Ilnicki, S., Jin, L., Krishnamoorthy, V., Shan, M.: Adaptive and dynamic service composition in eflow. In: Tech. Report, HPL-200039, Software Tech. Lab. (2000)
3. Zeng, L., Benatallah, B.and Dumas, M., Kalagnanam, J., Sheng, Q.: Quality driven web service composition. In: WWW'03:Proc. of 12th Int. World Wide Web Conf. (2003)
4. Piccinelli, G., Stefanelli, C., Trastour, D.: Trusted mediation for e-service provision in electronic marketplaces. In: Lecture Notes in Computer Science, 2232:39. (2001)
5. Mahbub, K., Spanoudakis, G.: A framework for requirements monitoring of service based systems. (In: ICSOC'04: In Proc. of the 2nd Int. Conf. on Service Oriented Computing)
6. Jurca, R., Faltings, B.: Reputation-based service level agreements for web services. (In: ICSOC'05: In Proc. of the 3rd International Conference on Service Oriented Computing)
7. Lux, K.D., May, M.J., Bhattad, N.L., Gunter, C.A.: WSEmail: Secure Internet messaging based on Web services. In: Int. Conf. on Web Services (ICWS '05), IEEE (2005)
8. Tsesmetzis, D., Roussaki, I.G., Papaioannou, I., Anagnostou, M.E.: Qos awareness support in web-service semantics. In: AICT-ICIW'06. (2006)
9. Dobson, G., Lock, R., Sommerville, I.: Qosont: a qos ontology for service-centric systems. In: EUROMICRO-SEAA'05. (2005)
10. Kagal, L., Paolucci, M., Srinivasan, N., Denker, G., Finin, T., Sycara, K.: Authorization and privacy for semantic web services. (In: AAAI'04: Workshop on Semantic Web Services)
11. Uszok, A., Bradshaw, J.M., Jeffers, R., Johnson, M., Tate, A., Dalton, J., Aitken, S.: Kaos policy management for semantic web services. In: IIS'04: IEEE Intelligent Systems. (2004)
12. AMPol-Q: website. `http://seclab.cs.uiuc.edu/ampol/AMPol-Q` (2006)
13. Sirin, E., Parsia, B., Hendler, J.: Filtering and selecting semantic web services with interactive composition techiques. In: IEEE Intelligent Systems, 19(4). (2004)

14. Pathak, J., Koul, N., Caragea, D., Honavar, V.G.: A framework for semantic web services discovery. In: WIDM05. (2005)
15. Shuping, R.: A model for web service discovery with qos. In: ACM SIGecom. (2003)
16. von Ahn, L., Blum, M., Hopper, N., Langford, J.: CAPTCHA: Using hard AI problems for security. In: Proceedings of Eurocrypt. (2003) 294–311
17. Juels, A., Brainard, J.: Client puzzles: A cryptographic defense against connection depletion attacks. In: NDSS99: Networks and Distributed Security Systems. (1999)
18. Dwork, C., Naor., M.: Pricing via processing or combatting junk mail. In Brickell, E.F., ed.: Proc. CRYPTO 92, Springer-Verlag (1992) 139–147
19. Boneh, D., Franklin, M.: Identity based ecncryption from the Weil pairing. SIAM J. of Computing **32**(3) (2003) 586–615
20. Afandi, R., Zhang, J., Hafiz, M., Gunter, C.A.: AMPol: Adaptive Messaging Policy. In: 4th IEEE European Conference on Web Services (ECOWS'06), Zurich, Switzerland, IEEE, IEEE Conference Publishing Services (2006)
21. Karastoyanova, D., Buchmann, A.: Development life cycle of web service-based business processes. enabling dynamic invocation of web services at run time. In: ICSOC'05: In Proc. of the 3rd International Conference on Service Oriented Computing. (2005)
22. Kiczales, G., Lamping, J., Mendhekar, A., Maeda, C., Lopes, C., Loingtier, J.M., Irwin, J.: Aspect-oriented programming. In Aksit, M., Matsuoka, S., eds.: Proceedings ECOOP '97. Volume 1241 of LNCS., Jyvaskyla, Finland, Springer-Verlag (1997) 220–242
23. Hürsch, W., Lopes, C.V.: Separation of concerns. Technical Report NU-CCS-95-03, College of Computer Science, Northeastern University, Boston, Massachusetts (1995)
24. Yu, T., Lin, K.: Service selection algorithms for composing complex services with multiple qos constraints. In: ICSOC'05: 3rd Int. Conf. on Service Oriented Computing. (2005)
25. Mukhi, N.K., Konuru, R., Curbera, F.: Cooperative middleware specialization for service oriented architectures. In: WWW '04, IEEE Computer Society (2004)
26. Mukhi, N., Plebanni, P., Silva-Lepe, I., Mikalsen, T.: Supporting policy-driven behaviors in web services: Experiences and issues. In: ICSOC '04, IEEE Computer Society (2004)
27. Baligand, F., Monfort, V.: A concrete solution for web services adaptability using policies and aspects. In: WISE'03: Proceedings of the Fourth International Conference on Web Information Systems Engineering, IEEE Computer Society (2004)
28. Bosloper, I., Siljee, J., Nijhuis, J., Hammer, D.: Creating self-adaptive service systems with dysoa. (In: ECOWS'05, Proceedings of the 3rd European Conference on Web Services)
29. Wohlstadter, E., Tai, S., Mikalsen, T., I.Rouvellou, Devanbu, P.: Glueqos: Middleware to sweeten quality-of-service policy interaction. In: ICSE '04: Proceedings of the 26th International Conference on Software Engineering, IEEE Computer Society (2004)
30. Bobba, R., Fatemieh, O., Khan, F., Gunter, C.A., Khurana, H.: Using attribute-based access control to enable attribute-based messaging. In: Annual Computer Security Applications Conference (ACSAC '06), Miami Beach, FL, Applied Computer Security Associates (2006)
31. Lee, A.J., Boyer, J.P., Olson, L.E., Gunter, C.A.: Defeasible security policy composition for web services. In: Formal Methods in Software Engineering (FMSE '06), Alexandria, VA, ACM (2006)

Adaptive Web Processes Using Value of Changed Information

John Harney and Prashant Doshi

LSDIS Lab, Dept. of Computer Science,
University of Georgia, Athens, GA 30602
{jfh, pdoshi}@cs.uga.edu

Abstract. Web process composition is receiving much attention as an important problem for the services oriented computing community. Most compositions built by planning methods use a pre-defined model of the process environment. These methods have assumed that the information in the models and consequently the compositions remain static and accurate throughout the life cycle of the Web process. We describe an approach that accounts for the dynamic nature of services by formulating a system that queries external sources intelligently. We give a method for measuring the value of change that revised information may potentially introduce in the Web process. We provide an algorithm that calculates and uses this value to optimally adapt the Web process to possible changes in the environment. Using two realistic scenarios, we show our idea and compare its performance to alternative approaches.

1 Introduction

Planning based approaches to Web process composition [1, 2, 3] rely on pre-specified models of the process environment to generate plans. For example, decision-theoretic planners such as Markov decision processes (MDPs) [2, 4] utilize a model, which describes the state-action transition probabilities and the costs of service invocations, to generate a policy that guides the composition. The optimality of the Web process is dependent on the accuracy with which the model captures the process environment. In volatile environments [5] where the characteristics of the process participants may change frequently, the Web process may become suboptimal if it is not updated with the changes. As an example, consider a supply chain scenario in which a manufacturer has the option of ordering goods from either its preferred or another supplier. The ordering of the manufacturer's actions depends on the probability with which the preferred supplier usually satisfies the orders and the cost of using the preferred supplier. If the preferred supplier's rate of order satisfaction drops suddenly (due to unforeseen circumstances), and the manufacturer does not revise its model to reflect this change, its Web process will continue to utilize that supplier over others.

A straightforward approach to address this problem is to query the model parameters periodically, update them if they have changed, and reformulate the

A. Dan and W. Lamersdorf (Eds.): ICSOC 2006, LNCS 4294, pp. 179–190, 2006.

Web process based on the updated model. [1] This approach does not account for the cost of querying the model parameters, which may be more expensive than using a suboptimal Web process. For example, finding out a supplier's current rate of order satisfaction may be more expensive than a reduction in expected cost that the new information will entail for the Web process.

In this paper, we introduce a method to intelligently adapt the Web process to volatile environments by computing the *value of changed information (VOC)*. In this method, we compute the tradeoff between the cost of querying for revised information and the expected value of the change in the Web process that the revised information will bring. We update the model parameters and compose the Web process again, only if the VOC is greater than the query cost. We adopt a *myopic* approach in that we query only one service provider at a time and utilize the revised information from that provider which leads to the maximum VOC. We show that, though myopic, the approach performs reasonably well in adapting the Web process to the changes in the environment. In particular, our experiments demonstrate that the VOC mechanism avoids "unnecessary" queries in comparison to the naive approach of periodic querying. This translates to a savings in overall costs for the Web process. For the purpose of evaluation, we utilize two scenarios - a supply chain and a clinical administrative pathway. Within our services-oriented architecture (SOA), we represent the manufacturer's and hospital's Web processes using WS-BPEL [6], and the provider services as well as a service for computing the VOC using WSDL [7].

We point out that the VOC computation shares its conceptual underpinnings with the value of perfect information (VPI) [8]. This is due to the fact that they are both special cases of the value of information idea, which attempts to determine if new information is indeed useful to a particular process. However, there is an important difference between the two concepts. VPI computes the value of *additional* information, while the VOC provides the value of *revised* information. Both quantities cannot be negative. The updated information may lead to a Web process whose total cost is greater than before. For example, if the preferred supplier's probability of meeting orders drops considerably, the manufacturer may be forced to drop the preferred supplier in favor of using a more expensive supplier. Nevertheless, as we show, the revised Web process incurs less total cost in the changed environment in comparison to the original Web process in this environment.

2 Related Work

Only recently have researchers turned their attention to managing processes in volatile environments. Au et al. [5] obtains current parameters about the Web process by querying specific Web service providers when the values expire. Plan recomputation is assumed to take place irrespective of whether the revised parameter values are expected to bring about a change in the composition. This

[1] In general, new information may require a complete recomposition of the Web process to remain optimal, though sometimes only local changes may be sufficient.

may lead to frequent unnecessary computations. Muller et al. [9] propose a workflow adaptation strategy based on pre-defined event-condition-action rules that are triggered when a change in the evironment occurs. While the rules provide a good basis for performing contingency actions, they are limited in the fact that they cannot account for all possible actions and scenarios that may arise in complex workflows. Additionally, the above works do not address long term optimality of process adaptation. [2] offers such a solution using a technique that manages the dynamism of Web process environments through Bayesian learning. The process model parameters are updated based on previous interactions with the individual Web services and the composition plan is regenerated using these updates. This method suffers from being slow in updating the parameters, and the approach may result in plan recomputations that do not bring about any change in the Web process.

3 Motivating Scenarios

In order to illustrate our approach we present two example scenarios:

Supply Chain. A manufacturer receives an order to deliver some merchandise to a retailer. The manufacturer may satisfy the order in one of several ways. He may satisfy the order from his own inventory if sufficient stock exists. The manufacturer may request the required parts from a preferred supplier. The manufacturer may also search for a new supplier of parts, or buy them on the spot market. A *costing analysis* reveals that the manufacturer will incur least cost if he is able to satisfy the order from his own inventory. The manufacturer will incur increasing costs as he tries to fulfill the order by procuring parts from his preferred supplier, a new supplier, and the spot market.

In Fig. 1, we depict the supply chain scenario. The manufacturer may choose from several processes. For example, the manufacturer may attempt to satisfy

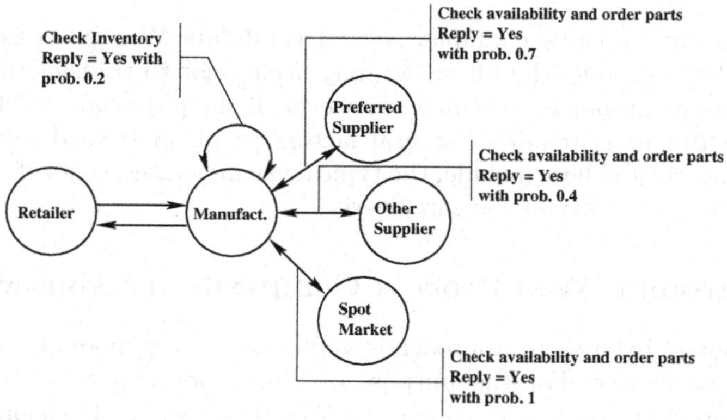

Fig. 1. Collaboration diagram showing interactions between the business partners in our motivating scenario. We have used example probability values to aid understanding.

the order from his inventory. If unable to do so, he may resort to order from the preferred supplier. Another process may involve bypassing the inventory check, since the manufacturer strongly believes that his inventory will not satisfy the order. He may then initiate a status check on his preferred supplier. These example processes reveal two important factors for selecting the optimal one. First, the manufacturer must accurately know the certainty with which his order will be satisfied by the various suppliers. Second, rather than selecting an action with the least cost at each stage, the manufacturer must select the action expected to be optimal over the long term.

Patient Transfer. A hospital receives a patient who has complained of a particular ailment. The patient is first checked into the hospital and then seen by one of the hospital's physicians. He may, upon examination, decide to transfer the patient to a secondary care provider for specialist treatment. We assume that the hospital has a choice of four secondary care givers to select from with differing vacancy rates and costs of treatment, with the preferred one having the best vacancy rate and least cost (see Fig. 2).

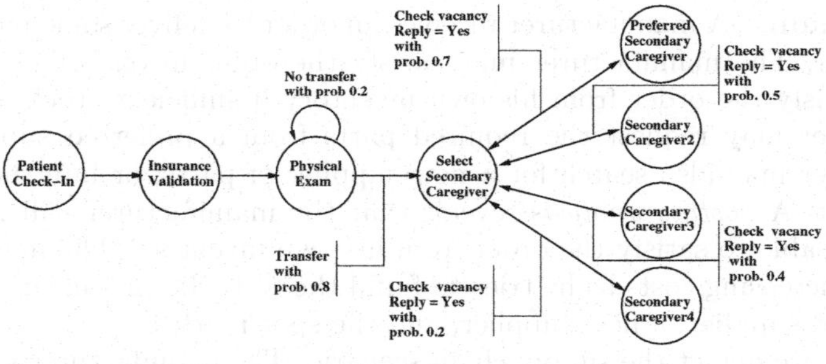

Fig. 2. The patient transfer clinical pathway for a primary caregiver. As before, we have used example probability values to aid understanding.

Similar to our previous example, several candidate Web processes present themselves. For example, the physician may decide not to transfer the patient, instead opting for in-house treatment. However, if the physician concludes that specialist treatment is required, several factors weigh in toward selecting the secondary care giver. These include, the typical vacancy rates, costs of treatment, and geographic proximity of the caregivers.

4 Background: Web Process Composition Using MDPs

As we mentioned before, our approach is applicable to any model based process composition technique. For the purpose of illustration, we select a decision-theoretic planning technique for composing Web processes [2]. Decision-theoretic planners such as MDPs model the process environment, WP, using a sextuplet:

$$WP = (S, A, T, C, H, s_0)$$

where $S = \Pi_{i=1}^{n} X^i$, where S is the set of all possible states factored into a set, X, of n variables, $X = \{X^1, X^2, \ldots, X^n\}$; A is the set of all possible actions; T is a transition function, $T : S \times A \rightarrow \Delta(S)$, which specifies the probability measure over the next state given the current state and action; C is a cost function, $C : S \times A \rightarrow \mathbb{R}$, which specifies the cost of performing each action from each state; H is the period of consideration over which the plan must be optimal, also known as the horizon, $0 < H \leq \infty$; and s_0 is the starting state of the process.

In order to gain insight into the functioning of MDPs, let us model the supply chain scenario as a MDP. The state of the workflow is captured by the random variables – **Inventory Availability**, **Preferred Supplier Availability**, **New Supplier Availability**, **Spot Market Availability**, **Order Assembled**, and **Order Shipped**. A state is then a conjunction of assignments of either *Yes*, *No*, or *Unknown* to each random variable. Actions are Web service invocations, A={Check Inventory Status, Check Preferred Supplier Status, Check New Supplier Status, Check Spot Market Status, Assemble Order, Ship Order}. The transition function, T, models the non-deterministic effect of each action on some random variable(s). For example, invoking the Web service Check Inventory Status will cause **Inventory Availability** to be assigned *Yes* with a probability of T(**Inventory Availability**= *Yes*|Check Inventory Status, **Inventory Availability**= *Unknown*), and assigned *No* or *Unknown* with a probability of (1-T(**Inventory Availability**= *Yes*|Check Inventory Status,**Inventory Availability**= *Unknown*)). The cost function, C, prescribes the cost of performing each action. This includes the financial as well as the infrastructural cost to the manufacturer of using a service. We let H be some finite value which implies that the manufacturer is concerned with getting the most optimal Web process possible within a fixed number of steps. Since no information is available at the start state, all random variables will be assigned the value *Unknown*.

Once our manufacturer has modeled its Web process composition problem as a MDP, he may apply standard MDP solution techniques to arrive at an optimal process. These solution techniques revolve around the use of stochastic dynamic programming [4] for calculation of the optimal policy using *value iteration*:

$$V^n(s) = \min_{a \in A} \; Q^n(s, a) \tag{1}$$

where:

$$Q^n(s, a) = \begin{cases} C(s, a) + \sum_{s' \in S} T(s'|a, s) V^{n-1}(s) & \text{n>0} \\ 0 & \text{n=0} \end{cases} \tag{2}$$

where the function, $V^n : S \rightarrow \mathbb{R}$, quantifies the minimum long-term expected cost of reaching each state with n actions remaining to be performed, and $Q^n(s, a)$ is the action-value function, which represents the minimum long-term expected cost from s on performing action a.

Once we know the expected cost associated with each state of the process, the optimal action for each state is the one which results in the minimum expected cost.

$$\pi^*(s) = \underset{a \in A}{argmin} \; Q^n(s, a) \tag{3}$$

In Eq. 3, π^* is the optimal policy which is simply a mapping from states to actions, $\pi^* : S \rightarrow A$. The Web process is composed by performing the WS invocation prescribed by the policy given the state of the process and observing the results of the actions. Details of the algorithm for translating the policy to the Web process are given in [2].

5 Value of Changed Information

Several characteristics of the process participants – service providers – may change during the life-cycle of a Web process. For example, the cost of using the preferred supplier's services may increase, and/or the probability with which the preferred supplier meets the orders may reduce. The former requires an update of the cost function, C, while the latter requires an update of the transition function, T, in the MDP model. In this paper, we focus on a change in the transition function T, though our approach is generalizable to fluctuations in other model parameters too.

Not all updates to the model parameters cause changes in the process composition. Furthermore, the change effected by the revised information may not be worth the cost of obtaining it. In light of these arguments, we need a method that will suggest a query, only when the queried information is *expected* to be sufficiently valuable to obtain. We provide one such methodology next.

5.1 Definition

As we mentioned before, we adopt a myopic approach to information revision, in which we query a single provider at a time for new information. In the supply chain example, this would translate to asking, say, only the preferred supplier for its current rates of order satisfaction, as opposed to both the preferred supplier and the other supplier, simultaneously. The revised information may change the following transition probabilities, T(**Preferred Supplier Availability** = Yes | Check Preferred Supplier Status, **Preferred Supplier Availability** = Unknown), and T(**Preferred Supplier Availability** = No | Check Preferred Supplier Status, **Preferred Supplier Availability** = Unknown).

Let $V_{\pi^*}(s|T')$ denote the expected cost of following the optimal policy, π^*, from the state s when the revised transition function, T' is used. Since the actual revised transition probability is not known unless we query the service provider, we average over all possible values of the revised transition probability, using our current belief distributions over their values. These distributions may be provided by the service providers through pre-defined service-level agreements or they could be learned from previous interactions with the service providers. Formally,

$$EV(s) = \int_{\mathbf{p}} Pr(T'(\cdot|a,s') = \mathbf{p}) V_{\pi^*}(s|T') d\mathbf{p} \tag{4}$$

where $T'(\cdot|a,s')$ represents the distribution that may be queried and subsequently may get revised, $\mathbf{p} = \langle p_1, p_2, \ldots, p_n \rangle$ represents a possible response to

the query (revised distribution), n is the number of values that the variable under question may assume, and $Pr(\cdot)$ is our current *belief* over the possible values. As a simple illustration, let us suppose that we intend to query the preferred supplier for its current rate of order satisfaction. Eq. 4 becomes,
$EV(s) = \int_{\langle p,1-p\rangle} Pr(T'$ (**Pref. Supp. Avail.**=Yes/No |Check Pref. Supp. Status, **Pref. Supp. Avail.** = Unknown)= $\langle p, 1-p\rangle)\ V_{\pi^*}(s|T')dp$
assuming that the random variable **Preferred Supplier Availability** assumes either *Yes* or *No* on checking the status of the preferred supplier.

Let $V_\pi(s|T')$ be the expected cost of following the original policy, π from the state s in the context of the revised model parameter, T'. We recall that the policy, π, is optimal in the absence of any revised information. We formulate the value of change due to the revised transition probabilities as:

$$VOC_{T'(\cdot|a,s')}(s) = \int_{\mathbf{p}} Pr(T'(\cdot|a,s') = \mathbf{p})[V_\pi(s|T') - V_{\pi^*}(s|T')]d\mathbf{p} \qquad (5)$$

The subscript to VOC, $T'(\cdot|a,s')$, denotes the revised information inducing the change. Intuitively, Eq. 5 represents how badly, on average, the original policy, π, performs in the changed environment as formalized by the MDP model with the revised T'.

Analogous to the value of perfect information, the following proposition holds for VOC.

Proposition 1. $\forall s \in S, \quad VOC(s) \geq 0$ *where* $VOC(\cdot)$ *is as defined in Eq. 5.*

Proof. The proposition follows trivially if we find that $\forall s, \mathbf{p}\ V_\pi(s|T') - V_{\pi^*}(s|T') \geq 0$. By definition (Eq. 3), π^* is an optimal policy for the revised model. This implies that for any other policy, $\pi' \in \Pi \backslash \pi^*$, where Π is the space of all policies, $\forall \mathbf{p} \quad V_{\pi'}(s|T') \geq V_{\pi^*}(s|T')$. This holds true over all the states. The required inequality obtains since π must either be in $\Pi \backslash \pi^*$, or be equal to π^*. □

Since querying the model parameters and obtaining the revised information may be expensive, we must undertake the querying only if we expect it to pay off. In other words, we query for new information from a state of the Web process only if the VOC due to the revised information in that state is greater than the query cost. More formally, we query if

$$VOC_{T'(\cdot|a,s')}(s) > QueryCost(T'(\cdot|a,s'))$$

where $T'(\cdot|a,s')$ represents the distribution we want to query.

5.2 Web Process Composition with VOC

In order to formulate and execute the Web process, we simply look up the current state of the Web process in the policy and execute the WS prescribed by the policy for that state. The response of the WS invocation determines the next state of the Web process. We adapt the composition of the Web process

```
Algorithm for adaptive Web process
   Input: π* //optimal policy, s0 //initial state
   s ← s0
   while goal state not reached
      if VOC*(s) > QueryCost(T'(·|a, s')
         Query service provider, a (Eq. 6), for new probabilities
         Form the new transition function, T'
         Calculate policy π* using the new MDP model
         with T'
      a ← π*(s)
      Execute the Web service a
      Get response of a and construct next state, s'
      s ← s'
   end while
end algorithm
```

Fig. 3. Algorithm for adapting a Web process to revised information and executing it

to fluctuations in the model parameters, by interleaving the formulation with VOC computations. The algorithm for the adaptive Web process composition is shown in Fig. 3.

For each state encountered during the execution of the Web process, we query a service provider for new information if the query is expected to bring about a change in the Web process that exceeds the query cost. For example, in the supply chain process, we select and query a supplier for its current rate of order satisfactions. Of all the suppliers, we select the one whose possible new rate of order satisfaction is expected to bring about the most change in the Web process, and this change exceeds the cost of querying that provider. In other words, we select the service provider associated with the WS invocation, a, to possibly query for whom the VOC is maximum:

$$a = \underset{a \in A}{argmax} \; VOC_{T(\cdot|a,s')}(s) \tag{6}$$

Let VOC*(s) represent the corresponding maximum VOC.

Our algorithm does not consider the cost of VOC computation in deciding whether to query a service provider. In particular, this would require knowing what the possible VOC computation cost could be, and a way to compare computation cost with WS invocation cost using inter-convertible units. We avoid these complications under the assumption that sufficient inexpensive computational resources are available to perform VOC computations.

6 Experiments

We first outline our SOA, in which we wrap the VOC computations in WSDL based internal Web services, followed by our experimental results on the performance of the adaptive Web process.

6.1 Architecture

The algorithm described in Fig. 3 is implemented as a WS-BPEL flow while all WSs were implemented using WSDL. To the WS-BPEL flow, we gave the optimal policy, π^*, and the start state as input. Our experiments utilized IBM's BPWS4J engine for executing the BPEL process. We show our SOA in Fig. 4.

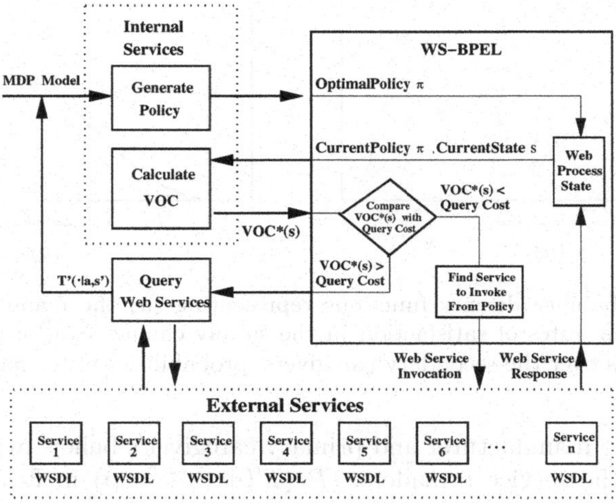

Fig. 4. SOA for implementing our adaptive Web process

Within our SOA, we provide internal WSs for solving the MDP and generating the policy, and computing the VOC. If the $VOC^*(s)$ exceeds the cost of querying a particular service provider (this cost is also provided as an input), the WS-BPEL flow invokes a special WS whose function is to query the service provider's WS for revised information. This information is used to formulate and solve a new MDP and the output policy is fed back to the WS-BPEL flow. This policy is used by the WS-BPEL flow to invoke the prescribed external WS and the response is used to formulate the next state of the process. This procedure continues until the goal state is reached.

6.2 Performance Evaluation

We experimentally compare the performance of our VOC based approach for adapting a Web process with two other methods, for both the supply chain and the patient transfer examples outlined in Section 3. The first method assumes that there is no adaptation to the volatile environment and uses the same policy for every execution of the process. A MDP model is formulated and solved before the first execution instance and the resulting policy is used for every instance then onwards. The second method implements a periodic querying strategy, in which a service provider is selected at random and queried for revised information at each state of the Web process. Using the new information, the policy is re-solved and the Web process continues to run using the new policy. For the supply chain example, we queried the inventory or the suppliers for their current percentage of order satisfaction [2], while in the patient transfer pathway, we queried the secondary caregivers for their current vacancy rates. [3]

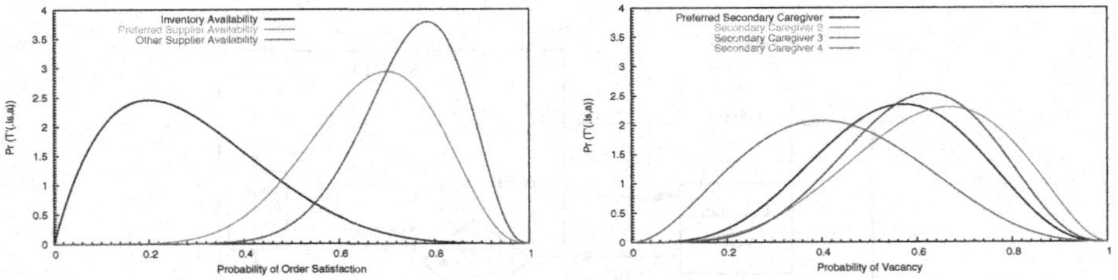

(*a*) (*b*)

Fig. 5. The probability density functions representing (*a*) the manufacturer's belief over the suppliers' rates of satisfaction in the supply chain scenario; (*b*) the primary caregiver's beliefs over the secondary caregivers' probabilities of having a vacancy

We model the manufacturer and primary caregiver's beliefs over the possible parameters of the service providers, ($Pr(T'(\cdot|a, s') = \mathbf{p})$ in Eq. 5) using *beta* density functions. Other density functions such as Gaussians or polynomials may also be used. Fig. 5(*a*) shows the beta densities that represent the manufacturer's distribution over the rate of order satisfaction by the inventory ie. $T'(\textbf{Inv. Avail.} = Yes|\textsf{Check Inv.}, \textbf{Inv. Avail.} = Unknown)$, and analogously for the preferred and other suppliers. Means of the densities reveal that the inventory tends to be less reliable in satisfying orders than other suppliers. Fig. 5(*b*) shows the density plots over the probability of a vacancy with the preferred and other secondary caregivers.

In Fig. 6 we compare the three strategies with respect to the average cost incurred from the execution of the Web process, as the cost of querying the service providers is increased. Our methodology consisted of running 100 independent instances of each process within a simulated volatile environment, where the queried parameters of the service providers were distributed according to the density plots in Fig. 5. We ensured that the processes using each of the three strategies received similar responses from the service providers.

Intuitively, as we increase the cost of querying, our VOC based approach performs less queries and adapts the Web process less. For large query costs, its performance is similar to using a Web process with a static policy strategy. In Fig. 6(*a*) and (*b*), we show the results for the supply chain and patient transfer

[2] In the real world, an example response by a supplier could be, "We are currently meeting 2 of every 3 orders".

[3] Of course, the rate of order satisfaction would depend on the quantity of the order and other factors; we assume that these will be provided to the suppliers.

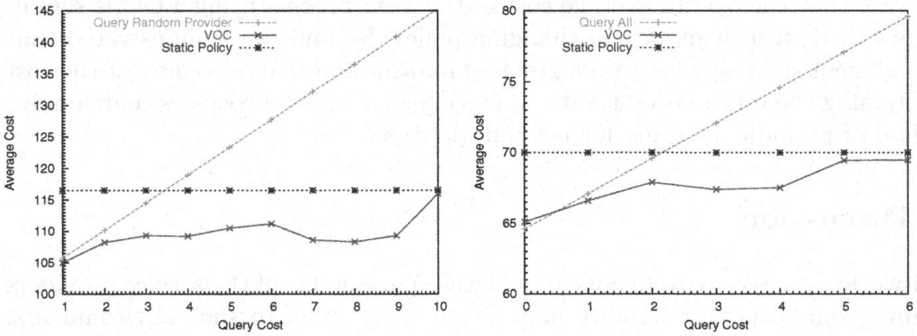

(*a*) (*b*)

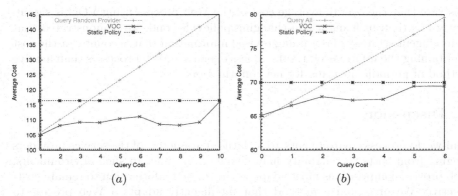

Fig. 6. Comparisons of the VOC based process composition with the static policy and periodic querying approaches for (*a*) supply chain, and (*b*) patient transfer scenarios

scenarios respectively. For smaller query costs, a VOC based approach will query frequently, though not as much as a strategy that always queries a provider. As we increase the query costs, the VOC based approach will allow a query for revised information only if its value exceeds the cost. Thus, a Web process that is adapted using VOC performs better (incurs less average cost) than periodic querying in a volatile environment because only significant changes to the Web process are carried out while simultaneously avoiding frequent costly queries.

We point out that the improvement in overall costs comes at a computational price, as illustrated by our execution time results in Table 1. Calculating the VOC as shown in Eq. 5 is computationally intensive. The probability $\mathbf{p}$ represents a revised probability of transition on performing an action. To calculate the VOC, we must compute $V_{\pi}(s|T')$ and $V_{\pi^*}(s|T')$ for all possible $\mathbf{p}$ and average over their difference based on our distribution over $\mathbf{p}$ (shown in Fig. 5). The revised value function $V_{\pi^*}(s|T')$ must be computed using the standard value iteration defined in Eq. 1. The integral in Eq. 5 is approximated using monte carlo sampling, which provides a faster evaluation technique and contains negligible error. Exploring additional efficient calculations of VOC is one avenue of future work.

Table 1. Execution times of Web processes using the VOC and query always approaches for the supply chain and patient transfer scenario

Problem	VOC	Query always
Supply Chain	1.43s	0.37s
Patient Transfer	18.6s	7.4s

Our experiments provide two conclusions: First, by augmenting Web process composition with VOC calculations, significant information changes in volatile environments are considered and used to make better decisions about which services to invoke next. The comparison of VOC and static policy implementations illustrate that the overall average cost of the Web process using VOC is significantly less than utilizing a non-changing policy. Second, we demonstrated that an intelligent strategy of obtaining revised information that accounts for the cost in obtaining the information results in less expensive Web processes than a naive method of periodic querying for new information.

7 Discussion

Real-world process environments are volatile–parameters of the service providers ranging from costs to reliability may change over time. In such environments, Web process compositions must adapt to the revised information to remain cost-effective. We presented a method that intelligently adapts a Web process to changes in parameters of service providers. Specifically, our approach measures the expected value of change that the revised information may bring to Web processes and compares it with the cost of obtaining the information. If the revised information is worth the cost of obtaining it, we query the providers for their current parameters and reformulate the Web process using the revised information. Using two example scenarios, we show that our approach results in Web processes that are more cost-effective than approaches that do not change the composition or use a simple periodic querying strategy. Our future line of work will involve attempting to compute the VOC more efficiently, and understand the trade off between VOC calculation accuracy and computational efficiency.

Acknowledgements. This research was supported by a grant from UGARF.

References

[1] Srivastava, B., Koehler, J.: Planning with workflows - an emerging paradigm for web service composition. (2004)
[2] Doshi, P., Goodwin, R., Akkiraju, R., Verma, K.: Dynamic workflow composition using markov decision processes. J of Web Services Research **2**(1) (2005) 1–17
[3] Wu, D., Parsia, B., Sirin, E., Hendler, J., Nau, D.: Automating daml-s web services composition using shop2. In: International Semantic Web Conference. (2003)
[4] Puterman, M.L.: Markov Decision Processes. John Wiley & Sons, NY (1994)
[5] Au, T.C., Kuter, U., Nau, D.S.: Web service composition with volatile information. In: International Semantic Web Conference. (2005) 52–66
[6] IBM: Business Process Execution Language for Web Services version 1.1. (2005)
[7] W3C: Web Services Description Language (WSDL) 1.1. (2001)
[8] Russell, S., Norvig, P.: Artificial Intelligence: A Modern Approach (Second Edition). Prentice Hall (2003)
[9] Muller, R., Greiner, U., Rahm, E.: Agentwork: a workflow system supporting rule-based workflow adaptation. J of Data and Knowledge Engg. **51**(2) (2004) 223–256

SCENE: A Service Composition Execution Environment Supporting Dynamic Changes Disciplined Through Rules

Massimiliano Colombo[1], Elisabetta Di Nitto[1,2], and Marco Mauri[1]

[1] CEFRIEL, Via Fucini 2, 20133 Milano – Italy
[2] Politecnico di Milano, Piazza Leonardo da Vinci, 32, 20133 Milano - Italy
mcolombo@cefriel.it, dinitto@elet.polimi.it, mmauri@cefriel.it

Abstract. Service compositions are created by exploiting existing component services that are, in general, out of the control of the composition developer. The challenge nowadays is to make such compositions able to dynamically reconfigure themselves in order to address the cases when the component services do not behave as expected and when the execution context changes. We argue that the problem has to be tackled at two levels: on the one side, the runtime platform should be flexible enough to support the selection of alternative services, the negotiation of their service level agreements, and the partial replanning of a composition. On the other side, the language used to develop the composition should support the designer in defining the constraints and conditions that regulate selection, negotiation, and replanning actions at runtime. In this paper we present the SCENE platform that partially addresses the above issues by offering a language for composition design that extends the standard BPEL language with rules used to guide the execution of binding and re-binding self-reconfiguration operations.

Keywords: service composition, autonomic behavior, self-reconfiguring systems, dynamic binding.

1 Introduction

Service-oriented approaches are capturing a growing interest not only as a mean for business to business integration, but also as the possible reference architecture to support the development of systems exposing autonomic and dynamically changing behavior [11]. Typical examples are the cases of applications able to reconfigure themselves and to contact different services depending on contextual information (e.g., the location of the final user), on QoS levels, on possible failures happening while a service is running, and so on.

The dynamic nature of such systems precludes the a-priori identification of the services defining the system and demands for run-time *discovery* and *selection* of such services. In particular, we argue that discovery and selection have to be supported at two different levels. On one side, the runtime platform executing systems built by composing services should be flexible enough to support the discovery and selection of alternative services, and the negotiation of their service level agreements. On the other side, the language used to develop the composition should support the

A. Dan and W. Lamersdorf (Eds.): ICSOC 2006, LNCS 4294, pp. 191 – 202, 2006.

designer not only in the definition of the way service invocations are sequenced in a workflow, but also in the definition of self-configuration policies that will discipline the selection of services and negotiation actions at runtime.

Through these policies, it should be possible, for instance, to express the fact that whenever a component service breaks the Service Level Agreement (SLA) [6] it has established with the system, an attempt to establish a new SLA is done and, if this fails, then the system will try to find an alternative component service, preferably offered by the same provider.

Industrial composition environments, typically BPEL-based [3], offer little support to dynamic changes [4] and do not support the explicit definition of self-configuration policies. If we look at service-oriented research initiatives, they tend to encapsulate self-configuration policies in some infrastructural components rather than to allow the designer to define them explicitly. In these cases, the degree of flexibility of the resulting system is often poor and designers have little control on the policies that are actually applied at runtime (see Section 6 for more details on some of these approaches).

In this scenario, we propose a composition language through which we describe service compositions in terms of two distinct parts: a process part, described using BPEL, that defines the main business logic of the composition, and a declarative part, described using ECA (Event Condition Action) rules. Rules are used to associate a BPEL workflow with the declaration of the policy to be used during (re)configuration. Rules can either be defined at design time or later before the execution of the system. Moreover, various sets of rules can coexist and be activated depending on the preferences of the system users.

A composition written in our language is executed by SCENE (*Service Composition ExecutioN Environment*). The current implementation of SCENE integrates an off-the-shelf BPEL executor called PXE [15] and a rule engine called Drools [9]. SCENE is part of a European project called SeCSE (*Service Centric Systems Engineering*) [17] aiming at providing methods, tools, and platform to support service-oriented engineering.

For the moment both language and runtime environment support the dynamic discovery and selection of services. We are currently working to provide support to the other self-configuration actions we have mentioned (e.g., negotiation of new SLAs and replanning of the composition).

The goal of this paper is to present the results we have achieved so far. Consistently, the paper is organized as follows: in Section 2 an example is shown to motivate our work. Section 3 briefly describes the main aspects of the composition language. Section 4 proposes the architecture of SCENE together with its execution semantics. Section 5 presents a preliminary evaluation of the approach, Section 6 presents the related approaches, finally, Section 7 concludes this paper and discusses about some possible future work.

2 Motivating Example

In this section we present an example that motivates the need for supporting dynamic changes in a composition. The example has been extracted from the scenarios defined by the industrial partners of the SeCSE project.

A car maker would like to equip its top level cars with a device allowing the end user to exploit a set of remote services all available through a portal offered by the car maker itself. One of the offered services, named *XTRIP*, helps the end user in keeping his/her schedule updated depending on the status of his/her travel. In particular, the service allows the user to plan a trip. Based on the plan and on a navigation system that allows the service to know the geographical position of the car, the service itself is able to automatically check the agenda of the user to make sure that he/she will be on time for the scheduled appointments. In case of problems, the service automatically establishes a telephone communication between the end user in the car and his/her secretary so that they can take actions to change the schedule as needed.

The process realizing the *XTRIP* service is composed of activities (see the activity diagram of Fig. 1) to get the data about the current position of the car (*plan trip*), to access the user's agenda (*check for conflicts* and *confirm commitments*) and to establish a telephone call when needed (*make call*).

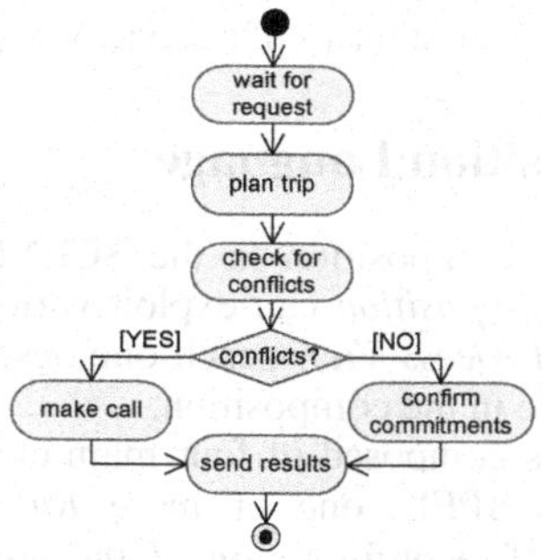

Fig. 1. The XTRIP process

The completion of these activities implies the invocation of operations to external services capable of fulfilling them. *check for conflicts* and *confirm commitments* activities are provided by the same service as they both operate on the end user agenda. The first one checks if some appointments for the period of interest are conflicting with the trip, and the second one confirms the appointments in case no conflict is detected.

Despite the simplicity of the example, its implementation should be dynamically adaptable to the way the service is actually used. In particular, the selection of the actual service for *plan trip* activity could be left open at design time and decided at runtime based on the geographical location of the user. This way, it is possible to take advantage of navigation systems specialized for specific areas. Moreover, the selection of the concrete service to complete both *check for conflicts* and *confirm commitments* activities should depend on the user which requests the service. Therefore, the service cannot be fixed at design time. Finally, the selection of the service to satisfy *make call* activity could depend on the telecom provider that offers the best rate to connect the traveler with his/her secretary and also on performance; these, again, are issues that cannot be addressed while designing the composition workflow.

By exploiting our composition approach, at design time all these choices can be left open, but, at the same time, rules can be defined that will guide all (re)configuration actions that will be taken at runtime.

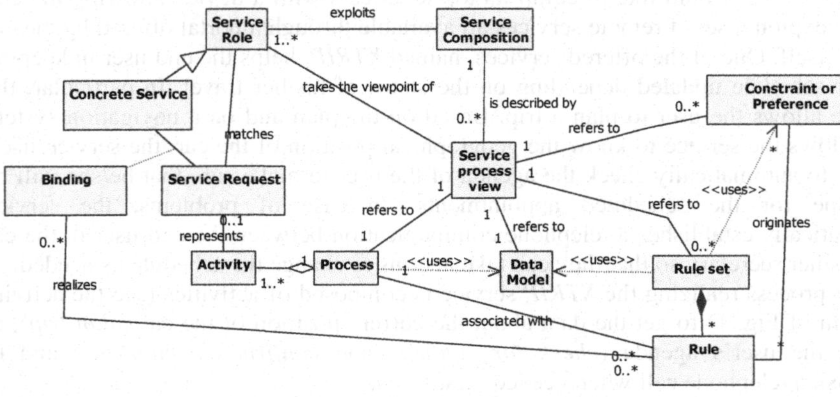

Fig. 2. The constituents of a service composition

3 The SCENE Composition Language

The constituents of a service composition in the SCENE composition language are shown in Fig. 2. A *Service Composition* can exploit various *Service Roles* and can be described by various *Service Process Views* each one describing the composition from the view point of a specific role in the composition.

The service process view is composed of four main elements: a *Process* that in our language is described using BPEL, one or more *Rule Sets* and *Constraints* and *Preferences* to control the self-reconfiguration of the composition at runtime, and a *Data Model* that includes all data types that are shared between the process and the rules. These include the structure of the input and output data used by the process part to communicate with the external services.

The process is composed of *Activities* that can be implemented as *Requests* to external services. These requests can be served by some service roles. At runtime, the rules are used to realize the *Bindings* between service requests and the concrete implementation of service roles (*Concrete Services*).

The decoupling between the process and the rules allows for a proper separation of concerns. The process is described in BPEL. We do not pose any restriction to the structure of the BPEL code describing the process. It defines the data and control flow among the various elements of the composition. The rules and the constraints and preferences define the policies used for self-organization. They, in fact, contain all it is needed to dynamically select/change services, possibly discovered on the fly.

Rules are aware of the state of the process. On the contrary, the process is completely agnostic of the existence of the rule part. As we will discuss in Section 4, at runtime, the execution environment is in charge of communicating to the rule part the state of the process and of modifying this state (and in the future work also the structure of the process) depending on the results provided by the execution of rules.

Rules do not have to be necessarily defined together with the process; they can also be introduced at any time before execution in order to account for the specific conditions in which the process is being executed. The notation we propose for rules is an extension of the XML rule language that is interpreted by Drools (see next section).

```
<!-- processInfo and eventList are global variables -->
<rule name="makeCall - prefix different from 33, 34, 38">
        <scope>
                <activity-name>make call</activity-name>
        </scope>
        <event>
                <name>bindingEvent</name>
                <type>rulelanguage.datamodel.events.ActivityBindingEvent</type>
        </event>
        <condition>
            !(bindingEvent.getInputVariableValue("CalledParty").equals("33") ||
              bindingEvent.getInputVariableValue("CalledParty").equals("34")  ||
              bindingEvent.getInputVariableValue("CalledParty").equals("38"))
        </condition>
        <consequence description="dynamic discovery and binding action request created and sent as an event payload">
                        DynamicDiscoveryBindingActionRequest actionRequest = new
                        DynamicDiscoveryBindingActionRequest(processInfo.getLocalBindingPreferences("makeCall"));
                        actionRequest.setActivityName("make call");
                        eventList.addExternalEvent(new Event(actionRequest));
        </consequence>
</rule>
```

Fig. 3. An example of dynamic discovery and binding rule

Fig. 3 shows an example of rule that refers to the case study described in Section 2. The rule can be activated while the composition process is executing the *make call* activity. The aim of the activity is to establish a phone call between the user in the car and his/her assistant. It exploits a Third Party Call Control (TPCC) service [20] offered by some telecom provider. The aim of the rule shown in Fig. 3 is to allow the activity to be dynamically bound to the most suitable TPCC service. More in detail, the rule is triggered by an event of type *ActivityBindingEvent* issued by the process execution environment whenever it realizes that the service request associated with some process activity is not bounded to any specific service. The condition that activates the rule requires that the phone number to be called through the TPCC service (this is the parameter of *bindingEvent*) does not start with some special numbers. These, in fact, are managed by a different rule (not shown for space reasons). In the action part a request for executing a dynamic discovery and binding operation is created (*actionRequest*) and this request is wrapped into an event that, in turn, is added to an event queue to be actually issued. The event queue is identified by the variable *eventList* that is defined as global and visible to all rules. Variable *processInfo* is global as well. It contains the defined self-reconfiguration preferences and constraints.

In general, rules can introduce some changes in the composition or they can delegate specific tasks to some infrastructural components. The rule sample presented above falls in this last category since it aims at activating the component able to identify new bindings (the Binder as explained in Section 4). This component receives as input some binding preferences through the variable *processInfo*. Fig. 4 shows a fragment of binding preferences stating that the service to be selected has to guarantee a price per minute of telephone conversation lower than 0.5 euros. Of course, in order to guarantee this preference, the selection of the concrete service to be bound has to be limited to all those exposing pricing information in their service specification.

The binding preferences fragment also provides information about the validity of each binding. In the example, the binding is valid for a single invocation. This means that it has to be renewed each time the corresponding process activity is executed. A determined binding can also be valid for the lifetime of the specific process instance or it can be associated with all new instances of the same process. In these last two cases, the *bindingValidity* tag takes the values *PROCESS INSTANCE* and *PERMANENT* respectively.

```
...
<local-binding-preferences>
        <discoveryPreferences> ... </discoveryPreferences>
        <selectionPreferences>
                <preference>
                        <key>singleQualityConstraint</key>
                        <value>PRICEPERMIN &lt; 0.5 (€) </value>
                </preference>
        </selectionPreferences>
        <bindingValidity>SINGLE INVOCATION</bindingValidity>
</local-binding-preferences>
...
```

Fig. 4. Binding preferences

Fig. 5 shows a sample of rule that triggers the reconfiguration of the composition in response to an event generated by a monitoring component. This reconfiguration can happen independently of the validity that has been set for bindings since it is used to deal with faulty situations: the event triggering the rule signals that some failure in a component service has occurred. The service that has failed is stored in a "blacklist" for future record and a *CacheUpdatingActionRequest* is issued (again, it is wrapped in a proper event) that causes any current binding to the failing service to be actually eliminated.

Rules can have either global or local scope. Rules having global scope can be activated any time during the execution of a composition. The service violation rule of Fig. 5 is an example of these kinds of rule. Rules with local scope are associated with some specific activities of the process that require interaction with external services. This means that these rules can be activated and can affect the composition only when the corresponding activity is being executed. The dynamic binding rule of Figure 3 has local scope (defined in the rule *scope* tag) since it is built to deal with a specific binding to a service offering a *makeCall* operation.

Fig. 6 shows some constraints defined on the *confirm commitments* activity. For each invoke activity the constraints specify if the activity is abstract, i.e., it has not been bound to a concrete service operation, if it is concrete, i.e., a binding for it has been finalized at design-time, and if any rule associated with that invoke activity is enabled. A relevant aspect concerns the presence of potential dependencies between activities.

```
<!-- processInfo and eventList are global variables -->
<rule name="service violation event">
        <scope>
                <all/>
        </scope>
        <event>
                <name>violationEvent</name>
                <type>rulelanguage.datamodel.events.ServiceViolationEvent</type>
        </event>
        <consequence description="the service endpoint is stored into the endpoint black list">
                processInfo.updateBlackList(violationEvent.getServiceDetails());
                CacheUpdatingActionRequest actionRequest = new CacheUpdatingActionRequest();
                actionRequest.setServiceEndpoint(violationEvent.getServiceDetails().getEndpoint());
                actionRequest.setMode("delete");
                eventList.addExternalEvent(new Event(actionRequest));
        </consequence>
</rule>
```

Fig. 5. Violation rule

In the specific example of Fig. 6, the dependency tag indicates that the activity under consideration (*confirm commitments*) has to rely on the same service exploited by the *check for conflicts* activity. Other kinds of dependencies can be expressed in terms of generic constraints (e.g., the service used in the current activity has to offer the same level of performance of the service used in some other activity).

```
<activity-info>
        <activity-name>confirm commitments</activity-name>
        <realization-info>ABSTRACT</realization-info>
        <binding-dependencies>
                        SAME SERVICE AS 'check for conflicts'
        </binding-dependencies>
        <rules-enabled>true</rules-enabled>
        <!--a rule will be auto-generated from this dependency-->
</activity-info>
```

Fig. 6. Dependencies between activities

4 Architecture of SCENE and Execution Model

The SCENE platform provides the runtime execution environment for compositions written in the SCENE language. The first prototype includes the following components (see Fig. 7):

- REDS [5], a publish-subscribe infrastructure that acts as integration middleware and supports both synchronous and asynchronous multicast communication.
- A process execution environment that, in turn, is composed of an open source BPEL engine, PXE, which is in charge of executing the process part of the service composition [15] and of a set of Proxies that decouple the BPEL engine from the logic needed to support reconfiguration (see below).
- An open source rule engine, Drools, responsible for running the ECA rules [9].
- The Binder, responsible for executing binding actions at runtime based on the directions defined in the rule language. This component is able to execute various policies for selecting the candidate services. For instance, the services could be selected from a predefined list or they could be selected in the "outside world" by exploiting some discovery mechanism. The selection could be based both on functional and non-functional attributes. More details on the Binder component can be found in [8].
- A monitoring system [1] is also connected to the bus and provides SCENE with the needed monitoring feedbacks.

Other components are being added to the platform to manage aspects such as dynamic negotiation and dynamic reconfiguration of a service composition.

In the following we briefly show how the SCENE platform supports the execution of a composition. We start from a situation where the designer has defined the composition process by using the standard BPEL constructs. He can have either defined all bindings to some concrete services or he can have left these undefined into the BPEL process. Also the designer might have defined some constraints to enable/disable the association of process activities with rules, to define dependencies between activities. When applicable, he defines rules and binding preferences that will be considered during the self-reconfiguration of the composition.

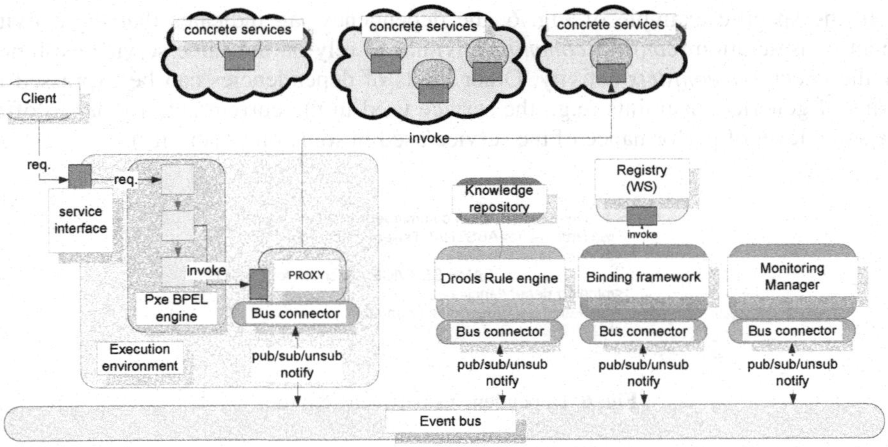

Fig. 7. The architecture of the SCENE platform

At deployment time, a SCENE composition is preprocessed. All activities in the BPEL process having the rule-enabled tag set to true are bound to specifically instantiated proxies. Moreover, additional rules are automatically generated that enforce the constraints defined as part of *processInfo*. For instance, the rule in Fig. 8 is generated to guarantee that the dependency relation defined between *confirm commitments* and *check for conflicts* activities is actually respected.

At runtime, when the execution of the process reaches the invocation of an external service, an operation offered by the proxy bound to that activity is actually called. The proxy has a well defined internal logic that works as follows: if the proxy refers to a valid concrete service, then it propagates the request directly to this service. In the opposite case, it emits on the bus an *ActivityBindingEvent*. The rule engine -- that has subscribed to this event -- receives it and activates a rule able to handle the missing binding (if this rule exists). If more than one rule can be activated, only one is non-deterministically selected (for the future we plan to add priorities to let the designer have an influence on this selection). The activated rule can take any decision, ranging from the activation of the binding procedure (as done by the rule in Fig. 3) to the immediate binding to some previously identified service (as done by the rule in Fig. 8), to the termination of the execution.

In all cases, when a new service is ready to be bound to the composition, or a decision to stop the composition is taken, an event is generated by the rule engine and received by the proxy that can then change its internal state, possibly invoke the proper operation on the bound service (if it has been identified), and then pass the control back to the BPEL execution environment. In the case a permanent binding has been identified, the rule engine will also load the files containing the process and change them by adding a concrete binding to the selected service.

When the monitoring infrastructure detects misbehavior of some service, it issues an event of type *ServiceViolationEvent*. Again, this is received by the rule engine and

```
<!-- processInfo and eventList are global variables -->
<rule name="autogenerated rule">
        <scope>
                <activity-name>confirm commitments</activity-name>
        </scope>
        <event>
                <name>bindingEvent</name>
                <type>rulelanguage.datamodel.events.ActivityBindingEvent</type>
        </event>
        <consequence description="">
                String endpoint = processInfo.getBinding("check for conflicts");
                ActivityBindingResultActionRequestactionRequest =
                                new ActivityBindingResultActionRequest();
                BindingResultInfo bindingInfo = new BindingResultInfo();
                bindingInfo.setAccessPoint(endpoint);
                actionRequest.setBindingInfo(bindingInfo);
                processinfo.updateBindingInfo_forActivity("confirm commitments", endpoint);
                eventList.addExternalEvent(new Event(actionRequest));
        </consequence>
</rule>
```

Fig. 8. Rule automatically generated to account for dependency between *confirm commitments* and *check for conflicts* activities

activates a violation rule. As in the previous case, various decisions can be defined in the rule to recover from the faulty situation. These range from simply disregarding the failure to change one or more bindings in the composition. In the forthcoming version of SCENE, we will manage also dynamic negotiation of SLAs and structural transformation of the composition itself.

5 Evaluation

We have developed some case studies to test the flexibility of the approach and its applicability to concrete cases. The examples we have considered so far have been defined within the SeCSE consortium and concern automotive and telecom domains. The example presented in Section 2 is one of these. For that example, besides the BPEL process sketched in Fig. 1, we have defined 15 rules. Some of the rules are those we have presented in the previous sections. The others have a similar structure and are not reported here for the sake of space.

The example, exploits some real services that are actually offered in a pre-operational environment by our partners. For instance, the TPCC service is offered by Telecom Italia and actually exploits the communication machinery of the company.

For the example we have developed two GUIs not shown here for space reasons. One of them is owned by the consumer of the XTRIP service and the other by the administrator. The consumer can start the execution of the composed service by requesting the system to plan a trip. Together with the request, the GUI has to pass to the composition some data about the user (his/her current position, the trip destination, the agenda service of the user, his phone number and the secretary's phone number). Through the administration interface can see the bindings and re-bindings that are computed during the execution of the composition can be monitored.

Our partners in the project are currently experimenting with the language and the platform and are providing feedbacks to us especially concerning the user friendliness of the language and its ability to capture their requirements. For the moment, this analysis has not revealed major weaknesses in the ability of the language to express the partners' needs, and we are constantly working on improving the intuitiveness and simplicity of the language.

As a final remark we highlight that the execution of a SCENE composition introduces some overhead with respect to the execution of a plain BPEL process. More in detail, referring to a specific invocation, this overhead varies depending on the following cases:

- The designer has disabled the usage of rules for the current invocation activity: in this case, there is no overhead introduced by SCENE since the invocation is executed directly by the BPEL engine.
- The usage of rules is enabled and the invoke activity that is being executed has associated a valid binding (this is stored into the corresponding proxy). In this case, the proxy acts as an intermediary between the BPEL engine and the actual services. Being the proxy fully dedicated to a single service, the overhead is mainly concerning the message exchange between the engine and the proxy. These two are installed on the same machine.
- The usage of rules is enabled and the invoke activity that is being executed does not have associated a valid binding. In this case, the proxy receiving the invocation request triggers the binding procedure by generating an event for the rule engine. In this case the overhead cannot be determined a priori, but it depends on the complexity of the rules that are triggered. Reasonably, this complexity is compensated, however, by the ability of the system to reconfigure itself.
- The monitoring system (that can exist independently of SCENE to monitor the execution of standard BPEL processes) signals a fault. This, again, triggers the execution of rules and, again, introduces, an overhead that is compensated by the fact that the system may be able to return in a correct state.

6 Related Work

Various approaches in the service-oriented domain tend to add some kind of dynamic binding features to service composition. MAIS [7] supports dynamic binding but the logic for selecting candidate services is predefined and cannot depend on user inputs as it happens with our binding rules.

Meteor-S [19] supports the execution of binding operations at design time, deployment time, and just before the execution. It also takes into account binding dependencies [18]. The composition is divided into scopes; semantic web languages are used to describe both domain constraints and services; matchmaking algorithms are used to associate each scope with the concrete set of services to invoke. While this approach requires that a semantic description is attached to each potential component service, our approach can work both using a complete description for services or a more lightweight one. Moreover, we support runtime bindings that do not seem to be addressed in Meteor-S.

The approach presented in [12] exploits DAML-S technologies to support semantic discovery of services and their runtime integration into the composition. In this case, however, the approach does not account for dependences between service invocations.

SELF-SERV [2] exploits a proprietary language for describing a composition and introduces the concept of service community. Binding is possible at runtime among the members of the community.

In [13] composition rules are used to govern the way a composition is built in a semiautomatic way. Our approach differs from this because more than exploiting rules to build a new composition, we use them to support its runtime self-configuration.

Combining rules with workflow languages in a service-oriented context has been already proposed in the literature as a way to define conditional business logic that is not directly captured by the workflow [16, 10]. Our rules, indeed, are not designed to encapsulate some business logic. Instead, they work at a lower level of abstraction to support the definition of policies for dynamic binding (and negotiation and replanning in the future).

As we have tried to convey in the previous sections, our approach aims at offering some autonomic features. In the research area of autonomic computing, the main idea behind the scene is to build applications capable of self-managing themselves, reflecting the behavior of biological systems. An autonomic application must own the following properties [14]: self-Awareness, self-Configuring, self-Optimizing, self-Healing, self-Protecting, Context-Awareness, Openness, Anticipatory behavior. We think at least three of the aforementioned characteristics are satisfied by our approach: rules associated with the process makes the composition self-configuring (e.g., a binding rule can re-configure the association between a process activity and a concrete service), self-healing (e.g., a service violation event can trigger a recovery action rule to avoid the use of services whose measured QoS properties deviate from our requirements), context-aware (e.g., service compositions can be executed by means of several external services, on the basis of the knowledge of the user input and the actual available services, obtainable only at run-time). Considering the differences between our work and the application computing view, rules we use are not applied only to re-establish the equilibrium between environment and application, but also to delay the association of the activities to be executed with the concrete services till runtime.

7 Conclusion

In this paper we have focused on the definition of proper linguistic and infrastructural mechanisms to support self-configuration of a service composition.

As future work we plan to extend the language and the platform to support dynamic negotiation of service level agreements with component services and to drive dynamic changes in the structure of the composition itself.

We also need to continue with the evaluation of the approach for what concern both performances and usability.

Acknowledgements

This work is framed within *SeCSE* [17], IST Contract No. 511680. We thank all our partners in the project for their valuable comments.

References

1. L. Baresi and S. Guinea, "Towards Dynamic Monitoring of WS-BPEL Processes", In the Proceedings of the 3rd International Conference of Service-oriented Computing (ICSOC'05). Amsterdam, The Netherlands, 2005.
2. B. Benatallah, M. Dumas, and Q. Z. Sheng, "Facilitating the Rapid Development and Scalable Orchestration of Composite Web Services", *Distributed and Parallel Databases*, 17(1): pp. 5-37, Jan. 2005.
3. BPEL. "Business Process Execution Language for Web Services Version 1.1", http://www.ibm.com/developerworks/library/ws-bpel/. May 2003.
4. S. Carey, "Part 3: Making BPEL Processes Dynamic", SOA Best Practices: The BPEL Cookbook, OTN Oracle Web Site.
5. G. Cugola, and G. P. Picco, REDS: A Reconfigurable Dispatching System. Technical report, Politecnico di Milano, 2005.
6. A. Dan, et al., "Web Services on demand: WSLA-driven Automated Management", *IBM Systems Journal*, Volume 43, Number 1, pages 136-158, IBM Corporation, March, 2004.
7. V. De Antonellis, M. Melchiori, L. De Santis, M. Mecella, E. Mussi, B. Pernici, P. Plebani, "A layered architecture for flexible e-service invocation", *Software-Practice & Experience*. ISSN: 0038-0644, John Wiley & Sons, 2005.
8. M. Di Penta, R. Esposito, M. L. Villani, R. Codato, M. Colombo, and E. Di Nitto, "WS Binder: a Framework to enable Dynamic Binding of Composite Web Services", in the Proceedings of the *ICSE Workshop on Service-Oriented Software Engineering* (IW-SOSE06), Shanghai China May 2006.
9. Drools. Java rule Engine. http://drools.org/.
10. K. Geminiuc, "Part 1: A Services-Oriented Approach to Business Rules Development", SOA Best Practices: The BPEL Cookbook, OTN Oracle Web Site.
11. IBM, "Autonomic computing: Enabling Self Managing Solutions", SOA and autonomic computing, IBM Whitepaper, Dec. 2005.
12. D. J. Mandell and S. A. McIlraith, "Adapting BPEL4WS for the Semantic Web: The Bottom-Up Approach to Web Service Interoperation", in the Proceedings of the Second International Semantic Web Conference (ISWC2003), Sanibel Island, Florida, 2003.
13. B. Orriens, J. Yang, and M.P. Papazoglou, "A Framework for Business Rule Driven Service Composition", in the Proceedings of the *3rd VLDB-TES Workshop*, Berlin, September 2003.
14. M. Parashar, and S. Hariri, "Autonomic Computing: An Overview", UPP 2004, Mont Saint-Michel, France, Editors: J.-P. Banâtre et al. LNCS, Springer Verlag, Vol. 3566.
15. PXE BPEL engine. http://www.fivesight.com/pxe.shtml.
16. F. Rosenberg, and S. Dustdar, "Towards a Distributed Service-Oriented Business Rules System", in the Proceedings of *IEEE European Conference on Web services* (ECOWS), 14-16 November 2005, IEEE Computer Society Press.
17. SeCSE Website: http://secse.eng.it/.
18. K. Verma, R. Akkiraju, R. Goodwin, P. Doshi, J. Lee, "On Accommodating Inter Service Dependencies in Web Process Flow Composition", in the Proceedings of *AAAI Spring Symposium on Semantic Web Services*, 2004.
19. K. Verma, K. Gomadam, A. P. Sheth, J. A. Miller, and Z. Wu, "The METEOR-S Approach for Configuring and Executing Dynamic Web Processes", Tech. Report 2005.
20. 3GPP, Technical Specification Group Core Network, Open Service Access (OSA), "Parlay X Web Services; Part 2: Third Party Call (Release 6)", 3rd Generation Partnership Project Technical Specification 29.199-2, v2.0.0 (2004-09).

A Self-healing Web Server Using Differentiated Services

Henri Naccache[1], Gerald C. Gannod[2,*,**], and Kevin A. Gary[3]

[1] Dept. of Computer Science & Engineering, Arizona State University
Box 878809, Tempe, AZ 85287
henri@asu.edu

[2] Dept. of Computer Science & Systems Analysis
Miami University, Oxford OH 45056
gannodg@muohio.edu

[3] Division of Computing Studies, Arizona State University
7001 E. Williams Field Rd., Mesa, AZ 85212
kgary@asu.edu

Abstract. Web-based portals are a convenient and effective mechanism for integrating information from a wide variety of sources, including Web services. However, since availability and performance of Web services cannot be guaranteed, availability of information and overall performance of a portal can vary. In this paper, we describe a framework for developing an autonomic self-healing portal system that relies on the notion of differentiated services (i.e., services that provide common behavior with variable quality of service) in order to survive unexpected traffic loads and slowdowns in underlying Web services. We also present a theoretical performance model that predicts the impact of the framework on existing systems. We demonstrate the framework with an example and provide an evaluation of the technique.

1 Introduction

In this paper we present a preliminary investigation into a self-healing framework implemented within a Java-based Web portal. As the load on the portal increases, and the response times surpass those set forth in the service level agreement (SLA), the framework directs the underlying adaptive-content aware components to lower their output resolution. The lowering of the output resolution of the components minimizes the service demands of the components on the system and allows for higher request loads to be handled within the same SLA.

Along with the preliminary implementation, we present a Queuing Network (QN) analytical model that shows the expected increase in request load handling that can be gained by implementing the self-healing framework. The sample

* This author supported by National Science Foundation CAREER grant No. CCR-0133956.

** Contact Author.

A. Dan and W. Lamersdorf (Eds.): ICSOC 2006, LNCS 4294, pp. 203–214, 2006.

portal implementation relies upon the database-driven nature of modern web applications.

The benefits of our framework are tangible when the site is hit with a higher than expected request load, usually the result of a *flash crowd* (the "Slashdot effect") [1] that would normally slow or stop a site from responding to requests. With our self-healing approach, the server can handle a much higher maximum load as it lowers the resolution of the web pages to just the minimum needed to convey the requested information. This approach requires a small investment in software that can reduce the cost of hardware needed to run a portal website. Normal capacity planning requires that the server support the peak load rather than the average load [2]. With our self-healing framework in place, the hardware requirements can be defined to meet the SLA of the average request load at full resolution and the peak load at the lowest resolution.

While admission control and queue management have been shown to improve throughput [3] and response times [4], the cost incurred is request refusal. We consider request refusal to be the worst experience an end-user can have. Most visitors in a flash crowd will be looking for the same information. In order for the site to survive the flash crowd it must allocate its resources optimally and only return the lowest feasible resolution of information while not refusing any valid requests.

The remainder of this paper is organized as follows. Section 2 describes background material on autonomic computing, adaptive content and QN models. The self-healing portal framework is presented in Section 3. An evaluation of that implementation is presented in Section 4. Section 5 discusses related work. Finally, Section 6 draws conclusions and suggests future investigations.

2 Background

This section describes background material in the areas of autonomic computing, adaptive content and QN models.

2.1 Self-healing Systems

The term *autonomic* comes from the autonomic nervous system found in mammals and other higher order creatures [5]. This aspect of the nervous system allows for necessary body functions to perform without conscious thought given to them. The fundamentals of autonomic computing revolve around self-managing components. In this context, inter-component collaboration is defined in a self-managing manner. The goals of autonomic computing are to minimize human intervention in system administration and to maximize reliability and system uptime. In order to do so, IBM has defined four fundamental features of components: *self-configuring, self-healing, self-optimizing and self-protecting* [6]. Self-healing systems "discover, diagnose, and react to disruptions". Self-healing systems must be able to recover from the failure of underlying components and services. The system must be able to detect and isolate the failed component, fix or replace the component, and finally reintroduce the repaired or replaced component without any apparent application disruption. Self-healing systems need to monitor components in order to predict problems and take action before complete component failure takes place. The objective of self-healing components is to minimize the number and duration of outages in order to maintain high levels of application availability.

An autonomic component consists of two integrated parts: a managed element, the underlying service or component, and an autonomic manager. [7] The manager is in charge of maintaining status information about the managed element and making sure that the managed element remains healthy.

Our research into differentiated services at the web application level is an example of a self-healing autonomic system.

2.2 Adaptive Content

An approach to QoS management at the web server level is to adapt the content in order to minimize bandwidth usage. The common approach is to re-encode multimedia files into lower-quality, and therefore smaller, files. This has been proposed by Bellavista [8] among others. The majority of this research was done in the early days of the internet before the current prevalence of dynamic database driven websites and the performance issues that come along with them.

Abdelzaher [9] offered an approach to minimize bandwidth requirements by providing two completely distinct websites on the same server. The sites offer the same base content, but each has a different resolution of content. This differs from the multimedia-only encoding in that it can also offer differentiated text-based content. In this system the two sites have to have similar file structures and file names, and have to be manually created by the webmaster. Depending on the current QoS level the server responds to a request with a file from either "tree".

We apply adaptive content techniques to dynamic multi-tiered web applications in order to maximize throughput at the server level.

2.3 QN Models

Analytic performance models are used to predict the response of a system to various configuration and design changes. They are composed of a set of computational algorithms that use actual workload parameters to compute the performance characteristics of a system. Using various analytic models, one can identify bottlenecks and estimate upper bounds on response times.

Queuing Network (QN) models are one way of creating an analytic performance model of a system. Menasce [10] defines a QN model as a collection of interconnected queues. Queues include both the resource providing the service and the waiting line to access that resource. The QN is used to model a system and estimate the performance impacts of design decisions. Two parameter types are used in creating QN models: workload intensity and service demands. Workload intensity provides an indication of the load of the system, and service demands are the average response times of specific resources in the system.

QN models can be used to represent multiclass systems. A multiclass system is one that supports more than one type of request. Services that output multiple resolutions can be modeled as multiclass systems. Open and closed networks represent two types of request arrival distributions. Open networks assume that request arrivals are uniformly distributed and throughput is used as a parameter to the model, while closed networks are used to model bulk or batch jobs where there is an assumption of a near constant number of requests in the system.

Response times R_c (Eq. 1 [10]) are calculated in a multiclass open QN based upon the utilization of each device (U_i) and the service demand of the user class on the device i: $D_{i,c}$.

$$R_c = \sum_{i=1}^{K} \frac{D_{i,c}}{1 - U_i} \tag{1}$$

Where the units for R_c are seconds, $D_{i,c}$ are seconds/request, c is the user class, i is the device and K is the total number of devices in the system. The total utilization of a device U_i is the sum of the utilizations due to all classes (Eq. 2). When $U_i = 1$ the device is fully utilized. The per class utilization is a product of arrival rates λ_c and service demands.

$$U_i = \sum_{c=1}^{C} U_{i,c} = \sum_{c=1}^{C} \lambda_c * D_{i,c} \tag{2}$$

In this paper we use a QN model with a modified response time formula to estimate the impact our framework will have on existing web applications.

3 Approach

This section describes the proposed framework for developing QN models with resolution factors and self-healing portal systems.

3.1 QN Model with Resolution Factors

In a QN model each device that impacts the performance of the system is modeled. Each device must have the service demands ($D_{i,c}$) measured for each class of request, where c is the user class, and i is the device. The service demands are represented as the time spent for the device to complete the request. The goal of the adaptive content framework is to lower the service demand on the most bottleneck-prone parts of the system. By reducing the resolution, the service demand on a device will go down by some factor.

We represent the impact of lowering the resolution as the resolution factor $F_{i,x}$, where x is the resolution level. For a full resolution request $F_{i,x} = 1$. The resolution factor is applied to the service demand in order to predict the response time R'_c for a given user class, as shown in Eq. (3).

$$R'_c = \sum_{i=1}^{K} \frac{D_{i,c} * F_{i,x}}{1 - U'_i} \tag{3}$$

Where c is the user class, i is the device and K is the total number of devices in the system. The total utilization of a device U_i' is the sum of the utilizations from all classes. The per class utilization is a product of arrival rates and service demands.

$$U_i' = \sum_{c=1}^{C} U_{i,c}' = \sum_{c=1}^{C} \lambda_c * D_{i,c} * F_{i,x} \tag{4}$$

Where λ is the arrival rate of requests of the class c. The first summation in Eq. (4) states that the utilization of a device is the sum of utilizations from all classes in the system. The second summation, which represents the per class utilization for a device, is the product of the arrival rates, the service demand and the resolution factor.

Our goal is to create a set of resolution factors that we can use to predict the impact of the self-healing framework on an existing web application. We will accomplish this by analyzing existing web applications, implementing our framework and measuring the impact on the service demands.

3.2 Portal System

We have developed a framework for developing self-healing portal systems based on monitoring service latency and overall system rendering performance. In contrast to the approach by Menasce et al. where QoS is managed by individual services [11], our approach places the burden of achieving a negotiated level of service on a portal application. As such, applications built within this framework provide user-level guarantees of QoS rather than component level guarantees, all of which can be managed dynamically at run-time.

Figure 1 shows the conceptual architecture of the approach that we have developed for creating self-healing portal systems that manage and monitor the use of several services. In the figure, the portal server is shown in the middle part of the diagram, clients on the left, and services, running on separate machines, shown on the right. As indicated in the diagram, a portal server in our framework is made up of a portal hosting system, autonomic monitor, and several self-healing portlet wrappers (one per service rendering portlet). The approach works as follows. The autonomic monitor continuously monitors the portal system state to determine whether the portal system is operating within certain specified parameters. The frequency of the checks typically corresponds with the frequency of client requests, but it may vary. When a request is made upon the portal, a QoS portlet wrapper checks the load on the system using a query to the monitor. Based on the load, the recent response times of the service, and the SLA for the user, the portlet wrapper potentially modifies the request and makes call to the corresponding service.

We have developed our approach with the following concerns in mind. First, we view services as potentially uncontrollable assets. The ability or inability to deliver specific levels of service is subject to network latency and load of the server or servers providing the service.

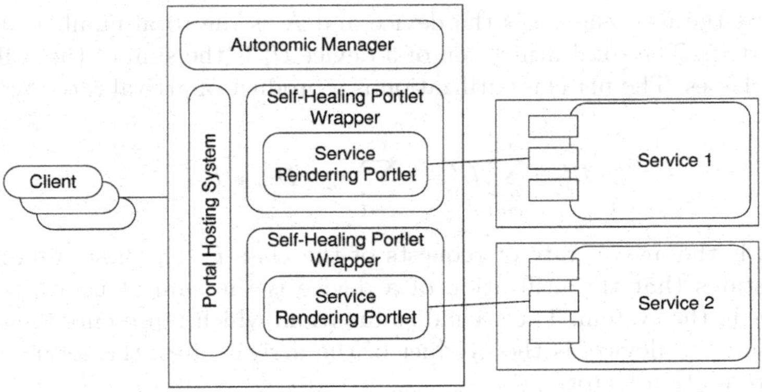

Fig. 1. Portal Conceptual Architecture

Second, for the end-server (i.e., the portal server providing some application), the potential variability in level of service caused by the aforementioned factors can be outweighed by the time to render the local application. That is, we take a global approach to providing an improved response time for an application by measuring time to render an application that utilizes services rather than optimizing individual services. As such, our approach for providing QoS-aware portal systems is based on the following concepts.

Monitoring: In order for an autonomic portal to properly meet service level agreements, it must be capable of monitoring its current load. Based on system upgrade and downgrade policies, this information is used to determine how information is requested from channels or service providers, and how that data is subsequently rendered in the portal.

Feedback: As stated by Bouch et al. [12], user experiences and acceptance of variations in performance are affected by feedback. In our approach, we use visual feedback to provide users with an indication of system state in order to provide explanations of why behaviors of services may differ over time.

Differentiation: We consider two forms of differentiation within our approach. First, at the user level, there are different user classes that each have different SLAs. The QoS levels that each user class receives are selected according the SLAs. Second, at the service level, we consider different service resolutions. The different resolutions are intended to affect the overall size of a package returned by a service as well as the amount of processing required to render a portal page.

4 Evaluation

In this section we describe the process by which we evaluated the self-healing portal system. Figure 2 provides an overview of the deployment of the portal

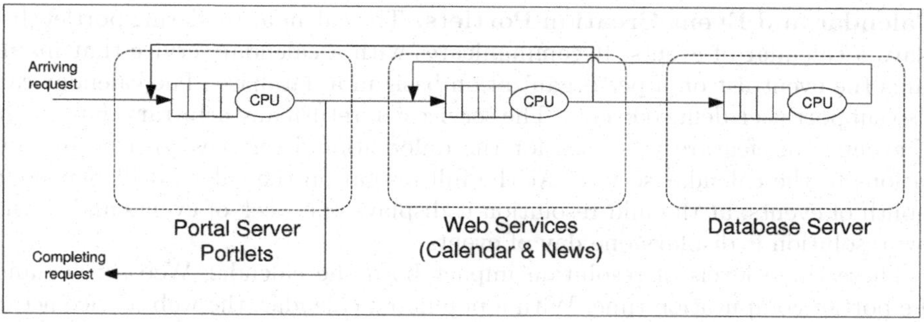

Fig. 2. 3-tiered Portal Application

system that we evaluated. The three CPUs and queues represent the devices for the QN model that we solved.

4.1 Performance Testing

All tests were run on three desktop-class computers running RedHat Fedora Core4. The database server was a 1Ghz Athlon with 512M of RAM, the web services server was a 1.7Ghz Pentium with 1G of RAM, and the portal server was a 2.6Ghz Pentium with 2G of RAM. The operating systems were not tuned in any way and other applications were running at the same time (standard desktop environment) but care was taken not to use the machine while the tests were underway. Apache Benchmark [13] was used to load test the portal container. This program allows you to configure either the number of requests it will make or the time spent on the test and the number of concurrent requests it will make at a given time. The response data was returned with the median response time, the mean response time and breakdown of what percentage of requests were returned within a given response time.

In order to bypass the HTTP-session based user authentication mechanism of Jetspeed, some extra parameters were passed along with the URL of the portal web page. These extra parameters were read by the outermost timing filter and used to populate the HTTP session with the user class and current service level that the QoSWrappers should use. These two parameters were used in order to be able to control the tests in a way that would have been impossible if the QoS monitor system was given full control of the differentiated service levels.

4.2 Portal Configuration and Resolutions

Three resolutions were defined for each of the portlets in the system. The services include a calendar service (for displaying scheduled events in a calendar), event service (for scheduling events in a calendar), and a news service (for displaying top news items). Each utilizes three QoS levels corresponding to high resolution, middle resolution, and low or minimum resolution data.

Calendar and Event Creation Portlets. The calendar rendering portlet displays a calendar of events. It communicates with a calendar service that maintains the event list on a per-organization basis in a database. The calendar can also support user-defined events. The service can return any arbitrary date range of events; this feature was used for the differentiated services with no modifications to the calendar service. At the full resolution the calendar displays one month of events, at the mid resolution it displays one week of events and at the low resolution it displays one day of events.

These three levels of resolution impact both the calendar Web service and the portlet computation time. With a populated calendar, the web service needs fewer database queries and less processing to respond to a request for fewer days. As the number of days is minimized, the portlet requires less processing time to loop through the number of days being displayed and render the HTML version of the calendar. While the total time is not impacted greatly in the portlet, the amount of memory used is, and the less memory you use per request in a Java Web server, the less often the memory garbage collection has to run, improving the overall performance of the web server.

The other calendar portlet is an event creation portlet. This portlet allows the user to create a new calendar event, which is processed by the portlet and then sent to the calendar web service. Depending on the user class and the current service level it may be either rendered or disabled.

News Portlet. The news portlet follows a similar architecture to that of the calendar. It talks to a news web service that stores the news items in the database and will return a requested number of news items for a given course. The three differentiated service levels for the news portlet follow the same approach as the calendar. For the full level of service, it renders the 10 most recent news items, for the mid level of service, it only renders the 3 most recent items and for the low level of service it only renders the most recent news item.

4.3 QN Model and Performance Testing Results

Using the Service Demand Law the service demands $D_{i,c}$ were computed for each device i and resolution c "as the average, for all requests, of the sum of the service times of that resource" [10]. The observed service demands are shown in Table 1. The impact of lowering the resolution is clearly visible in the service demands on the portal server and web services CPUs. The database was not taxed in this model; we believe this is because the data set was relatively small and

Table 1. Service Demands

	Portal CPU	Web Service CPU	Database CPU
Full Resolution	0.270	0.225	0.009
Mid Resolution	0.188	0.050	0.004
Low Resolution	0.171	0.018	0.004

could fit in memory. As the resolution is lowered, the service demand on the web services CPU drops drastically; we believe this is because much less data is being requested from the database, processed and converted into SOAP messages. Finally, the service demand on the portal server CPU remains high even as the resolution is lowered, due to the high per-request overhead in Jetspeed. Based on this initial investigation, the resolution factors at low resolution were 0.63 for the portal CPU device and 0.08 for the Web service CPU device.

Once the service demands were computed for the three resolutions, the QN model was solved with 3 seconds as the target response time. The first set of columns in Table 2 shows the predicted throughput of the portal system. The second set of columns shows the results of the performance testing. Performance tests were run for 60 seconds. The concurrency level was changed for each test until a 3 second response time was attained.

Table 2. QN Model and Performance Testing Results

	QN Model		Performance Tests	
	Req/Sec	Response Time	Req/Sec	Response Time
Full Resolution	3.52	3.01sec	4.33	2.99sec
Mid Resolution	4.98	3.01sec	5.11	3.03sec
Low Resolution	5.52	3.07sec	5.57	3.05sec

As one can see, the QN model we used did not perfectly predict the throughput necessary to create a 3 second response time. This may be because other programs impacted the measurement of the service demands. While the predicted QN model numbers are not exactly the same, they are quite close and follow the trend of the actual response times and throughput measured during the performance testing phase. The results of both the performance tests and QN model show that the self-healing system will, in this case, allow for a 33% increase in throughput without any changes to the hardware configuration and without reverting to refusing requests. When these tests were run on a single server-class multiprocessor computer the increase was 87%. We presented the results of the slower multiple server scenario to better show the QN model (the multiple CPUs on the server-class computer would be represented by a single device).

5 Related Work

Pradhan [14] took the approach of using the request file type as the criterion used to separate the requests into different queues. Each file type queue was assigned a weight, and as the load increased on the server, certain file types were given less priority. By doing so Pradhan shows that observation-based adaptation of the queues is advantageous compared to statically setting the QoS parameters. Urgaonkar [15] and others define and assign requests into multiple user classes to differentiate the service level per request. Their approaches classify the user class of the request and assign it to the appropriate queue. If the server approaches overload, the lower class requests are dropped or delayed in order to allow the higher user class requests to go through. Menasce [3] modifies the single request queue of the Apache web server in order to balance throughput and request times. By reducing the size of the incoming request queue, he limits the number of concurrent requests the server has to handle, thereby keeping the response time per request under a specified value. The trade-off here is that when the queue is shorter there are more rejected requests. Zhou [16] has a similar user class queuing approach, but also allows for lower class users to enter into the higher class queues if that will not impact the overall QoS of the higher classes. Urgaonkar et al [17] also describe a performance model for multi-tier dynamic websites that uses the Mean-Value Analysis algorithm for closed-queuing networks to estimate response times. They present two solutions to overload situations: dynamic capacity provisioning in order to respond to peak workloads without denying requests and policing requests with an admission control policy that refuses requests that would exceed the SLA.

Research into self-healing web service systems has included self-managing and self-recovering autonomic systems. The majority of the relevant self-managing systems used an autonomic manager to choose between equivalent services. Sadjadi et al. [18] address self-management of composite systems using autonomic computing. Their goal is to use two different equivalent web services (images from a surveillance system) in order to create a fault-tolerant system. Liao et al. [19] also use autonomic computing to manage composition of web services. They use a "federated multi-agent system for autonomic management of web services ... for autonomic service discovery, negotiation, and cooperation". They propose that the use of autonomic computing to manage the federation of agents will "simplify the control of web services composition, sharing and interaction". They offer some rules for selecting alternative web services in the case where the currently selected web service is no longer responding within its SLA. Maximilien [20] uses the term "self-adjusting" to describe the mechanism by which web service selection should be undertaken. Other research into self-healing systems has covered the total server failure scenarios [21] and transaction-based models for recovery of failed systems [22].

6 Conclusions and Future Investigations

The self-healing portal system presented in this paper is our initial investigation into autonomic systems. The system uses the ability of the underlying services to respond to requests at different resolutions in order to complete the end-user's request without breaking the SLA. As the load on the system increases, the responses become smaller, until they contain only the most critical information. We also presented a QN model with an added resolution factor to predict the response times and throughput of the portal application.

Using our framework, few changes are necessary in order to convert an existing web application system into a self-healing system. Either the underlying services are unchanged or a light-weight wrapper that will know how to respond to lower resolution requests needs to be written. Minor changes may be needed to the front-end components in order to render the lower resolution requests correctly. The benefits of the system are evidenced by increased throughput without increased response times. While this implementation does not cover some of the more familiar self-healing functionality (e.g., complete failure of a component or system), we do not foresee anything in the design or implementation that would hamper the co-existence of our self-healing system with other autonomic systems.

We plan on continuing this line of research by implementing our framework in existing open source web applications such as a blogging site, a discussion forum and an e-commerce site. Using the results of this work we will refine our set of resolution factors. We would like to be able to analyze an existing web application and accurately predict, using our knowledge base, the potential impact of the self-healing framework. Future investigations will cover a more robust autonomic manager and integration of other autonomic features and frameworks.

References

1. N. Feamster, J. Winick, and J. Rexford. A model of bgp routing for network engineering. In *SIGMETRICS 2004/PERFORMANCE 2004: Proceedings of the joint international conference on Measurement and modeling of computer systems*, pages 331–342, New York, NY, USA, 2004. ACM Press.
2. Virgilio A.F. Almeida and Daniel A. Menasce. Capacity planning: An essential tool for managing web services. *IT Professional*, 4:33 – 38, Jul/Aug 2002.
3. Daniel Menasce and Mohamed Bennani. On the use of performance models to design self-managing computer systems. In *Computer Measurement Group*, 2003.
4. Vikram Kanodia and Edward Knightly. Ensuring latency targets in multiclass web servers. *IEEE Transactions on Parallel and Distributed Systems*, 14:84–93, 2003.
5. Network world: Autonomic computing. http://www.networkworld.com/links/ Encyclopedia/A/842.html, November 2002.
6. A.G. Ganek and T.A. Corbi. The dawning of the autonomic computing era. Technical report, IBM, 2003.
7. A. Zeid and S. Gurguis. Towards autonomic web services. In *Computer Systems and Applications, 2005. The 3rd ACS/IEEE International Conference on*, pages 69–, 2005.
8. Paolo Bellavista, Antonio Corradi, Rebecca Montanari, and Cesare Stefanelli. An active middleware to control QoS level of multimedia services. In *IEEE Workshop on Future Trends of Distributed Computing Systems*, page IEEE, 2001.
9. Tarek F. Abdelzaher, Kang G. Shin, and Nina Bhatti. Performance guarantees for web server end-systems: A control-theoretical approach. *IEEE Trans. Parallel Distrib. Syst.*, 13(1):80–96, 2002.
10. Daniel A. Menasce, Virgilio A.F. Almeida, and Lawrence W. Dowdy. *Performance by Design*. Pretince Hall, 2004.
11. Daniel A. Menasce, Honglei Ruan, and Hassan Gomaa. A framework for qos-aware software components. In *Proceedings of the fourth international workshop on Software and performance*, pages 186–196. ACM Press, 2004.

12. Anna Bouch, Allan Kuchinsky, and Nina Bhatti. Quality is in the eye of the beholder: meeting users' requirements for internet quality of service. In *Proceedings of the SIGCHI conference on Human factors in computing systems*, pages 297–304. ACM Press, 2000.
13. Apache Software Foundation. Apache benchmark. [Online] Available http://httpd.apache.org/docs/programs/ab.html, March 2005.
14. P. Pradhan, R. Tewari, S. Sahu, C. Chandra, and P. Shenoy. An observation-based approach towards self-managing web servers. International Workshop on Quality of Service, 2002.
15. Bhuvan Urgaonkar and Prashant Shenoy. Cataclysm: policing extreme overloads in internet applications. In *WWW '05: Proceedings of the 14th international conference on World Wide Web*, pages 740–749, New York, NY, USA, 2005. ACM Press.
16. X. Zhou, Y. Cai, and G. Godavari. An adaptive process allocation strategy for proportional responsiveness differentiation on web servers. In *IEEE International Conference on Web Services ICWS 2004*, pages 142–149, 2004.
17. Bhuvan Urgaonkar, Giovanni Pacifici, Prashant Shenoy, Mike Spreitzer, and Asser Tantawi. An analytical model for multi-tier internet services and its applications. In *SIGMETRICS '05: Proceedings of the 2005 ACM SIGMETRICS international conference on Measurement and modeling of computer systems*, pages 291–302, New York, NY, USA, 2005. ACM Press.
18. S.M. Sadjadi and P.K. McKinley. Using transparent shaping and web services to support self-management of composite systems. In *Autonomic Computing, 2005. ICAC 2005. Proceedings. Second International Conference on*, pages 76–87, 2005.
19. Bei-Shui Liao, Ji Gao, Jun Hu, and Jiu-Jun Chen. A federated multi-agent system: autonomic control of web services. In *Machine Learning and Cybernetics, 2004. Proceedings of 2004 International Conference on*, volume 1, pages 1–6 vol.1, 2004.
20. E. Michael Maximilien and Munindar P. Singh. Toward autonomic web services trust and selection. In *ICSOC '04: Proceedings of the 2nd international conference on Service oriented computing*, pages 212–221, New York, NY, USA, 2004. ACM Press.
21. G. Candea, E. Kiciman, S. Zhang, P. Keyani, and A. Fox. Jagr: an autonomous self-recovering application server. In *Autonomic Computing Workshop, 2003*, pages 168–177, 2003.
22. G. Eddon and S. Reiss. Myrrh: A transaction-based model for autonomic recovery. In *Autonomic Computing, 2005. ICAC 2005. Proceedings. Second International Conference on*, pages 315–325, 2005.

Quality of Service Enabled Database Applications

S. Krompass, D. Gmach, A. Scholz, S. Seltzsam, and A. Kemper

TU München, D-85748 Garching, Germany
{krompass, gmach, scholza, seltzsam, alfons.kemper}@in.tum.de

Abstract. In today's enterprise service oriented software architectures, database systems are a crucial component for the quality of service (QoS) management between customers and service providers. The database workload consists of requests stemming from many different service classes, each of which has a dedicated service level agreement (SLA). We present an adaptive QoS management that is based on an economic model which adaptively penalizes individual requests depending on the SLA and the current degree of SLA conformance that the particular service class exhibits. For deriving the adaptive penalty of individual requests, our model differentiates between *opportunity costs* for underachieving an SLA threshold and *marginal gains* for (re-)achieving an SLA threshold. Based on the penalties, we develop a database component which schedules requests depending on their deadline and their associated penalty. We report experiments of our operational system to demonstrate the effectiveness of the adaptive QoS management.

1 Introduction

Future business software systems will be designed as service oriented architectures. These services are accessed via the Internet by a variety of different users – as exemplified by providers and vendors of Web-based business software, including RightNow Technologies, Salesforce.com, hosted SAP, and Oracle. This Web-based software is characterized by a multitude of services which invoke other enterprise services and ultimately submit requests to databases. The Web-based business software is made accessible for a multitude of customers, where each customer may have individual quality of service (QoS) requirements. The more customers access the services, the more they compete for system resources. In an uncontrolled environment this may lead to unpredictable and unacceptable response times. To prevent the customers from suffering bad performance in terms of response times of their invoked services, service level agreements (SLAs) are negotiated.

An SLA is a formal agreement between the service provider and a customer. The establishment of an SLA imposes obligations on the service provider regarding the service level of the provided services. If the constraints formulated in the SLA are violated after a certain time window, the *evaluation period*, the service provider is fined. The penalty depends on the severity of the SLA violation and

A. Dan and W. Lamersdorf (Eds.): ICSOC 2006, LNCS 4294, pp. 215–226, 2006.

is negotiated in the SLA. SLAs are typically only defined for services directly invoked by customers. Thus, the goal is to establish an end-to-end control for the quality of service, which covers all layers of the Web service architecture.

The contribution of this paper is to enable QoS for the bottom layer of a service infrastructure, where almost all services access a shared database. This is a very common scenario in mission-critical enterprise services that rely on an integrated database. For this scenario, we assume that an SLA for every service submitting requests to the database has been negotiated. Due to the multitude of services which access the database, the workload of the database consists of requests stemming from many different customers with different service classes, each having a dedicated SLA.

The challenge is to schedule incoming database requests in order to meet the performance goals specified in the SLAs. Scheduling is based on *adaptive priorities* which are derived from the current level of conformance with the request's SLA, that is, the percentage of timely requests, and the economic importance of this SLA relative to other pending requests' SLAs.

Current solutions in database systems, e.g., the Query Patroller for DB2 [7] or the Oracle Resource Manager [13], assign groups of customers to performance classes with static priorities. Thus, each request is assigned its priority depending solely on the client by whom it has been submitted. This *static prioritization* is used to schedule the requests, so that high-priority clients should complete faster on average than their low-priority counterparts.

This approach is sufficient to fulfill the requirements of particularly valuable customers. However, it cannot adequately manage overall SLA enforcement. Consider an SLA which requires 90% of all service requests to be processed within a certain time window. With static prioritization, SLAs for high-priority customers are likely to be overfulfilled by processing almost all requests in time. However, during peak-load times, it is likely that they overachieve their SLAs at the expense of lower-priority users. From a business-oriented point of view, it is desirable to provide only the service level which has been negotiated in the SLA. If SLAs are not overfulfilled, the additional free resources are used for satisfying SLAs that are violated with the static prioritization.

For this purpose, we developed a QoS management concept based on an economic model which adaptively prioritizes individual requests depending on the SLA and the current degree of SLA conformance that the particular service class exhibits. The core of the QoS management consists of *penalty-carrying requests*, that is, database requests which carry the requirements needed to fulfill the SLA constraints from the submitting service to the database.

The rest of the paper is organized as follows: Section 2 describes the two cost components, *marginal gains* and *opportunity costs*, of our QoS model in detail and presents the adaptive QoS management with which penalty-carrying requests are derived. Section 3 describes the system architecture and the implementation of our QoS management. The scheduling of the requests is in the focus of Section 4, followed by the evaluation results of our prototypical implementation in Section 5. An overview of related work is presented in Section 6.

Finally, in Section 7, we summarize the conclusions of our study and outline ongoing and future research on this subject.

2 Quality of Service Model

The central concept of our quality of service management is adaptive penalization of individual requests according to the current degree of *SLA conformance* c. The conformance is monitored per service class, that is, for each transaction type invoked by an individual customer and the associated SLA. We define c as

$$c = \frac{\text{Number of timely transaction invocations}}{\text{Total number of invocations of the transaction}}$$

In practice, so-called *step-wise SLAs* are commonly used to specify the QoS requirements of a service class. The SLAs consist of one or more *percentile constraints* and an optional *deadline constraint.* Percentile constraints require $n\%$ of all service requests to be processed within x seconds. If a percentile constraint is violated after the evaluation period, a penalty p for every m percentage points under fulfillment is due. Furthermore, p_{max} defines a maximum penalty for violating a percentile constraint. The deadline constraint – which does not incur any penalty – specifies an upper bound for the execution time of the service request. An example for a step-wise SLA with one percentile constraint d_1 and one deadline constraint d_2 is shown in the following:

> d_1: 90% in less than $5s$; p = \$900 per 10 percentage points of underfulfillment, p_{max} = \$1800; evaluation period: 1 month (e.g., end of month)
>
> d_2: Deadline $15s$

In general, SLAs contain additional constraints such as sizing constraints which restrict the maximum number of transaction invocations per time period. We concentrate on fulfilling response time constraints with the percentile and deadline constraints, assuming any additional SLA constraints are obtained.

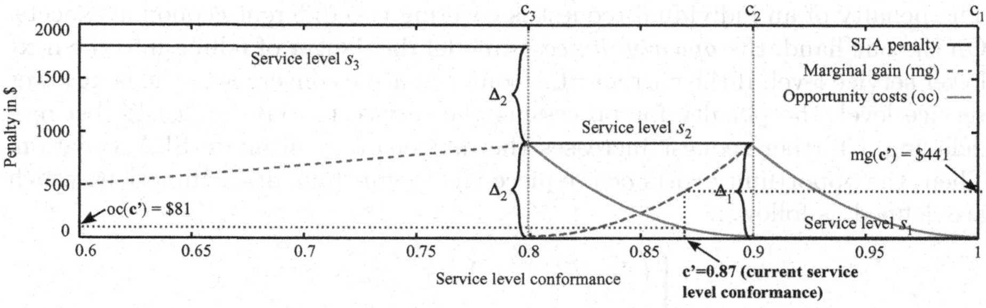

Fig. 1. Visualization of SLA constraint d_1

A percentile constraint in a fixed step-wise SLA implicitly defines an SLA penalty function with n steps. The penalty function for d_1 of our sample SLA is shown as the step function in Figure 1 (black solid lines). With c_i, $1 \leq i \leq n+1$, we denote the boundaries of the steps of the SLA penalty function. For the example in Figure 1, we have $c_4 = 0$ (not in the figure), $c_3 = 0.8$, $c_2 = 0.9$, and $c_1 = 1$.

Using the SLA penalty function, we define *service levels* as follows: For a penalty function with n steps, let $s_i, 1 \leq i \leq n$, denote the ith service level. This level is defined in the interval $[c_{i+1}, c_i[$, so that dropping to a lower service level corresponds to a higher penalty. Thereby, s_{i+1} denotes a lower service level than s_i, that is, the penalty incurred at s_{i+1} is higher than at s_i. We denote Δ_i as this cost difference between s_{i+1} and s_i.

As shown in Figure 1, our sample percentile constraint d_1 implicitly defines three service levels: Service level s_3 is defined in the interval $[0, 0.8[$, s_2 in $[0.8, 0.9[$, and s_1 in $[0.9, 1]$. The cost difference between service levels s_3 and s_2 is \$900 which is identical to the cost difference between s_2 and s_1.

2.1 Penalty-Carrying Requests

Penalty-carrying requests are queries with attached penalty information in a SQL-comment. For example, the penalty-carrying request for a `select`-Statement looks like this:

```
/* penalty ...
 * deadline ... */
select ... from ...
```

We use the SLA penalty function to compute these adaptive penalties for individual service requests. In the following section, we describe how to compute the adaptive penalty from the percentile constraint for an individual request. Then, we describe briefly the derivation of the deadline constraint for an individual query.

2.2 Deriving the Penalty for Individual Requests

The penalty of an individual request is covering two different economic aspects. On the one hand, the *opportunity costs* model the danger of falling into the next lower service level. If the current SLA conformance $\mathbf{c}$ converges to the next lower service level, the penalty for processing the service too late increases, because delaying a further request increases the danger of an ultimate SLA violation. Then, the opportunity costs oc are piece-wise defined quadratic functions which are defined as follows:

$$oc(\mathbf{c}) := \begin{cases} \left(\frac{c_{n-1}-\mathbf{c}}{c_{n-1}-c_n}\right)^2 \cdot \Delta_{n-1}, & c_n \leq \mathbf{c} < c_{n-1} \\ \dots & \\ \left(\frac{c_1-\mathbf{c}}{c_1-c_2}\right)^2 \cdot \Delta_1, & c_2 \leq \mathbf{c} < c_1 \\ 0, & \text{otherwise} \end{cases}$$

The rationale for choosing squared terms is given below. For the opportunity costs, we derive the decreasing parts of the parabolas as in Figure 1.

On the other hand, with *marginal gains*, we model the chance that a service class re-achieves a higher service level, that is, reaches s_i from s_{i+1}. If this appears to be "within reach", individual requests are penalized more and more to eventually achieve the higher level. The marginal gain mg is a piece-wise quadratic function:

$$mg(\mathbf{c}) := \begin{cases} \left(\frac{\mathbf{c}-c_{n+1}}{c_n-c_{n+1}}\right)^2 \cdot \Delta_{n-1}, & c_{n+1} \leq \mathbf{c} < c_n \\ \dots & \\ \left(\frac{\mathbf{c}-c_3}{c_2-c_3}\right)^2 \cdot \Delta_1, & c_3 \leq \mathbf{c} < c_2 \\ 0, & \text{otherwise} \end{cases}$$

Analogous to the opportunity costs, the rationale for choosing squared terms is given below. The marginal gain is depicted as increasing part of the parabolas in Figure 1.

If the SLA conformance of a request's service class is approaching the next lower service level, the chance for reaching the next higher service level is very small. Thus, the penalty of a request of this transaction is dominated by the opportunity costs. Similarly, the penalty is dominated by the marginal gain if the next higher service level is "within reach". Therefore, we define the penalty as the maximum of the computed opportunity costs and the marginal gain of this service request.

To define opportunity costs and marginal gains, we use a squared term – resulting in the parabolas – to weight the distance from the borders of neighboring service levels. If linear terms are used, requests stemming from SLAs with high penalties are almost always be handled with top priority, because there is only a very small area in the middle of a service level where the calculated penalties are low. This leads to overfulfillment and therefore an inferior overall performance. In contrast to that, if the order of the functions is chosen too high, the request has high priority only for SLA conformances near the borders of the next higher and next lower service level, respectively. So, if the opportunity costs are defined by higher order polynomials, there are only very few requests with high priority. If all of these requests are delayed, e.g., by waiting for database locks, the SLA conformance falls onto the next lower service level. To justify this rationale, we conducted extensive experimental studies, which cannot be reported here for space limitations. These studies have shown that squared terms were better suited to model the opportunity costs and marginal gains than linear order higher order terms.

2.3 Deriving the Deadline Constraint for Individual Requests

The time constraint of a deadline constraint x_d specifies an upper bound for the processing time of a transaction. We therefore need to derive the deadlines for individual requests of that transaction. Requests which have passed their deadline are scheduled with maximum priority. These requests most likely have a processing time that is less or equal to the observed average processing time as there are no requests with even higher priority. Note that the deadline is no guarantee, as high priority requests can still be delayed within the database if they access an object that is locked by a request with lower priority.

With enf_i, we denote the latest time at which a request r_i should be executed to be able to complete the respective transaction within the time constraint given by x_d. To compute enf_i, we monitor the execution times of requests already processed in the current transaction. In addition to that, we monitor previous invocations of the transaction and maintain the average processing time of each request. Thus, we derive the expected time to process the remaining requests by summing up the average response times of the requests. The time constraint enf_i for the current request is computed by subtracting the observed execution times and the expected time to process the remaining requests from x_d.

3 System Architecture and Implementation

To provide end-to-end quality of service for Web services, it is essential to incorporate all components of a Web service architecture, that is, the invoked service itself, all called sub-services and the databases at the bottom layer.

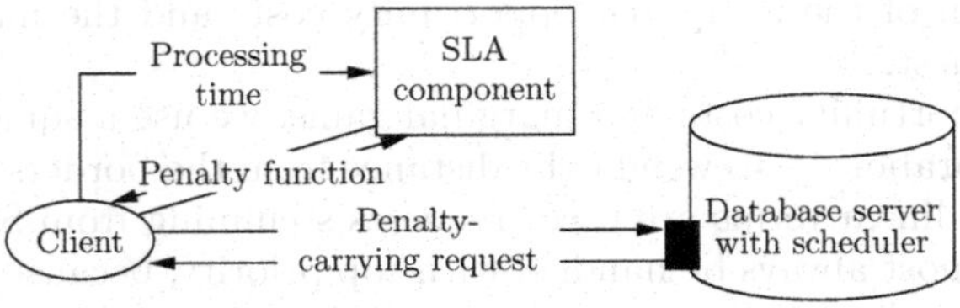

Fig. 2. Architecture Overview

A primary design goal for the implementation of the described concepts was to ease the future extension of the QoS management to entire Web service architectures. We therefore encapsulated all SLA-relevant functionality, including the monitoring of the SLA conformance and the generation of adaptive penalties, into a central entity, the *SLA component*. Figure 2 shows the resulting architecture. The SLA component can easily be extended to monitor the overall execution of Web service requests and not only derive adaptive penalties for the database layer, but also for all sub requests on the Web service layer. The adaptive penalties are piggybacked onto the corresponding requests and transported as penalty-carrying requests to the database. Upon completion of the database request, the SLA component is notified of the observed response time by the client and can thus update the current SLA conformance ratio.

The actual scheduling of requests is based on the adaptive penalties and is realized by a *scheduler*. The scheduler intercepts all arriving requests and carries out the admission control and the reordering of individual requests. The scheduler is architected as an external component so that it can be easily adapted to scheduling arbitrary service requests, besides the database requests exemplified here.

4 Request Scheduling

At the database server, the processing of a newly arriving penalty-carrying request works as follows. To prevent the database from being overloaded, the *admission control* limits the number of simultaneously executing requests. If the request it not immediately executed, it is *queued*. Prior to dequeueing a request, all queued requests are *scheduled*, that is, they are ordered by their priority. If there are sufficient system resources, requests are dequeued by the admission control.

In most current database systems, processes are assigned the same amount of resources, irrespective of the priority of the respective request. This implies that the available resources of the database are assigned in a round-robin manner to all active requests. In other words, all requests are equally important. To limit the database load it is therefore sufficient to restrict the number of concurrent queries, irrespective of their individual complexity [15].

As an alternative, we experimented with an admission control that is based on the optimizer costs of the requests that are currently being processed. However, our empirical studies, which cannot be shown here due to space restrictions, revealed that the query-complexity based admission control performed worse than simply controlling the multi-programming level by restricting the maximum number of concurrently processed requests.

Requests which are held back are put in one of two queues, as shown in Figure 3. Queue A holds requests which belong to running transactions, requests of transactions not yet started are maintained in queue B. Statements to be processed are chosen from queue A. Only if this queue is empty, new transactions are started by picking statements from queue B, so that running transactions are not unnecessarily delayed. Using this approach, we avoid the problem of *lock convoys* [6]. Lock convoys can arise if a transaction T_L which submits various requests to the database, exclusively locks a database object and there are pending requests of other transactions which intend to lock the same object. The queue of waiting objects does not shrink as long as the locking transaction is not finished. Before T_L releases the blocking lock, all of its requests need to be processed. Thus, intuitively, requests from active transactions are prioritized over requests from pending transactions.

Our goal is, prior to dequeuing a request, to create a schedule of the pending requests, such that the overall sum of incurred penalties is minimized. Thus, the requests are ordered in both queues according to their adaptive penalties. So, a request is inserted and removed, respectively, in $O(\log n)$ time by using a priority queue implementation, that is, the overhead for scheduling a request is negligible. For queue lengths of 150, which we observed in our benchmarks, the scheduling of a single request took about 0.28 milliseconds.

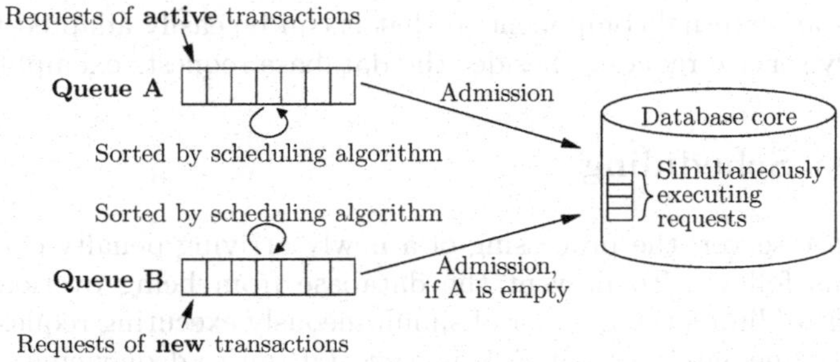

Fig. 3. Dual Queue Scheduling

5 Performance Evaluation

We performed comprehensive benchmarks using our prototype implementation to assess the effectiveness of the adaptive request-penalization. For the performance evaluation, we chose the TPC-C benchmark as a representative Online Transaction Processing (OLTP) workload.

5.1 Description of the Benchmarks

The TPC-C-benchmark models a company which is a wholesale supplier operating several warehouses which serve customers in geographically distributed sales districts. The database workload of the benchmark is centered around five principal business transactions of an order-entry environment. The transactions are invoked by *emulated users* whose behavior is controlled by *think times* and *keying times*. The detailed specification of the TPC-C benchmark can be found in [16].

The SLA for a transaction is based on the corresponding response time goal. For our experiments, we specified the SLAs using XML, similar to WS-Agreement [10], which is becoming a standard for establishing a service agreement between a service provider and a client. Our experiments are conducted with the step-wise SLAs introduced in Section 2. For each transaction, we define an SLA with a percentile and an deadline constraint. The percentile constraint requires 90% of the invocations to be processed in less than the corresponding response time requirement which is specified for each transaction in [16]. A violation of this constraint is fined with a penalty which depends on the terminal representing the client from which the transaction is invoked, that is, the SLA applies for the terminal and all transactions that are invoked from this terminal. In our test scenario, we chose a customer-mix where 15% of the terminals incur high ($1000), 35% incur medium ($200), and the remaining terminals incur low penalties ($40) if the corresponding SLA is violated. This customer mix models a service provider with a high number of regular customers that must be preferably processed compared to "normal" users. In order to avoid starvation of queued requests, we define an upper bound for the execution time of a transaction in our benchmark. The deadline for high-priority customers is three times the response time requirements. For medium- and low-priority customers, the deadline of the transactions is five and ten times of the response time requirement of that transaction.

For our experiments, we implemented our own version of the TPC-C benchmark based on MaxDB Version 7.5 [11]. The number of warehouses is held constant at 20, thus, the size of the database is about 2GB. As specified by the TPC-C, the number of terminals is ten times the number of warehouses, thus yielding a total number of 200 terminals during the benchmark.

For the benchmarks, we dimensioned the 100%-workload such that the required response times of the specification are met without any scheduling and admission control at all. Furthermore, we define a productive workload of 80%, as databases should not be operated at its limit due to possible load peaks. We control the workload by multiplying the keying and think times with a scaling factor.

A single benchmark consists of several phases. First, there is a "warmup" phase where the database is operated at 80% load for 15 minutes. Subsequently, 8 minute-periods of peak load (180% workload) alternate with "rest periods" (80% workload) which again last for 15 minutes. The benchmark terminated after an evaluation period of 65 minutes. After this time, the requests that have been accumulated in the second load peak, have been processed, so that the number of queued requests is reduced to the normal level again. The scheduler with admission control is configured such that the throughput is identical to the throughput of a benchmark with terminals directly connected to the database.

Our experiments are performed running the QoS-enabled database on a server with 1GB RAM and an Intel Xeon processor with 2.8GHz. The operating system is SUSE Linux Enterprise 9 based on kernel 2.6. All terminals run on another server with identical hardware and connect to the database via Gigabit-Ethernet using the MaxDB JDBC-driver.

5.2 Results

First, we present the analysis of the SLA conformance using static prioritization, that is, the priority of a customer remains constant throughout the entire benchmark. Figure 4 shows the SLA conformance for the NewOrder transaction which is the central transaction of the TPC-C benchmark. The values shown are the conformances at the end of the evaluation period for each of the terminals involved. The SLA conformances are ordered decreasingly, grouped by the priority of the terminals. With static prioritization, all SLAs for transactions stemming from high priority terminals are overfulfilled. 92% of the medium-priority terminals obtain their SLA, some of them with a conformance near 1. Only 6% of the low-priority terminals meet their SLA conformance requirements. The inequity between terminals having medium priority, i.e., terminals with the same SLA, arises if transactions from one terminal compete with more high-priority transactions than the other. Due to the lack of SLA awareness, the static prioritization cannot differentiate between a transaction stemming from a customer whose SLA is currently vastly overfulfilled and a transaction where the next higher service level is within reach.

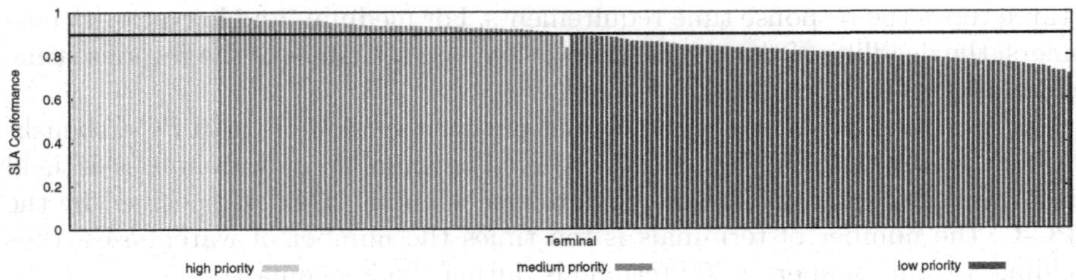

Fig. 4. SLA Conformance for all Terminals Using Static Prioritization

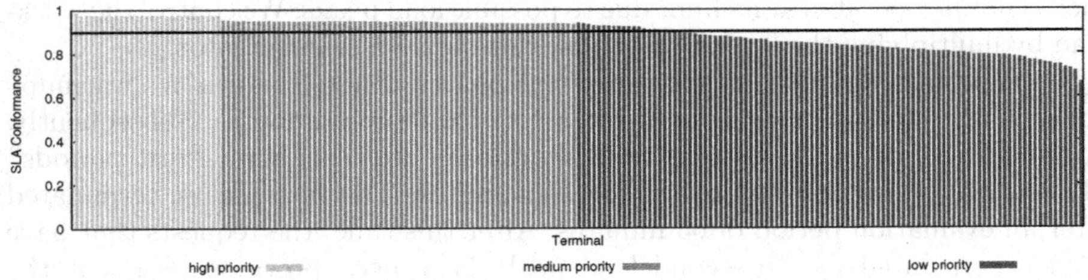

Fig. 5. SLA Conformance for all Terminals Using Adaptive Penalization

In contrast to this, the SLA conformance using adaptive prioritization is far more balanced within a group. Figure 5 shows the SLA compliance of all terminals using our novel adaptive penalization. Again, all high-priority terminals satisfy their SLAs. But the SLAs are not overfulfilled to the extent as with static prioritization, that is, the SLA conformance with static prioritization is 100% and with our adaptive prioritization between 97.3% and 98.8%. This adaptive "down-grading" of requests stemming from high-priority terminals is used to free resources for requests from low- and medium-priority terminals. Furthermore, as requests stemming from low-priority terminals do not have deadlines, these requests are delayed as long as possible to allow the prioritized execution of higher priority requests.

If the pending requests are statically prioritized, the reduction of costs induced by violating the SLAs of the terminals is due to favoring requests stemming from high-priority terminals to lower-priority requests. For our example configuration, the decrease of overall costs for all five transactions of the TPC-C is 53.5%, from \$17,600 using the static prioritization to \$8,180 with the adaptive penalization.

6 Related Work

Enabling QoS for Web service infrastructures is in the focus of our research group. Braumandl et al. [2] discuss distributed query processing systems on the Internet where the queries have different QoS demands. The paper presents an extension to the distributed query processing to support user QoS constraints. The query processor generates plans in such a way that its quality estimates are compliant with the user-defined quality constraints. Gmach et al. [5] present a fuzzy controller module which supervises services in a service oriented architecture. The controller executes appropriate actions to remedy overload, failure, and idle situations in the service architecture.

Quality of Service is an important issue for e-commerce and other e-services. Beeri et al. [1] analyze service compositions at compile-time stage to gain further information on the service's behavior. Selecting services which are dynamically bound to composite services at runtime to satisfy user QoS requirements is presented by Maximilien and Singh [12], and Gibelin and Makpangou [4]. However, these approaches are only applicable if there are several concrete services which implement the same interface. This is not necessarily true for enterprise services. Kraiss et al. [8,9] describe an analytical model for the HEART tuning tool for message oriented middleware. The tool assigns static priorities to different workload classes. The messages of the different classes are then processed by a priority based scheduling algorithm in the middleware. The approach differs from our work in three points. First, there is a fixed number of workload classes. Second, for each class, the workload parameters have to manually be specified by an administrator. Third, if the workload change, the priorities for the classes have to be recomputed.

An admission control and request scheduling for e-commerce Web sites is presented by Elnikety et al. [3]. Their work focuses on achieving stable behavior during overload and improved response times. Analog to our SLA based request management component they install a proxy between the Web service and the database. However, the optimization is not associated to the SLA conformance. As we have discussed in this paper, considering the conformance is an integral part of an adaptive QoS management.

Schroeder et al. [14] present a framework for providing QoS where the response time requirements are specified in an SLA. To meet the multiclass response time goals, the number of concurrently executing requests is dynamically adjusted using a feedback control loop which considers the available hardware resources and concurrently executing queries in the database. However, other than our approach their work is not based on an economic model that optimizes the overall system performance across different classes.

7 Conclusion and Future Work

In this paper, we presented and evaluated an adaptive QoS management that is based on an economic model which adaptively penalizes individual requests depending on the SLA and the current degree of SLA conformance. Our economic model differentiates between opportunity costs and marginal gains. Using this economic model, we compute adaptive penalties and annotate them to individual requests, thus creating penalty-carrying queries. Second, we described the architecture and the implementation of our QoS management. Third, we presented the scheduling of the requests which is based on an admission control. We integrated our research prototype of a QoS-enabled database into MaxDB. Using our prototype, we demonstrated the effectiveness of our proposed approach by performing comprehensive real-world studies using the TPC-C benchmark as OLTP workload.

Having shown the effectiveness of our approach for databases, we now move towards scheduling in multi-level service infrastructures.

References

1. C. Beeri, A. Eyal, S. Kamenkovich, and T. Milo. Querying Business Processes with BP-QL. In *Proceedings of the 31st International Conference on Very Large Data Bases*, Trondheim, Norway, September 2005.
2. R. Braumandl, A. Kemper, and D. Kossmann. Quality of Service in an Information Economy. *TOIT*, 3(4):291–333, 2003.
3. S. Elnikety, E. Nahum, J. Tracey, and W. Zwaenepoel. A Method for Transparent Admission Control and Request Scheduling in E-Commerce Web Sites. In *Proceedings of the 13th International Conference on WWW*, pages 276–286, New York, NY, USA, 2004. ACM Press.
4. N. Gibelin and M. Makpangou. Efficient and Transparent Web-Services Selection. In *Proceedings of the 3rd International Conference on Service Oriented Computing*, Lecture Notes in Computer Science (LNCS), Vol. 3826, pages 527–532, 2005.
5. D. Gmach, S. Krompass, S. Seltzsam, and A. Kemper. AutoGlobe: An Automatic Administration Concept for Service-Oriented Database Applications. In *Proceedings of the 22nd International Conference on Data Engineering (ICDE)*. IEEE Computer Society, 2006.
6. J. Gray and A. Reuter. *Transaction Processing: Concepts and Techniques*. Morgan Kaufmann, 1993.
7. IBM DB2 Query Patroller. `http://www-306.ibm.com/software/data/db2/querypatroller/`.
8. A. Kraiss, F. Schön, G. Weikum, and U. Deppisch. Towards Response Time Guarantees for E-Service Middleware. *IEEE Data Engineering Bulletin*, 24(1):58–63, 2001.
9. A. Kraiss, F. Schön, G. Weikum, and U. Deppisch. With HEART Towards Response Time Guarantees for Message-Based E-Services. In *Proceedings of the 8th International Conference on Extending Database Technology*, pages 732–735, London, UK, 2002. Springer.
10. H. Ludwig and Toshiyuki. WS-Agreement Concepts, Use, and Implementation. In *Tutorial at the ICSOC*, 2005.
11. MaxDB. `http://www.mysql.com/products/maxdb/`.
12. M. Maximilien and M. P. Singh. Toward Autonomic Web Services Trust and Selection. In *Proceedings of the 2nd International Conference on Service Oriented Computing*, pages 212–221, New York, NY, USA, 2004. ACM Press.
13. Oracle Database Resource Manager. `http://www.oracle.com/technology/deploy/availability/htdocs/rm_overview.html`.
14. B. Schroeder, M. Harchol-Balter, A. Iyengar, and E. Nahum. Achieving Class-Based QoS for Transactional Workloads. In *Proceedings of the 22nd International Conference on Data Engineering (ICDE)*. IEEE Computer Society, 2006.
15. B. Schroeder, M. Harchol-Balter, A. Iyengar, and E. Nahum. How to Determine a Good Multi-Programming Level for External Scheduling. In *Proceedings of the 22nd International Conference on Data Engineering (ICDE)*. IEEE Computer Society, 2006.
16. TPC Benchmark C, Standard Specification Version 5.4. `http://www.tpc.org/tpcc/`, April 2004.

A Model-Based Framework for Developing and Deploying Data Aggregation Services

Ramakrishna Soma[1], Amol Bakshi[2], V.K. Prasanna[2], and Will Da Sie[3]

[1] Dept of Computer Science, USC, Los Angeles, CA
[2] Dept of Electrical Engineering, USC, Los Angeles, CA
{rsoma, amol, prasanna}@usc.edu
[3] Chevron Corporation, San Ramon, CA
Will.DaSie@chevron.com

Abstract. Data aggregation services compose, transform, and analyze data from a variety of sources such as simulators, real-time sensor feeds, etc. This paper proposes a methodology for accelerating the development and deployment of data aggregation modules in a service-oriented architecture. Our framework allows existing semantic web-service techniques to be embedded into a programming language thereby leveraging ease of use and flexibility enabled by the former with the expressiveness and tool support of the latter. In our framework data aggregations are written as regular Java programs where the data inputs to the aggregations are specified as predicates over a rich ontology. Our middleware matches these data specifications to the appropriate web-service, automatically invokes it, and performs the required data serialization-deserialization. Finally the data aggregation program is deployed as yet another web-service. Thus, our programming framework hides the complexity of web-service development from the end-user. We discuss the design and implementation of the framework based on open standards, and using state-of-art tools.

1 Introduction

Data aggregation refers to the process of transforming, composing and analyzing data to produce information that is useful for decision making. Data aggregation workflows are especially important in an enterprise setting where data has to be acquired and aggregated from a variety of heterogeneous sources. Two major problems need to be addressed while creating data aggregation modules. The first problem of *how* the data is accessed is caused by the large diversity of interfaces and protocols presented by the data sources. The second problem of *what* data is being accessed is caused because the data produced by each source has its own syntax and semantics. Our goal is to address these two problems in order to allow domain experts with basic programming skills to easily create data aggregation components that can be plugged into a larger information management architecture.

The work described in this paper is a part of a larger effort on Integrated Asset Management (IAM) for smart oilfields [16]. We envision a framework that will provide a domain expert (in our case, a petroleum engineer or asset manager) simplified access to any piece of data, analysis, and functionality required for use in

A. Dan and W. Lamersdorf (Eds.): ICSOC 2006, LNCS 4294, pp. 227 – 239, 2006.

making a decision. To achieve this, we have made two key design choices: *service oriented architectures* (SOA) and *model based integration.* Service oriented architecture (SOA) is a style of architecting software systems by packaging functionalities as services that can be invoked by any service requester. Web services are becoming the *de facto* mechanism used for implementing service-oriented architectures and are also employed in our IAM framework. A model based integration framework is built around a shared set of formal models which define the *syntax* and *semantics* of the domain and data elements. All applications in the framework subscribe to these models by producing and consuming data which are compliant with these models. These two technologies in tandem enable data aggregation and application integration in general by standardizing the *how* and *what* of the data accessed.

In this paper we discuss how the problem of data aggregation is addressed in our IAM framework. We assume an enterprise setting where all sources of data are accessible as web-services. We also assume that the schemas of all the data produced and exchanged are known and agreed upon. This is a reasonable assumption in the light of the major thrust on standardization of XML-based data exchange schemas and APIs in the petroleum industry [10]. We build upon these assumptions to create a programming framework which accelerates authoring of data aggregation workflows. There are three main contributions of this paper:

- We present a novel framework for easing the development and deployment of data aggregation applications. The framework demonstrates the integration of techniques from the semantic web for service discovery and invocation into a programming language to provide a rich programming framework for the user.
- We describe the definition of a set of implementation-independent models and show how they are used for automatic service discovery and invocation.
- We discuss a prototype implementation of the framework built on open standards, and currently available tools.

The rest of the paper is organized as follows. Section 2 outlines a simple scenario for data aggregation, which will be the motivating example for the discussion in this paper. In Section 3, we survey existing methodologies and tools that are relevant to our problem and also discuss their shortcomings. An outline of our approach is provided in Section 4, followed by a description of a core set of models and how they are used for service discovery. Section 0 describes the implementation of our prototype service composition and deployment framework. We conclude in Section 6.

2 Motivating Example

To motivate our technique we examine a simple data aggregation workflow from the petroleum industry. Before we explain the workflow itself, we introduce the following terminology from the domain. A *well* is an entity that produces oil, water, and gas. A *block* is a set of wells. The production of a block is the sum of the production of its constituent wells. The oil, water, or gas production for a well or a block is often represented by a "recovery curve" or a "decline curve" for that well or block.

A decline curve is a plot of production volume versus time. Decline curves can also be plotted to show production volume versus the fraction of total oil in place recovered till that time step.

One of the inputs to our aggregation workflow is a data-structure called `WellProductionData`. This data structure holds the production information for a well and the data is produced by a simulator. However, higher-level tools require the aggregated production data at the *Block* level. We will refer to the aggregated data as `BlockProductionData`. To obtain the `BlockProductionData` from the `WellProductionData`, an additional data structure called `BlockData` is used. This data structure contains the information about a block, which contains information like what is the set of wells contained in a given block and some other pieces of data used for aggregation. It is generated either from a database or from another workflow i.e. is retrieved from another web-service. A simplified flow chart showing the workflow `BlockProductionData` from `WellProductionData` is shown below. Note that well-to-block aggregation is not a straightforward summation, and involves some complex calculations like finding moving averages.

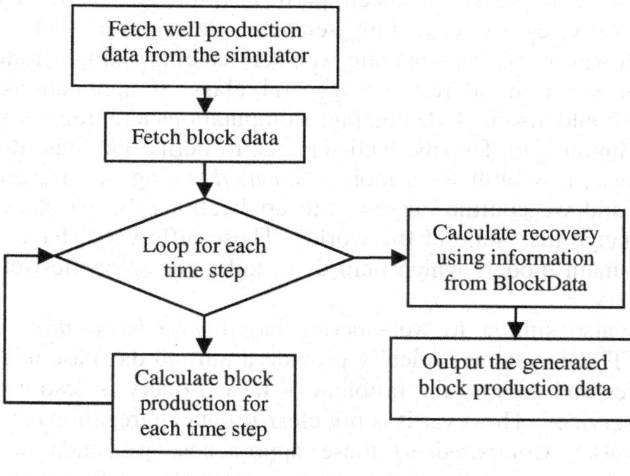

Fig. 1. Flowchart for the data aggregation workflow

We want the developer of this aggregation program to be unconcerned with the issues in web service development. These include service discovery, service invocation, and data serialization and de-serialization. The developer could also want the data aggregation program to be deployed into the IAM framework, so that it can be re-used in other aggregation workflows. Thus we require a framework that enables us to create and deploy shared data aggregation workflows without the complexity of understanding web-service standards and deployment issues.

3 State-of-the-Art Techniques and Their Limitations

WS-BPEL [1] is the W3C standard for writing web-service compositions. BPEL allows us to script composed services and exposes them as yet another web-service.

However, BPEL does not provide support to add complex computations within the composition - a key feature required to support aggregations. BPELJ[2] is a specification that addressed this shortcoming to some extent. It allowed *snippets* of java code to be embedded within the BPEL script. The main goal was to enable fairly simple calculations and transformations to be embedded within the compositions. It is not clear whether complex computations (such as integrating and invoking a third party tool) can be used. Creating BPEL scripts requires the user to have a good understanding of web-services specifications as well as the where the web-services are deployed. This conflicts with one of our key requirements.

SSIS [3] is a tool integrated with MSSQL server which allows the user to build such aggregation workflows. It consists of a visual composer, where data from various sources including web-services can be retrieved and aggregated. It also allows the user to specify complex transformations and aggregations in a .NET supported language. Although, the user need not write much web-service specific code, he still needs to be aware of the deployed services. The other problem with SSIS is that it is tightly integrated with the rest of the toolkit (.NET, SQL server) and thus integrating with it is not straight forward.

Much work in recent years has been performed on automatic discovery and composition web-services by providing semantic description of the constituent services [4][8]. However, typical semantic web-service composition frameworks like [5][7][11] do not seem to address the general class of applications where the composed service could also include complex computations and transformations. We have used the techniques to describe web-services to define facilitate discovery and invocation. Our system is built for a more *controlled* setting of an enterprise rather than the internet and we confine ourselves to applications that produce data rather those that also change the "state of the world". These differences have helped us to define focused domain models which help us to tailor the semantic-web techniques for our requirements.

Our system is also similar to web-service based *data integration* systems like Prometheus [9]. These systems typically provide a unified database abstraction to a set of web-services and address the problem of how a query is resolved to calls to appropriate web-services. However it is not clear if data aggregations can be defined in these frameworks. Compared to these approaches, we make a simplifying assumption that the produced by each source is a whole relation and thus do not concern ourselves with issues like view integration etc.

Data aggregation and similar workflows occur commonly in scientific workflows. Specialized frameworks like Kepler[17] and Chimera[18] (with concomitant service composition languages) have been employed for implementing such workflows. The major difference between our framework and the above mentioned frameworks is that they make the assumption that the modules containing the aggregation logic already exist and (only) provide methods to "wire" them together (using their special language). In our framework, the aggregation and wiring logic are both developed as part of a single program. This is consistent with one of the primary goals of our system, to avoid the need for the user to learn a new formalism.

Programming languages provide the right level of expressiveness and support we require to create aggregated services. Although the support for creating and consuming web-services in these platforms is becoming more and more seamless, the user still needs to have a good understanding of web-services, platforms and related issues like XML serialization, SOAP messaging /stub generation etc to be able author such services. Moreover, these languages do not address the problems of intuitive addressing and discovery of web-services. Our technique addresses some of these concerns by providing the user with an abstract data centric interface for writing aggregations. The hard tasks of discovering, invoking web-services are performed by our framework. In essence, our framework marries the expressiveness of programming languages with the semantic web-services idea of using service metadata to facilitate service discovery for authoring web-service compositions.

4 Our Approach

4.1 Overview

Consider a simplified version of the aggregation program from Section 2.

```
1. /**
2. * @iam.service
3. * @author Jane Smith
4. *
5. */
6. public class RecoveryCurveAggregator {
7.     /**
8.      * @iam.Operation
9.      * @iam.ServiceMetaData hasInput="blockName" hasOutput="RecoveryCurve"
10.     * @iam.SourceMetaData Producer="Aggregator"
11.     *                 hasRange="Block IN Block_A"
12.   * @return
13.     */
14.
15.    public Reccurve getRecoveryCurve(Object blockName)
16.    {
17.       try
18.       {
19.          DataFactory df = new DataFactory();
20.          WellProductionData csd = df.getData("WellProductionData",
                       "Block=Block_A && Producer="Simulation"", "date>1/1/2005 &&
                           date < 12/31/2006",null);
21.          BlockWellMap bwm = df.getData("BlockWellMap",
                       "Block=Block_A  Producer=Ontology", null, null);
22.          //Do the aggregation and return the aggregated object
23.          return(this.getReccurve(csd, bwn));
24.       }catch(Exception ex){
25.          System.out.println(ex.getMessage());
26.          ex.printStackTrace();
27.       }
28.          return null;
29.    }
30. }
```

Fig. 2. Code snippet for the example aggregation program

The most interesting part of this code snippet is Lines 19-21, which contains the code to obtain the data required for aggregation. The requests for the data are specified as calls the `DataFactory` which abstracts all the complexity of service discovery, service invocation and data serialization-deserialization. The parameters passed to the `DataFactory` are the type of the object required and a set of predicates that the data is required to have. The user in turn obtains a Java bean which is used to perform the aggregations.

The other important parts of this code snippet are the lines 1-5 and 7-13. These lines contain annotations with in the source code which specify the metadata used while deploying the aggregation program into our framework. The contents of the metadata descriptions are similar to those of a data request. It contains the type of object returned by the service and some predicates describing it.

Once this program is written, it is compiled, debugged as a normal program would be and deployed into our framework. The aggregation program becomes accessible as a web-service and can be similarly searched and invoked in other aggregation programs.

4.2 Modeling

At the heart of our framework is a set of three models which form the basis for a vocabulary for specifying data requests, service advertisements and matching services. These models are described below.

1. Domain model: This is an ontology that models the domain i.e. the entities in an oil-field and their inter-relationships. This model provides an intuitive query vocabulary for the user. For example a user may specify that the data required is the `WellProductionData` for all the *Wells* in a *Block* called Block_A. The notions of what a *Well, Block* and their relationship as a containment is defined in the domain model. A more detailed description of the domain model is out of the scope of this paper and is described elsewhere [15]. A simplified version which only considers parent-children relationships among entities of a domain model is currently used and is defined below.

A Domain object is a 4 tuple Do=<K, N_d, C, P> where:

- K is the kind/class of the domain object (for simplicity we assume here that it is a string),
- N_d is the name of the domain object,
- C = {Do_1,Do_2,...Do_n} is a set of domain objects that are contained by Do,
- P is the parent of the domain object.

A domain Configuration (or scenario) is a 2-tuple, DC=<Na, **D** > where

- Na is the name given to the configuration,
- **D** = {Do_1, Do_2,...Do_n} is the set of domain objects in the configuration.

A domain configuration is the context under which relationships between domain objects are defined. Thus a relationship between domain objects must also specify the configuration under which the relationship will be resolved (e.g. all *Wells* in *Config1.Block_A*).

2. Data Model: The data model is defined as an ontology of classes where each class is defined by a set of meta-data properties and a data schema. The meta-data properties in our system are similar to [13][14] and contains information to identify objects, track their audit trails etc. The schema of a class defines the various properties of the data object. Although the meta-data properties and the data schema are very similar (they define key-value pairs) and the difference between data and metadata is often tenuous, this distinction is very important to us because the metadata is defined and manipulated within our system where as the data schema is defined, stored and manipulated by "external" systems. This approach also allows us to reuse the data schemas published by standard bodies, software vendors etc.

More formally, a class is defined by a 4-tuple C = <N, R, M, S> where,

- N is the name of the class,
- R is the set of parent classes R= $\{C_1, C_2 \ldots C_k\}$,
- M is the set of metadata properties $\{p_{m1}, p_{m2}, \ldots p_{mn}\}$ where P_{mi} is given by a 2-tuple $<T, N_p>$ where T is the type of the parameter and N_p is the name of the property.
- S is the schema for the class (which defines its properties). S is given by a 2-tuple $<N_s, P>$ where N_s is the name of the schema and P is the set of properties given as 2-tuple $<T, N_p>$.

A special kind of class is called the *opaque* class where the class schema has only one property- its value i.e. P = {value}. This kind is used to represent binary and other legacy objects (like ASCII files) in the system.

An object is given by a 4-tuple $O = < C, V_{md}, V_d, \pi >$ where

- C is the class the object belongs to,
- $V_{md} = \{v_{m1}, v_{m2} \ldots v_{mn}\}$ is the set of values assigned to the meta-data fields where each v_i is a 2-tuple $<N_p, V_p>$, N_p is the name of the meta-data property and V_p is the value attribute,
- $V_d = \{v_{d1}, v_{d2} \ldots v_{dk}\}$ is the set of values attached to fields from the schema,
- $\pi = \{v\pi_1, v\pi_2 \ldots v\pi_w\}$ each $v\pi_i$ is a 2-tuple $<N_p, V_p>$; each $v\pi_i$ represents the set of parameters needed to create the object O.

Our framework models both *real* objects and *virtual* objects. Virtual objects are created by services and (in general) have $\pi \neq \emptyset$; on the other hand real objects already exist in some persistent store and have $\pi = \emptyset$. Thus to identify or create virtual objects we also need to specify the input parameters for the service i.e. π.

Finally, we define an ontology as a 3-tuple <C, D, O> where,

- C={ $DC_1, DC_2 \ldots DC_m$ } is a set of domain configurations
- D={$Do_1, Do_2 \ldots Do_n$} is a set of data objects
- O:S→bool is a function that takes a statement and informs whether that statement is entailed in the ontology or not.

3. Web-Service Model: The web-service model captures the semantics of the services- so that they can be advertised, discovered and invoked. Since all the web-services in our framework are data providers, the captured semantics of the web-services are all related to the data. In particular they describe the data provided by the web-service in terms of our data and domain ontology.

A service advertisement in our framework consists of the type of the output the service delivers, types of the input parameters, meta-data predicates that describes the output provided and the range of the data provided by the service defined as predicates over the fields of the output type. A predicate is given by a 3 tuple <P, op, val> where, P is the property asserted upon, op is a operation and val is the value. The expression values, defines a (possibly infinite) set of objects defining the range of objects catered by the service. It can be defined as expressions over primitive data types (int, float, Date etc) or objects/fields from the data and domain models. For the meta-data predicates, the *field* is from the data-model described above, while for the data predicates it is obtained from the schema where the output type is defined.

A service profile is given by a 4-tuple $S = < C_{out}^S,\ S, MP^S, DP^S >$ where,

- C_{out}^S is the type of the output of the service,
- $S = \{p_1, p_2 \ldots p_k\}$, where each p_i is a 2-tuple $<N_i,T_i>$ represents the input parameters of the service,
- MP^S is the set of predicates over the meta-data $\{mp_1, mp_2, \ldots, mp_m\}$.
- DP^S is the set of predicates over the fields from the schema of C_{out}^S which defines the range of data objects served by the service $\{dp_1, dp_2, \ldots, dp_m\}$.

4.3 Automatic Service Discovery

Service discovery in our framework involves matching service advertisements (profile) with requests. Please recall that the service advertisements are given by a 4-tuple $S = < C_{out}^S,\ \pi^S, MP^S, DP^S >$. Similarly, a request is a 4-tuple given by $R = <C_{out}^R,\ \pi^R,\ mp^R,\ dp^R>$. Note that a request tuple is quite similar to an object tuple; because the request identifies a set of objects needed for the aggregation.

Our matching algorithm matches the outputs (C_{out}^S, C_{out}^R) and input parameters (π^S, π^R) as described in [11]. The match is rated as *exact* ($C_{out}^S = C_{out}^R$) > *plugin* ($C_{out}^S \supset C_{out}^R$) > *subsumed* ($C_{out}^S \subset C_{out}^R$) > *fail.*

In addition to inputs and outputs, we also need to match the service and the request predicates. To define the predicate matching, we define a function:

$$INT{:}P_f \rightarrow D,\ D \subseteq range(f)$$

Intuitively, INT is an interpreter function that maps a predicate P over a field f to a set of values D. The set D is a subset of all the permissible values of f. We then say that a predicate P_f^S satisfies P_f^R iff $INT(P_f^R) \subseteq INT(P_f^S)$. This is written as $P_f^S \Rightarrow P_f^R$.

While matching the predicates of advertisements with those of a request, three cases occur:

1. *Perfect match*: $P_f^S \Rightarrow P_f^R$
2. *Failed match*: $\neg\ (P_f^S \Rightarrow P_f^R)$
3. *Indeterminate*: This occurs when for a predicate in the request P_f^R, the service does not advertise a predicate (P_f^S) over the same field. We make an open world assumption and consider an indeterminate match as a potential candidate.

Obviously the scoring function is ordered *perfect* > *indeterminate* > *fail*. All services with even one *fail* predicate match are discarded from being considered as possible candidates. This is intuitive because, if the user wants data from a Sensor (mp^R:*Producer*="Sensor"), it is not acceptable for her to get data from a Simulator (mp^S:*Producer*="Simulator"), even if it is for the same entity, and with the same timestamp. Thus a service is a match for a given request, if its outputs and inputs are *compatible* i.e. have an *exact* or *plugin* or *subsume* relations and the (metadata and data) predicates all match *perfect*ly or *indeterminate*ly.

Although the INT function is a good abstraction to define the notion of predicate satisfiability, from a more practical standpoint, it is checked by translating $P_f^S \Rightarrow P_f^R$ to an equivalent statement S that can be answered by the (oracle function O of the) ontology.

5 Implementation

The domain and data model are implemented using OWL in our prototype implementation. We have used the OWL-S [4] ontology to represent web-service descriptions. A OWL-S service description consists of three parts: the *service profile* which describes *what* a service does and is used for advertising and discovering services; the *service model* which gives a description of *how* the service works and the *grounding* which provides details on how to access a service. The OWL-S standard prescribes one particular realization of each of these descriptions, but also allows application specific service descriptions when the default ontologies are not sufficient. We have used this to define our own ontologies to describe web-services.

a. Service Profile: This ontology contains the vocabulary to describe service advertisements. We store the information described in the Web-service model here. As recommended in the OWL-S spec, we store these predicates as string literals in the owl description. In the next section, we describe how these advertisements are matched up with user specifications.

b. Service Model: The service model ontology describes the details of how a service works and typically includes information regarding the semantic content of requests, the pre-conditions for the service and the effects of the service.

In many data-producing services it is common that the parameters for the service actually define predicates over the data-type. For example a service that returns `WellProductionData` may contain parameters `startDate` and `endDate` that define the starting and ending dates for which the data is returned. We capture the semantics of such parameters as predicates over the fields. Thus the parameter `startDate` can be defined by the predicate "`WellProductionData.ProductionDate < startDate`". By doing this, we alleviate the need for the user to learn all the parameters of a service and rather let the user define the queries as predicates over the data object fields. Please note that not all parameters can be described as predicates over the data fields. For example, a fuzzy logic algorithm producing a report may require a parameter which describes the probability distribution function used. This parameter has no relation to the data being produced and is modeled here.

The default service model defined in the OWL-S standard, also defines the semantics of input parameters using the *parameterType* property which points to a specification of the class. Currently we do not model the pre-conditions and effects of the services. We do not model the effects of the service because of our assumption that the services are data producing services and do not change the state of the world. We do acknowledge that pre-conditions may be required in many cases and we intend to address this as part of our future work.

c. Service Grounding: The service grounding part of a model describes protocol and message formats, serialization, transport and addressing. We have used the *WsdlAtomicProcessGrounding* as described in the specification to store the service access related/WSDL data. This class stores information related to the WSDL document and other information that is required to invoke the web-services like the mapping of message parts in the WSDL document to the OWL-S input parameters.

Service advertisements are stored in a UDDI repository in our framework as described in [12]. Please recall from section 0 that a data request is programmed as a call to the `DataFactory`. A request in the program is handled by first inferring the closure of data-types that are compatible with the required data. This is used to query the UDDI store to retrieve the service profiles of all compatible services. These are matched according to the ranking criteria scheme described in the previous section and the best candidate is chosen. Currently our predicates can have one of the following operators {<, >, <>, ∈ } and values over basic data-types (Number types, String, Date) and domain objects. Predicate matching for basic types is quite trivial. For predicates involving domain objects the only operator allowed is ∈ , used to define the range of the data sources as (all or some) of the children of a domain object. For example the range of the objects served by a data source can be defined by assigning a meta-data field "`domainObject` = 'Well IN Config1.Block_A'". A query requesting for a data for Well_X i.e. with a predicate "`domainObject` = Well_X" can be resolved by querying the domain model. Please note that once the user has written the aggregations, she can debug it as a normal program. We think that during that process the request can be refined and the web-services are bound as she intended.

Once the candidate web-services are found, the information from the *Profile* and the *Grounding* part of the web-service model is used to construct a call to the appropriate web-service. Please note that some of the parameters are explicitly specified while some of them are a part of the predicates. The parameters which map to these predicates are constructed using the information in the *Profile*. To improve the performance of the system, we store all the Profile information and the Grounding information in the UDDI itself. Thus all required information can be retrieved with one call to the UDDI. We also "remember" the binding associated with a query, thus not incurring the overhead of a UDDI-access. When a call to the system fails (service may be un-deployed or re-deployed), the query is re-sent and the new service information is obtained.

5.1 Service Deployment

After the aggregation program is written it is deployed into a web-service engine. For a typical web-services engine like Apache Axis2[19], this involves creating deployment description document(s), packaging the classes and the dependant libraries as a jar file and copying it into in a specified directory. Apart from this, the OWL-S model for the aggregated service needs to be constructed and saved into a UDDI store. Most of the semantic information describing the service is provided as annotations in the source code by the author of the service. This style of embedding deployment specific information into the source code is a widely accepted technique in the Java programming community. So, after the author writes an aggregation service as plain java code with annotations, it is deployed by executing a pre-defined Ant script, which creates the deployment descriptors for the web-service engine as well as the OWL-S description documents. In the future we envisage a system with multiple web-service engines where service deployment additionally involves choosing the "best" server. For example an important factor to consider is to minimize the amount of data that needs to be moved. Thus it may be best to deploy an aggregated service on the same machine as (or one "nearest" to) the data producer.

A high-level view of the various elements of our framework and their relationships is summarized in the UML class diagram below[1].

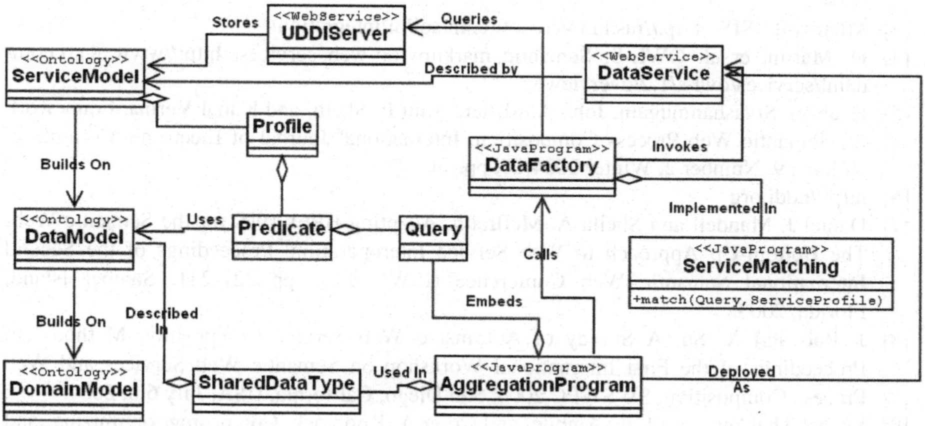

Fig. 3. Major elements of our framework and their interrelationships

6 Conclusions and Summary

In this paper we have presented a framework which eases the development and deployment of data aggregation workflows. The framework integrates techniques for automatic web-service discovery and invocation from the semantic web-services community into ordinary programming languages. This enables the user to write complex workflows in the programming language while using high-level, web-service agnostic specifications to gather the data required for the aggregations. The key element of our framework is the three models in our system: the domain model which

[1] The elements represented as classes in the diagram are not necessarily implemented as java classes- they are more coarse grained modules/data objects.

captures the semantics of the domain, the data model which captures the data-types and a rich set of meta-data associated with these data types and a service model which captures the semantics of the web services. The data and domain models form the vocabulary for defining the data required in the aggregations, as well as for advertising and matching the web services in the framework. We discussed how the OWL-S standard can be used to hold the information required for automatic discovery and invocation. Deployment of aggregation programs in our framework is aided by the use of meta-data embedded within the source code.

References

[1] F. Curbera, Y. Goland, J. Klein, F. Leymann, D. Roller, and S. Weerawarana. Business Process Execution Language for Web Services, Version 1.1. Specification, BEA Systems, IBM, Microsoft, SAP, Siebel, 05 May 2003.

[2] Michael Blow, Yaron Goland, Matthias Kloppmann, Frank Leymann, Gerhard Pfau, Dieter Roller, and Michael Rowley. BPELJ: BPEL for Java. Whitepaper, BEA and IBM, 2004.

[3] Microsoft SSIS: http://msdn.microsoft.com/sql/bi/integration/

[4] D. Martin, et al. OWL-S: Semantic markup for web services. http://www.ai.sri.com/daml/services/owl-s/1.2/overview/

[5] Kaarthik Sivashanmugam, John A. Miller, Amit P. Sheth, and Kunal Verma, Framework for Semantic Web Process Composition, International Journal of Electronic Commerce, Volume 9, Number 2, Winter 2004-05, pp. 71.

[6] http://uddi.org

[7] Daniel J. Mandell and Sheila A. McIlraith. Adapting BPEL4WS for the Semantic Web: The Bottom-Up Approach to Web Service Interoperation. Proceedings of the Second International Semantic Web Conference (ISWC2003), pp 227-241, Sanibel Island, Florida, 2003.

[8] J. Rao and X. Su. A Survey of Automated Web Service Composition Methods. In Proceedings of the First International Workshop on Semantic Web Services and Web Process Composition, SWSWPC 2004, San Diego, California, USA, July 6th, 2004.

[9] Snehal Thakkar, Jose Luis Ambite, and Craig A. Knoblock. Composing, optimizing, and executing plans for bioinformatics web services, VLDB Journal, Special Issue on Data Management, Analysis and Mining for Life Sciences, Vol. 14, No. 3, pp.330--353, Sep 2005.

[10] POSC, The Petrotechnical Open Standards Consortium, http://www.posc.org/

[11] K Sycara, M Paolucci, A Ankolekar, N Srinivasan. Automated Discovery, Interaction and Composition of Semantic Web Services, Journal of Web Semantics, 2003

[12] M. Paolucci, T. Kawamura, T. R. Payne, and K. Sycara. Importing the semantic web in UDDI. In Proceedings of E-Services and the Semantic Web Workshop, 2002

[13] Ewa Deelman, Gurmeet Singh, Malcolm P. Atkinson, Ann Chervenak, Neil P. Chue Hong, Carl Kesselman, Sonal Patil, Laura Pearlman, Mei-i Su. Grid-Based Metadata Services, 16th International Conference on Scientific and Statistical Database Management (SSDBM04), June 2004.

[14] Jun Zhao, Chris Wroe, Carole Goble, Robert Stevens, Dennis Quan and Mark Greenwood. Using Semantic Web Technologies for Representing e-Science Provenance In Proceedings of Third International Semantic Web Conference (ISWC2004), Hiroshima, Japan, November 2004. pp. 92-106, Springer-Verlag LNCS

[15] Cong Zhang, Viktor Prasanna, Abdollah Orangi, Will Da Sie, Aditya Kwatra, Modeling methodology for application development in petroleum industry, IEEE International Conference on Information Reuse and Integration, Las Vegas, 2005.
[16] CiSoft IAM project, http://indus.usc.edu/cisoft-iam/
[17] S. Bowers and B. Ludascher. Actor-oriented design of scientific workflows. In 24th Intl. Conf. on Conceptual Modeling (ER), 2005.
[18] I. Foster, J. Voeckler, M. Wilde, and Y. Zhao. Chimera: A Virtual Data System for Representing, Querying and Automating Data Derivation. In 14th Conference on Scientific and Statistical Database Management, Edinburgh, Scotland, July 2002.
[19] Apache Axis2: http://ws.apache.org/axis2/

A Distributed Approach for the Federation of Heterogeneous Registries

Luciano Baresi and Matteo Miraz

Politecnico di Milano,
Dipartimento di Elettronica e Informazione, Milano, Italy
{baresi, miraz}@elet.polimi.it

Abstract. Registries play a key role in service-oriented applications. Originally, they were neutral players between service providers and clients. The UDDI Business Registry (UBR) was meant to foster these concepts and provide a common reference for companies interested in Web services. The more Web services were used, the more companies started create their own "local" registries: more efficient discovery processes, better control over the quality of published information, and also more sophisticated publication policies motivated the creation of private repositories.

The number and heterogeneity of the different registries —besides the decision to close the UBR— are pushing for new and sophisticated means to make different registries cooperate. This paper proposes *DIRE* (DIstributed REgistry), a novel approach based on a publish and subscribe (P/S) infrastructure to federate different heterogeneous registries and make them exchange information about published services. The paper discusses the main motivations for the P/S-based infrastructure, proposes an integrated service model, introduces the main components of the framework, and exemplifies them on a simple case study.

1 Introduction

Service-oriented applications exploit *registries* to expose services to possible clients. Originally, the registry was a *neutral* actor between clients and providers; it was a "shared" resource aimed at facilitating their cooperation. This was the original mission of the first version of the UDDI (Universal Description, Discovery, and Integration, [11]) specification, which was the first market-supported standard that allowed companies to publish their services and interact with clients [2]. To this end, in September 2000, BEA, IBM, and Microsoft started *UBR* (UDDI Business Registry), a public UDDI-based registry, but also a common and neutral reference for all the companies interested in publishing and exploiting Web services.

The diffusion of Web services led to the need for "private" registries, directly controlled by the different companies, in parallel with the public one. Companies wanted to be able to control their registries to increase the efficiency of the discovery process, but they also wanted to manage private information —e.g., exclusive offers for their clients. These registries did not substitute the central

A. Dan and W. Lamersdorf (Eds.): ICSOC 2006, LNCS 4294, pp. 240–251, 2006.

one, which continued to be a universally-known reference. If a company was not able to serve a request internally, it could always access the central repository to find the services it needed.

Both the second version of the UDDI specification [11], and other approaches, like ebXML [5], took a more decentralized view and allowed for the creation of different separated registries. Moreover, January this year, the companies behind UBR decided to shut it down [6] since the original goal —the creation of a common sandbox to foster the diffusion of the service-oriented paradigm— was met. The new advice is to install a dedicated repository for each company. The complete control over published information allows the company to select and filter the information it wants to publish, organize it the way it prefers, and thus better tune the discovery process. Usually, companies manage their services, and those provided by their partners, but the lack of a common search space hinders the discovery of new services —supplied by providers with which the company is not used to cooperate. Companies interested in new services must a-priori select the companies that might provide them, and then search their proprietary registries, if allowed. Moreover, clients do not often know the services that fit their needs directly, but they would like to query the registries to find those that better fit their expectations. The more accurate the descriptions associated with services are, the more precise the discovery can be.

To overcome the lack of a centralized repository, and also to supply an extensible model to describe services, this paper proposes *DIRE* (DIstributed REgistry), a novel approach for the seamless cooperation among registries. *DIRE* proposes a decoupled approach based on the publish and subscribe (P/S) middleware *ReDS* [3]. A unique distributed dispatcher supports the information exchange among the different registries. Even if the dispatcher is logically unique, it provides a physically distributed communication bus to allow registries to publish information about their services, and clients —which may be other registries or suitable application interfaces— to receive it. According to the P/S paradigm, clients must subscribe to the services they are interested in and then the dispatcher forwards relevant data as soon as published. Moreover, *DIRE* supports the creation of dedicated *federations* to allow for the re-distribution of interesting information among the members even if they are not subscribed to it directly.

DIRE fosters the integration of repositories implemented using different technologies (currently, UDDI and ebXML) by means of dedicated plugs called *delivery managers*. They adopt a unique service model that both extends and abstracts the models used by the single registries, and provides a flexible means for the characterization of services. Delivery managers are also in charge of the interaction of registries with the P/S communication bus.

The rest of the paper is organized as follow. Section 2 surveys similar proposals and paves the ground to our approach. Section 3 sketches the approach. Section 4 describes the technology-agnostic service model defined to document services and provide delivery managers with a common base. Section 5 presents the delivery manager and digs down into the mechanisms offered to support flexible cooperations among registries. Section 6 demonstrates the approach on a simple case study and Section 7 concludes the paper.

2 Related Work

The different approaches for the cooperation and coordination among registries can be roughly classified in two main groups: approaches based on *selective replication* and approaches based on *semantic annotations*.

UDDI and ebXML belong to the first family. UDDI v.3 [12] extends the replication and distribution mechanisms offered by the previous versions to support complex and hierarchical topologies of registries, identify services by means of a unique key over different registries, and guarantee the integrity and authenticity of published data by means of digital signatures. The standard only says that different registries can interoperate, but the actual interaction policies must be defined by the developers.

ebXML [5] is a family of standards based on XML to provide an infrastructure to ease the online exchange of commercial information. Differently from UDDI, ebXML allows for the creation of federations among registries to foster the cooperation among them. The idea is to group registries that share the same commercial interests or are located in the same domain. A federation can then be seen as a single logical entity: all the elements are replicated on the different registries to shorten the time to discover a service and improve the fault tolerance of the whole federation. Moreover, registries can cooperate by establishing bilateral agreements to allow registries to access data in other registries.

Even if these approaches foster the cooperation among registries, they imply that all registries comply with a single standard and the cooperation needs a set up phase to manually define the information contributed by each registry. Moreover, given the way relations are managed by UDDI [8], the more registries we consider, the more complex the management of relations become, and the cost of publishing or discovering a service increases.

METEOR-S [13] and PYRAMID-S [7] are the two main representatives of the second family. They support the creation of scalable peer-to-peer infrastructures for the publication and discovery of services. METEOR-S only supports UDDI registers, while PYRAMID-S supports both UDDI and ebXML registries. Both the approaches adopt ontology-based meta-information to allow a set of registries to be federated: each registry is "specialized" according to one or more categories it is associated with. This means that the publication of a new service requires the meta-information needed to categorize the service within the ontology. This information can be specified manually or it can be inferred semi-automatically by analyzing an annotated version of the WSDL interface of the service. Notice that, if the same node of the ontology is associated with more than one registry, the publication of the services that "belong" to that node must be replicated on all the registries. Services are discovered by means of semantic templates. They give an abstract characterization of the service and are used to query the ontology and identify the registries that contain significant information.

The semantic infrastructure allows for the implementation of different algorithms for the publication and discovery of services, but it also forbids the complete control over the registries. Even if each registry can also be used as a stand-alone component, the selection of the registries that have to contain the description of a service comes from the semantic affinity between the service and the federated registries. For this reason, each node in a METEOR-S or PYRAMID-S federation must accept the publication of a service from any other member of the community. These approaches are a valid solution to the problem of federating registries, but the semantic layer imposes too heavy constraints on publication policies and also on the way federations can evolve dynamically.

3 DIRE

This section introduces the main elements of *DIRE* (DIstributed REgistry), which is our proposal to support loose interactions among registries. DIRE aims at fostering the communication among different proprietary registries by means of two elements: a distributed *communication bus* and a *delivery manager* associated with each registry. The former is introduced to interconnect the delivery managers, and is based on *ReDS* [3], a distributed publish and subscribe middleware. The latter acts as *facade*: it is the intermediary between the registry and the bus and manages the information flow in the two directions.

In P/S systems, components do not interact directly, but rather the communication is mediated by a *dispatcher*. Components send (*publish*) events (*messages*) to the dispatcher and decide the events they want to listen to (*subscribe*/*unsubscribe*). The dispatcher forwards (*notifies*) received events to all registered components.

DIRE allows registries to use the communication bus in two different ways:

- Registries (i.e., the companies behind them) declare their interest for particular services. This means that each publication —on a particular registry connected to the bus— is propagated to those registries that subscribed to it. Once the information is received, they can either discard it, or store it locally. The goal is to disseminate the information about services based on interests and requests, instead of according to predefined semantic similarities. This way, *DIRE* supports a two-phase discovery process. The registry retrieves the services the organization is interested in from the P/S infrastructure. The client always searches for the services it needs locally.
- Registries can be grouped in *federations* (communication groups, according to the P/S jargon) to allow for the re-distribution of interesting information among the elements of a federation even if they are not directly subscribed to it. To create a federation, some registries must declare their interest for a common *topic*. This means that when one of these registries is notified of new services, it re-distributes these data within the federation. Topics are not service types, but are abstract concepts, used to identify, for example, geographical areas, business organizations, or the parties involved in virtual enterprises. One registry can belong to different federations.

4 Service Model

The heterogeneity of considered registries and the need for a flexible means to describe services are the main motivations behind the *DIRE* service model. This model is conceived with three main goals: the compatibility with well-known standards, the unique identification of exchanged data, and the authentication of retrieved information. Currently, *DIRE* supports both UDDI and ebXML registries, but since we adopt JAXR (Java API for XML Registries, [9]), it is possible to easily integrate other types of registries. Our proposal (Figure 1) is in line with those approaches that tend to unify existing models (e.g., JAXR): we reuse the business elements, which are similar, and we introduce the concept of *facet* to allow for a more detailed and flexible management of the technical information associated with services.

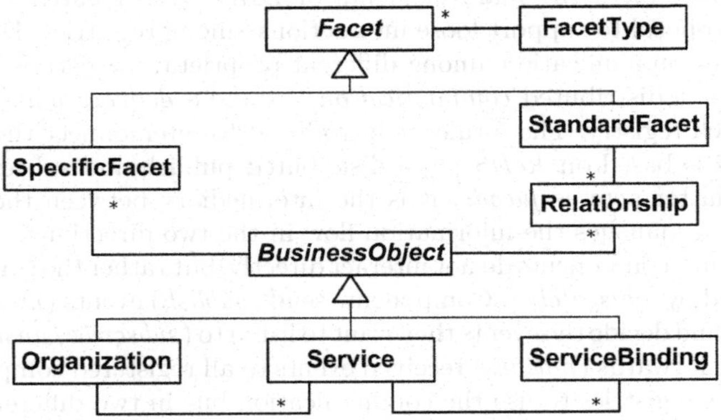

Fig. 1. *DIRE* information model

As far as business data are concerned, the lower part of Figure 1 describes the "shared" structure in terms of Organizations, Services, and ServiceBindings, with the meaning that these elements assume in existing registries.

The similarities vanish when we consider technical data. The different registries tend to provide predefined schemas to organize this information. In some cases, they also distinguish between references (stored in registries) and actual contents (put in repositories). *DIRE* integrates these elements and describes BusinessObjects by means of Facets. Each Facet addresses a particular feature of the BusinessObject by using an XML language. Facets are typed (FacetType) —based on the information they embed or the language they use— to ease the retrieval of services. For example, we can create *WSDL* Facets to describe the interfaces of a service, *RDF* Facets to add semantics, or *XMI* Facets to specify complex service behaviors through UML diagrams.

StandardFacets characterize recurring features (and are associated with BusinessObjects by means of Relationships). For example, they can specify the compliance with an abstract interface or the quality level according to a given certification authority. Given their meaning, we assume that StandardFacets are managed by special-purpose authorities that are in charge of linking the different services to these "certified" characteristics. StandardFacets are also a way to define the compatibility level between two services [11]. SpecificFacets describe what is peculiar to a given service. It can be the policies that must be used to charge users or the testing data that the provider wants to share with its possible clients. Some aspects require a combination of these two types: for the WSDL interfaces, we suggest to adopt the proposal presented in [1,4] and distinguish between the standard interface of a service and the properties of a given implementation: a StandardFacet describes the former and SpecificFacets deal with the latter.

Every user can attach a facet to a BusinessObject, even if it is not the service provider. This feature lets each company use its local registry as a blackboard, and allows a decoupled communication among the different elements of the service-centric system (e.g., runtime monitors might create facets that are then used by the dynamic binder). *DIRE* allows providers to sign and share these facets, thus allowing the receivers —if they trust the provider— to get a more detailed knowledge of the services in their registry.

The distributed setting behind *DIRE* requires that identification and authentication be carefully addressed. Since we can hardly understand the source of exchanged information, we use a digital signature to verify if received messages comply with sent ones and to identify the source of such messages.

5 Delivery Manager

The information distributed through the P/S middleware adopts the information model presented in Section 4. This is to allow for the integration of heterogeneous registries and also to support the creation of special-purpose filters to retrieve services efficiently. Heterogeneity and filters are managed by the *delivery manager*, that is, a *facade* element that standardizes the information flow. The delivery manager is responsible for the policies for both sharing the services in the registry and selecting the services that must be retrieved from the P/S infrastructure. Its adoption does not require modifications to the publication and discovery processes used by the different organizations behind the registries. They keep interacting with the repository they were used to, but published services are distributed through the P/S infrastructure, which in turn provides information about the services published by the others.

If adopted technology distinguishes between *registry* and *repository*, where the first contains references to the objects stored in the second, the delivery manager handle this distinction. It is also in charge of managing the federations the registry belongs to and of re-distributing significant data.

Service Publication. Services are published by providing the *delivery manager* with what should be shared. A company can choose to share data created on its registry or information retrieved from others. In both cases, the owner of published data remains the only subject able to update them. The manager simply retrieves what has to be published from the registry, transforms it into the right format, and then forwards it onto the P/S infrastructure.

Since *DIRE* is a decoupled distributed system, a registry can join and declare its interests at any time. The infrastructure guarantees that a registry can always retrieve the information it is interested in. For this purpose, the propagation of information is subject to *lease* contracts, a typical concept of many distributed systems (e.g., Jini [10]). When the lease expires, the information is not considered to be valid anymore; only a *renew*, which requires that the information be retransmitted, allows for extending its validity. The delivery manager can perform this operation automatically to guarantee that when the information is re-sent, all interested registries retrieve it.

The lease period τ is configurable at run-time; it guarantees that the information about services are re-trasmetted with a user-defined frequency. This means that τ is the maximum delay with which a registry is notified about a service. Moreover, if the description of a service changes, the lease guarantees that the new data are distributed to all subscribed registries within τ time units.

Service Selection. Because of commercial agreements between the parties, a client may know in advance the services it wants. In this case, the selection can be precise: the unique identifiers of interested elements are used by the delivery manager to create a filter and subscribe to them through the dispatcher. Since published information is refreshed periodically, the result is that all relevant data about selected services are stored in the client's registry.

When the client does not know the services it wants, *DIRE* allows the client to retrieve all the services whose descriptions comply with specified properties. If the property is encoded in a StandardFacet, the client can use the unique identifier of the facet and select all the services that have a Relationship with the selected property (facet). If the property is defined through a SpecificFacet, the client can express its requirements by using an XPath expression; the delivery manager wraps it into a filter and passes it to the dispatcher to subscribe to "relevant" services. This allows the delivery manager to receive the service descriptions that match desired properties. The delivery manager receives the unique identifiers associated with retrieved services and automatically create the filters to get them.

Notice that since the information is periodically re-transmitted, *DIRE* does not require any direct interaction between the registry that sends the information and those interested in it. Moreover, once data are received from other registries, the receiving actor (registry) cannot update them; it can only attach new SpecificFacets to further characterize retrieved services.

Federation Management. *DIRE* federates registries to allow them to "share" services. Each member of a federation can re-distribute the information it gets about a service to every registry of the federation. A registry can promote both proprietary services and services received from others.

Federations are treated as special-purpose subscriptions. Usually, we adopt *content-based* subscriptions, but federations exploit *topic-based* subscriptions.

Each federation is associated with a *topic* (that becomes the name of the federation). When a registry joins a federation, it must subscribe to the associated topic. This ensures that every time there is a message for that topic, it is received by all the participants of the federation, and thus we have a multicast communication group. Notice that if there are updates on services promoted in a federation, the registry that initially shared them must re-send the new information to the entire federation.

6 Case Study

This section introduces a simple case study to clarify how delivery managers help registries exchange information. The scenario, shown in Figure 2, considers four actors: *MyAirline*, *BigCompany*, *SmallCompany* and *TinyCompany*. The last two are subsidiaries of *BigCompany*: they are independent but federated entities, which need to efficiently communicate with the holding company. On the technical side, *MyAirline* has a UDDI registry, while the others use ebXML registries. In this context, *DIRE* fosters the collaboration between *BigCompany* and its subsidiaries, and enables the communication between *MyAirline* and its potential clients.

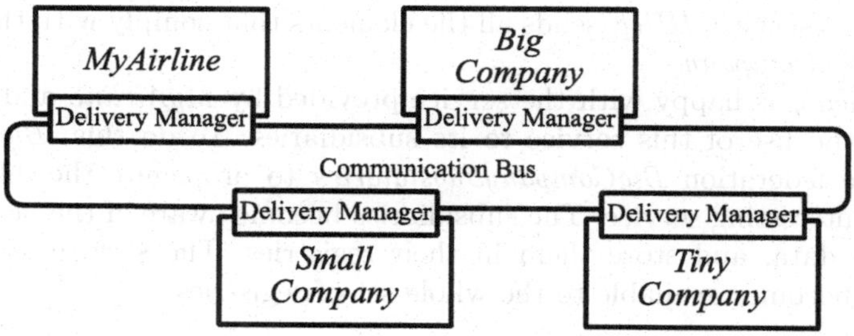

Fig. 2. Architecture of the scenario

MyAirline acts as service provider, and has two main services: one to compute the salaries of its employees and the other to sell airplane tickets on-line. The company wants to keep the first service private, while it wants to disseminate the second: if more companies discover the availability of such a service, *MyAirline* has the opportunity to increase its revenues.

As for the model presented in Section 4, we create one Organization element to describe the company (*MyAirline*), one Service to publish the online reservation service, and one ServiceBinding for each access point available for the offered service. To better advertise the service, *MyAirline* characterizes it through a set of facets. We use two StandardFacets, to identify the WSDL interface of the generic service, and to specify the ISO 9001 quality level of the company. Some SpecificFacets define the business data —like the semantic categorization, required commissions, and payment options— and identify the adopted transport protocol, encoding, and quality of service for each ServiceBinding. The relationship with the ISO 9001 facet is signed by an external company, which acts as certification authority, and thus the receivers can rely on its authenticity.

All this information (i.e., all these facets) are stored in the registry controlled by *MyAirline*. When the company decides to share the reservation service, the delivery manager can easily convert these data into our technology-agnostic format and publish them on the P/S infrastructure. Since *MyAirline* does not want to share the service to compute the salaries of its employees, it is kept private and no information is published. After the first publication, the delivery manager periodically re-sends the information about the service through the communication bus (i.e., through the *ReDS* dispatcher).

On the other side, *BigCompany* wants to optimize the purchase of airplane tickets. If *BigCompany* knows that *MyAirline* has a service that might be useful, it can subscribe to it directly. Otherwise, *BigCompany* can look for a service that complies with the interface of a generic online flight reservation service. As explained above, this property is rendered through a StandardFacet, and thus its unique identifier can be used to retrieve the set of services associated with that facet. As last option, *BigCompany* can exploit the semantic information associated with services to retrieve what it needs. It can create an XPath expression to search the content of RDF facets. All the options produce a subscription filter that embeds the requirements: when *MyAirline* renews the lease of the information about its service, *DIRE* sends all the elements that comply with the request (filter) to *BigCompany*.

BigCompany is happy with the service provided by *MyAirline* and wants to propagate the use of this service to its subsidiaries. To do this, *BigCompany* exploits the federation *BigCompanySubsidiaries* to propagate the information about the interesting service. The subsidiaries become aware of the new service, retrieve its data, and store them in their registries. The service supplied by *MyAirline* becomes available to the whole set of registries.

6.1 Experimental Assessment

The approaches described in Section 2 require that clients and information provider (i.e. *BigCompany* and *MyAirline* in our scenario) interact directly. Our methodology fully decouples the cooperation among registries, but requires the adoption of the lease mechanism: there is a periodical re-transmission of shared data, thus the exchange of messages, which is higher than with direct cooperation, might become the bottleneck of the whole approach.

Even if the use of *ReDS* in other domains gave encouraging results, we decided to conduct some empirical studies to assess the actual performance of *DIRE*. To analyze the scalability of the approach, we decided to particularly stress the communication bus and the delivery manager. In our tests, we exchanged 170,000 messages, that is, more than three times the entries in the UBR before its shutdown. Table 1 summarizes the results on the performance of the communication bus when we use simple filters, based on unique identifiers, and complex XPath ones. The 150,000 messages of the first column are handled with a mean time of

Table 1. Performances of the communication bus

	Simple filters	XPath filters
# of publications	150,000	20,000
# of subscriptions	40,000	10,000
Computation time	1 min 23 sec	9 min 04 sec
Mean time	0.55 ms	27.27 ms
Throughput	6,500,000 msg/h	132,000 msg/h

Table 2. Performances of the delivery manager

	New elements	Renewed elements
# of messages	50,000 msg	100,000 msg
Computation time	33 min 18 sec	26 min 3 sec
Mean time	39.96 ms	15.63 ms
Throughput	90,000 msg/h	230,000 msg/h
Standard deviation	6.32 ms	1.99 ms
99th percentile	76 ms	24 ms

0.55 ms, and thus a throughput of 6,500,000 publications per hour. The 20,000 messages of the second column are managed in 9.04 min, which implies a mean time of 27.27 ms. These figures highlight good results for managing simple filters and acceptable ones for complex XPath expressions.

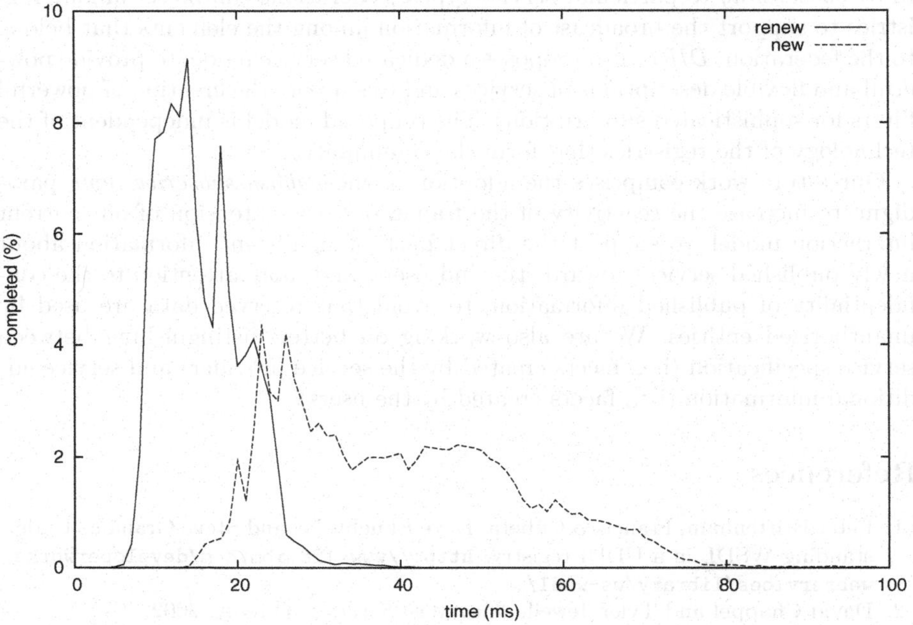

Fig. 3. Percentage of processed messages with respect to elaboration time

As for the delivery manager, we noticed that different messages impose different delays. Figure 3 plots the percentage of processed messages (y axis) with respect to elaboration time (x axis). There is a clear difference between the first time the delivery manager receives an element (dashed line) and subsequences renews (solid line). In particular, our experiments (Table 2) show a mean processing time of 39.96 ms for a new message and of 15.63 ms for a renew. The 99th percentile, that is, an estimation of the maximum time required to process a message, is very low (76 ms for a new element, 24 ms for e renewed one), and this indicates good global performance for the delivery manager. The low computational time required for processing renewed elements also demonstrates that the lease mechanism does not introduce a significant overhead. Our experiments suggested that a two-hour renew period is a good trade-off between a fast lookup and a non-saturated system. This threshold seems to be a very reasonable compromise for the effective deployment of *DIRE* in real settings.

7 Conclusions and Future Work

The paper presents *DIRE*, a framework for the cooperation and federation of distributed and heterogeneous registries based on the publish/subscribe paradigm. The *dispatcher* acts as common reference for the registries that want to communicate. Each entity is free to decide what information —and thus what services— it wants to share within the community by *publishing* it through the dispatcher. Similarly, registries can also decide the services they are interested in by *subscribing* to particular service types. Federations can be set among registries to support the broadcast of information among the elements that belong to the federation. *DIRE* also proposes a dedicated service model to provide powerful and flexible descriptions of services and to support the creation of powerful filters for sophisticated subscriptions. The proposed model is independent of the technology of the registries that form the community.

Our future work comprises the adoption of the *publish-subscribe-reply* paradigm, to increase the reactivity of the framework, the extension of our current interaction model, to support the direct push of significant information about newly published services towards the end users, and more attention to the confidentiality of published information, to avoid that reserved data are used by unauthorized entities. We are also working on better distinguishing between service specification (i.e., facets created by the service provider) and service additional information (i.e., facets created by the users).

References

1. Peter Brittenham, Francisco Cubera, Dave Ehnebuske, and Steve Graham. Understanding WSDL in a UDDI registry. `http://www-128.ibm.com/developerworks/webservices/library/ws-wsdl/`.
2. David Chappel and Tyler Jewell. *Java Web Services*. O'reilly, 2002.
3. Gianpaolo Cugola and Gian Pietro Picco. ReDS: A Reconfigurable Dispatching System. `zeus.elet.polimi.it/reds`.

4. Francisco Curbera, David Ehnebuske, and Dan Rogers. Using WSDL in a UDDI registry.
5. ebXML. ebXML: Electronic Business using eXtensible Markup Language. `http://www.ebxml.org/`.
6. IBM. UDDI Business Registry shutdown FAQ. `http://www-306.ibm.com/software/solutions/webservices/uddi/`.
7. T. Pilioura, G. Kapos, and A. Tsalgatidou. PYRAMID-S: A scalable infrastructure for semantic web services publication and discovery. In *RIDE-DGS 2004 14th International Workshop on Research Issues on Data Engineering, in conjunction with the IEEE Conference on Data Engineering (ICDE 2004)*, March 2004.
8. Cristina Schmidt and Manish Parashar. A peer-to-peer approach to web service discovery. *World Wide Web*, 7(2):211–229, June 2004.
9. Sun. Java Api for Xml Registries. `http://www.jcp.org/en/jsr/detail?id=93`.
10. Sun. Jini. `http://www.jini.org/`.
11. UDDI.org. Universal Description, Discovery and Integration version 2.0.
12. UDDI.org. Universal Description, Discovery and Integration version 3.0.2, October 2004.
13. Kunal Verma, Kaarthik Sivashanmugam, Amit Sheth, Abhijit Patil, Swapna Oundhakar, and John Miller. METEOR-S WSDI: A scalable P2P infrastructure of registries for semantic publication and discovery of web services. In *Information Technology and Management*, volume 6(1), pages 17 – 39, Jan 2005.

I-Queue: Smart Queues for Service Management

Mohamed S. Mansour[1], Karsten Schwan[1], and Sameh Abdelaziz[2]

[1] The College of Computing at Georgia Tech, Atlanta GA 30332, USA
{mansour, schwan}@cc.gatech.edu
[2] Worldspan, L.P., Atlanta GA 30339, USA
sameh.abdelaziz@worldspan.com

Abstract. Modern enterprise applications and systems are characterized by complex underlying software structures, constantly evolving feature sets, and frequent changes in the data on which they operate. The dynamic nature of these applications and systems poses substantial challenges to their use and management, suggesting the need for automated solutions. This paper considers a specific set of dynamic changes, large data updates that reflect changes in the current state of the business, where the frequency of such updates can be multiple times per day. The paper then presents techniques and their middleware implementation for automatically managing requests streams directed at server applications subjected to dynamic data updates, the goal being to improve application reliability in face of evolving feature sets and business data. These techniques (1) automatically detect input patterns that lead to performance degradation or failures and then (2) use these detections to trigger application-specific methods that control input patterns to avoid or at least, defer such undesirable phenomena. Lab experiments using actual traces from Worldspan show a 16% decrease in frequency of server restarts when using these techniques, at negligible costs in additional overheads and within delays suitable for the rates of changes experienced by this application.

1 Introduction

The complexity of modern enterprise systems and applications is causing renewed interest in ways to make them more reliable. Platform virtualization [1] and automated resource monitoring and management [2,3] are system-level contributions to this domain. Middleware developers have introduced new functionality like automated configuration management [4], improved operator interfaces like Tivoli's 'dashboards' [5], automated methods for performance understanding and display [6], and new methods for limiting the potential effects of failures [7,8]. Large efforts like IBM's Autonomic Computing and HP's Adaptive Enterprise initiatives are developing ways to automate complex management or configuration tasks, creating new management standards ranging from Common Base Events for representing monitoring information [3] to means for stating application-level policies or component requirements (e.g. WSLA[9]).

This paper addresses service failures in distributed applications. The failure model used is typical for distributed enterprise applications like web services,

A. Dan and W. Lamersdorf (Eds.): ICSOC 2006, LNCS 4294, pp. 252–263, 2006.

where 'failures' are not direct or immediate system or application crashes, but cause atypical or unusual application behaviors captured by distributed monitoring techniques [10]. Examples include returns of empty or insufficient responses, partially correct results, performance degradation causing direct or increasingly probable violations of delay guarantees specified by SLAs, and others.

Focusing on enterprise systems with reliable hardware infrastructure but potentially unreliable software, we investigate ways in which they can deal with unusual behaviors and eventually, failures caused by single or sequences of application requests, which we term *poison* request sequences. In earlier work, we identified and found ways to deal with a simple case observed by one of our industry partners, which concerned single requests, termed a 'poison message' that consistently caused unusual system and application responses [8]. In this paper, we tackle the more complex problem of sets or sequences of requests that cause such behaviors, and where such problems may depend on dynamic system conditions, such as which business rules are currently being run or to what current states they are being applied. The specific example studied is a global distribution system (GDS) that does transaction processing for the travel industry. To summarize, our assumption is that even with extensive testing applied to modern enterprise applications, it is difficult, if not impossible to ensure their correct operations under different conditions. This is not only because of the undue costs involved with testing such systems under all possible input sequences and application states, but also because the effects of poison message sequences can expose hidden faults that depend both on the sequence of input messages and on changes in system state or application databases. Examples of the latter include regular business data updates, evolving application databases, and system resources that are subject to dynamic limitations like available virtual memory, communication buffers, etc.

The particular problem considered in this paper is *poison requests* or request sequences arriving at a server system. These sequences lead to corrupted internal states that can result in server crash, erroneous results, degraded performance, or failure to meet SLAs for some or all client requests. To identify such sequences, we monitor each single server, its request sequences and responses, and its resource behavior. Monitoring results are used to dynamically build a library of sequence patterns that cause server failures. These techniques use dynamic pattern matching to detect poison sequences. While failure detection uses general methods, the techniques we use for failure prevention exploit application semantics, similar to what we have done in our earlier work on poison messages and more generally, in our 'Isolation-RMI' implementation of an improved communication infrastructure for Java-based enterprise infrastructures like Websphere or JBOSS [8]. As with solutions used to improve the performance of 3-tier web service infrastructures [11], we simply interpose a request scheduler between clients and server. In contrast to earlier work on load balancing [11], however, the purpose of our scheduler is to detect a potentially harmful request sequence and then change it to prevent the failure from occurring or at least, to delay its occurrence, thereby improving total system uptime. One specific prevention method used in this paper is to shuffle requests or change request order to defer (or eliminate) an imminent server crash. The idea is to dynamically apply different request shuffling methods within some time window, to prevent a failure or to at least, opportunistically defer it, thereby reducing the total time spent on system recovery or reboot.

Our motivation and experimental evaluation are based on a server complex operated by Worldspan, which is a leading GDS and the global leader in Web-based travel e-commerce. Poison message sequences and their performance effects were observed in a major application upgrade undertaken by the company in 2005, after a one man-year development effort for which its typical internal testing processes were used. The failures observed were degraded system performance resulting from certain message sequences, but system dynamics and concurrency made it difficult to reproduce identical conditions in the lab and identify the exact sequence and resource conditions that caused the problem. The current workaround being used is similar to the micro-reboot methods described in [12]. The experimental work described in this paper constitutes a rigorous attempt to deal with problems like these, using requests, business software, and request patterns made available to our group by this industry partner.

A concrete outcome of our research is the *I-Queue* request management architecture and software implementation. I-Queue monitors a stream of incoming Web Service requests, identifies potential poison message sequences, and then proactively manages the incoming message queue to prevent or delay the occurrence of failures caused by such sequences. The I-Queue solution goes beyond addressing the specific server-based problem outlined above, for multiple reasons. First, I-Queue is another element of the more general solution for performance and behavior isolation for distributed enterprise applications described in [8]. The basic idea of that solution is to embed performance monitoring and associated management functionality into key interfaces of modern enterprise middleware: (1) component interfaces, (2) communication substrates like RMI, and (3) middleware-system interfaces. Here, I-Queue is the messaging analogue of our earlier work on I-RMI [8]. Second, I-Queue solutions can be applied to any 3-tier web service infrastructure that actively manages its requests, an example being the popular RUBiS benchmark for which other research has developed request queuing and management solutions to better balance workloads across multiple backend servers. In that context, however, I-Queue's dynamic sequence detection methods would be embedded into specific end servers or into queues targeting certain servers rather than into the general workload balancing queue containing all requests in the system. Otherwise, substantial overheads might result from the need to sort requests by target server ID. Third, I-Queue solutions can be applied to request- or message-based systems, examples of the latter including event-based or publish-subscribe systems [13] or messaging infrastructures [14,15].

2 Motivating Scenario

Figure 1 shows an overview of the major components of Worldspan's distributed enterprise applications and systems. The airlines publish their fares, rules and availability information to clearing warehouses (CW). The CW in turn publishes the updates to several GDSs. The GDS implements several services which for a given travel itinerary searches for the lowest available fare across multiple airlines. It is estimated that the size of fare and pricing database at Worldspan, is currently at 10GB and is expected to increase by approximately 20% over the next few years. Worldspan receives an average of 11.5 million queries per day with contractual agreements to generate a reply within a predetermined amount of time. The high message volume coupled with constantly changing system state creates a real need for monitoring and reliability middleware that can learn the dynamically changing performance characteristics and adapt accordingly.

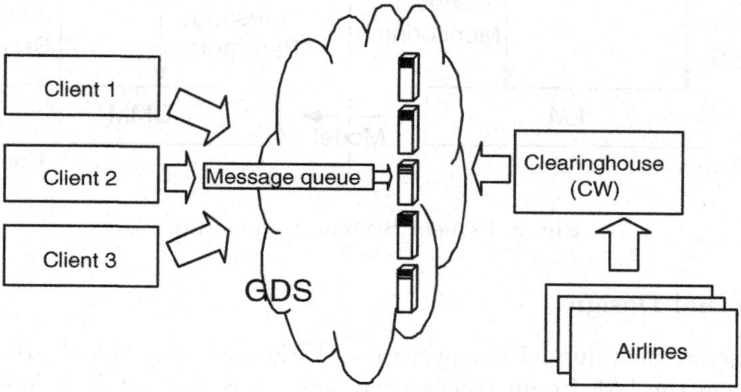

Fig. 1. General overview of message flows in air reservation systems

3 System Architecture

I-Queue uses a simple monitor-analyze-actuate loop similar to those described in previous adaptive and autonomic computing literature [16,17]. Our contribution is adding a higher level analysis module that monitors message traffic and learns the message sequences more likely to cause erratic behavior then apply application specific methods to prevent or reduce the likelihood of such problems.

The monitoring component observes inputs and outputs of the system. The analysis module in our system is the Learning Module (LM), which performs sensitivity analysis by correlating various system performance metrics and input message parameters. The goal of the Learning Module is to establish a set of parameter(s) that can act as good predictors for abnormal behaviors. The output is an internal model that can be used to predict performance behavior for incoming message streams. LM is modular and can use any machine learning algorithm suited for the problem at hand. This paper experiments with algorithms that use Markov Models.

The actuator component is the Queue Management Module (QMM). Using the internal performance model generated by LM, QMM prescans the incoming messages in a short window to see if they are likely to cause performance problems.

If a suspicious sequence is detected, QMM takes an application-specific action to prevent this problem from occurring, or at least, to defer it. The action used in this paper is to re-arrange the buffered messages to another sequence that is not known to cause performance problems, or that is known to cause fewer problems. Figure 2 shows an overview of the system architecture.

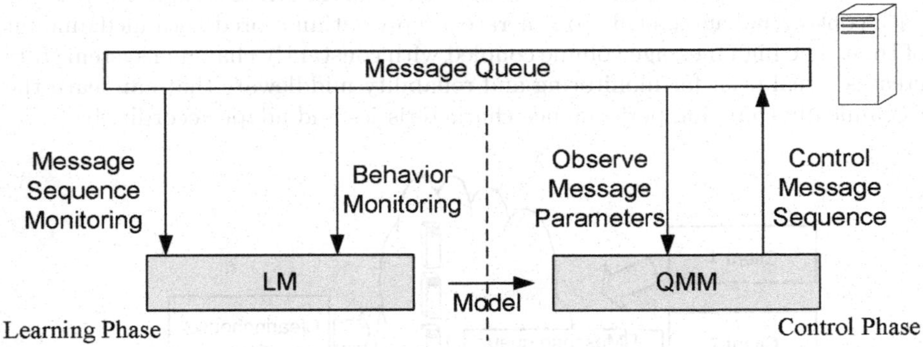

Fig. 2. I-Queue System Architecture

3.1 Internal Design

To demonstrate the value of I-Queue, we used Hidden Markov Models (HMMs) [18] to implement the LM. In our traces, each message is completely independent of other messages, and messages can be processed in any order without changing their semantics. During the learning phase, we construct transition matrices for each observed parameter(e.g., message size, internal message parameters, message interarrival time, ...). A transition matrix is a 2D matrix, for each message pair and a specific parameter, where the value of the parameter from the first message indicates the matrix column, and the value of the parameter from the second message indicates the matrix row. Analyzing message pairs leads to a first order model. For an N-order model, we check $N + 1$ messages, the concatenated parameter values from messages 1 to N indicate the column and the parameter value from message $N+1$ indicate the row. To reduce matrix size, we use a codebook to convert parameter values to a numeric index. For multi-valued parameters (i.e., list parameters), we use a two level codebook, where the first level encodes each value in the array, then we combine the array values for a message in sorted order and use that for a lookup into the second level codebook. N-dimensional parameters can be dealt with using $N + 1$ levels of codebooks.

We currently construct one transition matrix per parameter, but support for combinations of parameters can be added. For each message, we record all parameters as they arrive, and we observe system state after they are processed. If the system ends in a positive state, then we increment the corresponding cells in the transition matrices. If the server crashes or otherwise shows any performance misbehaviors, then we decrement the appropriate cells. During this training period, we also calculate a prediction error rate. This rate gives us an indication of the quality of a parameter as a predictor. It is calculated by counting the number of times the transition matrix for a certain parameter indicates strong likelihood of performance problems that do not actually occur (think of it as a false alarm rate).

An example of a transition matrix is shown in Table 1. For our experiments, we use a second order Markov Model. The rows of the matrix are labeled with the codes from 2 consecutive messages, the columns are labeled with the message that follows in sequence. The cell values give us an indication of server behavior as it executes a particular sequence of messages. A positive value indicates good behavior, e.g., message sequence *AAA* (first row by first column) and the higher the value the better, e.g., *AAA* is more preferable than *AAE* (first row by fifth column). A negative value indicates strong likelihood of poor server performance for a certain message sequence (e.g., *ADB*), the lower the negative value the worse. Sequences not observed in training are noted by a nil in the transition matrix. At the end of

Table 1. A portion of the transition matrix from the resource leakage experiment

	A	B	C	D	E	F...
AA	111	29	5	7	30	143
AB	17	26	2	5	7	9
AC	4	2	nil	2	2	12
AD	2	-2	-1	nil	-1	5
...						
BA	33	4	1	-1	3	36
BB	11	3	2	-2	4	15
BC	2	1	1	nil	1	-1
...						

the training period, we choose the parameter with the least prediction error rate as our predictor (multiple parameters with relatively close error rates require human evaluation). To account for system initialization and warm up effects, we also construct a separate set of matrices for tracking the first N messages immediately following a system restart. At the end of the learning phase, we have a transition matrix that is fed to QMM. QMM evaluates the buffered messages before releasing a message to the head of the queue. The performance score is calculated by enumerating all possible orderings of the messages and for each ordering examine the message pairs and add the corresponding value from the transition matrix. A higher score indicates a sequence that is less likely to cause performance problems a low score indicates a sequence that is very likely to cause performance problems. The ordering with the highest score is chosen and the queue is ordered accordingly. QMM also performs this reordering after a server restart.

4 Overview of Sample Applications

The experimental evaluation of I-Queue uses data traces obtained from Worldspan, a leading GDS and the global leader in Web-based travel e-commerce. Each message is a request for pricing a travel itinerary. Through contractual agreements with its customers, Worldspan needs to generate a reply message within a predefined time limit. It has been observed in the new server that it will occasionally slow down and fail to meet its delivery deadlines. To emulate this behavior, we utilize the Worldspan traces and build simple models of applications servers. In this paper, we report results obtained from experimenting with two server models, both based on known memory leak behaviors as well as other resource leak problems.

4.1 Basic Server Model

The specific subsystem managed by I-Queue is Worldspan pricing query service. The service is handled by a farm of 1500 servers. Query messages from various clients are placed in one of two global queues. Each server in the farm acts independently of the others. As a server becomes available for processing, it pulls a message from the queue, processes the message, and generates a corresponding response message forwarded to other parts of the system for further processing. The request message contains a set of alternative itineraries for which the lowest available fare is to be found by the server. The response message contains a list of fares for each itinerary sorted by fare. All request messages are independent, and the server should maintain an average memory usage level when idle.

4.2 Experimental Models

The I-Queue implementation built for the pricing server monitors server behavior and correlates it with request sequences. To evaluate it, we construct two models in our labs and apply the traffic traces obtained from Worldspan to both of these models. The goal is to evaluate the I-Queue approach with simple failure models using realistic traces. Our future work will evaluate the approach with Worldspans actual server (see the Conclusion section for more detail).

A class of failures used to evaluate I-Queue assumes a server with a small memory leak that is directly proportional to the size of the input message. The larger the input message, the more itineraries to process and hence, more work by the server which can lead to a larger leak. Memory leaks cause gradual degradation in server performance due to memory swapping and can eventually result in a server crash. To detect problems like these, the I-Queue prototype implements an early detection module to detect performance degradation early. The module utilizes the Sequential Partial Probability Test (SPRT) statistical method for testing process mean and variance. The server model is reset when SPRT raises an alarm indicating performance degradation significant enough to be detected. Real-time SPRT was developed in the 1980s based on Wald's original process control work back in 1947 [19]. SPRT features user-specified type I and type II error rates, optima detection times, and applicability to processes with a wide range of noise distributions. SPRT has been applied in enterprise systems for hardware aging problems [20] and for other anomaly detection [21].

5 Experimental Results

Experiments were run in Georgia Tech's enterprise computing laboratory, the model server were built in Java and run on an x345 IBM server (hostname: dagobah), a dual 2.8GHz Xeon machine with 4GB memory and 1GB/s NIC, running RedHat Linux kernel version 2.4.20. Sensitivity analysis and queue management code were also implemented in Java.

Our first experiment concerns sensitivity analysis using Worldspan's traffic traces. We model a server with a minor bug that leaks memory in proportion to the input message size. Figure 3 shows the results of our detection algorithm. The x-axis shows the different parameters we analyzed, the corresponding error rate is plotted on the y-axis. The error rate is a measure of the quality of a specific parameter as a predictor with lower error rates indicating a better predictor. As seen in the graph, the parameter MSG-SIZE has error rate of 0% which means it accurately predicts the failure 100% of the time. In the second part of the experiment, we engage the queue management module to reorder the messages. Figure 3 shows the reduction in number of server restarts as a function of the buffer length in our managed queue. We observe here that we do not get a significant improvement with larger buffer sizes. Instead, a buffer size of 5 is sufficient for giving us adequate results. The training phase for our system involves running a batch of messages and observing the system behavior for them. A training set is composed of 460 messages and in the real server environment, a message typically takes 4-16 seconds to process. Thus, in the best case scenario, we need 30 minutes to train the system (not counting the time needed to re-start the server). Given the cost of the learning phase of our system, we next evaluate the effectiveness of our algorithms for different training set sizes. Figure 4 shows system improvement measured as average reduction in number of crashes on the y-axis versus number of training sets on the x-axis. The training sets are generated by random re-ordering of the original set. The reduction rate is measured by counting the number of server restarts for the original batch

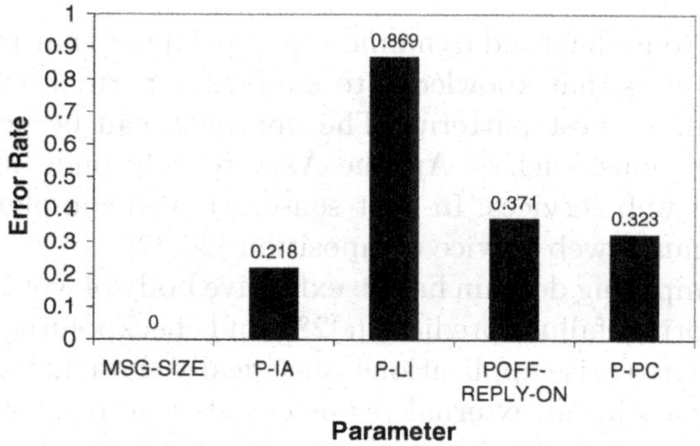

Fig. 3. Memory Leak Model: Sensitivity to various message parameters and message size

of messages with the managed vs. the unmanaged queue. It is a measure of the reduction in server faults we can achieve by using I-Queue, hence a higher reduction rate indicates more value in using I-Queue. The graph shows that we can get very good results with only a few training sets. This shows that I-Queue can be deployed with reasonable training time.

For brevity, we elide a second set of experimental results with a more complex failure model, termed the 'Connect Leak Model'. See [22] for more detail.

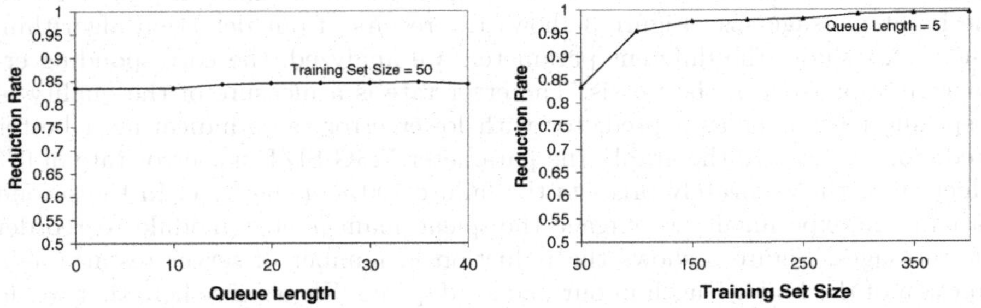

Fig. 4. Memory Leak Model: Error reduction measured for different queue length settings(left) and for different training set sizes (right)

6 Related Work

Our approach builds on established practice, in which machine learning techniques have been applied successfully to server and process monitoring. Application traces for detecting application faults are examined in [23,7,24,25]. These studies use application traces to detect a problem as it occurs and to recover the system by restarting the whole or parts of the system. Our approach differs in that we use application-defined methods to interpose and reschedule the message stream to minimize the number of system restarts and hence, increase system utility.

Our work aims to understand dynamic server behavior that results from client requests and then uses that knowledge to manage abnormal behaviors resulting from specific client request patterns. The approach can be embedded in Web service implementations, such as Apache Axis, to help build more reliable systems composed of web services. In that sense, we also complement other work in the area of dynamic web service composition [26,27].

The parallel computing domain has an extensive body of work on reliability using various monitoring, failure prediction [28], and checkpointing techniques [29]. Our work studies enterprise applications, specifically those in which system state is typically preserved in an external persistent storage (e.g., a relational database). In such systems, checkpointing the system state amounts to persisting the input event until it is reliably processed, and the cost of failures is dominated by process startup and initialization. In such environments, a reduction in the frequency of failures provides a tangible improvement to the system operators.

Additionally, the dynamic models we build (including the failure predictor) can prove valuable to system programmers as they try to troubleshoot the source of failure.

7 Conclusions and Future Work

This paper demonstrates a useful technique for automatically (1) detecting undesirable (i.e., poison) message sequences and then, (2) applying application-specific methods to achieve improved system performance and reliability. Future work includes conducting on-site experiments with the Worldspan search engine. We anticipate having more complex behaviors corresponding to multiple failure models interrelated in non-linear ways. We plan to approach this problem by using some of the well-studied clustering techniques (e.g., K-means analysis) to isolate the different behaviors and then apply our methods to each one separately.

Our longer term agenda is to use the monitoring and reliability techniques demonstrated in this paper in the context of service-oriented architectures. We are particularly interested in dynamically composed systems where users can create ad-hoc flows such as portal applications for high level decision support systems. In such systems, it is imperative to build middleware infrastructure to detect abnormal behaviors induced by certain component or service interactions and also, to impose 'firewalls' that can contain such behaviors and prevent them from further spreading into other parts of the system.

Acknowledgements. We gratefully acknowledge the help of James Miller in understanding the structure and parameters of the query messages. Many thanks also to Zhongtang Cai for directing us to the SPRT papers and algorithm.

References

1. Barham, P.T., Dragovic, B., Fraser, K., Hand, S., Harris, T.L., Ho, A., Neugebauer, R., Pratt, I., Warfield, A.: Xen and the art of virtualization. In: Proceedings of the 19th ACM Symposium on Operating Systems Principles (SOSP 2003), Bolton Landing, NY (2003) 164–177
2. Agarwala, S., Poellabauer, C., Kong, J., Schwan, K., Wolf, M.: System-level resource monitoring in high-performance computing environments. Journal of Grid Computing **1** (2003) 273 – 289
3. IBM: Common base event. `http://www.ibm.com/developerworks/library/specification/ws-cbe/` (2003) [online; viewed:5/24/2006].
4. Swint, G.S., Jung, G., Pu, C., Sahai, A.: Automated staging for built-to-order application systems. In: Proceedings of the 2006 IFIP/IEEE Network Operations and Management Symposium (NOMS 2006), Vancouver, Canada (2006)
5. IBM: IBM Tivoli monitoring. (`http://www.ibm.com/software/tivoli/products/monitor/`) [online; viewed: 5/24/2006].

6. Bodic, P., Friedman, G., Biewald, L., Levine, H., Candea, G., Patel, K., Tolle, G., Hui, J., Fox, A., Jordan, M.I., Patterson, D.: Combining visualization and statistical analysis to improve operator confidence and efficiency for failure detection and localization. In: ICAC '05: Proceedings of the Second International Conference on Automatic Computing, Washington, DC, USA, IEEE Computer Society (2005) 89–100
7. Roblee, C., Cybenko, G.: Implementing large-scale autonomic server monitoring using process query systems. In: ICAC '05: Proceedings of the Second International Conference on Automatic Computing, Washington, DC, USA, IEEE Computer Society (2005) 123–133
8. Mansour, M.S., Schwan, K.: I-RMI: Performance isolation in information flow applications. In Alonso, G., ed.: Proceedings ACM/IFIP/USENIX 6th International Middleware Conference (Middleware 2005). Volume 3790 of Lecture Notes in Computer Science., Grenoble, France, Springer (2005)
9. Keller, A., Ludwig, H.: The WSLA framework: Specifying and monitoring service level agreements for web services. J. Netw. Syst. Manage. **11** (2003) 57–81
10. Chen, M., Kiciman, E., Fratkin, E., Brewer, E., Fox, A.: Pinpoint: Problem determination in large, dynamic, internet services. In: Proceedings of the International Conference on Dependable Systems and Networks (IPDS Track), Washington D.C. (2002)
11. Jin, W., Chase, J.S., Kaur, J.: Interposed proportional sharing for a storage service utility. In: Proceedings of the joint international conference on Measurement and modeling of computer systems, ACM Press (2004) 37–48
12. Candea, G., Cutler, J., Fox, A.: Improving availability with recursive microreboots: a soft-state system case study. Perform. Eval. **56** (2004) 213–248
13. Kumar, V., Cai, Z., Cooper, B.F., Eisenhauer, G., Schwan, K., Mansour, M.S., Seshasayee, B., Widener, P.: IFLOW: Resource-aware overlays for composing and managing distributed information flows. In: Proceedings of ACM SIGOPS EUROSYS'2006, Leuven, Belgium (2006)
14. Sun Microsystems: Java message service (JMS). (`http://java.sun.com/products/jms/`) [online; viewed: 5/24/2006].
15. Tibco: Tibco Rendezvous. (`http://www.tibco.com/software/messaging/rendezvous.jsp`) [online; viewed: 5/24/2006].
16. Oreizy, P., Gorlick, M., Taylor, R., Heimbigner, D., Johnson, G., Medvidovic, N., Quilici, A., Rosenblum, D., Wolf, A.: An architecture-based approach to self-adaptive software. IEEE Intelligent Systems **14** (1999) 54–62
17. Hanson, J.E., Whalley, I., Chess, D.M., Kephart, J.O.: An architectural approach to autonomic computing. In: Proceedings of the First International Conference on Autonomic Computing (ICAC'04), Washington, DC, USA, IEEE Computer Society (2004) 2–9
18. Rabiner, L.R.: A tutorial on hidden Markov models and selected applications in speech recognition. (1990) 267–296
19. Wald, A.: Sequential Analysis. John Wiley & Sons, NY (1947)
20. Cassidy, K.J., Gross, K.C., Malekpour, A.: Advanced pattern recognition for detection of complex software aging phenomena in online transaction processing servers. In: DSN '02: Proceedings of the 2002 International Conference on Dependable Systems and Networks, Washington, DC, USA, IEEE Computer Society (2002) 478–482
21. Gross, K.C., Lu, W., Huang, D.: Time-series investigation of anomalous CRC error patterns in fiber channel arbitrated loops. In Wani, M.A., Arabnia, H.R., Cios, K.J., Hafeez, K., Kendall, G., eds.: ICMLA, CSREA Press (2002) 211–215

22. Mansour, M.S., Scwhan, K., Abdelaziz, S.: I-Queue: Smart queues for service management. Technical Report GIT-CERCS-06-11, CERCS (2006)
23. Fox, A., Kiciman, E., Patterson, D.: Combining statistical monitoring and predictable recovery for self-management. In: WOSS '04: Proceedings of the 1st ACM SIGSOFT workshop on Self-managed systems, New York, NY, USA, ACM Press (2004) 49–53
24. Lohman, G., Champlin, J., Sohn, P.: Quickly finding known software problems via automated symptom matching. In: ICAC '05: Proceedings of the Second International Conference on Automatic Computing, Washington, DC, USA, IEEE Computer Society (2005) 101–110
25. Jiang, G., Chen, H., Ungureanu, C., Yoshihira, K.: Multi-resolution abnormal trace detection using varied-length n-grams and automata. In: ICAC '05: Proceedings of the Second International Conference on Automatic Computing, Washington, DC, USA, IEEE Computer Society (2005) 111–122
26. Wohlstadter, E., Tai, S., Mikalsen, T.A., Rouvellou, I., Devanbu, P.T.: GlueQoS: Middleware to sweeten quality-of-service policy interactions. In: ICSE, IEEE Computer Society (2004) 189–199
27. Tai, S., Khalaf, R., Mikalsen, T.A.: Composition of coordinated web services. In: Proceedings ACM/IFIP/USENIX International Middleware Conference (Middleware 2004). Volume 3231 of Lecture Notes in Computer Science., Toronto, Canada, Springer (2004) 294–310
28. Li, Y., Lan, Z.: Exploit failure prediction for adaptive fault-tolerance in cluster computing. In: Proceedings of the Sixth IEEE International Symposium on Cluster Computing and the Grid (CCGRID'06), Los Alamitos, CA, USA, IEEE Computer Society (2006) 531–538
29. Coffman, E., Gilbert, E.: Optimal strategies for scheduling checkpoints and preventative maintenance. IEEE Trans. Reliability **39** (1990) 9–18

Optimizing Differential XML Processing by Leveraging Schema and Statistics

Toyotaro Suzumura, Satoshi Makino, and Naohiko Uramoto

Tokyo Research Laboratory, IBM Research
1623-14 Shimo-tsuruma Yamato-shi Kanagawa-ken, Japan, 242-8502
{toyo, mak0702, uramoto}@jp.ibm.com

Abstract. XML fills a critical role in many software infrastructures such as SOA (Service-Oriented Architecture), Web Services, and Grid Computing. In this paper, we propose a high performance XML parser used as a fundamental component to increase the viability of such infrastructures even for mission-critical business applications. We previously proposed an XML parser based on the notion of differential processing under the hypothesis that XML documents are similar to each other, and in this paper we enhance this approach to achieve higher performance by leveraging static information as well as dynamic information. XML schema languages can represent the static information that is used for optimizing the inside state transitions. Meanwhile, statistics for a set of instance documents are used as dynamic information. These two approaches can be used in complementary ways. Our experimental results show that each of the proposed optimization techniques is effective and the combination of multiple optimizations is especially effective, resulting in a 73.2% performance improvement compared to our earlier work.

Keywords: XML, Web Services, XML Schema, Statistics.

1 Introduction

Recently XML (Extensible Markup Language) has come to be widely used in a variety of software infrastructures such as SOA (Service-Oriented Architecture), Web Services, and Grid Computing. The language itself is used in various ways such as for protocols, for data formats, for interface definitions, etc. Even though the nature of the language gives us various advantages such as interoperability and self-description, its redundancy of expression leads to some performance disadvantages compared to proprietary binary data. Many methods [1][2][3] have been proposed for enhancing its performance, and these efforts are critical research areas in order to achieve the same or better performance and replace existing legacy infrastructures with XML-based infrastructures such as Web services. Our previous work [1] proposed an approach for realizing high performance XML processing by introducing the notion of differential processing. In this paper, we present an approach for improving the performance of our earlier approach by leveraging the knowledge given by XML schema and statistical information about instance documents.

The rest of the paper is organized as follows. In Section 2, we will explore optimized XML processing by reviewing our previous work. Section 3 describes the

A. Dan and W. Lamersdorf (Eds.): ICSOC 2006, LNCS 4294, pp. 264–276, 2006.

contributions of this paper, which enhance our previous work by leveraging two optimization techniques. Section 4 describes the optimization approach with schema languages. Section 5 describes the statistics-based optimization approach. Section 6 describes a performance evaluation. In Section 7, we introduce some related work using approaches with XML Schemas, and finally we conclude this paper with Section 8.

2 Improved Performance in Our Previous Work

In [1], we proposed a new approach called "Deltarser" to improve the performance of an XML parser based on the fundamental characteristics of Web services [1]. Next we give an overview of Deltarser and then discuss some of its limitations.

2.1 Overview of Deltarser

Deltarser is designed for efficiently processing XML documents similar to previously processed XML documents. The efficiency for similar documents is relevant in situations like Web service application servers, where middleware needs to process many similar documents generated by other middleware. In addition, the parsing of Deltarser is "safe" in the sense that it checks the well-formedness of the processed documents. From the viewpoint of users, Deltarser looks just like an XML parser implementation and has the same functionality as normal XML parsers such as the Apache Xerces implementation. The key ideas and technologies of Deltarser are summarized as follows: The main action of Deltarser is byte-level comparison, which is much faster than actual parsing. When feeding the actual XML document to the state machine described next, we have only to compare the byte sequence of each state and the incoming document. For efficiently remembering and comparing previously-processed documents, it remembers the byte sequence of the processed documents in a DFA (Deterministic Finite Automaton) structure. Each state transition in the DFA has a part of a byte sequence and its resultant parse event. It partially processes XML parsing only the parts that differ from the previously-processed documents. Each state of the DFA preserves a processing context required to parse the following byte sequences. It reliably checks the well-formedness of the incoming XML documents even though it does not analyze the full XML syntax of those documents. Deltarser's partial XML processing for differences checks whether or not the entire XML document is well-formed. It retains some contextual information needed for that processing. The experiments in [1] show the promising performance improvements such as being 106% faster than Apache Xerces [14] in a server-side use-case scenario and 126% faster in a client-side use-case scenario.

2.2 Observed Performance Limitations

Although our approach has promising performance benefits, some limitations were observed in our experiments with various performance evaluations. These limitations are twofold:

- **Startup overhead of creating state transitions.** Although byte sequence matching is much faster than regular XML processing, the initial cost of preparing an automaton cannot be ignored. The experiment conducted in [1] shows the comparison of Deltarser and other existing parsers such as open source fast XML parser, Piccolo, and a well-known XML parser, Xerces, but Deltarser is slower until 25 documents are processed. This initial overhead can be ignored for most XML applications, especially for long-running Web services that process large numbers of SOAP requests. However, considering the use of the differential processing approach for general purposes, it would be best if we could eliminate this initial overhead.
- **Runtime overhead for a series of state transitions.** An automaton is constructed by adding state transitions with a granularity corresponding to each SAX event. The graph shown in Figure 1 shows the average time for processing a 64-KB document while changing the number of constituent state transitions within the automaton. Obviously, as the number of state transition increases, the processing time increases. The line graph shows a case in which whitespace is represented as one state transition, and the number of state transitions is about 12,000, and it takes 3.25 ms for byte sequence matching.

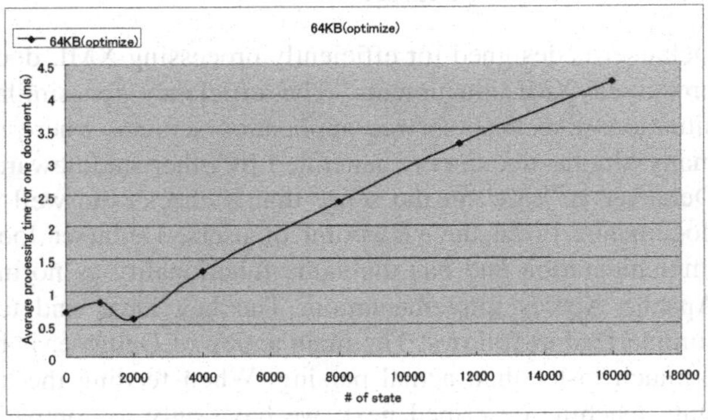

Fig. 1. Average processing time while changing the number of state transitions

When the whitespace is integrated with the other state transitions, the number decreases to about 8,000, and it takes 2.4 ms for byte sequence matching, which is 30% faster. As shown in this experiment, when there are fewer state transitions, there is less overhead incurred in differential processing. However this does not necessarily mean that the number of state transitions should be as small as possible. If the number is small and the automaton is compressed, then the probability of mismatching during the byte sequence matching will be high, and that results in the creation of many more new state transitions than needed for byte sequence matching.

3 Differential XML Parser with Optimized Automaton

To reduce the overhead mentioned in the previous section, we propose an approach that optimizes the internal automaton by leveraging some knowledge known before runtime as well as some runtime information. More precisely we leverage the following information:

- **XML Schema**
  An XML schema provides static information available before execution starts. The schema provides structural information as well as possible data values. By utilizing the schema information, it is possible to create an automaton even before the parser sees the target instance documents to be processed, and this results in the reduction of the startup overhead from the previous section. In addition, this can also be used for reducing the runtime overhead, since the schema gives the parser hints to design the shape of the state transitions.
- **Statistics**
  Statistical information is dynamic information obtained at runtime. By aggregating a set of instance documents, the parser obtains knowledge about the structural information as well as specific data values. This knowledge is similar to the kind of information provided by the XML schema, but the statistical approach can be used even if there is no schema, and it also provides more precise information than given by a schema.

These two approaches can be used in a complementary fashion. XML schema languages do not provide perfect information about instance documents. There are two reasons. One is because the languages themselves have some limitations in expressing all structures. These limitations are intentional to avoid too much complexity. The second reason is that users cannot always write a perfect schema before they have sufficient knowledge of the concrete documents. In addition, there may be situations where no XML schema is provided. Therefore, when the XML schema does not provide sufficient information, we can use the statistical approach. It may take some time to aggregate sufficient statistical data, but this can be more precise in expressing a class of instance documents compared to using an XML schema. In the following sections, we describe these two optimization approaches in more detail.

4 Optimization by XML Schema Language

This section describes an optimization approach leveraging the XML schema. Before describing the optimization approach, let us give a quick overview of the XML schema languages. An XML schema language is a formalization of the constraints, expressed as rules or as a model of a structure, that apply to a class of XML documents. Many schema languages have been proposed, such as XML DTD, W3C XML Schema, and RELAX NG. W3C XML Schema is the most common language and is widely used. Our approach does not depend on the specific XML schema language, but here we focus on using the set of schema representations used in W3C XML Schema.

The overall algorithm for optimizing state transitions is shown in Figure 1. First, our XML parser extracts one element and judges whether or not the element has attributes based on the schema information. When attributes exist, the parser fetches the attribute information from the schema. If any attribute is specified as a fixed value, the parser then executes Optimization 1 (Opt. 1), which is described in Section 4.1. Otherwise, it proceeds to the regular processing, which means that regular automaton creation is occurring.

When the element has no attributes, or after the attribute processing has been finished, the parser determines whether or not the element has child elements. If the answer is "no", processing continues with the next condition to check whether or not that element has default values. If the answer is "yes", the processing continues with Opt. 2 as described in Section 4.1. If the answer is "no", the regular processing will be executed.

In the branch where the element has child elements, the parser fetches the structural information from the schema. Then it branches on one of three paths depending on the type of the complex type. If the complex type is xsd:choice, then processing proceeds with Opt. 3 as described in Section 4.2. If the complex type is xsd:sequence, then processing checks whether the *maxOccurs* attribute equals to the *minOccurs* attribute, which leads to Opt. 4 as described in Section 4.2. If the schema provides a specific ordering, then processing continues with Opt. 5. Next we will describe each optimizations in detail.

Table 1. Excerpts from XML Schemas

Schema (1)	Schema (2)	Schema (3)
<xsd:simpleType name="schemaRecommendations"> <xsd:restriction base="xsd:string"> <xsd:enumeration value="A" /> <xsd:enumeration value="B"> </xsd:restriction> </xsd:simpleType>	<xsd:element name="X"> <xsd:complexType> <xsd:sequence> <xsd:elementname="A" xsd:type="xsd:int"/> <xsd:elementname="B" xsd:type="xsd:int"/> </xsd:sequence> </xsd:complexType> </xsd:element>	<xsd:complexType name="all"> <xsd:all> <xsd:element ref="A" /> <xsd:element ref="B" /> <xsd:element ref="C" /> </xsd:all> </xsd:complexType>

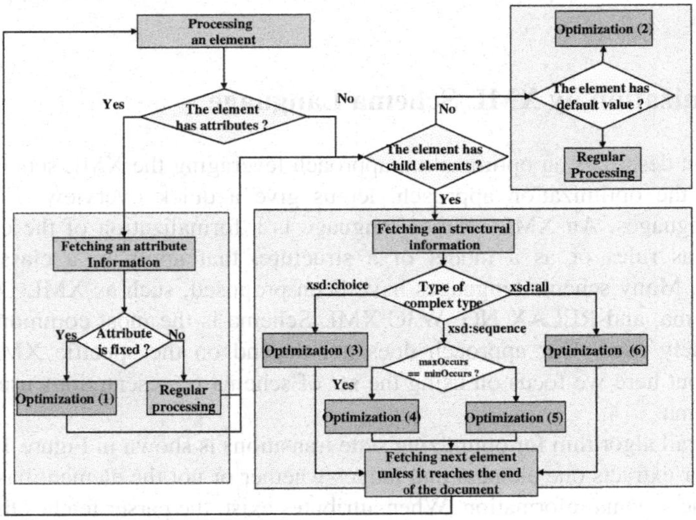

Fig. 2. Optimization Algorithms using XML Schema

4.1 Fixed Value or Enumerations

The xsd:enumeration is a facet that allows for definition of a list of possible values for the value of a specified data type. The example schema below shows a facet constraining the values. This enumerated information can be used for automaton creation.

I. Attribute (Opt. 1)
A fixed value of an attribute value is specified in the following schema fragment:

```
<xsd:attribute name="year" type="xsd:date" fixed="2004"/>
```

This allows a user to create one integrated state transition rather than creating a list of separate transitions.

II. Text Node (Opt. 2)
An element tag in the XML schema allows a user to write a fixed attribute. An example would be *<xsd:element name="name" type="xsd:string" fixed="IBM" />* and a sample instance document would be *<name> IBM </name>*. Using this schema, it is better to construct one integrated state transition containing one string, i.e. "*<name> IBM </name>*" rather than having three state transitions, "*<name>*", "*IBM*", and "*</name>*".

4.2 Compositors

Compositors such as xsd:choice, xsd:sequence, or xsd:all give hints to formulate optimized state transitions. However, such optimization tends to generate redundant state transitions that will never be used at runtime. For example, when creating all potential state transitions in advance using xsd:choice and xsd:all, the number of state transitions will be too large. This is a tradeoff depending on how much memory the users have available. Therefore this optimization should be controlled by some threshold given by the configuration of the implementation, or certain state transitions can be deleted by using a statistical approach at runtime, as described in Section 5.

- **xsd:choice (Opt. 3)**

The compositor xsd:choice defines a group of mutually exclusive particles. Only one can be found in the instance document per occurrence of an xsd:choice compositor. Since we know all of the possible elements that could appear in this schema fragment, it is possible to create the state transitions at startup time. This can be done at initialization time, not startup time.

- **xsd:sequence: Explicitly creating an expanded-type automaton using the maxOccurs and minOccurs attribute (Opt. 4)**

Some data-driven XML documents have repeating elements. For example, an XML document on customer data lists each customer's personal information. If these documents are expressed as one series of state transitions in a linear way, the automaton will become large. We call this type an "expanded-type state transition". In order to deal with these kinds of documents, it is possible to create "loop-type state transitions" in which backward state transitions are created to avoid the expansion of the same type state transitions. Loop-type state transitions have advantage over expanded-type ones in terms of memory consumption since the create automaton is more compressed, but in terms of processing cost, expanded-type state transitions could become faster since state machines have fewer choices to next states at each states. In order to determine which type of automaton is created, we can use the *maxOccurs* attribute and the *minOccurs* attribute within the xsd:sequence structure. Especially in the case the *maxOccurs* attribute equals to the *minOccurs* attribute, we can explicitly create an expanded-type automaton.

- **xsd:sequence: Specific ordering (Opt. 5)**

The following schema specifies the order of the child elements of the X element, saying that the A element should come first and B comes next. Suppose that an instance document is "<X><A>A</A><B>B</B></X>". Then the initial automaton would consist of 8 state transitions: "<X>", "<A>", "A", "</A>", "<B>", "B", "</B>", and "</X>". By leveraging the schema information, this automaton can be optimized as 5 state transitions. "<X><A>", "A", "</A><B>", "B", "</B>", reducing the number of state transitions. Speaking more technically, if there are N child elements and each child element has a text node (but not an empty element), then the number of state transitions is 3 * N + 2, and after being optimized, this will be 2 * N + 1, reducing the number of states by N + 1.

- **xsd:all (Opt. 6)**

The compositor xsd:all is used to describe an unordered group of elements whose number of occurrences may be zero or one. It is possible to create all of the state transitions that cover all of the combinations of the specified elements.

5 Optimization Using Statistics

In this section, we propose an algorithm to optimize the automaton statistically without considering any schema information. To determine which states are to be merged, a transition probability is assigned for the execution of each state transition.

Table 2. Examples of Automaton

<table>
<tr><td>Automaton I</td><td>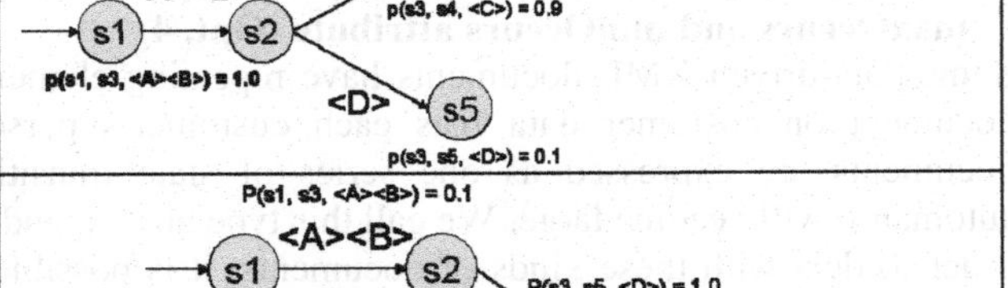
</td></tr>
<tr><td>Automaton II</td><td>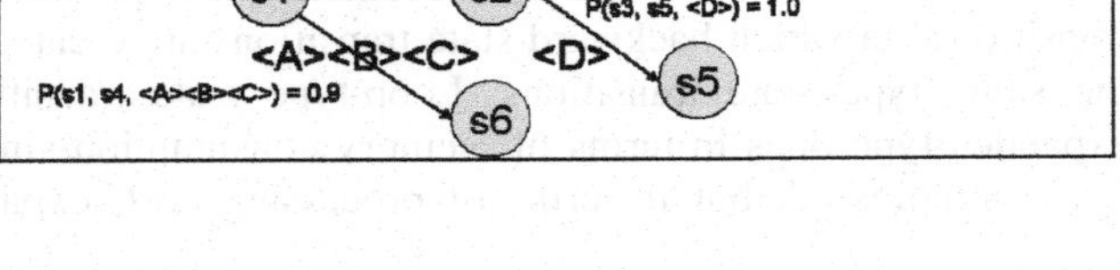
</td></tr>
<tr><td>Automaton III</td><td>
</td></tr>
</table>

Automaton I in Table 2 shows a sample automaton created after some parsing. For each transition, a transition probability *P* is assigned. This is calculated by counting the occurrences of that transition when the parser recognizes an XML element corresponding to the transition label. Automaton II in Table 2 shows that when the automaton recognizes the element <A>, the element <B> always appears next (the transition probability equals 1). The element <C> then appears in 90% of the processed XML documents. In the remaining 10%, the element <D> is next.

An automaton with transition probabilities is defined by {*S, Tr, P*} where S is a set of states, Tr is a set of transitions from one state to another state, and P is a set of transition probabilities. The transition probability $p(s_i, s_j, l)$ is the probability of a transition between states s_i to s_j upon recognizing a level string *l*.

The automaton shown in Automaton III of Table 2 is specified as follows:

S = (s1, s2, s3, s4, s5)
Tr = (s1, s2, <A>), (s2, s3, <B>), (s3, s4, <C>), (s3, s5, < D>))
P = (p(s1, s2, <A>)=1, p(s2, s3, <B>)=1, p(s3, s4, <C>)=0.9, p(s3, s5, <D>)=0.1

It is natural to merge a sequence of states with the transition probability *p=1* to minimize the number of states. It is plausible to merge a sequence with high transition probability (close to 1), but that may lead to an over-optimization that will cause

Table 3. Algorithm for optimizing the states of automaton

```
Suppose an automaton A = {S, Tr, P}.
For a list of states L = (s1, s2, ..., sn),
[Step 1]
// pop a state s from the list L.
s = pop(L);
[Step 2]
if ( si that satisfies p(s, si, l)) = 1 exists) then
  if (p(sj that satisfies p(si, sj, l') = 1 exists) then
    // sj is merged with si and removed from L and N
    delete (sj, L);
    delete (sj, S);
 delete(p(si, sj, l'), P);
 delete((si, sj, l'), Tr);
    // sets a new transition probability to from s to si
    add(p(s, si, append(l,l')), P), p(s, si, ll') = 1;.
    return to [Step 2]
  end if
else if (si that satisfies p(s, si, l)) > T exists) then
  if ( sj that satisfies P(si, sj, l') > T exists) then
    // create a new state
    add(s', S), add(p(s, s', ll');
    add((s, s', ll), Tr);
    p(s, s', ll') = p(s, si, l)*p(si, sj, l');
    // sj is merged with si and removed from L and N
    delete (sj, L);
    delete (sj, S); delete(p(si, sj, l'), P); delete((si, sj,l'), Tr);
    return to [Step 2]
  end if
end if
[Step 3]
return to [Step 1]
```

unnecessary recreation of merged states [1]. An algorithm which satisfies these conditions is shown in Table 3.

Let's examine the algorithm using the automaton shown in Table 2. First, pop the first state s_1 from the initial list L = {s_1, s_2, s_3, s_4, s_5} and set it as *s* (Step 1). Since the transition probabilities *p*(s_1, s_2, <A>) and *p* (s_2, s_3, <B>) equal 1, these two states are merged (Step 2). The result of the merging process is shown in Automaton II of Table 2. In this figure, the state s_3 is removed from the automaton and the label from s_1 to s_2 is changed to <A> <B>. Next, Step 2 is iterated and s_2 and s_4 are merged, since *p*(s_1, s_2,<A> <B>) is 1 and *p*(s_2, s_4, <C>) is 0.9 (supposing that T = 0.8). In this case, the state s_4 is removed from the automaton and a new state s_6 is created with the transition probability *p*(s_1, s_4, <A> <B> <C>) = 1 * 0.9 = 0.9. The result of this merging process is shown in Automaton III of Table 2. Now the optimized automaton has two paths, <A> <B> and < D>, and <A> <B> <C>. The states s_2 and s_5 are not merged, since the transition probability does not exceed the threshold *T*.

After the merging process, there are no states that satisfy the conditions in Step 2, so the process returns to Step 1 to set a new state for *s*[2].

6 Performance Evaluation

This section describes the effectiveness of each optimization technique proposed in this paper. To simplify the actual XML documents used in our experiment, we use the following type of XML document so that the element *c* is repeated more than once and *C* is a constant value:

<a><b>X</b><c>C</c><c>C</c>...<c>C</c></a>

In reality we used an XML document with the above form that represents a purchase order containing a shipping address, a billing address, and one or more purchase items with some properties such as a product name, quantity, price, and comment[3]. A purchased item corresponds to the element *c* in the above example.

To evaluate the optimization techniques, we performed a series of experiments using the following optimization techniques:

- No Optimization: The approach of the original Deltarser.
- Loop Expansion: Opt. 4 is applied.
- Concatenation: Opt. 5 is applied.
- Variable Fixation: Opt. 2 is applied.
- All Optimizations: Opt. 4, Opt. 5, and Opt. 2 are applied.

Note that in our experiments we did not measure the initial overhead as the basis of the statistical information, but we can understand the performance improvements based on the hypothesis that sufficient statistical information was obtained. Even with the optimizations by using the statistics described in Section 5, the above experiments

---

[1] Note that the parser parses any XML document correctly even in such case s . It simply means there is a cache miss.

[2] For the sake of simplicity, the case in which a state to be removed has incoming links. In this case, the state should not be removed.

[3] To reviewers: We could show the sample document, but we omitted it to save space.

are meaningful, since the same optimizations are applied. In order to measure the pure cost of byte sequence matching and state transitions, we did not produce any SAX events as in [1], so we can not compare our approach directly with Xerces and Piccolo. However the processing costs to be optimized are the dominant factor described in Section 2, and it is clear that the observed performance improvements are also applicable when measuring the system as a SAX parser and deserialization component in a SOAP engine.

The resulting automatons for each optimization are shown in Table 4. The columns *M*, *N*, and *L* refer to the number of states, the total number of branches to be summed up at each state, and the number of transitions with variables that need partial parsing, respectively.

Table 4. Generated Automaton by Each Optimization Techniques and its properties

Optimization	Formulated automaton	*M*	*N*	*L*
No Optimization	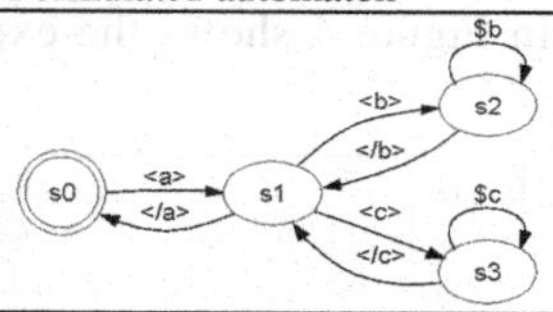	4	20	3
Loop Expansion	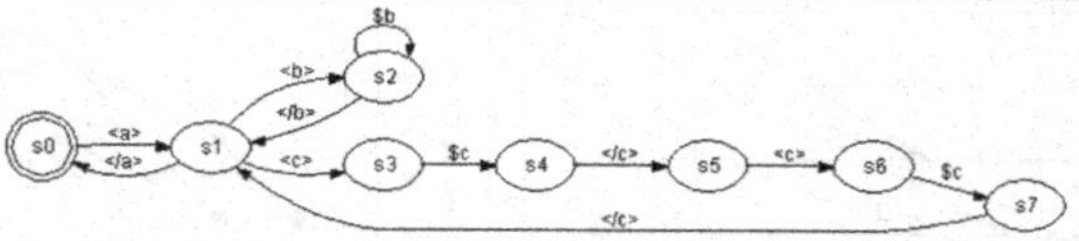	8	15	3
Concatenation	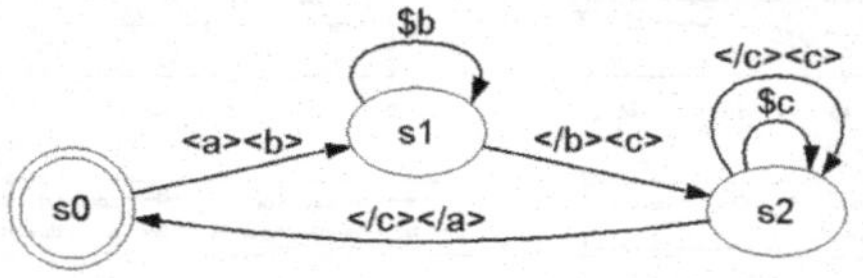	3	10	3
Variable Fixation	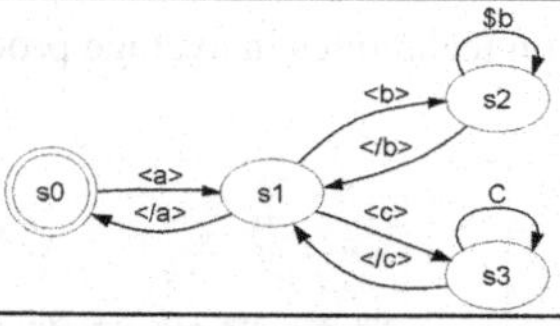	4	20	1
All Optimizations	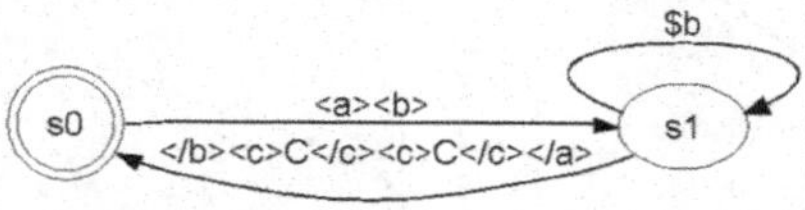	2	4	1

For the evaluation environment, we used Windows XP SP2 as the OS, IBM JDK 1.4.2 as the Java Virtual Machine running on an IBM ThinkPad X41 2525-E9J (CPU: 1.6 GHz, RAM: 1536 MB). The comparisons were measured by the average processing times for running 2,000 iterations after 10,000 warm-ups executions (to exclude the JIT compilation time).

The left graph shown in Figure 3 shows a comparison of average processing times for one document. The x-axis is the number of the element *item* that appeared. The element *item* corresponds to the element *c* in the previous example form and appears more than once. The y-axis is the average processing time for one document. The order of each optimization illustrated in the graph is "*No Optimization*" < "*Loop Expansion*" < "*Concatenation*" < "*Variable fixation*" < "*All Optimizations*" (Rightmost is the best). "*Loop Expansion*" obtains a performance improvement of 11.6% over "*No Optimization*" on average. "*Concatenation*" obtains a performance improvement of 31.1% on average. "*Variable Fixation*" obtains an average performance improvement of 26.2%. "*All Optimizations*" obtains has a performance improvement of 73.2%. We confirmed that the proposed optimization techniques are effective through the experiments. The right graph in Figure 3 is the same graph as the left one, but focuses on a small document.

The left graph in Figure 4 shows the memory consumption. Clearly the worst case is "*Loop Expansion*" and as the number of the element *items* grows, the memory consumption gets worse. The right graph in Figure 4 shows the experimental results

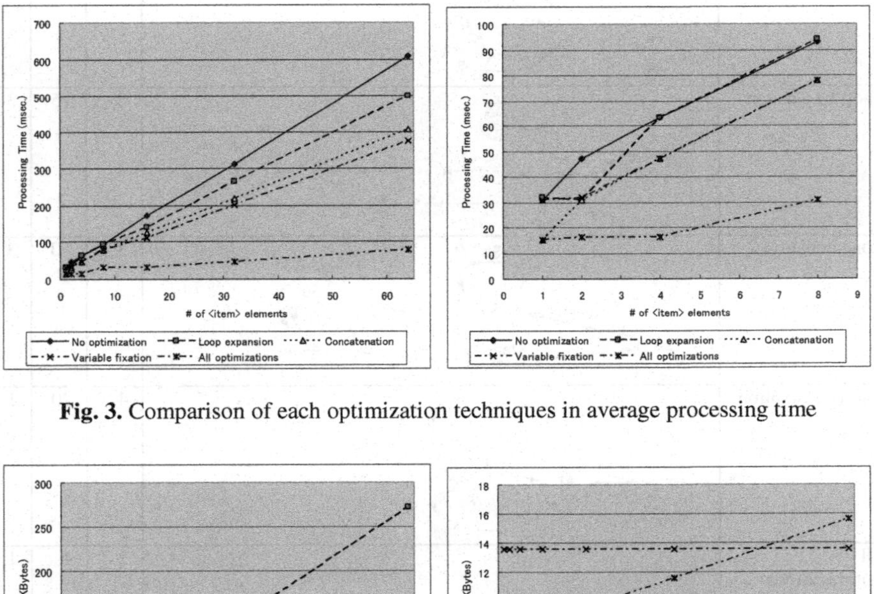

Fig. 3. Comparison of each optimization techniques in average processing time

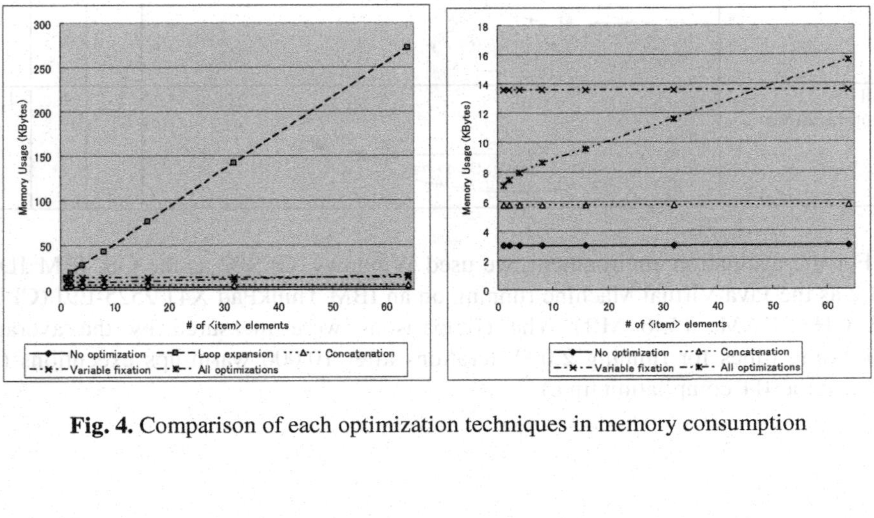

Fig. 4. Comparison of each optimization techniques in memory consumption

except for "*Loop Expansion*". The order of optimizations is "*All Optimizations*" < "*Variable Fixation*" < "*Concatenation*" < "*No Optimization*". "*All Optimizations*" consumes around 3.2 times more memory than "*No Optimization*", but considering the improvement in processing time, this number is acceptable.

Finally, we can conclude that each of these optimization techniques was quite effective, and the combination of multiple optimizations was especially effective in improving processing time with an acceptable level of memory consumption.

7 Related Work

[2][3] focus on the optimization of deserialization using the notion of differential processing. Meanwhile, our proposed XML parser is used not only for Web services but also for general XML-based infrastructures, insofar as it fulfills the condition that all of the processed XML messages are analogous to each other. Our optimization technique using XML schema can be compared with the work in [4], which proposes a parsing approach called schema-specific parsing. The validation of XML instances against a schema is usually performed separately from the parsing of the more basic syntactic aspects of XML. They posit, however, that schema information can be used during parsing to improve performance, using what they call schema-specific parsing. As mentioned earlier, statistical information can be complementary to the information that we can not obtain only from the XML schema, so there would be some situations where our approach has advantages. Currently there is no public implementation available, but it would be worthwhile to compare the performance between our approach and their approach.

8 Concluding Remarks

In this paper, we have presented an optimization approach to enhance XML parsing. Our approach is based on the notion of differential processing under the hypothesis that XML documents are similar to each other, and the proposed approach in this paper enhances our previous work [1] to achieve higher performance by leveraging static information as well as dynamic information. We use XML schema languages for static information that can be used for optimizing the internal state transitions. At the same time statistics for a set of instance documents are used as static information. These two approaches can be used in complementary ways. The experimental results show that all of the proposed optimization techniques are effective, and in particular the combination of multiple optimizations is most effective, yielding a 73.2% performance improvement compared to the original Deltarser. For future work, we will apply the proposed optimization approach to differential deserialization for the SOAP engine proposed in [2].

References

[1] Toshiro Takase, Hisashi Miyashita, Toyotaro Suzumura, and Michiaki Tatsubori. An Adaptive, Fast, and Safe XML Parser Based on Byte Sequences Memorization, 14th International World Wide Web Conference (WWW 2005)

[2] Toyotaro Suzumura, Toshiro Takase, and Michiaki Tatsubori. Optimizing Web Services Performance by Differential Deserialization, ICWS 2005 (International Conference on Web Services)
[3] Nayef Abu-Ghazaleh and Michael J. Lewis, Differential Deserialization for Optimized SOAP Performance, SC 2005
[4] Kenneth Chiu and Wei Liu, A Compiler-Based Approach to Schema-Specific XML Parsing, WWW 2004 Workshop
[5] Florian Reuter and Nobert Luttenberger. Cardinality Constraint Automata: A Core Technology for Efficient XML Schema-aware Parsers. www.swarms.de/publications/cca.pdf.
[6] Nayef Abu-Ghazaleh, Michael J. Lewis, Differential Serialization for Optimized SOAP Performance, The 13th IEEE International Symposium on High-Performance Distributed Computing (HPDC 13)
[7] Evaluating SOAP for High-Performance Business Applications: Real Trading System, In Proceedings of the 12th International World Wide Web Conference.
[8] Y Wang, DJ DeWitt, JY Cai, X-Diff: An Effective Change Detection Algorithm for XML Documents, 19th international conference on Data Engineering, 2003.
[9] Markus L. Noga, Steffen Schott, Welf Lowe, Lazy XML Processing, Symposium on Document Engineering, 2002.
[10] J van Lunteren, T Engbersen, XML Accelerator Engine, First International Workshop on High Performance XML
[11] M. Nicola and J.John, "XML parsing: a threat to database performance", 12th International Conference on Information and knowledge management, 2003.
[12] W3C XML Schema, http://www.w3.org/XML/Schema
[13] RELAX NG, http://www.oasis-open.org/committees/relax-ng/
[14] Apache Xerces http://xml.apache.org/

Optimized Web Services Security Performance with Differential Parsing

Masayoshi Teraguchi[1], Satoshi Makino[1], Ken Ueno[1], and Hyen-Vui Chung[2]

[1] Tokyo Research Laboratory, IBM Research
1623-14, Shimotsuruma, Yamato-shi, Kanagawa-ken, 242-8502 Japan
{teraguti, mak0702, kenueno}@jp.ibm.com
[2] IBM Software Group
11501 Burnet Rd. Austin, TX 78758-3415, USA
hychung@us.ibm.com

Abstract. The focus of this paper is to exploit a differential technique based on the similarities among the byte sequences of the processed SOAP messages in order to improve the performance of the XML processing in the Web Service Security (WS-Security) processing. The WS-Security standard is a comprehensive and complex specification, and requires extensive XML processing that is one of the biggest overheads in WS-Security processing. This paper represents a novel WS-Security processing architecture with differential parsing. The architecture divides the byte sequence of a SOAP message into the parts according to the XML syntax of the message and stores them in an automaton efficiently in order to skip unnecessary XML processing. The architecture also provides a complete WS-Security data model so that we can support practical and complex scenarios. A performance study shows that our new architecture can reduce memory usage and improve performance of the XML processing in the WS-Security processing when the asymmetric signature and encryption algorithms are used.

Keywords: Web Services, Web Services Security, Performance, XML parsing.

1 Introduction

Service-oriented architecture (SOA) is now emerging as the important integration and architecture framework in today's complex and heterogeneous enterprise computing environment. It promotes loose coupling so that Web services are becoming the most prevalent technology to implement SOA applications. Web services use a standard message protocol (SOAP [1]) and service interface (WSDL [2]) to ensure widespread interoperability even within an enterprise environment. Especially for the enterprise applications, securing these Web services is crucial for trust and privacy reasons and to avoid any security risks, such as malicious and intentional changes of the messages, repudiations, digital wiretaps, and man-in-the-middle attacks. The Web Services Security (WS-Security) specifications were released by OASIS in March 2004 [3].

They describe security-related enhancements to SOAP that provide end-to-end security with integrity, confidentiality, and authentication. As described in [7], WS-Security processing is categorized into two major operations: cryptographic processing

A. Dan and W. Lamersdorf (Eds.): ICSOC 2006, LNCS 4294, pp. 277 – 288, 2006.

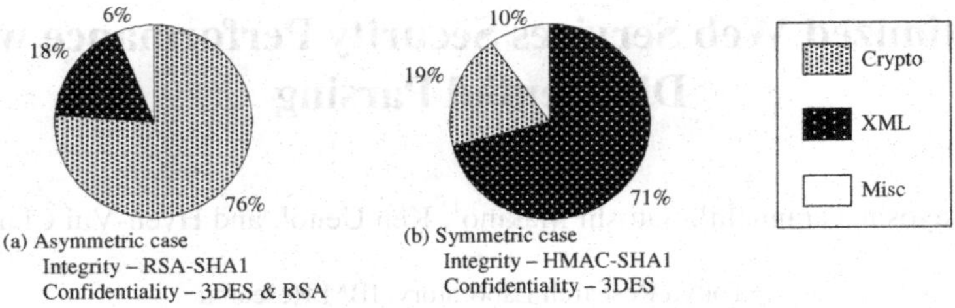

Fig. 1. Analysis of performance contribution of WS-Security processing on a DOM based implementation

and XML processing. In fact, we confirmed that these two operations contribute to the performance overhead of WS-Security processing through a preliminary experiment on a DOM based WS-Security implementation that we have developed using XML Security Suite technology [4] as the basis. The left side of Figure 1 shows the XML processing is the second constraint on performance when asymmetric algorithms are used. The right side of Figure 1 shows the XML processing is the primary limitation on throughput when symmetric algorithms are used.

An interesting characteristic of Web services is that all SOAP messages sent to a service have the almost same message structure. Based on this characteristic, some differential techniques that skip unnecessary XML processing, but which instead do only byte matching, have been proposed. [8][9] focus on reducing the general XML processing overhead (such as parsing, serialization, deserialization, and document tree traversal). In [8], only one template that memorizes the optimized basic structure of the message is constructed in advance. This template is used to extract only the differences between the input byte sequence and the data stored in the template. [9] also uses a single template, but it can be dynamically updated because the parser context is also stored in the template and this allows partial parsing. However it is difficult to apply these technologies to WS-security processing because WS-Security support is out of the scope of [9]. On the other hand, [10] considers improvements of the security-related XML processing (such as canonicalization and transformation). In [10], a message is divided into fixed parts and variable parts. A finite state automaton ("automaton" below) memorizes these parts as the basic structure of the message. But since the parser context is not stored in the automaton, it is impossible to partially parse the message or to optimize the data structure in the automaton.

In this paper, we address many of the problems in that previous works and describe a novel WS-Security processing architecture based on [10]. The architecture divides the byte sequence of a message into fixed parts and variable parts according to the XML syntax in the message and stores them in an automaton. The automaton consists of two parts: the states which store both the parser contexts and the WS-Security contexts, and the transitions which store the corresponding parts. Since the processor can extract the parser contexts from the automaton, it can resume a partial parsing and can dynamically update the data in the automaton without invoking another processor as in [10]. In addition, the data model in the automaton can be optimized even when the same structure appears repeatedly in the byte sequence. We also provide a more complete WS-Security data model relative to the one in [10], so we can support a

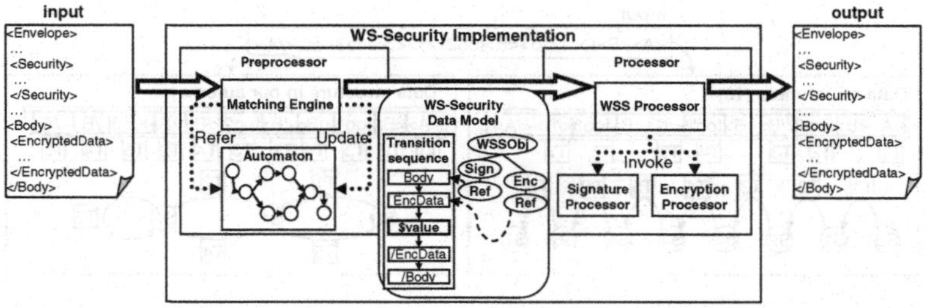

Fig. 2. Architecture of WS-Security processing with differential parsing

wider variety of practical scenarios than [10] covers. In this paper, we also conduct a performance study to evaluate memory usage and performance metrics. The performance study shows that our new architecture can reduce memory usage but retains almost same performance as the existing technology when the asymmetric algorithms are used, even though our method is more practical and more flexible.

The rest of the paper is organized as follows. We describe the details of our new architecture for WS-Security processing in Section 2. We introduce some related work using differential techniques in Section 3. We present our performance study in Section 4. Finally, we conclude the paper in Section 5.

2 WS-Security Processing with Differential Parsing

In this section, we describe a novel WS-Security processing architecture with differential parsing. Figure 2 shows the architecture of WS-Security processing. The architecture has two major components: the WSS preprocessor and the WSS processor. The WSS preprocessor manages an automaton, which has a more flexible and powerful internal data structure than the one described in [10]. It matches the byte sequence of an input SOAP message against the data that was previously processed and stored in the automaton, and constructs a new complete but still lightweight data model for the WS-Security processing. The WSS processor secures the SOAP message using the WS-Security data model. We can support a wider variety of practical scenarios than [10] supports by our new data model.

2.1 Internal Data Structure in an Automaton

Given a new input SOAP message as a byte sequence, the WSS preprocessor invokes its matching engine to match the byte sequence with the ones that were previously processed and stored in the automaton, without doing any analysis of the XML syntax in the message. If a part of the message (or the whole message) does not match any of the data stored in the automaton, then the matching engine parses only that part of the message and dynamically updates the automaton. When the matching engine parses the byte sequence, it is subdivided into the parts corresponding to the XML syntax in the message, according to the suggestion in [11]. Each divided part can be represented as either a fixed part or a variable part in the internal data structure. Figure 3 shows the internal data structure in the automaton. The data structure includes states (*Si* in

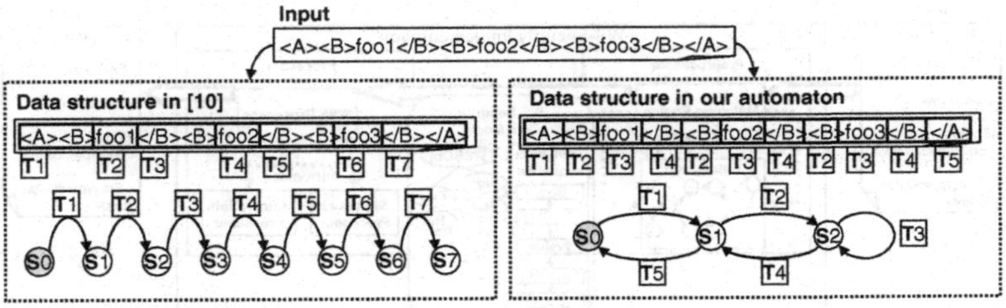

Fig. 3. The internal data structure in an automaton

Figure 3) and transitions (*Tj* in Figure 3). As shown in Figure 3, there is a difference between in the automaton in [10] and in our new automaton. In [10], it can't efficiently handle the same structure that appears repeatedly in the input because it doesn't consider the XML syntax. In Figure 3, the *<B>* elements appear repeatedly but they are stored as different transitions, such as T_1, T_3, T_5, and T_7. On the other hand, our new automaton can efficiently handle that. In Figure 3, the *<B>* elements are stored only in the transitions T_2 and T_4. In our new automaton, the state corresponds with the internal state in a parser and stores the parser context for partial parsing and the WS-Security context for construction of a WS-Security data model. The transition stores one fixed part or one variable part. The transition also stores a reference to the byte sequence, and the byte offset and the length of the snippet in order to get the original byte sequence without any additional concatenation, especially during encryption of the outbound message. The automaton doesn't allow two different states to have the same parser context and the same WS-Security context. This reduces the total memory usage even when same data structure appears repeatedly in the payload of a SOAP message. In Figure 3, we can merge two states into S_1 because there is no difference between the context after processing T_1 and the context after processing T_4. When the context before the processing of a transition is the same as after the processing, then the transition, such as T_3, can be a self-loop.

2.2 Lightweight WS-Security Data Model

[10] uses a very simple data model for WS-Security processing. But this makes it difficult to apply the data model to a wide variety of practical scenarios such as a model including multiple XML signatures, because it consists only of pairs of keys and WS-Security-relevant values. Therefore, we now define the more concrete and flexible, but still lightweight, WS-Security data model shown in Figure 4. The data model consists of two types of information: the WS-Security objects and the transition sequences. A WS-Security object includes all of the necessary information for the WS-Security processing done by the WSS processor. It is constructed in parallel as the WSS preprocessor matches the byte sequence with the data in the automaton. The logical structure of the WS-Security object is similar to the XML structure in the SOAP message secured by WS-Security. A transition sequence is a list of transitions that are traversed while matching the byte sequence with the data in an automaton. The transition sequence is used as the data representation of the input message instead of the byte sequence when the WSS processor secures the message based on the WS-Security data model.

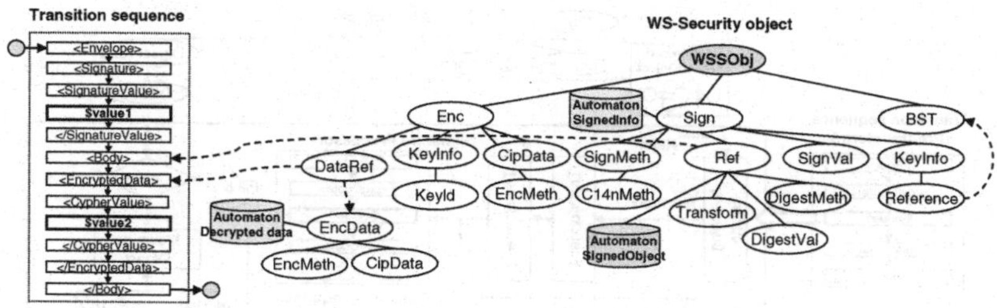

Fig. 4. The data model for WS-Security processing

2.3 WS-Security Processing Flow in the WSS Processor

In this section, we describe how the WSS processor applies WS-Security to the input SOAP message based on the WS-Security data model shown in the previous section. We use the following scenarios to simplify our explanations:

(1) For the inbound message, the WSS processor decrypts the contents of the SOAP body element first and then verifies the signature of the SOAP body element.
(2) For the outbound message, the WSS processor signs the SOAP body element first and then it encrypts the contents of the SOAP body element.

2.3.1 WS-Security Processing Flow for the Inbound Message

For the inbound message, the WSS processor invokes a decryption processor to decrypt the contents of the SOAP body element based on the WS-Security data model. The encryption processor extracts the cipher value including the octets of the encrypted data from the WSS object and invokes an encryption engine to decrypt the cipher value and to get the byte sequence of the real content of the SOAP body element. Then the encryption processor invokes its matching engine to match the decrypted byte sequence with those stored in the automaton and update the transition sequence for the subsequent WS-Security processing. The matching engine also dynamically updates the automaton if necessary. Figure 5 shows the processing flow of decryption for the SOAP body element. In Figure 5, the *<EncryptedData>* element is replaced with the actual content of the SOAP body element (the *<getQuote> element*).

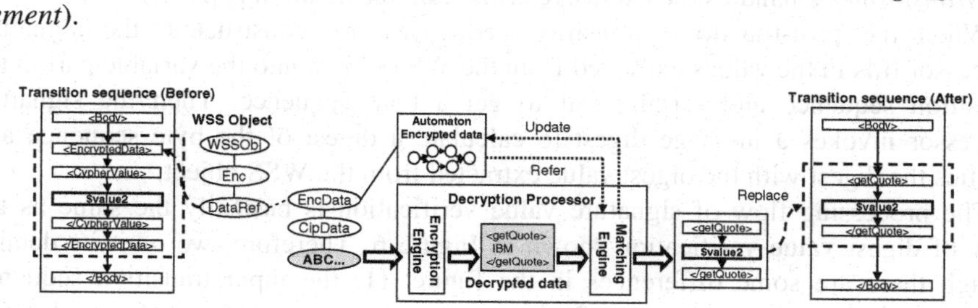

Fig. 5. Processing flow of decryption

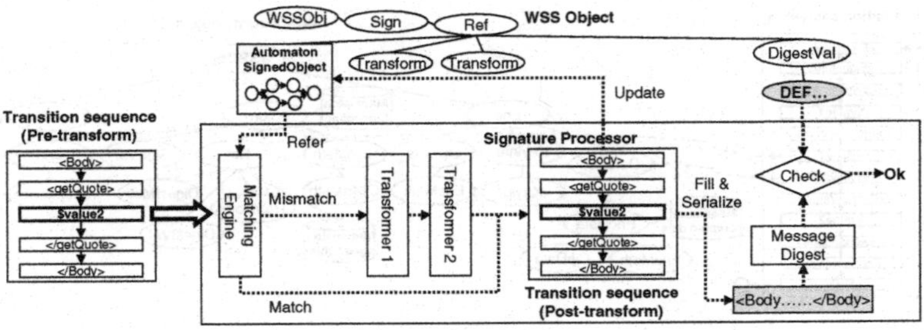

Fig. 6. Processing flow of digest value verification

After the decryption process is completed, the WSS processor invokes a signature processor to verify the signature of the SOAP body element based on the WS-Security data model. The signature verification process includes two steps: digest value verification and signature value verification. Figure 6 shows the processing flow for digest value verification. When the signature processor verifies the digest value, it first invokes the matching engine to match the input transition sequence with the ones stored in the automaton for the signed object, which means the SOAP body element in this case. The internal data structure in the automaton described here is slightly different from the one described in Section 3.1. This is because we avoid the same byte matching twice and reuse the input transition sequence to improve its performance. The state in the automaton for the signed object doesn't store the parser context since we don't use a parser in this case. The transition stores a transition T_i in the input transition sequence and another transition T_i' corresponding to T_i. T_i' is used to construct a post-transform transition sequence.

If there is a mismatch, the signature processor invokes the transformers for the corresponding transformation algorithm extracted from the WSS object, constructs the post-transform transition sequence, and dynamically updates the automaton. If the input matches, the signature processor can skip invocation of the transformers and automaton update because we can get the same post-transform transition sequence as would be constructed by the transformers. Figure 7 shows an example of transformations. In Figure 7, we assume that *transformer 1* handles XPath filter2 [5] and *transformer 2* handles the exclusive XML canonicalization [6].

When the post-transform transition sequences are constructed, the signature processor fills in the values extracted from the WSS object into the variable part in the transition sequence and serializes it to get a byte sequence. Then the signature processor invokes a message digest to calculate a digest of the byte sequence and verifies the digest with the digest value extracted from the WSS object.

The processing flow of signature value verification is basically the same as the flow of digest value verification shown in Figure 6. Therefore, we omit its details, though there are some differences in the figure: (1) the input transition sequence includes a *<SignedInfo>* element, (2) the automaton is for the *<SignedInfo>* element, (3) the transformers are changed to a canonicalizer, and (4) the message digest is changed to a signature engine.

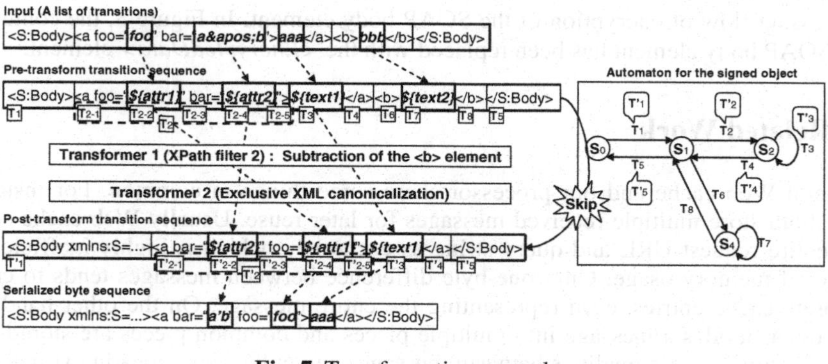

Fig. 7. Transformation example

2.3.2 WS-Security Processing Flow for the Outbound Message

For the outbound message, the WSS processor invokes a signature processor first to sign the SOAP body element based on the WS-Security data model. The signing process is a two-step process: digest value calculation and signature value calculation. The processing flow of digest value calculation is basically the same as the flow of digest value verification described in the previous section and details are not repeated. The only difference is that the signature processor for the outbound message stores the digest value in the WSS object after it invokes a message digester to calculate the digest value of the SOAP body element. The processing flow of the signature value calculation is also basically the same as the flow for signature value verification as described in the previous section, so we again skip the details. The only difference is that the signature processor for the outbound message stores the signature value in the WSS object after it invokes the signature engine to calculate the signature value of the *<SignedInfo>* element.

After signing, the WSS processor invokes an encryption processor to encrypt the content of the SOAP body element based on the WS-Security data model. The encryption processor extracts the original byte sequence of the content of the SOAP body element from the WSS object and invokes an encryption engine to encrypt the byte sequence. The WSS processor stores the encrypted cipher value in the WSS object, wraps the encrypted octet with the *<EncryptedData>* element, and updates the transition sequence for the subsequent WS-Security processing. Figure 8 shows the

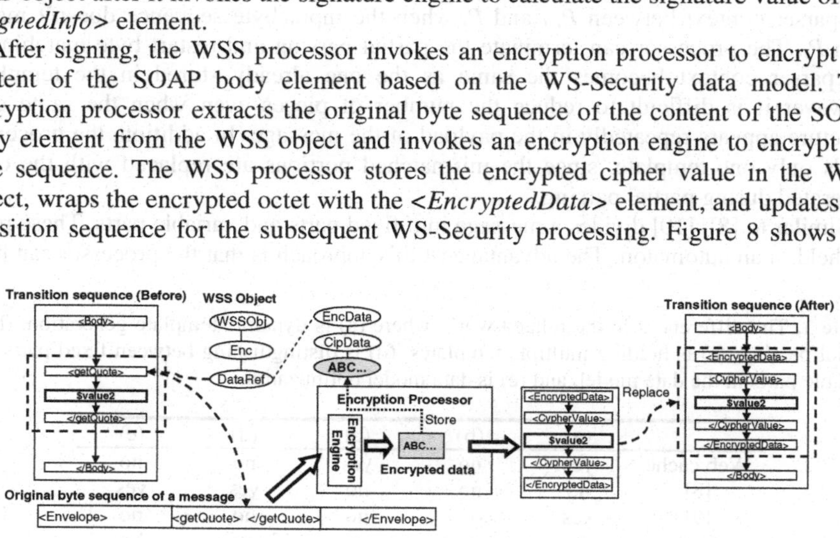

Fig. 8. Processing flow of encryption

processing flow of encryption of the SOAP body element. In Figure 8, the content of the SOAP body element has been replaced with the <*EncryptedData*> element.

3 Related Work

General Web cache and our processor share some things in common. For instance, they both store multiple received messages for later reuse. Usually Web cache stores the entire request URL and query string as cache key, which is highly inefficient in terms of memory usage. Only one-byte difference between messages tends to create separate cache entries, each representing the entire message. On the other hand, our processor divides a message into multiple pieces and common pieces are stored only once (merging commonalities between messages and collapsing repeating structure in one message), leading to an efficient data structure.

Some differential techniques, especially byte matching, have been proposed to avoid extensive XML processing in recent years. [8] assumes that a receiver knows in advance the structure of the SOAP messages (including the number of white spaces) to be exchanged. The receiver has to divide the message into two parts based on the XML syntax: fixed parts corresponding to element tags and variable parts corresponding to text nodes and attribute values, and hold them as a template before it processes the message. However this means that the entire message processing fails whenever any part mismatches the template, because the processor can't dynamically update the template. In addition, the processor can't hold more than one template at the same time.

In [9], an XML message was divided into fixed-length pieces. The pieces (P_1, ..., P_n) are held as a template. The template also stores the parser context at each boundary of the portions so that the processor can resume a partial parsing by using the parser context between P_{i-1} and P_i when the input byte sequence doesn't match with P_i. The processor can terminate the partial parsing and restart byte matching if the parser context becomes the same as the one already stored in the template. However it is difficult to reduce the number of pieces even when the same data structure appears repeatedly in the payload of the message. In addition, the processor holds only one template, since the mismatched portions are replaced with the ones generated during partial parsing.

Similar to [8], [10] divides a message into fixed parts and variable parts. These parts are held in an automaton. The advantage of this approach is that the processor can hold

Table 1. The differences in the related work, where (a) is dynamic template generation, (b) is partial parsing, (c) is holding multiple templates, (d) is distinguishing between fixed parts and variable parts in the data model, and (e) is data model optimization

	(a)	(b)	(c)	(d)	(e)
Web cache	yes	no	yes	no	no
[8]	no	no	no	yes	yes
[9]	yes	yes	no	no	no
[10]	yes	no	yes	yes	No
This paper	yes	yes	yes	yes	yes

multiple message templates in the automaton. However since the parser context is not stored, it is impossible to optimize the data structure in the automaton.

This paper addresses many of the problems in these systems. Our processor divides the message into fixed parts and variable parts according to the XML syntax in the input byte sequence and holds them in an automaton. The automaton also stores parser contexts. Therefore, the processor can resume a partial parsing and dynamically update the data in the automaton without invoking another processor as in [10]. In addition, the data model in an automaton can be optimized even when the same structure appears repeatedly in the byte sequence. Table 1 shows a summary of the differences in the related work, where Web cache can be regarded as holding multiple templates, each containing one large fixed part which representing the entire message..

4 Performance Study

This section describes a performance study that we conducted to evaluate the memory usage and performance of our differential technique. Section 4.1 presents the experiment in terms of memory usage and Section 4.2 shows the experiment in terms of performance.

4.1 Experiment in Terms of Memory Usage

We conducted an experiment to examine how the memory required for our data model differs from the memory needed for the data model in [10] on the service provider. We ran all of the tests on a ThinkPad[1] T42 (Intel Pentium[2] M 745 1.8 GHz, 1.5 GB RAM, Windows[3] XP Professional Edition). Five different services were used

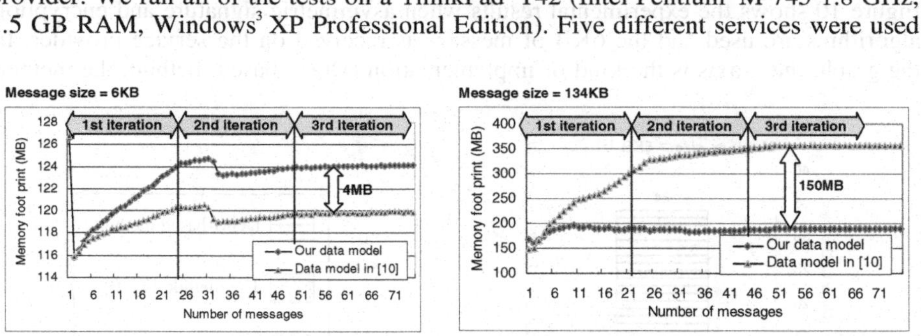

Fig. 9. Memory usage comparison between our data model and the data model in [10]

in the experiment. Then we prepared five different messages per service (for a total of 25 different messages). Each message included the same XML structure that appeared repeatedly in the payload of the SOAP body element. We sent them three times to the services with a Web services client. Therefore, the client sent a total of 75 messages

1 ThinkPad is a trademark of Lenovo in the United States, other countries, or both.

2 Intel and Pentium are trademarks of Intel Corporation in the United States, other countries, or both.

3 Windows is a trademark of Microsoft Corporation in the United States, other countries, or both.

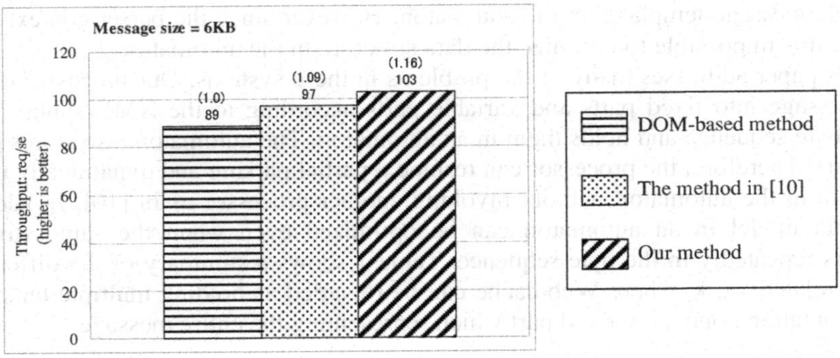

Fig. 10. Performance comparison between our method and the method in [10]

to the services. Figure 9 shows the experimental results. Figure 9 indicates that our data model can save about 150 MB of memory when sending the 13 KB of message though it required slightly more memory when sending the 6KB of message.

4.2 Experiments in Performance Number

We conducted an experiment to compare the performance of our method and the performance of the method in [10] on the service provider. We ran all of the tests with on an IBM xSeries[4] 365 (Intel Xeon[5] MP 3.0 GHz, 4-way, 4 MB L3 Cache, 8 GB RAM, with HyperThreading disabled, on Windows Server 2003 Enterprise Edition). Figure 10 shows the experimental results when asymmetric signature and encryption algorithms are used and the 6KB of message is received on the service provider. In the graph, the x-axis is the kind of implementation (DOM-based method, the method

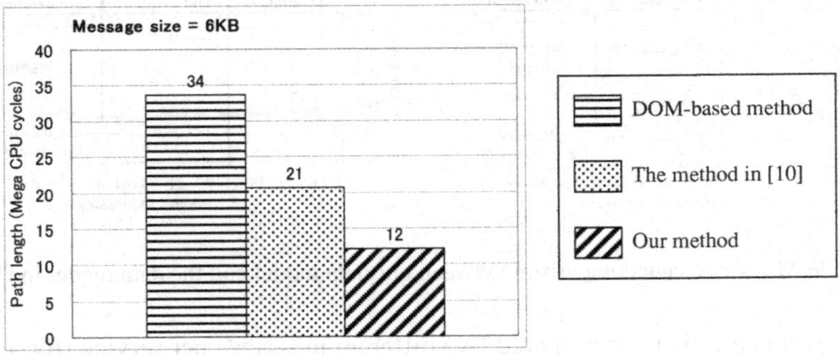

Fig. 11. Path length comparison between our method and the method in [10]

in [10], and our method) and the y-axis is throughput (requests/sec). Since the XML processing constitutes a second greater portion of the total WS-Security processing in

[4] IBM and xSeries are trademarks of International Business Machines Corporation in the United States, other countries, or both.

[5] Xeon is a trademark of Intel Corporation in the United States, other countries, or both.

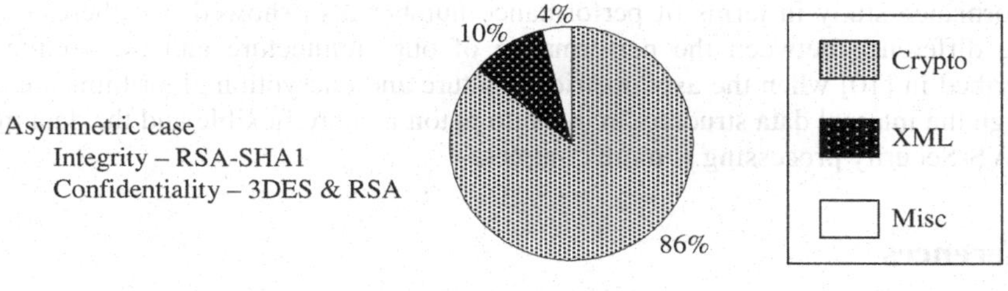

Fig. 12. Analysis of performance contribution in our method

the case using asymmetric algorithms, our method makes a contribution to performance improvement. Figure 10 also indicates that performance number of our method is faster than the method in [10], even though our method is more practical and more flexible.

We also conducted an experiment to examine the path lengths required for our processing method compared to the path lengths needed for the processing method in [10]. We ran all of the tests on an IBM xSeries 365 (Intel Xeon MP 3.0 GHz, 4-way, 4 MB L3 Cache, 8 GB RAM, with HyperThreading disabled, on Windows Server 2003 Enterprise Edition). In the experiment, we first used an internally developed tool to get a call graph. Then we analyzed the path lengths calculated from the call graph. Figure 11 shows the experimental results. Figure 11 indicates that our method can shorten path lengths required for the XML processing, compared with the method in [10].

Finally we conducted an experiment to analyze the performance contribution in our method. Figure 12 shows the experimental results. Figure 12 represents that our method can reduce the percentage of the XML processing in the while WS-Security processing compared with the percentage of the XML processing shown in the asymmetric case in Figure 1.

5 Concluding Remarks

In this paper, we have presented a new architecture for WS-Security processing with differential parsing to improve the XML performance in the WS-Security processing. In our architecture, the WSS preprocessor matches the byte sequence of an input SOAP message with the data that were previously processed and stored in an automaton. If the byte sequence completely matches with the data in the automaton, it means that we can skip all unnecessary XML processing in the WS-Security processing. On the other hand, if there is any mismatch, the processor can partially parse only the unmatched parts of the byte sequence of the message because the parser contexts are also stored in the automaton. While parsing the parts, it divides into the fixed parts and the variable parts according to the XML syntax in the message, and updates the automaton with the divided parts. We also proposed a more complete and more flexible data model for WS-Security processing so that we could support a wider variety of practical scenarios that [10] does not cover.

The performance study in terms of memory usage showed that our architecture requires less memory than needed for the architecture described in [10]. The performance study in terms of performance number also showed that there is not a large difference between the performance of our architecture and the architecture described in [10] when the asymmetric signature and encryption algorithms are used, though the internal data structure in the automaton is more flexible and the data model for WS-Security processing is more complete.

References

1. Simple Object Access Protocol (SOAP) Version 1.2, http://www.w3.org/TR/soap12/
2. Web Services Description Language (WSDL) 1.1, http://www.w3.org/TR/wsdl
3. Web Services Security: SOAP Message Security 1.1, http://www.oasis-open.org/committees/download.php/16790/wss-v1.1-spec-os-SOAPMessageSecurity.pdf
4. XML Security Suite, http://www.alphaworks.ibm.com/tech/xmlsecuritysuite
5. XML-Signature XPath Filter 2.0, http://www.w3.org/TR/xmldsig-filter2/
6. Exclusive XML Canonicalization Version 1.0, http://www.w3.org/TR/xml-exc-c14n/
7. Hongbin Liu, Shrideep Pallickara, and Geoffrey Fox, Performance of Web Services Security, Technical Report, 2004, http://grids.ucs.indiana.edu/ptliupages/publications/WSSPerf.pdf
8. Yoichi Takeuchi, Takashi Okamoto, Kazutoshi Yokoyama, and Shigeyuki Matsuda, "A Differential-analysis Approach for Improving SOAP Processing Performance," The 2005 IEEE International Conference on e-Technology, e-Commerce and e-Service (EEE'05), pp. 472-479, 2005
9. Nayef Abu-Ghazaleh and Michael J. Lewis, "Differential Deserialization for Optimized SOAP Performance," ACM/IEEE SC 2005 Conference (SC'05), pp. 21-31, 2005
10. Satoshi Makino, Michiaki Tatsubori, Kent Tamura, and Yuichi Nakamura, "Improving WS-Security Performance with a Template-Based Approach," IEEE International Conference on Web Services (ICWS'05), pp. 581-588, 2005
11. Toshiro Takase, Hisashi MIYASHITA, Toyotaro Suzumura, and Michiaki Tatsubori, "An adaptive, fast, and safe XML parser based on byte sequences memorization," The 14th international conference on World Wide Web (WWW 2005), pp. 692-701, 2005

Web Browsers as Service-Oriented Clients Integrated with Web Services

Hisashi Miyashita and Tatsuya Ishihara

IBM Research, Tokyo Research Laboratory, Japan
{himi, tisihara}@jp.ibm.com

Abstract. Web browsers are becoming important application clients in SOAs (Service-Oriented Architectures) because more and more Web applications are built from multiple Web Services. Therefore incorporating Web Services into Web browsers is of great interest. However, the existing Web Service frameworks bring significant complexities to traditional Web applications based on DHTML since such Web Service frameworks use RPC (Remote Procedure Call) or a message-passing model while DHTML is based on a document-centric model. Therefore Web application developers have to bridge the gaps between these two models such as an Object/XML impedance mismatch.

In our novel approach, in order to request Web Services, the application programs manipulate documents with uniform document APIs without invoking service-specific APIs and without mapping between objects and XML documents. The Web Service framework automatically updates the document by exchanging SOAP messages with the servers.

We show that in our new framework, WebDrasil, we can request a service with only one XPath expression, and then get the response using DOM (Document Object Model) APIs, an approach which is efficient and easily understood by typical Web developers.

1 Introduction

Service-Oriented Architecture (SOA) is an important technology to coordinate services across over multiple divisions in enterprise systems. These days, SOA on the client side is receiving attention for delivering services to end users [1], and many client frameworks are now supporting SOAs. For example, the Flex Framework by Adobe, the Eclipse based Rich Client Platform contributed by IBM, and the Mozilla Web browser [2] now support Web Services for SOA. Such a client having a close affinity to SOA is called an SOC (Service-Oriented Client) [1].

Of these clients, the Web browser is the most important platform for SOC. Recently, many websites or Web applications are combined using *mash-up* technology [3]. For example, HousingMaps (`http://www.housingmaps.com`) combines craigslist and Google maps and provides a totally new service to search for properties. This shift was triggered by the breakthrough technology, Ajax [4], which supports asynchronous access to distributed Web Services. Ajax allows a Web browser to be an intelligent client for Web Services by greatly improving the user experience. For example, Google provides Map and Calendar, and is now preparing a spreadsheet service by using Ajax.

A. Dan and W. Lamersdorf (Eds.): ICSOC 2006, LNCS 4294, pp. 289–301, 2006.

In line with the importance of Web browsers in service computing, supporting Web Services on Web browsers is becoming vital for SOA.

However, the existing Web Service frameworks such as JAX-WS (formerly JAX-RPC) [5] and Mozilla Web Service [2] do not fit with the programming model of Web browsers. These frameworks are designed not for Web browsers to present data for Web Services, but for native languages (JavaScript and Java) to easily access SOAP messages. Therefore, such frameworks are built on top of RPC (Remote Procedure Call) or a message-passing model. In contrast, Web browsers use a document-centric model. For example, in DHTML (Dynamic HTML) applications on Web browsers, scripts in the documents manipulate the in-memory tree structure, the *DOM (Document Object Model)*, to change the presentation. Since SOAP messages are now widely used as *document-literal* instead of *RPC/encoded* [1], they are viewed as XML documents, not as objects in Object-Oriented (OO) Programming. Therefore, introducing existing Web Services frameworks (from the OO world) into Web browsers (the XML world) doubles the gaps between these two models (as shown in Fig.1).

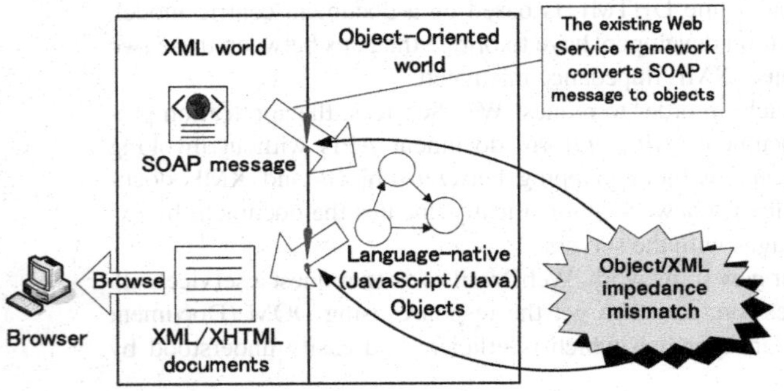

Fig. 1. The gaps by Web Services frameworks on Web browsers

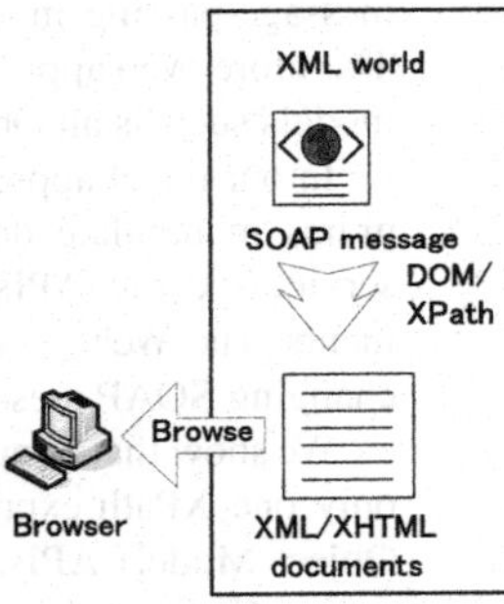

Fig. 2. Our approach

1.1 The Gaps in the Web Services Frameworks

Let us consider examples to clarify the gaps in a framework. In Fig. 3, we show a JavaScript code fragment that sends a request to Amazon.com Search Web Service on Mozilla using an RPC model. In this example, we construct an `searchRequest` object and then call the `KeywordSearchRequest` API to request the service. In contrast, to show the search results using DHTML, we write something like Fig. 4 using a document model. This code converts the `result` object to an HTML document, and inserts it into the DOM.

The gaps between the RPC and document models are twofold: 1) Non-uniform vs. uniform APIs and 2) Object/XML impedance mismatch [7].

For 1), in the RPC model, we invoke a service-specific API, `KeywordSearchRequest`. The names and arguments of such APIs differ from service to service. By comparison, in the document model, we use the uniform APIs, namely DOM APIs, to show the results. These same APIs can be used for services of any type.

[1] WS-I profile [6] does not support RPC/encoded for interoperability.

```
var searchRequest = new Object();
searchRequest.keyword=value;
searchRequest.page="1";
searchRequest.mode="books";
...
// proxy is Web Service Proxy object
proxy.KeywordSearchRequest(
                    searchRequest);
```

Fig. 3. Issue an Amazon search request (an RPC model)

```
var e = document.getElementById('resultid');
for (i = 0; i < result.Details.length; i++){
   e.innerHTML +="<p>"+
       result.Details[i].ProductName+"</p>";
}
```

Fig. 4. Show the search results in DHTML (a document model). The search results are stored in the `result` variable.

For 2), when we create an object to invoke a service, we have to manually convert the resulting object into a document written as HTML. To deal with this conversion, the developers have to understand how such language-native objects are mapped from SOAP messages. In other words, they have to know how the `result.Details[i].ProductName` object is translated from the `ProductName` element in the SOAP response that actually looks like:

```
... <ProductInfo>
      <Details url="...">
        <Asin>A00001O1XK</Asin>
        <ProductName> SOA Handbook </ProductName> ...
      </Details>
... </ProductInfo> ...
```

It is quite difficult for developers to understand how XML documents are mapped to language-native objects and how such objects should be converted to XML documents for presentation. In this example, it is not clear why `result.Details[0].ProductName` is correct, but `result.ProductInfo.Details.ProductName` is not correct. That depends on the specification of the Web Service framework.

As is shown by this example, in bridging the gaps between these two models, SOC application developers have to comprehend both programming and data models, which substantially increases development and maintenance costs for Web applications [7].

1.2 Document-Based Web Service Framework

We address the problems by introducing a new Web Service framework to integrate the programming models. In our approach, we can request services by manipulating documents (Fig. 2). For example, we can issue the same request to the Amazon.com Web Service with an XPath expression:

```
var request = webService.selectSingleNode(
 "./ws:Query[1]/ws:Request/aws:KeyWordSearchRequest\\
 [keyword='keyword' and page='1' and mode='books' ...]",
 namespaces);
```

Unlike existing Web Service stacks, our framework does not impose an object-XML mapping on the client applications. Rather, the client applications concentrate on manipulating documents by using uniform interfaces such as DOM and XPath. Our client framework translates such document manipulations into SOAP message exchanges, and then caches the requests and responses in the DOM tree appropriately. Thus, we store the results in XML documents, not in objects. This model is completely aligned with DHTML, and free from the Object/XML impedance mismatch. Actually, we can even directly present the responses from the XML by setting the styles with CSS without any XML transformation. Of course, we can directly extract data from the response with XPath. For example, we can access all the `ProductName` elements in the previous example by specifying something like:

```
var productNames = response.selectNodeList(
                   ".//Details/ProductName", namespaces);
```

By unifying the programming models of Web Services and Web browsers, we can achieve seamless integration between them. Developers can seamlessly deal with the usual Web applications and Web Service clients rather than fighting with various APIs introduced by individual Web Services.

In addition, in our approach we can efficiently integrate Web Service technology with powerful and successful Web standards such as HTML, XSLT, CSS, and XForms. Web Service solution providers can rely on the power of these technologies when they design service-specific XML messages. With reduced effort, they can build stylish and attractive clients by transforming the DOM tree with XSLT, defining styles with CSS, and using XForms to create forms.

The rest of this paper is organized as follows. In Section 2, we introduce the architecture design principles of our novel Web Service client framework. In Section 3, we present our Web Service client implementation named *WebDrasil*, and use some examples to show the efficiency of our client Web Service programming model. Finally, Sections 4 and 5 provide related work and our conclusions, respectively.

2 Web Service Architecture Based on Web Browsers

We propose a novel framework for Web Services suitable for Web Browsers that removes the gaps between DHTML applications and the existing SOAP stacks. Rather than explicitly sending SOAP messages or invoking new interfaces (typically generated from WSDL), we simply access a tree with a uniform API such as DOM. We show the mechanism in Fig. 5:(1) First, we insert a request message into a tree; (2) Try to get the result by accessing the location where the response message is to be inserted into the tree; (3)–(5) The client framework automatically exchanges the required messages with the server(s) and inserts the response into the tree; (6) Finally, we can access the response.

Let us explain these steps by using an example. Suppose we want to retrieve the cached page of `http://www.ibm.com` via the Google Web Service. In our framework, as Step (1), we place the request shown in Fig. 6 into the DOM tree by using the DOM or XPath APIs (the details are discussed in Section 2.1). In this example, we insert the request under the `ws:Query` element, as shown in Fig. 7. In Step (2), we access the DOM tree where the response message will be stored, that is, under the `ws:Response` element, as shown in the left panel of Fig. 8. In Step (3), when the client framework detects the changes in the DOM tree, the framework translates the message under the `ws:Request` element into a SOAP message and then sends it to the appropriate endpoint by using the WSDL definition of the service. In Step (4), the framework receives the SOAP response. In Step (5), the framework places the response from the SOAP message into the DOM tree, as shown in the right panel of Fig. 8. In Step (6), we find the required information in the `return` element, which should be the cached page of `http://www.ibm.com`. Notice that Steps (3)–(5) are automatically processed by the framework. Users can retrieve the result as though it already existed in the tree with this mechanism.

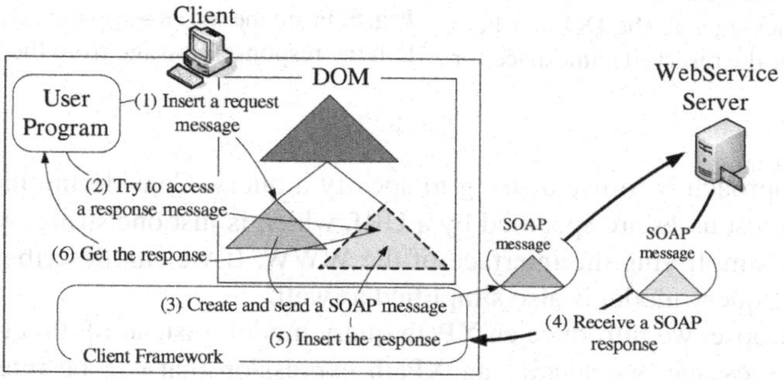

Fig. 5. The Mechanism of our Web Service Client Framework

```
<gws:doGetCachedPage xmlns:gws="urn:GoogleSearch">
  <key xsi:type="xsd:string">0000</key>
  <url xsi:type="xsd:string">http://www.google.com/</url>
</gws:doGetCachedPage>
```

Fig. 6. A request message of doGetCachedPage

In the rest of this section, we explain the details of our architecture. In the next subsection, we explain how we specify requests from a Web Service. We continue by discussing synchronous/lazy/asynchronous update modes and our cache mechanism. Finally, we discuss response transformations that help user programs be independent of the details of the Web Service interfaces.

2.1 Querying Services

In order to request a Web Service, we have to prepare a SOAP message from the request data, which we call a *query* in our framework (Fig. 5 (1)). That is, instead of invoking a method, we do a query to request a service.

We use the following steps to request a service: (a) create a SOAP body part for the query; (b) construct a SOAP envelope from the service specification and make a SOAP message by putting the body in the envelope; (c) select an endpoint for the service and send the SOAP message to it.

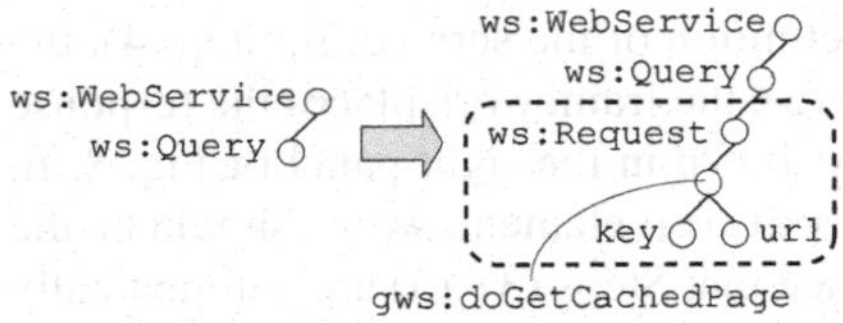

Fig. 7. The request message in the DOM. The `ws:WebService`, `ws:Query`, and `ws:Request` elements are introduced just for bundling messages in the DOM, where `ws` is a prefix of the reserved namespace for Web Service.

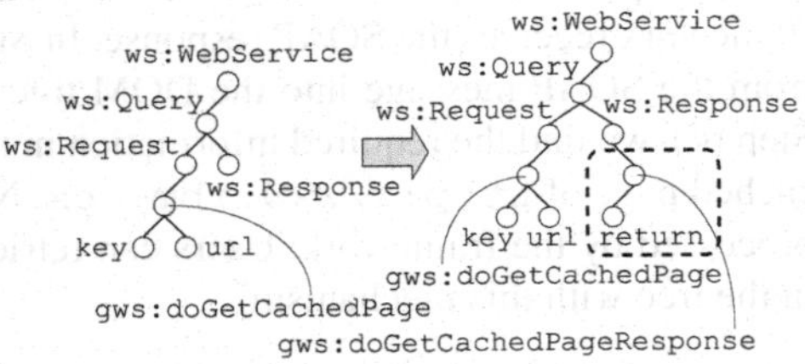

Fig. 8. From the `ws:Response` element, we obtain the response message from the Web Service

Another approach is to use a string to specify a query. Considering the WWW architecture, all resources are specified by a URI, which is just one string, which greatly contributes to simplifying the interface of the WWW. If we can describe a request in one string, our query model is also simplified as well.

For this purpose, we introduce an XPath query model. Instead of directly constructing an XML message, we specify an XPath expression that can be interpreted as a request message. Let us consider again the example shown in Fig. 6. In this example, the essential information to request the service is that the key is `0000` and the URL is `http://www.google.com/`. Therefore, we can specify these two in the following XPath expression.

```
doGetCachedPage[key='0000' and url='http://www.google.com/']
```

By extracting the type information from the WSDL definition, we can construct the request message in Fig. 6 from the above expression. That is, "`xsi:type`" attributes are automatically added by the WSDL definition.

More formally, this process requires translations from an XPath expression to an XML tree, which involves some challenging issues. Later, we explain our sample implementation in Subsection 3.2, and discuss the advanced topics in Section 5. Here, suffice it to say that we can convert some XPath expressions into XML trees, as long as they conform to the following restrictions:

- Every name test has a concrete QName (e.g., $\star$ or // is not allowed).
- All predicates are of the form:

$$[\mathit{PathExpr} = \mathit{Literal} \text{ and } \ldots \text{and } \mathit{PathExpr} = \mathit{Literal}],$$

  where the notations *PathExpr* and *Literal* are as defined in the XPath specification [8].

For Steps (b) and (c), since the service endpoints are described in WSDL, we can automatically generate a SOAP envelope to transfer the data, and then send the SOAP message to the specified endpoint.

2.2 Update Mode

Since SOAP communication takes considerable time, it is critical for applications to determine when we should send messages and when we should wait for the response. In our framework, we have the following three update modes for the timing of requests, which determines when we process requests for services (see Fig. 9).

Synchronous. Start the request when the request part is prepared in the DOM tree and wait until it finishes.

Lazy. Defer the request until the response part is accessed.

Asynchronous. Start the request when the request part is prepared in the DOM tree but do not wait for the completion at that time. When the response part is accessed, block the execution until the response is available.

Let us explain the differences of these three update modes by using examples. We suppose that we have just put a request message in the DOM tree (Step (1) in Fig. 5). In synchronous mode, we call the `send(element)` API, where `element` points at the `ws:Request` element in Fig. 7. Then the execution is blocked until the `ws:Response` part in the DOM (Fig. 8) is updated with the response message. In lazy mode, we do not have to explicitly call `send(element)`. Instead, we can directly access the `ws:Response` element. At that time, if we have not received the response message, the access is blocked until the `ws:Response` part is updated. In asynchronous mode, we explicitly call `send(element)`. But the execution is not blocked at that time. Then when we access the `ws:Response` element and if we have not received the response message, the access will be blocked as in the lazy mode.

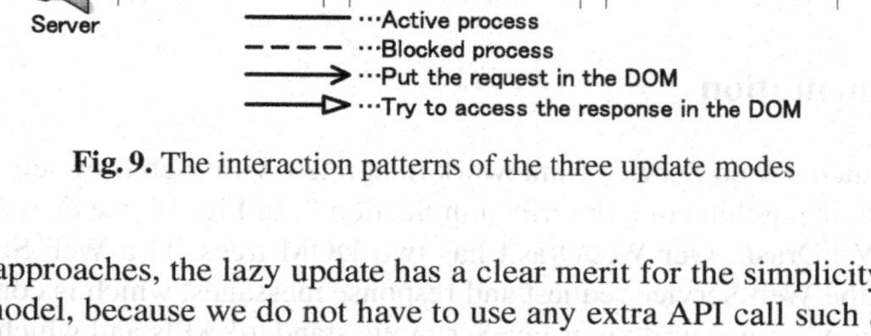

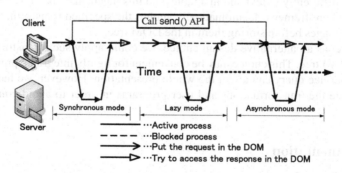

Fig. 9. The interaction patterns of the three update modes

Of these approaches, the lazy update has a clear merit for the simplicity of the programming model, because we do not have to use any extra API call such as `send()`. Therefore, the lazy update is the default mode in our framework.

For the other options, we have to explicitly specify when the request part in the DOM has been prepared. However, the asynchronous update is the preferred option considering the users' experience and is aligned with the Ajax style.

2.3 Cache Mechanism

Since the numbers of request and response messages are unlimited, we naturally require cache mechanisms in our framework, which stores request and response trees and evicts entries appropriately when the total cache size reaches the set limit.

We cache the response data associated with the corresponding request data. That means we assume the same request data always returns the same response data. This assumption is justified because a Web Service is usually designed in a stateless fashion, i.e., a request message contains all of the information required to invoke a service.

Note that we do require a "pin" mechanism for our cache system for lazy or asynchronous update modes. We have to pin the request data to prevent its eviction until the updating operation for the response data has been completed.

2.4 Response Transformation

The raw response data from a Web Service does not usually fit the requirements for browsing. In such cases, transforming the response data is desirable for client-side programs. This style agrees with separation of concerns. Ideally, the client-side programs concentrate on presentation issues and delegate the other parts to the transformation program. In addition, this architectural style is robust against changes of the Web Service interfaces. The design goal is that we will only have to update the transformation programs and that such changes will not affect the client user programs.

XSLT and XQuery are good candidates for performing this kind of XML transformation. In configurations of our client framework, we can specify these languages for each service. If we can apply different transformations to different locations in the DOM tree, it may be helpful for various presentations. For example, we may want to present stock prices differently in text and in a table, and this mechanism is convenient in such a case. The client framework automatically applies the specified transformations to the response messages before storing them in the DOM tree.

Otherwise, as an alternative design choice, we could apply such transformations to the entire DOM tree. This choice may be convenient for tightly integrated presentations, since each service query can affect the whole presentation. However, we have to carefully organize the transformations and user programs in order to avoid conflicts with each other.

3 Implementation

We implemented a Web Service framework integrated with Web browsers, *WebDrasil*, in accord with the architecture described in Section 2. In Fig. 10, we describe the components of WebDrasil. Our WebDrasil has two DOM trees: 1) a Web Service DOM representing the Web Service request and response messages, which is constructed using client user programs written in JavaScript via standard APIs and which is transparently updated with response messages; and 2) an HTML DOM representing an HTML document, which is provided by a special Web browser supporting the W3C DOM programming [9].

3.1 Applications on WebDrasil

A DHTML application supporting a Web Service is executed by following these steps (see Fig. 10): (1) WebDrasil sends the URI to the server to retrieve the application document; (2) The corresponding document is received from the server. The HTML DOM is created by parsing the HTML part of the retrieved document, and the JavaScript engine loads the received JavaScript code; (3) WebDrasil renders the constructed HTML DOM; (4), (5) If any event caused by user input is detected, the JavaScript function associated with that event is called; (6) To use a Web Service API, the Web Service DOM is updated by a JavaScript function using the DOM APIs, or by XPath functions; (7) When updating a Web Service DOM, a SOAP request is created and sent to the Web Service server; (8) Then a SOAP response message is sent to WebDrasil and the Web Service DOM is updated by examining the SOAP response message; (9),(10) The elements of the Web Service DOM that are necessary for updating the HTML DOM are retrieved, and the HTML DOM is updated based on them; (11) Finally WebDrasil renders the updated HTML DOM, and dynamically presents the changes.

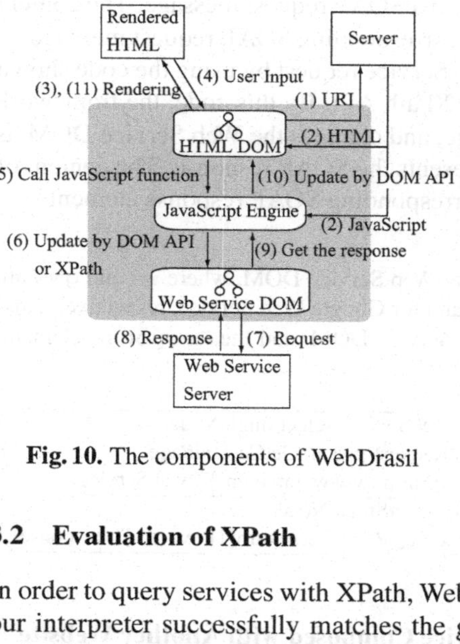

Fig. 10. The components of WebDrasil

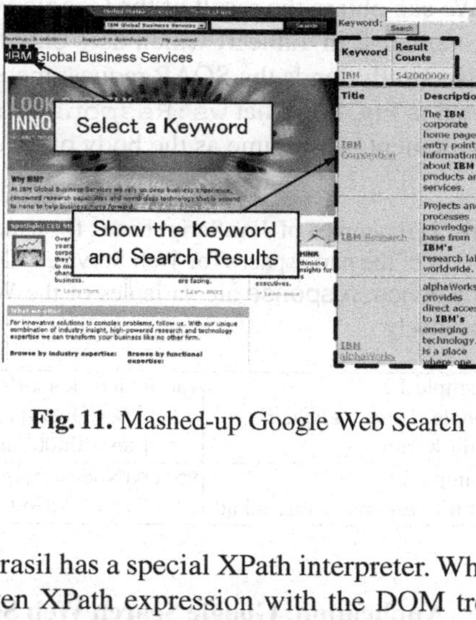

Fig. 11. Mashed-up Google Web Search

3.2 Evaluation of XPath

In order to query services with XPath, WebDrasil has a special XPath interpreter. When our interpreter successfully matches the given XPath expression with the DOM tree, it simply returns the matched part. Otherwise, our interpreter splits the XPath expression into location steps. For each location step, if the current context position is in a `ws:Request` element, our interpreter checks whether or not the matched node exists. Note that there is at most one matched node when the XPath expression obeys the restrictions in Subsection 2.1. If it does not exist, we create a new node from this location step. After evaluating all of the steps, we have an updated DOM tree that has a node that matches the given XPath expression.

We need to maintain the validity of the Web Service DOM after this update process. Our interpreter checks the validity of the updated DOM tree by using the schemas in the WSDL definitions. If it is not valid, our interpreter cancels the entire update.

3.3 JavaScript Examples for a Web Service

In Table 1, we show examples of JavaScript code for updating the Web Service DOM and invoking a Web Service. Even though these code samples include all of the essential steps to use the Web Service, they are written by using the XPath APIs, without using the service-specific interfaces.

The JavaScript code for updating `ws:Request` element by using the XPath API is Example 1 in Table 1. The request is created in the Web Service DOM as shown in Fig. 7. The `ws:WebService` is the root node of the Web Service DOM, and has the URL for the WSDL file as its attribute. The WSDL file is used for checking whether or not the DOM tree is valid. A node like `ws:Query` represents each query of the Web Service. Such a node has two children, an element for generating a SOAP request, and an element for storing a SOAP response corresponding to the request element. The node `ws:Request` holds the request as converted to a SOAP request message. The content of this element is the same as the body of the corresponding SOAP request message.

We can obtain the result of the Google Web Service request by using the code shown in Example 2 in Table 1, which uses only the XPath API. By this code, the framework transparently sends the SOAP request message, and changes the Web Service DOM as shown in Fig. 8, so that `ws:Response` represents the SOAP response. The content of this element is the same as the body of the corresponding SOAP response element.

Table 1. Examples of JavaScript codes for handling Web Service DOM, where `ws` and `gws` are prefixes of the namespaces for Web Service DOM and for Google Web Service, respectively; and **webService**, **response** are variables of the Web Service DOM, and the `Response` element, respectively

Example 1 : Update *Request element* using XPath	var doGetCachedPage =webService.selectSingleNode(".\/ws:Query[1]/ws:Request/gws:doGetCachedPage [key='0000' and url='http://www.ibm.com']", webService);
Example 2 : Get the response using XPath	var textNode = response.selectSingleNode("./gws:doGetCachedPageResponse/return[1]/text()[1]", response);

3.4 Application: Google Search Web Service Composed with Another Website

The DHTML application in Fig. 11 shows the benefits of using WebDrasil. This application has two visual components: (1) a web page, from which we can extract keywords, and (2) tables for showing the search history of keywords and the detailed search results. When the user selects a keyword from the web page, the search for the keyword is done with Google Web Service, and then the corresponding detailed results are shown in the detailed result table.

In this application, WebDrasil holds the response messages of the Google Web Service in the Web Service DOM. Because of this, the browser can change the presentation dynamically by updating or retrieving the Web Service DOM according to the user's input. This application is written using only HTML and JavaScript so that we can easily mash-up it with other websites as shown in Fig. 11.

By using the DOM and XPath APIs, Web developers can make smart and interactive Web Service DHTML applications such as this example.

4 Related Work

Our framework is built on top of various important studies in such areas as Web browser integration, Web and Web Service programming models, lazy DOM processing, and asynchronous interactions.

Web browsers are now such widespread components that integration with Web browsers is of great interest in various fields such as interactive programming environments [10] and collaboration tools [11]. Ponzo and Gruber integrated Web browser technologies with a rich client platform, Eclipse [9], for a better programming model. JSON (JavaScipt Object Notation)-RPC [12] is another service invocation method on Web browser. But it uses another data format familiar to JavaScript instead of XML.

There are some studies on Web Service programming models based on document processing. ActiveXML [13] introduced *dynamic XML documents* which consist of explicitly specified data and dynamic portions to be changed by querying Web services. Our work is similar to ActiveXML in that we use dynamically changing DOM. However, ActiveXML also proposed new query language and programming models. In contrast, we stick to use DOM and XPath fitting well with the DHTML programming model to integrate with Web browsers. Fox *et al.* proposed a collaborative Web Service [14] and Qui *et al.* proposed a collaboration framework using W3C DOM on top of their Web Service [15]. Their approach is somewhat similar to ours in that we use DOM for applications, but their framework is designed for collaboration by using the Web Service architecture, and does not provide a general Web Service programming model.

Asynchronous update mode involves asynchronous Web Service interactions. The correlation and coordination issues of asynchronous Web Services are studied in [16].

5 Conclusions and Future Work

We proposed a new client programming model for Web Services, a model which is document-centric and similar to that of Web browsers. In this programming model, we manipulate the document tree with uniform APIs such as DOM and XPath rather than by explicitly sending messages or by invoking non-uniform APIs. We prototyped a new Web Service client framework, WebDrasil, based on this architecture and provided some examples of client programs to show that the approach is intelligible and natural to Web developers.

Since this new programming model is based on many elementary technologies such as XML processing and distributed systems, we still have a lot of work to do:

XPath Query Model
In Subsection 2.1, we offered a rudimentary XPath-based query method for Web Services. However, we would like to have a more convenient and complete model for this purpose, one that would allow us to statically check or supplement XPath queries while considering the constraints of schemas. For example, if a schema specifies only one "key" element is allowed in the request message, then any XPath query for this service must contain a predicate only for that "key" element. We think match-identifying tree automata [17] could be used for this model.

Server-side Approach
In this paper, we introduced our framework on the client side of the Web applications, specifically in the Web browsers. However, our framework could also be applicable to the server side. For example, we could build a Web-Service-gateway server which feeds DHTML applications to the Web browsers and accepts requests from the browsers, and which then appropriately forwards them to external SOAP Web Service servers. By using such a gateway, Web browsers without support for SOAP Web Services could access those services. Also, in such a gateway, our framework would work well because the Web browsers would present XML documents rather than JavaScript objects.

Web Service Coordination and Security
When we use multiple services in our client framework, we need some coordination and security framework for reliable communications. Since, in our framework, we store the responses in one DOM tree, we require transactional cache mechanisms to maintain consistency and security mechanisms to prevent illegal accesses for DOM tree processing. Since our framework allows client-side scripting, such an access control mechanism is important to prevent XSS (Cross-Site Scripting) attacks.

Acknowledgments

We warmly thank to Makoto MURATA for helpful advises to improve this paper. This research was partly supported by the National Institute of Information and Communications Technology (NICT) of Japan as a part of the Multimedia Browsing Project for People with Visual Impairments.

References

1. J. Whatcott, "SOA's next wave: Service-oriented clients," May 2006, http://www.cio.com/weighin/column.html?CID=21201.
2. H. Dhurvasula and M. Galli, "Mozilla and web services," http://www.mozilla.org/projects/webservices/.
3. T. O'Reilly, "What is web 2.0," September 2005, http://www.oreillynet.com/pub/a/oreilly/tim/news/2005/09/30/what-is-web-20.html.
4. J. J. Garrett, "Ajax: A new approach to Web applications," February 2005, http://www.adaptivepath.com/publications /essays/archives/000385.php.
5. "Java api for xml web services (JAX-WS)," 2005, http://java.sun.com/webservices/jaxws/index.jsp.

6. K. Ballinger, D. Ehnebuske, M. Gudgin, C. K. Liu, M. Nottingham, and P. Yendluri, "WS-I basic profile version 1.1," http://www.ws-i.org/Profiles/BasicProfile-1.1-2004-08-24.html.
7. S. Loughran and E. Smith, "Rethinking the Java SOAP stack." in *ICWS*, 2005, pp. 845–852.
8. J. Clark and S. DeRose, "XML Path Language (XPath) Version 1.0," w3C Recommendation 16 November 1999, http://www.w3.org/TR/1999/REC-xpath-19991116.
9. J. Ponzo and O. Gruber, "Integrating Web technologies in Eclipse," *IBM Systems Journal*, vol. 44, no. 2, pp. 279–288, 2005.
10. M. Jambalsuren and Z. Cheng, "An interactive programming environment for enhancing learning performance," in *Databases in Networked Information Systems*, 2002, pp. 201–212.
11. K. M. Anderson and N. O. Bouvin, "Supporting project awareness on the www with the iscent framework," *SIGGROUP Bull.*, vol. 21, no. 3, pp. 16–20, 2000.
12. R. Barcia, "Build enterprise soa ajax clients with the dojo toolkit and json-rpc," http://www-128.ibm.com/developerworks/websphere/library/techarticles/0606_barcia/0606_barcia.html.
13. S. Abiteboul, A. Bonifati, G. Cobéna, I. Manolescu, and T. Milo, "Dynamic XML documents with distribution and replication," in *SIGMOD '03: Proceedings of the 2003 ACM SIGMOD international conference on Management of data*. New York, NY, USA: ACM Press, 2003, pp. 527–538.
14. G. Fox, H. Bulut, K. Kim, S.-H. Ko, S. Lee, S. Oh, S. Pallickara, X. Qiu, A. Uyar, M. Wang, and W. Wu, "Collaborative web services and peer-to-peer girds," in *Collaborative Technologies Symposium*, 2003.
15. X. Qiu, B. Carpenter, and G. Fox, "Internet collaboration using the w3c document object model." in *International Conference on Internet Computing*, 2003, pp. 643–647.
16. M. Brambilla, S. Ceri, M. Passamani, and A. Riccio, "Managing asynchronous web services interactions." in *ICWS*, 2004, pp. 80–87.
17. M. MURATA, "Extended path expressions for XML," in *PODS*, 2001, pp. 126–137.

Interaction Soundness for Service Orchestrations

Frank Puhlmann and Mathias Weske

Business Process Technology Group
Hasso-Plattner-Institute for IT Systems Engineering
at the University of Potsdam
D-14482 Potsdam, Germany
{puhlmann, weske}@hpi.uni-potsdam.de

Abstract. Traditionally, service orchestrations utilize services according to a choreography where they are a part of. The orchestrations as well as the choreographies describe pre-defined sequences of behavior. This paper investigates if a given orchestration can be enacted without deadlocks, i.e. is interaction sound, inside an environment made up of different services. In contrast to existing approaches, we utilize link passing mobility to directly represent dynamic binding as found in service oriented architectures. Thus, the sequences of interaction behavior are not statically pre-defined but rather depend on the possible behavior of the services in the environment.

1 Introduction

Service oriented architectures (SOA) comprise service orchestrations and choreographies [1]. While orchestrations resemble the internal processes of services, choreographies defines how different services should interact with each other. In this paper we focus on orchestrations that are enacted inside an environment of different services. Instead of reasoning on pre-defined sequences of interactions as given by a choreography, we would rather like to know if a certain orchestrations works seamlessly, i.e. without deadlocks, inside an environment made up of different services as possible interaction partners. The services are not statically connected to the orchestration, but are dynamically bound. For this dynamic binding to take place, we consider a service broker able to return semantically matching services that, however, might have different interaction behaviors. To cope with these different behaviors, we present an approach to determine if a certain orchestration is capable of interacting with a given set of dynamically bound services regardless of a pre-defined behavior.

The approach introduced, denoted as *interaction soundness*, utilizes lazy soundness for deciding deadlock freedom of orchestrations without considering interactions with the environment [3]. Interaction soundness extends lazy soundness by taking these interactions into account. As already motived in [1], the core of a SOA is dynamic discovery and binding of interaction partners. Lazy soundness has been chosen because it can be proven using bisimulation techniques of a process algebra, the π-calculus. The π-calculus in turn supports link passing mobility, a key feature

A. Dan and W. Lamersdorf (Eds.): ICSOC 2006, LNCS 4294, pp. 302–313, 2006.

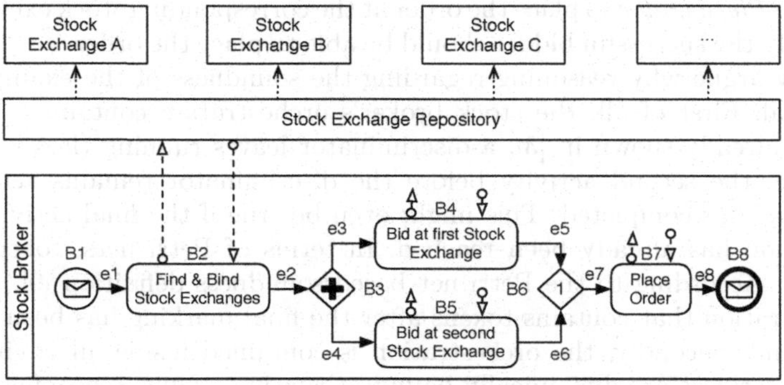

Fig. 1. Stock Exchange Choreography

required for representing dynamic binding [4]. An extended discussion on our motivation for using the π-calculus can be found in [5]. Furthermore, the paper builds on existing work on using the π-calculus for business process management and service oriented architectures [6,7].

The remainder of the paper is structured as follows. We first motivate the topic by introducing an example and refer to related work. Preliminaries are introduced, including π-calculus as well as the representation of orchestrations and choreographies in it. Based thereon, interaction soundness is defined. The paper concludes with a demonstration of existing tool support and a discussion of the achievements.

2 Motivation and Related Work

To motivate the topic, an example is shown in figure 1, denoted in a slightly extended variant of the Business Process Modeling Notation (BPMN). The example describes the orchestration of a *Stock Broker* service and its environment. The stock broker offers the ability of bidding at two different stock exchanges at the same time and place the order at the first stock exchange responding positive, i.e. where the order can be placed. This functionality is realized inside the orchestration using a discriminator pattern [8], denoted as a BPMN gateway containing the number of required incoming edges. Since there are many stock exchanges available with different properties such as fees, rates, and of course business hours, a *Stock Exchange Repository* is contained as a service in the environment. It is invoked as the first task of the stock broker, *Find & Bind Stock Exchanges.* The repository has knowledge about a number of *Stock Exchanges*, connected in the BPMN diagram using associations. Two of them matching the requested conditions are returned to the stock broker. The stock broker is now able to dynamically bind to the stock exchanges formerly unknown. This is denoted using in- and outgoing message flows at the activities *Bid at first Stock Exchange* and *Bid at second Stock Exchange.* Each stock exchange returns a special token if the bid has been accepted. This token is used inside *Place Order* to place the order at the corresponding stock exchange. Of course, only the successful bidder should be able to place the order.

We now argue why reasoning regarding the soundness of the example is far from trivial. First of all, the stock broker's orchestration contains a discriminator. As already shown in [3], a discriminator leaves running (lazy) activities behind, i.e. the second activity before the discriminator remains active after the first one has completed. This might even be true if the final activity of the orchestration has already been reached. In terms of Petri nets, token remain in the net. According to the Petri net based soundness definition [9], however, an orchestration that contains tokens after the final marking has been reached, is not sound. Secondly, the orchestration is contained inside an environment, where the services are dynamically bound at runtime. Thus, reasoning includes all combinations of services that can be potentially bound.

To overcome these problems, we propose adapting lazy soundness based on the π-calculus for interaction soundness. Lazy soundness takes care of lazy activities, thus solving the first problem (an extended discussion including other kinds of soundness can be found in [3]). More importantly, the π-calculus features link passing mobility, required for describing and reasoning on dynamic binding [4].

Related work comprises for instance Martens using Petri nets [10], Bordeaux and Salan using CCS [11], or Busi et al. using a proprietary process algebra [12]. However, these approaches do not adress dynamic binding. Recent research on interaction patterns by Barros et al. in general [13] and SOA in particular by Guidi and Lucci [14] showed that mobility is indeed required for service oriented architectures.

3 Preliminaries

This section introduces the π-calculus and the representation of orchestrations and environments in it.

3.1 The π-Calculus

The π-calculus is an algebra for the formal description and analysis of concurrent, interacting processes with support for link passing mobility. It is based on names and interactions used by processes defined according to [15].

Definition 1 (Pi Calculus). *The syntax of the π-calculus is given by:*

$$\begin{aligned} P &::= M \mid P|P' \mid \mathbf{v}zP \mid !P \mid P(y_1, \cdots y_n) \\ M &::= \mathbf{0} \mid \pi.P \mid M + M' \\ \pi &::= \overline{x}\langle\tilde{y}\rangle \mid x(\tilde{z}) \mid \tau \mid [x = y]\pi\ . \end{aligned}$$

P and M denote the processes and summations of the calculus. The informal semantics is as follows: $P|P'$ is the concurrent execution of P and P', $\mathbf{v}zP$ is the restriction of the scope of the name z to P, $!P$ is an infinite number of copies of P, and $P(y_1, \cdots, y_n)$ denotes parametric recursion. $\mathbf{0}$ is inaction, a process that can do nothing, $M + M'$ is the exclusive choice between M and M'. The actions of the calculus are given by π. The output prefix $\overline{x}\langle\tilde{y}\rangle.P$ sends a sequence of names $\tilde{y}$ over the co-name $\overline{x}$ and then continues as P. The input prefix $x(\tilde{z})$ receives a sequence of names over the name x and then continues as P with $\tilde{z}$ replaced by the received names (written as $\{^{\tilde{name}}/_{\tilde{z}}\}$). Matching input and output prefixes might communicate, leading to an interaction. The unobservable prefix $\tau.P$ expresses an internal action of the process, and the match prefix $[x = y]\pi.P$ behaves as $\pi.P$, if x is equal to y. Throughout this paper, upper case letters are used for process identifiers and lower case letters for names. The formal semantics of the π-calculus is based on a transition system. We only give short definitions of the required concepts and refer to [15,16] for details.

Definition 2 (Transition Sequence). *A sequence of interactions on names or unobservable actions is denoted as $P \xrightarrow{\alpha} P'$, where α describes the sequence of actions required to transform a process P to P'.* □

Thus, a transition sequence describes how a certain state P of a process is transfered to another denoted P'.

Definition 3 (Bound and Free Names). *The π-calculus has two operators for name binding, $x(z)$ and $\mathbf{v}zP$. In both cases the name z is* bound *inside process P. Names which are not bound by a name binding operator are called* free names *of a process.* □

Bound names can not be accessed from processes outside of P. Free names can be used for interactions between different processes. The free names of a processes can furthermore be observed outside of the process P for reasoning on bisimulation equivalence.

Definition 4 (Weak Open Bisimulation Equivalence). *Informally, two π-calculus processes P and Q are* weak open bisimulation equivalent, *denoted as $P \approx^o Q$, if they have the same observable behavior regarding their free names while abstracting from all internal actions.* □

Weak open bisimulation is used to prove interaction soundness later on. Formal details can be found in [16].

3.2 Orchestrations in the π-Calculus

Orchestrations can be formalized using set theory and π-calculus. The former is used to denote the static structure of the orchestration called *process graph*; the latter gives a formal semantics to a process graph. Since orchestrations are usually denoted graphically, a breakdown from graphical representations over process graphs up to π-calculus is possible.

Definition 5 (Process Graph). *A process graph is a four-tuple consisting of nodes, directed edges, types and attributes. Formally: $P = (N, E, T, A)$ with*

- *N is a finite, non-empty set of nodes.*
- *$E \subseteq (N \times N)$ is a set of directed edges.*

– $T : N \rightarrow 2^{TYPE}$ *is a function mapping nodes to sets of types.*
– $A : N \nrightarrow KEY \times VALUE$ *is a partial function mapping nodes to key/value pairs.* □

The nodes N of a process graph define the activities (incl. routing elements) of an orchestration, and the directed edges E define dependencies between activities. Each node can have none, one, or more types assigned by the function T. Furthermore, each node can hold optional attributes represented by key/values pairs assigned by the function A. Details will become more clear by looking at the process graph of the stock broker from figure 1. We now utilize the identifiers from the figure:

Example 1 (Process Graph of the Stock Broker Orchestration).

1. $N = \{B1, B2, B3, B4, B5, B6, B7, B8\}$
2. $E = \{(B1, B2), (B2, B3), (B3, B4), (B3, B5), (B4, B6), (B5, B6), (B6, B7), (B7, B8)\}$
3. $T = \{(B1, \{\text{Start Event}\}), (B2, \{\text{Task}\}), (B3, \{\text{AND Gateway}\}), (B4, \{\text{Task}\}), (B5, \{\text{Task}\}), (B6, \{\text{N-out-of-M-Join}\}), (B7, \{\text{Task}\}), (B8, \{\text{End Event}\})\}$
4. $A = \{(B6, (\text{continue}, 1))\}$ □

Each node of the orchestration is denoted as an element of N, whereas sequence flows between nodes are denoted in E. The types are simply represented as the textual name of the corresponding BPMN element in T. Other notations like *EPCs* or *UML2 Activity Diagrams* cause other types. The discriminator is denoted as a special kind of *n–out–of–m–join* with $n = 1$. This threshold is denoted in the set A.

However, since a process graph only denotes a static structure of an orchestration, in particular even with different types for the nodes, a formal semantics is given by mapping the process graph to π-calculus expressions. Therefore, we assume each node of the process graph to represent one of the workflow patterns [8]. The steps for mapping process graphs to π-calculus can then be sketched as follows (see [3] for a complete description).

Algorithm 1 (Sketch: Mapping Process Graphs to π-Calculus Processes). A process graph $P = (P_N, P_E, P_T, P_A)$ is mapped to the π-calculus as follows:

1. Assign all nodes of P a unique π-calculus process identifier $N1 \cdots N|P_N|$.
2. Assign all edges of P a unique π-calculus name $e1 \cdots e|P_E|$.
3. Define the π-calculus processes according to the π-calculus mapping of the workflow patterns found in [6,4] as given by the type of the corresponding node. Each functional part of an activity is represented by the unobservable prefix τ since it is abstracted from concrete realizations.
4. Define a global process $N = (\boldsymbol{\nu} e1, \cdots, e|P_E|) \prod_{i=1}^{|P_N|} Ni$. □

Section 5 contains a π-calculus mapping of the example.

3.3 Environments in the π-Calculus

Environments can be split into static ones with pre-defined bindings and such supporting dynamic binding. For static environments, a corresponding concept to a process graph, called *interaction graph IG*, can be introduced. An interaction graph relates several process graphs by *interaction flow*, according to *Message Flow* in BPMN.

However, the focus of this paper is on environments that support dynamic binding as given in the example. These environments are closely linked to the service interaction patterns by Barros et al. [13]. The patterns describe possible interaction behavior between services. To our knowledge, there exists no graphical notation that supports the representation of dynamic binding. Since a graphical representation is missing, we define the environments from scratch in π-calculus. This is done according to [4], where correlations and dynamic service invocation in π-calculus have been introduced. A synchronous service invocation is denoted in the π-calculus as:

$$A = \overline{b}\langle msg\rangle.A'$$
$$B = b(msg).B' \ ,$$

where A is the service requester and B is the service provider. The formalization leaves it open if A knows the link b at design time or acquired it during runtime. If the system is defined as

$$S = (\mathbf{v}b)(A \mid B) \ ,$$

A and B share the link b since design time. Using link passing mobility in π-calculus, we can model a repository $R = \overline{lookup}\langle b\rangle.R$ that transmits the link at runtime:

$$S = (\mathbf{v}lookup)(lookup(b).A \mid (\mathbf{v}b)(B \mid R)) \ .$$

An overview of formalizing more complex service interaction patterns in π-calculus including further references is given in [7].

4 Interaction Soundness

This section derives interaction soundness for orchestrations based on lazy soundness. Lazy soundness proves an orchestration containing lazy activities to be free of deadlocks and livelocks. Interaction soundness extends lazy soundness by incorporating the interactions between the orchestration and the environment.

4.1 Lazy Soundness

Lazy soundness requires *structural soundness* and *semantic reachability.* A process graph representing an orchestration is called structurally sound if it has exactly one initial node, exactly one final node and all nodes lie on a path from the initial to the final node.

Definition 6 (Structural Sound). *A process graph $P = (N, E, T, A)$ is structural sound if and only if:*

1. *There is exactly one initial node $N_i \in N$.*
2. *There is exactly one final node $N_o \in N$.*
3. *Every node is on a path from N_i to N_o.* □

Semantic reachability extends reachability by taking the semantics of the nodes into account.

Definition 7 (Semantic Reachability). *A node $N_1 \in N$ of a process graph $P = (N, E, T, A)$ is semantically reachable from another node $N_2 \in N$, denoted as $N_1 \rightsquigarrow N_2$, if and only if there exists a path leading from N_1 to N_2 according to the semantics of all nodes.*

Regarding the mapping of a π-calculus process from a process graph, a π-calculus process P_1 representing a node is semantically reachable from another π-calculus process P_2 representing a node, if and only if there exists a transition sequence from the functional abstraction τ of P_1 to the functional abstraction τ of process P_2. Lazy soundness is now defined as follows:

Definition 8 (Lazy Sound). *A structural sound process graph $P = (N, E, T, A)$ is lazy sound if and only if:*

1. *The final node N_o must be semantically reachable from every node $n \in N$ semantically reachable from the initial node until N_o has been reached for the first time. Formally: $\forall n \in N : N_i \rightsquigarrow n \rightsquigarrow N_o$ holds until N_o has been reached for the first time.*
2. *The final node N_o is reached exactly once.*

Definition 8 states that a lazy sound process graph representing a business process is deadlock and livelock free as long as the final node has not been executed (8.1). Once the final node has been executed, other nodes might still be executed, however they do not semantically reach the final node again (8.2). Lazy soundness can be proven by tracing the initial and the final activity of a process graph mapped to π-calculus processes.

4.2 Interaction Soundness for Service Orchestrations

Interaction soundness is defined for service graphs that enhance a process graph with interaction behavior.

Definition 9 (Service Graph). *A service graph extends a process graph by adding in- or outbound interaction edges used as a behavioral interface. Formally, $SG = (PS, C, L)$:*

- *$PS = (N_{PS}, E_{PS}, T_{PS}, A_{PS})$ is a structural sound process graph.*
- *$C \subseteq (N_{PS} \times \bot) \times (\bot \times N_{PS})$ is a set of directed interaction edges.*
- *$L \subseteq (C \times LABEL)$ is a set of labels of directed interaction edges.* □

PS is an orchestration describing the internal process of a service. Interactions with the environment are denoted by C, representing in- and outgoing communication (e.g. Message Flows in BPMN). The symbol $\perp$ is used as a connector to the environment. L attaches labels based on π-calculus names used to denote channels and data (examples can be found in section 5).

A counterpart to a service graph is given by an environment that can be utilized by the service graph.

Definition 10 (Environment). *Let SG be a service graph. An environment E for SG is given if E utilizes all in- and outgoing interaction edges C of SG by providing a matching process structure.*

Furthermore, a service graph SG unified with an environment E is denoted as $SG \uplus E$. Interaction soundness is now given by:

Definition 11 (Interaction Soundness). *A service graph SG is interaction sound regarding environment E if and only if $SG \uplus E$ is lazy sound.*

Interaction soundness states that a service graph representing an orchestration is deadlock and livelock free under consideration of all related interactions with the environment as long as the final activity of the orchestration has not been reached.

4.3 Reasoning on Interaction Soundness

Since interaction soundness is defined using service graphs and environments that do not yet have a formal semantics like process graphs, we now show how to enhance them for reasoning. First of all, the π-calculus mapping of the process graph contained in the service graph is annotated with π-calculus names used for interaction with the environment. This is done according to the labels and directed interaction edges of the service graph. Secondly, the environment is defined using π-calculus processes being able to interact with the π-calculus mapping of the service graph according to [4,7]. This is currently a manual task.

Once the π-calculus representation of a system consisting of the π-calculus mapping of a service graph and an environment has been defined, it can be enhanced for reasoning on lazy soundness as described in [3]. Basically the π-calculus process representing the initial activity of the orchestration is enhanced with the free name i and the π-calculus process representing the final activity is enhanced with the free name $\overline{o}$. Due to that, we are able to observe the occurrence of the initial activity and the final activity.

The distinction between interaction soundness and lazy soundness is given by the fact that not only the structure of the service graph is checked for conformance, but also the agile interaction with the environment using link passing mobility. For the π-calculus mapping of an orchestration and an environment to be interaction sound, i and $\overline{o}$ have to be observed exactly once for all possible transition sequences, including the ones between the participants. Thereby, i is just a helper to denote the start of the orchestration. The interesting part is $\overline{o}$. If $\overline{o}$ is not observed for all possible transition sequences, the orchestration contains a deadlock or livelock since property (1) of definition 8 is violated. If $\overline{o}$ is observed more then once, property (2) of definition 8 is violated, i.e. the orchestration contains uncontrolled loop or parallel process structures. To prove the π-calculus representation of an orchestrations and an environment to be interaction sound, it is compared for weak open bisimulation against a manually proved lazy sound π-calculus process given by $S_{LAZY} = i.\tau.\overline{o}.\mathbf{0}$.

Proposition 1. *A π-calculus representation SYS of a service choreography consisting of (1) a π-calculus mapping of an orchestration annotated with the free names i for the π-calculus process representing the initial and $\overline{o}$ for the π-calculus process representing the final activity of the orchestration, and (2) a π-calculus representation of a corresponding environment is interaction sound if and only if $CHO \approx^o S_{LAZY}$.*

5 Example and Tool Support

This section discusses how the theoretical results described in the last section can be applied using existing π-calculus tools like the Mobility Workbench (MWB) [17]. We utilize the example shown in figure 1.

The π-calculus representation of the stock broker's orchestration is generated from the BPMN diagram using a tool chain developed at our group.[1] The repository and different stock exchanges have been modeled manually, since their agile interaction behavior can not be modeled in BPMN. Interaction between the different participants is represented using π-calculus names. The π-calculus processes corresponding to figure 1 are printed below. To enable direct reasoning, the notation of the Mobility Workbench has been used, i.e. output prefixes are written as $'x$ instead of $\overline{x}$ and ^ denotes $\mathbf{v}$. Processes in the π-calculus are denoted as `agents`.

Example 2. Pi-Calculus Processes for the Stock Exchange Choreography.

```
agent SE_A(ch) = (^o)ch(b).t.'b<o>.o.SE_A(ch)
agent SE_B(ch) = (^o)ch(b).t.'b<o>.o.SE_B(ch)
agent SE_C(ch) = (^o)ch(b).t.'b<o>.o.SE_C(ch)

agent R(r,s1,s2,s3)=r(ch).'ch<s1>.r(ch).'ch<s2>.R(r,s1,s2,s3) +
      r(ch).'ch<s2>.r(ch).'ch<s3>.R(r,s1,s2,s3) + r(ch).'ch<s1>.r(ch).'ch<s3>.R(r,s1,s2,s3)

agent B(i,o,r)=(^e1,e2,e3,e4,e5,e6,e7,e8)( B1(e1,i) | B2(e1,e2,r) | B3(e2,e3,e4) | B4(e3,e5) |
      B5(e4,e6) | B6(e5,e6,e7) | B7(e7,e8) |B8(e8,o))
agent B1(e1,i)=i.t.'e1.0
agent B2(e1,e2,r)=(^ch)e1.'r<ch>.ch(s1).'r<ch>.ch(s2).t.('e2<s1,s2>.0 | B2(e1,e2,r))
agent B3(e2,e3,e4)=e2(s1,s2).t.('e3<s1>.0 | 'e4<s2>.0 | B3(e2,e3,e4))
agent B4(e3,e5)=(^b)e3(s).'s<b>.b(o).t.('e5<o>.0 | B4(e3,e5))
agent B5(e4,e6)=(^b)e4(s).'s<b>.b(o).t.('e6<o>.0 | B5(e4,e6))
agent B6(e5,e6,e7)=(^h,run)(B6_1(e5,e6,e7,h,run) | B6_2(e5,e6,e7,h,run))
agent B6_1(e5,e6,e7,h,run)=e5(o).'h<o>.0 | e6(o).'h<o>.0
agent B6_2(e5,e6,e7,h,run)=h(o).'run<o>.h(o).B6(e5,e6,e7) | run(o).t.'e7<o>.0
agent B7(e7,e8)=e7(o).'o.t.('e8.0 | B7(e7,e8))
agent B8(e8,o)=e8.t.'o.B8(e8,o)
```

[1] `http://bpt.hpi.uni-potsdam.de/twiki/bin/view/Piworkflow/Reasoner`

The first three lines of the example denote simple kinds of services that are used for reasoning. They simply create an order token o, wait for a connection via $ch(b)$, where b is a response channel used to signal back the o token. In between, however, complex computation takes place that is abstracted from by τ. Note that the different services do not differ in their interaction behavior right now, thus we could utilize each of them inside our orchestration.

The process R denotes a very simple kind of a repository that simply returns two arbitrary services. We omitted a complex structure based on lists that would allow arbitrary services to register and to de-register. The stock broker's orchestration is represented in the third block. B is a π-calculus process containing all activities of the stock broker, that in turn are represented according to figure 1 by $B1 \ldots B8$. Note the processes $B2$, where the stock exchanges are found at the repository (`'r<ch>.ch(s1).'r<ch>.ch(s2)`), $B4$ and $B5$, where the stock exchanges are dynamically bound and invoked (`'s<b>.b(o)`). Furthermore, the successful bidding activity forwards the order token to $B7$, where the order is finally placed. To allow activities of the orchestration to be observed according to lazy soundness, $B1$ and $B8$ are enhanced with `i` and `'o` accordingly. The process $SYS(i, o)$ places all participants into a system leaving only i and o as free names. SYS can then be compared to S_LAZY required for deciding lazy soundness.

The formalization given allows reasoning on the orchestration and the environment. The problems motivated in section 2 are solved using the π-calculus representation. Lazy (left–behind) activities before the discriminator are handled using lazy soundness. The π-calculus mapping of the discriminator, found in process $B6$, enables the outgoing sequence flow (denoted using $e7$) exactly once for the first incoming sequence flow (here $e5$ or $e6$). The second incoming sequence flow is simply captured. Furthermore, dynamic binding of different services is represented using link passing mobility as shown in the example. A tool session using MWB to prove interaction soundness is shown below:

```
MWB>weq SYS(i,o) S_LAZY(i,o)
The two agents are equal.
```

The orchestration of the stock broker inside the environment represented by SYS is weak open bisimulation equivalent to S_LAZY, hence the orchestration is interaction sound. Since the orchestration includes the interactions with the repository and stock exchanges, all possible behaviors of the services are acceptable and will not lead to a deadlock. But what happens if one of the possible interaction partners, e.g. one of the services, shows a different interaction behavior? This can be investigated for instance by changing the definition of $SE\_A(ch)$ to wait for a confirmation of the bidding via b before proceeding.

```
MWB>agent SE_A(ch) = (^o)ch(b).b(confirm).t.'b<o>.o.SE_A(ch)
MWB>weq SYS(i,o) S_LAZY(i,o)
The two agents are equal.
```

Once again, the orchestration is interaction sound. This is even true if the "defective" service represented by agent $SE\_A(ch)$ is dynamically bound to our orchestration. In this case, always the second service will be utilized (due to the discriminator). Hence, the orchestration will not deadlock even if a non-matching, defective service is contained in the environment. However, if we introduce a second defective service by changing $SE\_B(ch)$, the possibility of selecting and binding to two defective services exists, thus leading to a serious problem:

```
MWB>agent SE_B(ch) = (^o)ch(b).b(confirm).t.'b<o>.o.SE_A(ch)
MWB>weq SYS(i,o) S_LAZY(i,o)
The two agents are NOT equal.
```

The orchestration contained in the modified system is not interaction sound anymore, since there exist possible combinations of services in it that will lead to deadlock situations.

6 Conclusion

In this paper it has been shown how orchestrations that dynamically bind to services in a given environment can be proved to be interaction sound. The approach presented is generic in a sense that it is not limited to certain kinds of orchestrations or interactions. This is due to the possibility of representing all routing and interaction patterns, either workflow or service interaction ones, in a precise way in π-calculus [6,7]. Thus, existing orchestrations can be formalized and analyzed. The soundness criterion used for interaction soundness, lazy soundness, furthermore supports lazy activities. Since orchestrations can contain lazy activities, these do not disturb the reasoning.

The approach presented in this paper is a starting point for investigating formal properties of dynamic bindings. First of all, existing graphical notations like BPMN do not support the representation of systems containing dynamic binding. Without a graphical representation, user acceptance is limited. So one direction of further work is creating such a notation. Second, tool support for π-calculus is currently limited. The existing tools are not optimized for reasoning on service orchestrations. For instance, they use depth-first search strategies that cause problems regarding the detection of certain loop constructs.

References

1. Burbeck, S.: The Tao of E-Business Services. Available at: `http://www-128.ibm.com/developerworks/library/ws-tao/` (2000)
2. Aalst, W., ter Hofstede, A.H., Weske, M.: Business Process Management: ASurvey. In van der Aalst, W.M.P., ter Hofstede, A.H., Weske, M., eds.: Proceedings of the 1st International Conference on Business Process Management, volume 2678 of LNCS, Berlin, Springer-Verlag (2003) 1–12
3. Puhlmann, F., Weske, M.: Investigations on Soundness Regarding Lazy Activities. In Dustdar, S., Fiadeiro, J., Sheth, A., eds.: Proceedings of the 4th International Conference on Business Process Management (BPM 2006), volume 4102 of LNCS, Berlin, Springer Verlag (2006) 145–160

4. Overdick, H., Puhlmann, F., Weske, M.: Towards a Formal Model for Agile Service Discovery and Integration. In Verma, K., Sheth, A., Zaremba, M., Bussler, C., eds.: Proceedings of the International Workshop on Dynamic Web Processes (DWP 2005). IBM technical report RC23822, Amsterdam (2005)
5. Puhlmann, F.: Why do we actually need the Pi-Calculus for Business Process Management? In Abramowicz, W., Mayr, H., eds.: 9th International Conference on Business Information Systems (BIS 2006), volume P-85 of LNI, Bonn, Gesellschaft für Informatik (2006) 77–89
6. Puhlmann, F., Weske, M.: Using the Pi-Calculus for Formalizing Workflow Patterns. In van der Aalst, W., Benatallah, B., Casati, F., eds.: Proceedings of the 3rd International Conference on Business Process Management, volume 3649 of LNCS, Berlin, Springer-Verlag (2005) 153–168
7. Decker, G., Puhlmann, F., Weske, M.: Formalizing Service Interactions. In Dustdar, S., Fiadeiro, J., Sheth, A., eds.: Proceedings of the 4th International Conference on Business Process Management (BPM 2006), volume 4102 of LNCS, Berlin, Springer Verlag (2006) 414–419
8. Aalst, W., Hofstede, A., Kiepuszewski, B., Barros, A.: Workflow Patterns. Distributed and Parallel Databases **14** (2003) 5–51
9. Aalst, W.: Verification of Workflow Nets. In Azéma, P., Balbo, G., eds.: Application and Theory of Petri Nets, volume 1248 of LNCS, Berlin, Springer-Verlag (1997) 407–426
10. Martens, A.: Analyzing Web Service based Business Processes. In Cerioli, M., ed.: Proceedings of Intl. Conference on Fundamental Approaches to Software Engineering (FASE'05). Volume 3442 of Lecture Notes in Computer Science., Springer-Verlag (2005)
11. Bordeaux, L., Salaün, G.: Using Process Algebra for Web Services: Early Results and Perspectives. In Shan, M.C., Dayal, U., Hsu, M., eds.: TES 2004, volume 3324 of LNCS, Berlin, Springer-Verlag (2005) 54–68
12. Busi, N., Gorrieri, R., Guidi, C., Lucchi, R., Zavattaro, G.: Choreography and Orchestration: A Synergic Approach to System Design. In Benatallah, B., Casati, F., Traverso, P., eds.: Proceedings of the 3rd International Conference on Service-oriented Computing, volume 3826 of LNCS, Berlin, Springer-Verlag (2005) 228–240
13. Barros, A., Dumas, M., ter Hofstede, A.: Service Interaction Patterns. In van der Aalst, W., Benatallah, B., Casati, F., eds.: Proceedings of the 3rd International Conference on Business Process Management, volume 3649 of LNCS, Berlin, Springer-Verlag (2005) 302–318
14. Guidi, C., Lucchi, R.: Mobility mechanisms in Service Oriented Computing. In: Proc. of 8th International Conference on on Formal Methods for Open Object-Based Distributed Systems (FMOODS06). (2006 (to appear))
15. Sangiorgi, D., Walker, D.: The π-calculus: A Theory of Mobile Processes. Paperback edn. Cambridge University Press, Cambridge (2003)
16. Sangiorgi, D.: A Theory of Bisimulation for the Pi-Calculus. In: CONCUR '93: Proceedings of the 4th International Conference on Concurrency Theory, Berlin, Springer-Verlag (1993) 127–142
17. Victor, B., Moller, F., Dam, M., Eriksson, L.H.: The Mobility Workbench. Available at: `http://www.it.uu.se/research/group/mobility/mwb` (2005)

Modeling Web Services by Iterative Reformulation of Functional and Non-functional Requirements

Jyotishman Pathak, Samik Basu, and Vasant Honavar

Department of Computer Science
Iowa State University
Ames, IA 50011-1040, USA
{jpathak, sbasu, honavar}@cs.iastate.edu

Abstract. We propose an approach for incremental modeling of composite Web services. The technique takes into consideration both the functional and non-functional requirements of the composition. While the functional requirements are described using symbolic transition systems—transition systems augmented with state variables, function invocations, and guards; non-functional requirements are quantified using thresholds. The approach allows users to specify an abstract and possibly incomplete specification of the desired service (goal) that can be realized by selecting and composing a set of pre-existing services. In the event that such a composition is unrealizable, i.e. the composition is not functionally equivalent to the goal or the non-functional requirements are violated, our system provides the user with the causes for the failure, that can be used to appropriately reformulate the functional and/or non-functional requirements of the goal specification.

1 Introduction

With the recent advances in networking, computation grids and WWW, automatic Web service composition has emerged as an active area of research in both academia and industry (see [1,2] for a survey). The main objective of these approaches is to build and deploy new, value-added applications from existing ones in various domains such as e-Science, e-Business and e-Government.

Typically, automation in service composition relies on developers to formally describe a complete specification of the desired service (goal). In most situations, however, the task of developing such a complete functional description of a complex Web service is difficult and error prone as the developer is faced with the cognitive burden to deal with a large set of available components and their possible compositions. Furthermore, the existing techniques adopt a "single-step request-response" paradigm to service composition—that is, if the goal specification provided to a composition analyzer cannot be realized using the available component services, the entire process fails. Thus, it becomes the responsibility of the developer to identify the cause(s) for the failure of composition, which becomes a non-trivial task when modeling complex Web services. Additionally, baring a few approaches, most of the techniques for service composition focus only on the functional aspects of the composition. In practice, since there might be multiple component services that can provide the same functionality, it

A. Dan and W. Lamersdorf (Eds.): ICSOC 2006, LNCS 4294, pp. 314–326, 2006.

is of interest to explore the non-functional properties of the components to reduce the search space for determining compositions efficiently.

Towards this end, we introduce a framework for Modeling Service Composition and Execution (MoSCoE). Our approach allows the developer to start with an abstract, and perhaps incomplete specification of the goal (composite) service. In the event that the goal service is not realizable using the existing component services, the technique identifies the cause(s) for the failure of composition to help guide the developer in reformulating the goal specification and iterating the above process. In previous work, we modeled such a formalism for the iterative development of services in the context of sequential [3] and parallel [4] compositions of service functionalities. In this paper, we focus our attention on incorporating specification of non-functional requirements (e.g., Quality of Service) to the modeling of composite Web services in MoSCoE.

Specifically, given the component services $\texttt{STS}_1, \texttt{STS}_2, \ldots, \texttt{STS}_n$ and a goal service $\texttt{STS}_g$ as Symbolic Transition Systems (STSs), the objective is to generate a composition strategy $[\texttt{STS}_{i_1}, \texttt{STS}_{i_2}, \ldots, \texttt{STS}_{i_m}]$ (where $\texttt{STS}_{i_j}$ is deployed before $\texttt{STS}_{i_{j+1}}$), that satisfies both the functional and non-functional requirements. The non-functional requirements are quantified using *thresholds*, where a composition is said to conform to a non-functional requirement if it is below or above the corresponding threshold, as the case may be. For example, for a non-functional requirement involving the `cost` of a service composition, the threshold may provide an *upper-bound* (maximum allowable `cost`) while for requirements involving `reliability`, the threshold usually describes a *lower-bound* (minimum tolerable `reliability`). If more than one composition strategy meets the goal specifications, our algorithm generates all such strategies and ranks them. Strategies with higher rank are better than those with the lower rank in terms of meeting the non-functional requirements. For example, given two valid composition strategies A and B, if the `cost` of A is more than B, then A is ranked lower than B. It is left to the user's discretion to select the best strategy according to the requirements. Note that it is desirable to identify all the strategies, not just the best one, since the strategies are likely to be used multiple times in future to realize the goal service, and the component services that are part of the best strategy may become unavailable at the time of execution. In such situations, the user can select an alternate strategy from the generated set of alternative composition strategies.

The contributions of our work are:

1. A framework for incrementally composing complex Web services taking into consideration both the functional and non-functional requirements.
2. An algorithm for validating the conformance of composition to non-functional requirements. At its core, the algorithm relies on recursive forward-backward exploration of the search-space (various possible service compositions) to identify all possible compositions that meet the specified functional and non-functional requirements.
3. An approach to determine the causes of failures (due to violation of functional and/or non-functional requirements) of composition to assist the user in reformulation of functional and non-functional requirements of the goal specification.

The rest of the paper is organized as follows: Section 2 introduces an illustrative example used to explain the salient aspects our work, Sections 3 and 4 present a logical formalism and our algorithm for determining feasible composition strategies that meet the functional and non-functional requirements, Section 5 illustrates our approach for identifying the cause(s) for failure of composition, Section 6 briefly discusses related work, and finally Section 7 concludes with future avenues for research.

2 Illustrative Example

We present a simple example where a service developer is assigned to model a new Web service, `LoanApproval`, that allows potential clients to determine whether an amount of loan requested will be approved or not. The service takes as input the requested loan

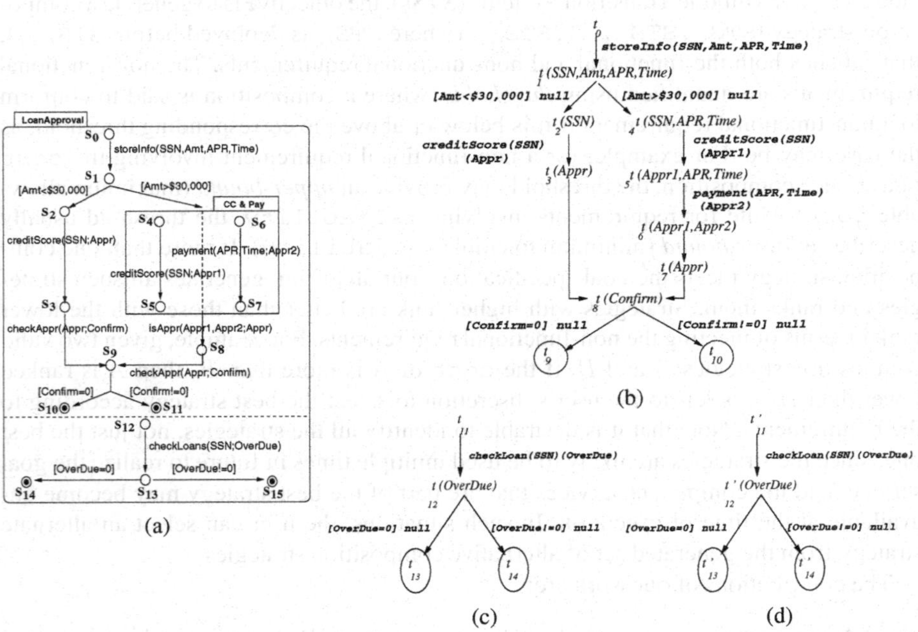

Fig. 1. (a) State machine representation of `LoanApproval` (b) STS representation of `Approver`, `cost`=\$100 (c) STS representation of `Checker`, `cost`=\$50 (d) STS representation of `Checker'`, `cost`=\$200

amount and social security number (SSN) of the client along with the annual percentage rate (APR) and payment duration (in months) for approval of the loan. Additionally, to assist in the decision-making process, the service also checks payment overdues of the client for his/her existing loans (if any). Figure 1(a) shows the state-machine representation of such a service. Each transition labeled by functions along with their input

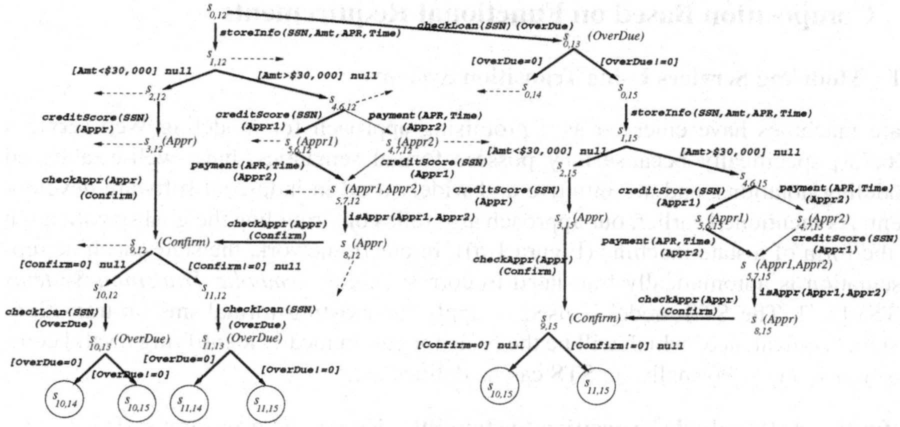

Fig. 2. Partial view of `LoanApproval` transition system

and output parameters (separated by ";"). Guards on transitions are enclosed in "[...]" and denote the conditions under which the transition is enabled. State machine representation is desirable because it allows the developer to present the functionality in a modularized and hierarchical fashion. For example, in Figure 1(a) the user modularizes the design of the desired service using composite states in the state machines; e.g. `CC & Pay` is present inside `LoanApproval`, and there are "and-" states where each partition is separated by dotted lines[1].

In MoSCoE, this goal state machine is internally translated into Symbolic Transition Systems (see Definition 1); the corresponding transition system of `LoanApproval` is presented in Figure 2. Transitions with no function invocation makes a call to a dummy function `null` and the dotted lines represent sequence of transitions (not shown) originating due to various interleaving choices of transitions in the and-partition (s_{12} in this case). Furthermore, the component services published by the service providers are also represented using STSs[2]. Figures 1(b) and 1(c) show the corresponding STS for component services `Approver` and `Checker`, respectively.

Our aim is to compose these component services to realize the goal service, thereby providing the desired capability. However, in reality, there might be multiple component services which provide the same functionality, but have different non-functional characteristics (e.g., `cost`). For example, consider services `Checker` (Figure 1(c)) and `Checker'` (Figure 1(d)), which provide the same functionality, but have different `cost` associated to their usage. Accordingly, depending on the user need, a valid composition is one which satisfies both functional and non-functional requirements. We formally describe present our approach to model such compositions in the remainder of this paper.

---

[1] An and-state represents the behavior where the transitions in its partition can interleave in any order.

[2] These specifications can be obtained from service descriptions provided in high-level languages such as BPEL or OWL-S by applying translators similar to those proposed in [5,6].

3 Composition Based on Functional Requirements

3.1 Modeling Services Using Transition Systems

State machines have emerged as a promising approach for modeling Web services [5,6,7,8] specifically because they possess formal semantics, have well-established modeling notations, and are intuitive and widely used in industrial software development. As mentioned earlier, our approach also relies on providing the goal specification in the form of a state machine (Figure 1(a)). In our framework, the state-machine representation is automatically translated to corresponding *Symbolic Transition Systems* (STS) [3,4]. The STS-model is used to apply the existing formalisms on transition-system "equivalence" which will be the basis for automatically identifying a valid composition strategy. Formally, an STS can be defined as:

Definition 1 (Symbolic Transition System [9]). *A symbolic transition system is a tuple* $(S, \longrightarrow, s0, S^F, A)$ *where* S *is a set of states represented by terms,* $s0 \in S$ *is the start state,* $S^F \subseteq S$ *is the set of final states and* $\longrightarrow$ *is the set of transition relations where* $s \xrightarrow{\gamma,\alpha,\rho} t$ *is such that*

1. γ *is the guard where,* $vars(\gamma) \subseteq vars(s)$
2. α *is a term representing service-functions of the form* $a(\boldsymbol{x})(y)$ *where* $\boldsymbol{x}$ *represents the input parameters and* y *denotes the return valuations*
3. ρ *relates* $vars(s)$ *to* $vars(t)$

Finally, A *is a set of non-functional attributes and the respective values corresponding to the service whose behavior is represented by the STS.*

Here, we assume that the values for non-functional attributes can be obtained from the "profiles" of the services [10] and can be mapped to a scale between 0 & 1 by applying standard mathematical maximization and minimization formulas depending on whether the attribute is *positive* or *negative*. For example, the values for attributes such as `latency` and `fault rate` need to be minimized, whereas `availability` need to be maximized. Figure 3 shows example STSs.

Semantics of STS. The semantics of STS is given with respect to substitutions of variables present in the system. A state represented by the term s is interpreted under substitution σ over the state variables ($s\sigma$). A transition $s \xrightarrow{\gamma,\alpha,\rho} t$ is said to be *enabled* from $s\sigma$ if and only if $\gamma\sigma = \texttt{true}$ and $\gamma \Rightarrow \rho$. The semantics of the transition under substitution σ is $s\sigma \xrightarrow{\alpha\sigma} t\sigma$.

3.2 Composition of Symbolic Transition Systems

A sequential composition of $\texttt{STS}_i$ and $\texttt{STS}_j$, denoted by $\texttt{STS}_i \circ \texttt{STS}_j$, is obtained by merging the final states of $\texttt{STS}_i$ with the start state of $\texttt{STS}_j$, i.e., every out-going transition of start state of $\texttt{STS}_j$ is also the out-going transition of each final state of $\texttt{STS}_i$. We say that given a goal service representation $\texttt{STS}_g$ and a set of component representations $\texttt{STS}_{1\ldots n}$, the former is said to be (partially) realizable from the latter

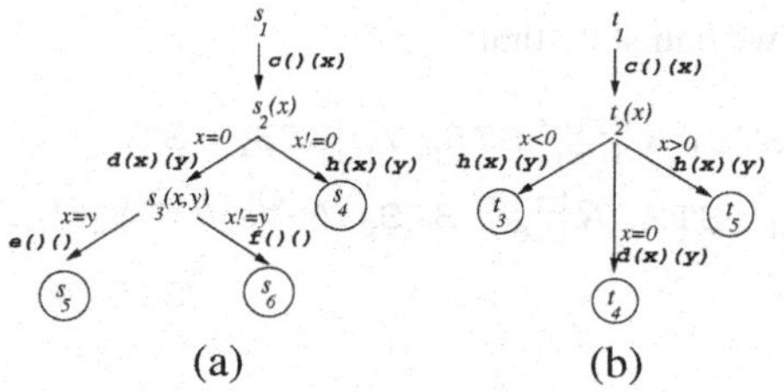

Fig. 3. Example Symbolic Transition Systems. (a) $\texttt{STS}_g$ (b) $\texttt{STS}_1$.

if there exists a composition of components such that $\texttt{STS}_g$ *simulates* $\texttt{STS}_i \circ \texttt{STS}_j \circ \ldots \texttt{STS}_k$. In essence, simulation relation ensures that the composition can 'mimic' the goal service functionality. We present the definition of simulation in the context of STSs.

Definition 2 (Late Simulation). *Given an STS $\mathcal{S} = (S, \longrightarrow, s0, S^F)$, late simulation relation with respect to substitution θ, denoted by $\mathcal{R}^\theta$, is a subset of $S \times S$ such that*

$$s_1 \, \mathcal{R}^\theta s_2 \Rightarrow (\forall s_1\theta \xrightarrow{\alpha_1} t_1\theta.\exists s_2\theta \xrightarrow{\alpha_2} t_2\theta.\forall\sigma.\alpha_1\theta\sigma = \alpha_2\theta\sigma \wedge t_1 \, \mathcal{R}^{\theta\sigma} t_2)$$

Two states, under the substitution θ over state variables, are equivalent with respect to simulation if they are related by the *largest* similarity relation $\mathcal{R}^\theta$. We say that an $\texttt{STS}_i$ is simulated by $\texttt{STS}_j$, denoted by $(\texttt{STS}_i \, \mathcal{R}^\theta \texttt{STS}_j)$ $\texttt{iff}$ $(s0_i \, \mathcal{R}^\theta s0_j)$.

For example, consider the STSs in Figure 3(a) and 3(b). If state t_1 is simulated by s_1, then $t_2(x)$ is simulated by $s_2(x)$ for all possible valuations of x. The above can be represented using logical expressions as follows:

$$\begin{aligned} t_1 \, \mathcal{R}^{\texttt{true}} \, s_1 &\Rightarrow \forall x.(t_2(x) \, \mathcal{R}^{[x]} \, s_2(x)) \\ &\Rightarrow (t_2(x) \, \mathcal{R}^{[x>0]} \, s_2(x)) \, (t_2(x) \, \mathcal{R}^{[x<0]} \, s_2(x)) \, \wedge \, (t_2(x) \, \mathcal{R}^{[x!=0]} \, s_2(x)) \\ &\Rightarrow (\forall y.(t_3 \, \mathcal{R}^{[x>0,y]} s_4)) \, \wedge \, t_4 \, \mathcal{R}^{[x=0,y]} s_3(x,y))) \, \wedge \, t_3 \, \mathcal{R}^{[x<0,y]} s_4)) \end{aligned} \quad (1)$$

Note that the simulation of the $\texttt{STS}_1$ by $\texttt{STS}_g$ leads the latter to the states $s_3(x,y)$ and s_4 with the constraints $x = 0$ and $x > 0 \vee x < 0$, respectively. In terms of sequential composition, it can be stated that a selected component (simulated by the goal) drives the goal to some specific states and the start state of the next component in the composition must be simulated by these goal states. These goal states and the corresponding constraints can be identified easily by expanding the simulation relation to also record the constraints and the goal-states that simulates the final state of the component under consideration (see [3] for details). We will use $\texttt{STS}_i \, \mathcal{R}^\theta_{[S_g\Delta]} \, \texttt{STS}_g$ to denote $\texttt{STS}_i$ being simulated by $\texttt{STS}_g$ under the constraint θ, which leads to the simulation of the final states of $\texttt{STS}_i$ by the goal states s_g under the constraint δ such $s_g\delta \in S_g\Delta$.

Therefore, the composition $[\texttt{STS}_1 \circ \texttt{STS}_2 \circ \ldots \circ \texttt{STS}_n]$ is said to (partially) replicate the goal $\texttt{STS}_g$ if and only if:

$$[\texttt{STS}_1 \circ \texttt{STS}_2 \circ \ldots \circ \texttt{STS}_n] \, \mathcal{R}^{\texttt{true}}_{S_g\Delta} \, \texttt{STS}_g \text{ such that } S_g \subseteq S^F_g$$

Proceeding further, we can state that:

$$\forall s_1\theta_1 \in S_1\Theta_1 : \texttt{STS}_1\ \mathcal{R}^{\texttt{true}}_{S_1\Theta_1}\ \texttt{STS}_g\ \wedge\ [\texttt{STS}_2 \circ \texttt{STS}_3 \circ \ldots \circ \texttt{STS}_n]\ \mathcal{R}^{\theta}_{S_g\Delta}\ s_1$$

$$\Leftrightarrow \quad \forall s_1\theta \in S_1\Theta_1 : \texttt{STS}_1\ \mathcal{R}^{\texttt{true}}_{S_1\Theta_1}\ \texttt{STS}_g\ \wedge\ \forall s_2\theta \in S_2\Theta_2 : \texttt{STS}_2\ \mathcal{R}^{\theta_1}_{S_2\Theta_2}\ s_1\ \wedge$$

$$[\texttt{STS}_3 \circ \ldots \circ \texttt{STS}_n]\ \mathcal{R}^{\theta_2}_{S_g\Delta}\ s_2$$

$$\text{such that } S_g \subseteq S_g^F$$

4 Composition Based on Non-functional Requirements

In order to determine a suitable ordering of the available components, it is necessary to select the appropriate components from the pool of candidates. This becomes challenge with the increasing size of the search space of available component services. Hence, we consider non-functional aspects (e.g., QoS) to winnow components (thereby reducing the search space) and composition strategies which violate the requirements desired by the user. We assume the existence of a shared controlled vocabulary [10] which is needed to specify the non-functional attributes of the component services. These attributes can be either domain-dependent or domain-independent, and are used to compose a quality matrix comprising of a set of quality attribute-values, such that each row of the matrix corresponds to the value of a particular QoS attribute and each column corresponds to a particular component service. Next, we describe an algorithm that considers both the functional and non-functional user requirements to determine feasible composition strategies as illustrated in Section 3.

4.1 Algorithm for Service Composition

The algorithm for determining feasible composition strategies (Figure 4) that are "equivalent" to the goal service works as follows: the procedure `forwardSearch([], v, g, F, OP)` is invoked by providing the threshold value `v` of a desired non-functional attribute[3] (e.g., `cost` of using the composite service should be less than $150), the start state `g` of the goal STS, an optimization function `F` that corresponds to maximization/minimization[4] of the non-functional attribute under consideration, and the composition operator `OP` for the specific optimization function. The initial composition strategy `prefixStrat` is incrementally built as the algorithm proceeds recursively by performing forward-backward traversals: The forward traversal tries to identify a feasible composition (by applying the simulation relation, Definition 2) that comply to the user-specified non-functional requirements; the backward traversal tries to explore alternate compositions (if any). If multiple compositions are identified, then it is left at user's discretion to select one amongst them.

More specifically, given a state g of the goal STS as input, the procedure `forward Search` selects a component from the available set of components `CompSet`, such

[3] In this paper, we consider only one non-functional attribute at a time for determining feasible compositions; considering multiple attributes simultaneously is part of our on-going work.

[4] Assuming that `F` is a minimization function, `F(x,y) = 1`, if `x < y`.

```
/*
 vO is the user-defined threshold value, prefixStrat is the valid strategy obtained so far
 v is non-functional attribute-value prefixStrat, g is the current goal state,
 F is optimization function, OP is the composition operation for a specific optimization,
 CompSet is the set of components
*/
1: proc forwardSearch(prefixStrat, v, g, F, OP) {
2:   if (g is not final goal-state) {
3:     select c_i ∈ CompSet s.t. ∀ c_j ∈ CompSet, j ≠ i : F(v_ci, v_cj) = 1 and
4:         c_i is simulated by g to reach g';
5:     /* update the attribute-value */
6:     v = v OP v_ci;
7:     if (F(v,vO)≠ 1) { backwardSearch(prefixStrat, F, OP); return; }
8:     /* add the component with the goal-state */
9:     prefixStrat = prefixStrat + (c_i,g);
10:    forwardSearch(prefixStrat, v, g', F, OP);
11:  }
12:  else /* if the goal state is final, strategy is achieved */ {
13:    assertPath(prefixStrat projection on components, v);
14:    backwardSearch(prefixStrat, F, OP);
15:  }
16: }

17: proc backwardSearch(prefixStrat, F, OP) {
18:   if (prefixStrat = ∅) return;
19:   prefixStrat = [(c_1, g_1), (c_2, g_2), ..., (c_n, g_n)];
20:   select c_i ∈ CompSet s.t. ∀ c_j ∈ CompSet, j ≠ i, F(v_cj, v_cn) ≠ 1 : F(v_ci, v_cj) = 1 and
21:       c_i is simulated by g_n to reach g';
22:   /* update the value and begin the forward search */
23:   v = vO OP v_c1 OP v_c2 OP ... OP v_ci;
24:   if (F(v_ci,v) = 1)
25:     forwardSearch([(c_1, g_1), (c_2, g_2), ..., (c_k, g_i)], v, g', F, OP);
26:   backwardSearch([(c_1, g_1), (c_2, g_2), ..., (c_{n-1}, g_{n-1})], F, OP)
27: }
```

Fig. 4. Algorithm for Identifying Compositions Satisfying Functional & Non-Functional User Requirements

that its value for the non-functional attribute under consideration (e.g., `cost`) is maximum/minimum (depending on `F`) and verifies whether the component state is "simulation equivalent" to the goal state g (`line 3`). If no such component exists, then an exception causing a failure of composition is raised and the user is notified (Section 5). On the other hand, if such a component is available, the value of the desired non-functional property is appropriately updated (`line 6`) and the component that simulates the goal state is added to the composition strategy (`line 9`). The procedure is recursively invoked with the updated non-functional attribute-value and a new goal state g', until the final state of the goal STS is reached; after which the corresponding composition strategy is stored with the associated non-functional attribute-value of the composition (`line 13`). This value will be either below or above the threshold v_0 (`line 7`), depending on composition optimization function `F`. Once this step is executed, the algorithm backtracks to determine alternate composition strategies that are feasible. Note that, the `forwardSearch` procedure is a local greedy approach for finding out a feasible composition and essentially identifies at least one path (beginning at the start and ending at the final state of the goal STS) in the composition graph that can be realized using the available component services.

When there are multiple components that provide the same functionality, it is possible to generate more than one composition strategy to realize the composite service. `backwardSearch` achieves this by replacing one component at a time (beginning with the last component in the composition strategy, `line 20`) with an "equivalent" component and then invokes `forwardSearch` to determine if the replacement violates the non-functional requirement under consideration (`line 24--25`). If there is no such violation, then the derived strategy is stored with its associated value of the corresponding non-functional attribute. The procedure proceeds further by recursively backtracking (`line 26`) until all feasible composition strategies are determined. However, if the replacement violates the non-functional requirements, then the replaced component as well as the corresponding composition strategy are disregarded. Thus, eliminating composition strategies (and components) that violate non-functional requirements yield significant reduction in the size of the search space.

4.2 Modeling `LoanApproval` Composite Service

We now show how to model the `LoanApproval` composite service introduced in Section 2 using the algorithm and the formalisms described above. Figures 2, 1(b) & 1(c) show the transition system of the goal (`LoanApproval`) and the component services (`Approver` and `Checker`, respectively). To determine whether `LoanApproval` can be realized from `Approver` and `Checker` services, we need to find out if $\mathtt{STS}_{\mathtt{LA}}$ simulates the composition of $\mathtt{STS}_{\mathtt{App}}$ and $\mathtt{STS}_{\mathtt{Chck}}$ as well as whether the non-functional requirements are met or not. Assume that the non-functional attribute we are interested is `cost`, and we want that the `cost` of the composite service is less than or equal to $150 (i.e., minimization of `cost`).

From Figure 4, if the algorithm selects component `Approver` first, it can be seen that $\mathtt{STS}_{\mathtt{App}}$ is *late*-simulated by $\mathtt{STS}_{\mathtt{LA}}$. The path starting from $s_{0,12}$ in `LoanApproval` simulates the paths in `Approver` such that $s_{10,12}$ and $s_{11,12}$ are the states in $\mathtt{STS}_{\mathtt{LA}}$ that are simulation equivalent to final states t_9 and t_{10} of $\mathtt{STS}_{\mathtt{App}}$ under a `true` constraint. Also, the `cost` of $\mathtt{STS}_{\mathtt{App}}$ is less than the threshold value of $150. Thus, this component is added to the composition strategy being constructed. Proceeding further, $\mathtt{STS}_{\mathtt{Chck}}$ is also simulated by states $s_{10,12}$ and $s_{11,12}$ of $\mathtt{STS}_{\mathtt{LA}}$, and the corresponding `cost` of $\mathtt{STS}_{\mathtt{Chck}}$ is $50, which makes the total `cost` of the composition strategy equal to the threshold value. Thus, the composition of $\mathtt{STS}_{\mathtt{App}} \circ \mathtt{STS}_{\mathtt{Chck}}$ realizes the goal service $\mathtt{STS}_{\mathtt{LA}}$. Note that, there is another solution to the above problem where `Checker` service is followed by `Approver` service.

Once this strategy is identified, the backward traversal procedure is invoked. Here, we try to replace $\mathtt{STS}_{\mathtt{Chck}}$ with $\mathtt{STS}_{\mathtt{Chck'}}$ (Figure 1(d)) since it can also be simulated by $\mathtt{STS}_{\mathtt{LA}}$. However, replacing $\mathtt{STS}_{\mathtt{Chck}}$ by $\mathtt{STS}_{\mathtt{Chck'}}$ violates the `cost` requirement.

5 Reformulation of Goal Specification

The composition of a goal service from available component services using the process outlined above will fail when some aspect of the goal specification cannot be realized using the available component services. When this happens, our approach seeks to provide to the user, information concerning the cause of the failure in a form that can be used to further refine the goal specification. In our framework, the reason for failure of an attempted composition to simulate a component by single or multiple states in the goal is obtained by examining the simulation relation $\mathcal{R}$:

$$s_1\, \overline{\mathcal{R}}^{\theta}\, s_2 \Leftarrow \exists s_1\theta \xrightarrow{\alpha_1} t_1\theta . \forall s_2\theta \xrightarrow{\alpha_2} t_2\theta . \exists\sigma.(\alpha_1\theta\sigma = \alpha_2\theta\sigma) \Rightarrow t_1\, \overline{\mathcal{R}}^{\theta\sigma}\, t_2 \quad (1)$$

Two states are said to be *not* simulation equivalent if they are related by the least solution of $\overline{\mathcal{R}}$. We say that $\mathtt{STS}_i\ \overline{\mathcal{R}}^{\theta}\ \mathtt{STS}_j$ iff $s_i^0\, \overline{\mathcal{R}}^{\theta}\, s_j^0$. From Equation 1, the cause of the state s_1 *not* simulated by s_2 can be due to:

1. $\exists\sigma.\alpha_1\theta\sigma \neq \alpha_2\theta\sigma$ (i.e., that actions do not match), or
2. $\exists\sigma.\alpha_1\theta\sigma = \alpha_2\theta\sigma$ and the subsequent states are related by $\overline{\mathcal{R}}^{\theta\sigma}$, or
3. $\exists s_1\theta \xrightarrow{\alpha_1} t_1\theta$, but there is no transition enabled from s_2 under the substitution θ.

For example, consider the STSs in Figure 5(a) & 5(b). The component STS is not simulated by the first $\mathtt{STS}_g$ (rooted at s_1) as there exists a transition from $t_2(x)$ to t_4 when the x is not equal to zero, which is absent from the corresponding state $s_2(x)$ in the goal. The state t_1 is also not simulated by state s_4 of $\mathtt{STS}_{g'}$ as the state $t_2(x)$ is not simulated by $s_5(y)$. This is because x and y may not be unified as the former is generated from the output of a transition while the latter is generated at the state. In fact, a state which generates a variable is not simulated by any state if there is a guard on the generated variable. Such generated variables at the states are *local* to that transition system and hence, cannot be 'mimicked' by another transition system. In our example, $t_2(x)$ is not simulated by $s_5(y)$.

Note that in some cases, the failure to realize a feasible composition can also be due to non-compliance of non-functional requirements specified by the user. In essence, this refers to argument `prefixStrat` of procedure `forwardSearch` (Figure 4) being `null` after exploring all possible composition strategies. When such a situation arises, the framework identifies the particular non-functional requirement (v_0) that cannot be met using the available components, and provides this information to the service developer such that it can be used for appropriate refinement of the requirement.

Failure-Cause Analysis for `LoanApproval`. Returning to our example from Section 2, assume that we replace the `Checker` component service (Figure 1(c)) with another service for determining client payment overdues (`NewChecker` Figure 5(c)), which

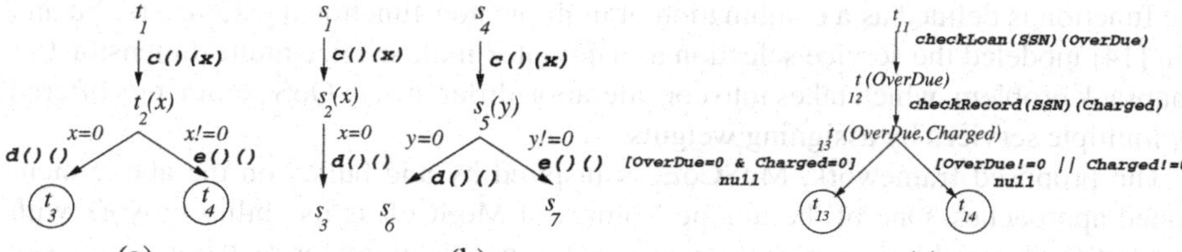

Fig. 5. (a) Component STS (b) Goal STSs $\mathtt{STS}_g$ & $\mathtt{STS}_{g'}$ (c) STS for `NewChecker`

functions exactly like `Checker`, but additionally checks the criminal record of the client. The service first checks whether the client has payment overdues for the existing loans (if any) and then determines if the client has been previously charged for a criminal act. Since, the 'additional' criminal verification transition is not present in $\mathtt{STS}_{\mathtt{LA}}$,, the component start state t_{11} is not simulated by states $s_{10,12}$, $s_{11,12}$ or $s_{0,12}$. On the other hand, assuming that we replace `Checker` with `Checker'` (Figure 1(d)), even though the functional requirements are satisfied (due to equivalence), the non-functional requirements are violated. Note that such failure-cause information can be provided to the user which can be used for refining the goal specification in an iterative manner. In this case the user can add the criminal verification transition (with appropriate parameters) to the goal specification or change the threshold value of the non-functional attribute `cost` and try to determine a feasible composition strategy. These steps can be iterated until such a strategy is found or the user decides to abort.

6 Related Work

A number of approaches have been proposed in the literature which adopt a transition-system based framework to service composition. Fu et al. [11] model Web services as automata extended with a queue, and communicate by exchanging sequence of asynchronous messages, which are used to synthesize a composition for a given specification. Their approach is extended in Colombo [8] which deals with infinite data values and atomic processes. Colombo models services as labeled transition systems and define composition semantics via message passing, where the problem of determining a feasible composition is reduced to satisfiability of a deterministic propositional dynamic logic formula. Pistore et al. [5,6] represent Web services using non-deterministic state transition systems, which also communicate through messaging. Their approach relies on symbolic model checking techniques to determine a parallel composition of all the available component services and then generates a plan that controls the services, based on user-specified functional requirements.

Several techniques have also been developed which consider non-functional requirements for service composition. Cardoso et al. [12] describe a model that allows prediction of quality of service for workflows based on individual QoS attributes for the component services. Their technique allows compensation of composition deficiency if many services with compatible functions exist. Benatallah et al. [7,13] consider service selection task as a global optimization problem and apply linear programming to find solution that represents service composition optimizing a target function, where the function is defined as a combination of multiple non-functional parameters. Yu and Lin [14] modeled the service selection as a complex multi-choice multi-dimension 0-1 knapsack problem, which takes into consideration difference in QoS parameters offered by multiple services by assigning weights.

The proposed framework, MoSCoE, is inspired by and builds on the above mentioned approaches. One of the unique features of MoSCoE is its ability to work with abstract (and possibly incomplete) goal service specifications for realizing composite services, and in the event of failure of composition, determining the cause(s) for the failure. In addition, provides an approach to consider both functional and non-functional characteristics of services simultaneously to determine feasible composition strategies. We believe that such a technique holds the promise of efficiently modeling complex composite Web services; empirically verifying this claim is part of our current work.

7 Summary and Discussion

We introduce a novel approach for automatically developing composite services by the applying the techniques of abstraction, composition and reformulation in an incremental fashion. The framework provides a goal-directed approach to service composition and adopts a symbolic transition system-based approach for computing feasible composition strategies. Our formalism allows us to identify and validate all possible composition strategies that meet the user-specified functional and non-functional requirements. However, in the event that a composition cannot be realized using the existing set of candidate services, the technique determines the cause(s) for the failure (due to violation of functional and/or non-functional requirements), and assists the user in reformulation of those requirements in the goal specification.

Our on-going work is aimed at developing heuristics for hierarchically arranging failure-causes to reduce the number of refinement steps typically performed by the user to realize a feasible composition. We also plan to explore approaches to reducing the number of candidate compositions that need to be examined e.g., by exploiting domain specific information to impose a partial order over the available services. Other work in progress is aimed at automatic translation of the composition strategy into BPEL process flow code that can be executed to realize the composite service. Of particular interest to us is a systematic evaluation of scalability and efficiency of the proposed approach on a broad class of benchmark service composition problems [15]. More details about our framework can be obtained from `http://www.moscoe.org`.

Acknowledgment. This research has been supported in part by the NSF-ITR grant 0219699 to Vasant Honavar and NSF grant 0509340 to Samik Basu. The authors would like to thank Robyn Lutz for her help in preparing this manuscript.

References

1. Hull, R., Su, J.: Tools for Composite Web Services: A Short Overview. SIGMOD Record **34**(2) (2005) 86–95
2. Dustdar, S., Schreiner, W.: A Survey on Web Services Composition. International Journal on Web and Grid Services **1**(1) (2005) 1–30
3. Pathak, J., Basu, S., Lutz, R., Honavar, V.: Selecting and Composing Web Services through Iterative Reformulation of Functional Specifications. In: 18th IEEE International Conference on Tools with Artificial Intelligence. (2006)
4. Pathak, J., Basu, S., Lutz, R., Honavar, V.: Parallel Web Service Composition in MoSCoE: A Choreography-based Approach. In: 4th IEEE European Conference on Web Services. (2006)
5. Pistore, M., Traverso, P., Bertoli, P.: Automated Composition of Web Services by Planning in Asynchronous Domains. In: 15th Intl. Conference on Automated Planning and Scheduling. (2005) 2–11

6. Traverso, P., Pistore, M.: Automated Composition of Semantic Web Services into Executable Processes. In: 3rd Intl. Semantic Web Conference, Springer-Verlag (2004) 380–394
7. Benatallah, B., Sheng, Q., Dumas, M.: The Self-Serv Environment for Web Services Composition. IEEE Internet Computing **7**(1) (2003) 40–48
8. Berardi, D., Calvanese, D., Giuseppe, D.G., Hull, R., Mecella, M.: Automatic Composition of Transition-based Semantic Web Services with Messaging. In: 31st Intl. Conference on Very Large Databases. (2005) 613–624
9. Basu, S., Mukund, M., Ramakrishnan, C.R., Ramakrishnan, I.V., Verma, R.M.: Local and Symbolic Bisimulation Using Tabled Constraint Logic Programming. In: Intl. Conference on Logic Programming. Volume 2237., Springer-Verlag (2001) 166–180
10. Pathak, J., Koul, N., Caragea, D., Honavar, V.: A Framework for Semantic Web Services Discovery. In: 7th ACM Intl. Workshop on Web Information and Data Management, ACM press (2005) 45–50
11. Fu, X., Bultan, T., Su, J.: Analysis of Interacting BPEL Web Services. In: 13th Intl. conference on World Wide Web, ACM Press (2004) 621–630
12. Cardoso, J., Sheth, A., Miller, J., et al.: Quality of Service for Workflows and Web Service Processes. Journal of Web Semantics **1**(3) (2004) 281–309
13. Zeng, L., Benatallah, B.: QoS-Aware Middleware for Web Services Composition. IEEE Transactions on Software Engineering **30**(5) (2004) 311–327
14. Yu, T., Lin, K.: Service Selection Algorithms for Composing Complex Services with Multiple QoS Constraints. In: International Conference on Service Oriented Computing, LNCS 3826 (2005) 130–143
15. Oh, S.C., Kil, H., and, D.L.: WSBen: A Web Services Discovery and Composition Benchmark. In: 4th International Conference on Web Services, IEEE Press (2006) 239–246

SOCK: A Calculus for Service Oriented Computing*

Claudio Guidi, Roberto Lucchi, Roberto Gorrieri,
Nadia Busi, and Gianluigi Zavattaro

Department of Computer Science, University of Bologna, Italy
{cguidi, lucchi, gorrieri, busi, zavattar}@cs.unibo.it

Abstract. Service oriented computing is an emerging paradigm for designing distributed applications where *service* and *composition* are the main concepts it is based upon. In this paper we propose SOCK, a three-layered calculus equipped with a formal semantics, for addressing all the basic mechanisms of service communication and composition. The main contribute of our work is the development of a formal framework where the service design is decomposed into three fundamental parts: the behaviour, the declaration and the composition where each part can be designed independently of the other ones.

1 Introduction

Service oriented computing (SOC) is an emerging paradigm for designing distributed applications where *service* and *composition* are the main concepts it is based upon. A service can be seen as an application which performs a certain task when it is invoked. A composition of services can be seen as a group of services that, by means of collaborating message exchanges, fulfills a more complex task than those performed by the single services it is composed of. The key fact is that a suitable *composition of services is a service.* The most credited service oriented technology is the Web Services. A lot of industries and consortia in the world like Microsoft, IBM, W3C, OASIS (just to mention a few) have developed standards which define Web Services interfaces such as WSDL [Wor] and composition languages such as WS-BPEL [OAS]. Such a kind of languages are based on XML and are not equipped of a formal semantics.

In this paper, we propose SOCK, Service Oriented Computing Kernel, which is a process calculus equipped with a formal semantics, for addressing all the basic mechanisms of service communication and composition that takes inspiration from Web Services specifications. Our approach aims at dealing with different service features by considering them separately and in an orthogonal way. We distinguish among *service behaviour*, *service declaration*, *service engine* and *services system.* The service behaviour deals with the internal behaviour of the service and communication primitives, the service declaration is a description of the service deployment, the service engine is the execution environment where

* Research partially funded by EU Integrated Project Sensoria, contract n. 016004.

A. Dan and W. Lamersdorf (Eds.): ICSOC 2006, LNCS 4294, pp. 327–338, 2006.

the service is actually deployed and the services system is the composition of service engines. The main contribute of our work is the development of a formal framework where the service design is decomposed into three fundamental parts: the behaviour, the declaration and the composition. Each part can be designed independently of the other ones. We present a three-layered calculus which is an evolution of those proposed in our previous work [BGG+05, BGG+06, GL06]. It is formed by three calculi: the *service behaviour calculus*, the *service engine calculus* and the *services system calculus*. The former allows for the design of service behaviours by supplying computation and external communication primitives inpired to Web Services operations and workflow operators such as sequence, parallel and choice. The second calculus is built on top of the former and it allows for the specification of the service declaration where it is possible to design in an orthogonal way three main characteristics: *execution modality*, *persistent state* flag and *correlation sets*. The execution modality deals with the possibility to execute a service in a sequential order or in a concurrent one; the persistent state flag allows to declare if each session (of the service engine) has its own independent state or if the state is shared among all the sessions of the same service engine; the correlation sets is the mechanism for distinguishing sessions initiated by different dialoguers by means of the values received within some specified variables. Finally, the services system calculus allows for the definition of the whole system including all the involved services that interact each others.

The paper is organized as follows. In Section 2 we present the SOCK calculi: the service behaviour calculus, the service engine calculus and the services system one. In Section 3 conclusions and future research are reported.

2 SOCK

In this section we present calculi of SOCK for representing service behaviours, service engines and services system. They are an extension of those presented in our previous work [BGG+05, BGG+06] even if, for the sake of brevity, here we do not model asynchronous communications[1]. The semantics of the calculi are defined in terms of labelled transition systems (lts for short) [Kel76] and they are organized as follows. There are five lts layers: the *service behaviour lts layer*; the *service engine state lts layer*; the *service engine correlation lts layer*; the *service engine execution modality lts layer* and the *services system lts layer*. The first layer is the lower one. Each lts layer catches the actions raised by the underlying one and will enable or disable them. If an action is enabled by an lts layer it will be raised to the overlying one. The service behaviour lts layer describes all the possible execution paths generated by a session behaviour. The service engine state lts layer defines the rule for joining a service behaviour with a service engine local state. The service engine correlation lts layer deals with correlation set mechanism and the service engine execution modality lts layer represents rules for executing sessions concurrently or in a sequential order. Finally, the

[1] The reader interested to asynchoronous modelling in this setting may consult [BGG+06].

services system lts layer deals with a composed service engine system. A SOCK example can be found in [GLZ+].

2.1 Service Behaviour Calculus

Before introducing the calculus we discuss some important issues such as the external input and output actions and the service locations. The external input and output actions deal with those actions that are exploited by the service behaviour for communicating with other services. The primitives related to such a kind of actions are called *operations* and they are inspired to those of Web Services. Each operation is described by a name and an *interaction modality*. There are four kinds of peer-to-peer interaction modalities divided into two groups:

- Operations which supply a service functionality, *Input operations*:
  - *One-Way*: it is devoted to receive a request message.
  - *Request-Response*: it is devoted to receive a request message which implies a response message to the invoker.
- Operations which request a service functionality, *Output operations*:
  - *Notification*: it is devoted to send a request message.
  - *Solicit-Response*: it is devoted to send a request message which requires a response message.

The input operations are published by a service behaviour in order to receive messages on them. The output operation, on the contrary, are exploited for sending messages to the input ones exhibited by the service behaviour to invoke. Here we group the operations into *single message operations* and *double message operations.* The former ones deal with the One-Way and the Notification operations whereas the latter with the Request-Response and the Solicit-Response ones. Let $\mathcal{O}$ and $\mathcal{O}_R$ be two disjoint sets of operation names where the former represents the single message operation names and the latter the double message ones. Let $Sup = \{(o, ow) \mid o \in \mathcal{O}\} \cup \{(o_r, rr) \mid o_r \in \mathcal{O}_R\}$ be the set containing all the input operations where ow and rr indicate One-Way and Request-Response operations, respectively. Let $Inv = \{(o, n) \mid o \in \mathcal{O}\} \cup \{(o_r, sr) \mid o_r \in \mathcal{O}_R\}$ be the set containing all the output operations where n and sr denote Notification and Solicit-Response operations. Let $Op = Sup \cup Inv$ be the set of all the possible operations. In our framework, locations represent the address (let it be a logical or a physical one) where a service is located. In order to perform an output operation it is fundamental to explicit both the operation name and the location of the receiver in order to achieve a correct message delivery. In the following, locations will appear into the output operation primitives of the service behaviour calculus and, since they deal with the external communication, they will be exploited into the services system calculus for synchronizing external inputs with the corresponding output ones. Formally, let Loc be a finite set of location names ranged over by l.

The Syntax. In the following we present the syntax of the calculus devoted to represent services. Let $Signals$ be a set of signal names exploited for synchronizing processes in parallel within a service behaviour. Let Var be a set of variables ranged over by x, y, z and Val, ranged over by v, be a generic set of values on which it is defined a total order relation. We exploit the notations $\boldsymbol{x} = \langle x_0, x_1, ..., x_i \rangle$ and $\boldsymbol{v} = \langle v_0, v_1, ..., v_i \rangle$ for representing tuples of variables and values respectively. Let k range over $Var \cup Loc$ where $Var \cap Loc = \emptyset$. The syntax follows:

$$P, Q ::= \mathbf{0} \mid \overline{\epsilon} \mid \epsilon \mid x := e \mid \chi ? P : Q \mid P; P \mid P|P \mid \textstyle\sum^{+}_{i \in W} \epsilon_i; P_i \mid \chi \rightleftharpoons P$$
$$\epsilon ::= s \mid o(\boldsymbol{x}) \mid o_r(\boldsymbol{x}, \boldsymbol{y}, P)$$
$$\overline{\epsilon} ::= \overline{s} \mid \overline{o} @ k(\boldsymbol{x}) \mid \overline{o_r} @ k(\boldsymbol{x}, \boldsymbol{y})$$

We denote with SC the set of all possible processes ranged over by P and Q. $\mathbf{0}$ is the null process. Outputs can be a signal $\overline{s}$, a notification $\overline{o}@k(\boldsymbol{x})$ or a solicit-response $\overline{o_r}@k(\boldsymbol{x}, \boldsymbol{y})$ where $s \in Signals$, $o \in \mathcal{O}$ and $o_r \in \mathcal{O}_R$, $k \in Var \cup Loc$ represents the receiver location which can be explicit or represented by a variable[2], $\boldsymbol{x}$ is the tuple of the variables which store the information to send and $\boldsymbol{y}$ is the tuple of variables where, in the case of the solicit-response, the received information will be stored. Dually, inputs can be an input signal s, a one-way $o(\boldsymbol{x})$ or a request-response $o_r(\boldsymbol{x}, \boldsymbol{y}, P)$ where $s \in Signals$, $o \in \mathcal{O}$ and $o_r \in \mathcal{O}_R$, $\boldsymbol{x}$ is the tuple of variables where the received information are stored whereas $\boldsymbol{y}$ is the tuple of variables which contain the information to send in the case of the request-response; finally P is the process that has to be executed between the request and the response. $x := e$ assigns the result of the expression e to the variable x. For the sake of brevity, we do not present the syntax for representing expressions, we assume that they include all the arithmetic operators, values in Val and variables. $\chi ? P : Q$ is the *if-then-else* process, where χ is a logic condition on variables whose syntax is: $\chi ::= x \leq e \mid e \leq x \mid \neg\chi \mid \chi \wedge \chi$. It is worth noting that conditions such as $x = v$, $x \neq v$ and $v_1 \leq x \leq v_2$ can be defined as abbreviations; P is executed only if the condition χ is satisfied, otherwise Q is executed. $P; P$ and $P \mid P$ represent sequential and parallel composition respectively whereas $\sum^{+}_{i \in W} \epsilon_i; P_i$ is the non-deterministic choice restricted to be guarded on inputs. Such a restriction is due to the fact that we are not interested to model internal non-determinism in service behaviour. Our calculus indeed aims at supplying a basic language for designing service behaviours where designers have a full control of the internal machinery and the only non-predictable choices are those driven by the external message reception. Finally, $\chi \rightleftharpoons P$ is the construct to model guarded iterations. As far as the semantics is concerned, here we consider the extension of SC which includes also the the terms $\bar{o_r}@l(\boldsymbol{x}), \bar{o_r}@z(\boldsymbol{x})$ and $o_r(\boldsymbol{x})$. These terms allows us to reduce the semantics rules for the Request-Response message exchange mechanism. In the semantics indeed, we will consider the response message as a One-Way message exchange as well. It is worth noting that the service behaviour calculus does not deal with the actual values of variables and locations but it models all the possible execution paths for all the possible variable values and locations. The semantics follows this idea by means of an infinite set of actions where external

[2] It is worth noting that the receiver location is contained within the variable z in order to fullfil location mobility. The reader interested to this topic may consult [GL06].

inputs, external outputs and assignment actions report all the value substitutions for both variables and locations except the actions $\bar{o}@l(\boldsymbol{v}/\boldsymbol{x}), \bar{o_r}@l(\boldsymbol{v}/\boldsymbol{x})$ and $\overline{o_r}@l(\boldsymbol{v}/\boldsymbol{x},\boldsymbol{y})$ where locations are defined. Formally, let ω range over $\mathcal{O} \cup \mathcal{O}_R$ and let Act be the set of actions, ranged over by γ, defined as follows:
$Act = In \cup Out \cup Internal$

$$In = \{\omega(\boldsymbol{v}/\boldsymbol{x}), o_r(\boldsymbol{v}/\boldsymbol{x},\boldsymbol{y},P)@l\}$$
$$Out = \{\bar{\omega}@l/z(\boldsymbol{v}/\boldsymbol{x}), \bar{\omega}@l(\boldsymbol{v}/\boldsymbol{x}), \overline{o_r}@l/z(\boldsymbol{v}/\boldsymbol{x},\boldsymbol{y}), \overline{o_r}@l(\boldsymbol{v}/\boldsymbol{x},\boldsymbol{y})\}$$
$$Internal = \{s, \bar{s}, x := v/e, \chi?, \neg\chi?\}$$

We define $\rightarrow \subseteq SC \times Act \times SC$ as the least relation which satisfies the axioms and rules of Table 1 and closed w.r.t. $\equiv$, where $\equiv$ is the least congruence relation satisfying the axioms at the end of Table 1. The rules are divided into axioms and rules for defining composition operators that are quite standard. Rules ONE-WAYOUTLOC and REQ-OUTLOC deals with output operations where the location l is explicit whereas rules ONE-WAYOUT and REQ-OUT deal with output operations where the location is represented by the variable z. Rule REQIN produces a process which executes P and then performs a notification joined with the sender location l. It is worth noting that the actual location will be joined at the level of the services system lts layer where synchronizations among service engines are defined. Rule SYNCHRO defines the synchronization between signals which allows us to exploit them for synchronizing parallel processes of the same service behaviour. Finally, rules ITERATION and NOT ITERATION model iteration in a way which resembles that of imperative programming.

Definition 1. ***(Well-formedness)*** *Let $P \in SC$ be a service behaviour calculus process. Let Ψ the set of all the possible external input operation terms. We say that P is a well-formed process if:*
$\exists \gamma_1, ..., \gamma_n \in \Psi, \exists Q_1, ..., Q_n \in SC, P = \gamma_1; Q_1 + ... + \gamma_n; Q_n$
We denote the set of all the well-formed processes with the symbol X_{SC}.

Definition 2. *Let $P \in X_{SC}$, a trace γ^* of P is a session iff $P \xrightarrow{\gamma^*} \boldsymbol{0}$.*

The condition of Definition 1 states that a service behaviour process is well-formed if it is formed by a set of processes, composed by means of an alternative choice, which start with an external input operation. By defintion it follows that $X_{SC} \subseteq SC$.

2.2 Service Engine Calculus

This section is devoted to present the service engine calculus. Before presenting its syntax, we introduce some basic concepts such as *state*, *correlation sets* and *service declaration*. In a service engine indeed, all the executed sessions of a service behaviour are joined by a state and a correlation set. Furthermore, a service engine always executes sessions by following the specifications defined within the service declaration. A state is represented by a function $\mathcal{S} : Var \rightarrow Val \cup \{\bot\}$ from variables to the set $Val \cup \{\bot\}$ ranged over by w. Val, ranged

Table 1. Rules for service behaviour lts layer

(In) $s \stackrel{s}{\rightarrow} \mathbf{0}$ (Out) $\bar{s} \stackrel{\bar{s}}{\rightarrow} \mathbf{0}$ (One-WayOut) $\bar{\omega}@z(\boldsymbol{x}) \stackrel{\bar{\omega}@l/z(\boldsymbol{v}/\boldsymbol{x})}{\longrightarrow} \mathbf{0}$ (One-WayOutLoc) $\bar{\omega}@l(\boldsymbol{x}) \stackrel{\bar{\omega}@l(\boldsymbol{v}/\boldsymbol{x})}{\longrightarrow} \mathbf{0}$ (One-WayIn) $\omega(\boldsymbol{x}) \stackrel{\omega(\boldsymbol{v}/\boldsymbol{x})}{\rightarrow} \mathbf{0}$

(Assign) $x := e \stackrel{x:=v/e}{\rightarrow} \mathbf{0}$ (Req-Out) $\overline{o_r}@z(\boldsymbol{x},\boldsymbol{y}) \stackrel{\overline{o_r}@l/z(\boldsymbol{v}/\boldsymbol{x},\boldsymbol{y})}{\longrightarrow} o_r(\boldsymbol{y})$ (Req-OutLoc) $\overline{o_r}@l(\boldsymbol{x},\boldsymbol{y}) \stackrel{\overline{o_r}@l(\boldsymbol{v}/\boldsymbol{x},\boldsymbol{y})}{\longrightarrow} o_r(\boldsymbol{y})$

(Req-In) $o_r(\boldsymbol{x},\boldsymbol{y},P) \stackrel{o_r(\boldsymbol{v}/\boldsymbol{x},\boldsymbol{y},P)@l}{\longrightarrow} P;\bar{o}_r@l(\boldsymbol{y})$ (If then) $\chi?P:Q \stackrel{\chi?}{\rightarrow} P$ (Else) $\chi?P:Q \stackrel{\neg\chi?}{\rightarrow} Q$

(Iteration) $\chi \rightleftharpoons P \stackrel{\chi?}{\rightarrow} P;\chi \rightleftharpoons P$ (Not Iteration) $\chi \rightleftharpoons P \stackrel{\neg\chi?}{\rightarrow} \mathbf{0}$ (Synchro) $\dfrac{P \stackrel{s}{\rightarrow} P', Q \stackrel{\bar{s}}{\rightarrow} Q'}{P \mid Q \stackrel{\tau}{\rightarrow} P' \mid Q'}$

(Sequence) $\dfrac{P \stackrel{\gamma}{\rightarrow} P'}{P;Q \stackrel{\gamma}{\rightarrow} P';Q}$ (Parallel) $\dfrac{P \stackrel{\gamma}{\rightarrow} P'}{P \mid Q \stackrel{\gamma}{\rightarrow} P' \mid Q}$ (Choice) $\dfrac{\epsilon_i \stackrel{\gamma}{\rightarrow} \mathbf{0} \quad i \in I}{\sum^{+}_{i\in I} \epsilon_i;P_i \stackrel{\gamma}{\rightarrow} P_i}$

Structural Congruence

$$P \mid Q \equiv Q \mid P \qquad P \mid \mathbf{0} \equiv \mathbf{0} \qquad P \mid (Q \mid R) \equiv (P \mid Q) \mid R \qquad \mathbf{0}; P \equiv P$$

over by v, is a generic set of values on which it is defined a total order relation[3]. We use $\mathcal{S}[v/x]$, whose definition follows, to denote the variable state update:

$$\mathcal{S}[v/x] = \mathcal{S}' \qquad \mathcal{S}'(x') = \begin{cases} v & \textit{if } x' = x \\ \mathcal{S}(x') & \textit{otherwise} \end{cases}$$

Conditions can be evaluated over states. We exploit the notation $\mathcal{S} \vdash \chi$ for denoting that the state $\mathcal{S}$ satisfies the condition χ. The satisfaction relation for $\vdash$ is defined by the following rules, where e denotes an expression and $e \hookrightarrow_{\mathcal{S}} v$ denotes that, when the state is $\mathcal{S}$, the expression e is evaluated into the value v or, when some variables within the expression are not instantiated, into the symbol $\perp$:

1. $e \hookrightarrow_{\mathcal{S}} v, \mathcal{S}(x) \leq v \Rightarrow \mathcal{S} \vdash x \leq e$ 2. $e \hookrightarrow_{\mathcal{S}} v, v \leq \mathcal{S}(x) \Rightarrow \mathcal{S} \vdash e \leq x$
3. $\mathcal{S} \vdash \chi' \wedge \mathcal{S} \vdash \chi'' \Rightarrow \mathcal{S} \vdash \chi' \wedge \chi''$ 4. $\neg(\mathcal{S} \vdash \chi) \Rightarrow \mathcal{S} \vdash \neg\chi$

Sessions often require to be distinguished and accessed only by those dialoguers which hold some specific references. In the object oriented paradigm such a reference is the object reference guaranteed by the object oriented framework. In service oriented computing in general, we cannot assume the existence of an underlying framework which guarantees references management. Correlation sets, which are a mechanism defined within WS-BPEL, allows us to address such an

[3] We extend such an order relation on the set $Val \cup \{\perp\}$ considering $\perp < v$, $\forall v \in Val$.

issue. A correlation set is a set of variables called *correlated variables.* Formally, let $CSet = \mathbf{P}(Var)$ be the set of all the correlation sets ranged over by c. In a service engine a session is identified by the values assigned to the correlated variables by the current state. The session identification issue is raised when a message is received on an input operation. Since there should be several sessions that are waiting on the same input operation indeed, the right session to which the message is delivered is identified by means of the correlated variables values. Given a variable x, two values v and w where the former is the value which is willing for being replaced within the variable x and the latter is the actual value of x and a correlation set c, we say that v is correlated to x coherently with c, $v/x \vdash_c w$, if: the variable x belongs to c and its actual value is $w = v$;the variable x belongs to c and its actual value is $w = \perp$; the variable x does not belong to c. Formally we exploit the following notation:

$$v/x \vdash_c w \iff (x \in c \wedge (v = w \vee w = \perp)) \vee x \notin c$$

We extend such a definition to vector of variables and values:

$$\boldsymbol{v}/\boldsymbol{x} \vdash_c \boldsymbol{w} \iff \forall x_i, v_i/x_i \vdash_c w_i$$

As far as the service declaration is concerned, it contains all the necessary information for executing sessions. In particular, it specifies: the service behaviour whose sessions are executed by the service engine; if each session has its own state or if there is a common state shared by all the sessions (in the former case the state is renewed each time the execution of a session starts and it expires when the session terminates: we say that the state is *not persistent* whereas in the latter case, the state is never renewed and the variables hold their values after the termination of the sessions: we say that the state is *persistent*); the correlation set which guards the executed sessions; if the sessions are executed in a sequential order or in a concurrent one. The syntax follows:

$$U ::= P_\times \mid P_\bullet \qquad W ::= c \triangleright U \qquad D ::= !W \mid W^*$$

where $P \in X_{SC}$ is a service behaviour, flag $\times$ denotes that P is equipped with a not persistent state and flag $\bullet$ denotes that P is equipped with a persistent one. c is the correlation set which guards the execution of the sessions, $!W$ denotes a concurrent execution of the sessions and W^* denotes the fact that sessions are executed in a sequential order. D is a service declaration.

The Service Engine Calculus Syntax. Here we present the service engine calculus syntax:

$$Y ::= D[H] \qquad H ::= c \triangleright P_S \qquad P_S ::= (P, \mathcal{S}) \mid P_S \mid P_S$$

where D is a service declaration, P is a service behaviour process and $\mathcal{S}$ is a state. Y is a service engine and it is composed of a service declaration D and an execution environment H. H represents the actual sessions which are running on the service engine modelled as the parallel composition of service behaviour process coupled with a state $(P, \mathcal{S})$. All the couples are guarded by the same correlation set c; it is worth noting that a service engine is not correlated when $c = \emptyset$. We denote with HC the set of all the possible processes ranged over by Y. The semantics is defined in terms of different label transition system layers

Table 2. Rules for service engine state lts layer

(In)
$$\frac{P \xrightarrow{s} P'}{(P,\mathcal{S}) \xrightarrow{s} (P',\mathcal{S})}$$

(Out)
$$\frac{P \xrightarrow{\bar{s}} P'}{(P,\mathcal{S}) \xrightarrow{\bar{s}} (P',\mathcal{S})}$$

(Synchro)
$$\frac{P \xrightarrow{\tau} P'}{(P,\mathcal{S}) \xrightarrow{\tau} (P',\mathcal{S})}$$

(One-WayOut)
$$\frac{P \xrightarrow{\bar{\omega}@l/z(\boldsymbol{v}/\boldsymbol{x})} P', \mathcal{S}(z) = l, \mathcal{S}(\boldsymbol{x}) = \boldsymbol{v}}{(P,\mathcal{S}) \xrightarrow{\bar{\omega}@l(\boldsymbol{v})} (P',\mathcal{S})}$$

(One-WayOutLoc)
$$\frac{P \xrightarrow{\bar{\omega}@l(\boldsymbol{v}/\boldsymbol{x})} P', \mathcal{S}(\boldsymbol{x}) = \boldsymbol{v}}{(P,\mathcal{S}) \xrightarrow{\bar{\omega}@l(\boldsymbol{v})} (P',\mathcal{S})}$$

(One-WayIn)
$$\frac{P \xrightarrow{\omega(\boldsymbol{v}/\boldsymbol{x})} P'}{(P,\mathcal{S}) \xrightarrow{\omega(\boldsymbol{v}/\boldsymbol{x})\mapsto\mathcal{S}(\boldsymbol{x})} (P',\mathcal{S}[\boldsymbol{v}/\boldsymbol{x}])}$$

(Req-In)
$$\frac{P \xrightarrow{o_r(\boldsymbol{v}/\boldsymbol{x},\boldsymbol{y},P)@l} P'}{(P,\mathcal{S}) \xrightarrow{o_r(\boldsymbol{v}/\boldsymbol{x},\boldsymbol{y},P)@l\mapsto\mathcal{S}(\boldsymbol{x})} (P',\mathcal{S}[\boldsymbol{v}/\boldsymbol{x}])}$$

(Req-Out)
$$\frac{P \xrightarrow{\overline{o_r}@l/z(\boldsymbol{v}/\boldsymbol{x},\boldsymbol{y})} P', \mathcal{S}(z) = l, \mathcal{S}(\boldsymbol{x}) = \boldsymbol{v}}{(P,\mathcal{S}) \xrightarrow{\overline{o_r}@l(\boldsymbol{v},\boldsymbol{y})} (P',\mathcal{S})}$$

(Req-OutLoc)
$$\frac{P \xrightarrow{\overline{o_r}@l(\boldsymbol{v}/\boldsymbol{x},\boldsymbol{y})} P', \mathcal{S}(\boldsymbol{x}) = \boldsymbol{v}}{(P,\mathcal{S}) \xrightarrow{\overline{o_r}@l(\boldsymbol{v},\boldsymbol{y})} (P',\mathcal{S})}$$

(Assign)
$$\frac{P \xrightarrow{x:=v/e} P', e \hookrightarrow_{\mathcal{S}} v}{(P,\mathcal{S}) \xrightarrow{\tau} (P',\mathcal{S}[v/x])}$$

(Satisfaction)
$$\frac{P \xrightarrow{\chi?} P', \chi \vdash \mathcal{S}}{(P,\mathcal{S}) \xrightarrow{\tau} (P',\mathcal{S})}$$

(Not Satisfaction)
$$\frac{P \xrightarrow{\neg\chi?} P', \chi \nvdash \mathcal{S}}{(P,\mathcal{S}) \xrightarrow{\tau} (P',\mathcal{S})}$$

presented in Tables 2,4 and 5. Table 2 deals with the rules for the service engine state lts layer which defines the semantics for a couple of a service behaviour process and a state, Table 4 deals with the rules for service engine correlation lts layer where it is defined the semantics for managing correlation sets and Table 4 deals with the service engine execution modality lts layer which defines the semantics for executing sessions in a concurrent or in a sequential way. As far as Table 2 is concerned, an action is enabled if the current state contains variables values which correspond to those reported into the action. An action is disabled, i.e. it is not raised to the overlying lts layer, when the variables values into the state do not correspond to those reported into the action. The enabled action, when raised to the overlying lts layer, will be modified in order to forward only the needed information. Table 3 reports the one-to-one mapping from the service behaviour lts layer actions to the service engine state lts layer ones. Actions a), b) are not altered since they do not deal with the state whereas actions g) are replaced with a τ action because they do not carry any information needed by the overlying layer. Actions c) and e) are related to the output operations and, when enabled, they resolve the values of the variables and locations. Indeed, if we consider rules One-WayOut and Req-Out they contain the conditions $\mathcal{S}(z) = l$ and $\mathcal{S}(\boldsymbol{x}) = \boldsymbol{v}$ which allows for the verification of the actual values of the variables within the current state. In particular, rules One-WayOutLoc and Req-OutLoc do not resolve locations because they are explicitly represented.

Actions d) and f) deal with the input operations (rules ONE-WAYIN, REQ-IN) and, when enabled, they do not resolve the values of the variables but they forward the actual values of the variables involved into the action ($\mapsto \mathcal{S}(\boldsymbol{x})$). This is due to the fact that some variables could be correlated and it will be necessary to verify if they satisfy the current correlation set. Such a control will be done in the overlying layer whose rules, closed w.r.t. the structural congruence, are reported in Table 4. Also in this case the actions, if enabled, will be modified and raised for the overlying layer[4]. In Table 4 rules CORRELATEDONE-WAYIN and CORRELATEDREQ-IN deal with the actions d) and f) of Table 3 where the values of the variables are resolved only if the condition on correlation set is satisfied ($\boldsymbol{v}/\boldsymbol{x} \vdash_c \boldsymbol{w}$). As far as Table 5 is concerned, the actions are enabled at the level of the service engine (rule EXECUTION) and session execution modalities, concurrent or sequential with a persistent or a not persistent state, are defined (rules CONCURRENTNOTPERSISTENT, CONCURRENTPERSISTENT, SEQUENTIALNOTPERSISTENT and SEQUENTIALPERSISTENT). Rule CONCURRENTNOTPERSISTENT deals with a concurrent execution of the sessions and with a not persistent state. In particular, each session has its own state, that is initially fresh ($\mathcal{S}_\perp$), and it is executed concurrently with the other ones. It is worth noting that condition $\nexists \ \mathcal{S}_i \in P_S \ c \rhd (P, \mathcal{S}_i) \xrightarrow{\gamma} c \rhd (P', \mathcal{S}_i')$[5] states that it is not possible to start a new session with a set of values for the correlated variables that belong to another running session. Rule CONCURRENTPERSISTENT deals with the concurrent execution of sessions which share a common state. Rule SEQUENTIALNOTPERSISTENT deals with the sequential execution of sessions which have their own state. In this case there is always no more than one executed session at a time. The state is not persistent and it is renewed each time a new session is spawned. Finally, rule SEQUENTIALPERSISTENT deals with the sequential execution of the sessions where the state is shared and it does not expire after session termination.

2.3 Services System Calculus

Here we present the services system calculus which is based on the service engine one and it allows for the composition of different engines into a system. The service engines are composed in parallel and they are equipped with a location that allows us to univocally distinguish them within the system. The calculus syntax follows:

$$E ::= Y_l \ \mid \ E \parallel E$$

A service engine system E can be a located service engine Y_l, where l is a location, or a parallel composition of them. The semantics is defined in terms of a labelled transition system whose rules are described in Table 6 and closed w.r.t. the structural congruence. At the level of services system there are only

[4] For the sake of brevity, we do not report the mapping table for the actions. It is easy to extract it from the rules of Table 4.

[5] We abuse of the notation $\mathcal{S}_i \in P_S$ for meaning that it exists a couple $(P, \mathcal{S}_i)$ within the term P_S.

Table 3. Enabled action mapping

	Service behaviour actions	Service engine state actions
a)	s	s
b)	$\overline{s}$	$\overline{s}$
c)	$\overline{\omega}@l/z(\boldsymbol{v}/\boldsymbol{x}), \overline{\omega}@l(\boldsymbol{v}/\boldsymbol{x})$	$\overline{\omega}@l(\boldsymbol{v})$
d)	$\omega(\boldsymbol{v}/\boldsymbol{x})$	$\omega(\boldsymbol{v}/\boldsymbol{x}) \mapsto \mathcal{S}(\boldsymbol{x})$
e)	$\overline{o_r}@l/z(\boldsymbol{v}/\boldsymbol{x},\boldsymbol{y}), \overline{o_r}@l(\boldsymbol{v}/\boldsymbol{x},\boldsymbol{y})$	$\overline{o_r}@l(\boldsymbol{v},\boldsymbol{y})$
f)	$o_r(\boldsymbol{v}/\boldsymbol{x},\boldsymbol{y},P)@l$	$o_r(\boldsymbol{v}/\boldsymbol{x},\boldsymbol{y},P)@l \mapsto \mathcal{S}(\boldsymbol{x})$
g)	$\chi?, \neg\chi?, x := v/e, \tau$	τ

Table 4. Rules for service engine correlation lts layer

(NOT CORRELATED)
$$\frac{P_S \xrightarrow{\gamma} P'_S}{c \rhd P_S \xrightarrow{\gamma} c \rhd P'_S}\ \gamma \neq \begin{cases} o(\boldsymbol{v}/\boldsymbol{x}) \mapsto \boldsymbol{w} \\ o_r(\boldsymbol{v}/\boldsymbol{x},\boldsymbol{y},P)@l \mapsto \boldsymbol{w} \end{cases}$$

(PARALLEL)
$$\frac{c \rhd P_S \xrightarrow{\gamma} c \rhd P'_S}{c \rhd P_S \mid Q_S \xrightarrow{\gamma} c \rhd P'_S \mid Q_S}$$

(CORRELATEDONE-WAYIN)
$$\frac{P_S \xrightarrow{\omega(\boldsymbol{v}/\boldsymbol{x})\mapsto(\boldsymbol{w})} P'_S,\ \boldsymbol{v}/\boldsymbol{x} \vdash_c \boldsymbol{w}}{c \rhd P_S \xrightarrow{\omega(\boldsymbol{v})} c \rhd P'_S}$$

(CORRELATEDREQ-IN)
$$\frac{P_S \xrightarrow{o_r(\boldsymbol{v}/\boldsymbol{x},\boldsymbol{y},P)@l\mapsto(\boldsymbol{w})} P'_S,\ \boldsymbol{v}/\boldsymbol{x} \vdash_c \boldsymbol{w}}{c \rhd P_S \xrightarrow{o_r(\boldsymbol{v},\boldsymbol{y})@l} c \rhd P'_S}$$

STRUCTURAL CONGRUENCE

$$P_S \mid Q_S \equiv Q_S \mid P_S \qquad P_S \mid (Q_S \mid R_S) \equiv (P_S \mid Q_S) \mid R_S \qquad P_S \mid (\mathbf{0}, \mathcal{S}) \equiv P_S$$

Table 5. Rules for service engine execution modality lts layer

(CONCURRENTNOTPERSISTENT)
$$\frac{(P, \mathcal{S}_\perp) \xrightarrow{\gamma} (P', \mathcal{S}'), \nexists\ \mathcal{S}_i \in P_S\ c \rhd (P, \mathcal{S}_i) \xrightarrow{\gamma} c \rhd (P', \mathcal{S}'_i)}{!c \rhd P_\times[c \rhd P_S] \xrightarrow{\gamma} !c \rhd P_\times[c \rhd P_S \mid (P', \mathcal{S}')]}$$

(CONCURRENTPERSISTENT)
$$\frac{c \rhd (P, \mathcal{S}) \xrightarrow{\gamma} c \rhd (P', \mathcal{S}')}{!c \rhd P_\bullet[c \rhd (Q, \mathcal{S})] \xrightarrow{\gamma} !c \rhd P_\bullet[c \rhd (Q \mid P', \mathcal{S}')]}$$

(SEQUENTIALNOTPERSISTENT)
$$\frac{c \rhd (P, \mathcal{S}_\perp) \xrightarrow{\gamma} c \rhd (P', \mathcal{S}')}{(c \rhd P_\times)^*[c \rhd (\mathbf{0}, \mathcal{S}'')] \xrightarrow{\gamma} (c \rhd P)^*_\times[c \rhd (P', \mathcal{S}')]}$$

(SEQUENTIALPERSISTENT)
$$\frac{c \rhd (P, \mathcal{S}) \xrightarrow{\gamma} c \rhd (P', \mathcal{S}')}{(c \rhd P_\bullet)^*[c \rhd (\mathbf{0}, \mathcal{S})] \xrightarrow{\gamma} (c \rhd P)^*_\bullet[c \rhd (P', \mathcal{S}')]}$$

(EXECUTION)
$$\frac{H \xrightarrow{\gamma} H'}{D[H] \xrightarrow{\gamma} D[H']}$$

two kinds of action label: τ and $\tilde{\tau}$ where the former represents synchronizations among service engines and the latter represents not observable internal actions of service engines (rule INTERNAL). Rules ONE-WAYSYNC and REQ-SYNC describe synchronizations among different service engines. The former models a One-Way

Table 6. Rules for services system lts layer

(ONE-WAYSYNC)

$$\frac{Y_l \stackrel{\overline{\omega}@l'(v)}{\longrightarrow} Y'_l \;,\; Z_{l'} \stackrel{\omega(v)}{\longrightarrow} Z'_{l'}}{Y_l \parallel Z_{l'} \stackrel{\tau}{\rightarrow} Y'_l \parallel Z'_{l'}}$$

(REQ-SYNC)

$$\frac{Y_l \stackrel{\overline{o_r}@l'(v,y)}{\longrightarrow} Y'_l \;,\; Z_{l'} \stackrel{o_r(v,y)@l}{\longrightarrow} Z'_{l'}}{Y_l \parallel Z_{l'} \stackrel{\tau}{\rightarrow} Y'_l \parallel Z'_{l'}}$$

(PAR-EXT)

$$\frac{E_1 \stackrel{\gamma}{\rightarrow} E'_1}{E_1 \parallel E_2 \stackrel{\gamma}{\rightarrow} E'_1 \parallel E_2}$$

(INTERNAL)

$$\frac{Y_l \stackrel{\gamma}{\rightarrow} Y'_l}{Y_l \stackrel{\tilde{\tau}}{\rightarrow} Y'_l} \quad \gamma \neq \begin{cases} \overline{o}@l(v) \\ o(v) \\ \overline{o_r}@l(v,y) \\ o_r(v,y)@l \end{cases}$$

(STRUCTURAL CONGRUENCE OVER E)

$$E_1 \parallel E_2 \equiv E_2 \parallel E_1 \qquad E_1 \parallel (E_2 \parallel E_3) \equiv (E_1 \parallel E_2) \parallel E_3$$

message exchange and the latter models the request message exchange in the case of a Request-Response. It is worth noting that the response message exchange, in the case of a Request-Response, is modelled by the former rule indeed, by means of rules of Table 1, Request-Response operations can be externally seen as two One-Ways.

3 Conclusion

In this paper we have proposed a set of process calculi for dealing with service design and composition. There are other works which exploit formal models for representing services and service composition. In general, they use different models for representing service behaviours and service composition and they do not deal with service deployment features. In [DD04] the authors use Petri Nets for describing service behaviours but they focus only on workflow aspects without distinguishing among the different kind of operations. In [LM] a semantics of WS-BPEL is defined in terms of pi-calculus processes but correlation sets are not considered. In [MC06] the authors present a language, called *Orc*, where services are considered as functions and a service invocation is expressed by a function call. Finally, as far as correlation sets are concerned, in [Vir04] Viroli propose a first formalization of the mechanism specified within BPEL4WS specification.

Our work must be considered within a wider framework context we are working on where we have analyzed orchestration and choreography calculi for addressing system design issues. The relationship between the two views has been given by exploiting a notion of conformance based on bisimulation. Jointly with the formal investigation, we are developing a Java interpreter for the orchestration language called JOLIE (Java Orchestration Language Interpreter Engine) [MGLZ]. At the present, JOLIE is able to intepret the service behaviour calculus and it allows us to compose different JOLIE services over the Internet. In the future, we intend to extend it in order to interpret the service engine calculus.

References

[BGG+05] N. Busi, R. Gorrieri, C. Guidi, R. Lucchi, and G. Zavattaro. Choreography and orchestration: A synergic approach for system design. In *ICSOC'05*, volume 3826 of *LNCS*, pages 228–240, 2005.

[BGG+06] N. Busi, R. Gorrieri, C. Guidi, R. Lucchi, and G. Zavattaro. Choreography and orchestration conformance for system design. In *Proc. of 8th International Conference on Coordination Models and Languages (COORDINATION'06)*, volume 4038 of *LNCS*, pages 63–81, 2006.

[DD04] R. Dijkman and M. Dumas. Service-oriented Design: a Multi-viewpoint Approach. *Int. J. Cooperative Inf. Syst.*, 13(4):337–368, 2004.

[GL06] C. Guidi and R. Lucchi. Mobility mechanisms in service oriented computing. In *Proc. of 8th International Conference on on Formal Methods for Open Object-Based Distributed Systems (FMOODS'06)*, volume 4037 of *LNCS*, pages 233–250, 2006.

[GLZ+] C. Guidi, R. Lucchi, G. Zavattaro, N. Busi, and R. Gorrieri. Technical Report UBLCS-2006-20, Dep. of Computer Science, Univ. of Bologna [http://www.cs.unibo.it/research/reports/], 2006.

[Kel76] R. M. Keller. Formal verification of parallel programs. *Commun. ACM*, 19(7):371–384, 1976.

[LM] R. Lucchi and M. Mazzara. A pi-calculus based semantics for WS-BPEL. *Journal of Logic and Algebraic Programming.* Elsevier Press. To appear.

[MC06] J. Misra and W. Cook. Computation orchestration, a basis for wide-area computing. *Journal of Software and Systems modeling*, 2006. To appear.

[MGLZ] F. Montesi, C. Guidi, R. Lucchi, and G. Zavattaro. JOLIE: a Java Orchestration Language Interpreter Engine. In *CoOrg06*, volume to appear of *ENTCS*.

[OAS] OASIS. *Web Services Business Process Execution Language Version 2.0, Working Draft.* [http://www.oasis-open.org/committees/download.php/10347/wsbpel-specification-draft-120204.htm].

[Vir04] M. Viroli. Towards a Formal Foundation to Orchestration Languages. In *Proc. of 1st International Workshop on Web Services and Formal Methods (WS-FM 2004)*, volume 105 of *ENTCS*. Elsevier, 2004.

[Wor] World Wide Web Consortium. *Web Services Description Language (WSDL) 1.1.* [http://www.w3.org/TR/wsdl].

A Priori Conformance Verification for Guaranteeing Interoperability in Open Environments*

Matteo Baldoni, Cristina Baroglio, Alberto Martelli, and Viviana Patti

Dipartimento di Informatica — Università degli Studi di Torino
C.so Svizzera, 185 — I-10149 Torino, Italy
{baldoni, baroglio, mrt, patti}@di.unito.it

Abstract. An important issue, in open environments like the web, is guaranteeing the interoperability of a set of services. When the interaction scheme that the services should follow is given (e.g. as a choreography or as an interaction protocol), it becomes possible to verify, before the interaction takes place, if the interactive behavior of a service (e.g. a BPEL process specification) respects it. This verification is known as "conformance test". Recently some attempts have been done for defining conformance tests w.r.t. a protocol but these approaches fail in capturing the very nature of interoperability, turning out to be too restrictive. In this work we give a representation of protocol, based on message exchange and on finite state automata, and we focus on those properties that are essential to the verification of the interoperability of a set of services. In particular, we define a conformance test that can guarantee, a priori, the interoperability of a set of services by verifying properties of the single service against the protocol. This is particularly relevant in open environments, where services are identified and composed on demand and dynamically, and the system as a whole cannot be analyzed.

1 Introduction

In this work we face the problem of verifying the interoperability of a set of peers by exploiting an abstract description of the desired interaction. On a hand, we will have an interaction protocol (possibly expressed by a choreography), capturing the global interaction of a desired system of services; on the other, we will have a set of service implementations which should be used to assemble the system. The protocol is a specification of the desired interaction, as thus, it might be used for defining several systems of services [3]. In particular, it contains a characterization of the various *roles* played by the services [6]. In our view, a role specification is not the exact specification of a process of interest, rather it identifies a *set of possible processes*, all those whose evolutions respect the dictates given by the role. In an open environment, the introduction of a new peer in an execution context will be determined provided that it satisfies the

* This research has partially been funded by the European Commission and by the Swiss Federal Office for Education and Science within the 6th Framework Programme project REWERSE number 506779 (cf. http://rewerse.net), and it has also been supported by MIUR PRIN 2005 "Specification and verification of agent interaction protocols" national project.

A. Dan and W. Lamersdorf (Eds.): ICSOC 2006, LNCS 4294, pp. 339–351, 2006.

protocol that characterizes such an execution context; as long as the new entity satisfies the rules, the interoperability with the other components of the system is guaranteed.

In the literature it is possible to find works that tackle the composition of *specific* entities (or services). In this context the issue of verifying that the desired services can actually interact is crucial. For instance, in [20] the aim is to verify the existence of a partner that is able to interact with a service of interest. This property is called "controllability". In [9], instead, the problem that is faced consists in verifying if there is a composition of certain web services that respects a partial sequence of actions given by a client. Works in this line of research differ from ours in the fact that we consider the choreography, which is given a priori, as a model. This allows the distribution of the verification in time and among the various candidate players. A candidate player can autonomously check its conformance to the model independently from the others because it only compares its behavior to the role that it means to play. To do this it is not necessary to have the implementations of the other roles. In our framework, the verification of the correctness of the model is supposed to preceed the verification of the interoperability of the various players. This *modularity* meets the requirements given by interaction protocol engineering: in fact, the expected properties of the composition are captured by the model, defined at design time, which preceeds the verification of the conformance of the peers to be composed. On the contrary, in works where the compatibility of a set of peers is studied, the verification of the designer's specifications is to be done *after* the composition is made.

The computational model of web services shows some analogies with of *method-invocation* over objects [17], in the sense that as an object cannot refuse to execute a method, which is invoked on it and that is contained in its public interface, a service cannot refuse to execute over an invocation that respects its public interface (although it can refuse the answer). This, however, is not the only possible model of execution. In multi-agent systems, for instance, an agent sending a request message to another agent cannot be certain that it will ever be answered, unless the interaction is ruled by a protocol. The protocol plays, in a way, the role of the public interface: an agent conforming to a protocol must necessarily answer and must be able to handle messages sent by other agents in the context of the protocol itself. The difference between the case of objects and the case of protocols is that the protocol also defines an "execution context" in which using messages. Therefore, the set of messages that it is possible to use varies depending on the point at which the execution has arrived. In a way, the protocol is a *dynamic interface* that defines messages in the context of the occurring interaction, thus ruling this interaction. On the other hand, the user of an object is not obliged to use all of the methods offered in the public interface and it can implement more methods. The same holds when protocols are used to norm the interaction. Generally speaking, only part of the protocol will be used in an entity's interaction with another, moreover, an entitycan understand more messages than the one forseen by the protocol. Moreover, we will assume that the initiative is taken from the entity that plays as a sender, which will commit to sending a specific message out of its set of alternatives. The receiver will simply execute the reception of the message. Of course, the senders should send a message that its counterpart can understand. For all these reasons, performing the conformance test is analogous to verifying at compilation time (that is, a priori) if a class implements an interface in a correct way and to execute a static typechecking.

Sticking to a specification, on the other hand, does not mean that the service must do *all* that the role specification defines; indeed, a role specification is just a formal definition of what is lawful to say or to expect at any given moment of the interaction. Taking this observation into account we need to define some means for verifying that a single service implementation comforms to the specification of the role in the protocol that it means to play [16]. The idea is that if a service passes the conformance test it will be able to interact with a set of other services, equally proved individually conformant to the other roles in the protocol, in a way that respects the rules defined in the protocol itself.

A typical approach to the verification that a service implementation respects a role definition is to verify whether the execution traces of the service belong to the protocol [1,14,7]. This test, however, does not consider processes with different branching structures. Another approach, that instead takes this case into account, is to apply bisimulation and say that the implementation is conformant if it is bisimilar to its role or, more generally, that the composition of a set of policies is bisimilar to the composition of a set of roles [10,24]. Bisimulation [21], however, does not take into account the fact that the implementor's decisions of cutting some interaction path not necessarily compromise the interaction. Many services that respect the intuitions given above will not be bisimilar to the specification but it would be very restrictive to say that they are not conformant (see Section 3.1). Thus, in order to perform the conformance test we need a softer test, a test that accepts all the processes contained in a space defined by the role. Moreover, (bi)simulation does not take into account the *asymmetry* between messages that are sent (outgoing messages) and messages that are, instead, received (incoming messages) [5]. In this work we provide such a test (Section 3). This proposal differs from previous work that we have done on conformance [7,8] in various aspects. First of all, we can now tackle protocols that contain an arbitrary (though finite) number of roles. Second, we account also for the case of policies and roles which produce the same interactions but have different branching structures. This case could not be handled in the previous framework due to the fact that we based it exclusively on a trace semantics.

2 Protocols, Policies, and Conversations

A *conversation policy* is a program that defines the communicative behavior of an interactive entity, e.g. a service, implemented in some programming language [3]. A conversation *protocol* specifies the desired communicative behavior of a set of interactive entities. More specifically, a conversation protocol specifies the sequences of messages (also called speech acts) that can possibly be exchanged by the involved parties, and that we consider as lawful.

In languages that account for communication, speech acts often have the form $m(a_s, a_r, l)$, where m is the kind of message, or performative, a_s (sender) and a_r (receiver) are two interactive entities and l is the message content. In the following analysis it is important to distinguish the incoming messages from the outgoing messages w.r.t a role of a protocol or a policy. We will write m? (*incoming message*) and m! (*outgoing message*) when the receiver or the utterer and the content of the message is clear from the context or they are not relevant. So, for instance, $m(a_s, a_r, l)$ is written as m? from the point of view of a_r, and m! from the point of view of the sender. By the term *conversation* we will, then, denote a sequence of speech acts that is a dialogue of a set of parties.

Both a protocol and a policy can be seen as sets of conversations. In the case of the protocol, it is intuitive that it will be the set of all the possible conversations allowed by its specification among the partners. In the case of the single policy, it will be the set of the possible conversations that the entity can carry on according to its implementing program. Although at execution time, depending on the interlocutor and on the circumstances, only one conversation will actually be expressed, in order to verify conformance *a priori* we need to consider them all as a set. It is important to remark before proceeding that other proposal, e.g. [2], focus on a different kind of conformance: *run-time* conformance, in which only the ongoing conversation is checked against a protocol. In this line also [23] where data mining techniques are used to compare event logs to a desired business process.

Let us then introduce a formal representation of policies and protocols. We will use *finite state automata* (FSA). This choice, though simple, is the same used by the well-known verification system SPIN [18], whose notation we adopt. FSA will be used for representing individual processes that exchange messages with other processes. Therefore, FSA will be used both for representing the *roles* of a protocol, i.e. the abstract descriptions of the interacting parties, as well as for representing the policies of specific entities involved in the interaction. In this work we do not consider the translation process necessary to turn a protocol (e.g. a WS-CDL choreography) or an entity's policy (e.g. a BPEL process) in a FSA; our focus is, in fact, conformance and interoperability. It is possible to find in the literature some works that do this kind of translations. An example is [14].

Definition 1 (Finite State Automaton). *A finite state automaton is a tuple* (S, s_0, L, T, F)*, where* S *is a finite set of states,* $s_0 \in S$ *is a distinguished initial state,* L *is a finite set of labels,* $T \subseteq (S \times L \times S)$ *is a set of transitions,* $F \in S$ *is a set of final states.*

Similarly to [18] we will denote by the "dot" notation the components of a FSA, for example we use $A.s$ to denote the state s that belongs to the automaton A. The definition of run is taken from [18].

Definition 2 (Runs and strings). *A run* σ *of a FSA* (S, s_0, L, T, F) *is an ordered, possibly infinite, set of transitions (a sequence)* $(s_0, l_0, s_1), (s_1, l_1, s_2), (s_2, l_2, s_3), \ldots$ *such that* $\forall i \geq 0$, $(s_i, l_i, s_{i+1}) \in T$*, while the sequence* $l_0 l_1 \ldots$ *is the corresponding string* $\overline{\sigma}$.

Definition 3 (Acceptance). *An accepting run of a finite state automaton* (S, s_0, L, T, F) *is a finite run* σ *in which the final transition* (s_{n-1}, l_{n-1}, s_n) *has the property that* $s_n \in F$*. The corresponding string* $\overline{\sigma}$ *is an accepted string.*

Given a FSA A, we say that a state $A.s_1 \in A.S$ is *alive* if there exists a finite run $(s_1, l_1, s_2), \ldots, (s_{n-1}, l_{n-1}, s_n)$ and $s_n \in A.F$. Moreover, we will write $A_1 \subseteq A_2$ iff every string of A_1 is also a string of A_2.

In order to represent compositions of policies or of individual protocol roles we need to introduce the notions of *free* and of *synchronous* product. These definitions are an adaptation to the problem that we are tackling of the analogous ones presented in [4] for Finite Transition Systems.

Definition 4 (Free product). *Let A_i, $i = 1, \ldots, n$, be n FSA's. The* free product $A_1 \times \cdots \times A_n$ *is the FSA $A = (S, s_0, L, T, F)$ defined by:*

- *S is the set $A_1.S \times \cdots \times A_n.S$;*
- *s_0 is the tuple $(A_1.s_0, \ldots, A_n.s_0)$;*
- *L is the set $A_1.L \times \cdots \times A_n.L$;*
- *T is the set of tuples $((A_1.s_1, \ldots, A_n.s_n), (l_1, \ldots, l_n), (A_1.s'_1, \ldots, A_n.s'_n))$ such that $(A_i.s_i, l_i, A_i.s'_i) \in A_i.T$, for $i = 1, \ldots, n$; and*
- *F is the set of tuples $(A_1.s_1, \ldots, A_n.s_n) \in A.S$ such that $s_i \in A_i.F$, for $i = 1, \ldots, n$.*

We will assume, from now on, that every FSA A has an *empty* transition (s, ε, s) for every state $s \in A.S$. When the finite set of labels L used in a FSA is a set of *speech acts*, strings will represent *conversations*.

Definition 5 (Synchronous product). *Let A_i, $i = 1, \ldots, n$, be n FSA's. The* synchronous product *of the A_i's, written $A_1 \otimes \cdots \otimes A_n$, is the FSA obtained as the free product of the A_i's containing only the transitions $((A_1.s_1, \ldots, A_n.s_n), (l_1, \ldots, l_n), (A_1.s'_1, \ldots, A_n.s'_n))$ such that there exist i and j, $1 \leq i \neq j \leq n$, $l_i = \mathsf{m}!$, $l_j = \mathsf{m}?$, and for any k not equal to i and j, $l_k = \varepsilon$.*

The synchronous product allows a system that exchanges messages to be represented. It is worth noting that a synchronous product does not imply that messages will be exchanged in a synchronous way; it simply represents a message exchange without any assumption on how the exchange is carried on.

In order to represent a protocol, we use the synchronous product of the set of FSA's associated with its roles (each FSA represents the communicative behavior of the role). Moreover, we will assume that the automata that compound the synchronous product have some "good properties", which meet the commonly shared intuitions behind protocols. In particular, we assume that for the set of such automata the following properties hold:

1. *any message that can possibly be sent, at any point of the execution, by a role to another, will be handled by that interlocutor;*
2. *whatever point the conversation has reached, there is a way to bring it to an end.*

An arbitrary synchronous product of n FSA's might not meet these requirements, which can, however, be verified by using automated systems, like SPIN [18].

Note that protocol specification languages, like UML sequence (activity) diagrams and automata [22], naturally follow these requirements: an arrow starts from the lifeline of a role, ending into the lifeline of another role, and thus corresponds to an outgoing or to an incoming message depending on the point of view. Making an analogy with the computational model of distributed objects, one could say that the only messages that are sent are those which can be understood. Moreover, usually protocols contain finite conversations.

We will say that a conversation is *legal w.r.t. a protocol* if it respects the specifications given by the protocol, i.e. if it is an accepted string of the protocol.

3 Interoperability and Conformance Test

We are now in position to explain, with the help of a few simple examples, the intuition behind the terms "conformance" and "interoperability", that we will, then, formalize. By *interoperability* we mean the capability of a set of entities of actually producing a conversation when interacting with one another [5]. Interoperability is a *desired property* of a system of interactive entities and its verification is fundamental in order to understand whether the system works. Such a test passes through the analysis of all the entities involved in the interaction. In an open system, however, it is quite unlikely to have a global view of the system either because it is not possible to read part of the necessary information (e.g. some services do not publish their behavior) or because the interactive entities are identified at different moments, when necessary. Protocols are adopted to solve such problems, in fact, having an interaction schema allows the *distribution of the tests in time*, by checking a single entity at a time against the role that it should play. The protocol, by its own nature guarantees the interoperability of the roles that are part of it. One might argue why we do not simply verify the system obtained by substituting the policy in place of its corresponding role within the protocol and, then, check whether any message that can be sent will be handled by some of the interlocutor roles, bringing to an end the conversations. Actually, this solution presents some flaws, as the following counter-example proves. Let us consider a protocol with three roles: A_1 sends m_1 to A_2, A_2 waits for m_1 and then waits for m_2, and A_3 sends m_2 to A_2. Let us know substitute to role A_2 the policy which, first, waits for m_2 and then it waits for m_1. The three partners will perfectly interoperate and successfully conclude their conversations but the conversation that is produced is not legal w.r.t. the protocol. In protocol-based systems, the proof of the interoperability of an entity with others, obtained by checking the communicative behavior of the entity against the rules of the system (i.e. against an *interaction protocol* itself), is known as *conformance test*. Intuitively, this test must guarantee the following *definition of interoperability*.

Definition 6 (Interoperability w.r.t. an interaction protocol). *Interoperability w.r.t. an interaction protocol is the capability of a set of entities of producing a conversation that is legal w.r.t. the protocol.*

Let us now consider a given service that should play a role in a protocol. In order to include it in the interaction we need to understand if it will be able to interact with the possible players of the other roles. If we assume that the other players are conformant to their respective roles, we can represent them by the roles themselves. Roles, by the definition of protocol, are interoperable. Therefore, in order to prove the interoperability of our service, it will be sufficient to prove for it the "good properties" of its role. First of all, we should prove that its policy does not send messages that the others cannot understand, which means that it will not send messages that are not accounted for by the role. Moreover, we should prove that it can tackle every incoming message that the other roles might send to it, which means that it must be able to handle all the incoming messages handled by the role. Another important property is that whatever point of conversation has been reached, there is a way to bring it to an end. In practice, if a role can bring to an end a conversation in which it has been engaged, so must do the service. To summarize, in order to check a service interoperability it will be sufficient to check its *conformance w.r.t. the desired role* and this check will guarantee that the service will be able to interact with services equally, and separately, proved conformant to the other roles. This, nevertheless, does not mean that the policy of the service must be a precise "copy" of the role.

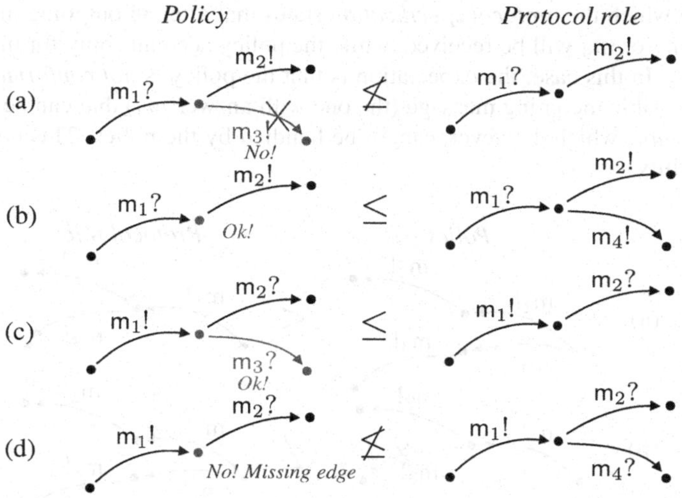

Fig. 1. A set of cases that exemplifies our expectations about a conformant policy: cases (b) and (c) do not compromise interoperability, hence they should pass the conformance test; cases (a) and (d) instead should not pass the conformance test

3.1 Expectations for Interoperability

Let us now discuss some typical cases in which a policy and a role specification that differ in various ways are compared in order to decide if the policy conforms to the role so as to guarantee its interoperability with its future interlocutors that will play the other roles in the protocol. With reference to Figure 1, let us begin with considering the case reported at row (a): here, the service can possibly utter a message m_3 that is not foreseen by the role specification. Trivially, this policy is *not conformant* to the protocol because the service might send a message that cannot be handled by any interlocutor that conforms to the protocol. The symmetric case in which the policy accounts for less outgoing messages than the role specification (Figure 1, row (b)) is, instead, legal. The reason is that at any point of its conversations the entity will anyway always utter only messages that the entities playing the other roles will surely understand. Hence, interoperability is preserved. The restriction of the set of possible alternatives (w.r.t. the protocol) depends on the implementor's own criteria.

Let us now consider the case reported in Figure 1, row (c). Here, the service policy accounts for two conversations in which, after uttering a message m_1, the entity expects one of the two messages m_2 or m_3. Let us also suppose that the protocol specification only allows the first conversation, i.e. that the only possible incoming message is m_2. When the entity will interact with another that is conformant to the protocol, the message m_3 will never be received because the other entity will never utter it. So, in this case, we would like the a priori conformance test to accept the policy as *conformant* to the specification.

Talking about incoming messages, let us now consider the symmetric case (Figure 1, row (d)), in which the *protocol specification* states that after an outgoing message m_1, an answer m_2 or m_4 will be received, while the policy accounts only for the incoming message m_2. In this case, the expectation is that the policy is *not conformant* because there is a possible incoming message (the one with answer m_4) that can be enacted by the *interlocutor*, which, however, cannot be handled by the policy. This compromises interoperability.

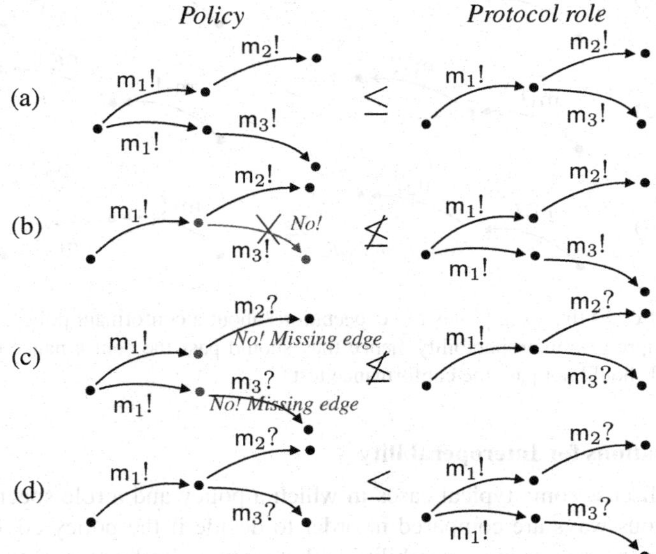

Fig. 2. A set of cases that exemplifies our expectations about a conformant policy: differently than in Figure 1, for every row, the policy and the role produce the same conversations but the structure of their implementations differ

To summarize, at every point of a conversation, we expect that a conformant policy never utters speech acts that are not expected, according to the protocol, and we also expect it to be able to handle any message that can possibly be received, once again according to the protocol. However, the policy is not obliged to foresee (at every point of conversation) an outgoing message for every alternative included in the protocol but it must foresee at least one of them if this is necessary to proceed with the conversation. Trivially, in the example of row (b), a policy containing only the conversation m_1? (not followed either by m_2! or by m_4!) would not be *conformant*.

Let us now consider a completely different set of situations, in which the "structure" of the policy implemented and the structure of the role specification are taken into account. These situations are taken from the literature on communicating processes [15]. Figure 2 reports a set of cases in which the role description and the policy allow the *same conversations* but their structure differs: in rows (a) and (c) the policy decides which message to send (receive, respectively) after m_1 from the very beginning, while in the protocol this decision is taken after m_1 is sent. In row (b) and (d) the situation is inverted.

The case of row (a) does not compromise conformance in the same way as the case reported at row (b) of Figure 1 does not: after a non-deterministic choice the set of alternative outgoing messages is restricted but in both cases only legal messages that can be handled by the interlocutor will be sent. The analogous case reported in row (c), concerning incoming messages, instead, compromises the conformance. In fact, after the non-deterministic step the policy might receive a message that it cannot handle, similarly to row (d) of Figure 1.

The case of row (b), Figure 2, compromises the conformance because after the non-deterministic choice the role specification allows a single outgoing message with no alternatives. The policy, instead, might utter one out of two alternative messages (similarly to row (a) of Figure 1). Finally, the case of row (d) does not compromise the conformance, following what reported in Figure 1, row (c).

3.2 Conformance and Interoperability

In this section we define a test, for checking conformance, that is derived from the observations above. A first consideration is that a conformance test *is not an inclusion test* w.r.t. the set of possible conversations that are produced. In fact, for instance, in row (d) of Figure 1 the policy produces a subset of the conversations produced by the role specification but interoperability is not guaranteed. Instead, if we consider row (c) in the same figure, the set of conversation traces, produced by the policy, is a superset of the one produced by the protocol; despite this, interoperability is guaranteed. A second consideration is that a conformance test is not a bisimulation test w.r.t. the role specification. Actually, the (bi)simulation-based test defined in concurrency theory [21] is too strict, and it imposes constraints, that would exclude policies which instead would be able to interoperate, within the context given by the protocol specification. In particular, all the cases reported in Figure 2 would not be considered as conformant because they are all pairs of processes with different branching structures. Despite this, we would like our test to recognize cases (a) and (d) as conformant because they do not compromise interoperability.

The solution that we propose is inspired by (bi)simulation, but it distinguishes the ways in which incoming and outgoing messages are handled, when a policy is compared to a role. In the following, we will use "$A_1 \leq A_2$" to denote the fact that A_1 conforms to A_2. This choice might seem contradictory after the previous discussion, in fact, in general $A_1 \leq A_2$ does not entail $A_1 \subseteq A_2$. However, with symbol "$\leq$" we capture the fact that A_1 will actually produce a subset of the conversations forseen by the role, *when interacting with entities that play the other roles in the protocol* (see Propositions 1 and 2). This is what we expect from a conformant policy and from our definition of interoperability.

Definition 7 (Conformant simulation). *Given two FSA's A_1 and A_2, A_1 is a* conformant simulation *of A_2, written $A_1 \leq A_2$ iff there is a binary relation $\mathcal{R}$ between A_1 and A_2 such that*

1. *$A_1.s_0 \mathcal{R} A_2.s_0$;*
2. *for every outgoing message $\mathsf{m}! \in A_1.L$ and for every state $s_i \in A_1.S$, for every $s_j \in A_2.S$ such that $s_i \mathcal{R} s_j$ and $(s_i, \mathsf{m}!, s_{i+1}) \in A_1.T$, then there is a state $s_{j+1} \in A_2.S$ such that $(s_j, \mathsf{m}!, s_{j+1}) \in A_2.T$ and $s_{i+1} \mathcal{R} s_{j+1}$;*
3. *for every incoming message $\mathsf{m}? \in A_2.L$ and for every state $s_j \in A_2.S$, for every $s_i \in A_1.S$ such that $s_i \mathcal{R} s_j$ and $(s_j, \mathsf{m}?, s_{j+1}) \in A_2.T$, then there is a state $s_{i+1} \in A_1.S$ such that $(s_i, \mathsf{m}?, s_{i+1}) \in A_1.T$ and $s_{i+1} \mathcal{R} s_{j+1}$.*

Particularly relevant is the case in which A_2 is a role in a protocol and A_1 is a policy implementation. Notice that, in this case, conformance is defined only w.r.t. the role that the single policy implements, *independently* from the rest of the protocol. As anticipated above, Definition 7 does not imply the fact that "$A_1 \leq A_2$ entails $A_1 \subseteq A_2$". Instead, the following proposition holds.

Proposition 1. *Let $A_1 \otimes \cdots \otimes A_i \otimes \cdots \otimes A_n$ be a protocol, and A'_i a policy such that $A'_i \leq A_i$, then $A_1 \otimes \cdots \otimes A'_i \otimes \cdots \otimes A_n \subseteq A_1 \otimes \cdots \otimes A_i \otimes \cdots \otimes A_n$.*

This proposition catches the intuition that a conformant policy is able to produce a subset of the legal conversations defined by the protocol but only when it is executed in the context given by the protocol.

The above proposition can be generalized in the following way. Here we consider a set of policies that have been individually proved as being conformant simulations of the various roles in a protocol. The property states that the dialogues that such policies can produce will be legal *w.r.t. the protocol.*

Proposition 2. *Let $A_1 \otimes \cdots \otimes A_n$ be a protocol and let $A'_1, \ldots, A'_n$ be n policies such that $A'_i \leq A_i$, for $i = 1, \ldots, n$, then $A'_1 \otimes \cdots \otimes A'_n \subseteq A_1 \otimes \cdots \otimes A_n$*

In order to prove interoperability we need to prove that our policies will actually produce a conversation when interacting, while so far we have only proved that if a conversation will be generated, it will be legal. By assumption, in a protocol it is always possible to conclude a conversation whatever the point at which the interaction arrived. We expect a similar property to hold also for a set of policies that have been proved conformant to the roles of a protocol. The relation $\leq$ is too weak, so we need to introduce the notion of *complete conformant simulation*.

Definition 8 (Complete conformant simulation). *Given two FSA's A_1 and A_2 we say that A_1 is a* complete conformant simulation *of A_2, written $A_1 \trianglelefteq A_2$, iff A_1 is a conformant simulation of A_2 under a binary relation $\mathcal{R}$ and*

– *for all* $s_i \in A_1.F$ *such that* $s_i \mathcal{R} s_j$*, then* $s_j \in A_2.F$*;*
– *for all* $s_j \in A_2.S$ *such that* s_j *is alive and* $s_i \mathcal{R} s_j$*,* $s_i \in A_1.S$*, then* s_i *is alive.*

Now, we are in the position to give the following fundamental result.

Theorem 1 (Interoperability). *Let* $A_1 \otimes \cdots \otimes A_n$ *be a protocol and let* $A'_1, \ldots, A'_n$ *be* n *policies such that* $A'_i \trianglelefteq A_i$*, for* $i = 1, \ldots, n$*. For any common string* $\overline{\sigma'}$ *of* $A'_1 \otimes \cdots \otimes A'_n$ *and* $A_1 \otimes \cdots \otimes A_n$ *there is a run* $\sigma'\sigma''$ *of the protocol such that* $\overline{\sigma'\sigma''}$ *is an accepted string of* $A'_1 \otimes \cdots \otimes A'_n$*.*

Intuitively, whenever two policies, that have independently been proved conformant to the two roles of a protocol, start an interaction, thanks to Proposition 2, they will be able to conclude their interaction producing a legal accepted run. Therefore, Theorem 1 implies Definition 6 (interoperability).

4 Conclusions and Related Works

In this work we have given a definition of conformance and of interoperability that is suitable to application in open environments, like the web. Protocols have been formalized in the simplest possible way (by means of FSA) to capture the essence of interoperability and to define a fine-grain conformance test.

The issue of conformance is widely studied in the literature in different research fields, like multi-agent systems (MAS) [11] and service-oriented computing (SOA). In particular, in the area of MAS, in [7,5] we have proposed two preliminary versions of the current proposal, the former, based on a trace semantics, consisting in an inclusione test, the latter, disregarding the case of different branching structures. The second technique was also adapted to web services [8]. Both works were limited to protocols with only two roles while, by means of the framework presented in this paper we can deal with protocols with an arbitrary finite number of roles. Inspired to this work the proposal in [1]: here an abductive framework is used to verify the conformance of services to a choreography with any number of roles. The limit of this work is that it does not consider the cases in which policies and roles have different branching structures. The first proposal of a formal notion of conformance in a declarative setting is due to Endriss *et al.* [13], the authors, however, do not prove any relation between their definitions of conformance and interoperability. Moreover, they consider protocols in which two partners strictly alternate in uttering messages.

In the SOA research field, conformance has been discussed by Foster *et al.* [14], who defined a system that translates choreographies and orchestrations in labeled transition systems so that it becomes possible to apply model checking techniques and verify properties of theirs. In particular, the system can check if a service composition complies with the rules of a choreography by equivalent interaction traces. Violations are highlighted back to the engineer. Once again, as we discussed, basing on traces can be too much restrictive. In [10], instead, “conformability bisimulation” is defined, a variant of the notion of bisimulation. This is the only work that we have found in which different branching structures are considered but, unfortunately, the test is too strong. In fact, with reference to Figure 1, it excludes the cases (b) and (c), and it also excludes cases (a) and (d) from Figure 2, which do not compromise interoperability. A recent proposal, in this same line, is [24], which suffers of the same limitations. In other approaches, like [19,12], bisimulation is used to check that an implementation respects its specification, given at design time; in this case there is no reuse of software.

References

1. M. Alberti, F. Chesani, M. Gavanelli, E. Lamma, P. Mello, and M. Montali. An abductive framework for a-priori verification of web services. In *Principles and Practice of Declarative Programming, PPDP'06)*. ACM Press, 2006.
2. M. Alberti, D. Daolio, P. Torroni, M. Gavanelli, E. Lamma, and P. Mello. Specification and verification of agent interaction protocols in a logic-based system. In *ACM SAC 2004*, pages 72–78. ACM, 2004.
3. G. Alonso, F. Casati, H. Kuno, and V. Machiraju. *Web Services*. Springer, 2004.
4. André Arnold. *Finite Transition Systems*. Pearson Education, 1994.
5. M. Baldoni, C. Baroglio, A. Martelli, and Patti. Verification of protocol conformance and agent interoperability. In *Post-Proc. of CLIMA VI*, volume 3900 of *LNCS State-of-the-Art Survey*, pages 265–283. Springer, 2006.
6. M. Baldoni, C. Baroglio, A. Martelli, and V. Patti. Reasoning about interaction protocols for customizing web service selection and composition. *J. of Logic and Algebraic Programming, special issue on Web Services and Formal Methods*, 2006. To appear.
7. M. Baldoni, C. Baroglio, A. Martelli, V. Patti, and C. Schifanella. Verifying protocol conformance for logic-based communicating agents. In *Proc. of CLIMA V*, number 3487 in LNCS, pages 192–212. Springer, 2005.
8. M. Baldoni, C. Baroglio, A. Martelli, V. Patti, and C. Schifanella. Verifying the conformance of web services to global interaction protocols: a first step. In *Proc. of WS-FM 2005*, volume 3670 of *LNCS*, pages 257–271. Springer, September, 2005.
9. Daniela Berardi, Giuseppe De Giacomo, Maurizio Lenzerini, Massimo Mecella, and Diego Calvanese. Synthesis of underspecified composite -services based on automated reasoning. In *ICSOC*, pages 105–114, 2004.
10. N. Busi, R. Gorrieri, C. Guidi, R. Lucchi, and G. Zavattaro. Choreography and orchestration: a synergic approach for system design. In *Proc. of 4th International Conference on Service Oriented Computing (ICSOC 2005)*, 2005.
11. Amit K. Chopra and Munindar P. Singh. Producing compliant interactions: Conformance, coverage, and interoperability. In M. Baldoni and U. Endriss, editors, *Declarative Agent Languages and Technologies IV: Fourth International Workshop, DALT 2006*, LNAI. Springer, Hakodate, Japan, 2006. To appear.
12. G. Decker, J. M. Zaha, and M. Dumas. Execution semantics for service choreographies. In M. Bravetti, M. Núñez, and G. Zavattaro, editors, *Proc. of WS-FM 2006*, volume 4184, pages 163–177. 2006.
13. U. Endriss, N. Maudet, F. Sadri, and F. Toni. Logic-based agent communication protocols. In *Advances in agent communication languages*, volume 2922 of *LNAI*, pages 91–107. Springer-Verlag, 2004. invited contribution.
14. H. Foster, S. Uchitel, J. Magee, and J. Kramer. Model-based analysis of obligations in web service choreography. In *Proc. of IEEE International Conference on Internet&Web Applications and Services 2006*, 2006.
15. R.J. van Glabbeek. Bisimulation. Encyclopedia of Distributed Computing (J.E. Urban & P. Dasgupta, eds.), Kluwer, 2000. Available at `http://Boole.stanford.edu/pub/DVI/bis.dvi.gzz`.

16. F. Guerin and J. Pitt. Verification and Compliance Testing. In H.P. Huget, editor, *Communication in Multiagent Systems*, volume 2650 of *LNAI*, pages 98–112. Springer, 2003.
17. B. Heckel. *Thinking Java.* Prentice Hall, 2005.
18. Gerard J. Holzmann. *The SPIN Model Checker : Primer and Reference Manual.* Addison-Wesley Professional, 2003.
19. R. Kazhamiakin and M. Pistore. Choreography conformance analysis: Asynchronous communications and information alignment. In M. Bravetti, M. Núñez, and G. Zavattaro, editors, *Proc. of WS-FM 2006*, volume 4184, pages 227–241. 2006.
20. Niels Lohmann, Peter Massuthe, Christian Stahl, and Daniela Weinberg. Analyzing Interacting BPEL Processes. In *Business Process Management, 4th International Conference, BPM 2006, Vienna, Austria, September 5-7, 2006, Proceedings*, volume 4102 of *Lecture Notes in Computer Science*, pages 17–32. Springer-Verlag, September 2006.
21. R. Milner. *Communication and Concurrency*. Prentice Hall, 1989.
22. OMG. Unified modeling language: Superstructure, 2005.
23. W.M.P. van der Aalst. Business alignment: Using process mining as a tool for delta analysis and conformance testing. *Requirements Engineering Journal*, 10(3):198–211, 2005.
24. X. Zhao, H. Yang, and Z. Qui. Towards the formal model and verification of web service choreography description language. In M. Bravetti, M. Núñez, and G. Zavattaro, editors, *Proc. of WS-FM 2006*, volume 4184, pages 273–287. 2006.

A Business-Aware Web Services Transaction Model

Mike P. Papazoglou and Benedikt Kratz

Tilburg University, Infolab
P.O. Box 90153, 5000 LE Tilburg, The Netherlands
{mikep, B.Kratz}@uvt.nl

Abstract. Advanced business applications typically involve well-defined standard business functions such as payment processing, shipping and tracking, managing market risk and so on, which apply to a variety of application scenarios. Although such business functions drive transactional applications between trading partners they are completely external to current Web services transaction mechanisms as they are only expressed as part of application logic. To remedy this situation, this paper proposes a business aware Web services transaction model and support mechanisms. The model allows expressing and blending business and QoS aware transactions on the basis of business agreements stipulated in SLAs and business functions.

1 Introduction

As enterprises follow the path to e-business, business processes are becoming increasingly complex and integrated both within internal corporate business functions (e.g., manufacturing, design engineering, sales and marketing, and enterprise services) and across the external supply chain. In this environment there is a clear need for advanced business applications to coordinate multiple Web services into a multi-step business transaction. This requires that several Web service operations or processes attain transactional properties reflecting business semantics, which are to be treated as a single logical (atomic) unit of work. For example, consider, a manufacturer that develops Web service based solutions to automate the order and delivery business functions with its suppliers as part of a business transaction. The transaction between the manufacturer and its suppliers may only be considered as successful once all products are delivered to their final destination, which could be days or even weeks after the placement of the order, and payment has ensued.

In contrast to Web service transactions, which are driven by purely technical requirements such as coordination, data consistency, recovery, and so on, business transactions are driven by economic needs and their objective is accomplished only when the agreed upon conclusion among trading parties is reached, e.g., payment in exchange for goods or services.

This approach requires distilling from the structure of a business collaboration the key capabilities that must necessarily be present in a business transaction

A. Dan and W. Lamersdorf (Eds.): ICSOC 2006, LNCS 4294, pp. 352–364, 2006.

and specifying them accurately and independently of any specific implementation mechanisms. The business transaction then becomes the framework for expressing detailed operational business semantics.

Conventional approaches to business transactions, such as Open EDI (http://www.iso.org) and more recently ebXML, focus only on the documents exchanged between partners, and ignore important constituents in a business transaction such as business operations and their behavioral semantics. A more natural approach to business transactions is to make common business operational requirements and operational level relationships between trading partners first class tenets in a business transaction. This requires providing a common core of well-understood business operational principles (or business transaction functions) such as ordering, transport, distribution and payment that can be rationalized and appropriately combined across any supply chain to create semantically enhanced business transactions. Developers can then build transactional applications by using, combining, and, possibly specializing, these constructs in a similar way that abstract data types are used in programming languages.

This paper focuses on introducing an advanced business transaction model and on providing operational business principles for specifying and modeling business transactions along with their QoS characteristics. The approach taken mimics business operation semantics and does not depend upon underlying technical protocols and implementations. The paper also presents a Business Transaction Model Language (BTML) that is used at design time to specify the elements of a business transaction. Run-time support for this environment is provided by conventional Web services standards such as BPEL, WS-Coordination and WS-Transaction and will be briefly highlighted in the context of a reference architecture. Detailed descriptions of the run-time environment as well as run-time transformations between the BTML and equivalent constructs supported by Web services transaction standards are outside the scope of this paper.

2 The Business Transaction Model

An important requirement in making cross-enterprise business process automation happen is the ability to describe the collaboration aspects of the business processes, such as business commitments, mutual obligations and exchange of monetary resources, in a standard form that can be consumed by tools for business process implementation and monitoring. This gives raise to the concept of a *business transaction model* that encompasses a set of business transaction functions and several standard business primitives and conventions that can be utilized to develop complex business applications involving transactional and monetary exchanges.

Central to the business transaction model is the notion of a business transaction. Business transactions cover many domains of activity that businesses engage in, such as request for quote, supply chain execution, purchasing, manufacturing, and so on. A *business transaction* is defined as a trading interaction between possibly multiple parties that strives to accomplish an explicitly shared business objective, which extends over a possibly long period of time and which is terminated successfully only upon recognition of the agreed conclusions between the interacting parties. A business transaction is driven by well-defined business tasks and events that directly or indirectly contribute to generating economic value, such as processing and paying an insurance claim. If a business transaction completes successfully then each participant will have made consistent state changes, which, in aggregate, reflect the desired outcome of the multi-party business interaction. The purpose of a business transaction is to facilitate specifying common business procedures and practices in the form of business application scenarios that allow expressing business operational semantics and associated message exchanges as well as the rules that govern business transactions. Such rules include operational business conventions, agreements, and mutual obligations. The combination of all these factors characterizes the nature of business relationships among the parties involved in a business transaction. It enforces trading parties to achieve a common semantic understanding of the business transaction and the implications of all messages exchanged.

The business transaction is initiated by a single organization and brings about a consistent change in the state of a business relationship between two or more trading parties. A *business relationship* is any distributed state held by the parties, which is subject to contractual constraints agreed by those parties. A business transaction needs to express features like the parties that are involved in the transaction; the entities under transaction; the destination of payment and delivery; the transaction time frame; permissible operations; links to other transactions; receipts and acknowledgments; and finally, the identification of money transferred outside national boundaries.

The previous definition of a business transaction has been derived from (classical) commerce models and serves as a common high-level, non-technical view of how business organizations interact with each other. The definition emphasizes the operational business view of a transaction. There are four key components in a business transaction model that help differentiate it from (general) message exchange that business processes involve. These are: (1) commitment exchange; (2) the party (or parties) that has the ability to make commitments; (3) business constraints and invariants that apply to the message exchanged between the interacting parties; and (4) business objects (documents) that are operated upon by business activities (transactional operations) or by processes. These terms are introduced and explained below, while Fig. 1 represents them and their inter-relationships in UML.

A *commitment exchange* occurs between two or more interacting *parties* and concerns tasks or functions to be carried out and usually involves formal trading partner agreements. A commitment exchange identifies such things as the overall business process, the partner roles, the business documents used, message and document flow, legal aspects, security aspects, business level acknowledgments and status, and so on. Partners inside a transaction have distinct roles (such as *buyer* and *seller*) and the ability to make commitments, being held responsible for, having rights and obligations, in the context of the business transactions.

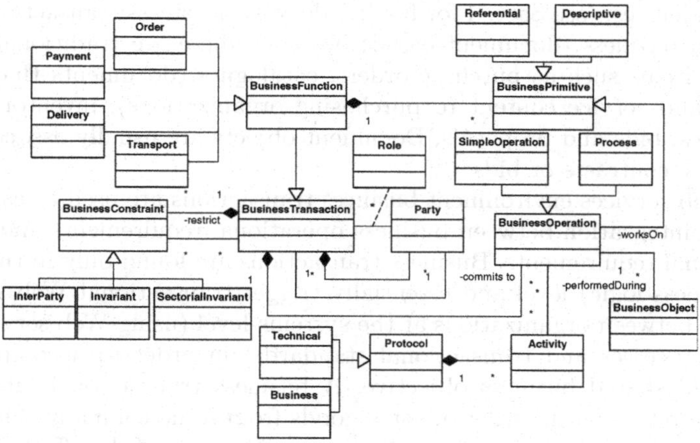

Fig. 1. UML view of a business transaction

One party can act as the initiator of the transaction while the others can act as responders.

A *business transaction constraint* is defined as an explicitly stated rule that prescribes, limits, or specifies any aspect of a business transaction that forms part of the commitment(s) mutually agreed to among the interacting parties. *Business invariants* are constraints external to constraints agreed by interacting parties in a transaction and include universal legal requirements, commercial and/or international trade and contract terms, public policy (e.g., privacy/data protection, product or service labeling, consumer protection), laws and regulations that are applicable to parts of a transaction. Invariants ensure the nature of the business transaction and/or the goods or services delivered while guaranteeing that no regulations are compromised. Business invariants are universal (or horizontal) in nature and apply regardless of the type of business or sector within which the business occurs. There are, however, constraints external to parties that are of a sectorial nature called *Sectorial invariants* which can be found in sectors such as telecommunications, transportation and delivery, financial/banking, and so on. Universal and sectorial invariants can be combined with inter-party business constraints for building application use scenarios. It is important to understand that in such situations invariants take precedence over internal constraints in a business transaction.

Business transactions may be characterized by universally acceptable business operational primitives (or simply business functions), which represent functions that are critical to the conduct of business. A *business function* is a description of a well-defined and commonly acceptable critical business principle, e.g., payment or delivery of goods or services, that transforms business values and causes state changes to transaction participants, e.g., transforms an unpaid order to paid order. To achieve this the business function uses contextually aware polymorphic business operations, e.g., cancel an order or cancel a payment, constraints and dependencies, (see Sect. 4 for further details). Business transactions usually operate on business (document-based) objects. These are traditionally associated with items such as purchase orders, catalogues (documents that describe products and service content to purchasing organizations), inventory reports, ship notices, bids and proposals. Document objects are usually associated with agreements, contracts or bids.

In a Web services environment business transactions are used to capture and define the integration between business operational requirements and technical transactional requirements. Business transactions are found only in the application (business-logic) level and essentially trigger transactional Web service interactions between organizations at the systems-level (using Web services-based business processes and transactional standards) in order to accomplish some well-defined shared business objective. A business transaction in its simplest form could represent an order of some goods from some company. The completion of an order results in a consistent change in the state of the affected business: the back-end order database is updated and a document copy of the purchase order is filed. More complex business transactions may involve activities such as payment processing, shipping and tracking, determining new product offerings, granting/extending credit, and so on.

At run-time the business transaction model requires support from systems-level transactional frameworks provided by Web Services standards that include the Web Services Coordination and Transaction [1,2,3] and the Web Services Composite Application Framework (WS-CAF) [4]. Objective of systems-level transactional support is to automate the internal flow of transaction processing, spanning multiple disparate applications provide solutions for reliable, consistent, and recoverable composition of back-end services. Important systems-related aspects of a business transaction include features like the ability to support long-running interactions; to specify exceptional conditions; to support compensatible and contingency transactions; to make use of alternate transactions; to reconcile and link transactions with other transactions; to support secure transactions and to allow transactions to be monitored, audited/logged and recovered.

3 Integrated Logistics Example

In this section we present a simple integrated logistics example based on standard business protocol RosettaNet PIPs [5], which we shall enhance in subsequent sections with transactional functions and business operational semantics as well as QoS features.

Fig. 2 depicts an integrated logistics scenario involving a customer, suppliers and a logistics service provider. This logistics model consists of forecast notification, forecast acceptance, inventory reporting, shipment receipt, request and fulfil demand, consumption and invoice notification processes provided by RosettaNet PIPs. In Fig. 2 PIP 4A2 supports a process in which a forecast owner sends forecast data to a forecast recipient. PIP 4A5 provides visibility of available

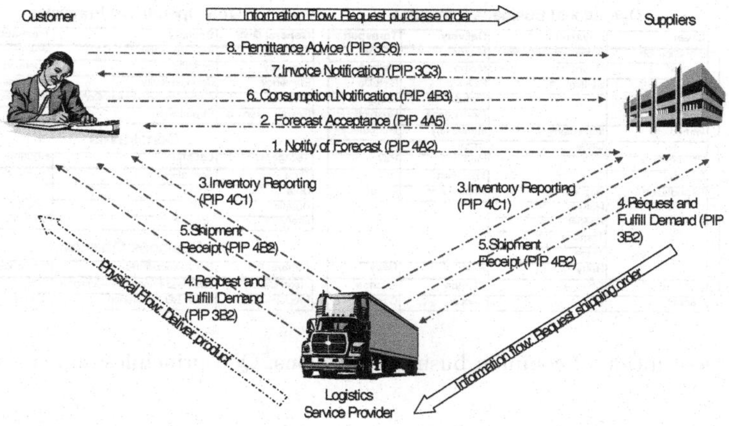

Fig. 2. Integrated logistics example using RosettaNet PIPs

forecasted product quantity between two trading partners. PIP 4C1 supports a process in which an inventory information provider reports the status of the inventory to an inventory user. The inventory report can include any product, active or inactive, held in inventory. PIP 3B2 allows a shipper to notify a receiver that a shipment has been assigned. This notification is often a part of the shipment process. PIP 4B2 supports a process used by a consignee to report the status of a received shipment to another interested party, such as a shipper. The customer then issues an invoice notification (PIP 4B3) to communicate material consumption to the supplier, allowing the supplier to trigger invoicing for the consumed material. PIP 3C3 enables a provider to invoice another party, such as a buyer, for goods or services performed. Finally, PIP 3C6 enables a payer to send remittance advice to a payee (in this case the supplier) which indicates which payables are scheduled for payment.

4 Operational Business Principles and QoS Functions

In the previous we argued for the identification of functional capabilities necessary to support business transactions and introduced the concept of critical business functions. Figure 3 describes the elements of the business functions in the business transaction model which is described schematically in Fig. 1. Note that Fig. 3 due to reasons of brevity depicts only constraints and not invariants. In particular, this figure illustrates that the business transaction model divides trade into four broad areas - ordering, paying, delivery and transportation, which are referred to as *operational business principles* (or business functions) in this figure. These areas represent common business functions that are generic, industry neutral and re-usable and can be used to develop business transactions in a multiplicity of business scenarios. In this way we remove excess complexity from the business transaction, allowing common business functions such as ordering,

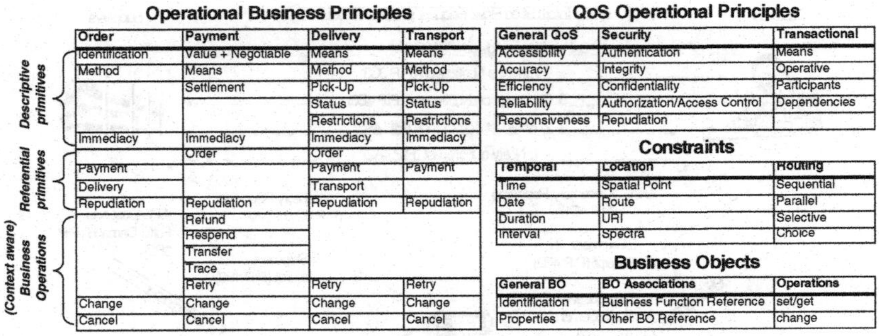
Operational Business Principles
QoS Operational Principles
Descriptive primitives
Referential primitives
(Context aware) Business Operations
Order
Payment
Delivery
Transport
Identification
Value + Negotiable
Means
Means
Method
Means
Method
Method
Settlement
Pick-Up
Pick-Up
Status
Status
Restrictions
Restrictions
Immediacy
Immediacy
Immediacy
Immediacy
Order
Order
Payment
Payment
Payment
Delivery
Transport
Repudiation
Repudiation
Repudiation
Repudiation
Refund
Respend
Transfer
Trace
Retry
Retry
Retry
Change
Change
Change
Change
Cancel
Cancel
Cancel
Cancel
General QoS
Security
Transactional
Accessibility
Authentication
Means
Accuracy
Integrity
Operative
Efficiency
Confidentiality
Participants
Reliability
Authorization/Access Control
Dependencies
Responsiveness
Repudiation
Constraints
Temporal
Location
Routing
Time
Spatial Point
Sequential
Date
Route
Parallel
Duration
URI
Selective
Interval
Spectra
Choice
Business Objects
General BO
BO Associations
Operations
Identification
Business Function Reference
set/get
Properties
Other BO Reference
change

Fig. 3. Description of common business functions, QoS principles and constraints

distribution and payment to be expressed in a form analogous to abstract data types and rationalizing them across an integrated supply chain.

Figure 3 shows that each business function uses a number of *descriptive primitives* (or attributes) that describe a certain business function, e.g., the means of payment. There are also *referential primitives* that refer to other business functions, e.g., payment refers to an associated order. Finally, the *context aware business operations* introduce a set of polymorphic business operations that collectively transform business values and cause state changes to the business transaction participants.

Business functions not only help streamline and rationalize common business practices across an integrated supply chain, they also help enforce participant commitments. They introduce a mandatory set of four *business level atomicity criteria* that reflect the operational semantics the four standard business functions (ordering, payment, delivery and transportation). For instance, payment atomicity affects the transfer of funds from one party to another in the transaction. This means that the transaction would fail if payment is not made within a pre-specified time period that was agreed between a supplier and a customer. Delivery atomicity, on the other hand, implies that the right goods will be delivered to a customer at the time that has been agreed.

Each atomicity criterion is treated as a single indivisible logical unit of work, which determines a set of viable outcomes for a business transaction. The outcomes of a business transaction may involve non-critical partial failures, or selection among contending service offerings, rather than the strict *all-or-nothing* assumption of conventional ACID transactions, and govern the duration and character of participation in a transaction. They also allow provisional results to be revealed deliberately to allow such business activities as probabilistic inventory management. Atomicity criteria can be characterized as *vital* or *non-vital*. If a business level atomicity criterion is characterized as vital and fails then the transaction aborts at the system-level. If, however, the atomicity criterion is characterized as non-vital then a contingency activity may be issued in case that a given atomicity criterion, e.g., transportation, fails. For instance, using another shipper in case that the chosen one fails to deliver. The above characteristics give

```
Means <!- The means of the delivery (depends on nature of goods) -->
•setMeans
        •setChannel
                •Online <!- intangible goods --> / offline <!- tangible goods -->
        •setDeliveryMeans
                •Air / Sea / Ground / Combinations
Method <!- Method of the delivery -->
•setDeliveryMethod <!- How will goods be delivered (e.g., batch, all in once, etc) -->
        •setNumberOfDeliveries <!- How often will goods be delivered (if in batches) -->
•setDeliveryOptions
        •Express
                •Type
                        •Next day / Two day / ...
                        •Boolean Delivery_Signature_Required
•setTransportCompany <!- Which company is responsible for the transport -->
        •setTransportCompanyDetails
•setDeliveryPeriod
        •Temporal
```

Fig. 4. Describing the *delivery* business function attributes

the ability to a business transaction to explicitly describe business operational semantics, specify the proper behavior of common business functions and their implications in case of success or failure.

The business transaction model not only expresses the purpose of each business collaboration interaction but is also capable of capturing the timing and sequence of message exchanges. The model has fixed sequencing semantics which require that *ordering* occurs first and is followed by *transport* and *delivery*. *Payment* can happen before or after the *delivery* function. For instance, in the integrated logistics scenario described in the previous section, there might be an implicit or explicit agreement that the delivery of goods must take place before the payment and that payment always follows the confirmation of an order. This situation is depicted by the following code snippet that uses BTML:

```
<BTx>
 <name>LogisticsScenario</name> ...
 <sequence>
  <BF> <name>Order</name> </BF>
  <BF> <name>Delivery</name> </BF>
  <BF> <name>Payment</name> </BF> ...
 </sequence>
</BTx>
```

By using these constructs, each participant can understand and plan for conformance to the business protocol being employed.

Figure 4 shows two of the attributes of the *delivery* business function. These are *means* and *method* which describe the means and method of delivery, respectively. The *delivery* business function is seen from Fig. 3 to also use referential primitives to refer to such other functions as *payment*, and *transport*. It also uses context aware polymorphic business operations, such as *retry* to retry a failed delivery, *change* to change a delivery and *cancel* to cancel a delivery. All attributes and operations in Fig. 3 have been defined and formalized and are available on request.

Finally, an important element of the business model is the quality of service required from the functional capabilities for the business transactions. For instance, one of the referential primitives used in business functions such as ordering, payment, transport and delivery, is the issue of non-repudiation using digital signatures, see Fig. 3. In this way business transactions can also become QoS-aware and QoS principles can be blended with constraints and business requirements enforced by the business functions. Other QoS primitives that can be attached to a business transaction and govern its behavior may include general QoS primitives such as desired performance rates, mean time to respond, accessibility periods, time-to-repair a service that has failed, desirable security protocols and tokens, and so on. These are also depicted in Fig. 3. QoS criteria can be registered in a Service Level Agreement, which specifies the agreements and commitments of trading partners involved in a business transaction. More specifically, they form part of the agreed service-level objectives, which define the levels of service that both the service customers and the service providers agree on, and usually include a set of service level indicators, like availability, performance and reliability.

5 Business Transaction Reference Architecture

The reference architecture that supports the business transaction model is depicted in Fig. 5. Application scenarios are specified by using the business related aspects of the model, e.g., business principles, constraints, QoS criteria, and so forth. Both the business aspects of the model are connected to a runtime infrastructure providing the system-level support for executing a business transaction. Each business level construct is appropriately mapped to a corresponding infrastructure primitive(s) that that can be found in Web services standards, such as BPEL, WS-Coordination, WS-AtomicTransaction and WS-BusinessActivity. For instance, constructs such as activities, sequences and roles map directly to BPEL constructs as presented in [6], while vital business level atomicity criteria map directly to WS-AtomicTransaction and non-vital atomicity criteria map to WS-BusinessActivity. Currently, the above set of Web services standards is used to implement business transactions. This infrastructure is based on open an source implementation framework provided by JBoss Transactions (http://www.jboss.org) which supports the latest Web services transactions standards, providing all of the components necessary to build interoperable, reliable, multi-party, Web services-based applications quickly and easily.

Figure 5 also shows how QoS criteria can be registered in an SLA. An SLA contains several entries that are related to a business transaction. These include the scope of the agreement (the services covered in the agreement), penalties (sanctions should apply in case the service provider under-performs and is unable to meet the objectives specified in the SLA), optional services (any services that are not normally required by the user, but might be required in case of an exception) and exclusion terms (specify what is not covered in the SLA). QoS criteria in the context of a business transaction are expressed as assertions by an assertion sub-language of BTML. This assertion language is an extension of the WS-Policy assertion language [7] thereby reusing existing functionality like

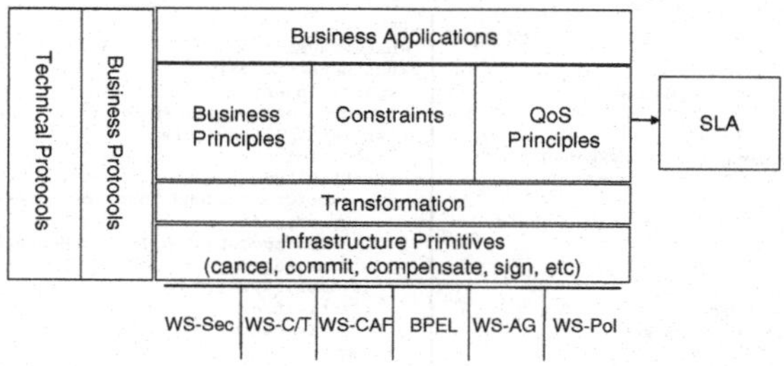

Fig. 5. Business transaction reference architecture

normal form, referential and combined policies. BTML's assertion language also contains context specific assertion definitions for a business transaction. This part of the BTML can then be incorporated as guarantee terms into agreements templates specified by WS-Agreement [8] to enable the specification, negotiation and acceptance of SLAs that are used to drive business transactions.

Finally, the reference architecture supports the use of business and technical protocols in the context of the business transaction model. Currently, the architecture supports one business protocol namely, RosettaNet, and one technical protocol, the Secure Electronic Transactions (SET) [9]. In the following section we however concentrate on illustrating how to semantically enhance the RosettaNet business protocol, which lacks the notion of a business transaction as defined in Sect. 2, by injecting into it business functions, explicit sequencing of interactions, partner commitments and constraints.

6 Emulating Business and Technical Protocols

In this section we will illustrate how we can supplant transactional primitives into the integrated logistics scenario in Fig. 2 to semantically enhance the operational characteristics of the interacting RosettaNet processes.

This procedure is performed according to the following steps. We start first by grouping the individual PIPs into related sets that realize a specific common business function. We observe that PIPs 4A2, 4A5 and 4C1 are all part of the *order* business function. PIP 3B2 is part of the *transport* function and PIPs 4B2 and 4B3 are part of the *delivery* function. The *payment* function is covered by PIPs 3C3 and 3C6.

Following this we need to capture the message and commitment exchange requirements between any trading partners, identifying the timing and sequence of message exchanges. We assume that the trading partners have agreed on a business protocol (developed on the basis of RosettaNet) which requires that *payment* follows *order* and *delivery*. This is specified in BTML as shown in Sect 4. Subsequently, we can specify the business functions using BTML. We assume that in the integrated logistics example the customer and the supplier have agreed on an all or nothing express delivery method, which specifies that

Listing 1

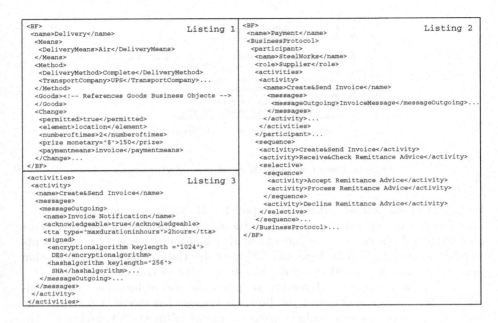

```
<BF>
 <name>Delivery</name>
  <Means>
   <DeliveryMeans>Air</DeliveryMeans>
  </Means>
  <Method>
   <DeliveryMethod>Complete</DeliveryMethod>
   <TransportCompany>UPS</TransportCompany>...
  </Method>
  <Goods><!-- References Goods Business Objects -->
  </Goods>
  <Change>
   <permitted>true</permitted>
   <element>location</element>
   <numberoftimes>2</numberoftimes>
   <prize monetary="$">150</prize>
   <paymentmeans>invoice</paymentmeans>
  </Change>...
</BF>
```

Listing 2

```
<BF>
 <name>Payment</name>
 <BusinessProtocol>
  <participant>
   <name>SteelWorks</name>
   <role>Supplier</role>
   <activities>
    <activity>
     <name>Create&Send Invoice</name>
      <messages>
       <messageOutgoing>InvoiceMessage</messageOutgoing>...
      </messages>
     </activity>...
    </activities>
   </participant>...
   <sequence>
    <activity>Create&Send Invoice</activity>
    <activity>Receive&Check Remittance Advice</activity>
    <selective>
     <sequence>
      <activity>Accept Remittance Advice</activity>
      <activity>Process Remittance Advice</activity>
     </sequence>
     <activity>Decline Remittance Advice</activity>
    </selective>
   </sequence>...
  </BusinessProtocol>...
</BF>
```

Listing 3

```
<activities>
 <activity>
  <name>Create&Send Invoice</name>
  <messages>
   <messageOutgoing>
    <name>Invoice Notification</name>
    <acknowledgeable>true</acknowledgeable>
    <tta type="maxdurationinhours">2hours</tta>
    <signed>
     <encryptionalgorithm keylength ="1024">
      DES</encryptionalgorithm>
     <hashalgorithm keylength="256">
      SHA</hashalgorithm>...
   </messageOutgoing>...
  </messages>
 </activity>
</activities>
```

Fig. 6. Listings of BTML snippets

if the goods are ready for transport the delivery should not take more than two days (which requires delivery by air). The specification in BTML can be found in Listing 1 of Fig. 6. Listing 1 also specifies that the delivery location is changeable at most twice at a cost of 150 $ per time and that the fees will be added to the original invoice. Listing 2 of the same figure specifies part of a simple payment protocol seen from the vantage point of the supplier. Finally, Listing 3 adds QoS properties to the elements of the business transaction. In particular, we may wish to indicate that the InvoiceNotification process (PIP 3C in Fig. 2) requires that the time to acknowledge an Invoice Notification message send from the Create&Send Invoice activity of the Supplier to the Receive Invoice activity of the Customer is no longer then 2 hours. This property can be specified using the Responsiveness primitive in the General QoS field in Fig. 3. The QoS Responsiveness primitive has an operator called setAcknowledgeable that specifies whether a particular message should or should not be acknowledgeable and also the time frame for this to happen. We may also wish to add other QoS constraints on messages or message parts. For example we may wish to specify further security primitives indicating whether or not a message or message part should be non-reputable or signed with a particular hash and encryption function. All of this can be specified in BTML as shown in Listing 3 of Fig 6.

Another important aspect of the business reference architecture is that it can blend business with technical protocols. For instance, the business application that we sketched in the previous does not have any concrete way to handle the actual payment so that it can transfer funds using a financial service provider.

This situation also holds for the RosettaNet PIPs. To remedy this situation we also extended the payment part of the business transaction described in the previous with a technical protocol, such as SET, that guarantees secure payments [10].

7 Related Work

Automated business transactions are a new category of research, wider than historical data-centric local, distributed of federated transactions. This *third generation* of transaction management builds out from core transactional technology, particularly the concept of a open nested transactions and multi-phase distributed outcomes (*two-phase commit* in conventional database/messaging transactions). Research in this paper was inspired by the work found in [11], which motivates the need for using transactions that mimic real business exchanges and presents an overview of several technologies and protocols that may support a business transaction framework. Research in the business transactions area is also related to the creation of meta-models for Web service transaction models. In [12], a meta-modeling approach to transaction management is proposed; that approach however focuses on the modeling and representation of transaction models driven purely from database technology perspective without taking into account business and workflow requirements. To support our implementation efforts, the work found in [13] is used, where the authors propose to combine multiple transaction models as WS-C coordination types into BPEL specifications that can support transactional workflows. The work reported in this paper can also benefit from other ongoing research in the SOC domain. Of particular interest is the work on SLAs reported in [14]. Here, the authors define a template-based approach that enables automated service provisioning. This provisioning can be guided by the WS-Agreement [8] protocol. Finally, the work reported in [15] is quite relevant as it describes many non-functional properties applicable for Web services that can also benefit business transactions.

8 Summary

In the previous we have described a business transaction model, business transaction specification language and associated reference architecture. Key characteristics of this model is that it sharply distinguishes between a business related and a systems related view of transactions. At the business-level, the transactions of our model are weaved around commonly standard business functions that apply to a variety of application scenarios and can represent business exchanges, the sequencing and timing, business agreements stipulated in SLAs, liabilities and dispute resolution policies, and blends these transactions with QoS criteria. Business transactions in the systems-level retain the driving ambition of consistency and provide support for conventional ACID as well as open-nested long-running transactions. Implementation of the systems-level services is currently provided by Web services standards like BPEL, WS-Coordination, and WS-Transaction.

The potential benefits of this approach arise largely from its ability to standardize common business functions, better align business processes with business objectives and provide information to enable monitoring and troubleshooting of problems and delays. Business decisions can be made at every step of the business transaction to align it with business objectives and to alleviate undesirable conditions. For example, in case of a purchase order cancellation due to a faulty part, an order transaction can automatically reserve a suitable replacement product and notify the billing and inventory processes of the changes. When all interactions between the various business processes have been completed and the new adjusted schedule is available, the purchase order Web service notifies the customer sending her an updated invoice.

References

1. Cabrera, L.F., et al.: Web Services Coordination (2005)
2. Cabrera, L.F., et al.: Web Services Atomic Transaction (2005)
3. Cabrera, L.F., et al.: Web Services Business Activity Framework (2005)
4. Bunting, D., et al.: Web Services Composite Application Framework (2003)
5. RosettaNet: Standards required to support xml-based b2b integration (2001) http://xml.coverpages.org/rosettanetStandardsForIntegration.pdf.
6. Khalaf, R.: From rosettanet pips to bpel processes: A three level approach for business protocols. In BPM, Proceedings. Volume 3649 of LNCS (2005) 364–373
7. Bajaj, S., et al.: Web Services Policy 1.2 - Framework (WS-Policy). W3C (2006) http://www.w3.org/Submission/WS-Policy/.
8. Andrieux, A., et al.: Web Services Agreement Specification (WS-Agreement). TR, Grid Resource Allocation Agreement Protocol (GRAAP) WG (2005)
9. Merkow, M.S., et al.: Building SET Applications for Secure Transactions. Wiley & Sons, USA (1998)
10. Kratz, B.: Emulating SET in BTML. ITRS 30, Infolab, Tilburg University (2006)
11. Papazoglou, M.: Web services and business transactions. World Wilde Web: Internet and Web Information Systems **6**(1) (2003) 49–91
12. Hrastnik, P., Winiwarter, W.: Using advanced transaction meta-models for creating transaction-aware web service environments. International Journal of Web Information Systems **1**(2) (2005) 89–99
13. Tai, S., et al.: Transaction policies for service-oriented computing. Data & Knowledge Engineering **51** (2004) 59–79
14. Ludwig, H., et al.: Template based automated service provisioning supporting the agreement driven service life-cycle. In ICSOC 2005, Proceedings. Volume 3826 of LNCS (2005) 283–295
15. O'Sullivan, J., et al.: Formal description of non-functional service descriptions. TR, QUT (2005) http://www.bpm.fit.qut.edu.au/about/docs/non-functional.jsp.

Licensing Services: Formal Analysis and Implementation

G.R. Gangadharan and Vincenzo D'Andrea

Department of Information and Communication Technology,
University of Trento,
Via Sommarive, 14, Trento, 38050 Italy
gr@dit.unitn.it, dandrea@dit.unitn.it

Abstract. The distribution of services spanning across organizational boundaries raises problems related to intellectual value that are less explored in service oriented research. Being a way to manage the rights between service consumers and service providers, licenses are critical to be considered in services. As the nature of services differs significantly from traditional software and components, services prevent the direct adoption of software and component licenses. We propose a formalisation of licensing clauses specific to services for unambiguous definition of a license. We extend Open Digital Rights Language to implement the clauses of service licensing, making a service license compatible with all the existing service standards.

1 Introduction

Service oriented computing (SOC) is an emerging distributed systems paradigm referring to systems structured as networks of loosely coupled, communicating services [1]. While software behaves as a stand-alone application, services intend making network-accessible operations available anywhere and anytime.

In contrast to traditional software components [2], the functionality of a service resides and runs at the provider's host in a distributed way beyond organizational boundaries, and consumers are not required to download the service executable for consuming the service. While components encapsulate coarse grained functionalities, the granularity of services could range from finer to coarse. Further, services allow the applications to be constructed on-the-fly and to be reused everywhere.

As service oriented applications are rapidly penetrating the society, there arises a need for governing their access and distribution. Although services are software fragments, the distinguishing characteristics of services preclude them to be licensed under traditional software / component licenses. While we do not intend to discuss the similarities and differences between services and components in general, we explicate the significant differences of services with respect to the components from the perspective of licensing. In case of components, the provider of a component is responsible for functionality of the component. Components are downloaded and executed in the environment of clients, within

A. Dan and W. Lamersdorf (Eds.): ICSOC 2006, LNCS 4294, pp. 365–377, 2006.

an organization. Services could span across different participating organizations. Services run through provider and the responsibility for operations of a service is more complex than that of components. We have explored in [3] the dimensions of services inducing a new paradigm of licensing. Nevertheless, being services accessed and consumed in a number of ways, there is the need to carefully define a set of licenses suitable for services.

Researches focus mainly on the expression of functional as well as non-functional properties of services. There exists an obvious paucity of licensing clauses for a service and embedding a license within a service. In order to fulfill this gap, we study the strategy of implementing licenses within a service. The salient features of our approach are:

- Formal representation of licensing clauses to unambiguously describe a service license.
- Extension of Open Digital Rights Language (ODRL) to encompass the service licensing clauses.

As licenses form the basis for distribution of services, in this paper, we elucidate a formal analysis of service licenses together with an implementation scenario of expressing the licensing terms in services. We describe by presenting various examples how a service interface and realization could be exploited by other services in Section 2. Section 3 compares various languages illustrating functional and non-functional properties of services as complementary to WSDL and elucidates their lack of expressiveness in describing the clauses of licensing. The formal description of licenses are presented in Section 4. We implement some of the service licensing clauses by extending ODRL in Section 5. Finally, we illustrate licensing of a service by extended ODRL in Section 6.

2 Exploring Service Licensing Clauses

A service is represented by an interface part defining the functionality visible to the external world and an implementation part realizing the interface [4]. In this section, we will analyze some of the prominent combinations of reproduction (or not) of the service interface, relationship between services (compositional properties), and derivation (or not) from the source code.

As service interfaces (WSDL) together with bindings are publicly available, several services could be created with the same interface. These services can vary in their performance and Quality of Service (QoS) issues. However, copying and using the interface with or without modifications are twined with intellectual values.

By the following example, we show how a service could simply be reused by an other service copying the interface directly: Let S_A be a service providing a spell checking operation for words, say, $Spell(word)$. Consider S_A provides this service by wrapping a proprietary word processor (PWP) spell checker API. As the WSDL interface of this service is publicly available, any service, say S_B could copy this interface and the interface of S_A could be used by S_B with or without modifications. Thus, S_B is an another independent service, wrapping an other proprietary word processor (QWP) spell checker API, created by replicating the WSDL of the S_A. Albeit S_A and S_B are performing spell checking, S_A and S_B are two different services, executed separately.

The prominent scenarios on ***reproduction*** of interface with modifications are as follows:

1. The interface of a service could be modified by changing the name of some operations such as for translation i.e. the expression of a service in a language other than that of the original version.
2. The interface of a service could be modified by some changes in the service parameters such as for data translation or by some pre-processing and/or post-processing of the service.

Following the styles of [5] for representing figures, services are denoted by the shadowed rectangular boxes. An operation of a service interface is represented as an Unified Modeling Language package marked by a stereotype $<< desc >>$. The wrapped application for the service is shown on the left side of the service.

The reproduction by interface translation is illustrated in Figure 1. The interface of S_A is translated by S_B to provide a spell checking operation in Italian language, say $Ortografia(parole)$. In this case, S_B translates the interface of S_A and results in the Italian version of S_A as an independent service.

We refer to ***composition*** as the federation of a service with other remote services. In other words, the operations of a composite service relies on the availability of services being composed [6].

Let S_B be a service providing a spell checking operation $Spell(sentence)$ for sentences, that could compose internally operations for spelling of words with a parser. S_B could be designed in such a way (See Figure 2) that $Spell(word)$ of S_B directly invokes the operation of S_A, executing on the host of S_A. In the absence of S_A, S_B fails to perform.

A service could deny or allow to use and/or modify the service realization. A service could allow to use its realization as an executable in an other service. For example, a service S_A could allow its realization to be used as an executable by an other service S_B. However, S_A could restrict S_B not to modify the operations of S_A.

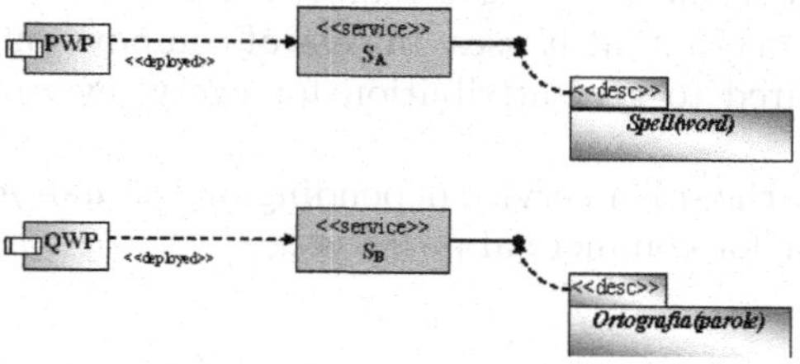

Fig. 1. Reproduction

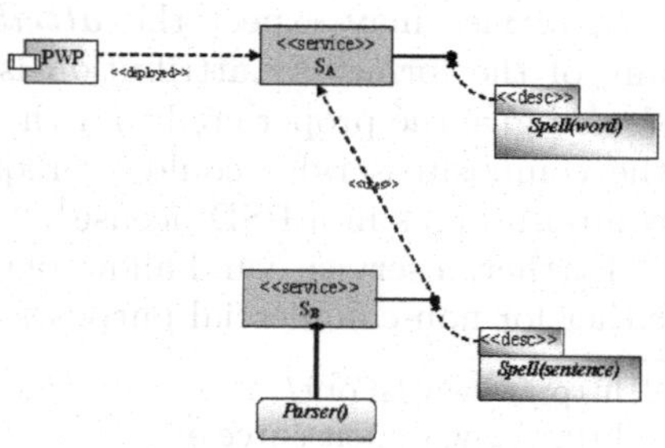

Fig. 2. Composition of Services

A service could allow to modify its realization by other service. The modification of a service realization, termed as ***derivation*** of a service, is an inspiration by Free[1] and Open Source[2] Software (FOSS) movement.

Consider a service S_A providing $Spell(word)$ operation for spell checking of a word. A new service S_B, performing spell checking for a sentence, could be derived from S_A. The derived service S_B contains an operation for parsing $Parser()$ in addition to the operation of S_A. In this case (See Figure 3), S_B significantly modifies the operation of S_A and thus S_B is a derivative service of S_A.

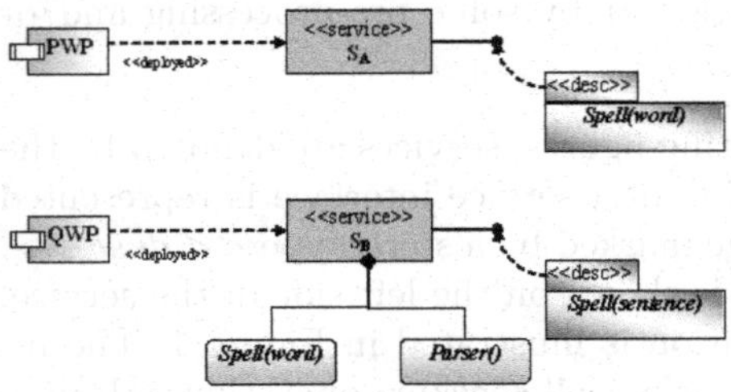

Fig. 3. Normal Derivation

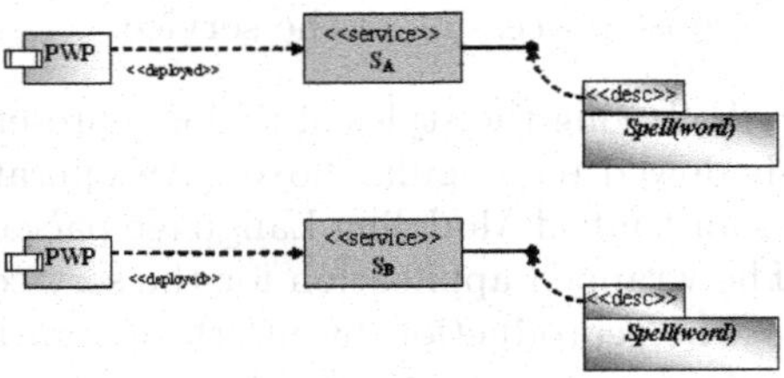

Fig. 4. Replica Derivation

Making replica of a service uses the service realization and service interface. If the WSDL interface as well as realization of a service allows copying, replica services (See Figure 4) are created. Consider S_B as an independent service created by replicating/mirroring the source code of realization and WSDL of S_A. Though S_A and S_B are performing the same operations, S_A and S_B are two different services, executed separately. Theoretically, there will be no differences (may include network delays!) in performances of both the services. Thus, derived service is a manifestation of 'Free Culture'.

Beyond these aspects, a service may expect certain moral rights [7] to be satisfied. A service, S_A, could expect the service, say S_B, being composed / derived / reproducing the interface to reflect the ***same terms and conditions*** of the S_A (Similar to 'Sharealike' of CreativeCommons [8] or Copyleft of GNU[3]).

A service may expect the ***attribution*** for its use by the other service in any of the forms. As attribution is considered a basic requirement, a service should give the proper credit for the service that it uses. In case of composition, the composite service could be required to give attribution for every level of composition as in a BSD license[4].

Further, a service could allow/deny the other service depending on the ***usage*** either for non-commercial purposes or for commercial purposes.

[1] http://www.fsf.org/
[2] http://www.opensource.org/
[3] http://www.gnu.org/copyleft/
[4] http://www.openbsd.org/policy.html

3 Licensing Clauses in Service Descriptions Languages

WSDL is the standard way to describe what a service does. Researches focusing on languages to enhance and to complete the description provided by WSDL are continually in progress. These languages being complementary to WSDL address functional/non-functional properties and business/management information of services with varying levels of details.

Web Service Level Agreement (WSLA): The WSLA framework [9] describes the complete life cycle of a Service Level Agreement (SLA) including SLA establishment by negotiation (signing of a SLA by signatory parties for a given service offering), SLA deployment (checking the validity of the SLA and distributing it), Service level measurement and reporting (configuring the run-time system to meet a set of SLAs and comparing measured SLA parameters against the thresholds defined in the SLA), Management actions (determining SLA violations and corrective management actions to be taken), and SLA termination (specifying the conditions for termination). The WSLA framework enables to specify and monitor a wide variety of SLAs for web services. Based on XML, the WSLA language defines a type system for the various SLA artifacts. A SLA in WSLA is comprised of parties (identifying all the contractual parties), service description (specifying the characteristics of service and the observable parameters like service availability, throughput, or response time), and obligations (defining various guarantees and constraints to be imposed on SLA parameters).

The WSLA language is a general purpose way to express performance characteristics of web services.WSLA encompasses the agreed performance characteristics and the way to evaluate and measure them. However, WSLA does not focus on the rights to be associated with service provider and service consumer.

SLA Notation generator (SLAng): SLAng [10] is a XML based language, for describing Service Level Specifications in the domain of distributed systems and e-business. This language has been modeled by Object Constraints Language (OCL) and Unified Modeling Language (UML) in order to define SLA precisely. SLAng formally defines SLA vocabulary in terms of the behaviour of the services and clients involved in service usage, with reference to a model of service usage. A SLA described in SLAng comprises information on parties involved (end point description of contractors), contractual statements (defining the agreement), and QoS description with the associated metrics (service level specifications). Further, SLAng supports the inter-service composition of SLAs as a description of relationship between possible service behaviors.

Although SLAng has a broader scope beyond web services enabling different types of SLAs, SLAng is silent about the intellectual rights associated with services.

Web Service Offering Language (WSOL): WSOL [11], a language for specifying constraints, management information, and service offering, provides different service levels defined by several classes of services. The same WSDL description with differing constraints (functional, non-functional, and access right) and managerial statements (price, penalty, and responsibility) is referred as 'classes of service' of a web service in WSOL. Consequently, different classes of services could vary in prices and payment models. WSOL offers several reusability elements to enable easier derivation of a new service offering from the existing offerings.

The value of WSOL lies in the simplicity of the negotiation process and the simplified management infrastructure of WSOL.However, WSOL misses the syntax of business and legal contents of contracts.

WS-Policy: WS-Policy [12] provides a general framework to specify and communicate (publish) policies for web services. It is a model for expressing the capabilities, requirements, and general characteristics of a web service as policies. WS-Policy provides a base set of constructs that can be used and extended by other web services specifications to describe a broad range of service requirements, preferences, and capabilities.

WS-Policy defines a policy as a collection of policy alternatives. In turn, each policy alternative comprises a collection of policy assertions. Each policy assertion indicates an individual requirement, capability or other property of a behaviour. WS-policy is one of the fundamental works for specifying policies for web services. However, WS-Policy does not detail the specification of functional constraints, QoS policies, and other related management information.

We have analysed the current attempts by some of the web service languages to describe functional and/or non-functional properties and managerial information of services. Every language describes certain properties of services entirely. Generally, all the standards focus on the QoS and the terms and conditions agreed by the provider and consumer. However, in our view, none of them intensively describe the distribution aspects and the ownership clauses of licensing. The business and legal contractual information are not focused in detailed level by the services research community. The issues of copyrights and moral rights [13] are unexplored by the currently available service description standards. We think, there is a need to be considered to enable a broad usage of service that preserves certain rights of the owner and presents certain rights to the consumer.

From a different perspective, few languages and models capable of expressing a range of licenses are existing in the domain of Digital Rights Management (DRM) [14] for digital contents and multimedia. In the pioneering work of [15], a mathematical model for describing payment and rendering events is described. In [16], the properties of licenses are stated and proved by using deontic logic. LicenseScript [17] based on multi-set rewriting, expresses dynamic conditions of audio/video contents. As these models and languages restrict themselves within the domain of digital contents and multimedia, they could not be adaptable for describing services. Copyrights and other related rights are also not formalised in all these models.

4 Formalising the Service Licenses

A service could allow/deny itself to be used by other services. Further, a service could allow/deny to reuse its interface with or without modification. Allowing or denying composition and derivation influences reuse of services significantly. For drafting a family of machine readable licenses, the clauses of a service license should be unambiguous. We will formalise the clauses of rights detailed in Section 2 to avoid ambiguity in describing service licenses.

Let $\{\text{op}(S_A)\}$ be the set of operations offered by a service S_A. We refer to each clause ($\mathcal{C}$) of the license for service S_A as $\mathcal{C}_{S_A}$.

We define Interface Expressive Power ($\mathcal{E}$) as the degree to which a service interface is explainable, described by the number of operations involved and the number and type of parameters of operations[5]. We define $\mathcal{E}$ as,

$$\mathcal{E} = n + \sum_{i=1}^{n} \left(\frac{\sum_{j=1}^{m} \delta_j}{m} \right)$$

where n is the number of operations of an interface and for each operation, m is the number of parameters. δ_j is the measure of the complexity of the data type. Following WSDL definitions, we consider the values for simple, derived, and complex data types as 1, 2, and 3 respectively.

Derivation (D): Derivation of a service, inspired by FOSS, is a new aspect of creating a new service from existing service, modifying the WSDL interface and implementation. We define a service as a Free/Open Service [18] if the service provides its WSDL interface as well as source code freely available for creating a new and independent service. The open service allows the new service to use a modified version of the original source code. A service S_B is said to be derived from S_A if $\{\text{op}(S_B)\} \supseteq \{\text{op}(S_A)\}$ on satisfying the following two conditions: (i) To exist S_B, S_A should be a Free/Open Service and (ii) S_A and S_B are independent in execution. Normal Derivation (See Figure 3) is represented formally as $\{\text{op}(S_B)\} \supset \{\text{op}(S_A)\}$. Replica Derivation (See Figure 4) is represented by $\{\text{op}(S_B)\} \equiv \{\text{op}(S_A)\}$. In any case of derivation, the $\mathcal{E}$ of the derived service is always higher than or equal to the $\mathcal{E}$ of the service used for derivation. Thus, $\mathcal{E}(S_B) \geq \mathcal{E}(S_A)$. However, network latency issues in delivery of S_A and S_B could exist.

Reproduction (R): Reproduction signifies making a new independent service from an existing service interface. If a service S_A is reproduced as an other independent service S_B, then $\{\text{op}(S_B)\} \neq \{\text{op}(S_A)\}$ and S_A and S_B are independent in execution.

Weyuker's property number 8 of software complexity [19] explicitly states that if a program is a straight renaming of another program, its complexity would be

[5] The interface expressive power of services could be defined based on several metrics. We have considered a few relevant metrics and we do not claim this as an optimal solution. Nevertheless, our general line of thought is not affected by the interface expressive power computation.

same as the original program. Observing this property for a reproduction that unmodifies the interface, the $\mathcal{E}$ of the reproduced service remains unchanged: $\mathcal{E}(S_B) = \mathcal{E}(S_A)$. In case of a reproduced service changing the interface, the $\mathcal{E}$ of the reproduced service could differ from the service being reproduced: $\mathcal{E}(S_B) \neq \mathcal{E}(S_A)$.

Composition (C): Composition is a form of integration of services with value addition provided a composite service could be further composable [20]. Composition of services specifies the participating services, the invocation sequence of services and the methods for handling exceptions [21]. A service S is said to be composite if $\{\text{op}(S)\} \supset \{O_f : O_f \in \{\text{op}(S_i)\}\}$ and $\exists\, S \mid S_i,\, i = [1, .., n]$. O_f could be a single operation or a set of operations adding value addition by combining all or some of the operations of S_i.

Based on Weyuker's properties (property numbers 5 and 9) of software complexity, we propose the $\mathcal{E}$ of a composite service differing from the $\mathcal{E}$ of the composing services obviously. Thus, $\mathcal{E}(\text{S}) \neq \mathcal{E}(S_i,\, S_j)$. Though the underlying assumption of SOC is composition, a service can deny or limit other services to use itself in a composition.

Attribution (A): Attribution means to ascribe a service to the entity responsible for its creator. If a service S_B uses a service S_A, then the attribution to S_A could be formally represented as $A_{S_B} \supset A_{S_A}$. The levelled attribution as in BSD styled service licensing is represented by $A_{S_C} \supset A_{S_B} \supset A_{S_A}$ where the service S_C uses S_B and S_B uses S_A.

Similar Terms (T): A service S_B may expect another service S_A (which uses S_B) to have the same terms as of S_B. In other words, $L(S_A) = L(S_B)$ where S_B uses S_A and $L(S)$ is the service license defined as below.

Non-Commercial Use (N): A service S_B could deny its use for commercial purposes. $N_{S_B} = 1$ implies that an other service S_A could use S_B if S_A is not commercial.

Now, we define the license L of a service S as[6]

$L(S) = (D, R, C, A, T, N)$.

The combinations of these licensing clauses define a family of licenses for services ranging from the most restrictive to the most unrestrictive.

5 Implementing Licenses in Services

Instead of proposing a new language for describing the licensing aspects of services, we could draft the terms and agreements of license using existing rights expression languages. XrML [23] is a comprehensive right expression language,

[6] Further, a service license comprises the financial terms, warranties, indemnification and limitation of warranties, and other clauses [22]. These terms are integral for a legally enforceable license. In this paper, we are primarily concerned with the clauses directly associating the scope of rights of a service license.

created by the ContentGuard Inc.[7], currently the basis of MPEG-21[8]. ContentGuard has a portfolio of patented technologies, covering the distribution and use of digital works and the use of a grammar in connection with the distribution of digital works. Though the terms are not specific to XrML, XrML is restricted to be used for a context covered by the patents. Hence, to obviate any kinds of patent infringements, we avoid XrML for implementing the terms of licenses in services.

Open Digital Rights Language (ODRL) [24] is an open standard language for the expressions of terms and conditions over assets, in open and trusted environments. The models for the ODRL language and data dictionary contain the structure and core semantics for the expressions. These models provide the overall framework for the expressions into which elements can be applied. The core entities of ODRL are as follows:

- *Assets:* a resource being licensed (to be identified uniquely), for instance, a web service.
- *Rights:* rules concerning permissions (the actual usages or activities allowed over the assets), constraints (limits to these permissions), requirements (the obligations needed to exercise the permission), and conditions (the specifications of exceptions that, if become true, expire the permissions and re-negotiation may be required).
- *Parties:* information regarding the service provider, consumer, broker etc.,

With these three entities, ODRL expresses offers (proposals from rights holders for specific rights over their assets) and agreements (contracts or deals between the parties, with specific offers). These core entities together allow for a wide and flexible range of ODRL expressions to be declared.

Our motivations for ODRL as an appropriate rights expression language for describing machine readable licensing agreements for services are as follows:

- ODRL is an open standard language, for expressing rights information.
- Being defined in XML, ODRL provides syntactic and semantic interoperability.
- ODRL is extensible and capable of incorporating specific clauses related to service licenses.
- Several business scenarios across various domains are expressable in ODRL.
- Being published in the World Wide Web Consortium (W3C), ODRL has a wide acceptance
- ODRL is supported by several industries and consortia like the Dublin Core Metadata Initiative (DCMI)[9] and the Open Mobile Alliance (OMA)[10].

With this proposal, we extend ODRL to define the clauses of a service license $L(S)$, by creating a new data dictionary that imports the ODRL expression language schema (See Table 1) to describe the scope of rights of services.

[7] http://www.contentguard.com/
[8] http://www.chiariglione.org/mpeg/standards/mpeg-21/mpeg-21.htm
[9] http://dublincore.org/
[10] http://www.openmobilealliance.org/

Table 1. ODRL/$L(S)$ Data Dictionary Semantics and Schema

ODRL Element	Identifier	Description
Permission	Derivation (D)	The service may be derived.
`<xsd:element name="Derivation" type="o-ex:permissionType" substitutionGroup="o-ex:permissionElement"/>`		
Permission	Reproduction (R)	The service may be reproduced.
`<xsd:element name="Reproduction" type="o-ex:permissionType" substitutionGroup="o-ex:permissionElement"/>`		
Permission	Composition (C)	The service may be composed.
`<xsd:element name="Composition" type="o-ex:permissionType" substitutionGroup="o-ex:permissionElement"/>`		
Requirement	Attribution (A)	The use of service must always include attribution of the service.
`<xsd:element name="Attribution" type="o-ex:requirementType" substitutionGroup="o-ex:requirementElement"/>`		
Constraints	SimilarTerms (T)	The license terms should be same without changed when used/reused.
`<xsd:element name="SimilarTerms" type="o-ex:constraintType" substitutionGroup="o-ex:constraintElement"/>`		
Constraints	NonCommercialUse (N)	The service is for non-commercial purposes.
`<xsd:element name="NonCommercialUse" type="o-ex:constraintType" substitutionGroup="o-ex:constraintElement"/>`		

ODRL/$L(S)$[11] Data Dictionary Semantics expresses the core $L(S)$ semantics in the ODRL.

6 A Scenario of Service Licensing

In order to illustrate our approach, we consider a simple scenario where R is a restaurant service providing the following operations (and parameters): R_0, information on location and opening hours ($address$: $complex$; $hours$: $complex$); R_1, the facility for reserving table ($seats$: $simple$; $name$: $simple$; $reservedTable$: $simple$); R_2, a catalogue of specialty cuisines ($menuType$: $simple$; $listing$: $complex$); R_3, a daily recipe for one of the specialty cuisine ($ingredients$: $complex$; $difficulty$: $simple$; $timeforPreparation$: $simple$; $preparation$: $complex$). In this scenario, the interface expressive power ($\mathcal{E}$) of

[11] Though few semantics of ODRL/$L(S)$ resembles to the ODRL Creative Commons Profile [25], the underlying clauses of a service license and the proposal of implementation within the WSDL of a service differ entirely. The meanings and motivations of ODRL/$L(S)$ data dictionary are related to the field of SOC. To the best of our knowledge, there exists no previous works on the aspects of service licenses using ODRL.

R is given by,

$$\mathcal{E} = n + \sum_{i=1}^{n} \left(\frac{\sum_{j=1}^{m} \delta_j}{m} \right) = 4 + \left(\frac{(3+3)}{2} + \frac{(1+1+1)}{3} + \frac{(1+3)}{2} + \frac{(3+1+1+3)}{4}\right) = 12$$

Consider R having the following clauses of licensing:

1. The license clauses of R may deny the provision of R_3 to other services intended for providing recipe information exclusively that means the service R denies reproduction.
2. R requires a service to be licensed same as R.
3. R allows composite works for noncommercial purposes.

The above clauses could be represented in ODRL/$L(S)$ as follows:

```
<!-- Namespace Declarations -->
<o-ex:offer>
    <o-ex:asset>
        <o-ex:context>
            <o-dd:uid>............</o-dd:uid>
        </o-ex:context>
    </o-ex:asset>
    <o-ex:permission>
        <ls:Composition/>
    </o-ex:permission>
    <o-ex:constraint>
        <ls:NonCommercialUse/>
        <ls:SimilarTerms/>
    </o-ex:constraint>
    <o-ex:requirement>
        <o-dd:attribution/>
    </o-ex:requirement>
</o-ex:offer>
```

From the given licensing clauses of R, it is perceptible that R denies reproduction. A new service could not be created by directly using R. However R allows composition. Assuming R as a non-open service, R forbids derivation.

Another service, F, a restaurant finder service uses R, for the following operations: F_1, a restaurant locator giving a list of restaurants close to a given location and using R_0 (as well as similar operations for other restaurants); F_2, for intermediating table reservation, using R_1; F_3, a daily recipe randomly selected among the recipes provided by the restaurants listed using F (in the case of R, it will use operation R_3). F can use R in a composition even the reproduction is prohibited. R expects SimilarTerms license for F that is using R. In this case, the license terms of F will have to comply with R, for the request and deny provision of F_3 to other services intended to provide the recipe information exclusively (See Table 2).

Table 2. ODRL/$L(S)$ Clauses and Values for Service R

Identifier	Value	Line numbers in ODRL/$L(S)$ listing
Derivation (D)	No	(*Denied*)
Composition (C)	Yes	7 - 9
Reproduction (R)	No	(*Denied*)
Attribution (A)	Yes	14 - 16
SimilarTerms (T)	Yes	10 - 13
NonCommercialUse (N)	Yes	10 - 13

7 Concluding Remarks

Being a way to enable widespread use of services and to manage the rights between service consumers and service providers, licenses are critical to be considered in services. We have proposed a formal representation of licensing clauses to describe the licenses in machine understandable form that would be recognizable by services. We have extended ODRL to define the licensing clauses of services, as ODRL licenses are compatible with all service standards. We have focused on the aspects of copyrights and moral rights in this paper, introducing a free culture of services.

As composition federates independently developed services into a more complex service, the license proposed for the composed service should be consonant with the implemented licenses of individual services. In our future work, we intend to propose a framework to compare the service licenses, iterating over the licensing clauses of services to be composed. Based on the comparison of the rights expressed on services to be composed, the framework would also be able to suggest dynamically a license(s) for the composed service, yet legally enforceable.

Acknowledgements

We are grateful to Dr. Renato Ianella for his suggestions on enhancing ODRL for services. We acknowledge Prof. Michael Weiss and Prof. Fabio Casati for their suggestions. We thank anonymous reviewers for their helpful comments.

References

1. Foster, I.: Service Oriented Science. Science **308** (2005) 814–817
2. Szyperski, C.: Component Software: Beyond Object Oriented Programming. ACM Press, New York (1998)
3. D'Andrea, V., Gangadharan, G.R.: Licensing Services: The Rising. In: Proceedings of the IEEE Web Services Based Systems and Applications (ICIW'06), Guadeloupe, French Caribbean. (2006) 142–147

4. Papazoglou, M., Georgakopoulos, D.: Service Oriented Computing. Communications of the ACM **46**(10) (2003) 25–28
5. Heckel, R., Lohmann, M., Thone, S.: Towards a UML Profile for Service Oriented Architectures. In: Proceedings of the Workshop on Model Driven Architecture: Foundations and Applications (MDAFA) . (2003)
6. Hamadi, R., Benatallah, B.: A Petri Net-based Model for Web Services Composition. In: Proceedings of the Fourteenth Australasian Database Conference on Database Technologies. (2003) 191–200
7. Goldstein, P.: International Copyright Principles, Law, and Practice. Oxford University Press (2001)
8. Fitzgerald, B., Oi, I.: Free Culture: Cultivating the Creative Commons. Media and Arts Law Review (2004)
9. Keller, A., Ludwig, H.: The WSLA Framework: Specifying and Monitoring Service Level Agreements for Web Services. Journal of Network and Systems Management **11**(1) (2003)
10. Skene, J., Lamanna, D., Emmerich, W.: Precise Service Level Agreements. In: Proc. of 26th Intl. Conference on Software Engineering (ICSE). (2004)
11. Tosic, V., Pagurek, B., Patel, K., Esfandiari, B., Ma, W.: Management Applications of the Web Service Offerings Language. In: Proc. of the 15th CAiSE. (2003)
12. Jeffrey Schlimmer (Ed.): Web Services Policy Framework (WS-Policy). http://www-128.ibm.com/developerworks/webservices/library/ specification/ws-polfram/ (2004)
13. World Intellectual Property Organization: WIPO Copyright Treaty (WCT). http://www.wipo.int/treaties/en/ip/wct/trtdocs_wo033.html (1996)
14. Rosenblatt, B., Trippe, B., Mooney, S.: Digital Rights Management: Business and Technology. M & T Publishers, New York (2002)
15. Gunter, C., Weeks, S., Wright, A.: Models and Languages for Digital Rights. In: Proceedings of the HICSS-34. (2001)
16. Pucella, R., Weissman, V.: A Logic for Reasoning about Digital Rights. In: IEEE Proceedings of the Computer Security Foundations Workshop. (2002)
17. Chong, C., Corin, R., Etalle, S., Hartel, P., Law, Y.: LicenseScript: A Novel Digital Rights Language. In: Proceedings of the International Workshop for Technology, Economy, Social and Legal Aspects of Virtual Goods. (2003)
18. D'Andrea, V., Gangadharan, G.R.: Licensing Services: An "Open" Perspective. In: Open Source Systems (IFIP Working Group 2.13 Foundation Conference on Open Source Software), Vol. 203, Springer Verlag. (2006) 143–154
19. Weyuker, E.: Evaluating Software Complexity Measures. IEEE Transactions on Software Engineering **14**(9) (1988) 1357–1365
20. D'Andrea, V., Fikouras, I., Aiello, M.: Interface Inheritance for Object Oriented Service Composition Based on Model Driven Configuration. In: Proceedings of ICSOC (Short Papers). (2004) 66–74
21. Alonso, G., Casati, F., Kuno, H., Machiraju, V.: Web Services Concepts, Architectures, and Applications. Springer Verlag (2004)
22. World Intellectual Property Organization: Successful Technology Licensing. WIPO Publishers, Geneva, Switzerland (2004)
23. ContentGuard Inc.: XrML: The Digital Rights Language for Trusted Contents and Services. http://www.xrml.org/ (Accessed on May 2006)
24. Renato Iannella (Ed.): Open Digital Rights Language (ODRL) Version 1.1. http://odrl.net/1.1/ODRL-11.pdf (2002)
25. Renato Ianella (Ed.): ODRL Creative Commons Profile. http://odrl.net/Profiles/CC/SPEC.html (2005)

QoS Assessment of Providers with Complex Behaviours: An Expectation-Based Approach with Confidence

Gareth Shercliff, Jianhua Shao, W. Alex Gray, and Nick J. Fiddian

School of Computer Science, Cardiff University, UK

Abstract. Service Level Agreements (SLAs) define a set of consumer expectations which must be met by a provider if a contract is not to be broken. Since providers will potentially be providing many different services to thousands of different consumers, they must adopt an efficient policy for resource management which differentiates consumers into service ranges. Existing approaches to QoS assessment of providers assume that the policy of a provider with respect to consumers is handled on an individual basis. We maintain that such approaches are ineffective when providers adopt a policy based on service differentiation and in response introduce and evaluate an expectation-based approach to QoS assessment which presupposes the classification of consumers into ranges defined by their expectation. As well as carrying out assessment to determine the likely future behaviour of a provider for a given consumer expectation, we attach a confidence value to our assessment to indicate the level of certainty that the result is accurate. Our results suggest that our confidence-based approach can help consumers make better informed decisions in order to find the providers that best meet their needs.

1 Introduction

Before a consumer and provider enter into an instance of service provision, a set of mutually agreeable criteria must be defined in the form of an SLA[2] in order that both sides are aware of their commitments and of what they should expect from the other party. In such an agreement, the consumer's commitments are usually limited in number and trivial in enaction. Conversely, the commitments of a provider to an individual consumer may be numerous and complex. Consumers may specify QoS parameters such as availability, throughput and response time[9] and there may be interrelationships between particular clauses of the contract. A provider may concurrently be providing several service types, interacting with thousands of consumers and having to efficiently manage resources[11][7] in order that their commitments to each individual SLA are met.

Service differentiation[7] is a generally accepted solution to dealing with the complexity of resource management in flexible domains such as service oriented environments[6]. Taking this approach, consumers are classified into performance classes, where each class represents a set of consumers with particular SLA-defined expectations and commitments. Consumers within the same performance

A. Dan and W. Lamersdorf (Eds.): ICSOC 2006, LNCS 4294, pp. 378–389, 2006.

class can be expected to be treated equally - that is, consumers with similar expectations and commitments will be treated in a similar way by the provider. The policy adopted in classifying and managing consumers in performance classes will differ from provider-to-provider and it can be assumed that providers will not publish details of their policy. Hence, providers are unlikely to advertise each service level as a separate service - to consumers and third-parties it will appear as if all service levels are actually one offering. This presents a challenge to third-party services such as QoS Assessment tools and reputation brokers that attempt to evaluate the likely future performance of a provider, and exposes inadequacies in existing approaches.

Our contribution, which we present in this paper, is an approach to QoS assessment which presupposes that an individual provider may be offering a set of functionally identically services differentiated only by QoS but which are advertised as a single service. We previously introduced an approach to assessment which recognised this differentiation of services[13]. Here we build on our approach by taking into account confidence in the assessment process as an indicator of how likely it is that our assessment is accurate. In this paper we outline our improved approach and demonstrate cases where the confidence in an assessment result may be a discriminating factor in evaluating and choosing between providers.

The remainder of this paper is structured as follows. In Section 2 we briefly discuss existing work similar to our own, identifying points of difference and similarity between the approaches. This is followed in Section 3 by a brief formalisation of the concepts and processes of a model SOC environment that we refer to in our work. In Section 4, we provide a description of our expectation-based approach to assessment, focussing on the incorporation of confidence into our model. In Section 5, we provide evidence of and discuss a set of experiments that we have carried out in order to verify the effectiveness of our approach compared to a non-confidence based equivalent. Finally, in Section 6, we present our conclusions.

2 Related Work

Our work falls into the area of QoS Aware Service Discovery and Selection (QoSDS) the goal of which is to develop techniques to determine the likely future behaviour of a provider based on information that may be provided as ratings[5] or by directly monitoring services[1]. Whilst having the same overall goal, our approach can be distinguished from the majority in taking an expectation-based approach by recognising that the level of service delivered by a provider is partially dependent upon the expectation of the consumer. We previously developed such an approach based upon consumer ratings[4]. An expectation-based approach is also adopted by Scherchan et al.[12] who concur with our assertion in using similar expectation as a discriminating factor in selecting relevant past provision instances for use in assessment. However, we maintain that when delivered values are used instead of ratings, simply choosing past instances of provision where expectation is similar is ineffective when providers adopt a differentiated services approach to service provision[13].

The research into trust and reputation has developed techniques to choose the best provider to meet a consumer's needs, though the emphasis in this case is on *how likely* the provider will be to keep to contractually agreed levels of service[10], rather than determining the actual level of service that can be expected. In [8] Maximillien and Singh provide a comprehensive approach to establishing reputation of providers taking into account both rated and recorded levels of service.

3 Problem Statement

We here provide a brief formalisation of the concepts and processes of a service-oriented environment relevant to our work, concluding the section with a statement of the problem addressed by our approach.

3.1 Quality

We adhere to the conformance view of quality, used commonly in the literature[5][3] - specifically, we take the approach that conformance is the act of meeting consumer expectation.

Definition 1 (Quality). *Let Q be the degree of conformance of the service delivered (D) by a service provider to a consumer's expectation (E).*

We assume that the definition of quality above is used rationally by both consumers and providers in their environment. That is, consumers are happier when their expectations are being met and providers believe that they are able to keep consumers happy by minimising the distance between the level of service they are providing and the consumer's expectation.

3.2 Service Provider Behaviour

We assume a problem space within an SOC environment, in which a set of service providers $PSet = \{P_1, ..., P_n\}$ offer functionally identical services. Each individual service provider will adopt a policy to resource management by classifying consumers based on their expectation - effectively dividing the range of consumer expectation into partitions such that the whole range of expectation is covered. We refer to each partition as a *service range* (SR). The ranges are defined by an upper and lower expectation - all consumers with expectation falling into a particular range will be treated similarly by the provider.

Within each service range, at a given point in time, we assume that a provider has a target level of service that they attempt to provide (denoted D_t) though generally they will not be able to maintain performance at exactly this level. We represent the actual level of service delivered at any point as consisting of D_t and an error, ε. D_t may change over time dependent on other factors such as a change in the amount of resources allocated by a provider to a particular service range.

Definition 2 (Target Service Level). *Let D_t be the level of service which a provider attempts to meet for all consumers classified within a single expectation-delimited service range and ε be the difference between the level of service received by the consumer at any point and D_t.*

It is important to reiterate at this point that explicit knowledge about a provider's target service levels or the extent of the service ranges remains unavailable to anyone except the provider.

3.3 Collection and Utilisation of QoS Information

When a service is provided to a consumer, we assume that data about the instance is collected. We refer to all QoS information about a single instance as a quality datum QD, and the set of all quality datum as the quality database (QDB):

$$QDB = \{QD_0, ..., QD_p\}$$
$$QD_i = (time_i, P_i, exp_i, del_i)$$

Where $time_i$ was the time that the service instance terminated, P_i was the provider that provided the service (from PSet), exp_i was the consumer's expectation and del_i was the average level of service provided (measured on the same scale as exp_i). For simplicity and ease of presentation, we assume that exp and del are normalised onto a scale of (0..1).

Definition 3 (Quality Assessment). *Given a consumer expectation E_c, a provider $P \in PSet$ and the contents of QDB, the goal of QoS assessment is to determine the likely behaviour of P if he were to agree to provide E_c.*

In carrying out such an assessment, it is necessary to consider both the effect of differing expectation of consumers - two individuals with different expectations may gain a different utility from the same delivered level of service (from Definition 1); and the behaviour of individual providers in relation to a consumer's expectation - providers will adopt different policies with respect to defining and adhering to service levels and these are not explicitly available to the assessment service (from Definition 2).

3.4 Notation

We can consider the data from the QDB regarding a single provider as being a set of tuples (e,d). In order to illustrate our approach, we utilise a graphical notation (Figure 1) in which we define two interconnected spaces: e-space and d-space; containing tuple data with a one-to-one mapping between spaces. That is, each tuple corresponds to exactly one point in each space.

4 An Expectation-Based Approach with Confidence

In this section we describe our approach to QoS assessment. A more comprehensive overview of our intial approach is provided in [13]. Here, we concentrate on identifying the factors which will affect the confidence of our assessment,

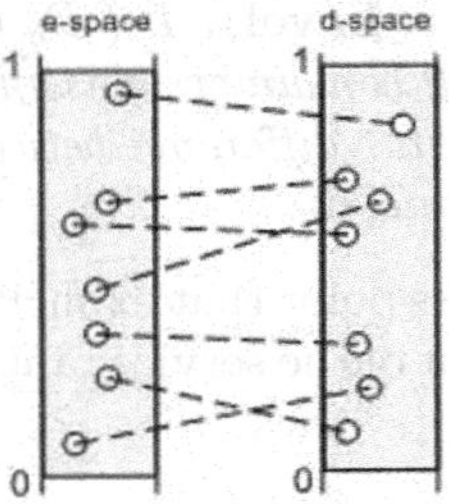

Fig. 1. Quality Spaces: e-space and d-space

formalising their calculation and describing how they are used to improve the effectiveness of our approach.

We consider our approach as consisting of four main phases (Figure 2) which we describe below.

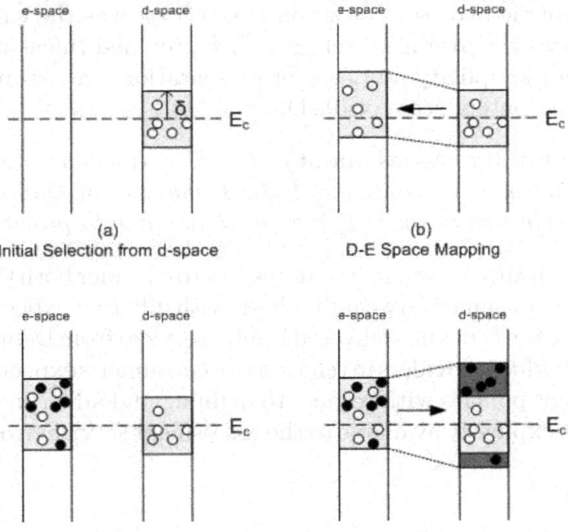

Fig. 2. Stages of the Approach - Mapping, Selection and Aggregation

Initial Selection from D-Space (Figure 2(a)). In order to ascertain whether it is possible for a provider (P_i) to meet the consumer's expectation (without constraining the circumstances under which this might happen), we attempt to find past instances in which the delivered level of service is similar to that of the consumer's expectation. We define similarity through the use of a threshold value δ - the range delimited by E_c and δ specifying a range of provided level of service for which we assume the consumer will be satisfied (with E_c at the centre of the range).

$$ProviderData = \{pd \mid pd \in QDB, pd.prov = P_i\}$$

$$SimilarInstances = \{sim \mid sim \in ProviderData, E_c - \delta \leq sim.del < E_c + \delta\}$$

If any similar instances are found this is an indication that the provider is capable (or has been capable) of providing service at the level desired by the consumer. However, the instances of provision which have been selected may have been provided as a result of a consumer having a different expectation to E_c - for instance, if a provider consistently over- or under-provides. In the next step, we identify whether this is the case.

D-Space to E-Space Mapping (Figure 2(b)). In order to determine the level of consumer expectation which results in E_c being provided, we identify the corresponding e-space points for each element of SimilarInstances, determining the lower and upper range of expectation covered by the points - denoted as lowerExp and upperExp respectively.

If E_c is in the range delimited by lowerExp and upperExp this should increase our confidence that the provider is capable of delivering a level of service similar to E_c when asked to do so. i.e. the provider has a high degree of conformance when asked for E_c. At this stage, however, we must still consider the fact that the provider's level of service is not constant over time. That is, for other instances with consumer expectation in the range identified, the provider may have delivered different values in the past - if this were the case, it would lower our confidence in our provider's ability to maintain a consistent behaviour at the level E_c.

In general, the confidence that the points identified in e-space are relevant to our assessment is inversely proportional to the distance of E_c from the mean of the expectation identified.

$$conf_{exp} = 1 - \mid E_c - \mu_{exp} \mid$$

E-Space Selection (Figure 2(c)). We now select *all* points in e-space where the consumer's expectation in each instance falls into the range delimited by lowerExp and upperExp. The points identified now cover all data that is potentially relevant to the result of our assessment.

$$PotentiallyRelevant = \{ran \mid ran \in ProviderData, lowerExp \leq ran.exp < upperExp\}$$

E-Space to D-Space Mapping (Figure 2(d)). Finally, we aggregate the values from the corresponding points from d-space in order to determine the predicted behaviour of the provider. As indicated above, the set of data used to carry out the final aggregation and thus predict the performance of the provider contains all past instances which are *potentially* relevant. In an ideal situation, the points used in the final aggregation will fall into a single service range of the provider (Figure 3 (a)). If this is the case, by aggregating the delivered values we should obtain a prediction which falls into the same range and is thus a good indication of performance. However, in other situations the instances which we identify may fall across multiple service ranges (Figure 3 (b)). In this case, aggregating the delivered values will produce a prediction which falls between the ranges identified and is thus unlikely to be accurate.

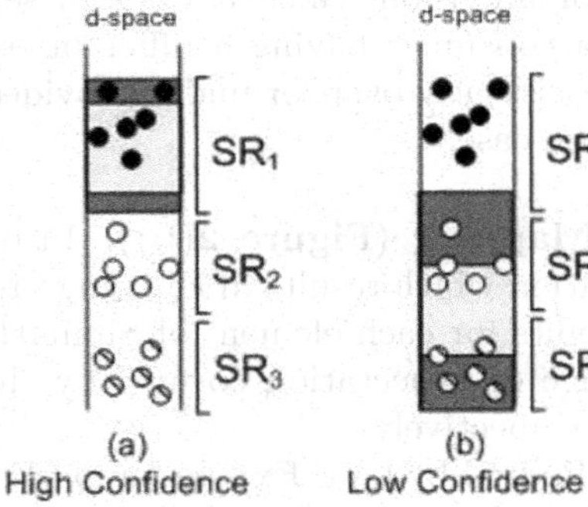

Fig. 3. Confidence in data used for final aggregation

To quantify the level of confidence we have in the data we consider the likely distribution of data within each of the service ranges. As discussed in Section 3.2, a provider will attempt to meet a target level D_t but in each instance will generally miss this objective by an error defined as ε. It is reasonable to assume that in each case, the probability of ε being small is greater than the probability of ε being large - that is, in general the provider is likely to miss D_t by a small amount more often than a large amount. We can therefore consider the distribution of recorded delivered values in each service range as being normal, with D_t as the mean.

The confidence which we can have in the data is proportional to the probability that the data we have found falls into a single service range. We use likelihood estimation to determine the probability of the observed data being generated as the result of a normal distribution (whose mean and variance are derived from the data). The higher the likelihood, the more likely that our data falls into a single range.

$$\mu = \frac{\sum_{i=1}^{n} del_i}{n} \tag{1}$$

$$\sigma^2 = \frac{\sum_{i=1}^{n} del_i^2 - (\sum_{i=1}^{n} del_i)^2/n}{n-1} \tag{2}$$

$$conf_{del} = P(RelevantInstances|M_{\mu,\sigma}) = \Pi_{i=1}^{n} P(relevantinstances_i.del|M_{\mu,\sigma}) \tag{3}$$

Where M is a model of a normal distribution defined by μ and σ.

Overall Confidence and Result Calculation. The overall confidence in assessment is defined as the product of the two separate confidences from d-space and e-space. The predicted value of performance for the provider is taken as the mean of the final set of points identified in d-space.

$$conf = conf_{exp} * conf_{del} \tag{4}$$

$$prediction = \frac{\sum_{i=1}^{n} del_i}{n} \tag{5}$$

Once overall confidence and the predicted performance for the provider have been determined, both values are passed back to the consumer.

5 Evaluation

We have created a discrete-time event simulator which allows fine-grained control over the parameters of a model SOC environment described in Section 3. The simulator allows the modelling of provider behaviour in terms of service levels and QoS delivered over time; service discovery and provision in which expectation and delivered values are recorded in a QDB; and provides a scripting language for the description and simulation of specific scenarios. We used this simulator in order to carry out a number of experiments in order to validate our assertions and to verify the effectiveness of our approach.

5.1 Empirical Results

In the first experiment, we observed the behaviour of our approach in terms of how well the performance of a single provider could be predicted. Figure 4 illustrates the behaviour of a single provider over time. Here, the provider's policy divides the expectation space into two ranges - the provider giving a level of service of around 0.55 for exp > 0.35 and a level of service of around 0.4 for exp < 0.35. The performance of the approach can be evaluated by observing how far the predicted value falls from the actual delivered level of service. The bars for each point on the graph indicate the confidence in the result - the larger the bar, the higher the confidence.

In our second experiment, we compared the performance of non-confidence and confidence based approaches in selecting between two providers. In this case, the graphs (Figure 5) illustrate the behaviour of each provider for the consumer's expectation. For each approach, we plot a point at each assessment during the simulation to indicate which provider was chosen by each algorithm. At any point in the simulation, the best provider (and hence the one that should be selected by the algorithm) is the one whose delivered level of service is closest to E_c.

Experiment 1 - Confidence as an Indicator of Uncertainty. We defined a provider behaviour in which the delivered values for each service range both intersect the range defined by $E_c \pm \delta$ i.e. from 0.4 - 0.6. In this case, the actual delivered level of service which would be received for E_c is defined by the upper service range (since $E_c > 0.35$). However, in this instance we are providing the assessment algorithm with a behaviour in which the delivered values for both service ranges overlap the range defined by $E_c \pm \delta$. We are therefore concerned with both how the effectiveness of prediction is affected and the level of confidence that the algorithm has in its assessment. The results of this experiment are illustrated in Figure 4.

Figure 4 shows that initially the confidence-based algorithm predicts a default value for the provider (this is to be expected as the algorithm has not yet

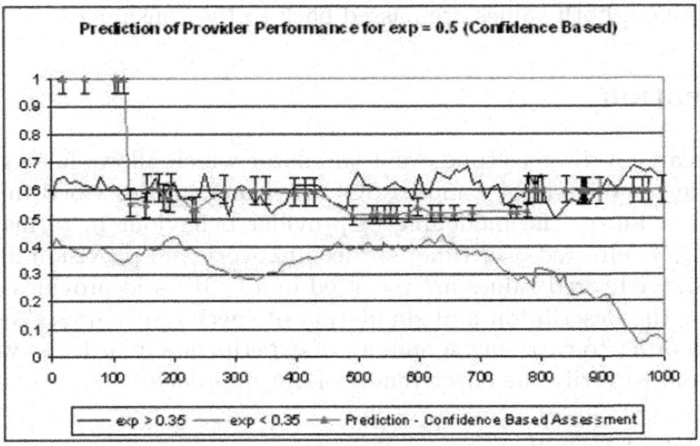

Fig. 4. Experiment 1 - Confidence as an Indicator of Uncertainty

observed any provision in the range defined by $E_c \pm \delta$). From t=100 to t=400, the algorithm correctly predicts performance in accordance with the upper service range. However, between t=450 and t=750 the level of service delivered by the lower service range falls into the range $E_c \pm \delta$. In this case, the assessment algorithm predicts a level of service between the two service ranges, though the confidence in the assessment is now substantially reduced. As the delivered level of service for the ower service range drops towards t=1000, both the predictive accuracy and confidence of the assessment return to normal. This experiment illustrates that the inclusion of confidence within the assessment has the desired effect. When the predictive performance of the approach is affected by an overlap in the performance of the provider's service levels, confidence in the assessment falls appropriately.

Experiment 2 - Choosing between multiple providers. In our second experiment, we defined behaviour for two providers. Provider 1 has a single behaviour which begins providing service at 0.6, but drops to about 0.4 (E_c in this case) later in the simulation. Provider 2 has multiple service ranges - in this simulation, the level of service offered to consumers requesting $E_c = 0.4$

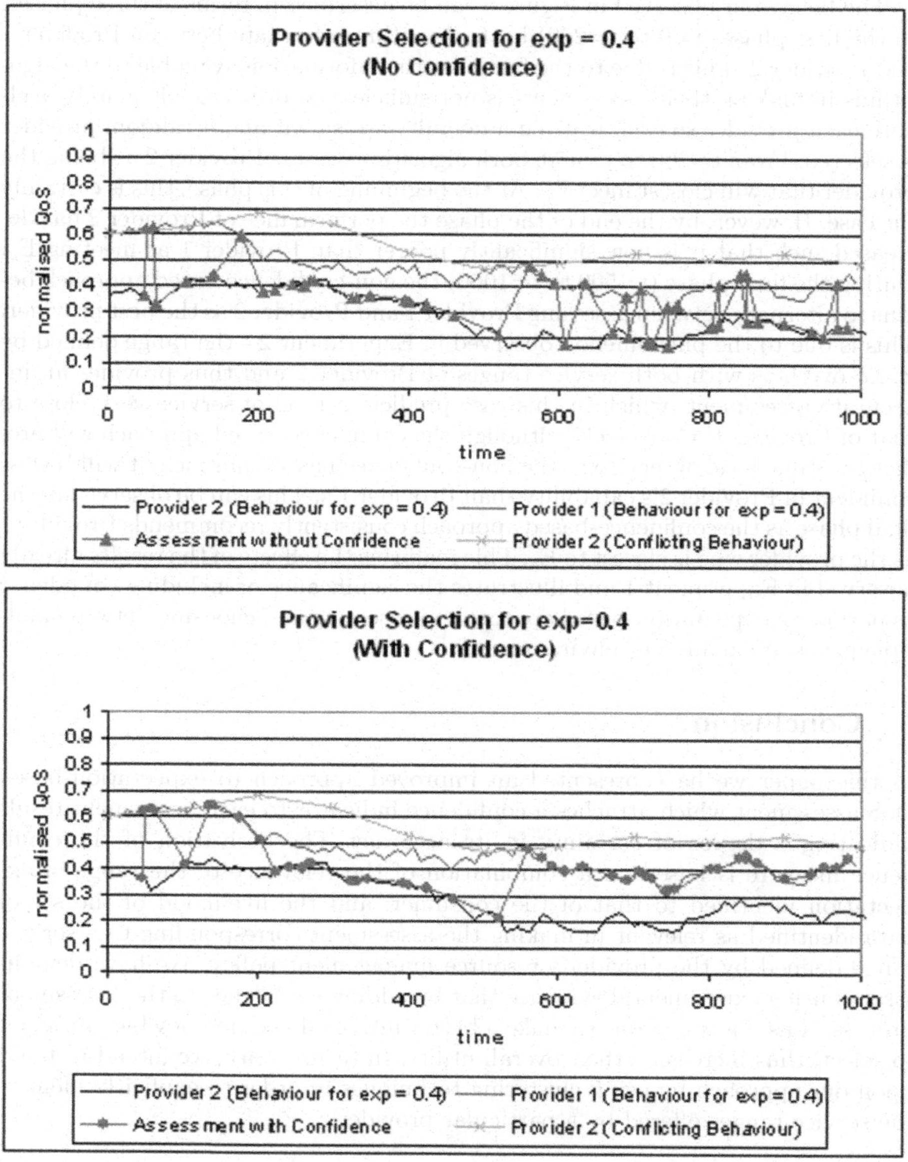

Fig. 5. Experiment 2 - Choosing between Multiple Providers

begins at 0.4, but falls to 0.2 later in the simulation. The second behaviour of Provider 2 would be received from the provider for $E_c \neq 0.4$, and as such should be irrelevant to our assessment.

The behaviour observed in Figure 5 can be described in terms of three phases. In the first phase (t=0 to t=200) both algorithms alternate between Provider 1 and Provider 2. This is due to the fact that the information available to the algorithms in making their assessments is not sufficient in order to adequately evaluate each provider so each is given a default assessment and a random provider is selected. From t=200 to t=450, both algorithms assess Provider 2 as being the provider that will closest meet E_c. At the beginning of this phase, this is certainly the case. However, by the end of the phase the performance of Provider 2 has decreased such that it is now significantly poorer than Provider 1 at meeting E_c. During the final phase (t=500 to t=1000) the non-confidence based approach begins to alternate between assessing Provider 1 and Provider 2 as the best provider. This is due to the phenomenon observed in Experiment 2 - the range defined by $E_c \pm \delta$ overlaps with both service ranges of Provider 2 and thus provides an inaccurate assessment, which in this case predicts a level of service very close to that of Provider 1. Conversely, although the confidence-based approach will predict the same level of service as the non-confidence based approach, it will be less confident in Provider 2's capability than Provider 1's. This can be observed in the final phase as the confidence-based approach consistently recommends Provider 1 as the provider who is closest to E_c. This reaffirms the effects of the results already observed in Experiment 1 and illustrates the significance of including confidence as part of an expectation-based approach to assessing and choosing between multiple providers in an SOC environment.

6 Conclusion

In this paper we have presented an improved approach to expectation-based QoS assessment which attaches a confidence indicator to each assessment result indicating a degree of certainty in its accuracy. The derivation of the confidence measure is based on a combination of the relevance of the range of expectation identified to that of the consumer; and the likelihood of the set of data identified as relevant in making the assessment corresponding to a service range defined by the provider's resource management policy. We have demonstrated using experimental evidence that by adding confidence to the assessment process, consumers are able to make a better informed decision of which provider to select, thus increasing their overall utility. In future work, we intend to build upon our approach by using clustering techniques in order to explicitly identify the service ranges offered by a particular provider.

References

1. Rashid J. Al-Ali, Omer F. Rana, and David W. Walker. G-QoSM: Grid Service Discovery Using QoS Properties. *Journal of Computing and Informatics*, 2003.
2. A. Dan, D. Davis, R. Kearney, R. King, A. Keller, D. Kuebler, H. Ludwig, M. Polan, M. Spreitzer, and A. Youssef. Web Services on Demand: WSLA-Driven Automated Management. *IBM Systems Journal, Special Issue on Utility Computing*, 43(1):136–158, March 2004.

3. V. Deora, J. Shao, W.A. Gray, and N.J. Fiddian. A Quality of Service Management Framework Based on User Expectations. In *Lecture Notes in Computer Science*, volume 2910, pages 104–114, January 2003.
4. Vikas Deora, Jianhua Shao, W. Alex Gray, and Nick J. Fiddian. Expectation based quality of service assessment. *to appear in International Journal on Digital Libraries*, 2006.
5. Sravanthi Kalepu, Shonali Krishnaswamy, and Seng Wai Loke. Reputation = f(User Ranking, Compliance, Verity). In *Proceedings of the IEEE International Conference on Web Services (ICWS'04)*. IEEE Computer Society, 2002.
6. Ronald M. Levy, Jay Nagarajarao, Giovanni Pacifici, Mike Spreitzer, Asser N. Tantawi, and Alaa Youssef. Performance Management for Cluster Based Web Services. In Germán S. Goldszmidt and Jürgen Schönwälder, editors, *Integrated Network Management*, volume 246 of *IFIP Conference Proceedings*, pages 247–261. Kluwer, 2003.
7. Heiko Ludwig. Web Services QoS: External SLAs and Internal Policies or: How do we deliver what we promise? In *Fourth International Conference on Web Information Systems Engineering Workshops (WISEW'03)*, pages 115–120, 2003.
8. E. Michael Maximilien and Munindar P. Singh. Toward Autonomic Web Services Trust and Selection. In *ICSOC '04: Proceedings of the 2nd International Conference on Service Oriented Computing*, pages 212–221. ACM Press, 2004.
9. Daniel A. Menasce. QoS Issues in Web Services. *IEEE Internet Computing*, 6(6):72–75, November 2002.
10. Sarvapali D. Ramchurn, Dong Hunyh, and Nicholas R. Jennings. Trust in Multi-Agent Systems. *Knowledge Engineering Review*, 2004.
11. A. Sahai, J. Ouyang, V. Machiraju, and K. Wurster. BizQoS: Specifying and Guaranteeing Quality of Service for Web Services through Real Time Measurement and Adaptive Control. HPL-2001-134. Technical report, HP Labs, 2001.
12. Wanita Sherchan, Shonali Krishnaswamy, and Seng Wai Loke. Relevant Past Performance for Selecting Web Services. In *QSIC '05: Proceedings of the Fifth International Conference on Quality Software*, pages 493–445, Washington, DC, USA, 2005. IEEE Computer Society.
13. Gareth Shercliff, Jianhua Shao, W. Alex Gray, and Nick J. Fiddian. A Multiple Quality-Space Mapping Approach to Qos. In *CIT 2006: Proceedings of the Sixth IEEE International Conference on Computer and Information Technology [to appear]*. IEEE Computer Society, September 2006.

A QoS-Aware Selection Model for Semantic Web Services

Xia Wang[1], Tomas Vitvar[1], Mick Kerrigan[2], and Ioan Toma[2]

[1] Digital Enterprise Research Institute(DERI)
IDA Business Park, Lower Dangan Galway, Ireland
[2] Digital Enterprise Research Institute (DERI),
Leopold-Franzens Universität Innsbruck, Austria
{xia.wang, tomas.vitvar, michael.kerrigan, ioan.toma}@deri.org

Abstract. Automating Service Oriented Architectures by augmenting them with semantics will form the basis of the next generation of computing. Selection of service still is an important challenge, especially, when a set of services fulfilling user's capabilities requirements have been discovered, among these services which one will be eventually invoked by user is very critical, generally depending on a combined evaluation of qualities of services (Qos). This paper proposes a QoS-based selection of services. Initially we specify a QoS ontology and its vocabulary using the Web Services Modeling Ontology (WSMO) for annotating service descriptions with QoS data. We continue by defining quality attributes and their respective measurements along with a QoS selection model. Finally, we present a fair and dynamic selection mechanism, using an optimum normalization algorithm.

1 Introduction

Web services with well-defined semantics, called semantic Web services (SWS), provide interoperability between Web services by describing their own capabilities in a computer-interpretable way [10, 11]. The greatest advantage of SWS is that they enable machines to automatically perform complex tasks by manipulating a series of heterogeneous Web services based on semantics. Most aspects of SWS, such as automatic discovery, selection, composition, invocation, or monitoring of services are tightly related to the quality of these services (Qos). QoS as part of the service description is an especially important factor for service selection [5] and composition [14].

In order to discover services, a service requester provides some requirements on the capability of a requested service. Furthermore, many service providers publish their services by advertising the service capabilities. Hence a service discovery engine can be used to match requirements of a user against advertised capabilities of service providers. In such a case that several similar services are yielded by the discovery process, which has carried out the matchmaking of the non-functional and functional properties of services. Of these similar services, the one which will be finally invoked by the user depends mostly on the qualities of services.

A. Dan and W. Lamersdorf (Eds.): ICSOC 2006, LNCS 4294, pp. 390–401, 2006.

In the literature, this issue has not been thoroughly addressed, due to the complexity of QoS metrics. Sometimes, the quality of a service is dynamic or unpredictable. Moreover, most of the current work focuses on the definition of QoS ontology, vocabulary or measurements and to a lesser extent on an uniform evaluation of qualities. In our former work, we defined a selection model for semantic services [12][1], in which we specified details of quality-based selection algorithm. This paper will go on to elaborate the synthetical evaluation of the multiple and diverse qualities of services for selection of service.

The Web Service Modeling Ontology (WSMO) [13] is a conceptual model for describing Web services semantically, and defines the four main aspects of semantic Web service, namely Ontologies, Web services, Goals and Mediators. With respect to WSMO, only a small amount of work has been carried out on the selection of services, mainly in [3], which introduces a number of generic selection mechanisms to be used conjunction with WSMO. In this paper, we use the WSMO model and features to describe a QoS model, specific quality metrics, value attributes, and their respective measurements. Furthermore, we propose an algorithm to normalize different quality attributes, providing a dynamic and fair evaluation of services. This is done by considering users' quality requirements together with a set of quality advertisements provided by a service provider. Then we synthetically evaluate all of the metrics closeness in quality attributes by normalization. A weight matrix is applied to obtain the final evaluation.

The paper is structured as follows, Section 2 provides an overview on the current related work. In Section 3, a QoS ontology language designed for the needs of Web services is defined in the context of WSMO, and a QoS model for service selection is presented. Our QoS-based service selection algorithm is evaluated in Section 4. In Section 5 experimental results are presented to show the validity of the algorithm.

2 Related Work

Most of the related work in using QoS for service selection focuses on the development of QoS ontology languages and vocabularies, as well as on the identification of various QoS metrics and their measurements with respect to semantic services. For example, [9] and [4] emphasized the definition of QoS aspects and metrics. In [9], all of the possible quality requirements were enumerated and organized into several categories, including runtime-related, transaction support related, configuration management and cost-related QoS, and security-related QoS. Also, they shortly present their definitions or possible determinants. Unfortunately, they failed to present quantifiable measurements.

In [8] and [2], the authors focused on the creation of QoS ontology models, which proposed QoS ontology frameworks aiming to formally describe arbitrary QoS parameters. From their on-going work, we know that they did not consider, yet, QoS-based service matching. Additionally, the work [5], [6], and [7]

[1] This research was supported by FernUniversitaet, in Hagen and by DAAD, the German Academic Exchange Service.

tries to attempt to conduct a proper evaluation and proposes QoS-based service selection, despite the authors failing to present a fair and effective evaluation algorithm.

Especially, the work was presented in [5], which is also similar to ours. There are, however, some differences to our approach: 1) The measurement of linguistic-based qualities was not considered; 2) The algorithm uses average ranking, neglecting nuances in different quality properties; 3) A possible maximum value is used to normalize the QoS matrix, although such kind of value is worth deliberating; 4) Upon analyzing the experimental data, after normalization, the final result looks as $G' = (\{0.769, 1.429, 1.334, 1.111\}, \{0.946, 0.571, 0.666, 0.889\})$. For their way of normalisation, it is hard to make a fair evaluation of all qualities, because the metrics do not have the same range. One quality attribute even has a higher weight, while its real impact is decreased by its smaller value. Therefore, our approach is to normalize each quality metric into values between 0 and 1 by specifically defined measurements, which are fair to each quality metric. That means, we propose a different normalization algorithm.

Additionally, [17] focused on augmenting QoS classes and properties to extend the DAML-S [1] profiles. [16] defined a QoS ontology for DAML+OIL using description logic notions to express different QoS templates. [9] incorporated QoS into UDDI and SOAP messages [4] to improve the service discovery process. This paper however emphasizes the extension of WSMO with a QoS ontology class.

3 QoS Ontology Language and Vocabulary in WSMO

The Web Service Modeling Ontology (WSMO) [13] is a conceptual model for describing various aspects related to semantic Web services. WSMO is made up of four top level elements, namely ontologies, web services, goals and mediators. Briefly, *ontologies* provide the terminology and formal semantics for the other elements of WSMO. *Web services* define a semantic description of services including their functional and non-functional properties. *Goals* specify the requesters requirements for a Web Service. And *mediators* resolve the heterogeneity problem by implementing ooMediators (between ontologies), ggMediators (between goals), wgMediators (between web services and goals), and wwMediators (between services).

In WSMO, quality aspects are part of the non-functional information of a Web service description and are simply defined as: *Accuracy*, *Availability*, *Financial*, *Network-related QoS*, *Performance*, *Reliability*, *Robustness*, *Scalability*, *Transactional* and *Trust*. Such kinds of QoS definition are neither expressive nor flexible enough for QoS attributes. Therefore in this paper, for the purpose of selecting services, we introduce a new class, QoS concept classes, that refines the non-functional properties class in WSMO. Furthermore, we define a QoS model following the same syntax to extend the WSMO model. The defined QoS model may be referred to by the *web service* and *goal* entities, and quality factors can adequately be considered during the process of service selection.

We will specify a QoS upper ontology named WSMO-QoS. It is a complementary ontology that provides detailed quality aspects about services. Developers benefit from WSMO-QoS for QoS-based matchmaking and QoS measurement.

3.1 QoS Ontology and Vocabulary

Based on [2, 6, 8], we define a new class *QoS* (Table. 1) which is a subclass of *nonFunctionalProperties* class already defined in WSMO. Class *QoS* can be attached to class *webService* or *Goal*. Please notice that the current WSMO conceptual model remains unchanged, we however simply refine the class *nonFunctionalProperties*.

Table 1. QoS Ontology in WSMO

```
Class QoS sub-Class nonFunctionalProperties
  hasMetricName type string
  hasValueType type valueType
  hasMetricValue type value
  hasMeasurementUnit type Unit
  hasValueDefinition type logicalExpression
    multiplicity = single-valued
  isDynamic type boolean
  isOptional type boolean
  hasTendency type {small, large, given}
  isGroup type boolean
  hasWeight type string
```

Each QoS metric is generally described by *MetricName*, *ValueType*, *Value* (given or calculated at service run-time), *MeasurementUnits* (e.g. $, millisecond), *ValueDefinition* (how to calculate the value of this metric), and *Dynamic/Static*. For the purpose of QoS-based selection, there are four additional features defined, namely: *isOptional*, *hasTendency*, *isGroup*, and *hasWeight*. The following is an simple interpretation of every property in Table. 1:

- Types of the parameter *valueType* may be *linguistic*, *numeric* (int, float, long), *boolean* (0/1, True/False) or other. Therefore, there will be different forms of preprocessing according to the different value types.
- The property *MetricValue* defines a metric's values which are either real ones or a string such as *'calculate'*. If $MetricValue =' calculate'$, then this attribute should refer to its $valueDefinition$ for a dynamic value calculation.
- The property *MeasurementUnit* specifics the concrete unit of every quality metric, with possible types such as $Unit = \{\$, millisecond, percentage, kpbs, times, ...\}$. In addition, class *Unit* has a conversion function between different measurement units, e.g., to transform second to millisecond.

- Parameter $hasValueDefinition$ is either a logical expression defined as in [13] or the string $'NULL'$. If $hasValueDefinition =' NULL'$, then this value definition cannot explicitly extracted from the context of service description, but must dynamically be invoked from its service provider. In this case this quality attribute must be dynamic, that is $isDynamic = True$.
- Through property *isDynamic*, the nature of a quality is defined as static or dynamic. For a static quality, its values are given by a priori, and can be directly used during the selection process. If $isDynamic = True$, this quality metric must be dynamically invoked and obtained from its service provider, and its values must be calculated at run-time.
- If *isOption* $= 0$, this attribute, assumed to be noted as q_k, is necessary, such that $q_k \in Q_N$, where Q_N is the necessary quality set. This property is described in Subsection 3.2.
- $hasTendency$ is an object property representing the expected tendency of the value from the user's perspective. For example, the price of a service is expected to be as low as possible, so that its $hasTendency =' low/small'$. On the contrary, the quality of *security* of a service should be as high as possible, i.e., $hasTendency =' high/large'$. When $hasTendency =' given'$, the user expects the value of this quality to be as close the given value as possible. Also, in a quality inquiry, $hasTendency = \{low/small, high/large, given\}$ denotes, respectively, that $\{\geq, \leq, =\}$ for its $MetricValue$.
- *isGroup* indicates if this quality attribute is defined by a group of other qualities or not. For example, *security* is composed of *nonRepudiatior*, *DataEncryption*, *Authorisation*, *Authentication*, *Auditability*, and *Confidentiality* [2]. Hence, *isGroup* $= True$ means that in the preprocessing stage, the group value must be calculated first.
- Finally, $hasWeight$ is a value denoting the weightiness of the property, especially when synthetically measuring several metrics. In this context we define the weight value either ranges in $[0, 10]$ or 'NULL', different end users have different weight values for their service requirements. Note, in this paper, this property is used only by a WSMO *goal*, which describes user's desire; In the description of a WSMO *web service*, its value is 'NULL'.

During the selection process, when a QoS profile is parsed, in order to obtain a metric's value for which $hasMetricValue =' calculate'$ holds, its $hasValueDefinition$ property must be checked to determine how to calculate it. If $hasValueDefin ition =' NULL'$ and $isDynamic = 1$, then the invocation function is to inquire the real-time value, otherwise an error is encountered. If $isDynamic = 0$, its corresponding $hasMetricValue$ is an existing value, or again an error occurs.

In [15,4,9], all of the possible QoS requirements for Web services were defined, mainly including: performance, reliability, scalability, capacity, robustness, exception handling, accuracy, integrity, accessibility, availability, inter-operability, security and network-related QoS requirements. Fig. 1 gives a simple view on QoS vocabulary, which consists of many general QoS attributes and the scalable domain-specific QoS subset used; for example, to define the hotel category for a hotel service. The definition and the discussion of concrete measurement of qualities is out of this paper's scope.

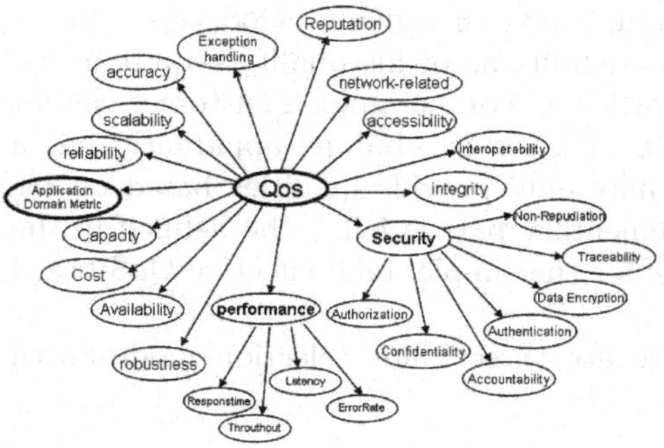

Fig. 1. QoS ontology and vocabulary

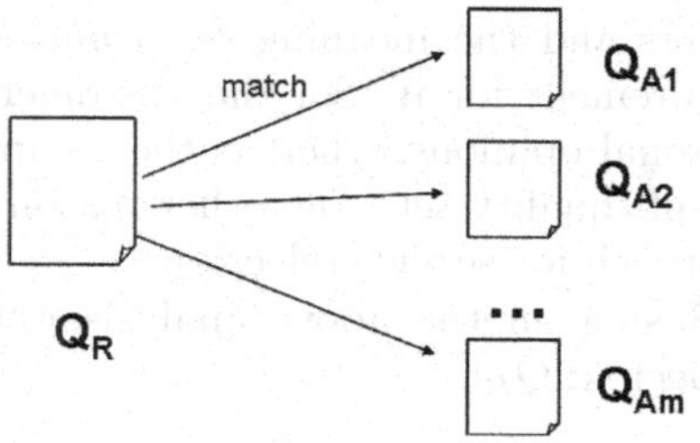

Fig. 2. QoS-based selection of services

3.2 QoS Selection Model

The scenario of QoS-based service selection is described as follows. The user provides his requirements (including non-functional, functional, and quality properties) for the expected service, which are formed into a requirement profile, noted as $s_R = (NF_R, F_R, Q_R, C_R)$, where the denotations are the identifers of Non-Functionality, Functionality, Quality and Cost (the details of such selection model can be found in [12]). On the other side, there can be thousands of available services published in either a service repository or a kind of peer-to-peer service environment. The advertisement of a service s is denoted as $s_A = (NF_A, F_A, Q_A, C_A)$, similarly.

The first filter of service selection matches s_R with any available s_A on the basis of non-functional-NF (bascially only the service name and service category) and functional-F (including inputs, outputs, preconditions and effects) features of services. We assume that m similar services are yielded, namely, $S = \{s_1, s_2, ..., s_m\}$, $m \in \mathcal{N}$.

The second filter synthetically considers all quality features to select the service among S satisfying the user's requirements best. This matchmaking takes place between the pair of the QoS requirements Q_R and a quality profile Q_A of a candidates service $s_A \in S$, as illustrated in Fig. 2.

For the purpose of matching, a QoS selection model is defined, in which metrics are defined both from the perspectives of users and providers of web services. We assume that $Q = \{q_1, q_2, ..., q_i\}$, $i \in \mathcal{N}$, and Q_I denotes the quality set. Thus,

- Q_N is the necessary quality set for each service defaulted by machine, and $Q_N \subseteq Q_I$;
- Q_O is the optional quality set of the service defined as $Q_O = Q_I \setminus Q_N$; and
- Q_D is the default quality set of the service. When user does not explicitly give any quality requirements, i.e., when $Q_R = \emptyset$ and $Q_D \subseteq Q_I$, then Q_D will be taken as Q_R, i.e., $Q_R = Q_D$, where Q_R are the user's quality requirements. Generally, $Q_N \subseteq Q_D$.

There are two reasons for distinguishing between different QoS sets. One is to free the customer from multifarious definitions of his quality requirements, which sometimes need professional knowledge. For example, a customer cannot understand the meaning of *availability* of a service, but he apparently has a requirement for it. So, the customer may only provide qualities based on his personal opinions, whereas the complementary part is left to be defined in the default quality set. The other reason is for the simple, high effective QoS-based approach for service selection.

Basing on the above analysis, there are three kinds selection modes with respect to Q_R:

- Default mode. When $Q_R \neq \emptyset$, Q_R is redefined as union of the original user requirements and the default ones about service performance, as $Q_R := Q_R \cup Q_N$;
- Totally based on the user's requirements, and $Q_R \neq \emptyset$;
- Totally based on default definitions, if $Q_R = \emptyset$.

Further, for purposes of efficient and flexible service selection and from the user's perspective, in our model only several qualities are defined in the necessary set, viz., Q_N={*cost, responseTime, reliability, accurary, security, reputation*}, and similarly Q_D={*cost, responseTime, reliability, accuracy, security, reputation, executionTime, exceptionHandling*}. Of course, the definitions are extendable and changeable for specific application system.

There are many approaches to collect values of quality metrics:

- Directly from the service descriptions, e.g., sometimes the price of invoking a service is given a priori.
- Simple calculation of a quality value based on the defining expression in the service description.
- Collection through active monitoring, e.g., execution duration defined in [5].
- Dynamical inquiry from the current server.
- Periodical update of quality values for statistical purposes in a log.
- Obtaining the customers' feedbacks on quality characteristics, e.g., *Reputation* of a service [5] .

Not only are the collection of quality requirements dynamic, unpredictable, and even difficult during run-time, but the value characteristics of quality metric can be concluded approximately as:

- Numerical metric, denoted by a number but with different value ranges.
- Ordinal and linguistic-based metric, denoted by a term from an ordered finite collection of terms, e.g., the reputation of a service may be evaluated by $\{Low, veryLow, Medium, veryHigh, High\}$.
- Regional metric, denoted by a numerical region $[min, max]$.
- Graded metric, e.g., rank of a hotel service in $\{1, 2, 3, 4, 5\}$.
- Boolean value numeric or enumerative scales.

It is worth noting that this QoS model is easy to extend or customize. The user may customize his/her Q_N, Q_D, Q_I at will. The detailed definition of all quality attributes is out of this paper's scope. Instead, we focus mainly on the QoS foundation of the selection model, and the combined evaluation of the quality attributes.

4 Selection Algorithm

QoS-based selection of services is very complex, not only due to the diversity of multifarious quality metrics with different value types, value range, and measurements, but also since an effective algorithm, which evaluates all metrics in combination, is missing.

We assume that $Q_R = \{r_1, r_2, ..., r_k\}$ expresses the profile of a user's quality requirements, which includes k quality metrics. Similarly, the quality profile of m candidate services in set S is denoted as $Q_S = \{Q_{A_1}, Q_{A_2}, ..., Q_{A_m}\}$, where $Q_{A_i} = \{q_{i1}, q_{i2}, ..., q_{ij}\}$, $i, j \in \mathcal{N}$. It defines that the advertisement of service S_i has j quality metrics provided.

It is well-known that there are two cases during the matchmaking,

- $Q_R = \emptyset$, then $Q_R := Q_D$;
- $Q_R \neq \emptyset$, then $Q_R := Q_R \cup Q_N$. The Q_R is matched with each Q_{Ai}, $i \in \mathcal{N}$.

It is quite obvious that it is rather unlikely that any Q_R or Q_{A_i} will have the same number of quality metrics. So, in the first preprocessing step, we take Q_R as benchmark for alignment with every Q_{A_i}. This process includes:

1. To re-arrange the metrics of Q_{Ai} in the same order.
2. If Q_{A_i} is lacking a quality, then one can add a metric and set its value to 0.
3. To tailor the qualities which are not listed in Q_R.

Therefore, the matrix of QoS for service matchmaking $M_Q = \{Q_R, Q_{A_1}, Q_{A_2}, ..., Q_{A_m}\}$ looks like:

$$M_Q = \begin{pmatrix} r_1 & r_2 & r_3 & \cdots & r_k \\ q_{11} & q_{12} & q_{13} & \cdots & q_{1k} \\ q_{21} & q_{22} & q_{23} & \cdots & q_{2k} \\ \cdots & \cdots & \cdots & \cdots & \cdots \\ q_{m1} & q_{m2} & q_{m3} & \cdots & q_{mk} \end{pmatrix}_{(m+1)\times k}$$

Here, M_Q is a $(m+1) \times k$ matrix, with the quality requirements Q_R in the first row, and the quality information of candidates services in the other rows. Each column contains values of the same quality property. For uniformity, matrix M_Q has to be normalized with the objective to map all real values to a relatively small range, i.e., the elements of the final matrix are real numbers in the closed interval $[0, 1]$. The main idea of the algorithm is to scale the value ranges with the maximum and minimum values of each quality metric for thousands of current candidate services. Accordingly, the maximum and minimum values are mapped to the uniform values 1 and 0, respectively, depending totally on their definition of $hasTendency$.

For instance, a user searches a flight constraining the ticket price to be below \$300, and three service providers ask for \$250, \$280, and \$260, respectively. In this case the minimum and maximum are \$250 and \$280. Then, the calculation of relative closeness for this quality metric reads as $(1-\frac{250-250}{280-250}) = 1$, $(1-\frac{280-250}{280-250}) = 0$, and $(1-\frac{260-250}{280-250}) = 0.667$.

The second preprocessing step is uniformity analysis. We distinguish different quality metrics with their value features. In our QoS model, we take the information of $hasTendency$ as a quality metric $r_i, i \in k$:

1. if $hasTendency =' given'$, then we calculate the ratio by

$$q'_{ij} = \begin{cases} 1 - \frac{q_{max} - q_{ij}}{q_{max} - q_{min}} & \text{if } r_j \geq q_{max} \\ \frac{q_{ij} - q_{min}}{q_{max} - q_{min}} & \text{if } r_j \leq q_{min} \\ 1 - (|\frac{|q_{ij} - r_j| - m}{n - m}|) & \text{if } r_j \in (q_{min}, q_{max}) \end{cases} \tag{1}$$

2. if $hasTendency =' small/low'$, then the ratio is calculated by

$$q'_{ij} = (1 - \frac{q_{ij} - q_{min}}{q_{max} - q_{min}}) \tag{2}$$

3. if $hasTendency =' large/high'$, then the ratio is calculated by

$$q'_{ij} = (1 - \frac{q_{max} - q_{ij}}{q_{max} - q_{min}}) \tag{3}$$

where $q_{max} = \max\{q_{ij}\}$, $q_{min} = \min\{q_{ij}\}$, $n = \max\{|q_{ij} - r_{ij}|\}$, and $m = \min\{|q_{ij} - r_{ij}|\}$, $i \in k, j \in m$. In Fig. 3, three cases of matchmaking are shown, and the area from the left to the right of the scale line corresponds to the growing values, whose tendency is *small/low*, *given*, and *large/high*, respectively. Also the value of $r_j,\ j \in k$ is scattered either among $q_{ij},\ i \in m$ or the right side or the left side of the candidates values. Formula 1-3. present their algorithms.

By taking the Formula 1. as an example, it describes the case that a user requires the value of a quality to be as close to his given value as possible. We assume r_j with its value as u_j and the other quality $\{q_a, q_b, ..., q_h\}$ with their value as $\{v_a, v_b, ..., v_h\}$. There are also three cases in Formula 1. First, when $u_j \geq q_{max}$, just as the candidate set is $\{q_a, q_b, q_d, q_d\}$, then by Formula 1 we know q_d gets the best ratio as 1. A similar situation occurs when $u_j \leq q_{min}$. When r_j scatters in $\{q_c, q_d, q_e, q_f\}$, the range of scale should be first defined by $(n - m)$, then ratios are calculated following the third case of Formula 1.

The weighted value for each quality metric is defined in the parameter of $hasWeight$. These are brought into the form of a diagonal matrix as $W = \{w_1, w_1, ..., , w_k\}$. Here, we assume that $\sum_{i=1}^{n} w_i = 10$ (which is not defined as 1,

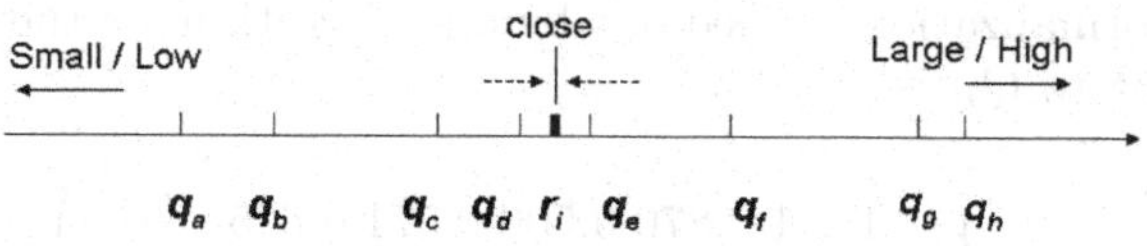

Fig. 3. Quality Measurement

for the reason of magnifying the effect of experiments). Then, W is applied to matrix M_Q yielding

$$M_{Q'} = M_Q \times W = \sum_{i=1}^{m} (q'_{ij} \times w_i) \tag{4}$$

Finally, we can calculate the evaluation result for each quality metric by summing the values of each row. These abstract values are taken as a relative evaluation of each service's QoS.

5 Experiments

For reasons of comparison and simplification we borrowed test data from [5]. In their experiments, they implemented a hypothetical phone service (UPS) registry, which provides various phone services such as long distance, local, wireless, and broadband. They simulated 600 users to collect the experimental data. Especially, two phone services' test data are presented with seven quality criteria, including *Price*, *Transaction*, *Time Out*, *Compensation Rate*, *Penalty Rate*, *Execution Duration*, and *Reputation*. Their corresponding value types are \$, 0/1, microsecond, percent, percent, microsecond, and rank value in $[0, 5]$.

In order to be applied into our selection mode, we assume a requirement of a service customer and another two services for testing, then the M_Q is as Table.2.

Table 2. Experiment Data

Data	Pri	Trans	TimeOut	ComRat	PenRat	Execu	Repu
R	30	1	80	0.4	0.8	120	4.0
ABC	25	1	60	0.5	0.5	100	2.0
BTT	40	1	200	0.8	0.1	40	2.5
A_1	28	1	140	0.2	0.8	200	3.0
A_2	55	1	180	0.6	0.4	170	4.0

The first row is the supposed Q_R, the next two rows are taken from [5], and the last two ones are also hypothetical candidates services. From the definitions of each quality criterion of that example, we know that *Price* and *Execution Duration* are expected to be smaller, *Compensation Rate*, *Penalty Rate*, and *Reputation* are to be bigger, and *Time Out* is required to be as close as possible.

The result of normalization carried out by our algorithm for the four candidate services referring to Q_R is:

$$Q' = \begin{pmatrix} 1 & 1 & 0.870 & 0.500 & 0.571 & 0.625 & 0 \\ 0.500 & 1 & 1 & 1 & 0 & 1 & 0.250 \\ 0.900 & 1 & 0.522 & 0 & 1 & 0 & 0.500 \\ 0 & 1 & 0 & 0.667 & 0.429 & 0.188 & 1 \end{pmatrix}$$

Assuming $W = \{4, 0, 0, 2, 1, 1, 2\}$, we apply Formula 4. to obtain a quality evaluation set, named $Q'' = \{6.196, 5.500, 5.600, 3.951\}$. That is, in case of putting a high weight on price, service s_1 is the best choice, the order of the results is in line with human intuition, see Fig. 4, and the result is consistent with [5], too.

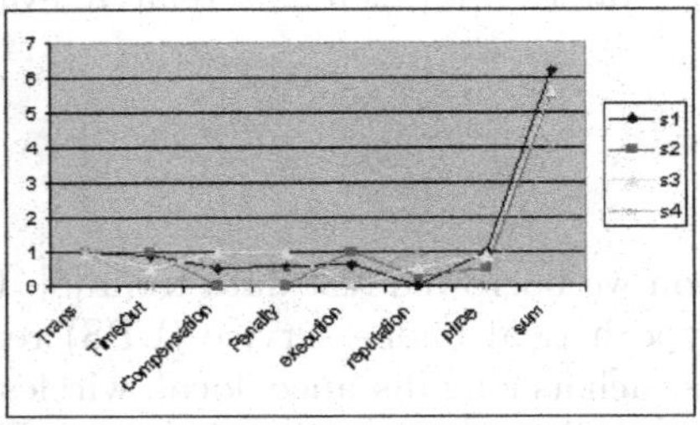

Fig. 4. Combined evaluation of qualities

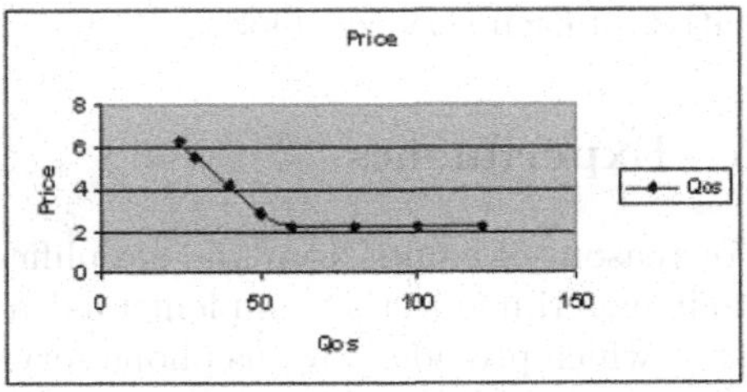

Fig. 5. Combined evaluation of qualities

Here a short discussion is presented. Our Qos-based model is dynamic and real-time, which is fully adapted to the current distributed network environment, and which is kept a well relativity and up-to-date, it is also fair on this point. Since it is always basing on the current available services to compare their current integrative capability. If services are added or deleted, the evaluation should be updated.

Also, in a certain relatively stable service environment, a service provider may consider to change one of its property, it is easy to forecast its constraint for value. For instance, we take the service s_1 (the service *ABC* in Table. II) as an example to analysis the effect of the price on its QoS. From Fig. 5., we knew that if its price were to go beyond the current maximum, it will lose its competition on price and keep an invariable QoS value.

6 Conclusion

This paper proposed a QoS-based approach for web service selection, by presenting a fair and simple algorithm for evaluating multiple quality metrics in combination. First, we specified a QoS ontology and its vocabulary in order to augment the QoS information in WSMO. Furthermore, various quality attributes, their respective measurements, and a QoS selection model were defined in detail. Finally, a fair and dynamic selection mechanism was presented, which uses a normalization algorithm oriented at optimal value range. This approach was validated by a case study for a kind of phone service.

Acknowledgment. This material is based upon work supported by the Science Foundation Ireland under Grant No. 02/CE1/I131, and the European projects KnowledgeWeb (FP6-507482), and Adaptive Services Grid (FP6-C004617).

References

1. DAML-S Coalition, DAML-S: Web Service Description for the Semnatic Web. In Proc. Internatioal Semantic Web Conference (ISWC02), 2002.
2. D.T. Tsesmetzis, I.G. Roussaki, I.V. Papaioannou and M.E. Anagnostou, QoS awareness support in Web-Service semantics, AICT-ICIW06, 2006, pp.128-128.
3. M. Kerrigan, Web Service Selection Mechanisms in the Web Service Execution Environment (WSMX), In Proceedings of the 21st Annual ACM Symposium on Applied Computing (SAC), Apr 2006, Dijon, France.
4. K. Lee, J. Jeon, W. Lee, S. Jeong and S. Park, QoS for Web Services: Requirements and Possible Approaches, W3C Working Group Note 25, 2003.
5. Y. Liu, A.H.H. Ngu and L. Zeng, QoS Computation and Policing in Dynamic Web Service Selection. Proceeding 13th International Conference World Wide Web, 2004.
6. Y. Mou, J. Cao, S.S. Zhang, J.H. Zhang, Interactive Web Service Choice-Making Based on Extended QoS Model, CIT 2005, pp.1130-1134.
7. D.A. Menasce, QoS Issues in Web Services. IEEE Internet Computing, 2002, 6(6).
8. I.V. Papaioannou, D.T. Tsesmetzis, I.G. Roussaki, and E.A. Miltiades, QoS Ontology Language for Web-Services, AINA2006.
9. S.P. Ran, A Model for Web Services Discovery with QoS. SIGecom Exchange, 2003, 4(1):1-10.
10. S. McIlraith, T.C. Son and H. Zeng, Semantic Web Services, IEEE Intelligent Systems, Special Issue on the Semantic Web, 2001, 16(2):46–53.
11. S. McIlraith and D. Martin, Bringing Semantics to Web Services, IEEE Intelligent Systems, 2003, 18(1):90–93.
12. X. Wang, Y. Zhao, B.K. Kraemer and H. Wolfgan, Representation and Discovery of Intelligent E-Services. In: *E-Service Intelligence – Methodolgies, Technologies and Applications*, Lu, J., Ruan,D., and Zhang, G.(Eds.) 2006.
13. D. Roman, H. Lausen, and U. Keller, D2v1.1. Web Service Modeling Ontology (WSMO), WSMO Final Draft 10 February 2005.
14. L.Z. Zeng, B. Benatallah, H.H.Ngu Anne, M. Dumas, J. Kalagnanam and H. Chang, QoS-Aware Middleware for Web Services Composition, IEEE Transaction Software Engineer, 2004, 30(5):311-327.
15. A. Mani and A. Nagarajan, Understanding Quality of Service for Web Services, IBM Developerworks, 2002.
16. C. Zhou, L.T. Chin and B.S. Lee, DAML-QoS Ontology for Web Services. In International Conference on Web Services (ICWS 2004), 2004, pp.472-479.
17. C. Zhou, L.T. Chia and B.S. Lee, Semantics in Service Discovery and QoS Measurement, IT Professional, 2005, 7(2):29–34.

UML-Based Service Discovery Framework

Andrea Zisman and George Spanoudakis

Department of Computing
City University
Northampton Square, London EC1V 0HB, UK
{a.zisman, gespan}@soi.city.ac.uk

Abstract. The development of service centric systems, i.e software systems constructed as compositions of autonomous services, has been recognised as an important approach for software system development. Recently, there has been a proliferation of systems which are developed, deployed, and consumed in this way. An important aspect of service centric systems is the identification of web services that can be combined to fulfill the functionality and quality criteria of the system being developed. In this paper we present the results of the evaluation of a UML-based framework for service discovery. This framework supports the identification of services that can provide the functionality and satisfy properties and constraints of service centric systems as specified during their design. Our approach adopts an iterative design process allowing for the (re-) formulation of the design models of service centric systems based on the discovered services. A prototype tool has been developed and includes (a) a UML integration module, which derives queries from behavioural and structural UML design models and integrates the results of the queries; and (b) a query execution engine, which performs queries against service registries based on similarity analysis.

1 Introduction

Service centric systems (SCS) has been recognised as an important paradigm for software system development in which service integrators, developers, and providers need to create methods, tools, and techniques to support cost-effective development and use of dependable services and service oriented applications. In the SCS paradigm software systems are constructed based on the composition of autonomous web services. Moreover, this paradigm centres on the creation, discovery, and composition of autonomous services that can fulfil various functional and quality requirements. Recently, software systems are being developed, deployed, and consumed in this way. The emergence of important standards in the last years has enabled the SCS vision. However, new processes, methods and tools are necessary to support the engineering of complex and dependable SCS.

Our interest relies in the engineering of hybrid service centric systems, i.e. software systems that are composed of services, but may also use legacy code or software components when no services can be found to fulfil the requirements and functionalities of the system. To assist the engineering of hybrid SCS, we developed a

A. Dan and W. Lamersdorf (Eds.): ICSOC 2006, LNCS 4294, pp. 402–414, 2006.

UML-based framework supporting service discovery. This framework allows the identification of services that can provide the functionality and satisfy properties and constraints of SCS specified during the design phase of the development life-cycle. It also supports the design of SCS by allowing for the (re-)formulation and amendment of the design models based on the services that have been discovered. Our framework uses UML to specify structural and behavioural design models of an SCS being developed and includes two main components: (a) a *UML 2.0 integration module*, which derives queries from UML design models and integrates back the results of the queries, and (b) a *query execution engine*, which performs the queries against service registries. The execution of queries is based on a two-stage approach. In the first stage, services that satisfy certain functional and quality criteria are located. In the second stage, the similarity of these services against additional functional and quality discovery criteria is assessed based on a similarity analysis algorithm [23].

The use of UML as a basis for our approach is due to several reasons: (a) UML is the de facto standard for designing software systems and can effectively support the design of SCS as it has been argued in [5][7][16]; (b) the use of services as well as legacy code and software components in the system; and (c) the expressive power of UML to represent the design models necessary in our approach and to specify queries to identify the services.

Our framework addresses important challenges and requirements that have been identified by industrial partners in the areas of telecommunications, automotive, and software in an integrated European project on service centric systems engineering (SeCSE [21]).

This paper focuses on the evaluation of our UML-based framework in terms of its precision. This evaluation has been conducted by three users with substantial knowledge in the areas of service centric engineering and object oriented modelling. In the evaluation, a total of 48 query iterations with various level of complexity have been performed in two different scenarios. These queries have been executed against a service registry with 97 real services and a total of 1028 operations with different numbers of parameters, data types associated with the parameters, and complexity. The results of the evaluation are encouraging and well accepted by our industrial partners, as described in the paper.

The remainder of this paper is structured as follows. In Section 2, we present an overview of the UML-based framework. In Section 3, we describe the evaluation of the framework and present the results of the experiments. In Section 4 we present some related work. Finally, in Section 5, we conclude and discuss future work.

2 Overview of UML-Based Service Discovery Framework

The UML-based service discovery framework adopts an iterative process in which the service discovery activity relies on the ongoing design of SCS and the available services identified during this process can be used to amend and reformulate the design models of the system. The reformulation of the design models may trigger new service discovery iterations. The result of this iterative process is a complete specification of the SCS structural and behavioural design models. In the framework, queries are derived from system design models and support the identification of services that can subsequently be integrated into these models. The framework uses structural (SySM) and behavioural (SyBM) models of SCS expressed in UML as sequence and class diagrams, respectively.

Figure 1 shows an overview of the iterative process. The process starts from the construction of initial system structural (SySM) and behavioural (SyBM) models by the system designers. The SyBM model describes interactions between operations of an SCS that can be provided by web services, legacy systems or software components. The SySM model specifies the types of the parameters of the operations in SyBM, and constraints for these operations and their parameters (e.g., variants, pre- and post-conditions). When the result of the discovery process is not adequate, designers may decide to reformulate their queries and run the process again. It is also possible, that during the process the designers realise that parts of the system cannot be fulfilled by available services. In this case, designers may alter the design of the system to reflect the fact that the relevant part will be realised by existing legacy code and components, or by the development of new software code. Designers may terminate the process at any time or when further queries cannot discover services that match the existing design models.

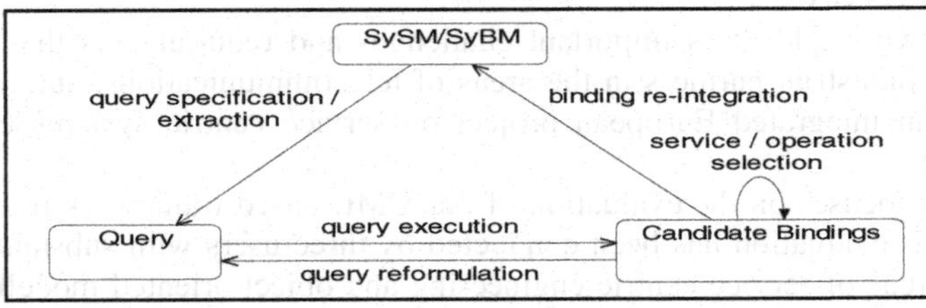

Fig. 1. Process overview

The interactions in SyBM and classes and interfaces in SySM are used to specify queries which are used to identify candidate services and operations that can fulfil parts of (or all) the functionality of the system. Designers may select some of the discovered services and operations and bind them to the design models. This binding results in a reformulation of both the SyBM and the SySM models. The new versions of these models may be used to specify further queries to discover other services that can satisfy more elaborated functionality, properties, and constraints of the system. When the results of the queries are not adequate, designers may reformulate their queries and execute them again.

The UML-based framework is composed of two main components. The *UML 2.0 integration module* component is combined with a UML CASE tool and is responsible for (a) extracting queries specifying the service functionality, properties, and constraints from the design models, based on the designer's selections, and (b) integrating the discovered candidate services back into the design models. The *query engine* component executes the queries by searching for services in different service registries. The search is based on a graph-matching algorithm [23] that computes similarities between queries and service specifications. We assume that service specifications are composed of parts, called *facets*, which describe different aspects of services. Facets include information stored in service registries based on standard UDDI and ebXML technologies such as service interface specifications expressed in WSDL [29], behavioural service specifications expressed as BPEL4WS [4] or OMML [8], semantic service specifications expressed in OWL [19], WSMO [31], or WSML [30], quality of service information, and other information types (e.g., textual description) described in XML format.

Query Specification and Result. Queries are specified by system designers who select an interaction I from SyBM, create a copy of I called *query interaction* (*I'*), select the messages in *I'* that should be realised by operations of services to be discovered, and specify various constraints on these operations or the interaction as a whole.

A query and its results are specified by using a UML 2.0 profile that we have developed. The profile defines a set of stereotypes for different types of UML elements that may be found in (a) query interaction (e.g., messages), (b) results of query execution (e.g. messages, services), or (c) SySM model of a system that are referenced by elements of the query interaction (e.g., operations, classes that define the types of the arguments of interaction messages) or result parameters. The profile also contains metamodels of the facets that may be used for specifying services. A query is represented as a UML package stereotyped as <<asd_query_package>>[1]. A detailed description of the profile can be found in [15].

The messages of the interaction may be stereotyped as: (i) query messages <<asd_query_message>> that indicate the service operations that should be discovered; (ii) context messages <<asd_context_message>> that imply additional constraints for the query messages (e.g. if a context message has a parameter p1 with the same name as a parameter p2 of a query message, then the type of p1 should be taken as the type of p2); and (iii) bound messages <<asd_bound_message>> that are bound to concrete operations that have been discovered by executing the queries in previous iterations. All the messages in a query interaction, which are not stereotyped by any of the above stereotypes, are treated as unrelated messages in I'. These messages should not restrict the services to be discovered in any way and do not play any role in the query execution apart from being copied back to the results of a query execution. The operations corresponding to the query messages are stereotyped as <<asd_query_operation>>. The Profile also defines stereotype properties, which are used to specify parameters and constraints for the elements to which the stereotypes containing these properties are applied. Both <<asd_query_package>> and <<asd_query_message>> stereotypes can specify query parameters.

Query parameters are used to limit the search space and the amount of information returned by the query execution engine (e.g., the number of services to be returned), and are specified as scalar values. Query constraints stereotyped as <<asd_constraint>> provide specific selection criteria for choosing services based on their various characteristics. The constraints may be formulated in terms of UML metamodel or facets metamodel.

A constraint includes (a) a type (hard or soft), (b) an OCL [18] expression, and (c) an optional weight if the constraint is soft (real value between 0.0 and 1.0). Hard

[1] The stereotype names used in the profile have prefix "asd" indicating the name of the UML-based framework in the SeCSE project (Architecture-driven Service Discovery-ASD).

constraints must be satisfied by all the discovered services and operations. Soft constraints influence the identification of the best services/operations but may not be satisfied by all the services/operations that are discovered. The use of OCL is motivated by the fact that OCL is the standard formal language for specifying constraints for UML models and, therefore, queries which are based on these models. Apart from functional constraints, OCL expressions can be used to describe quality of service constraints in our framework.

Following the specification of a query interaction, the framework generates a query package that contains the context and query messages of the query, the classes that define the types of the parameters of these messages, as well as other classes that may be directly or indirectly referenced by these classes.

The result of a query identified by the query execution engine (see below) is also specified by using the profile and is represented as a UML package stereotyped as <<asd_results_package>>. The result package contains a refinement of the query interaction used by the designer to create the query together with the structural model for the elements in the interaction, and various UML service packages, for each candidate service identified by the query execution engine.

The service packages contain elements representing concrete discovered services together with all data types used in the XSD schemas reversed engineered from the WSDL specification of the services. The attributes and relationships of these data types are represented as a class diagram. The operations in the service packages can be *bound*, *candidate*, or *uncharacterised*. A bound operation signifies the service operation with the best match to a query message. A candidate operation reflects another possible result for the query message, but not necessarily the best match. The uncharacterised operations are other operations in the services WSDL specifications.

The framework allows the designer to analyse the results of a query and select candidate operations to become bound operations. After a particular service from the returned candidates is selected, the structural model in the results package is automatically updated with concrete data of the chosen service, and the interaction is modified to reflect the binding of the services and operations. The result package can be used as a basis for a new iteration.

Query Execution Engine. The query package is submitted to the query execution engine to be processed. The execution of queries is a two-stage process. In the first stage (*filtering*), the query execution engine searches service registries in order to identify services with operations that satisfy the *hard* constraints of a query and retrieves the specifications of such services. In the second stage (*best operation matching*), the query execution engine searches through the services identified in the filtering phase, to find operations that best match the soft constraints of the query.

Detection of the *best possible matching* between the operations required by a query and the candidate service operations identified in the filtering stage is formulated as an instance of the *assignment problem* following the approach proposed in [23]. More specifically, an *operation matching graph* G is constructed with (a) two disjoint sets of vertices: one set of vertices represent operations required by a query and another set of vertices represent the service operations identified in the filtering stage; and (b) edges that connect each of the operations in the query with all the operations of the retrieved services, and vice versa. Each edge *e(vi,vj)* in graph G is weighted by a measure that indicates the overall distance between vertices vi and vj. This measure has a value between [0.0, 1.0] and is computed as the weighted sum of a set of *partial distances* quantifying the semantic differences between vi and vj, with respect to each facet F in the description of vi and vj.

Following the computation of the distances between the vertices, the matching between the operations in the query and the operations in the candidate services is detected in two steps. In the first step, a subset S of the edges in graph G is selected, such that S is a total morphing between the vertices in G and has the minimal distance values (this subset is selected by applying an assignment problem algorithm [23])[1]. In the second step, the subset S is restricted to include edges with distances that do not exceed a certain threshold value.

The partial distances are computed based on functions that take into consideration the distance of the signature of two operations. These functions account for the linguistic distance of the names of the operations and distance between the set of input and output parameters. The distance between the set of parameters is computed by finding the best matching between the structures of the data types of these parameters.

The best matching is identified by comparing edges in the graphs representing the structure of the data types of the input and output parameters. The graph of the input and output parameters of an operation is constructed taking into consideration both primitive data types and non-primitive data types. In the graph, the operation name is represented as the root of the graph with immediate $input_{\_pi}$ and $output_{\_po}$ children nodes, for each input and output parameter in the operation, respectively. The data type associated with an input parameter or output parameter is added to the graph as a child node of the respective $input_{\_Pi}$ node or $output_{\_po}$ node ($datatype_{\_pi}$ and $datatype_{\_po}$ nodes). The name of the input and output parameters are represented in the graph as the name of the edges between $input_{\_pi}$ and $datatype_{\_pi}$, and $ouput_{\_po}$ and $datatype_{\_po}$. In the case of a data type $datatype_{\_i}$ that is a non-primitive type, a subgraph for this data type is constructed such that each data type of the attributes in the class representing $datatype_{\_i}$ is added to the graph as a child of $datatype_{\_i}$ with the name of the attribute as the name of the respective edge. If the data type of an attribute is also non-primitive the process is repeated for this data type. The process terminates when all the node edges of the graph has only primitive data types.

An example of graphs of parameter data types is shown in Figure 2 for a query operation *getBusinessInfo(business:Business):string* (represented in white) and service operation *getStockDailyValueByValueXML(getstockdailyvalue:GetStockDailyValue): string* (represented in grey). In the figure, the dashed lines represent the matching of edges of the input and output parameters in both operation graphs based on the similarity of the names of the edges and their respective data types. For instance, edge exchange of complex type *Stock* is matched to edge *strStockExchange* in complex type *GetStockDailyValue*.

The matching process can support modifications to the set of facets F for service specifications. When new facets are added, the matching process can be extended by incorporating partial distance functions for enabling operation comparisons with respect to the new facets. A detailed description of the process with the distance functions is presented in [15].

[1] When the number of operations is not the same between the query and candidate services, special vertices are added in the graph representing dummy operations, in order to make the number even.

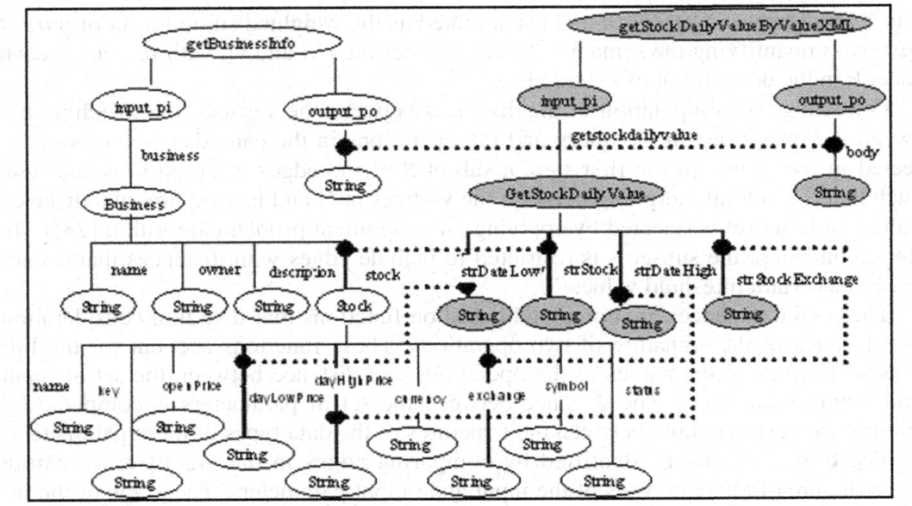

Fig. 2. Examples of data type graphs

3 Evaluation of UML-Based Service Discovery Framework

To evaluate our UML-based service discovery framework, we conducted a set of experiments using descriptions of real services that were identified in the Internet and queries that were constructed as part of two different design scenarios. The objectives of these experiments were to: (i) evaluate the service discovery precision that can be achieved using our framework, and (ii) investigate the effect of different factors on this precision including the complexity of queries, the number of query messages, the use of OCL constraints in them, the use of iterative queries incorporating context messages.

Precision was measured according to its standard definition in the information retrieval literature [6], i.e: $Precision_i = | SO \cap UO_i| / |SO|$, where SO is the set of service operations returned for a query Q; UO_i is the set of the retrieved operations for query Q (SO) that a user i considered to be adequate candidate answers for the query (i.e., relevant operations); and $|X|$ is the cardinality of set X.

3.1 Experimental Set Up

Service Registry. In our experiments, we used a service registry containing descriptions of 97 real services that were taken from various service providers including Across Communications [1], Arc Web [3], ViaMichelin [26], WebServiceX [27], Woogle [28], and Xignite [33]. Eighty two of these services were: (a) communication services (i.e., services that perform communication activities such as sending a fax, making a phone call, sending a text message); (b) location services (e.g., services identifying points of interest, verifying postal addresses, identifying best routes between locations); and (c) business services (e.g.. services providing stock information and market news). The remaining 15 services in the registry were not related to any of the above categories. The services in the registry had a total of 1028 operations of different complexity (see Section 3.2 below).

Queries. The queries used in our experiments were specified in reference to two SCS design scenarios. The first scenario (*AirportTrip*) was concerned with the design of a global positioning SCS offering its users various functionalities including: (i) identification of certain locations and airports in different cities, (ii) identification of best route to airports, (iii) checks for traffic problems in certain routes, (iv) displaying of maps, news reports and weather forecasts, and (v) translation of news reports between different languages. The second scenario (*BrokerInfo*) was concerned with the design of SCS stock purchasing system allowing users to: (a) purchase shares in different stock exchanges, (b) get stock market news, (c) get information about different companies, (d) find present and historical information about stocks, (e) get equity option information, (f) get information about exchange rates, and (g) send transaction documents by fax.

For each of the above scenarios we created a behavioural model (SyBM) of the intended system interactions and a structural model (SySM) defining the data types used in the behavioural model. These models can be found in [25]. Based on these models we specified 24 different service discovery queries for each of the scenarios. These queries were constructed in a way that ensured their variability with respect to four different characteristics that were introduces to investigate whether different types of queries may affect the precision of the results obtained for them and are described below.

(a) *Query complexity*: We used queries of *low* and *medium-high* complexity. The complexity of a query was measured by the number of edges in the graph of the data types of the parameters of the query messages in the query (see Section 2). Based on this measure, low and medium-high complexity queries were defined as queries that had query messages whose data type graphs had up to 10 edges and more than 10 edges, respectively. The threshold distinguishing between the *low* and *medium-high* complexity queries was identified by an analysis of the complexity of the service operations in the registry. This analysis shown that 49% of the service operations had data type graphs with less than 10 edges, 39% of the service operations had data type graphs with 10 to 19 edges, and 12% of the service operations had data type graphs with 20 or more edges. To have query complexity categories representative of the complexity of the operations in the registry, we set the threshold complexity value to 10 representing the median complexity of the operations in the registry.
(b) *Number of query messages*: We used queries with one, two and three query messages.
(c) *Existence or absence of context messages*: We used queries with no context messages and queries with one context message.
(d) *Existence or absence of OCL expressions*: We used queries with no OCL constraints and queries with one OCL constraint. The same type of OCL constraint was used for all the queries of the latter type. This constraint was global and restricted the services that should be returned by a query to be offered by a particular service provider (the form of the constraint was *self.description.Provider.contains('nameOfProvider')*).

Table 2 shows a summary of the different types of queries used in the experiment. The numbers (1) to (24) in the cells of the table represent a different query type. A specific query was created for each query type in each of the two scenarios. Furthermore, we set the number of candidate service operations that should be returned for each query message in a query to be three. This number was fixed to guarantee that precision would be measured in a consistent way across all queries. The value three was selected as it

Table 2. Different types of queries used in the experiment

		No Context Message						With Context Message					
#Query Msg		1		2		3		1		2		3	
OCL		N	Y	N	Y	N	Y	N	Y	N	Y	N	Y
Complexity	Low	1	2	5	6	9	10	13	14	17	18	21	22
	Med/High	3	4	7	8	11	12	15	16	19	20	23	24

was the average number of returned relevant service operations in a sample of queries that we executed prior to the main experiment and, therefore, it would allow for the retrieval of all relevant operations in a query. The complete list of the queries used in the experiment is presented in [25].

Users. In the experiments three different users indicate whether the operations discovered by each query were relevant to the corresponding query message. These users had substantial knowledge in the areas of service centric engineering and object oriented modelling. Each user provided relevance assessments for all 48 queries executed across the scenarios.

3.2 Experimental Results

Tables 3 and 4 show an overview of the precision that we observed in our experiments. More specifically, Table 3 presents the average precision that was recorded for all the queries executed for each of the scenarios and users, and the general precision across all scenarios, queries and users. These results show that on average the precision of the service discovery results for all users in all scenarios is 67%. Also the average measures recorded for the different scenarios were not significantly different: 68% for *AirportTrip* scenario, 67% for *BrokerInfo* scenario. Although some differences were observed for the different users, there was no specific trend for the different scenarios.

Table 4 shows the precision for the different types of queries averaged across the different scenarios and users. As shown in the table (*#Query Mes / Total AVG* row), queries with a larger number of query messages had slightly higher precision than queries with fewer messages (precision ranged from 60% in queries with 1 message to 65.7% in queries with 2 messages and 68.8% in queries with 3 messages). Also, we observed that queries of low complexity had a lower precision than queries of medium/high complexity (60.7% and 70%, respectively, as shown in row *Complexity / Total AVG*). Both these observations confirmed the expectation that as the specification of a query becomes more elaborated (more query messages, messages with more complex data types), precision improves as the models provide a basis for computing more fine-grain distance measures. This trend, however, was not confirmed in the case of OCL constraints where queries with no OCL constraints had higher precision than queries with OCL constraints (69.2% and 60%, respectively as shown in row *OCL / Total AVG*). This was a consequence of the form of the constraint used, which restricted results to services provided by a specific provider and in some queries the required provider did not offer any service with operations relevant to the queries.

The detailed results of our experiments for each scenario and each user with the distance measures of the operations can be found in tables presented in [25].

Our experiments have also demonstrated that the average distance of a discovered service operation that is considered to be relevant to a query message is less than the

Table 3. Summary of precision results

Scenario	User	Average per User and Scenario	
AirportTrip	U1	0.71	AVG: 0.68
	U2	0.68	
	U3	0.64	
BrokerInfo	U1	0.65	AVG: 0.67
	U2	0.65	
	U3	0.70	
		Total Average	0.67

Table 4. Summary of precision results by query characteristics

	No Context Message							
	No OCL				With OCL			
	1	2	3	AVG	1	2	3	AVG
Low Complexity	0.34	0.84	0.68	0.61	0.34	0.69	0.78	0.60
Med/High Complexity	0.84	0.72	0.81	0.79	0.84	0.47	0.57	0.62
Average	0.59	0.78	0.74	0.7	0.59	0.58	0.675	0.61
	With Context Message							
	No OCL				With OCL			
	1	2	3	AVG	1	2	3	AVG
Low Complexity	0.44	0.86	0.76	0.68	0.44	0.69	0.48	0.54
Med/ High Complexity	0.78	0.5	0.74	0.67	0.78	0.67	0.70	0.72
Average	0.61	0.59	0.75	0.67	0.61	0.68	0.59	0.63
#Query Mes / Total AVG	1		0.600	2		0.657	3	0.688
Complexity / Total AVG	Low		0.607	Med/High		0.700		
OCL / Total AVG	No OCL		0.692	With OCL		0.620		
Context /Total AVG	No Context		0.660	With Context		0.653		

average distance of a discovered service operation that is considered not to be relevant to a query message. Furthermore, the difference between these two average distances is statistically significant. This is evident from Table 5 which shows the average distances between operations which were considered to be relevant and not relevant to a query message. The average distances shown in this table have been calculated across the different query scenarios for the individual users who participated in the experiments. The table also shows the standard deviation of the distances of relevant and not relevant operations to query messages and the number of observed cases.

The statistical significance of the difference between the average distance of relevant service operations and query messages and the average distance between not relevant service operations and query messages was checked using the *t-test* assuming samples with non equal variances [24]. The values of the t-statistic that were calculated for the three different users are also shown in Table 5 (row *t-value*) and demonstrate that the probability of the difference in the average distances be incidental was almost 0. Thus, the differences in the averages can be considered as statistically significant (at $\alpha=0.01$). It should also be noted that the average distance of relevant operations to query messages was less than the average distance of non-relevant operations to query messages. These two observations demonstrate that the distance functions which underpin the querying process implemented by the framework produce distance measures which can differentiate between relevant and not relevant operations in a way that is compliant with assessments provided by designers.

Table 5. Average distances of relevant and irrelevant operations

	U1		U2		U3	
	Relevant Ops	**Not relevant Ops**	**Relevant Ops**	**Not relevant Ops**	**Relevant Ops**	**Not relevant Ops**
AVG distance	0.1326	0.1660	0.1342	0.1655	0.1320	0.1687
Standard deviation	0.0233	0.3567	0.0250	0.0383	0.0220	0.0402
# observations	276	155	274	159	257	174
t-value	10.46		-9.225		-10.986	
d-f	229		237		243	

Overall, the average precision measured in our experiments (i.e., 67%) is an encouraging result. Our results are comparable to the results achieved in [32]. An evaluation of the approach in [32] has shown precision measures between 42% and 62% for similarity analysis of names and types of parameters of service operations (*interface similarities*). Furthermore, the UML-based framework is supposed to be used in an interactive process in which the discovery activity relies on the ongoing development of the design of an SCS and the available services identified during the process can be used to amend and reformulate the design models of the system by the SCS engineer. Thus, in our view a precision of 67% provides a good basis for obtaining more precise results in subsequent discovery queries defined using amended and more elaborated design models by SCS designers.

4 Related Work

Semantic matchmaking approaches have been proposed to support service discovery based on logic reasoning of terminological concept relations represented on ontologies [2][10][12][14][17]. The METEOR-S [2] system adopts a constraint driven service discovery approach in which queries are integrated into the composition process of a SCS and represented as collections of tuples of *features*, *weight*, and *constraints*. In our approach, the queries contain information about features, weights, constraints, and parts of the design models of the SCS being developed. In [10] the discovery of services is addressed as a problem of matching queries specified as a variant of Description Logic (DL). The work in [14] extends existing approaches by supporting explicit and implicit semantic by using logic based, approximate matching, and IR techniques. Our work differs from the above approaches since it supports the discovery of services not only based on the linguistic distances of the query and service operations and their input and output parameters, but also on the structure of the data type graphs of these parameters. Moreover, our approach is not restrictive to return exact matches, but instead it returns a set of best matches for a request. These best matches give the designer the opportunity to choose the most adequate service and become more familiar with the available services and, therefore, design the system based on this availability. Matching based on the structure of data types is important during the design phase of (hybrid) SCS since they specify the functionality and constraints of the system being constructed during design phase.

Hausmann et al. [9] propose the use of graph transformation rules for specifying both queries and services. The matching criteria in our work are more flexible and are based on distance measures quantifying similarities between the graphs. Another approach that uses graph-matching is [11] although details of the matching algorithm are not described. The approach in [13] focuses on interface queries where operation signature checking is based on string matching and cannot account for changes in the order or names of the parameters. In [8] the authors advocate the use of (abstract) behavioural models of service specifications in order to increase the precision of service discovery process. Similarly, in [22], the authors propose to use service behaviour signatures to improve service discovery. We plan to conduct new evaluations using behavioural specifications, as proposed in [8].

Some specific query languages for web services have been proposed [20][34], although they cannot be integrated with UML-based system engineering design process. The use of UML to support SCS has been advocated in [5][7][16]. However, none of these approaches combines service discovery as part of the UML-based design process of SCS. When comparing to the existing discovery approaches, our UML-based service discovery framework has demonstrated that UML can be used to support design of SCS and service discovery.

5 Conclusions

In this paper we have presented the results of the evaluation of a UML-based framework to support service discovery in terms of its precision. Our UML-based framework adopts an iterative design process for service centric systems (SCS) and allows the (re-)formulation and amendment of design models of SCS based on discovered services. The framework identifies services based on queries derived from UML behavioural and structural models of SCS. The results of our experiments have shown that on average the precision of the UML-based framework is around 67%. The experiments have also demonstrated that the average distance between relevant discovered service operations and query messages was less than the average distance between not relevant discovered service operations and query messages, and that the difference between these average distances was statically significant. We are conducting new evaluations of our framework that take into consideration behavioural service models and quality constraints.

Acknowledgements. The work reported in this paper has been funded by the European Commission under the Information Society Technologies Programme as part of the project SeCSE (contract IST-511680).

References

[1] Across Communications, http://ws.acrosscommunications.com/
[2] Aggarwal R., Verma K., Miller J., Milnor W. "Constraint Driven Web Service Composition in METEOR-S", IEEE Int. Conf. on Services Computing, 2004.
[3] Arc Web, http://www.esri.com/software/arcwebservices/
[4] BPEL4WS. "Business Process Execution Language for WS", http://www.106.ibm.com/developerworks/library/ws-bpel.
[5] Deubler M., Meisinger M., and Kruger I. "Modelling Crosscutting Services with UML Sequence Diagrams", ACM/IEEE 8th International Conference on Model Driven Engineering Languages and Systems, MoDELS 2005, Jamaica, October 2005.

[6] Faloutsos C. and Oard D. "A Survey of Information Retrieval and Filtering Methods", Tech. Report CS-TR3514, Dept. of Computer Science, Univ. of Maryland, 1995.
[7] Gardner T., "UML Modelling of Automated Business Processes with a Mapping to BPEL4WS", 2nd European Workshop on OO and Web Services (ecoop), 2004.
[8] Hall R.J. and Zisman A. "Behavioral Models as Service Descriptions", 2nd Int. Conference on Service Oriented Computing, ICSOC 2004, New York, November 2004.
[9] Hausmann, J. H., Heckel, R. and Lohmann, M., "Model-based Discovery of Web Services", IEEE International Conference on Web Services (ICWS'04), USA, 2004.
[10] Horrocks, I., Patel-Schneider, P.F. and van Harmelen, F. "From SHIQ and RDF to OWL: The making of a Web ontology language", J. of Web Semantics, 1(1), 7-26, 2003.
[11] Hoschek W. "The Web Service Discovery Architecture", IEEE/ACM Supercomputing Conf., Baltimore, USA, 2002.
[12] Keller U., Lara R., Lausen H., Polleres A., and Fensel D. "Automatic Location of Services", Proc. of 2nd European Semantic Web Conference (ESWC), Greece, 2005.
[13] Klein M. and Bernstein A. "Toward High-Precision Service Retrieval". IEEE Internet Computing, 30-36, January 2004.
[14] Klusch M., Fries B, and Sycara K. "Automated Semantic Web Service Discovery with OWLS-MX", 5th Int. Conf. on Autonomous Agents and Multiagent Systems (AAMAS), Japan, 2006
[15] Kozlenkov A., Spanoudakis G., Zisman A., Fasoulas V., and Sanchez F. "A Framework for Architecture Driven Service Discovery". International Workshop on Service Oriented Software Engineering – IW-SOSE'06, in conjunction with ICSE'06, Shanghai, May 2006.
[16] Kramler G., Kapsammer E., Kappel G., and Retschitzegger W. "Towards Using UML 2 for Modelling Web Service Collaboration Protocols", Proc. Of the 1st Conference on Interoperability of Enterprise Software and Applications (INTEROP-ESA '05), 2005.
[17] Li L. and Horrock I. "A Software Framework for Matchmaking based on Semantic Web Technology", 12th Int. WWW Conference Workshop on E-Services and the Semantic Web, 2003
[18] OCL. http://www.omg.org/docs/ptc/03-10-14.pdf
[19] OWL-S. http://www.daml.org/services/owl-s/1.0, 2003.
[20] Papazoglou M., Aiello M., Pistore M., Yang J. "XSRL: A Request Language for web services" http://citeseer.ist.psu.edu/575968.html
[21] SeCSE, http://secse.eng.it/pls/secse/ecolnet.home.
[22] Shen, Z. and Su, J. "Web Service Discovery Based on Behavior Signature". IEEE International Conference on Services Computing, SCC 2005, USA, July 2005.
[23] Spanoudakis G, Constantopoulos P., "Elaborating Analogies from Conceptual Models", International Journal of Intelligent Systems, 11(11), pp917-974, 1996.
[24] Swinscow T.D.V., "Statistics at Square One", BMJ Publishing Group 1997,: http://bmj.bmjjournals.com/collections/statsbk/index.shtml
[25] UML-based Framework.. http://www.soi.city.ac.uk/~zisman/ASD_Evaluation
[26] ViaMichelin, http://ws.viamichelin.com/wswebsite/gbr/jsp/prs/MaKeyFeatures.jsp
[27] WebServiceX, http://www.webservicex.net/WS/default.aspx
[28] Woogle, http://haydn.cs.washington.edu:8080/won/wonServlet
[29] WSDL. http://www.w3.org/TR/wsdl.
[30] WSML. http://www.wsmo.org/wsml/wsml-syntax
[31] WSMO.http://www.w3.org/Submission/2005/SUBM-WSMO-20050603.
[32] Wu J. and Wu Z. "Similarity-based Web Service Matchmaking". IEEE International Conference on Services Computing, SCC 2005, USA, July 2005.
[33] Xignite, http://www.xignite.com/
[34] Yunyao L.Y., Yanh H., and Jagadish H. "NaLIX: an Interactive Natural Language Interface for Querying XML", SIGMOD 2005, Baltimore, June 2005.

BPEL-Unit: JUnit for BPEL Processes

Zhong Jie Li and Wei Sun

IBM China Research Lab, Beijing 100094, China
{lizhongj, weisun}@cn.ibm.com

Abstract. Thanks to unit test frameworks such as JUnit, unit testing has become a common practice in object-oriented software development. However, its application in business process programming is far from prevalent. Business process unit testing treats an individual process as the unit under test, and tests its internal logic thoroughly by isolating it from the partner processes. This types of testing cannot be done by current web service testing technologies that are black-box based. This paper proposes an approach to unit testing of Business Process Execution Language for Web services (BPEL4WS, or WS-BPEL as the new name), and introduces a tool prototype named BPEL-Unit, which extends JUnit. The key idea of this approach is to transform process interaction via web service invocations to class collaboration via method calls, and then apply object-oriented test frameworks. BPEL-Unit provides the following advantages: allow developers simulate partner processes easily, simplify test case writing, speed test case execution, and enable automatic regression testing. With BPEL-Unit, BPEL process unit testing can be performed in a standardized, unified and efficient way.

1 Introduction

Over the last decade, businesses and governments have been giving increasing attention to the description, automation, and management of business processes using IT technologies. This interest grows out of the need to streamline business operations, consolidate organizations, and save costs, reflecting the fact that the process is the basic unit of business value within an organization.

The Business Process Execution Language for Web Services [1] (BPEL4WS, or WS-BPEL as the new name, abbr. BPEL) is an example of business process programming language for web service composition. Other languages include: BPMN, WfXML, XPDL, XLANG, WSFL [2], etc. They all describe a business process by composing web services. Generally speaking, a business process is defined in terms of its interactions with partner processes. A partner process may provide services to the process, require services from the process, or participate in a two-way interaction with the process.

Mission-critical business solutions need comprehensive testing to ensure that it performs correctly and reliably in production. However, in current industrial practice, business process testing focuses on system and user acceptance testing, whereas unit testing [3] has not gained much attention. This is strange, given the fact that unit testing has been prevalent in object-oriented software development

A. Dan and W. Lamersdorf (Eds.): ICSOC 2006, LNCS 4294, pp. 415–426, 2006.

[4]. We expect that business process, e.g. BPEL process, unit testing will draw more attention along with the maturation and adoption of SOA and BPEL specification. BPEL unit testing treats an individual BPEL process as the unit under test, and tests its internal logic thoroughly.

Current web service testing methods and tools like [5][6] (open source) and [7][8] (commercial) are not applicable to business process unit testing, as they are black-box based, and only deal with simple request-response interaction patterns between a web service and its client. [9] presents a BPEL unit test framework that uses a proprietary approach, specially, a self-made test specification format in xml and the associated test execution.

We show in this paper how to use, adapt and extend current object-oriented unit test frameworks (specially, JUnit [10] and MockObjects [11]) to support BPEL process unit testing. The key idea is to transform process interaction via web service invocations to class collaboration via method calls, and then apply object-oriented test framework and method. The proposed method has been implemented in a tool prototype named BPEL-Unit, an extension of JUnit.

This paper is organized as follows. Section 2 introduces some preliminary knowledge, including JUnit, MockObjects and a BPEL process example. Section 3 describes BPEL unit test method in an abstract view. Section 4 presents the BPEL-Unit tool implementation in detail. Section 5 concludes the paper with future work prediction.

2 Preliminaries

2.1 JUnit

JUnit is an open source Java testing framework used to write and run repeatable tests. Major JUnit features include: assertions for testing expected results, test fixtures for sharing common test data, test suites for easily organizing and running tests, graphical and textual test runners. For a quick tour, please go to http://junit.sourceforge.net/doc/faq/faq.htm.

2.2 MockObjects

MockObjects is a generic unit testing framework that supports the test-first development process. It is used to simulate the collaborator class or interface dynamically in order to test a class in isolation from its real collaborators. A mock implementation of an interface or class mimics the external behavior of a true implementation. It also observes how other objects interact with its methods and compares actual behavior with preset expectations. Any discrepancy will be reported by the mock implementation. EasyMock [12] is a specific MockObjects implementation that is adopted in BPEL-Unit.

2.3 Example BPEL Process

Through this paper, we'll use the purchase process in the BPEL specification as the running example. It is shown graphically in Figure 1.

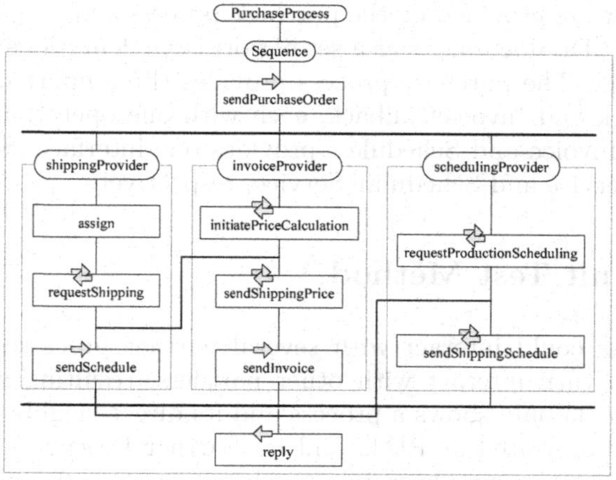

Fig. 1. Purchase process example

The purchase process runs as follows. On receiving a purchase order from a customer (*sendPurchaseOrder*), the process communicates with three partner processes - ShippingProvider, InvoiceProvider and SchedulingProvider - to carry out the work. It initiates three tasks concurrently: requesting for shipment (*requestShipping*), calculating the price for the order (*initiatePriceCalculation*), and scheduling the production and shipment for the order (*requestProduction-Scheduling*). While some of the processing can proceed concurrently, there are control and data dependencies between the three tasks. In particular, the shipping price is required to finalize the price calculation (as is indicated by the link between *requestShipping* and *sendShippingPrice*), and the shipping date is required for the complete fulfillment schedule (as is indicated by the link between *sendSchedule* and *sendShippingSchedule*). When the three tasks are completed, invoice processing can proceed and the invoice is sent to the customer (*reply*).

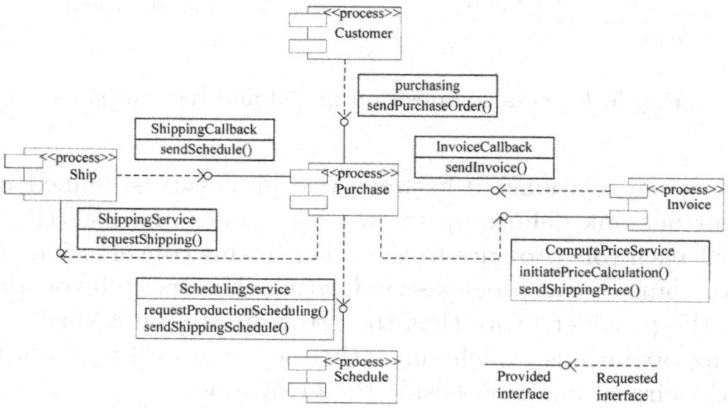

Fig. 2. Service contract between the purchase process and its partners

Interfaces that are provided by the purchase process and its partner processes are defined in WSDL documents as a set of portType definitions. They are visualized in Figure 2. The purchase process provides three interfaces: Purchasing, ShippingCallback and InvoiceCallback, each with one operation. Each partner process - Ship, Invoice and Schedule - provides one interface: ShippingService, ComputePriceService and SchedulingService, respectively.

3 BPEL Unit Test Method

A BPEL process could interact with several partner processes (partners, for short), which in turn interact with other partners, resulting in a network of processes. Figure 3a only shows a process and its direct neighbors. The Process Under Test is abbreviated as PUT, and its Partner Process is abbreviated as PP. A partner may be a simple stateless web service, or a complex process that choreographs several web services / processes and exposes one or several web service interfaces to the caller process. Treating a partner as a generic process makes the method applicable for general cases.

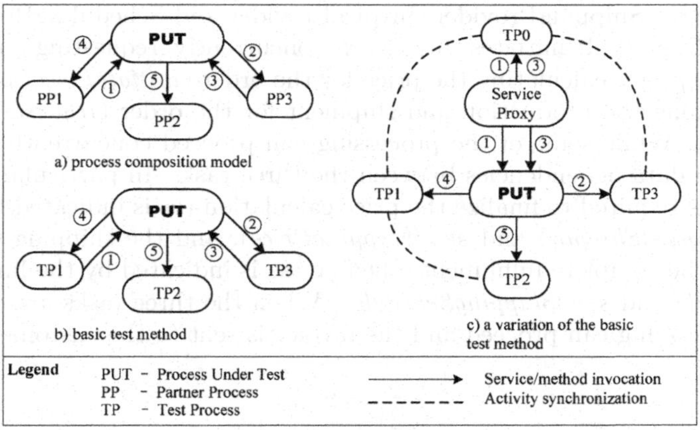

Fig. 3. Process composition model and test methods

A conversational relationship between two processes is defined in a partner link. Each partner link defines up to two *role* names and lists the web service interfaces that each role provides to the other in this conversation. Thus we use arrow lines to connect two processes, indicating the service invocation from the consumer to the provider. Note that the arrow lines do not specify the type of the web service operations, which may either be 1-way or 2-way. For the present, let's ignore the circled numbers beside the arrow lines.

Figure 3b shows a basic unit test method for the process composition model in Figure 3. A Test Process (TPi, i=1,2,3) is used to simulate the behavior of each

Partner Process (PPi). A variation of this method is used in [3] and implemented in a tool prototype named B2B, where test processes are specified in BPEL and executed in a BPEL engine.

Comparatively, this paper uses a different variation of the basic test method as shown in Figure 3c, wherein test processes are simulated by mock objects in Java code and executed in any Java runtime. In this method, each test process (TPi) only describes one direction of interactions - service invocation from the PUT to its partners. This fact can be seen from the direction of the arrow lines between the PUT and TPi. The other direction of invocation - service invocation from the partner processes to the PUT - is delegated to a Service Proxy. Thus the invocations of PUT services that are originally made in partner processes are now made in the Service Proxy to execute in testing. This decision is made based on the fact that a mock object can only specify how its methods are invoked, but not how it calls other methods. There is a special test process named TP0, which describes the expected service invocations into the PUT and its expected responses. The requests and responses are used by the service proxy to actually invoke PUT services and verify the actual responses. In addition, the dashed lines between test processes indicate activity synchronization between test processes. This will be explained in more detail later.

4 BPEL-Unit Implementation

The implementation of BPEL-Unit is centered around the following idea: transform process interaction using web service invocations to class collaboration using method calls, then apply object-oriented testing techniques.

Web service definitions are described in WSDL files and optionally XSD files. The structure of a typical WSDL file is shown in Figure 4 which contains the following elements: type, message, portType, binding, and service. The portType groups a set of operations that can be invoked by a service requester, type and message definitions provide the data model of the operation. Binding gives protocol and data format specification for a particular portType, and service declares the addressing information associated with defined bindings.

Figure 4 also shows the implementation details: how to map web service elements to Java equivalents, how to simulate partner interfaces with mock objects, how to use partner stubs to connect the PUT to the simulated partners, and how to write the test logic inside mock objects based on the PUT behavior. Each is described in a separate section below.

4.1 Web Service to Java Interface Mapping

For the purpose of writing Java tests, firstly the WSDL elements should be mapped to Java language equivalents. Specially, each web service interface definition of the involved processes is mapped to a Java interface definition. As Figure 4 shows, this consists of two parts: a web service interface (denoted as A) maps to a Java interface (denoted as C); and web service types and messages

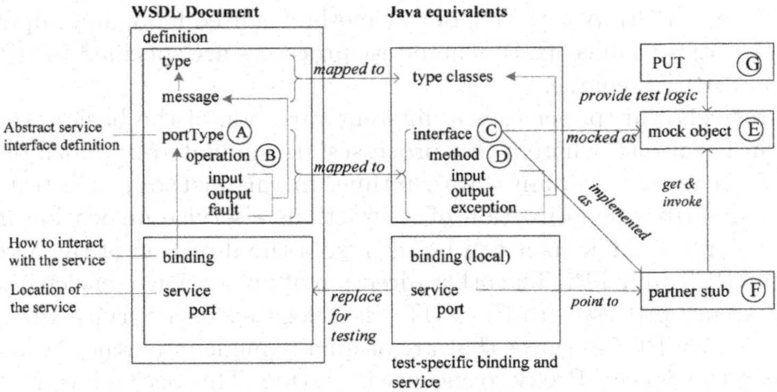

Fig. 4. Method details

map to Java data type classes. Java data type classes will be used to define test data. A Java interface will be used to generate a mock object (or simply called *mock*, denoted as E) of the interface, and a partner stub of the interface (denoted as F, introduced later). Each WSDL operation (denoted as B) will have a correspondent Java method (denoted as D).

The following code snippet illustrates the mapping between the ShippingService portType of the purchase process example and a Java interface.

```
<portType name="ShippingService">
    <operation name="requestShipping">
        <input message="wsdl:ShippingRequest"/>
        <output message="wsdl:ShippingInfo"/>
        <fault message="wsdl:ShippingFault" name="fault"/>
    </operation>
</portType>
-->
public interface ShippingService {
    public ShippingInfo requestShipping(ShippingRequest
    shippingRequest) throws java.lang.Exception;
}
```

4.2 Mock Objects

With a mapped Java interface (denoted as C in Figure 4), a mock implementation (a mock control and a mock object, denoted as E in Figure 4) can be created to simulate that interface, as exemplified in Section 2.2.

Each portType (defining a web service interface) of the PUT and its partner processes has a mock implementation. Therefore, a process may correspond to several mock objects, one for each portType. For the purchase process example, there will be six mock objects: three for the purchase order process (Purchasing, InvoiceCallback and ShippingCallback), one for each partner process - ShippingService, ComputePriceService and SchedulingService.

A mock object for a process sets the expected invocations on the process as well as the return values, and verifies at runtime that the expected invocations occur with the correct parameters. For example, say that *mockShip* is the mock object of ShippingService, we use *mockShip.requestShipping(shipRequest)* to set the expectation of the invocation of requestShipping with a parameter shipRequest, and use *setReturnValue("ShippingService", shipInfo)* to set the return value *shipInfo* of the invocation. Therefore, a mock object simulates the services provided by a non-existent partner process. The mock objects for partner processes will be called by the PUT at run time by relay of partner stubs.

However, mock objects for the PUT are handled differently. We use mock objects for the PUT not to simulate its behavior, but to tell the service proxy to make an invocation to the PUT and then check if the return value of the invocation is correct. Let's see the following example. *mockPurchasing* is the mock object of the PUT Purchasing interface. The first statement tells the service proxy that it should invoke the *sendPurchaseOrder* operation with the specified parameters, and the second statement tells the service proxy to check that the PUT should return invoice as the response.

```
mockPurchasing.sendPurchaseOrder(po, customerInfo);
setReturnValue("Purchasing", invoice);
```

The service proxy does so on behalf of the relevant partner process which makes the invocation originally, because the MockObjects framework does not allow specifying outgoing call behavior in a mock object. The service proxy also invokes the mock object when it invokes the PUT. This is a unified way of expressing test logic, allowing all the interactions to be verified by the MockObjects built-in verification function, no matter it is from the PUT to a partner process or reverse. Nevertheless, this may bring in some confusion on the semantics of mock objects. A simple cure for this problem is to treat the PUT as nonexistent process too in writing test cases.

4.3 Partner Stubs

In a process execution, how to interact with a service, and the address of that service are described in the WSDL binding and service elements. The original WSDL binding and service definitions of a partner process may be varied: SOAP, JMS, EJB, etc. For unit testing, all the partner processes will be simulated as local services implemented in Java. So we should define test-specific WSDL Java binding and service endpoints.

In testing, each service endpoint of a partner process should be a Java class. As we know, mock objects are dynamically created Java artifacts and cannot serve this purpose. So we decide to define a separate stub Java class for each web service interface and name it "partner stub". A partner stub class (denoted as F in Figure 4) implements an interface (C). The implementation of each method (D) in a stub class is simple: it dynamically gets the mock object (E) that simulates the service and calls the mock object's correspondent method (D), collects the return value (if not void) and returns that value. In this way, the partner stub is essentially a simple wrapper of the real service provider implementation in mock (E), and doesn't contain any test logic. The exact behavior of the mock objects can be defined dynamically in test cases. The partner stubs are stateless and independent of test behaviors, and can be automatically generated. For the purchase process example, the ShippingServiceStub is shown below.

```
public class ShippingServiceStub implements ShippingService{
    public ShippingInfo requestShipping(ShippingRequest
    shippingRequest) {
      ShippingService service = MockUtil.getMockObject("ShippingService");
      ShippingInfo result = service.requestShipping(shippingRequest);
      return result;  }
}
```

The address of the partner stubs will be referenced in the correspondent WSDL service endpoint definition so that the invocation of a web service operation (B) will go to the correct method (D) of a correct partner stub (F). In this way, a partner stub and its associated mock object collectively implement a simulated partner process. For the purchase process example and the ShippingServiceStub, the service endpoint information is shown below.

```
<service name="ShippingServiceJavaService">
 <port binding="ShippingServiceJavaBinding" name="ShippingServiceJavaPort">
    <java:address className="ShippingServiceStub"/>
 </port>
</service>
```

The java:address specifies that ShippingServiceStub is the service endpoint. Note that this binding and service information should replace the original one in deploying the process under test to test it. Therefore, these artifacts should be taken as part of the test resource and thus managed as such in the project.

This is different from current use of stub processes in that stub processes contain the real test logic, and are connected to the process under test directly, so that we have to write and maintain a lot of stub processes, redeploy and restart the processes for each test scenario. Through a separation of responsibilities onto a partner stub and a mock object, only one partner stub is needed, and also dynamic changing of test logic without redeploying and restarting is supported.

4.4 Test Logic Specification

Test logic specifies the behavior of the process under test and the simulated partner processes. As aforementioned, test logic will be written in the mock objects that simulate the partner processes.

The first question is where to get the behavior of each partner process. The answer is the process under test. It may have many execution scenarios that are resulted from different decision-making in the control flow. Each of these execution scenarios consists of a set of activities, which are either internal or external. The external activities are those related to service invocation, including invoke, receive, reply and so on. These external activities form a service invocation sequence, which can be used as a test scenario. From a test scenario, interactions with different partners can be separated and used to specify the partner behaviors in mock objects.

Then in a test case, in each mock object of a partner, we record a sequence of calls that the correspondent partner process is expected to receive from the PUT, and prescribe the return values. If the PUT makes a wrong invocation at runtime (including method call with wrong parameters, wrong call numbers or sequencing), the verification mechanism of MockObjects will report the error.

Concurrency and synchronization. In a BPEL process, the service composition follows certain sequencing, which is expressed using programming control structures. BPEL defines the following control structures among others: *sequence*, *flow*, *while* and *switch*. A *flow* construct creates a set of concurrent activities directly nested within it. It further enables expression of synchronization dependencies between activities that are nested within it using *link*.

Therefore, in test processes that simulate real processes, we need similar control structures to express the original activity ordering constraints. Note that complex test logic is not encouraged in unit testing, whereas fast-written, simple, correct, and easy to read/maintain test logic is favored. Applying this principle in BPEL unit testing, a piece of test logic should simply describes an execution path of the PUT; complex behaviors like branching should be avoided as far as possible. However, concurrency and synchronization is a common kind of ordering constraints put on an execution path, so it's unavoidable and must be supported in test behavior description. In Figure 3c, activity synchronization is denoted by dashed lines. It only shows synchronization dependencies between test processes. Actually, the synchronization can also occur inside a test process. Figure 5 shows both cases. Figure 5a specifies: op1, op3, op6 are concurrent activities; op1 must be invoked before op4; op5 must be invoked after op2 and op4. Figure 5b specifies: op1 must be invoked before op5; otherwise is a violation.

With such synchronization capabilities provided, the service interaction ordering indicated in Figure 3a is supported in the test logic as Figure 3c shows. For example, the logic "firstly a PUT service is invoked, then a TP3 service is invoked" could be supported.

Test logic support in MockObjects implementations. Usually a MockObjects implementation provides some flexible behavior description and verification mechanism. For example, EasyMock has three types of MockControl. The *normal* one will not check the order of expected method calls. Another *strict* one will check the order of expected method calls. For these two types, an unexpected method call on the mock object will lead to an AssertionFailedError. The remaining *nice* one is a more loose version of the *normal* one, it will not check the

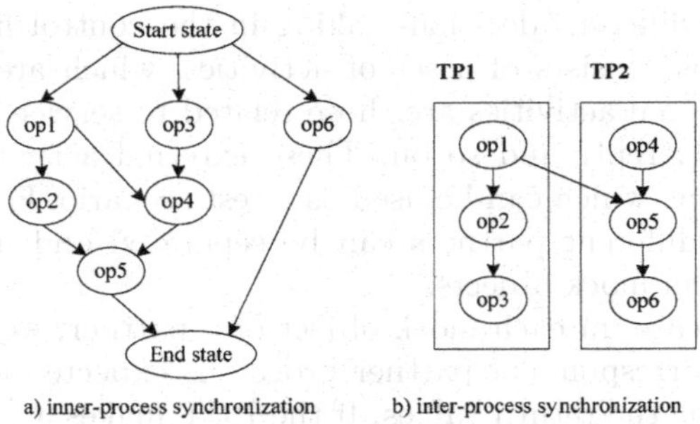

Fig. 5. Activity synchronization

order of expected method calls, and an unexpected method call will return an empty value (0, null, false).

These preset and special MockControl types could be used to express two basic types of control logic / method call ordering: sequence and random (unordered). Take the purchase process as an example. If we want to ensure that several service invocations from the PUT to another process occur in the right sequential order as specified, the strict MockControl could be used to create the mock implementation of that process. Besides sequence and random, there is generic control logic such as alternative (*switch*), *timer* operations (start, cancel, timeout), and concurrency that probably haven't been supported by existing MockObjects implementations. Ideally, the testing of business processes requires the MockObjects implementation to support generic control logic. Practically, the MockObjects implementation should support the concurrency and synchronization logic described previously.

For this purpose, extension to current MockObjects implementation may be necessary. For example, a possible extension is to allow testers specify a successive relation on several methods, say, by an API *syncMethods(m1, m2, ...)* that specifies the occurrence order of the methods m1, m2, etc. This extension has been implemented on EasyMock in BPEL-Unit.

Then for inner-process concurrency and synchronization shown in Figure 5a, the logic could be expressed as follows: use normal MockControl to create the mock implementation so that the method calls will be unordered, then the ordering constraints are expressed by the *syncMethods()* API like this: *syncMethods(op1, op2, op5)*; *syncMethods(op3, op4, op5)*; *syncMethods(op1, op4)*.

For inter-process concurrency and synchronization shown in Figure 5b, the logic could be expressed as follows: use strict MockControl to create the mock implementations for TP1 and TP2 so that the method calls on each mock object will be checked for their correct ordering, e.g. op1 before op2 before op3, then use *syncMethods(op1, op5)* to designate the synchronization between TP1 and TP2. Note that different mock objects are independently invoked at run time so their behaviors are pure concurrent unless explicit synchronization is specified.

4.5 BUTestCase

BUTestCase extends JUnit TestCase class. It is implemented to add business process testing specific APIs and override JUnit APIs to facilitate business process unit test case design. For example, the tearDown() method is overrode to include MockObjects verification logic. For each test method of a test case, tearDown() will be automatically called after the test method is run, thus saving the tester's effort to write verification logic in each test method.

The code below shows a test case for the example purchase process, named PurchaseTest, which extends BUTestCase. In the test case, firstly variables for mock objects and test data objects are declared. Then the variables are initialized in the setUp() method. There can be many test methods defined in a test case, one for each test scenario. The example test method testNormal() checks a complete execution of the purchase process: from the submission of a purchase order to the reply of an invoice. In this method, firstly we set the process input and predict the output. Note that *mockPurchasing* is a mock object of the PUT. The *sendPurchaseOrder*() operation tells the service proxy to start the process, and the *invoice* specified in *setReturnValue*() is used to verify the response of the PUT. Then *mockShip*, *mockPrice* and *mockSchedule* object will receive method calls in parallel. If the method has a return, the return value is set using the *setReturnValue*() method. Finally, the possible synchronization relationship between activities are expressed using the *syncMethods*() API.

```
public class PurchaseTest extends BUTestCase {
  // variables for mock objects and data objects
  public void setUp() {
    // get mock objects & read Process Data Objects
  }
  public void testNormal() throws Exception {
    // Process Input/Output
    mockPurchasing.sendPurchaseOrder(po, customerInfo);
    setReturnValue("Purchasing", invoice);
    // Interaction with Shipping Provider
    mockShip.requestShipping(shipRequest);
    setReturnValue("ShippingService", shipInfo);
    mockShipCallBack.sendSchedule(scheduleInfo);
    //Interaction with Invoice Provider
    mockPrice.initiatePriceCalculation(po, customerInfo);
    mockPrice.sendShippingPrice(shipInfo);
    mockInvoiceCallBack.sendInvoice(invoice);
    // Interaction with Scheduling Provider
    mockSchedule.requestProductionScheduling(po, customerInfo);
    mockSchedule.sendShippingSchedule(scheduleInfo);
     // Synchronization
    MethodSynchronizer.syncMethods(new String[] {
        "ShippingService.requestShipping(ShippingRequest)",
        "ShippingCallback.sendSchedule(ScheduleInfo)" });
    ...}
}
```

5 Conclusion and Future Works

With the increasing attention to business processes in the e-business age, business process testing is becoming more and more important. Lack of unit test tools has resulted in inefficient practices in developing, testing and debugging of automated business processes, e.g. BPEL processes. To address this problem, this paper proposed a BPEL test framework - BPEL-Unit that extends JUnit.

BPEL-Unit has several advantages in supporting BPEL process unit testing.

1. Does not rely on the availability of partner processes. BPEL-Unit provides an easy way to simulate partner processes using mock objects. Thus a single process can be easily tested in isolation.
2. Simplify test case writing. Most developers are already familiar with the JUnit test framework. BPEL-Unit allows process interaction to be programmed in object-oriented flavor. With this tool, developers will no longer be concerned with XML document manipulation, interface, binding and service details in testing.
3. Speed test execution. BPEL-Unit allows "one-deploy, multiple tests". The process under test is deployed only once to run all the test cases associated with this process. This is compared to those methods using stub processes to simulate the partner processes, in which any modification of the stub processes mandates the process redeployment and server restart.
4. Enable automatic regression testing. Process testing is automated by encapsulating all the required test logic and data in formal JUnit test cases. Each time the process under test is modified, its test cases can be re-run (after possible modification) to detect potential function break due to modification.

Currently, we are working on automatic unit test case generation for BPEL processes, which includes searching various execution scenarios, and giving proper test data to enable the execution scenario. The generated BPEL tests can be concretized into BUTestCase format and run in BPEL-Unit.

References

1. http://www.ibm.com/developerworks/library/ws-bpel
2. Process Markup Languages. http://www.ebpml.org/status.htm
3. Z. J. Li, W. Sun, Z. B. Jiang, and X. Zhang. Bpel4ws unit testing: framework and implementation. ICWS2005, volume 1, pages 103 C 110, 11-15 July 2005.
4. Test Driven Development. http://www.testdriven.com
5. WS-Unit. The Web Service Testing Tool. https://wsunit.dev.java.net/
6. ANTEater. Ant based functional testing. http://aft.sourceforge.net/
7. WebServiceTester. http://www.optimyz.com
8. SOAPtest. http://www.parasoft.com/soaptest
9. Philip Mayer and Daniel Lubke. Towards a BPEL unit testing framework. TAV-WEB'06, Pages: 33-42.
10. JUnit. http://www.junit.org
11. MockObjects. http://www.mockobjects.com
12. EasyMock Projects. http://www.easymock.org/EasyMock1_2_Java1_3_Documentation.html

A User Driven Policy Selection Model

Mariagrazia Fugini, Pierluigi Plebani, and Filippo Ramoni

Politecnico di Milano, Dipartimento di Elettronica e Informazione
{fugini, plebani, ramoni}@elet.polimi.it

Abstract. This paper introduces a model for expressing quality according to both applications and human users perspectives. Such a model, compliant with the WS-Policy framework, not only mediates between the application and human user perspectives, but is also capable of considering the different importance that the user can assign to a quality dimension. In addition, the paper introduces a policy selection model based on the adopted quality model. So a human user expresses its requirements according to a high level language and such requirements are matched against a lower level service quality specification.

1 Introduction

Web service selection plays a crucial role in Service Oriented Computing, since it is responsible for identifying which is the best Web service among a set of available Web services with respect to the user needs. It is worth noting that service selection can be performed by two kind of users: applications and human being with different perspectives. For example, technical parameters such as throughput, bandwidth, latency, framerate could be comprehensible by applications and developers but not by final users: the latter have not skills to define the quality by technical parameter but they need a set of higher level dimensions such as video quality and audio quality defined according to discrete scales such as, for instance, *good*, *average*, and *worst*. The aim of this paper is twofold. On one hand, it introduces a model for expressing the quality of service according to both applications and human users perspectives, also considering the different importance that the user can assign to a given quality dimension. On the other hand, the paper introduces a policy selection model based on the adopted quality model. According to this selection model, a human user can express its requirements according to a high level language and such requirements are matched against to the Web service quality specification expressed through a more technical language. Both models are based on AHP (Analytical Hierarchical Process) developed by T.L. Saaty [6].

2 Quality Dimension Model

In the literature [1] several quality models have been proposed. In our opinion they are able to express the non-functional properties of a service, but they do not

[1] see http://www.cs.uni-magdeburg.de/∼ rud/wsqos-links.html

A. Dan and W. Lamersdorf (Eds.): ICSOC 2006, LNCS 4294, pp. 427–433, 2006.

deal with the difference between user and service perspective. In the same way, not all the quality dimensions have the same importance and such importance depends on both the application domain and the service users.

The quality of Web service model we propose in this work aims at dealing with this aspect and it is based on three main elements: a quality dimension model, a quality of Web service definition model, and a quality evaluation model.

A *quality dimension*, also known as *quality parameter*, is a non-functional aspect related to an entity that we are describing. Thus, the quality dimension is close to the application domain we are taking into account and it can be directly measured or estimated starting from other dimensions. We identify two classes of quality dimensions, namely, *primitive* and *derived*. A *primitive quality dimensions* (*pqd* hereafter) is a directly measurable quality dimension and it is defined as follows:

$$pqd =< name, values > \tag{1}$$

- *name*: uniquely identifies the quality dimension (e.g., framerate, bandwidth).
- *values*: defines the domain of values of the dimension. The domain can be either continue (e.g., 0..100) or discrete (e.g., high, medium, low).

On the other hand, a *derived quality dimension* (*dqd* hereafter) is not directly measurable but it depends on other quality dimensions:

$$dqd =< name, f(pqd_i, dqd_j) > \quad i = 0..n, \ j = 0..m \tag{2}$$

- *name*: uniquely identifies the quality dimension.
- $f(pqd_i, dqd_j)$: the *dependency function* stating the influence of other quality sub-dimension (both *pqd* or *dqd*). The nature of the function may vary from a simple expression to a composite function.

2.1 Quality of Web Service Definition Model

Quality of Web service can be defined as the set of quality dimensions which express the non-functional aspects of a Web service. Due to the strong dependency of a quality dimension of the considered application domain, in our quality model we include an actor called *quality designer* that is in charge of collecting and organizing the relevant quality dimensions. Since the quality designer is a domain expert, he is also able to state if a quality dimension is primitive or derived. As stated above a *dqd* depends on both *pqd*s and *dqd*s, thus the work of the quality designer results in a tree named *quality tree* (QT) (see Figure 1):

$$\begin{aligned} QT &= < dqd_{QoS}, tree\_node_k > \quad k = 1..p \\ tree\_node &= [< pqd > \mid < dqd, v(pqd_i, dqd_j), w(pqd_i, dqd_j) >] \\ & \quad i \leq n, j \leq m, domain(f_{dqd}) \supseteq domain(g) = domain(w) \end{aligned} \tag{3}$$

A QT refers to a given application domain and it includes and organizes all the relevant quality dimensions identified by the quality designer. Given a class

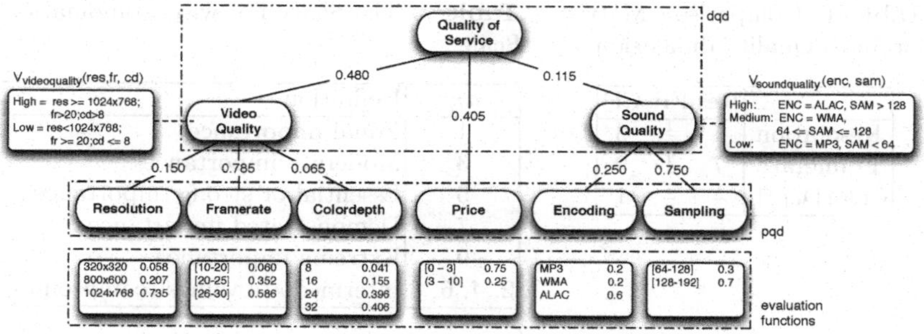

Fig. 1. Quality tree for video-on-demand Web services

of Web services (e.g.: video-on-demand, flight booking), both service providers and users will rely on the related QT tree to describe the offered and desired quality. So, the tree offers a common knowledge for reasoning about quality.

About the structure of a QT, the root is a *dqd* named *QoS*, leaves refers to *pqd*s, and internal nodes are *dqd*s. The function $v(pqd_i, dqd_j)$ derives from $f(pqd_i, dqd_j)$ and returns the value of a *dqd* with respect to the quality dimensions which the *dqd* depends on. The domain of f might contain the domain of v since the quality designer can decide to include in the quality tree only some of the dependent quality dimensions which usually define a given *dqd*.

In addition to the function v, a tree node is also specified by a weigth function w expressing the importance of the quality dimensions which the *dqd* depends on: the higher the weight value, the higher the importance of the quality dimension. The weight assignment is a quite critical activity and we decide to adopt the *AHP (Analytic Hierarchy Process)* approach, developed by T.L. Saaty [6], to perform such an activity. This is a decision-making technique that assigns to each sub-dimension a score that represents the overall performance with respect to the different parameters. AHP is suitable for hierarchical structure as QT and proposes to user some pairwise comparisons between sub-dimensions.

According to this approach, given a *dqd* the quality designer should fill tables like the one shown in Table 1. The first column and the first row are populated with the name of the sub-dimensions influencing the given *dqd*. For each cell, the quality designer assigns a number in $[\frac{1}{9}..9]$ range according to the meaning defined in Table 2 which is the usually adopted one in AHP. About our example, the eigenvector of the matrix in Table 1 is $\{0.150; 0.785; 0.065\}$. This motivates the values reported in QT of Figure 1.

2.2 Quality Evaluation Model

In some case, e.g., bandwidth, lower value means lower quality; in some other cases, e.g., latency, higher value means lower quality. For this reason, nearby the QT, the quality designer also defines, for each quality dimensions in QT, an *evaluation function* which captures the quality trend with respect to the quality dimension value.

Table 1. Comparison Matrix for VideoQuality dimension

	Res	FR	CD
Resolution	1	$\frac{1}{7}$	3
Framerate	7	1	9
ColorDepth	$\frac{1}{3}$	$\frac{1}{9}$	1

Table 2. The Saaty Pairwise Combination Scale

a_{ij}	Definition
1	Equal importance
3	Moderate importance
5	Essential or strong importance
7	Demonstrated importance
9	Extreme importance
2, 4, 6, 8	Intermediate values (compromise)

The evaluation function has different forms with respect to the kind of quality dimension. In case of *pqd*, the evaluation function – $e_{pqd}(values)$ – is a punctual function required to state how a quality value is close or far to the best quality value. Such values can be obtained exploiting the AHP approach.

In case of *dqd*, the evaluation function – $e_{pqd}(QT, pqd_i, dqd_j)$ – is a linear combination of the quality dimensions which influence such a *dqd* according to the considered QT (i.e., $domain(e) = domain(v_{pqd})$). In particular, since the influencing quality dimensions can be both primitive or derived, the evaluation function of a *dqd* will be:

$$e_{dqd}(QT, pqd_i, dqd_j) = \sum_{i=0..n} e_{pqd}(pqd_i.values) * w(pqd_i) + \tag{4}$$

$$+ \sum_{j=0..m} e_{dqd}(QT, domain(g_{dqd_i})) * w(dqd_i)$$

2.3 Policy Model

A policy is a document stating the requirements or the offering of a Web service. Following the quality dimension model, a policy document collects a set of relevant quality dimensions included in a QT and defines the admissible values for each of them. According to WS-Policy specification and the model introduced in [5], a policy P can be defined by a set of mutually exclusive alternatives A:

$$P(QT) = \bigoplus_{k=1..l} A_k(QT) \tag{5}$$

where an alternative A is defined as a set of assertions a:

$$A_k(QT) = \bigwedge_{pqd_i \in QT} a(pqd_i) \tag{6}$$

An assertion $a(pqd)$ is a specialization of a quality dimension with a restricted admissible value set, i.e., $a(pqd) =< pqd.name, values \subseteq pqd.values >$.

At the provider side, we have a service policy document $SP(QT)$ (SP hereafter) which specifies the quality of service with respect to several configurations, i.e. alternatives. At user side we have both a user policy document $UP(QT)$ and the user quality tree (UQT), a version of QT customized by the user.

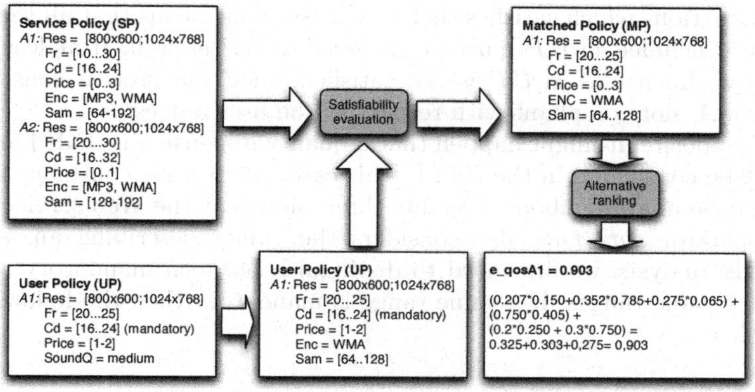

Fig. 2. Example of SP, UP and quality evaluation

3 Policy Selection Model

Given a user request and a set of Web service policies, the policy selection is in charge of figuring out the best Web service policy with respect to the user preferences. The policy selection considers Web services of the same type so, the related quality tree (QT) can be obtained by the quality designer for the given application domain.

The selection process starts when an input of type SP, UP and UQT [2] is received. The process output is a revised policy (RP) where the alternatives included in SP are sorted from the alternative which best matches the user requirements to the worst one.

The selection process is composed by two main steps: *Satisfiability evaluation* and *Alternative ranking*. Figure 2 exemplifies the process considering the video-on-demand scenario.

3.1 Satisfiability Evaluation

Given a $A_i \in SP$, the satisfiability evaluation aims at stating if

$$\forall u_j \in UP, \exists s_i \in A_i \mid s_i \; satisfies \; u_j \tag{7}$$

The operator *satisfies* considers both the name and the values of a quality dimensions. About the former:

$$s_i \quad satisfies \quad u_j \Rightarrow s_i.name = u_j.name \tag{8}$$

Roughly speaking, during this activity, the selection process verifies that, for all the service requests expressed in UP, there exists at least one of the service

[2] For the sake of simplicity, we only describe the matching between a UP and a single SP where the latter expresses several configurations. In addition, we assume that the user does not modify the QT so $UQT = QT$. The general scenario where a set of SPs are considered and $UQT \neq QT$ can be simply derived.

offering assertions which satisfies such a request. This means that all the quality dimensions included in UP must be included in SP as well. If at least one of the quality dimensions in UP is not satisfied, then the process considers the alternative A_i not compliant with respect to the user request.

At the opposite, it might happen that a quality dimension included in the SP could not be considered in the UP. In this case, the process continues since the user might be unaware about a quality dimension that the Web service offers.

The operator *satisfies* also considers the values describing an assertion. About this analysis, we first need to distinguish between mandatory and non-mandatory value ranges. If a value range is mandatory then the following definition holds:

$$s_i \quad satisfies \quad u_j \Rightarrow s_i.value \supseteq u_j.value \tag{9}$$

Instead, if a user defines a non-mandatory value range then:

$$s_i \quad satisfies \quad u_j \Rightarrow s_i.value \cap u_j.value \neq \emptyset \tag{10}$$

The satisfiability evaluation results in a MP (matched policy), a revised version of SP where the structure remains the same of SP and the value ranges are redefined according to the user request:

$$\begin{aligned} MP = \bigoplus A_m \mid & (\forall A_m, \exists A_k \in SP \mid \\ & (\forall s_i \in A_k,\ \exists m_i \in A_m \mid \\ & (m_i.name = s_i.name = u_j.name \wedge \\ & m_i.values = s_i.values \cap u_j.values))) \end{aligned} \tag{11}$$

3.2 Alternative Ranking

The second step of the selection process has to sort the alternatives included in MP taking into account the importance assigned by the user to the quality dimensions. So, the inputs of the alternative ranking phase are both MP and UQT whereas the output is the final policy RP (Ranked Policy).

Similarly to what done during the satisfiability evaluation, RP has the same structure of MP and is defined as follows:

$$\begin{aligned} RP = \bigoplus A_r \mid & (\forall A_r, \exists A_m \in MP | A_r = A_m) \wedge \\ & (\forall A_i, A_j \in RP, i < j \Rightarrow \\ & e_{qosA_i}(UQT, domain(g_{qosA_i})) \geq e_{qosA_j}(UQT, domain(g_{qosA_j})) \end{aligned} \tag{12}$$

The quality of an alternative that we need to rank is calculating using the evaluation functions of the assertions composing the alternatives. An alternative in MP, in fact, is expressed in terms of assertions related to *pqd* which, in turns, are the leaves of the quality tree associated to the alternative as well. Actually, during the quality calculation we do not consider the original quality tree but UQT, i.e., the version that the user customizes.

$$quality(A, UQT) = e_{qos}(pqd_i) \;\; pqd_i.name \in UQT = a_k.name \in A \tag{13}$$

4 Concluding Remarks

In this work we have proposed an approach for selecting Web services by analyzing the offered quality. A quality definition and evaluation model are introduced to allow both Web service providers and users to specify, namely, the offered and desired quality. Such models also deal with the different levels of details in expressing quality by these two actors.

Based on this model, the selection process we propose is capable of automatically matching user and provider policies and ranking several quality alternatives to identify the best Web service. A prototype implementing our approach is under development.

Comparable approaches are given by WSOL [7] and WSLA [2], which provide some description model which our work can use to express *pqd*. Focusing on the selection process, in [4] the dynamics selection of the services is discussed proposing a solution based on agents, using the Web Services Agent Framework (WSAF), that includes an ontology for the QoS and a *ad-hoc* language to specify quality. The proposed approach only evaluate services with feedback assigned from the user that have already used the service, and does not consider the actual users' needs. In [3], the proposed utility theory uses utility functions to estimate every quality parameter without any focus on the dynamic creation and personalization of the dimensions. In our work we have adopted *WS-Policy* as policy language; other languages, such as *Features and Properties (F&P)*, are also available. Different work, like [1], show the substantially equivalence between the two languages, finding the differences at the syntax level.

References

1. G. Daniels. Comparing Features & Properties and WS-Policy. *W3C Workshop on Constraints and Capabilities for Web Services*, 2004.
2. A. Keller and H. Ludwig. The WSLA Framework: Specifying and Monitoring Service Level Agreements for Web Services. Technical Report RC22456(W0205-171), IBM Research Division, T.J. Watson Research Center, May 2002.
3. S. Lamparter and S. Agarwal. Specification of Policies for Web Service Negotiations. *Semantic Web and Policy Workshop, Galway*, November 2005.
4. E. M. Maximilien and M. P. Singh. A Framework and Ontology for Dynamic Web Services Selection. *IEEE Internet Computing*, September-October 2004.
5. T. Mikalsen, N. K. Mukhi, P. Plebani, and I. Silva-Lepe. Supporting Policy-driven behaviors in Web services: Experiences and Issues. *ICSOC-04*, 2004.
6. T. L. Saaty. *The Analytic Hierarchy Process.* Mc Graw Hill, New York, 1980.
7. V. Tosic, K. Patel, and B. Pagurek. WSOL - Web Service Offerings Language. In *Web Services, E-Business and the Semantic Web, CAiSE 2002 International Workshop (WES 2002)*, Toronto, Canada, May 2002.

Abstract Transaction Construct: Building a Transaction Framework for Contract-Driven, Service-Oriented Business Processes*

Ting Wang, Paul Grefen, and Jochem Vonk

Information Systems Subdepartment,
Department of Technology Management,
Eindhoven University of Technology,
P.O. Box 513, 5600 MB Eindhoven, The Netherlands
{t.wang, p.w.p.j.grefen, j.vonk}@tm.tue.nl

Abstract. Transaction support is vital for reliability of business processes which nowadays can involve dynamically composed services across organizational boundaries. However, no single transaction model is comprehensive enough to accommodate various transactional properties demanded by these processes. Therefore we develop the Business Transaction Framework, which is built on Abstract Transactional Constructs (ATCs). ATCs are abstract types of existing transaction models that can be composed and executed in a service-oriented transaction framework according to the ATC algebra. By selecting and composing ATCs on demand, flexible and reliable process execution is guaranteed.

1 Introduction

With the expanding scale and scope of business process collaboration, the complexity and dynamism of a business process has been dramatically increased. Today's business processes may involve a huge amount of activities, resources and business relationships thus impose a big challenge to compose and manage such processes. Service-Oriented Architecture (SOA) allows distributed applications to be loosely coupled into a cross-organizational business process. E-contracting technology provides an efficient and effective way to ensure trustworthiness between the business parties. Therefore, contract-driven service-oriented processes have been emerging in mission-critical business paradigms (e.g. outsourcing).

Transaction management, which has been widely used in information systems for exception handling and fault tolerance, guarantees reliable and robust process execution. However, the traditional approach of transaction management by locking and afterwards releasing the shared resources per access is not applicable in today's complex and long-lasting processes. Driven by the growing need of reliable service composition and execution in complex business environment, a lot

* The research reported in this paper has been conducted as part of the eXecution of Transactional Contracted Electronic Services (XTC) project (No. 612.063.305) funded by the Dutch Organization for Scientific Research (NWO).

A. Dan and W. Lamersdorf (Eds.): ICSOC 2006, LNCS 4294, pp. 434–439, 2006.

of research efforts have been made from both industry and academia. For example, within the CrossFlow project, the X-transaction model for contract-driven enterprise processes in outsourcing paradigms has been proposed[1]. Within the ADAPT project, support for multiple different transaction models for basic and composed services is created [2]. In addition, Web services transaction protocols [3,4] have been proposed by different standardization bodies. These attempts usually address the transaction issues in a very specific application or business environment that are not comprehensive and flexible enough.

According to [5], a solution towards a general transaction support for service-oriented processes is to orchestrate loosely coupled services into a single business transaction by guaranteeing coordinated, predictable outcomes for the participating partners. Following this thought, the XTC (eXecution of Transactional Contracted Electronic Services) project was proposed to develop a Business Transaction Framework (BTF) that provides comprehensive and flexible transaction support for contract-driven, service-oriented business processes. The basic idea of the BTF is to abstract existing transaction models into Abstract Transaction Constructs (ATCs) and compose proper ATCs into a transaction scheme to provide on-demand transaction support. We specify three phases along the BTF life cycle. During the definition phase, the ATC templates are designed. Then during the second composition phase, the needed ATCs are selected to build a transaction scheme according to the process specification. The transaction scheme can be adjusted to accommodate the changes that might take place later on. Last, during the execution phase, real business transactions are instantiated and executed.

In this paper, we introduce and elaborate the novel concept of ATCs, which are the building blocks of the BTF to achieve both comprehensiveness and flexibility. We apply XTraCalm (Cross-organizational Transaction and Contract Algebra and Logic Method) for correct ATC composition and specification. We propose to use e-contracts to specify the Transactional Quality of Service (Tx-QoS) of ATCs. Thus reliable and robust process execution is guaranteed by the ATC-based BTF with Tx-QoS specifications. Due to the page limit, we briefly present our work here and more detailed explanations and examples can be found in [6].

2 Abstract Transaction Construct (ATC) Concept

ATCs are a series of abstract constructs representing the existing transaction models. In fact, they are transactional services that encapsulate transactional semantics and behaviors. ATCs are created during the design phase and the ATC templates exist in the ATC library for later configuration and enactment. We define an ATC as an artifact with the below characteristics:

An ATC has an internal structure. We identify four types of ATC structures: Flat(no internal structure), Sequence, Complex and Tree. A flat ATC is a basic unit representing an ACID transaction. A sequence ATC has the internal structure corresponding to chained or Saga transactions. A complex ATC has the internal structure of the mixed type of arbitrary sequences and parallels, which roughly corresponds to some complex workflow transaction models. A tree ATC has the internal structure like a tree, which corresponds to nested or similar transaction models. Please note that the tree-like ATCs have the structure of parent-child relationship with no control flow between the nodes. By abstracting existing models with various structures, we mean a semantic abstraction and do not consider their implementation details (e.g. the underlying transaction processing systems).

ATCs are composed in a recursive manner. When viewed from multiple layers, a top-level ATC can be decomposed into several second-level ATCs and the decomposition can go further if necessary. We regard a business process as a single transaction. In service-oriented environment, the component services within a process are regarded as sub-transactions, connecting with each other horizontally or vertically. This way, the whole business transaction can be abstracted as a top-level ATC, while each sub-transaction is abstracted as a second-level ATC and this may go on to get the Nth-level ATCs. For example, Figure 1-b illustrates an ATC ‘A’, consisting of the second-level ATCs of ‘B’, ‘C’, ‘D’, ‘E’ and ‘F’. ‘F’ represents a complex process operated by another party, therefore it needs to be assigned as a complex ATC type and may have many levels of decomposition inside. The complexity of the ATC composition within ‘F’ depends on the transparency level agreed by the two parties. In our example, only one sub-level in ‘F’ is relevant. This multi-level view of ATC recursion allows a comprehensive transaction scheme that supports complex cross-organizational business processes.

Each ATC guarantees specific transactional qualities. We define these qualities as Transactional Quality of Service (Tx-QoS). In a service-oriented environment, Tx-QoS can be enclosed in the service description files or service agreements. With the unambiguous specification of transactional qualities, process reliability can be enhanced. We define two sets of Tx-QoS: customer-oriented Tx-QoS representing the transactional requirements in a business context, and provider-oriented Tx-QoS representing the system capacity and technical ability from the service provider. With a mapping between these two sets, the service consumers can expect what Tx-QoS can be offered by the service provider thus can better choose services or partners. Meanwhile the service providers can make use of the Tx-QoS specifications for better monitoring and management of their service quality. In Section 4, an algebra and logic method for specifying ATC composition for Tx-QoS specifications is introduced.

An ATC has a parameterizable interface. Like the description file of a service, the interface of each ATC contains the information of the above characteristics. First the names of the parameters in the ATC specifications are defined while the assignment of these parameters take place the next. There are three types of parameters. The first type of parameters specify the internal structure of an ATC e.g. the specific structure type. The second type of parameters specify the composition information of an ATC such as its predecessors, successors and parallels. The third type of parameters specify the transactional qualities

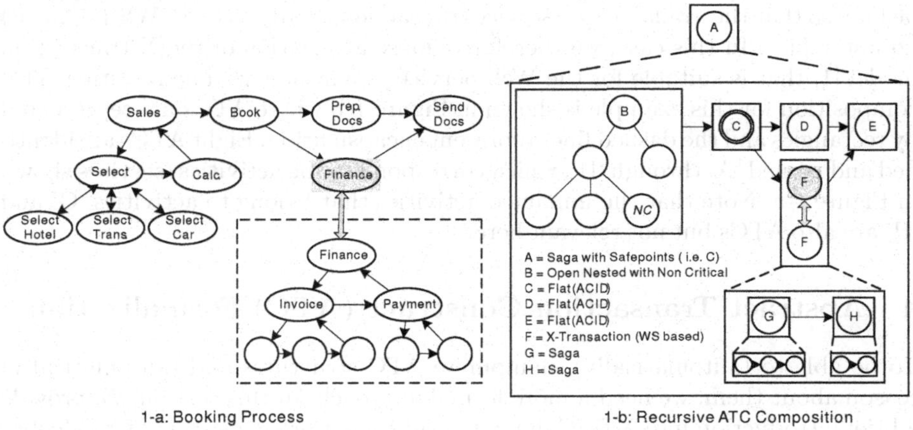

Fig. 1. Example Travel Agency

e.g. atomicity, consistency. When necessary, the composer can assign the recursion level and further refer to other ATCs.

3 Abstract Transaction Construct (ATC) Composition

Upon receiving a process specification, proper ATCs are selected from the ATC library and recursively composed into a top-level ATC for later enactment. To illustrate the ATC concept and especially the composition, we use a variation of the well-known example of a travel agency, shown in Figure 1-a. Customers can create a trip by selecting a hotel, transportation, and an optional rental car (in parallel), after which the costs are calculated and the trip can be booked. Then in parallel the required documents are prepared and the financial issues are dealt with (i.e., invoicing and payment checking), after which the documents are sent to the customer. Being a small travel bureau, the financial dealings are outsourced to a specialized organization, which offers this function through a Web Service. The internal of this Web service consists of invoicing and payment activities, which in turn consist of other activities not relevant for the example.

Assigning certain ATCs, or by redividing the process over ATCs, the transactional behavior will be different depends on the composer's choice upon a particular process specification. As the example process is a long-running one, the entire process might best be supported by a Saga-like transaction model that comprises 'sales', 'book', 'prep. docs', 'finance' (the grayed-out one), and 'send docs'. The selection activities can be supported by an (variation of the) open nested transaction model, as these tasks can be done in parallel. The Web Service needs to be executed under some Web Services transaction model, while the internals of this Web Service, i.e., 'invoice' and 'payment' can be supported by a Saga again. As the Web Service cannot run in isolation, the travel agency might need to see intermediate results when its customers ask for status information, but needs to run in an atomic fashion so that the available web service transaction protocols (e.g., WS-BA in [4]) do not suffice. In this case, we therefore choose a variation of the X-transaction model [1] that is suitable for the Web Services environment. The resulting ATC composition for this example is shown in Figure 1-b where ATCs are represented by rectangles and the dashed lines represent encapsulation. Eight ATCs are identified and named 'A' through 'H', which correspond to the activities/services shown in Figure 1-a. Note that the unnamed activities that belong to activities 'G' and 'H' are also ATCs but not relevant here.

4 Abstract Transaction Construct (ATC) Formalization

To be able to (automatically) manipulate ATC structures and (automatically) reason about them, we need a more formal approach. In this section, we provide a brief introduction into XTraCalm, a hybrid framework consisting of an algebra and a first order logic. The algebra component of XTraCalm is used to specify ATC structures, the logic component to specify characteristics of (constraints over) ATC structures. As such, XTraCalm forms the basis for Tx-QoS specification in electronic service contracts. For reasons of brevity, this paper only presents a brief glance of XTraCalm and more details can be found in [6].

ATC graphs form the structure of ATC compositions where the XTraCalm algebra is defined. We take A as the domain of ATCs. An element of G is a directed graph of which the nodes are ATCs. Consequently, we can define G as follows: $G = \langle N, E \rangle, \quad N = a \in A, \quad E = \{\langle a, a \rangle \in A \times A\}$. The second level of the ATC structure of the example as shown in Figure 1 can be specified as:$\langle \{B, C, D, E, F\}, \{\langle B, C \rangle, \langle C, D \rangle, \langle C, F \rangle, \langle D, E \rangle, \langle F, E \rangle\} \rangle$.

XTraCalm algebra is used to manipulate elements in G. It is a true algebra in the mathematical sense: it consists of operators that take one or more operands of type G and result type G (it is a closed mathematical system). Currently, we have formally defined operators to combine (both composition resulting forests and concatenation resulting connected graphs) and subtract ATC graphs, as well as operators to extract subgraphs (various forms of chopping and slicing). For example, the *nodes* and *edges* functions result in the nodes and the edges of an ATC graph respectively. The *heads* and *tails* functions result in the sets of ATCs without incoming and outgoing edges respectively. Using the composition (+) and concatenation ($\oplus$) operators, we can construct the example graph A introduced above as follows: $\langle B, \emptyset \rangle \oplus \langle C, \emptyset \rangle \oplus (\langle D, \emptyset \rangle + \langle F, \emptyset \rangle) \oplus \langle E, \emptyset \rangle$. Apart from these horizontal operators (operating on graphs at the same aggregation level), we have operators to wrap and unwrap ATC graphs to deal with recursive refinement of ATCs: the wrap operator inserts an ATC graph into a higher-level singleton graph, the unwrap operator results the ATC graph encapsulated in a singleton graph.

XTraCalm logic allows to specify characteristics of ATCs. It is a first-order logic with predicates over A. Using the constructs of the XTraCalm algebra, characteristics over complex ATC structures can be specified. The basis of the logic is formed by base predicates that specify transactional properties of ATCs.

Examples of these base predicates are: *atomic*(a) that asserts ATC a is strictly atomic and *savepoint*(a) that asserts ATC a is a savepoint in a saga-like structure. If, for example, we want to specify that in an example graph g, all second 'steps' (in our example case only ATC C) must be atomic and that at least one savepoint must be contained, we can use the following logic expression ($\downarrow$ represents a graph slicing operator): $(\forall a \in g \downarrow 2)(atomic(a)) \wedge (\exists a \in g)(savepoint(a))$. The XTraCalm logic now has a mathematical notation only.

5 Summary and Future Work

To provide flexible and comprehensive transaction support for contract-driven, service-oriented business processes, we have developed the ATC-based BTF. As the building blocks of the BTF, ATCs are encapsulated, parameterizable, composable transactional services, which abstract existing transaction models as reusable constructs. Our main contribution of such a transaction framework lies in three folds. First, it achieves flexibility by selecting and composing ATCs on demand. Second, it uses contractual agreements to specify transactional qualities for processes thereby guaranteeing business trustworthiness. Third, a hybrid transactional algebra and logic for composition and execution is developed to guarantee correctness.

In our future work, the ATC specification will be refined to accommodate even more advanced transactional semantics, which then also requires extending the ATC language. XTraCalm will be extended further to cope with the additional transactional semantics so that reasoning about them, also in compositions with other ATCs, in terms of Tx-QoS is possible. For example, more predicates are needed for full expressions of possible transactional semantics. Moreover, we have to extend the BTF design to specifically cover the cross-organizational aspect that is left out by our present architecture design.

References

1. Vonk, J., Grefen, P.: Cross-organizational transaction support for e-services in virtual enterprises. Distributed and Parallel Databases **14** (2003) 137–172
2. Sorrosal, F.P., no Martínez, M.P., Peris, R.J.: Prototype of the transactional engine, deliverable d4, adapt project (2004) `http://adapt.ls.fi.upm.es/`.
3. Bunting, D., et al.: Web Services Composite Application Framework. available at http://developers.sun.com/techtopics/webservices/wscaf/primer.pdf (2003)
4. Cabrera, L.F., et al.: Web Services Transactions. Available at http://www-128.ibm.com/developerworks/library/specification/ws-tx/ (2005)
5. Papazoglou, M.: Web services and business transactions. World Wide Web: Internet and Web Information Systems **6** (2003) 49–91
6. Wang, T., Vonk, J., Grefen, P.: Analysis on a contract-driven workflow process from a transactional perspective. XTC working document, Eindhoven University of Technology (2006)

Securing Web Service Compositions: Formalizing Authorization Policies Using Event Calculus

Mohsen Rouached and Claude Godart

LORIA-INRIA-UMR 7503
BP 239, F-54506 Vandœuvre-les-Nancy Cedex, France
{mohsen.rouached, claude.godart}@loria.fr

Abstract. This paper presents a formal model for composing security policies dynamically to cope with changes in requirements or occurrences of events. We address one particular issue - that of authorization within a Web services composition. In particular, we propose a dynamic authorization model which allows for complex authorization policies whilst ensuring trust and privacy between the components services.

1 Introduction

Service Oriented Computing (SOC) is gaining prominence as the technology of choice for integrating applications in diverse and heterogeneous distributed environments. It is widely recognized that one of the barriers preventing widespread adoption of this technology is a lack of products that support non-functional features of applications, such as security, transactionality and reliability. Such properties are of utmost importance for Web service composition languages to keep their promises. Security is a challeging aspect of Web service composition that has not been so far deeply investigated despite its importance [2,3]. For instance, a first challenge is the definition, the verification, and the enforcement of security policies as the complexity of composite Web services grows. To cope with this complexity, it is useful to design a conceptual model that gives a structured way to think about security policies. Another challenge is that non-functional concerns should be addressed by external specifications for a better separation of concerns and for more modular composition specification. For example, if we extend WSBPEL with new constructs for each non-functional concern of the composition, it would evolve into a very complex language, which in turn would limit its acceptance. Furthermore, mixing the specification of the core logic of the composition with specifications of security features and other non-functional concerns into one unit would make the composition specification too complex and hard to maintain and evolve.

In this paper, we propose to use a formalism based on the Event Calculus ($\mathcal{EC}$) [5] to specify authorization policies Web services compositions. $\mathcal{EC}$ is interesting because it supports the direct representation of events that are used in such policies, and the advantage of such a formalism is that it allows for having a common representation for different security models, every service having its own security model.

A. Dan and W. Lamersdorf (Eds.): ICSOC 2006, LNCS 4294, pp. 440–446, 2006.

In the rest of the paper, we introduce in Section 2 the notion of authorization in the context of Web services composition. In Section 3, we present how we specify the policies using the $\mathcal{EC}$, and how the consistency can be checked. Section 4 is dedicated to related works. Finally, Section 5 concludes the paper and outlines some future directions.

2 Formalizing Authorization for Composite Web Services

Service Oriented Architecture allows for considerably more complex interaction models than the classical client/server model, including symmetric peer-to-peer interactions where both parties want to check authorisations, or multi-party composed services where authorization is an issue for each component service. Therefore, an appropriate authorization framework is needed to smooth the flow of a transaction between multiple services whilst respecting the privacy of the data used. This is a complex task since each individual service may have its own authorization requirements

2.1 Basic Notations and Definitions

In this work, we use two booleans $autho^+$ and $autho^-$ to model positive and negative authorizations respectively. Therefore a positive authorization is denoted by $autho^+(s, o, a)$, where s, o, and a stand for subject, object, and action respectively. This authorization holds if the value of $autho^+(s, o, a)$ equals true and does not hold otherwise. Similarly, $autho^-(s, o, a)$ models a negative authorization. Positive and negative authorizations are used at the specification level to state who is or is not allowed to do what. As we will show, the use of signed (i.e positive/negative) authorizations gives more flexibility in handling authorization rules.

Given a Web service, we distinguish between two states according to its role in the request. The first one is given by s_{src} to express that the service s represent the source (who submit the request). The second type is denoted by s_{targ} to precise that the service s is the target (who receive the request). To summarize, a service is seen as a resource that is provided within the system, to which access is controlled. A service can also request other services and is actively involved in computation.

2.2 Authorization Model

To provide a formal specification of the authorization policies, we adapt a simple classical logic form of the $\mathcal{EC}$, whose ontology consists of (i) a set of time-points isomorphic to the non-negative integers, (ii) a set of time-varying properties called fluents, and (iii) a set of event types (or actions). The logic is correspondingly sorted, and includes the predicates $Happens$, $Initiates$, $Terminates$ and $HoldsAt$, as well as some auxiliary predicates defined in terms of these. $Happens(a, t)$ indicates that event (or action) a actually occurs at time-point t. $Initiates(a, f, t)$ (resp. $Terminates(a, f, t)$) means that if event a were to occur at t it would cause fluent f to be *true* (resp. *false*) immediately afterwards. $HoldsAt(f, t)$ indicates that fluent f is true at t.

To achieve a complete specification that supports formal reasoning in $\mathcal{EC}$, the following elements must be represented in the model.

- Separation between source services (s_{src}) and target services (s_{targ}) depending on the role of the service when performing or receiving the effect of an operation.
- Functions that can be used as parameters in the basic predicate symbols of $\mathcal{EC}$. We define these functions as events that may occur during the composition execution. Below, the introduced events are explained. In these formulas, V_p represents the set of parameters values for the operations supported by services.
  - $operation(s, Action(V_p))$: used to denote the operations specified in a policy function or event (see below).
  - $requestAction(s_{src}, operation(s_{targ}, Action(V_p)))$: represents the event that occurs whenever a service source attempts to perform an operation on a target service. Therefore, this is the event that will trigger a permission (or denial) decision to be taken by the target service's access controller.
  - $doAction(s_{src}, operation(s_{targ}, Action(V_p)))$: represents the event of the action specified in the operation term being performed by the service s_{src} on the service s_{targ}.
  - $rejectAction(s_{src}, operation(s_{targ}, Action(V_p)))$: the event that occurs after the enforcement decision to reject the request by a particular source service to perform an action is taken.
  - $permit(s_{src}, operation(s_{targ}, Action(V_p)))$: represents the permission granted to a source service to perform the action defined in the operation on the target service.
  - $deny(s_{src}, operation(s_{targ}, Action(V_p)))$: used to denote that the source service, s_{src}, is denied permission to perform that action on the target service s_{targ}.
- In addition to the described $\mathcal{EC}$ predicates, we add specific predicate symbols. Indeed, in our case many of the function definitions above contain the tuple $(s_{src}, operation(s_{targ}, Action(V_p))$. To check if the members of this tuple are consistent with the specification of the Web service composition, we define the $isValidComp$ predicate. As such it must be used in any rule where functions with the tuple $(s_{src}, operation(s_{targ}, Action(V_p))$ are involved.

Having specified these elements, it is now possible to explain how the various symbols defined above can be incorporated into rules that represent the different types of information required to specify authorization policies able to support Web service composition requirements in terms of security. The complete authorization enforcement model is illustrated in Figure 1. As shown, once the service source makes a request to perform an action on the service target, the target service's access controller processes it. To do this, the access controller evaluates the request by referring to the policy repository and the access control model. If the action is permitted, the access control model will proceed to do the requested action. Otherwise, if the action should be denied, the access control system will reject the action. We precise that the scheme is symmetric, i.e each of the two services could be target, source, or target and source at the same time. As shown in Figure 1,

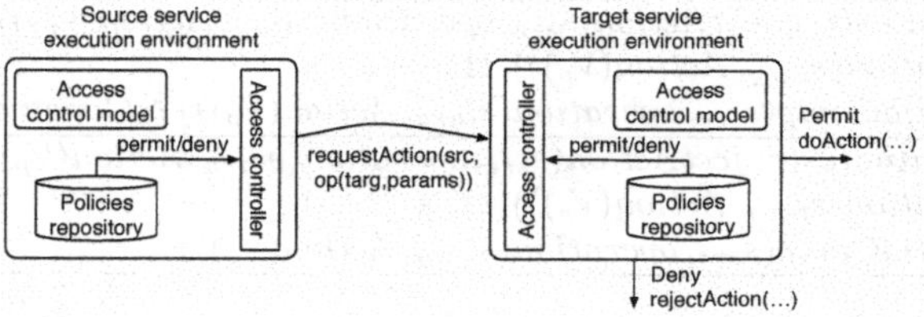

Fig. 1. Authorization Enforcement Model

we distinguish two scenarios to represent the enforcement model. The first scenario models the behaviour of the target service's access controller, generating a *doAction* event when an action is permitted. This event would trigger the relevant service behaviour rules thus causing the composition state to change according to the specification. The second one models a target service's access control monitor rejecting the action to prevent a denied operation from being performed.

2.3 Authorization Specification

In order to correctly interact with the enforcement model described above, each policy specification rule should initiate the appropriate policy function symbol (permit, deny) for each of the events. So for example, a positive authorization policy rule should specify that $permit(s_{src}, Operation(s_{targ}, Action(V_p)))$ holds when the $requestAction(s_{src}, Operation(s_{targ}, Action(V_p)))$ event occurs and the constraints that control the applicability of the policy hold. Additionally, the fluent $permit(s_{src}, Operation(s_{targ}, Action(V_p)))$ should cease to hold once the action has been performed thus making it possible to re-evaluate the policy rule on subsequent requests to perform the action. The $\mathcal{EC}$ representation of this functionality is indicated in the $auto^+$ specification shown in Figure 2. This also shows how each of the other policy types would be represented by rules in the formal notation. For each rule, the terms, s_{src}, s_{targ}, *Action* and *Constraint*, can be directly mapped to the source service, target service, action, *constraint* and event clauses used when specifying policies. The *Constraint* predicate is introduced to specify the pre- and post-conditions for each operation. It can be represented by a combination of $HoldsAt$ terms.

The $autho^-$ specification shown in Figure 2 represents a negative authorization policy by stating that, if the *Constraint* holds and the event requesting the action is performed happens, the action is denied. The second part of the rule shows how the *deny* fluent will be terminated once the decision to reject that action has been

Policy	Specification
$autho^+$	$Initiates(requestAction(s_{src}, operation(s_{targ}, Action(V_p))), permit(s_{src}, operation(s_{targ}, Action(V_p))), t1) \leftarrow isValidComp(s_{src}, operation(s_{targ}, Action(V_p))) \wedge Constraint$
	$Terminates(doAction(s_{src}, operation(s_{targ}, Action(V_p))), permit(s_{src}, operation(s_{targ}, Action(V_p))), t1) \leftarrow isValidComp(s_{src}, operation(s_{targ}, Action(V_p)))$
$autho^-$	$Initiates(requestAction(s_{src}, operation(s_{targ}, Action(V_p))), deny(s_{src}, operation(s_{targ}, Action(V_p))), t1) \leftarrow isValidComp(s_{src}, operation(s_{targ}, Action(V_p))) \wedge Constraint$
	$Terminates(rejectAction(s_{src}, operation(s_{targ}, Action(V_p))), deny(s_{src}, operation(s_{targ}, Action(V_p))), t1) \leftarrow isValidComp(s_{src}, operation(s_{targ}, Action(V_p)))$

Fig. 2. Event Calculus Specification for Authorization Policies

taken, thus allowing the specification to be re-evaluated on subsequent requests. Note that the termination parts for these policies do not have any constraints and can be generically specified for the whole service composition.

2.4 Conflicts

In order to detect conflicts involving authorization policies, i.e. those that arise when it exists two policies defined for the same source, target and action: one being an authorization and the other one being a prohibition, we introduce the *authConflict* predicate that holds if an authorization conflict is detected. This predicate is defined as:

$$HoldsAt(authConflict(s_{src}, operation(s_{targ}, Action(V_p))), t1) \leftarrow$$
$$HoldsAt(permit(s_{src}, operation(s_{targ}, Action(V_p))), t1) \wedge$$
$$HoldsAt(deny(s_{src}, operation(s_{targ}, Action(V_p))), t1)$$

Let consider a typical example of authorization conflict, which arises when the same service is assigned to two roles that have opposite authorization permissions. To enable a complete specification of the different conflict cases that may arise, we introduce a further set of predicates, events, and fluents.

The additional predicates are $Service(name)$, $Action(name)$, $Role(name)$, and $ContradictoryRoles(r1, r2, t, a)$. $Service(name)$ denotes a service with a name *name*. $Action(name)$ defines an action with a name *name* that a source can process on a target. $Role(name)$ determines a role with the name *name*. $ContradictoryRoles(r1, r2, t, a)$ describes that roles $r1$ and $r2$ have opposite permissions for processing an action a at t.

Then, the events introduced are $AssignServiceRole(s, r)$ that denotes a request of a service s for assignment to a role r, $RolePermitAction(r, a)$ that specifies a request for permission of an action a for a role r, and $RoleDenyAction(r, a)$ that defines a request for denial of action a for a role r.

Finally, three fluents are specified: $Assigned(s, r)$ indicates that service s is assigned to a role r, $RoleHavePermission(r, a)$ defines that a role r is permitted to process action a, and $AuthorizationConflict(r1, r2)$ denotes that there is an authorization conflict in the composition (a service is assigned to contradictory roles).

Considering the elements described above, it is possible to define rules that can be used to recognise conflicting situations in the authorization policy specification. These rules are formalized as shown in Figure 3.

Rule	Specification
R1	$Initiates(RoleHavePermission(r, a), RolePermitAction(r, a), t) \leftarrow Happens(RolePermitAction(r, a), t) \wedge (\neg HoldsAt(RoleHavePermission(r, a), t))$
R2	$Terminates(RoleHavePermission(r, a), RoleDenyActivity(r, a), t) \leftarrow Happens(RoleDenyActivity(r, a), t) \wedge HoldsAt(RoleHavePermission(r, a), t)$
R3	$Initiates(Assigned(s, r1), AssignUserRole(s, r1), t) \leftarrow Happens(AssignUserRole(s, r1), t) \wedge (\neg HoldsAt(AuthorizationConflict(r1, r2), t))$
R4	$ContradictoryRoles(r1, r2, t, a) \leftarrow (HoldsAt(RoleHavePermission(r1, a), t) \wedge (\neg HoldsAt(RoleHavePermission(r2, a), t)))\mid(HoldsAt(RoleHavePermission(r2, a), t) \wedge (\neg HoldsAt(RoleHavePermission(r1, a), t)))$
R5	$Happens(conflictEvent, t) \wedge Initiates(AuthorizationConflict(r1, r2), conflictEvent, t) \leftarrow HoldsAt(Authorized(s, r2), t) \wedge Happens(Authorize-Request(r1, s), t) \wedge ContradictoryRoles(r1, r2, a, t)$

Fig. 3. Rules for Authorization Conflicts

The first rule initiates the fluent $RoleHavePermission(r, a)$ when the event $RolePermitAction(r, a)$ happens if this fluent is currently not true. The second rule implements deny for role r to process the action a as a termination of fluent $RoleHavePermission(r, a)$ when $RoleDenyActivity(r, a)$ event happens. The third rule assigns service s to the role r when $AssignUserRole(s, r)$ event happens if $AuthorizationConflict(r1, r2)$ between the role $r1$ and some other role $r2$ is not presented in the composition process. The fourth rule defines two roles, one of which has and another one does not have permission for some action. Here we note that we not fix which role has positive permission and which role has negative permission. Thus, $ContradictoryRoles$ is symmetrical regarding $r1$ and $r2$. Finally, the fifth rule defines a notion of authorization conflict: the user requested the assignment for the second of two contradictory roles.

3 Related Work

There are few papers on security in the context of Web service compositions. We are aware only of the work presented in [4], which presents an access control framework for business processes in BPEL. Like our's, this framework is specific to the authorization problem. Our proposal is more formalized and it can be easily applicable to more security facets in Web service compositions (confidentiality, integrity, and authentication). In [7] the authors present a tool giving a simplified, business-policy-oriented view to its users, who are configuring secure Web services in their systems. They also based their proposal on WS-Security and WS-Policy but their tool does not support composite Web services.

In the project SECTINO[1], a system architecture for local and global workflow system is proposed based on the XACML[6] and SAML. Security concerns are defined in OCL(Object Constraint Language) with model-driven UML tools. XACML is good for specifying policy in a specified domain. But it is not semantic rich enough for cross-organisational orchestration and high-level security requirements.

AO4BPEL[1] proposes an aspect-oriented extension to BPEL. It uses aspects-oriented concept to modularize cross-cutting concerns like security and performance in business processes. Although the AO4BPEL framework offers the modularity and dynamic adaptability to the Web service composition, it lacks semantic description of security aspects, business processes and business rules. This make conflicts detection and policy negotiation infeasible for securing the Web service composition.

4 Conclusion

In this paper, we presented a framework for managing authorization policies for Web service compositions. Specifically, we have described the use of Event Calculus and abductive reasoning for developing a language that supports specification and analysis of authorization policies for Web service composition. A complete implementation and an EC plug-in for Web service were developed and tested using test cases.

References

1. A. Charfi and M. Mezini. Aspect-oriented web service composition with ao4bpel. In *ECOWS*, volume 3250 of *LNCS*, pages 168–182. Springer, 2004.
2. D. Geer. Taking steps to secure web services. *IEEE Computer*, 36(10):14–16, 2003.
3. P. Hung, E. Ferrari, and B. Carminati. Towards standardized web services privacy technologies. In *Proc of the IEEE International Conference on Web Services (ICWS'04)*, San Diego, CA, USA, July 2004.
4. H. Koshutanski and F. Massacci. An access control framework for business processes for web services. In *XMLSEC '03: Proceedings of the 2003 ACM workshop on XML security*, pages 15–24, New York, NY, USA, 2003. ACM Press.
5. R. Kowalski and M. J. Sergot. A logic-based calculus of events. *New generation Computing 4(1)*, pages 67–95, 1986.
6. T. Moses. Extensible access control markup language (xacml) version 2.0 3, Feb 2005.
7. M. Tatsubori, T. Imamura, and Y. Nakamura. Best-practice patterns and tool support for configuring secure web services messaging. In *ICWS '04: Proceedings of the IEEE International Conference on Web Services (ICWS'04)*, page 244, Washington, DC, USA, 2004. IEEE Computer Society.

[1] http://qe-informatik.uibk.ac.at

Supporting QoS Monitoring in Virtual Organisations

Patrick J. Stockreisser, Jianhua Shao, W. Alex Gray, and Nick J. Fiddian

School of Computer Science
Cardiff University, UK
{p.j.stockreisser, j.shao}@cs.cf.ac.uk

Abstract. There are methods proposed for managing various aspects of quality of service (QoS) in service oriented computing environments, but existing effort tends to adopt a provider-centric perspective, aiming largely at optimising and guaranteeing QoS for service delivery. In this paper, we consider QoS monitoring from a service user's perspective. We describe an approach in which monitoring requirements are expressed as queries in a simple language and are processed against continuously arriving QoS data streams.

1 Introduction

In recent years there has been considerable interest in the service oriented computing paradigm. The goal of this research is to create a large-scale distributed computing environment [6] where flexible resource sharing and dynamic collaboration among autonomous individuals are made possible. One particular form of such collaboration is the idea of virtual organisation (VO), where some service providers may team up, at some point in time, to form an alliance in order to respond to or exploit a particular market opportunity [5].

In this paper, we consider one important supporting mechanism for the effective operation of a VO – the monitoring of quality of services (QoS). Typically, a VO manager will establish some measurable, agreed-to performance targets for the service providers in the VO and record them in a Service Level Agreement (SLA) [7]. It is easy to see that in order for an SLA to be truly useful, the ability to monitor the level of QoS that is actually delivered is essential. To achieve this, the following issues need to be addressed:

- As many types of service may exist, a VO manager must be allowed to specify a variety of monitoring requirements.
- The use of different monitoring metrics must be supported to enable different interpretations of a QoS attribute.
- Efficiency and scalability must be considered due to the potentially vast number of services and monitoring requests to be handled.

While some methods have been proposed for managing various aspects of QoS in service oriented computing environments, existing effort tends to adopt

A. Dan and W. Lamersdorf (Eds.): ICSOC 2006, LNCS 4294, pp. 447–452, 2006.

a provider-centric perspective, aiming largely at optimising and guaranteeing QoS for service delivery. In this paper, we consider QoS monitoring from a service user's perspective. More specifically, we propose a simple language for VO managers to express various monitoring requests concisely, independent of any specific application domains, and we adopt a data stream [1] based approach to processing such requests efficiently as continuous queries over potentially-unbounded streams of observed QoS data.

The rest of this paper is structured as follows. In Section 2, we describe related work. Section 3 discusses QoS monitoring requirements and introduces our language. In Section 4, we consider the processing of monitoring requests using a data stream based approach. Finally, we conclude in Section 5.

2 Related Work

Various languages exist for describing services and SLAs. WSDL (Web Service Description Language) allows the functionality of a service as well as its invocation details to be described, but it does not support SLA specifications. More recently, Web Service Level Agreement Language (WSLA) [8], WS-Agreement [4] and the Web Services Management Framework (WSMF) [2] have been developed which allow, in addition to functional specifications, SLA elements such as QoS agreements, monitoring metrics and actions to take when agreements are violated to be included. In terms of supporting QoS monitoring, the language that we propose in this paper can be considered similar to WSLA. That is, both have a similar goal to achieve. However, our language is designed and intended to be used as a query language that treats each monitoring request expressed in it as a query to be continuously answered against the observed QoS data stream.

Much work exists in monitoring, optimising and guaranteeing QoS for specific application domains, for example, optimising network traffic, delivering audio and video over distributed networks, running services on mobile networks and establishing participants' reputation in e-commerce applications. These techniques are rather limited in their applicability. Typically, QoS parameters to be monitored are fixed and there is little need to express different monitoring requirements in such applications. In contrast, our proposal attempts to develop techniques that support QoS monitoring in an application independent manner.

Another area of study related to our work is that of data stream processing pursued by the database community in recent years [1]. Different data stream models, such as sliding windows [3], have been considered, some advanced techniques for maintaining summary data structures over potentially-unbounded, seen-once-only data sequences, such as histograms, wavelets and sketches, have been developed, and the results from these studies have been applied to a number of monitoring application domains, e.g. sensor networks, stock market tickers and network traffic management. We treat monitored QoS data sequences as data streams and use existing stream processing models and techniques, such as sliding windows and approximate aggregations, in our work, but configure them specifically for processing QoS monitoring requests.

3 Expressing QoS Monitoring Requirements

In this section, we describe how QoS monitoring requests are expressed through examples. The reader is referred to [10] for details. We refer to each provision of a service from a service provider (SP) to a service user (SU) as a *service instance*, and we assume that for each service instance relevant QoS data is collected in the following form: `Observation(SIID, QoSAttribute, Value, Time)` where `SIID` identifies the service instance, `QoSAttribute` is the QoS attribute being monitored, `Value` is the observed value of the QoS attribute (nomalised to values in $[0, 1]$), and `Time` is the time at which the observation was made.

The collected QoS data is then streamed into the *Monitoring Component* in our system, where QoS monitoring requests, expressed by VO managers as queries in a simple language that we propose in this paper, will be processed. The design of our language has been influenced by what is expressible in WSLA, and it consists of five main components as shown in the following template:

```
REPORT      <items>
FOR         <instance>
ON          <content>
AT EVERY    <frequency>
DURING      <period>
```

and a query expressed in it is to be interpreted as a request for monitoring the `<instance>` in terms of the `<content>` during the `<period>`, and reporting the `<items>` of interest with a specified `<frequency>`.

The `ON` clause is most significant and allows different types of monitoring to be specified. The simplest is *direct* monitoring of an attribute, as demonstrated by the following example:

```
REPORT observation
FOR    ServiceProvider = "SP1",
       ServiceUser = "SU7",
       Service = "MovieService",
       SIID = "MS234"
ON     "Availability"
DURING [2005-12-12T12:30:00,2005-12-12T14:45:00];
```

Here, the `REPORT` clause indicates that it is the value (`observation`) generated by the `ON` clause that will be returned to the requester. Since the `ON` clause contains a single attribute, it will simply return each received measure of `Availability` as the value for output by the `REPORT` clause. As the `AT EVERY` clause is not present in this case, a default reporting frequency (returning every value generated by the `ON` clause to the requester) is assumed. Direct monitoring is useful in cases where the requester prefers to perform its own analysis of the raw monitored data. However, such monitoring can result in excessive network traffic.

To support more efficient monitoring, we allow *selective* and *aggregative* monitoring to be specified in the `ON` clause. A selective monitoring clause considers a single observation at a given point in time to check if it satisfies a required condition for reporting. The following is a selective monitoring request which asks the Monitoring Component to report if the `Reliability` of the service instance `MS234` drops below 0.8, from start (`SOS`) to end (`EOS`) of the service:

```
REPORT "Reliability", Timestamp
FOR    SIID = "MS234"
ON     "Reliability" < 0.8
DURING [SOS ,EOS];
```

Here, the `REPORT` clause indicates that it is the value of the attribute (`Reliability`) together with the associated timestamp that will be returned to the requester. Different from direct monitoring, however, the value of `Reliability` will only be reported to the requester when the condition specified in the `ON` clause is satisfied. Generally speaking, we can regard the `ON` clause as a conditional statement for the `REPORT` clause - report the items when the `ON` clause is true - if a non-conditional `ON` clause is assumed to be always true.

Aggregative monitoring is another form of summative monitoring that is supported in our language. With this monitoring, observations made at several points over a given period are aggregated to a single measure. The following is an example of an aggregative monitoring which requires the Monitoring Component to report the average Framerate over 10 observations every 30 seconds for the movie service MS234 from start to end of the service:

```
REPORT   observation
FOR      SIID = "MS234"
ON       AVG("Framerate", 10)
AT EVERY 00:00:30
DURING   [SOS,EOS];
```

The `AT EVERY` clause declares a time interval for which a monitoring report is to be sent. Here, a report will be sent every 30 seconds with the most current reading. Note that when selective monitoring is specified in the `ON` clause, the `AT EVERY` clause is ignored.

What we have introduced so far (direct, selective and aggregative monitoring) may be regarded as primitive requirements. It is also possible to use a combination of them in a single query. For example, it is possible to use `COUNT(AVG("Framerate",5) < 24,100)` in an `ON` clause, which will report the number of times within 100 observations that the average Framerate over 5 observations has dropped below 24 to the requester. The reader is referred to [10] for further discussion on the proposed language.

4 Processing QoS Monitoring Requests as Data Streams

In this section, we discuss how monitoring requests expressed as queries in our language are processed. Note that such queries are of a "continuous" nature, that is, they are evaluated not once but continuously as new observations arrive. Processing such requests poses two key challenges: we only have limited time and memory capacity to process the data.

To address these challenges, we adopt data stream techniques in the heart of our query processing engine. More specifically, we use a sliding window model which enables response to queries to be made based on statistics gathered over recently observed data elements, rather than the actual data items themselves [3]. We have implemented two generic algorithms as part of our Monitoring Component for evaluating aggregate functions allowed in our language. SUM, COUNT and AVERAGE are calculated by maintaining statistics of a data stream using exponential histograms [3], and MAX and MIN are computed using a Treap structure [9].

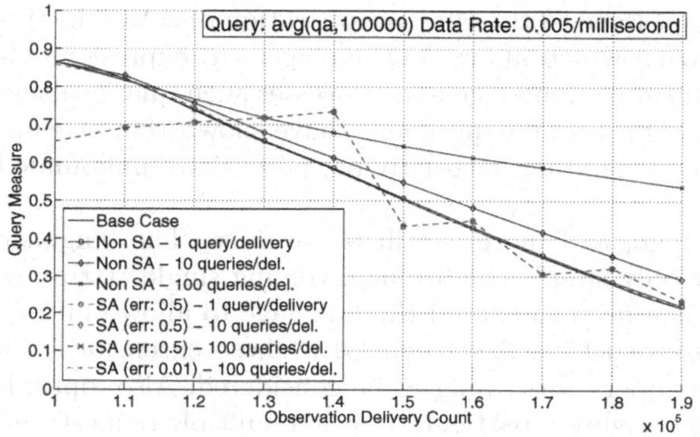

Stream Based			
N	*EM*	*M*	*ID*
1	0.5	88	79
10	0.5	88	81
100	0.5	88	107
100	0.01	1764	921
Non-Stream Based			
N	*EM*	*M*	*ID*
1	n/a	100000	1770
10	n/a	100000	20602
100	n/a	100000	91249

Fig. 1. Experiment Results

We have implemented our Monitoring Component as part of the CONOISE-G project [5]. Figure 1 shows the result of one set of experiments we performed. We ran our experiments with a simple query $avg(qa, 100000)$ (an internal representation of an aggregative monitoring query which has qa as a QoS attribute and a span of 100000 observations), over an input data stream of 200000 observations with a varying number of queries to be handled simultaneously. We set the sliding window size to be 100000 and simulated a data generation rate of one new observation every 200ms.

As can be seen from Figure 1, the non-stream-based method (averaging observations over a span each time when a new observation is received) performed well when the number of queries handled by the system was small. However, when more queries were handled, the measured average deviated substantially away from the expected average (the base case in Figure 1). This is because as the number of queries to be handled increased, more time was required to compute them and computation could not keep up with the rate of data arrival. Consequently, some data was lost resulting in errors in measures. This is explained in the table on the right in Figure 1.

As we can see the amount of items dropped (*ID*) got increasingly severe as the number of queries (*N*) to be handled increased. In contrast, the stream-based method (maintaining exponential histograms) handled the workload much better - the performance was largely independent of the varying number of queries. This is because the stream-based method can “guess” the outcome using the data synopsis maintained on the stream. However, the quality of stream-based method depends on the allowed error margin (*EM*). When the allowed error margin was set to 0.01, a more accurate result was produced than that of 0.5. However, a lower error margin requires more memory space (*M*) in computation, hence some tradeoff must be exercised in practice.

5 Conclusions and Future Work

QoS monitoring is an important issue to the effective operation of a VO. In this paper, we described an approach which allows VO managers to express monitoring requests as queries in a simple language and processes such queries using data stream based algorithms. Our initial experiments have shown that stream-based operations are effective in handling fast-arriving, potentially unbounded sequences of QoS data.

Our work is at an early stage, and more is still to be done. The language is still quite primitive in that only simple conditions involving single attributes have been considered. There is a need to extend the language to allow multiple attributes and logical operators such as AND and OR. These extensions will however require more complex query processing to be considered. Also, optimisation strategies need to be investigated, particularly when multiple requests are handled at the same time.

References

1. B. Babcock, S. Babu, M. Datar, R. Motwani, and J. Widom. Models and Issues in Data Stream Systems. In *Proc. of PODS*, pages 1–16. ACM Press, 2002.
2. N. Catania, P. Kumar, B. Murray, H. Pourhedari, W.Vambenepe, and K.Wurster. Overview: Web Services Management Framework. Technical report, HP, July 2003.
3. M. Datar, A. Gionis, P. Indyk, and R. Motwani. Maintaining Stream Statistics Over Sliding Windows. *SIAM Journal on Computing*, 31(6):1794–1813, 2002.
4. A. Andrieux et al. Web Services Agreement Specification (WS-Agreement). Technical report, Global Grid Forum, 2006.
5. J. Patel et al. Agent-Based Virtual Organisations for the Grid. *Intl. J. of Multi-Agent and Grid Systems*, 1(4):237–249, 2005.
6. I. Foster, C. Kesselman, and S. Tuecke. The Anatomy of the Grid: Enabling Scalable Virtual Organizations. *Intl. J. Supercomputer Applications*, 15(3), 2001.
7. A. Keller and H. Ludwig. The WSLA Framework: Specifying and Monitoring Service Level Agreements for Web Services. *J. Net. Sys. Mngt.*, 11(1), 2003.
8. H. Ludwig, A. Keller, A. Dan, R. King, and R. Franck. Web Service Level Agreement (WSLA) Language Specification. Technical report, IBM, 2003.
9. R. Seidel and C. R. Aragon. Randomized Search Trees. *Algorithmica*, 16(4-5):464–497, 1996.
10. P. J. Stockreisser, J. Shao, W. A. Gray, and N. J. Fiddian. Supporting QoS Monitoring in Virtual Organisations. Technical report, Cardiff University, 2006.

Event Based Service Coordination over Dynamic and Heterogeneous Networks

Gianluigi Ferrari[1], Roberto Guanciale[2], and Daniele Strollo[1,2]

[1] Dipartimento di Informatica,
Università degli Studi di Pisa, Italy
{giangi, strollo}@di.unipi.it
[2] Istituto Alti Studi IMT Lucca, Italy
{roberto.guanciale, daniele.strollo}@imtlucca.it

Abstract. This paper describes the design and the prototype implementation of a programming middleware for coordinating services distributed over dynamic and heterogeneous networks without a public addressing schema (i.e. service addresses are not always public available). We illustrate the problems posed by relaxing the public addressing schema in the context of service orchestration. We discuss the design choices of our middleware. Then, we discuss the actual network technologies underlying the prototype implementation and the formal foundations that drive our approach.

1 Introduction

Modern distributed systems demand not only heterogeneity but also a higher degree of adaptability. The so called Service Oriented Architectures (SOAs) provide evidence of this issue. In the SOA approach, applications are developed by coordinating the behavior of autonomous components distributed over an overlay network. Several research and implementation efforts are currently devoted to design and to implement middleware for coordinating distributed services (see ORC [6], BPEL [8] and WS-CDL [10] to cite a few). These efforts have focused on overlay networks based on a public addressing schema, namely the *address* of each service is directly visible and reachable from any part of the network. Indeed, very few approaches address coordination of services over overlay networks where services reside on hosts without a public address or are hosted behind a firewall hiding their addresses. Other modern distributed systems raise similar demands with respect to the visibility of addresses. Illustrative examples are peer-to-peer networks. Coping with these issues is therefore a challenging task for the SOA paradigm.

This paper attempts to explore the features of the SOA approach within computing environments without a public addressing schema where visibility of service addresses is not always guaranteed. Our goal is twofold. First, we describe the design and the implementation of a programming middleware for service coordination where identification of services endpoints is more structured while preserving, at the same time, independence from the underlining network technologies. Second, we aim at developing a formal model that drive our implementation choices. In our approach, the primitives of the calculus represent the basic programming constructs supplied by the middleware.

A. Dan and W. Lamersdorf (Eds.): ICSOC 2006, LNCS 4294, pp. 453–458, 2006.

The starting point of our work is the event-notification paradigm where service behaviors are coordinated through the exchange of (typed) signals. This coordination model has been adopted for developing a middleware for service choreography called JSCL (Java Signal Core Layer [9]). To cope with the event notification paradigm within a formal setting, in [4] we introduced the Signal Calculus (SC). The SC calculus has driven the design and the prototype implementation of JSCL. The JSCL prototype has been used in [1] for implementing a framework for programming Long Running Transactions (LRTs) [2]. In this paper we extend the JSCL framework to deal with partial visibility of services. Services have no public addresses and their visibility over an overlay network is obtained through intermediate entities called *gateways*. Gateways are directly reachable from the network, and communication from services to gateways can be performed (e.g. by using SOAP). However, services can open a "channel" with several gateways by exploiting registration facilities, and can receive messages from other services through gateways. We discuss how JSCL has been extended to accommodate the new features. In particular, we investigate how the addressing of private services can be implemented by exploiting the SOAP binding proposed in 3.1, preserving the ability to support different coexisting bindings. Then we provide the formal semantic characterization for the operations that SC makes available to handle the new model.

2 Java Signal Core Layer

JSCL is a Java middleware to implement the choreography of distributed services exploiting the event notification style. JSCL has been originally proposed in [4] to deal with services with a public addressing schema (e.g. each service is directly reachable from the network). To abstract from the particular underlaying network adopted, the middleware has been programmed with a pluggable part, the Inter Object Communication Layer (*iocl*), which provides an unique interface to deal with communication primitives (e.g. message exchange, addressing, etc.).

The main concepts of JSCL are *signals*, *components*, *gateways*, *input ports* and *signal links*. The messages exchanged among participants are modeled as signals that are uniquely identified by a name and are tagged with a *topic*, that represents the event class to which they belong to. A JSCL component represents an autonomous service deployed over at least one overlay network. Here we assume that the public addressing schema of components is relaxed. Hence, to supply service visibility, we introduce intermediate entities called *gateways*. Gateways have a unique public name and are directly reachable from each service. In order to receive signals, a component must join a gateway that acts like bridge among different heterogeneous networks (using several *iocl* instances). To avoid centralization, while allowing interoperability among networks, the same component can join with more gateways. The JSCL component interface is structured into *input ports* and *signal links*. *Input ports* describe component behavior and the parameters bound upon signal reception. Indeed, the reception of a signal acts like a trigger that activates the execution of a new computation within the component. Orchestration among components is implemented through *signal links* that connect outgoing signals to input ports of other components. Signal links, on their turn, are strictly related to a particular topic thus offering the possibility to express different topologies of connectivity, depending on the topic of the outgoing signals. Both input ports and signal links can be dynamically modified by the components.

3 Implementation Overview

In this section, we outline the design choices adopted for implementing the JSCL extension supporting the two level addressing. Gateways become the unique public visible entities in the global network. Having several *iocl* plugins, one for each network overlay, gateways need to make available on the *iocls* they are interested to operate in. In the following we only deal with two kinds of overlay networks: SOAP with standard HTTP binding and SOAP with the binding proposed in 3.1. Depending on the protocol used to identify a component or a gateway, JSCL instantiate the proper *iocl* (e.g. to *rhttp* corresponds the *iocl* with multipart, etc.). Communication from a gateway to a public service hosted on the same "domain" can be obtained through HTTP binding or through more scalable and efficient ad-hoc solutions (e.g. JMS).

3.1 X-Mixed-Replace SOAP Binding

We propose an alternative SOAP binding for HTTP 1.1 to supply an envelope transport mechanism for services that cannot open local *tcp* ports (e.g. firewalled applications), or that are executed on machines without public address (e.g. internet applications) or that are hosted in an environment that disallows socket management (e.g. Ajax and Comet applications inside a Web Browser). The proposed binding is based on the X-MIXED-REPLACE [7] mimetype and is structured as follows. *(Step1)* The service opens a HTTP 1.1 connection to a potential requester and performs a GET request specifying the information needed for the publication. *(Step2)* The requester sends back a response having mimetype X-MIXED-REPLACE. Usually, this mimetype informs a client that the server will send a stream of multiple versions of the same document. The client and the server must keep opened the HTTP connection, until the server terminates to deliver the stream. *(Step3)* When the requester wants to send a SOAP request to a previously published service, it sends a SOAP envelope over the active HTTP connection, as a new version of the multipart document. *(Step4)* When a new version of the multipart document is received, the SOAP envelope is extracted and the local service is invoked.

As we will see in section 3.2, the first and second steps are performed by the *gateway.register* method, which creates the *virtual channel* between the gateway and the component, and the third and forth steps are performed for routing signals from the gateway to the component.

3.2 JSCL Implementation Outline

The *UML-like sequence diagram* (Figure 1) illustrates the steps performed by JSCL to implement the component registration to a gateway (*block* 1) and the signal exchanging between two components (*blocks* 2, 3 and 4). In the following we will use the notation P_X^S to represent proxies for an entity S (a component or a gateway) communicating through the network via protocol X. Analogously, A_X^S represents an address of the entity S over the network via protocol X.

The *block* 1, defined in Figure 1, describes the steps performed by the component S_1, hosted on $Host_1$, to activate a registration on the gateway G, located on $Host_2$. S_1 demands to the *iocl* to create a proxy P_X^G for the gateway G, having address A_X^G, which will be encapsulated into the proxy instance. The registration method is invoked on the proxy which makes an HTTP request, specifying the encapsulated gateway address and the component identifier (see Step 1 in section 3.1). The request is received by the *iocl* on the $Host_2$ that creates the local proxy P_X^{S1} for the component requester. Notice that the connection ($socket$) established with P_X^G and the component identifier $S_1.id$ are stored into the component proxy. The gateway stores, into the table H, the association between the component identifier and the proxy bound to it. Finally, the *iocl* sends back an HTTP response to declare that further messages will be send on that stream (see Step 2 of section 3.1). As result of a signal emission, the component S_2 retrieves the set of component link descriptors of the form $(A_H^G, S1_{id})$. For each component, S_2 requests a proxy for the intermediate gateway (P_H^G), then invokes its method $spawn$ (*block* 2). The gateway proxy sends a HTTP Post request, containing the signal and the target component identifier, using standard SOAP HTTP binding. At the reception of the message, the *iocl* on $Host_2$ retrieves the proper gateway and invokes its method $spawn$. The gateway retrieves, from the table H, the proxy for the target component that has been created at the registration phase (*block* 3). The component proxy forwards the signal through the multipart stream using the previously encapsulated connection with P_X^G (see Step 3 of section 3.1). Finally, in *block* 4, the gateway proxy retrieves the locally registered component and demands to it the signal handling (see Step 4 of section 3.1).

4 Signal Calculus

SC is a process calculus in the style of [5, 3] introduced in [4] as foundational model of the JSCL middleware. In this section we describe the extension of SC introduced to formal represent the network model considered in this paper.

Component behaviors (B) are defined by the following grammar:

$$B ::= 0 \mid +R[x : \tau \rightarrow B] \mid +F[\tau \triangleright g[a]] \mid \triangleright g \mid \bar{s} : \tau.B \mid B|B \mid !B$$

Behaviors represent JSCL computations executed inside a component, while the set of primitives represents the JSCL programmer API. The flow update ($+F[\tau \triangleright g[a]]$) represents the JSCL API to create a new outgoing signal link, it extends the component flow, appending the gateway g handling all signal communications of schema τ with component named a. The gateway join ($\triangleright g$) represents JSCL API to publish the component, it opens a *channel* between the service and the gateway g, suppling the addressing schema for the service. A gateway body contains a tuple (possibly empty) of envelopes to route to the joined components. Gateway bodies (G) are defined by the following grammar:

$$S ::= \emptyset \mid S|S \mid < s@a : \tau >$$

Networks (N) are defined by the following extended grammar:

$$N ::= \emptyset \mid a[B]_{(R,F,g)} \mid g[S]_{(a)} \mid N \| N \mid < s@g[a] : \tau >$$

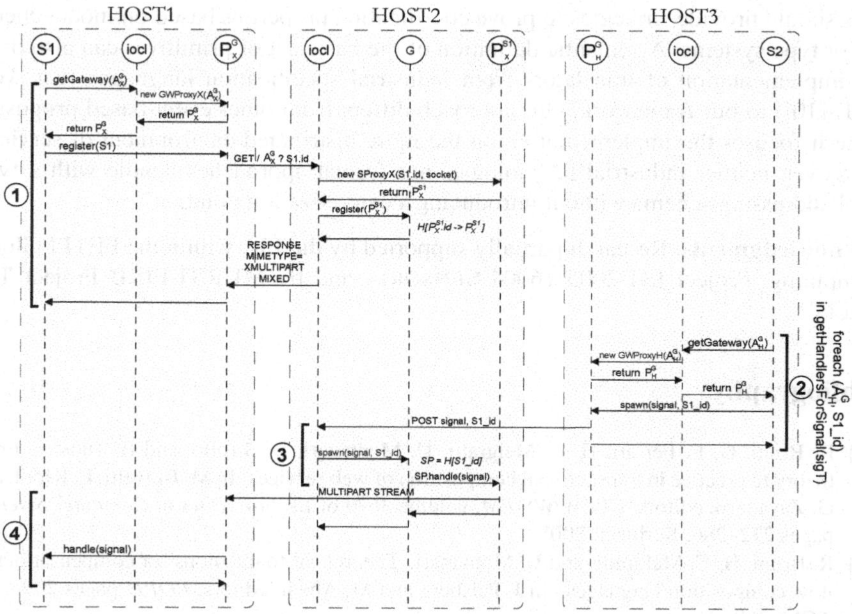

Fig. 1. Registration and signal emission protocol

A network describes the component and gateway topologies, and it is an abstraction of the set of JSCL *iocls* shared among services and gateways. The new primitive gateway ($g[S]_{(\boldsymbol{a})}$) describes a public gateway. The set $\boldsymbol{a}$ identifies the set of component names that have joined the gateway. The component primitive ($a[B]_{(R,F,\boldsymbol{g})}$) has been extended with the tuple ($\boldsymbol{g}$) of gateway names to which the component is linked. Analogously, the signal envelope primitive ($< s@g[a] : \tau >$) has been adapted to contain the gateway g that will effectively deliver the message.

SC components and gateways are closely related to the notion of *Ambient* [3], but enriched with mechanisms to control the interaction policies among ambients. The SC semantics is defined in a reduction style. Hereafter, we simply provide an example of the reduction rules.

$$\frac{a \in \boldsymbol{a} \quad g \in \boldsymbol{g} \quad R \downarrow_{s:\tau} = (\sigma, B)}{g[< s@a : \tau > |S]_{(\boldsymbol{a})} \| a[Q]_{(R,F,\boldsymbol{g})} \rightarrow g[S]_{(\boldsymbol{a})} \| a[\sigma B|Q]_{(R,F,\boldsymbol{g})}} \; (IN)$$

This rule allows an envelope contained into the gateway to react with the component whose name is specified inside the envelope (see step 4 in Figure 1).

5 Concluding Remarks

We have introduced a framework to program coordination policies of distributed services with a two level addressing schema. Unlike current industrial coordination technologies (e.g. BPEL [8]), our solution is based on top of a clear foundational approach.

This should provide strategies to prove coordination properties based on model checking or type systems. A semantic definition of the basic set of primitives can also drive the implementation of translators from industrial specification languages (e.g. WS-CDL [10]) to our framework. Our approach differs from other event based proposals, since it focuses the implementation on the more distributed environment of services. Moreover, neither industrial technologies nor formal approaches handle with a two-level addressing schema without introducing a centralization point.

Acknowledgments. Research partially supported by the EU, within the FETPI Global Computing, Project IST-2005-16004 SENSORIA and by MURST-FIRB Project TOCAI.IT

Bibliography

[1] R. Bruni, G. L. Ferrari, H. C. Melgratti, U. Montanari, D. Strollo, and E. Tuosto. From theory to practice in transactional composition of web services. In M. Bravetti, L. Kloul, and G. Zavattaro, editors, *EPEW/WS-FM*, volume 3670 of *Lecture Notes in Computer Science*, pages 272–286. Springer, 2005.

[2] R. Bruni, H. C. Melgratti, and U. Montanari. Theoretical foundations for compensations in flow composition languages. In J. Palsberg and M. Abadi, editors, *POPL*, pages 209–220. ACM, 2005.

[3] L. Cardelli and A. D. Gordon. Mobile ambients. In M. Nivat, editor, *FoSSaCS*, volume 1378 of *Lecture Notes in Computer Science*, pages 140–155. Springer, 1998.

[4] G. Ferrari, R. Guanciale, and D. Strollo. JSCL: a Middleware for Service Coordination. In *Proc. FORTE'06*, Lecture Notes in Computer Science, 2006. To appear.

[5] R. Milner. The polyadic π-calculus: A tutorial. In F. L. Bauer, W. Brauer, and H. Schwichtenberg, editors, *Logic and Algebra of Specification, Proceedings of International NATO Summer School (Marktoberdorf, Germany, 1991)*, volume 94 of *Series F*. NATO ASI, 1993. Available as Technical Report ECS-LFCS-91-180, University of Edinburgh, October 1991.

[6] J. Misra. A programming model for the orchestration of web services. In *SEFM*, pages 2–11. IEEE Computer Society, 2004.

[7] Netscape. An Exploration of Dynamic Documents. `http://wp.netscape.com/assist/net_sites/pushpull.html`, 1999.

[8] OASIS Bpel Specifications. OASIS - BPEL. `http://www.oasis-open.org/cover/bpel4ws.html`.

[9] D. Strollo. Java Signal Core Layer (JSCL). Technical report, Dipartimento di Informatica, Università di Pisa, 2005. Available at `http://www.di.unipi.it/~strollo`.

[10] W3C. Web Services Choreography Description Language (v.1.0). Technical report.

Implicit vs. Explicit Data-Flow Requirements in Web Service Composition Goals

Annapaola Marconi, Marco Pistore, and Paolo Traverso

ITC-irst
Via Sommarive 18, Trento, Italy
{marconi, pistore, traverso}@itc.it

Abstract. In this paper we compare two different approaches to specify data-flow requirements in Web service composition problems, i.e., requirements on data that are exchanged among component services. *Implicit* data-flow requirements are a set of rules that specify how the functions computed by the component services are to be combined by the composite service. They implicitly define the required constraints among exchanged data. *Explicit* data-flow requirements are a set of explicit specifications on how the composition should manipulate messages and route them from/to components. In the paper, we compare these two approaches through an experimental evaluation, both from the point of view of efficiency and scalability and from that of practical usability.

1 Introduction

Service composition is one of the fundamental ideas underlying service-oriented applications: composed services perform new functionalities by interacting with component services that are available on the Web. In most real-world applications, service compositions must be at the "process-level", i.e., they must take into account that component services are stateful processes [1] and that they require to follow complex interaction protocols specified in language such as WS-BPEL [2], The automated synthesis of composed services is one of the key tasks that supports the design and development of service oriented applications: given a set of available component services and a composition goal, the task corresponds to the synthesis of a composition, e.g., a new service, or a set of constraints on the behaviors of existing services, which satisfies the requirements expressed by the composition goal.

Recent works address the problem of the automated synthesis of composed services at the process level, see, e.g., [1,3,4,5,6,7]. However, most of them do not take into account a key aspect of the composition problem: the specification of *data-flow requirements*, i.e. requirements on data that are exchanged among component services. This is a significant and challenging problem, since, in real life scenarios, business analysts and developers need a way to express complex requirements on the exchanged data. Moreover, to make the automated composition an effective and practical task, the requirements specification should be easy to write and to understand for the analyst. Surprisingly, very little effort has been devoted in the literature to address this problem.

In this paper we compare two different approaches to the specification of data-flow requirements for the automated synthesis of composed services specified in WS-BPEL.

A. Dan and W. Lamersdorf (Eds.): ICSOC 2006, LNCS 4294, pp. 459–464, 2006.

The first approach is based on *implicit data-flow requirements* [7]. It exploit the functions that define the tasks carried out by the component services, and that annotate their WS-BPEL descriptions. Composition goals contain references to such functions that implicitly define constraints on data flows. Consider, for instance, a virtual travel agency (VTA from now on) that composes two component services, a Flight and a Hotel reservation service. The implicit data-flow requirement stating that the cost offered to the Customer is a specific function (prepare_cost) of the costs of the Hotel and of the Flight can be specified as follows:

$$\text{C.cost} = \text{prepare\_cost}(\text{H.costOf}(\text{C.loc},\text{C.date}),\text{F.costOf}(\text{C.loc},\text{C.date}))$$

We assume that the cost functions F.costOf and H.costOf appear as "semantic" annotations in the WS-BPEL processes of the flight and hotel components, respectively. This requirement implicitly specifies a data flow from the messages of the components to the composed service. The composition task should determine from this specification which messages and which data should be sent from a service to another. In [7] it is shown how the framework for process-level composition defined in [5,6] can be exploited to generate the composition starting from implicit data-flow requirements.

The second approach is based on *explicit data-flow requirements*. In this case, composition goals contain constraints that define the valid routings and manipulations on the messages of the component services, i.e., these constraints specify how the output messages of the composed service are obtained by manipulating and combining in suitable ways the input messages obtained from the component services. In the VTA example, the explicit data flow requirement is the following:

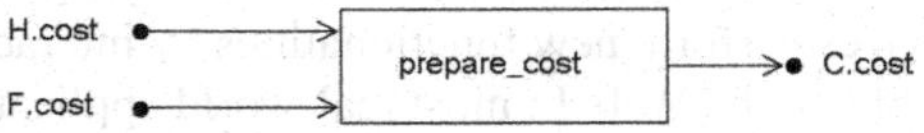

It directly specifies that the VTA must apply its internal function prepare_cost on the costs received from the Hotel and from the Flight, to obtain the cost to be sent in the offer to the Customer. In [8] it is shown that explicit data-flow requirements can be described in a graphical way, as *data-nets*. It is also shown how to adapt the composition framework of [5,6] to the case of explicit data-flow requirements.

2 Comparison of the Two Approaches

We now compare the two proposed approaches for modeling data-flow requirements from a technical point of view, from the point of view of the performance, and for what concerns usability.

The two approaches present some similarities. First of all, both of them extend the automated composition framework proposed in [6,5]. Moreover, the analysis of the approaches described in [7] and in [8] shows that they adopt the same strategy to encode data manipulation and exchange at an abstract level in the composition domain: introducing goal variables (which model variables of the new composite process) and encoding data-flow requirements as constraints on the operations that can be performed on goal variables. Another similarity is that both approaches do not require to enumerate the values that these variables can assume; this task would be impossible since variables often require very large or infinite ranges that prevent an explicit enumeration — consider for instance the variables representing the costs in the VTA example. The main difference lies in the way the two approaches reason on goal variables. The implicit approach reasons on what is "known" about the goal variables in the states of the composition domain (e.g., H.costOf(C.loc, C.date) becomes a goal variable, and the composition approach reasons on whether the value of this variable is "known"), and uses this information to check whether the goal is satisfied. The explicit approach does not encode at all data within the composition domain: its states simply model the evolution of the processes, and data-flow constraints are modeled as additional "services" (e.g. the requirement in the VTA example is modeled as a 'service' that transforms the flight and hotel cost into the cost for the customer). This difference is reflected in the size of the obtained composition domain, which in the implicit approach is much larger.

In order to test the performance of the proposed approaches, we have conducted some experiments on a scalable domain. Since we wanted to compare the two approaches on realistic domains, we consider here a real e-commerce scenario, the Virtual Online Shop (VOS from now on). The VOS consists in providing an electronic purchase and payment service by combining a set of independent existing services: a given number of e-commerce services Shops and a credit-card payment service Bank. This way, the Customer, also described as a service, may directly ask the composite service VOS to purchase some given goods, which are offered by different Shops, and pay them via credit-card in a single payment transaction with the Bank. For the Bank we modeled a real on-line payment procedure offered by an Italian bank. Such a process handles several possible failures: it checks both the validity of the target bank account (the Store's one in our case) and the validity of the credit card, it checks whether the source bank account has enough money and whether the owner is authorized for such a money transfer. The Shop models a hypothetical e-commerce service, providing a complex offer negotiation and supporting a transactional payment procedure. This composition problem requires a high degree of interleaving between components (to achieve the goal, it is necessary to carry out interactions with all component services in an interleaved way) and both the implicit and explicit models of data-flow requirements are pretty complex (due to the number of functions and to the need of manipulating data in a complex way). To evaluate the scalability of the two approaches when the number of (complex) component services grows, we increased the number of stores participating to the composition. The following table reports the experimental results.

	Implicit					**Explicit**						**WS-BPEL**
	domain			**time (sec.)**		**domain**				**time (sec.)**		num complex activities
	goal vars	nr. of states	max path	model construction	composition & emission	goal vars	data constr.	nr. of states	max path	model construction	composition & emission	
VOS	6	1357	54	11.937	3.812	14	6	390	26	1.612	0.218	52
VO2S	9	8573	64	185.391	84.408	20	9	1762	32	1.796	0.688	84
VO3S	12	75289	74	M.O.	-	26	12	12412	38	1.921	2.593	109
VO4S	-	-	-	-	-	32	15	122770	44	2.218	12.500	136
VO5S	-	-	-	-	-	38	18	1394740	50	2.547	26.197	165
VO6S	-	-	-	-	-	44	21	16501402	56	2.672	246.937	196

For each considered scenario the table shows some parameters that characterize the complexity of the composition domain, the automated composition time, and the size of the generated composite process. The complexity of the implicit approach is given in terms of the number of goal variables that encode the pieces of "knowledge" that the composite process acquires while interacting with the component services and manipulating messages (see [7] for the details). For what concerns the explicit approach, we consider the number of data-flow constraints and the number of goal variables (as shown in [8], the variables correspond to number of nodes of the data net obtained by combining all the data-flow constraints). To complete the characterization of the complexity of the composition domain, for both approaches we report the number of states and the number of transitions of the longest path in the composition domain that is passed as input to the automated generation techniques of [5,6]. These measures characterize the size of the search space for the composed service.

The complexity of the composition task can also be deduced from the size of the new composite WS-BPEL process, which is reported in the last column of the table. We remark that we report the number of WS-BPEL basic activities (e.g. `invoke`, `receive`, `reply`, `assign`, `onMessage`) and do not count the WS-BPEL structured activities that are used to aggregate basic activities (e.g. `sequence`, `switch`, `flow`). Indeed, the former activities are a better measure of the complexity of the generated process, while the latter are more dependent on the coding style used in the composite WS-BPEL process. Notice that we report only one measure for the composite process. Indeed, the processes generated by the two approaches are basically identical: they implement the same strategy, handle exceptions and failures in the same way and present the same number of activities. The only difference is the way in which such activities are arranged, e.g. the order of invocation of the different shops or of the assignments when preparing different parts of a message to be sent.

The composition times have been obtained on a Pentium Centrino 1.6 GHz with 512 Mb RAM of memory running Linux. We distinguish between model construction time and composition and emission time. The former is the time required to obtain the composition domain, i.e., to translate the WS-BPEL component services into a finite state domain and to encode the composition goal. The latter is the time required to synthesize the controller according to [5,6] and to emit the corresponding WS-BPEL process. The experiments show that the implicit approach has worse performances both for the model construction time and for the composition time. In particular, the implicit approach is not able to synthesize the VOS scenario with three shops: a memory out is obtained in model construction time. In the case of the explicit approach, instead, the time required to generate the composition domain is very low for all the scenarios, and also the performance for the composition scales up to very complex composition scenarios: the VO6S example (6 Stores, 1 Bank and 1 Customer) can be synthesized in about 4 minutes. We remark that this example is very complex, and requires several hours of work to be manually encoded: the corresponding WS-BPEL process contains about 200 non-trivial activities! We also remark that the number of states in the implicit domain for the VO6S example is much larger than the number of states of the VO3S example in the explicit approach. The fact that the former composition has success while the latter has not shows another important advantage of the explicit approach: the domain is very modular, since each data-flow constraint is modeled as a separated "service", which allows for a very efficient exploitation of the techniques implemented by [5,7].

For what concerns usability, the judgment is not so straightforward, since the two approaches adopt very different perspectives. From the one side, modeling data-flow composition requirements through a data net requires to explicitly link all the messages received from component services with messages sent to component services. Moreover, a second disadvantage is that component services are black boxes exporting only input and output ports: there is no way to reason about their internal data manipulation behaviors. From the other side, data nets models are easy to formulate and understand through a very intuitive graphical representation. It is rather intuitive for the designer to check the correctness of the requirements on data routings and manipulations. Also detecting missing requirements is simple, since they usually correspond to WS-BPEL messages (or part of messages) that are not linked to the data net. Finally, the practical experience with the examples of the experimental evaluations reported in this section is than the time required to specify the data net is acceptable, and much smaller that the time required to implement the composite service by hand. In the case of the VO6S scenario, for instance, just around 20 minutes are sufficient to write the requirement, while several hours are necessary to implement the composite service.

The implicit approach adopts a more abstract perspective, through the use of annotations in the process-level descriptions of component services. This makes the goal independent from the specific structure of the WS-BPEL processes implementing the component services, allowing to leave out most implementation details. It is therefore less time consuming, more concise, more re-usable than data nets. Moreover, annotations provide a way to give semantics to WS-BPEL descriptions of component services, along the lines described in [9], thus opening up the way to reason on semantic annotations capturing the component service internal behavior. Finally, implicit knowledge level specifications allow for a clear separation of the components annotations from the composition goal, and thus for a clear separation of the task of the designers of the components from that of the designer of the composition, a separation that can be important in, e.g., cross-organizational application domains. However, taking full advantage of the implicit approach is not obvious, especially for people without a deep know-how of the exploited composition techniques. There are two main opposite risks for the analysts: to over-specify the requirements adding non mandatory details and thus performing the same amount of work required by the explicit approach; to forget data-flow requirements which are necessary to find the desired composite service. Moreover, our experiments have shown that, while the time required to write the implicit data-flow requirements *given* the annotated WS-BPEL processes is much less than the time to specify the data net, the time required to write the requirements *and* to annotate the WS-BPEL processes is much more (and the errors are much more frequent) than for the data net.

3 Conclusions and Related Works

We have compared two different approaches to the definition of data flow requirements for the automated synthesis of process-level compositions for component services described in WS-BPEL. Implicit requirements [7] compose functions that annotate

WS-BPEL descriptions of component services. Explicit requirements [8] directly specify the routing and manipulations of data exchanged in the composition. Both approaches have their pros and cons. Explicit models allow for much better performances, due to the very modular encoding of requirements. Moreover, they are rather easy to write and to understand for the analyst. Implicit requirements allow for a higher degree of re-use and abstraction, as well as for a clear separation of the components annotations from the composition goal.

Most of the works that address the problem of the automated synthesis of process-level compositions do not take into account data flow specifications. This is the case of the work on synthesis based on automata theory that is proposed in [1,3], and of work within the semantic web community, see, e.g., [10]. Some other approaches, see, e.g., [11], are limited to simple composition problems, where component services are either atomic and/or deterministic.

The work closest to ours is the one described in [4], which proposes an approach to service aggregation that takes into account data flow requirements. The main difference is that data flow requirements in [4] are much simpler and at a lower level than in our framework, since they express direct identity routings of data among processes, and do not allow for manipulations of data. The examples reported in this paper clearly show the need for expressing manipulations in data-flow requirements and higher level requirements.

References

1. Hull, R., Benedikt, M., Christophides, V., Su, J.: E-Services: A Look Behind the Curtain. In: Proc. PODS'03. (2003)
2. Andrews, T., Curbera, F., Dolakia, H., Goland, J., Klein, J., Leymann, F., Liu, K., Roller, D., Smith, D., Thatte, S., Trickovic, I., Weeravarana, S.: Business Process Execution Language for Web Services (version 1.1) (2003)
3. Berardi, D., Calvanese, D., Giacomo, G.D., Mecella, M.: Composition of Services with Nondeterministic Observable Behaviour. In: Proc. ICSOC'05. (2005)
4. Brogi, A., Popescu, R.: Towards Semi-automated Workflow-Based Aggregation of Web Services. In: Proc. ICSOC'05. (2005)
5. Pistore, M., Traverso, P., Bertoli, P., A.Marconi: Automated Synthesis of Composite BPEL4WS Web Services. In: Proc. ICWS'05. (2005)
6. Pistore, M., Traverso, P., Bertoli, P.: Automated Composition of Web Services by Planning in Asynchronous Domains. In: Proc. ICAPS'05. (2005)
7. Pistore, M., Marconi, A., Traverso, P., Bertoli, P.: Automated Composition of Web Services by Planning at the Knowledge Level. In: Proc. IJCAI'05. (2005)
8. Marconi, A., Pistore, M., Traverso, P.: Specifying Data-Flow Requirements for the Automated Composition of Web Services. In: Proc. SEFM'06. (2006)
9. Pistore, M., Spalazzi, L., Traverso, P.: A Minimalist Approach to Semantic Annotations of Web Processes. In: Proc. of ESWC'05. (2005)
10. McIlraith, S., Son, S.: Adapting Golog for Composition of Semantic Web Services. In: Proc. KR'02. (2002)
11. Ponnekanti, S., Fox, A.: SWORD: A Developer Toolkit for Web Service Composition. In: Proc. WWW'02. (2002)

Light-Weight Semantic Service Annotations Through Tagging

Harald Meyer and Mathias Weske

Hasso-Plattner-Institute for IT-Systems-Engineering at the University of Potsdam
Prof.-Dr.-Helmert-Strasse 2-3, 14482 Potsdam, Germany
{harald.meyer, mathias.weske}@hpi.uni-potsdam.de

Abstract. Discovering and composing services is a core functionality of a service-oriented software system. Semantic web services promise to support and (partially) automate these tasks. But creating semantic service specifications is a difficult, time-consuming, and error prone task which is typically performed by service engineers. In this paper, we present a community-based approach to the creation of semantic service specifications. Inspired by concepts from emergent semantics and folksonomies, we introduce semantic service specifications with restricted expressiveness. Instead of capturing service functionality through preconditions and effects, services are tagged with categories. An example illustrates the pragmatic nature of our approach in comparison to existing approaches.

1 Introduction

The goal of service orientation is the alignment of the IT infrastructure to the business goals of a company [1,2,3]. Service-oriented architecture (SOA) defines the elements and relations of such an IT infrastructure. Two of the core tasks in a SOA are discovering services and composing services into new services to fulfill complex tasks [4,5]. In the presence of hundreds or thousands of services, both tasks become challenging. Semantic web services [6] are a promising approach to find services based on functionality. Service functionality is described through preconditions and effects. Creating them and writing queries to find services according to preconditions and effects is a complex task.

In this paper, we present a novel approach towards service semantics for service discovery and composition. Instead of assuming fully automated discovery and composition, we want to assist users with these tasks. For this, preconditions and effects are not necessary. Service users (process designers, etc.) tag services with keywords. These tags enable them to find services. While a service engineer can provide an initial categorization for a service, users can refine categorizations incrementally. This helps capturing real world aspects of service usage and bridging the gap between service description and real world service usage.

The approach presented is similar to *service categories* in OWL-S [7] and WSDL-S [8]. But service categories are static. During development, the service engineer assigns suitable service categories to the new service. A strict separation between service development and service usage prevents changes by people

A. Dan and W. Lamersdorf (Eds.): ICSOC 2006, LNCS 4294, pp. 465–470, 2006.

other than the service engineer. Systems like NAICS (North American Industry Classification System), UNSPSC (United Nations Standard Products and Services Code), or RosettaNet have defined processes for changes to their taxonomies. Adding new concepts may take up to 5 years (for NAICS). Categories are statically assigned: it rarely makes sense to change a service categorization in UNSPSC from *4410260214* (Retail of Printers) to *4410310314* (Retail of Toners). Instead one would remove the existing service and publish a new one.

Our work is inspired by the recent advent of emergent semantics and folksonomies. Both approaches do not depend on a-priori semantical commitments. Instead, semantic commitment is achieved incrementally. In the next section we go into more details of emergent semantics and present a formalization for tags. This formalization serves as the foundation for our application of emergent semantics to service discovery in Section 3. The paper concludes with a summary and an outlook on future work.

2 Emergent Semantics

Technologies for semantic annotation originate in the annotation of documents. Recently, these technologies are also used to specify service functionality [6]. When annotating documents, annotations are created either by dedicated professionals or the authors of the documents [9,10]. Professionally created annotations are of high-quality, but their creation is costly and rarely scales for large amounts of documents. Author-created annotations overcome this problem. But in both approaches the actual users are detached from the creation of the annotations. Annotations might therefore not match the actual usage of the documents. If the usage of document changes or it is used in unintended ways, the annotations cannot reflect this.

Emergent semantics [11] replaces a-priori agreements by incremental, local agreements. The recent rise in *folksonomies* can be seen as an application of emergent semantics. The term *folksonomy* is a composition of folk and taxonomy. In a folksonomy annotations for documents are created by the users of the system through tagging. The most prominent examples for systems based on folksonomy are del.icio.us (`http://del.icio.us/`) and flickr (`http://flickr.com/`) bookmark and photo management systems. When adding a bookmark in del.icio.us you can add multiple tags or categories to the bookmark. Later, tags can be used to find the bookmark again. Another feature of folksonomies is their community orientation. Bookmarks and tags are shared among all users. Hence, a user cannot only find all the bookmarks he tagged with a given tag, but he can also find all the bookmarks tagged with the same tag by all other users.

The freedom resulting from the usage of tags leads to problems illustrated by Golder and Huberman [12]. It is possible that a tag has multiple homonymous or polysemous meanings. Synonyms can appear as well. Such synonyms can be especially complicated in a tagging-based system as user using one tag, will not find documents tagged with the other tag. User do not need to adhere to a naming convention. This is problematic as it is unclear whether a tag should be in singular (e.g. *book*) or in plural (e.g. *books*). How tags consisting of more than one words are composed is also undefined: write them as one word, separate them with underscore, or two tags. Similar problems occur on the level of message-level heterogeneities when Web services exchange data [13,14] and in multidatabase systems [15,16]. Michlmayer [17] identifies spamming as an additional problem. The assumption why these problems do not interfere with the actual usability of existing systems, is that most of them do not matter if only enough users participate. For example, the problems with synonyms is that two different tags for the same meaning lead to separated document landscapes. But if enough users participate, chances are high that most documents get tagged with both tags.

As a last point in this section we describe a formalization for emergent semantics introduced by Mika [18]. This formalization will later serve us as the basis for our formalization of emergent semantics for service annotation. A folksonomy:

Definition 1. *A folksonomy $F \subseteq A \times T \times O$ is hypergraph G(F)=(V,E) with*

- *$V = A \cup T \cup O$ as the vertices. The disjoint sets $A = \{a_1, ..., a_k\}$, $T = \{t_1, ..., t_m\}$, $O = \{o_1, ..., o_n\}$ are the set of actors, the set of tags, and the set of objects.*
- *$E = \{\{a, t, o\} | (a, t, o) \in F\}$ as the hyperedges connecting an actor a who tagged an object o with the tag t.*

3 Emergent Semantics for Service Annotation

To find services it is important to annotate them with a description of their functionality. Existing author-created or professionally created semantic annotations, are costly to produce and have the risk of not matching the actual usage of the service. Hence, we will apply the concept of tagging in this section as a light-weight approach towards semantic service annotations. As a first step we introduce service landscapes:

Definition 2. *A service is a discrete business functionality. It is described by a service description. A service landscape is the set of available services described by service descriptions $\mathcal{S} = \{s_1, s_2, ..., s_n\}$.*

In the upcoming semantic web service *standards* OWL-S [7] and WSMO [19] services are described through preconditions and effects. WSMO also introduces assumptions and postconditions. It distinguishes between information space and world space. SAWSDL [20] explicitly excludes "expression of Web services constraints and capabilities, including precondition and effect". The precondition defines if a service is invokable in the current state. A formal specification of the functional description of services can be found in [21]. If the precondition is satisfiable by the current state, the service is invokable. The effect describes the changes to the current state that result from invoking the service. With our approach preconditions and effects are no longer necessary. Instead tagging is applied to semantic services:

Definition 3. *A tagging-based semantic service system with a service landscape $\mathcal{S}$ is a folksonomy where the objects are the service landscape: $F \subseteq A \times T \times \mathcal{S}$.*

This means service descriptions are tagged to express service functionality. The actors in such an environment are for example process designers, service landscape managers, and service engineers.

3.1 Example

This example will from now on serve as an illustration for our findings. The example is about leave requests by employees. Two different kinds of leave requests can be distinguished: vacation and sabbatical. Figure 1 shows the service landscape $S = \{s_1, s_2, s_3, s_4, s_5, s_6\}$. On the left side of each service the input parameters and on the right side the output parameters are denoted. The services s_1, s_2, and s_3 deal with vacation requests. After requesting a vacation (s_1), the request's validity (e.g. whether enough vacation days are left) is checked (s_2), and finally the vacation is approved or rejected (s_3).

Services s_4 and s_5 are the respective services for sabbatical requests. In contrast to vacation requests, no automated validity check is performed. Instead the supervisor needs to manually check the eligibility of the employee to go on a sabbatical. Finally, service s_6 is used to update the information about sabbaticals and vacations of employees in the human resources system. The human resources system then publishes the information to the project planning tools so that no work is planned for employees, who are on leave.

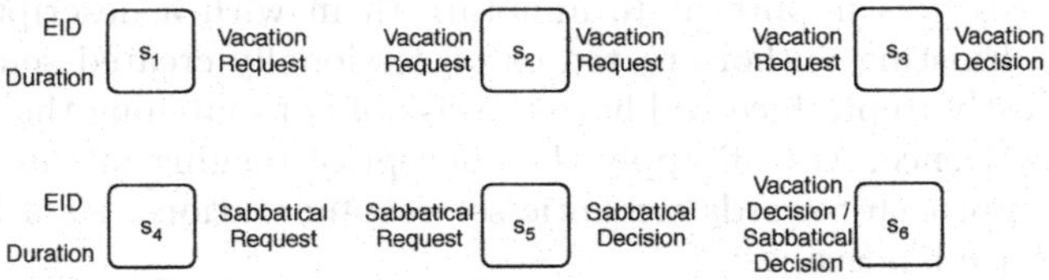

Fig. 1. Employee leave request: service landscape

Pete and Mary are process designers. Pete is the first one to model a process. He wants to model a process for vacation request approval. As no tags exist, he needs to browse the service landscape to find the required services s_1, s_2, s_3, and s_6. To help him and other persons in finding these services in the future, he tags them with the new tag *vacation*. This leads to the following folksonomy: $F = \{(Pete, vacation, s_1), (Pete, vacation, s_2), (Pete, vacation, s_3), (Pete, vacation, s_6)\}$. Mary works in another department that currently not tracks spent vacation days in the human resources system. Instead, the head of department uses a spreadsheet for this purpose. Hence, she does not need to use service s_2. As she sees Pete's *vacation* tag, she can easily figure out all useful services. The system does not store relations between services, so Mary has to model the process manually without the usage of s_2. While she found Pete's tags useful, she thinks fine granular tags are better. Hence, she introduces *vacation_request* to tag s_1, *vacation_approval* to tag s_3, and *update_leave_info* to tag s_6. She also models a new process for sabbatical requests using services s_4, s_5, and s_6. The folksonomy now is (Figure 2): $F = \{(Pete, vacation, s_1), (Pete, vacation, s_2), (Pete, vacation, s_3), (Pete, vacation, s_6), (Mary, vacation\_request, s_1), (Mary, vacation\_approval, s_3), (Mary, update\_leave\_info, s_6), (Mary, sabbatical\_request, s_4), (Mary, sabbatical\_approval, s_5)$.

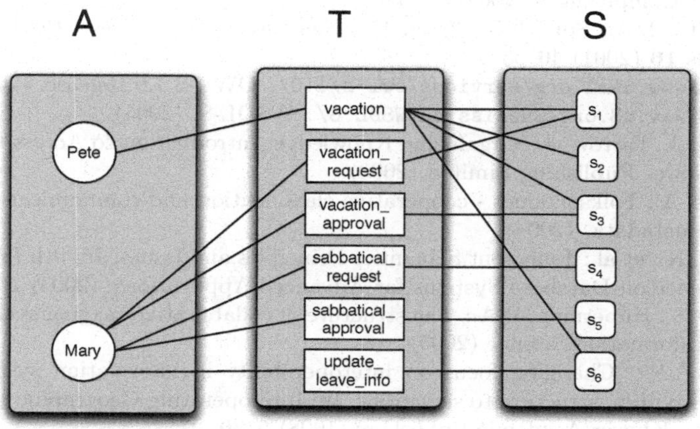

Fig. 2. Service Folksonomy

4 Conclusion

In this paper we presented a novel approach to service semantics. Instead of modeling service semantics up-front by service engineers, they are incrementally refined by the users. Existing Folksonomy implementations like del.icio.us are positive examples how the problems of community-based tagging can be solved. Systems like del.icio.us overcome these problems through their large user base. In comparison to several thousand users using such web-based system, we have to deal with a significantly smaller user base. In an intra-enterprise scenario maybe only a few dozen users use the system. While the user group is smaller, it is also of higher quality. Users have a direct gain in their daily work and have responsibility for their doings.

We already implemented a preliminary prototype for the displayed functionality. The next step is to integrate this functionality into an existing BPM suite and UDDI repository. As a part of this work, experiments will be conducted to prove the applicability and usefulness in real world process modeling.

References

1. Burbeck, S.: The tao of e-business services. IBM developerWorks (2000)
2. Papazoglou, M.P., Georgakopoulos, D.: Service-oriented computing: Introduction. Communications of the ACM **46** (2003) 24–28

3. Alonso, G., Casati, F., Kuno, H., Machiraju, V.: Web Services – Concepts, Architectures and Applications. Data-Centric Systems and Applications. Springer (2004)
4. Curbera, F., Khalaf, R., Mukhi, N., Tai, S., Weerawarana, S.: The next step in web services. Communications of the ACM **46** (2003) 29–34
5. Milanovic, N., Malek, M.: Current solutions for web service composition. IEEE Internet Computing **8** (2004) 51–59
6. McIlraith, S.A., Son, T.C., Zeng, H.: Semantic web services. IEEE Intelligent Systems **16** (2001) 46–53
7. `http://www.daml.org/services/owl-s/1.0/`: OWL-S 1.0 Release. (2003)
8. `http://www.w3.org/Submission/WSDL-S/`: WSDL-S. (2005)
9. Rowley, J., Farrow, J.: Organizing Knowledge: Introduction to Access to Information. Gower Publishing Limited (2000)
10. Mathes, A.: Folksonomies - cooperative classification and communication through shared metadata. (2004)
11. Aberer, K., et al.: Emergent Semantics Principles and Issues. In: 9th International Conference on Database Systems for Advanced Applications. (2004) 25–38
12. Golder, S., Huberman, B.A.: The structure of collaborative tagging systems. Journal of Information Science (2005)
13. Sheth, A.P.: Changing focus on interoperability in information systems: From system, syntax, structure to semantics. In: Interoperating Geographic Information Systems, Kluwer Academic Publishers (1998) 5–30
14. Nagarajan, M., Verma, K., Sheth, A.P., Miller, J.A., Lathem, J.: Semantic interoperability of web services – challenges abd experiences. In: Proceedings of the 4th IEEE Intl. Conference on Web Services. (2006) (to appear).
15. Sheth, A.P., Kashyap, V.: So far (schematically) yet so near (semantically). In: Conference on Semantics of Interoperable Database Systems. (1992) 283–312
16. Kim, W., Choi, I., Gala, S.K., Scheevel, M.: On resolving schematic heterogeneity in multidatabase systems. Distributed and Parallel Databases **1** (1993) 251–279
17. Michlmayr, E.: A Case Study on Emergent Semantics in Communities. In: Proceedings of the Workshop on Social Network Analysis, International Semantic Web Comference (ISWC). (2005)
18. Mika, P.: Ontologies are us: A unified model of social networks and semantics. In: Proceedings of the 4th International Semantic Web Conference (ISWC2005). Number 3729 in LNCS, Springer (2005) 522–536
19. `http://wsmo.org`: Web Service Modeling Ontology. (2005)
20. `http://www.w3.org/2002/ws/sawsdl/`: SAWSDL Working Group. (2006)
21. Keller, U., Lausen, H., Stollberg, M.: On the semantics of functional descriptions of web services. In: Proceedings of the 3rd European Semantic Web Conference (ESWC2006) (to appear). (2006)

Service-Oriented Model-Driven Development: Filling the Extra-Functional Property Gap*

Guadalupe Ortiz and Juan Hernández

Quercus Software Engineering Group
University of Extremadura
Computer Science Department
Spain
{gobellot, juanher}@unex.es

Abstract. Although vendors provide multiple platforms for service implementation, developers demands approaches for managing service-oriented applications at all stages of development. In this sense, approaches such as *Model-Driven Development* (MDD) and *Service Component Architecture* (SCA) can be used in conjunction for modeling and integrating services independently of the underlying platform technology. Besides, WS-Policy provides a XML-based standard description for extra-functional properties. In this paper we propose a cross-disciplinary approach, in which the aforementioned MDD, SCA and WS-Policy are assembled in order to develop extra-functional properties in web services from a platform independent model.

Keywords: Extra-Functional property, web service, model-driven development, aspect oriented techniques, WS-policy, service component architecture.

1 Introduction

Web Services provide a successful way to communicate distributed applications, in a platform independent and loosely coupled manner. Although development middlewares provide a splendid environment for service implementation, methodologies for earlier stages of development, are not provided in a cross-disciplinary scope. At present, academy and industry are beginning to focus on the modeling stage; two representative approaches are described below:

To start with, SCA provides a way to define interfaces independently of the final implementation [3]. This proposal allows the developer to define a high level model; however, it does not face how to integrate this definition with other stages of development. As the second trend, many proposals are emerging where MDA is being applied to service development. MDA solves the integration of the different stages of development, but it does not provide a specific way to do so for service technology.

Let us consider now that we want to provide our modeled services with extra-functional properties; the way to do so has not been considered yet neither by SCA approach nor by model-driven ones. On the other hand, WS-Policy provides a

* This work has been developed thanks to the support of MEC under contract TIN2005-09405-C02-02.

A. Dan and W. Lamersdorf (Eds.): ICSOC 2006, LNCS 4294, pp. 471 – 476, 2006.

standardized way for describing extra-functional service capabilities; however, it does not determine how the properties are to be modeled or implemented.

Closely related to this is the aim of this paper, which consists on offering a model-driven methodology in order to deal with extra-functional properties, that is, additional functionality which should not be part of the system's main functionality.

The rest of the paper is organized as follows: *Section 2* gives an overview of the whole process followed in this approach. *Section 3* shows how the PIM should be implemented; then, *Section 4* explains the PSM stage. *Section 5* explains the rules used to obtain code from PSMs. Other related approaches are examined in *Section 6*, whereas the main conclusions are presented in *Section 7*.

2 Model-Driven Transformations

In this section we provide and depict (*Figure 1*) a general overview of the presented approach: The first thing to be done is to define the metamodel to be followed by the platform independent model. In this sense, we propose to use a UML profile (MOF compliant) for the platform independent model, consequently the UML metamodel is our PIM's metamodel. Afterwards, three different metamodels are proposed in this approach for PSM stage, which will be explained later on.

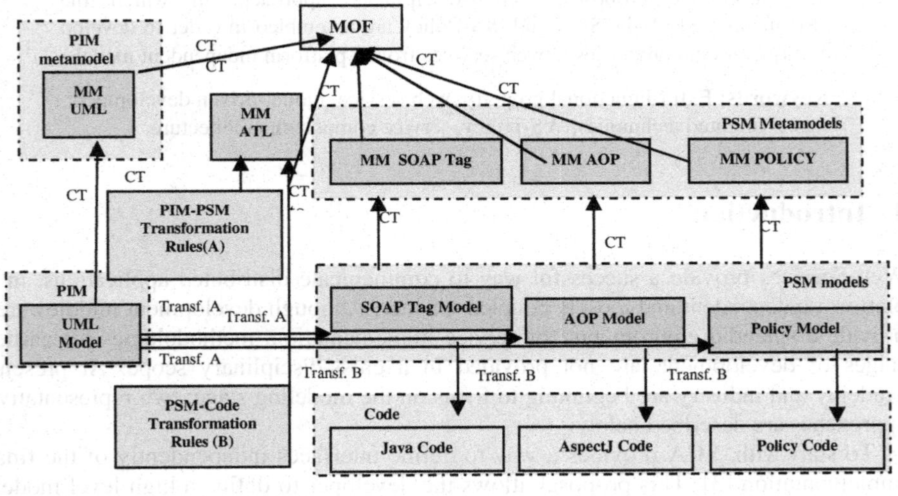

Fig. 1. ATL transformation process

Subsequently the transformation from the PIM to the PSMs has to be defined. We used *ATL* tool, which provides an Eclipse plugin and which has its own model transformation language. The ATL transformation file will define the correspondence between the elements in the source metamodel (PIM) and the target ones (PSMs) and will be used to generate the target model based on the defined rules and the input model. Finally, once we have obtained the specific models, we will transform them into code automatically by using additional transformation rules.

3 Extra-Functional Property PIM

In order to maintain our system loosely coupled when adding extra-functional properties to the model, we propose the profile in *Figure 2,* whose elements will be explained as follows and are deeply detailed in [9]:

- First of all, we define the stereotype *extra-functional property*, which extends *operation metaclass* or *interface metaclass*: when applied to an interface the property will be applied to all the operations in it. The stereotype provides five attributes: *actionType* indicates whether the property behavior will be performed *before*, *after* or *instead of* stereotyped operation's execution – or if no additional behavior is needed it will have the value *none,* only possible in the client side, which is out of the scope of this paper. Secondly, *optional* will indicate whether the property is performed optionally or compulsorily. *ack*, when *true* it means that it is a well-known property and its functionality code can be generated at a later stage; it will have the value *false* when it is a domain-specific property and only the skeleton can be generated. Finally, *PolicyId* will contain the name to be assigned to generated policy; *policyDoc* will be the url where the policy will be available.
- In order to define *actionType*, an *enumeration* is provided with four alternative values: *before*, *after, instead* or *none*.
- If the property is applied in an offered interface, then it will be implemented when the stereotyped operations are executed. If the property is applied in a required interface, it will be performed when the operations are invoked; in this case the service is acting as a client, which is beyond the purpose of this paper.

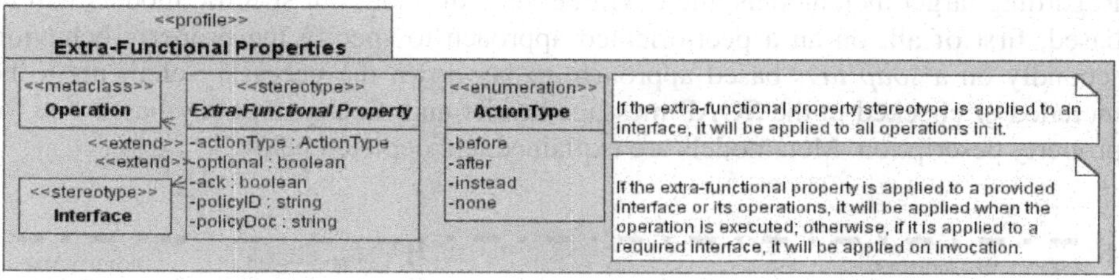

Fig. 2. Extra-functional property profile

Consider now we have a tourist information service. We will represent this service as a component, stereotyped as *serviceComponent*, which will offer a provided interface. Let us imagine now that we want to include some extra-functional properties to the *touristInformation* service model. We have devised three different sample properties:

- First of all, a *Log* property, which will be applied to all the operations offered by the service to record information related to all received invocations.
- Secondly, *RealTime* will be required discretionarily by the client when invoking *weatherInformation*: subject to a different pricing, the real time weather in a city may be obtained; under the regular price the average weather will be obtained.

- Finally, a *Login* property, used to control access to *RentingCar*, since it will only be possible to rent a car for those who have a username and a password.

We have to extend the extra-functional property stereotype with the specific properties to be applied, as shown in *Figure 3*. Properties are added then to *touristServiceInterface*. In order to provide all the operations with *Log*, we have stereotyped the interface with *log*, whose attributes indicate that the property will be performed *after* any operation in the interface is executed (not optional); information will be recorded in *logFile*; it is a well-known property; *policyID* is *Log* and *policyDoc* is null. *RealTime* and *Login* would also be interpreted similarly.

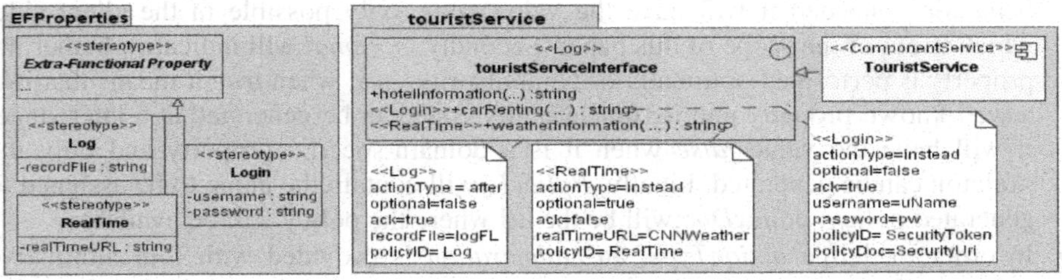

Fig. 3. PIM with extra-functional properties

4 Extra-Functional Property PSMs

Regarding target metamodels, there will be three of them: our specific models will be based, first of all, on an aspect-oriented approach to specify the property behavior, secondly on a *soap tags*-based approach, to lay down the necessary elements to be included or checked in the SOAP message header and, finally, a policy-based one for property description. Metamodels are explained and depicted below:

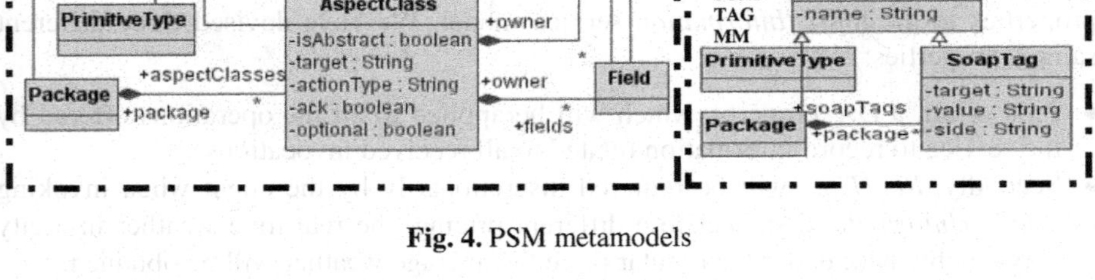

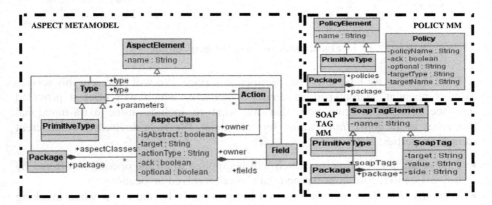

Fig. 4. PSM metamodels

- Every *aspectClass* will have an attribute *target* which indicates the method or interface for the property to be applied; *actionType* informs of when the property has to be applied; *ack* indicates whether the property is well-known or not and, finally, an *action* provides the corresponding functionality. All additional characteristics from the particular property will be included as attributes.
- New tags are included in the SOAP Header to select –client - or to check –service - the properties to be applied, when optional, or to deliver additional information [8]. Every Soap tag element will have a *target* which will instruct the method or interface for the property to be applied, *value,* to indicate the tag to be included; and *side*, which indicates whether it is included from the client or service side.
- A policy will be generated for every property. The policy will contain the policy *name*, whether the property is *optional* or not, well-known o domain-specific (*ack*); *targetType* indicates if the policy is to be applied to a *portType* or to an *operation* and *targetName* gives the name of the specific element.

Once the transformation rules are applied to the PIM, the specific models containing information about the properties are obtained, which are going to be described. Due to space restrictions only one characteristic element from each metamodel has been described: Log is applied to the interface, thus one aspect will be generated for each operation in the interface. The aspect would be named *TS_hotelInformation_Log*; *target* and *actionType* would have the values *touristServiceInterface.hotelInformation* and *after*, respectively, and *action* would be also included. Additionally, *ack* would have the *true* value. Regarding the policy element, *name* would be *http://aop4ws/Log*; *optional* would be *false*. Finally, for *policyAttachment, targetType* would take *portType* and *targetName touristServiceInterface*. The *RealTime* transformation would be similar, but being *optional*, a new attribute would be included in the SOAP Handler.

5 Code Layer: Extra-Functional Property Generated Code

In the last transformation stage, Java code will be generated to check if soap tags are included in the SOAP message and AspectJ code will be created for the aspects, , thus maintaining properties decoupled from the services implemented and the transparency in the property selection by the client [8]. With regard to description, it is proposed to generate the WS-Policy [1] documents for each property, which are integrated with the aspect-oriented generated properties [10]. This allows properties to remain decoupled not only at modeling stage, but also in during implementation.

ATL tools have also been used for code generation, where the transformation rules identify the different elements in the specific models and generate code from them. Transformation rules will generate skeleton code for the three model elements:

An AspectJ aspect will be generated for each aspect class in our model. Pointcuts will be determined by the execution of the target element. Regarding the advice, depending on the *actionType* attribute value, *before*, *after* or *instead*, the advice type will be *before*, *after* or *around*, respectively. Regarding property description, an xml file based on the WS-Policy standard is generated and attached to the service by the file based on the WS-PolicyAttachment standard. Code for the inclusion of SOAP Tags will be generated for every SOAP Tag Class in the model.

6 Related Work

As regards Web Service modeling proposals, the research presented by J. Bezivin et al. [4] is worth a special mention; in it Web Service modeling is covered in different levels, using *Java* and *JWSDP* implementations in the end. It is also worth mentioning the paper from M. Smith et al. [11], where a model-driven development is proposed for Grid Applications based on the use of Web Services. Our work provides the possibility of adding extra-functional properties to the services and is not oriented to the service modeling itself; thus it could be considered as complementary to them.

Concerning proposals which focus on extra-functional properties, we can especially mention the one from D. Fensel et al. [7], where extra-functional properties are modeled as pre and post conditions in an ontology description. Secondly, L. Baresi et al. extend WS-Policy by using a domain-independent assertion language in order to embed monitoring directives into policies [2]. Both are interesting proposals, however they do not follow the UML standard, which we consider essential for integrating properties in future service models.

7 Conclusions

This paper has shown a model-driven approach to including extra-functional capabilities in web service development in a loosely coupled manner. Properties are included in the PIM by using a UML profile. The initial PIM has been converted into three specific models which conform to three provided metamodels, based on the soap tags information, aspect oriented elements and policy based ones. All the code related to extra-functional property has been automatically generated from PSMs.

References

[1] Bajaj, S., Box, D., Chappeli, D., et al. Web Services Policy Framework (WS-Policy), ftp://www6.software.ibm.com/ software/developer/library/ws-policy.pdf, September 2004
[2] Baresi, L. Guinea, S. Plebani, P. WS-Policy for Service Monitoring. VLDB Workshop on Technologies for E-Services, Trondheim, Norway, September 2005
[3] Beisiegel, M., Blohm, H., Booz, D.,et al. Service Component Architecture. Building Systems using a Service Oriented Architecture. http://download.boulder.ibm.com/ibmdl/pub/software/dw/specs/ws-sca/SCA_White_Paper1_09.pdf, November 2005
[4] Bézivin, J., Hammoudi, S., Lopes, D. et al. An Experiment in Mapping Web Services to Implementation Platforms. N. R. I. o. Computers: 26, 2004
[5] Fensel, D., Bussler, C. The Web Service Modeling Framework WSMF. http://informatik.uibk.ac.at/users/c70385/ wese/wsmf.bis2002.pdf
[6] Ortiz G., Hernández J., Clemente, P.J.How to Deal with Non-functional Properties in Web Service Development, Proc. Int. Conf. on Web Engineering, Sydney, Australia, July 2005
[7] Ortiz G., Hernández J., Toward UML Profiles for Web Services and their Extra-Functional Properties, Proc. Int. Conf. on Web Services, Chicago, EEUU, September 2006.
[8] Ortiz, G., Leymann, F. Combining WS-Policy and Aspect-Oriented Programming. Proc. of the Int. Conference on Internet and Web Applications and Services, Guadeloupe, French Caribbean, February 2006.
[9] Smith, M., Friese, T. Freisbelen, B. Model Driven Development of Service-Oriented Grid Applications. Proc. of the Int. Conference on Internet and Web Applications and Services, Guadeloupe, French Caribbean, February 2006

WSMX: A Semantic Service Oriented Middleware for B2B Integration*

Thomas Haselwanter[1], Paavo Kotinurmi[1,2], Matthew Moran[1], Tomas Vitvar[1], and Maciej Zaremba[1]

[1] Digital Enterprise Research Institute
University of Innsbruck, Austria
National University of Ireland in Galway, Ireland
firstname.lastname@deri.org
[2] Helsinki University of Technology, Finland

Abstract. In this paper we present a B2B integration scenario building on the principles of Semantic Web services. For this scenario we show the benefits of semantic descriptions used within the integration process to enable conversation between systems with data and process mediation of services. We illustrate our approach on the WSMX – a middleware platform built specifically to enact semantic service oriented architectures.

1 Introduction

Although Business-to-Business (B2B) standards such as RosettaNet, EDI and ebXML have brought new value to inter-enterprise integration, they still suffer from two drawbacks. All partners must agree to use the same standard and often the rigid configuration of standards makes them difficult to reconfigure, reuse and maintain. In order to overcome some of the difficulties of B2B integration, semantic technologies offer a promising potential to enable more flexible integration that is more adaptive to changes that might occur over a software system's lifetime [4]. There remains, however, very few realistic publicly implemented scenarios demonstrating the benefits of this technology. In this respect, we aim to showcase how Semantic Web service (SWS) technology can be used to facilitate the dynamics for B2B integration. We base our work on specifications of WSMO[5], WSML[5] and WSMX[3] providing a conceptual framework, ontology language and execution environment for Semantic Web services. In addition, we make use of the RosettaNet B2B standard – an industry standard providing definition of intercompany choreographies (e.g. PIP3A4 Request Purchase Order (PO)) as well as structure and semantics for business messages. In this paper we show how these technologies are used in a real-world scenario involving (1) semantic representation of XML schema for RosettaNet as well as a proprietary purchase order using the WSML ontology language, (2) semantic representation of services provided

* This work is supported by the Science Foundation Ireland Grant No. SFI/02/CE1/I131, and the EU projects Knowledge Web (FP6-507482), DIP (FP6-507483) and ASG (FP6-C004617).

A. Dan and W. Lamersdorf (Eds.): ICSOC 2006, LNCS 4294, pp. 477–483, 2006.

by partners using WSMO, (3) executing a conversation between partner services using the WSMX integration middleware, and (4) application of data and process mediation between heterogeneous services where necessary.

2 Architecture

In figure 1, a fictitious trading company called Moon uses two back-end systems to manage its order processing, namely, a Customer Relationship Management system (CRM) and an Order Management system (OMS). Moon has signed agreements to exchange purchase order messages with a partner company called Blue using the RosettaNet PIP 3A4. We use SWS technology to facilitate conversation between all systems, to mediate between the PIP 3A4 and the XML schema used by Moon, and to ensure that the message exchange between both parties is correctly choreographed. Following is a description of the basic blocks of the architecture.

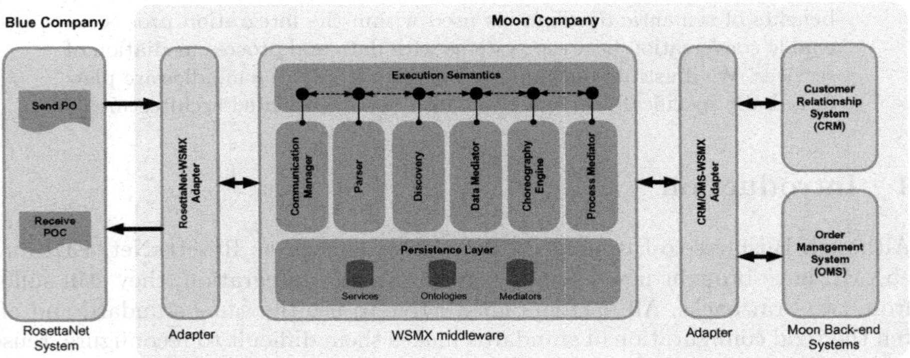

Fig. 1. Architecture Overview

- **Existing Systems.** The existing systems are Moon's back-end applications including CRM and OMS systems as well as Blue's RosettaNet system. Each system communicates using different formats, i.e. Blue's RosettaNet system communicates according to the RosettaNet PIP 3A4 PO, whereas communication with the CRM and OMS systems is proprietary, specified in their WSDL descriptions.
- **Adapters.** Since WSMX internally operates on the semantic level (WSML), adapters facilitate *lifting* and *lowering* operations to transform between XML and WSML. In addition, it also identifies the WSMO Goal that corresponds to a PO request and sends it to WSMX.
- **WSMX.** WSMX is the integration platform which facilitates the integration process between different systems. The integration process is defined by the WSMX execution semantics, i.e. interactions of middleware services including discovery, mediation, invocation, choreography, repository, etc.

There are two phases to the integration of the Blue and Moon partners: (1) *integration setup phase* and (2) *integration runtime phase*. During the setup phase, the development of adapters, WSMO ontologies and services, rules for lifting/lowering, mapping rules between ontologies are carried out for RosettaNet, OMS and CRM systems. The focus of this paper is on the runtime phase describing interactions between Blue and Moon systems.

2.1 Activity Diagram

In this section we describe interactions between the Blue and Moon systems facilitated by WSMX through its middleware services as depicted in the figure 2. We refer to parts of the figure using numbers before title of each subsection.

1 – Sending Request. A PIP3A4 PO message is sent from the RosettaNet system to the entry point of the RosettaNet-WSMX adapter. On successful reception of the message by the adapter, an acknowledgment is sent back to the RosettaNet system. In the RosettaNet-WSMX adapter, the PO XML message is lifted to WSML according to the PIP3A4 ontology and rules for lifting using XSLT. Finally, a WSMO Goal is created from the PO message including the definition of the desired capability and a choreography. The capability of the requester (Blue company) is used during the discovery process whereas the Goal choreography describes how the requester wishes to interact with the environment. After the goal is created, it is sent to WSMX through the *AchieveGoal* entrypoint. In return, a *context* is received containing the identification of the *conversation* – this information is used in subsequent asynchronous calls from the requester.

2 – Discovery and Conversation Setup. The *AchieveGoal* entrypoint is implemented by the WSMX Communication Manager – the WSMX middleware service, which facilitates the inbound and outbound communication with the WSMX environment. After receipt of the goal, the Communication Manager initiates the *execution semantics* which manages the whole integration process. The Communication Manager sends the WSML goal to the instance of the execution semantics, which in turn invokes the WSMX Parser returning the Goal parsed into an internal system object. The next step is to invoke the discovery middleware service in order to match the requested capability of the Goal with the capabilities of services registered in the WSMX repository. Since we do not concentrate on the discovery in this paper, we use a very simplified approach when only one service in the repository (CRM/OMS service) can be matched with the goal. After discovery, the execution semantics registers both the requester's and the provider's choreography with the Choreography Engine (these choreographies are part of the goal and service descriptions respectively). Both choreographies are set to a state where they wait for incoming messages that could fire a transition rule. This completes the conversation setup.

3 – Conversation with Requester. The instance data for the goal is sent from the RosettaNet-WSMX adapter to the WSMX asynchronously by invoking the

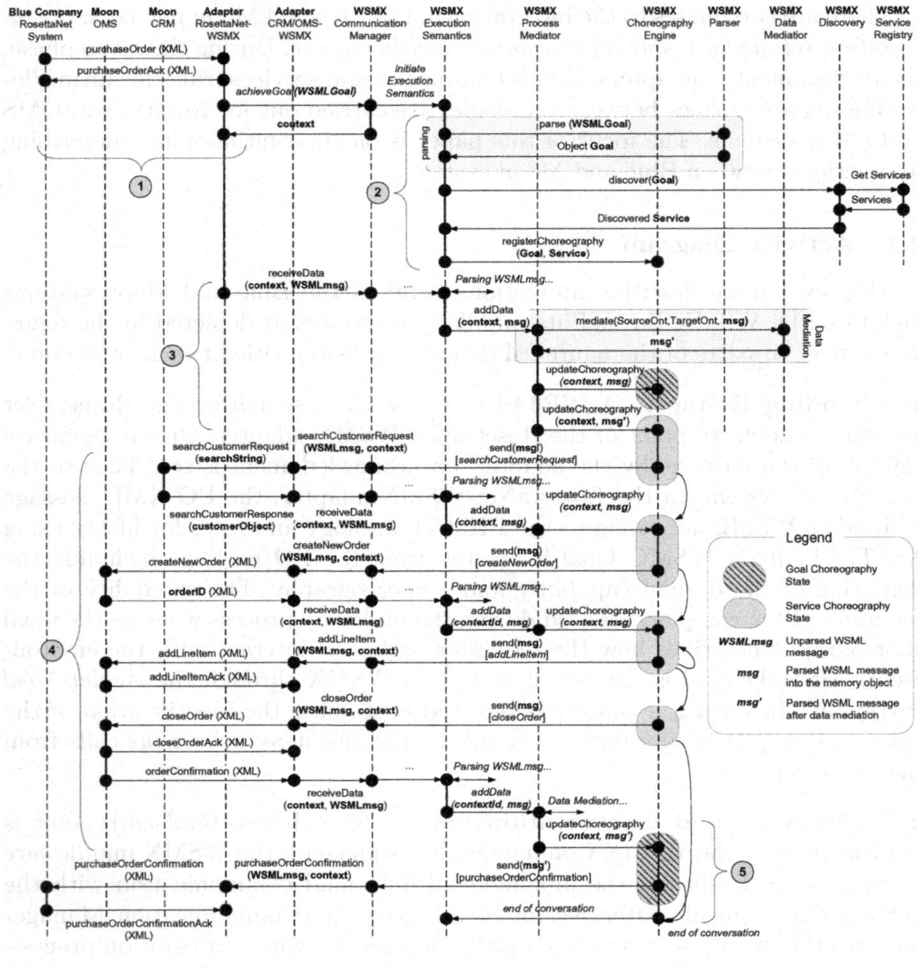

Fig. 2. Activity Diagram

receiveData entrypoint. The data in WSML (WSMLmsg) is passed through the Communication Manager to the execution semantics, they are parsed and sent to the WSMX Process Mediator. The first task of the WSMX Process Mediator is to decide, which data will be added to requester's or provider's choreography[1] – this decision is based on analysis of both choreographies and concepts used by these choreographies. Process Mediator first updates the memory of the requester's choreography with the information that the PO request has been sent. The Process Mediator then evaluates how data should be added to the memory of the provider's choreography – data must be first mediated to the ontology used by the provider. For this purpose, the source ontology of the requester, target

[1] Choreographies of WSMO services are modeled as Abstract State Machines [2].

ontology of the provider and the instance data are passed to the WSMX Data Mediator. Data mediation is performed by execution of mapping rules between both ontologies (these mapping rules are stored within WSMX and have been created and registered during the integration setup phase). Once mediation is complete, the mediated data is added to the provider's choreography.

4 – Conversation with Provider (Opening Order, Add Line Items, Closing Order). Once the requester's and provider's choreographies have been updated, the Choreography Engine processes each to evaluate if any transition rules could be fired. The requester's choreography remains in the waiting state as no rule can be evaluated at this stage. For the provider's choreography, the Choreography Engine finds the rule shown in the listing 1.1 (lines 14-21). Here, the Choreography Engine matches the data in the memory with the the antecedent of the rule and performs the action of the rule's consequent. The rule says that the message *SearchCustomerRequest* with data *searchString* should be sent to the service provider (this data has been previously added to the choreography memory after the mediation - here, *searchString* corresponds to the *customerId* from the requester's ontology). The Choreography Engine then waits for the *SearchCustomerResponse* message to be sent as a response from the provider. Sending the message to the service provider is initiated by Choreography Engine passing the message to the Communication Manager which, according to the grounding defined in the choreography, passes the message to the *searchCustomer* entrypoint of the CRM/OMS-WSMX Adapter. In the adapter, lowering of the WSML message to XML is performed using the lowering rules for the CRM/OMS ontology and the CRM XML Schema. After that, the actual service of the CRM system behind the adapter is invoked, passing the parameter of the *searchString*. The CRM system returns back to the CRM/OMS Adapter a resulting *customerObject* captured in XML. The XML data is lifted to the CRM/OMS ontology, passed to the WSMX, parsed, evaluated by the WSMX Process Mediator and added to the provider's choreography memory. Once the memory of the provider's choreography is updated, the next rule is evaluated resulting in sending a *createNewOrder* message to the Moon OMS system. This process is analogous to one described before. As a result, the *orderID* sent out from the OMS system is again added to the memory of the provider's choreography. After the order is created (opened) in the OMS system, the individual items to be ordered need to be added to that order. These items were previously sent in one message as part of order request from Blue's RosettaNet system (i.e. a collection of *ProductLineItem*) which must be now sent to the OMS system individually. As part of the data mediation in the step 3, the collection of items from the RosettaNet order request have been split into individual items which format is described by the provider's ontology. At that stage, the Process Mediator also added these items into the provider's choreography. The next rule to be evaluated now is the rule of sending *addLineItem* message with data of one *lineItem* from the choreography memory. Since there is more then one line item in the memory, this rule will be evaluated several items until all line items from the ontology have been sent to the OMS system. When all line items have been sent, the next rule is to close the order in the OMS system. The *closeOrder* message is sent out from the WSMX to the OMS system and since no additional rules from the provider's choreography can be evaluated, the choreography gets to the end of conversation state.

The listing 1.1 shows the fragment of the provider's choreography and the first selected rule from the requester's choreography described above. The choreography is described from the service point of view thus the rule says that the service expects to receive the *SearchCustomerRequest* message and send the reply *SearchCustomerResponse* message. The choreography is part of the service definition which in addition also contains definition of *non-functional properties* and *capability*. For brevity, these elements are not included in the listing.

```
...
choreography MoonWSChoreography
    stateSignature _"http://www.example.org/ontologies/sws−challenge/MoonWS#statesignature"
      importsOntology {_"http://www.example.org/ontologies/sws−challenge/Moon",
                  _"http://www.example.org/ontologies/choreographyOnto" }

      in moon#SearchCustomerRequest withGrounding { _"http://intranet.moon.local/wsmx/services/
            CRMOMSAdapter?WSDL#wsdl.interfaceMessageReference(CRMOMSAdapter/CRMsearch
            /in0)" }
      ...
      out moon#SearchCustomerResponse
      ...
      controlled oasm#ControlState

transitionRules _"http://www.example.org/ontologies/sws−challenge/MoonWS#transitionRules"
  forall {?controlstate, ?request} with (
      ?controlstate[oasm#value hasValue oasm#InitialState] memberOf oasm#ControlState and
      ?request memberOf moon#SearchCustomerRequest
    ) do
      add(?controlstate[oasm#value hasValue moonc#SearchCustomer])
      delete(?controlstate[oasm#value hasValue oasm#InitialState])
      add(_# memberOf moon#SearchCustomerResponse)
  endForall
  ...
```

Listing 1.1. Requester's Service Choreography

5 – Conversation with Requester (Order Confirmation, End of Conversation). When the order in OMS system is closed, the OMS system replies with *orderConfirmation*. After lifting and parsing of the message, the Process Mediator first invokes the mediation of the data to the requester's ontology and then adds the data to the memory of the requester's choreography. The next rule of the requester's choreography can be then evaluated saying that *purchaseOrderConfirmation* message needs to be sent to the RosettaNet system. After the message is sent, no additional rules can be evaluated from the requester's choreography, thus the choreography gets to the end of conversation state. Since both requester's and provider's choreography are in the state of end of conversation, the Choreography Engine notifies the execution semantics and the conversation is closed.

3 Conclusion and Future Work

This work addresses the fact that although research into the area of Semantic Web services is well established, there is a scarcity of implemented use cases demonstrating the potential benefits. Existing approaches to dynamic or semantic B2B integration such as [1], [4], [6] are mostly conceptual with lack of demonstration and evaluation of real-world case scenarios. The system presented here has been implemented according to the scenario from the SWS Challenge[2] addressing data and process heterogeneities in a B2B integration. It has been evaluated how our solution adapts to changes of back-end systems with needs to change the execution code (success level 1), data/configuration of the system (success level 2), no changes in code and data (success level 3)[3]. For data mediation we had to make some changes in code due to forced limitations of existing data mediation tools. For process mediation we changed only description of service interfaces (choreographies) according to the changes in back-end systems. Ultimately, we aim to the level when our system adapts without changes in code and configuration – the adaptation will be purely based on reasoning over semantic descriptions of services, their information models and interfaces. We also plan to expand our solution to cover more B2B standards and to integrate key enterprise infrastructure systems such as policy management, service quality assurance, etc.

References

1. N. Anicic, N. Ivezic, and A. Jones. An Architecture for Semantic Enterprise Application Integration Standards. In *Interoperability of Enterprise Software and Applications*, pp. 25–34. Springer, 2006.
2. E. Brger and R. Strk. *Abstract State Machines: A Method for High-Level System Design and Analysis*. Springer-Verlag, 2003.
3. A. Haller, *et al.* WSMX – A Semantic Service-Oriented Architecture. In *Proc. of the 3rd Int. Conf. on Web Services*, pp. 321 – 328. IEEE Computer Society, 2005.
4. C. Preist, *et al.* Automated Business-to-Business Integration of a Logistics Supply Chain using Semantic Web Services Technology. In *Proc. of 4th Int. Semantic Web Conference*. 2005.
5. D. Roman, *et al.* Web Service Modeling Ontology. *Applied Ontologies*, 1(1):77 – 106, 2005.
6. K. Verma, *et al.* The METEOR-S Approach for Configuring and Executing Dynamic Web Processes, available at http://lsdis.cs.uga.edu/projects/meteor-s/techRep6-24-05.pdf. Tech. rep., 2005.

[2] http://www.sws-challenge.org

[3] http://sws-challenge.org/wiki/index.php/Workshop_Budva

Top Down Versus Bottom Up in Service-Oriented Integration: An MDA-Based Solution for Minimizing Technology Coupling

Theo Dirk Meijler, Gert Kruithof, and Nick van Beest

Information Systems, Faculty of Management and Organization
{t.d.meijler, g.h.kruithof}@rug.nl,
n.r.t.p.van.beest@student.rug.nl

Abstract. Service-oriented integration typically combines top-down development with bottom-up reverse engineering. Top-down development starts from requirements and ends with implementation. Bottom-up reverse engineering starts from available components and data sources. Often, the integrating business processes are directly linked to the reverse-engineered web services, resulting in a high degree of technology coupling. This in turn leads to a low level of maintainability and low reusability. The Model-Driven Architecture (MDA) provides an approach aimed at achieving technology independency through full top-down development. However, this approach does not handle the bottom-up reverse-engineered components very well. In this paper, an approach is introduced that combines top-down with bottom-up realization, while minimizing the technology coupling. This is achieved by an explicit buffer between top-down and bottom-up. "High-level" web services are derived through top-down development, whereas "Low-level" web services are reverse-engineered, and a mapping is created between the two. The approach focuses on engineering web services reversely, while retaining the advantages of the MDA with respect to platform independency, maintainability and reusability.

Topics: Business Service Modeling, Service Assembly.

Scientific Area: Service-oriented software engineering.

1 Introduction

Various approaches have been proposed for developing enterprise information systems (EISs) in a top-down manner [1],[2]. An important characteristic of a pure top-down development approach is that it starts from the desired business situation (rather than from the current situation) and finally results in the implementation of a new system. In the approaches adopted by [1],[2] the Model-Driven Architecture (MDA) plays an important role. Models serve as a better form of communication with the domain expert than code does, and so the domain expert can be given a bigger role in the development process. A Service-Oriented Architecture (SOA) [3] can also play an important role in the top-down development of reconfigurable business processes. A bottom-up approach, in contrast, starts from a system's existing components

A. Dan and W. Lamersdorf (Eds.): ICSOC 2006, LNCS 4294, pp. 484–489, 2006.

(including data sources). The SOA enables publishing of legacy components into the standard form of web services. An effective combination of top-down and bottom-up development is clearly required because enterprises both need to reuse their legacy components and work toward a desired business situation.

According to the standard SOA integration approach top-down development results in process realizations. These processes are directly linked to the web services that result from the bottom-up reverse engineering of legacy components. Changes in the relatively autonomous legacy components have an impact on the business processes. Thus, due to this form of technology coupling, the process model no longer reflects the "real" business process and becomes less understandable to the domain expert, making it more difficult for him/her to maintain. So, linking top-down and bottom-up development in this way undermines flexibility.

This paper presents an alternative approach to the linking of top-down and bottom-up development in a SOA on the basis of which technology decoupling is achieved. This approach improves the integration of MDA and SOA, as already presented by other authors [4][5].

2 Example from the Financial Sector

Generally, banks already have several components and data sources at their disposal, and they may integrate these by adopting a SOA approach. This example represents a highly simplified process of loan provision. The main legacy component is a data source. The schema of the initial database contains two tables: client and loan (Fig. 1a). Fig. 1 also shows the bottom-up reverse-engineered web services that represent this data source.

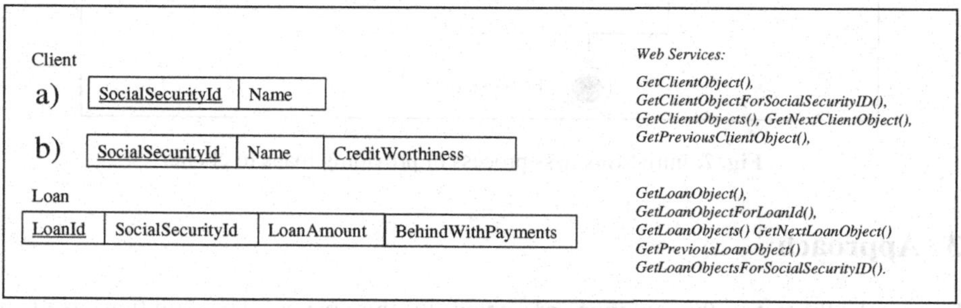

Fig. 1. Initial data structure and some web services

Fig. 2 shows a part of the business process model. The business process invokes the web service GetClientForSocialSecurityID() directly from an activity in the process. The SocialSecurityID of the Client has to be passed on to the LoanProvision subprocess, which can only continue if the client is creditworthy. The second activity in the process therefore involves the calculation of creditworthiness by iterating over all loans to assess whether in one of these loans the value of the "BehindWithPayments" property is set to true.

Now, the bank may decide to add a new "CreditWorthiness" property to the Client table (Fig. 1b). From the perspective of the business process, it is irrelevant whether creditworthiness is calculated in advance and stored as a Client attribute, or calculated at the time it is being requested in the process. However, the process will be strongly impacted by this change: the additional activity of calculating creditworthiness is no longer required.

This example shows that in a standard top-down and bottom-up integration, changes in the structure of the data sources of the bottom-up web services have an undesired impact on the structure of the business process.

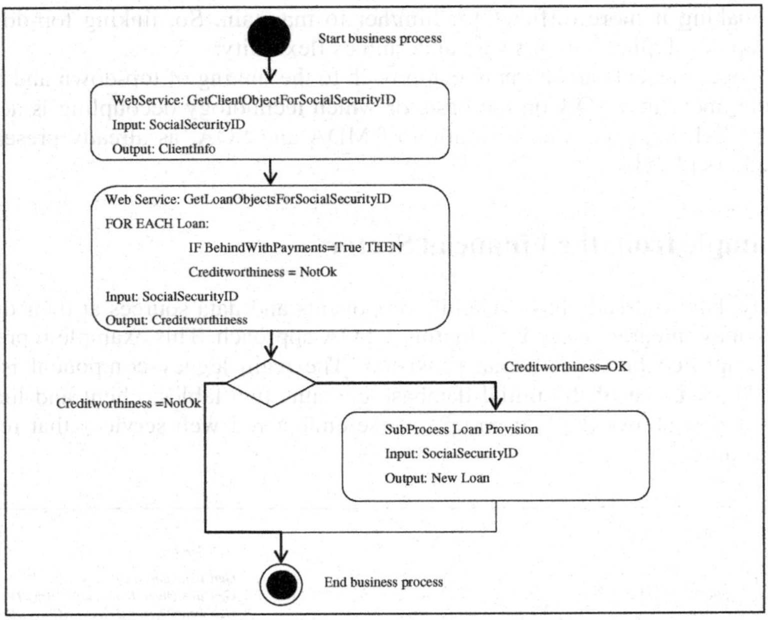

Fig. 2. Initial Business process of providing loans to clients

3 Approach

Figure 3 illustrates the solution presented in this paper. The solution itself is represented in the middle of the figure. Figure 3a, b and c are used to indicate the application of the solution to the example. The solution contains the following main components:

1. The solution applies the standard MDA subdivision between PIM (Platform Independent Model), PSM (Platform Specific Model) and Implementation. The lowest implementation part is represented by BPEL and WSDL files for the executable business process and web services that can be invoked. In a PSM a process is modeled in a SOA-specific way, indicating which activities call which web services, where these are located etc. (See [4] for a SOA specific UML

profile). A PIM may be a process model invoking interfaces that map to web services (See also [5]); Figure 3a depicts the PIM process model in our example, which abstracts from the implementation of creditworthiness.

2. New in comparison to other approaches to integrating MDA and SOA [4][5] is that the PIM not only contains a process model but also a data model. While the PIM process model serves to do top-down development of the BPEL process implementation, the PIM data model serves to do a top-down development of a set of so-called "high-level" (abbreviated: hl) web services (abbreviated: ws). Figure 3b shows the PIM data model and corresponding high-level web services. Thus, the addition of a data-model serves to enable a full-fledged *top-down* derivation of an implementation.

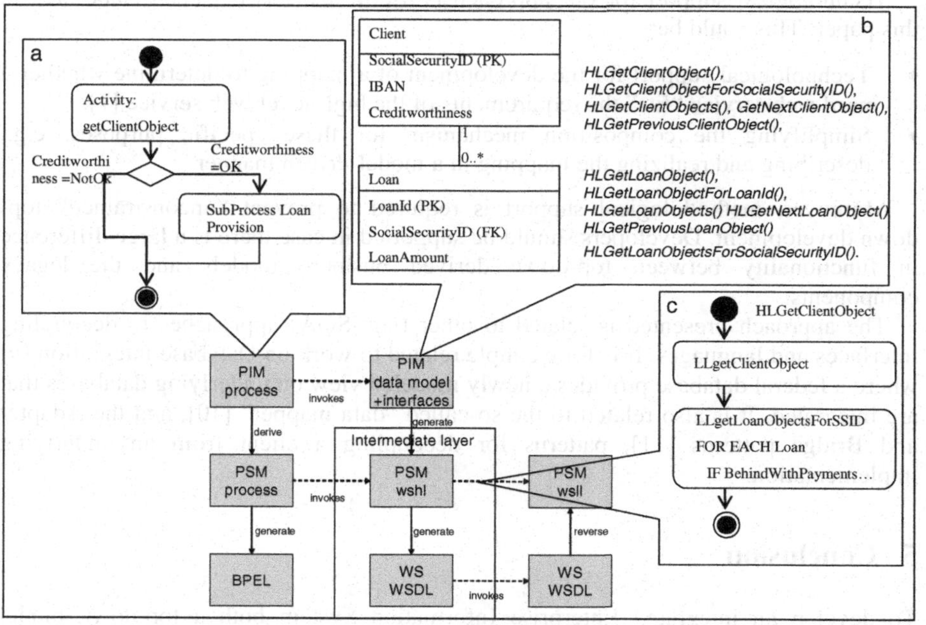

Fig. 3. Illustration of the approach

3. Another new element is the use of an intermediate decoupling layer between the top-down derived high-level web services and the web service that have been bottom-up reverse-engineered on the basis of legacy components. These web services will be called the "low-level" (abbreviated: ll) web services. The intermediate layer has been implemented by means of a simple design-time composition. In figure 3c the mapping is presented between high-level web services based on the data model of b, and the web services based on the database schema as presented in Fig. 1a. This mapping itself is presented and realized by means of a process model. The high-level low-level mapping can absorb unwanted changes from bottom-up to top-down. Thus, changing the database to the one presented in Fig. 1b does not affect the process. The mapping can, moreover, hide semantic heterogeneity aspects and integrate the results of different low-level web services.

4 Related Work and Future Research

Both technology decoupling as well as web services composition for the purpose of heightening the level of abstraction are well-known in SOA literature. Aspects such as automatic composition [6], matching the Quality of Services to what is requested and what is provided [7] and dynamic composition, e.g. on the basis of semantic information [8] have generated quite some interest.

Due to the focus on integrated EIS, the reuse of existing components and the creation of right mappings are more important than automatic composition and dynamism [8]. Furthermore, dynamic matching undermines performance, which should be avoided in this context.

Technological support for our approach is useful and has not been elaborated in this paper. This could be:

- Technological support for the development of a mapping to determine whether a used web service "fits" the requirements of the high-level web service [7].
- Simplifying the composition mechanism for these specific purposes, e.g., describing and realizing the mapping in a model-driven manner.

Moreover, methodological support is required to prevent "unconstrained" top-down development. Developers should be supported in case there is a large difference in functionality between top-down derived business models and the legacy components.

The approach presented is related to other (non-SOA) approaches to decoupling interfaces and languages. It is for example related to work on Database integration [9] where a federal database provides a newly modeled view on underlying databases that are integrated. It is also related to the so-called "data mapper" [10], and the Adapter and Bridge patterns [11], patterns for decoupling a client from an underlying implementation.

5 Conclusion

To develop an integrated Enterprise Information System both a top-down model driven development approach is needed as well as a bottom-up development. A standard top-down bottom-up linking however breaks the principle of top-down model driven development, as the process model is partly determined by the availability of components and data sources. Thus, a technology coupling is introduced that impairs the understandability and maintainability of the process model.

This paper introduces a decoupling between full-fledged top-down development following the Model-driven Architecture (MDA) and bottom-up development in the context of a SOA. Full-fledged top-down development consists of a platform independent process model as well as a data model as normal in the MDA. The data-model is used to generate so-called "high-level" web services. Thus a process model invokes these high-level web services and is no longer dependent of the availability of the bottom-up derived "low-level" web services of which the change can also not be controlled. The high-level web services are mapped using a simple design-time composition to the bottom-up derived low-level web services. The mapping can buffer the unwanted impact of change. The simplicity of a design-time composition enables its direct application in industrial setting, this while more complex dynamic composition mechanisms are neither needed nor optimal for these purposes.

Acknowledgements

This work is framed the project "Software Mass Customization" and is paid by the Dutch ministry of Economic Affairs. We thank Cordys, one of the partners of this project for their time and giving us access to their platform. We furthermore thank Bart Orriëns and Douwe Postmus for valuable comments.

References

[1] R. Hubert Convergent Architecture, Wiley Computer Publishing, ISBN 0-471-105600 2002

[2] D.S. Frankel Model Driven Architecture Applying MDA to Enterprise Computing, OMG Press – Wiley Publishing, ISBN 0-471-31920-1 2003

[3] T. Erl. A Field Guide to Integrating XML and Web Services, Pearson Education, Publishing as Prentice Hall Technical Reference, ISBN 0-13-142898-5 2004

[4] D. Skogan, R. Groenmo, I. Solheim, Web service composition in UML Proceedings of the Eighth IEEE International Enterprise Distributed Object Computing Conference, (EDOC 2004) IEEE 2004

[5] B. Orriëns, J. Yang and M.P. Papazoglou, Model Driven Service Composition, Service-Oriented Computing - ICSOC 2003 Eds. M. E. Orlowska, S. Weerawarana, M. P. Papazoglou, J. Yang LNCS 2910 / 2003, ISBN 3-540-20681-7 2003

[6] M. Aiello, M. Papzoglou, J. Yang, M. Carman, M. Pistore, L. Serafini, P. Traverso, A request language for web-services based on planning and constraint satisfaction, Proceedings of the VLDB workshop on Technologies for E-Services, Hongkong, China, 2002

[7] J. Cardoso, A. Sheth, J. Miller, J. Arnold, K. Kochut, Quality of Service for Workflows and Web Service Processes, Journal of Web Semantics, Elsevier, Vol. 1, No. 3, pp. 281-308, Amsterdam, The Netherlands, 2004

[8] P. Rajasekaran, J. Miller, K. Verma, A. Sheth, Enhancing Web Services Description and Discovery to Facilitate Composition, International Workshop on Semantic Web Services and Web Process Composition, 2004 (Proceedings of SWSWPC 2004)

[9] H. Balsters, E.O. de Brock, An object-oriented framework for managing cooperating legacy databases; 9th International Conference Object-Oriented Information Systems; Lecture Notes in Computer Science LNCS 2817, Springer, September 2003

[10] M. Fowler, Patterns of Enterprise Application Architecture, Eddison Wesley Pearson Education, ISBN 0-321-12742-0, 2003

[11] E. Gamma, R. Helm, R. Johnson, J. Vlissides, Design patterns: elements of reusable object-oriented software, Addison-Wesley Longman Publishing Co., Inc., Boston, MA ISBN 0-201-63361-2 1995

Semantic Service Mediation

Liangzhao Zeng[1], Boualem Benatallah[2], Guo Tong Xie[3], and Hui Lei[1]

[1] IBM T.J. Watson Research Center, Yorktown Heights, NY 10598
{lzeng, hlei}@us.ibm.com
[2] School of Computer Science and Engineering University of New South Wales, Sydney, Australia
boualem@cse.unsw.edu.au
[3] IBM China Research Laboratory
Building 19, Zhongguancun Software Park, ShangDi, Beijing, 100094, P.R. China
xieguot@cn.ibm.com

Abstract. The service mediation that decouples service interactions is a key component in supporting the implementation of SOA solutions cross enterprises. The decoupling is achieved by having the consumers and providers to interact via an intermediary. The earliest service mediations are keyword and value-based, which require both service providers and consumers to adhere same data formats in defining service interfaces and requests. This requirement makes it inadequate for supporting interactions among services in heterogeneous and dynamic environments. In order to overcome this limitation, semantics are introduced into service mediations, for more flexible service matchings. In this paper, we proposed a novel semantic service mediation. Different from existing semantic service mediations, our system uses ontologies not only for one-to-one service matchings, but also for one-to-multiple service matchings. By performing service correlation systematically as part of the service mediation, services can be composted automatically, without any programming efforts (neither composition rules nor process models). We argue that a service mediator like ours enables more flexible and on-demand mediation among services.

1 Introduction

The service mediation enables decoupling among the service providers and consumers, which is a key component in Enterprise Service Bus (ESB) for supporting SOA solutions cross enterprises. Typically, the service mediation system contains three roles: (1) *service providers*, who publish services; (2) *service consumers*, who request services, (3) *service mediators*, who are responsible for service repository management, service matching, service invocation and invocation result delivery. The earliest service mediations are keyword and value-based (e.g., UDDI [6]). There are two major limitations in such service mediations: (i) the service discovery is keyword-based; (ii) service invocations are based on value of exchanged messages. For example, a service request is about retrieving a sports car's insurance quote, where the input parameter is `SportsCar` and output parameter is `CarPremium`. For the value-based service mediation, only the services that have input parameter `SportsCar` and output parameter `CarPremium` can match the request. In case service request and service interfaces' input/output parameters are not exactly matched, then data format mapping needs to be provided.

A. Dan and W. Lamersdorf (Eds.): ICSOC 2006, LNCS 4294, pp. 490–495, 2006.

Consequently, as an improvement to keyword and type-based solutions, semantics are introduced into service mediations [1,5], wherein ontologies enable richer semantics in service publication and more flexible matchings. However, current semantic service mediations only support one-to-one service matchings. Any sophisticate one-to-multiple services matchings (i.e., composing a collection of services to fulfill a service request) requires either defining knowledge base (e.g., composition rules) or creating process models [7,8]. In order to overcome these limitations, in our semantic service mediation, one-to-multiple matchings are enabled using correlation-based composition, by utilizing the semantics derived from service interface definitions. In particular, proposed correlation-based composition is transparent to service consumers, i.e., requires neither defining service composition knowledge bases nor creating process models. It should be noted that our correlation-based solution is complementary to those knowledge-based and process-based solutions. With our correlation-based solution, either knowledge-based or process-based service composition developers can focus on high level business logic to develop composition services, without understanding extraordinary details of service interfaces. In the case of the expected service interfaces that defined in knowledge bases or process models are not currently available, the service mediator can locate multiple services and correlate them to a "virtual service" to fulfill the service request.

The remainder of this paper is organized as follows: Section 2 introduces some important concepts. Section 3 presents the overview of the semantic service mediation. Section 4 discusses the correlation-based service composition. Finally, Section 5 discusses some related work and Section 6 provides concluding remarks.

2 Preliminaries

In our system, we adopt an object-oriented approach to the definition of ontology, in which the type is defined in terms of *classes* (See Definition 1) and an instance of a class is considered as an *object* (See Definition2). It should be noted that this ontology formulation can be easily implemented using OWL [4] and IODT [3]. We will present details on how to use ontologies to perform semantic matchings and correlation matchings in following sections.

Definition 1 (*Class*). A class C is defined as the tuple $C = \langle N, S, P, R \rangle$, where

- N is the name of the class;
- S is a set of synonyms for the name of class, $S = \{s_1, s_2, ..., s_n\}$;
- P is a set of properties, $P = \{p_1, p_2, ..., p_n\}$. For $p_i \in P$, p_i is a 2-tuple in form of $\langle T, N_p \rangle$, where T is a basic type such as integer, or a class in an ontology, N_p is the property name. p_1 ($p_1 \in P$) is the key property for identification;
- R is a set of parent classes, $R = \{C_1, C_2, ..., C_k\}$. □

In the definition of class, the *name*, *synonyms*, and *properties* present the connotation of a class; while *parent classes* specify relationships among the classes, i.e., present the denotation of a class. A class may have parent classes for which it inherits attributes. For example, class `sportsCar`'s parent class is `Car`, so the class `sportsCar` inherits all the attributes in class `Car`.

Definition 2 (***Object***)**.** An object o is a 2-tuple$\langle N_c, V\rangle$, o is an instance of a class C, where

- N_c is the class name of C;
- $V = \{v_1, v_2, ..., v_n\}$, are values according to the attributes of the class C. For $v_i \in V$, v_i is a 2-tuple in form of $\langle N_p, V_p\rangle$, where N_p is the property name, V_p is the property value. □

A service interface is denoted as $I_s(P_{in}, P_{out})$, where P_{in} ($P_{in} = \langle C_1, C_2, ..., C_n\rangle$) indicates input parameter classes, and P_{out} ($P_{out} = \langle C_1, C_2, ..., C_m\rangle$) indicates output parameter classes. An example of a service s's interface can be I_s ($P_{in}\langle\texttt{SportsCar}\rangle$, $P_{out}\langle\texttt{CarInsurance, CarFinance}\rangle$), which contains one input parameter and two output parameters.

A service request is denoted as $Q(O_{in}, E_{out})$, where O_{in} ($O_{in} = \langle o_1, o_2, ..., o_n\rangle$) indicates input objects, and E_{out} ($E_{out} = \langle C_1, C_2, ..., C_m\rangle$) indicates expected output parameters from the services. An example of a service request can be $Q(O_{in}\langle\texttt{car}\rangle$, $E_{out}\langle\texttt{CarInsurance, CarFinance}\rangle)$, which contains one input object `car` and expects a service provides two outputs: `CarInsurance` and `CarFinance`.

Table 1. Examples

Entity	Example
service request	$Q_1(O_{in}\langle\texttt{sportsCarA}\rangle, E_{out}\langle\texttt{CarInsurance, CarFinance}\rangle)$
candidate service's interface	I_s ($P_{in}\langle\texttt{Car}\rangle$, $P_{out}\langle\texttt{CarInsurance, CarFinance}\rangle$)
interface set	$\mathbb{I}_k$=$\{I_1, I_2\}$, where I_1 ($P_{in}\langle\texttt{Car}\rangle$, $P_{out}\langle\texttt{CarInsurance}\rangle$), I_2 ($P_{in}\langle\texttt{Car}\rangle$, $P_{out}\langle\texttt{CarFinance}\rangle$)

3 Service Matching in Semantic Service Mediation

By introducing ontologies into the service mediation, other than *exact matching*, we extend the service matching algorithm with two extra steps: *semantic matching* and *correlation matching*. Therefore, three steps are involved in our matching algorithm:-

Step 1. Exact Matching. The first step is to find exact matches, which returns service interfaces that have exactly the same parameter (input and output) classes as the service request;

Step 2. Semantic Matching. The system searches service interfaces that have parameter classes that are semantically compatible with the service request. In our system, the semantic matching is based on the notion of *Semantic Compatibility*.

Definition 3 (***Semantic Compatibility***)**.** Class C_i is semantically compatible with class C_j, denoted as $C_i \stackrel{s}{=} C_j$, if in the ontology, either (i) C_i is the same as C_j (same name or synonym in an ontology) , or (ii) C_j is a superclass of C_i. □

By adopting the definition of semantic compatibility, we say a class C semantically belongs to a class set $\mathbb{C}$ (denoted as $C \in_s \mathbb{C}$) if $\exists C_i \in \mathbb{C}$, $C \stackrel{s}{=} C_i$. Using the notion of semantic compatibility, we define a *Candidate Service Interface* as a service interface that can accept service request's input objects and provide all outputs that are semantically compatible with the outputs required by the service request. For example (see Table 1), with regard to the service query Q, the interface I_s can be invoked by the service request as the input object `sportsCarA` "is a" `Car` (semantic compatibility). At the same time, I_s can provide all the outputs required in Q since two output parameters are exactly matched. Therefore, I_s is a candidate service interface for Q.

Step 3. Correlation Matching. The system searches a set of service interfaces that can accept the input object from service request and be correlated to provide expected output for the service request. It is worth noting that the type-based service mediation only performs step 1. Most of the semantic service mediations perform semantic matching which is step 2. In our semantic service mediation, we also consider correlation matchings, which are unique to our semantic service mediation. In this paper, we assume that both service consumers and providers use the same ontology for a domain. If a consumers and providers use different ontologies for a domain, then a common ontology can be created. Detailed discussion on creating a common ontology is outside the scope of the paper. Therefore, by engineering ontologies, our system allows different services to exchange information using their native information format to define interfaces and request. The cost of engineering ontologies is much less than that of developing object adaptors for value-based service mediations as ontologies are declaratively defined. Further, ontologies are reusable, while developing object adaptors requires case by case programming efforts.

4 Correlation-Based Service Composition

Obviously, multiple service interfaces can be correlated to one if they have share some input parameters and different output parameters. For example, two service interfaces I_1 and I_2 in $\mathbb{I}_k$ (see Table 1) can be correlated as they both have the field `Car` as the input parameter. Therefore, when the service mediator performs the correlation matching, in order to compose a service interface that can provide all the required outputs for the service request, it first searches a *correlation service interface set*, i.e., a set of service interfaces that are correlatable by a key input parameter that is specified by the service request and can provide all the outputs required by the service request. The formal definition of correlation interface set is shown as follows.

Definition 4 (*Correlation Interface Set*). $\mathbb{I}$ ($\mathbb{I} = \{I_1, I_2, ..., I_n\}$) is a set of service interfaces, $\mathbb{C}_{Pin_i}$ is the class set consists of all the input parameter classes in interface I_i; $\mathbb{C}_{Pout_i}$ is the class set that consists of output parameter classes in I_i; Q is the service request where $\mathbb{C}_{Oin}$ is the class set consists of the input object classes, $\mathbb{C}_{Eout}$ is the class set that consists of expected output parameter classes; o_k is an input object for correlation key. $\mathbb{I}$ is a ***Correlation Service Interface Set*** of Q iff:

1. $\forall C \in \mathbb{C}_{Pin}, C \in_s \mathbb{C}_{Oin}$, where $\mathbb{C}_{\mathbb{P}in}$($\mathbb{C}_{\mathbb{P}in} = \cup_{i=1}^{n} \mathbb{C}_{Pin_i}$) is union of all the input parameter class sets in $\mathbb{I}$;
2. $\forall C \in \mathbb{C}_{Eout}, C \in_s \mathbb{C}_{\mathbb{P}out}$, where $\mathbb{C}_{\mathbb{P}out}$($\mathbb{C}_{\mathbb{P}out} = \cup_{i=1}^{n} \mathbb{C}_{Pout_i}$) is union of all the output parameter class sets in $\mathbb{I}$;

3. $\forall \mathbb{C}_{Pin_i}, \exists C_k', C_k \stackrel{s}{=} C_k'$, where C_k is class for key object o_k;
4. $\forall \mathbb{C}_{Pout_i}, \exists C, C \in (\mathbb{C}_{Pout_i} - (\cup_{j=1}^{i-1} \mathbb{C}_{Pout_j} \bigcup \cup_{j=i+1}^{n} \mathbb{C}_{Pout_j}))$ and $C \in_s \mathbb{C}_{Eout}$.

□

In this definition, four conditions need to be satisfied when correlating a set of service interfaces to fulfill a service request: condition 1 indicates any outputs required by the service request can be provided; condition 2 indicates the service request can provide all the required input for each interface in the set; condition 3 implies all the interfaces have the key field as an input parameter, therefore, are correlatable; condition 4 evinces any interfaces in the set contributes at least one unique output. It should be noted that both condition 1 and 2 are necessary condition of the definition, while condition 3 and 4 are the sufficient conditions for the definition. Using above example, the aggregation of I_1 and I_2 provides all the required outputs for the service request, which satisfy condition 1; and their input can be provided by the service request, which satisfies condition 2. These two interfaces have the input parameter `Car` and `Car` is ancestor of `SportsCar`, the key class in service request Q, which satisfies condition 3. Also, I_1 (resp. I_2) provides unique output `CarInsurance` (resp. `CarFinance`), which satisfied condition 4. Therefore, I_1 and I_2 compose a correlation service interface set for the service request.

5 Related Work

Service mediation is a very active area of research and development. In this section, we first review some work in area of service discovery (matching), and then we look at some service composition prototypes.

Service discovery and matching is one of the cornerstones for service mediation. Current Web service infrastructure have limitation on providing flexibility of choose selection criteria along multiple dimensions. For instance, UDDI provides limited search facilities that allows only keyword-based search of services. To overcome this limitation, semantic technology [1] is used to support multiple dimensions searching criterions for services. In [1], a flexible matchmaking between service description and request by adopting Description Logics (DLs). However, most of existing semantic solutions focus on one-to-one matchings. In our service mediation, semantic information in service descriptions and request enables one-to-multiple service matchings, which initiates an other type of automatic service composition.

It should be noted that our correlation-based service composition is different from existing industrial and academic service composition framework. The industrial solution typically does not provide explicit goals of the composition and does not describe the pre- and post-conditions of individual services. A service is viewed as a remote procedure call.A service composition is quite often specified as a process model (e.g. BPEL4WS [2]) though a richer process specification is needed. The composition itself is mostly done manually by IT specialists in an ad-hoc manner. Our approach, using a semantic ontology and a correlation based composition, enables us to construct a composed service based on the semantics of service interfaces, without much programming efforts.

6 Conclusion

In this paper, we propose a novel semantic service mediation, which is another step forward in the development of current service mediation systems. We introduce semantics to understand the interface of service. Our system not only considers single service interface for a service request, but also automatically correlates multiple interfaces for a service request when there is not exactly matched interface. Unlike knowledge-based or process-based solution, the service correlation in our system is transparent to developers. We argue that the proposed service mediation is essential to enable cooperative service interactions in service-oriented computing. Our future work includes optimization of semantic service matching and correlation, and a scalability and reliability study of the system.

References

1. B. Benatallah, M.-S. Hacid, A. Leger, C. Rey, and F. Toumani. On automating web services discovery. *The VLDB Journal*, 14(1):84–96, 2005.
2. Business Process Execution Language for Web Services, Version 1.0, 2000. http://www-106.ibm.com/developerworks/library/ws-bpel/.
3. IBM Integrated Ontology Development Toolkit, 2006. http://www.alphaworks.ibm.com/tech/semanticstk.
4. OWL, 2006. http://www.w3.org/TR/owl-ref/.
5. M. Paolucci, T. Kawmura, T. Payne, and K. Sycara. Semantic Matching of Web Services Capabilities. In *First International Semantic Web Conference*, 2002.
6. Universal Description, Discovery and Integration of Business for the Web, 2005. http://www.uddi.org.
7. L. Zeng, B. Benatallah, H. Lei, A. Ngu, D. Flaxer, and H. Chang. Flexible Composition of Enterprise Web Services. *Electronic Markets - The International Journal of Electronic Commerce and Business Media*, 2003.
8. L. Zeng, B. Benatallah, A. H. H. Ngu, M. Dumas, J. Kalagnanam, and H. Chang. QoS-Aware Middleware for Web Services Composition. *IEEE Transactions on Software Engineering*, 30(5):311–327, 2004.

Examining Usage Protocols for Service Discovery

Rimon Mikhaiel and Eleni Stroulia

Computing Science Department, University of Alberta, Edmonton AB, T6G 2H1, Canada
{rimon, stroulia}@cs.ualberta.ca

Abstract. To date, research on web-service discovery has followed the tradition of signature matching based on the interface description captured in WSDL. WSDL specifications, however, can be information poor, with basic data types, and unintuitive identifiers for data, messages and operations. The nature of the usage of the WSDL component in the context of a BPEL composition can be an extremely useful source of information in the context of service discovery. In this paper, we discuss our method for service discovery based on both interface and usage matching, exploiting the information captured in the WSDL and BPEL specifications. Our approach views both WSDL and BPEL as hierarchical structures and uses tree alignment to compare them. We illustrate our method with an example scenario.

Keywords: service discovery, WSDL matching, BPEL matching, process matching.

1 Motivation and Background

Service discovery is an essential task in the process of developing service-oriented applications. In a typical service-discovery scenario, the service requester has specific expectations about the candidate service. In general, there are three types of desiderata for a service: it has (a) to be *capable* of performing a certain task, i.e., maintain a shopping cart, (b) to expose a particular *interface*, i.e., provide view, add-product and remove-product, and (c) to *behave* in a certain manner, i.e., ignore any request for product removals if no product additions have been performed yet. Such expectations motivate and guide the developers' searches through web-services repositories, as they try to discover and select the service that best matches their needs.

When not all these dimensions are considered in concert, the precision of the discovery process tends to be limited. For example, applying only a capability matching method between a service and a request does not guarantee that they are interoperable. Additionally, even when the interface of a service matches a request's interface, it is not necessarily clear how exactly its data and operations match the requestor's specification, especially when the parameter types are simple. Furthermore, in some cases, interface matching may get confused because the operation signatures are not significantly distinct.

In this paper, we propose an integrated service matching approach that is based on both interface and behavioral matching. For example, a WSDL [5] (interface) specification of a complex web service may be associated with a BPEL [1]

A. Dan and W. Lamersdorf (Eds.): ICSOC 2006, LNCS 4294, pp. 496 – 502, 2006.

(behavioral) specification that provides semantic information about the usage protocol of the provided operations and the overall usage patterns of the data types. In the proposed integrated matching approach, WSDL components are matched not only in a syntactic manner, but also in a way that complies with their BPEL's usage protocols.

Our method involves two steps: First, relevant information from the WSDL and BPEL descriptions of the desired and candidate services is parsed and represented in a special-purpose tree representation. Next, the tree representing the desired service is compared against the trees representing each of the candidate services to select the most similar one and to precisely identify how the data and operations offered by the candidate map to the requestor's needs in a way that respects their usage protocols.

The rest of this paper is organized as follows. Section 2 reviews related research on service discovery. Section 3 discusses a case study illustrating the insufficiency of WSDL for effective service discovery and the relevance of BPEL and usage-protocol information to the task. Section 4 presents our service-matching method based on tree alignment. Section 5 shows how the presented method resolves the issues raised in Section 3. Finally, Section 6 concludes with the essential ideas of our work.

2 Related Research

According to the literature, there are three categories of service discovery approaches. *Capability matching* examines whether a published service can satisfy the requested needs. UDDI matching is an example of such an approach. However, such capability matching is not enough to establish a real interaction; it does not specify the ontology of the involved data types nor the operations applicable for this service. *Interface matching* is based on signature matching between the published operations and the requested ones [8], [9], [10], [11]. However, this approach suffers from two drawbacks: first, interface matching does not guarantee a successful interaction because interfaces do not usually specify the usage conditions of the operations involved. Hence, an improper usage of the published operations may lead to an interaction failure. Second, interface matching may easily get confused when the services specifications are not distinctive; because it relies on documentation and operation signatures, when the data types are simple and there is not much documentation there is not enough information on the basis of which to assess (dis)similarity. Finally, *behavior matching* examines whether both the requested and provided service behave according to a similar interaction protocol. This approach is only concerned about either control-structure matching (like Petri nets [4], and π-calculus [7]), or message-flow matching (like WSDL [2] [3], and BPEL finite state machines [12]).

Our method integrates ideas from both interface and behavior matching. In this paper, we demonstrate that such integration is essential not only to enhance the matching quality but also to resolve ambiguities that may occur when each approach is applied separately. Additionally, this method requires a capability-matching step to be performed to maintain a set of candidate services, out of which this method selects the best inter-operable service.

3 The Service-Discovery Problem in an Example

In general, when looking for a service, a developer has in mind both the signatures of the operations desired and some behavioral scenarios, in which the candidate service is expected to participate. Discovery based simply on WSDL matching is concerned with the matching of the operations desired and provided. However, given a candidate service, there usually exist multiple likely mappings between the desired operations and the ones provided by the candidate service. Unambiguously selecting one of these mappings is often impossible, when neither the syntactic types nor the identifiers and documentation are distinctive.

For example, consider the case illustrated in Fig. 1, when the provided service performs an asynchronous task. The consumer is expected to first submit the task, to obtain a receipt, and then to return (after a while) asking for the results associated to that receipt; if, at that time, the task is completed the results are returned to the consumer otherwise an exception is returned. Fig. 1 illustrates the WSDL specifications of a provided and a requested service, both involving such a task-submission service. However, it is not clear how the two published operations can be mapped to the consumer's expected ones; both accept a string parameter and return a string parameter. Applying WSDL matching only cannot unambiguously select a mapping of their operations.

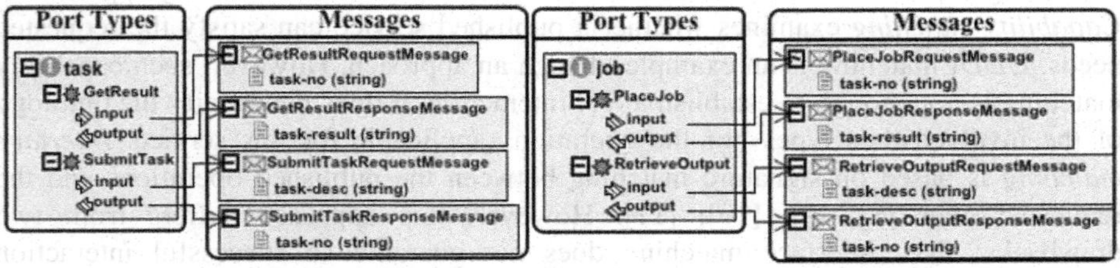

(a) A published WSDL description **(b) A requested WSDL description**

Fig. 1. A visual representation of two WSDL descriptions showing each operation, connected to its associated *input* and *output* messages. Each message description includes its associated *parameter name* and *type*.

4 The Method

The specific research question that our method is designed to address is: "how should service components be matched in a way that respects both their interface description and usage protocols?". Its underlying intuition is that both these aspects of a service description provide information that can be useful when considering a candidate service as a potential match for a requested one. More specifically, ambiguities in operations' mapping can be resolved by examining the behaviors in which these operations are involved. Consequently, our method is based on a two-level comparison of the corresponding service aspects, where a specialized tree-alignment approach is adopted for each level. First, the BPEL behavioral specification of the provided service is compared against the behaviors expected of the requested service. Second, the WSDL operations of the desired and the candidate services are compared, using a cost function that is based on the results of the first step.

4.1 Web-Service Matching as Tree-Edit Distance

Both BPEL and WSDL descriptions are expressed in terms of XML documents that can be represented as ordered labeled trees, where the attributes of the XML elements are represented as their children.

For each of the two steps in the service aspects' comparison, we adopted the SPRC [6] tree-alignment algorithm, developed in the context of our work in RNA structure alignment. This algorithm is based on the Zhang-Shasha's tree-edit distance [13] algorithm, which calculates the minimum edit distance between two trees given a cost function for different edit operations (e.g. change, deletion, and insertion). In addition, SPRC uses an affine–cost policy and reports all the alignment solutions that are associated with the calculated tree edit distance. Additionally, in a post-processing step, SPRC applies a simplicity-based filter to discard the more unlikely solutions from the solution set produced by the SPRC tree-alignment phase.

4.2 A Usage-Aware Cost Function

The usage similarity between two components is the similarity of how they are referenced by higher-order descriptions. For example, the result of BPEL matching should be considered while performing a WSDL operation-matching step. If the BPEL references to two operations are similar, then the cost of mapping them in the WSDL-matching step is reduced, proportionally to their *degree of mapping* (DOM). The degree of mapping between two operations is defined as double the number of mappings between the references two the two operations divided by the total sum of their references. Incorporating the DOM ratio of a BPEL-matching step into the WSDL-matching step effectively incorporates the usage similarity of the components references with their signature matching.

5 The Example Revisited

Fig. 2(a) shows the BPEL description of the published service where the service provider describes how that service is supposed to be used, while Fig. 2(c) shows the expected scenario from the consumer point of view. Additionally, Fig. 2(b) and Fig. 2(d) show the tree representation of the published and requested services, respectively.

The result of aligning the BPEL descriptions of Fig. 2(a) and Fig. 2(c) is shown in Fig. 2(b) and Fig. 2(d): the receive action named "receive task" associated with the operation named `SubmitTask` is mapped to the receive action named "place a job" associated with the operation named `PlaceJob`. Additionally, the send action named "Send task-no" is mapped to "Reply with Job ID". Hence, the two (out of two) references to the operation `SubmitTask` are mapped to two (out of two) references to the operation `PlaceJob`, which leads to a DOM ratio of (2*2)/(2+2)=1. Similarly, Fig. 2(b) and Fig. 2(d) show that 3 (out of 4) references to the operation `GetResult` are mapped to the three (out of three) references to the operation `RetrieveOutput` and vice versa, which also results in DOM ration (2*3)/(4+3)=0.86. Therefore, the cost function for the subsequent alignment step is advised to reduce the mapping cost for both (`SubmitTask`, `PlaceJob`) and (`GetResult`, `RetrieveOutput`) by 100% and 86%, respectively. Thus, there is no longer any ambiguity for how the operations and messages of the two WSDL specifications should be mapped.

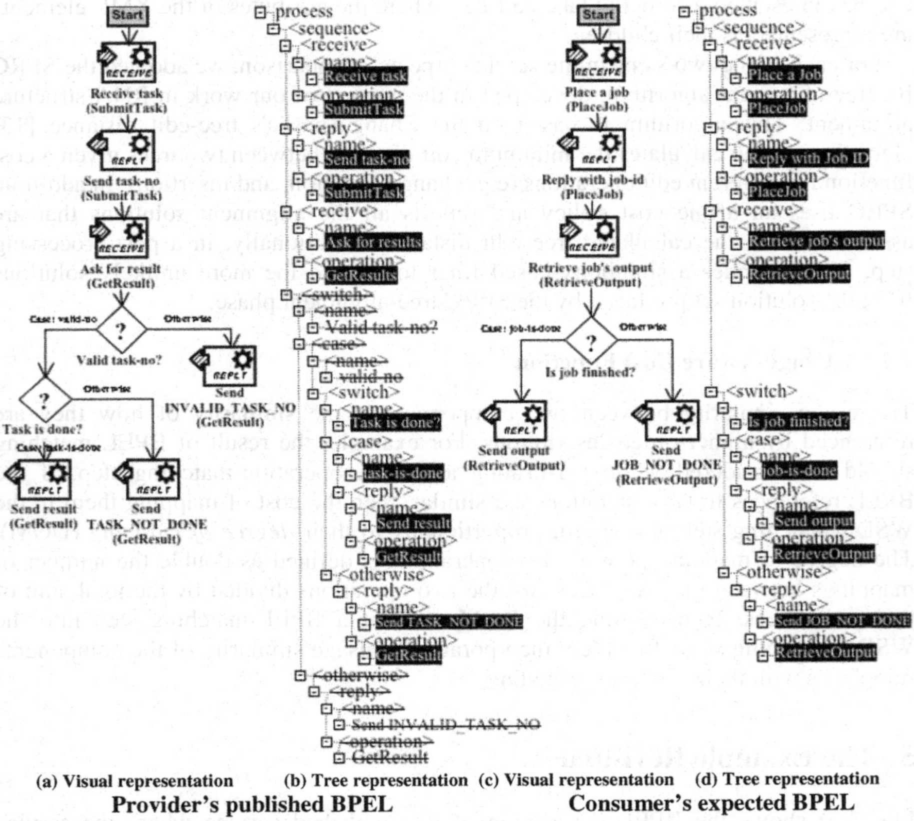

Fig. 2. BPEL descriptions of the published and requested services. Figures (a) and (c) are visual representations showing two types of actions *receive* and *send* actions; each of them is accompanied by the associated operation name. Figures (b) and (d) are annotated tree representations, e.g. a strike labels refer to deleted nodes, while highlighted labels refer to changed nodes.

It is interesting to note that the BPEL description of the published service imposes the pre-condition that a call to `SubmitTask` is to be invoked before a call to `GetResult`. Similarly, according to the requester BPEL description, the consumer expects to invoke an operation that has a semantic like `PlaceJob` before invoking an operation that has the semantic of `RetrieveOutput`. This is exactly the information that our method is designed to respect.

6 Conclusions

In this paper, we discussed our approach for resolving ambiguities in the mapping of published service elements to those of the requested service, by examining the usage of these elements in the context of BPEL-specified behavioral specifications of the service in action. The basic intuition underlying our work is to match operations usage references in order to get a measure of how a certain published operation is used similarly to a requested one. Our service discovery method is based on tree-alignment of the two corresponding specifications (BPEL and WSDL), with results from the BPEL matching step feeding into the WSDL matching step. It is designed to match the semantics implicitly embedded in the BPEL description in order to enhance the quality of the WSDL signature matching, and to resolve any possible ambiguities. Although BPEL specifications of services may not yet be widely used, their potential usefulness, as outlined in this paper, should motivate service providers to develop BPEL descriptions for their services, in order to improve the potential quality of automated discovery methods.

Acknowledgements

This research was supported by ICORE and the Alberta IBM CAS.

References

[1] Andrews, T., Curbera, F., Dholakia, H., Goland, Y., Klein, J., Leymann, F., Liu, K., Roller, D., Smith, D., Thatte, S., Trickovic, I., and Weerawarana, S. "Business Process Execution Language for Web Services." version 1.1, 2003, http://www-128.ibm.com/developerworks/library/specification/ws-bpel/

[2] Blanchet, W., Elio, R., Stroulia, E. "Conversation Errors in Web Service Coordination: Run-time Detection and Repair". Proc. International Conference on Web Intelligence (WI), 2005.

[3] Blanchet, W., Elio, R., Stroulia, E. "Supporting Adaptive Web-Service Orchestration with an Agent Conversation Framework". Proceedings of the third IEEE International Conference on Web Services (ICWS), 2005.

[4] Brockmans, S., Ehrig, M., Koschmider, A., Oberweis, A., and Studer, R., "Semantic Alignment of Business Processes". In 8th International Conference on Enterprise Information Systems, 2006.

[5] Christensen, E., Curbera, F., Meredith, G., Weerawarana, S., "The web services description language WSDL." http://www.w3.org/TR/wsdl

[6] Mikhaiel, R., Lin, G., Stroulia, E., "Simplicity in RNA Secondary Structure Alignment: Towards biologically plausible alignments". In Post Proceedings of the IEEE 6th Symposium on Bioinformatics & Bioengineering (BIBE 2006), October 16 - 18, 2006

[7] Milner, R., Parrow, J., and Walker, D., "A Calculus of Mobile Processes, Part I+II". Journal of Information and Computation, September 1992, 1--87.

[8] Payne, T.R., Paolucci, M., and Sycara, K., "Advertising and Matching DAML-S Service Descriptions". Semantic Web Working Symposium (SWWS), 2001.

[9] Syeda, T., Shah, G., Akkiraju, R., Ivan, A., and Goodwin, R., "Searching Service Repositories by Combining Semantic and Ontological Matching". ICWS, 2005, 13--20.
[10] Stroulia, E., and Wang, Y., "Structural and Semantic Matching for Assessing Web-Service Similarity", Int. Journal of Cooperative Information Systems, 14(4):407-437, June 2005.
[11] Wang, Y., Stroulia, E. "Flexible Interface Matching for Web-Service Discovery". 4th International Conference on Web Information Systems Engineering, 2003, pp. 147-156, IEEE Press.
[12] Wombacher, A., Fankhauser, P., and Neuhold, E. "Transforming BPEL into Annotated Deterministic Finite State Automata for Service Discovery." ICWS, 2004, 316--323.
[13] Zhang, K., Stgatman, R., and Shasha, D. "Simple fast algorithm for the editing distance between trees and related problems." SIAM Journal on Computing, 18(6), 1989, 1245--1262.

Sliver: A BPEL Workflow Process Execution Engine for Mobile Devices

Gregory Hackmann, Mart Haitjema,
Christopher Gill, and Gruia-Catalin Roman

Dept. of Computer Science and Engineering, Washington University in St. Louis

Abstract. The Business Process Execution Language (BPEL) has become the dominant means for expressing traditional business processes as workflows. The widespread deployment of mobile devices like PDAs and mobile phones has created a vast computational and communication resource for these workflows to exploit. However, BPEL so far has been deployed only on relatively heavyweight server platforms such as Apache Tomcat, leaving the potential created by these lower-end devices untapped. This paper presents Sliver, a BPEL workflow process execution engine that supports a wide variety of devices ranging from mobile phones to desktop PCs. We discuss the design decisions that allow Sliver to operate within the limited resources of a mobile phone or PDA. We also evaluate the performance of a prototype implementation of Sliver.

1 Introduction

In today's world, there is an ever-growing need for collaboration among teams of people on complex tasks. The *workflow* model offers a powerful representation of groupware activities. This model is defined informally as "the operational aspect of a work procedure: how tasks are structured, who performs them, what their relative order is, how they are synchronized, how information flows to support the tasks and how tasks are tracked" [1]. In other words, workflow systems coordinate and monitor the performance of tasks by multiple active agents (people or software services) towards the realization of a common goal.

Many traditional business processes — such as loan approval, insurance claim processing, and expense authorization — can be modeled naturally as workflows. This has motivated the development of Web standards, such as the Business Process Execution Language [2] (BPEL), which describe these processes using a common language. Each task in a BPEL process is represented as a service that is invoked using the Simple Object Access Protocol [3] (SOAP). A centralized BPEL server composes these services into complex processes by performing an ordered series of invocations according to the user's specifications. Because BPEL builds on top of standards like XML and SOAP that are already widely deployed, it has been accepted readily in business settings.

The ubiquity of inexpensive mobile and embedded computing devices, like PDAs and mobile phones, offers a new and expanding platform for the deployment and execution of collaborative applications. In 2004, over 267 million Java-capable mobile phones were deployed worldwide, and Sun estimates that up to

A. Dan and W. Lamersdorf (Eds.): ICSOC 2006, LNCS 4294, pp. 503–508, 2006.

1.5 billion will be deployed by the end of 2007 [4]. Though each device is individually far less powerful than a standalone server, their aggregate computation and communication potential is remarkable, and has yet to be fully realized.

Many collaborative applications, such as those described in [5], could incorporate such devices advantageously. These applications can benefit greatly from Web standards like BPEL and SOAP. By defining a common language for interservice interactions and data flow, these standards encourage the composition of simple services into powerful distributed applications.

Unfortunately, these applications pose several important challenges that the current state-of-the-art in SOAP and BPEL systems cannot meet. First, typical mobile devices feature severely constrained hardware requiring a very lightweight software infrastructure. Second, in the absence of a stable Internet connection, it may be impossible, impractical, or too expensive for mobile devices to contact centralized servers. Finally, wireless network links among mobile devices may be disrupted frequently and unpredictably. These challenges necessitate a lightweight, decentralized Web service middleware system which can perform on-the-fly replanning, reallocation, and/or reconfiguration in the face of network failure. Addressing these issues is a significant software engineering challenge.

In this paper, we describe Sliver, our first milestone in this long-term effort. Sliver supports the execution of SOAP services and BPEL processes on mobile devices like mobile phones and PDAs. Because Sliver builds on existing Web standards, it can be used in conjunction with a wide array of existing development tools. We emphasize that Sliver is not intended to *replace* existing SOAP and BPEL middleware: rather, it extends the Web services paradigm to new devices which did not previously support it. In Section 2, we discuss the fundamental characteristics of mobile devices that compel a new kind of middleware. Section 3 provides an overview of Sliver's architecture. The resulting prototype implementation is evaluated in Section 4. Finally, we give concluding remarks in Section 5.

2 Problem Statement

Today, developers can choose from a wide variety of support platforms for SOAP services and BPEL processes. Unfortunately, there are several practical issues that prevent existing SOAP and BPEL middleware packages from being deployed on mobile devices. The first issue is the combined footprint of the middleware and its support layers. For example, the open-source ActiveBPEL [6] engine depends on the Java Standard Edition 1.4.2 runtime and Apache Tomcat [7] application server, with a total footprint of 92 MB of disk space and 22 MB of RAM. While this requirement is reasonable for desktop computers and servers, only a handful of the highest-end mobile phones and PDAs can support systems with such large footprints.

The second issue is that these middleware frameworks and their support layers are often designed with Java 2 Standard Edition (J2SE) in mind. Generally, J2SE runtimes are not available for mobile devices. These devices support a more limited Java runtime, such as one based on the Mobile Information Device Profile (MIDP) standard. Such runtimes support only a fraction of the features provided by a full J2SE runtime. Among other features, MIDP 2.0 does not offer most of J2SE's abstract data structures; its support for runtime reflection is minimal; and it features a unified API for file and network I/O that is incompatible with J2SE's I/O APIs.

Finally, existing BPEL systems typically use HTTP for all communication between hosts. However, this protocol is not a reasonable choice for many mobile devices. Because of network restrictions, many mobile devices (such as most mobile phones) cannot accept incoming TCP/IP sockets, and hence cannot serve HTTP requests. Incoming requests are often restricted to less-conventional transports, such as SMS messages, which current systems do not support.

Thus, if a SOAP or BPEL execution engine is to be deployed on mobile devices, it must embody three major traits: (1) it must have a suitably small storage and memory footprint, including all the libraries on which it depends; (2) it must depend only on the Java APIs that are available on all devices; and (3) it must support a wide variety of communication media and protocols flexibly. In the next section, we discuss how these traits influenced our design and implementation of Sliver.

3 Design and Implementation

Sliver exhibits several architectural decisions which fit the traits described above. Sliver uses a pluggable component architecture, as shown in Figure 1. This architecture provides a clean separation between communication and processing. Communication components can therefore be interchanged without affecting the processing components, and vice versa. In place of a heavyweight, general-purpose XML parser, Sliver uses a series of hand-written parsers developed using the lightweight kXML [8] and kSOAP [9] packages. These packages are designed with mobile devices in mind: they have a small combined footprint (47 KB of storage space) and operate on most available Java runtimes.

Excluding the communication components, Sliver is implemented using the features that J2SE, Java Foundation Profile, and MIDP 2.0 have in common. Sliver can be deployed on devices which support any of these standards, which includes most mobile phones and PDAs sold today. Sliver's streamlined API allows users to deploy an embedded SOAP or BPEL server in under 15 lines of Java code. Further information on Sliver's architecture and implementation, including sample code, can be found in [5].

4 Evaluation

Sliver currently supports BPEL's core feature set and has a total code base of 114 KB including all dependencies (excluding an optional HTTP library). Sliver supports all of the basic and structured activity constructs in BPEL, with the exception of the *compensate* activity, and supports basic data queries and transformations expressed using the XPath language [10]. Sliver also supports the use of BPEL Scopes and allows for local variables and fault handlers to be defined within them. However, Sliver does not currently support some of BPEL's

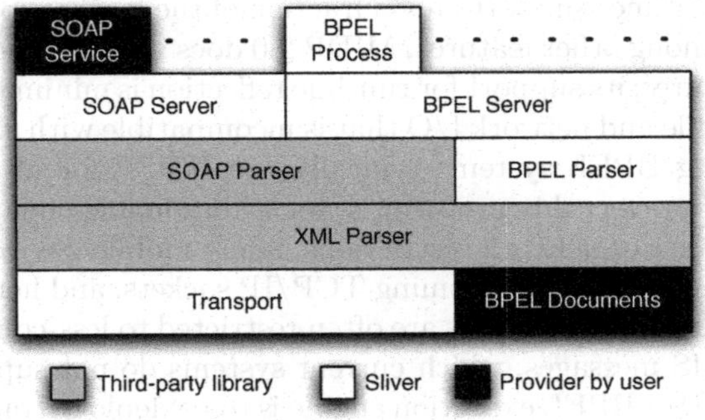

Fig. 1. The architecture of the Sliver execution engine

most advanced features, including *Serializable Scopes* and *Event Handlers*. In future work, we will extend Sliver to support these features.

In order to provide an adequate evaluation of Sliver, it is important not only to benchmark its performance against an existing BPEL engine, but also to examine to what extent the expressive power of BPEL is preserved by Sliver. A framework has been proposed which allows for the analysis of workflow languages in terms of a set of 20 commonly reoccurring workflow patterns [11]. A study of the BPEL language in terms of this framework shows that BPEL can support in full 16 of these 20 workflow patterns, and partially supports one other pattern [12]. Sliver currently supports all but 2 of these 17 patterns.

Our performance benchmark consists of 12 of the 20 patterns listed in [11]. The Multi-Merge, Discriminator, and Arbitrary Cycle patterns are excluded because BPEL does not support them. Sliver also does not presently support all of the BPEL features used by the one of the Multiple Instances patterns and the Interleaved Parallel Routing pattern. The Multiple Instances without Synchronization pattern is not a practical benchmark, since it creates child processes which may continue executing even after the parent process has completed. Finally, the Deferred Choice and Milestone patterns are non-deterministic and therefore do not make practical benchmarks.

In Figure 2, we compare Sliver's execution of these 12 patterns versus the combination of ActiveBPEL 2.0.1.1 and Apache Axis 1.4, popular open source engines for BPEL and SOAP respectively[1]. Our test platform for this comparison is a desktop computer equipped with a 3.2 GHz Pentium 4 CPU, 512 MB of RAM, Linux 2.6.16, and Sun Java 1.5.0_07. Both ActiveBPEL and Apache Axis are hosted on Apache Tomcat 5.5.15. Additionally, this figure shows Sliver's performance running these processes on a Dell Axim X30 PDA which is equipped with a 624 MHz XScale CPU, Windows Mobile 2003, and IBM WebSphere Micro

[1] We once again emphasize that Sliver is not intended to replace feature-rich SOAP and BPEL engines on capable hardware, but rather to support the execution of BPEL processes on resource-limited devices. Our comparison is only intended to provide a metric for acceptable performance.

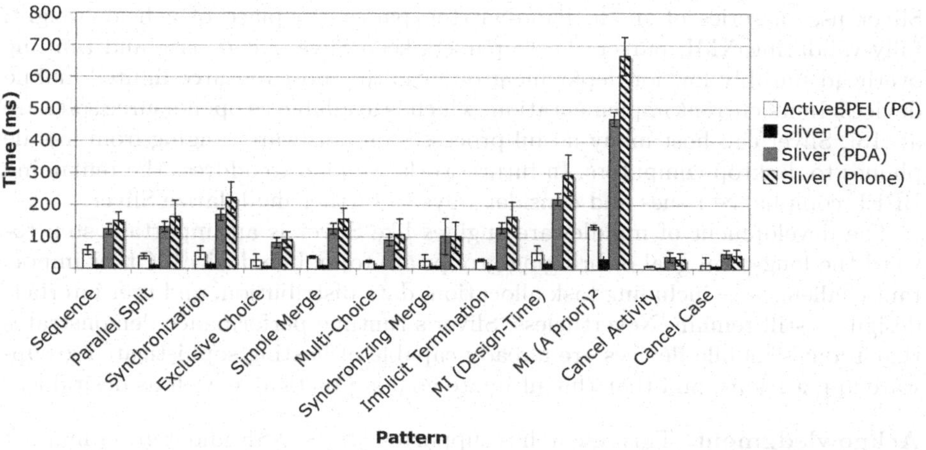

Fig. 2. The cost of executing BPEL patterns; results are the mean of 100 runs

Environment 5.7; and on a Nokia 6682 mobile phone which is equipped with a 220 MHz ARM9 CPU, Symbian OS 8.0a, and a bundled MIDP 2.0 runtime. To isolate the cost of process execution from network delays, the BPEL process and SOAP service are colocated.

Where not noted otherwise, 105 runs of each benchmark were used to generate Figure 2. The first few runs of each benchmark have unusually high costs (often 5 to 10 times the mean) due to class loading, etc. For this reason, we discarded the first 5 runs of each benchmark and computed the mean of the remaining 100 runs. The error bars indicate the standard deviation.

These results demonstrate that it is feasible to deploy BPEL processes on limited hardware. Even on the resource-limited PDA and phone platforms, the cost of carrying out most processes is on the order of 100 ms. (The only exceptions are the Multiple Instances patterns, which contain loops that make them inherently slower than the other patterns.) As noted above, in order to isolate the costs of the BPEL engine, we evaluated processes which invoke a trivial SOAP service located on the same host. Realistically, the cost of executing non-trivial SOAP services (including network delays) is expected to dwarf the cost of supporting the BPEL process in Sliver.

5 Conclusion

In this paper, we have presented Sliver, a middleware engine that supports BPEL process execution on mobile devices. Our design flexibly supports many different communication protocols and media, while still maintaining a minimal footprint.

[2] Due to the complexity of the MI (A Priori) pattern, and very limited hardware resources, the Nokia 6682 is unable to perform 100 runs of this benchmark consecutively. 50 consecutive runs of this pattern were used on the Nokia platform.

Sliver uses a series of small, hand-written parsers in place of a heavyweight, fully-validating XML parser. These parsers keep Sliver's code size and runtime overhead suitably low for deployment on even the most resource-limited mobile devices. In its current implementation, which is available as open-source software at [13], Sliver can host many useful processes on hardware ranging from mobile phones to desktop computers. In future work, we plan to address the remaining BPEL compliance issues and consider ways to further modularize Sliver.

The development of middleware engines like Sliver is an important step toward the long-term goal of bringing groupware to mobile devices. Other important challenges — including task allocation, data distribution, and user interface design — still remain. Nevertheless, Sliver's runtime performance demonstrates that today's mobile devices are already capable of hosting sophisticated groupware applications, and that this ultimate goal is practical as well as desirable.

Acknowledgment. This research is supported by the NSF under grant number IIS-0534699. Any opinions, findings, and conclusions expressed in this paper are those of the authors and do not necessarily represent the views of the research sponsors.

References

1. Wikipedia: Workflow. *http://en.wikipedia.org/wiki/Workflow* (2006)
2. OASIS Open: OASIS web services business process execution language (WSBPEL) TC. *http://www.oasis-open.org/committees/tc_home.php?wg_abbrev=wsbpel* (2006)
3. Box, D., et al.: Simple object access protocol (SOAP) 1.1. Technical Report 08 May 2000, W3C (2000)
4. Ortiz, C.E.: J2ME technology turns 5! *http://developers.sun.com/techtopics/mobility/j2me/articles/5anniversary.html* (2004)
5. Hackmann, G., Haitjema, M., Gill, C., Roman, G.C.: Sliver: A BPEL workflow process execution engine for mobile devices. Technical Report WUCSE-06-37, Washington University, Department of Computer Science and Engineering (2006)
6. ActiveBPEL LLC: ActiveBPEL engine. *http://www.activebpel.org/* (2006)
7. Apache Software Foundation: Apache tomcat. *http://tomcat.apache.org/* (2006)
8. Haustein, S.: kXML 2. *http://kxml.sourceforge.net/kxml2/* (2005)
9. Haustein, S., Seigel, J.: kSOAP 2. *http://ksoap.org/* (2006)
10. Clark, J., DeRose, S.: XML path language (XPath) version 1.0. Technical Report 16 November 1999, W3C (1999)
11. van der Aalst, W.M.P., ter Hofstede, A.H.M., Kiepuszewski, B., Barros, A.P.: Workflow patterns. Distributed and Parallel Databases **14**(1) (2003) 5–51
12. Wohed, P., et al.: Pattern based analysis of BPEL4WS. Technical Report FIT-TR-2002-04, Queensland University of Technology (2002)
13. Hackmann, G.: Sliver. *http://mobilab.wustl.edu/projects/sliver/* (2006)

Automated Discovery of Compositions of Services Described with Separate Ontologies*

Antonio Brogi[1], Sara Corfini[1], José F. Aldana[2], and Ismael Navas[2]

[1] Department of Computer Science
University of Pisa, Italy
[2] Departamento de Lenguajes y Ciencias de la Computación
Universidad de Málaga, Espãna

Abstract. We present a matchmaking system that exploits ontology-based (OWL-S) service descriptions to discover service compositions capable of satisfying a client request. Efficiency is achieved by pre-computing off-line a (hyper)graph that represents the functional dependencies among different (sub)services. The notion of Semantic Field [1] is employed to cross different ontologies.

1 Introduction

The synergy between Web services and the emerging area of the Semantic Web [2] is promoting the development of so-called *semantic Web services*. A semantic Web service is a software service which self-describes its functionalities by annotating them with (instances of) concepts defined by means of ontologies.

The development of fully-automated, semantics-based service discovery mechanisms constitutes a major open challenge in this context, and it raises several important issues. One of them is the ability of coping with different ontologies, as different services are typically described in terms of different ontologies. Another important feature is the capability of discovering service compositions rather than single services. Indeed it is often the case that a client query cannot be fulfilled by a single service, while it may be fulfilled by a suitable composition of services. Last, but not least, efficiency is obviously an important objective of service discovery mechanisms.

In this perspective, we proposed in [3] an algorithm for the composition-oriented discovery of (semantic) Web services. The algorithm in [3], as well as its evolved version described in [4], takes a client query, specifying inputs and outputs of the desired service (composition), and performs a flexible matching over a registry of OWL-S advertisements to determine whether there exists a service (composition) capable of satisfying the query. A limitation of [3,4] is that they do not properly address the problem of crossing ontologies: in [3] all services are (unrealistically) assumed to share the same ontology, while in [4] multiple ontologies are (inefficiently) crossed at query-time.

* Work partially supported by the SMEPP project (EU-FP6-IST 0333563) and by the project TIN2005-09098-C05-01 (Spanish Ministry of Education and Science.

A. Dan and W. Lamersdorf (Eds.): ICSOC 2006, LNCS 4294, pp. 509–514, 2006.

In this paper, we extend [3] and [4] by presenting a semantic-based composition-oriented discovery system which employs the notion of Semantic Fields [1] to cross different ontologies, and it achieves efficiency by pre-computing off-line all the query-independent tasks (viz., to determine the dependencies within/among services as well as the relationships among ontologies). The proposed system is the first one – at the best of our knowledge – that addresses all the previously described issues, namely, composition-oriented discovery, ontology crossing and efficiency. The matchmaking system consists of two main modules: the *hypergraph builder*, which builds a hypergraph representing intra-service and inter-service data relationships, and the *query solver*, which analyses the hypergraph, given a client query that specifies the set of inputs and outputs of the desired service (composition).

The *hypergraph builder* and the *query solver* are described in Sections 2 and 3, respectively. Some concluding remarks are drawn in Section 4.

2 Hypergraph Builder

The hypergraph builder analyses the ontology-based descriptions of the registry-published services in order to build a labelled directed hypergraph, which synthesises all the data dependencies of the advertised services. Although this module performs a time consuming task, it does not affect the efficiency of the matching process, as the hypergraph construction is completely query independent and can be pre-computed off-line before query answering time.

According to [5], a *directed hypergraph* $H = (V, E)$ is a pair, where V is a finite set of vertices and E is a set of directed hyperedges. A directed hyperedge is an ordered pair (X, Y) of (possible empty) disjoint subsets of V, where X and Y denote the tail and the head of the hyperedge, respectively.

The vertices of the hypergraph constructed by the hypergraph builder correspond to the concepts defined in the ontologies employed by the analysed service descriptions, while the hyperedges represent relationships among such concepts. More precisely, an hyperedge has one of the following three types:

- $E_{\subset} = (D, \{c\}, nil)$ – *subConceptOf relationship*. Let c be a concept defined in an ontology O and let $D \in O$ be the set of the (direct) subconcepts of c. Then, there is a $E_{\subset}$ hyperedge from D to c.
- $E_{\equiv} = (\{e\}, \{f\}, sim)$ – *equivalentConceptOf relationship*. Let e, f be two concepts defined in two separate ontologies and let sim be the similarity between e and f, i.e., the probability that e is (semantically) equivalent to f. As we will see, if sim is above a given similarity threshold, there is a $E_{\equiv}$ hyperedge from e to f labelled by sim.
- $E_S = (I, O, \{s\})$ – *intra-service dependency*. Let s be (a profile of) a service and let I be the set of inputs that s requires to produce the set O of outputs. Then, there is a E_S hyperedge from I to O labelled by s.

The hypergraph builder updates the hypergraph whenever a new service s is added to the registry. More precisely, the hypergraph builder firstly adds to the hypergraph the concepts defined in the ontologies employed by s (independently of whether they directly occur in the specification of s). Next, it draws the hyperedges representing the *subConceptOf* relationships, the *equivalentConceptOf* relationships, and the *intra-service* dependencies between the newly added ontology concepts.

As mentioned in the Introduction, in order to cope with different ontologies, the hypergraph builder exploits the notion of Semantic Fields [1,6], which are groups of interrelated ontologies that may be relevant to a given information request. To find Semantic Fields we firstly compute the similarity between pairs of concepts and next we calculate the distance between pairs of ontologies (i.e., how similar two ontologies are). The Semantic Field Tool[1] (SemFiT) determines mappings between concepts by combining the results of individual matchers which analyse the similarity between pairs of concepts with different strategies: *exact match*, *same prefix*, *same suffix*, *synonyms* in wordNet *v*.1.7 and *similar path* in the ontology. The hypergraph builder determines the *subConceptOf* and *equivalentConceptOf* relations by suitably exploiting the SemFiT methods.

Consider now the intra-service dependencies of s. As one may expect, several intra-service dependencies can be drawn out from a service description, as a service may behave in different ways and feature different functionalities. The different *profiles* of s can be determined by analysing the OWL-S[2] process model which describes the behaviour of s. The hypergraph builder inserts in the hypergraph a intra-service dependency for each profile of s.

Finally, it is worth observing that the *inter-service dependencies* are directly represented by the hypergraph and they are automatically updated whenever a service is added to the registry. Indeed, an inter-service dependency between two services s and t occurs if there exists (at least) a concept which belongs both to the head of a s-labelled E_S hyperedge and to the tail of a t-labelled E_S hyperedge. Note that there is a inter-service dependency between s and t also if there exist two concepts c_s and c_t linked together by means of $E_{\subset}$ and/or $E_{\equiv}$ hyperedges, where c_s belongs to the head of the s-labelled E_S hyperedge and c_t belongs to the tail of the t-labelled E_S hyperedge.

We present next an example which illustrates the behaviour of the hypergraph builder. Let us consider an empty registry where we add the hotelService and the conferenceService. The former allows a client to search for and/or to reserve hotels, and the latter allows a client to register to academic events. Figure 1 depicts the OWL-S process models of hotelService and conferenceService, which employ three different ontologies, namely `hotel`, `e-commerce` and `event`[3].

The hypergraph builder firstly adds to the hypergraph all the concepts defined in the `hotel`, `e-commerce` and `event` ontologies together with the *subConceptOf* and the *equivalentConceptOf* relationships returned by SemFiT. Then, it computes and inserts also the *intra-service* dependencies of HotelService and ConferenceService. The resulting hypergraph is shown in Figure 2.

---

[1] Available through a Web Service at `http://khaos.uma.es/SemanticFieldsWS/services/SemFieldsConceptHierarchy?-wsdl`

[2] OWL-S: Semantic Markup for Web Service. http://www.daml.org/services/owl-s

[3] Available at `http://khaos.uma.es/esp/ont/br/[hotel,e-commerce,event].owl`

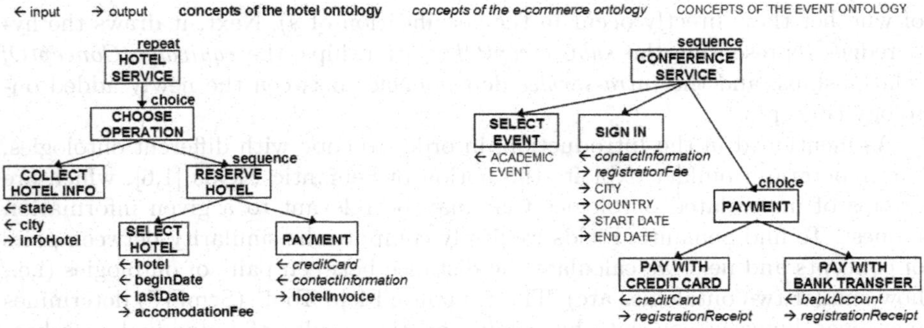

Fig. 1. Process models of HotelService and ConferenceService

3 Query Solver

The query solver takes as input a client query specifying the set of inputs and outputs of the desired service (composition), and next it analyses the hypergraph in order to discover the (compositions of) services capable of satisfying the client request. The formulation of the query is eased by a suitable interface that displays the available concepts (e.g., with an expandable tree structure) and highlights the (computed) equivalences between concepts.

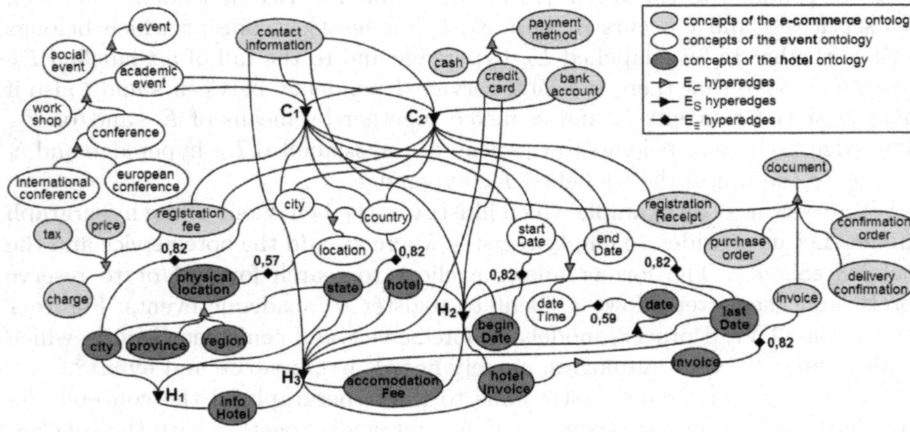

Fig. 2. A simple dependency hypergraph

The query solver explores the hypergraph, by suitably considering the intra-service and inter-service dependencies to address the discovery of (compositions of) services as well as by considering the *subConceptOf* and *equivalentConceptOf* relationships to cope with (different) ontologies. Before describing in more details the behaviour of the query solver, let us extend the notion of *subConceptOf* between two concepts c, d defined in two given (possibly equivalent) ontologies. c is *subConceptOf* d if and only if in the dependency hypergraph there exists a path from c to d which consists of *subConceptOf* relationships and/or *equivalentConceptOf* relationships.

The query solver starts by choosing an output o from the goal set (initially the query outputs). A new instance of query solver is generated for each service s which produces (a sub-concept of) o. If there exists no service yielding o, the query solver fails. Each instance updates the goal set by removing the concepts that are now available (i.e., the outputs of s) and by adding the inputs of s which are not contained in the query inputs nor produced by some previously selected service. If the goal set is empty, the query solver returns the set of services selected so far (i.e., a successful composition), otherwise it continues recursively. The efficiency of the query solver can be improved by enumerating the non-deterministic generation of the possible solutions in order to return the first successful service (composition) only. Moreover, the large number of services taken into account by the query solver can be reduced by introducing a suitable service pre-selection phase (e.g., using UDDI to filter services not belonging to certain service categories), and by selecting services which produce a needed output with respect to some heuristics (e.g., the number and/or on the quality of the produced outputs) in order to consider the "most promising" services only.

Let us continue the example introduced at the end of Section 2. Consider now a client wishing to plan its participation in an international conference by registering to the conference and by booking her hotel accomodation, and receiving the conference and hotel confirmations. The client query may be composed by the following parameters:

- **inputs** – `event#internationalConference`, `hotel#hotel`, `e-commerce#contactInformation`, `e-commerce#creditCard`
- **output** – `e-commerce#registrationReceipt`, `e-commerce#invoice`.

As one may note, neither hotelService nor conferenceService satisfies the given query by itself. Yet, the query can be fulfilled by suitably composing the two available services. Indeed, after visiting the hypergraph in Figure 2, the query solver returns two successful service compositions, represented by the hyperedges $\{H_2, C_1\}$ and $\{H_3, C_1\}$, while it discards compositions $\{H_2, C_2\}$ and $\{H_3, C_2\}$, as `e-commerce#bankAccount` cannot be produced by any available service.

4 Concluding Remarks

We have presented a new fully-automated semantic-based matchmaking system for discovering (compositions of) services capable of satisfying a given client request. As already mentioned in the Introduction, our proposal addresses three main issues of service discovery, namely, composition-oriented discovery, crossing different ontologies and efficiency.

Given the increasing availability of Web services, several composition-oriented discovery systems have been recently proposed, such as [7,8,9], which address the discovery of service compositions by operating in the domain of hypergraphs, finite state automata and interface automata, respectively. Although [7,8,9] deal with ontology-based service descriptions, they do not address the task of crossing ontologies. A composition-oriented discovery algorithm capable of coping with different ontologies has been presented in [10], however, it crosses ontologies at query time, hence severely affecting the efficiency of the whole procedure. An interesting approach for discovering semantic Web services has been proposed in [11], where efficiency is achieved by pre-processing the available ontologies and by pre-classifying the registry-published services before query answering time. Still, [11] does not address the discovery of service compositions.

Our plan for future work includes: to develop fresh indexing and/or ranking techniques to sensibly improve the efficiency of the query solver, to complete our system by employing a behavioural analyser module to determine whether the candidate services can really be composed together and satisfy the query without dead-locking, and finally, to extend SemFiT by employing other existing matching tools in order to achieve better results for the ontology matching problem. Our long-term goal is to develop a well-founded methodology to support an efficient and fully-automated discovery and composition of Web services.

References

1. Navas-Delgado, I., Sanz, I., Aldana-Montes, J.F., Berlanga, R.: Automatic Generation of Semantic Fields for Resource Discovery in the Semantic Web. In: 16th Int. Conf. on Database and Expert Systems Applications. LNCS *3588*. (2005)
2. Berners-Lee, T., Hendler, J., Lassila, O.: The Semantic Web. In: Scientific American. (2001)
3. Brogi, A., Corfini, S., Popescu, R.: Composition-oriented Service Discovery. In Gschwind, T., Aßmann, U., Nierstrasz, O., eds.: Software Composition. LNCS *3628*, Springer-Verlag (2005) 15–30
4. Brogi, A., Corfini, S.: Behaviour-aware discovery of Web service compositions. In: University of Pisa, Department of Computer Science - Tech. Rep. TR-06-08. (2006)
5. Gallo, G., Longo, G., Nguyen, S., Pallottino, S.: Directed hypergraphs and applications. Discrete Applied Mathematics **42** (1993) 177–201
6. Aldana-Montes, J.F., Navas-Delgado, I., del Mar Roldan-Garcia, M.: Solving Queries over Semantically Integrated Biological Data Sources. In: Int. Conf. on Web-Age Information Management (WAIM 2004). LNCS *3129*. (2004)
7. Benatallah, B., Hacid, M.S., Rey, C., Toumani, F.: Request Rewriting-Based Web Service Discovery. In Goos, G., Hartmanis, J., van Leeuwen, J., eds.: The Semantic Web - ISWC 2003, LNCS 2870, Springer-Verlag (2003) 242–257
8. Mokhtar, S.B., Georgantas, N., Issarny, V.: Ad Hoc Composition of User Tasks in Pervasive Computing Environment. In Gschwind, T., Aßmann, U., Nierstrasz, O., eds.: Software Composition, LNCS 3628, Springer-Verlag (2005)
9. Hashemian, S., Mavaddat, F.: A Graph-Based Approach to Web Services Composition. In IEEE Computer Society, ed.: SAINT 2005, CS Press (2005) 183–189
10. Aversano, L., Canfora, G., Ciampi, A.: An Algorithm for Web Service Discovery through Their Composition. In Zhang, L., ed.: IEEE International Conference on Web Services (ICWS'04), IEEE Computer Society (2004) 332–341
11. Mokhtar, S.B., Kaul, A., Georgantas, N., Issarny, V.: Towards Efficient Matching of Semantic Web Service Capabilities. In: Proceedings of WS-MATE 2006. (2006)

Dynamic Web Service Selection and Composition: An Approach Based on Agent Dialogues

Yasmine Charif-Djebbar and Nicolas Sabouret

Laboratoire d'Informatique de Paris 6.
8, rue du Capitaine Scott. 75015 Paris
{yasmine.charif, nicolas.sabouret}@lip6.fr

Abstract. In this paper, we are motivated by the problem of automatically and dynamically selecting and composing services for the satisfaction of user requirements. We propose an approach dealing with requirements freely expressed by the user, and in which agents perform service composition through unplanned interactions. Our architecture is based on agents that offer semantic web services and that are capable of reasoning about their services' functionalities. We propose to provide such agents with an interaction protocol that allows them, through dialogues, to select and compose appropriate services' functionalities in order to fulfill a complex set of requirements specified by a user.

Keywords: Service Composition, Service Selection, Agent-based SOA, Interaction Protocol, Agents' Dialogues.

1 Introduction

Service-Oriented Architectures have been recognized as advantageous architectural styles for future enterprise and scientific applications. However, on top of already available middleware layers, many problems regarding service engineering and management, such as service composition [8], have been identified as open issues.

In recent years, web service composition in service-oriented architectures has been actively investigated in the database and semantic web communities. Some of the existing approaches propose to specify manually the composition process [3,9,10]; others need a designer's assistance in a semi-automated approach to composition [6,7]; and others tackle this problem as a planning task [1,15]. However, these approaches present recurring limitations:

- Most of them require the user to have low-level knowledge of the composition process; *e.g.* in the case of [9,10], the user is expected to set up a workflow at the XML level, and the tools proposed in [6,7] propose to the user low-level semantic suggestions. Consequently, these approaches cannot be handled by ordinary users of the web.
- In some of these approaches, *e.g.* [11,16], the user is not free to express his or her requirements and is rather constrained to choose a "generic goal" in a predefined list, *e.g. "Making the travel arrangements for the ICSOC conference trip"*.

A. Dan and W. Lamersdorf (Eds.): ICSOC 2006, LNCS 4294, pp. 515–521, 2006.

– Automated service composition requires handling the discovery and selection of services. Solutions that are proposed for these tasks are based on semantic annotations, which does not guarantee (on its own) the provision of the service that fulfills all the user's request. For instance, suppose that a service has been annotated as providing a sports coach and a user expresses the query *"I would like to engage a sports coach starting 4 July"*. A service discovery process based on semantic annotations may encounter scalability problems, as it will propose all the sports coach services, while the user needs a more specific service available from 4 July.
– Most of these approaches assume that the services to compose are elementary since they only propose solutions to compose the overall services and not the specific functionalities required [1,15].

These drawbacks lead us to propose a new approach for a **dynamic** service selection and composition. In such an approach, services are selected and composed on the fly according to requirements freely expressed by the user [12]. Therefore, this is the suitable approach for end-user applications in the web where available components are dynamic and expected users may vary.

The composition approach we are developing is based on multi-agent systems (MAS). Indeed, dynamic service selection and composition can benefit from solutions provided by research in MAS. For instance, service composition can be performed dynamically through agent collaboration, without predefining abstract plans. In addition, agent technology offers well-developed approaches to formally express and utilize richer semantic information, such as nonfunctional characteristics of web services or qualitative constraints on the results proposed by a service. On another hand, local and reactive processing in MAS can avoid centralized systems' bottlenecks and improve scalability.

Overview of Our Composition Approach

In our approach, we define semantic web services provided by interactive agents capable of reasoning about their services' functionalities. Our overall approach can be broadly decomposed into three steps (see figure 1):

1. Formalize and decompose the user's requirements into one or several interdependent requests, which are sent to a mediator agent responsible for the discovery of candidate services;
2. Discover and retrieve the candidate services from a registry using keywords extracted from the user's requests;
3. Select and compose the services' functionalities through the interactions of the mediator agent and the agents providing the candidate services, until the user's requirements are satisfied.

In this paper, we assume that the first two phases have been performed and we focus on the service composition phase by defining *an interaction protocol* allowing agents/services to dialogue so as to respond to a complex query requiring the coordination of several services. Three features distinguish our proposal

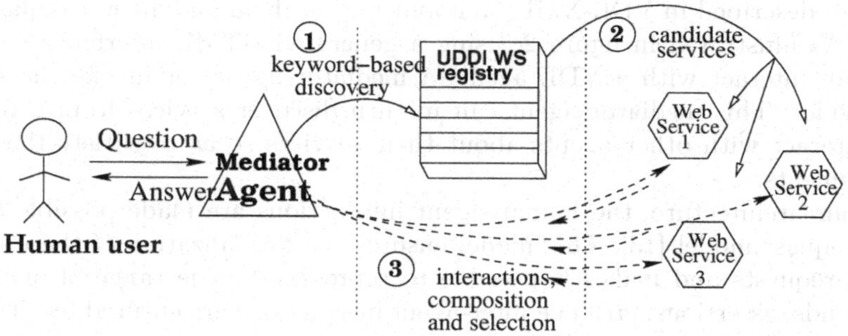

Fig. 1. Overview of our Agent-based Composition Approach

from other work in the area. First, in our approach web services are pro-active and can thus engage in complex conversations, instead of just simple invocation and response with a result or error. Second, since it is performed through a dialogue model, our composition process is dynamic and doesn't require predefined plans or a predefined order of invocation of the services' operations. Finally, the use of agent technology allows for the expression of global constraints, making it possible to select services according to specific user requirements.

In the rest of this paper, we present briefly our web service architecture based on MAS in section 2. We describe in section 3 the interaction protocol making it possible for agents/services to manage their dialogues so as to select and compose the appropriate services with respect to user's requests and constraints. Finally, in section 4 we discuss the limitations of our current work, and place it in perspective.

2 A Web Service Architecture Based on MAS

The aim of our research is to take draw on solutions provided in MAS to propose an approach for service selection and composition. To this end, we implemented a web service architecture following the definition given by the W3C [5] where a service is viewed as part of an agent. Our web service architecture is thus based on interactive agents that are capable of providing semantic web services and reasoning about them.

We designed these agents as the combination of three layers. *A concrete agent* reasoning about its offered service and processing the inter-agent communication issues; *an abstract service* representing an XML-based declaration of the functionalities offered by the service, associated to an ontology defining the concepts and actions it handles; and *a web service* which is the WSDL interface of the abstract service deployed on the web. To model such agents, we propose to use the VDL formalism. VDL (for View Design Language) [14] is a programming language for autonomous agents capable of interacting with the human user and other agents. VDL allows to implement agents able to offer semantic web services, described in VDL-XML, to about reason them and answer requests for them. As illustrated in figure 2, using a generated HTML interface, a human user can interact with a VDL agent (a mediator agent) or invoke the service it provides. This mediator agent can in turn discover services from a registry and interact with other agents about their services so as to satisfy the user's requirements.

In our architecture, the human-agent interactions are made possible by the VDL request model [13]. This model ensures the formalization of the user and agents requests and makes it possible to represent a wide range of questions, commands, assertions, *etc.* The inter-agent interactions are ensured by the agent communication language (ACL) encompassing requests about services into structured messages. The content of each message is a set of requests among which dependencies can be raised. Services can then either be invoked by SOAP or, as we previously mentioned, accessed via the agent offering it through the ACL.

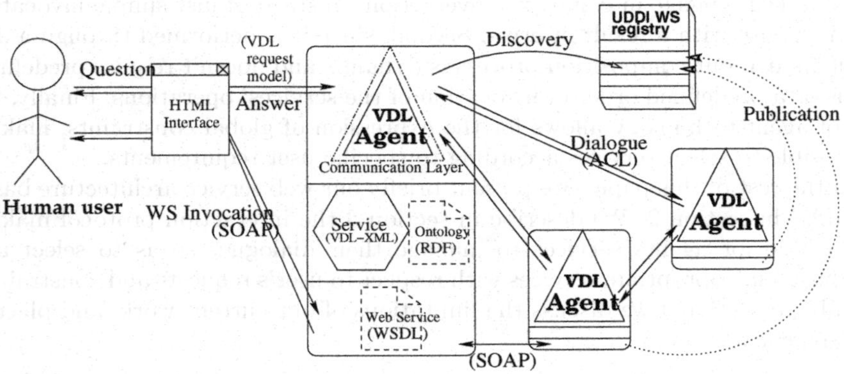

Fig. 2. Our Agent-based SOA

3 The Agent's Interaction Protocol

In our approach, the user's requirements are formalized as a set of (dependent) requests, *e.g. "I want to buy and have delivered a piano, and remove my old wardrobe"*, plus a set of constraints about the services discovered, *e.g.* QoS or trust parameters, or constraints about the results they provide, *e.g. "I want to pay less than $300 for both the wardrobe removal and the piano delivery"*. These requests and constraints are stored within the mediator agent in a record (gathering the information related to a composition goal), comprising also the set of messages exchanged with other services to satisfy the user's requests. Such a record is stored within a history table, provided for each agent, containing all the information related to an agent interactions.

To design our protocol, we consider that an agent has not only to answer to a message according to its services' functionalities, but also to take the initiative whenever the message comprises requests requiring the coordination of several services. More precisely, the agent tries to discover services that may be composed so as to fulfill the user's needs. This composition and selection mechanism is performed following three main phases supported by three algorithms we defined. For each phase, agents' behaviors have been defined according to their role (mediator agent, or participant agent providing a candidate service).

3.1 Processing Triggering Messages

The mediator agent starts by broadcasting the triggering message, *i.e.* the message containing the user's requests, to the discovered services. When a participant agent, providing a service, receives such a message, it builds an answer to each request following its service's functionalities and knowledge using its request processing module (RPM) [13]. This module builds for each request range (assertion, command, *etc*) the corresponding answer according to the service's functionalities. The agent then returns the answering message to the sender.

Suppose in our example that the mediator agent discovered a music equipment service, a removal service, a delivery service, and another delivery service offering to remove equipments under certain conditions. In this step, each service answers according to its functionalities and knowledge. For instance, the music equipment service sends a proposal for a piano specifying its characteristics and price, and one of the delivery services informs the mediator agent that it can't answer to the delivery request as long as it hasn't been sent information related to the piano (the delivery cost could for instance depend on the value and weight of the equipment to deliver).

3.2 Message Composition

The processing of a non triggering message depends on the role of the agent receiving it. If this agent is the mediator agent, it analyzes it together with the stored messages in order to relaunch the interaction if needed. For instance, if one of the services sent an answer stating that it needs a variable value, and if the received message provides an assertion about this variable, the mediator agent builds a composed message containing this assertion and invokes the specific service requiring it. If a participant agent receives a non triggering message, in addition to it's service's functionalities and knowledge, it uses the assertions contained in the received messages as knowledge to solve the received requests.

In our example, the delivery service needs information related to the piano that the music equipment service sent to the mediator agent. Following the second step of our protocol, the mediator agent sends a composed message containing the assertion about the piano characteristics and invokes the delivery service needing it.

3.3 Service Selection

The mediator agent is provided with a timeout value over which, if no more message arrives, it proceeds to service selection. This step aims at selecting services that best fit to the user's constraints among those which could answer to the user's requests.

To perform this selection, the mediator agent builds for each triggering request (composing the triggering message) a candidate answers list storing the ids and answers of the services that could respond to this request. For each stored constraint, for instance `deliveryCost+removalCost<$300`, the mediator agent builds the corresponding expression using the services answers. In our example, the mediator agent build the expression `deliveryCost+removalCost` and assesses it first with the first delivery service and the removal service answers (where the expression is assessed to `$350`), then the second delivery service which offers equipments removal (where the expression is assessed to `$280`). Comparing the obtained results with respect to the constraint, the mediator agent removes from the candidate answers list the services that don't respect the constraint. In our example, the first delivery service and the removal service are removed from the candidate answers lists. The mediator agent then returns to the user, for each triggering request, the corresponding service and the answer it provided.

4 Conclusion and Future Work

We have proposed in this paper a dynamic approach to performing web service selection and composition using unplanned agent-based dialogues. Our approach rests on a web service architecture that supports pro-active and interactive web services provided by agents. We have specified an interaction protocol that allows agents interacting about their services functionalities so as to satisfy a composition goal with respect to requests and constraints freely expressed by the user. This protocol specifies the agents' behaviors according to their role (mediator or participant) in the composition process and allows them to coordinate so as to solve dependent requests. As a result, the mediator agent performs a selection over the proposed answers with respect to the user constraints and provides the user with the set of services, together with their answers, that could respond to both his requests and constraints.

However, even though our interaction protocol performs well in the presented example, in future work we need to consider several improvements in order to achieve greater scalability in the composition and selection techniques. For instance, if a user constraint involves the results of several services, as in the presented scenario, the service selection step should try different answer combinations. We propose to use MAS algorithms for negotiation [2] during this step to retrieve the best combinations of answers respecting complex constraints. Moreover, we also envision for our interaction protocol to consult with the human user whenever more information is needed by a service to answer a request, or to solve conflicts or multiple choice situations. On another hand, rule-based policies [4] might condition the evolution of the conversation, *e.g.* the requester might require a certificate to be sent by the service provider in order to disclose his credit card details. Finally, we plan to study (both theoretically and empirically) the performance of our system, so as to provide a quantitative demonstration of the benefit to our system's scalability from the use of MAS techniques.

References

1. R. Aggarwal, K. Verma, J. Miller, and W. Milnor. Constraint Driven Web Service Composition in METEOR-S. In *Special Issue of the International Journal of Electronic Commerce (IJEC)*, 2004.
2. S. Aknine. Improving Optimal Winner Determination Algorithms Using Graph Structures. In *Proc. Agent Mediated Electronic Commerce*, 2004.
3. B. Benatallah, Q.Z. Sheng, and M. Dumas. The Self-Serve Environment for Web Services Composition. *IEEE Internet Computing*, 7(1):40–48, 2003.
4. P. A. Bonatti, N. Shahmehri, C. Duma, D. Olmedilla, W. Nejdl, M. Baldoni, C. Baroglio, A. Martelli, P. Coraggio V. Patti and, G. Antoniou, J. Peer, and N. E. Fuchs. Rule-based Policy Specification: State of the Art and Future Work. Technical report, Project deliverable D1, Working Group I2, EU NoE REWERSE, Sep 2004.
5. D. Booth, H. Haas, F. McCabe, E. Newcomer, M. Champion, C. Ferris, and D. Orchard. Web Services Architecture. Technical report, W3C Working Group Note 11, 2004.
6. L. Chen, N.R. Shadbolt, C. Goble, F. Tao, S.J. Cox, C. Puleston, and P. Smart. Towards a Knowledge-based Approach to Semantic Service Composition. In *Proc. 2nd International Semantic Web Conference*, 2003.
7. J. Domingue and S. Galizia. Towards a Choreography for IRS-III. In *Proc. of the Workshop on WSMO Implementations (WIW 2004)*, 2004.
8. A. Gustavo, F. Casati, H. Kuno, and V. Machiraju. Web Services. Concepts, Architectures and Applications, 2004.
9. IBM Alphaworks. BPWS4J. `http://www.alphaWorks.ibm.com/tech/bpws4j`, 2002.
10. N. Kavantzas, D. Burdett, G. Ritzinger, T. Fletcher, and Y. Lafon. Web Services Description Language (WS-CDL). Technical report, W3C, 2004.
11. S. McIlraith and T.C. Son. Adapting golog for Composition of Semantic Web Services. In *Proc. of the 8th International Conference on Knowledge Representation and Reasoning (KR'02)*, 2002.
12. T. Osman, D. Thakker, and D. Al-Dabass. Bridging the Gap between Workflow and Semantic-based Web services Composition. In *Proc. of the Web Service Composition Workshop WSCOMPS05*, 2005.
13. N. Sabouret. A model of requests about actions for active components in the semantic web. In *Proc. STAIRS 2002*, pages 11–20, 2002.
14. N. Sabouret. Representing, requesting and reasoning about actions for active components in human-computer interaction. Technical Report 2002-09, LIMSI-CNRS, 2002.
15. P. Traverso and M. Pistore. Automated Composition of Semantic Web Services into Executable Processes. In *Proc. of the 3rd International Semantic Web Conference, Hiroshima, Japan (ISWC'04)*, pages 380–394, 2004.
16. M. Vallée, F. Ramparany, and L. Vercouter. Flexible Composition of Smart Device Services. In *Proc. of the 4th International Conference on Pervasive Computing*, pages 91–96, 2006.

Leveraging Web Services Discovery with Customizable Hybrid Matching

Natallia Kokash[1], Willem-Jan van den Heuvel[2], and Vincenzo D'Andrea[1]

[1] DIT - University of Trento, Via Sommarive, 14, 38050 Trento, Italy
{kokash, dandrea}@dit.unitn.it
[2] Infolab, Tilburg University, 5000 LE, PO Box 90158, Tilburg, The Netherlands
wjheuvel@uvt.nl

Abstract. Improving web service discovery constitutes a vital step for making a reality the Service Oriented Computing (SOC) vision of dynamic service selection, composition and deployment. Matching allows for comparing user requests with descriptions of available service implementations, and sits at the heart of the service discovery process. This paper firstly evaluates the efficacy of several key similarity metrics for matching syntactic, semantic and structural information from service interface descriptions, using a uniform corpus of web services. Secondly, it experiments with a hybrid style of matching that allows for blending various matching approaches and makes them configurable to cater service discovery given domain-specific constraints and requirements.

1 Introduction

Service Oriented Architectures (SOAs) offer tantalizing possibilities for enterprizes by allowing large-scale reuse of loosely-coupled services, defining service description, discovery and composition at heart of its paradigm. Web services has become the preferred implementation technology for realizing the SOA promise of service sharing and interoperability. By now, a stack of standards and specifications supports the description, discovery, invocation, composition, security and deployment of web services, and many tools to develop applications from web services have become commercially available. However, the vision of dynamic composition of heterogeneous web services still seems far away.

Web service discovery is generally perceived a key step to reach automation of service composition, and further realizing the SOA vision. It is concerned with locating web services that match a set of functional and non-functional criteria. Discovery involves three interrelated phases: (1) matching, (2) assessment and (3) selection. During the first phase, the description of a service is matched to that of a set of available resources. Next, the result of matching (typically a set of ranked web services) is assessed, filtered by a set of criteria. Finally, services are actually selected so they may be subsequently customized and combined with others. This paper focuses on the first phase of service discovery - matching.

In [1] we present the overview of the existing approaches to web service matching. Unfortunately, in many cases an evaluation of the proposed matching techniques is lacking. And, if available, each experimental evaluation uses its own

A. Dan and W. Lamersdorf (Eds.): ICSOC 2006, LNCS 4294, pp. 522–528, 2006.

corpus, making an objective judgement about their efficacy very cumbersome. To analyze their merits, it is useful to classify the existing algorithms as uniform or hybrid. Uniform approaches refer to atomic matching techniques that can not be further decomposed in finer-grained methods. Hybrid approaches on the other hand may combine various matching methods into a composite algorithm.

In Section 2, we introduce a web service matching approach that serves to highlight the basic workings of hybrid matching and compare several similarity measures using a similar WSDL corpus. Based on these evaluations, Section 3 proposes a customizable approach towards hybrid service matching. Section 4 concludes this paper by summarizing our main findings and exploring new research areas.

2 The WSDL Matching Method (WSDL-M2)

We present a matching algorithm, named WSDL-M2, that was inspired by several existing discovery methods. It is oriented to work with incomplete web service specifications and combines two techniques: *lexical matching* to calculate the linguistic similarity between concept descriptions, and *structural matching* to evaluate the overall similarity between composite concepts.

All WSDL specifications are parsed in order to allow extraction of their structured content. The parsed document is tagged to enable lexical analysis. The implementation of the method considers five WSDL concepts that are supposed to contain meaningful information: *services*, *operations*, *messages*, *parts* and *data types*. Each element has a *description*, i.e., a vector that contains semantic information about this element extracted from the specification.

The tagged WSDL specifications can be further analyzed and subsequently indexed using different IR models. The most widely-used IR technique constitutes the Vector-Space Model. It weights indexed terms to enhance retrieval of relevant WSDL documents and then computes a similarity coefficient after which they may be ranked. Traditionally, term weights are assigned using the *tf-idf (term frequency-inverse document frequency)* measure. After this assignment, the similarity between descriptions is determined using associative coefficients based on the inner product of the description vectors. To address the major shortcoming of VSM, the fact that VSM considers words at the syntactic level only, our method expands both the query and the WSDL concept descriptions using synonyms that are extracted from WordNet. Next, we compare the obtained word tuples as in VSM. Finally, we used a measure that reflects the semantic relation between two concepts using the WordNet lexicon[1]. Formally, it is defined as $sim(c_1, c_2) = 1 - \big(ic_{wn}(c_1) + ic_{wn}(c_2)\big)/2 + \max_{c \in S(c_1,c_2)} ic_{ws}(c)$, where $ic_{wn}(c)$ denotes information content value of a concept c and $S(c_1, c_2)$ is a set of concepts that subsume c_1 and c_2. More details of this method are outlined in [2]. In principle, any other algorithm could have been chosen instead.

[1] Java implementation of the algorithm that defines the semantic similarity of two terms is available on `http://wordnet.princeton.edu/links.shtml`.

Using these metrics, the matching phase then continues with the comparison of service descriptions and the set of service operations, which are later combined in a single-number measure. The similarity between operations, in their turn, is assessed based on the descriptions of operations and their input/output messages. To compare message pairs we again evaluate similarity of their descriptions and parts. Since one part with a complex data type or several parts with primitive data types can describe the same concept, we compare message parts with subelements of complex data types as well. We rely on "relaxed" two-level structural matching of data types since too strict comparison can significantly reduce recall. At the first level, description of complex types are compared. At the second one, all atomic subelements of the complex type are compared. For each element, names of higher-level organizational tags such as `complexType` or `simpleType` and composers such as `all` or `sequence` are included in the element description. Order constraints are ignored since parser implementations often do not observe them. This does not harm well-behaved clients and offers some margin for errors.

The structural matching is treated as *Maximum Weight Bipartite Matching* problem that can be solved in polynomial time using, for example, Kuhn's Hungarian method. We use this method for two purposes: (i) to calculate semantic similarity between concept descriptions, (ii) to compute similarity of complex WSDL concepts taking into account their constituents (sub-types). Weight w_{ij} of each edge is defined as a lexical similarity between elements i and j. The total weight of the maximum weight assignment depends on the dimensions of the graph parts. There are many strategies to acquire a single-number dimension-independent measure in order to compare sets of matching pairs. The simplest of them is to calculate the matching average. Alternatively, we can consider two elements $i \in X$, $j \in Y$ to be similar if $w_{ij} > \gamma$ for some parameter $\gamma \in [0, 1]$. In this case, Dice, Simpson, and Jaccard coefficients may be applied. Due to space reasons, we are not able to include the entire formal details of the matching algorithm. We refer to [3] for a detailed formal treatment.

We have conducted a series of experiments to evaluate the efficacy of the presented matching method. We have compared the efficacy of the *tf-idf* heuristic, its WordNet-based extension and the semantic similarity metric described above. We ran our experiments using two web service collections presented in [4] and [5][2]. For each service we queried the complete data set for the relevant services (i.e., services classified in the same group). The similarity assigned to different files with respect to the query can be treated as a level of the algorithm *confidence*. It ranges from 0 (no match) to 1 (WSDL documents contain all concepts from the query regardless of the order). To avoid dependency from the chosen similarity threshold, the efficacy of the matching algorithm was accessed by *average precision* that combines precision, relevance ranking, and overall recall [6].

For the first collection of the classified web services WSDL-M2 proved to be very effective (46-100%). For several categories of the second collection average

[2] Stroulia and Wang describe a collection of 814 services. However, we excluded a group of 366 unclassified WSDL specifications and 1 WSDL file was not parsed correctly.

precision was dramatically low (15-40%) reaching 100% for the other groups in the same time. This can be explained by the fact that the most categories in the corpus were very coarse-grained and too generic in nature. Further, our experimental results have shown that the VSM was the most effective method for the overwhelming majority of the queries despite the fact that it is limited to syntactic matching only. Application of the *tf-idf* heuristic applied on the WSDL specifications enriched with synonyms from the WordNet lexicon, did not improve the quality of the matching results for the first collection. For the second data set the Wilcoxon signed rank tests indicate that these two approaches are significantly different (p-value $= 0.00693 < 0.01$) and prove that the average precision of the VSM is consistently better (p-value $= 0.003465 < 0.01$). The semantic correlations between WSDL concepts found with the help of the WordNet-based semantic similarity measure in most cases are wrong or too weak. As a result many irrelevant files for the query have a high similarity score. At the same time, WordNet is restricted to a fixed set of six semantic relationships (including: hypernyms, synonyms, entailment, etc.) when the similarity measure that we need is the relation "can be converted" rather than the general lexical (synonymy) similarity. Aside from the efficacy of this particular application of *tf-idf*, the semantic matching approach has a significantly lower performance than the previous two approaches.

Due to the absence of a standard corpus in combination with the usage of different data models, WSDL-M2 cannot be compared quantitatively with the existing approaches for which some empirical validations are available, notably, [4][5][7]. A challenging anomaly occurs: groups with better precision in [4] correspond to the groups with worse average precision in our experiments. This may be caused by a different proportion (weight) of structure vs. semantic similarity impact on the final similarity score.

The above provides empirical evidence that one of the key factors that influence on the performance of the matching methods that we studied this far, is the quality of the vocabulary used in description of various services. These observations point towards the idea that a *customizable hybrid* matching is needed to increase confidence in matching results. For example, hybrid matching can help to reduce the processing time of semantic matching using structural matching to reduce the number of WSDL documents to be compared.

3 Customizable Hybrid Matching Approaches

In this section, we introduce a *customizable hybrid approach* towards matching of web services. The significance of customization lies in the fact that it caters for composition of a new hybrid approach from various existing techniques. Hence, this approach may in fact be perceived as a *meta-matching strategy*, which is very flexible as it is not restricted to any matching technique, but enables adhoc composition of several (pre-existing) matching approaches.

It is of critical importance to make matching methods *customizable* so that they may be tailored to meet organization-, domain- and/or context-specific constraints and needs, including, (non-)absence of domain-specific taxonomies, quality of the request/available web service descriptions, availability of textual descriptions, number of available services, usage of topic-specific terminology and the such. For example, hybrid matching seems a viable solution in case one has more confidence in structural than semantic matching due to the fact that WSDL labels carry poor semantics and service descriptions are lacking. The level of confidence may be expressed by parameterizing the hybrid algorithm so that more weight can be assigned to structural and less weight to semantic matching.

Let us illustrate our approach using a simple example. Suppose that two kinds of matching algorithms are available: Sy, which compares service descriptions using syntax driven techniques and Se, that relies on semantic matching. Let $sim^{Sy}(q, x)$ designate a similarity score between query q and web service (operation) x defined by the syntactic matching algorithm, and $sim^{Se}(q, x)$ be a similarity score between query q and web service (operation) x defined by the semantic matching algorithm. Given query q and threshold $\gamma > 0$, let $X^A(q, \gamma) = \{x|sim^A(q, x) > \gamma\}$ denote a set of services (operations) found by the algorithm A. Now, we propose three compositional operators to combine matching approaches:

- *Mixed* - a series of matching techniques are executed in parallel. In fact, these matching techniques may be homogenous (e.g., all of them of the same type) or heterogenous (various types of matching, e.g., a mixture of semantic and syntactic matching). This type of composition combines sets of services found by the different matching techniques in a single list. For example, syntactic and semantic matching algorithms are grouped in a single ranking list, i.e., $X^{H1a}(q, \gamma) = \{x|sim^{H1a}(q, x) > \gamma\}$, where $sim^{H1a}(q, x) = f\{sim^{Sy}(q, x), sim^{Se}(q, x)\}$ such that $f = \{max, min\}$. Alternatively, the results of the two approaches are fused based on weights allocated to each matching constituent, i.e., $X^{H1b}(q, \gamma) = \{x|sim^{H1b}(q, x) > \gamma\}$ such that $sim^{H1b}(q, x) = w_1 sim^{Sy}(q, x) + w_2 sim^{Se}(q, x) \,|\, w_1 + w_2 = 1, 0 \leq w_1, w_2 \leq 1$.
- *Cascade* - each matching technique that is part of the composite matching algorithm reduces the searching space of relevant service specifications. In other words, each subsequent matching algorithm refines the matching results of the previous one. For example, given a set of services found by the syntactic matching algorithm, choose those services whose similarity that is computed by the semantic matching algorithm is higher than a predefined threshold, i.e., $X^{H2a}(q, \gamma_1) = \{x|sim^{H2a}(q, x) > \gamma_1\}$, where $sim^{H2a}(q, x) = sim^{Sy}(q, x) \,|\, x \in X^{Se}(q, \gamma_2)$. Alternately, from the set of services found by the semantic matching algorithm, we select those services whose syntactic similarity is higher than a predefined threshold, i.e., $X^{H2b}(q, \gamma_2) = \{x|sim^{H2b}(q, x) > \gamma_2\}$, where $sim^{H2b}(q, x) = sim^{Se}(q, x) \,|\, x \in X^{Sy}(q, \gamma_1)$.
- *Switching* - this category of composition allows to switch between different matching algorithms. In principle, the decision to switch to another matching technique is driven by predefined criteria. For example, based on the number of the found services for a query after using a uniform algorithms we can alter between cascade and mixed combinations.

Parametrization entails a prime mechanism to allow for customization. Principally, the weights may be applied to hybrid matching techniques, being assembled using mixed, cascading and switching styles of composition. In fact, configuration of hybrid matching may not only be achieved at the level of matching techniques, but also at the level of the data models underlying them. There exist two fundamental choices to combine data-models underpinning hybrid matching:

- *Combination* - different data models are combined by a single algorithm.
- *Augmentation* - various data-models are used sequentially to enrich the information that serves as an input to the matching process. This style of data-model combination is most effective for cascading or switching style of composition. Typically, this strategy involves interaction with the service requester and/or information that is gathered from a service monitor.

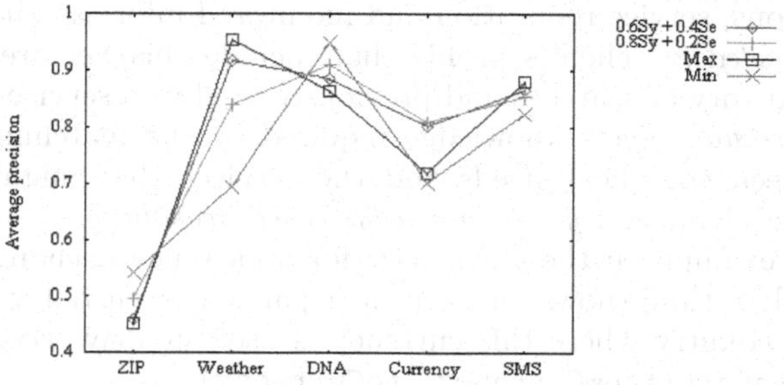

Fig. 1. Average precision of four hybrid algorithms on the first data set

We have experimented with a combination of the approaches presented in Section 2 to increase confidence in matching results and demonstrate the potential of parameterizing hybrid matching more in general. Some preliminary experiments using the same corpus as before, yielded the outcome drawn in Figure 1. Four mixed algorithms were tested: in the first two approaches, different weights for syntactic matching were assigned, 60% and 80% correspondingly. Other two methods experimented with ranking of the retrieved services using maximum and minimum similarity scores between those assigned by the semantic and syntactic uniform algorithms. First two hybrid approaches over-performed the purely semantic matching, while two others showed both increases and decreases in average precision for different categories of web services.

4 Conclusions and Outlook

Web service discovery plays a pivotal role in the SOC paradigm. In this paper we have introduced the WSDL-M2 matching algorithm that was implemented in a prototypical toolset. We have conducted a comparative analysis of WSDL-M2 with three lexical similarity measures: *tf-idf* and two WordNet-based metrics, using a uniform corpus.

To leverage WSDL matching, we have proposed a multi-dimensional composition model, having matching techniques and data models as its main constituents. The research findings that were presented in this paper are core results in nature. More research is needed in various directions. Though promising in nature, empirical evidence for hybrid matching is in need of experimentation in larger settings. We intend to conduct more experiments with hybrid matching approaches, equipping them with learning strategies.

Also, we believe that the augmentation strategy towards data model composition of matching approaches is a promising research direction. This composition model assumes that extra information may be gathered from monitoring tools. In particular, we plan to scrutinize application of the following types of knowledge:

- *Service knowledge* - knowledge about the existing services and their features, such as service documentation, interface description, ontology-based semantic extensions, service reputation and monitored information.
- *Client knowledge* - client's profile that includes his/her area of expertise, location, history of searches and previously used web services.
- *Functional knowledge* - knowledge required by the matching algorithm to map between the client needs and the services that might satisfy those needs. The chain *query* $\rightarrow$ *knowledge-based reasoning* $\rightarrow$ *response* is implied. For example, if the client asks for a currency exchange web service, and the algorithm knows that given a particular currency the client can define the country where this currency is used, it may recommend service `conversionRate(fromCurrency, toCurrency)`.

Additionally, in future work we are going to consolidate and extend our current empirical study with other IR models.

References

1. Kokash, N., van den Heuvel, W.J., D'Andrea, V.: Leveraging web services discovery with customizable hybrid matching. Technical Report DIT-06-042, DIT-University of Trento, Italy (2006)
2. Seco, N., Veale, T., Hayes, J.: An intrinsic information content metric for semantic similarity in wordnet. In: Proceedings of the ECAI, IOS Press (2004) 1089–1090
3. Kokash, N.: A comparison of web service interface similarity measures. In: Proceedings of the STAIRS, IOS Press (2006) 220–231
4. Wu, Z., Wu, Z.: Similarity-based web service matchmaking. In: Proc. of the IEEE Int. Conference on Services Computing. Volume 1. (2005) 287–294
5. Stroulia, E., Wang, Y.: Structural and semantic matching for accessing web service similarity. Int. Journal of Cooperative Information Systems **14**(4) (2005) 407–437
6. Buckley, C., Voorhees, E.M.: Evaluating evaluation measure stability. In: Proc. of SIGIR. (2000) 33–40
7. Dong, X., Halevy, A., Madhavan, J., Nemes, E., Zhang, J.: Similarity search for web services. In: Proceedings of the VLDB Conference. (2004) 372–383

Assembly of Business Systems Using Service Component Architecture

Anish Karmarkar[1] and Mike Edwards[2]

[1] Oracle, 1211 SW 5th Ave, Suite 900, Portland, OR, USA
[2] IBM Corporation, Hursley Park, Winchester, SO21 2JN, UK
anish.karmarkar@oracle.com,
mike_edwards@uk.ibm.com

Abstract. Service Component Architecture (SCA) is a set of specifications which provide a programming model for the creation and assembly of business systems using a service oriented architecture. SCA uses service components as the building blocks of business systems. SCA supports service components written using a very wide range of technologies, including programming languages such as Java, BPEL, C++ and also declarative languages such as XSLT.

SCA also provides a composition model for the assembly of distributed groups of service components into a business solution, with composites used to group collections of components and wires modeling the connections between components. SCA aims to remove "middleware" concerns from the programming code, by applying infrastructure concerns declaratively to compositions, including aspects such as Security and Transactions.

SCA is being evolved by an industry collaboration, with the aim of eventual submission to a standards body.

Keywords: SOA, SCA, service assembly, composition, integration, service component architecture.

1 Introduction

Service Component Architecture (SCA) is a set of specifications [1] which define a model for building applications and systems using a Service-Oriented Architecture.

In SCA, services are provided by *service components*, which may in turn use services provided by other components. Multiple service components can be configured and assembled into groupings called *composites,* to provide specific business capabilities, which model connections between components through *wires*.

SCA supports the creation and reuse of service components using a wide variety of implementation technologies. Components can be built with programming languages such as Java, C++, PHP, COBOL, and BPEL [2]. Components using frameworks such as Java Enterprise Edition [3] and the Spring Framework [4] are also supported. SCA enables the use of declarative languages such as XSLT [5] and SQL for components. Integration of both new and existing components is a key feature of SCA assemblies, including the ability to assemble existing components that are not SCA-aware.

SCA provides for the use of a wide range of specific protocols, transports and infrastructure capabilities when configuring and assembling components and services

A. Dan and W. Lamersdorf (Eds.): ICSOC 2006, LNCS 4294, pp. 529 – 539, 2006.

within composites. Examples include access methods or bindings such as SOAP-based [6] Web services, REST web services, JMS [7], EJB (RMI-IIOP) [8] and JCA [9]. SCA aims to make the protocol used for communication transparent to the implementation code within components.

The set of SCA specifications consists of the following:

1. SCA Assembly specification. The SCA Assembly Model defines the configuration of an SCA system in terms of service components which implement and/or use services and composites which describe the assembly of components into packages of function, including the connections between components, the configuration of component properties and how services and references are exposed for use.
2. SCA Policy Framework. The SCA Policy Framework provides a framework to support specification of constraints, capabilities, and Quality of Service (QoS) expectations from component design through to concrete deployment. The SCA Policy Framework allows the specification of interaction and implementation policies such as those related to security, reliability and transactions.
3. SCA Client and Implementation specifications. The SCA Client and Implementation specifications each specify how SCA components and service clients can be built using a particular language or framework, including language- or framework-specific APIs and annotations. Examples of current language specifications are-Java, C++ and BPEL. Examples of supported frameworks include Java Enterprise Edition (EJBs), the Spring Framework and JAX-WS [10].
4. SCA Binding specifications. The SCA Binding specifications each describe how services can be accessed and references can be satisfied using a particular access method, protocol or transport. Examples include SOAP-based Web services, JMS and EJB (RMI-IIOP).

The next section gives a simple example of how an application can be assembled and implemented using SCA. This paper then goes on to explain the assembly model for configuring and connecting components, services and references; a brief overview of SCA bindings; SCA Client and Implementation models; and the SCA Policy Framework. The paper ends with a description of ongoing and future work and describes the collaboration which is continuing to enhance the specifications.

2 SCA Assembly Example

"A picture is worth a thousand words" as the saying goes – and so it is with SCA. While the formal content of an SCA assembly is captured as a set of XML files and possibly also as annotations in code artifacts, SCA also has a graphical representation of components and composites, which is designed to provide an "at a glance" picture of the relationship of the services and components which make up an SCA business solution. This section starts the description of the SCA model by looking at an example diagram of a service assembled from a set of business components.

First, an explanation of some of the elements in the assembly diagrams. An SCA component appears like this:

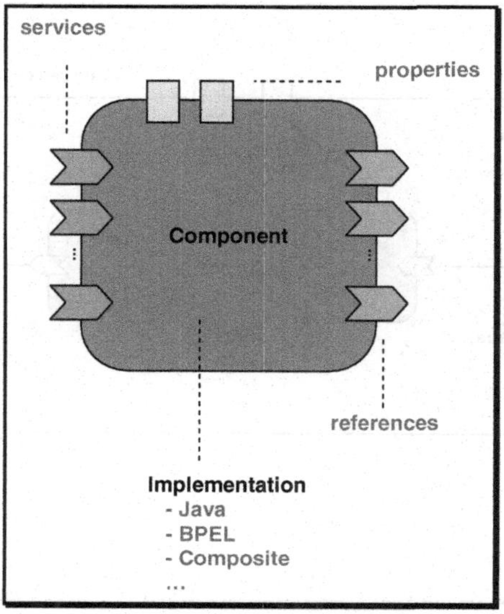

Fig. 1. Diagram of SCA component

The chevrons on the left (pointing in) each represent a service offered by the component. The chevrons on the right (pointing out) each represent a reference that this component makes to a service supplied elsewhere (ie the component uses those services to perform its business function). The small boxes at the top represent settable property values that the component has that may be configured. The “middle” of the component represents some implementation code – this may be any of the implementation types supported by SCA.

Groups of components can be assembled into composites. Composites can be used to create particular business capabilities from the assembled components, with wiring used to connect the components in the right way – each wire represents the connection of a reference of one component to the service of another – alternatively, services and references may be exposed out of the composite for use in “higher level” compositions. This is useful in structuring and organizing larger business solutions. A simple example of a composite is shown in figure 2:

Composites can provide services and make references to other services. They can also have settable properties. These all relate to some aspects of the components contained in the composite.

Having introduced the general form of SCA diagrams, next is a simple example of a business service built from a series of components to give a flavor of how SCA is used in practice. The example is an order processing service. The function provided by the service is to take an order for products. This involves information about the products being ordered, information about the customer placing the order such as payment information and dispatch address.

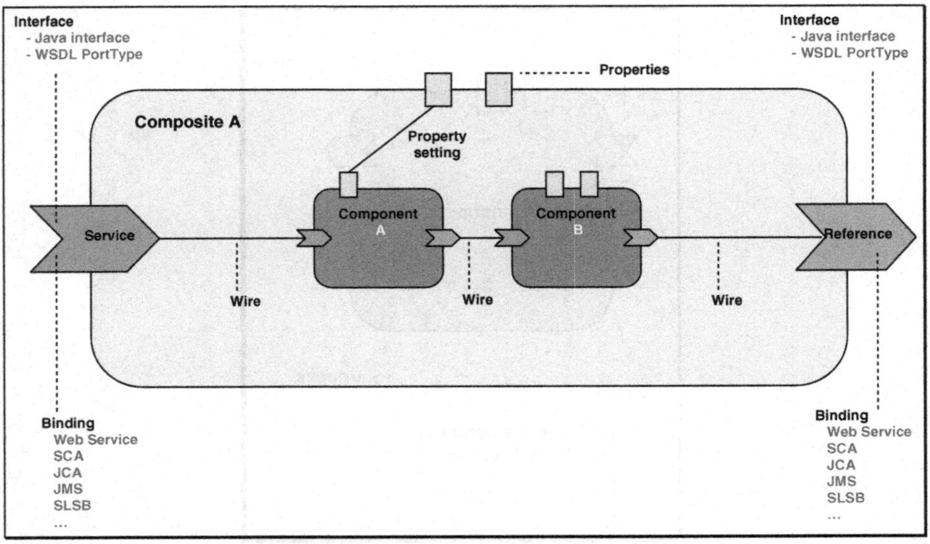

Fig. 2. SCA Diagram for a composite

In the Assembly diagram for the ordering system, the Order Processing Service is the large chevron on the left – this represents the external service endpoint, for example a Web service endpoint, which is available for calling by external customers of the business. The order processing service is implemented by the Order Processing Component. The Order Processing component in turn uses a series of other services to perform the order processing service – these are signified by the three references that the Order Processing Component has. These services are

- Payment Service – for taking the payment associated with the order
- Warehouse service - for checking availability of the ordered goods and for getting the goods dispatched to the customer
- Logging service – for recording details of the services invoked

The payment service is provided by the Accounts Composite, while the Warehouse service is provided by the Warehouse Composite. The Event logging service is relatively simple so that it is provided by a simple component – the EventLog component.

The Accounts Composite provides a payment service using a Payments component working in alliance with an Accounts Ledger component and with a reference to a Banking service which is an external service provided by the bank used by the business (eg this service may provide credit card services for collecting payments). In a real business, it is likely that the Accounts composite would be much larger, with a wide range of services available of which the payments service is just one.

The Warehouse composite provides the Warehouse service using a Warehouse broker component, which is able to talk with the Warehouse component representing the warehouse within the business, but also with external Warehouse services provided by other businesses, represented by the External Warehouse reference on the right. The broker can make queries to the warehouse services to find stock of

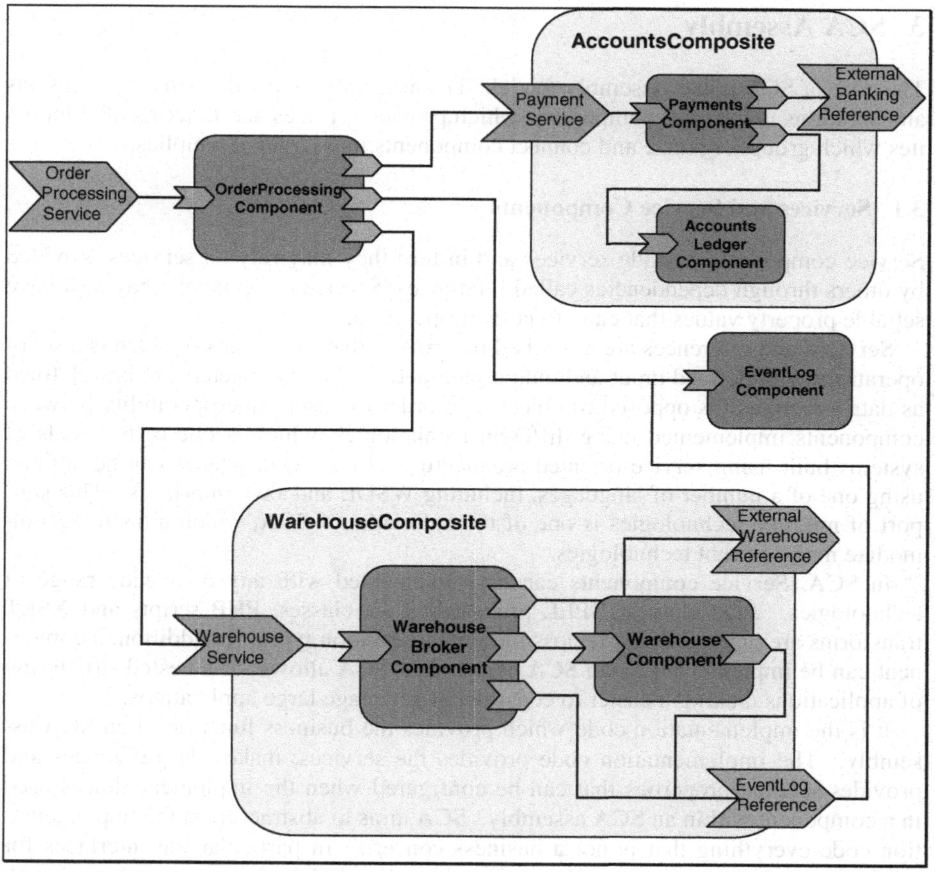

Fig. 3. SCA Assembly Diagram of an Order Processing System

products and also to request dispatch of those products. The components in the Warehouse composite make use of the Event Logging service, which is again connected to the EventLog component.

To summarize, the Assembly model shows which services are offered from our business for others to use. It also models those references that our business makes to services provided by others. The model also shows how particular services are implemented by specific components – and shows that these components may in turn have references that need to be satisfied by services provided by other components – or by services provided outside our business system by other businesses.

Note that an SCA assembly models the set of components that are used to make a particular business function and it models the way in which they are connected. It does ***not*** model the time sequences involved in executing particular service operations. Such business process sequencing can be provided by specialized component implementations such as BPEL processes.

3 SCA Assembly

The core of SCA is the Assembly model. The assembly model describes applications and solutions in terms of components which provide services and in terms of composites which group, organize and connect components into larger assemblies.

3.1 Services and Service Components

Service components provide services and in turn they may rely on services provided by others through dependencies called references. Service components may also have settable property values that can affect their operation.

Services and references are described in terms of their interfaces – which is a set of operations with defined input and output parameters. The parameters are best defined as data structures (as opposed to objects), in order to ensure interoperability between components implemented using different technologies, which is one of the goals of systems built using service-oriented architecture. In SCA, interfaces can be defined using one of a number of languages, including WSDL and Java interfaces. This support of multiple technologies is one of the hallmarks of SCA, which aims to accommodate many current technologies.

In SCA, Service components can be implemented with any of a wide range of technologies. Java classes, BPEL processes, C++ classes, PHP scripts and XSLT transforms are just a few of the possible implementation types. In addition, a component can be implemented by an SCA composite. SCA allows for a nested structuring of applications making it easier to construct and manage large applications.

It is the implementation code which provides the business function of an SCA assembly. The implementation code provides the services, makes the references and provides settable properties that can be configured when the implementation is used in a component within an SCA assembly. SCA aims to abstract from the implementation code everything that is not a business concern. In particular the interfaces for services and for references are business oriented and should not be concerned with technical details such as the communication mechanisms used to invoke services or of which component satisfies a particular reference. These details are left to the configuration applied in the composites which use the implementation code within service components.

3.2 Composites and the Assembly Process

The assembly of components into a larger solution is described in SCA in terms of composites. Composites contain service components which are configured through the setting of values for their properties and through the connecting of services to references through wires. The wires represent communication between components - they resolve which service gets called when a component invokes a reference and they represent messages flowing back and forth between a service consumer and the service.

A composite can control which services are made available for use outside the composite, through service elements on the composite itself. Similarly, the composite can define which references are satisfied outside the composite, through reference elements on the composite.

Part of the configuration which the composite can specify is which mechanism to use for a wire, for example Web services or JMS messaging. The composite can also provide configuration details about the endpoint at which a service is made available. The composite can also apply policies to components, services and references. Policies can be used to apply infrastructure capabilities such as message encryption and user authentication.

SCA has a formal language which is used to describe composites and their contents. This is an XML dialect. An example of a composite follows:

```
<composite name="AccountsComposite">

  <service name="PaymentService">
    <interface.wsdl interface=
      "http://example.org/Payment#wsdl.interface(pay)" />
    <binding.ws>
      <soapbinding version="1.1"/>
    </binding.ws>
    <reference>PaymentsComponent</reference>
  </service>

  <component name="PaymentsComponent">
    <implementation.java class="org.example.MyImpl"/>
    <property name="currency">USD</property>
    <reference name="Banking">
      ExternalBankingReference
    </reference>
    <reference name="Accounts">
      AccountsLedgerComponent
    </reference>
  </component>

  <component name="AccountsLedgerComponent">
    ...
  </component>

  <reference name="ExternalBankingReference">
    <interface.wsdl interface=
      "http://example.org/bank#wsdl.interface(credit)"/>
    <binding.ws endpoint=
      "http://example.org/bank#wsdl.endpoint(svc/port)"/>
  </reference>
</composite>
```

Example 1. Composite file for AccountsComposite

This example corresponds to the AccountsComposite of the Order Processing System shown in Figure 3. It shows the two components, PaymentsComponent and AccountsLedgerComponent, the service PaymentService and the reference ExternalBankingReference. The wires connecting these elements are defined by the <reference…/> subelements of the service and the components.

Composites can be used as implementations within components of other composites. This nesting of composites provides for structured assembly of larger systems avoiding the need to place a large number of components into a single composite and supporting the design concept of high-level, coarse grained services (such as our Order Processing example) being implemented by lower level more fine grained services that deal with specific aspects of the high level service.

4 Client and Implementation - Languages and Frameworks

SCA aims to support a wide range of technologies for the implementation of service components. This includes not only specific programming languages but also frameworks and other extensions built using those programming languages. SCA does this so that it can support the integration of existing applications and components into an assembly with minimal effort. SCA also aims to appeal to many different programming communities since building service components can be done in many languages.

There are SCA specifications which deal with implementing components in a range of programming languages and a set of frameworks, but this is not meant to imply that SCA is limited to supporting only those technologies. SCA is explicitly extensible to include other technologies and it is expected that additional languages and frameworks will be covered by new SCA specifications.

The current SCA specifications cover BPEL, C++ and Java as implementation languages. There are additional Java specifications that describe the use of components written using Enterprise Java Beans (versions 2.1 and 3.0); using the Spring Framework and using the JAX-WS specification.

The general principle of the SCA client and implementation specifications is to reduce the use of special "middleware" APIs to a minimum. The focus is to identify and call the service interface(s) offered by a component and to provide business interfaces for the service references that the component needs to invoke. For example, in Java, it is possible to provide all necessary property values and reference objects via injection.

5 Communication Mechanisms – SCA Bindings

SCA Bindings apply to SCA services and SCA references. Bindings allow services to be provided, and references to be satisfied, via particular access methods, protocols or transports. Bindings are typically added to an SCA assembly late in the development process – often during the deployment steps when the assembly is made available in the runtime system. This late attachment of Bindings gives the deployer great flexibility in adapting the business solution to new requirements, such as the need to change the supplier of an external service, who may use a different protocol from a previous supplier.

There are four standard SCA bindings currently being developed: Web service binding, Messaging/JMS binding, EIS/JCA binding, and EJB binding. Bindings can be added to SCA and it is likely that other bindings will be added in the near future.

Web service bindings expose an SCA service or allow access to an external reference using Web services technologies. Web services provide an interoperable way to access the service components. The Web service binding provides the glue between an SCA system and other services that are external to the SCA system but are used by composites within the SCA system.

Messaging and JMS bindings provide for communication between service consumers and service implementations using messaging protocols. JMS bindings apply to messaging made available through the Java JMS API. The messaging bindings provide more general access to messaging protocols such as WebSphere MQ.

The EIS/JCA Bindings allow access from the SCA runtime to the services provided by the Enterprise Information Systems residing outside the SCA system. The JCA Binding is the specialization of the EIS Binding, where the access to the external services is provided via Java JCA Resource Adapter.

The EJB binding allows references to access to services provided by stateless and stateful EJBs implemented using the Java EJB 2.1 or the EJB 3.0 technologies, via the RMI-IIOP protocol.

6 SCA Policy Framework

The SCA Policy Framework provides a solution to the problem of applying infrastructure capabilities to an SOA composite application. The kinds of capabilities include features such as security, reliability and transactions.

SCA aims to apply these infrastructure capabilities declaratively to components and the wires that connect them. This approach removes the need for the developer to code complex features into service components, allowing her to concentrate on business capabilities. The infrastructure capabilities are then applied by the SCA runtime in the ways defined in the assembly.

The policy framework defines two kinds of policy types –

1. Interaction policies, which apply to services, references and the wires between them. An example is the encryption of the messages sent between service consumer and the service implementation.
2. Implementation policies, which apply to components. An example is the security role which must apply when a component runs.

Detailed *policies*, which define fine-grained features of the way in which infrastructure capabilities are applied at runtime, are held in *policy sets*. An example of a detailed policy is the specific encryption method to use for confidentiality purposes when transmitting messages when a service is invoked. Policy sets are typically closely related to specific bindings used for a service and will be applied to an assembly at the time that the binding is chosen, possibly at deployment time.

SCA also provides a mechanism that the component developer can use to indicate the general capabilities required by a service or a component, in the case where the developer does not know in advance which bindings will be used with the component, or where multiple bindings might be used. These are high-level *intents*, which can be used to select an appropriate policy set at the later time when bindings and policy sets are applied to an assembly containing the component.

An example of a high level intent is 'confidentiality', which is a security intent applying to a service or a reference requesting that messages should be sent with a level of encryption to ensure that no one but the intended recipient can read the message. The presence of this intent means that at runtime a policy set must be chosen for the service which includes an appropriate level of message encryption. For some intents, it may not be possible to find a policy set for every binding that will provide the capability requested by the intent – this is an indication to the deployer that they must choose a different binding in order to meet the needs expressed by the intent.

6.1 Infrastructure Capabilities – Security, Transactions, Reliability

The SCA policy framework defines general mechanisms for attaching intents and policies to components, services and references. In principle, the policy framework can accommodate a very wide range of policy statements. In practice, SCA defines policies relating to infrastructure capabilities in the areas of Security, Transactions and Reliability.

Reliability refers to the reliable delivery of messages with various delivery assurances such as "once and only once". This is not true for all protocols. SCA provides the means for a service to indicate that it requires reliable delivery of its messages.

"Security" is a catch-all term that covers a range of capabilities. Examples include authentication and authorization of users and encryption of messages. SCA supports these capabilities.

Transactions refers to transactional behavior of components and in particular the ability to commit or to roll back a series of updates. SCA supports transactional capabilities.

7 Ongoing and Future Work

The SCA specification set is being developed under the aegis of Open Service Oriented Architecture (OSOA) collaboration [11]. The OSOA collaboration is a group of vendors who have come together to develop specifications for Service Oriented Architecture. The first version of the specification set is expected to contain:

1. SCA Assembly Model
2. SCA Policy Framework
3. SCA Client and Implementation Model for Spring Framework
4. SCA Client and Implementation Model for EJB
5. SCA Client and Implementation Model for JAX-WS
6. SCA Client and Implementation Model for BPEL
7. SCA Client and Implementation Model for Java
8. SCA Client and Implementation Model for C++
9. SCA Web Service Binding
10. SCA EJB Binding
11. SCA Messaging/JMS Binding
12. SCA EIS/JCA Binding

These specifications are expected to be completed by the end of this year and are expected to be submitted to a standards development organization for standardization in an open forum.

A subsequent version of the SCA specification set is expected to contain:

1. SCA Eventing Model
2. SCA Client and Implementation Model for PHP
3. SCA Client and Implementation Model for COBOL

Extensibility is built into the SCA model as a design principle. Therefore, it is expected that SCA will be extended by vendors and users to accommodate various implementation- and binding-specific technologies and needs.

There are several ongoing implementations of SCA by various vendors participating in the OSOA collaboration. In addition, there are two open source projects: Apache Tuscany [12] and Eclipse SOA Tools Platform [13] that implement and support the SCA specifications.

References

[1] Service Component Architecture (SCA) Specifications http://www.osoa.org/display/Main/Service+Component+Architecture+Specifications
[2] "Web Services Business Process Execution Language Version 2.0," A. Alves et al, 23rd August 2006, OASIS Public Review Draft, http://docs.oasis-open.org/wsbpel/2.0/wsbpel-specification-draft.pdf
[3] "Java™ Platform, Enterprise Edition (Java EE) Specification, v5," Bill Shannon, 28th April 2006, Final Release, http://jcp.org/aboutJava/communityprocess/final/jsr244/index.html
[4] Spring Framework, http://www.springframework.org
[5] "XSL Transformations (XSLT) Version 1.0," James Clark, 16th November, 1999, W3C Recommendation, http://www.w3.org/TR/1999/REC-xslt-19991116
[6] "SOAP Version 1.2 Part 1: Messaging Framework," M. Gudgin et al, 24th June 2003, W3C Recommendation, http://www.w3.org/TR/2003/REC-soap12-part1-20030624/
[7] "Java Message Service version 1.1," M. Hapner et al, 12th April, 2002, http://java.sun.com/products/jms/docs.html
[8] "JSR 220: Enterprise JavaBeansTM,Version 3.0," L. DeMichiel et al, 2nd May, 2006, Final Release, http://jcp.org/aboutJava/communityprocess/final/jsr220/index.html
[9] "J2EE™ Connector Architecture Specification, Version 1.5," November, 2003, Final Release, http://jcp.org/aboutJava/communityprocess/final/jsr112/index.html
[10] "The Java API for XML-Based Web Services (JAX-WS) 2.0," R. Chinnici et al, April 19, 2006, Final Release, http://jcp.org/aboutJava/communityprocess/final/jsr224/index.html
[11] Open Service Oriented Architecture (OSOA) Collaboration http://www.osoa.org/display/Main/Home
[12] Tuscany Apache Incubator project, http://incubator.apache.org/tuscany/
[13] Eclipse SOA Tools Platform Project http://www.eclipse.org/stp/

The End of Business as Usual: Service-Oriented Business Transformation

Andy Mulholland

Capgemini, 76 Wardour Street, London W1F 0UU, UK
andy.mulholland@capgemini.com

Abstract. Service-Oriented Architecture (SOA) is a new approach for organizing and isolating application functionality, built on a flexible and reusable foundation of services. It has the capacity to expand the reach of the enterprise by enabling services to define and transform relationships and, in so doing, expand the scope of what Information Technology can make possible. Above all, service orientation focuses on the business imperative and offers opportunities to approach business issues in a different way. In short, SOA means the end of business as usual. This paper briefly outlines some of the key challenges businesses need to overcome in order to become Service-Oriented Enterprises. For more in depth discussion on the topic, read the book *Mashup Corporations: The End of Business as Usual.*

Keywords: Service-Oriented Architecture, Information and Communications Technology, shadow IT, mashups, composite applications, web services, governance, compliance.

1 Introduction

Services-Oriented Architecture (SOA) is a new structure and a set of mechanisms for organizing and isolating application functionality, built on a flexible and reusable foundation of services. But services are not drivers of business change in and of themselves. The transformations promised by SOA will never take place unless a new culture and innovative business models take shape around it. SOA will gradually expand the scope of what Information Technology (IT) can make possible, but only if leaders possess the imagination to make use of it.

Unlike most discussions of SOA that focus on its mechanisms—services, modeling, patterns, messaging, events—we will explore the shape and value of a service-enabled business and how you can lead your company through the necessary cultural transformation. You will hear quite a bit about mashups because they demonstrate the power of utilizing SOA capabilities. But mashups are the thin end of a larger wedge of change that SOA will bring about, while SOA represents a new era in computing evolution.

In simplest terms, SOA expands the reach of the enterprise by allowing services to define and transform relationships. We will examine the five kinds of relationships upon which SOA will make the most impact:

A. Dan and W. Lamersdorf (Eds.): ICSOC 2006, LNCS 4294, pp. 540 – 544, 2006.

- The relationships between a company and customer-focused innovators inside and outside the company.
  How can you harness the ideas and energy of outsiders eager to help?
- The relationships between a company and its customers.
  How can you bring your customers closer to your core business processes?
- The relationships between a company and its suppliers.
  How can you strengthen the connection between yourself and your suppliers? How can you create a win-win relationship instead of an adversarial one?
- The relationships between the IT department and the larger company.
  How can IT support employee initiatives instead of stifling them? How can innovation break new ground while protecting critical data?
- The relationships amongst the IT professionals within a company.
  How can you best structure your IT resources to reflect the needs and new capabilities of SOA? How can SOA help IT balance demands (e.g. security and ease-of-use)?

The culture that meshes best with SOA is one of empowerment and flexibility. For SOA to achieve its potential, many assumptions that have ruled business and IT must be abandoned. New rules will govern the creation of an SOA business culture, a culture that is focused on putting as much power as possible in the hands of those closest to the customer in order to create and discover new markets and to unlock value that had never previously been accessible.

It's a culture of change and experimentation, and for IT to keep up, some reorganization will be necessary. Before that happens, however, forces that are currently driving deep structural changes within companies must be acknowledged and harnessed. A partial list of those challenges follows.

2 ICT Versus IT

A new term: Information and Communications Technology (ICT) is rapidly being adopted to refer to a larger world of possibilities and techniques that have developed since the term Information Technology (IT) was born. Here and there, where we are speaking about the future and technology, we use ICT. Primarily, we will stick with the term IT in this book referring to the IT Department itself or because for the most part we are referring to the commonly held understanding of IT, which is the application of technology in an enterprise or large organization.

3 "Shadow IT" and the IT Generation Gap

In the history of enterprise computing, up until this moment, IT was mostly a world unto itself, whether centralized or decentralized. The willful isolation of IT into a narrow focus on recording transactions shaped several generations' attitudes toward the role of IT within the larger context of the organization. For older executives (defined for our purposes as 45 years old and older), the traditional mode of dealing with IT involved creating requirements and then asking IT to do what needed to be done.

But in the last decade, since the advent of the Internet era, a generational split has occurred. Employees under the age of 35 (and including many who are older) entered the workplace and took for granted plentiful bandwidth, desktop productivity tools, open source software, and a wealth of networks, including social networking, peer-to-peer technologies, and other beneficiaries of Metcalfe's Law. The members of this generation seized the tools of IT production for themselves as they configured their email, cell phones, instant messaging, wikis, and blogs to help them transact business. This do-it-yourself capability has become known as Shadow IT. To maximize the impact and breadth of use of services, Shadow IT must be encouraged, supported, and officially recognized as a critical component of day-to-day operations.

For SOA to work, Shadow IT must be acknowledged and supported.

4 The Architectural Shift Toward Mashups and Composites

It's no longer enough to simply be on the Web. The browser window is increasingly competitive real estate, and relying on advertising-infused HTML invites uncontrollable interruptions. Head to a travel web site, for example, and the first thing you're likely to notice are popup ads for the site's competitors. Such is the dark side of the Web's ongoing shift to ad-supported models.

But the pioneering efforts of independent developers in tandem with services provided by companies like Google, Amazon.com, and many others, have enabled the assembly of simple composite applications commonly called "mashups" to appear on the scene.

Mashups may run inside browsers or in new, richer environments called composite applications. They aren't based exclusively on HTML delivered by a server. Instead, mashups use services typically delivered in XML from many different sites to knit together a useful experience for the customer. Perhaps the best-known mashups marry the basic functionality of Google or Yahoo!® Maps with specialized data sets to create customized, searchable maps.

This mashup environment is self-contained and controlled. And its ease of use heralds the next generation of flexibly recombined services.

For SOA to work, services to support mashup/composite applications must be made available.

5 User-Driven Innovation

Mashups aren't invented during the IT department's annual offsite meetings, except for the rare exception in which an IT organization is promoting the reuse of commonly used corporate services. Instead, they spring from the minds of entrepreneurial virtuosos who are continually sifting through the services they discover on the Internet and imagining the emergent possibilities.

Companies that "get" SOA do everything in their power to turn their value-creating processes into services and then place them in the hands of their most innovative thinkers whose efforts become the company's bridge to new customers. To the outside world, the company becomes increasingly defined by the services it offers others to use as a springboard for innovation and creating new kinds of business relationships.

For SOA to work, companies must remove barriers to innovation and put tools in the hands of innovators.

6 Transformed Business Models

Providing services to innovators, inside the company and out, profoundly changes the way it appears to customers, partners and competitors. Some of these new business processes create markets where none existed before; others change the role the company plays within the value chain. Most of these processes feel completely unnatural at fi rst and arrive with a complete checklist of objections and excuses explaining why they will never work.

Lightweight, reusable services offer the perfect building blocks for inexpensive experiments that may fail, as expected, or may create a massive opportunity.

For SOA to work, new and imperfect business models must be implemented so they can be debugged and perfected.

7 Incremental, Agile Development

Applications based on services frequently use better, more user friendly development tools that expand the pool of potential developers far beyond the boundaries of the IT department. Ideas for new solutions will arrive in the form of half-baked applications created by lay users who start down a path toward a solution, but lack the expertise to finish it. To exploit the full potential of SOA, the development lifecycle must accept partial solutions from wherever they originate and nudge them toward completion so that their potential can be fully measured. Agile development methods are suspicious of requirements gathered in a vacuum and promote an incremental approach in which applications are built, deployed, and then improved in a succession of rapid steps. The best solutions will ultimately emerge from these small steps forward, with the final step representing the sum total of accumulated experience.

For SOA to work, development methods must allow rapid cycles based on learning from experience.

8 Governance, Security, and Operational Stability

Exposing services to the outside world inevitably places power in the hands of outsiders who are directed by their own self-interest.

What are those outsiders allowed to do? How much power do they need to innovate? How can abuse be discouraged? And how can the services be created to embed rules for governance, security, and operational stability? Policies governing all of these issues and more must be created in parallel with technical efforts to build an SOA, and in many cases, will be built into the services themselves.

For SOA to work, governance, security, and operational stability must be designed into services.

9 Conclusion

SOA means the end of business as usual. However, it can only be achieved if leaders possess the knowledge, the imagination and the roadmap to make optimal use of it. Services are not drivers of business change. The transformations promised by service orientation will not happen without the adoption of a new culture and innovative business models.

A Service Oriented Reflective Wireless Middleware

Bora Yurday[1] and Halûk Gümüşkaya[2]

[1] TUBITAK-MAM, ETCBASE Yazılım
Gebze, Turkey
bora.yurday@etcbase.com
[2] Department of Computer Engineering, Fatih University
34500 Istanbul, Turkey
haluk@fatih.edu.tr

Abstract. The role of middleware has become increasingly important in mobile computing, where the integration of different applications and services from different wired and wireless businesses and service providers exist. The requirements and functionalities of the wireless middleware can be achieved by Service Oriented Computing which can be an ideal paradigm for mobile services. Reflective middleware responses are optimized to changing environments and requirements. In this paper a Service Oriented Reflective Wireless Middleware (SORWiM) is proposed. It provides basic (Event, Messaging, Location, and Redirection) and composite services for efficient and reliable information discovery and dissemination in ad hoc mobile environments. One of the primary goals of this research is to investigate how the construction of mobile services can benefit from the Service-Oriented paradigm.

1 Introduction

Middleware is distributed software that sits above the operating system and below the application layer and abstracts the heterogeneity of the underlying environment [1]. It provides integration and interoperability of applications and services running on heterogeneous computing and communications devices, and simplifies distributed programming. Middleware can be decomposed into multiple layers such as host infrastructure middleware (Java Virtual Machine (JVM)), distribution middleware (Java RMI, CORBA, Simple Object Access Protocol (SOAP)), common middleware services (J2EE, .NET), and domain-specific middleware services (developed for particular domains, such as telecom, or e-commerce) [2]. Conventional middleware technologies, such as CORBA and RMI have been designed and used successfully with fixed networks. However, there are significant challenges to design and optimize middleware for mobile computing. Since conventional middleware platforms are not appropriate for mobile computing, because, first of all, they are too big and inflexible for mobile devices. Mobility, quality of service, security, management of services, service discovery, ad hoc networking and dynamic configuration are main middleware issues for mobile computing. It is therefore essential to devise new middleware solutions and capabilities to fulfill the requirements of emerging mobile technologies.

A. Dan and W. Lamersdorf (Eds.): ICSOC 2006, LNCS 4294, pp. 545 – 556, 2006.

Service-Oriented Computing (SOC) [3] is a distributed computing paradigm based on the Service-Oriented Architecture (SOA) [4], which is an architectural style for building software applications that use services. SOC and SOA are not completely new concepts; other distributed computing technologies like CORBA and RMI have been based around similar concepts. SOA and SOC are merely extensions of the existing concepts and new technologies, like XML, and Web Services, are being used to realize platform independent distributed systems.

The SOA appears to be an ideal paradigm for mobile services. However, it is currently focused only on enterprise and business services. In addition, most of SOA research has been focused on architectures and implementations for wired networks. There are many challenges that need to be addressed by wireless middleware based on SOA. Wireless middleware will play an essential role in managing and provisioning service-oriented applications. In this paper a Service Oriented Reflective Wireless Middleware (SORWiM) is proposed. It provides a set of services for efficient and reliable information discovery and dissemination in ad hoc mobile environments. One of the primary goals of this research is to investigate how the construction of mobile services can benefit from the Service-Oriented paradigm.

This paper is structured as follows. In section 2, the properties affecting the design of wireless middleware and why conventional middleware platforms are not appropriate for mobile computing are presented. In section 3, the service oriented approach to wireless middleware and SORWiM are introduced. In section 4, the detailed architecture and services are given. In section 5, service orchestration and mobile application scenarios are introduced. In section 6, the performance evaluation of SORWiM is presented, and finally in section 7, our future work is given.

2 Wireless Middleware for Mobile Computing

Limited resources, heterogeneity, and a high degree of dynamism are the most common properties that usually exist in mobile devices such as pocket PCs, PDAs, sensors, phones, and appliances. Although limited resource availability varies from device to device; mobile devices generally don't have powerful CPUs, large amount of memory and high-speed I/O and networking compared to desktop PCs. Different hardware and software platforms, operating systems imply changes in some parameters such as byte ordering, byte length of standard types, and communication protocols. The degree of dynamism present in ubiquitous computing does not exist in traditional servers and workstations. A PDA, for example, interacts with many devices and services in different locations, which implies many changing parameters such as the type of communication network, protocols, and security policies. Therefore, because we can't predict all possible combinations, the software running on a PDA device must be able to adapt to different scenarios to cope with such dynamism.

All these properties affect the design of the wireless middleware infrastructure required for mobile computing. Conventional middleware platforms are not appropriate, because, first of all, they are too big and inflexible for mobile devices [5], [6]. A wireless middleware should be lightweight as it must run on hand-held, resource-scarce devices. Conventional middleware platforms expect static connectivity, reliable channels, and high bandwidth that are limited in resource-varying wireless networks.

Wireless middleware should support an asynchronous form of communication, as mobile devices connect to the network opportunistically and for short periods of time. It should be built with the principle of awareness in mind, to allow its applications to adapt its own and the middleware behavior to changes in the context of execution, so as to achieve the best quality of service and optimal use of resources. Hiding network topologies and other deployment details from distributed applications becomes both harder and undesirable since applications and middleware should adapt according to changes in location, connectivity, bandwidth, and battery power.

New wireless network middleware is required to increase performance of applications running across potentially mixed wireless networks (from GPRS to WLANs), supporting multiple wireless devices, providing continuous wireless access to content and applications, as well as to overcome periods of disconnection and time-varying bandwidth delivery. Wireless middleware could also ensure end-to-end security and dependability from handheld devices to application servers.

We cannot customize existing middleware platforms manually for every particular device. It is not flexible or suitable for coping with dynamic changes in the execution environment. Reflective middleware presents a comprehensive solution to deal with ubiquitous computing [7]. Reflective middleware system responses are optimized to changing environments or requirements, including mobile interconnections, power levels, CPU/network bandwidth, latency/jitter, and dependability needs. Reflection is the ability of a program to observe and possibly modify its structure and behavior. In the SORWiM architecture, reflection was used in the service level. A fully reflective middleware was not implemented initially; instead we worked on reflective services that take decisions according to context information.

Principles and guidelines for designing middleware for mobile computing have been published in literature [5], [6], [7], [8], and some wireless middleware projects have been developed for some specific areas, such as sensor networks [9], [10]. A few researchers have also published service oriented computing imperatives for wireless environments [11], [12]. To the best of our knowledge, there are no or a few real implemented wireless middleware platforms based on SOA.

3 A Service Oriented Approach to Wireless Middleware

A SOA-based service is self-contained, i.e., the service maintains its own state [4]. A service consists of an interface describing operations accessible by message exchange. Services are autonomous, platform-independent and can be described, published, dynamically located, invoked and (re-)combined and programmed using standard protocols. SOA promotes loose coupling between software components.

The building block of SOA is the SOAP [13]. SOAP is an XML-based messaging protocol defining standard mechanism for remote procedure calls. The Web Service Description Language (WSDL) [14] defines the interface and details service interactions. The Universal Description Discovery and Integration (UDDI) protocol supports publication and discovery facilities [15]. Finally, the Business Process Execution Language for Web Services (BPEL4WS) [16] is exploited to produce a service by composing other services.

The high level architecture of SORWiM using the reference model of the web services standards stack is shown in Fig 1. There are four services, Event (Notification), Messaging, Location, and Redirection. These are some of the first important and basic services in a typical wireless environment. We have also developed some example composite services using these basic services in our implementation.

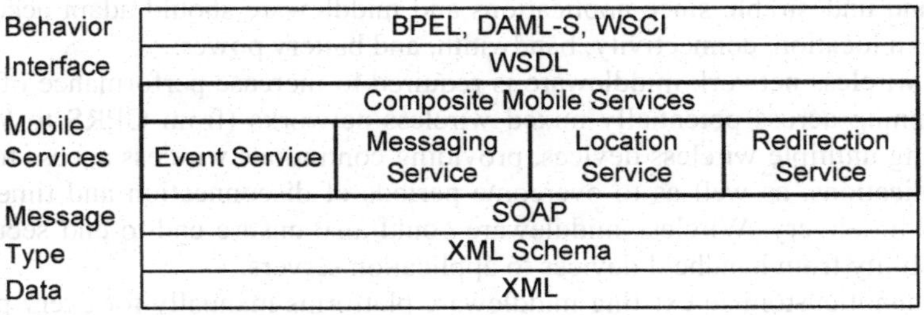

Fig. 1. The high level architecture of SORWiM based on the Web Services Standards Stack

4 The Architecture of SORWiM and Its Services

The architecture of SORWiM is shown in Fig 2. Each service is depicted by a WSDL document, which describes service accessing rules. Web services are registered to the central UDDI database. The client searches the UDDI to find out the service it needs, fetches the WSDL file, and generates the stub with the WSDL to stub code generator provided by the web service toolkit, and starts calling remote methods.

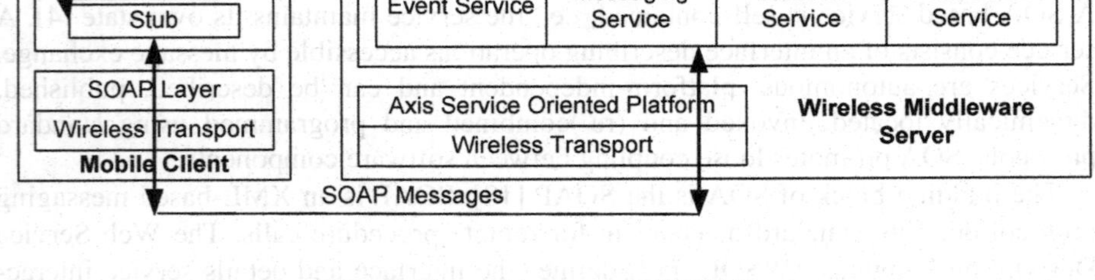

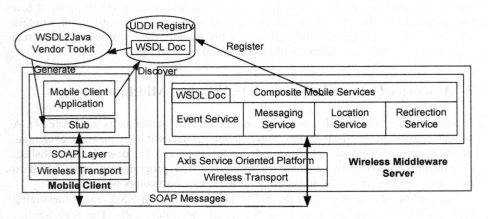

Fig. 2. The architecture of SORWiM

The package diagrams of SORWiM basic services are shown in Fig 3. A package describes a stateless service which can communicate with other services through service interfaces. That is there is no dependency between services which is one of the primary goals of SOA. By defining relations between services we create composite services that form new application scenarios in our wireless framework. We extensively used the design patterns [17] in the implementation of the SORWiM architecture. Design patterns codify design expertise, thus providing time-proven solutions to commonly occurring software problems in certain contexts [17], [18].

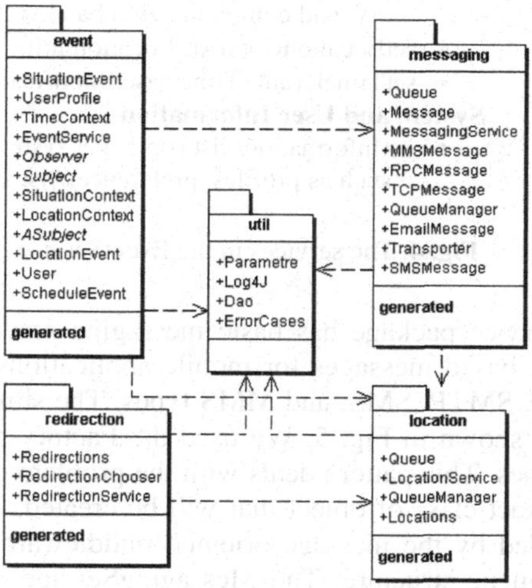

Fig. 3. The UML package diagrams of SORWiM basic mobile services

All basic services use the util package which organizes logging, error cases, database operations, initializing parameters. Since we need single instances of the classes in this package and a global point of access to them, the Singleton pattern [17] is used in the implementation.

A mobile client application, TestPad, which aims to test the basic services, was written using the PocketBuilder, the Sybase's the rapid application development tool for building mobile and wireless applications running on Microsoft Pocket PC devices [19]. In the middleware implementation we used the Apache Axis which is a proven service oriented platform to develop Java web services [20]. In the following, first, the basic services are explained. Then how composite services are orchestrated using these basic services are presented.

The EventService is one of the first basic services of SORWiM. It provides an interface schema for four main functions, authentication, profiles and preferences, notification (alert), and system and user information as shown in Fig. 4. A behavioral pattern, the Observer pattern [17], is used in the implementation of the notification engine. This pattern defines a one-to-many dependency between a subject object and any number of observer objects so that when the subject object changes state, all its observer objects are notified and updated automatically.

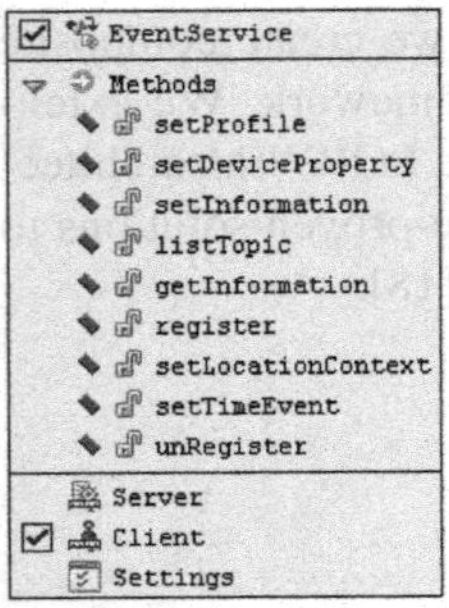

Mobile services implemented in the Axis 1.2

Authentication
- register: Mobile user logs in the system
- unRegister: Log off the system

Profiles and Preferences
- setProfile: Detailed user profile and preferences

Notification
- setDeviceProperty: Device info such as battery power, memory, and communication bandwidth
- setLocationContext: Location info
- setTimeEvent: Time based-notification event

System and User Information
- getInformation/ listTopic: get system and user information such as profiles, preferences/list a topic

Fig. 4. The services in the EventService

The MessagingService package has basic messaging services to create, send, receive and read XML based messages for mobile applications. This service can send messages using RPC, SMTP, SMS, and MMS types. The simplified class diagram of MessagingService is shown in Fig. 5. We used the Factory pattern [17] for creating different message types. This pattern deals with the problem of creating objects without specifying the exact class of object that will be created. The asynchronous communication is provided by the message oriented middleware approach of SORWiM using a messaging queue structure. The MessagingService class provides the functionality of the Facade pattern [17] for the messaging service package. It decouples the other classes of the MessagingService package from its clients and other subsystems, thereby promoting service independence and portability.

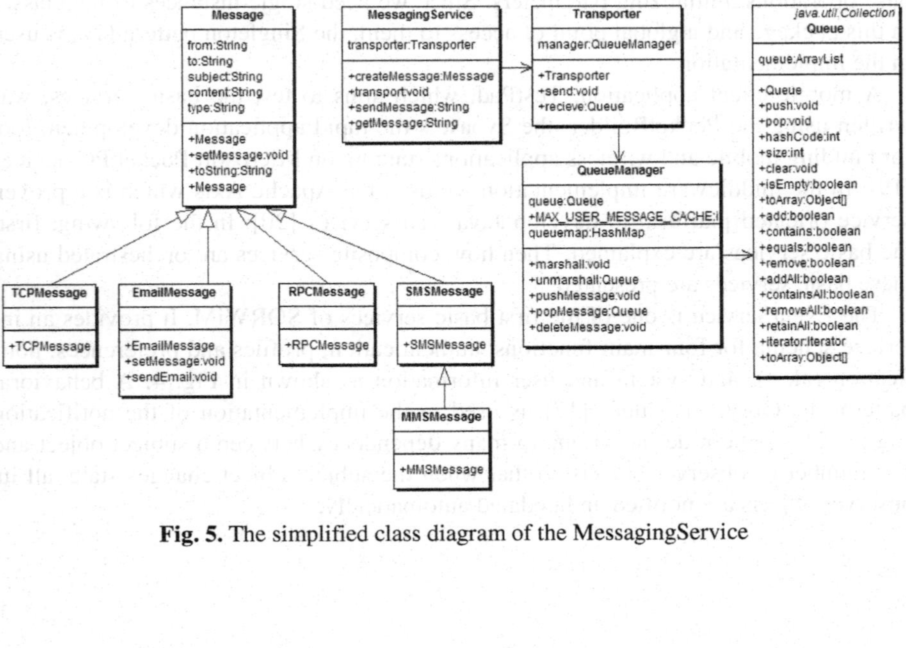

Fig. 5. The simplified class diagram of the MessagingService

The Location Service handles the problem of searching and updating locations of mobile nodes in a wireless network. This service is also used by other services for giving decisions and providing active context-awareness that autonomously changes the application behavior according to the sensed location information.

We designed and implemented an indoor positioning system, WiPoD (Wireless Position Detector), which locates and tracks a user having an IEEE 802.11 supported device across the coverage area of a WLAN [21]. With high probability, WiPoD can estimate a user's location to within a few meters of his/her actual location. The location information for the SORWiM indoor applications will be provided by WiPoD.

The services such as redirectionRequest and replicationRequest in the Redirection package are responsible for client redirection to different servers and server reference translation. There are two main problems dealt with in redirection: Address migration and data replication, both provide migration transparency. Migration transparency allows components to change their location, which is not seen by a client requesting these components. Server translation and redirection can be done transparently or non transparently. The Redirection Service needs to be aware of the state of connectivity and the location of the client at any point in time. The steps of redirection:

- Request- sent from a client to a server to signal that the client wishes to carry out a request on the server
- Response-sent from the server to a client in response to a request
- Redirection – Sent from a server to a client signaling that the client should send its request to another server whose reference will be embedded in redirection response.

In an asynchronous replication one server acts as the master, while one or more other servers act as slaves. The master server writes updates to log files, and maintains an index of the files to keep track of log rotation. These logs serve as records of updates to be sent to any slave servers. The slave receives any updates that have taken place, and then blocks and waits for the master to notify it of new updates. These replication functions are provided by the replication servers of different vendors.

5 Service Orchestration and Mobile Application Scenarios

Composite services provide standardized interfaces for state transfer between basic services. The first step in SORWiM Services was to create the stateless basic services as Event, Messaging, Location and Redirection, and their descriptions (WSDL) as explained above. The second step was to aggregate the functionality provided by each independent service and create the composite services which receive client requests, make the required data transformations and invoke the component web services.

The basic services and their usage in service composition are shown in Fig 6 using two example composite services, Location Based Redirection Composite Service (LBRCS) and Context Aware Notification Delivery Composite Service (CANDCS). To evaluate the development of mobile applications on SORWiM, TestPad was implemented to emulate several wireless application scenarios. The TestPad screen for basic services is shown in Fig 7(a).

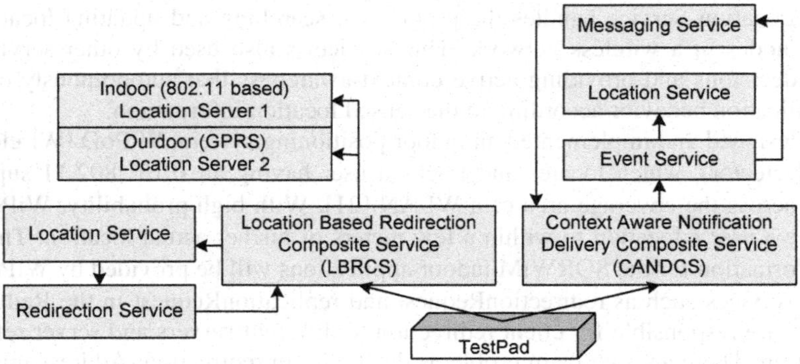

Fig. 6. Two example composite mobile services in service orchestration

LBRCS maintains transparent redirection according to changes in the mobile location using basic Location and Redirection services. This service first obtains the device location (Location Service) and redirects to the available addresses (Redirection Service). We will give a scenario to explain how LBRCS can be used in a mobile application. In this scenario, there are three locations. These are the user's home and user's office which both are covered by a Wireless LAN, and the outdoor location between the home and office where GPRS connection is available. In all these three locations the user can connect to these networks using Pocket PCs or laptops. When the user has left his/her office and moved out from the office WLAN coverage area, his mobile device keeps connected to SORWiM through the GPRS connection. The WLAN-to-GPRS handover is generally initiated by the mobile user. In our approach, the mobile user sets the location information based on the local measurement of WLAN signal quality. When LBRCS decides that a WLAN-to-GPRS handover is required, it sends a handover-required message and an available endpoint (IP, port number, and service name) of the server to the mobile device. The mobile user then performs a handover and switches from the WLAN connection to the GPRS connection. When the user arrives in home, and discovers a wireless access point, the mobile device sends the location information to LBRCS through the GPRS connection. SORWiM then sends the response of the endpoint of the server that is accessible in the office. The user performs a handover again and switches from GPRS to the WLAN connection again. The TestPad screen for this last scenario is shown in Fig 7(b). The user sets the new location as Home and gets a response message from SORWiM. The response is a new connection end point for the WLAN network. The old and new end points are also shown in the lower part of the screen in Fig 7(b).

CANDCS which composes the services of Messaging, Event and Location, notifies all registered users who are interested in a specific event. Imagine the following scenario using this composite service: Haluk is waiting for Bora's arrival and types in his Pocket PC as "notify me as soon as Bora appears on the campus". This message is sent to SORWiM using the Pocket PC's window shown in the upper part of the screen in Fig 7(c). When Bora arrives and enters the campus, immediately a notification is sent to Haluk's Pocket PC as a message or SMS as shown in the lower part of the screen in Fig 7(c).

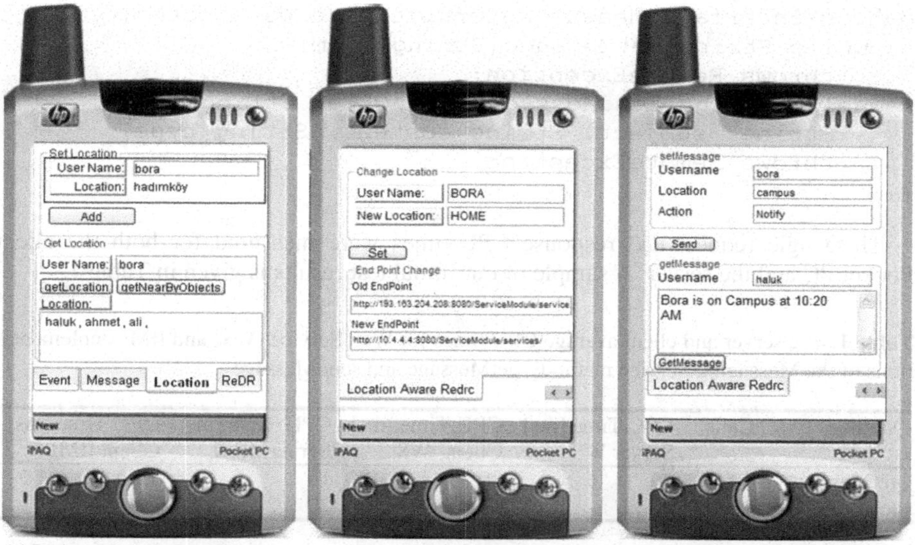

(a) Basic services: Event, Message, Location and Redirection (ReDR)

(b) Location Based Redirection Composite Service (LBRCS)

(c) Context Aware Notification Delivery Composite Service (CANDCS)

Fig. 7. Basic services and composite services TestPad screens

CANDCS makes a decision using three basic services for requests similar to "I want to be registered for notifications about whether person X is in Y location". The Event Service provides an interface for registering the notifications. The Location Service gives location information and can query the nearby objects as shown in Fig 7(a). The Messaging Service that has the ability of sending different types of messages is responsible for delivering the notification messages.

6 Performance Evaluation of SORWiM

There are a number of research studies for the performance evaluations of web services and SOAP compared to middleware technologies, including Java RMI, CORBA. In these studies, a comparison is made based on the performance of a web service implementation that calls a simple method and an RMI, CORBA, or other implementation that calls the same method [22], [23], [24], [25], [26], [27].

We performed similar benchmarking tests to measure the performance of SORWiM to see if its performance is acceptable for a wireless middleware. The technologies used in this study were: Jakarta Tomcat 5.0.25, Axis 1.2, Java RMI from Java 1.4 SDK. The server specification is Intel Pentium M Processor 1.6 GHz 591 Mhz. 504 MB RAM. The client is an HP IPAQ h6340 Pocket PC. The Messaging Service in SORWiM is implemented using two middleware technologies, RMI and Web Service. The remote interface for performance tests is given below:

```
public interface MessagingService extends Remote {
  public String getMessage(String from)
      throws RemoteException;
  public String sendMessage(String to, String from,
      String  subject, String content, String type)
      throws RemoteException;
}
```

The single request and response CPU-times were measured for both the client Pocket PC and the server. A sample of our initial test results is given in Table 1.

Table 1. The server and client average CPU times for Web Service (WS) and RMI implementations of the Messaging Service methods, getMessage and sendMessage

Method	Calls	CPU Time [ms] Server WS	CPU Time [ms] Client WS	CPU Time [ms] Server RMI	CPU Time [ms] Client RMI
getMessage	10	30	80	10	20
sendMessage	10	50	180	20	30

Our test results and other research studies showed that web services implementations performed slower than a Java RMI implementation. The large amount of XML metadata contained in SOAP messages is the main reason that Web services will require more network bandwidth and CPU times than RMI. We have concluded that although the web service implementations are slower, the performance is acceptable for many real time operations of a wireless middleware. The performance can be made better and improved if the following issues are known and taken into consideration in middleware server designs.

All numeric and other data in web services are converted to text. Meta-data, defining structure, are provided as XML mark-up tags. XML parsers allow client and server implementations to construct their distinct but equivalent representations of any data structures The use of HTTP, and XML text documents, supports increased interoperability but also represents a significant increase in run-time cost for web service solutions as compared with Java-RMI solutions. The XML formatted documents are inherently more voluminous than the binary data traffic of the other approaches. More data have to be exchanged across the network, and more control packets are required.

When considering performance alone, web services provide value when the overhead of parsing XML and SOAP is outweighed by the business logic or computation performed on the server. Although web services generally don't provide value in performance, but do provide a convenient way to provide user interface, automatic firewall protection (because they use HTTP for transport and HTTP traffic can normally pass through firewalls), mobility and heterogeneity of applications, transparent proxies, and thin clients. The most natural designs for distributed objects are easy to use but scale poorly, whereas web services have good scaling properties.

The performance studies in literature generally measure RPC-style communication and do not consider the possibilities of document-oriented designs that demonstrate the strengths of web services [28]. Web services are not intended to be used RPC-style like other distributed object technologies. Web services provide a literal encoding that can be used in a document-centric paradigm rather than an RPC-centric one. If the document-centric nature of web services is used in implementations, web services can outperform other traditional implementations when compared with an RPC-centric approach. According to [28] the pure-object RMI or CORBA implementation is faster for small batches of documents and low-latency networks, but performance degrades rapidly with larger batches and higher latency. The web services have a high initial cost, but show little or no change with larger batches. Higher latency creates a greater initial cost, but performance is still independent of batch size. As latency increases, the performance benefits of the document-oriented approach increase significantly. This is relevant when in some real world wireless communication scenarios, latency may even be minutes, or hours, as for disconnected or asynchronous operations.

7 Conclusion

In this paper the design issues of a SOA based reflective wireless middleware, SORWiM have been presented. We will work on the research and development problems of different mobile location based services (LBS) applications based on service oriented computing using the basic and composite services provided by the middleware. SORWiM currently has four basic services and two composite services which can be used as building blocks of such wireless applications. We need develop some more new basic and composite services for more complex mobile applications and LBS.

The integration of SORWiM and WiPoD will be also one of our next projects. The WiPoD client application currently has a decentralized architecture and does not need a server. It will be connected to the SORWiM server to provide the indoor location information for the mobile user.

References

1. Schantz, R., Schmidt, D.: Middleware for Distributed Systems: Evolving the Common Structure for Network-Centric Applications. In Encyclopedia of Software Engineering, J. Marciniak, J., Telecki, G., (Eds): John Wiley & Sons, Inc., New York (2001)
2. Schmidt, D.: Middleware for Real-Time and Embedded Systems. Communications of the ACM, Vol. 45, No: 6 June (2002)
3. Papazoglou, M. P., Georgakopoulos, D.: Service-Oriented Computing. Communications of the ACM. Vol. 46, No: 10 (2003)
4. Papazoglou, M. P., Heuvel, W. J. van den: Service Oriented Architectures: Approaches, Technologies and Research Issues. The VLDB Journal (2005) Available at: http://infolab.uvt.nl/pub/papazogloump-2005-81.pdf
5. Mascolo, C., Capra, L., Emmerich, W.: Mobile Computing Middleware. Lecture Notes In Computer Science, Advanced Lectures on Networking, Vol. 2497. Springer-Verlag (2002) 20–58
6. Vaughan-Nichols, S. J.: Wireless Middleware: Glue for the Mobile Infrastructure. IEEE Computer, Vol. 37, No. 5 (2004) 18–20
7. Roman, M., Kon, F., Campbell, R.: Reflective Middleware: From your Desk to your Hand. IEEE Communications Surveys, 2 (5) (2001)

8. Mascolo, C., Capra, L., Emmerich, W.: Principles of Mobile Computing Middleware. In Middleware for Communications, Wiley (2004)
9. Heinzelman, W. B., Murphy, A. L., Carvalho, H. S., Perillo, M. A. Middleware to Support Sensor Network Applications. IEEE Network, January/February (2004) 6 – 14
10. Yu, Y., Krishnamachari, B, PrasannaIssues, V. K.: Designing Middleware for Wireless Sensor Networks. IEEE Network, January/February (2004) 15 – 21
11. Sen, R., Handorean, R., Roman, G.-C., Gill, C.: Service Oriented Computing Imperatives in Ad Hoc Wireless Settings. Service-Oriented Software System Engineering: Challenges And Practices, Stojanovic, Z. and Dahanayake, A., eds., Idea Group Publishing, Hershey, USA, April, (2005) 247 – 269
12. Thanh, D., Jørstad, I.: A Service-Oriented Architecture Framework for Mobile Services. IEEE Proceedings of the Advanced Industrial Conference on Telecommunications/Service Assurance with Partial and Intermittent Resources Conference/ELearning on Telecommunications Workshop, September (2005)
13. Box, D., Ehnebuske, D., Kakivaya, G., Layman, A., Mendelsohn, M., Nielsen, H., Thatte, S., Winer, D.: Simple Object Access Protocol 1.1. , available at http://www.w3.org/
14. Chinnici, R., Gudgina, M., Moreau, J., Weerawarana, S.: Web Service Description Language (WSDL), version 1.2. Technical Report (2002)
15. W3C. UDDI Technical White Paper. Technical Report (2000)
16. Andrews, T. et al. Business Process Execution Language for Web Services (BPEL4WS), ver. 1.1. Technical Report (2003)
17. Gamma, E., Helm, R., Johnson, R., Vlissides, J., Design Patterns, Elements of Reusable Object-Oriented Software. Addison-Wesley (1995)
18. Schmidt, D., Stal, M., Rohnert H., Buschmann, F. Pattern-Oriented. Software Architecture: Patterns for Concurrent and Networked Objects. John Wiley (2000)
19. PocketBuilder: http://www.sybase.com/products/developmentintegration/pocketbuilder
20. Apache Axis web site: http://ws.apache.org/axis/
21. Gümüşkaya, H., Hakkoymaz, H.: WiPoD Wireless Positioning System Based on 802.11 WLAN Infrastructure. Proceedings of the Enformatika, Vol. 9 (2005) 126–130
22. Davis, D., Parashar, M.: Latency Performance of SOAP Implementations. IEEE Cluster Computing and the Grid (2002)
23. Demarey, C., Harbonnier, G., Rouvoy, R., Merle, P.: Benchmarking the Round-Trip Latency of Various Java-Based Middleware Platforms. Studia Informatica Universalis Regular Issue, Vol. 4, No. 1, May (2005) 724–
24. Elfwing, R., Paulsson, U., Lundberg, L.: Performance of SOAP in Web Service Environment Compared to CORBA. in APSEC. IEEE Computer Society (2002) 84–
25. Juric, M. B., Kezmah, B., Hericko, M., Rozman, I., Vezocnik, I.: Java RMI, RMI Tunneling and Web Services Comparison and Performance Analysis. SIGPLAN Not., vol. 39, no. 5, (2004) 58–65
26. Gray, N. A. B.: Comparison of Web Services, Java-RMI, and CORBA Service Implementations. Fifth Australasian Workshop on Software and System Architectures (ASWEC 2004), Melbourne, Australia, April (2004)
27. Juric, M. B., Rozman, I., Brumen, B., Colnaric, M., Hericko M.: Comparison of Performance of Web Services, WS-Security, RMI, and RMI–SSL. The Journal of Systems and Software 79 (2006) 689–70
28. Cook, W. R., Barfield, J.: Web Services versus Distributed Objects: A Case Study of Performance and Interface Design, Proc. of the IEEE International Conference on Web Services (ICWS), September 18-22 (2006)

Procedures of Integration of Fragmented Data in a P2P Data Grid Virtual Repository*,**

Kamil Kuliberda[1,4], Jacek Wislicki[1,4], Tomasz Kowalski[1,4], Radoslaw Adamus[1,4], Krzysztof Kaczmarski[2,4], and Kazimierz Subieta[1,3,4]

[1] Technical University of Lodz, Lodz, Poland
[2] Warsaw University of Technology, Warsaw, Poland
[3] Institute of Computer Science PAS, Warsaw, Poland
[4] Polish-Japanese Institute of Information Technology, Warsaw, Poland
{kamil, jacenty, tkowals, radamus}@kis.p.lodz.pl,
kaczmars@mini.pw.edu.pl, subieta@pjwstk.edu.pl

Abstract. The paper deals with integration of distributed fragmented collections of data, being the basis for virtual repositories in the data grid or P2P architecture. The core of the described architecture is based on the Stack-Based Query Language (SBQL) and virtual updateable SBQL views. Our virtual repository transparently integrates distributed, heterogeneous and fragmented data producing conceptually and semantically coherent result. In the background the system is based on the P2P architecture. We provide three examples of data integration procedures, for either horizontal and vertical fragmentation. The procedures are implemented under the integrator prototype.

1 Introduction

A *virtual repository* becomes an increasingly popular concept in database environments as a mean to achieve many forms of transparent access to distributed resources applicable, in particular, in e-Government, e-University or e-Hospital. Data must be accessible from anywhere, at any time, regardless of its location and a form it is stored in. There are many approaches attempting to realize such an idea. Some of them are based on semantic data description and ontology usage extended with logic-based programs striving to understand users needs, collect data and transform it to a desired form (RDF, RDFQL, OWL). Commercial systems like Oracle-10G offer a flexible execution of distributed queries but they are still limited by a data model and SQL, not quite efficient and convenient for the case. Our novel system offers features necessary to build such a virtual repository. It keeps programming very simple. The main idea is based on P2P networks as a model for connecting clients and repositories combined with a powerful viewing system [2] enabling users to access data exactly in a desired form [8]. This viewing system also allows an easy-to-operate mechanism for integration of fragmented data collections into a consistent virtual whole.

---

* This work is supported by European Commission under the 6th FP project e-Gov Bus, IST-4-026727-ST.

** This work has been supported by European Social Fund and Polish State in the frame of "Mechanizm WIDDOK" programme (contract number Z/2.10/II/2.6/04/05/U/2/06).

A. Dan and W. Lamersdorf (Eds.): ICSOC 2006, LNCS 4294, pp. 557 – 568, 2006.

The rest of the paper is organized as follows. Section 2 presents the idea of a data grid based on a virtual repository. Section 3 presents a virtual network basis for a data grid. Section 4 presents integration details and section 5 three examples of integration. Section 6 concludes.

2 Distributed Data in Virtual Repository

The main difficulty of the described virtual repository concept is that neither data nor services can be copied, replicated and maintained in the centralized server. They are to be supplied, stored, processed and maintained on their autonomous sites [6, 7]. The external resources should be easily pluggable into the system as well as users can appear and disappear unexpectedly. Such a system, by a similarity to an electric grid, is called a grid database or a data grid [1, 9].

A user as well as a resource provider may plug into a virtual repository and use its resources according to his or her requirements, availability of the resources and assigned privileges. The goal of our research is to design a platform where all users and providers are able to access multiple distributed resources and to work on the ground of a global schema for all the accessible data and services. A virtual repository should present a middleware supplying a fully transparent access to distributed, heterogeneous and fragmented resources from its clients [8].

In the system we distinguish two kinds of data schemata. The first one, named *contributory schema*, is the description of a local resource acceptable for the virtual repository. A virtual repository can deal only with the data that is exported by the decision of a local administrator. Another reason for limited access to local resources is some consortium agreement, which is established for the virtual repository. The agreement has certain business goals and need not to accept any data from any provider [3, 5].

The second schema, named *grid schema* or *user schema*, describes global data and services available for clients. The task of a virtual repository system is to transform data from local contributory schemata into a global user schema. The transformation can perform more sophisticated homogenization of data and integration of fragmented collections. This is done by updateable views that are able to perform any data transformation and support view updates with no limitation that are common in other similar systems. Our views have the full algorithmic power of programming languages, thus are much more powerful than e.g. SQL views.

The global infrastructure is responsible for managing grid contents through access permissions, discovering data and resources, controlling location of resources and indexing whole grid attributes. The design and implementation challenge is a method of combining and enabling free bidirectional processing of contents of local clients and resource providers participating in the global virtual store [8].

Each resources provider possesses a view which transforms its local share into an acceptable contribution, a *contributory view*. Providers may also use extended wrappers to existing DBMS systems [6, 7]. Similarly, a client uses *a grid view* to consume needed resources in a form acceptable for his or her applications. This view is performing the main task of data transformation and its designer must be aware of data fragmentation, replication, redundancies, etc. [3, 5] This transformation may be described by an *integration schema* prepared by business experts or being a result of automatic semantic-based analysis. The problem is how to allow transparent plugging in new resources and incorporate them into existing and working views. This question is discussed in the next section.

3 Virtual Network for Distributed Resources

The idea of a database communication in a grid architecture relies on transparent processing data from all database engines plugged to a virtual repository. Our approach deals not only with an architecture and features of the network, but also with additional mechanisms to ensure: (1) users joining, (2) transparent integration of resources, (3) trust infrastructure for contributing participants. The general architecture of a virtual network concept solves the above issues through a middleware platform mechanisms designed for an easy and scalable integration of a community of database users. It creates an abstraction method for a communication in a grid community, resulting in an unique and simple database grid, processed in a parallel *peer-to-peer* (P2P) architecture [8] realized with the JXTA package [14].

Our investigations concerning distributed and parallel systems like Edutella [10] and OGSA [11] have led us to conclusion that a database grid should be independent of TCP/IP stack limitations, e.g. firewalls, NAT systems and encapsulated private corporate restrictions. The network processes (such as an access to the resources, joining and leaving the grid) should be transparent for the participants.

User's grid interfaces – in this proposal database engines – are placed over the P2P network middleware. DBMS-s work as heterogeneous data stores, but in fact they are transparently integrated in the virtual repository. Users can process their own local data schemata and also use business information from global schema available for all contributors. This part of a data grid activity is implemented with top-level user applications available through database engines and SBQL query language [12, 13], see *OODBMS Engines Layer* in Figure 1. In such an architecture, databases connected to the virtual network peer applications arrange unique parallel communication between physical computers for an unlimited business information exchange.

Our virtual network has a centralized architecture whose crucial element is a *central management unit* (CMU) – see Figure 1. In the virtual network there can exist only one CMU peer being responsible for a data grid's lifetime. Besides, it manages the virtual repository integrity and resource accessibility. Inside the P2P network level, the CMU is responsible for creating and managing the grid network – this means that CMU creates a *peer group* which is dedicated to linking data grid participants. The CMU also maintains this peer group. For regular grid contributors the virtual network is equipped with participant's communication peers. They are interfaces to the virtual repository for OODBMS user's engines. Each database has its unique name in local and global schemata which is bound with the peer unique name in the virtual network. If a current database IDs are stored in the CMU, a user can cooperate with the peer group and process information in the virtual repository (according to a trust infrastructure) through a database engine with a transparent peer application. Unique peer identifiers are a part of P2P implementation of JXTA platform [14, 15]. A peer contains a separate embedded protocol for a local communication with OODBMS engine and separate ones for cooperating with an applicable JXTA mechanism and whole virtual network. All exceptions concerning a local database operation, a virtual network availability and a TCP/IP network state are handled by a peer application responsible for a local part of grid maintenance. Notice that in one local environment there are residing two separate applications (a P2P virtual network application and a database engine) composing (in grid aspects) one logical application [8].

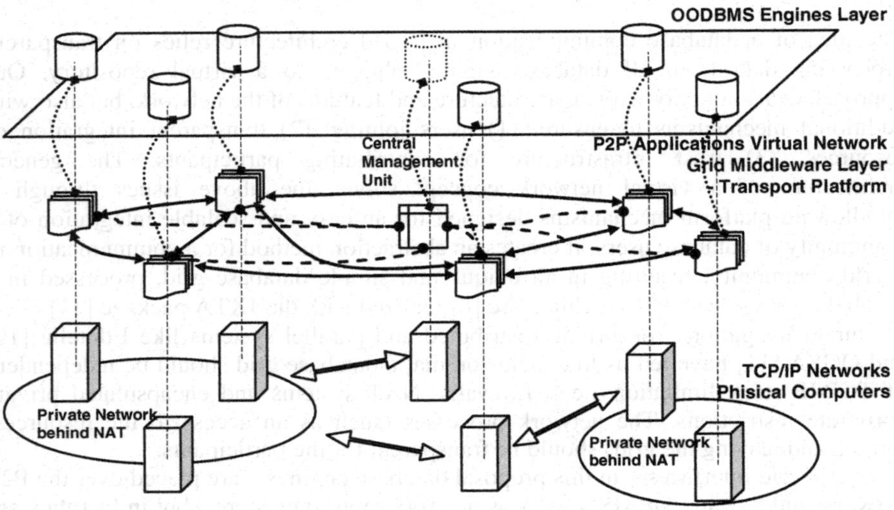

Fig. 1. Data grid communication layers and their dependencies

4 Transparent Integration Via Viewing System and Global Index

The presented virtual repository based on a P2P networking must be permanently updated and this is the most important aspect of its operation. For an easy management of the virtual repository's content, we have equipped the CMU with a *global index* mechanism, which covers technical networking details, management activities and also is a tool for efficient programming in a dynamically changing environment. The global index not necessarily has to be really centralized as there are many ways to distribute its tasks. The system needs this kind of additional control and it does not matter how it is organized. Its tasks are: (1) controlling grid views available for users, (2) keeping information on connected peers, (3) keeping network statistics, (4) registering and storing information on available resources.

The global index is a complex object which can be accessed with SBQL syntax (as a typical database object) on every database engine plugged into the virtual repository. This means that we can evaluate the queries on its contents. There is however one substantial difference from processing typical virtual repository's objects – as a result of an expression evaluation CMU can return only an actual content of index, like a list of on-line grid participants.

The global index is the basic source of knowledge about the content of the virtual repository. Basing on indexed information referring the views' system we can easily integrate any remote data inside the virtual repository. If the data have been indexed already, it can be transparently processed without any additional external interference. The *global index* has a specified structure which is a reflection of a *global schema* and contains mainly additional objects for characterizing the type of a data fragmentation. These objects are dynamically managed through the views' systems whenever a virtual repository contents undergoes a change (e.g. when a resource joins or disconnects). The *global index* keeps also dependencies between particular objects (complexity of the objects, etc.) as they are established in the *global schema*.

Each indexed object in the global index is equipped with a special object called *HFrag* (horizontal fragmentation) or *VFrag* (vertical fragmentation). Each of them keeps a special attribute named *ServerName*, whose content is a *remote object* – an identifier of a remote data resource (see fig. 5 and 7). If any new resource appears in a virtual repository, there will be added a suitable *ServerName* into the global index automatically with appropriate information about it.

Accessing the remote data can be achieved by calling the *global index* with:

GlobalIndex.Name_of_object_from_global_scheme.(Name_of_subobject).
HFrag_or_VFrag_object.ServerName_object;

Because every change of the virtual repository's content is denoted in the global index, accessing data in this way is the only correct one.

Since every reference to a remote object must explicitly contain its location (a server it resides on), such a procedure would be too complicated for grid participants. Moreover, it would not accomplish with transparency requirements and would complicate an automation of multiple resources integration process. Thus, we have decided to cover this stage together with automation of integration process behind a special procedure exploiting updatable object views mechanism [4]. The process is described in the next section.

5 Examples of Integrators Action

We introduce examples showing how our automatic integration procedure works. The basic mechanism we utilize during the integration process is presented by object updatable views. Figure 2 depicts the virtual repository objects accessible through self-operating integrators on a distributed databases. Basing on this object structure we create our integrator examples. As the first one we introduce the easiest type of an integration of fragmented objects – a horizontal fragmentation, as the second we present more complicated type of fragmentation – a vertical one. After these two examples we describe an example from a real life – a mixed fragmentation which is a composition of two above.

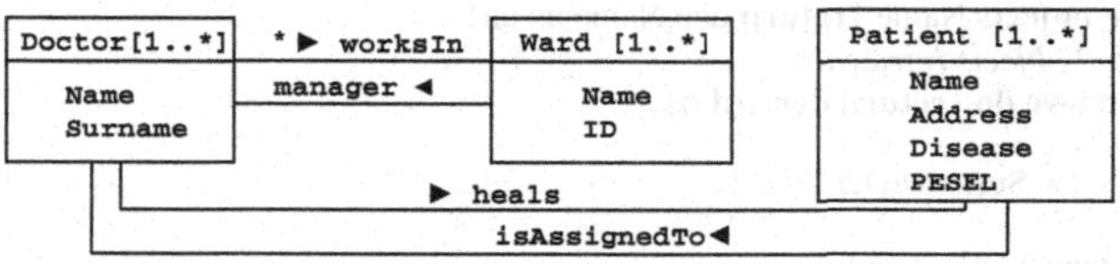

Fig. 2. Virtual repository data schema

In all examples we create virtual objects explicitly, what implies that a grid designer must be aware of fragmented objects in the grid schema. He or she doesn't need any knowledge of the fragmentation details, but must know which objects are fragmented. The rest of the integration process is executed automatically through SBQL [12, 13] syntactic transformations.

5.1 Horizontal Fragmentation Case

The first example realizes a transparent integration process concerning a horizontal fragmentation of Doctor and Ward objects (Figure 2). These complex objects are stored on two different servers, but the data structure for each sever is the same (see Figure 3), and the corresponding global index content is presented in Figure 7 (see part of GlobalIndex object and subobjects Ward and Doctor).

The situation where data is horizontally fragmented in distributed resources forces merging all data as a one virtual structure, transparently achieved by all grid's clients. This process can be done by employment the *union* operator (like in [2]) in updatable object views. Because in the current example we call GlobalIndex objects, this operation is performed automatically. Thus we do not need this operator explicitly. The logical schema of this operation is presented in Figure 3.

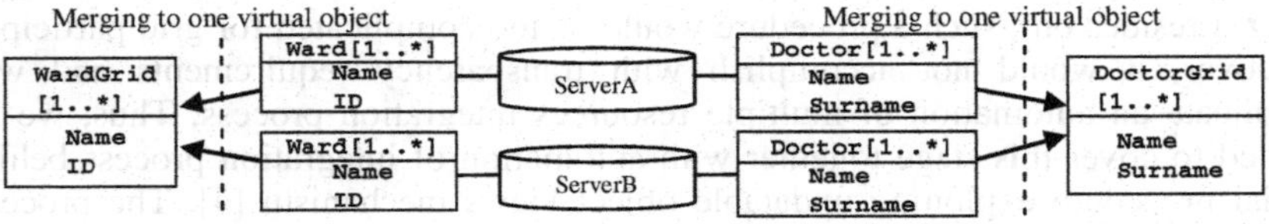

Fig. 3. Integration of distributed databases (with identical data structure) into one virtual structure for virtual repository

The following query presents the use of the defined view (*names of all doctors working in the cardiac surgery ward*):

(DoctorGrid **where** *WorksIn.WardGrid.Name = "cardiac surgery").Name;*

The DoctorGrid and WardGrid virtual objects definitions are as follows:

```
create view DoctorGridDef {
  virtual_objects DoctorGrid {
//create and return remote not fragmented objects doc
        return (GlobalIndex.Doctor.HFrag.ServerName).Doctor as doc};
//the result of virtual objects retrieval
   on_retrieve do {return deref(doc)};
        create view NameDef {
//create a virtual subobjects Name of DoctorGrid object
        virtual_objects Name {return doc.Name as dn};
//the result of virtual objects retrieval
         on_retrieve do {return deref(dn)};};

        create view SurnameDef {//...};

        create view worksInDef {
           virtual_pointers worksIn { return doc.WorksIn as wi};
           on_retrieve do {return deref(wi)};};
};
```

```
create view WardGridDef {
  virtual_objects WardGrid {
        return (GlobalIndex.Ward.HFrag.ServerName).Ward as war};
  on_retrieve do {return deref(war)};
        create view NameDef {
          virtual_objects Name {return war.Name as wn};
          on_retrieve do {return deref(wn)};
        create view IDDef {//...};
};
```

5.2 Vertical Fragmentation Case

The second example depicts a transparent integration process concerning vertical fragmentation, which is more complicated, because we must join different data structures stored on physically separated servers. For solving this problem we use the *join* operator with a *join predicate* specific for appropriate integration of distributed objects. The database schema (according to the global schema) is presented in Figure 2, where the complex object Patient is placed on three different servers and the data structure of stored objects is different, Figure 4. The corresponding global index content is presented in Figure 5.

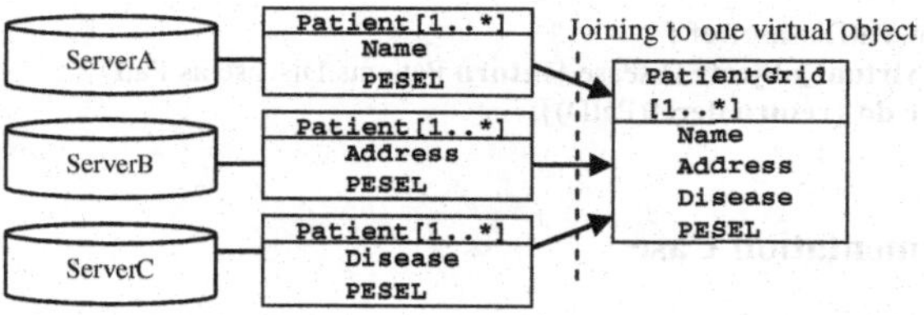

Fig. 4. Integration of distributed databases (with different data structure) into one virtual structure for a virtual repository

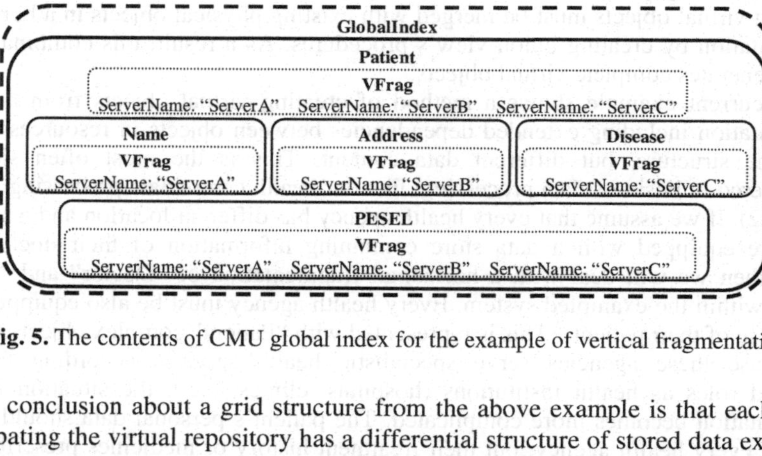

Fig. 5. The contents of CMU global index for the example of vertical fragmentation

The conclusion about a grid structure from the above example is that each server participating the virtual repository has a differential structure of stored data except for the PESEL object (the unique patient person identifier) which has an identical content on each server. We utilize the knowledge about the PESEL object and its content to make a "join" on the fragmented Patient object. The PESEL attribute is an unique identifier (predicate) for joining distributed objects into a virtual one.

This integration for a vertical fragmentation can be exemplified with the query evaluation where we *retrieve names of all patients suffering from cancer*: *(PatientGrid **where** Disease = "cancer").Name;*

The PatientGrid virtual objects definitions (through object views) are following:

```
create view PatientGridDef {
//create and return remote not fragmented  Patient objects
        virtual_objects PatientGrid {
          return { (((GlobalIndex.Patient.VFrag.ServerName).Patient as pat).(
          ((pat where exist(Name)) as pn) join
          ((pat where exist(Address)) as pa where pa.PESEL = pn.PESEL) join
          ((pat where exist(Disease)) as pd where pd.PESEL = pn.PESEL)).(
                    pn.Name as Name, pn.PESEL as PESEL, pa.Address as Address,
                    pd.Disease as Disease)) as Patients };
  //the result of virtual objects retrieval
        on_retrieve do {return deref(Patients)};

        create view PatNameDef {
                  virtual_objects Name {return Patients.Name as PatN};
        on_retrieve do {return deref(PatN)};

        create view PatDiseaseDef {
                  virtual_objects Disease {return Patients.Disease as PatD};
        on_retrieve do {return deref(PatD)};
  };
```

5.3 Mixed Fragmentation Case

Basing on approaches presented, defining an integration mechanism for objects fragmented horizontally and vertically together is easy. In order to do so, we must combine them into a specific model. If we mix above examples, at first, we must define a joining procedures for vertical fragmentations in views. After this, the resulting virtual objects must be merged with existing physical objects in a horizontal fragmentation by creating union view's procedures. As a result, this combination of views generates complete virtual objects.

The current example shows a method of creating virtual objects from a mixed fragmentation including extended dependencies between objects in resources having the same structure, but different data content. This is the most often situation encountered in business data processing, like our health centre data processing system (Figure 2). If we assume that every health agency has different location and a some of them are equipped with a data store containing information of their doctors and wards, then we will deal with a horizontal fragmentation of "Doctor" and "Ward" objects within the exampled system. Every health agency must be also equipped with a database of their patients. This is represented with "Patient" complex objects.

Because these agencies serve specialistic health services according to their specified roles as health institutions (hospitals, clinics, etc.), the situation in data fragmentation becomes more complicated. The patient's personal data should be the same in every health agency, but their treatment history or medicines prescribed are different in every place. Moreover, in the system also stores separately the archival

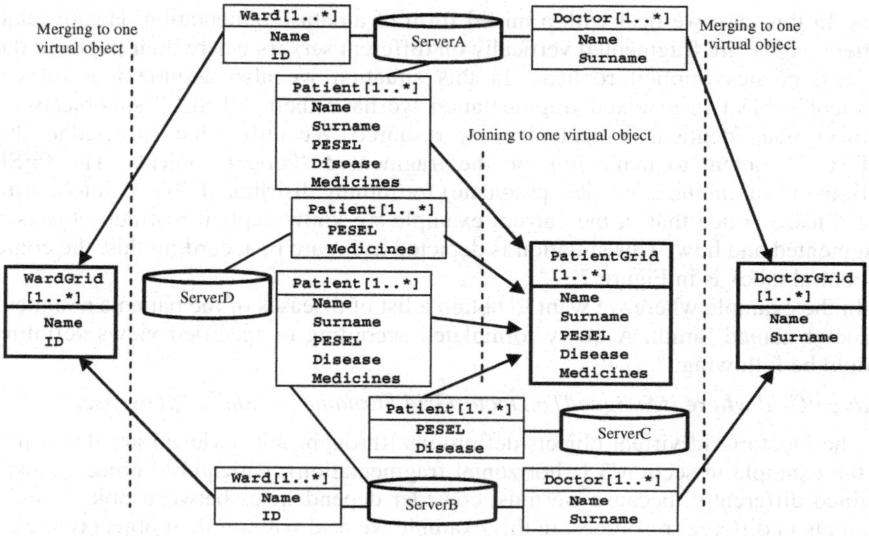

Fig. 6. Integration of distributed databases (with mixed object fragmentation) into one virtual structure for a virtual repository

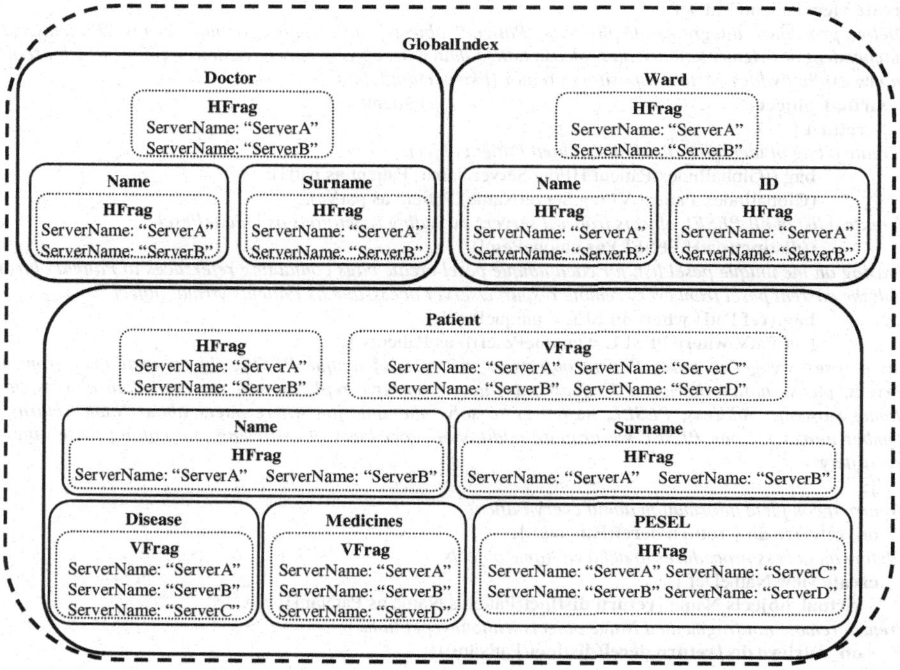

Fig. 7. The contents of CMU global index for example of mixed fragmentation

data. In this case we deal with a mixed form of a data fragmentation. Health-related patient's data are fragmented vertically on different servers where their personal data, in fact, creates implicit replicas. In this situation we also assume that for each "Patient" object in a mixed fragmentation we have their "PESEL" subobjects – id number with identical content in every resource. We utilize the knowledge about "PESEL" content to make *join* on the fragmented "Patient" objects. The PESEL attribute is an unique identifier (predicate) for joining distributed objects into a virtual one. Please notice that in the current example we know explicitly which objects are fragmented and how. This situation is depicted in Figure 6, according this, the content of central index is in Figure 7.

In the example where we want to obtain a list of diseases of the patients assigned to a doctor named Smith. A query formulated according to specified views definitions should be following:

*(PatientGrid **where** isAssignedTo.DoctorGrid.Surname = "Smith").Disease;*

The DoctorGrid virtual objects definitions (through object views) are the same as in the example in section 5.1 (horizontal fragmentation), PatientGrid objects must be defined differently, because we must consider dependencies between objects and its contents in different resources, in this example we deal with implicit object replicas:

```
create view DoctorGridDef {
//as in the example of a horizontal fragmentation, section 5.1
};

create view PatientGridDef {
//below procedure integrates all physical "Patient" objects into complete virtual objects "PatientGrid"
independent of fragmentation issues, please notice that some objects may have data replicas which are not
known explicitly for a virtual repository creator (like personal data)
  virtual_objects                                   PatientGrid                                   {
    return {
//create a bag of identifiers to all distributed Patient objects
        bag ((GlobalIndex.Patient.HFrag.ServerName).Patient as patH),
        (GlobalIndex.Patient.VFrag.ServerName).Patient as patV)).
//create a list of all PESEL objects from all servers excluding repetitions as uniquePesel
        ((distinct(patH.PESEL) as uniquePesel).
//basing on the unique pesel list, for each unique pesel create bags containing references to Patient objects
with the current pesel from every remote resource/server accessible as Patients virtual object
        bag((ref PatH where PESEL = uniquePesel),
        (ref PatV where PESEL = uniquePesel))) as Patients };
//as a result we get as many Patient objects as instances of unique PESEL objects available from all
servers, please notice that some PatientGrid objects can have replicas with personal data objects such
Name, Surname, Address, PESEL, moreover to solve the situation where query about Name returns a
number names for one PESEL we propose additional procedures of retrieving and calling these objects
separately.
    };
//return a complete information about every Patient
  on_retrieve do { return deref(Patients) };
//define an access procedures to achieve Name objects
  create view NameDef {
    virtual_objects Name {return distinct(Patients.Name as PatNam};
//return remote not fragmented Name objects without repetitions
      on_retrieve do {return deref(distinct(PatNam))};
  };

//define an access procedures to achieve Disease objects
  create view DiseaseDef {
```

```
    virtual_objects Disease {return distinct(Patients.Disease as PatDis};
//return remote not fragmented Disease objects without repetitions
    on_retrieve do {return deref(distinct(PatDis))};
  };

//here should be situated subview definitions for following objects: Surname, Address, Medicines, PESEL

//here is a virtual pointer definition for Patients and their assigned Doctors
  create view isAssignedToDef {
    virtual_pointers isAssignedTo {return Patients.isAssignedTo as iat};
    on_retrieve do {return deref(iat)};
  };
};
```

The above example is shortened so that it demonstrates only the necessary procedures of integrating vertically fragmented objects. There are no limitations in designing a fully automatic integration process by extending the above views with the integration routines (like for "Disease" and "Name" objects) for every object indexed in the CMU global index.

6 Conclusions and Future Work

In this paper we have presented an implemented prototype technology addressing integration of distributed, heterogeneous and fragmented resources through a virtual repository based on the P2P paradigm. Due to the paper size limits we are unable to illustrate all the cases, combinations and issues of a transparent integration of resources, however we will do our best to present more solutions in future publications. We have proposed the methodology to accomplish the process of integration and we have implemented virtual repository software supporting this methodology. The results are illustrated through examples of different data fragmentation. Our solution utilizes a consistent combination of several technologies, such as P2P networks (JXTA), SBA object-oriented databases and their query language SBQL with virtual updatable views. Our preliminary implementation solves a very important issue of independence between technical aspects of a distributed data structure management (including additional issues such as participants incorporation, resource contribution) and a logical virtual repository content scalability (business information processing). We expect that the presented methods of integration of fragmented data will be efficient and fully scalable. These factors will be tested within our implemented prototype.

The future work is oriented on extending the presented idea with new functionalities permitting solving more complex situations, in particular, when distributed resources have additional challenges, such as replicas and redundancies.

References

1. Foster I., Kesselman C., Nick J., Tuecke S.: The Physiology of the Grid: An Open Grid Services Architecture for Distributed Systems Integration. Global Grid Forum, 2002.
2. Kaczmarski K., Habela P., Kozakiewicz H., Subieta K.: Modeling Object Views In Distributed Query Processing on the Grid. OTM Workshops 2005, Springer LNCS 3762, 2005, pp.377-386

3. Kaczmarski K., Habela P., Subieta K.: Metadata in a Data Grid Construction. 13th IEEE International Workshops on Enabling Technologies (WETICE 2004), IEEE Computer Society 2004, pp. 315-326
4. Kozankiewicz H.: Updateable Object Views. PhD Thesis, 2005, http://www.ipipan.waw.pl/~subieta/, Finished PhD-s
5. Kozankiewicz H., Stencel K., Subieta K.: Implementation of Federated Databases through Updateable Views. Proc. EGC 2005, Springer LNCS 3470, 2005, pp.610-619
6. Kuliberda K., Wislicki J., Adamus R., Subieta K.: Object-Oriented Wrapper for Relational Databases in the Data Grid Architecture. OTM Workshops 2005, Springer LNCS 3762, 2005, pp.367-376
7. Kuliberda K., Wislicki J., Adamus R., Subieta K.: Object-Oriented Wrapper for Semistructured Data in a Data Grid Architecture. 9th International Conference on Business Information Systems 2006, LNI vol. P-85, GI-Edition 2006, pp.528-542
8. Kuliberda K., Kaczmarski K., Adamus R., Błaszczyk P., Balcerzak G., Subieta K.: Virtual Repository Supporting Integration of Pluginable Resources, 17th DEXA 2006 International Workshops - (GRep 2006), IEEE Computer Society, to appear.
9. Moore R., Merzky A.: Persistent Archive Concepts. Global Grid Forum GFD-I.026. December 2003.
10. Nejdl W., Wolf B., Qu C., Decker S., Sintek M., Naeve A., Nilsson M., Palmer M., Risch T.: EDUTELLA, a P2P networking infrastructure based on RDF. Proc. Intl. World Wide Web Conference, 2002.
11. Open Grid Services Architecture, Data Access and Integration Documentation, http://www.ogsadai.org.uk
12. Subieta K.: Theory and Construction of Object-Oriented Query Languages. Editors of the Polish-Japanese Institute of Information Technology, 2004 (in Polish)
13. Subieta: Stack-Based Approach (SBA) and Stack-Based Query Language (SBQL). http://www.ipipan.waw.pl/~subieta, Description of SBA and SBQL, 2006
14. The JXTA Project Web site: http://www.jxta.org
15. Wilson B.: JXTA Book, http://www.brendonwilson.com/projects/jxta/

Towards Facilitating Development of SOA Application with Design Metrics

Wei Zhao, Ying Liu, Jun Zhu, and Hui Su

IBM China Research Lab,
Beijing 100094, P.R. China
{weizhao, aliceliu, junzhu, suhui}@cn.ibm.com

Abstract. Applications based on service-oriented architecture (SOA) are intended to be built with both high cohesion and low coupling. The loosely coupled services bring forth the lower costs of development and maintenance as well as the higher reusability and extensibility. To implement each SOA application with such intention, designs play an important role for the success of the whole project. The services and the relationships among them represented in a design are two critical factors to decide the quality of an SOA application in terms of modularity. At the mean while, they are valuable indicators for guiding the following development and maintenance phases to progress in a cost-effective way. In this paper, we present that measurement of designs for SOA applications can objectively judge the quality and further facilitate the development and maintenance of SOA applications through employing two specific metrics. We also performed an experimental study on an ongoing SOA project. In this study, we applied these two metrics to the design of this project to acquire judgments and make estimations. The data in CVS were retrieved to reflect the genuine project situations. The analysis on these data shows that adopting the measurement in the early stage of SOA projects may avoid wasting efforts and delaying schedule as well as acquire a deep grasp and an effective control on the issues in the following phases.

Keywords: SOA, modular design, service design measurement, metrics.

1 Introduction

Modular architectures solve the problem of complexity of the business by decomposing complex services into modules so that service providers can design and deliver them independently [1]. These business service modules are implemented by the corresponding service modules and components (within the implementation context, service components are programming entities with finer granularity than service modules) at IT level under the service-oriented architecture (SOA) and the supporting programming model (e.g. service component architecture, SCA) as an SOA application. The descriptions of which service modules and components construct an SOA application and how they are interrelated to provide the business services are regarded as the architecture design of an SOA application. Accordingly, these service modules and components at IT level should hold the similar modular

A. Dan and W. Lamersdorf (Eds.): ICSOC 2006, LNCS 4294, pp. 569 – 580, 2006.

properties in finer granularity to satisfy the modular design of business services. That is to say, SOA applications consisting of various service modules and components are intended to be built by showing both high cohesion and low coupling [2]. The architecture of an SOA application with higher cohesion as well as lower coupling indicates a better design in terms of modularity. A well-modularized design of an SOA application brings forth potential benefits in multiple aspects, such as acceleration of development, reduction of maintenance cost, as well as the enhanced flexibility and reusability.

The quality of the modular designs for SOA applications often heavily relies on the experiences and expertise of specific designers. In addition, the best practices and design patterns as well as frameworks, which are summarized from accumulated experiences, can be a useful guidance for a better design. However, these facilities are still kinds of informal aids to modular design and the achieved effectiveness from them still heavily depends on the experiences and expertise of individual designers to some extent.

There are no any practical reports in industry to employ measurement technologies to evaluate whether a certain design of an SOA application is well modularized than another or to guide the activities in the following development and maintenance phases through design metrics. Actually, to employ measurement to judge the modularity of software designs is not new. Many efforts have been dedicated to judge and reorganize the structural designs of software systems according to the modularized degrees (e.g. [3] and [4]). However, with the intention to acquire the loosely coupled SOA applications, service-oriented architecture does provide a framework to model the constructive entities (i.e. interfaces, service components, and service data objects) and their interrelationships more explicitly at a higher abstract level, but it does not mean that any application based on SOA holds the loose coupling and tight cohesion inherently.

In this paper, we report an initial exploration of measurement on SOA designs. We present that measurement of designs for SOA applications can quantitatively evaluate the quality of modular designs through a comparative way and also can facilitate the development and maintenance of applications.

We performed an experimental study on an ongoing SOA project. In this study, we employed two metrics on the design of this project to acquire judgments and make estimations. The corresponding data in CVS were retrieved to reflect the genuine project situations. The analysis on these data shows that adopting the design metrics in the early stage of SOA projects may avoid wasting efforts and delaying the schedule as well as acquire an early grasp and effective control on the issues in the following phases.

The remainder of this paper is organized as follows. Section 2 introduces the goals we want to achieve through measuring designs for SOA applications and the corresponding design metrics we used. An experimental study on an ongoing SOA application is presented in section 3 to validate the effectiveness of the metrics and imply their indicating and aiding roles. Section 4 summarizes this paper.

2 Goals and Design Metrics

2.1 Goals

A measurement program identifies and defines metrics to support an organization's business goals [5]. These metrics provide insights into the critical quality and management issues that the organization concerns for its success. During the establishment of a measurement program, the organization selects metrics traceable to its business goals. This "goal-driven" approach assures that measurement activities stay focused on the organization's objectives.

Because the well modularized designs of SOA applications bring multiple benefits such as reducing the development and maintenance cost and increasing the reusability as mentioned above, one of our goals is to quantify the modular designs of SOA applications in terms of the estimated relative development cost and maintenance cost in an early stage (i.e. right after acquiring the designs of applications). The design metrics in this paper refer to these quantitatively estimated indicators for the costs of following development and maintenance activities based on the design information. Although we aim to acquire the quantitative insights on how well a modular design is, it should be noted that we examine such merit through a comparative way. That is to say, we cannot claim that a specific SOA application is well designed enough in terms of modularity even with the quantitative metrics. However, given the two candidate designs for a certain application, we can quantitatively judge that one is better (or worse) than the other in terms of modularity and make a choice for lower development and maintenance costs.

In addition to the quantitative evaluation of the whole design, the comparison based on the design metrics can also be carried out within a specific SOA application design to pinpoint the modular characteristics of each service module and component. For a determined design of an SOA application, further scrutinizing each service module and component based on the design metrics provides the valuable insights to the following development and maintenance phases. This is the other goal we expect to pursue through the design metrics.

2.2 Metrics Definition

We adopt a technique called Design Structure Matrix (DSM) [6] to analyze the designs of SOA applications. A DSM is a tool that highlights the inherent structure of a design by examining the dependencies that exist between its component elements using a symmetric matrix.

The component elements in the design of an SOA application are service components. As service modules are composed of service components, the metrics of a service module can be acquired through calculating the service components belonging to it. As a result, the service modules' corresponding metrics will not be omitted although they are not explicitly represented in the design structure matrix. To construct the design structure matrix based on the service components of an SOA application's design, we follow Parnas's "information hiding" criterion [7] to mark the dependencies among the service components which are further used to measure and judge the modularity of an SOA application's design. In more detail, for the design of an SOA application, each service component may operate (i.e. *create*, *update*, *read* and *delete*) some data objects. Due to the dependent operations on the same data objects, the service components are interrelated among others. These dependencies are the key factors to identify how well the investigated design is modularized according to the "information hiding" principle from the perspective of the operated data.

Based on the constructed design structure matrix presented above, we employ two DSM-based metrics originally proposed by MacCormack et. al. to estimate the phenomena with which the design structure of software are associated [3]. MacCormack et. al.'s work focuses on the predication through an overall design to compare the modularity of two candidate designs. Since we aim at not only providing a quantitative cognition of a current modular design but also facilitating the subsequent development and maintenance activities, we further employ these two metrics to scrutinize the designs in the finer granularity. The definitions of these two metrics, change cost and coordination cost, are introduced as follows:

Change Cost

Change cost is a metric which determines the impact of a change to each service component, in terms of the percentage of other service components that are potentially affected. It is an indicator of the efforts needed for the maintenance activities of an SOA project. Obviously, the higher the change cost, the worse the design is modularized. In MacCormack et. al.'s work, this metric is computed only for the overall design of software. We also scrutinize this metric for each service component of a specific design. Actually, change cost of the overall design is an average of all service components' change costs.

	A	***B***	***C***	***D***	***E***	***F***
A	0	1	1	0	0	0
B	0	0	0	1	0	0
C	0	0	0	0	1	0
D	0	0	0	0	0	0
E	0	0	0	0	0	1
F	0	0	0	0	0	0

Fig. 1. An example design structure matrix

To acquire the change cost of a service component or an SOA application (change cost of a service module consisting of service components can be acquired through the same way as the SOA application), a matrix is constructed firstly to represent the structure of the design of an SOA application as described above. If an SOA application is composed of *n* service components, the size of the matrix is *n*×*n*. Each cell of this matrix indicates the modular dependency between the service components in the corresponding column and row based on the "information hiding" principle from the perspective of the operated data as mentioned above.

The computation of change cost is illustrated by the following example. Considering the relationships among service components displayed in the design structure matrix in Fig. 1, it can be seen that *service component A* depends on *service component B* and *C*. Therefore any change to *service component B* may have a direct impact on *service component A*. Similarly, *service component B* and *C* depend on *service component D* and *service component E* respectively. Consequently, any change to *service component D* may have a direct impact on *service component B*, and may have an indirect impact on *service component A*, with a "path length" of 2.

Obviously, the technique of matrix multiplication can be used to identify the impacted scope of any given service component for any given path length. Specifically, by raising the matrix to successive powers of *n*, the results show the direct and indirect dependencies that exist for successive path lengths. By summing these matrices together, the matrix *V* (which is called as the visibility matrix) can be derived, showing the dependencies that exist for all possible path lengths up to *n*. It should be noted that this calculating process includes the matrix for *n*=0 (i.e., a path length of zero) when calculating the visibility matrix, implying that a change to a service component will always affect itself. Fig. 2 illustrates the calculation of the visibility matrix for the above example.

M0	*A*	*B*	*C*	*D*	*E*	*F*	M1	*A*	*B*	*C*	*D*	*E*	*F*	M2	*A*	*B*	*C*	*D*	*E*	*F*
A	1	0	0	0	0	0	*A*	0	1	1	0	0	0	*A*	0	0	0	1	1	0
B	0	1	0	0	0	0	*B*	0	0	0	1	0	0	*B*	0	0	0	0	0	0
C	0	0	1	0	0	0	*C*	0	0	0	0	1	0	*C*	0	0	0	0	0	1
D	0	0	0	1	0	0	*D*	0	0	0	0	0	0	*D*	0	0	0	0	0	0
E	0	0	0	0	1	0	*E*	0	0	0	0	0	1	*E*	0	0	0	0	0	0
F	0	0	0	0	0	1	*F*	0	0	0	0	0	0	*F*	0	0	0	0	0	0
M3	***A***	***B***	***C***	***D***	***E***	***F***	**M4**	***A***	***B***	***C***	***D***	***E***	***F***	**V**	***A***	***B***	***C***	***D***	***E***	***F***
A	0	0	0	0	0	1	*A*	0	0	0	0	0	0	*A*	1	1	1	1	1	1
B	0	0	0	0	0	0	*B*	0	0	0	0	0	0	*B*	0	1	0	1	0	0
C	0	0	0	0	0	0	*C*	0	0	0	0	0	0	*C*	0	0	1	0	1	1
D	0	0	0	0	0	0	*D*	0	0	0	0	0	0	*D*	0	0	0	1	0	0
E	0	0	0	0	0	0	*E*	0	0	0	0	0	0	*E*	0	0	0	0	1	1
F	0	0	0	0	0	0	*F*	0	0	0	0	0	0	*F*	0	0	0	0	0	1

Fig. 2. Successive powers of the design structure matrix and visibility matrix

From the visibility matrix, the change cost metric can be acquired to give the insight for each service component and the whole SOA application. Firstly, for each service component, the change cost is obtained by summing along the column of the visibility matrix, and dividing the result by the total number of service components. A service component with higher change cost possibly affects more service components while changing it. In the above example, *service component F* has a change cost of 4/6 (or 66.67%) which means a change on it may affect other 4 service components in the system.

The average change cost of all service components need to be computed for the whole design. The resulting metric is the change cost for the overall design of a given SOA application. Intuitively, this metric reflects the percentage of service components affected on average when a change is made to a certain service component in the application. In the example above, we can calculate the change cost of the overall design as [1/6+2/6+2/6+3/6+3/6+4/6] divided by 6 service components = 41.67%.

Coordination Cost
Coordination cost is a metric to evaluate how well the proposed design of an SOA application in terms of the coordinating efforts needed in the procedure of developing it in the future. It is an indicator of the efforts needed for the development activities of an SOA project. The higher the coordination cost, the worse the design is modularized. Different from the change cost, the coordination cost is not only determined by the dependencies between the constructing service components but also affected by how these service components are organized into different service modules. The calculation of coordination cost metric operates by allocating a cost to each dependency between service components firstly. Specifically, for an SOA application, when considering a dependency between service components *A* and *B*, the cost of the dependency takes one of following two forms:

$$CoordCost\ (A \rightarrow B | \text{in same module}) = (A \rightarrow B)^{cost\_dep} \times size\ of\ module^{cost\_cs} \quad (1)$$

$$CoordCost\ (A \rightarrow B | \text{not in same module}) = (A \rightarrow B)^{cost\_dep} \times sum\ size\ of\ two\ modules^{cost\_cs} \quad (2)$$

Where ($A \rightarrow B$) represents the strength of the dependency (that is, the number of correlations between *service component* A and *B*) and *cost_dep* and *cost_cs* are user-defined parameters that reflect the relative weights given to the strength of dependencies versus the size of the modules.

For each service component, the corresponding coordination cost is determined through summing up all *CoordCost* between it and all its dependent service components. The coordination cost of the overall design of an SOA application can be acquired from summarizing the coordination costs of all the service components in the design.

3 Experimental Study

3.1 Experimental Method

Rifkin and Cox performed case studies on software measurement programs of different corporations and reported that the most successful programs they observed supported experimentation and innovation [8]. Following the similar point of view, we performed a pilot experimental study to validate effects of adopted metrics and initiate the measurement program on the designs of SOA applications for some particular project goals.

The subject system in our study is an SOA project as a proof of concept for early convincing the customers. The specific requirements on this project include implementing the basic functionalities as customer needed within a short time as well as low cost. Although the scope of this project is not big enough as a real SOA project, it does represent the key factors and characteristics of an SOA application. It should be noted that we did the experimental study not through applying the design metrics we introduced above to guide the development and maintenance activities of this project. We adopted a way using the project data without affected by the design metrics to provide the evidences whether the design metrics make the right estimates and whether the estimates can provide the effective advices for the following stages to help achieve the goals of this project.

3.2 Data Analysis and Observations

The subject SOA project is composed of five service modules each of which are further implemented by service components. Due to the confidential consideration, we use *ModuleA*, *ModuleB*, *ModuleC*, *ModuleD* and *ModuleE* designating these five service modules. An overall implementation situation of the subject system is listed in Table 1. As we can see, *ModuleA* includes 6 service components which provide services (each service component implements one service) to be consumed by end users directly or by other services. Each service component is implemented by an entrance class as well as other related classes. All these 6 services have 11 operations to perform the specific tasks provided by these services. Methods of entrance class correspond to each service's operations. *ModuleA* is implemented by 13 Java files including 6 entrance classes for 6 services respectively and 7 related classes (We do not further include those supporting classes since they are not the interferential factors for the analysis).

Table 1. Modules, services, operations and Java files of subject system

Modules	Services	Operations	Java files
ModuleA	6	11	13
ModuleB	2	4	10
ModuleC	3	10	3
ModuleD	6	13	33
ModuleE	18	26	47

		A1	A2	A3	A4	A5	A6	B1	B2	C1	C2	C3	D1	D2	D3	D4	D5	D6	E1	E2	E3	E4	E5	E6	E7	E8	E9	E10	E11	E12	E13	E14	E15	E16	E17	E18
ModuleA	ServiceA1	X	1	1	1	1	1	1	1			1	1		1	1	1						1		1	1	1						1			
	ServiceA2	1	X				1																													
	ServiceA3	1		X			1					1	1			1							1			1							1			
	ServiceA4	1			X		1																													
	ServiceA5	1				X	1																													
	ServiceA6	1	1	1	1	1	X	1																												
ModuleB	ServiceB1	1					1	X	1			1	1			1							1			1							1			
	ServiceB2	1							X			1	1			1		1					1			1							1			
ModuleC	ServiceC1									X			1																							
	ServiceC2										X				1																					
	ServiceC3	1		1				1	1			X	1		1	1	1	1					1		1	1	1						1			
ModuleD	ServiceD1	1		1				1		1			X	1	1	1	1	1					1		1	1	1						1			
	ServiceD2												1	X	1	1	1	1					1										1			
	ServiceD3	1		1				1		1		1	1	1	X	1		1					1			1							1			
	ServiceD4	1		1				1	1				1	1	1	X	1	1					1		1	1	1						1			
	ServiceD5	1										1	1	1		1	X	1					1			1										
	ServiceD6							1					1	1	1	1	1	X					1													
ModuleE	ServiceE1																		X	1	1	1	1													
	ServiceE2	1																		X																
	ServiceE3	1																			X															
	ServiceE4	1																				X														
	ServiceE5	1		1				1	1				1	1	1	1	1	1	1				X	1	1	1	1						1			
	ServiceE6																						1	X	1	1									1	1
	ServiceE7	1										1	1		1	1							1		X	1	1	1	1	1	1		1		1	1
	ServiceE8	1		1				1	1				1	1	1	1	1						1		1	X	1	1	1	1	1		1		1	1
	ServiceE9	1										1	1		1	1							1		1	1	X	1	1	1	1		1			
	ServiceE10																								1	1	1	X	1	1	1					
	ServiceE11																								1	1	1	1	X		1					
	ServiceE12																								1	1	1	1		X	1					
	ServiceE13																								1	1	1	1	1	1	X					
	ServiceE14																															X	1			
	ServiceE15	1		1				1	1				1	1	1	1	1						1		1	1	1					1	X	1		
	ServiceE16																																1	X		
	ServiceE17																							1	1	1									X	1
	ServiceE18																						1	1	1	1									1	X

Fig. 3. Design structure matrix of subject system

According to the descriptions of the construction of the design structure matrix in section 2, we acquired the DSM of the subject system which can be seen in Fig. 3. The dependencies among the service components of the subject system were picked out and filled in the matrix through the analysis on the dependent operations on data

Table 2. Change cost and coordination cost of service components and the overall system

Service components	Change cost (%)	Coordination cost
ServiceA1	60	229
ServiceA2	9	18
ServiceA3	29	123
ServiceA4	9	18
ServiceA5	9	18
ServiceA6	20	44
ServiceB1	31	101
ServiceB2	23	99
ServiceC1	9	12
ServiceC2	3	12
ServiceC3	26	181
ServiceD1	49	197
ServiceD2	26	84
ServiceD3	37	152
ServiceD4	46	196
ServiceD5	29	99
ServiceD6	26	68
ServiceE1	6	90
ServiceE2	6	42
ServiceE3	6	42
ServiceE4	6	42
ServiceE5	54	358
ServiceE6	11	108
ServiceE7	46	315
ServiceE8	6	406
ServiceE9	37	279
ServiceE10	20	126
ServiceE11	17	108
ServiceE12	17	108
ServiceE13	20	126
ServiceE14	6	36
ServiceE15	46	334
ServiceE16	6	36
ServiceE17	14	90
ServiceE18	14	108
Overall	24	4405

objects based on the "information hiding" principle. It can be seen from this figure that *ServiceA1* of *ModuleA* depends on *ServiceA2, A3, A4, A5* and *A6* of *ModuleA*, *ServiceB1*, *B2* of *ModuleB*, *ServiceC3* of *ModuleC*, *ServiceD1*, *D3*, *D4* and *D5* of *ModuleD*, and *ServiceE5*, *E7*, *E8*, *E9* and *E15* of *ModuleE*. According to the definitions of two metrics presented in section 2.2, change costs and coordination costs of the overall SOA application and each service component in this application were acquired correspondingly in Table 2. The change cost of the overall SOA application is 24% and the coordination cost is 4405. We assigned the value "1" to the *cost_dep* and *cost_cs* just for the simplicity of the calculation. Although we do not have another candidate design of the subject system as a counterpart to validate the metrics for the overall design, the following analysis based on each service component does validate the metrics and present the potential spaces where the measurement of design could help for the development and maintenance.

As introduced above, *ModuleA* includes 6 service components which implement 6 services. Fig. 4 shows the development data of each service component in *ModuleA* acquired from the project's CVS database, where Axis-X indicates the working days passed while the project progresses and Axis-Y indicates the working efforts consumed until a particular working day. We simply use the lines of code (LOC) to denote the working efforts since the subject system of our experimental study was at its initial stage and the complexity of components does not affect much on working efforts. As a result, in Fig. 4, each service component in *ModuleA* has a corresponding pillar when its implementation source code was checked in the CVS database. The height of a pillar means how many lines of code have been added, deleted or modified since the beginning rather than the lines of code of current source files checked in for each service component.

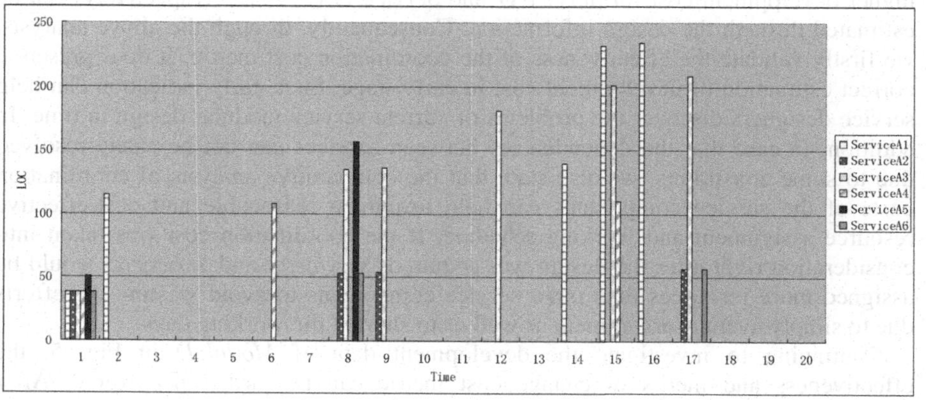

Fig. 4. Development data of ModuleA acquired from CVS

Combining the spent working days and working efforts we can acquire the cognition of the development cost and the schedule of each service component in *ModuleA*. As we can see that the implementations of all service components in *ModuleA* began at the same day. Except *ServiceA1* and *ServiceA3*, the other service

Table 3. Sizes of service components in ModuleA

Services in ModuleA	Size (LOC)
ServiceA1	213
ServiceA2	54
ServiceA3	134
ServiceA4	110
ServiceA5	157
ServiceA6	54

components in *ModuleA* finished the initial versions in 9 days. The working efforts on *ServiceA4* at the 15th day as well as *ServiceA2* and *ServiceA6* at the 17th day were due to fixing the bugs discovered through the integration testing. *ServiceA1* and *ServiceA3* spent 6 more days than others to accomplish their initial versions at the 15th day. Although the size of *ServiceA1* (the lines of code of the finally implemented service component) is larger than other service components as shown in Table 3, the differentiation at such order of magnitude is not a critical factor for the additional six working days. Moreover, the size of *ServiceA3* is even less than *ServiceA5*, but it still costs more. Actually, such situation was caused by the average assignment of resources for each service component since the different working efforts were not carefully taken into considered for the schedule. However, as we can see from the acquired metrics of service components in *ModuleA* in Table 2, due to *ServiceA1* and *ServiceA3* hold the dependencies to the service components in all the other modules (which can be seen in Fig. 3), the implementation of *ServiceA1* and *ServiceA3* has to coordinate with the implementation of other service components and therefore the higher development cost for *ServiceA1* and *ServiceA3* (229, 123 respectively) can be estimated through the design information. Consequently, through the above analysis, we firstly validate the effectiveness of the coordination cost metric. It does present a correct estimation of development cost in early stage. Such early indication can help service designers discover the problems of current service modular design in time. In addition, in case that the dependencies between services can not be easily resolved due to some constraints, we also state that the comparative analysis of coordination costs of the service components can help acquire a reasonable and cost-effective resource assignment and working schedule. If the coordination cost was taken into consideration right after the design was acquired, *ServiceA1* and *ServiceA3* would be assigned more resources than other service components to avoid wasting the efforts due to simply average assignment as well as to shorten the working days.

Continuing to investigate the development data of *ModuleD* in Fig. 5, the effectiveness and merits of change cost metric can be further discovered. After finishing the first version of *ModuleD* (at the 17th working day), there was a change request to *ServiceD4* from customers. However, the individual developers did not know that *ServiceD1* and *ServiceD3* depend on *ServiceD4* and the change was performed to *ServiceD4* only at first. The modifications on *ServiceD1* and *D3* were only accomplished two days later triggered by the testing. From the acquired change cost metric in Table 2, potential change impacts are estimated for each service component. Although current project data does not provide the proof to validate this metric through comparing the costs due to changes on two different service

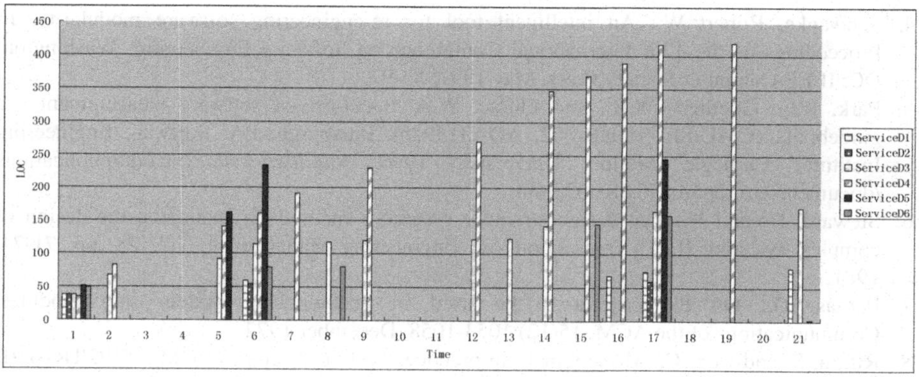

Fig. 5. Development data of ModuleD acquired from CVS

components, change cost metric does provide a quantitative and conservative estimate for potentially affected service components according to the case of a change request to *ServiceD1*. It is obvious that such metric is an effective aid for the maintenance activities. Besides, we can further acquire the specific service components potentially affected through checking the service design structure and therefore provide the effective guidance for specific change requests to service components.

4 Summary

In this paper, we present that measurement of the designs for SOA applications can evaluate the quality of modularity and facilitate the development and maintenance of SOA applications with high efficiency. We performed an experimental study on an ongoing SOA project. In this study, we employed two metrics (change cost and coordination cost) on the design of this project to acquire judgments and make estimations. The project data in CVS was retrieved to reflect the genuine situations of its implementation, integration and testing. The analysis on these data shows that adopting the design metrics in early stage of SOA projects may avoid wasting efforts and delaying the schedule as well as acquire a deep grasp and effective control on the issues in following phases.

References

1. Bohmann, T. and Loser, K.U.: Towards a service agility assessment - Modeling the composition and coupling of modular business services. In Proceedings of the 7th IEEE International Conference on E-Commerce Technology Workshops, 2005: 140-148.
2. Brocke, J. and Lindner, M.A.: Service portfolio measurement: a framework for evaluating the financial consequences of out-tasking decisions. In Proceedings of 2nd International Conference on Service-Oriented Computing, November 15-19, 2004: 203-211.
3. MacCormack, A., Rusnak, J. and Baldwin, C.: Exploring the structure of complex software designs: an empirical study of open source and proprietary code. Harvard Business School Working Paper, Number 05-016, 2004.

4. Schwanke, Robert W.: An intelligent tool for re-engineering software modularity. In Proceedings of the 13th International Conference on Software Engineering. Washington, DC: IEEE Computer Society Press, May 1991: 83-92.
5. Park, R.E., Goethert, W.B., and Florac, W.A.: Goal-driven software measurement - a guidebook. (CMU/SEI-96-HB-002, ADA313946). Pittsburgh, PA: Software Engineering Institute, Carnegie Mellon University, 1996. http://www.sei.cmu.edu/publications /documents/96.reports/96.hb.002.html
6. Steward, Donald V.: The design structure system: a method for managing the design of complex systems. IEEE Transactions on Engineering Management, vol. 28, pp. 71-74, 1981.
7. Parnas, D.: On the criteria to be used in decomposing system into modules. Communications of the ACM, 15(12):1053-1058, December 1972.
8. Rifkin, S. and Cox, C.: Measurement in practice. Technical report of CMU SEI, TR16.91, July, 1991.

Dynamic Service Oriented Architectures Through Semantic Technology

Suzette Stoutenburg[1], Leo Obrst[2], Deborah Nichols[2], Ken Samuel[2], and Paul Franklin[1]

[1] The MITRE Corporation, 1155 Academy Park Loop
Colorado Springs, Colorado 80910
[2] The MITRE Corporation, 7515 Colshire Drive
McLean, Virginia 22102
{suzette, lobrst, dlnichols, samuel, pfranklin}@mitre.org

Abstract. The behavior of Department of Defense (DoD) Command and Control (C2) services is typically embedded in executable code, providing static functionality that is difficult to change. As the complexity and tempo of world events increase, C2 systems must move to a new paradigm that supports the ability to dynamically modify service behavior in complex, changing environments. Separation of service behavior from executable code provides the foundation for dynamic system behavior and agile response to real-time events. In this paper we show how semantic rule technology can be applied to express service behavior in *data*, thus enabling a *dynamic* service oriented architecture.

Keywords: Dynamic Service Oriented Architectures, Integrated ontology and rules, Knowledge Management, Semantic rules, Web services.

1 Introduction

In this paper, we describe an implementation that applies a proposed standard rule language with ontologies to construct dynamic net-centric web services. We successfully show that rules for service behavior can be expressed in XML-based languages with formal semantics. This greatly simplifies the service code and allows rules for behavior to be changed dynamically with no code modifications, thus achieving an agile service architecture.

We modeled a military convoy traveling through an unsecured area under changing conditions. The World Wide Web Consortium (W3C) standard Web Ontology Language (OWL) [1] was used to describe the battlespace domain and the proposed W3C Semantic Web Rule Language (SWRL) [2] was used to capture recommended operating procedures for convoys in theater. We translated the ontologies and rules into a logical programming language to produce an integrated knowledge base that derives alerts and recommendations for the convoy commander. In our experiment, two sets of rules were used: one set models rules of engagement for favorable visibility conditions on the battlefield, and the other models rules of engagement for poor visibility conditions. When a dynamic event, such as an unexpected sandstorm,

A. Dan and W. Lamersdorf (Eds.): ICSOC 2006, LNCS 4294, pp. 581 – 590, 2006.

occurs, this causes the latter set of rules of engagement to be applied to the service to guide the convoy to safety. In this paper, we provide a description of our approach and outline the architectural options for constructing dynamic services. We briefly describe the semantic-based approach utilizing the ontologies and rules that we developed. We conclude with our findings and recommendations.

2 Use Case

To demonstrate the potential power of agile services, we selected a convoy support scenario for our use case. In this scenario, a convoy moves through enemy territory. As the convoy approaches potential threats, a web service consults an integrated knowledge base (consisting of ontologies and rules) to generate alerts and recommendations for action. These alerts and recommendations are provided to the convoy commander for decision support. The integrated knowledge bases can be switched dynamically, thus achieving instantaneous change in service behavior. In particular, we implemented an approach in which dynamic events, such as an unexpected sandstorm, automatically trigger the swapping of knowledge bases, thus effecting dynamic services. With this scenario, we demonstrate agility in a dynamic battlefield, a current real mission need, with application to mission challenges of the Army, Air Force, Joint Forces and others.

3 Implementation Overview

The high-level design of the application is shown in Figure 1. The components of the system include the following.

- Enterprise Service Bus (ESB)
- Google Earth[1] Client
- AMZI Prolog Logic Server[2]
- Knowledge Base
- Convoy Service
- Adapter
- Message Injector

We selected Mule[3] as the ESB solution to manage the interactions of the components in our solution. The ESB detects messages moving between components, including events that cause the swapping of knowledge bases. ESB technology also applies translations when appropriate, by using the XSLT capabilities of the Adapter.

We chose Google Earth as the client, since it offers seamless integration of multiple data sources via its Keyhole Markup Language (KML). We were able to show that structured data from heterogeneous sources can be translated to KML and easily rendered, thus offering the potential for dynamic, user-defined displays.

[1] http://earth.google.com/
[2] http://www.amzi.com/
[3] http://mule.codehaus.org/

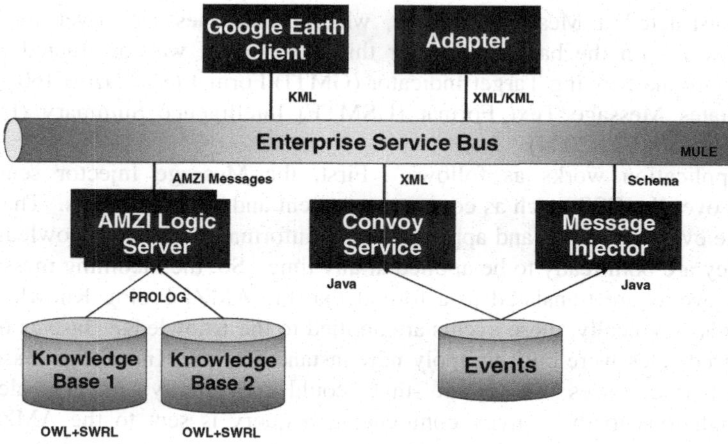

Fig. 1. High-Level Application Design

AMZI's Prolog Logic Server was selected as the platform on which to host the integrated ontologies and rule base. Prolog was selected because it is based on formal logic and therefore supports the notion of proof.

The Knowledge Base consists of integrated ontologies, rules and instances. Ontologies were constructed in the Web Ontology Language (OWL) and the rules in the Semantic Web Rule Language (SWRL). These were then translated to one Knowledge Base in Prolog. Two knowledge bases were modeled, each reflecting slightly different service behavior; that is, each knowledge base had different rules of engagement that are applied when queried by services.

We constructed the Convoy Service, a software service that detects events (message exchanges over the ESB), consults the knowledge base, and delivers appropriate alerts and recommendations to the convoy commander via Google Earth clients. Events can be object movement, changes in weather, changes in alert conditions, etc.

The service operates under a very basic set of instructions:

> ***"Something moved on the battlefield.***
> ***What does that mean for the convoy?"***

To determine the answer, the Convoy Service queries the integrated knowledge base to determine what new events mean to the convoy. So, the rules for behavior of the Convoy Service are in fact, expressed in data, thus allowing for agile response to real-time events. The Convoy Service also detects when the rules of behavior should change (based on message exchanges over the ESB) and triggers the swapping of rules on the AMZI Logic Server.

The Adapter comprises a set of XSLTs that are invoked by the ESB to translate messages to the appropriate format as they move between components. XSLTs have been developed to convert from OWL, SWRL and RuleML[4] to Prolog.

---

[4] http://ruleml.org

We constructed a Message Injector, which sends messages over the ESB to simulate events on the battlefield. For this experiment, we constructed messages using the Ground Moving Target Indicator (GMTI) Format (STANAG 4607) and the United States Message Text Format (USMTF) Intelligence Summary (INTSUM) message format (3/31/2004).

The application works as follows. First, the Message Injector sends event messages over the ESB, such as convoy movement and weather events. The Adapter detects the event messages and applies the new information to both knowledge bases, so that they are both ready to be applied at any time. So, the incoming messages that report on events are translated to a format that the AMZI Prolog Knowledge Base understands. Typically, these events are applied to the Knowledge Base as instances. Custom predicates were built to apply new instances to the Knowledge Base. If the Convoy Service sees an event that could potentially impact alerts and recommendations to the convoy commander, a query is sent to the AMZI Prolog Logic Server, requesting the latest alerts and recommendations. The Google Earth client then presents them to the convoy commander.

Certain events are recognized by the Convoy Service as events that should trigger a change in rule sets. For example, if a weather report is issued indicating reduced visibility on the battlefield, the Convoy Service stops querying the high-visibility knowledge base, switching to the low-visibility knowledge base. More details on the separation of rules from software are provided in section 5.

Note that this paper reflects work performed on a research project. The focus on the research was not to secure the system, but to show how semantic rule languages could be used to build agile services. If we do transition this capability to operations in the future, we would investigate use of the Gateway Security Model [3] in which all incoming requests would be verified through a single gateway before being processed on the ESB. Regarding scalability, note that Mule 1.2 uses the Staged Event Driven Architecture (SEDA) processing model [4] to increase the performance and throughput of events. Mule allows pooling of objects and providers to allow multiple threads to process events concurrently. Therefore, we believe that this overall application, while simplistic and focused on a particular research issue, can form the basis for a secure, scalable architecture in the future.

4 Architecture Options for Dynamic Services

There are a number of issues that must be considered when developing an integrated knowledge base to support dynamic service behavior. These include design decisions such as how to structure the rule bases (which impacts how to trigger and implement the swapping of rules), and whether to store instances in an ontology or a database.

One approach to structuring knowledge bases is to build fully separate knowledge bases designed to handle different environments or situations. For example, we chose to build two independent rule sets, one to handle favorable visibility on the battlefield and one to handle poor visibility on the battlefield. If this approach is used, triggers to invoke the applicable knowledge base could be handled by services or through a set of meta-rules in the knowledge base, as shown in Figures 2 and 3 respectively.

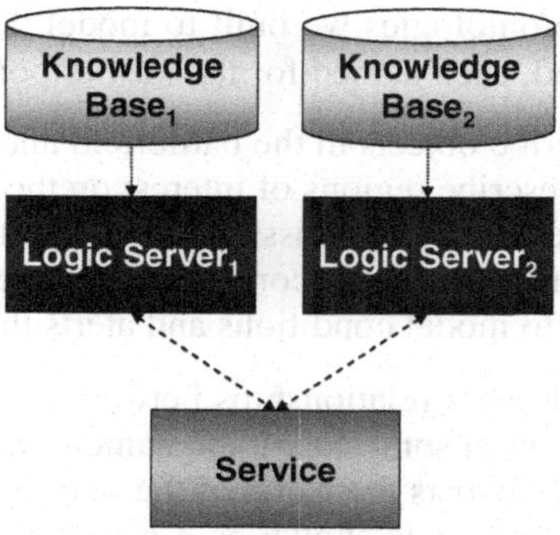

Fig. 2. Option for Dynamic Services: Service Triggers Knowledge Base Swap

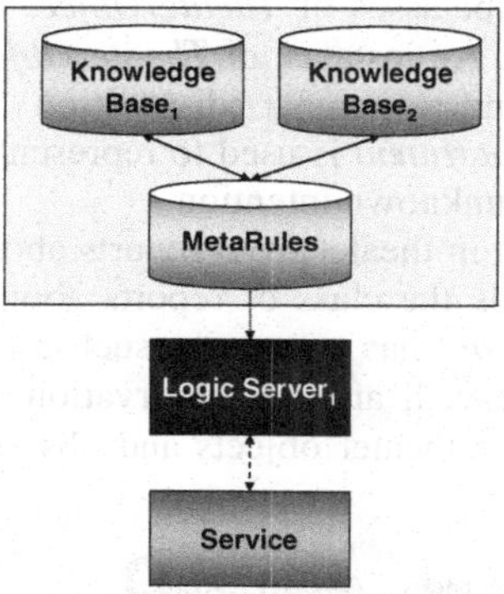

Fig. 3. Option for Dynamic Services: Meta-rules Trigger Knowledge Base Swap

We selected the former case to simplify the rule set necessary to model the use case. This approach also reduces the risk of unintended interactions of rules. By instantiating a different logic server for each rule set, each knowledge base is ready to be swapped at any time, allowing us to change service behavior instantly, whenever a real-time event is detected. The disadvantage of this approach, however, is that the burden of detection is on the service, which reduces agility. Applying meta-rules, on the other hand, offers more flexibility, since these are expressed in data and can therefore be changed without change in code.

Another design decision involves whether to store instances in a database or ontology. We chose to store instances in the ontology to simplify the overall approach. However, since we planned to swap between logic servers in real-time, we found we had to keep both knowledge bases updated with instance information and synchronized at all times. This didn't pose any performance problems and in fact, worked well in the AMZI environment. Finally, if instances are stored in a database, then tools for linking database tables to ontological concepts must be used.

5 Ontologies

To understand how we separated rules from service behavior, it is necessary to have a basic understanding of the ontologies we built to model the use case. The following ontologies were constructed, each named for its most important class.

- TheaterObject – to describe objects in the battlefield and reports about them.
- RegionOfInterest – to describe regions of interest on the battlefield.
- Convoy –to describe the convoy, its mission, components, etc.
- ConvoyRoute – to describe routes the convoy might take.
- ConditionsAndAlerts – to model conditions and alerts that affect the convoy.

Figure 4 shows the high level relationships between the five major ontologies and their key concepts. Note that in some cases, the name of an ontology is also the name of a class. For example, *Convoy* is the name of the ontology but it is also the name of a class in the ontology. Thus, it is shown as a subclass of *MilitaryUnit*. This was done to show the high level structure of the ontology set.

The heart of the model is the class *TheaterObject*, representing objects in theater (i.e., on the battlefield.) Subclasses of *TheaterObject* include *MilitaryUnit*, *Sniper*, *RoadObstacle*, and *Facility*. An instance of *TheaterObject* has a location, and it may have a speed, heading, and a combat disposition (*combatIntent*), among other features. The property *combatIntent* is used to represent whether an object in theater is friendly, hostile or has an unknown intention.

To distinguish the objects in theater from reports about them, we created the class *ObservationArtifact*, which is the class of reports about objects in the theater. An instance of *ObservationArtifact* has properties such as the time and location of the observation, the object observed, and the observation source and/or platform. We found the distinction between theater objects and observations to be very important,

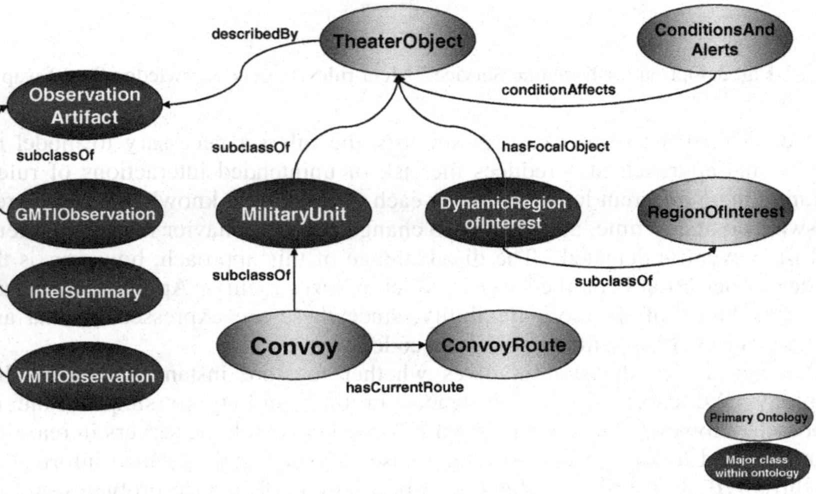

Fig. 4. Ontology Overview

as it allows inferencing over multiple reports about the same object in theater. This provided the foundation for using rules to fuse information from multiple sources. The distinction required that we build rules to transfer, or derive, property values from an instance of *ObservationArtifact* to a corresponding instance of *TheaterObject*. We modeled subclasses of *ObservationArtifact*, including *GMTIObservation* and *IntelSummary*, based on the message formats referenced above.

The *RegionOfInterest* (ROI) ontology models the class of geospatial areas of special interest surrounding theater objects. Each *TheaterObject* is the focal object of a *DynamicROI*, since most theater objects move on the battlefield. An ROI is centered on the position of its focal object. An ROI has shape, dimensions and area, which may depend on the type of threat or interest. For example, ROIs are used to define a "safety zone" around a convoy which must not be violated by hostile or suspicious objects. Also, ROIs are used to define the area around a reported hostile track that delineates the potential strike area of the threat. Currently, the rules can handle any ROI shape, but we are limited by the Google Earth visualization client to simply circles.

The *Convoy* ontology models the class of organized friendly forces moving on the ground. This ontology allows specification of the mission, components and personnel associated with a convoy. *Convoy* is a subclass of *TheaterObject*. The *ConvoyRoute* ontology provides a representation of possible paths of a convoy, including critical points on primary and alternate routes. Recommended routes can change based on application of rules.

The *ConditionsAndAlerts* ontology provides a description of situations on the battlefield based on aggregations of events and actions of theater objects. As the knowledge base grows, a set of conditions is constructed based on events on the battlefield, which can result in alerts and recommendations to friendly forces. Conditions, alerts and recommendations are generated through the application of rules.

6 Rules

Rules were used to specify the behavior of the Convoy Service by incrementally constructing a knowledge base of the situation on the battlefield from which alerts and recommendations could be derived and made available to the convoy commander. To that end, rules were applied in numerous ways. First, we used rules to construct a conceptualization of the battlespace for enhanced situational awareness. This was done in two major ways. First, rules were used to transfer the characteristics of *ObservationArtifacts* to *TheaterObjects*. If a location, speed, combatIntent, etc., are reported by (or inferable from) an observation, those characteristics must be transferred to the observed object, as shown in Example Rule 1 below. Note that this design positions the model to reason over multiple messages in the future, a potential mechanism for sensor fusion.

Example Rule 1.

If there is a GMTI report about a mover,
then the velocity of the mover is assigned the velocity in the GTMI report.

The second way the battlespace was conceptually constructed using rules was to establish regions of interest (ROIs) around each theater object and derive characteristics about those ROIs. For example, if the object is hostile, then we classify its ROI as an *AreaOfRedForceActivity*. See Example Rules 2 and 3 below. This also builds the basis for future enhancements, such as defining the ROI radius size based on the capability of the threat. For example, a dirty bomb would result in a much wider ROI than a sniper.

Example Rule 2.

If there is a TheaterObject,
then there exists a RegionOfInterest that surrounds that object.

Example Rule 3.

If the TheaterObject is hostile,
then classify its RegionOfInterest as anAreaOfRedForceActivity.

Rules were also used to synthesize information from multiple sources, for greater situational awareness. For example, the convoy's "safety zone," derived from GMTI tracking, is correlated with threat locations reported by human intelligence, allowing convoy commanders to be alerted.

Example Rule 4.

If an AreaOfThreatActivity intersects with the convoy's RegionOfInterest,
then alert the convoy commander of the threat.

Rules are also used for logical processing of real-time events. Specifically, as updated information modifies the picture of the battlespace, rules are used to derive new knowledge relevant to the convoy's safety. Example Rule 5 ensures that a new intel report of a threat (such as a mortar emplacement) along the planned convoy route will result in that route being flagged as unsafe.

Example Rule 5.

If a threat has a range that intersects with planned convoy route,
then classify that route as unsafe.

Accumulated events result in a build-up of conditions that may lead to alerts and recommendations to the convoy. Examples are provided below.

Example Rule 6.

If a convoy's planned route is unsafe, then recommend change of route.

Example Rule 7.

If threat is approaching from behind,
then recommend that convoy proceed at maximum speed.

Note that there are currently no good tools to detect inconsistences in a knowledge base of ontologies and rules expressed in W3C standards. Thus, inconsistency in the knowledge base is a risk.

7 Convoy Service Design

The design of the Convoy Service is very simple. The service basically monitors the ESB for messages that provide information about events on the battlefield. When the service detects that a relevant event has occurred that may impact the convoy, the service queries the knowledge base to determine if new alerts and recommendations may have been generated by the new event. The query is a semantic one, using the ontologies and rules modeled in the integrated knowledge base. For example, consider the case in which a track of unknown intent is moving on the battlefield. The Convoy Service detects the event and queries the knowledge base, basically querying for the concept of "unknown and hostile movers" and "alerts and conditions". The data source of instances of these concepts does not matter, since the query is semantic; that is, over the *concepts* not the tables. The query triggers a set of rules to fire, including rules to apply the new position of the unknown mover, determine the size and location of the region of interest around that mover, and whether or not the mover is now within proximity of the convoy. If the unknown mover is within proximity, additional rules fire to construct conditions that lead to the generation of alerts and conditions.

The Convoy Service also controlled which Logic Server was consulted when battlefield events were detected. Recall that we implemented two sets of rules; one was used to model rules of engagement for favorable visibility conditions and the other set modeled rules of engagement for poor visibility conditions. When the Convoy Service detected particular weather events, in particular, an unexpected sandstorm, the service would switch logic servers. Subsequent queries would be launched to the logic server instantiated with the more conservative (poor visibility) rule set.

8 Findings and Conclusions

First, we found that expressing service behavior in structured data is a feasible solution for constructing dynamic services. By separating the rules from the executable code, and expressing service behavior in *data*, we show that dynamic services can be constructed. So, given a real time event, we can swap rules sets, thus delivering services that can be agile in real time. We were able to design a generic set of instructions for the service (i.e., "Something moved on the battlefield, what does that mean for the convoy?) then express the particular behaviors (which alerts and recommendations apply?) in data, that is, in SWRL. We were able to build a demonstration that supported sub second response time, rendering alerts and recommendations to the Google Earth client.

We believe that a standard XML-based language with formal semantics, such as SWRL, is the best choice for expressing service behavior since this allows the rules to be "understandable" by machines, building the foundation for a Machine-to-Machine Enterprise. Also, since the languages are established or proposed standards, they are more likely to be used widely. OWL, in particular, is *inherently extensible, since it offers a standard way of expressing* meaning, So, as other ontologies and rule sets are developed using standards, they can potentially be linked and reused for a richer knowledge model. We also found that ontologies are useful to bridge the "dialects" of each data source, allowing querying over *concepts*, thus freeing the application from having to understand the many ways of representing an event.

Regarding the richness of the W3C semantic languages, we found that OWL is expressive and meets the majority of identified DoD requirements. However, OWL should be extended to support uncertainty, *n*-ary predicates (n > 2) and individual-denoting functions. We found that neither SWRL (nor RuleML) supports some of the more important DoD requirements identified in this use case, such as reasoning with uncertainty, non-monotonic reasoning, assertion of the existence of new instances, triggers to execute external code, and *n*-ary predicates. Extensions to these languages will be proposed to support the DoD.

We found that the state of tools for expressing rules in W3C proposed standards are immature or non-existent. We believe that an integrated framework of tools and capabilities is needed to support dynamic service development, particularly in the DoD. First, we need tools to allow the expression of semantic rules that support the emerging W3C standards. Further, an integrated approach to specifying ontologies and rules is needed. For example, we would like to see drop down lists of imported OWL classes and properties while rules are being built, similar to how XML Spy and other tools offer drop down lists of valid XML schema entries. We would also like to see integrated validation of ontologies and rules when rules refer to ontologies or data sources, and in particular, inconsistency detection. The standard framework should include tools for specification, validation, translation, execution and debugging. The GUI should hide the complexity of rule constructs. Most importantly, integrated reasoning engines to operate over ontologies and rules, with knowledge compilation for performance, are required.

References

[1] McGuinness, Deborah L; Frank van Harmelen. *Web Ontology Language (OWL)*, W3C Recommendation, 10 February, 2004. http://www.w3.org/TR/owl-features/

[2] Horrocks,Ian. Peter F. Patel-Schneider; Harold Boley; Said Tabet; Benjamin Grosof; Mike Dean. *SWRL: A Semantic Web Rule Language Combining OWL and RuleML.* W3C Member Submission, 21 May, 2004. http://www.w3.org/Submission/SWRL/

[3] Goldstein, T. *The Gateway Security Model in the Java Electronic Commerce Framework.* JavasSoft, November 1996.

[4] Welsh, Matt; David Culler; Eric Brewer. *SEDA: An Architecture for Well Conditioned, Scalable Internet Services.* 18th Symposium on Operating System Principles, Banff, Canada, 21 October 2001.

A Service Oriented Architecture Supporting Data Interoperability for Payments Card Processing Systems

Joseph M. Bugajski[1], Robert L. Grossman[2], and Steve Vejcik[2]

[1] Visa International, P.O. Box 8999, Foster City, CA 94128
[2] Open Data Group, 400 Lathrop Ave, Suite 90, River Forest IL 60305
JBugajsk@visa.com, rlg1@opendatagroup.com, vejcik@opendatagroup.com

Abstract. As the size of an organization grows, so does the tension between a centralized system for the management of data, metadata, derived data, and business intelligence and a distributed system. With a centralized system, it is easier to maintain the consistency, accuracy, and timeliness of data. On the other hand with a distributed system, different units and divisions can more easily customize systems and more quickly introduce new products and services. By data interoperability, we mean the ability of a distributed organization to work with distributed data consistently, accurately and in a timely fashion. In this paper, we introduce a service oriented approach to analytics and describe how this is used to measure and to monitor data interoperability.

Keywords: data quality, data interoperability, service oriented architectures for analytics, payments card processing systems.

1 Introduction

VisaNet is the largest private payment data network in the world. The annual total payment volume on VisaNet recently exceeds USD $4 trillion. The network can handle about 10,000 payment messages per second. It supports every payment card brand including approximately 1.0 billion Visa cards. It permits card holders to make secure payments in 120 countries and most currencies through over 20 million businesses, who operate over 100 million point-of-sales acceptance devices. Above all, member banks that own Visa require that all the transactions be completed among all the member banks error free and with extremely high system reliability.

The systems that comprise VisaNet were, until recently, controlled by one information technology division. That division assured data interoperability. They enforced a rule that permitted only one source for defining and modifying payment transaction record format and semantic definitions. The computing and network infrastructure ran on IBM TPF and IBM MVS mainframe computers. Each mainframe ran an identical code base in one of several processing centers strategically situated around the world. Hence, data interoperability was assured because all data in VisaNet, and all processes that operated on data, were always the same.

A. Dan and W. Lamersdorf (Eds.): ICSOC 2006, LNCS 4294, pp. 591 – 600, 2006.

The current guaranteed "uniformity" system environment for data interoperability comes at a not insignificant price with respect to time to market capability and cost effectiveness for faster growing economies; e.g., the Asia Pacific and Latin American regions. Visa determined that the old model for interoperability had to change to meet the demands of its member banks for quicker market entry for product modification and entirely new types of payment products.

In this paper, we describe an approach to measuring and monitoring data interoperability using large numbers of baseline models that are each individually estimated. These are examples of what, in the context of data interoperability, we call Key Interoperability Indicators or KIIs. The first contribution of this paper is the introduction of baseline models as an effective procedure for measuring and monitoring data interoperability.

The second contribution of this paper is the introduction of a service oriented architecture for computing the analytics required for estimating, updating, and scoring using these baseline models.

Section 2 contains background and related work. Section 3 discusses data interoperability and baseline models. Section 4 describes a service oriented architecture supporting baseline models. Section 5 describes a deployed application based upon a service oriented architecture for analytical models and which is scalable enough to support millions of baseline models.

2 Background and Related Work

Loosely speaking, the interoperability of data and services means that data and services can be defined and used independently of the application, programming language, operating system, or computing platform which implements them. Interoperability has a long history in computing. Major phases include: Electronic Data Interchange, object models, virtual machines, and web services, which we now describe briefly.

Electronic Data Interchange (EDI). EDI introduced a standard syntax and a standard set of messages for various common business transactions. EDI began by introducing standard formats for purchase orders, invoices, and bills of lading so that these could be processed without human intervention. In other words, EDI approached interoperability by requiring all applications using purchase orders to use a standard structured format. Each different business document had its own structured format.

Object Models. With the introduction of object models, interfaces for both data and methods became formalized. A wide variety of object models have been introduced, including Microsoft's COM and DCOM, Sun Microsystems Java Beans and Enterprise Java Beans, and the Object Management Group's (OMG) Object and Component Models. OMG's Common Object Request Broker Architecture or CORBA is an architecture providing interoperability for objects across different languages, operating systems, and platforms. For more details, see [4].

Virtual Machines. Java popularized the idea of supporting interoperability by mapping a language to an intermediate format (byte code) which could be executed on any machine which had an interpreter for byte code (virtual machine). In this way, the same code could be executed on different operating systems and platforms. Note though that the same language (Java) must be used.

Service Oriented Architectures. More recently, web services and service oriented architectures have popularized the use of XML to define data and message formats. In particular the Web Services Description Language or WSDL provides a way to define services that can be bound to different programming languages (e.g. Java, Perl, C/C++) and protocols (http, smtp, etc.)

Our approach to data interoperability is based upon a service oriented architecture that is specifically designed to support statistical and other analytical models, as well as various services employing them.

3 Data Interoperability

Not all data in a complex, distributed system needs to be interoperable. In this section, we distinguish between data that must be interoperable, which we call global data, and other data, which we call local data.

Our approach is based upon introducing two new primitive concepts: a new class of data called *global data* and a new class of services called *global services*. Data that is not global and services that are not global are called *local*. Not all data and not all services are expected to be global; rather, in general data and services are local and only when they need to interoperate across the enterprise are then required to be global. Global data and global services are designed so that different applications storing, accessing, querying or updating global data using global services can easily interoperate.

In our approach, the interoperability of global data is measured using statistical models called Key Interoperability Indicators or KIIs. In the remainder of this section, we define global data and global services, as is usual for service based architectures.

3.1 Global Data

Global data is any data with the following properties:

- The schema is defined using UML® or XML.
- Data is accompanied by XML based metadata.
- Associated metadata must be accessible through a metadata repository and discoverable through discovery services.
- Associated metadata must also specify one or more access mechanisms. Access mechanisms include service-based mechanisms, message-oriented mechanisms, or data protocol based mechanisms.
- Permitted values for individual field elements are also stored using XML and corresponding discovery services

3.2 Global Services

Global services are any services or functions with the following properties:

- Global services operate on data through interfaces. By inspecting the interface, a service can specify the operation it wants to perform and marshal the arguments it needs to send. Interfaces are independent of programming languages; on the other hand, to be useful, interfaces, such as J2EE or the Web Service's Web Service Description Language (WSDL), have mappings or bindings to common programming languages, such as C, C++, Java, Python, Perl, etc.
- Global services transport data using an agreed upon wire protocol. For example, web service based global services use the protocol specified in the WSDL corresponding to the service.
- Global services are registered. For example, web services may be discovered through Universal Description, Discovery & Integration (UDDI) services.
- Global services follow from UML descriptions of requisite functionality to remove details concerning implementation in the matter of the Model Driven Architecture (MDA®) and Meta-Object Facility (MOF®), both defined by the Object Management Group (OMG)[1].

Interoperability is achieved in several ways. First, separating interfaces from implementations facilitates interoperability. Services can inspect interfaces but not implementations. In this way, multiple languages can be bound to the same interface and implementations can be moved to a different platform. Second, by supporting multiple wire protocols, global services can improve their interoperability. Third, registration provides a mechanism for a client application to obtain sufficient metadata to ensure that it is bound to the correct global service.

3.3 Key Interoperability Indicators (KIIs)

Our approach to measuring the interoperability of global data is to measure and monitor a number of indicators of interoperability using statistical baseline models.

- We measure whether the values of fields and tuples of field values change unexpectedly as transactions move from one system to another.
- We measure whether the values of fields and tuples of field values change unexpectedly after changes and updates to the processing system and components of the processing system.
- We measure whether the values of fields and tuples of field values are correlated to various exception conditions in the system's processing of data.

These measurements are done by establishing baseline behavior with a statistical model, and then each day measuring changes and deviations from the expected baseline. Here is a simple example. A table of counts characterizing certain behavior in a specified reference baseline period can be measured. Counts during an observation period can then be computed and a test used to determine whether a

[1] UML, MDA, MOF and OMG are registered trademarks of the Object Management Group, Inc.

difference in counts is statistically significant. If so, an alert can be generated, and used as a basis by subject matter experts for further investigation.

Value	%
00	76.94
01	21.60
02	0.99
03	0.27
04	0.20
Total	100.00

Value	%
00	76.94
01	20.67
02	0.90
03	0.25
04	1.24
Total	100.00

Table 1. The distribution on the left is the baseline distribution. The distribution on the right is the observed distribution. In this example, the value 04 is over 6x more likely in the observed distribution, although the two dominant values 00 and 01 still account for over 97% of the mass of the distribution. This example is from [1].

4 A Service Based Architecture for Analytics

In the last section, we gave relatively standard definitions, from a service oriented architecture point of view, of types of data and services (global) that are designed to be the basis of data interoperability across an enterprise. In this section, we introduce a service based architecture for analytics based upon four types of services: services for preparing data, services for producing analytical models, services for scoring, and services for producing OLAP reports.

4.1 Services for Preparing Data

In practice, extracting, aggregating, and transforming data in various ways represents a significant fraction of the cost of developing complex enterprise applications. In addition, small differences in the transformations can result in the lack of interoperability of an application. For these reasons, our model singles out services for preparing or transforming data from one format to another. Data preparation and transformations are generally comprise much of the work of developing analytical models.

More formally, *derived data* is the result of applying global services implementing one or more of a class of predefined transformations. For our applications, we used the transformations defined by the Data Mining Group [2]. These include:

- Normalization: A normalization transformation maps values to numbers. The input can be continuous or discrete.
- Discretization: A discretization transformation maps continuous values to discrete values.
- Value mapping: A value mapping transformation maps discrete values to discrete values.
- Aggregation: An aggregation transformation summarizes or collects groups of values, for example by computing counts, sums, averages, counts by category

The Data Mining Group's Predictive Model Markup Language or PMML allows these types of data transformations to be defined in XML. Although these four types of transformations may seem rather restrictive, in practice, a surprisingly large class of transformations can be defined from these.

4.2 Services for Producing Models

In our service-oriented approach to analytical processes, services operate on data and derived data to produce rules, statistical models and data mining models, which we refer to collectively as analytics. See Figures 1 and 2.

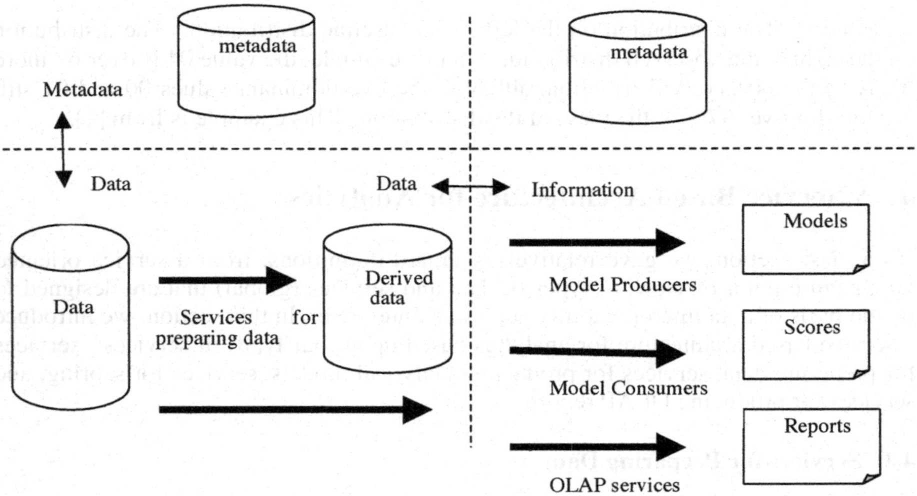

Fig. 1. Specialized global services applied to global data produces global derived data, which in turn produces global information such as analytical models, scores, and reports

The DMG's PMML markup language captures the most common analytical models [2]. These include statistical models for regression, clustering, tree based regression and classification models, association rules, neural networks, and baseline models. So, to be very concrete, analytical services for producing models can be thought of as operating on data and derived data to produce PMML models. Because of this, these types of analytical services are sometimes called Model Producers.

4.3 Services for Scoring

Given an analytical model described in PMML, a scoring service processes a stream of data, computes the required inputs to the analytical models, and then applies the analytical model to compute scores.

Sometimes scoring services are called Model Consumers since they consume analytical models to produce scores, in contrast to Model Producers, which consume data sets, viewed as learning sets, to produce analytical models.

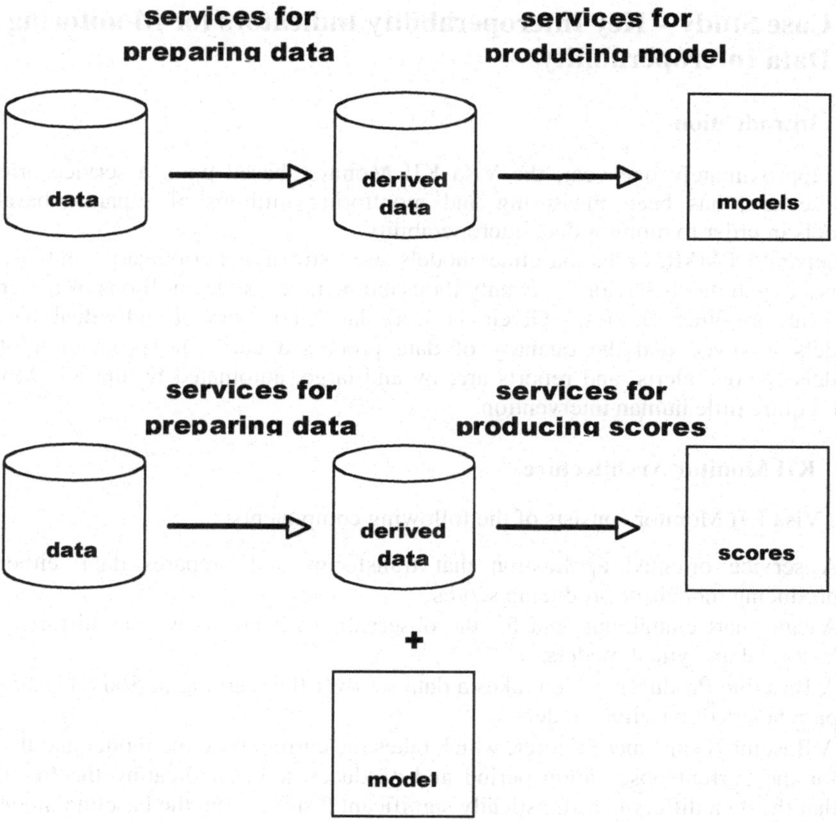

Fig. 2. This diagram illustrates three types of services used in our service oriented architecture for analytics: services for preparing data, services for producing models (model producers), and services for producing scores (model consumers)

One of the main advantages of a service oriented architecture for analytics, is that it is very common for the model producers and consumers to be deployed on different systems, with quite different requirements. For example, in the case study described in Section 5 below, the model producer can be deployed on several systems, while the model consumer must run on an operational system with very stringent security requirements.

For many applications, including the application described in Section 5 below, these scores are then post-processed using various rules to produce reports and alerts.

4.4 Services for Reports

In the same way, although outside of the scope of this paper, one can define OLAP services as services that operate on global data and global derived data to produce OLAP reports.

5 Case Study – Key Interoperability Indicators for Monitoring Data Interoperability

5.1 Introduction

For approximately one year, the Visa KII Monitor, based upon a service oriented architecture, has been measuring and monitoring millions of separate baselines models in order to monitor data interoperability.

Separate PMML-based baseline models are estimated periodically and used to monitor each day behavior for twenty thousand member banks, millions of merchants and various other entities. Given the very large numbers of individual baseline models involved and the quantity of data processed each, the production of the models, scores, alerts, and reports are, by and large, automated by the KII Monitor and require little human intervention.

5.2 KII Monitor Architecture

The Visa KII Monitor consists of the following components:

- A service oriented application that transforms and prepares data, either for producing models or producing scores.
- A data mart containing data for the observation period, as well as historical and historical analytical models.
- A Baseline Producer, which takes a data set over the learning period and estimates parameters of baseline models.
- A Baseline Consumer / Scorer, which takes the current baseline model and the data for the current observation period and produces scores indicating the likelihood that the data differs in a statistically significant fashion from the baseline model.
- A service oriented application that produces alerts and reports by analyzing the scores produced by the Baseline Consumer and applying certain rules.

5.3 Baseline Models

The Visa KII Monitor measures a large number of different baselines, including the following.

- The KII Monitor measures whether the values of payment fields change in unexpected manners as transactions move from one system to another.
- The KII Monitor measures whether the values of payment fields change in unexpected manners after changes and updates to the processing system and components of the processing system.
- The KII Monitor measures whether the values of payment fields are correlated to declines and other exceptions to the normal processing of transactions.

Separate baselines are computed for each member bank, and for merchant, and for various other entities. This results in millions of individual baselines being computed and monitored.

5.4 KII Alerts and Reporting

Here is an overview of the basic steps that the KII Monitor uses to generate alerts and reports.

First, parameters used for segmenting baseline models are selected. These include the time period, the region, the specific payment field values being monitored, and the various logical entities, such as banks, merchants, etc. For each separate segment, a baseline model is estimated and periodically updated.

Using the baseline model, during each observation period, usually a day or a week, the following steps are performed.

1. Scores that represent statistically significant deviations from baselines are generated by the Baseline Consumer / Scorer.
2. The approximate business value for the scenario associated with the baseline is estimated. If the business value is above a threshold, a report containing one or more alerts is generated.
3. The report is passed to a subject matter expert for investigation, and, if appropriate, for remediation.
4. The scenarios are monitored for future compliance.

5.5 Standards

The Visa KII Monitor described in this section was one of the motivating examples for a proposal for baseline models that is currently under consideration by the Predictive Model Markup Language Working Group of the Data Mining Group [3] for inclusion in PMML version 3.2.

6 Summary and Conclusion

In this paper, we have described how Visa used service oriented architecture to measure and monitor payment data interoperability. The interoperability of payment data has emerged as a key requirement as Visa introduces its distributed computing environment where six operating regions have more local control of their computing environments.

Data interoperability was defined by introducing the concepts of global data and global services, which can be defined relatively easily using the standard concepts of a service oriented architecture.

In this paper, we used baseline models to measure data interoperability and a service oriented analytics architecture to produce baseline models, as well as alerts and reports based upon them.

Working with the KII Monitor during the past year has taught us several lessons concerning data interoperability and the implementation of a service oriented architecture for analytics:

1. Baseline models are effective for uncovering certain important data interoperability and data quality problems for complex, distributed systems, such as the payments card processing system described above.

2. An important practical consideration when using baseline models for monitoring data interoperability is to select a sufficient number of segments and appropriate threshold levels so that the number of alerts produced have business meaning and relevance, but not so many different segments that so many alerts are produced that they are not manageable.
3. An important design decision for the project was to use the Predictive Model Markup Language (PMML) to represent baseline models.
4. Once PMML was chosen, it was natural to design the system using services for preparing data (using PMML-defined transformations), services for producing PMML models, PMML-based services for scorings, and services for producing alerts and reports.

For the past year, this service oriented architecture for analytics has provided a solid foundation for the weekly alerts that are produced by the KII Monitor.

References

1. Joseph Bugajski, Robert Grossman, Eric Sumner, Tao Zhang, A Methodology for Establishing Information Quality Baselines for Complex, Distributed Systems, 10th International Conference on Information Quality (ICIQ), 2005
2. Data Mining Group, retrieved from http://www.dmg.org on June 10, 2006.
3. Data Mining Group, PMML 3.1 - Baseline Model, RFC Version 5.2.7, retrieved from www.dmg.org on June 10, 2006.
4. Aniruddha Gokhale, Bharat Kumar, Arnaud Sahuguet, Reinventing the Wheel? CORBA vs. Web Services, The Eleventh International World Wide Web Conference, retrieved from http://www2002.org/CDROM/alternate/395/ on June 20, 2003.
5. Web Services Interoperability Organization, retrieved from http://ws-i.org/ on June 20, 2003.

Services-Oriented Computing in a Ubiquitous Computing Platform

Ji Hyun Kim[1], Won Il Lee[1], Jonathan Munson[2], and Young Ju Tak[1]

[1] IBM Ubiquitous Computing Laboratory, Seoul
[2] IBM T. J. Watson Research Center, Hawthorne, New York
jihkim@kr.ibm.com, wilee@kr.ibm.com, jpmunson@us.ibm.com, yjtak@kr.ibm.com

Abstract. Current telematics services platforms are tightly integrated, relatively fixed-function systems that manage the entire end-to-end infrastructure of devices, wireless communications, device management, subscriber management, and other functions. This closed nature prevents the infrastructure from being shared by other applications, which inhibits the development of new ubiquitous computing services that may not in themselves justify the cost of an entire end-to-end infrastructure. Services-oriented computing offers means to better expose the value of such infrastructures. We have developed a services-oriented, specification-based, ubiquitous computing platform called TOPAZ that abstracts common ubiquitous computing functions and makes them accessible to any application provider through Web-service interfaces. The nature of the TOPAZ services, as enabling long-running sessions between applications and remote clients, presents peculiar challenges to the generic issues of service metering and resource management. In this paper we describe these challenges and discuss the approach we have taken to them in TOPAZ. We first motivate and describe the TOPAZ application model and its service set. We then describe TOPAZ's resource management and service metering functions, and its three-party session model that forms the basis for them.

Keywords: Ubiquitous computing, telematics, resource management, service metering.

1 Introduction

The term "ubiquitous computing" is often applied to the applications that serve mobile users such as drivers, healthcare workers, and emergency personnel. They typically link personal or embedded devices with centrally operated services, using information (context) gathered from the devices. These applications are particularly popular in the automotive world, having millions users worldwide, and are now appearing in other domains as well. In the Republic of Korea, for example, several municipalities are launching ubiquitous computing initiatives under the collective name "u-City." The term encompasses a general vision where information systems for healthcare, education, and even private residences are responsive to collective contextual data, and these information systems have a pervasive presence in homes, streets, buildings, and public places such as convention centers.

A. Dan and W. Lamersdorf (Eds.): ICSOC 2006, LNCS 4294, pp. 601 – 612, 2006.

Meeting the diverse and changing needs of these user communities can be prohibitively expensive given the cost of developing, building, and operating ubiquitous computing systems serving millions of users, over wireless networks, using a diverse set of devices. Organizations that could provide valuable services to telematics or other ubiquitous-computing consumers face a high barrier of entry, because they must either integrate their service with an existing service provider, or provide their own end-to-end solution. As a result, business models that can be supported in this kind of ecosystem are limited.

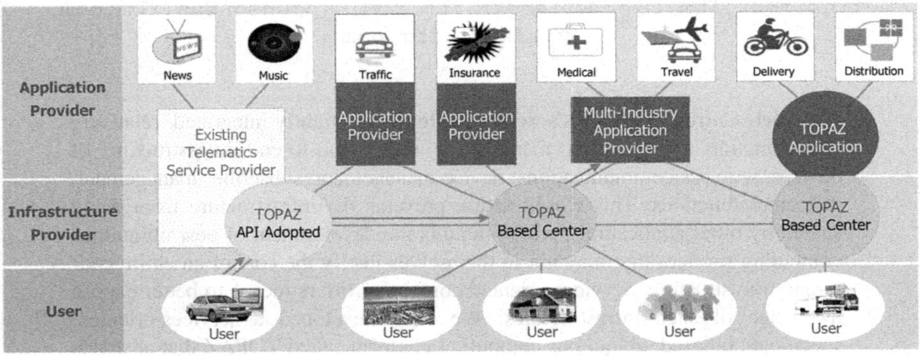

Fig. 1. The role of TOPAZ in the ubiquitous computing applications marketplace

We envision a marketplace in which application providers are able to easily compete for the business of users and user communities. They would be able to inexpensively develop, operate, and maintain the applications, and they would be able to quickly make them available to end users. In this paper we describe a ubiquitous computing framework named TOPAZ that we designed to enable this kind of marketplace. TOPAZ is a platform of core services for ubiquitous-computing applications, the purpose of which is to factor out the telematics-intensive parts of telematics applications and make them available in a uniform way to all application providers, through public applications-programming interfaces. The TOPAZ service set is provided by TOPAZ Platform Operators (TPOs), who make the services available to any application provider. Fig. 1 illustrates.

We designed TOPAZ based on this vision and the technology of services-oriented computing. At the outset of the project we identified services-oriented computing as the model that would enable us to realize our vision of a new kind of ubiquitous computing marketplace. Service interfaces would allow us to abstract out ubiquitous-computing infrastructure functions and provide them to applications through standards-based interfaces. Web services, in particular, would enable us to clearly separate the execution environments of the TOPAZ Platform Operator and the application providers, and enable TPOs to provide their services to any application provider on the Internet.

The position of TOPAZ with respect to applications and ubiquitous-computing clients (e.g., cell phones, telematics devices) is illustrated in Fig. 2.

The services that TOPAZ provides include managing content flows from the applications to the clients; managing user-interaction flows from the clients to the applications; managing the flow of sensor data from clients to applications; detecting application-specific situations involving clients; and supporting peer-to-peer flows of data and content among clients. All of these services are accessed through industry-standard Web-service interfaces. Like other Web-service-based platforms of application services, TOPAZ has the same concerns of service metering, quality of service guarantees, and resource management. However, while we have been able to use some existing models for these functions, we have had to adapt them to the peculiar nature of our services, and we have had to develop our own implementations of them. In this paper we describe the nature of our specific application model and discuss the particular services our platform offers. We then describe our approaches to the utility-computing issues of resource management, quality-of-service guarantees, and service metering.

2 TOPAZ Application Services

The set of application services offered by TOPAZ was defined by a process of requirements gathering and factoring. We sought to define a platform that met the needs of a wide range of applications with a relatively small number of services. Automotive and fleet telematics was the applications domain of initial focus. We began by compiling a large set of application scenarios through surveying a number of existing telematics systems and industrial telematics consortia. Then, through analyzing their requirements, we factored out a set of core services that would support the applications. The services are implemented as WSDL-based Web services.

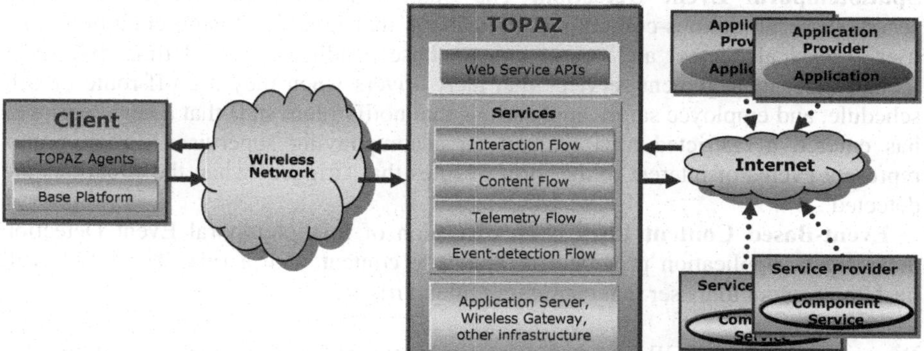

Fig. 2. TOPAZ in End-to-end System

TOPAZ services are in general concerned with facilitating and managing data flows between applications and clients or between peer clients, where the data may be content flowing from applications to clients, or data and events from clients to applications. The services include Telemetry Subscription, Content Push, Client-to-Client Communication, Spatiotemporal Event Detection, and Event-Based Content Push. We describe these services in more detail below.

Telemetry Subscription. This service enables service providers to receive dynamic vehicle data (a.k.a. telemetry data) from individual vehicles or groups of vehicles. Service providers specify the data that is to be sampled, simple conditions under which the data is to be sent, the period at which the conditions are to be evaluated, and an address of a Web service that will receive the data. A TOPAZ Telemetry Agent fulfils the subscription at the vehicle end and sends to a TOPAZ telemetry receiver server. The server collects the telemetry from multiple vehicles for a short time and then forwards it to the requesting application.

Content Push. The Content Push service enables application providers to push multimedia messages, map features, Web forms, and other content to customers' in-vehicle displays. This may be used, for example, by real-time navigation applications to push routes, route information, and just-in-time turn instructions to drivers. The Content Push service offers different priority levels and different reliability levels to the application programmer. Content received from multiple applications concurrently is aggregated for delivery to the client, for greater efficiency in wireless networks.

Client-to-Client. TOPAZ also provides a service enabling application providers to connect groups of users directly, for message- or connection-oriented communications. This service enables applications to link communication applications with the interactive viewers provided by a TOPAZ client, and it eliminates the need for them to act as their own communications hub.

Spatiotemporal Event Detection. The Spatiotemporal Event Detection Service serves those ubiquitous-computing applications that involve sensing conditions in a user's physical context and responding to those conditions in real time. Examples include fleet-management services that alert drivers when they are off-route or off-schedule, and employee safety applications that notify plant staff that a new employee has entered a restricted area without an accompanying supervisor. Programmers represent events of interest in the form of rules that "trigger" when the situations are detected.

Event-Based Content Push is an extension of Spatiotemporal Event Detection that enables application providers to associate content with a rule. The ECPS will push the content to a user that caused the rule to trigger.

Resource Services. TOPAZ provides several services for managing specific kinds of resources. The User Group service enables applications (and application providers, through a portal) to create groups and assign users to groups. Each of the services above allows groups, as well as individual users, to be subjects of service calls. The Rule Resource service enables applications to create, update, and delete data objects (such as geographical polygons) that are referenced in rules of the Spatiotemporal Event Detection service. The User/Device Resources service enables applications to associate arbitrary data with a user or device, for general-purpose use.

Application Example. A typical TOPAZ application is one offering drivers turn-by-turn driving instructions to a given destination. Use of the application by a client involves three flows: one for application requests from the user to the application, another for telemetry data (the vehicle's position) from the vehicle to the application, and another for content from the application to the user: routes and turn instructions. Fig. 3 illustrates. Execution begins with a request from the user to start navigation, the request including the destination. The request takes the form of an HTTP Post, using an HTML form provided by the application.

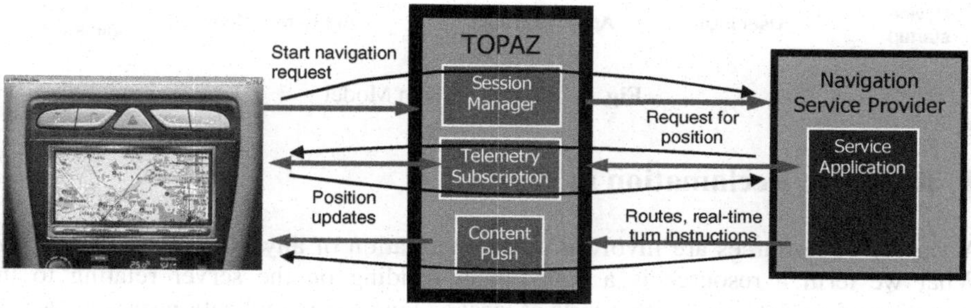

Fig. 3. Application execution using Telemetry Subscription and Content Push services

When the application receives the request, it invokes the Telemetry Subscription service, which initiates the second flow, of position data from the vehicle to the application.

When the application decides it needs to notify the driver of an upcoming turn, or if it has determined that the driver is off-route, and it needs to send the driver new instructions, it will compose the content and invoke the Content Push service to do so. These pushes constitute the third flow.

3 TOPAZ Session Model

The data flows (of content, application requests, telemetry data, and rule-triggering events) managed by TOPAZ services take place in the context of sessions. TOPAZ provides a multi-layered session model, shown in Fig. 4. A session may be a device session, user session, or application session. Each session has a parent session. For application sessions, the parent session is a user session; for user sessions, the parent session is a device session. For device sessions, the parent session is the System session, not shown. Parent relationships of the sessions in Fig. 4 are shown by the tree in the figure.

A device session is created when a device first connects to a TOPAZ Session Manager. The Session Manager automatically creates a user session for the device owner. Then the Session Manager will start any device-dependent auto-startup applications, creating application sessions for them. Normal user sessions are started when users log in. Non-device-dependent applications set for auto-startup are then started at this time. Users can manually start and stop applications at any time following this. When a device is shutdown, all children sessions of the device session are closed.

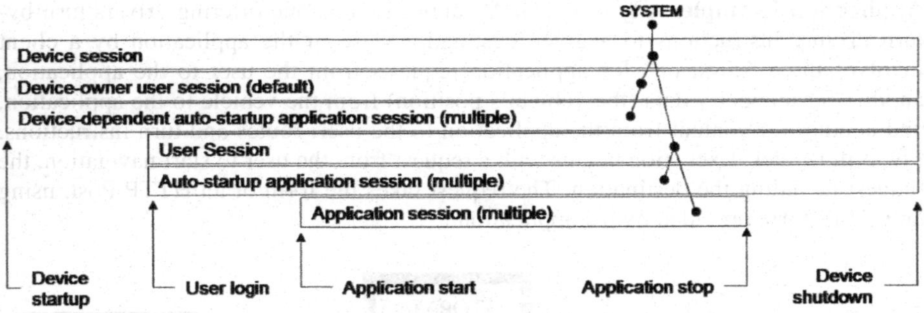

Fig. 4. TOPAZ Session Model

4 Resource Reclamation in TOPAZ

A variety of resources are involved in the facilitation of any given flow in TOPAZ. What we term a resource is a data object residing on the server relating to the operation of an application, that lasts at least as long as an application session. A user group is an example of a resource, as is the internal record of a telemetry subscription. Resources may be created explicitly through service invocations, such as user groups created through calls to the User Group Service, or may be created implicitly by services, such as when telemetry subscriptions are created as the result a rule subscription to the Spatiotemporal Event Detection Service. Resources may be passive data objects, such as telemetry subscription records, or they may be active objects, such as the objects in the Content Push Service that manage content pushes to individual clients. Applications can elect to manage the lifetimes of resources themselves, or they can allow TOPAZ to manage the lifetime for them.

Table 1. Resource lifetimes

Lifetime Name	Duration
DEVSESSION	The life of the associated device session.
USERSESSION	The life of the associated user session.
APPSESSION	The life of the associated application session.
APPLICATION	The life of the application that created the resource.
PROVIDER	The life of the provider of the application that created the resource.

Automatic resource reclamation is an important function in TOPAZ because forcing applications to do it explicitly is too great a burden on programmers. They may not properly clean up; the client or the application may quit unexpectedly, or clients or applications may suffer long periods of disconnection. Without automatic resource reclamation, dead resources would grow continuously with no way to reclaim them.

Table 2. Resource types

Service	Resources	Allowable Lifetimes
Telemetry Subscription	Telemetry subscriptions	APPSESSION or APPLICATION, chosen by application
	Per-client subscription optimizers	DEVSESSION
Content Push	Per-client content-push priority managers	DEVSESSION
User Group	User groups	APPSESSION, APPLICATION, or PROVIDER, chosen by application
Client-To-Client	Telemetry subscriptions	APPSESSION
Spatiotemporal Event Detection	Rules	APPSESSION or APPLICATION, chosen by application
	Rule subscriptions	APPSESSION or APPLICATION, chosen by application
	Telemetry subscriptions	APPSESSION or APPLICATION, chosen by application
Rule Resources	Rule resources	APPLICATION
	User rule resources	APPSESSION or APPLICATION, chosen by application
Event-based Content Push	Rules	APPLICATION
	Rule subscriptions	APPLICATION
	Telemetry subscriptions	APPLICATION
	Event/content table	APPLICATION
User/Device Resources	User/device resources	APPLICATION

To facilitate the reclaiming of resource objects, each resource is associated with the lifetime of a session, an application, or a provider. Table 1 lists the possible resource lifetimes. Programmers declare the lifetime of resources they create explicitly, while TOPAZ services declare the lifetime of resources that are created implicitly, as the result of creation of other resources.

Modular Resource Management. The model for resource management in TOPAZ is that each application service manages its own set of resources. Each service module is notified of lifetime events (e.g., session ended), and each module performs the appropriate resource-management functions. The table below lists the resources managed by each service.

The lifetime events that each module uses to dispose of resources (and in some cases create them) originate with the Session Manager, the Applications Manager, and the Provider Registration Manager. The Resource Manager is a component on the server that acts as a central clearinghouse for these events, distributing them to the other server-side modules that require them.

Internally, the Resource Manager uses an asynchronous messaging mechanism (J2EE Message-Driven Beans) to decouple the callers of the Resource Manager from the execution of the management logic at the receivers of the Resource Manager's lifetime events.

Table 3. Quality of Service Parameters in TOPAZ Services

Service	Parameter	Description
Telemetry Subscription Service	Sampling interval	Applications specify the sampling interval of the requested telemetry data.
	Report aggregation	Applications can request that the telemetry reports be delivered in as large batches as practically possible.
Content Push Service	Push priority	Applications set the priority of content delivery, on a per-push basis.
User Group Service	None	
Client-To-Client Service	Same as Telemetry Subscription Service	
Spatiotemporal Event Detection Service	Rule evaluation interval	Applications specify how frequently rules are evaluated.
Rule Resources Service	None	
Event-based Content Push Service	Same as STED Service and Content Push Service	
User/Device Resources Service	None	

5 Quality-of-Service in TOPAZ

The conventional notion of quality-of-service in Web services is the response time of a service invocation. However, since TOPAZ services are client-session-oriented, not request/response oriented, its notions of quality-of-service are correspondingly different. Rather than requesting a certain response time, TOPAZ service callers specify certain qualities of the client session, on a per-session, or finer, basis. Table 3 lists the quality-of-service parameters offered by each service.

In the sections following we discuss the quality-of-service parameters offered by the Telemetry Subscription Service and the Content Push Service.

QoS for the Telemetry Subscription Service. The Telemetry Subscription Service offers two parameters related to quality of service, sampling interval and report aggregation.

Sampling Interval. Applications express the sampling interval of a telemetry subscription as minimum and maximum intervals between any two samples of the telemetry requested. In order to make most efficient use of its bandwidth to the TOPAZ server, a TOPAZ client will attempt to send the data for multiple subscriptions at the same time, and so allowing some variance in the sampling period of subscriptions is helpful.

Applications choose a maximum interval according to the response-latency requirements of their application. The shorter the interval, the more quickly the application can respond to changes in the client's context. Applications set the minimum interval to a level high enough to avoid unnecessary expenses due to too-frequent telemetry reports (because more frequent telemetry result in increased service charges from the TOPAZ platform operator). However, the usage fee structure for the Telemetry Subscription service encourages applications to set a reasonably wide range between the minimum and maximum intervals.

Report Aggregation. Group telemetry subscriptions offer a "maximize aggregation" parameter, which, when true, instructs TOPAZ to aggregate client telemetry destined to a single application as much as possible. This will result in fewer telemetry transmissions to the application, each one aggregating more client reports. The resulting load on the application server handling subscriber telemetry should therefore be lower. However, the cost of transmitting data from clients may increase because TOPAZ has less flexibility in scheduling transmissions from clients to the TOPAZ servers. Thus the TOPAZ platform operator's service charges to the application provider may increase.

The mechanism for doing this is to approximately synchronize the sampling and transmission of the application's requested telemetry data at all clients in the group. TOPAZ synchronizes (roughly) the telemetry streams by telling each client to start sampling at a common UTM-specified time and to sample at a common interval thereafter. Clients who miss the start time can synchronize with the group by beginning sampling at any multiple of the specified maximum sampling interval.

Whether or not clients synchronize their sampling, the Telemetry Subscription Service will buffer their telemetry reports for a short time before forwarding them together to the application.

QoS for the Content Push Service. The Content Push service offers two parameters related to quality of service: the priority of a push, and the reliability required for the push.

Priority. The Content Push Service is used for content that is time-sensitive, such as a message from a real-time navigation service instructing a user turn right in 50 meters, and for content that is not time-sensitive, such as telemetry requests. Because it must handle content push requests from multiple applications simultaneously, it must therefore make decisions about which content goes first. A simple first-come, first-served approach would mean that time-sensitive content may unnecessarily wait for non-time-sensitive content. Therefore, in order to serve applications more effectively, the Content Push Service offers a "push priority" parameter that can take on the values URGENT and NORMAL. Callers use URGENT for content that represents a time-sensitive communication. NORMAL delivery should be used for all other content. Content sent with NORMAL delivery may experience slight delays for efficiency reasons. Content sent as URGENT will not suffer these delays, but will be charged a higher rate.

Reliability. Not all content has the same importance, and the Content Push Service offers two levels of reliable delivery: BESTEFFORT and ASSURED. With BESTEFFORT delivery, the CPS will attempt delivery a limited number of times before it gives up and discards the push request. With ASSURED delivery the CPS will retry delivery unless it is clear that delivery is not possible (e.g., user has unsubscribed from the application).

6 Service Metering

TOPAZ does not mandate a particular business model used by a TOPAZ Platform Operator, but it does provide models for service metering that a TPO can use as a basis for its business model. We expect a typical business model for a TPO to be one in which it charges users for subscriptions to applications, and it charges application providers for the use of TOPAZ application services. TOPAZ's service metering models provide a basis for a TPO's charges to an application provider.

Rather than metering per service invocation, as do some Web-services platforms (for example, ESRI's ArcWeb services [6]), or using monthly or annual fees (for example Microsoft's MapPoint services [11]) TOPAZ's metering models are based on the aggregated cost of providing flows. In this section we describe how this orientation toward flows has determined out metering models. Our work in this area is not complete; we are currently refining our models and determining the various constants in them empirically.

Each application service has its own metering model, according to how flows in the service consume system resources. A service's metering model is a function whose inputs are the parameters used in invoking the service that generated the flow and any statistics recorded for the flow, and whose outputs are abstract "cost units". These cost units translate directly to monetary charges. The terms in the formulas for the models reflect how invocation parameters impact the consumption of particular system resources.

In this section we focus on two services, Telemetry Subscription and Content Push.

Metering Telemetry Subscription. The various parameters used in invoking the Telemetry Subscription service impact its consumption of system resources in various ways, but the most important are the minimum and maximum sampling intervals. For each telemetry report received by the server, it must allocate a thread and a database connection. Relatively few CPU cycles are consumed in processing the data. In order to not block the client while sending the data to the application, the TSS decouples the process of receiving the telemetry from the process of sending it, but this means the service must allocate another thread for sending. In order to reduce the number of threads required for this, the service will batch reports together for a short time before sending them to the application.

The initial TSS metering model we are working with now charges application providers according to how their subscriptions consume bandwidth, modified by how the subscriptions impact other system resources. The charge to any one application for a telemetry session is a simple summation of the charges for handling each report, where the charge for each report is a product of the size of the report and the sampling parameters in the application's subscription. Applications reduce their charges by specifying a generous tolerance between minimum and maximum sampling intervals, thus allowing the client more flexibility in combining telemetry reports destined for different applications in the same message sent to the server. Therefore the server needs to allocate only one thread and one database connection to process multiple reports. This is reflected in the metering model by applying a discount to the per-report charges, where the discount is a function of the range between minimum and maximum sampling intervals.

Metering Content Push. Threads are the primary resources consumed by the Content Push service. For each URGENT push a thread must be allocated to invoke the transport mechanism that will carry the data. NORMAL pushes, however, are queued for a short time before the entire queue is emptied and sent to the client. Therefore, the metering model for Content Push is a function of the priority used, as well as the size of the content pushed.

7 Related Work

Our technique for resource reclamation is similar to the "soft state" approach used in management of network-entity state in Internet protocols[5, 13, 14], RMI and Jini [12], and more recently the Open Grid Services Architecture [8], in that each reclaimable resource is associated with a lifetime. In our technique, however, the lifetime is not an actual time, but instead a link to the lifetime of an entity in the system—a session, application, or application provider. Resources are known to be reclaimable when the entity to which they are associated has ceased to exist. In this respect our technique is similar to reference counting in a distributed system [2], except that references point in the other direction. Thus, knowing the ID of a deceased entity, we can query a resource set directly for resources whose lifetime is associated with it.

Work in quality of service for Web services—how to specify it, measure it, and monitor it—focuses, for performance metrics, on generic qualities such as response time, throughput, availability, and reliability [3, 10]. However, our flow-oriented services require different performance metrics, such as sampling regularity in the Telemetry Subscription service. In this respect our concerns are more nearly aligned with multimedia systems, but with looser real-time constraints. See [4].

The abstract cost units our metering models are based on are similar to the credits used by ESRI's ArcWeb Services [6]. Our cost units, however, are based on how a particular service's flows consume critical resources, and the cost of providing those resources. We have based our models partly on the modeling of thread and database connection resources in [7]. While we have implemented our own metering subsystem, we could also use metering services such as that in the UMI utility infrastructure [1].

8 Conclusions

TOPAZ is a Web-services-based platform of services designed to facilitate a marketplace of ubiquitous computing applications, by making these applications radically less expensive to develop, deploy, and operate. As with any utility-computing infrastructure, it faces challenges on how to manage the objects and resources consumed in the delivery of its services, how to meter the use of its services, and what quality-of-service parameters to offer to applications. We have presented our own approaches to these challenges, which take into account the nature of TOPAZ services as providing "flows" of content, data, and event-detection between clients and applications. We continue to refine our metering models based on observations of our system's runtime characteristics.

We have developed a number of applications for TOPAZ, and external developers have developed others. We are currently in the process of measuring the performance of TOPAZ when serving large numbers of clients.

References

1. Albaugh, V., Madduri, H., The Utility Metering Service of the Universal Management Infrastructure. IBM Systems Journal, Vol. 43, No. 1, 2004, 179–189.
2. Bevan, D.I., Distributed Garbage Collection Using Reference Counting. In *Parallel Architectures and Languages Europe*, 1987, Springer-Verlag, LNCS 259, 176–187.
3. Bhoj, P., Singhal, S., Chutani, S., SLA Management in Federated Environments. In *Proceedings of the Sixth IFIP/IEEE Symposium on Integrated Network Management (IM '99)*, IEEE, 1999, 293–308.
4. Campbell, A., Coulson, G., Garcia, F., Hutchison, D., Leopold, H., Integrated Quality of Service For Multimedia Communications. In *Proceedings of the 12th Annual Joint Conference of the IEEE Computer and Communications Societies - IEEE INFOCOM '93*; 1993, 732–739.
5. Clark, D.D. The Design Philosophy of the DARPA Internet Protocols. In *SIGCOMM Symposium on Communications Architectures and Protocols*, 1988, ACM Press, 106–114.
6. ESRI ArcWeb Services. http://www.esri.com/software/arcwebservices/index.html
7. Ferrari, G., Ezhilchelvan, E., Mitrani, I. Performance Modeling and Evaluation of E-Business Systems. CS-TR 954, School of Computing Science, University of Newcastle, March 2006.
8. Foster, I., Kesselman, C., Nick, J.M., Tuecke, S. Grid Services for Distributed Systems Integration. *Computer*, Vol. 35, No. 6, 2002.
9. Frølund, S., Koistinen, J. 1998. Quality-of-Service Specification in Distributed Object Systems, Distributed System Engineering 5: 179–202.
10. Keller, A., Ludwig, H., The WSLA Framework: Specifying and Monitoring Service Level Agreements for Web Services. Journal of Network and Systems Management, Vol. 11, No. 1, March 2003, 57–81.
11. Microsoft MapPoint. http://www.microsoft.com/mappoint/default.mspx
12. Oaks, S., and Wong, H. *Jini in a Nutshell.* O'Reilly, 2000.
13. Sharma, P., Estrin, D., Floyd, S., Jacobson, V., Scalable Timers for Soft State Protocols. In *IEEE Infocom '97*, 1997, IEEE Press.
14. Zhang, L., Braden, B., Estrin, D., Herzog, S., Jamin, S., RSVP: A New Resource Reservation Protocol. In *IEEE Network*, 1993, 8–18.

SCA Policy Association Framework

Michael Beisiegel[1], Nickolas Kavantzas[2], Ashok Malhotra[2], Greg Pavlik[2], and Chris Sharp[1]

[1] IBM
[2] Oracle
mbgl@us.ibm.com, nickolas.kavantzas@oracle.com, ashok.malhotra@oracle.com, greg.pavlik@oracle.com, sharpc@uk.ibm.com

Abstract. SCA (Service Component Architecture) is a collaborative effort by the leading vendors in the enterprise software space to define an architecture for building applications and systems using a Service-Oriented Architecture. SCA allows developers to define components that implement business logic, which offer their capabilities through services and consume functions offered by other components through references in a relatively abstract manner. This paper discusses how infrastructure and Quality of Service constraints and capabilities can be associated with SCA artifacts either as abstract desires or as concrete policies.

Keywords: SCA, QoS, Policy.

1 Introduction

SCA (Service Component Architecture) is a collaborative effort by the leading vendors in the enterprise such as Web Services [1]. The collaboration started in 2005 and is ongoing. Another paper in this conference describes the SCA framework in detail.

SCA encourages an SOA organization of business application code based on components that implement business logic, which offer their capabilities through service-oriented interfaces called services and which consume functions offered by other components through service-oriented interfaces, called references. SCA software space to define an architecture for building applications and systems using a Service-Oriented Architecture. SCA extends and complements prior approaches to implementing services, and builds on open standards divides the steps in building a service-oriented application into two major parts:

The **implementation** of components which provide services and consume other services

The **assembly** of sets of components to build business applications, through the **wiring** of references to services.

SCA emphasizes the decoupling of service implementation and of service assembly from the details of Quality of Service (QoS) or infrastructure capabilities and from the details of the access methods used to invoke services. SCA components operate at a business level and use a minimum of middleware APIs.

A. Dan and W. Lamersdorf (Eds.): ICSOC 2006, LNCS 4294, pp. 613 – 623, 2006.

SCA supports service ***implementations*** written using any one of several programming languages including conventional object-oriented and procedural languages such as Java™, PHP, C++, COBOL; XML-centric languages such as BPEL and XSLT; and declarative languages such as SQL and XQuery. SCA also supports a range of programming styles, including asynchronous and message-oriented, in addition to the synchronous call-and-return style.

SCA supports ***bindings*** to a wide range of access mechanisms used to invoke services. These include Web services, Messaging systems and CORBA IIOP. Bindings are handled declaratively and are independent of the implementation code. Infrastructure capabilities, such as Security, Transactions and the use of Reliable Messaging are also handled declaratively and are separated from the implementation code.

The capture and expression of non-functional requirements is an important aspect of service definition, and has impact on SCA throughout the lifecycle of components and compositions. SCA provides a framework to support specification of infrastructure capabilities constraints and Quality of Service (QoS) expectations, from component design through to concrete deployment. Specifically, this paper describes the SCA policy association framework that allows policies and policy subjects specified using WS-Policy[2] and WS-PolicyAttachment[3] and possibly other policy languages to be associated with interactions between SCA components as well as with component implementations.

DISCLAIMER: This paper describes the SCA Policy Attachment Framework in its current state of design. Work on the framework is continuing and so the details are likely to change.

2 Policy Framework

2.1 Overview

The SCA policy framework defines the following key concepts:

Intents

... allow the SCA developer to specify abstract Quality of Service capabilities or requirements independent of their concrete realization.

Profiles

... allow the SCA developer to express collections of abstract QoS intents.

Policy Set

... collects together concrete policy and policy subject pairings, potentially from different policy domains, and declares which intents that they realize collectively.

Intent Maps

... are a set of alternative concrete policy and policy subject pairs for a single policy domain that appear in a Policy Set

… declare defaults and fixed values for alternatives in a single domain

The SCA policy framework utilizes the following key concepts from the SCA assembly model:

Binding
...some bindings may support intents implicitly through the nature of the protocols they implement
...other bindings may be configurable to provide support for intents through extension

(...SCA bindings may be configured using a combination of intents (via profiles) and concrete policies via policySets)

2.2 Framework Model

SCA Framework model comprises of Intents, Profiles and Policy sets. These concepts are defined below.

2.2.1 Intents

An intent is an abstract capability or requirement that is expressed independent of its realization.

Intent names are represented as case-sensitive strings in the SCA Policy Framework. The name typically designates the name of a policy domain. It may also contain an additional qualifier separated from the domain name by a "/". It is possible to use a "." In a domain name as a convention to indicate scoping. For example, "sec.confidentiality" names the confidentiality domain within the security area as an intent. Qualified intents designate an additional level of specificity. When the intent contains a qualifier (i.e. is a qualified intent), the value preceding the separator "/" designates the name of the intent and the value after the separator designates the specific qualifier.

A qualified intent is a member of a qualified intent set. A qualified intent set is the union of qualified intents formed from a single intent. As an example, the sec.confidentiality intent may be qualified with a qualifier from the following qualifier set: {"message", "transport"}. The qualified intent set, therefore, is as follows: {"sec.confidentiality/message", "sec.confidentiality/transport"}.

To ensure a minimum level or portability, SCA will normatively define a set of core intents that all SCA implementations are expected to provide a concrete realization for. Users of SCA may define new intents, or extend the qualifier set of existing intents.

2.2.2 Profiles

Profile elements aggregate intent names. A set of intents (qualified or non-qualified) may be expressed by a profile element using the @intents attribute. This takes a space-separated list of intent names as its value.

For example:

```
<sca:profile intents="sec.authentication
          rel.reliability
  sec.confidentiality/message" />
```

The first two intents state that policies providing authentication and reliability are required. Although sec.authentication has a qualifier set it has been used in its unqualified form here. This means that some form of authentication is required, but the SCA developer has not specified the particular type of authentication mechanism used to be used. The third intent is used in its qualified form and states that a policy for a specific capability, "message", in the confidentiality domain is required.

The intents specified in the profile are mapped to concrete policies specified in policySets before deployment. An unqualified intent maps to a policySet that provides a policy or policies for the domain of the intent. If a given policySet provides multiple policies, corresponding to members of the qualified intent set for that domain, the default policy is selected. The specific algorithm used to map intents to PolicySets is outside the scope of this specification.

2.2.3 Policy Sets

A policySet element is used to define a set of concrete policies that correspond to a set of intents. The structure of the PolicySet element is as follows:

- It must contain a @name attribute that declares a name for the policy set. The value of the @name attribute is a QName.
- It may contain a @binding attribute. The value of the @binding attribute indicates the binding to which the policySet applies.
- It may contain a @provides element which is a space-separated list on intent names. The values in @provides indicate the intents (qualified or unqualified) that the policySet provides policies for.

A policySet can contain the following element children:

- intentMap element
- policySetReference element
- wsp:PolicyAttachment element
- xs:any extensibility element

Any mix of the above types of elements, in any number, can be included as children. The extensibility elements may be from any namespace and may be intermixed with the other types of child elements. The pseudo schema for policySets is shown below:

```
<sca:policySet name="xs:QName"
          provides="... list of intent names... "?
          bindings="binding names"?
       xmlns="http://www.osoa.org/xmlns/sca/1.0
       xmlns:wsp="http://schemas.xmlsoap.org/ws/2004
  /09/policy">
```

```
        <sca:policySetReference name="xs:QName"/>*
            <sca:intentMap/>*
        <wsp:PolicyAttachment>*
        <xs:any>*
  </sca:policySet>
```

As an example, the policySet element below declares that it provides "sec.authentication/basic" and "rel.reliability" using the @provides attribute, for the "binding.ws" SCA binding.

```
  <sca:policySet name="SecureReliablePolicy"
            provides="sec.authentication
      rel.reliability"
      bindings="sca:binding.ws"
            xmlns="http://www.osoa.org/xmlns/sca/1.0"
                  xmlns:wsp=
      "http://schemas.xmlsoap.org/ws/2004/09/policy">
      <wsp:PolicyAttachment>
            <!-- policy expression and policy subject
            for "basic authentication" -->
      </wsp:PolicyAttachment>
      <wsp:PolicyAttachment>
      <!-- policy expression and policy subject for
            "reliability" -->
      </wsp:PolicyAttachment>
  </sca:policySet>
```

2.2.3.1 IntentMaps. Intent maps given below contain concrete policies and policy subjects for a named policy domain in the policySet. The pseudo-schema for intentMaps is shown below:

```
  <sca:intentMap provides="xs:QName"
            default="xs:string">
            <sca:qualifier name="xs:string">*
                        <wsp:PolicyAttachment>*
                              ...
                        </wsp:PolicyAttachment>
            </sca:qualifier>
      <xs:any>*
  </sca:intentMap>
```

If a policySet contains intentMaps, each intentMap provides alternative policies for a single policy domain. The intent contained in the @provides of the intent map must be included in the @provides of the policySet. All intents in the @provides of the policySet must appear in the @provides of an intentMap.

An intentMap element must contain qualifier element children. Each qualifier element corresponds to a qualified intent where the unqualified form of that intent is included in the @provides attribute value of the parent intentMap.

A qualifier element in an intentMap designates a set of concrete policy attachments that correspond to a qualified intent. Concrete policy attachments may be specified using wsp:PolicyAttachment[3] element children or by using extensibility elements specific to a policy domain.

The default attribute of an intentMap must correspond to one of the qualifier elements of its child qualifier elements. It represents the default choice of qualifier, when only the unqualified form of the intent has been specified as a requirement in a profile element.

As an example, the policySet element below declares that it provides "sca:confidentiality" using the @provides attribute. It contains a single intentMap. The qualifiers (transport and message) each specify the policy and policy subject they provide. The default is "transport".

```
<sca:policySet name="SecureMessagingPolicies"
          provides="sca:confidentiality"
    bindings="sca:binding.ws"
          xmlns="http://www.osoa.org/xmlns/sca/1.0"
    xmlns:wsp=
    "http://schemas.xmlsoap.org/ws/2004/09/policy">
    <sca:intentMap provides="confidentiality"
                default="transport">
      <sca:qualifier name="transport">
          <wsp:PolicyAttachment>

          <!--  policy  expression  and  policy  subject
                for    "transport"    alternative     -->

          </wsp:PolicyAttachment>
          <wsp:PolicyAttachment>
                    ...
          </wsp:PolicyAttachment>
      </sca:qualifier>
      <sca:qualifier name="message">
          <wsp:PolicyAttachment>

          <!--  policy  expression  and  policy  subject
                for "message" alternative" -->

          </wsp:PolicyAttachment>
      </sca:qualifier>
    </sca:intentMap>
</sca:policySet>
```

2.2.3.2 Direct Use of Attachments within Policy Sets. If a policySet contains a complete policy without the need for defaults or overriding, it can contain policy attachment elements directly without the use of intentMaps. In this case, there are two ways of including attachments within a policySet element. Either wsp:policyAttachment elements may be included directly as children or deployment specific extension elements (using xs:any) that designate concrete policy attachments may be included as children.

When a policySet element contains wsp:policyAttachment children, it is assumed that the set of ALL policy attachments specified as children satisfy the intents expressed using the @provides attribute value of the policySet element. This assumption also applies to deployment specific representation of concrete policies.

2.2.3.3 Policy References. A policySet may refer to other policySets by using a PolicySetReference element. This provides a recursive inclusion capability for intentMaps, policy attachments or other specific policies from different domains.

When a policySet element contains policySetReference element children, the @name attribute of the policySetReference element designates a policySet with the same value for its @name attribute.

The binding attribute of a referenced policySet must be compatible with that of the policySet referring to it. Compatibility, in the simplest case, is string equivalence of binding names.

The @provides attribute of a referenced policySet must include intent values that are compatible with one of the values of the @provides attribute of the referencing policySet. A compatible intent either is a value in the referencing policySet's @provides attribute values or is a qualified value of one of the intents of the referencing policySet's @provides attribute value.

The use of a policySetReference element indicates that a copy of the element content children of the policySet that is being referred is included within the referring policySet. If the result of inclusion results in a reference to another policySet, inclusion is repeated until the contents of a policySet do not contain any references to other policy sets.

Note that, since the attributes of a referenced policySet are effectively removed/ignored by this process, it is the responsibility of the author of the referring policySet to include any necessary intents in its @provides attribute if they wish that policySet to correctly advertise its aggregate capabilities.

The default values when using this aggregate policySet come from the defaults in the included policySets. A single intent (or all qualified intents that comprise an intent) in a referencing policySet must only be included once by using references to other policySets.

The following example illustrates the inclusion of two other policy Sets in a policySet element:

```
<sca:policySet
    name="BasicAuthMsgProtSecurity"
    provides="authentication confidentiality"
                        bindings="binding.ws"
    xmlns="http://www.osoa.org/xmlns/sca/1.0">
    <sca:policySetReference
                  name="AuthenticationPolicies"/>
    <sca:policySetReference
                  name="ConfidentialityPolicies"/>
</sca:policySet>
```

The above policySet refers to two other policySets for authentication and message protection and, by reference, provides policies and policy subject alternatives in these domains.

2.3 Attachment of SCA Policy Artifacts

This section describes the mechanisms used to associate profiles or policySets with SCA artifacts. It describes the various attachment points and semantics for profile elements and their relationship to other SCA elements within their scope of influence, and how profiles relate to policySets in these contexts.

2.3.1 Services and References

The SCA developer may declare any requirements that should be satisfied for interactions with their components by attaching a profile element as a child of a service or reference. The meaning of this attachment is that, for all interactions with the service (or via the reference), the intents listed by the profile element should be concretely realized, irrespective of the specific binding that may be chosen.

The following is a pseudo schema for attachment to services and references:

```
<sca:service> or <sca:reference>
    ...
    <sca:interface.interface-type/>
    <sca:profile intents="xs:string"/>?
        ...
</sca:service> or </sca:reference>
```

An example of this is:

```
<sca:service name="mySpecialService">
        <sca:interface.wsdl    portType="..."      />
        <sca:profile
              intents="sec.authentication
                        rel.reliabilty"/>
</sca:service>
```

Here, the developer is indicating that it is essential to the operation of mySpecialService that all interactions with it are authenticated and reliable.

Thus, the presence of a profile element, guides the choice of binding that may be used for the service/reference concerned. The selected binding must satisfy the requirements indicated by the profile. In the above example, therefore, any binding element used with the mySpecialService should be capable of realizing authentication and reliability.

Bindings may realize intents either natively by virtue of the kind of transport technology they implement (e.g. an SSL binding would natively support confidentiality automatically) or through configuration using concrete policy artifacts, contained in policySets. The following section looks at the relationship between these three elements (profiles, bindings and policySets) in more detail.

2.3.2 Bindings

Profiles may also be associated with bindings to indicate that the intents specified in the profile are mapped to concrete policies contained in policySet elements that are compatible with those bindings. Bindings may also be directly associated with a policySet and the policies specified by it.

The following is a pseudo schema for attachment to a binding:

```
<sca:service> or <sca:reference>
        ...
   <sca:binding.binding-type >*
              <sca:profile intents="xs:string"/>?
   <sca:/binding.binding-type>

        ...
</sca:service> or </sca:reference>
```

2.3.2.1 Associating Profiles with Bindings. When a profile element is in scope of a binding element (i.e. it is either a sibling or child of that binding) then it should be used to ensure that the binding will satisfy the intents specified by the profile. In other words, it is "profiling" the usage of the binding in this instance.

To ensure this, any policySet that may be used to configure that binding (i.e. that declares the binding in question as a value of its binding attribute) should include all the intents expressed by the profile element in its provides list:

An intent that is unqualified in the profile element may be qualified in the policySet @provides attribute.

When an intent is both unqualified in the profile element and the policySet, it may be subsequently qualified by an intentMap/qualifier element contained within the policySet.

An intent that is qualified in the profile element may be unqualified in the @provides attribute of the policySet if and only if that policySet contains an intentMap/qualifier element for that qualified form of the intent.

In this manner, the profile element designates a selection of concrete policies specified by a policySet element (thus overriding the defaults specified in the policySet, should the policySet contain intentMaps).

Although an intentMap typically contains a number of concrete policies to represent different qualified intents, only one of the qualified intents relating to a given unqualified intent may be selected and enforced in a given usage of the policySet. The choice of which qualified intent to use is influenced by the use of profile elements, but sometimes a profile element may not be specific enough to list the particular qualified form of the intent. To ensure one and only one qualified form is chosen a default must be specified.

2.3.2.2 Associating Policy Sets with Bindings. A binding element may specify one or more policySets to indicate the specific policies that will be used to configure the binding. The binding element indicates the name of the policy sets by using the @policySet attribute. This attribute can contain a space separated list of policySet names.

As is the case where a profile element is in scope of a binding element, a profile element that is a child of a binding element with a @policySet attribute may specify an attribute named @intents that contain a list of qualified intent values. When used, the value of @intents attribute specifies a set of intents that override the default intents provided by the policySets. This overriding is only possible when the policySet contains intentMaps. For example:

```
<sca:binding.ws policySet="MyEnterprisePolicy">
   <sca:profile intents="sec.authentication/cert
               sec.confidentiality/message"/>
</sca:binding.ws>
```

A child profile element adds to or further qualifies the intents specified on profile elements specified for service of reference elements that are a peer to binding elements. The following example shows child profile elements that further qualifies the sca.authentication intent that was specified as a peer to the binding element.

```
<sca:service>
   <sca:profile intents="sec.authentication
                          rel.reliability"/>
         <sca:binding.ws>
               <sca:profile
               intents="sec.authentication/cert"/>
         </sca:binding.ws>
         <sca:binding.ejb>
               <sca:profile
         intents="sec.authentication/kerberos"/>
   </sca:binding.ejb>
</sca:service>
```

2.3.3 Implementation Policies

Abstract QoS requirements may be associated with SCA components to indicate implementation policies as shown in the following example.

```
<sca:component name='myComponent'>
         <sca:profile intents="logging"/>
</sca:component>
```

This indicates that all messages to and from the component must be logged. The technology used to implement the logging is unspecified. Specific technology is selected when the intent is mapped to a policySet.

Alternatively, one or more policySets may be specified directly by associating them with the component.

```
<sca:component name="myComponent">
   policySet="StandardImplementationPolicy"/>
```

In this usage, the default intents for each intentMap in the policySet are used.

If the default intents in the policySet(s) need to be overridden, this can be accomplished by specifying the overriding intents by name.

```
<sca:component name="myComponent">
   policySet="StandardImplementationPolicy"/>
         <sca:profile
               intents="Access/restricted"/>
</sca:component>
```

References

1. Service Component Architecture (SCA) http://www.osoa.org
2. Web Services Policy (WS-Policy) http://www.w3.org/TR/2006/WD-ws-policy-20060731
3. Web Services Policy Attachment (WS-PolicyAttachment) http://www.w3.org/TR/2006/WD-ws-policy-attachment-20060731

A Model-Driven Development Approach to Creating Service-Oriented Solutions

Simon K. Johnson and Alan W. Brown

IBM Rational, 3039 Cornwallis Road, P.O. Box 12195, RTP, NC 27709, USA
{skjohn, awbrown}@us.ibm.com

Abstract. Many challenges face organizations as they describe their business domains from a services perspective and transform that understanding of their business into a specific realization targeting a solution infrastructure. However, one of the most pressing problems involves helping organizations to effectively transition to service-oriented design of applications. Great benefit could be gained by using a well-defined, repeatable approach to the modeling of business domains from a services perspective that supports the application of automated approaches to realize a service-based solution. In this paper we explore model-driven approaches to the realization of service-oriented solutions. We describe a services-oriented design approach that utilizes a UML profile for software services as the design notation for expressing the design of a services-oriented solution. We describe how a services model expressed in this UML profile can be transformed into a specific service implementation, and describe the design-to-implementation mapping. We then comment on how these technology elements play in an overall MDD approach for SOA.

Keywords: Software design, Model-driven development, Service-oriented Architecture, Unified Modeling Language.

1 Introduction

Many organizations are struggling to improve the flexibility and reduce the maintenance cost of the enterprise solutions that run their businesses. To help them in their task they are looking for ways to move toward solutions that are more readily assembled from existing capabilities, and to develop new capabilities that enable reuse. An approach gaining a lot of support in the industry today is based on viewing enterprise solutions as federations of services connected via well-specified contracts that define their service interfaces. The resulting system designs are frequently called ***Service Oriented Architectures (SOAs)***. Systems are composed of collections of services making calls on operations defined through their service interfaces. Many organizations now express their solutions in terms of services and their interconnections. The ultimate goal of adapting an SOA is to achieve flexibility for the business and within IT.

A number of important technologies have been defined to support an SOA approach, most notably when the services are distributed across multiple machines and connected over the Internet or an intranet. For example web service approaches

A. Dan and W. Lamersdorf (Eds.): ICSOC 2006, LNCS 4294, pp. 624–636, 2006.

rely on intra-service communication protocols such as the Simple Object Access Protocol (SOAP), allow the web service interfaces (expressed in the Web Services Definition Language – WSDL) to be registered in public directories and searched in Universal Description, Discovery and Integration (UDDI) repositories, and share information in documents defined in the eXtensible Markup Language (XML) and described in standard schemas.

Of course, SOA is more than a set of standards and service descriptions. Indeed, it is possible to create an SOA that does not use web services technology, and it is possible to use web services technology in a way that would not be considered service-oriented. There is a great deal more that needs to be explored to understand why a service-oriented viewpoint adds value to the business, and how service-oriented solutions are designed, implemented, deployed, and managed. However, one of the most pressing areas involves helping organizations to effectively transition to service-oriented design of applications. Many challenges face organizations as they describe their business domains from a services perspective and transform that understanding of their business into a specific realization targeting a solution infrastructure. Industry analysts such as Gartner [1] and CBDi [2] place poor services design and the difficulties of educating software practitioners in the techniques of service design at the top of their list of inhibitors to success with developing SOA solutions.

Great benefit could be gained by using a well-defined, repeatable approach to the modeling of business domains from a services perspective that supports the application of automated approaches to realize a service-based solution. Fortunately, we have a rich tradition of modeling and model-driven approaches to software development on which we can draw. Models, modeling, and model transformation form the basis for a set of software development approaches that are known as ***Model-Driven Development (MDD)***. Models are used to reason about the problem domain and the solution domain for some area of interest. Relationships between these models provide a web of dependencies that record the process by which a solution was created, and help to understand the implications of changes at any point in that process. In fact, we can be quite prescriptive in the use of models in a software development process. If we define the kinds of models that must be produced, and apply some rigor to the precise semantics of these models, we can define rules for:

- Automating many of the steps needed to convert one model representation to another;
- Tracing between model elements;
- Analyzing important characteristics of the models.

This style of MDD is called Model-Driven Architecture (MDA). Standards are emerging to support this approach. The primary driving force behind MDA approaches based on a standardized set of models, notations, and transformation rules is the Object Management Group (OMG). They provide an open, vendor-neutral basis for system interoperability via OMG's established modeling standards: Unified Modeling Language (UML), Meta-Object Facility (MOF), and Common Warehouse Meta-model (CWM). Platform-independent descriptions of enterprise solutions can be built using these modeling standards and can be transformed into a major open or proprietary platform, including CORBA, J2EE, .NET, XMI/XML, and Web-based platforms [3].

In this paper we explore model-driven approaches to the realization of service-oriented solutions. We describe a services-oriented design approach that utilizes a UML profile for software services as the design notation for expressing the design of a services-oriented solution. We describe how a services model expressed in this UML profile can be transformed into a specific service implementation, and define the design-to-implementation mapping. We then comment on how these technology elements play in an overall MDD approach for SOA.

2 Model-Driven Generation of Services and Service-Oriented Solutions

Defining and applying model transformations are critical techniques within any model-driven style of development. Model transformations involve using a model as one of the inputs in the automation process. Possible outputs can include another model, or varying levels of executable code. In practice there are three common model transformations: refactoring transformations, model-to-model transformations, and model-to-code transformations [4, 5].

1. *Refactoring transformations* reorganize a model based on some well-defined criteria. In this case the output is a revision of the original model, called the refactored model. An example could be as simple as renaming all the instances where a UML entity name used, or something more complex like replacing a class with a set of classes and relationships in both the metamodel and in all diagrams displaying those model elements.
2. *Model-to-model transformations* convert information from one model or models to another model or set of models, typically where the flow of information is across abstraction boundaries. An example would be the conversion of one type of model into another, such as the transformation of a set of entity classes into a matched set of database schema, Plain Old Java Objects (POJOs), and XML-formatted mapping descriptor files.
3. *Model-to-code transformations* are familiar to anyone who has used the code generation capability of a UML modeling tool. These transformations convert a model element into a code fragment. This is not limited to object-oriented languages such as Java and C++. Nor is it limited to programming languages: configuration, deployment, data definitions, message schemas, and others kinds of files can also be generated from models expressed in notations such as UML. Model-to-code transformations can be developed for nearly any form of programming language or declarative specification. An example would be to generate Data Definition Language (DDL) code from a logical data model expressed as a UML class diagram.

2.1 Applying Model Transformations

Having described different kinds of model transformations, we also note that in practice there are several ways in which model transformations can be applied. In model-driven approaches there are four categories of techniques for applying model transformations:

- *Manual*. The developer examines the input model and manually creates or edits the elements in the transformed model. The developer interprets the information in the model and makes modifications accordingly.[1]
- *Prepared Profile*. A profile is an extension of the UML semantics in which a model type is derived. Applying a profile defines rules by which a model is transformed.
- *Patterns*. A pattern is a particular arrangement of model elements. Patterns can be applied to a model and results in the creation of new model elements in the transformed model.
- *Automatic*. Automatic transformations apply a set of changes to one or mode models based on predefined transformation rules. These rules may be implicit to the tools being used, or may have been explicitly defined based on domain-specific knowledge. This type of transformation requires that the input model be sufficiently complete both syntactically and semantically, and may require models to be marked with information specific to the transformations being applied.

The use of profiles and patterns usually involves developer input at the time of transformation, or requires the input model to be "marked". A marked model contains extra information not necessarily relevant to the model's viewpoint or level of abstraction. This information is only relevant to the tools or processes that transform the model. For example, a UML analysis model containing entities with String types may be marked variable or fixed length, or it may be marked to specify its maximum length. From an analysis viewpoint just the identification of the String data type is usually sufficient. However, when transforming a String typed attribute into, say, a database column type, the additional information is required to complete the definition.

2.2 Models and Transforms

Transformations such as these can be used to enable efficient development, deployment and integration of services and services-oriented solutions. Practitioners create models specific to their viewpoint and needs which are used as the basis of analysis, consistency checking, integration, and automation of routine tasks. Model-driven approaches allow developers to create services and service-oriented solutions by focusing on logical design of services and to apply transformations to the underlying SOA technologies. Furthermore, as illustrated in the examples later in this paper, substantial improvements in the quality and productivity of delivered solutions is possible by automating substantial aspects of these transformations to service implementations.

3 Model-Driven Service Specification and Design

The Unified Modeling Language (UML) is the standard modeling notation for software-intensive systems [6]. Originally conceived over a decade ago as an integration of the most successful modeling ideas of the time, the UML is widely used by organizations, and supported by more than a dozen different product offerings. Its evolution is managed through a standards process governed by the Object Management Group (OMG).

---

[1] Apart from raw speed, the significant difference between manual and automated transformations is that automation is guaranteed to be consistent, while a manual approach is not.

One of the reasons for the success of UML is its flexibility. It supports the creation of a set of models representing both the problem domain and solution domain, can capture and relate multiple perspectives highlighting different viewpoints on these domains, enables modeling of the system at different levels of abstraction, and encourages the partitioning of models into manageable pieces as required for shared and iterative development approaches. In addition, relationships between model elements can be maintained across modeling perspectives and levels of abstraction, and specialized semantics can be placed on model elements through built-in UML extension mechanisms (i.e., stereotypes and tagged values bundled into UML profiles).

One recent effort at IBM has been to create a UML profile for software services, a profile for UML 2.0 which allows for the modeling of services, service-oriented architecture (SOA), and service-oriented solutions.[2] The profile has been implemented in IBM Rational Software Architect, used successfully in developing models of complex customer scenarios, and used to help educate people about the concerns relevant to developing service-oriented solutions. This profile is used as the basis for a model-driven approach in which services and service interactions are

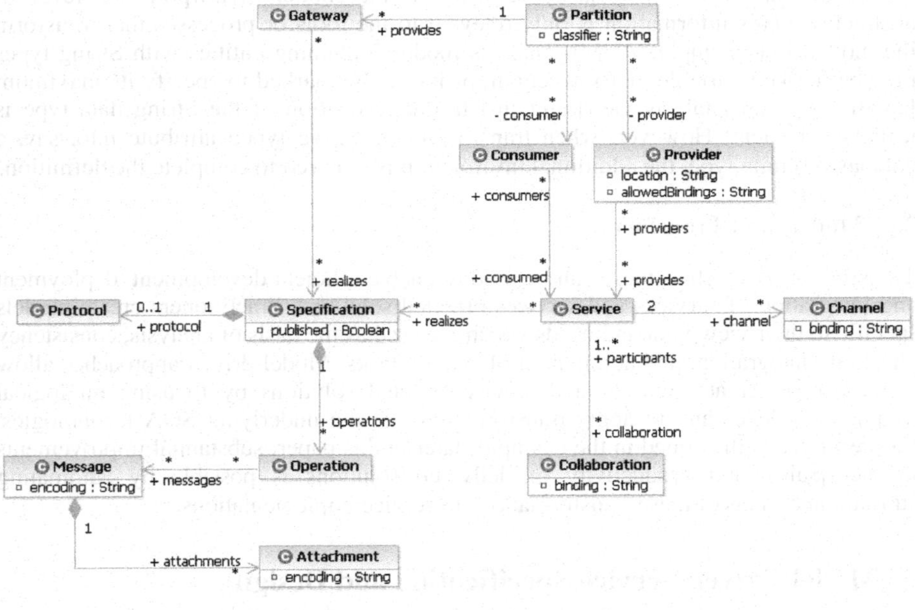

Fig. 1. Conceptual Model

described using the UML profile, and realizations of those services are then generated through an automated model transformation to Web Services Definition Language (WSDL), a standard language for web services implementation.

[2] Details of this UML profile and a downloadable version of the profile for Rational Software Architect are available at http://www.ibm.com/developerworks/rational/library/05/419_soa.

3.1 The UML Profile for Software Services

The UML profile for software service provides a common language for describing services that covers a number of activities through the development lifecycle and also provides views of those services to different stakeholders [7]. So, for example, the profile provides capabilities for the architect to map out services early in the lifecycle using logical partitions to describe the entire enterprise-wide service portfolio. This view is further detailed by designers who develop the service specifications, both structural and behavioral that act as the contracts between the service clients and implementers. The message view provides the ability for designers to reuse information models for common service data definitions. The profile has been implemented in Rational Software Architect and used successfully in developing models of complex customer scenarios and also in educating people to the concerns relevant to development of service-oriented solutions.

Figure 1 is a model showing the concepts important in modeling services. As you can see the number of concepts is relatively small and should be reasonably familiar to anyone having worked on service-oriented solutions.

Note, however that although the profile is a realization of this model a number of the concepts are not explicit stereotypes in the profile. For example there is no stereotype for operation or for protocol as these are existing notions in the UML 2.0 that the profile reuses without any ambiguity or further constraint.

The following table lists the elements of the UML 2.0 meta model that are used as meta classes for stereotypes in the UML Profile.

UML 2.0 Meta Class	Stereotypes
Class	Message, Service Partition, Service Provider
Classifier	Service Consumer
Collaboration	Service Collaboration
Connector	Service Channel
Interface	Service Specification
Port	Service, Service Gateway
Property	Message Attachment

3.2 The Profile Defined

To describe the concepts supported by the UML profile for software services we can begin by looking at the details of the profile itself. Figure 2 is a UML 2.0 profile diagram, it illustrates the details of the profile with each stereotype, its meta class using the extension notation (filled arrow head). Additionally, a number of constraints in the model are described, particularly those co-constraints between profile elements.

By reference to Figure 2 we can review the key elements of how services and service interactions are defined in the profile, and some of the expected uses and constraints when modeling services and service interactions using the profile.

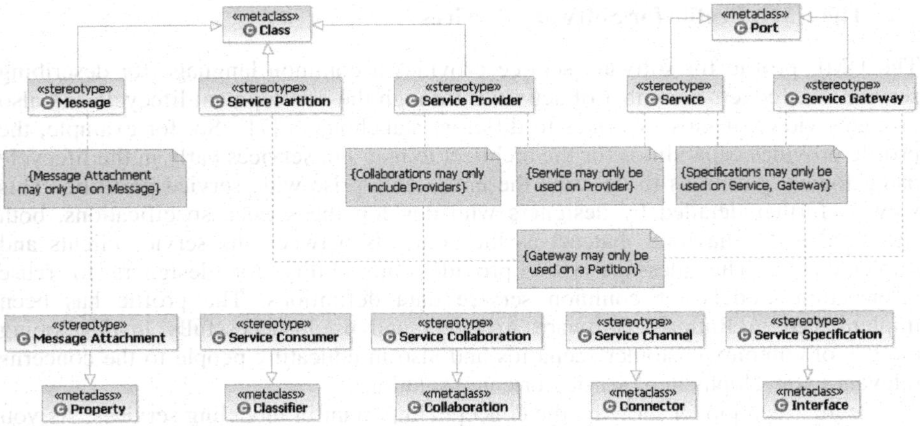

Fig. 2. UML 2.0 profile

- **Message:** A message represents the concept of a container for actual data which has meaning to the service and the consumer. A message may not have operations, it may have public properties and associations to other classes (one assumes classes of some domain model). A message stereotype has a property to denote it's assumed encoding form (i.e. "SOAP-literal", "SOAP-rpc", "ASN.1", etc.). The use of this element may be optional in a tool for two reasons. Firstly the modeler may simply wish to use elements from a domain model directly as the parameters to an operation rather than specifying a message. Secondly the modeler may wish to use the convention of specifying a set of input and output messages on an operation, in which case the modeling tool would have to construct an input and output message matching the parameters when generating service descriptions in WSDL.
- **Message Attachment:** This is used to denote that some component of a message is an attachment to the message as opposed to a direct part of the message itself. In general this is not likely to be used greatly in higher level design activities, but for many processes attached data is important to differentiate from embedded message data. A message attachment stereotype may only be used on properties owned by classes stereotyped as message. The stereotype also has a property to denote its assumed encoding form (i.e. "SOAP-literal", "SOAP-rpc", "ASN.1", etc.). For example, a catalog service may return general product details as a part of the structured message but images as attachments to the message; this also allows us to denote that the encoding of the images is binary as opposed to the textual encoding of the main message.
- **Service:** The service model element provides the end-point for service interaction (in web service terminology) whereas the definition of these interactions is a part of the service specification. In the model a service not only identifies the provided interface, but may also identify required interfaces (such as callback interfaces). This stereotype may only be used on ports owned by Classes or Components stereotyped as Service Provider. A service has an additional property that denotes the binding to be used, such as "SOAP-HTTP", "SOAP-JMS", etc.

- **Service Channel:** A channel represents the communication path between 2 services, importantly it is the channel over which interaction may occur and does not represent any particular interaction. In the web services world each service denotes the binding(s) associated with it so that a client may access it. In the modeling profile we denote binding on the communication between services or between a service and consumers. In this way we can be flexible in understanding the binding requirements. The stereotype has a "channel" property denoting the platform binding mechanism to use in generating the service binding in WSDL; examples might be SOAP-RPC, SOAP-Doc, HTTP-Get, and so on.
- **Service Collaboration:** A service collaboration is a way of specifying the implementation of a service as a collaboration of other services. From a web services point of view this corresponds to the use of BPEL4WS in specifying service implementation. A service collaboration is used as the behavior of a service and, if it is intended to generate to a language such as BPEL it may have other implementation-specific constraints. Participants in a Service Collaboration may be Service Consumers, Service Providers or Service Specifications.
- **Service Consumer:** Any classifier (Class, Component, etc.) may act as the consumer of a service, and that includes another service. While this stereotype is most definitely optional it may be useful in identifying elements of a model that are not services themselves as clients of services. On the other hand it may be overhead and not used.
- **Service Gateway:** A service gateway looks like a service but is only available for use on partitions and not service providers. A gateway acts as a proxy service and can be used to mediate protocols or denote the interface available to a partition. This stereotype may only be applied to a port owned by a Service Partition. For example, we might denote that although a number of services are implemented within a partition only some are available for use outside the partition and so gateways are provided for these services. This disallows other services or partitions from communicating to services that are not exposed via gateways.
- **Service Model:** The Service Model is an architectural view of an SOA highlighting the major elements of a system based on an SOA style.
- **Service Partition:** A service partition represents some logical or physical boundary of the system. It is optional to model partitions, but frequently this concept is very useful. For example, partitions could be used to represent the web, business and data tiers of a traditional n-tier application. Partitions might also be used to denote more physical boundaries such as my primary data center, secondary site, customer site, partners etc. in which case the crossing of partitions may have particular constraints for security, allowed protocols, bandwidth and so on. A partition may only have properties that represent nested parts, be they services or other partitions (this is a constraint - no other elements may currently be represented in a partition). A partition may not have any owned properties, operations or behaviors. It may have parts that are either Service Providers or Service Specifications. This stereotype also has a property "classifier" which is used to group partitions that represent similar concepts. A partition also has the notion of being "strict", if a partition denotes that all communication between it and other partitions must be directed through typed gateways then it is said to be a strict partition.

- **Service Provider:** The Service Provider is a software element that provides one or more services. In modeling terms one would most usually expect to see a UML component here, however such a restriction seems arbitrary and so the metaclass is noted as Class for more flexibility. A service provider has a property that captures information about its location although the meaning of this is implementation dependent. The Class acting as the service provider may not expose any attributes or operations directly, only public ports may be provided (stereotyped as service) and these are typed by service specifications (or classes realizing service specifications).
  A Service Provider may not have any directly owned properties, operations or behaviors. All operations are provided through the ports on the provider. The location property, while implementation/platform specific is useful in generating service endpoint names. For example with WSDL the location may be `http://svc.myco.com/` and a service might be called CustInfo, in which case the endpoint name for the service could be generated as `http://svc.myco.com/CustInfo`.
- **Service Specification:** The use of an interface denotes a set of operations provided by a service; note that a service may implement more than one interface. By convention it is possible to attach a protocol state machine or UML 2.0 Collaboration to such a specification to denote the order of invocation of operations on a service specification. With such a behavioral specification any implementing service can be validated against not only a static but dynamic specification of its structure and behavior. Note that the service specification may only provide public operations. The service specification may not have owned properties and all operations shall be public. The stereotype also has a property "published" that denotes whether the service is assumed to be published into a service repository; this is a different notion from the public/private property provided by UML.

4 The Role of a Service Model in MDD

A description of services and service assemblies using the UML profile for software services is useful in that it provides:

- A consistent set of concepts, notations, and semantics for modeling services and service interactions.
- A first-class "domain-specific language" for service modeling to support designers of SOAs as they design and reason about their solution.
- A language that can act as the target for transformations from more abstract, business-focused analysis models that will result in a logical service design model used as the basis for a service-oriented solution.
- A consistent basis for generating service realizations from the logical service model.

These observations are particularly important in terms of supporting a model-driven approach to service-oriented solutions. The classical approach of mapping from Computation Independent Model (CIM) to Platform Independent Model (PIM) to Platform Specific Model (PSM) can be instantiated by equating these three levels to a business analysis model, services model, and services implementation, respectively. Mappings between these models can be defined as the basis for automation in the form of model transformations. Here, we briefly discuss the CIM-PSM mapping before a more offering a more detailed concrete example of a PIM to PSM mapping for model-driven design of services-oriented solutions.

4.1 Generation of a Service Model from an Analysis Model

In many projects detailed business-level analysis takes place to understand the business context within which any IT solution must operate. The resulting business analysis model is useful as documentation of the business needs and goals. However, in addition service models can be generated from business analysis models. A simple example of a business analysis model consistent with the business modeling discipline defined in the Rational Unified Process (RUP) is illustrated in Figure 3.

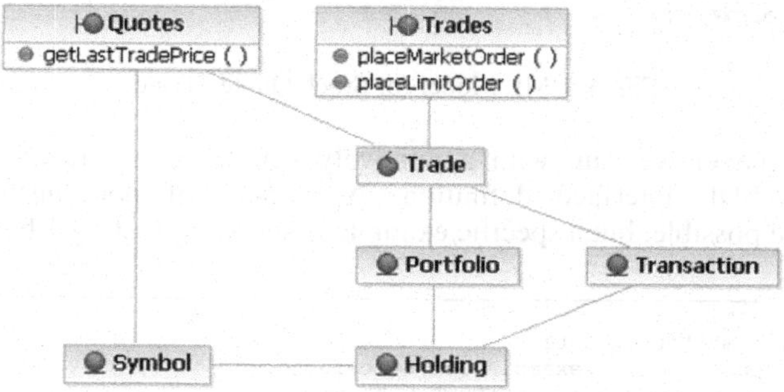

Fig. 3. RUP Analysis Model for Stock Portfolio

A transformation from this model to the service model shown later in Figure 4 is relatively easy to specify. A number of interesting aspects of that transformation are of note. For example, the transformation crosses abstraction boundaries and so we would expect transformations of types and some structures. In this case we would expect the boundary elements to be transformed to service specifications and service providers with Entities that are operation parameters being transformed as messages. Control elements and internal Entities would not be transformed to the service model, they are appropriate to the implementation of the service and not its specification.

4.2 Generation of WSDL from the Service Model

Based on this profile we are able to define specific model transformations that convert service models expressed using the profile into various target languages for service realization. Of particular interest is the Web Services Definition Language (WSDL), a standard maintained by the World Wide Web Consortium (W3C). WSDL is "an XML format for describing network services as a set of endpoints operating on messages containing either document-oriented or procedure-oriented information."[3] Improvements

[3] See the WSDL description at the W3C website: http://www.w3.org/TR/wsdl.

in the design of service implementations can be gained by being able to model the logical design of services-oriented solutions and generating the WSDL service specifications from these models by applying a well-defined set of model transforms.

Figure 4 illustrates a simple stock quote service example (derived from an example discussed in the WSDL specification document). In this example the Service Specification provides the structural interface specification, the Message elements model the types of the structures passed into and returned from the operations, and a service provider realizing the specification.

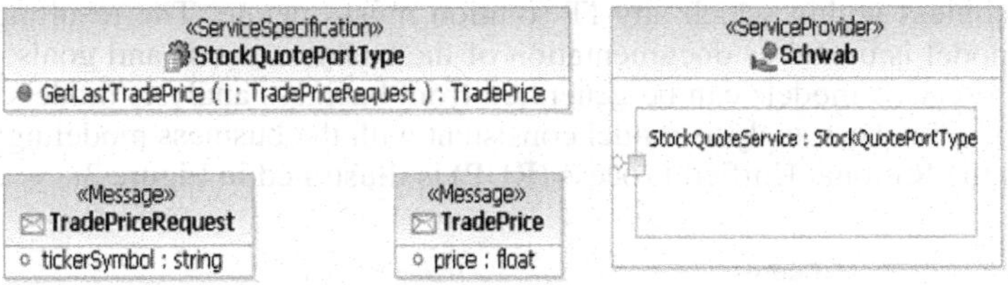

Fig. 4. UML Model for Stock Quote Service

From this model we can, with a relatively simple set of transformation rules, generate a WSDL interface definition. A number of possible transformation approaches are possible, but a specific example is shown in Listing 1 below.

```
<?xml version="1.0"?>
<definitions name="StockQuote"
  targetNamespace="http://example.com/stockquote.wsdl"
  xmlns:tns="http://example.com/stockquote.wsdl"
  xmlns:xsd1="http://example.com/stockquote.xsd"
  xmlns:soap="http://schemas.xmlsoap.org/wsdl/soap/"
  xmlns="http://schemas.xmlsoap.org/wsdl/">

  <types>
    <schema targetNamespace="http://example.com/stockquote.xsd"
      xmlns="http://www.w3.org/2000/10/XMLSchema">
      <element name="TradePriceRequest">
        <complexType>
          <all>
            <element name="tickerSymbol" type="string"/>
          </all>
        </complexType>
      </element>
      <element name="TradePrice">
        <complexType>
          <all>
            <element name="price" type="float"/>
          </all>
        </complexType>
      </element>
    </schema>
  </types>

  <message name="GetLastTradePriceInput">
    <part name="body" element="xsd1:TradePriceRequest"/>
  </message>
```

Listing 1. Generated WSDL for Stock Quote Service

```
  <message name="GetLastTradePriceOutput">
    <part name="body" element="xsd1:TradePrice"/>
  </message>

  <portType name="StockQuotePortType">
    <operation name="GetLastTradePrice">
      <input message="tns:GetLastTradePriceInput"/>
      <output message="tns:GetLastTradePriceOutput"/>
    </operation>
  </portType>

  <binding name="StockQuoteSoapBinding" type="tns:StockQuotePortType">
    <soap:binding style="document"
        transport="http://schemas.xmlsoap.org/soap/http"/>
      <operation name="GetLastTradePrice">
        <soap:operation soapAction="http://example.com/GetLastTradePrice"/>
        <input>
          <soap:body use="literal"/>
        </input>
        <output>
          <soap:body use="literal"/>
        </output>
      </operation>
    </binding>

    <service name="StockQuoteService">
      <documentation>My first service</documentation>
      <port name="StockQuotePort" binding="tns:StockQuoteBinding">
        <soap:address location="http://example.com/stockquote"/>
      </port>
    </service>

</definitions>
```

Listing 1. *(Continued)*

The mapping demonstrated here relies on some relatively simple translation rules that can readily be automated using a model transformation engine, such as the one embedded in the IBM Rational Software Architect product:

- The Service Provider is used to denote a logical grouping of services and therefore it provides the scope for the outer WSDL definitions element.
- Each Service Specification becomes a WSDL port type, all operations are transformed to WSDL operations defined for the port type.
- All UML2 ports on the service provider become WSDL service definitions, the port types already derived above.
- A single message is created for input parameters and a single message created for returned data; each message has a single associated XML Schema element that aggregates any parameters on the original operation. Best practice is still to define a single class in the model for all information required by an operation (using the Message stereotype).

The example above does not demonstrate how the WSDL bindings are derived – these are derived from the connectors between services or services and their consumers modeled with UML collaborations.

5 Summary

Creating solutions for SOA means rethinking the kinds of systems being built today, reconsidering the skills in an organizations, and redefining the ways in which members of teams collaborate. Most importantly, adopting a service-oriented to development of solutions requires a broader review of its impact on how solutions are designed, what it means to assemble them from disparate services, and how deployed services-oriented applications are managed and evolved.

In this paper we have focused on UML profile offering a common notation and semantics for software service modeling, and the use of this profile for generating service implementations in WSDL. This technology is part of a much broader set of best practices for creating service-oriented solutions, captured as process guidance in the Rational Unified Process (RUP), and supported though automated tools in the IBM Rational Software Development Platform. As we gain experience in the design and realization of service-oriented solutions, we are continually documenting them for external validation (e.g., [8, 9]), adding new modeling support for service design in IBM products, and describing new techniques that help organizations repeatably deliver high quality solutions.

References

1. Daryl Plummer, "Six Missteps That Can Result in SOA Strategy Failure", Gartner Research Report, June 2005.
2. John Dodd, "Practical Service Specification and Design", CBDi Series, www.cbdiforum.com, May 2005.
3. OMG, "MDA Guide v1.0.1", Available at http://www.omg.org/docs/omg/03-06-01.pdf 12th June 2003.
4. A.W. Brown, J. Conallen, D. Tropeano, "Models. Modeling, and Model Driven Development", in *Model-Driven Software Development*, pages 1-17, S. Beydeda, M. Book, V. Gruhn (Eds.), Springer Verlag, 2005.
5. A.W. Brown, J. Conallen, D. Tropeano, "Practical Insights into MDA: Lessons from the Design and Use of an MDA Toolkit", in *Model-Driven Software Development*, pages 403-432, S. Beydeda, M. Book, V. Gruhn (Eds.), Springer Verlag, 2005.
6. Jim Rumbaugh, Grady Booch, Ivar Jacobsen, "The UML 2.0 Reference Manual", Second Edition, Addison-Wesley, 2005.
7. S. Johnston, "Modeling Service-oriented Solutions", IBM Developerworks, http://www.ibm.com/developerworks/rational/library/jul05/johnston/, July 2005.
8. A.W. Brown, S. Iyengar, S.K. Johnson, "A Rational Approach to Model-Driven Development", IBM Systems Journal, pages 463-480, Vol. 44, #4, July 2006.
9. A.W. Brown, M. Delbaere, P. Eeles, S. Johnston, R. Weaver, "Realizing Service oriented Solutions with the IBM Software Development Platform", IBM Systems Journal, pages 727-752, Vol. 44, #4, October 2005,

Towards Adaptive Management of QoS-Aware Service Compositions – Functional Architecture*

Mariusz Momotko[1], Michał Gajewski[1], André Ludwig[2],
Ryszard Kowalczyk[3], Marek Kowalkiewicz[4], and Jian Ying Zhang[3]

[1] Rodan Systems S.A., ul. Puławska 465, 02-844 Warsaw, Poland
{Michal.Gajewski, Mariusz.Momotko}@rodan.pl
[2] University of Leipzig, Marschnerstr. 31, 04109 Leipzig, Germany
ludwig@wifa.uni-leipzig.de
[3] Swinburne University of Technology, PO Box 218 Hawthorn, Victoria 3122, Australia
{jyzhang, rkowalczyk}@it.swin.edu.au
[4] Poznan University of Economics, Al. Niepodleglosci 10, 60-967 Poznan, Poland
M.Kowalkiewicz@kie.ae.poznan.pl

Abstract. Service compositions enable users to realize their complex needs as a single request. Despite intensive research, especially in the area of business processes, web services and grids, an open and valid question is still how to manage service compositions in order to satisfy both functional and non-functional requirements as well as adapt to dynamic changes. In this paper we propose an (functional) architecture for adaptive management of QoS-aware service compositions. Comparing to the other existing architectures this one offers two major advantages. Firstly, this architecture supports various execution strategies based on dynamic selection and negotiation of services included in a service composition, contracting based on service level agreements, service enactment with flexible support for exception handling, monitoring of service level objectives, and profiling of execution data. Secondly, the architecture is built on the basis of well know existing standards to communicate and exchange data, which significantly reduces effort to integrate existing solutions and tools from different vendors. A first prototype of this architecture has been implemented within an EU-funded Adaptive Service Grid project.

1 Introduction

Users want to realize their needs as simply as possible and, therefore, look for sophisticated services that would handle compound needs related to their life events or business activities as a single request. One of the most promising approaches for such sophisticated services is to implement them as compositions of other, simpler services (referred further to as atomic services).

* This work is partially supported by the European Union FP6 Integrated Project on Adaptive Services Grid (EU-IST-004617) and the International Science Linkages programme under the Australian Government's innovation statement, Backing Australia's Ability on Adaptive Service Agreement and Process Management project (AU-DEST-CG060081).

A. Dan and W. Lamersdorf (Eds.): ICSOC 2006, LNCS 4294, pp. 637 – 649, 2006.

In the last decade, a huge effort has been put into developing solutions targeting management of service composition, especially in the area of web services and grids. As its result, a number of new standards on various aspects of service composition management have been defined. In Web Service Business Process Execution Language (WS-BPEL) OASIS standardised a language to define service compositions. In Web Service Quality Model (WSQM) OASIS also proposed a quality model and a set of quality factors for web services. One of the recent OASIS standards is Web Service Distributed Management (WSDM) which enables management applications to be built using web services, allowing resources to be controlled (and monitored) by many managers through a single interface. Currently, OASIS is working on Web Service Quality Description Language (WS-QDL) which will describe WSQM in a standardised type of XML representation. At the same time, IBM Corporation has defined Web Service Level Agreement (WSLA) – a language to represent service level agreement (SLA) for web services. Recently, GRAAP working group of the Global Grid Forum has prepared a draft version of a WS-Agreement specification which describes domain-independent elements of a simple contracting process, extensible by domain specific elements.

Focusing on adaptive management of service compositions, several intensive research works have been carried out recently. The *eFlow* project at HP labs [3] proposes an adaptive and dynamic approach to manage service compositions focusing on their functional aspects such as dynamic service discovery and ad-hoc changes. The *QUEST* framework ([6]) extends the work done on eFlow introducing quality of service (QoS) provisioning. In that framework, contracting of service compositions and atomic services is done by SLA documents. The MAIS project ([5]) focused on negotiation of web service QoS parameters with the ability to use different negotiation strategies. In the area of SLA-based contracting and monitoring, there are several advanced approaches and frameworks such as those presented in [2] and [9].

Recently, the Adaptive Services Grid (ASG) project proposed a comprehensive approach towards adaptive management of QoS-aware service compositions. This approach integrates well known concepts and techniques and proposes various **execution strategies** (see [8] for further details) based on dynamic selection and negotiation of services included in a service composition, contracting based on service level agreements, service enactment with flexible support for exception handling, monitoring of service level objectives, and profiling of execution data. Due to the various execution strategies, the approach is able to cope with dynamic changes related to the contracted atomic services, re-negotiate a contract in case of QoS constraint violation, and re-select dynamically another atomic service that satisfies QoS constraints. In addition, the approach also considers service profiling and historical execution data and therefore is able to optimise its way of working.

In this paper we define an **(functional) architecture** that can support various execution strategies for service compositions. This architecture includes specification of software components, definition of their public interfaces and detailed description of interaction among them according to the basic tasks common for all execution strategies. Most of the data exchange formats and interaction protocols between components are based on standards as WS-BPEL , WS-Agreement, and WSQM. This approach gives the architecture appropriate flexibility and makes it open for implementations of different components from various software vendors.

The paper is organised as follows. Section 2 introduces the concept of execution strategies for adaptive service compositions management identifying a set of basic tasks common for all execution strategies and presenting briefly the main strategies. Section 3 provides an overview of an (functional) architecture that may support the described execution strategies. This architecture is described in terms of software components and their public interfaces. The next three sections focus on basic tasks organised in various ways within the individual execution strategies. Section 4 describes selection and contracting of atomic services. Section 5 presents enactment and monitoring of an atomic service. Section 6 provides detailed information on exception handling. The paper closes with a conclusion and an outlook of future work.

2 Execution Strategies for Service Compositions

There are many possible strategies for executing a service composition. However, there is a common feature of all possible strategies - they are built on the top of basic tasks. These tasks[1] concern a single atomic service and are specified in **Table 1.**

Table 1. Basic tasks used in all execution strategies

Basic task	***Main responsibility***
Service Selection and Contracting (SC)	Select and contract a concrete atomic service based on its functional (service type) and non-functional (QoS constraints) requirements. In some execution strategies, SC task is done for the whole composition (all atomic services included) before enactment and monitoring. In the other strategies, SC task is intertwined with enactment and monitoring of the individual atomic services according to the service composition specification.
Service Enactment and Monitoring (EM)	Enact (invoke) a concrete atomic service and monitor its execution (w.r.t QoS constraints). Enactment is done according to the service composition specification given as a WS-BPEL process.
Exception handling (Ex)	Three steps to handle exceptions have been identified: 1) renegotiate the contract with the current atomic service provider (and possibly with other service providers affected by the exception); if not possible then 2) re-select a replacement from other atomic service providers that match the service specification and new requirements; otherwise 3) re-plan the whole service composition.

The number of basic tasks used in a strategy depends on the strategy itself, and on the number of atomic services included in a given service composition. As usual, there is no one optimal strategy. Every strategy focuses on different aspects of service executions and has both advantages and disadvantages. Two basic (quite opposite) execution strategies (see also [11] for more details) and three intermediate execution strategies are described in the consecutive sections.

[1] The tasks which are not directly related to execution of a service composition have been omitted (e.g. registration or un-registration of an atomic service).

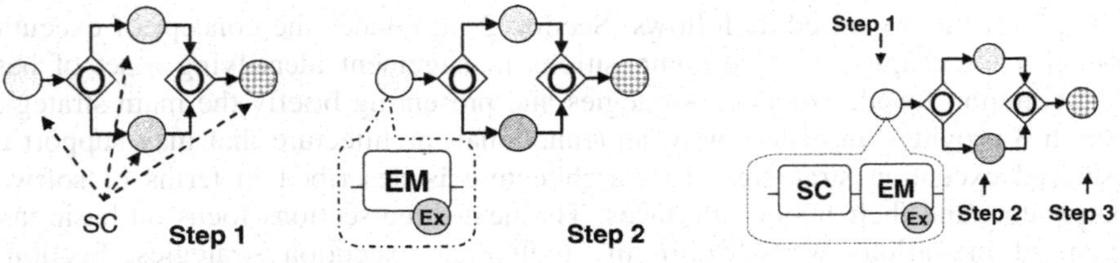

Fig. 1. The concept of the basic strategies: first-contract-all-then-enact (left) and step-by-step-negotiate-and-enact (right)

2.1 First-Contract-All-Then-Enact Strategy

This strategy assumes (see figure 1, left hand side) that selection and contracting of all atomic services included in the service composition (actual execution) is done before its execution (step 1). Execution and monitoring of the individual atomic services is done step by step according to the control flow defined for the service composition. (step 2) Any failure reported during service execution is handled by exception handling mechanism described in the previous section.

This strategy makes it possible to guarantee non-functional requirements for the whole service composition (global level). Since contracting is done before execution, concurrent selection and negotiation is allowed. As a result, it is possible to consider aggregated concessions and preferences (e.g., if the same provider provides services for several atomic services, then some discount may be regarded), so that the service composition QoS parameters can be optimised.

On the contrary, in this strategy all the activities on conditional branches need to be selected and contracted although some of them may never be enacted. A reservation mechanism is needed. Also service implementations registered during service execution cannot be selected. Finally, the strategy requires coordinated negotiation mechanisms with a coordination agent and a set of negotiation agents.

2.2 Step-by-Step-Contract-and-Enact Strategy

This strategy assumes (see figure 1, right hand side) that selection and contracting is done just before atomic service execution. The order of the executed services is determined by definition of the composition. That means that the first atomic service in the service composition can be executed and monitored when its SLA document is established (see figure 1, step 1, first SC then EM). After completion of this atomic service, the selection and contracting is carried out for each subsequent atomic service and followed by its execution (steps 2 and 3). Any failure occurred during service execution is handled by exception mechanism described in the previous sections.

This strategy allows for 'on-the-fly' selection and contracting based on actual QoS values of services that have been executed. This will lead to more accurate and efficient contracting (esp. negotiation) since it is based on what it had been done for the executed services. Only the invoked atomic services are contracted. Services included in the composition but not executed (i.e. included in conditional branches that have not been chosen) are not considered. In addition, selection is able to use atomic services registered after starting execution of the service composition.

On the contrary, the strategy mainly optimises QoS for atomic services which are about to be invoked (local level). Optimisation of the global QoS parameters is hard. Instantiation and execution of the whole service composition can not be guaranteed (i.e. a service implementation is executed but it may be impossible to select and contract a subsequent service implementation) thus failing the whole service composition and wasting already executed services (a need for un-doing the services).

2.3 Other Strategies

The **late-contracting-then-enact strategy** assumes that the selection and contracting of atomic services is done before their execution, as soon as it is sure that they will be executed within a given composition. If, for example, there are two alternative branches, as soon as it is known which of them will be taken, all atomic services on the satisfied branch are selected and contracted. Execution of the atomic services is carried out according to the control flow definition. This strategy is similar to the first-contract-all-then-enact strategy but minimises the risk in contracting services which will never be executed. The risk to not satisfy the global QoS requirements is less than for the mentioned strategy but still exists.

The **first-contract-plausible-then-enact strategy** tries to select and contract first (before service composition execution) all atomic services that belong to the composition path which is the most likely to be executed. The path is predicted on the basis of historical data from previous executions of the service composition. The services that belong to other paths are not selected and contracted. Execution of the atomic services is carried out according to the control flow definition. This strategy minimises the risk of a) contracting services that with high probability of not being executed, b) satisfying the global QoS requirements. However, it will work properly only for that cases in which execution concerns the most probable path in the composition. For the other paths it will have similar problems as the step-by-step-contract-and-enact strategy.

The **first-contract-critical-then-enact strategy** selects and contracts before execution only those atomic services which are hard to be contracted dynamically. 'Hard' in this context means that the number of service candidates for those service specifications is significantly lower than the number of candidates for the other services included. This strategy is similar to the step-by-step-contract-and-enact strategy but reduces the risk of not satisfying the global QoS requirements. On the other hand, it has similar problems with branches which will never be executed.

2.4 Representations for Service Compositions

Specification of a service composition is provided at the design phase of adaptive management of service compositions. This specification describes the composition in terms of control flow (i.e. the order of the invoked atomic **services**) and data flow (mapping between input and output parameters of atomic services). This specification operates on classes of atomic services, instead of concrete services. Basically, such a specification provides a solution to satisfy all (static) functional requirements (classes of atomic services that together satisfy them) and leaves flexibility during processing a request (i.e. execution of the composed service) to select and contract concrete atomic services of given service classes that also satisfy its (dynamic) non-functional requirements.

Making the service composition specification generic is very useful, but on the other hand it prevents from using standard execution engines that process WS-BPEL processes. In order to cope with this problem we propose an intermediate solution based on the concept of generic workflows proposed in [1]. We represent the specification as a **WS-BPEL process** and, instead of invoking concrete atomic services, we invoke concrete **brokers (services) for atomic service classes**. Every atomic service class has its own broker. Such a broker has input and output parameters as every concrete service of this class. In addition, it receives as an input parameter a set of non-functional requirements that makes it possible to choose an appropriate atomic service of a given class.

The way of using service composition specification at the execution phase depends on the applied execution strategy. For the execution strategies which carry out contracting of more than one atomic service before their enactment (e.g. first-contract-then-enact), the specification will be analysed by service selection and contracting component (based on WS-BPEL) in order to contract appropriate atomic services. After that, the input parameter representing non-functional requirements will be replaced with information of the selected atomic service and a reference to the agreed contract (SLA document). For the other execution strategies, which intertwine contracting and enactment, the specification will be interpreted by service enactment component (again based on WS-BPEL) which will invoke appropriate service class brokers. These brokers will be responsible for organising selection and contracting by themselves and then assure appropriate invocation and monitoring.

History from execution of a service composition is represented as a **service composition execution**. This includes basic information about service composition and invoked atomic services (transformed information from invocation of service class brokers) in the form of a workflow log. This log is used for service profiling.

3 Architecture Overview

On the basis of the execution strategies briefly presented in the previous sections we present a functional architecture of an adaptive service composition management subsystem (i.e. part of a larger system to manage service compositions, for example Adaptive Service Grid platform [7]). In general, this architecture aims at implementation of all previously described strategies.

The subsystem provides two public interfaces (see figure 2): *scEnactment* and service *scMonitoring*. The first interface includes just one method *enact* which is responsible for execution of a service composition. As the input this method requires specification of a service composition (given as a WS-BPEL process), input data and non-functional constraints (e.g. maximal duration). In the first step, the subsystem determines the best strategy to execute the composition. This strategy is determined on the basis of composition specification (static) as well as profiling data (dynamic, given for concrete service but also for service type). The next steps are specific for individual execution strategies and are related to basic tasks described earlier.

In the first-contract-all-then-enact strategy, all abstract atomic services (i.e. service type brokers) included in the composition are used to select concrete atomic services and to contract one of their composition that is able to satisfy all QoS constraints. Within service specification all abstract services are replaced by concrete already contracted atomic services. In the next stage such composition defined as a WS-BPEL process is executed. In the step-by-step-contracting-and-enactment strategy the composition is executed step by step. The composition is represented as a WS-BPEL process which instead of concrete services includes calls to service type brokers. When a broker is executed it first triggers selection and contracting for a given abstract service and then, having concrete atomic service, executes it.

The second subsystem interface, namely *scMonitoring* is responsible for monitoring and administration of the executed service compositions. It provides methods to get information about execution history of a given composition (in a form of execution log), to visualise its execution or to do some administration tasks such as suspending or resuming.

The subsystem requires three interfaces from atomic service providers: one (optional) for negotiation of the contract between the service composition provider and a given atomic service provider, one for invocation of the atomic service (obligatory), and one for (also optional) gathering the values of QoS parameters agreed to be monitored by the service provider.

The subsystem consists of six software components: Execution Coordinator, Service Selection & Negotiation Manager, Service Level Agreement Manager, Service Enactment Engine, Service Monitor, and Dynamic Service Profiler.

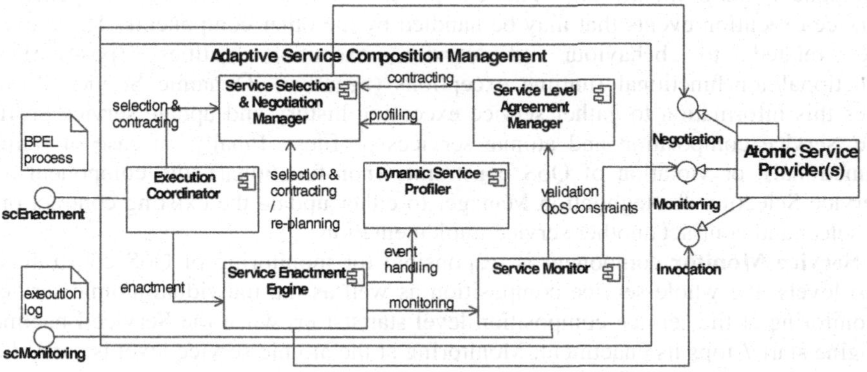

Fig. 2. The functional architecture for adaptive service composition management

Execution Coordinator is responsible for selection of the best execution strategy for a given service composition. To do that it analyses specification of service composition and uses profiling data. It also validates strategy selection rules checking what strategy satisfies the greatest number of the rules.

Service Selection & Negotiation Manager is responsible for selection and contracting atomic service implementations that may be invoked within a given service composition. This selection is done for individual service specifications and is based on both functional as well as non-functional requirements. On the basis of a generic process (i.e. WS-BPEL process which invokes service type brokers, extended of information required to select service implementations), it makes a concrete process replacing atomic service type brokers with the most appropriate atomic service implementations. The component also provides negotiation features that support the service composition provider with possibility to negotiate some/all non-functional requirements that were not satisfied initially by the selected services. The contracts used during negotiation and contracting are taken from SLA Manager. To negotiate with atomic services it uses *Negotiation* interface provided by their providers and FIPA Iterative Contract Net Protocol. Profiling data are extracted from Dynamic Service Profiler.

Service Level Agreement Manager (SLA Manager) is responsible for management of SLA documents compliant with WS-Agreement (XML format). The SLA Manager creates SLA templates that are used during negotiation and contracting, and stores the agreed SLA documents. In addition, it verifies SLA documents (i.e. QoS constraints) during invocation of respective atomic services. Meaning of QoS parameters is defined in WSQM standard.

Service Enactment Engine is responsible for enactment of a service composition represented as a WS-BPEL process. According to the process definition, the component invokes either individual atomic services (first contract then enact strategies) or service type brokers (step by step strategies) passing appropriate input data and gathering the invocation results. For atomic services (described in WSDL) such invocation is done by calling *Invocation* interface provided by the service provider (or any additional invocation layer). When a service invocation begins, the component starts monitoring. The component is also responsible for generating service execution events that may be handled by the other components. These events are related to behaviour of service execution entities (positive) or functional/non-functional runtime exceptions (negative). Dynamic Service Profiler uses this information to gather service execution history and update service profiles (i.e. service composition and atomic services profiles). Finally, in case of failures (functional), or violation of QoS constraints (non-functional), the component asks Service Selection & Negotiation Manager to either update the existing contract or to re-select and contract another service implementation.

Service Monitor component is responsible for monitoring of QoS constraints at two levels: the whole service composition as well as the individual atomic services. Monitoring at the service composition level starts/stops when the Service Enactment Engine starts/stops its enactment. Monitoring at the atomic service level is carried out for every invoked service. By analogy, it starts/stops atomic service monitoring when the atomic service starts/stops its invocation. For every atomic service there is one monitoring rule, which is triggered periodically (the resolution for this activity is determined on the basis of previous executions as well as required QoS parameters related to its duration). When it is triggered, Service Monitor asks the atomic service provider via *Monitoring* interface to provide the values for the QoS parameters defined as 'monitored by the provider' in respective SLA document. These QoS parameters are completed with other QoS parameters monitored by the subsystem itself and included in the SLA document. This document is then verified against QoS constraints by *Validation* interface provided by SLA Manager. If there is any violation of QoS constraint, it is reported to Service Enactment Engine.

Dynamic Service Profiler is responsible for gathering data describing basic QoS parameters and, on their basis, calculating more advanced QoS parameters. To collect all basic QoS parameters it listens to service execution events.

4 Selection and Contracting

The detailed scenario for selection and contracting of an atomic activity is presented in figure 3. *Service Selection & Negotiation Manager* finds all atomic services of a given type (steps 1, 2). In addition, for all returned services the component asks Dynamic Service Profiler for profiling data that may be used in further validation of QoS constraints (steps 3, 4).

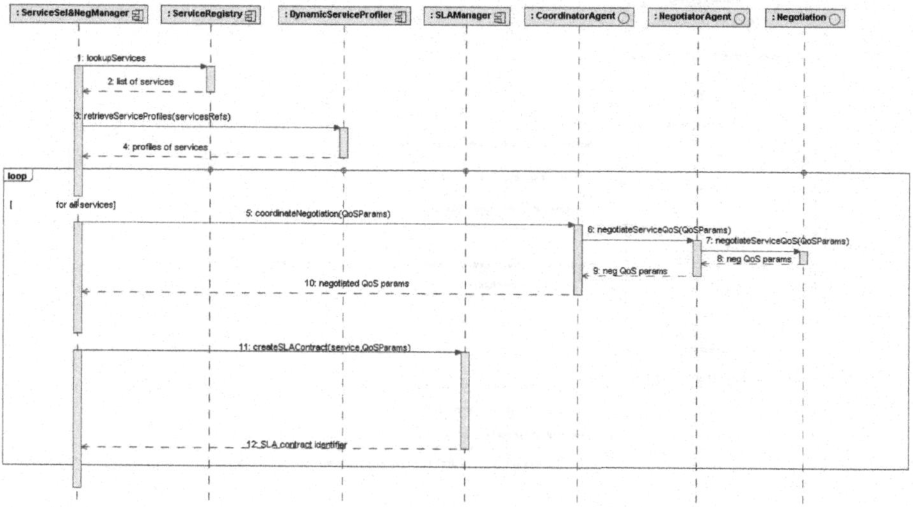

Fig. 3. Selection and contracting services by iterative negotiation

Then an iterative process of service selection starts (steps from 5 to 12). This process is organised by a Coordination agent and usually based on negotiation techniques [3]. This agent starts and then coordinates all negotiation agents which are responsible for negotiation QoS parameters with individual service providers (steps from 6 to 9). Negotiation may be iterative. In general, there are some configuration parameters which describe how many iterations is possible, and what is the weighted value of the negotiated QoS parameters. If this value is acceptable (i.e. between minimum and maximum required values) then the selection process is completed and the selected atomic service is contracted. To contract it, *Service Selection & Negotiation Manager* asks *SLA Manager* to create a contract with the agreed QoS parameters. This contract is represented as a SLA document and managed by *SLA Manager*. Reference to the SLA document is added to service composition specification. This gives an opportunity to verify actual QoS values against expected QoS ones for every invoked atomic service.

5 Enactment and Monitoring

The detailed scenario for (positive) enactment and monitoring of an atomic activity is presented in figure 4. Based on the atomic service implementation reference *Service Enactment Engine* calls *Invocation interface* (of *Atomic Service Provider*) to retrieve a service instance.

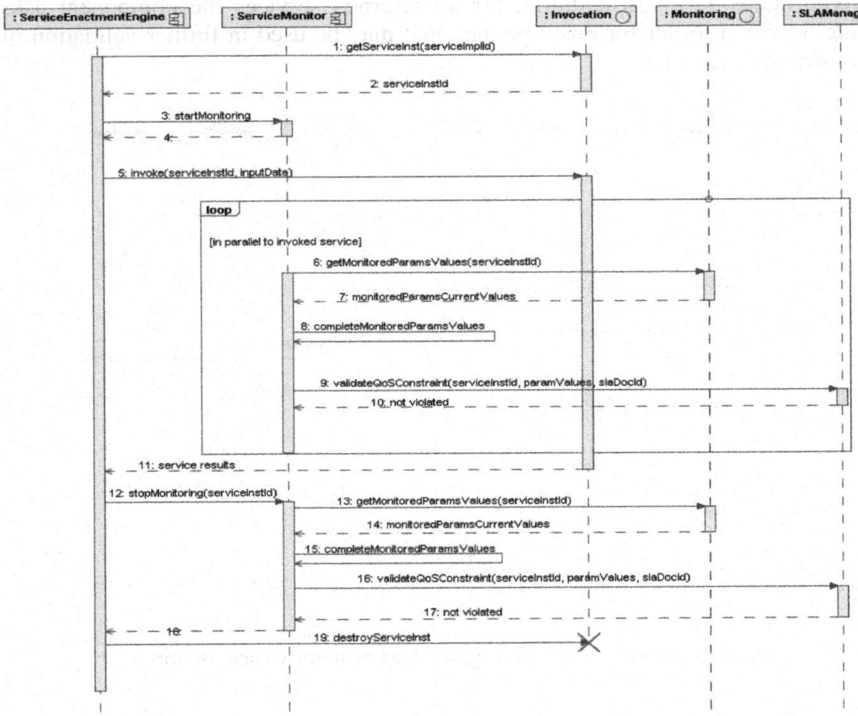

Fig. 4. The positive scenario of an atomic service execution

After that it uses *Service Monitor* to run monitoring for this particular service instance. Then again *Service Enactment Engine* calls *Invocation* interface to invoke the service instance passing its input data. Service invocation and monitoring are conducted in parallel. With the assumed resolution (i.e. how often the monitor verifies a QoS constraint) *Service Monitor* gathers current values of monitored parameters through *Monitoring* interface and verifies them against QoS constraint (for the service) using *SLA Manager*. The resolution can be expressed via different strategies – once the whole service execution, as often as possible or service profile value, which is the default choice that is equal to the half of the minimal service execution time (assigned a priori and adjusted periodically after real executions). When the service instance finishes its execution, *Service Enactment Engine* stops monitoring and the post-execution QoS validation is conducted. Additionally *Service Monitor* performs composed level QoS validation i.e. it checks whether (even positive) result of the currently finishing atomic service does not harm the overall (at composed level) QoS constraints. At the end *Service Enactment Engine* calls *Invocation* interface to destroy the service instance.

6 Exception Handling

During execution *Service Monitor* must be prepared to deal with different exceptional situations, which are caused either by QoS violations or any other runtime exceptions. Figure 5 presents a (negative) atomic service execution scenario where *Service Monitor* is informed by *SLA Manager* about QoS constraint violation. In such case the first step is to suspend execution of the whole composition. Then *Service Enactment Engine* calls *Service Selection and Negotiation Manager* (*SS&NM*) to re-plan the composed service passing a composed service execution log (i.e. history of execution together with the current state).

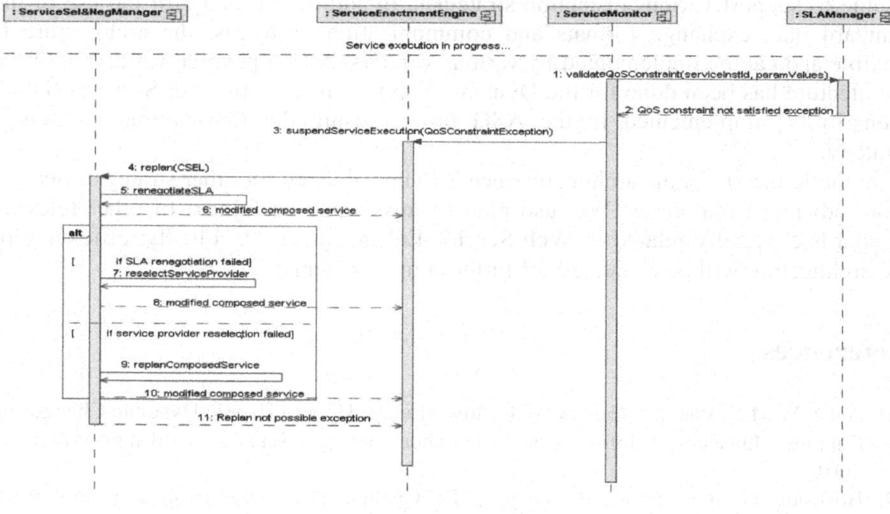

Fig. 5. Exception handling in case of QoS violation

The latter component tries to resume service execution using the following approaches. First it tries to re-renegotiate the contract with the existing service (i.e. increase its cost using spare money and decrease its duration). If it is not possible, the in the second step the component checks if a given atomic service may be replaced by another atomic service of the same type. Such verification is carried out as a standard selection & contracting procedure. The only difference is the set of atomic service candidates which excludes service(s) that already failed. If it is also impossible then final possibility is to re-plan the whole service composition that will meet the overall request requirements. This process involves a service re-composer and is described more in detail in [10].

If all of the mentioned steps fail, *SS&NM* throws an exception. In the aftermath of it *Service Enactment Engine* is not able to continue service execution and reports it to the service composition provider. Otherwise *SS&NM* delivers a modified composed service so that *Service Enactment Engine* could continue the execution.

7 Conclusions

Adaptive management of service compositions is an area of web services research that has recently been attracting more and more attention. The most important questions stimulating research in this area include proper management of service compositions in order to satisfy not only functional requirements, but also non functional ones. Another important issue is adaptation to dynamic changes in the service environment, which so far has not been researched to a satisfactory extent, and there is still a clear need for improvement of current methods and tools.

The work described in this paper aims at defining an (functional) architecture towards adaptive management of QoS aware service compositions. This architecture is able to support various execution strategies. In addition, because of the use of the standard data exchange formats and communication protocols, the architecture is flexible and can be implemented by various vendors. A first positive validation of the architecture has been done for the Dynamic Supply Chain of Internet Services (DSC) scenario [7] implemented in the ASG project using the first-contract-then-enact strategy.

In the future steps, the architecture needs to be validated for other strategies and yet more advanced real cases. We also plan to investigate usefulness of other relevant standards especially related to Web Service Enhancement 2.0. Finally, efficiency of the architecture will be evaluated for further improvements.

References

1. Aalst, W.M.P. Van der: Generic Workflow Models: How to Handle Dynamic Change and Capture Management Information? Computer Systems, Science and Engineering, 15, 2001.
2. Boström, G., Giambiagi, P., Olsson, T.: Quality of Service Evaluation in Virtual Organizations Using SLAs. submitted to 1st Workshop on Interoperability Solutions to Trust, Security, Policies and QoS for Enhanced Enterprise Systems, 2006.
3. Braun, P., J. Brzostowski, J., Kersten, G., Kim, J., Kowalczyk, R., Strecker, S., Vahidov, R.: E-Negotiation Systems and Software Agents Methods, Models, and Applications. In i-DMSS: Foundations, Applications and Challenges. UK, 2005.
4. Casati, F., Ilnicki, S., Jin, L., Krishnamoorthy, V., Ming-Chien Shan, M., Ch.: Adaptive and Dynamic Service Composition in eFlow. HP technical Report HPL-2000-39, March.
5. Comuzzi, M., Penrici, B., An Architecture for Flexible Web Service QoS Negotiation, EDOC, 2005.

6. Gu, X., Nahrstedt, K., Chang, R., Ward, and C.: QoS-assured service composition in managed service overlay networks. Proc. of Distributed Computing Systems, 2003.
7. Integrated Project "Adaptive Services Grid", http://asg-platform.org
8. Momotko, M., Gajewski, M., Ludwig, A., Kowalczyk, R., Kowalkiewicz, M., Zhang, J. Y.: Towards Adaptive Management of QoS-aware Service Compositions, International Journal on Multiagent and Grid Systems, volume 2:2, Sept 2006 (to appear).
9. Salle, A., Bartolini, C.: Management by Contract, HPL-2003-186, HP labs, 2004.
10. Weske, M., Gajewski, M., Momotko, M., Mayer, H., Schuschel, H.: Dynamic Failure Recovery of Generated Workflows. DEXA'2005, BPMPM Workshop, 2005.
11. Zeng, L., Benatallah, B., Lei, H., Ngu, A., H., H., Flaxer, D., and Chang, H.: Flexible composition of enterprise web services. Electronic Markets - Web Services, 2003.

Author Index

Lecture Notes in Computer Science

For information about Vols. 1–4237

please contact your bookseller or Springer

Vol. 4337: S. Arun-Kumar, N. Garg (Eds.), FSTTCS 2006: Foundations of Software Technology and Theoretical Computer Science. XIII, 430 pages. 2006.

Vol. 4333: U. Reimer, D. Karagiannis (Eds.), Practial Aspects of Knowledge Management. XII, 338 pages. 2006. (Sublibrary LNAI).

Vol. 4331: G. Min, B. Di Martino, L.T. Yang, M. Guo, G. Ruenger (Eds.), Frontiers of High Performance Computing and Networking – ISPA 2006 Workshops. XXVII, 1141 pages. 2006.

Vol. 4329: R. Barua, T. Lange (Eds.), Progress in Cryptology - INDOCRYPT 2006. X, 454 pages. 2006.

Vol. 4326: S. Göbel, R. Malkewitz, I. Iurgel (Eds.), Technologies for Interactive Digital Storytelling and Entertainment. X, 384 pages. 2006.

Vol. 4325: J. Cao, I. Stojmenovic, X. Jia, S.K. Das (Eds.), Mobile Ad-hoc and Sensor Networks. XIX, 887 pages. 2006.

Vol. 4318: H. Lipmaa, M. Yung, D. Lin (Eds.), Information Security and Cryptology. XI, 305 pages. 2006.

Vol. 4313: T. Margaria, B. Steffen (Eds.), Leveraging Applications of Formal Methods. IX, 197 pages. 2006.

Vol. 4312: S. Sugimoto, J. Hunter, A. Rauber, A. Morishima (Eds.), Digital Libraries: Achievements, Challenges and Opportunities. XVIII, 571 pages. 2006.

Vol. 4311: K. Cho, P. Jacquet (Eds.), Technologies for Advanced Heterogeneous Networks II. XI, 253 pages. 2006.

Vol. 4307: P. Ning, S. Qing, N. Li (Eds.), Information and Communications Security. XIV, 558 pages. 2006.

Vol. 4306: Y. Avrithis, Y. Kompatsiaris, S. Staab, N.E. O'Connor (Eds.), Semantic Multimedia. XII, 241 pages. 2006.

Vol. 4305: A.A. Shvartsman (Ed.), Principles of Distributed Systems. XIII, 441 pages. 2006.

Vol. 4304: A. Sattar, B.-H. Kang (Eds.), AI 2006: Advances in Artificial Intelligence. XXVII, 1303 pages. 2006. (Sublibrary LNAI).

Vol. 4302: J. Domingo-Ferrer, L. Franconi (Eds.), Privacy in Statistical Databases. XI, 383 pages. 2006.

Vol. 4301: D. Pointcheval, Y. Mu, K. Chen (Eds.), Cryptology and Network Security. XIII, 381 pages. 2006.

Vol. 4300: Y.Q. Shi (Ed.), Transactions on Data Hiding and Multimedia Security I. IX, 139 pages. 2006.

Vol. 4296: M.S. Rhee, B. Lee (Eds.), Information Security and Cryptology – ICISC. XIII, 358 pages. 2006.

Vol. 4295: J.D. Carswell, T. Tezuka (Eds.), Web and Wireless Geographical Information Systems. XI, 269 pages. 2006.

Vol. 4294: A. Dan, W. Lamersdorf (Eds.), Service-Oriented Computing – ICSOC 2006. XIX, 653 pages. 2006.

Vol. 4293: A. Gelbukh, C.A. Reyes-Garcia (Eds.), MICAI 2006: Advances in Artificial Intelligence. XXVIII, 1232 pages. 2006. (Sublibrary LNAI).

Vol. 4292: G. Bebis, R. Boyle, B. Parvin, D. Koracin, P. Remagnino, A. Nefian, G. Meenakshisundaram, V. Pascucci, J. Zara, J. Molineros, H. Theisel, T. Malzbender (Eds.), Advances in Visual Computing, Part II. XXXII, 906 pages. 2006.

Vol. 4291: G. Bebis, R. Boyle, B. Parvin, D. Koracin, P. Remagnino, A. Nefian, G. Meenakshisundaram, V. Pascucci, J. Zara, J. Molineros, H. Theisel, T. Malzbender (Eds.), Advances in Visual Computing, Part I. XXXI, 916 pages. 2006.

Vol. 4290: M. van Steen, M. Henning (Eds.), Middleware 2006. XIII, 425 pages. 2006.

Vol. 4289: M. Ackermann, B. Berendt, M. Grobelnik, A. Hotho, D. Mladenič, G. Semeraro, M. Spiliopoulou, G. Stumme, V. Svatek, M. van Someren (Eds.), Semantics, Web and Mining. X, 197 pages. 2006. (Sublibrary LNAI).

Vol. 4288: T. Asano (Ed.), Algorithms and Computation. XX, 766 pages. 2006.

Vol. 4286: P. Spirakis, M. Mavronicolas, S. Kontogiannis (Eds.), Internet and Network Economics. XI, 401 pages. 2006.

Vol. 4285: Y. Matsumoto, R. Sproat, K.-F. Wong, M. Zhang (Eds.), Computer Processing of Oriental Languages. XVII, 544 pages. 2006. (Sublibrary LNAI).

Vol. 4284: X. Lai, K. Chen (Eds.), Advances in Cryptology – ASIACRYPT 2006. XIV, 468 pages. 2006.

Vol. 4283: Y.Q. Shi, B. Jeon (Eds.), Digital Watermarking. XII, 474 pages. 2006.

Vol. 4282: Z. Pan, A. Cheok, M. Haller, R.W.H. Lau, H. Saito, R. Liang (Eds.), Advances in Artificial Reality and Tele-Existence. XXIII, 1347 pages. 2006.

Vol. 4281: K. Barkaoui, A. Cavalcanti, A. Cerone (Eds.), Theoretical Aspects of Computing - ICTAC 2006. XV, 371 pages. 2006.

Vol. 4280: A.K. Datta, M. Gradinariu (Eds.), Stabilization, Safety, and Security of Distributed Systems. XVII, 590 pages. 2006.

Vol. 4279: N. Kobayashi (Ed.), Programming Languages and Systems. XI, 423 pages. 2006.

Vol. 4278: R. Meersman, Z. Tari, P. Herrero (Eds.), On the Move to Meaningful Internet Systems 2006: OTM 2006 Workshops, Part II. XLV, 1004 pages. 2006.

Vol. 4277: R. Meersman, Z. Tari, P. Herrero (Eds.), On the Move to Meaningful Internet Systems 2006: OTM 2006 Workshops, Part I. XLV, 1009 pages. 2006.

Vol. 4276: R. Meersman, Z. Tari (Eds.), On the Move to Meaningful Internet Systems 2006: CoopIS, DOA, GADA, and ODBASE, Part II. XXXII, 752 pages. 2006.

Vol. 4275: R. Meersman, Z. Tari (Eds.), On the Move to Meaningful Internet Systems 2006: CoopIS, DOA, GADA, and ODBASE, Part I. XXXI, 1115 pages. 2006.

Vol. 4274: Q. Huo, B. Ma, E.-S. Chng, H. Li (Eds.), Chinese Spoken Language Processing. XXIV, 805 pages. 2006. (Sublibrary LNAI).

Vol. 4273: I. Cruz, S. Decker, D. Allemang, C. Preist, D. Schwabe, P. Mika, M. Uschold, L. Aroyo (Eds.), The Semantic Web - ISWC 2006. XXIV, 1001 pages. 2006.

Vol. 4272: P. Havinga, M. Lijding, N. Meratnia, M. Wegdam (Eds.), Smart Sensing and Context. XI, 267 pages. 2006.

Vol. 4271: F.V. Fomin (Ed.), Graph-Theoretic Concepts in Computer Science. XIII, 358 pages. 2006.

Vol. 4270: H. Zha, Z. Pan, H. Thwaites, A.C. Addison, M. Forte (Eds.), Interactive Technologies and Sociotechnical Systems. XVI, 547 pages. 2006.

Vol. 4269: R. State, S. van der Meer, D. O'Sullivan, T. Pfeifer (Eds.), Large Scale Management of Distributed Systems. XIII, 282 pages. 2006.

Vol. 4268: G. Parr, D. Malone, M. Ó Foghlú (Eds.), Autonomic Principles of IP Operations and Management. XIII, 237 pages. 2006.

Vol. 4267: A. Helmy, B. Jennings, L. Murphy, T. Pfeifer (Eds.), Autonomic Management of Mobile Multimedia Services. XIII, 257 pages. 2006.

Vol. 4266: H. Yoshiura, K. Sakurai, K. Rannenberg, Y. Murayama, S. Kawamura (Eds.), Advances in Information and Computer Security. XIII, 438 pages. 2006.

Vol. 4265: L. Todorovski, N. Lavrač, K.P. Jantke (Eds.), Discovery Science. XIV, 384 pages. 2006. (Sublibrary LNAI).

Vol. 4264: J.L. Balcázar, P.M. Long, F. Stephan (Eds.), Algorithmic Learning Theory. XIII, 393 pages. 2006. (Sublibrary LNAI).

Vol. 4263: A. Levi, E. Savaş, H. Yenigün, S. Balcısoy, Y. Saygın (Eds.), Computer and Information Sciences – ISCIS 2006. XXIII, 1084 pages. 2006.

Vol. 4262: K. Havelund, M. N\'u\~nez, G. Ro\csu, B. Wolff (Eds.), Formal Approaches to Software Testing and Runtime Verification. XXXXXX, 24555555 pages. 2006.

Vol. 4261: Y. Zhuang, S. Yang, Y. Rui, Q. He (Eds.), Advances in Multimedia Information Processing - PCM 2006. XXII, 1040 pages. 2006.

Vol. 4260: Z. Liu, J. He (Eds.), Formal Methods and Software Engineering. XII, 778 pages. 2006.

Vol. 4259: S. Greco, Y. Hata, S. Hirano, M. Inuiguchi, S. Miyamoto, H.S. Nguyen, R. Słowiński (Eds.), Rough Sets and Current Trends in Computing. XXII, 951 pages. 2006. (Sublibrary LNAI).

Vol. 4257: I. Richardson, P. Runeson, R. Messnarz (Eds.), Software Process Improvement. XI, 219 pages. 2006.

Vol. 4256: L. Feng, G. Wang, C. Zeng, R. Huang (Eds.), Web Information Systems – WISE 2006 Workshops. XIV, 320 pages. 2006.

Vol. 4255: K. Aberer, Z. Peng, E.A. Rundensteiner, Y. Zhang, X. Li (Eds.), Web Information Systems – WISE 2006. XIV, 563 pages. 2006.

Vol. 4254: T. Grust, H. Höpfner, A. Illarramendi, S. Jablonski, M. Mesiti, S. Müller, P.-L. Patranjan, K.-U. Sattler, M. Spiliopoulou, J. Wijsen (Eds.), Current Trends in Database Technology – EDBT 2006. XXXI, 932 pages. 2006.

Vol. 4253: B. Gabrys, R.J. Howlett, L.C. Jain (Eds.), Knowledge-Based Intelligent Information and Engineering Systems, Part III. XXXII, 1301 pages. 2006. (Sublibrary LNAI).

Vol. 4252: B. Gabrys, R.J. Howlett, L.C. Jain (Eds.), Knowledge-Based Intelligent Information and Engineering Systems, Part II. XXXIII, 1335 pages. 2006. (Sublibrary LNAI).

Vol. 4251: B. Gabrys, R.J. Howlett, L.C. Jain (Eds.), Knowledge-Based Intelligent Information and Engineering Systems, Part I. LXVI, 1297 pages. 2006. (Sublibrary LNAI).

Vol. 4250: H.J. van den Herik, S.-C. Hsu, T.-s. Hsu, H.H.L.M. Donkers (Eds.), Advances in Computer Games. XIV, 273 pages. 2006.

Vol. 4249: L. Goubin, M. Matsui (Eds.), Cryptographic Hardware and Embedded Systems - CHES 2006. XII, 462 pages. 2006.

Vol. 4248: S. Staab, V. Svátek (Eds.), Managing Knowledge in a World of Networks. XIV, 400 pages. 2006. (Sublibrary LNAI).

Vol. 4247: T.-D. Wang, X. Li, S.-H. Chen, X. Wang, H. Abbass, H. Iba, G. Chen, X. Yao (Eds.), Simulated Evolution and Learning. XXI, 940 pages. 2006.

Vol. 4246: M. Hermann, A. Voronkov (Eds.), Logic for Programming, Artificial Intelligence, and Reasoning. XIII, 588 pages. 2006. (Sublibrary LNAI).

Vol. 4245: A. Kuba, L.G. Nyúl, K. Palágyi (Eds.), Discrete Geometry for Computer Imagery. XIII, 688 pages. 2006.

Vol. 4244: S. Spaccapietra (Ed.), Journal on Data Semantics VII. XI, 267 pages. 2006.

Vol. 4243: T. Yakhno, E.J. Neuhold (Eds.), Advances in Information Systems. XIII, 420 pages. 2006.

Vol. 4242: A. Rashid, M. Aksit (Eds.), Transactions on Aspect-Oriented Software Development II. IX, 289 pages. 2006.

Vol. 4241: R.R. Beichel, M. Sonka (Eds.), Computer Vision Approaches to Medical Image Analysis. XI, 262 pages. 2006.

Vol. 4239: H.Y. Youn, M. Kim, H. Morikawa (Eds.), Ubiquitous Computing Systems. XVI, 548 pages. 2006.

Vol. 4238: Y.-T. Kim, M. Takano (Eds.), Management of Convergence Networks and Services. XVIII, 605 pages. 2006.